T0375321

Repeated Games

Three leading experts have produced a landmark work based on a set of working papers published by the Center for Operations Research and Econometrics (CORE) at Université Catholique de Louvain in 1994, under the title "Repeated Games," which holds almost mythic status among game theorists. Jean-François Mertens, Sylvain Sorin, and Shmuel Zamir have significantly elevated the clarity and depth of presentation with many results presented at a level of generality that goes far beyond the original papers – many written by the authors themselves. Numerous results are new, and many classic results and examples are not to be found elsewhere. Most remain state of the art in the literature. This book is full of challenging and important problems that are set up as exercises, with detailed hints provided for their solution. A new bibliography traces the development of the core concepts up to the present day.

The late Jean-François Mertens (11 March 1946–17 July 2012) was professor at the Université Catholique de Louvain (where he earned his PhD) and a member of the CORE. One of the world's leading experts in game theory and economic theory, Mertens is the author of seminal papers on equilibrium selection in games, formulation of Bayesian analysis, repeated and stochastic games, general equilibrium, social choice theory, and dynamic general equilibrium. A Fellow of the Econometric Society, he was also a founding member of the Center for Game Theory in Economics at the State University of New York at Stony Brook.

Sylvain Sorin is a member of the Mathematics Department at the Université Pierre et Marie Curie. He was previously professor at Université L. Pasteur, Strasbourg, and Université Paris X-Nanterre. He has been an affiliated member of the Département de Mathématiques, École Normale Supérieure (Paris); the Laboratoire d'Econométrie, École Polytechnique, Palaiseau; and the Center for Game Theory in Economics, State University of New York at Stony Brook. He is a Fellow of the Econometric Society and was a charter member of the Game Theory Society and editor-in-chief of the *International Journal of Game Theory*.

Shmuel Zamir, author of the textbook *Game Theory* (with M. Maschler and E. Solan, Cambridge 2013), is professor emeritus at the Hebrew University of Jerusalem and a founding member of the Center for the Study of Rationality there. He is professor of economics at the University of Exeter Business School, UK. Zamir is a Fellow of the Econometric Society, a charter member and a former council member of the Game Theory Society, and an affiliated member of the Center for Game Theory in Economics at the State University of New York at Stony Brook. Since 2008, he has been the editor-in-chief of the *International Journal of Game Theory*.

Econometric Society Monographs

The Econometric Society is an international society for the advancement of economic theory in relation to statistics and mathematics. The Econometric Society Monograph series is designed to promote the publication of original research contributions of high quality in mathematical economics and theoretical and applied econometrics.

Other Titles in the Series:

G. S. Maddala, *Limited dependent and qualitative variables in econometrics*, 9780521241434, 9780521338257

Gerard Debreu, *Mathematical economics: Twenty papers of Gerard Debreu*, 9780521237369, 9780521335614

Jean-Michel Grandmont, *Money and value: A reconsideration of classical and neoclassical monetary economics*, 9780521251419, 9780521313643

Franklin M. Fisher, *Disequilibrium foundations of equilibrium economics*, 9780521378567

Andreu Mas-Colell, *The theory of general equilibrium: A differentiable approach*, 9780521265140, 9780521388702

Truman F. Bewley, Editor, *Advances in econometrics – Fifth World Congress (Volume I)*, 9780521467261

Truman F. Bewley, Editor, *Advances in econometrics – Fifth World Congress (Volume II)*, 9780521467254

Hervé Moulin, *Axioms of cooperative decision making*, 9780521360555, 9780521424585

L. G. Godfrey, *Misspecification tests in econometrics: The Lagrange multiplier principle and other approaches*, 9780521424592

Tony Lancaster, *The econometric analysis of transition data*, 9780521437899

Alvin E. Roth and Marilda A. Oliviera Sotomayor, Editors, *Two-sided matching: A study in game-theoretic modeling and analysis*, 9780521437882

Wolfgang Härdle, *Applied nonparametric regression*, 9780521429504

Jean-Jacques Laffont, Editor, *Advances in economic theory – Sixth World Congress (Volume I)*, 9780521484596

Jean-Jacques Laffont, Editor, *Advances in economic theory – Sixth World Congress (Volume II)*, 9780521484602

Halbert White, *Estimation, inference and specification*, 9780521252805, 9780521574464

Christopher Sims, Editor, *Advances in econometrics – Sixth World Congress (Volume I)*, 9780521444590, 9780521566100

Christopher Sims, Editor, *Advances in econometrics – Sixth World Congress (Volume II)*, 9780521444606, 9780521566094

Roger Guesnerie, *A contribution to the pure theory of taxation*, 9780521629560

David M. Kreps and Kenneth F. Wallis, Editors, *Advances in economics and econometrics – Seventh World Congress (Volume I)*, 9780521589833

David M. Kreps and Kenneth F. Wallis, Editors, *Advances in economics and econometrics – Seventh World Congress (Volume II)*, 9780521589826

David M. Kreps and Kenneth F. Wallis, Editors, *Advances in economics and econometrics – Seventh World Congress (Volume III)*, 9780521580137, 9780521589819

Donald P. Jacobs, Ehud Kalai, and Morton I. Kamien, Editors, *Frontiers of research in economic theory: The Nancy L. Schwartz Memorial Lectures*, 1983–1997, 9780521632225, 9780521635387

A. Colin Cameron and Pravin K. Trivedi, *Regression analysis of count data*, 9780521632010, 9780521635677

Steinar Strom, Editor, *Econometrics and economic theory in the 20th century: The Ragnar Frisch Centennial Symposium*, 9780521633239, 9780521633659

Continued following the index

Repeated Games

Jean-François Mertens

Sylvain Sorin
Université Pierre et Marie Curie, France

Shmuel Zamir
The Hebrew University of Jerusalem, Israel, and the University of Exeter, UK

CAMBRIDGE
UNIVERSITY PRESS

32 Avenue of the Americas, New York NY 10013-2473, USA

Cambridge University Press is part of the University of Cambridge.

It furthers the University's mission by disseminating knowledge in the pursuit of education, learning and research at the highest international levels of excellence.

www.cambridge.org
Information on this title: www.cambridge.org/9781107030206

First published 2015

A catalogue record for this publication is available from the British Library

Library of Congress Cataloguing in Publication data
Mertens, Jean-François, 1946–
Repeated games / Jean-François Mertens, Sylvain Sorin, Shmuel Zamir.
pages cm. – (Econometric society monographs ; 55)
Includes bibliographical references and index.
ISBN 978-1-107-03020-6 (hardback) – ISBN 978-1-107-66263-6 (paperback)
1. Game theory. 2. Stochastic processes. I. Sorin, Sylvain. II. Zamir, Shmuel. III. Title.
HB144.M47 2014
519.3 – dc23 2014006953

ISBN 978-1-107-03020-6 Hardback
ISBN 978-1-107-66263-6 Paperback

Contents

Part C: Further Developments

List of Figures

Foreword

Robert J. Aumann

John von Neumann reportedly said that pure and applied mathematics have a symbiotic relationship: not only does applied math draw heavily on the tools developed on the pure side, but, correspondingly, pure math cannot exist in the rarefied atmosphere of abstract thought alone; if it is not somehow rooted in the real world, it will wither and die.

The work before us – which certainly qualifies as beautiful, subtle, pure mathematics – is a case in point. It originated half a century ago, at the height of the Cold War between the United States and the Soviet Union, indeed as a direct result of that conflict. The US and SU were trying to keep the Cold War from getting hot; to minimize the damage if it did; and to cut down the enormous expenses that the nuclear arms race entailed. To that end, they met repeatedly in Geneva to negotiate mutual reductions in their nuclear arsenals. Regarding these arsenals, both sides were in the dark. Neither knew how many weapons the other had; and clearly, it was the number retained, rather than destroyed, that mattered. In Princeton, Oskar Morgenstern and Harold Kuhn had just founded the mathematics consulting firm "Mathematica." The United States Arms Control and Disarmament Agency (ACDA) was responsible for conducting the Geneva negotiations for the US; it turned to Mathematica to see whether the Theory of Games – created two decades earlier by John von Neumann and Oskar Morgenstern (the same as the Mathematica principal) – could help in addressing the strategic issues raised by these negotiations. Mathematica responded by assembling a team of theorists that included Gerard Debreu, John Harsanyi, Harold Kuhn, Mike Maschler, Jim Mayberry, Herb Scarf, Reinhard Selten, Martin Shubik, Dick Stearns, and the writer of these lines. Mike and I took charge of the informational aspect (Dick joined us later): whether one side could glean any information about the size of the other's nuclear arsenal from its tactics in previous negotiation rounds. To get a handle on this problem, we started by looking at the simplest possible analogues: very simple-looking two-person zero-sum repeated games, in which one player knows the payoff matrix while the other does not, and each observes the action of the other at each stage of the repetition. In such games, can the uninformed player glean any information about the payoff matrix from the informed player's actions at previous stages? Answering this question, even for the simplest 2×2 games, turned out to be surprisingly difficult – and challenging, fun! I vividly remember feeling that we were not working on a contrived, artificial problem, but were exploring the mysteries of the real world, like an astronomer or biologist. Thus was born the theory of repeated games of incomplete information.

What developed from that early work certainly *cannot* be considered applied math. To be sure, some insights may have been useful; for example, that in the context of a long series of repetitions, one cannot make use of information without implicitly revealing it. As a very practical corollary, we told the ACDA that it might be advisable to withhold some information from the ACDA's own negotiators. But the lion's share of the theory did not become directly useful, neither at that time nor subsequently. It really is pure mathematics: though *inspired* by experience – by the real world – it is of no direct use, at least to date.

The theory born in the mid to late sixties under the Mathematica-ACDA project started to grow and develop soon thereafter. For many years, I was a frequent visitor at CORE – the Center for Operations Research and Econometrics – founded in the late sixties by Jacques Drèze as a unit of the ancient university of Leuven-Louvain in Belgium. Probably my first visit was in 1968 or '69, at which time I met the brilliant, flamboyant young mathematician Jean-François Mertens (a little reminiscent of John Nash at MIT in the early fifties). One Friday afternoon, Jean-François took me in his Alfa-Romeo from Leuven to Brussels, driving at 215 km/hour, never slowing down, never sounding the horn, just blinking his lights – and indeed, the cars in front of him moved out of his way with alacrity. I told him about the formula, in terms of the concavification operator, for the value of an infinitely repeated two-person zero-sum game with one-sided incomplete information – which is the same as the limit of values of the n-times repeated games. He caught on immediately; the whole conversation, including the proof, took something like five or ten minutes. Those conversations – especially the vast array of fascinating, challenging open problems – hooked him; it was like taking a mountain climber to a peak in the foothills of a great mountain range, from where he could see all the beautiful unclimbed peaks. The area became a lifelong obsession with him; he reached the most challenging peaks.

At about the same time, Shmuel Zamir, a physics student at the Hebrew University, asked to do a math doctorate with me. Though a little skeptical, I was impressed by the young man, and decided to give it a try. I have never regretted that decision; Shmuel became a pillar of modern game theory, responsible for some of the most important results, not to speak of the tasks he has undertaken for the community. One problem treated in his thesis is estimating the error term in the above-mentioned limit of values; his seminal work in that area remains remarkable to this day. When Maschler and I published our Mathematica-ACDA reports in the early nineties, we included postscripts with notes on subsequent developments. The day that our typist came to the description of Zamir's work, a Jerusalem bus was bombed by a terrorist, resulting in many dead and wounded civilians. By a slip of the pen – no doubt Freudian – she typed "terror term" instead of "error term." Mike did not catch the slip, but I did, and to put the work in its historical context, purposely refrained from correcting it; it remains in the book to this day.

After finishing his doctorate, Shmuel – like many of my students – did a postdoctoral stint at CORE. While there, he naturally met up with Jean-François, and an immensely fruitful lifelong collaboration ensued. Together they attacked and solved many of the central unsolved problems of Repeated Game theory.

One of their beautiful results concerns the limit of values of n-times repeated two-person zero-sum games with incomplete information on *both* sides – like the original repeated Geneva negotiations, where neither the US nor the SU knew how many nuclear weapons the other side held. In the Mathematica-ACDA work, Maschler, Stearns, and I had shown that the infinite repetition of such games need not have a value: the minmax may be strictly greater than the maxmin. Very roughly, that is because, as mentioned above, using information involves revealing it. The minmax is attained when the maximizing player uses his information, thereby revealing it; but the minimizing player refrains from using her information until she has learned the maximizing player's information, and so can use *it*, in addition to her own. The maxmin is attained in the opposite situation, when he waits for her. In the infinitely repeated game, no initial segment affects the payoff, so each side waits for the other to use its information; the upshot is that there is *no* value – no way of playing a "long" repetition optimally, if you don't know *how* long it is.

But in the n-times repeated game, you can't afford waiting to use your information; the repetition will eventually end, rendering your information useless. Each side must use its information gradually, right from the start, thereby gradually revealing it; simultaneously, each side gradually learns the information revealed by the other, and so can – and does – use it. So it is natural to ask whether the values converge – whether one can speak of the value of a "long" repetition, without saying *how* long. Mike, Dick, and I did not succeed in answering this question. Mertens and Zamir did: they showed that the values indeed converge. Thus one *can* speak of the *value* of a "long" repetition without saying how long, even though one cannot speak of optimal *play* in such a setting. This result was published in the first issue – Vol. 1, No. 1 – of the *International Journal of Game Theory*, of which Zamir is now, over forty years later, the editor.

The Mertens–Zamir team made many other seminal contributions. Perhaps best known is their construction of the complete type space. This is not directly related to repeated games, but rather to all incomplete information situations – it fully justifies John Harsanyi's ingenious concept of "type" to represent multi-agent incomplete information.

I vividly remember my first meeting with Sylvain Sorin. It was after giving a seminar on repeated games (of complete information, to the best of my recall) in Paris, sometime in the late seventies, perhaps around 1978 or '79. There is a picture in my head of standing in front of a grand Paris building, built in the classical style with a row of Greek columns in front, and discussing repeated games with a lanky young French mathematician who actually understood everything I was saying – and more. I don't remember the contents of the conversation; but the picture is there, in my mind, vividly.

There followed years and decades of close cooperation between Sylvain, Jean-François, Shmuel, and other top Israeli mathematical game theorists. Sylvain and Jean-François came to Israel frequently, and the Israelis went to France and Belgium frequently. One winter, Sylvain and his family even joined me and my family for a few days of skiing in the Trois Vallées. During those years, Sylvain succeeded in attracting an amazing group of students, which became today's magnificent French school of mathematical game theory. One summer, he came to the annual game theory festival at Stony Brook University with twelve doctoral students; "Sylvain and his apostles" were the talk of the town.

Of the book's three authors, only Sylvain actually conducted joint research with the writer of these lines. We conjectured a result during the conference on repeated games organized by Abraham Neyman at the Israel Academy of Sciences in the spring of 1985; concentrated work on it started at the 1985–6 emphasis year in Math Econ and Computation organized by Gerard Debreu at the Mathematical Sciences Research Institute in Berkeley, in which we both participated; it continued by correspondence after we each returned to our home bases; finally, we succeeded in proving the conjecture, and in 1989 published it as the first paper in Vol.1, No.1, of the journal *Games and Economic Behavior*. The result concerns endogenous emergence of cooperation in a repeated game, and perhaps that is a good place to wrap up this preface. The book before us has been in the making, in one sense or another, for close to half a century; so its production may well be viewed as a repeated – or dynamic – game. And, both the production of the book itself, and the work described therein, have been highly cooperative ventures, spanning decades and continents.

The above has been a highly personal account of my involvement with the people and the work that made this extraordinary book happen. I have not done justice to the book itself. Perhaps the best way to do so is to quote from the reports of the anonymous readers who were asked by the publisher to report on the book. These reports are uniformly excellent and highly enthusiastic – I wish my work got reports like that. We here content ourselves with the opening paragraph of just one of those reports; the enthusiastic tone is typical:

> The results and proofs in this text are the foundations on which modern repeated-game theory is built. These are results that apply to zero-sum games, stochastic games, repeated games of incomplete information, spaces of beliefs, stochastic processes and many many other topics. It is impossible to find these results together in one place except in this volume. Existing texts and monographs cover some of them, but none covers anything like all of these topics. However, it is not the coverage of foundational material that makes this text one of a kind; it is the generality and the breadth of vision that is its most special feature. In virtually every section and result the authors strive

> to establish the most powerful and most general statement. The intellectual effort required to produce this work is huge. It was an enormous undertaking to have brought these results together in this one place. This makes the work as a whole sound leaden and dull; however, it is anything but that. It is filled with an intellectual *joie de vivre* that delights in the subject. This is epitomized by the astonishing links between disparate topics that are casually scattered throughout its pages – the Minmax Theorem used to prove the Peron–Frobenius Theorem; the Normal distribution arising in repeated games with incomplete information; the use of medial limits as a way of describing payoffs. . . .

It should be added that the book provides encyclopedic coverage of the area of repeated games – with and without complete information – as well as of stochastic and other dynamic games. The main emphasis is on developments during the classical period – the second half of the twentieth century – during which the theory took shape. Later developments – right up to the present – are also thoroughly covered, albeit more briefly.

In short, the work before us is an extraordinary intellectual tour de force; I congratulate and salute the authors, and wish the reader much joy and inspiration from studying it.

Jerusalem, January 2014

Preface

This book presents essentially the content of the CORE discussion papers (DP) 9420, 9421, and 9422 published as "Repeated Games," Parts A, B, and C in 1994. It may be appropriate to recall first the preface to those discussion papers:

> These notes represent work in progress, and far from its final form. An earlier version was circulated previously, and has been cited in various places. In view of this, we felt that the time had come to make it more widely available, in the form of discussion papers. We hope eventually to publish it in a more polished format. Remarks and suggestions are most welcome.
>
> Louvain-la-Neuve, June 1993

Unfortunately, the more polished published form was not realized, and the CORE discussion papers were out of print at some point. The objective of this book is to make this material accessible. Although several subsequent versions of this work have been available and were circulated, the material presented here is basically identical to that in the discussion papers with no intention to add new and recent material. We do, however, provide a more detailed presentation of the content, and in Appendix D we briefly introduce further developments after the DP version, along with the corresponding complementary bibliography.

Very sadly, this book is being published when Jean-François Mertens is no longer with us. He passed away on July 17, 2012. We obviously dedicate the book to him as a modest expression of our appreciation of his invaluable contributions to this project and to the underlying research in repeated games of incomplete information that led us to this book.

Sylvain Sorin
Shmuel Zamir
February 26, 2014

Acknowledgments

Our first acknowledgments are due to R. J. Aumann and the late M. Maschler, who, besides being among the founders of this research field of *repeated games with incomplete information*, were those who suggested this project to Shmuel Zamir and Jean-François Mertens more than thirty years ago . . . and from then on they persistently encouraged and even "pushed" the authors to terminate and publish it. As a matter of fact, it was Aumann's suggestion to publish it temporarily as a CORE discussion paper. Here we are happy to quote the following acknowledgment from the CORE discussion papers version:

> Support of CORE, and of numerous other institutions over the years, is gratefully acknowledged. So is Fabienne Henry's invaluable help in typing draft after draft.

We thank G. Mailath for suggesting this publication with Cambridge and for being patient enough to get the agreement and cooperation of the three of us. We are very grateful to B. von Stengel for helping us with some of the figures and to Ilan Nehama for his great help in dealing with the LaTeX software.

Finally, we are grateful to Mike Borns for proofreading the manuscript.

Sylvain Sorin
Shmuel Zamir
February 26, 2014

Acknowledgments

Presentation of the Content

Part A collects basic results that will be used in the book.

In view of the large variety of games that are introduced and studied, it is necessary to present a general setup that will cover all cases (in the normal and extensive forms).

Chapter I deals with normal form games.

The first three sections (I.1, I.2, I.3) offer a comprehensive treatment of the minmax theorem. We start with an analysis of the case of pure strategies, basically Sion's theorem (Theorem I.1.1 in this volume) and some variants. We further treat the case of mixed strategies (Proposition I.1.9). The basic tool is the separation theorem, which is briefly studied. Then we present extensions corresponding to topological regularization (continuity, compactness), measurability requirements leading to the general "mixed form" (Theorem I.2.4), and purification of mixed strategies (Proposition I.2.7). Next we study the case of ordered fields (Theorem I.3.6), and the elementary finite approach is presented in I.3 Ex.[1]

The next section (I.4) is devoted to Nash equilibria (Theorem I.4.1), and several properties (manifold of equilibria, being semi-algebraic, fictitious play, etc.) are studied in I.4 Ex.

Chapter II defines extensive form games and treats successively the following topics:

Section II.1: The description of the extensive form, including the definition of pure, mixed, and behavioral strategies, linear games, and perfect recall (see also II.1 Ex.); Dalkey, Isbell, and Zermelo's theorems; and the measurable version of Kuhn's theorem (Theorem II.1.6).

Section II.2: The case of infinite games, first with perfect information, including Gale and Stewart's analysis and Martin's theorem (II.2.3) and then Blackwell's games (imperfect information) (Proposition II.2.8).

[1] "Ex." is short for exercise. Thus, "1.3 Ex." means the exercises in Chapter I, Section 3. See the paragraph on enumeration at the end of this Presentation (p. xxviii) for a more detailed explanation of the book's numbering system.

Section II.3: The notion of correlated equilibria, its properties (Aumann's theorem [Theorem II.3.2]), and several extensions: first, extensive form correlated equilibria, then communication equilibria (general formulation and properties; specific representation for finite games).

Section II.4: Games with vector payoffs and Blackwell's theorem (Theorem II.4.1).

The purpose of Chapter III is to study the interaction at the informational level, namely, the belief space.

We present a construction of the universal belief space (III.1) leading to Theorem III.1.1 (an alternative construction is in III.1 Ex. 2); its main properties (III.2 and III.3) such as belief subspaces, consistency, and relation with an information scheme (Theorem III.2.4) and the approximation (Theorem III.3.1).

In Section III.4 we describe the general model of games with incomplete information. First, we recover Harsanyi's model (Theorem III.4.1); then we prove, in the framework of two-person zero-sum games, regularity properties of the value. Proposition III.4.4 will be crucial for the recursive structure and the comparison of information (Proposition III.4.5). Further properties of extended approachability and convexity/concavity with respect to the information structure are then developed in Sections III.4.c and d.

Chapter IV is a presentation of the general class of repeated games.

After an exposition of the model (IV.1) including the (strong) notions of maxmin, minmax, and uniform equilibrium, we describe alternative representations (IV.2).

We then present the underlying recursive structure (IV.3) for the two-person zero-sum case leading to the basic Theorem IV.3.2.

The next section (IV.4) is devoted to supergames, that is, repeated games with complete information. We study Nash equilibria in the standard signaling case: uniform, discounted, and finite frameworks leading to Theorems IV.4.1, IV.4.2, and IV.4.4, respectively (perfect equilibria are treated in IV.4 Ex); then we give properties of uniform equilibrium payoffs for games with partial monitoring; and finally we study correlated and communication equilibrium payoffs.

Section IV.5 studies recursive games.

Part B treats the central results of the book: games with incomplete information (V and VI) and stochastic games (VII).

Chapter V deals with "repeated games with lack of information on one side." This corresponds to a two-person zero-sum repeated game where one of the players (Player 1) is fully informed and the other (Player 2) has no information.

Section V.1 proves concavity properties and the famous splitting procedure (Proposition V.1.2).

Section V.2 is devoted to the full monitoring case. We introduce the notion of posterior probabilities generated by the strategies and the bounds on the L^2 and L^1 variations of this martingale. Then we establish the basic lemma (V.2.3) relating the distance to the set of non-revealing strategies to the variation of the posteriors. The fundamental result is the $\mathsf{Cav}\, u$ Theorem V.2.10. Finally the approachability strategy of the noninformed player is described in Section V.2.c.

Section V.3 covers the general case of a signaling structure. We first describe the non-revealing game, then the extension of the $\mathsf{Cav}\, u$ Theorem V.3.3 and of the construction of an optimal strategy for player 2 in Section V.3.d. Sections V.3.e–3.i expose a general procedure for approachability in function spaces to be applied to the case of a continuum of types of Player 1.

Section V.4 develops the links between the recursive formula for the value, the maximal variation of the martingale, and the appearance of the normal law (Theorem V.4.1 and Theorem V.4.3).

Section V.5 studies the speed of convergence of v_n to its limit, first for the state-independent signaling case, then for state-dependent signaling.

Chapter VI covers "repeated games with lack of information on both sides." This corresponds to two-person zero-sum games where each player has some private information.

Section VI.2 presents the new $\mathsf{Cav}_{\mathrm{I}}$ and Vex_{II} operators and the extensions of the tools of Section V.2.

Section VI.3 studies the uniform approach and determines the maxmin and minmax of the infinite undiscounted game (Theorem VI.3.1).

Section VI.4 is concerned with the limit of the value v_n of the n-stage repeated game leading to the MZ system (Proposition VI.4.10).

Section VI.5 deals with further properties of the MZ equations.

Section VI.6 is devoted to the analysis of the speed of convergence of v_n to its limit, and Section VI.7 studies several examples in detail.

Chapter VII presents a general analysis of stochastic games.

Section VII.1 offers an analysis of the discounted case: first for zero-sum games (Propositions VII.1.4 and VII.1.5), then for (subgame perfect) equilibria in the n-person case, and for stationary strategies in the finite case (Proposition VII.1.7 and Theorem VII.1.8).

The algebraic approach is studied in Section VII.2.

Section VII.3 covers the main result dealing with the uniform approach (Theorem VII.3.1).

Section VII.4 considers two-person non-zero-sum absorbing games: we compare the different approaches in an example and prove the existence of equilibria (Theorem VII.4.6).

After Section VII.5, which is devoted to exercises (Shapley operator, $\lim v_n$, correlated equilibria, $\limsup$ payoffs, etc.), Section VII.6 offers a reminder about dynamic programming.

The last Part C presents further developments.

Chapter VIII is devoted to extensions and further results in a zero-sum framework.

Section VIII.1 deals with the case where the players have the same information and describes the reduction to absorbing games.

Section VIII.2 studies games with no signals. The analysis for the minmax and the maxmin is done through the construction of an auxiliary game in normal form that mimics the infinite game. The proof for $\lim v_n$ uses a sequence of games played by blocks.

Section VIII.3 introduces a game with lack of information on both sides with state-dependent signaling matrices. The analysis is conducted with the help of a family of auxiliary stochastic games and shows the link between the two fields of incomplete information and stochastic games.

Section VIII.4 is explicitly devoted to stochastic games with incomplete information and introduces new tools for the study of the minmax, maxmin, and $\lim v_n$.

Chapter IX is concerned with two-person non-zero-sum games with incomplete information on one side.

Section IX.1 gives an existence proof of uniform equilibrium in the case of two states of nature (Theorem IX.1.3), and a characterization of this set via "bi-martingales" (Theorem IX.1.4), which are explicitly studied in Section IX.2.

Section IX.3 introduces several communication devices and characterizes communication and "noisy channel" equilibrium payoffs.

Finally, Appendix A deals with analytic sets and Appendix B with historical notes.

Enumeration

Theorems, propositions, lemmas, corollaries, definitions, remarks, and examples are enumerated so that they can be easily referred to. The first part of the number is the chapter and section. Within each chapter two counters start from 1, 2, ..., where theorems, propositions, lemmas, and corollaries use the same counter (thus for example, Proposition I.1.5 in Chapter I, Section 1, is followed by Theorem I.1.6). Similarly the second counter is for definitions, remarks, and examples (thus, for example, Remark III.2.9 in Chapter III, Section 2, is followed by Definition III.2.10).

Exercise enumeration is just 1, 2, ... in each section. The reference to exercises is by indication of the chapter, section, and exercise number and part. For example: II.1, Ex. 9b is part b of Exercise 9 in Section 1 of Chapter II.

Figures are enumerated by chapter and counter (with no indication of section), e.g., Figure II.4.

Thanks

The material in Chapters V and VI is largely due to Robert J. Aumann, M. Maschler, and R. Stearns. Shapley's work is basic for Chapter VII.

We also rely heavily on the works of F. Forges in II.3.c and IX.3, E. Lehrer in IV.4.b, and S. Hart in IX.1.b and IX.2.

Further acknowledgments can be found in the historical notes.

PART A

BACKGROUND MATERIAL

CHAPTER I

Basic Results on Normal Form Games

Non-cooperative games (or strategic games) are mainly studied through two models: normal form or extensive form. The latter will be presented in Chapter II. The former describes the choice spaces of each player and the result of their common choices. This is evaluated in terms of the players' von Neumann–Morgenstern utilities (i.e., the utility of a random variable is its expected utility (von Neumann and Morgenstern, 1944, Chapter I, 3.5)), and hence the following definition:

A **normal form** game is defined by a set of **I**, **strategy** spaces S^i, $i \in \mathbf{I}$, and real **payoff functions** F^i, $i \in \mathbf{I}$, on $S = \prod_i S^i$.

It is finite (or a **bi-matrix game** if #**I** = 2) if **I** and all S^i are finite.

Under suitable measurability conditions one defines the **mixed extension** of a game $G = (\mathbf{I}, (S^i, F^i)_{i \in \mathbf{I}})$ as the game $\Gamma = (\mathbf{I}, (\Sigma^i, \phi^i)_{i \in \mathbf{I}})$, where Σ^i is the set of probabilities on S^i and $\phi^i(\sigma) = \int_S F^i(s) \prod_{i \in \mathbf{I}} \sigma^i(ds^i)$. An element of S^i will be called a **pure strategy**, while an element of Σ^i will be called a **mixed strategy** (of player i). Unless explicitly specified (or self-evident), the following definitions are always used on the mixed extension of the game.

> s^i is a **dominant strategy** of player i if $F^i(s^i, s^{-i}) \geq F^i(t^i, s^{-i})$ for all t^i in S^i, and $s^{-i} \in S^{-i} = \prod_{h \neq i} S^h$.
>
> s^i is **dominated** (resp. strictly dominated) if there exists t^i with $F^i(t^i, s^{-i}) > F^i(s^i, s^{-i})$ for some s^{-i} (resp. all s^{-i}) and $F^i(t^i, \cdot) \geq F^i(s^i, \cdot)$.
>
> s^i is an (ε-)**best reply** to s^{-i} if $F^i(s^i, s^{-i}) \geq F^i(t^i, s^{-i})$ $(-\varepsilon)$ for all $t^i \in S^i$.

An (ε-)**equilibrium** is an **I**-tuple s such that for every i, s^i is an (ε-)best reply to s^{-i}.

A **two-person zero-sum game** (or a **matrix game** if the strategy sets are finite) is a normal form game with **I**= {I, II}, $S^{\mathrm{I}} = S, S^{\mathrm{II}} = T$, $F^{\mathrm{I}} = g = -F^{\mathrm{II}}$. One defines then the **minmax** $\overline{v}(g) = \inf_{t \in T} \sup_{s \in S} g(s, t)$ and the **maxmin** $\underline{v}(g) = \sup_{s \in S} \inf_{t \in T} g(s, t)$.

If they are equal the game has a **value** $v(g)$.

s is an (ε-)**optimal strategy** for player I if $g(s, t) \geq \underline{v}(g)$ $(-\varepsilon)$ for all $t \in T$.

I.1. THE MINMAX THEOREM

A minmax theorem gives conditions under which a two-person zero-sum game $(S, T; g)$ has a value. We allow here the payoff function g to map $S \times T$ to $\overline{\mathbb{R}}$. All minmax theorems in this paragraph will be derived from Theorem I.1.1. Proposition I.1.3 uses additional convexity assumptions to weaken continuity requirements, and Proposition I.1.9 applies the previous result to the mixed extension of the game.

I.1.a. Definitions and Notations

We start by introducing basic definitions and notations.

Definition I.1.1. A convex set is a convex subset of a vector space on the reals.

Definition I.1.2. An admissible topology on a convex set S is a topology such that, for each n, and for every $n-$ tuple $x_1, \ldots, x_n$ of points in S, the mapping $\phi_{x_1,\ldots,x_n}$ from the $n-1$-dimensional simplex $\{ p = (p_1, \ldots, p_n) \mid p_i \geq 0, \sum_i^n p_i = 1 \}$ to S, which maps p to $\sum_{i=1}^n p_i x_i$, is continuous, when the simplex is endowed with its usual topology (i.e., the topology induced by the Euclidian norm).

Definition I.1.3. A convex topological space is a convex set endowed with an admissible topology.

Remark I.1.4. Any convex subset of a linear topological (or topological vector) space is a convex topological space.

Remark I.1.5. A compact space is assumed not to be Hausdorff (T_2), unless explicitly stated.

Definition I.1.6. For a topological space S, a function $f\colon S \to \mathbb{R} \cup \{-\infty\}$ is **upper semi-continuous (u.s.c.)** iff $\{f \geq x\}$ is closed for every x. f is **lower semi-continuous (l.s.c.)** iff $(-f)$ is u.s.c.

Remark I.1.7. On a completely regular space, the u.s.c. functions that are bounded from above are the infima of a family of bounded continuous functions.

Definition I.1.8. For a convex set S, $f\colon S \to \overline{\mathbb{R}}$ is **quasi-concave** iff $\{f \geq x\}$ is convex for every x. f is **quasi-convex** iff $(-f)$ is quasi-concave. f is **concave** (resp. **convex, affine**) iff $f(\alpha x_1 + (1-\alpha)x_2) \leq \alpha f(x_1) + (1-\alpha) f(x_2)$ (resp. $\geq$, $=$) whenever the right-hand member is well defined $(0 < \alpha < 1)$.

I.1.b. A Basic Theorem

Theorem I.1.1. *(Sion, 1958) Assume S and T are convex topological spaces, one of which is compact. Assume that, for every real c, the sets $\{ t \mid g(s_0, t) \leq c \}$ and $\{ s \mid g(s, t_0) \geq c \}$ are closed and convex for every $(s_0, t_0) \in S \times T$. Then:*

$$\sup_{s \in S} \inf_{t \in T} g(s, t) = \inf_{t \in T} \sup_{s \in S} g(s, t).$$

If S (resp. T) is compact, then sup *(resp.* inf*) may be replaced by* max *(resp.* min*), i.e., the corresponding player has an* **optimal** *strategy.*

Proof. Obviously, one always has:

$$\sup_{s \in S} \inf_{t \in T} g(s, t) \leq \inf_{t \in T} \sup_{s \in S} g(s, t).$$

Suppose that, contrary to the theorem, for some real number c:

$$\sup_{s \in S} \inf_{t \in T} g(s, t) < c < \inf_{t \in T} \sup_{s \in S} g(s, t).$$

Assume, for instance, that S is compact. The sets $A_t = \{ s \in S \mid g(s, t) < c \}$ form an open covering of S; thus, there exist $t_1, \ldots, t_n$ such that the sets A_{t_i} $(1 \leq i \leq n)$ cover S. We can restrict T to the convex hull of the set T_0 of points t_i $(1 \leq i \leq n)$ and work now on the $(n-1)$-simplex, using the admissibility of the topology. All our assumptions are still valid. We can now do the same operation with the sets $B_s = \{ t \in T \mid g(s, t) > c \}$, so that both S and T become simplices with vertex sets S_0 and T_0, and with the property that, for any $s \in S$, there exists $t \in T_0$ such that $s \in A_t$ and that, for any $t \in T$, there exists $s \in S_0$ such that $t \in B_s$. We can further assume that S_0 and T_0 are minimal for this property, eventually eliminating some additional points from S_0 and T_0.

Let s_i $(1 \leq i \leq n)$ be the points in S_0, and for each i, $T_i = \{ t \in T \mid g(s_i, t) \leq c \}$. The sets T_i are compact convex, satisfy $\bigcap_{i=1}^n T_i = \emptyset$, and, by the minimality property, for every j, $\bigcap_{i \neq j} T_i \neq \emptyset$. The next lemma will show that this implies that $\bigcup_{i=1}^n T_i$ is not convex. Thus there exists $t_0 \in T$ such that, for all i, $t_0 \notin T_i$, we have, for each i, $g(s_i, t_0) > c$, and thus, for each $s \in S$, $g(s, t_0) > c$. The same argument would show dually that there exists $s_0 \in S$ such that, for each $t \in T$, $g(s_0, t) < c$; we thus have both $g(s_0, t_0) < c$ and $g(s_0, t_0) > c$, the desired contradiction.

The replacement of sup by max is possible due to the u.s.c. of $g(\cdot, t)$ on the compact set S (for each $t \in T$). ∎

To complete the proof, we shall prove the following lemma:

Lemma I.1.2. *Let T_i $(1 \leq i \leq n)$ be compact convex subsets of a Hausdorff locally convex topological vector space, such that $T = \bigcup_i T_i$ is convex and such that, for every i, $\bigcap_{h \neq i} T_h \neq \emptyset$. Then $\bigcap_i T_i \neq \emptyset$.*

Remark I.1.9. For a simpler and more general result, cf. I.4, Ex. 19, p. 56. Here the only "sport" is to obtain Theorem I.1.1 using just the separation theorem, and in fact only for polyhedra in finite dimensional space.

Proof. The proof goes by induction on n. We assume that the lemma is proved up to $n-1$ and is false for n. Then $\bigcap_{i<n} T_i$ and T_n are two disjoint compact convex sets and can therefore, by the Hahn–Banach theorem (cf. I.1.e, p. 9), be strongly separated by a closed hyperplane, whose (compact convex) intersection with T we denote by $\tilde{T}$. Let $\tilde{T}_i = T_i \cap \tilde{T}$; the $\tilde{T}_i$ are compact convex, $\tilde{T}_n = \emptyset$, and $\bigcup_{i<n} \tilde{T}_i = \tilde{T}$.

Further, for any $j < n$, $\bigcap_{i \notin \{n,j\}} T_i$, which is convex, has, by assumption, a non-empty intersection both with T_n and with $\bigcap_{i<n} T_i$, which lie on opposite sides of the hyperplane; therefore, $\bigcap_{i \notin \{n,j\}} T_i$ has a non-empty intersection with the hyperplane. Thus $\bigcap_{i \notin \{n,j\}} \tilde{T}_i \neq \emptyset$.

It follows by the validity of the lemma for $n-1$ that $\bigcap_{i<n} \tilde{T}_i \neq \emptyset$, i.e., $(\bigcap_{i<n} T_i) \cap \tilde{T} \neq \emptyset$; this yields the contradiction. ■

I.1.c. Convexity

Proposition I.1.3. *Assume S is a compact convex topological space, T is a convex set, and, for every real c, and for every $(s_0, t_0) \in S \times T$, the sets $\{ s \in S \mid g(s, t_0) \geq c \}$ are closed and convex, and $g(s_0, t)$ is convex in t, and $g < +\infty$. Then:*

$$\max_{s \in S} \inf_{t \in T} g(s,t) = \inf_{t \in T} \max_{s \in S} g(s,t).$$

Proof. As in the proof of the theorem, we can reduce the discussion to the case where T is a simplex with vertices $(t_1, \ldots, t_k)$ and where:

$$\sup_{s \in S} \inf_{i} g(s, t_i) < c < \inf_{t \in T} \sup_{s \in S} g(s,t).$$

Then, for every $s \in S$, the function $g(s, \cdot)$ is continuous on the interior of the simplex T, being convex. If t_i^n are interior points, $\lim_{n \to \infty} t_i^n = t_i$, then, for every s, $\lim_{n \to \infty} g(s, t_i^n) \leq g(s, t_i)$ by the convexity of g. Therefore, the sets $A_{i,n} = \{ s \mid g(s, t_i^n) < c \}$, $1 \leq i \leq k$, $n = 1, 2, \ldots$, form an open covering of S; extracting a finite subcovering, we see that we can replace T by some compact polyhedron $\tilde{T}$ contained in the interior of T: now we have the continuity and convexity in t of $f(t,s)$ for every $s \in S$, and we can apply Theorem I.1.1, p. 5, to yield a contradiction. ■

I.1.d. Mixed Strategies

Definition I.1.10. A **regular measure** on a topological space X is a positive bounded measure μ on the Borel sets (σ-algebra generated by the open sets) such that $\mu(A) = \sup\{ \mu(B) \mid B \subseteq A,\ B \text{ closed and compact} \}$. It is the smallest closed subset with a negligible complement. The set of those measures that have total mass 1 is denoted by $\Delta(X)$.

Definition I.1.11. $\Delta(X)$ is endowed with the **weak* topology**, defined as the weakest topology for which the mapping $\mu \mapsto \mu(f) = \int f d\mu$ is u.s.c. for all bounded u.s.c. f.

Definition I.1.12. $f: X \to Y$ is **Lusin-measurable** if $\forall \varepsilon > 0, \exists K$ closed, compact with $\mu(K) > 1 - \varepsilon$, and $f_{|K}$ continuous.

Remark I.1.13. The regularity of a measure is equivalent to the Lusin-measurability of all Borel maps with values in separable metric spaces.

Proposition I.1.4. *$\Delta(X)$ is always T_1, and is Hausdorff, resp. compact, resp. completely regular, if X is so. Further, if X is completely regular, then, using the integral of bounded continuous functions, the above definition coincides with the usual one.*

Proof.

- For the T_1 property, i.e., points are closed. If $\mu_1 \neq \mu_2$, by regularity there exists an open set O with $\mu_1(O) > t > \mu_2(O)$ and μ_2 does not belong to $W(\mu_1) = \{\, \mu \mid \mu(O) > t \,\}$.
- For the Hausdorff property, assume $\mu_1 \neq \mu_2$. Given a Borel set B with $\mu_1(B) > \mu_2(B)$, choose (regularity) two compacts C_1 (included in B) and C_2 (in its complement) satisfying $\mu_1(C_1) + \mu_2(C_2) > 1$. Then there exist disjoint open sets $O_i,\ C_i \subseteq O_i,\ i = 1, 2$ and real numbers α_i, $\alpha_1 + \alpha_2 > 1$ with $\mu_i(O_i) > \alpha_i$. Thus the following are disjoint neighborhoods: $V_i(\mu_i) = \{\, \mu \mid \mu(O_i) > \alpha_i \,\}$.
- For the compactness, cf. I.1, Ex. 10, p. 15.
- For the completely regular case, the above remark (sub I.1.a, p. 4) on u.s.c. functions implies that it is enough to show that $\int f\, d\mu = \inf\{ \int g\, d\mu \mid g$ continuous, bounded, and above $f \}$. This in turn follows from the fact that f is Lusin-measurable and from Dini's theorem. ■

Proposition I.1.5. *(Dudley, 1968) If X is metrizable and separable, so is $\Delta(X)$ with the metric $d(\mu, \nu) = \sup\{ |\mu(f) - \nu(f)| \mid f$ Lipschitz with constant 1 and bounded by $1 \}$. Moreover, if X is complete, so is $\Delta(X)$.*

For more properties, cf. Appendix A.9.

Fubini's Theorem I.1.6. *Given positive bounded regular measures μ_1 and μ_2 on two topological spaces E_1 and E_2, there exists a unique regular measure μ on $E = E_1 \times E_2$ such that $\mu(K_1 \times K_2) = \mu_1(K_1)\mu_2(K_2)$ for any closed compact subsets K_i of E_i, and then for any non-negative μ-measurable function f on $E_1 \times E_2$, $\int_{E_2} f d\mu_2$ is μ_1-measurable and $\int f d\mu = \int d\mu_1 \int f d\mu_2$.*

Proof. For existence, extract an increasing sequence of closed compact subsets C_i^n from E_i that carry most of the mass. Let μ_i^n be the corresponding restriction of μ_i. By the validity of the theorem in the compact case (Mertens, 1986,

Proposition 2), we obtain corresponding regular measures $\mu^n = \mu_1^n \otimes \mu_2^n$ on $C^n = C_1^n \times C_2^n \subseteq E$. Clearly the μ_i^n are increasing, and so their limit μ is a regular measure on E for which our condition is easily verified. For any such μ, observe that the regularity of μ_1 and μ_2 implies then the validity of our product formula when the K_i are μ_i measurable. Hence the product $\mathscr{E}_1 \otimes \mathscr{E}_2$ of the σ-fields $\mathscr{E}_i$ of μ_i-measurable sets is contained in the μ-measurable sets, and μ coincides with the product measure there. It follows immediately that μ is uniquely determined on closed compact subsets of E, since those have a basis of neighborhoods (regularity) that belong to the product of the Borel σ-fields (compactness). Therefore (regularity again), μ is unique. ■

Remark I.1.14. The above applied inductively yields the existence of a product also for n factors, and the uniqueness proof remains identical, and so the product is "associative."

Proposition I.1.7. *The product of regular probabilities is a continuous map from $\Delta(X) \times \Delta(Y)$ to $\Delta(X \times Y)$.*

Proof. For O open in $X \times Y$ and $\mu \in \Delta(X)$, $f(\mu, y) = \mu(O_y)$ is l.s.c. on $\Delta(X) \times Y$: choose K_0 closed compact $\subseteq O_{y_0}$ with $\mu_0(K_0) \geq \mu_0(O_{y_0}) - \varepsilon$; then O^1 and O^2 open in X and Y respectively with $K_0 \subseteq O^1$, $y_0 \in O^2$, $O^1 \times O^2 \subseteq O_0$. Then:

$$\liminf_{\mu \to \mu_0, y \to y_0} \mu(O_y) \geq \liminf_{\mu \to \mu_0, y \to y_0} \mu(O^1)\mathbb{1}_{O^2}(y) \geq \mu_0(O^1) \geq \mu_0(O_{y_0}) - \varepsilon.$$

Hence $f(\mu, y) = \sum_{i=1}^n \alpha_i \mathbb{1}_{U^i}$ up to a uniform ε, with $\alpha_i > 0$ and U^i open in $\Delta(X) \times Y$. Hence (Fubini) $(\mu \otimes \nu)(O) = \int f(\mu, y)\nu(dy) = \sum_{i=1}^n \alpha_i \nu(U_\mu^i)$ up to ε, and $\nu(U_\mu^i)$ is l.s.c. on $\Delta(X) \times \Delta(Y)$ by our previous argument. ■

Proposition I.1.8. *Let X and Y be topological spaces, with Y Hausdorff, μ be a regular measure on X, and f be a Lusin-measurable function from X to Y.*

(1) *The image of μ by f, $\mu \circ f^{-1}$, is a regular measure on Y. Further, if f is continuous, the mapping $\overline{f}$ from $\Delta(X)$ to $\Delta(Y)$: $\mu \mapsto \mu \circ f^{-1}$ is continuous (and also denoted by $\Delta(f)$).*
(2) *Let $(X_k, \rho_{k,\ell})$ be a projective system of Hausdorff spaces ($\rho_{k,\ell} : X_k \to X_\ell$ being the continuous projection for $\ell \leq k$), with projective limit (X, ρ_k). Given a consistent sequence of regular measures μ_k on X_k (i.e., with $\overline{\rho}_{k,\ell}(\mu_k) = \mu_\ell$) there exists a unique regular measure μ on X with $\overline{\rho}_k(\mu) = \mu_k$, the **projective limit** of the sequence μ_k.*

Proof. The first point is clear. For the second, cf. Bourbaki (1969, §4, no. 3, Théorème 2). ■

In the sequel, we denote by Σ (resp. $\mathscr{T}$) the space $\Delta(S)$ (resp. $\Delta(T)$), and by $\mathscr{T}_f$ the space of all probability measures with finite support on T (points in Σ or $\mathscr{T}$ are **mixed strategies**, points in $\mathscr{T}_f$ mixed strategies with finite support).

Proposition I.1.9. *Let S be a compact topological space, T any set. Assume that, for each t, $g(\cdot, t)$ is u.s.c. in s. Then:*

$$\max_{\sigma\in\Sigma}\inf_{\tau\in\mathscr{T}_f}\int g(s,t)\,d(\sigma\otimes\tau) = \inf_{\tau\in\mathscr{T}_f}\max_{\sigma\in\Sigma}\int g(s,t)\,d(\sigma\otimes\tau).$$

Proof. Σ with the weak* topology is compact convex (I.1.4), and $F(\sigma,\tau)$, defined on $\Sigma\times\mathscr{T}_f$ by:

$$F(\sigma,\tau)=\int g(s,t)d(\sigma\otimes\tau)=\int_T d\tau\int_S g(s,t)d\sigma=\int_S d\sigma\int_T g(s,t)d\tau,$$

is affine in each variable and upper semi-continuous in σ. We can therefore apply Proposition I.1.3, p. 6, to yield the equality. ∎

Remark I.1.15. With an appropriate redefinition of regular measure the above remains true even if S is countably compact instead of compact (Mertens, 1986, pp. 243–246, and Remark 3, p. 247).

I.1.e. Note on the Separation Theorem

The Hahn–Banach theorem was used in the first lemma, in some exercises below, and in many other circumstances. Here follows a short refresher.

In the following statements, E is a real topological vector space, all subsets considered are convex, U denotes an open subset, and letters f are linear functionals.

The basic result is:

Proposition I.1.10. *If $0\notin U$, $\exists f\colon f(U)>0$ (f is then clearly continuous).*

Proof. Apply Zorn's lemma to the open convex subsets disjoint from 0. ∎

The basic technique for separating two convex sets is to separate their difference from zero, that is:

Proposition I.1.11. *If $A\cap U=\emptyset$, $\exists f\colon f(A)\cap f(U)=\emptyset$.*

(With obvious "refinements": B has an interior point, and A is disjoint from the interior of B; also: $\exists f\neq 0$, continuous, $f(A)\geq 0$ iff there exists a non-empty open convex cone disjoint from A: cf. I.3, Ex. 12, p. 42, for the necessity of the interior point.)

One can always obtain an "algebraic" statement from the above by using the strongest locally convex topology defined as follows: A is radial at $x\in A$ iff $\forall y\in E, \exists\varepsilon>0\colon x+\varepsilon y\in A$; then U is open iff it is radial at each of its points. Therefore:

Proposition I.1.12. *If p is a sublinear functional ($p(\lambda x)=\lambda p(x)$ for $\lambda\geq 0$, $p(x)\in\mathbb{R}$, $p(x+y)\leq p(x)+p(y)$), V a subspace, $f\colon V\to\mathbb{R}$, $f(v)\leq p(v)$; then $\exists\overline{f}\colon E\to\mathbb{R}$, $\overline{f}\leq p$, $\overline{f}(v)=f(v)$ for $v\in V$.*

Proof. Apply I.1.11 in $E \times \mathbb{R}$ to the subsets $U = \{ (x, \varphi) \mid \varphi > p(x), x \in E \}$ and $A = \{ (v, f(v)) \mid v \in V \}$. ■

Henceforth E will be locally convex, subsets closed, and linear functionals continuous and non-zero.

Proposition I.1.13. *If* $0 \notin A, \exists f \colon f(A) \geq 1$.

Proof. Apply Proposition I.1.11, where U is a neighborhood of zero. ■

Corollary I.1.14. *Finite dimensional convex subsets with disjoint relative interiors (i.e., their interiors in the affine subspace they generate) can be separated.*

Proof. It suffices to separate from zero the difference D of their relative interiors. For example, by Proposition I.1.12, we can assume E is spanned by D. If 0 is not in the closure of D, apply Proposition I.1.13; otherwise D has a non-empty interior and apply Proposition I.1.10. ■

Otherwise, to apply I.1.13 one needs conditions for the difference $B - C$ of two closed convex sets to be closed. This is true if one is compact; more generally, $A_B = \bigcap_{\varepsilon > 0} \varepsilon(B - b)$ does not depend on the choice of $b \in B$ and is called the **asymptotic cone** of B. Then:

Proposition I.1.15. *If* $A_B \cap A_C = \{0\}$, *and* B *or* C *is locally compact, then* $B - C$ *is closed, and* $A_{B-C} = A_B - A_C$.

Proposition I.1.16. *Assume* B *and* C *are cones, one of them locally compact, and* $B \cap C = \{0\}$. *Then* $\exists f \colon f(B) \geq 0, f(C) \leq 0$.

Taking for B *the polar* P^0 $(= \{ b \mid \langle b, \varphi \rangle \geq 0 \ \forall \varphi \in P \})$ *of some closed convex cone* P *in the dual, one obtains the alternative: either* $\exists c \in C - \{0\}$, $\langle c, \varphi \rangle \geq 0 \ \forall \varphi \in P$, *or* $\exists \varphi \in P - \{0\}$, $\langle c, \varphi \rangle \leq 0 \ \forall c \in C$, *and thus this alternative holds as soon as one of the cones* C, C^0, P, P^0 *is locally compact.*

Proof. Apply Proposition I.1.15 to B and $C - b$ for $b \in B - \{0\}$. ■

Corollary I.1.17. *If in Proposition I.1.16 both* B *and* C *are locally compact and contain no straight lines, then* $\exists f \colon f(B \setminus \{0\}) > 0 > f(C \setminus \{0\})$.

Proof. Indeed, $D = B - C$ has then the same properties, which imply that the sets $\{ d \in D \mid f(d) \leq 1 \}$, for f in the dual, form a basis of neighborhoods of zero in D. Choose then an f yielding a compact neighborhood. ■

EXERCISES

The first series of exercises investigates the general properties of the value operator. For short, we let, for any sets S and T, and any function $g(s, t)$ (with values in $\mathbb{R} \cup \{+\infty\}$ or in $\mathbb{R} \cup \{-\infty\}$)

$$\overline{v}(g) = \inf_{\tau \in \mathcal{T}_f} \sup_{\sigma \in \Sigma_f} g(\sigma, \tau), \quad \underline{v}(g) = \sup_{\sigma \in \Sigma_f} \inf_{\tau \in \mathcal{T}_f} g(\sigma, \tau),$$

where $g(\sigma, \tau) = \int g(s,t)d(\sigma \otimes \tau)$, and we write $v(g)$ when they are equal. We start for the record with the obvious properties.

1. $\overline{v} \geq \underline{v}$ and both are **positively homogeneous** of degree one (i.e., $\overline{v}(tg) = t\overline{v}(g)$ for $t \geq 0$), monotone, and invariant under translation by constant functions (i.e., $\overline{v}(g+\lambda) = \overline{v}(g) + \lambda$). The latter two properties imply they are **non-expansive**, i.e., $|\overline{v}(f) - \overline{v}(g)| \leq \|f - g\|$ with $\|f - g\| = \sup_{s,t} |f(s,t) - g(s,t)|$ (and with the convention $|\infty - \infty| = 0$).

2.

a. Under the assumptions of Proposition I.1.9, p. 9, the common value asserted there equals $\overline{v}(g)$. We will then use the notation $\Sigma(g)$ for $\{\sigma \in \Sigma \mid g(\sigma, t) \geq \overline{v}(g)\ \forall t \in T\}$ (and similarly for $\mathscr{T}(g)$ under dual assumptions). $\Sigma(g)$ is closed (hence compact), convex, and non-empty.

b. If a decreasing net g_α satisfies the assumptions of Proposition I.1.9, then:

(1) $g = \lim g_\alpha$ does also.
(2) $\overline{v}(g) = \lim \overline{v}(g_\alpha)$.
(3) If $\sigma_\alpha \in \Sigma(g_\alpha)$, or if only $g_\alpha(\sigma_\alpha, t) \geq \overline{v}(g) - \varepsilon_\alpha$, $\forall t \in T$, with $\varepsilon_\alpha \to 0$, then for any limit point σ of σ_α we have $\sigma \in \Sigma(g)$.
(4) If $\tau \in \mathscr{T}_f$ is ε-optimal for g, it is also so for all g_α with α sufficiently large.

HINT. Point (1) is obvious, and (2) and (3) follow from the fact that if f_α is a decreasing net of real-valued u.s.c. functions on the compact space S converging to f, and σ_α s.t. $f_\alpha(\sigma_\alpha) \geq \lambda - \varepsilon_\alpha$ with $\varepsilon_\alpha \to 0$, then $f(\sigma) \geq \lambda$ for any limit point σ. This follows in turn from the u.s.c. of the f_α on the compact space Σ, and from $f_\alpha \to f$ on Σ.

3. Continuity
Let S and T be compact. Denote by C the convex cone of real-valued functions on $S \times T$, which are u.s.c. in s and l.s.c. in t. If f_α is a net in C, let:

$$\varphi_{\alpha_0}(s_0, t_0) = \limsup_{s \to s_0} \left[\sup_{\alpha \geq \alpha_0} f_\alpha(s, t_0) \right],$$

$$\psi_{\alpha_0}(s_0, t_0) = \liminf_{t \to t_0} \left[\inf_{\alpha \geq \alpha_0} f_\alpha(s_0, t) \right].$$

Define the following concept of convergence on C: $f_\alpha \to f$ iff φ_α and ψ_α converge pointwise to f. Assume $f_\alpha \to f$.

a. Then $\forall t, \exists \alpha_0 : \varphi_\alpha(s,t) < +\infty$, $\forall s \in S$ and $\forall \alpha \geq \alpha_0$, and similarly for ψ.

b. The convergence is compatible with the lattice structure and with the convex cone structure:

(1) $f_\alpha \to f$ and $g_\alpha \to g$ imply $f_\alpha \wedge g_\alpha \to f \wedge g$, $f_\alpha \vee g_\alpha \to f \vee g$, and $f_\alpha + g_\alpha \to f + g$.
(2) $\lambda_\alpha \geq 0$, $\lambda_\alpha \to \lambda$, and $f_\alpha \to f$ imply $\lambda_\alpha f_\alpha \to \lambda f$.

HINT. For point (2), it suffices to prove, e.g., convergence from above, and hence to fix $t_0 \in T$. Using I.1, Ex. 3a, subtract then an appropriate constant to reduce (by (1)) to the case where $f_\alpha(s, t_0) \leq 0\ \forall \alpha, \forall s$. Let $\mu_{\alpha_0} = \inf_{\alpha \geq \alpha_0} \lambda_\alpha$: then $\mu_\alpha \varphi_\alpha(s, t_0)$ are u.s.c., $\geq \lambda_\alpha f_\alpha(s, t_0)$, and decrease to $\lambda f(s, t_0)$.

c. Assume $v(f)$ exists and $f_\alpha \to f$. Then:

(1) $\overline{v}(f_\alpha)$ and $\underline{v}(f_\alpha)$ converge to $v(f)$.
(2) Any limit point of ε_α-optimal strategies for f_α ($\varepsilon_\alpha \to 0$) belongs to $\Sigma(f)$.
(3) Any ε-optimal strategy with finite support for f is so for all f_α (α sufficiently large).

HINT. Point 1 allows us to use I.1, Ex. 2b.

d. If S and T are Hausdorff (or just "locally compact," i.e., such that every point has a basis of compact neighborhoods), the convergence concept is topological, i.e., derives from a "locally convex" Hausdorff topology on C.

HINT. Take as subbase of open sets the sets $V_{t,\lambda,K} = \{ g \in C \mid g(s,t) < \lambda \text{ for } s \in K \}$ and $W_{s,\lambda,K'} = \{ g \in C \mid g(s,t) > \lambda \text{ for } t \in K' \}$ with $\lambda \in \mathbb{R}$, K and K' compact.

4. I.1, Ex. 3b shows that $f_\alpha^i \to f^i$, $\lambda_\alpha^i \to \lambda^i$, $\lambda_\alpha^i \geq 0$ implies $\sum_1^n \lambda_\alpha^i f_\alpha^i \to \sum_1^n \lambda^i f^i$. Even under the best circumstances, the restriction to $\lambda_\alpha^i \geq 0$ cannot be dispensed with.

a. Let $S = \{s_0\}$, $T = [0,1]$, $f_1(t) = \mathbb{1}_{t>0}$, $f_2(t) = t^{-1}$ for $t > 0$, $f_2(0) = 0$: f_1 and f_2 belong to C and are ≥ 0, and $-f_1 + \varepsilon f_2$ belongs to C for $\varepsilon > 0$ but not for $\varepsilon = 0$: we have a monotone straight line whose intersection with C is not closed.

b. Consider $g_\varepsilon = (1 - \varepsilon f_2)^2 = (1 - 2\varepsilon f_2 + \varepsilon^2 f_3)$: this is a nice curve in a fixed plane, with this time $g_\varepsilon \in C$ for all $\varepsilon \geq 0$. Yet $v(g_\varepsilon) = 0$ for $\varepsilon > 0$, $v(g_0) = 1$.

c. Nevertheless, prove that the intersection of C with a finite dimensional affine function space A is closed, and that on this intersection the convergence in C coincides with the usual in A, if any difference of two functions in A is separately bounded (i.e., bounded in each variable, the other being fixed).

5. To show that monotonicity and compactness in I.1, Ex. 2 cannot be dispensed with:

a. Let $S = \overline{\mathbb{N}}$, $T = \{0\}$, $g_k = \mathbb{1}_k$: the g_k are a sequence of positive continuous functions converging weakly to zero ($\sum g_k \leq 1$), yet $v(g_k) = 1$ does not converge to zero.

b. On any infinite compact Hausdorff space S, the above example can be reduplicated (thus: g_k continuous, $\|g_k\| = 1$, $g_k \geq 0$, $g_k(s) > 0 \Longrightarrow g_n(s) = 0 \; \forall n \neq k$).

HINT. Show that one can find in S two disjoint compact sets with a non-empty interior, one of which is infinite, and use this inductively.

c. Even with monotonicity, one cannot dispense with compactness: e.g., $S = \mathbb{N}$, $g_k(n) = \mathbb{1}_{n \geq k}$.

d. Cf. also II.2, Ex. 1, p. 96.

6. Differentiability

We keep the notation of I.1, Ex. 3. Denote by G the convex cone of functions g having an unambiguous, u.s.c.-l.s.c. extension $g(\sigma, \tau)$ to $\Sigma \times \mathscr{T}$, i.e., $g(s, \tau) < +\infty$ is u.s.c. on S for each τ, $g(\sigma, t) > -\infty$ is l.s.c. on T for each σ, and

$$\int g(s,\tau)\, \sigma(ds) = \int g(\sigma, t)\, \tau(dt) \text{ for each } (\sigma, \tau).$$

Let also $V = \{ f \in C \mid v(f) \text{ exists} \}$.

For $f \in V$, $g \in G$, $g_{|\Sigma(f)\times\mathscr{T}(f)} \in V$ (e.g. by Theorem I.1.1); denote the value of this game by $v_f(g)$. We deal with differentiability first along straight lines, then along differentiable curves.

Remark I.1.16. Theorem I.1.1, p. 5, and Proposition I.2.4, p. 21, give sufficient conditions for $f \in V$. I.1, Ex. 7, p. 14, and I.2, Ex. 1, p. 24, give sufficient conditions for $g \in G$.

a. For $f + \varepsilon g \in V$, $g \in G$, $\lim_{\varepsilon \gtrsim 0}[v(f+\varepsilon g) - v(f)]/\varepsilon = v_f(g)$.

HINT. (cf. Mills, 1956). For $\tau \in \mathscr{T}(f)$, σ_ε an ε^2-optimal strategy with finite support in $f + \varepsilon g$, one has $v(f+\varepsilon g) \le f(\sigma_\varepsilon, \tau) + \varepsilon g(\sigma_\varepsilon, \tau) + \varepsilon^2$ and so $(v(f+\varepsilon g) - v(f))/\varepsilon \le g(\sigma_\varepsilon, \tau) + \varepsilon$. Then $g \in G$ implies that $\limsup_{\varepsilon \gtrsim 0}(v(f+\varepsilon g) - v(f))/\varepsilon \le \max_{\tilde\sigma} g(\tilde\sigma, \tau)$, where $\tilde\sigma$ ranges over the limit points of σ_ε. I.1, Ex. 3b, and I.1, Ex. 3c, p. 11, imply $\tilde\sigma \in \Sigma(f)$. Thus $\limsup_{\varepsilon \gtrsim 0}(v(f+\varepsilon g) - v(f))/\varepsilon \le \min_{\tau \in \mathscr{T}(f)} \max_{\tilde\sigma \in \Sigma(f)} g(\tilde\sigma, \tau) = v_f(g)$.

b. If $f + \varepsilon g$ is real-valued and satisfies the assumptions of Theorem I.1.1 for $0 \le \varepsilon \le \varepsilon_0$ (e.g., is concave in s and convex in t), one does not need $g \in G$: the above argument holds also in pure strategies, where the results $\Sigma(f)$ and $\mathscr{T}(f)$ are interpreted as pure strategy sets.

HINT. Since $\Sigma(f)$ and $\mathscr{T}(f)$ are compact convex, $(f+\varepsilon g)_{|\Sigma(f)\times\mathscr{T}(f)}$ also satisfies the assumptions of Theorem I.1.1. But f is constant on $\Sigma(f) \times \mathscr{T}(f)$, and so $g_{|\Sigma(f)\times\mathscr{T}(f)}$ satisfies them. Let now $h = f + \varepsilon_0 g$, and use the arguments of I.1, Ex. 6a for $f + \varepsilon h$, plus the above remark and homogeneity.

c. Assume that $h_\varepsilon \in V$ and $(h_\varepsilon - h_0)/\varepsilon \to g \in G$, in the sense that, like in I.1, Ex. 3, p. 11, there exists, for each σ and τ, $\varphi_\varepsilon(s, \tau)$ u.s.c. in s and decreasing to $g(s, \tau)$ and $\psi_\varepsilon(\sigma, t)$ l.s.c. in t and increasing to $g(\sigma, t)$ such that $h_\varepsilon(s, \tau) \le h_0(s, \tau) + \varepsilon\varphi_\varepsilon(s, \tau)$ and $h_\varepsilon(\sigma, t) \ge h_0(\sigma, t) + \varepsilon\psi_\varepsilon(\sigma, t)$. Then $\left[v(h_\varepsilon) - v(h_0)\right]/\varepsilon \to v_{h_0}(g)$.

HINT. Argue as in I.1, Ex. 6a.

d.

- One can use in I.1, Ex. 6c the homogeneity as was done in I.1, Ex. 6b, using the conditions $h_\varepsilon(s, \tau) \le (1 - \varepsilon A)h_0(s, \tau) + \varepsilon\varphi_\varepsilon(s, \tau)$ and $h_\varepsilon(\sigma, t) \ge (1 - \varepsilon A)h_0(\sigma, t) + \varepsilon\psi_\varepsilon(\sigma, t)$ (A arbitrary) instead of the above with $A = 0$, to obtain $(v(h_\varepsilon) - v(h_0))/\varepsilon \to v_{h_0}(g) - Av(h_0)$ (since $h_0(\sigma, \tau)$ is not necessarily defined, even on $\Sigma_{h_0} \times \mathscr{T}_{h_0}$, one does not obtain as in I.1, Ex. 6b that this limit equals $v_{h_0}(g - Ah_0)$).
- Similarly, I.1, Ex. 6b can be extended: if f_ε satisfies the assumptions of Theorem I.1.1, p. 5, for $0 \le \varepsilon < \varepsilon_0$, and if for A sufficiently large, $(f_\varepsilon - f_0)/\varepsilon + Af_0 \to g + Af_0$ (in the sense of I.1, Ex. 3), then $[v(f_\varepsilon) - v(f_0)]/\varepsilon \to v_{f_0}(g)$.

e. In fact, closer inspection of the proof shows that much less is needed: assume $f_\varepsilon(s, t)$ and $g(s, t)$ are real-valued, such that f_ε (for $0 \le \varepsilon < \varepsilon_0$) satisfies the assumptions of Theorem I.1.1, and such that (letting O denote an open set):

$$\forall t,\ \forall s_0,\ \forall \delta > 0,\ \exists \varepsilon_0 > 0,\ \exists O : s_0 \in O \subseteq S,\ \exists A > 0 :\ \forall s \in O,\ \forall \varepsilon < \varepsilon_0$$

$$[f_\varepsilon(s, t) - f_0(s, t)]/\varepsilon < g(s_0, t) + A[\max_x f_0(x, t) - f_0(s, t)] + \delta$$

and the dual condition. Then $g_{|S(f_0)\times T(f_0)}$ satisfies the assumptions of Theorem I.1.1, and $[v(f_\varepsilon) - v(f_0)]/\varepsilon \to v_{f_0}(g)$.

HINT. Establish the first statement, and that $f_\varepsilon \to f_0$ (I.1, Ex. 3), and that there exist $\varphi_{\varepsilon,A}(s,t)$ that are u.s.c. in s, decreasing in ε ($\varepsilon \to 0$) and A ($A \to +\infty$), such that $(f_\varepsilon(s,t) - f_0(s,t))/\varepsilon + Af_0(s,t) - Av(f_0) \le \varphi_{\varepsilon,A}(s,t)$, and such that for $t \in T(f_0)$ $\lim_{\substack{\varepsilon\to 0\\ A\to+\infty}} \varphi_{\varepsilon,A}(s,t) \le g(s,t)$. Finally show $[v(f_\varepsilon) - v(f_0)]/\varepsilon \le [f_\varepsilon(s_\varepsilon,t) - f_0(s_\varepsilon,t)]/\varepsilon + Af_0(s_\varepsilon,t) - Av(f_0)$, for $\varepsilon A \le 1$, $t \in T(f_0)$ and $s_\varepsilon \in S(f_\varepsilon)$, and argue as above.

Remark I.1.17. Thus I.1, Ex. 6e is by far the "best" result, and I.1, Ex. 6c and I.1, Ex. 6d should be applied only in cases where I.1, Ex. 6e is not applicable, a.o. because the mixed extension of the game is not defined or lacks the proper u.s.c.-l.s.c. properties. The next exercise shows such cases are bound to be very rare.

7. Let S and T be compact metric spaces, f a bounded real-valued function on $S \times T$ such that $f(\cdot, t)$ is u.s.c. for each t and $f(s, \cdot)$ is l.s.c. for each s.

a. Show that f is Borel-measurable. (Hence $f(\sigma, \tau)$ is unambiguous, and the assumptions of Proposition I.2.4, p. 21, are satisfied.)

HINT. Find an increasing sequence of functions converging pointwise to f, where for each function in the sequence there is some partition of T with the function being constant in t on each partition element.

b. Show that $f(\sigma, \tau)$ is u.s.c. on Σ for each $\tau \in \mathscr{T}$ and l.s.c. on $\mathscr{T}$ for each $\sigma \in \Sigma$.

HINT. Use Fubini's theorem and Fatou's lemma.

c. If measurability is known, I.1, Ex. 7b also follows without the metrizability assumption, but by assuming just strict semi-compactness (the closure of a subset is the set of limit points of convergent sequences in the subset). Most compact subsets of topological vector spaces have this property (Grothendieck, 1953).

8. Often, the result of I.1, Ex. 6 strengthens itself in the following way. Assume, e.g., we are working on a finite dimensional subspace of games, and we know (e.g., by I.1, Ex. 1) that the function v is Lipschitz on this subspace. Then we have: if a Lipschitz function $f\colon \mathbb{R}^n \to \mathbb{R}$ is such that $f'_x(y) = \lim_{\varepsilon \gtrsim 0}\big(f(x+\varepsilon y) - f(x)\big)/\varepsilon$ exists for all x and y, then $f'_x(\cdot)$ is Lipschitz and is a "true" differential, i.e., $F(y) = f(x+y) - f(x) - f'_x(y)$ is differentiable at zero (with zero differential: $\lim_{\varepsilon\to 0}\sup_{0<\|y\|\le\varepsilon} |F(y)| \,/\, \|y\| = 0$).

9.

a. The Lipschitz condition in I.1, Ex. 8 is necessary: on $[0,1]^2$, $F(x,y) = x^3y/(x^4 + y^2)$ is analytic except at zero, and is Lipschitz at zero: $0 \le F(x,y) \le \frac{1}{2}\|(x,y)\|$, and has all its directional derivatives zero (thus linear) at zero, yet $F(t,t^2) = \frac{1}{2}t$: F is not differentiable at zero.

b. u.s.c.-l.s.c. functions occur quite easily, e.g., on $[0,1]^2$: $F(0,0) = 0$, $F(x,y) = (y-x)/(y+x)$.

c. The boundedness condition in I.1, Ex. 7b is really needed: even with separate continuity (where the metrizability condition in I.1, Ex. 7 become superfluous, cf. I.2, Ex. 1, p. 24), define F on $[0,1]^2$ by $F(0,0) = 0$, $F(x,y) = xy/(x^3 + y^3)$. Show that the mixed extension (which always exists by I.1, Ex. 7a using just positivity), although being jointly lower semi-continuous (F being so), is not separately u.s.c.

Show also that, for real-valued measurable functions, boundedness of the function is equivalent to finiteness of the mixed extension (i.e., (absolute) integrability for every product probability).

10. Compactness of $\Delta(X)$ for compact X. (Mertens, 1986)
Denote by C the convex cone of bounded l.s.c. functions on a compact space X and let $E = C - C$. Denote by P the set of monotone functions on C satisfying:

- $p(tf) = tp(f)$ for $t \geq 0$ and
- $p(f + g) \leq p(f) + p(g)$.

P is ordered in the usual way. Let $M(X)$ be the set of minimal elements of P.
a. $\forall p \in P, \exists \mu \in M(X) : \mu \leq p$.

HINT. Given $\alpha \leq 0$, $f \geq \alpha$ and $q \leq p$, one has $p(f) \geq q(f) \geq q(\alpha) \geq -q(-\alpha) \geq -p(-\alpha)$, and hence the set of possible values for $q(f)$ is a bounded interval: use Zorn's lemma.

b. Any μ in $M(X)$ can be identified with a positive linear functional on E satisfying:

$$\mu(f) = \inf\{\, \mu(g) \mid g \in C,\ g \geq f \,\}.$$

HINT. $\widetilde{\mu}$ defined by the above right-hand member satisfies *i*) and *ii*) and coincides with μ on C. Use Hahn–Banach to get a positive linear functional $\zeta \leq \widetilde{\mu}$. This ζ is unique, otherwise μ would not be minimal on C, and hence, using again Hahn–Banach, coincides with $\widetilde{\mu}$.

c. $M(X)$ is the set of regular Borel measures on X.

HINT. Follows from a Daniell-type extension:

If f_n is an increasing sequence in C, $\mu(\lim f_n) = \lim \mu(f_n)$, (use Dini, cf. Meyer (1966, X.6) and I.1, Ex. 10b). Define μ^* on the set F of real bounded functions on X by $\mu^*(f) = \inf\{\, \mu(g) \mid g \in C,\ g \geq f \,\}$. Then:

$$\mu^*(f + g) \leq \mu^*(f \vee g) + \mu^*(f \wedge g)) \leq \mu^*(f) + \mu^*(g),$$

and if f_n is an increasing sequence in F, $\mu^*(\lim f_n) = \lim \mu^*(f_n)$.

Define $L = \{\, f \in F \mid \mu^*(f) + \mu^*(-f) \leq 0 \,\}$. L is a vector space and μ^* a linear functional on it. Given O and U open in X, $\mathbb{1}_O$ and $\mathbb{1}_{O \cap U}$ are in L, hence also $\mathbb{1}_{O \setminus U}$ with: $\mu^*(O) = \mu^*(O \cap U) + \mu^*(O \setminus U)$, and hence for any subset A: $\mu^*(A) \geq \mu^*(A \cap U) + \mu^*(A \setminus U)$, so that any open set U is μ^*-measurable; hence all Borel sets are also μ^*-measurable.

Finally since $\mu^*(A) = \sup\{\, \mu(F) \mid F \subseteq A,\ F \text{ closed} \,\}$, and X is compact, μ^* defines a regular Borel measure (unique since equal to μ on open sets).

d. For all $t > 0$, the sets $\{\, \mu \mid \mu \in \Delta(X),\ \mu(1) = t \,\}$ and $\{\, \mu \mid \mu \in \Delta(X),\ \mu(1) \leq t \,\}$ are closed and compact (recall Proposition I.1.4).

HINT. It suffices to prove the compactness of the second set. Given an ultrafilter on it, let φ denote its point-wise limit in the set of positive linear functionals on E. By I.1, Ex. 10a, there exists $\nu \in \Delta(X)$ with $\nu \leq \varphi$ on C: ν is a limit point in $\Delta(X)$.

I.2. COMPLEMENTS TO THE MINMAX THEOREM

This section gives a number of more specialized "how to use" tricks and other complements to the minmax theorem of Section I.1 and to its "usual" form (Proposition I.2.4, p. 21).

I.2.a. The Topology on S

Since there is no Hausdorff requirement, Proposition I.1.9 just asks that S be compact when endowed with the coarsest topology for which the functions $f(\cdot, t)$ are u.s.c. This is equivalent (Mertens, 1986, Remark 1, p. 247) to asking that any pointwise limit of pure strategies, i.e., of functions $f(s, \cdot)$, be dominated (i.e., smaller on T) by some pure strategy. Using the "countably compact" version, this can even be further weakened to: for any countable subset T_0 of T, and any sequence $s_i \in S$, there exists $s_0 \in S$ such that, for all $t \in T_0$, $\liminf_{i\to\infty} f(s_i, t) \leq f(s_0, t)$ (Mertens, 1986, Remark 3, p. 247).

I.2.b. Lack of Continuity: Regularization

Here we consider the case where the u.s.c. or compactness condition is not met.

Definition I.2.1. Let $(\Omega, \mathscr{A})$ denote a measurable space, and Σ a class of probability measures on $(\Omega, \mathscr{A})$. The "support function" $\phi_{\mathscr{F}}(\sigma)$ of a class $\mathscr{F}$ of extended real-valued functions on Ω is defined on Σ by

$$\phi_{\mathscr{F}}(\sigma) = \inf_{f\in\mathscr{F}} \int_{\star} f \, d\sigma,$$

where $\int_\star$ denotes the lower integral ($\int_\star f\,d\sigma = \sup\{ \int h\,d\sigma \mid h \leq f, h$ measurable and bounded from above $\}$).

Definition I.2.2. Let, for each measurable set B, $\mathscr{F}_B = \{ f_{|B} \mid f \in \mathscr{F} \}$. Denote by $co(\mathscr{F})$ the convex hull of the set of bounded functions minorated by some element of $\mathscr{F}$, and by $m(\mathscr{F})$ the "monotone (decreasing) class" generated by $\mathscr{F}$, i.e., the smallest class of functions containing $\mathscr{F}$ and containing the limit of every decreasing sequence in $m(\mathscr{F})$. Let finally $D(\mathscr{F})$ (or $D_\Sigma(\mathscr{F})$) be such that:

$$D(\mathscr{F}) = \{f \text{ bounded from above} \mid \forall\sigma\in\Sigma, \exists B\in\mathscr{A} : \sigma(B) = 1, f_{|B}\in m(co(\mathscr{F}_B))\}$$

$D(\mathscr{F})$ stands for the decreasing class generated by $\mathscr{F}$.

Lemma I.2.1. *$D(\mathscr{F}) \subseteq \{ g$ bounded from above $\mid \int_\star g\,d\sigma \geq \phi_{\mathscr{F}}(\sigma)\ \forall\sigma \in \Sigma \}$, with equality if:*

(1) *all functions in $\mathscr{F}$ are σ-measurable and σ-a.e. bounded from above, for all $\sigma \in \Sigma$,*
(2) *Σ contains every probability measure that is absolutely continuous w.r.t. some $\sigma \in \Sigma$.*

Proof. We first show inclusion. It suffices to show that:

$$g \in m(co(\mathscr{F})) \implies \int_\star g\,d\sigma \geq \phi_{\mathscr{F}}(\sigma)$$

(applying then this result to some set B with $\sigma(B) = 1$). This follows from the standard properties of the lower integral (note that any decreasing sequence in $m(co(\mathscr{F}))$ is uniformly bounded from above).

We turn now to the other inclusion. It will be sufficient to prove that, for bounded g satisfying $\int_\star g\, d\sigma \geq \phi_{\mathscr{F}}(\sigma)$ for all $\sigma \in \Sigma$, one has $g \in D(\mathscr{F})$, since, for any other g, one will then have $g \vee (-n) \in D(\mathscr{F})$ for all n, hence, $g \in D(\mathscr{F})$, $D(\mathscr{F})$ being a monotone class. (In fact, assume $g_n \in D(\mathscr{F})$ decreases to g; let $\sigma(B_n) = 1$, $h_n \in m(co(\mathscr{F}_{B_n})) : h_n \leq g_{n|B_n}$. For $B = \bigcap_n B_n$, one has $\sigma(B) = 1$ and $m(co(\mathscr{F}_B)) \supseteq [m(co(\mathscr{F}_{B_n}))]_{|B}$, so $h_{n|B} \in m(co(\mathscr{F}_B))$ and, for some constant K, $h_{n|B} \leq g_{n|B} \leq K$, so $h = \lim_{k\to\infty} \sup_{n\geq k} h_{n|B} \in m(co(\mathscr{F}_B))$ and $h \leq g_{|B}$.)

Now fix σ, and let $\tilde{g} \in L_\infty(\sigma)$ stand for the (σ-)essential supremum of the measurable functions smaller than g. Note that, for any non-negative measure μ in $L_1(\sigma)$, i.e., bounded and absolutely continuous w.r.t. σ: $\int \tilde{g}\, d\mu \geq \inf_{f\in\mathscr{F}} \int f\, d\mu$ since, by assumption, $(\mu/\|\mu\|) \in \Sigma$.

Now, if $\mu \in L_1(\sigma)$ has a non-zero negative part μ^-, consider the Hahn decomposition $\mu = \mu^+ - \mu^-$, $\mu^+ \geq 0$, $\mu^- \geq 0$, $\mu^+(B_-) = 0$, $\mu^-(B_+) = 0$, B_+ and B_- measurable, $B_+ \cap B_- = \phi$. Fix $f_0 \in \mathscr{F}$ ($f_0 \leq K$ μ-a.e.), and let $f_n = f_0^+ + n\mathbb{1}_{B_-}$; we have $f_n \in \mathscr{L}_\infty(\sigma)$, $f_n \geq f_0 \in \mathscr{F}$, and $\mu(f_n) = \mu(f_0^+) + n\mu^-(B_-) \to -\infty$. Therefore, if $G = \{\, g \in \mathscr{L}_\infty(\sigma)$ and is bounded below $\mid \exists f \in \mathscr{F} : f \leq g \,\}$, we have, for all $\mu \in L_1(\sigma)$, $\int \tilde{g}\, d\mu \geq \inf_G \int g\, d\mu$. Thus, $\tilde{g}$ belongs, by the Hahn–Banach theorem (I.1.e), to the $\sigma(L_\infty, L_1)$-closed convex hull of G. Denote by G^c the convex hull of G, and by $G^{c,m}$ the "monotone class" spanned by G^c, i.e., the smallest class of functions containing G^c and such that $f_n \in G^{c,m}$, f_n decreasing to f, f bounded below imply $f \in G^{c,m}$ (thus $G^{c,m}$ consists of those functions of $m(G^c)$ that are bounded below). Note that $G^{c,m}$ is convex, and $G^{c,m} + \mathscr{L}_\infty^+(\sigma) \subseteq G^{c,m}$.

Denote by H the image of $G^{c,m}$ in $L_\infty(\sigma)$, i.e., the set of equivalence classes of $G^{c,m}$. H is still convex, $H + L_\infty^+(\sigma) \subseteq H$, and $f_n \in H$, $\sup_n \|f_n\|_{L_\infty} < +\infty$ implies $\limsup_{n\to\infty} f_n \in H$. Indeed, if $g_n \in G^{c,m}$ belongs to the equivalence class of f_n, if $M = \sup_n \|f_n\|_{L_\infty}$, if $B_n = \{\, s \mid g_n(s) > M \,\}$, and if $h_n = (\sup_{k\geq n} g_k) \vee (-M)$, then h_n decreases everywhere to some element h of the equivalence class $\limsup_{n\to\infty} f_n$, h is bounded from below, and $\{h_1 > M\} \subseteq B = \bigcup_n B_n$. Since $\sigma(B) = 0$ and since $h_n \geq g_n \in G^{c,m}$, we have indeed $h_n \in G^{c,m}$ and thus $h \in G^{c,m}$, so $\limsup f_n \in H$.

We have seen that $\tilde{g}$ belongs to the weak*, i.e., $\sigma(L_\infty, L_1)$-closure of H. We will now show that H is weak*-closed, so it will follow that $\tilde{g}$ is the equivalence class of some element $\overline{g}$ of $G^{c,m}$: there exists $\overline{g} \in G^{c,m}$, $\overline{g} \leq g$, except on a σ-negligible set.

We want thus to show that a convex subset H of L_∞ is weak*-closed if ($f_n \in H, \sup_n \|f_n\|_{L_\infty} < +\infty$ implies $\limsup f_n \in H$). By the Krein–Smulian theorem on weak*-closed convex sets (Kelley et al., 1963, p. 212), since H is convex in the dual L_∞ of the Banach space L_1, it is sufficient to show that the intersection of H with any ball is weak*-closed: we can assume that $\sup_{f\in H} \|f\|_\infty = R < +\infty$. Further, it is sufficient to prove that H is

$\tau(L_\infty, L_1)$-closed (Kelley et al., 1963, p. 154, Th. 17.1). But the Mackey topology $\tau(L_\infty, L_1)$ is finer than any L_p topology, hence a fortiori finer than the topology of convergence in measure. (In fact, they coincide on bounded subsets of L_∞; cf. I.2, Ex. 12, p. 28). Since this topology is metrizable, and since, from any sequence that converges in probability, one can extract an a.e. convergent subsequence, it is sufficient to show that if a sequence f_n in H converges a.e. to f then f (= $\limsup f_n$ a.e.) belongs to H, which is our basic property of H. Thus, for some $\overline{g} \in G^{c,m}$, and some measurable set B_0 with $\sigma(B_0) = 1$, we have $\overline{g} \leq g$ everywhere on B_0.

Note now that, given a set G of functions, the union of the monotone classes generated by all countable subsets of G is a monotone class (because a countable union of countable subsets is still countable) and hence is the monotone class spanned by G. Thus $\overline{g}$ belongs to the monotone class spanned by a sequence $g_n \in G^c$, and each g_n is a convex combination of finitely many $g_{n,i} \in G$. Since $g_{n,i} \in \mathscr{L}_\infty(\sigma)$, there exists $B_{n,i} \in \mathscr{A}$ with $\sigma(B_{n,i}) = 1$ such that $g_{n,i|B_{n,i}}$ is bounded and $\mathscr{A}$-measurable. Choose also $f_{n,i} \in \mathscr{F}$, $f_{n,i} \leq g_{n,i}$: for $B = B_0 \cap (\bigcap_{n,i} B_{n,i})$; we have $B \in \mathscr{A}$, $\sigma(B) = 1$, $g_{n,i|B}$ is bounded, measurable, and $\geq f_{n,i|B}$: thus $g_{n|B} \in co(\mathscr{F}_B)$ and $\overline{g}_{|B} \in m(co(\mathscr{F}_B))$ with $\overline{g}_{|B} \leq g_{|B}$. Since such a construction is possible for each $\sigma \in \Sigma$, we have indeed $g \in D_\Sigma(\mathscr{F})$. ■

Given a function g on $S \times T$, let, for all $\tau \in \mathscr{T}_f$, $\phi_\tau(s) = \limsup_{s' \to s} g(s', \tau)$, and let $D(g) = D\{\phi_\tau \mid \tau \in \mathscr{T}_f\}$. We define similarly $I(g)$ (I for increasing), reversing the roles of S and T and the order on the reals.

Proposition I.2.2. *Let S be a compact topological space, T any set. Assume, for all $t \in T$, $g(\cdot, t) \in D(g)$. Then:*

$$\max_{\sigma \in \Sigma} \inf_{\tau \in \mathscr{T}_f} \int g(s,t)\, d(\sigma \otimes \tau) = \inf_{\tau \in \mathscr{T}_f} \sup_{\sigma \in \Sigma} \int g(s,t)\, d(\sigma \otimes \tau)\,.$$

Proof. Proposition I.1.9 can be applied to the game $\phi_\tau(s)$; one obtains pure strategies τ because $\phi_\tau(s)$ is convex in τ. Lemma I.2.1 yields then that the same optimal strategy σ guarantees the same amount against g, hence the result. ■

Remark I.2.3. The convexity in τ of $\phi_\tau(s)$ implies that the convexification in the definition of D will be superfluous: one would equivalently obtain D if, instead of using $m(co(\mathscr{F}))$, one just stabilized the set of functions $\{\phi_\tau \mid \tau \in \mathscr{T}_f\}$ under the $\limsup$ of sequences that are uniformly bounded from above.

Remark I.2.4. When the payoff function g is uniformly bounded from above, as in many applications, one does not even have to stabilize: one could equivalently just define $G = \{\limsup_{n\to\infty} \phi_{\tau_n} \mid \tau_n \in \mathscr{T}_f\}$, and $D = \{h \mid \forall \sigma \in \Sigma,\ \exists f \in G\colon f \leq h\ \sigma\text{-a.e.}\}$. Indeed, take $f \in m(co(\mathscr{F}_B))$, $f \leq h_{|B}$, $\sigma(B) = 1$. Then, clearly f belongs to the closure of $co(\mathscr{F}_B)$ for the topology of convergence in measure; i.e., since $\sigma(B) = 1$, the equivalence class of f belongs to the closure of $co(\mathscr{F})$. Thus, f is the limit in measure of a sequence in $co(\mathscr{F})$, hence the limit of a σ-a.e. convergent sequence $f_n \in co(\mathscr{F})$. Each

f_n is minorated by some ϕ_{τ_n}, hence $\limsup_{n\to\infty} \phi_{\tau_n} \leq h \quad \sigma -$ a.e. Since the payoff function is uniformly bounded from above, the sequence ϕ_{τ_n} is also.

Remark I.2.5. Further, in most actual applications (cf. Exercises), the σ-a.e. aspect in the definition of D is not needed. Thus this is the form in which the criterion is most often used: show that, for each $t \in T$, there exists a sequence $\tau_n \in \mathscr{T}_f$ such that $\limsup_{n\to\infty} \phi_{\tau_n}(\cdot) \leq g(\cdot, t)$ (and such that $\phi_{\tau_n}(\cdot)$ is uniformly bounded from above if g is not).

Remark I.2.6. Only the "obvious part" (monotone convergence theorem) of the lemma was needed. The hard part shows that the above simple use of the monotone convergence theorem (or of Fatou's lemma) is as powerful as the more sophisticated closure methods, as used for instance in (Karlin, 1950). Indeed, any such closure method will only yield functions satisfying, for all σ, $\int_\star f\, d\sigma \geq \inf_\tau \int \phi_\tau\, d\sigma$.

I.2.c. Lack of Compactness: Approximation

When also S is not necessarily compact, the previous ideas can be combined with an old idea going back to Wald (1950) that compactness is not really necessary, but is only an appropriate form of precompactness (but in the uniform topology), and in fact a one-sided form, as was later observed.

Since, however, our typical assumptions are much weaker than a joint continuity of the payoff function, the typical compactness that we have is not in the uniform topology, not even a one-sided form, so we retain from this precompactness only the one-sided uniform approximation by another game with a compact (and not necessarily finite) strategy space: we will let the function ϕ vary with ε and use compact subsets Σ_ε of Σ.

Proposition I.2.3. *Assume that, for all $\varepsilon > 0$, there exists a compact convex subset Σ_ε of Σ, and a function $\phi_\varepsilon : S \times \mathscr{T}_f \to \mathbb{R} \cup \{-\infty\}$ such that:*

(1) *$\phi_\varepsilon(s, \tau)$ is u.s.c. in s and convex in τ.*
(2) *For all $t \in T$, $g(\cdot, t) \in D_{\Sigma_\varepsilon}\{\phi_\varepsilon(\cdot, \tau) \mid \tau \in \mathscr{T}_f\}$.*
(3) *For all $s \in S$, there exists $\sigma_s \in \Sigma_\varepsilon$ such that $g(s, \tau) \leq \int \phi_\varepsilon(\cdot, \tau)\, d\sigma_s + \varepsilon$, for all τ.*

Then:

$$\sup_{\Sigma} \inf_{\mathscr{T}_f} \int g(s,t)\, d(\sigma \otimes \tau) = \inf_{\mathscr{T}_f} \sup_{\Sigma} \int g(s,t)\, d(\sigma \otimes \tau).$$

Proof. Apply Proposition I.1.3, p. 6, to ϕ_ε, on $\Sigma_\varepsilon \times \mathscr{T}_f$; let v_ε, σ_ε, and τ_ε be the corresponding value and optimal strategies. By (2) and Lemma I.2.1, σ_ε still guarantees v_ε against $\mathscr{T}_f$ in the game g. By (3), τ_ε guarantees $v_\varepsilon + \varepsilon$ against S in g. This being true for all ε, the value v exists and σ_ε and τ_ε are ε-optimal strategies. ∎

Remark I.2.7. Typically one thinks of Σ_ε as the set of probabilities on a compact subset S_ε of S.

Remark I.2.8. The previous proposition was the particular case where σ_s was the unit mass at s and ϕ_ε was independent of ε.

Remark I.2.9. Point (3) and the compactness of Σ_ε, together with the upper semi-continuity of ϕ_ε, imply that any limit of functions $g(s,\cdot)$ on $\mathscr{T}_f$ is ε-dominated by some function $\phi_\varepsilon(\sigma,\cdot)$.

Remark I.2.10. This last condition (together with (2)) is in principle sufficient, barring some measurability problems: use first Proposition I.1.9, p. 9, to solve the game where player I's strategy set is the set of all limits of functions $g(s,\cdot)$. Let σ_0 be his optimal strategy in this game and v the value. If one could select in a measurable way for each limit function a σ such that $\phi_\varepsilon(\sigma,\cdot)$ ε-dominates the function, one could use this selection to map σ_0 to some $\tilde{\sigma}_0 \in \Sigma$, which guarantees in the game ϕ_ε at least $v-\varepsilon$. By (2), $\tilde{\sigma}_0$ will also guarantee $v-\varepsilon$ in g, hence will be an ε-optimal strategy in g.

Even without such a measurable selection, one might, e.g., attempt to define a mixed strategy as some auxiliary probability space (here σ_0), together with a map from there to the strategy space (here an arbitrary, non-measurable selection), such that player I guarantees himself $v-\varepsilon$ in the sense of lower integrals.

I.2.d. Measurability: Symmetric Case

The right-hand member (and thus the left-hand member) in the equality of the above propositions is not increased if Σ is replaced by the space $\tilde{\Sigma}$ of all order-preserving linear functionals of norm 1 on the cone of functions on S generated by the functions $g(\cdot,t)$ and the constants. That is to say that this quantity is an unambiguous upper bound for any evaluation of the game (because symmetrically player II's strategies are of the most restricted type (finite support)). Denote by $\mathscr{T}_B$ the set of all probability measures on some σ-field B on T, and let $F(\sigma,\tau)=\int_T d\tau \int_S g(s,t)\,d\sigma$, where the integral on T is understood to be a lower integral. Then:

$$\max_{\sigma\in\Sigma}\inf_{\tau\in\mathscr{T}_B} F(\sigma,\tau)=\inf_{\tau\in\mathscr{T}_f}\sup_{\sigma\in\tilde{\Sigma}} F(\sigma,\tau).$$

Thus the possible discrepancy between upper and lower bounds apparently depends more on the order of integration than on the allowed strategy spaces.

Although those propositions are a basic tool in proving that a game has a value, the above shows well why they do not assert per se that the game in question has a value: the value might in general depend on the order of integration, or, in other words, on the greater or lesser generality of mixed strategies allowed for each player. The next propositions show some cases where this ambiguity can be relieved completely. (A less "complete" (cf. I.2, Ex. 11, p. 27) way of relieving it would be to add to the previous assumptions some measurability requirement and use Fubini's theorem to obtain the minmax theorem directly on the mixed extension.) Obviously one would very much prefer to be able to dispense with the hypotheses in the next theorem; cf. Mertens (1986) for the importance of this question, and why this would yield a completely "intrinsic" theorem.

Theorem I.2.4. *Assume S and T are compact, and g is real-valued and bounded from below or from above. Assume further that $g(s,\cdot)$ is lower semi-continuous on T for each $s \in S$, and $g(\cdot,t)$ is upper semi-continuous on S for each $t \in T$. Then under any one of the following three hypotheses:*

(1) *g is $\mu \otimes \nu$ measurable for any regular product probability on the Borel sets of $S \times T$,*
(2) *one of the two spaces has a countable basis,*
(3) *one of the two spaces is Hausdorff,*

one has:

$$\sup_{\sigma \in \Sigma_f} \inf_{t \in T} \int g(s,t)\, d\sigma = \inf_{\tau \in \mathscr{T}_f} \sup_{s \in S} \int g(s,t)\, d\tau.$$

Further, each player obviously has an optimal strategy in the form of a regular probability.

Proof. In case (1), Proposition I.1.9, p. 9, applied both ways, yields the existence of an upper value $\overline{v}$ that player I can guarantee with a regular probability μ and player II with probabilities with finite support, and of a lower value $\underline{v}$ that player II can guarantee with a regular probability ν and player I with probabilities with finite support. $\int_S g(s,t)\,\mu(ds) \geq \overline{v}$ implies $\int_T \nu(dt) \int_S g(s,t)\,\mu(ds) \geq \overline{v}$ and, similarly, $\int_T g(s,t)\,\nu(dt) \leq \underline{v}$ implies $\int_S \mu(ds) \int_T g(s,t)\nu(dt) \leq \underline{v}$. By the measurability and boundedness assumptions of g, we can apply Fubini's theorem: $\overline{v} \leq \int_T d\nu \int_S g\, d\mu = \int_S d\mu \int_T g\, d\nu \leq \underline{v}$. But, by their very definition $\underline{v} \leq \overline{v}$ (they are $\sup\inf$ and $\inf\sup$ of the game played in strategies with finite support), the proof is complete in this case.

Suppose now that (2) holds; we shall prove that in this case g is Borel and so (1) applies. Assume that T has a countable basis O_n, and define:

$$f_n(s,t) = \begin{cases} -\infty, & \text{for } t \notin O_n \\ \inf_{t' \in O_n} f(s,t'), & \text{otherwise.} \end{cases}$$

Then f_n is Borel (since u.s.c. in s) and $g_n = \max_{k \leq n} f_n$ is an increasing sequence converging to f (since l.s.c. in t).

It remains to consider case (3). Hence assume T Hausdorff. We will first construct a countable set of best replies. Let $\mathscr{T}_n = \{\, \tau \in \mathscr{T}_f \mid \#\operatorname{Supp}(\tau) \leq n \,\}$. Denote by Φ_0 the set of continuous functions φ on T such that there exists $s \in S$ with $f(s,\cdot) \geq \varphi(\cdot)$ on T. Since $\overline{v} \leq \inf_{\tau \in \mathscr{T}_n} \sup_{\varphi \in \Phi_0} \int \varphi\, d\tau$, the following sets:

$O_{\varphi,k,n} = \{\tau \in \mathcal{T}_n \mid \int \varphi d\tau > \overline{v} - 1/k\}$, form for $\varphi \in \Phi_0$ and each fixed n and k, an open covering of the compact space $\mathcal{T}_n$. Denote by $\Phi_{k,n}$ the indices of a finite subcovering. Then $\Phi = \bigcup_{k,n} \Phi_{k,n}$ is a countable subset of Φ_0, such that $\overline{v} = \inf_{\tau \in \mathcal{T}_f} \sup_{\varphi \in \Phi} \int \varphi d\tau$. We now reduce the situation to one where (2) applies. If φ_i enumerates Φ, let us consider the function d on $T \times T$, defined by $d(t_1, t_2) = \sum_i 2^{-i} |\varphi_i(t_1) - \varphi_i(t_2)| / \|\varphi_i\|$. d defines a metrizable quotient space $\widetilde{T}$ of T, such that, if ψ denotes the quotient mapping, any $\varphi \in \Phi$ can be written as $g \circ \psi$, for some $g \in \Psi$, where Ψ denote the set of all g continuous on $\widetilde{T}$, such that for some $s \in S$, $g \circ \psi(.) \leq f(s, .)$ on T. Define $\widetilde{f}$ on $S \times \widetilde{T}$ by $\widetilde{f}(s, \widetilde{t}) = \sup\{ g(\widetilde{t}) \mid g \in C(\widetilde{T}), g \circ \psi(.) \leq f(s, .)\}$. Then we have:

$$\overline{v} \leq \inf_{\tau \in \mathcal{T}_f} \sup_{\varphi \in \Phi} \int \varphi \, d\tau \leq \inf_{\tau \in \mathcal{T}_f} \sup_{g \in \Psi} \int g \circ \psi(t) \, d\tau(t) \leq \inf_{\widetilde{\tau} \in \widetilde{\mathcal{T}}_f} \sup_{s \in S} \int \widetilde{f}(s, \widetilde{t}) \, d\widetilde{\tau}(\widetilde{t}).$$

Obviously $\widetilde{f}$ is l.s.c. on $\widetilde{T}$ for each $s \in S$, and is the largest such function satisfying $\widetilde{f}(s, \psi(t)) \leq f(s, t)$. Let $h(s, \widetilde{t}) = \inf\{ f(s, t) \mid t \in \psi^{-1}(\widetilde{t})\}$: to prove that $\widetilde{f}$ is u.s.c. on S, we will show that $\widetilde{f} = h$. This in turn follows from $h(s, .)$ being l.s.c. on $\widetilde{T}$ for each $s \in S$. In fact, $\widetilde{T}$ being metrizable, let $\widetilde{t}_i$ be a sequence converging to $\widetilde{t}$. Choose t_i such that $\psi(t_i) = \widetilde{t}_i$ and $f(s, t_i) \leq h(s, \widetilde{t}_i) + 1/i$, and let t be a limit point of the sequence t_i: we have $\psi(t) = \widetilde{t}$ and $h(s, \widetilde{t}) \leq f(s, t) \leq \liminf f(s, t_i) \leq \liminf h(s, \widetilde{t}_i)$, hence the required property. We then use the result under case (2) for $\widetilde{f}$ on $S \times \widetilde{T}$. It follows that $\overline{v} \leq \sup_{\sigma \in \Sigma_f} \inf_{\widetilde{t} \in \widetilde{T}} \int \widetilde{f}(s, \widetilde{t}) d\sigma(s) \leq \sup_{\sigma \in \Sigma_f} \inf_{t \in T} \int f(s, t) d\sigma(s)$, since $\widetilde{f}(s, \psi(t)) \leq f(s, t)$. This completes the proof of the proposition. ■

Remark I.2.11. When g is continuous in each variable no further assumptions are needed: either by using I.2, Ex. 1, p. 24, to show that condition (1) is satisfied or reducing to (3), by using, e.g., on S the coarsest topology for which all functions $g(\cdot, t)$ are continuous (and going to the quotient space) (cf. I.2, Ex. 11, p. 27, for an example showing that, even under such assumptions, compactness on both sides is really needed).

We obtain now the analogues to Propositions I.2.2, p. 18, and I.2.3, p. 19.

Proposition I.2.5. *Let S and T be compact. Assume $g(s, \cdot)$ and $g(\cdot, t)$ are bounded from below and from above resp. for all $s \in S$ and for all $t \in T$. Assume there also exists $f : S \times T \to \overline{\mathbb{R}}$, measurable for any regular product probability and bounded either from below or from above, and such that:*

$$f(s, \cdot) \in I(g) \qquad \forall s \in S$$

$$f(\cdot, t) \in D(g) \qquad \forall t \in T.$$

Then g has a value, and both players have ε-optimal strategies with finite support.

Proof. Is the same as the proof of Theorem I.2.4, but using Proposition I.2.2 instead of Proposition I.1.9. ■

Remark I.2.12. One usually takes f to be (some regularization of) g; cf. Exercises.

With the same proof as above one obtains:

Proposition I.2.6. *Assume, for all $\varepsilon > 0$, there exist compact, convex subsets Σ_ε and $\mathcal{T}_\varepsilon$ of Σ and $\mathcal{T}$ and functions $\phi_\varepsilon\colon S \times \mathcal{T}_f \to \mathbb{R} \cup \{-\infty\}$, $\psi_\varepsilon\colon \Sigma_f \times T \to \mathbb{R} \cup \{+\infty\}$, $f_\varepsilon\colon S \times T \to \overline{\mathbb{R}}$ such that:*

(1) *ϕ_ε is u.s.c. in s and convex in τ; ψ_ε is l.s.c. in t and concave in σ;*
(2) *f_ε is measurable for any regular product measure, and bounded from below or from above;*
(3) *for all $s \in S$, there exists $\sigma_s \in \Sigma_\varepsilon$ such that, for all $\tau \in T_f$,*

$$g(s, \tau) \leq \phi_\varepsilon(\sigma_s, \tau) + \varepsilon$$

and, for all $t \in T$, there exists $\tau_t \in \mathcal{T}_\varepsilon$ such that, for all $\sigma \in \Sigma_f$,

$$g(\sigma, t) \geq \psi_\varepsilon(\sigma, \tau_t) - \varepsilon;$$

(4) *$f_\varepsilon(\cdot, t) \in D_{\Sigma_\varepsilon}(\phi_\varepsilon)$ for all $t \in T$ and $f_\varepsilon(s, \cdot) \in I_{\mathcal{T}_\varepsilon}(\psi_\varepsilon)$ for all $s \in S$.*

Then g has a value, and both players have ε-optimal strategies with finite support.

Remark I.2.13. Theorem I.2.4 and Propositions I.2.5 and I.2.6 imply that each player has ε-optimal strategies that are safe against any type of mixed strategy of the other player (even finitely additive ones) no matter in what order the integrations are performed. Further, those mixed strategies are really "playable" in the sense that one can obviously realize the mixing with a finite number of coin tosses. That is why we say the game has a value.

I.2.e. Pure Optimal Strategies

Definition I.2.14. Call a function f defined on $S \times T$ **concave-like** (resp. **convex-like**) if, for any α $(0 < \alpha < 1)$ and for any s_1 and s_2 (resp. t_1 and t_2), there exists s_0 (resp. t_0) such that, for all t, $f(s_0, t) \geq \alpha f(s_1, t) + (1 - \alpha) f(s_2, t)$ (resp., for all s, $f(s, t_0) \leq \alpha f(s, t_1) + (1 - \alpha) f(s(t_2))$.

Proposition I.2.7. *Assume, in addition to the hypotheses of Proposition I.1.9, that g is concave-like (resp. convex-like). Then any strategy in Σ (resp. $\mathcal{T}_f$) is dominated by a pure strategy. In particular the (ε-)optimal strategy σ (resp. τ) may be taken as a point mass. In particular, if g is concave-like, there is an unambiguous value.*

Proof. It is sufficient to prove the first statement. Induction on the number of pure strategies used in a mixed strategy with finite support shows immediately that any mixed strategy with finite support is dominated by a pure strategy. This proves the proposition in case g is convex-like. If g is concave-like, consider a regular probability μ on S, and a finite subset T_0 of T: for any $\varepsilon > 0$, there exists a probability μ_{ε,T_0} with finite support on S, such that, for all $t \in T_0$, $\int_S g(s,t)\,d\mu_{\varepsilon,T_0} \geq \int_S g(s,t)\,d\mu - \varepsilon$; this follows, for instance, from the strong law of large numbers. But we know that μ_{ε,T_0} is dominated by a point mass, say, at s_{ε,T_0}: for all $t \in T_0$, $g(s_{\varepsilon,T_0},t) \geq \int_S g(s,t)\,d\mu - \varepsilon$. For all $t \in T$, let $S_{\varepsilon,t} = \{\, s \in S \mid g(s,t) \geq \int_S g(s,t)\,d\mu - \varepsilon \,\}$; thus the $S_{\varepsilon,t}$ are compact subsets of S, and we have just shown that any finite intersection of them is non-empty: therefore they have a non-empty intersection. Let $s_\mu \in \bigcap_{\varepsilon,t} S_{\varepsilon,t}$; for all $t \in T$, we have $g(s_\mu,t) \geq \int_S g(s,t)\,d\mu$; the strategy μ is thus dominated by the pure strategy s_μ. ■

Remark I.2.15. When g is both concave-like and convex-like, the above result is often referred to as Fan's theorem (1953). One could have deduced Proposition I.1.9 from it.

Remark I.2.16. Similarly, if g satisfies only the hypotheses of Proposition I.2.2, in addition to being concave-like (resp. convex-like), then σ (resp. τ) may still be taken as a point mass. Indeed, the above argument, taking μ as the optimal strategy σ, still yields that the sets $S_{\varepsilon,t} = \{\, s \in S \mid f(s,t) \geq \overline{v} - \varepsilon \,\}$ have non-empty finite intersections ($\overline{v}$ being the (upper) value given in Proposition I.2.2). Therefore, the compact sets $\overline{S}_{\varepsilon,t} = \{\, s \in S \mid \phi_t(s) \geq \overline{v} - \varepsilon \,\}$ have a non-empty intersection: let $s_0 \in \bigcap_{\varepsilon,t} \overline{S}_{\varepsilon,t}$; then, for all $t \in T$, $\phi_t(s_0) \geq \overline{v}$. Therefore, for all $g \in D(\phi)$, $g(s_0) \geq \overline{v}$, and s_0 is an optimal pure strategy.

EXERCISES

1.

a. Let S and T be two topological spaces, g a real-valued function defined on $S \times T$, continuous in each variable separately. Then g is μ-measurable for any regular probability measure μ on the Borel sets of $S \times T$.

HINT. It is sufficient to consider the case of bounded g, and by regularity the case of compact S and T, and further to consider that the topology on S (resp. T) is the coarsest for which every function $g(\cdot,t)$ (resp. $g(s,\cdot)$) is continuous.

Let F be any subset of T, and t_0 in the closure of F: then there exists (Kelley et al., 1963, th. 8.21) a sequence $t_i \in F$ converging to t_0. Therefore, $\int_S g(\cdot,t_i)\,d\mu \to \int_S g(\cdot,t_0)\,d\mu$ uniformly over every weakly (i.e., $\sigma(M,M^\star)$) compact subset of the space M of all bounded regular measures on S (using Dunford–Pettis' (e.g., Dunford and Schwartz, 1958, IV.8.11 and V.6.1) equi-integrability criterion for those subsets). Thus the mapping ϕ from T to the space $C(S)$ of continuous functions on S mapping $t \to g(\cdot,t)$ is injective and such that $\phi(\overline{F}) = \overline{\phi(F)}$ when $C(S)$ is endowed with the topology $\kappa(C(S),M)$ of uniform convergence on $\sigma(M,M^\star)$ compact subsets of M: ϕ is continuous, and $\phi(T)$ compact.

For any fixed probability $\mu \in M$, and every $f \in L_1(\mu)$, let $\psi(f) \in C(T)$ be defined by $[\psi(f)](t) = \int f(s)g(s,t)\,d\mu(s)$. Since the measures $f\,d\mu$ form a $\sigma(M,M^\star)$ compact subset of M when f ranges in the unit ball of $L_\infty(\mu)$, ψ will, by Ascoli's theorem, map the balls of $L_\infty(\mu)$ into norm-compact subsets of $C(T)$. Those being separable, and $L_\infty(\mu)$ being dense in $L_1(\mu)$, ψ will map $L_1(\mu)$ into a separable subspace of $C(T)$, i.e., in a space $C^\mu(T)$ of all continuous functions for some weaker pseudo-metrizable topology on T.

Let $S_\mu = \{\, s \mid g(s,\cdot) \in C^\mu(T) \,\}$, so that S_μ is a compact (pseudo-) metric subset of S. Let s_0 be any point in the support of μ; let O_α be the decreasing net of open neighborhoods of s_0, and $\mu_\alpha(A) = \mu(A \cap O_\alpha)/\mu(O_\alpha)$; we thus have $\lim_\alpha \int g(s,t)\,d\mu_\alpha = g(s_0,t)$ pointwise, and therefore weakly since each integral is in the closed convex extension of $\phi(T)$, which is weakly compact. Each approximating measure being in $\psi(L_1(\mu))$ and thus in the weakly closed space $C^{\mu}(T)$, we have $g(s_0, t) \in C^{\mu}(T)$; the support of μ is thus contained in S_{μ}. Now $C^{\mu}(T)$ is a Polish space (cf. Appendix A.5) in the norm topology, and thus its Borel subsets for the strong topology and for the weak topology coincide (cf. Appendix A.5.f). Thus μ can be considered as a measure on the Borel subsets of $C^{\mu}(T)$ with the strong topology. This being Polish, there exists a norm-compact subset K_{ε} of $C^{\mu}(T)$ with $\mu(K_{\varepsilon}) \geq 1-\varepsilon$. The set $K_{\varepsilon}^{\mu} = \{ s \mid g(s, \cdot) \in K^{\varepsilon} \}$ is a compact metric subset of S, with $\mu(K_{\varepsilon}^{\mu}) \geq 1-\varepsilon$, and the functions $g(s, \cdot)$, $s \in K_{\mu}^{\varepsilon}$, are equicontinuous on T (Ascoli's theorem): the restriction of g to $K_{\varepsilon}^{\mu} \times T$ is jointly continuous. For an arbitrary measure μ on $S \times T$, conclude by considering its marginal $\tilde{\mu}$ on S.

b. The above proof showed in particular that, if furthermore S is compact, g bounded, and μ a regular measure on T, then $\int g(s,t)d\mu$ is continuous on S.

HINT. Apply the proof in case T is furthermore compact.

c. Deduce from I.2, Ex. 1a, and I.2, Ex. 1b, that, if S and T are compact, and g bounded and separately continuous, the mixed extension $g(\sigma, \tau)$ is well defined, separately continuous, and bi-linear.

HINT. Use Fubini's theorem.

d. If S and T are compact, and f_{α} is a net of bounded separately continuous functions decreasing pointwise to zero, the mixed extension $f_{\alpha}(\sigma, \tau)$ does also.

HINT. Use I.2, Ex. 1b.

e. Conclude from I.2, Ex. 1d, that products of regular measures extend naturally to the σ-field generated by the limits of increasing nets of positive, separately continuous functions.

HINT. Consider first the case of S and T compact, and use the proof of Riesz's theorem (Kelley et al., 1963, p. 127).

2. Can one replace "convex" in Proposition I.1.3, p. 6, by convex-like? (Possibly with additional topological assumptions?)

3. Let S and T be compact metric spaces, g a bounded measurable function defined on $S \times T$, such that, if $E = \{ (s_0, t_0) \mid g(\cdot, t_0)$ is not continuous in s at s_0 or $g(s_0, \cdot)$ is not continuous in t at $t_0 \}$, then, for each s_0 and t_0, the sets $\{ t \mid (s_0, t) \in E \}$ and $\{ s \mid (s, t_0) \in E \}$ consist of at most one point (cf. I.2, Ex. 1, and I.2, Ex. 4, for the measurability requirement). For any $(s_0, t_0) \in S \times T$, let $\phi_1(s_0, t_0) = \limsup_{s \to s_0, s \neq s_0} g(s, t_0)$, $\phi_2(s_0, t_0) = \liminf_{t \neq t_0} g(s_0, t)$. If $\min(\phi_1, \phi_2) \leq g \leq \max(\phi_1, \phi_2)$, then Proposition I.2.5, p. 22, applies, with $f = g$ (using Remark I.2.5, p. 19). For examples of this type, cf. Karlin (1950, examples 1, 2, 3, and Remark 3). Even if this last condition does not hold, Proposition I.2.5 still applies, with $f = \max(\min(\phi_1, \phi_2), \min(g, \max(\phi_1, \phi_2))$ (or any f such that $\min(\phi_2, \max(g, \phi_1)) \leq f \leq \max(\phi_1, \min(g, \phi_2))$). The general game of timing of class II (Karlin, 1959, Vol. II, Chapter V, Exercise 20) falls into this category.

4. Let S and T be two topological spaces, g a real-valued function on $S \times T$, and denote by E the set of points of discontinuity of g. If, for every $(s_0, t_0) \in S \times T$, the sets $\{ s \mid (s, t_0) \in E\}$ and $\{ t \mid (s_0, t) \in E \}$ are at most countable, then g is measurable for any regular product probability $\sigma \otimes \tau$ on the Borel sets of $S \times T$.

HINT. Note that the set of points of discontinuity of a function is always an F_{σ}, a countable union of closed sets.

5. Let both S and T be the unit interval with its usual topology. Let g be a bounded real-valued function on $S \times T$ satisfying the condition of I.2, Ex. 4, and such that for each $t_0 \in T$, $g(\cdot, t_0)$ is lower semi-continuous from the left in s: $\liminf_{s \lesssim s_0} g(s, t_0) \geq g(s_0, t_0)$; for each $s_0 \in S$, $g(s_0, \cdot)$ is upper semi-continuous from the left in t: $\limsup_{t \lesssim t_0} g(s_0, t) \leq g(s_0, t_0)$; $g(0, t)$ is lower semi-continuous in t; and $g(s, 0)$ is upper semi-continuous in s. Then Proposition I.2.5, p. 22, applies (with $f = g$). Example 4 of Karlin (1950) is in this category.

6. I.2, Ex. 5, remains true when S and T are compact convex sets in Euclidian space, if $s < s_0$ (resp. $t < t_0$) is understood coordinatewise, and if we require the lower semi-continuity in t of $g(s_0, t)$ for all minimal s_0 (those for which $\{ s \in S \mid s < s_0 \}$ is empty), and similarly for the upper semi-continuity in s of $g(s, t_0)$. Those requirements of semi-continuity can be dropped for those minimal s_0 such that $f(s_0, t)$ is dominated. Similarly, Proposition I.2.5 applies to the general silent duel (Restrepo, 1957) (even when the accuracy functions $P(t)$ and $Q(t)$ are only assumed to be upper semi-continuous and left continuous (and with values in $[0, 1]$, $P(0) = Q(0) = 0$)).

7. (Sion and Wolfe, 1957)
Let $S = T = [0, 1]$, and let:

$$f(s,t) = \begin{cases} -1 & \text{if } s < t < s + \frac{1}{2}\,, \\ 0 & \text{if } t = s \text{ or } t = s + \frac{1}{2}\,, \\ 1 & \text{otherwise.} \end{cases}$$

Show that $\sup_\sigma \inf_t \int f(s,t)\, d\sigma = \frac{1}{3}$ and $\inf_\tau \sup_s \int f(s,t)\, d\tau = \frac{3}{7}$.

8. Let $S = T = [0, 1]$, and let:

$$f(s,t) = \begin{cases} 0 & \text{for } 0 \leq s < \frac{1}{2} \text{ and } t = 0, \text{ or for } \frac{1}{2} \leq s \leq 1 \text{ and } t = 1, \\ 1 & \text{otherwise.} \end{cases}$$

Then f satisfies all conditions of Theorem I.1.1 except the upper semi-continuity in s at $t = 1$ and $\sup_s \inf_t f = 0$, $\inf_t \sup_s f = 1$ (Sion, 1958). Let $g(s,t) = tf(s,1) + (1-t)f(s,0)$; $g(s,t)$ is linear in t, satisfies all conditions of the theorem, except the upper semi-continuity in s for $t > \frac{1}{2}$ and $\sup_s \inf_t g = 0$, $\inf_t \sup_s g = \frac{1}{2}$.

9. Dual machine gun duel. (Karlin, 1959, Vol. II, pp. 225ff.)
Players I and II, possessing quantities α and β of ammunition, approach each other without retreating, using quantities $\mu(ds)$ and $\nu(ds)$ of ammunition at a distance between s and $s + ds$ ($\int_0^\infty d\mu = \alpha$, $\int_0^\infty d\nu = \beta$, $\mu \geq 0$, $\nu \geq 0$). The probability of scoring a hit at a distance between s and $s + ds$, provided they are still alive in this interval, is given by $\xi(s)\mu(ds)$ and $\eta(s)\nu(ds)$, respectively.

Strategies of the players are the measures μ and ν, and the payoff to player I is 1 if II is destroyed without I being destroyed, r in case of double survival, r' in case both players are destroyed, and -1 if I is destroyed without II being ($-1 \leq r, r' \leq 1$). Assume that $\limsup_{h \gtrsim 0} \xi(s+h) \geq \xi(s)$, $\limsup_{h \gtrsim 0} \eta(s+h) \geq \eta(s)$, and that ξ and η are upper semi-continuous and bounded.

a. Show that, whatever a player can guarantee against non-atomic strategies of the other player, he can guarantee against any strategy of the other player (i.e., the "monotone class," $D(\cdot)$, generated by the non-atomic strategies, contains all strategies).

Show that, if μ and ν are non-atomic, the probability that both players are still alive when at a distance s apart is given by $Q_{\tilde{\mu}}(s)Q_{\tilde{\nu}}(s)$, where $Q_{\tilde{\mu}}(s) = \exp(-\tilde{\mu}(I_s))$, $Q_{\tilde{\nu}}(s) = \exp(-\tilde{\nu}(I_s))$, $I_s =]s, \infty[$, $\tilde{\mu}(ds) = \xi(s)\mu(ds)$, $\tilde{\nu}(ds) = \eta(s)\nu(ds)$. In particular, $\tilde{\mu}_i \to \tilde{\mu}_0$ implies $Q_{\tilde{\mu}_i}(s) \to Q_{\tilde{\mu}_0}(s)$ at every point of continuity of $Q_{\tilde{\mu}_0}$. Further, $Q_{\tilde{\mu}}$ is a convex function of $\tilde{\mu}$.

Show that, if μ and ν have no common atom, the probability that both players are destroyed is zero. If both are non-atomic, the probability that II is destroyed is $P(\tilde{\mu}, \tilde{\nu}) = \int_0^\infty Q_{\tilde{\nu}}(s)Q_{\tilde{\mu}}(ds)$. Note that $P(\tilde{\mu}, \tilde{\nu})$ is continuous in one variable as soon as the other is non-atomic.

Show that, for any $\tilde{\mu}$, $P(\tilde{\mu}, \tilde{\nu})$ is a convex function of $\tilde{\nu}$.

Show also that $P(\tilde{\mu}, \tilde{\nu}) = 1 - Q_{\tilde{\mu}}(0-)Q_{\tilde{\nu}}(0-) - P(\tilde{\nu}, \tilde{\mu})$, when either $\tilde{\mu}$ or $\tilde{\nu}$ is non-atomic, and conclude that, for $\tilde{\nu}$ non-atomic, $P(\tilde{\mu}, \tilde{\nu})$ is a concave and continuous function of $\tilde{\mu}$. For any bounded positive measure σ on the real line and every Borel A, let $\sigma_+^\varepsilon(A) = \mathsf{E}(\sigma(A - \eta))$ and $\sigma_-^\varepsilon = \mathsf{E}(\sigma(A + \eta))$ where η is a random variable uniform on $[0, \varepsilon]$ (E is expectation). For any μ, ν, we have $P(\mu, \nu) = \lim_{\varepsilon \to 0} P(\mu, \nu_-^\varepsilon)$, $P(\mu, \nu_-^\varepsilon) = \lim_{\eta \to 0} P(\mu_+^\eta, \nu_-^\varepsilon)$, where both limits are decreasing. The mappings $\sigma \to \sigma_+^\varepsilon$ and $\sigma \to \sigma_-^\varepsilon$ are linear and continuous for the weak topology on σ and the norm topology on σ_+^ε (resp. σ_-^ε).

Show first that this implies that $R(\mu, \nu) = P(\tilde{\mu}, \tilde{\nu})$ is upper semi-continuous on the product space, and concave in μ for any ν (and convex in μ for any ν). Show also that it implies that whatever be μ and ν, $P(\tilde{\mu}, \tilde{\nu})$ is the probability that II will be destroyed. Since I needs to consider only non-atomic strategies of II, he is faced with the payoff function $f(\mu, \nu) = (1 - r)P(\tilde{\mu}, \tilde{\nu}) - (1 + r)P(\tilde{\nu}, \tilde{\mu}) + r$, which is concave and continuous in $\tilde{\mu}$, $\tilde{\nu}$ being non-atomic. Thus I has a pure optimal strategy, say, $\tilde{\mu}_0$ (Proposition I.1.3, p. 6). Similarly, II is faced with the same payoff function, and thus has a pure optimal strategy, say, $\tilde{\nu}_0$.

Conclude that the game has a value, and both players have optimal strategies, none of which depend on r'.

b. The above solution is for the case of a "silent" duel: neither of the players is informed in the course of the game about the quantity of ammunition spent by the other player.

Conclude that the solution remains the same in the noisy duel.

c. Show also that both players have ε-optimal strategies that have a bounded density with respect to Lebesgue measure.

d. The above results remain a fortiori true if an additional restriction, say, an upper bound on the speed of firing (as used by Karlin), is imposed on the strategy spaces (this restriction may look natural in our interpretation of the model, but may be less natural in an interpretation, e.g., in terms of an advertising campaign). What do our results for the unbounded case imply about the behavior of the value in the bounded case when the bounds get large?

e. What happens to the above results when the accuracy functions ξ and η are not necessarily bounded (for instance, $\lim_{s \gtrsim 0} \xi(s) = \lim_{s \gtrsim 0} \eta(s) = +\infty$)?

10. Use the results of the present section (notably part I.2.b)) to improve those of I.1, Ex. 2–I.1, Ex. 6, p. 11. In particular, the convergence concept should allow for convergence of the games $\exp[-n(s - t)^2]$ to the zero game, not only to the indicator of the diagonal.

11. (Kuhn, 1952, p. 118)

Player I picks a number x in $[0, 1]$, player II a continuous function f from $[0, 1]$ to itself with $\int_0^1 f(t)\, dt = 1/2$. The payoff is $f(x)$. Thus, I's strategy space is compact metric, II's strategy space is complete, separable, and metric, and the payoff function is jointly uniformly continuous. Nevertheless, if player I is restricted to mixed strategies with finite support, he can guarantee himself only zero, and otherwise $1/2$ (and player II guarantees himself $1/2$ with a pure strategy).

12. (Grothendieck, 1953)
The Mackey topology $\tau(L_\infty, L_1)$ coincides on bounded subsets of L_∞ with the topology of convergence in measure.

HINT. One direction is given in the text in the proof of Lemma I.2.1, p. 16. For the other direction, show first that it is sufficient to prove that a uniformly bounded sequence that converges in measure converges uniformly on weakly compact subsets of L_1. To obtain this, just use Dunford–Pettis' equi-integrability criterion.

The next series of exercises concerns applications of the minmax theorem, i.e., the separation theorem, to the problem of how to assign a limit to non-converging sequences, i.e., how to define the payoff function in an infinitely repeated game.

13. Banach limits.
A Banach limit $\mathscr{L}$ is a linear functional on ℓ_∞, such that:

$$\mathscr{L}((x_n)_{n\in\mathbb{N}}) \leq \limsup_{n\to\infty} x_n \ .$$

We will also write $\mathscr{L}(x_n)$.

a. Show (see Proposition I.1.12, p. 9) that Banach limits exist.

b. Banach limits are positive linear functionals of norm 1.

c. Banach limits can equivalently be defined as regular probability measures on the Stone–Čech compactification (Kelley, 1955, p. 152) $\beta(\mathbb{N})$ of the integers, assigning probability zero to $\mathbb{N}$.

d. If C is a compact, convex subset of a locally convex Hausdorff space, and $x_n \in C$ for all n, there exists a unique $\mathscr{L}(x_n) \in C$ such that, for each continuous linear functional ϕ, $\langle \phi, \mathscr{L}(x_n)\rangle = \mathscr{L}(\langle \phi, x_n\rangle)$.

e. In particular, if X_n is a uniformly integrable sequence of random variables, there exists a unique random variable $X_\infty = \mathscr{L}(X_n)$ such that, for each measurable set A, $\int_A X_\infty = \mathscr{L}(\int_A X_n)$.

f. Similarly, if X_n is a sequence of r.v. with values in a compact convex subset C of $\mathbb{R}^k$, there exists a unique r.v. X_∞ with values in C such that $\mathscr{L}\,\mathsf{E}\langle X_n, Y\rangle = \mathsf{E}\langle X_\infty, Y\rangle$ for all $Y \in (L_1)^k$.

14. A separation theorem. (Meyer, 1973)

a. Let X be a compact convex subset of a locally convex vector space V. μ will stand for an arbitrary regular probability measure on X. Any μ has a barycenter $b_\mu \in X$ (defined to be such that, for any continuous affine functional u on X, $u(b_\mu) = \int u \, d\mu$). If u_1 and u_2 are two u.s.c. concave functions on X, one of them bounded, show that their least upper bound in the set of all concave functions is bounded and u.s.c. Show also (I.1.13, p. 10) that $u_1(b_\mu) \geq \int u_1 d\mu$. Denote by Γ_- the set of bounded concave functions u on X that are the least upper bound of a sequence of u.s.c. concave functions, and let $\Gamma_+ = -\Gamma_-$. Show that the sequence can, without loss of generality, be assumed monotone, and that:

$$u(b_\mu) \geq \int u \, d\mu. \qquad (\star)$$

b. Let $u \in \Gamma_-$, $v \in \Gamma_+$, $u \le v$. Show that, for all μ, there exist $u' \in \Gamma_-$ and $v' \in \Gamma_+$ such that $u \le u' \le v' \le v$ and $u' = v'$ a.e.

HINT. Let u_n u.s.c. concave and bounded increase strictly to u, and dually for v_n and v. Let $A_n = \{\phi \mid \phi$ affine continuous, $u_n \le \phi \le v_n\}$. A_n decreases and is non-empty (Proposition I.1.13) and convex, so that its closure $\overline{A}_n$ in $L_1(\mu)$ is weakly closed and thus (boundedness) weakly compact. Let $\phi \in \bigcap_n \overline{A}_n$ s.t. $\|\phi - \phi_n\|_1 \le 2^{-n}$ with $\phi_n \in A_n$; thus $\phi_n \to \phi$ μ-a.e. Let $u' = \liminf_{n\to\infty} \phi_n$, $v' = \limsup_{n\to\infty} \phi_n$. Note further that u' and v' can be assumed to be in the cones Γ_- and Γ_+ for some metrizable quotient space $\tilde{X}$ (consider the weak topology on V generated by the functions ϕ_n).

c. Call a bounded function w on X strongly affine if, for any μ, w is μ-measurable and $w(b_\mu) = \int w\, d\mu$. Let $u \in \Gamma_-$, $v \in \Gamma_+$, $u \le v$. Assume the continuum hypothesis, and show that there exists a strongly affine w such that $u \le w \le v$.

HINT. By I.2, Ex. 14b) X can, without loss of generality, be assumed metrizable. The set of all probabilities on X, being compact metric, has the power of the continuum. Let thus μ_α be an indexing of it by the set of all countable ordinals (continuum hypothesis). Construct by transfinite induction $u_\alpha \in \Gamma_-$ and $v_\alpha \in \Gamma_+$ such that $\alpha < \beta$ implies $u \le u_\alpha \le u_\beta \le v_\beta \le v_\alpha \le v$ and $u_\alpha = v_\alpha$ μ_α-a.e. (point I.2, Ex. 14b). Since all point masses ε_x are among the μ_α, the u_α and the v_α have a common limit w, which is strongly affine by ($\star$).

15. Medial limits (Mokobodzki). (cf. Meyer, 1973)

a. Show that, under the continuum hypothesis, there exist positive linear functionals ℓ ("medial limits") of norm 1 on ℓ_∞ such that, if x_n is a convergent sequence, $\ell(x_n) = \lim_{n\to\infty} x_n$, and such that, for any uniformly bounded sequence of random variables $Z_n(\omega)$, $\ell(Z_n(\omega))$ is measurable and $\mathsf{E}[\ell(Z_n(\omega))] = \ell[\mathsf{E}(Z_n(\omega))]$.

Show that ℓ can even be chosen so as to satisfy $\ell(x_n) = x_\infty$ for any sequence x_n converging to x_∞ in Cesàro's sense (or equivalently Abel's sense (cf. I.2, Ex. 16, and I.2, Ex. 17)). This would, in particular, imply that ℓ is translation invariant: $\ell(x_n) = \ell(x_{n+1})$.

Even stronger: one can choose ℓ such that, for any $x \in \ell_\infty$, $\ell(x) = \ell(\overline{x})$, where $\overline{x}_n = \frac{1}{n}\sum_{i=1}^n x_i$.

HINT. Take $X = [-1,1]^{\mathbb{N}}$. For any $x \in \ell_\infty$, let $\phi(x) = (x - \overline{x})/2$. $\phi(X)$ is a compact convex subset of X. Let $V_n = \{(t,x) \mid 1 \ge t \ge \sup_{i\ge n} x_i\ ,\ x \in X\}$, and U_n the convex hull of $-V_n$ and $[-1,0] \times \phi(X)$, $u_n(x) = \max\{t \mid (t,x) \in U_n\}$, $v_n(x) = \min\{t \mid (t,x) \in V_n\}$.

Prove that $u_n \le v_n$ (show that $[V_n + (\varepsilon,0)] \cap [U_n - (\varepsilon,0)] = \phi$). Let $u = \lim_{n\to\infty} u_n$, $v = \lim_{n\to\infty} v_n$: $\liminf_{i\to\infty} x_i \le u(x) \le v(x) = \limsup_{i\to\infty} x_i$, and $x \in \phi(X)$ implies $u(x) \ge 0$. Apply I.2, Ex. 14c, to get ℓ strongly affine $u \le \ell \le v$. Show that $\ell(0) = 0$, and extend ℓ by homogeneity to a linear functional on ℓ_∞. Show that ℓ is positive, of norm 1, and satisfies, for any $x \in \ell_\infty$, $\liminf_{n\to\infty} x_n \le \ell(x) = \ell(\overline{x}) \le \limsup_{n\to\infty} x_n$. By homogeneity, one can assume that Z_n is an X-valued random variable Z. The barycenter of the distribution μ_z of Z on X is the sequence $(\mathsf{E}(Z_n))$. The formula $\mathsf{E}[\ell(Z_n(\omega))] = \ell[\mathsf{E}(Z_n(\omega))]$ is thus equivalent to the strong affinity of ℓ.

b. Using I.2, Ex. 13c, ℓ can be extended to all sequences x_n such either $(\overline{x})^+$ or $(\overline{x})^-$ is ℓ-integrable. Show that:

(1) If a sequence of random variables $X_n(\omega)$ is bounded in L_1, then $\ell(X_n(\omega))$ exists a.e. and is in L_1.
(2) If the sequence is uniformly integrable, then $\mathsf{E}[\ell(X_n(\omega))] = \ell[\mathsf{E}(X_n(\omega))]$.
(3) In particular, if $X_n(\omega)$ converges weakly in L_1 to $X(\omega)$, then $\ell(X_n(\omega)) = X(\omega)$ a.e.

(4) If a sequence of random variables converges in probability to a real-valued random variable $X(\omega)$, then $\ell(X_n(\omega)) = X(\omega)$ a.e.

16. Abelian theorems.

a. If $x_n \in \ell_\infty$, $y_n = \sum_i p_{n,i} x_i$, $p_{n,i} \geq 0$, $\sum_i p_{n,i} = 1$, and if $\lim_{n\to\infty} p_{n,i} = 0$, then $\limsup y_n \leq \limsup x_n$.

b. In particular, if also $p_{n,i} \geq p_{n,i+1}$, then $\limsup y_n \leq \limsup \overline{x}_n$.

HINT. Rewrite the y_n as convex combinations of the $\overline{x}_n$, and use I.2, Ex. 16a.

c. In particular, $\limsup_{\lambda\to 0} \lambda \sum_n (1-\lambda)^n x_n \leq \limsup_{n\to\infty} \overline{x}_n$ (the $\limsup$ in Abel's sense is smaller than the $\limsup$ in Cesàro's sense).

d. Denote by P_t^α $(0 \leq \alpha \leq 1)$ the one-sided stable distribution of index α (Feller, 1966, Vol. II, XIII.6) (i.e., with Laplace transform $\exp(-t\lambda^\alpha)$). Observe that $\int_0^\infty P_s^\alpha(\cdot) P_t^\beta(ds) = P_t^{\alpha\beta}(\cdot)$ (subordination, e.g. Feller (1966, Vol. II, XIII, 7.e)). Given a bounded measurable function $x(t)$ on $\mathbb{R}_+$, let $p_\alpha(x) = \limsup_{t\to\infty} \int_0^\infty x(s) P_t^\alpha(ds)$. Conclude from the subordination property and from I.2, Ex. 16a, that $\alpha \leq \beta \Longrightarrow p_\alpha(x) \leq p_\beta(x)$. In particular, $p_0(x) = \lim_{\alpha\to 0} p_\alpha(x)$ is a well-defined sublinear functional: more precisely $p_0(x+y) \leq p_0(x) + p_0(y)$, $p_0(\lambda x) = \lambda p_0(x)$ for $\lambda \geq 0$, p_0 is monotone, $p_0(1) = 1$, $p_0(-1) = -1$. And $p_0 \in \Gamma_+$ (cf. I.2, Ex. 14), say, on the unit ball X of L_∞.

Remark I.2.17. Observe that p_0 is fully canonical, given the additive semigroup structure and the multiplication by positive scalars on $\mathbb{R}_+$, or equivalently, given the additive semigroup structure and the topology. There is also a fully canonical way of transforming a problem of limit of sequences to a problem on $\mathbb{R}_+$ (as a topological semigroup) (provided one uses on $\mathbb{R}_+$ only limits ℓ satisfying $\ell(f(\lambda t)) = \ell(f(t))$ for all $\lambda > 0$ and f bounded). This uses the Poisson process: if P_t denotes the Poisson distribution on $\mathbb{N}$ at time t, map first the bounded sequences x_n to the function $P_t(x) = \sum_n P_t(n) x_n$.

Remark I.2.18. One might wish to add further requirements to a "uniform distribution" on the integers $\mathscr{L}$, such as $\mathscr{L}(x_n) \leq \limsup_{\lambda\to 1}(1-\lambda)\sum_n \lambda^n x_n$, or such as the fact that the quotient and the rest of a uniform random number upon division by k are also uniform and independent (given the shift invariance, which is guaranteed by any other requirement, the latter requirement amounts to $\mathscr{L}(x_n) = k\mathscr{L}(y_n)$ if (y_n) is obtained from (x_n) by inserting $(k-1)$ zeros between two successive values).

Remark I.2.19. What type of limit operations do those considerations lead to? In particular, is there any relationship with the sublinear functional $q(x) = \limsup_{n\to\infty} (1/\ln n)(\sum_{i=1}^n x_i/i)$? What is the relation between such Banach limits (i.e., satisfying $\mathscr{L}(x) \leq q(x)$) and those for which $\mathscr{L}(x_n) = \mathscr{L}(\overline{x}_n)$?

17. Hardy and Littlewood's Tauberian theorem.

This provides a partial converse to I.2, Ex. 16c. Assume the sequence x_n is bounded from below. If $\lim_{\lambda\to 1}(1-\lambda)\sum_n x_n \lambda^n = \ell$ exists, then $\lim \overline{x}_n = \ell$.

HINT. By adding a constant, we can assume $x_n \geq 0$; and also $\ell = 1$ by normalization.

Show that $\lim_{\lambda\to 1}(1-\lambda)\sum_{n=0}^\infty x_n \lambda^n P(\lambda^n) = \int_0^1 P(t)\,dt$ first for $P(t) = t^k$, then for a polynomial, then a continuous function, and finally, for a bounded function whose set of discontinuities has Lebesgue measure zero.

Apply this to $P(t) = 0$ $(0 \leq t \leq e^{-1})$, $P(t) = t^{-1}$ $(t > e^{-1})$, $\lambda = \exp(-1/n)$.

I.3. THE MINMAX THEOREM FOR ORDERED FIELDS

Definition I.3.1. An **ordered field** K is a (commutative) field K together with a subset of positive elements P such that: P is closed under addition and multiplication; for any element $x \in K$, one and only one of the following holds: $x \in P$, $x = 0$, $-x \in P$. For two elements x and y of K, we write $x > y$ iff $x - y \in P$ and similarly for $\geq$, $<$, $\leq$.

An ordered field is called **real closed** if it has no ordered algebraic extension. An ordered field is contained in a minimal real closed field, called its **real closure** (Jacobson, 1964, Th. 8, p. 285).

Ordered fields arise naturally in studying the asymptotic behavior of repeated games, e.g., the field of Puiseux series or the real closure of the field of rational fractions in the discount factor λ when studying the asymptotic behavior of v_λ for stochastic games. Since because of those applications we will have to work with such real closed fields we will use related tools rather than remaining systematically with the elementary methods of ordered fields.

Definition I.3.2. A K-**polynomial system** (resp. linear) $\mathscr{S}$ is a finite number of polynomial (resp. linear) equations and inequalities ($P = 0$, $P > 0$, $P \neq 0$) with coefficients in K.

A **semi-algebraic set** in K^n (K being a real closed field) is a finite (disjoint) union of sets defined by a K-polynomial system. Observe that semi-algebraic sets form a Boolean algebra (spanned by the sets $\{ x \mid P(x) > 0 \}$ where P is a polynomial).

A **semi-algebraic function** (correspondence) is one whose graph is semi-algebraic.

Theorem I.3.1. (Tarski, cf. Jacobson, 1964, Th. 16, p. 312) *Given a $\mathbb{Q}$-polynomial system $\mathscr{S}$ in $n + m$ variables, there exists a finite family of $\mathbb{Q}$-polynomial systems in n variables, $\mathscr{T}_i$, such that for any real closed field K the projection on K^n of the semi-algebraic set in K^{n+m} defined by $\mathscr{S}$ is the semi-algebraic set in K^n defined by the $\mathscr{T}_i$'s.*

Corollary I.3.2. *The projection on K^n of a semi-algebraic set in K^{n+m} is semi-algebraic. Equivalently one can also allow quantifiers (over variables in K) in the sentences defining semi-algebraic sets (besides any logical connectives).*

Corollary I.3.3. *Images and inverse images of semi-algebraic sets by semi-algebraic functions (correspondences) are semi-algebraic. The closure and the interior of semi-algebraic sets in $\mathbb{R}^n$ are semi-algebraic.*

Corollary I.3.4. *If a semi-algebraic set in K^{n+m} defined by $\mathbb{Q}$-polynomial systems $\mathscr{S}_i$ has a projection on K^n equal to K^n, then on every real closed field the semi-algebraic set defined through the $\mathscr{S}_i$'s has the same property.*

Theorem I.3.5. *Let $\tilde{K}$ be an ordered field and K a subfield. If a K-linear system has a solution in $\tilde{K}$, it has a solution in K.*

Proof. Denote by F_i, $i = 1, \ldots, n$ the linear equalities and inequalities in m unknowns $x_1, \ldots, x_m$ and coefficients in K. Note that for any $x \in \tilde{K}$, $x > 0$, there exists $\varepsilon \in K$ such that $0 < \varepsilon < x$. Consider now a solution $x^0 = (x_1^0, \ldots, x_m^0)$ in $\tilde{K}^m$: replace any $\geq$ (resp. $\leq$) sign in the F_i by "$>$" (resp. "$<$") or "$=$" in such a way that x^0 will still be a solution. Replace now any "$>$" (resp. "$<$") in the conditions by "$\geq \varepsilon$" (resp. "$\leq -\varepsilon$") with $\varepsilon > 0$ in K in such a way that x^0 will still be a solution. Take any solution y^1 in K^m of the equalities of the system. If y^1 does not satisfy the inequalities, then there exists $\gamma \in \tilde{K}$ such that $x^1 = \gamma y^1 + (1-\gamma)x^0$ is still a solution, but one of the $\geq$ (or $\leq$) becomes an equality at x^1. Repeat the procedure with x^1. Since the number of inequalities decreases at every repetition, at some stage k, y^k will satisfy the system, if only because no inequalities are left. ■

Remark I.3.3. For a more elementary approach to the above and the next results, cf. Remarks I.3.9 and I.3.10 after I.3, Ex. 4, p. 34. For more powerful versions of the next result, cf. I.4, Ex. 4, p. 46, and I.4, Ex. 8, p. 48.

Theorem I.3.6. *Let $A = (a_{\ell m})$ be an $L \times M$-matrix with elements $a_{\ell m}$ in an ordered field K. Then, there exists a unique element v of K and there exists $x_1, \ldots, x_L$ and $y_1, \ldots, y_M$ in K such that $x_\ell \geq 0$ $\forall \ell$ $1 \leq \ell \leq L$, $\sum_{\ell=1}^{L} x_\ell = 1$, $y_m \geq 0$ $\forall m$ $1 \leq m \leq M$, $\sum_{m=1}^{M} y_m = 1$, and*

$$\sum_{\ell=1}^{L} x_\ell a_{\ell m} \geq v \,, \forall m \,, 1 \leq m \leq M \,,$$

$$\sum_{m=1}^{M} y_m a_{\ell m} \leq v \,, \forall \ell \,, 1 \leq \ell \leq L \,.$$

Proof. Theorem I.1.1, p. 5, implies that the result is true when K is the real number field. Corollary I.3.4 implies that it remains true for any real closed field. Hence the system of $2(L + M + 1)$ linear equalities and inequalities in (x_ℓ, y_m, v) with coefficients in K has a solution in its real closure $\tilde{K}$ (with unique v). Theorem I.3.5 implies that it has a solution in K. ■

EXERCISES

1. Farkas's lemma.

A finite system of linear equations and inequalities (on a vector space on an ordered field) is inconsistent (i.e., has no solution) iff there is an inconsistency proof by a linear combination.

Remark I.3.4. This is understood modulo the usual rules for inequalities: equalities are preserved after multiplication by any scalar, weak or strict inequalities are preserved (or change sign, or turn into an equality) according to the sign of the scalar, and sums of equations and weak and strict inequalities also follow the usual rules. An inconsistency proof means that one obtains in this way either $0 \geq 1$ or $0 > 0$.

Remark I.3.5. One reason for allowing both weak and strict inequalities is to be able to express frequent statements of the type "the system $f_i(x) \geq a_i$ implies $f(x) \geq a$" by statements of the type "the system $f_i(x) \geq a_i$ and $f(x) < a$ is inconsistent."

Remark I.3.6. The other reason is that then the "dual" of the system $f_i(x) \geq a_i$, $g_j(x) > b_j$, $h_k(x) = c_k$, i.e., the system expressing its inconsistency, is the system of the same form:

$$\begin{aligned}
&\sum \lambda_i f_i + \sum \mu_j g_j + \sum \nu_k h_k &&= 0, \qquad \lambda_i \geq 0,\ \mu_j \geq 0,\\
&\sum \lambda_i a_i + \sum \mu_j b_j + \sum \nu_k c_k &&\geq 0,\\
&\sum \lambda_i a_i + \sum \mu_j b_j + \sum \nu_k c_k + \sum \mu_j > 0.
\end{aligned}$$

Remark I.3.7. The duality terminology is justified by the fact that the second dual of a system is the system itself: let $(e_\alpha)_{\alpha \in A}$ be the inverse images in our vector space E of a basis of the finite dimensional quotient of E by the map (f, g, h). Then the equalities in our dual system translate to $\sum \lambda_i f_i(e_\alpha) + \sum \mu_j g_j(e_\alpha) + \sum \nu_k h_k(e_\alpha) = 0\ \forall \alpha \in A$. Thus the second dual is of the form $\sum \lambda_i f_i(x) + \sum \mu_j g_j(x) + \sum \nu_k h_k(x) + \sum u_i \lambda_i + \sum v_j \mu_j + w[\sum \lambda_i a_i + \sum \mu_j b_j + \sum \nu_k c_k] + r(\sum \lambda_i a_i + \sum \mu_j b_j + \sum \nu_k c_k + \sum \mu_j) = 0$, with $x = \sum x_\alpha e_\alpha$, $u_i \geq 0$, $v_j \geq 0$, $w \geq 0$, $r > 0$. The equation yields $f_i(x) + u_i + w a_i + r a_i = 0$, $g_j(x) + v_j + w b_j + r b_j + r = 0$, $h_k(x) + w c_k + r c_k = 0$, thus $f_i(x) + (w + r) a_i \leq 0$, $g_j(x) + (w + r) b_j \leq -r$, $h_k(x) + (w + r) c_k = 0$. Let $y = -x/(w + r)$ (note $w + r > 0$): we have $f_i(y) \geq a_i$, $g_j(y) \geq b_j\ + r/(w + r)$, $h_k(y) = c_k$: it expresses that there exists $x \in E$ and $\varepsilon (= r/w + r) > 0$ such that $f_i(x) \geq a_i$, $g_j(y) \geq b_j + \varepsilon$, $h_k(y) = c_k$.

The lemma states then that a system is inconsistent iff its dual is consistent.

Hint. It suffices to prove that, if the system is inconsistent, the dual has a solution. As seen in Remark I.3.7 above, it suffices to consider a finite dimensional vector space over the field K. One gets rid of the equations easily, replacing them by the pair of opposite weak inequalities; this leads in effect to the same dual system. We make the system homogeneous by multiplying the right-hand member by an additional variable x_0, and adding the inequality $x_0 > 0$: the system and its dual remain equivalent to the original.

We now take advantage of the homogeneity to replace all inequalities $g_j(x) > 0$ by $g_j(x) \geq z$, $z \geq 1$. Both systems are still equivalent and are now of the form $\tilde{f}_i(x) \geq 0$, $x_0 \geq 1$, and $\sum \tilde{\lambda}_i \tilde{f}_i(x) + x_0 = 0$, $\tilde{\lambda}_i \geq 0$. Fixing a basis in the finite dimensional vector space, the $\tilde{f}_i$ are given by a matrix F with elements in the ordered field K (and also $\tilde{a}_i \in K$). We can assume K real closed (Theorem I.3.5, p. 31) and then, for any fixed dimensions of F, uses Tarski's principle (Corollary I.3.4, p. 31): it suffices to deal with real vector space.

The fact that the system is inconsistent means that the subspace $V = \{(x_0, \tilde{f}_i(x))_{i=1}^{k-1} \mid x \in E\} \subseteq \mathbb{R}^k$ satisfies $V \cap Q = \emptyset$, with $Q = (1, 0, 0, \dots) + \mathbb{R}_+^k$. This implies $\delta = d(V, Q) > 0$: otherwise choose a sequence $x^n \in V$, $y^n \in Q$ with $\|x^n - y^n\| \leq n^{-1}$ and $\|y^n\|$ minimal under those constraints. The fact that V and Q are closed and disjoint implies $\|x^n\| \sim \|y^n\| \to +\infty$. The minimality implies $y_0^n = 1$. Extracting a subsequence, we get that $x^n / \|x^n\|$ and $y^n / \|y^n\|$ converge, say, to z, with $z_0 = 0$, $\|z\| = 1$, $z \in \mathbb{R}_+^k$, and $z \in V$. Hence, for n sufficiently large, $x^n - z \in V$ and $y^n - z \in Q$ contradict the minimality of $\|y^n\|$. Thus V is still disjoint from the open convex set $Q^\delta = \{ y \mid d(y, Q) < \delta \}$. Separation then yields the result (Proposition I.1.11).

2. Strong complementarity. (Bohnenblust et al., 1950)

a. If strategy sets are finite, there exists an optimal strategy pair such that every best reply is used with positive probability.

Hint. Let (σ, τ) be an optimal pair with maximal support, and assume w.l.o.g. that $v(g) = 0$ and that $g(\sigma, t_0) = 0 = \tau(t_0)$. Thus, the system of linear inequalities in σ: $[g(\sigma, t) \geq 0]_{t \in T}$ and $\sigma \geq 0$ implies $g(\sigma, t_0) \leq 0$; hence, by I.3, Ex. 1, there exist $\lambda_t \geq 0$ such that $g(s, t_0) + \sum_t \lambda_t g(s, t) \leq 0$ for all $s \in S$; i.e., $(1 + \lambda_0, \lambda_1, \lambda_2, \dots)/1 + \sum \lambda_t$ is an optimal strategy $\tilde{\tau}$ of player II with $\tilde{\tau}(t_0) > 0$.

Alternative: reduce to a symmetric game (antisymmetric matrix A), and express by I.3, Ex. 1, the inconsistency of $xA \geq 0$, $x \geq 0$, $xA + x > 0$: this yields the existence of $y \geq 0$, $z \geq 0$, $z \neq 0$ s.t. $A(y + z) + z \leq 0$. Make a scalar product with $y + z$.

b. Hence every pair in the relative interior of the optimal strategy sets has this property (in particular the barycenter, which has all the symmetries of the game). And conversely every pair with this property is a relative interior pair.

3. Examples.

a. In the game $\begin{pmatrix} x & -x^2 \\ -1 & 0 \end{pmatrix}$, where player I chooses $x \in [0, 1]$ or Bottom, both players have unique optimal strategies, and both have a best reply that is used with probability zero: finiteness of both strategy sets is essential, even for strong complementarity to hold for a single player.

I.4, Ex. 9 p. 48, provides a striking example, where both pure strategy sets are $[0, 1]$, and both players have unique optimal strategies, whose support is nowhere dense, while every pure strategy is a best reply. Even better is the polynomial game $st(t - s)$.

b. The "Cobb–Douglas" cone $C = \{(x, y, z) \mid z^2 \leq xy, x + y \geq 0\} \subseteq \mathbb{R}^3$ is closed, convex, and disjoint from the straight line $D = \{(x, 0, 1)\}$, yet for any linear functional φ one has $\varphi(C) \cap \varphi(D) \neq \emptyset$: there is no hope of obtaining anything like I.3, Ex. 1, in the non-polyhedral case, and the explicit use of the structure of $\mathbb{R}^k_+$ is necessary at the end of that proof.

4. Structure of polyhedra.

A (closed, convex) polyhedron is a finite intersection of closed half spaces (in a finite dimensional vector space E over an ordered field K).

a. The projection (hence (by finite dimensionality) any affine image) of a polyhedron is a polyhedron (and clearly so are the inverse images).

Hint. Since the projection is from (x, y)-space to x-space, express by I.3, Ex. 1, that x does not belong to the image, so as to obtain a description of the inequalities of the projection as those convex combinations of inequalities of the polyhedron that are independent of y. Alternatively, eliminating one coordinate at a time is completely elementary.

b. The product of two polyhedra is a polyhedron.

c. The sum (hence the difference) of two polyhedra is a polyhedron, and so is the intersection. (Use I.3, Ex. 4a, and I.3, Ex. 4b.)

d. Define the dual P^0 of a polyhedron P as $\{(a, b) \in E^* \times K \mid \langle a, x \rangle \geq b, \ \forall x \in P\}$. The dual is a polyhedral cone (in $E^* \times K$).

Hint. It suffices to consider a non-empty polyhedron. Expressing then the inconsistency of $Mx \geq m$ with $ax < b$ yields (I.3, Ex. 1), $a = (y_1, \dots, y_k)M$, $b = (y_1, \dots, y_k)m - y_0$ for $y \geq 0$; use now I.3, Ex. 4a.

e. The convex hull of two polyhedra cannot be expressed as the set of solutions to a system of linear inequalities, even allowing for strict inequalities: consider a line and a point. But the closed convex hull of two polyhedra is a polyhedron: consider the intersection I.3, Ex. 4c, of their duals I.3, Ex. 4d. In particular, the convex hull of finitely many compact polyhedra is a polyhedron (cf. I.3, Ex. 10d, p. 40).

f. A polyhedral cone is defined by finitely many inequalities $Ax \geq 0$. (If $Ax \geq b$, necessarily $b \leq 0$, and $Ax \geq 0$.) Conclude that a dual cone is of the form $\{(a, b) \mid aX_1 \geq 0, aX_2 \geq b\}$, where X_1 and X_2 are columns of vectors in E. (Note that $(0, -1)$ is in the dual cone.)

g. The polyhedra are the sums of a compact polyhedron and a polyhedral cone.

HINT. I.3, Ex. 4c, yields one direction. For the other one, use I.3, Ex. 4f, and I.3, Ex. 1, to express the polyhedron as the set of vectors $\sum \lambda_i x_i^1 + \sum \mu_j x_j^2$ with $\lambda_i \geq 0, \mu_j \geq 0, \sum \mu_j = 1$.

h. The compact polyhedra are the convex hull of their finitely many extreme points, and the polyhedral cones are spanned by finitely many vectors (which can also be chosen extreme (rays) if the cone contains no straight line). (Cf. I.3, Ex. 4g. Remove from the x_j^2 the non-extremal ones. Use I.3, Ex. 4a, for the opposite direction.) In general, polyhedral cones can be decomposed to the sum of a subspace $(P \cap (-P))$ and of a pointed polyhedral cone (the quotient), which in turn has a unique decomposition in terms of extreme rays.

i. In $\mathbb{R}^n$, show that for any convex set $B(\neq \emptyset)$ that is the set of solutions of a (finite or infinite) system of (weak or strict) linear inequalities, its asymptotic cone A_B (cf. I.1.14, p. 10) is a closed convex cone, independent of b.

j.

α. The polyhedral cone in any decomposition of a polyhedron P is A_P, as in I.3, Ex. 4g.

β. To make the decomposition unique, one can specify the compact polyhedron, when P contains no straight line, as the convex hull of the extreme points of P.

For $x \in P$, define the dual face F_x^0 of x as $\{(a, b) \in P^0 \mid \langle a, x\rangle = b\}$, and the face F_x of x as $\{y \in P \mid \langle a, y\rangle = b, \forall (a, b) \in F_x^0\}$.

k. Show that F_x^0 is the convex cone spanned by the vectors (A_i, b_i) with $A_i x = b_i$ if $P = \{x \mid Ax \geq b\}$.

l. Show that $F_x = \{y \in P \mid x + \varepsilon(x - y) \in P \text{ for some } \varepsilon > 0\}$.

m. Show that $\dim F_x + \dim F_x^0 = \dim E$.

HINT. For example, choose x as origin, and as basis vectors first $e_1, \ldots, e_n \in F_x$, with $n = \dim F_x$, then $f_1, \ldots, f_k \in P$ with $k + n = \dim(P)$, and finally $g_1, \ldots, g_\ell$, with $\ell = \dim E - \dim P$. The inequalities of P in this basis must have the form $P = \{\sum_i u_i e_i + \sum_j v_j f_j + \sum w_h g_h \mid Au + Bv \leq 1, Cv \geq 0, w = 0\}$, where C has full column rank; otherwise one would have $(0, v, 0) \in F_x$ for some $v \neq 0$. Thus $\dim\{\mu C \mid \mu \geq 0\} = k$, so, by I.3, Ex. 4k, $\dim F_x^0 = k + \ell$. Alternatively, use induction on $\dim F_x$, starting with $F_x = P$.

n. P has finitely many dual faces (I.3, Ex. 4k), hence by definition finitely many faces. If one adds $\emptyset$ as a face with P^0 as a dual face, there is a lattice structure (stability under intersections). (To preserve I.3, Ex. 4m, take the dimension of the empty face to be one less than the dimension of the minimal non-empty faces).

o. The faces of P are the sets of minimizers of linear functionals. Alternatively, they are the intersections of P with affine subspaces, whose complement in P is convex.

p. The dual faces of P are the faces of P^0.

q. For simplicity (in order not to deal with K-valued distances and Lipschitz constants), think of K as being the reals. The distances used on vector spaces are assumed to derive from some norm.

If f is an affine map from a polyhedron P to a vector space, then f^{-1} is Lipschitz as a map from $f(P)$ to closed (convex) subsets of P, endowed with the Hausdorff metric $d(S_1, S_2) = \max\left[\max_{x \in S_1} d(x, S_2), \max_{x \in S_2} d(x, S_1)\right]$. (All norms on finite dimensional vector spaces are equivalent.)

HINT. The statement is clearly equivalent to the Lipschitz character of the map f^{-1} from closed subsets of P to closed subsets of $f^{-1}(P)$, and this property is stable under composition. Assume thus the kernel of f is one-dimensional: P is a polyhedron in $\mathbb{R}^n \times \mathbb{R}$, and f the projection to $\mathbb{R}^n$. Consider the $\overline{\mathbb{R}}$-valued functions on $f(P)$: $\overline{u}(x) = \sup\{ y \mid (x, y) \in P \}$, $\underline{u}(x) = \inf\{ y \mid (x, y) \in P \}$. $\overline{u}$ is the minimum of a finite number (possibly zero) of linear functions (look at the inequalities determining P), hence Lipschitz, and similarly $\underline{u}$.

Remark I.3.8. I.3, Ex. 4c, immediately implies that two disjoint polyhedra can be strictly separated. Similarly, I.3, Ex. 4a, I.3, Ex. 4b, and I.3, Ex. 4c, are still true if some of the half spaces in the definition of a polyhedron are allowed to be open, so two such generalized polyhedra P_1 and P_2 that are disjoint can be separated by a linear function f with $f(P_1) \cap f(P_2) = \emptyset$ (applying I.3, Ex. 1, to $P_1 - P_2$ and $\{0\}$). However I.3, Ex. 1, yields both those separations directly, with the additional information that f can be selected to belong to the convex hull of both A_1 and A_2 ($P_1 = \{ x \mid A_1 x \geq b_1 \}$, $P_2 = \{ x \mid A_2 x \leq b_2 \}$).

Remark I.3.9. The alternative argument of I.3, Ex. 4a, used for generalized polyhedra, yields a quantifier elimination algorithm for the logic having the linear inequalities as elementary sentences, plus quantifiers and propositional calculus (cf. Remark I.3.3, p. 32).

Remark I.3.10. It also provides an elementary route to Farkas' lemma and the following exercises, without relying on Tarski's theorem. (At the end of I.3, Ex. 1, take the image of Q under the quotient mapping by V, and apply I.3, Ex. 4a.)

Remark I.3.11. Walkup and Wets (1969) have shown that I.3, Ex. 4q, in fact characterizes the polyhedra among all closed convex subsets.

5. Linear programming.

Consider the general linear program $\underline{v} = \sup\{ xc \mid xA \leq b, x \geq 0 \}$, where b and x are row vectors, c a column vector, and A a matrix (equality constraints can be changed to a pair of inequality constraints, the sign of "$\geq$" inequalities changed, and unrestricted variables x replaced by $x^+ - x^-$ to obtain this form). (If $E = \emptyset$: $\sup E = -\infty$, $\inf E = +\infty$.)

Consider also the "dual" program $\overline{v} = \inf\{ by \mid Ay \geq c, y \geq 0 \}$ (note that from first principles $\underline{v} \leq \overline{v}$) and the symmetric matrix game:

$$M = \begin{pmatrix} 0 & -A & c \\ A^t & 0 & -b^t \\ -c^t & b & 0 \end{pmatrix}.$$

Apply the strong complementarity property in M (I.3, Ex. 2):

a. Start by applying it to the last strategy, to deduce that either there is an optimal strategy (x, y, t) with $t > 0$ in which case $\overline{v} = \underline{v} \in \mathbb{R}$ and x/t and y/t solve $\underline{v} = xc, xA \leq b, x \geq 0$ and $\overline{v} = by$, $Ay \geq c$, $y \geq 0$ or $\overline{v} = \underline{v} = +\infty$, or $\overline{v} = \underline{v} = -\infty$, or $\overline{v} = +\infty, \underline{v} = -\infty$.

HINT. Note that $\overline{v} = +\infty$ is equivalent to $\sup\{xc \mid xA \leq 0, x \geq 0\} = +\infty$.

b. Then apply it to the other strategies, to obtain the strong complementarity relations for linear programs (Tucker, 1956).

c. Consider a polyhedral game (Wolfe, 1956), i.e., player I's and player II's strategy sets are polyhedra $X = \{ x \mid xC \leq c \}$ and $Y = \{ y \mid By \geq b \}$, and the payoff function is xAy. Let $\overline{v}$ and $\underline{v}$ denote the $\inf\sup$ and the $\sup\inf$, respectively. Show that either $\overline{v} = \underline{v}$, and then there exist optimal strategies if this value is finite, or $\overline{v} = +\infty, \underline{v} = -\infty$.

HINT. The case is clear if X or Y or both are empty. Assume thus otherwise. For a given strategy y of player II, player I wants to solve the linear program $\max\ xAy$ in $xC \leq c$, whose dual is $\min cv$ in $Cv = Ay$, $v \geq 0$ (there is no sign restriction on x), with the same value (cf. I.3, Ex. 5a), since $X \neq \emptyset$. Thus y guarantees this quantity to player II, and he wants to solve the program $\min cv$ in $Cv = Ay$, $v \geq 0$, $By \geq b$ and play the corresponding y. Similarly player I wants to solve $\max ub$ in $uB = xA$, $u \geq 0$, $xC \leq c$. Observe that those two programs are themselves dual (cf. I.3, Ex. 5d) and apply I.3, Ex. 5a. (Note also that $\overline{v}$ and $\underline{v}$ in the sense of the dual programs are always the same as those for the game.)

d. In general, the "dual" of a linear program ($\underline{v} = \max\ xc$, subject to a system of equality and inequality constraints) is the expression that $\underline{v} = \min\{\, r \mid xc > r$ and the system is inconsistent$\,\}$, where the condition is expressed by means of I.3, Ex. 1, p. 32, assuming the system itself to be consistent. Verify that this indeed yields the duals used in I.3, Ex. 5a, and I.3, Ex. 5c, above.

(It is this unverified assumption that causes the possibility of $\overline{v} \neq \underline{v}$, as in ($\max x$ in $y \geq 1, -y \geq 1$), while the dual in the sense of I.3, Ex. 1, always gives a full diagnostic about the original system.)

e. In a polyhedral game, cf. I.3, Ex. 5c, above, with finite value v,

(1) the sets of optimal strategies $\tilde{X}$ and $\tilde{Y}$ of players I and II are polyhedra,
(2) (Strong Complementarity) the face (I.3, Ex. 4) $\tilde{F}$ of X spanned by $\tilde{X}$ (or by a point in the relative interior of $\tilde{X}$) equals $\{\, x \in X \mid xAy \geq v\ \forall y \in \tilde{Y}\,\}$, and similarly for the face $\tilde{G}$ of Y spanned by $\tilde{Y}$.

HINT. Use the dual programs of I.3, Ex. 5c, above, together with I.3, Ex. 4a, for (1) and I.3, Ex. 5b, above for (2).

f. $\operatorname{codim}_{\tilde{F}}(\tilde{X}) = \operatorname{codim}_{\tilde{G}}(\tilde{Y})$ (same notations as in I.3, Ex. 5e).

HINT. Item (2) implies that, if strategy sets are restricted to $\tilde{F}$ and $\tilde{G}$, resp., $\tilde{X}$ and $\tilde{Y}$ increase while keeping the same dimensions. Assume thus $\tilde{F} = X$, $\tilde{G} = Y$: in the affine spaces spanned by those sets, put the origin at some interior optimal strategies: we get a new polyhedral game of the form $By \geq -1$, $xC \leq 1$, with payoff $= xAy + \alpha y + x\beta + \gamma$; $(0, 0)$ being optimal implies $\alpha = \beta = 0$, and so the payoff is xAy. Thus $\tilde{X} = \{\, x \in X \mid xA = 0\,\}$, $\tilde{Y} = \{\, y \in Y \mid Ay = 0\,\}$, $\operatorname{codim}(\tilde{X}) = \operatorname{codim}(\tilde{Y}) = \operatorname{rank}(A)$.

6. Von Neumann's model of an expanding economy. (Thompson, 1956)

I is the set of production processes (activities), J the set of commodities. The $I \times J$ matrices A and B describe by a_{ij} (resp. b_{ij}) the input (resp. output) of commodity j corresponding to a unit intensity of process i. One wants a stationary growth path, i.e., a growth factor $\lambda (\geq 0)$, an interest factor $r > 0$, an intensity (row-)vector $x \geq 0$, and a price (column-) vector $p \geq 0$ such that:

$xB \geq \lambda xA$ (the outputs of the current period suffice as inputs for the next period),

$(xB - \lambda xA)p = 0$ (goods in excess supply carry a zero price),

$x[Bp - rAp] \geq \sup_{\tilde{x} \geq 0} \tilde{x}[Bp - rAp]$ (profit maximization: $Bp - rAp$ gives the net profit from each activity at p and r).

This last condition thus immediately yields $Bp \le rAp$ and $xBp = rxAp$. We assume that $A \ge 0$, $\sum_j a_{ij} > 0$ (no free lunch), and $v(B) > 0$ (there is some combination of activities by which every good can be produced). We require finally that the value of total input be non-zero, to avoid the completely degenerate solutions: $xAp > 0$.

a. The above requirements imply $r = \lambda$ and are equivalent to: $x(B - \lambda A) \ge 0$, $(B - \lambda A)p \le 0$, $xAp > 0$, i.e.: $f(\lambda) = v(B - \lambda A) = 0$, with x and p being optimal strategies (after normalization).

(Hence one could equivalently impose in addition (by I.3, Ex. 2) $x(B - \lambda A) + p^t > 0$, $(\lambda A - B)p + x^t > 0$.)

b. The assumptions imply $f(\lambda)$ is decreasing, $f(0) > 0 > f(+\infty)$, and thus $\{\lambda \mid f(\lambda) = 0\} = [\underline{\lambda}, \overline{\lambda}]$, $0 < \underline{\lambda} \le \overline{\lambda} < +\infty$.

c. To show existence of a solution, show that a strongly complementary pair of optimal strategies (I.3, Ex. 2) at $\overline{\lambda}$ (or at $\underline{\lambda}$) yields $xAp > 0$ (hence also $xBp > 0$).

HINT. Order the strategies so that those used with positive probability are first. The matrix $B - \lambda A$ then takes the form $\left(\begin{smallmatrix} Q & T \\ R & S \end{smallmatrix}\right)$, where Q is identically zero in A if $xAp = 0$. The strong complementarity property yields $x\left(\begin{smallmatrix} T \\ S \end{smallmatrix}\right) > 0$: thus x still guarantees zero in $B - (\lambda + \varepsilon)A$.

d. There exists at most $\min(\#I, \#J)$ solutions λ.

HINT. Consider two solutions, $\lambda^1 < \lambda^2$. For some $j = j_2$, we have $p_j^2 > 0$, $xB_j = \lambda^2 xA_j > 0$. Then $xB_j > \lambda^1 xA_j$, and since x is still optimal at λ^1, we have $p_j^1 = 0$: any j_1 must be different.

e. Assume w.l.o.g. that the solutions (x^i, p^i) selected at λ^i satisfy the strong complementarity relations, and set, as in (d),

$$J_0^2 = \{j \mid p_j^2 > 0, x^2B_j > 0\},\ J_1^2 = \{j \mid p_j^2 > 0, x^2B_j = 0\},\ J_2^2 = \{j \mid p_j^2 = 0\},$$

and similarly for J_0^1, J_1^1, J_2^1 at λ^1, and sets I_0^1, etc., for player I (e.g., $I_0^1 = \{i \mid x_i^1 > 0, B_i p^1 > 0\}$).

α. Show that, on $I_0^k \times J_0^k$, every row and every column contain some $a_{ij} > 0$, and $a_{ij} = 0$ elsewhere on $(I_0^k \cup I_1^k) \times (J_0^k \cup J_1^k)$, $k = 1, 2$. The same conclusions hold for B if $B \ge 0$.

β. Show that $J_0^1 \cup J_1^1 \subseteq J_0^2 \cup J_1^2$, and similarly $I_0^2 \cup I_1^2 \subseteq I_0^1 \cup I_1^1$.

HINT. p^1 is optimal in $B - \lambda^2 A$

γ. Show that $J_0^2 \cup J_2^2 \subseteq J_2^1$, and $I_2^1 \cup I_0^1 \subseteq I_2^2$.

HINT. Cf. I.3, Ex. 6d, for J_0^2: use strong complementarity for J_2^2.

δ. Deduce from the two last points that $J_0^1 \cup J_1^1 \subseteq J_1^2$, $I_0^2 \cup I_1^2 \subseteq I_1^1$.

ε. Conclude from the above, putting the solutions λ^i in increasing order, and using an appropriate ordering on activities and commodities, that A has the following structure: if there are n roots λ^i, there exist n special blocks, any element to the left or below (or both) any special block being zero, while in the special blocks every row and every column contains a positive element. If $B \ge 0$, it has the same structure, with the same special blocks. The support of the ith solution is the ith special block, together with everything to the left and below.

7. Examples on I.3, Ex. 6

a. $A = \left(\begin{smallmatrix} 0 & 1 \\ 1 & 0 \end{smallmatrix}\right)$, $B = \left(\begin{smallmatrix} 2 & 0 \\ 0 & 1 \end{smallmatrix}\right)$ yields $\lambda = \sqrt{2}$: the problem needs a real closed field.

b. $\#I = \#J = n$, $a_{ij} = b_{ij} = 0$ for $i \ne j$, $a_{ii} = 1$, $b_{ii} = i$: there are n solutions, $\lambda = 1, 2, \ldots, n$: the upper bound of I.3, Ex. 6d, is attained.

c. The following examples (with two goods) show that there is no extension to a continuum of activities. In that case one represents simply the set of all feasible input-output vectors (x, y) by a closed convex cone in $\mathbb{R}^2 \times \mathbb{R}^2$.

(1) First Example. $x_i \geq 0$, $y_i \geq 0$, $x_1(x_2 - y_2) \geq y_2^2$, $x_1 + x_2 \geq y_1$.
(2) Second Example. Replace the last inequality in Example 1 by the stricter inequality $x_1(x_2 + y_1) \geq y_1^2$.

Check that both examples describe convex (cf. below), closed cones C in $(\mathbb{R}^2_+)^2$, which are comprehensive $[(x, y) \in C, x' \geq x, y' \leq y \Longrightarrow (x', y') \in C]$, contain an interior point of $\mathbb{R}^4_+$, say $P_\varepsilon = (1, \varepsilon(1 + \varepsilon); 1 + \varepsilon, \varepsilon)$; (check for 2, after having verified that $C_2 \subseteq C_1$), and offer no free lunch ($x = 0 \Longrightarrow y = 0$; check for 1).

Their efficient frontiers are described, for Example 1, by replacing the last two inequalities by equalities, and, for Example 2, by $(0, 0, 0, 0)$ and $\{x_1 = y_1 - y_2 > 0, x_1 x_2 = y_1 y_2, y_2 \geq 0\}$, which is thus not closed (cf. also I.4, Ex. 12, p. 49, and I.4, Ex. 13, p. 50, for more classical, but infinite dimensional, examples of a non-closed efficient frontier). For the closure, put a weak inequality, and add $x_2 \geq 0$. They describe a map (one-to-one for Example 2) from efficient inputs ($x_1 > 0, x_2 \geq 0$ or $(0, 0)$ for Example 2) to efficient outputs ($y_1 > y_2 \geq 0$ or $(0, 0)$ for Example 2). In Example 2, $x_1(y) = y_1 - y_2 > 0, x_2(y) = y_2 + y_2^2/x_1(y)$: since $x_1(y)$ is linear, and y^2/x convex, we indeed obtain that for an average output, one needs less than the average input, hence the convexity of the comprehensive hull. Use a similar argument for the convexity in the first example.

Yet, for both cones C, there is no solution $[\lambda, \mu, p, (x^*, y^*)] \in \mathbb{R} \times \mathbb{R} \times \mathbb{R}^2 \times C$ of $\lambda y^* \geq \mu x^*$, $\langle p, \lambda y - \mu x\rangle \leq 0, \forall (x, y) \in C$, $\langle p, y^*\rangle > 0$ (resp. $\langle p, x^*\rangle > 0$) and $(\lambda, \mu) \neq (0, 0)$ (resp. $\mu = 0 \Longrightarrow \lambda > 0$).

HINT. $\lambda \leq 0$ or $\mu \leq 0$ is trivial: $\mu < 0 \Longrightarrow p \leq 0$ (free disposal of outputs), $\mu = 0 < \lambda \Longrightarrow p \leq 0$ (free disposal and feasibility of strictly positive output), $\mu > 0 \geq \lambda \Longrightarrow y^* = x^* = 0$ (no free lunch), and $\lambda < 0 = \mu \Longrightarrow y^* = 0$. Assume thus $\lambda = 1$, $\mu > 0$. In Example 1 (a fortiori Example 2) $y \geq x$ implies $y_1 = x_1$, $y_2 = x_2 = 0$. Thus $\mu > 1$ implies $y^* = x^* = 0$. Also (free disposal) $\langle p, y - \mu x\rangle \leq 0$ implies $p \geq 0$. And in Example 2 (a fortiori Example 1) $\langle p, y - x\rangle \leq 0\ \forall (x, y) \in C$ then implies $p_1 = 0$ (use P_ε). Since (P_ε again) $y_2 - \mu x_2$ can be > 0 for $\mu < 1$, it follows that $p = 0$ for $\mu < 1$: in every case $\langle p, y^*\rangle = 0$.

8. Block decomposition. (Kemeny, cf. Thompson, 1956)

Consider the matrix game $M = \left(\begin{smallmatrix} O & P \\ Q & R \end{smallmatrix}\right)$, in block decomposition, where the first block consists of zeros only.

a. If $v(M) = 0$, then player I has an optimal strategy carried by the first block iff $v(P) \geq 0$, and similarly for player II iff $v(Q) \leq 0$. Also $v(P) \geq 0 \geq v(Q) \Longrightarrow v(M) = 0$.

b. Denote by $\tilde{v}(R)$ the value of R when players I and II are both restricted to optimal strategies in Q and P respectively (compare I.1, Ex. 6, p. 12).

Assume $v(P) \geq 0 \geq v(Q)$. Then player I has an optimal strategy in M that is not carried by the first block only iff $v(Q) = 0$ and either $v(P) > 0$ or $\tilde{v}(R) \geq 0$. (Use I.3, Ex. 2, p. 33, for the sufficiency of the condition). In particular, both players can use strategies in their second block iff $v(P) = v(Q) = \tilde{v}(R) = 0$.

c. Conclude from I.3, Ex. 8a, and I.3, Ex. 8b, that every optimal strategy in M is carried by the first block iff $v(P) > 0 > v(Q)$.

9. Perron–Frobenius theorem.

a. In I.3, Ex. 6, p. 37, take for B a matrix P of transition probabilities ($P_{ij} \geq 0; \sum_j P_{ij} = 1$) and $A = I$: one obtains the existence of an invariant probability distribution. (One could rescale so as to drop $\sum_j P_{ij} = 1$, cf. I.3, Ex. 9b.)

However, this does not require the strong complementarity, so a direct application of the minmax theorem yields more:

b. Assume S is compact, and, $\forall s \in S$, P_s is a non-negative regular measure on S with $P_s(f) = \int f(x)P_s(dx)$ continuous whenever f is continuous. Then there exists a probability measure μ on S with $\int P_s(A)\mu(ds) = \int_A P_s(1)\mu(ds)$, for all Borel A.

HINT. Apply Proposition I.1.9, p. 9, to the game where T is the space of continuous functions on S, and the payoff is $P_s(t) - t(s)P_s(1)$; consider the minimizer s_0 of t.

10.

a. *Carathéodory.* Any point in the convex hull of a subset S of $\mathbb{R}^n$ is a convex combination of $n+1$ points of S.

HINT. For $k = 1, \ldots, n$, let $\sum_{i=1}^{n+m} \lambda_i x_k^i = a_k$, $\sum_{i=1}^{n+m} \lambda_i = 1$ be the equations: if $m > 1$, there are more equations than unknowns, so the set of solutions λ meets the boundary $\min_i \lambda_i = 0$ of the simplex. Proceed by induction.

b. *Fenchel.* Assume S has at most n components; then n points suffice.

HINT. Assume p is interior to the simplex $\{x_1, \ldots, x_{n+1}\}$, x_i in S. Consider the reflection of this simplex in p (i.e., $y_i = 2p - x_i$) and the cones C_i based at p with vertices $(y_1, \ldots, y_{i-1}, y_{i+1}, y_{n+1})$. $\bigcup_1^{n+1} C_i$ contains S and one point of S belongs to the boundary of some C_i.

c. (cf. I.3, Ex. 14, p. 43). Carathéodory extends to continuous averages: for a convex subset C of $\mathbb{R}^n$, the expectation of any integrable C-valued random variable belongs to C.

Remark I.3.12. Since C is not necessarily measurable for the distribution μ of X, the above statement is preferable to one that involves the barycenter of measures on C.

HINT. Assume the expectation $b \notin C$, and separate: for a linear functional φ we have $\varphi(b) \geq \alpha = \sup_{x \in C} \varphi(x)$. But $\varphi(b) = \mathsf{E}(\varphi(X))$, so a.s. $\varphi(X) = \alpha = \varphi(b)$: X is carried by the convex set $C_1 = \{x \in C \mid \varphi(x) = \varphi(b)\}$. Proceed by induction on the dimension. More precisely the proof shows that

- the expectation belongs to the relative interior of the convex hull of the support of the distribution,
- this relative interior is included in C.

d. The convex hull of a compact subset of $\mathbb{R}^n$ is compact (use I.3, Ex. 10), just as is in general the convex hull of finitely many compact convex subsets.

11. Linear programming and polyhedral games (continued).

Consider the program: maximize xb in $xA \leq c$, $x \geq 0$, and its dual: minimize cy in $Ay \geq b$, $y \geq 0$. Assume $\overline{v} \in \mathbb{R}$.

a. The solution sets X and Y are polyhedra and have an extreme point.

HINT. I.3, Ex. 5a, p. 36, yields $X \neq \emptyset$, $Y \neq \emptyset$. I.3, Ex. 4c, p. 34, yields that they are polyhedra. The constraints $x \geq 0$, $y \geq 0$ ensure the existence of an extreme point (I.3, Ex. 4j, p. 35).

b. The pairs of extreme points (x, y) of X and Y are the feasible points such that, for some subsets I of the rows and J of the columns, one has A^{IJ} non-singular and $x^I = c^J(A^{IJ})^{-1}$, $y^J = (A^{IJ})^{-1}b^I$, $x_i = 0$ for $i \notin I$, and $y_j = 0$ for $j \notin J$ (where x^I, y^J, A^{IJ}, etc., denote the restrictions to the corresponding sets of indices). And then $v = c^J(A^{IJ})^{-1}b^I$. (The 0×0 matrix is non-singular by convention, in which case $v = 0$ as it is an empty sum).

HINT. Optimality for such a pair (x, y) follows from $xb = cy$. If $x = \frac{1}{2}(x^1 + x^2)$, x^k feasible $(k = 1, 2)$, then $x_i^k = 0$ $(i \notin I)$ and $x^{k,I}A^{IJ} = c^J$, hence $x^k = x$ by the independence of the rows of A^{IJ}. Similarly y is extreme. Conversely, for an extreme pair (x, y), let $I_1 = \{ i \mid x_i > 0 \}$, $J_1 = \{ j \mid y_j > 0 \}$, $I_2 = \{ i \mid A_i y = b_i \}$, $J_2 = \{ j \mid xA_j = c_j \}$: $I_1 \subseteq I_2$ and $J_1 \subseteq J_2$. Further the rows of $A^{I_1J_2}$ and the columns of $A^{I_2J_1}$ are linearly independent by the extremality of x and y resp.; cf. supra. Extend thus I_1 (resp. J_1) to a basis I (resp. J) of the rows (resp. columns) of $A^{I_2J_2}$. Conclude that A^{IJ} is itself non-singular.

c. Particularize I.3, Ex. 11b, to a characterization of the extreme points of a polyhedron $P = \{ x \mid xA \le b \}$.

HINT. Rather than first trying to find a system of coordinates, using the extreme points, where $P \subseteq \mathbb{R}^n_+$, a more direct approach uses I.3, Ex. 4m, p. 35, and I.3, Ex. 10, p. 40.

d. (Shapley and Snow, 1950) If A is a matrix game with value v, a pair of optimal strategies is an extreme pair iff, for some subsets I and J of rows and columns, one has, writing $\tilde{B}$ for the adjoint of $B = A^{IJ}$, and 1^I, 1^J, for appropriate vectors of ones, that $1^J\tilde{B}1^I \neq 0$, and $x^I = \frac{1^J\tilde{B}}{1^J\tilde{B}1^I}$, $y^J = \frac{\tilde{B}1^I}{1^J\tilde{B}1^I}$. And then $v = \det(B)/(1^J\tilde{B}1^I)$.

HINT. Assume first $v > 0$. Then $\xi = x/v$ and $\eta = y/v$ are the solutions of the following dual programs: minimize $\xi \cdot 1$ in $\xi A \ge 1$, $\xi \ge 0$, and maximize $1 \cdot \eta$ in $A\eta \le 1$, $\eta \ge 0$. Apply I.3, Ex. 11b, to those, and that $M^{-1} = [\tilde{M}/\det(M)]$. For other values of v, reduce to the case where $v > 0$ using the fact that adding a constant c to the entries of A does not change the solutions x and y, and adds c to v; and that, if M' is obtained by adding c to all entries of M, then $1 \cdot \tilde{M}' = 1 \cdot \tilde{M}$, $\det(M') = \det(M) + c[1 \cdot \tilde{M} \cdot 1]$. Those equations follow from the previous case for completely mixed matrices M with $v > 0$: indeed, the determinant is clearly an affine function of c, (i) either geometrically, as a volume of a parallelepiped, whose volume is clearly bounded by $K(1 + |c|)$, and whose determinant is polynomial; (ii) or analytically, subtracting the first column from the others and expanding. Since $v = v_0 + c$, the equation for v yields then that $1\tilde{M}1$ must be a polynomial of degree 0 in c, hence constant. Therefore the constancy of x and y yields that of $1\tilde{M}$ and of $\tilde{M}1$. Since those equations for the adjoints and determinants are proved on an open subset of matrices, and since they are polynomial, they hold everywhere.

Remark I.3.13. The procedure used in the first sentence of the hint is the efficient way to solve a matrix game by linear programming.

e.

α. $\{ c \mid \underline{v}(b, c) > -\infty \} = \{ c \mid \exists x \ge 0, xA \le c \}$ is a polyhedral cone $\underline{P}$, independent of b; cf. I.3, Ex. 9a, p. 40. Similarly $\overline{P} = \{ b \mid \overline{v}(b, c) < +\infty \}$.

β.

A. $\underline{v}(b, c)$ and $\overline{v}(b, c)$ are convex in b, concave in c, and non-decreasing.

B. $v(b, c)$ is positively homogeneous of degree one (with $0 \cdot \infty = 0$) in c for $b \in \overline{P}$ and in b for $c \in \underline{P}$.

C. On $\overline{P} \times \underline{P}$, $v \in \mathbb{R}$; on $\overline{P} \times \underline{P}^c$, $v = -\infty$; on $\overline{P}^c \times \underline{P}$, $v = +\infty$; on $\overline{P}^c \times \underline{P}^c$, $\overline{v} = +\infty$ and $\underline{v} = -\infty$.

γ. On $\overline{P} \times \underline{P}$, v is piecewise bi-linear in the sense that there exist subdivisions of $\overline{P}$ and $\underline{P}$ into finitely many simplicial cones, such that the restriction of v is bi-linear on any product of two such cones.

HINT. By I.3, Ex. 11b, for fixed pair (I, J), v is bi-linear. I.3, Ex. 11b, is applicable because of I.3, Ex. 11a. This formula is applicable as long as the corresponding vectors x and y are feasible, which translates into a finite system of homogeneous linear inequalities in b and another one in c. The union over all possible (I, J) of those lists of linear functionals cuts up $\overline{P}$ into finitely many polyhedral cones, add the coordinate mappings to those lists to be sure each of those cones is pointed. A further subdivision (e.g., barycentric) then yields simplicial cones. Similarly for $\underline{P}$.

δ. For some $K > 0$, v is, on $\overline{P} \times \underline{P}$, Lipschitz in c with constant $K \|b\|$ and in b with $K \|c\|$. (Use I.3, Ex. 11eγ.)

f. The results of I.3, Ex. 11e, remain verbatim true for the inf sup $\overline{v}$ and the sup inf $\underline{v}$ of the polyhedral games of I.3, Ex. 5c, p. 36.

HINT. Rewrite the primal-dual programs of the hint of I.3, Ex. 5c, in the form used in the present exercise, replacing y and x by differences of non-negative vectors $y_1 - y_2$ and $x_1 - x_2$, and equations by pairs of opposite inequalities.

g. Those results still remain true, except for the monotonicity, if the strategy polyhedra of the polyhedral games have the most general presentation $X = \{x \mid xC_1 \leq c_1, xC_2 \geq c_2, xC_3 = c_3\}$ and similarly for Y.

HINT. Rewriting the constraints in the standard way yields $x\overline{C} \geq \overline{c}$, where $\overline{c} = (c_1, -c_2, c_3, -c_3)$ is a linear function of the vector $c = (c_1, c_2, c_3)$.

h. Allow now further the payoff function of the polyhedral game to be bi-affine rather than bi-linear, i.e., of the form $(1, x)\ A\ (1, y)$. Then $\overline{v}$ is piecewise bi-linear and concave convex in $(A_{0,\cdot}, c)$ and $(A_{\cdot,0}, b)$ respectively.

HINT. Introduce u_j and v_i as additional parameters of the strategies of players I and II, fixed by constraints to the values $A_{0,j}$ and $A_{i,0}$ respectively: the payoff becomes $u_0 v_0 + \sum_{j \geq 1} u_j y_j + \sum_{i \geq 1} v_i x_i + \sum_{i,j \geq 1} x_i A_{ij} y_j$ (and apply g).

Remark I.3.14. In the case of polyhedral games, the solution set may have no extreme points. Their analogue would be minimal faces, i.e., faces that are an affine subspace.

Remark I.3.15. This case includes the general linear programming model (without restrictions), which is obtained by taking a one-point polyhedron for one of the players.

12. To illustrate the need for the internal point conditions in the separation theorems (cf. Proposition I.1.11 above), even without continuity requirements and with the best of the other conditions, consider the following example:

a. Denote by $E = \mathbb{R}[x]$ the vector space of polynomials in x with real coefficients, ordered by the positive polynomials, that is, polynomials whose coefficient of highest degree is positive. The positive cone P satisfies $P \cup (-P) = E$, $P \cap (-P) = \{0\}$, i.e., the order is total, yet any non-negative linear function is zero.

b. Deduce that, on any ordered field extension of the reals, there is no positive (i.e., non-negative non-null) linear functional.

c. Show more generally, in part by the above argument, that this still holds for any ordered field extension $\overline{K}$ of an ordered field K (viewed as an ordered K-vector space).

13. (Weyl, 1950)
Give a direct proof of Theorem I.3.6, p. 32.

14. Jensen's inequality.
a. Let f be a convex function from $\mathbb{R}^n$ to $\mathbb{R} \cup \{+\infty\}$, and X an integrable random variable on $(\Omega, \mathscr{A}, P)$ with values in $\mathbb{R}^n$. Then $\int_* f(X(\omega))P(d\omega) \geq f(\mathsf{E}(X))$. (Recall that $\int_*$ denotes lower integral; cf. Section I.2.b, p. 16.)

HINT. Reduce first to the case where $\mathsf{E}(X) = 0$, and where X is not carried by any strict subspace. In $\mathbb{R}^n \times \mathbb{R}$, consider then the convex set $\overline{C} = \{(x, t) \mid t \geq f(x)\}$ and any point $(0, \alpha)$ with $\alpha < f(0)$: both are disjoint, there thus exists a linear functional φ and $\lambda \in \mathbb{R}$ such that $\varphi(x) + \lambda t \geq \lambda\alpha$ for $(x, t) \in \overline{C}$ (if $\overline{C} = \emptyset$ there is nothing to prove), and $\|\varphi\| + |\lambda| > 0$. Note that $\lambda \geq 0$, and if $\lambda > 0$ then $f(x) \geq \alpha - \frac{1}{\lambda}\varphi(x)$ yields the desired inequality. So one can assume $\lambda = 0$, i.e., $f(x) < \infty \Longrightarrow \varphi(x) \geq 0$. But since X is not carried by any strict subspace, $\mathsf{E}(X) = 0$ yields that $P\{\omega \mid \varphi(X(\omega)) < 0\} > 0$, hence $f(x) = +\infty$ on a set of positive (inner) measure: the inequality will also hold, as soon as one obtains an integrable bound for $f^-(x)$: for this, reduce again first to the case where zero is in the interior of $\{x \mid f(x) < +\infty\}$, and separate as above.

Remark I.3.16. For C convex, let $f(x) = 0$ for $x \in C$, $= +\infty$ otherwise, and thus obtain I.3, Ex. 10c, p. 40. The same shows there would be no gain in allowing f to be defined only on a convex subset of $\mathbb{R}^n$.

b. *Conditional versions*

Remark I.3.17. For conditional versions, we need somewhat stronger measurability requirements, e.g., even in the framework of I.3, Ex. 10c, we do not know whether $\mathsf{E}(X \mid \mathscr{B}) \in C$ with inner (or even just outer) probability one, for an integrable random variable X with values in a convex set C and $\mathscr{B} \subseteq \mathscr{A}$. Thus:

α. Assume $\mathscr{B} \subseteq \mathscr{A}$, X is an integrable random variable on $(\Omega, \mathscr{A}, P)$ with values in $\mathbb{R}^n$, and $g(\omega, x)$ maps $\Omega \times \mathbb{R}^n$ in $\mathbb{R} \cup \{+\infty\}$, is convex in x for each ω, and is μ-measurable, μ being the distribution of the random variable $(\omega, X(\omega))$ on $(\Omega, \mathscr{B}) \otimes (\mathbb{R}^n$, Borel sets). Assume also $g^-(\omega, X(\omega))$ is integrable. Then $\mathsf{E}[g(\cdot, X(\cdot)) \mid \mathscr{B}](\omega) \geq g[\omega, \mathsf{E}(X \mid \mathscr{B})(\omega)]$ a.s.

HINT. Show first that $g(\omega, X(\omega))$ is measurable, so that both conditional expectations are well defined. Let then (as in II.1, Ex. 9, p. 68) $\mu(dx \mid \omega)$ be a regular version of the conditional distribution of X given $\mathscr{B}$, chosen such that $\int \|x\| \, \mu(dx \mid \omega) < +\infty$ everywhere. Show that the measurability conditions on g assure that $\mathsf{E}(g(\cdot, X(\cdot)) \mid \mathscr{B})(\omega) = \int g(\omega, x)\mu(dx \mid \omega)$ a.e., and that the right-hand side is everywhere well defined. By (A), $\int g(\omega, x)\mu(dx \mid \omega) \geq g(\omega, y(\omega))$, with $y(\omega) = \int x\mu(dx \mid \omega)(= \mathsf{E}(X \mid \mathscr{B})(\omega)$ a.e.).

β. The measurability requirement on g can always be relaxed without changing the conclusion by adding to $\mathscr{B}$ all negligible subsets of $(\Omega, \mathscr{A}, P)$. Show however that one cannot add, on $\Omega \times \mathbb{R}^n$, all negligible subsets of the distribution of $(\omega, X(\omega))$ in $(\Omega, \mathscr{A}) \otimes (\mathbb{R}^n$, Borel sets). (The "argument" "just replace Ω by $\Omega \times \mathbb{R}^n$ with that distribution" does not work.)

HINT. Consider some g taking only the values 0 and $+\infty$.

γ. Show that the convexity assumption on g in I.3, Ex. 14bα, can be weakened to: $g(\omega, x)$ has a convex restriction to some convex set C_ω, where, for some (and then for any) regular version $\mu(dx \mid \omega)$ of the conditional distribution of X given $\mathscr{B}$, a.e. C_ω has $\mu(dx \mid \omega)$-outer measure 1.

HINT. In the proof of I.3, Ex. 14bα, you must have shown that a.e. $g(\omega, x)$ is $\mu(dx \mid \omega)$-measurable, so $\int g(\omega, x)\mu(dx \mid \omega) = \int_{C_\omega} g(\omega, x)\mu^*(dx)$, where $\mu^*(dx)$ is the trace of $\mu(dx \mid \omega)$ on C_ω, $(\mu^*(B \cap C_\omega) = \mu(B \mid \omega))$. Apply thus (A) with (C_ω, μ^*) as probability space, modifying g to $+\infty$ outside C_ω.

Remark I.3.18. Versions like I.3, Ex. 14bα, above will be needed in Chapter IX, Section IX.2. A version with varying C_ω (like in I.3, Ex. 14bγ) will be used in Lemma VI.2.14, p. 338. For versions with values in infinite dimensional spaces (e.g., Lemma VI.2.2, p. 328), one has to impose lower semi-continuity of the convex function, in order to use the Hahn–Banach theorem. Corresponding conditional versions (as in the use of Lemma VI.2.2 in Lemma VI.3.4, p. 340) can often be obtained by the same technique as above (regular conditionals), e.g., in the present case, because a (Bochner) integrable random variable with values in a Banach space has (a.e.) its values in a separable subspace, which is Polish. (Other techniques involve (1) using the same proof as in the unconditional case, e.g., when the convex function is already the upper bound of a countable family of continuous linear functionals, or (2) conceivably relying on versions of the martingale convergence theorem, approximating $\mathscr{B}$ by an increasing sequence of countable partitions $\mathscr{B}_n$, e.g., such that $\mathsf{E}(g(X) \mid \mathscr{B})$ is bounded on each partition element, and using the lower semi-continuity in the right-hand side.)

15. Real-valued convex functions.

a. A real-valued convex function on a polyhedron is u.s.c.

b. On the space of continuous, real-valued convex functions on a compact polyhedron, the topologies of pointwise convergence and of uniform convergence coincide.

HINT. Prove first, using the idea of I.3, Ex. 15a, plus compactness, that if $f_\alpha \to f$ pointwise, then $(f_\alpha - f)^+$ converges uniformly to zero. So one can assume $f_\alpha \le f$. Next, by Dini's theorem, $g_\beta \to f$ uniformly, where g_β denotes the increasing filtering family of all maxima of finitely many affine functions that are strictly smaller than f. Thus we can assume that $f > 0$, and it suffices to show that $f_\alpha \ge 0$ for $\alpha \ge \alpha_0$. Let $f_\alpha(x_\alpha) \le 0$. Then with b an interior point, and $y_\alpha = (1 - \varepsilon)x_\alpha + \varepsilon b$, we have $f_\alpha(y_\alpha) \le \varepsilon f(b)$. Choose $\varepsilon > 0$ such that $f(x) > \varepsilon f(b)\ \forall x$, and subtract $\varepsilon f(b)$ from f: we have $f > 0$, $f_\alpha(y_\alpha) \le 0$, and y_α is bounded away from the boundary. Thus, for $M = \max_x f(x)$, we can set φ_α the convexification of the function which is zero at y_α and M elsewhere: $\varphi_\alpha \ge f_\alpha$ so $\liminf \varphi_\alpha \ge f > 0$, and the φ_α are Lipschitz, since y_α is bounded away from the boundary. Conclude.

c. Define the "lower topology" on the space of convex $\overline{\mathbb{R}}$-valued functions on a convex set C by the neighborhood system $V_\varepsilon(f) = \{g \mid \varepsilon + g \ge f\}$. Show that this defines a topology. Prove that, if C is a compact, convex polyhedron and if a net of convex functions f_α converges pointwise to an u.s.c. function f, then $f_\alpha \to f$ in the lower topology.

HINT. We claim that $\varepsilon_\alpha = \max_{p \in C}[f(p) - f_\alpha(p)]$ converges to zero. We can prove this by induction on the dimension, and hence assume that the maximum on the boundary converges to zero. Hence, if the claim were not true, we would have, at least for some subnet, p_α in the interior and $f_\alpha(p_\alpha) \le f(p_\alpha) - 3\varepsilon$ for some $\varepsilon > 0$ (and hence f would be finite everywhere, hence bounded). Extracting a further subnet, we can assume $p_\alpha \to p_\infty$. Denote by $\overline{f}$ the (convex) extension by continuity of f from the interior to the boundary (i.e., $\overline{f}(p_\infty) = \lim_{\alpha \to \infty} f(p_\alpha)$). Let g be the (continuous) convexification of the function with value $\overline{f}(p_\infty) - 2\varepsilon$ at p_∞, and $\overline{f}$ elsewhere. Denote by q_∞ some interior point with $g(q_\infty) < f(q_\infty) - \varepsilon$: we have $q_\infty = tq + (1 - t)p_\infty$, with $0 < t < 1$, q interior, and $tf(q) + (1 - t)[\overline{f}(p_\infty) - 2\varepsilon] < f(q_\infty) - \varepsilon$. Let $q_\alpha = tq + (1 - t)p_\alpha$: $q_\alpha \to q_\infty$, by convexity $f_\alpha(q_\alpha) \le tf_\alpha(q) + (1 - t)f_\alpha(p_\alpha) \le tf_\alpha(q) + (1 - t)f(p_\alpha) - 3(1 - t)\varepsilon$, and the right-hand member converges to $tf(q) + (1 - t)\overline{f}(p_\infty) - 3(1 - t)\varepsilon$; hence for

α sufficiently large $f_\alpha(q_\alpha) \le tf(q) + (1-t)[\overline{f}(p_\infty) - 2\varepsilon] < f(q_\infty) - \varepsilon$. But the sequence $q_\alpha \to q_\infty$, being compact in the interior, is included in some compact, convex polyhedron P in the interior of C. On P, the functions f_α and f are continuous, hence $f_\alpha \to f$ implies that $f_\alpha \to f$ uniformly on P (by I.3, Ex. 15b), contradicting our inequality which implies that, for α sufficiently large, $f_\alpha(q_\alpha) < f(q_\alpha) - \varepsilon$.

I.4. EQUILIBRIUM POINTS

Theorem I.4.1. *(Nash, 1950; Glicksberg, 1952) Let $S^1, \dots, S^n$ be compact topological spaces, $F^1, \dots, F^n$ continuous real-valued functions on $\prod_{i=1}^n S^i$. Then, using regular probability measures for mixed strategies, there exists an equilibrium point.*

The same result holds true in pure strategies if the sets S^i are compact convex subsets of locally convex linear spaces and if, for every i and every real α, the sets $A^\alpha(s^j)_{j\neq i} = \{ s^i \mid F^i(s^1, \dots, s^n) \ge \alpha \}$ are convex.

Proof. There is no loss in assuming the S^i to be Hausdorff: first, map S^i to its compact Hausdorff image $\overline{S}^i$ in the space of continuous $\mathbb{R}^n$-valued functions on $\prod_{j\neq i} S^j$, do the proof on the $\overline{S}^i$, and finally extend the resulting $\overline{\sigma}^i$ on $\overline{S}^i$ to regular probability measures σ^i on S^i; such extensions always exist. Let Σ^i be the (convex) set of all regular probabilities on S^i, endowed with the (compact) topology of weak convergence. Let Φ^i be the real-valued function defined on $\Sigma = \prod_i \Sigma^i$ by $\Phi^i(\sigma^1, \dots, \sigma^n) = \int_{\prod_j S^j} F^i d \prod_j \sigma^j$. Obviously, Φ^i is multilinear. It is continuous by Proposition I.1.7, p. 8. So $\Sigma^1, \dots, \Sigma^n$ and $\Phi^1, \dots, \Phi^n$ satisfy the conditions of the second part of the theorem. Thus there remains only to prove it.

Let T be the **best-reply correspondence**:

$$T(s^1, \dots, s^n) = \prod_{i=1} \{ \tilde{s} \in S^i \mid F^i(s^1, \dots, s^{i-1}, \tilde{s}, s^{i+1}, \dots, s^n) = \max_{s \in S^i} F^i(s^1, \dots, s^{i-1}, s, s^{i+1}, \dots, s^n) \}.$$

We know that $T(s^1, \dots, s^n)$ is a non-empty, compact, and convex subset of $S = \prod_i S^i$. Further, the continuity of the F^i ensures that T has a closed graph (i.e., $G = \{ (s,t) \in S^2 \mid t \in T(s) \}$ is closed in S^2). By Fan's fixed point theorem (Fan, 1952) (cf. also Glicksberg (1952), and I.4, Ex. 17, p. 54), the mapping T has a fixed point. This completes the proof. ∎

EXERCISES

1. Symmetric equilibria.

a. (Nash, 1951) In the finite case, prove the existence of an equilibrium invariant under all symmetries of the game, i.e., permutations of the player set accompanied by one-to-one mappings between the pure strategy sets of corresponding players, leaving the payoff functions (or merely the best-reply correspondence) invariant.

HINT. Let X be the set of symmetric n-tuples of mixed strategies (i.e., invariant under all above symmetries of the game). Prove that X is convex, compact, and non-empty. Show that the set of best replies to a point in X intersects X (consider its barycenter).

b. Under the conditions of Theorem I.4.1, p. 45, assume that $S^i = S$ and $F^i(s^1, \ldots, s^n) = F^{\theta(i)}(s^{\theta(1)}, \ldots, s^{\theta(n)})$ for all i and all θ permutation on $\{1, \ldots, n\}$. Prove that there exists a symmetric equilibrium. (Use Fan's theorem on $\Phi(\tau) = \{\sigma \mid F^1(\sigma, \tau, \ldots, \tau) \geq F^1(\sigma', \tau, \ldots, \tau),\ \forall \sigma'\}$.)

2. Under the assumptions of Theorem I.4.1, show that, if for some player i, F^i is "strictly concave-like," i.e., any convex combination of two distinct pure strategies of him is strictly dominated by one of his pure strategies, then he uses a pure strategy in any equilibrium point.

3. Let S and T be two compact topological spaces, and $f(s, t)$ a continuous real-valued function on $S \times T$. Deduce the minmax theorem for $f(s, t)$ from Theorem I.4.1.

4. The manifold of Nash equilibria. (Kohlberg and Mertens, 1986)

a. We assume finite strategy sets S^i, and keep the notations of Theorem I.4.1. Let $\Gamma^i = \mathbb{R}^S$ (space of payoff functions of i); then $\Gamma = \prod_i \Gamma^i$ is the space of games. Let also $E = \{(G, \sigma) \in \Gamma \times \Sigma \mid \sigma \text{ is an equilibrium of } G\}$ (the equilibrium graph). Denote by $\overline{L}$ the one-point compactification of a locally compact space L, and by $\overline{p}\colon \overline{E} \to \overline{\Gamma}$ the continuous extension of the projection $p\colon E \to \Gamma$ with $\overline{p}(\infty) = \infty$. Prove that $\overline{p}$ is homotopic to a homeomorphism (under a homotopy mapping ∞ to ∞ and E to Γ).

HINT. Let $T^i = \prod_{h \neq i} S^h$; reparameterize Γ^i, the set of all $S^i \times T^i$-payoff matrices $G^i_{s,t}$ by $G^i_{st} = \tilde{G}^i_{s,t} + g^i_s$ with $\sum_t \tilde{G}^i_{st} = 0$; letting $z^i_s = \sigma^i_s + \sum_{t \in T^i} G^i_{s,t} \prod_{j \neq i} \sigma^j_{t_j}$, $(\tilde{G}, z)$ can be viewed as belonging to Γ. Show that $(G, \sigma) \to (\tilde{G}, z)$ is a homeomorphism ϕ from E to Γ (let $v^i = \min\{\alpha \mid \sum_{s \in S^i} (z^i_s - \alpha)^+ \leq 1\}$; then $\sigma^i_s = (z^i_s - v^i)^+$ and $g^i_s = z^i_s - \sigma^i_s - \sum_{t \in T_i} \tilde{G}^i_{s,t} \prod_{j \neq i} \sigma^j_{t_j}$). Then $p_t(G, \sigma) = (\tilde{G}, tz + (1 - t)g)$, and $p_t(\infty) = \infty$ is the desired homotopy; for the continuity at ∞, show that $\|z - g\| \leq \|\tilde{G}\| + 1$ in the maximum norm.

b. Deduce that the number of equilibria is generically finite and odd.

5.

a. Assume the sets S^i are finite, and the functions F^i have values in an ordered field K. If $N > 2$, assume K is real closed. Show that Theorem I.4.1, p. 45, remains valid, the μ^i being a vector $(p^i_1, \ldots, p^i_{\#S}) \in K^{\#S^i}$ such that $p^i_s \geq 0$ and $\sum_{s \in S^i} p^i_s = 1$.

HINT. cf. Section I.3, p. 31.

Remark I.4.1. This implies the result of Section I.3 (cf. I.4, Ex. 3).

b. In the following three-person game with integral payoffs (I chooses the rows, II the columns, III the matrix):

$$\begin{pmatrix} 0,0,0 & 2,1,2 \\ 1,2,2 & 0,0,0 \end{pmatrix} \qquad \begin{pmatrix} 2,0,1 & 1,1,0 \\ 0,1,1 & 0,0,0 \end{pmatrix},$$

there is a unique equilibrium with irrational payoff.

HINT. Consider the golden number as probability of the first strategy and as payoff.

c. The symmetric three-person game

$$\begin{pmatrix} 0,0,0 & 2,1,2 \\ 1,2,2 & 0,0,0 \end{pmatrix} \qquad \begin{pmatrix} 2,2,1 & 0,0,0 \\ 0,0,0 & 1,1,1 \end{pmatrix}$$

has nine different equilibria, of which three are symmetric, four are pure, and two are completely mixed with the same payoff.

6. Under the assumptions of Theorem I.4.1 or of I.4, Ex. 5, show that the support of μ^i is contained in the closed set of pure best replies:

$$\Big\{ s \in S^i \mid \int_{\prod_{h \neq i} S^j} F^i(s^1, \ldots, s^{i-1}, s, s^{i+1}, \ldots, s^n)\, d \prod_{h \neq i} \mu^h$$

$$= \max_{\tilde{s} \in S^i} \int_{\prod_{h \neq i} S^h} F^i(s^1, \ldots, s^{i-1}, \tilde{s}, s^{i+1}, \ldots, s^n)\, d \prod_{h \neq i} \mu^h \Big\}.$$

In particular, the μ^h $(h \neq i)$ are "equalizing" for all pure strategies that are in the support of μ^i.

7. Linear complementarity problem.

This concerns the computation of equilibria of bi-matrix games and related problems in operations research (cf. Lemke and Howson (1964) for corresponding algorithms).

a. *Reduction to symmetric games.* Let (A, B) be a bi-matrix game. Add constants to the payoffs such as to have $\max_x \min_y xAy > 0$, $\max_y \min_x xBy > 0$, (i.e., each player can guarantee himself a positive amount). Denote by (S, S^t) the symmetric game $\begin{pmatrix} 0,0 & A,B \\ B^t, A^t & 0,0 \end{pmatrix}$. Show that there is a one-to-one correspondence between equilibria of (A, B) and symmetric equilibria of (S, S^t).

b. Let $T = K - S$, for some constant matrix K larger than the payoff $x\,S\,x$ of any symmetric equilibrium x of S. In terms of T, the symmetric equilibria of S are characterized by the linear complementarity problem, where z is a symmetric equilibrium strategy x divided by $x\,T\,x$:

$$Tz = \tilde{1} + u, \qquad z \geq 0,\ u \geq 0,\ \langle z, u \rangle = 0,$$

"$\tilde{1}$" being a column of ones. Show that our assumption on K can be rewritten in terms of T as:

$$Tz^+ - z^- = \lambda \cdot \tilde{1}, \qquad \lambda \leq 0 \Longrightarrow z = \lambda \cdot \tilde{1}.$$

c. Denote by $\mathscr{S}$ the class of $n \times n$-matrices S such that, for some non-negative, non-singular diagonal matrix D, one has:

$$z \geq 0,\ z \neq 0 \Longrightarrow z^t(SD)z > 0.$$

α. Show that, if D_1 and D_2 are non-negative, non-singular diagonal matrices, then $S \in \mathscr{S} \Longrightarrow D_1 S D_2 \in \mathscr{S}$, and $S^t \in \mathscr{S}$.

β. $\mathscr{S}$ contains all sums of a positive definite matrix, a non-negative matrix, and an antisymmetric matrix.

γ. For $T \in \mathscr{S}$, the condition in I.4, Ex. 7b, is satisfied.

δ. For $T \in \mathscr{S}$, let $F: x \to Tx^+ - x^-$. Show that $F(\mathbb{R}^n)$ contains the interior of the positive orthant.

HINT. Use I.4, Ex. 7cα, to perform a rescaling from the result of I.4, Ex. 7b.

d. *A direct approach; compare with I.4, Ex. 4.* For $T \in \mathscr{S}$, the map $F: x \to Tx^+ - x^-$ (with $F(\infty) = \infty$) is of degree one (homotopic to the identity); in particular $F(\mathbb{R}^n) = \mathbb{R}^n$.

HINT. For $F_t: x \to (1-t)x + tF(x)$ to be a homotopy, one needs that $\forall M, \exists K: \|x\| \geq K \Longrightarrow \|F_t(x)\| \geq M, \ \forall t \in [0,1]$. By homogeneity (and extracting subsequences), this is equivalent to $F_t(x) = 0 \Longrightarrow x = 0$, i.e., to $[x \geq 0, x^t x = 1, Tx \geq (x^t Tx) \cdot x] \Longrightarrow x^t Tx > 0$ or equivalently $x^- = (T + \lambda I)x^+, \lambda \geq 0 \Longrightarrow x = 0$, which clearly holds for $T \in \mathscr{S}$. More generally, this holds for all matrices in the connected component of I in the open set of matrices M satisfying $Mx^+ = x^- \Longrightarrow x = 0$. (Same argument: prove openness directly, and use semi-algebraicity to deduce the equivalence of connectedness with pathwise connectedness and the existence of finitely many connected components.) Show that there is more than one connected component (consider $-I$, at least for n odd.).

e. By rescaling, I.4, Ex. 7b, implies that if $F_i(z) < 0, \ \forall i$ implies $z_i < 0, \ \forall i$, and if $F(z) = 0$ implies $z = 0$, then $F(z) = a$ has a solution whenever $a_i > 0, \ \forall i$. Verify that the condition $x^- = (T + \lambda I)x^+, \lambda \geq 0 \Longrightarrow x = 0$ in I.4, Ex. 7d, above, is weaker.

f. The above existence result remains true over any ordered field.

8. Let K be a real closed field. Call a subset A of K^ℓ bounded if there exists $m \in K$ such that, for all $x \in A$, $x = (x_1, \ldots, x_\ell)$, and for all i $(1 \leq i \leq \ell)$, $|x_i| \leq m$. Call a semi-algebraic subset of K^ℓ closed if it can be described using only weak inequalities (i.e., $\geq$ or $\leq$).

Assume each set S^i is a closed bounded semi-algebraic subset of K^{ℓ_i}, which is a union of closed algebraic subsets A^i_j $(j = 1, \ldots, n_i)$. Assume the restriction of each F^i to $\prod_{i=1}^n A^i_{j_i}$ (for all j_i: $1 \leq j_i \leq n_i$) is a polynomial in the coordinates with coefficients in K. Show that the game has an equilibrium point in algebraic strategies, i.e., mixed strategies with finite support, the weights of the distinct points in the support being in K (i.e., as in I.4, Ex. 5).

HINT. Use first Corollary I.3.4, p. 31, to reduce the problem to the case $K = \mathbb{R}$. Show then that the assumptions of Theorem I.4.1, p. 45, are satisfied, so that there exists an equilibrium point in mixed strategies $\mu^1, \ldots, \mu^n$. Note then that the restriction of μ^i to A^i_j intervenes only through a finite number of its moments, so (I.3, Ex. 10, p. 40) each μ^i may be taken with finite support (with at most N points, N depending only on the number of A^i_j's and on the degrees of the polynomials appearing in the F^j's: this is needed to justify the use of Tarski's theorem).

9. (Gross, 1957)

Let $S = T = [0,1]$, and let $f(s,t) = \sum_{n=0}^{\infty} 2^{-n}[2s^n - (1 - \frac{s}{3})^n - (\frac{s}{3})^n][2t^n - (1 - \frac{t}{3})^n - (\frac{t}{3})^n]$. Show that $f(s,t)$ is a rational payoff function without singularities on the unit square, i.e., can be written as the ratio of two polynomials with integer coefficients in s and t, the denominator of which vanishes nowhere in the unit square.

Show that the value of the corresponding two-person zero-sum game is zero, and that both players have the Cantor distribution $C(x)$ as a unique optimal strategy.

HINT. Note that $C(x)$ is the unique monotone solution of $C(x) + C(1 - x) = 1$ and $C(x) = 2C(\frac{x}{3})$. Deduce that, for any continuous real-valued function $h(x)$, $\int_0^1 [2h(x) - h(1 - \frac{x}{3}) - h(\frac{x}{3})] \, dC(x) = 0$. There only remains to show the uniqueness of the solution. Let μ be any optimal strategy of player I. Then $\int_0^1 f(s,t)\mu(ds)$ is an analytical function of t (integrate the series term by term) that has to vanish on the (infinite) support of the Cantor distribution: it vanishes everywhere. Thus $\int_0^1 f(s,t)\,\mu(ds)\,\mu(dt) = 0 = \sum_0^\infty 2^{-n}(\mu_n)^2$, so that, for all n, $\int_0^1 [2s^n - (1-\frac{s}{3})^n - (\frac{s}{3})^n]\,\mu(ds) = \mu_n = 0$. This determines inductively in a unique way all moments $\int_0^1 s^n\,\mu(ds)$ $(n \geq 1)$, and thus the distribution μ itself.

Remark I.4.2. This shows that the solution may be a singular continuous distribution. Glicksberg and Gross (1953) show how to construct rational games over the square whose solutions are purely atomic and have dense support. In view of the importance of the possibility of reducing to mixtures with finite support in the proof of I.4, Ex. 8, it is not surprising to find (Glicksberg and Gross, 1953) the following example of a rational game over the square with transcendental value, which therefore definitely excludes the possibility of an algebraic solution of rational games.

10. Let $S = T = [0,1]$, and $f(s,t) = (1+s)(1+t)(1-st)/(1+st)^2$.

Show that the value of the corresponding two-person zero-sum game is $4/\pi$, and that each player's optimal strategy is given by the cumulative distribution function on $[0,1]$: $F(x) = \frac{4}{\pi}\arctan\sqrt{x}$.

11. Can you get similar results to I.4, Ex. 8, that would include Karlin's (1959) "generalized convex games" and/or "bell-shaped games"?

12. Bertrand competition.

Two firms compete in price over the sale of a product. Assume that production costs are zero (if only by subtracting mentally a constant from prices). Assume the demand $D(p)$ at any price $p \geq 0$ satisfies $0 \leq D(p) < +\infty$, and $\limsup_{q \lessgtr p} D(q) \geq D(p) \geq \limsup_{q \gtrless p} D(q)$ for $p > 0$. Typically the demand is decreasing, which implies those relations. We also assume that demand is not identically zero in a neighborhood of zero. The firm announcing the lowest price serves the whole demand, at that price. If the announced prices are equal, consumers decide indifferently what share of their demand to allocate to each firm. Profit is pd, if p is the announced price and d the demand served, and firms want to maximize expected profits.

a. Show that $(0,0)$ is a Nash equilibrium.

b. Let $G(p) = \max_{q \leq p} qD(q)$. Show that $G(p)$ is continuous, except possibly at $p = 0$.

c. Show that $\{\, p \mid pD(p) < G(p) \,\}$ is a countable union of disjoint intervals, open on the right.

d. For any Nash equilibrium, denote by π_i the expected profit of player i, and by $F_i(p)$ the probability that his announced price is $\geq p$, i.e., $F_j(p) = \sigma_j([p,+\infty])$.

α. Show that, if $\pi_1 = 0$ or $\pi_2 = 0$, we have only the equilibrium, I.4, Ex. 12b. Henceforth we assume $\pi_1 > 0, \pi_2 > 0$.

β. Show that $\pi_1 < +\infty$ and $\pi_2 < +\infty$.

γ. Show that $F_i(p) \leq \pi_j H(p)$, $\forall p$, with $H(p) = 1/G(p)$ $(i \neq j)$.

δ. Let $T_j = \{\, p \mid F_i(p) = \pi_j H(p) \,\}$. Show that T_j is closed, except possibly at zero, and that $\sigma_j(T_j) = 1$.

e. Show that $T_1 = T_2 (= T)$.

HINT. The complement of T_1 is a countable, disjoint union of open intervals $[\alpha_k, \beta_k]$ (with possibly $\beta_1 = +\infty$), plus either $\{0\}$ or $[0, \beta_0]$. On $[\alpha_k, \beta_k]$, and on $[0, \beta_0]$, we have

$F_1(p) = F_1(\beta_k) \le \pi_2 H(\beta_k)$ (with $F(\infty) = H(\infty) = 0$ by convention), and $\pi_1 H(p) > F_2(p) \ge F_2(\beta_k) = \pi_1 H(\beta_k)$. Thus $\pi_2 H(p) > F_1(p)$, hence $[\alpha_k, \beta_k] \cap T_2 = \emptyset$. And certainly $0 \notin T_1$, $0 \notin T_2$.

f. Show that any Nash equilibrium is symmetric (thus $\pi_1 = \pi_2 = \pi, \sigma_1 = \sigma_2 = \sigma$, $F_1 = F_2 = F$).

HINT. Let $\tilde{H}(p) = \sup\{ H(q) \mid q \in T, q \ge p \}$, with $\sup(\emptyset) = 0$. By I.4, Ex. 12d, and I.4, Ex. 12e, $F_i(p) = \pi_j \tilde{H}(p)$. And $F_i(0) = 1$.

g. Show that any Nash equilibrium (other than (0, 0)) is non-atomic.

HINT. By I.4, Ex. 12f, every atom is common to both players, and is > 0. Use then Bertrand's "undercutting" argument.

h. Conclude that either $T = [a, +\infty]$ with $a > 0$ or $T = [0, +\infty]$. In particular, let $\overline{G}(p) = G(p)$ for $p > 0$, $\overline{G}(0) = \lim_{\varepsilon \gtrsim 0} G(\varepsilon)$, then $F(p) = 1 \wedge (\overline{G}(a)/\overline{G}(p))$ for some $a \ge 0$ with $0 < \pi = \overline{G}(a) < +\infty$.

i. Conclude that, for the existence of equilibria $\neq (0, 0)$, one needs both $\overline{G}(\infty) = \infty$, i.e., $\limsup_{p \to \infty} pD(p) = +\infty$, and $\overline{G}(0) < +\infty$, i.e., $\limsup_{p \to 0} pD(p) < +\infty$.

j. Show that, for any $F(p)$ as in I.4, Ex. 12h, one has

(1) $(pD(p))F(p) \le \pi, \quad \forall p \ge 0$ and
(2) $\sigma\{ p \mid (pD(p))F(p) < \pi \} = 0$.

HINT. For the second point, use I.4, Ex. 12c.

k. Deduce from I.4, Ex. 12j, that the condition in I.4, Ex. 12i, is also sufficient: any such F is an equilibrium; hence the equilibria different from (0, 0) are under that condition in one-to-one correspondence with the profit levels $\pi > 0, \pi \ge \limsup_{p \to 0} pD(p)$.

In particular, if possible profits are bounded in this market, there is a unique equilibrium, (0, 0), which involves strategies that are dominated by every other strategy. The next exercise considers better-behaved examples of the same situation.

13. Variations on Bertrand competition.

a. Players I and II choose, respectively, x and y in [0, 1], and get, respectively, as payoffs $f(x, y) = y^2 x/(2x^2 + y^2)$ and $f(y, x)$.

α. The payoff is continuous, even Lipschitz.

β. Show that (0, 0) is the unique Nash equilibrium.

HINT. Observe that, for $y > 0$ fixed, $f(x, y)$ decreases after its maximum at $y/\sqrt{2} < y$. Do not forget any type of mixed or mixed versus pure equilibrium.

γ. Yet those strategies are dominated by every other strategy: for any other mixed strategy of the opponent, any other mixed strategy of the player is strictly better than the equilibrium strategy.

b. Show that, in any game with continuous payoff function on compact metric strategy spaces, there is some equilibrium whose strategies are limits of undominated strategies. (In particular, the above example of Bertrand's "undercutting" argument is probably the best known case of a limit of undominated points being dominated; cf. also I.3, Ex. 7, p. 38.)

HINT. Show that each player has a strategy with full support. Show that the perturbed game where each player's choice is played with probability $1 - \varepsilon$ (independently of the other players), while a fixed strategy with full support is played otherwise, satisfies the usual conditions for existence of equilibria. Then let $\varepsilon \to 0$.

c. Show that the phenomenon in example I.4, Ex. 13a, cannot occur when f is polynomial, or, more generally, with separable payoffs $f(x, y) = \sum_1^n g_i(x)h_i(y)$ (when the g_i and h_i are continuous functions on compact strategy spaces). In other words, for such payoff functions there cannot be a unique equilibrium that is dominated by every other strategy.

HINT. The requirement implies the equilibrium is pure, say (x_0, y_0). Subtract $f(x_0, y)$ from player I's payoffs $f(x, y)$, and similarly for II's payoffs: this preserves the separability and the equilibria: let $\varphi_y(x) = f(x, y)$, and $\varphi_x(y) = f(y, x)$; then we have $\varphi_y(x_0) = 0$, $\varphi_{y_0}(x) = 0$, $\varphi_y(x) \geq 0$, and $\|\varphi_y\| > 0$ for $y \neq y_0$ (if $\|\varphi_y\| = 0$, then (x_0, y) would be another equilibrium, since $\psi_{x_0}(y) = 0$). The functions φ_y vary in a finite n-dimensional space, where all norms are equivalent, and where the unit sphere is compact: construct thus a new game with I's payoff function $G(x, y) = [\varphi_y(x)] / \|\varphi_y\|$, for $y \neq y_0$, and take for the strategy space of player II the closure of those functions (for computing player II's payoff, points in the closure are sent to y_0). Do now the same with the payoff function of II. The new game is still continuous (on compact strategy spaces), but now since $\max_x G(x, y) = 1$, $\forall y$, player I's minmax payoff is > 0 (strategy with full support). Hence an equilibrium of this game assigns zero probability to x_0 and to y_0 ($G(x_0, y) = 0$). By the separability, the equilibrium can be chosen with finite support (I.3, Ex. 10, p. 40). Reconstruct from this an equilibrium of the original game, with the same support.

d. Let $F_1(x, y) = y[x^3 - (1 + 2y)x^2 + (2y + \frac{1}{2}y^2)x]$, $F_2(x, y) = F_1(y, x)$ ($(x, y) \in [0, 1]^2$) be the payoff functions of players I and II. As polynomials, the payoffs are a bi-linear function of the first three moments $(\sigma_1, \sigma_2, \sigma_3)$ ($\sigma^i = \int_0^1 x^i \sigma(dx)$) of the strategy σ of I, and of (τ_1, τ_2, τ_3), given by the payoff matrix:

$$\begin{array}{c} \\ \sigma_1 \\ \sigma_2 \\ \sigma_3 \end{array} \begin{array}{c} \begin{array}{ccc} \tau_1 & \tau_2 & \tau_3 \end{array} \\ \begin{pmatrix} 0, 0 & 2, -1 & 1/2, 1 \\ -1, 2 & -2, -2 & 0, 0 \\ 1, 1/2 & 0, 0 & 0, 0 \end{pmatrix} \end{array},$$

where $(\sigma_1, \sigma_2, \sigma_3)$ and (τ_1, τ_2, τ_3) are to be selected in the compact convex "moment space" C in $\mathbb{R}^3$ given by:

$$C = \{ (\mu_1, \mu_2, \mu_3) \mid \mu_2^2 \leq \mu_1\mu_3, (\mu_1 - \mu_2)^2 \leq (1 - \mu_1)(\mu_2 - \mu_3)$$
$$\text{together with } 0 \leq \mu_3 \leq 1 \}.$$

Show that indeed $C = \{ \int_0^1 (x, x^2, x^3)\mu(dx) \mid \mu \in \Delta([0, 1]) \}$.

HINT. A direct proof may go by characterizing by hand the supporting affine functionals, hence the extreme rays of the cone of third-degree polynomials that are non-negative on $[0, 1]$.

Alternatively, write a polynomial as $A^t \cdot X$, all vectors being column vectors, with A the vector of coefficients and X the successive powers of the variable x. Then $A^t X X^t A$ is the square of a polynomial, hence non-negative; since μ is carried by $[0, 1]$, this remains true if XX^t is multiplied by powers of x and/or of $1 - x$, yielding a matrix Y. Thus the expectation of Y is positive semi-definite. Hence the validity of the inequalities.

Conversely, observe first that on C, we have $0 \leq \mu_3 \leq \mu_2 \leq \mu_1 \leq 1$; and that $\{ \mu \in C \mid \mu_2^2 = \mu_1\mu_3 \}$ is the set of convex combinations of $(0, 0, 0)$ and a point on the curve (x, x^2, x^3), and similarly for the other inequality and the point $(1, 1, 1)$. Conclude that the whole of C belongs to the convex hull of the curve.

More generally, the converse may go by showing that the polynomials we considered span indeed the cone of polynomials non-negative on $[0, 1]$: polynomials that are non-negative on $[0, 1]$

can be factored in a product of quadratic factors that are everywhere non-negative, and of linear factors that are of the form $(x + a)$ or $(a + 1 - x)$ for $a \geq 0$. Decompose the quadratic factors as sums of two squares, and the linear factors into the sum of the constant non-negative polynomial a (a square) and either x or $1 - x$: our whole polynomial is now rewritten as a sum of products of a square with powers of x and of $1 - x$.

e. Show that the game defined in I.4, Ex. 13d, has a unique Nash equilibrium, (0, 0), while strategy 0 is dominated by 1, with strict inequality for all strategies of the opponent different from the equilibrium strategy.

HINT. The dominance is clear. The statement does not depend on the factor y in $F(x, y)$. Let $\varphi_y(x) = F_1(x, y)/y$. For $y > 0, \varphi_y'(0) > 0, \varphi_y'(y) < 0$, there is a local maximum $x(y)$ in $[0, y]$, with $\varphi_y(x(y)) > \varphi_y(y)$. Also $\varphi_y(y) - \varphi_y(1) \geq 0$, thus $x(y) < y$ is the global maximum. By symmetry, conclude that there is no equilibrium where one player's strategy is pure and $\neq 0$. And if the pure strategy is zero, since it is as good a reply as 1, it means the opponent also uses zero with probability one. Thus there only remains to consider equilibria where no player uses a pure strategy. For any such strategy of II, player I's payoff function is of the form $Ax^3 + Bx^2 + Cx$, with $A > 0, C > 0$: thus if the maximum is not unique, it is a set of the form $\{x_0, 1\}$ with $0 < x_0 < 1$. Thus also II uses a mixture on $\{y_0, 1\}$ with probabilities q and $1 - q$, with $0 < y_0 < 1, 0 < q < 1$: in player I's payoff we have $B = -1 - 2(qy_0 + 1 - q)$. On the other hand, since I is indifferent between x_0 and 1, we have $Ax^3 + Bx^2 + Cx = (x - x_0)^2(x - 1) + \text{constant}$, hence $B = -1 - 2x_0$. Thus $x_0 > y_0$, and dually $y_0 > x_0$.

f. In $\begin{pmatrix} x, 0 & -x^2, x & 0, 0 \\ 0, 1 & 0, 0 & 1, 0 \end{pmatrix}$ player I also has to choose $x \in [0, 1]$ if he selects the top row. This game also has a unique Nash equilibrium, where player I uses a dominated strategy. Further the game is "almost strictly competitive": the unique equilibrium strategies are also dominant strategies in the game where each player would instead try to minimize his opponent's payoff; thus we are as close to the zero-sum situation and to finite games as one could possibly get (cf. I.4, Ex. 13g, and I.4, Ex. 13h)). But the game no longer has the flavor of Bertrand's "undercutting"; player II's strategy is not dominated (cf. I.4, Ex. 13b, and I.4, Ex. 13g), and the dominating strategy of player I is no longer strictly better for every strategy different from the equilibrium strategy (cf. I.4, Ex. 13i).

Remark I.4.3. As defined by Aumann (1961a), "almost strictly competitive" means:

- Equilibrium payoffs in (g_1, g_2) and $(-g_2, -g_1)$ are the same.
- The sets of equilibria in (g_1, g_2) and $(-g_2, -g_1)$ intersect.

Then there exists (s, t) such that s realizes $\max_s \min g_1$ and $\min_s \max g_2$ (and similarly for t). s is not a dominant strategy.

g. If player I has a finite strategy set, his set of undominated mixed strategies is closed and is a union of faces. Indeed, if σ is dominated, say, by $\tilde{\sigma}$, then any convex combination $\alpha\sigma + (1 - \alpha)\tau$ $(0 < \alpha < 1)$ is also dominated by $\alpha\tilde{\sigma} + (1 - \alpha)\tau$. Thus, in a finite dimensional vector space ordered by an arbitrary positive cone, the set of admissible points of a compact polyhedron is a union of faces (cf. Arrow et al., 1953).

h. In the zero-sum case, say under the assumptions of Theorem I.2.4, p. 21, there always exist undominated optimal strategies.

HINT. Under those assumptions, show that every strategy is dominated by an undominated strategy. (Use Zorn's lemma or an equivalent.)

i. If player II's strategy set is finite, player I's is compact, and the payoff continuous, and if there is an equilibrium where I's strategy is dominated by another one that is strictly better for every strategy of II different from the equilibrium strategy, then there is another equilibrium.

HINT. Since player I maximizes, the dominating strategy will then dominate a neighborhood of his equilibrium strategy. Apply then I.4, Ex. 13b; only II's strategy has to be perturbed.

14. (Dasgupta and Maskin, 1986)

Let $S^i = [0, 1]$ for all i and let $\mathscr{F}$ be a finite family of one-to-one continuous mappings from $[0, 1]$ to $[0, 1]$. Let $A(i) = \{ s \mid \exists j \neq i, \exists f \in \mathscr{F} : s^j = f(s^i) \}$. Assume that F^i is continuous on $(B(i))^c$ for all i, with $B(i) \subseteq A(i)$.

a. Define G_n as the initial game restricted to $S^i_n = \{ k/n \mid k = 0, 1, \dots, n \}$ for all i and let σ_n be a corresponding equilibrium such that σ_n converges (weak*) to $\overline{\sigma}$ and $F^i(\sigma_n)$ converges to some $\overline{F^i}$, $i = 1, \dots, n$. Prove that there are at most countably many points s^i such that $F^i(s^i, \overline{\sigma}^{-i}) > \overline{F^i}$. (Prove first that for such an s^i one has $\overline{\sigma}^{-i}(\{ s^{-i} \mid (s^i, s^{-i}) \in A^i \}) > 0$ and that this implies: $\exists j \neq i, \exists f \in \mathscr{F}, \sigma^j(f(s^i)) > 0$.)

b. Assume moreover $\sum_{i=1}^n F^i$ u.s.c. and that each F^i satisfies the following: for all $s^i \in B_i(i)$: $\exists \lambda \in [0, 1]$ such that for all s^{-i} with $s = (s^i, s^{-i}) \in B(i)$, $\lambda \liminf_{t^i \nearrow s^i} F^i(t^i, s^{-i}) + (1 - \lambda) \liminf_{t^i \searrow s^i} F^i(t^i, s^{-i}) \geq F^i(s)$. Prove that $\overline{\sigma}$ is an equilibrium with payoff $\overline{F}$.

c. Extend the result to S^i compact convex in some $\mathbb{R}^m$.

d. Consider the two-person symmetric game with

$$F^1(s^1, s^2) = \begin{cases} 0, & \text{if } s^1 = s^2 = 1, \\ s^1, & \text{otherwise.} \end{cases}$$

(Note that $F^1 + F^2$ is not u.s.c. at $(1, 1)$.)

15. Fictitious play. (Robinson, 1951)

"Fictitious play" is the procedure where each player chooses at every stage a best reply against the distribution of his opponent's past choices. We prove here that, for zero-sum games, the frequency of moves converges to the optimal strategies.

Given an $m \times n$ real payoff matrix A, write A^i for the row i and A_j for the column. Call admissible a sequence $(\alpha(t), \beta(t))$ in $\mathbb{R}^n \times \mathbb{R}^m$, $t \in \mathbb{N}$ satisfying:

(1) $\inf_j \alpha_j(0) = \sup_i \beta_i(0)$.
(2) $\forall t \in \mathbb{N}, \exists i : \alpha(t + 1) = \alpha(t) + A^i$, with $\beta_i(t) = \sup_k \beta_k(t)$.
(3) $\forall t \in \mathbb{N}, \exists j : \beta(t + 1) = \beta(t) + A_j$, with $\alpha_j(t) = \inf_k \alpha_k(t)$.

Say that i (resp. j) is useful in (t_1, t_2) if there exists t in $\mathbb{N}$ with $t_1 \leq t \leq t_2$ and $\beta_i(t) = \sup_k \beta_k(t)$ (resp. $\alpha_j(t) = \inf_k \alpha_k(t)$).

a. Prove that if all j are useful in $(s, s + t)$; then:

$$\sup_j \alpha_j(s + t) - \inf_j \alpha_j(s + t) \leq 2t \, \|A\| .$$

Defining $\mu(t)$ as $\sup_i \beta_i(t) - \inf_j \alpha_j(t)$, prove that if all i and j are useful in $(s, s + t)$; then:

$$\mu(s + t) \leq 4t \, \|A\| .$$

b. Prove by induction that for every matrix A and $\varepsilon > 0$, there exists s in $\mathbb{N}$ such that $\mu(t) \leq \varepsilon t$ for all $t \geq s$ and all admissible sequences.

HINT. Let r be such that $\mu'(t) \leq \varepsilon t$ for all $t \geq r$ and all admissible sequences associated to a (strict) submatrix A' of A, with corresponding μ'. Prove that if i is not useful in $(s, s + r)$ one has $\mu(s + r) \leq \mu(s) + \varepsilon r$. Finally given $t = qr + s$ with $s < r$, let p be the largest integer $\leq q$ such that all i, j are useful in $((p - 1)r + s, pr + s)$, and 0 if this never occurs. Show that $\mu(t) \leq \mu(pr + s) + \varepsilon(q - p)r$ and conclude.

c. Prove that for all admissible sequences:

$$\lim_{t\to\infty} (\sup_i \beta_i(t)/t) = \lim_{t\to\infty} (\inf_j \alpha_j(t)/t) = v(A)$$

(where $v(A)$ is the value of A).

16. (Shapley, 1964)
Consider fictitious play in the following two-person game: $S_1 = S_2 = \{1, 2, 3\}$ and

$$F_1 = \begin{pmatrix} a_1 & c_2 & b_3 \\ b_1 & a_2 & c_3 \\ c_1 & b_2 & a_3 \end{pmatrix}, \qquad F_2 = \begin{pmatrix} \beta_1 & \gamma_1 & \alpha_1 \\ \alpha_2 & \beta_2 & \gamma_2 \\ \gamma_3 & \alpha_3 & \beta_3 \end{pmatrix}$$

with $a_i > b_i > c_i$ and $\alpha_i > \beta_i > \gamma_i$ for all i.

a. Assume the first choice is $(1, 1)$. Prove that the sequence of $(1, 1)$ will be followed by a sequence of $(1, 3)$, which will be followed by a sequence of $(3, 3)$, then of $(3, 2)$, then of $(2, 2)$, then of $(2, 1)$, and back to $(1, 1)$, etc.

b. Denote by r_{11} the length of a sequence of $(1, 1)$ and by r_{13} the length of the following sequence of $(1, 3)$. Show that $r_{13} \geq r_{11}(a_1 - c_1)/(a_3 - b_3)$ and deduce inductively, if r'_{11} is the length of the next sequence of $\{1, 1\}$, that:

$$r'_{11} \geq \prod_i \left(\frac{a_i - c_i}{a_i - b_i}\right)\left(\frac{\alpha_i - \gamma_i}{\alpha_i - \beta_i}\right) r_{11}.$$

c. Deduce that the empirical strategies do not converge. Furthermore, no subsequence converges to the (unique) equilibrium pair.

17. On fixed points.
Note that the quasi-concavity assumption in Theorem I.4.1, p. 45, was not used in its full force; only the convexity of the best reply sets was used. But even this is too much: given an upper semi-continuous correspondence T from a compact convex set S to itself, the condition for T to have a fixed point should be purely topological. This is the aim of the present exercise. In fact, it will be more convenient to argue in terms of a compact Hausdorff space X (e.g., the graph of T), together with two (continuous) maps f and g from X to S (e.g., the two projections). We look then for a solution of $f(x) = g(x)$, and the best-reply sets are the sets $f^{-1}(s)$.

We assume also that S is Hausdorff, that f is onto, and that $\tilde{H}^q(f^{-1}(s)) = 0$ for all $q \geq 0$ and $s \in S$, where $\tilde{H}$ denotes reduced Čech-cohomology with coefficients in a module G (Spanier, 1966). We express this condition in short by saying that f is (G)-acyclic: this is a purely topological condition on the best-reply sets, satisfied as soon as each of them is contractible (homotopy invariance). Similarly we call an upper semi-continuous correspondence Γ from X to S acyclic if the projection from its graph to X is so, i.e., if $\forall x \in X$, $\tilde{H}^q(\Gamma(x)) = 0$ and $\Gamma(x) \neq \emptyset$.

a. Prove that, when S is a finite dimensional convex set, there exists a solution (of $f(x) = g(x)$).

HINT. Denote by ∂S the boundary of S, and let $\partial X = f^{-1}(\partial S)$. Apply the Vietoris–Begle mapping theorem (Spanier, 1966, VI.9.15) to $f\colon X \to S$ and to $f\colon \partial X \to \partial S$ to conclude by the "five lemma" (Spanier, 1966, IV.5.11) and exactness (Spanier, 1966, V.4.13) that $f\colon (X, \partial X) \to (S, \partial S)$ is an isomorphism in Čech-cohomology. If $f(x) \neq g(x)$ for all x, construct (as in Spanier, 1966, IV.7.5) a map $\tilde{f}\colon X \to \partial S$ that is homotopic to f. Conclude with a contradiction.

b. To show that acyclic maps are the "right" class of maps for this problem, prove that if $f\colon X \to Y$ and $g\colon Y \to Z$ (all spaces compact) are (G)-acyclic, so is $g \circ f$.

HINT. Clearly $g \circ f$ is onto. Let $S = g^{-1}(z) : \tilde{H}^q(S) = 0$. Since f as a map from $\tilde{X} = f^{-1}(S)$ to S is acyclic, $f^*\colon \tilde{H}^q(S) \to \tilde{H}^q(\tilde{X})$ is an isomorphism (cf. a)): $\tilde{H}^q(\tilde{X}) = 0$ for all sets $\tilde{X} = (g \circ f)^{-1}(z)$.

c. A continuous affine map f on a compact convex subset X of a Hausdorff topological vector space is acyclic to $f(X)$.

HINT. Use the above-mentioned contractibility criterion.

d. Assume S is a compact convex subset of a topological vector space, such that points of S are separated by continuous affine functionals on S (henceforth a compact convex set for short). Prove that there exists a solution.

HINT. By the separation property on S and compactness of X it suffices to show that $(p \circ f)(x) = (p \circ g)(x)$ has a solution for every continuous affine map $p\colon S \to \mathbb{R}^k$. Use I.4, Ex. 17b, and I.4, Ex. 17c, to show that $p \circ f$ and $p \circ g$ satisfy the conditions in I.4, Ex. 17a.

e. If S is a retract of a compact convex set Y, there exists a solution.

HINT. The assumption means that there are continuous maps $i\colon S \to Y$ and $r\colon Y \to S$ such that $(r \circ i)(s) = s,\ \forall s \in S$. Let then $\tilde{X} = \{(x, y) \in X \times Y \mid f(x) = r(y)\}$; denote by p_1 and p_2 the two projections, and apply I.4, Ex. 17d, to $\tilde{f} = p_2$ and $\tilde{g} = i \circ g \circ p_1$.

·At this stage we have a purely topological statement. To see that those are the right assumptions, note that the statement remains true, but without additional generality, if g is replaced by an acyclic correspondence Γ from X to S. Slightly more generally, since f^{-1} is an acyclic correspondence from S to X, we have:

f. Let X_i $(i = 0, \ldots, n)$ be compact Hausdorff spaces, with $X_0 = X_n$ being a retract of a compact convex set. Let $\Gamma_i (i = 1, \ldots, n)$ be (G)-acyclic correspondences from X_{i-1} to X_i. Then their composition Γ has a fixed point $x \in \Gamma(x)$. $[(\Gamma_1 \circ \Gamma_2)(x_0) = \bigcup_{x_1 \in \Gamma_1(x_0)} \Gamma_2(x_1)]$.

HINT. Let $Y_j = \{(x_0, \ldots, x_j) \in \prod_{i \le j} X_j \mid x_i \in \Gamma_i(x_{i-1}) \text{ for } 0 < i \le j\}$, with projection f_j to Y_{j-1}. Then the f_j are acyclic, and their composition $f\colon Y_n \to X_0$ is also acyclic (by I.4, Ex. 17b). Let also $g\colon Y_n \to X_n (= X_0)$ denote the projection to the last coordinate, and apply I.4, Ex. 17e.

This proof shows, in other words, that the class of correspondences that are the composition of a (G)-acyclic correspondence with a continuous map is stable under composition.

g. Reverting to our context of games, use Künneth's formula (Spanier, 1966, VI.Ex.E) to show that, if G is a field, the best-reply correspondence will be acyclic if and only if any best reply set B of any single player satisfies $\tilde{H}^q(B) = 0$.

Remark I.4.4. The above appears as the "correct" formulation for this type of fixed-point theorem. Nevertheless, one sees that the crux of the problem lies in the case where S is an n-dimensional compact convex set; and there the assumption on f is used only to ensure that the map f^* from $\tilde{H}^n(S, \partial S)$ to $\tilde{H}^n(X, \partial X)$ is non-zero (and hence that f is not homotopic to a map to ∂S). This assumption is much too stringent for that, and other much more flexible tools are available to prove such things (e.g., homotopy invariance of f^*). But for proving existence of (pure strategy) Nash equilibria, this is already a reasonably good tool.

18. Knaster–Kuratowski–Mazurkiewicz theorem.
Consider the n-simplex Δ with its faces $F_i = \{ x \in \Delta \mid x_i = 0 \}$ $(i = 0, \ldots, n)$. Let C_i be closed subsets, with $F_i \subseteq C_i$, $\bigcup_i C_i = \Delta$. Then $\bigcap_i C_i \neq \emptyset$.

HINT. Let $f_i(x) = d(x, C_i)$, $f(x) = \sum_0^n f_i(x)$, $\varphi(x) = (f_i(x)/f(x))_{i=0}^n : \varphi$ is a continuous map from Δ to $\partial\Delta$, with $\varphi(F_i) \subseteq F_i$. View now Δ as the unit ball: the map $x \to -\varphi(x)$ is a continuous map from Δ to itself without a fixed point. Apply I.4, Ex. 17.

Remark I.4.5. Observe that the last part of the proof also shows that the sphere is not a retract of a compact convex set (otherwise $x \to -x$ contradicts I.4, Ex. 17).

19. Deduce Lemma I.1.2, p. 5, from I.4, Ex. 18.

HINT. Select the extreme point e_i of Δ in $\bigcap_{j \neq i} T_j$.

20. Also the continuity assumption in Theorem I.4.1, p. 45, was not the right one, even in the more general framework of I.4, Ex. 17: it is sufficient to assume for each player i that his payoff function F^i is upper semi-continuous on $\prod_j S^j$, and is, for each fixed $s^i \in S^i$, continuous in the other variables jointly, and, if one wants a mixed strategy version, like Theorem I.4.1, and not a pure strategy version like I.4, Ex. 17, to assume furthermore that F^i is bounded and the S^i strictly semi-compact (I.1, Ex. 7c, p. 14), or F^i continuous in s^i using I.2, Ex. 1c, p. 25.

HINT. For simplicity, we write S^i for S, T for $\prod_{j \neq i} S^j$, and F for $F^i : S \times \prod_{j \neq i} S^j \to \mathbb{R}$. Let $R = \{ (s, t) \mid F(s, t) = \max_{\tilde{s} \in S} F(\tilde{s}, t) \}$. Show that R is closed under the above assumptions. This yields the pure strategy version of I.4, Ex. 17. For the mixed strategy version, upper semi-continuity and boundedness imply that the mixed extension is well defined. Use then the stated exercises.

21. Teams.
A team problem (game with finite strategy spaces where all players have the same payoff function) has finitely many equilibrium payoffs.

HINT. It suffices to show that there are finitely many payoffs to completely mixed equilibria. Show that, at such an equilibrium, the gradient of the payoff function is zero, and use Sard's theorem (e.g. Milnor, 1969, p. 16) to deduce that the set of completely mixed equilibrium payoffs has Lebesgue measure zero. The semi-algebraicity of this set (Corollary I.3.2, p. 31) implies it is a finite union of intervals.

22. Games with payoff correspondence. (Simon and Zame, 1990)
Consider an N-person game with strategy spaces S^i and a correspondence Q from S to $\mathbb{R}^n$. Assume each S^i compact Hausdorff, and Q non-empty compact convex-valued and u.s.c. (IX.3). Prove the existence of a Borel selection q of Q such that the game $(S^i, i = 1, \ldots, N; q)$ has an equilibrium.

HINT. For any finite game (S^i_α finite and included in S^i and q_α an arbitrary selection of the graph of Q above S_α) choose equilibrium strategies $\mu_\alpha = (\mu^i_\alpha)$. Let μ_α and $q_\alpha d\mu_\alpha$ converge weakly (along some ultrafilter refining the increasing net of all finite subsets S^i_α) to μ and ν and note that ν is absolutely continuous w.r.t. μ. Let q be μ-measurable with $q d\mu = d\nu$. Then $\mu\{s \mid q(s) \notin Q(s)\} = 0$; otherwise choose $a, b \in \mathbb{Q}$ and $x \in \mathbb{Q}^N$ such that $V = \{s \mid \langle q(s), x\rangle > a > b > \langle t, x\rangle, \quad \forall t \in Q(s)\}$ has positive measure. Use then the regularity of μ and Urysohn's lemma to get a contradiction. Change q on a set of μ measure 0 to get a Borel selection and let us still write q for the mixed extension. Show (as above) that $T^i = \{s^i \in S^i \mid q^i(s^i, \mu^{-i}) > q^i(\mu)\}$ has μ^i measure 0. To get an equilibrium we finally modify q as follows: let $p[i]$ be a selection of Q minimizing i's payoff and define:

$$\overline{q}(s) = \begin{cases} p[i](s), & \text{if } s^i \in T^i, s^j \notin T^j, j \neq i; \\ q(s), & \text{otherwise.} \end{cases}$$

Note that $\overline{q}^i(\mu) = q^i(\mu)$ and $\overline{q}^i(\cdot, \mu^{-i}) = q^i(\cdot, \mu^{-i})$ on $S^i \setminus T^i$. Finally, on T^i, since Q u.s.c. implies $p[i]^i$ l.s.c., one has: $\overline{q}^i(t^i, \mu^{-i}) = p[i]^i(t^i, \mu^{-i}) \leq \liminf_\alpha p[i]^i(t^i_\alpha, \mu^{-i}_\alpha) \leq \liminf_\alpha q^i_\alpha(t^i_\alpha, \mu^{-i}_\alpha) \leq \liminf_\alpha q^i_\alpha(\mu_\alpha) \leq q^i(\mu)$.

CHAPTER II

Basic Results on Extensive Form Games

II.1. THE EXTENSIVE FORM

The extensive form is the most commonly used way to describe or to define a game. We give here a rather general description with some typical variants. The aim is, among others, to have finite extensive forms, e.g., for repeated games (cf. Remark II.1.4 below), so as to be able to define them effectively in this way. The flexibility is also needed to describe the solutions of some repeated games with incomplete information as the solutions of auxiliary *finite* games (Chapter VIII, Section VIII.2, p. 433; also VIII.4, Ex. 2, p. 475).

II.1.a. Definitions

Definition II.1.1. An **extensive form** game consists of:

(1) a player set $\mathbf{I} = \{1, \ldots, \mathbf{I}\}$,
(2) a space of **positions** Ω,
(3) a **signal** space A and a function α from Ω to (probabilities on) A,
(4) a partition $(A^i)_{i \in \mathbf{I}}$ of A,
(5) an **action** space S and a function q from $\Omega \times A \times S$ to (probabilities on) Ω,
(6) for each i, a payoff function g^i from Ω^∞ to $\mathbb{R}$,
(7) an initial position ω_1.

Of course, when dealing with probabilities in (3) and (5), appropriate precautions will have to be taken; cf. II.1.c below. Also when there are no probabilities, the factor A in (5) is redundant.

Each player $i \in \mathbf{I}$ has to decide what action $s \in S$ to choose when he is told a in A^i, i.e., to define a function σ^i from A^i to S. The game is then played as follows: at stage n, a_n will be chosen according to $\alpha(\omega_n)$, and if it belongs to A^{i_n}, the next position ω_{n+1} will be chosen according to $q(\omega_n, a_n, \sigma^{i_n}(a_n))$. In other words, if a_n belongs to A^i, player i has the move: in that case, he is told the signal or message a_n and nothing else: he does not remember his past information or his past choices and not even the stage n itself, if they are not explicitly included in the message. He selects then an action s_n as a function of this signal, and the new position ω_{n+1} is selected using $q(\omega_n, a_n, s_n)$. Each player i receives at the end of the game the payoff $g^i(\omega_1, \omega_2, \dots)$. In some sense, each player i decides, at the beginning of the game on σ^i, "the program of his machine," and the game then proceeds purely automatically. σ^i is called player i's **pure strategy**. Signals (in the deterministic case) are often identified with their inverse images in the sets of positions, called **information sets**.

Variants of the Model

The model can be adapted to incorporate the following variants:

(1) When ω_1 is chosen at random, add an additional initial state ω_0, and extend q and α appropriately.
(2) Often a set of **terminal positions** is needed, where the game stops. This can be formalized by leaving those positions fixed under q, whatever be the action s in S. Conversely, if after a position only one sequence of positions is possible, we can replace it by a terminal position.
(3) Usually, for any signal a in A, only a (non-empty) subset of actions in S is allowed. This can be taken care of either by allowing in the definition for an S-valued correspondence on A and then defining q only on the relevant set, or by keeping the above definition and extending q and g outside this set in a proper way, say, by duplication: any additional move is equivalent to some fixed strategy. But the second trick cannot be used when discussing perfect recall and behavioral strategies (cf. below): indeed, if one does not inform the player of which duplicate was used, one loses the perfect recall property, and if one does, one introduces in the new game additional behavioral strategies, which are not behavioral strategies of the original game, but mixed (or "general") strategies (cf. below for the terminology). Hence in those cases we will write $\overline{S}$ for the S-valued correspondence on A, i.e., its graph in $A \times S$ (thus: $\overline{S}_a$ for its value at a). q is then defined on $\Omega \times \overline{S}$.
(4) Another formulation that leads to deterministic signals is: take $\Omega^* = \Omega \times A$ and define q^* from $\Omega^* \times S$ to probabilities on Ω^* using first q and then α. α^* is then the deterministic projection from Ω^* to A, or simply a σ-field $\mathscr{C}$ on Ω^*. The partition $(A^i)_{i\in \mathbf{I}}$ becomes then a $\mathscr{C}$-measurable partition Ω_i^* of Ω^*, and σ_i $\mathscr{C}$-measurable on Ω_i^*.

Let $\Omega' = \Omega \times A \times S$ (or $\Omega \times \overline{S}$ in the case of variable action sets), and denote by Ω'_n the nth copy of Ω'. Let $H_\infty = \prod_1^\infty \Omega'_n$ be the set of **plays**, while the set H of **histories** is the set of (finite, possibly empty) initial segments of plays.

Remark II.1.2. There is no need to allow, like in (3), for position-dependent sets of possible signals, or similarly for variable sets of possible new positions.

Indeed, the transition probabilities q and α already describe in some sense what is possible, so one would add a new primitive concept that duplicates to a large extent the information already available in the model. Further, here there is no problem in using the full containing space A (or Ω), extending the transition probability q in an arbitrary way when its arguments are not feasible.

The only drawback is that we will in general not have a meaningful definition of a set of **feasible plays**, since it will depend on this "containing space" A. The set can be defined meaningfully only when all probabilities in the model are purely atomic: then one should define the set as consisting of those plays such that each of their initial segments has positive probability under some strategy vector. Hence, in the general definition below of linear games and of (effectively) perfect recall, we will have to avoid using this concept of feasible play.

II.1.b. The Finite Case

Here we consider games where there are finitely many different (feasible) plays. As defined above, a **pure strategy** for i is a mapping from A^i to S. A **mixed strategy** will be a probability distribution on those. A **behavioral strategy** is a mapping from A^i to probability distributions on S. Finally, a **general strategy** will be a probability distribution on the (compact) set of behavioral strategies. (For the solution of such games, cf. II.1, Ex. 3, p. 65.)

An **I**-tuple of (general) strategies defines a probability distribution on plays. Two strategies of a player are **equivalent** if they induce the same distribution on plays whatever be the strategies of the other players. The **normal form** of the game associates with every strategy vector the corresponding vector of expected payoffs (thus, in general, normal form can be in pure, mixed, or behavioral strategies).

The above definition of the extensive form does not exclude that a play may produce the same message twice. There could even be two identical positions at two different stages along the same play. We call the game **linear** (Isbell, 1957) (for player i) if, a.e. for every strategy vector, every message of player i occurs at most once along every play. (All the games that we will study in this book will be linear; however, some finite, non-linear games will occur as auxiliary games to solve a class of repeated games with incomplete information; cf. Chapter VIII.) The term "linear" is related to the following property:

Theorem II.1.1. *(Isbell, 1957) In a linear game (for player i), every general strategy of i is equivalent to a mixed strategy.*

Proof. In fact, given a behavioral strategy τ of player i, we will construct a mixed strategy inducing the same probability on plays, whatever be the other players' strategies. Let μ be defined on each pure strategy σ by:

$$\mu(\sigma) = \mathsf{Pr}_{\mu}(\sigma) = \prod_{a^i \in A^i} \tau(a^i)\{\sigma(a^i)\}.$$

It is then clear that, given any strategies of the other players, the probability of the corresponding sequence of moves in S will be the same under τ and μ. Obviously, the same result holds for general strategies, taking the expectation w.r.t. to τ. ■

To see the need for the assumption "linear," cf. II.1, Ex. 2, p. 65. For a more general case, cf. II.1, Ex. 10d, and II.1, Ex. 10e, p. 72.

The game is said to have **(effectively) perfect recall** for player i if (knowing the pure strategy he is using) he can deduce from any signal he may get along some feasible play the sequence of previous messages he got along that play. (All the games we study will have effectively perfect recall.) Observe that a game with effectively perfect recall for i is necessarily linear for i. In other words, to have perfect recall, every message must in particular recall both the last message and the last action, while, to have effectively perfect recall, it is sufficient that the player be able to reconstruct the last message, in which case he can also, knowing his pure strategy, reconstruct his last action, and so on: this shows inductively that he can do as well as if he had remembered also his past actions. Formally we have:

Theorem II.1.2. *(Dalkey, 1953) In a game with effectively perfect recall for player i, his pure strategy set is essentially the same (i.e., except for duplication) whether or not he recalls, in addition to his current information, his own past signals and moves.*

Proof. A pure strategy of player i when he recalls his own past signals and choices is of the form: $\{s_n = \sigma(a_1, \ldots, a_n; s_1, \ldots, s_{n-1})\}$ for $n \geq 1$, where $(a_1, \ldots, a_n)$ denotes the sequence of signals from A^i he has heard, $(s_1, \ldots, s_{n-1})$ is the sequence of his past choices in S^i, and s_n in S^i is the move to be chosen. Define, by induction on the number n of signals previously heard, a strategy ϕ that depends only on the current signal: roughly, for each initial signal a in A^i, $s_1 = \phi(a) = \sigma(a)$. Inductively, given a signal a, deduce from a and ϕ the previous signals, say, $a_1, \ldots, a_n$, and let $\phi(a) = \sigma(a_1, \ldots, a_n, a; \phi(a_1), \ldots, \phi(a_n))$. Whatever be the strategy of the other players, the pure strategy ϕ results in the same probability distribution on plays as the pure strategy σ; hence the proof is complete. ■

For more details and/or more generality, cf. II.1, Ex. 14, p. 82.

Remark II.1.3. Observe that, since the set of strategies ϕ is clearly smaller than the set of strategies σ by our construction, several strategies σ will be mapped to the same strategy ϕ. This is the duplication of strategies mentioned above.

Remark II.1.4. From our previous definitions, it appears that, for a game with effectively perfect recall, we need a very large space of positions, essentially H. But it follows from the above that, to specify a game with effectively perfect recall, it is sufficient to describe each player's incremental information every time he has to play. This can be arbitrary; in particular, it does not have to remind him of his last move. This is the way we will describe all our models in this book from Chapter IV on: the signal $a \in A^i$ will be player i's incremental information. (That is, his true signals, in the previous general model, are finite sequences in A^i.) Therefore we will still be able to use small (finite) sets of positions.

The main advantage of games with perfect recall is the following:

Theorem II.1.3. *(Kuhn, 1953) In a game with perfect recall for player i, general, mixed, and behavioral strategies are equivalent for i.*

Proof. By Theorem II.1.1, p. 60, it is enough to represent any mixed strategy μ by a behavioral strategy τ. In fact, given μ (a probability distribution on pure strategies), compute first, for every initial signal a_1 (cf. II.1, Ex. 8, p. 68), the marginal distribution μ_{a_1} on "strategies after a_1," and compute then from μ_{a_1} the marginal distribution τ_{a_1} of s_1 and the conditional distribution μ_{a_1,s_1} on "strategies for the future" given s_1. Continue then with μ_{a_1,s_1} as before with μ. ■

As a corollary, by Dalkey's theorem, one can also study games with effectively perfect recall by using behavioral strategies in the corresponding game with perfect recall.

A game is said to have **perfect information** if the position at each stage in a feasible play determines all the previous positions along the play and moreover the signal determines the position. In other words, when he has to play, each player knows the whole past history.

Theorem II.1.4. *(Zermelo, 1913) In a game with perfect information, there exists an equilibrium in pure strategies.*

Proof. The proof is very simple using **backwards induction**: replace each position that is followed only by terminal positions by a terminal position with, as payoff, the payoff corresponding to an optimal choice of action of the player having the move at that position. ■

II.1.c. A Measurable Setup

We consider now a game where the spaces Ω, A, and S are measurable as well as the partition $(A^i)_{i\in\mathbf{I}}$, the graph $\overline{S}$, and the map g; α and q are transition probabilities. A pure strategy, say, for player i, is then a measurable selection from $\overline{S}$ defined on $(A^i, \mathscr{A}^i)$. Similarly, a behavioral strategy will be a transition probability from $(A^i, \mathscr{A}^i)$ to $(S, \mathscr{S})$, assigning probability one to $\overline{S}$. Note that there is no adequate measurable structure on those sets; hence it is more appropriate to define a mixed strategy as a measurable selection from S defined on $(X^i \times A^i, \mathscr{X}^i \otimes \mathscr{A}^i)$, where $(X^i, \mathscr{X}^i, Q^i)$ is an auxiliary probability space. One similarly defines general strategies as transition probabilities from $(X^i \times A^i, \mathscr{X}^i \otimes \mathscr{A}^i)$ to $(S, \mathscr{S})$, assigning probability one to $\overline{S}$.

Proposition II.1.5. *An* I-tuple *of general strategies induces a unique probability distribution on plays.*

Proof. Use Ionescu Tulcea's theorem (Neveu, 1970, Proposition V.1.1) with $(\Omega \times A \times S)^\infty$, then show that $(\Omega \times \overline{S})^\infty$ has probability one. ■

Hence, the normal form will be well defined (so one can speak of equilibria), e.g., as soon as g is bounded from below or from above. Since for each $x \in \prod_i X^i$ we also have a vector of strategies, the corresponding payoff $g(x^1, x^2, \ldots)$ is also well defined, and, by the cited theorem, it will be a measurable function on $\prod_i X^i$, with $g(Q^1, Q^2, \ldots) = \int g(x^1, x^2, \ldots) \prod_{i \in \mathbf{I}} dQ^i$.

It also follows that the definition of the equivalence of strategies extends to this case. In particular, if general strategies are shown to be equivalent to mixed strategies (cf. II.1, Ex. 10d, p. 72) a strategy vector is an equilibrium iff no player has a profitable pure strategy deviation.

Definition II.1.5. A game has **(effectively) perfect recall** for player i if (for every pure strategy of i) there exists a measurable map φ from A^i to $(A^i \times S^i) \cup \{\iota\}$ such that, for every strategy vector of i's opponents, a.s. $\varphi(a^i) = \iota$ means that a^i is the first signal to this player; otherwise $\varphi(a^i)$ is the previous signal to him and the action he took upon it. (For a justification of this definition, cf. II.1, Ex. 12, p. 74.)

Theorem II.1.6. *Assume player i has perfect recall and $(S, \mathscr{S})$ is standard Borel (cf. Appendix A.6). Every general strategy of player i is equivalent to a mixed strategy and to a behavioral strategy.*

Proof. To prove the inclusion of general strategies in the set of mixed strategies, represent $(S, \mathscr{S})$ as $[0, 1]$ with the Borel sets; then a general strategy yields a family of cumulative distribution functions $F_{x,a}(s)$ jointly measurable in x, a, and s (Remark II.1.15, p. 69). The perfect recall assumption implies there is a measurable map $n(a)$ (II.1, Ex. 10, p. 70) from A_i to $\mathbb{N}$ that increases strictly along every play. Let then u_n be an independent sequence of uniform random variables on $[0, 1]$, and define $\mu(u, x, a) = \min\{ s \mid F_{x,a}(s) \geq u_{n(a)} \}$: μ is a mixed strategy with as auxiliary space the product $(X^i, \mathscr{X}^i, Q^i) \times ([0, 1], \mathscr{B}, \lambda)^{\mathbb{N}}$, where λ denotes Lebesgue measure on the Borel sets $\mathscr{B}$ of $[0, 1]$. And $\Pr(\mu \leq s \mid x, a, \text{past}) = \Pr(u_{n(a)} \leq F_{x,a}(s) \mid x, a, \text{past}) = F_{x,a}(s)$, so μ induces clearly the same probability distribution on plays as the general strategy.

The proof of the second part is given in II.1, Ex. 10, p. 70. ■

Actually, the above is the proof of a different statement; cf. II.1, Ex. 10d. In II.1, Ex. 10a, and II.1, Ex. 10b, we give a full proof of Theorem II.1.6; part II.1, Ex. 10a, is there only to justify the "clearly" in the last sentence of the proof above.

Remark II.1.6. When A^i is countable (cf. also II.1, Ex. 14, Remark II.1.30, p. 84), a behavioral strategy can be identified with a point in $[S^*]^{A_i}$, where

S^* denotes the set of probability distributions on S. The σ-field $\mathscr{S}$ induces a natural σ-field on S^* (requiring that the probability of every measurable set be a measurable function on S^*), and hence on $[S^*]^{A^i}$. Thus general (resp. mixed) strategies are naturally defined as probability distributions on $[S^*]^{A^i}$, resp. S^{A^i}. Those definitions are clearly equivalent to the former (without any standard Borel restrictions): given a probability distribution P on $[S^*]^{A^i}$, use $([S^*]^{A^i}, [\mathscr{S}^*]^{A^i}, P)$ as $(X^i, \mathscr{X}^i, Q^i)$; this also reduces to the former case the question of how to define the probability distributions induced on plays by those new strategies. Conversely, given $(X^i, \mathscr{X}^i, Q^i)$, there is an obvious measurable map to $([S^*]^{A^i}, [\mathscr{S}^*]^{A^i})$ defining a P (and similarly for mixed strategies). It is clear that this transformation preserves the probability distribution induced on plays. This probability distribution is clearly the average under P of the distributions induced by the underlying behavioral (resp. pure) strategies. Thus we are led back, at least for linear games (cf. II.1, Ex. 10c, p. 72), to the general concept (Chapter I) of a mixed strategy as a probability distribution over pure strategies and the corresponding normal forms.

Remark II.1.7. When A is countable, and topologies on Ω and S (often discrete topologies) are given for which q and α are continuous, the induced mapping from pure strategies (S^A with the product topology) to plays (product topology) will be continuous too, so that continuity properties of g translate immediately into the same (joint) continuity properties of the normal form payoff function (and compactness of S yields compactness of S^A).

EXERCISES

1.

a. Show that a game as defined in Section II.1.a, p. 58, can also be represented by a deterministic one, i.e., α and q functions, by adding nature as player zero (which uses a fixed behavioral strategy).

Remark II.1.8. This modification is frequently useful in specific situations, because it allows us to have a smaller and more manageable set of (feasible) plays, by giving variable action sets to nature as well as to the other players.

b. Observe that, in such a game with moves of nature, one can always redraw the tree such that the game starts with a move of nature, and is deterministic afterwards; i.e., the only randomness is in the selection of the initial position. (To get a mixed strategy for player zero, use Theorem II.1.3, p. 62, or its generalization in II.1, Ex. 10, p. 70, below.)

c. Similarly, one can also redraw the tree so as to let nature postpone as much as possible its choices (thus histories of the form $(a_1, s_1, a_2, s_2, a_3, s_3, \dots)$), this time by obtaining a behavioral strategy for player zero.

Remark II.1.9. This transformation is often important: e.g., in Chapter VIII, it will reduce a class of games with symmetric information to stochastic games.

2. (Isbell, 1957)
In the two-person zero-sum game of Figure II.1, show that:

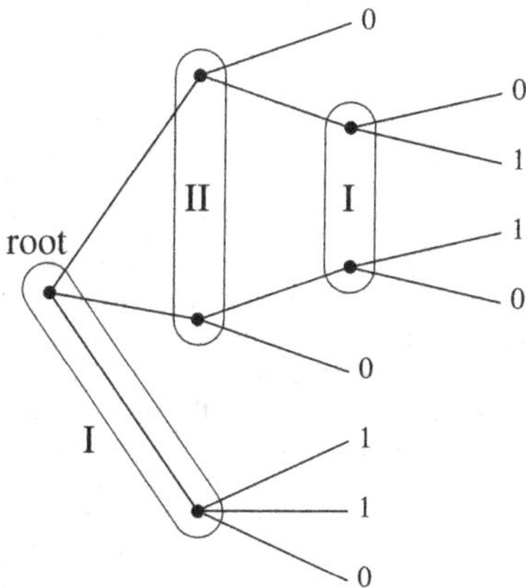

Figure II.1. A non-linear game.

- By randomizing $(1/2, 1/2)$ between $(3/4, 0, 1/4; 0, 1)$ and $(0, 3/4, 1/4; 1, 0)$ player I can guarantee $9/16$.
- He cannot guarantee more than $1/2$ with mixed strategies.
- He cannot guarantee more than $25/64$ with behavioral strategies.

3. Polynomial payoff functions

a. Prove that, in a game with finitely many different feasible plays, the payoff is polynomial in behavioral strategies.

b. Show that any polynomial payoff function on a product of compact, convex strategy polyhedra can be obtained in this way.

HINT. Reduce first to the case of strategy simplices. Show then how to construct a sum, and reduce thus the problem to the case of the same payoff function to all players, which is a single monomial.

See I.4, Ex. 8, p. 48, to show that such games have "finite" solutions.

4. An n-dimensional moment problem

a. Let $P(x)$ be a polynomial, with $P(x) > 0$ for $x > 0$. Show that, for n sufficiently large, all coefficients of $(1+x)^n P(x)$ are positive.

HINT. The binomial formula yields the n-step distribution of a random walk. Use the corresponding asymptotic approximations. In a more elementary fashion, factor first P into linear and quadratic factors of the form $x+q$ and $(x-p)^2+q$, with $q>0$, so as to reduce the problem to $P(x) = (x-p)^2 + q$, $p>0$, $q>0$, which can then be handled in a fully elementary way, remaining within the realm of second-degree equations.

b. Let $P(x_1, y_1; x_2, y_2; \dots)$ be a polynomial, homogeneous in each pair $(x_i, y_i)(1 \leq i \leq k)$. Assume $P > 0$ whenever $x_i \geq 0$, $y_i \geq 0$, $x_i + y_i > 0$, for all i. Show that, for n sufficiently large, all coefficients of $[\prod_i (x_i + y_i)^n] P(x, y)$ are positive.

HINT. Induction on k. For fixed values $x_i \geq 0$, $y_i \geq 0$ for $i \geq 2$ $(x_i + y_i > 0)$, apply II.1, Ex. 4a, to the resulting polynomial in x_1/y_1. By continuity of the coefficients, they will still be positive in the neighborhood of $z = \{(x_i, y_i) \mid i \geq 2\}$; use compactness.

c. Let the polynomial P be positive on $\Delta_k = \{x \in \mathbb{R}_+^{k+1} \mid \sum x_i = 1\}$. Then there is a homogeneous polynomial T of degree d, where every possible monomial of degree d has a positive coefficient, and with $P(x) = T(x)$ for $x \in \Delta_k$. If P is homogeneous, then $T = [\sum_i x_i]^n P$.

HINT. Make first P homogeneous by multiplying each monomial by the appropriate power of $\sum x_i$; add then $\varepsilon[1 - \sum_i x_i]$ for $\varepsilon > 0$ sufficiently small (compactness), so as to have $P(x) > 0$ on the unit cube. Obtain now $Q(x, y)$ by replacing in $P(x)$ every x_i^h by $x_i^h(x_i + y_i)^{d_i - h}$, where d_i is the maximal power of x_i in P: for $x \in \Delta_k$, $y_i = \sum_{j \neq i} x_j$, $Q(x, y)$ still equals the original $P(x)$. Apply II.1, Ex. 4b, to $Q(x, y)$, and let $R(x, y) = [\prod_i (x_i + y_i)^n] Q(x, y)$: we still have $R = P$ on Δ_k, and all terms of R are non-negative, hence this remains so when replacing all y_i by $\sum_{j \neq i} x_j$ and expanding to obtain $T(x)$, which is clearly homogeneous, say, of degree d. And the coefficients of x_i^d are necessarily strictly positive. If some other coefficients are still zero, multiplying T by an appropriate power $[(k-1)d]$ of $\sum x_i$ will make them all positive. For the last sentence, set n equal to the difference in degrees: the two polynomials are then equal on $\mathbb{R}_+^{k+1}$, hence are identical.

d. Let K be a compact convex polyhedron in $\mathbb{R}^n$ (cf. I.3, Ex. 4, p. 34) defined by the inequalities $f_i(x) \geq 0$ $(i = 1, \ldots, k)$, where the f_i are affine functionals. Any positive polynomial function P on K can be written as a sum with positive coefficients of all monomials of some degree d in $f_1, \ldots, f_k$.

HINT. If K is a singleton, take $d = 0$. Since K is compact, the f_i separate points. Let $f = (f_i)_{i=1}^k : \mathbb{R}^n \to \mathbb{R}^k$: $f(K)$ is the intersection of $\mathbb{R}_+^k$ with an affine subspace, say, with equations $\varphi_i(y) = 0$ $(i = 0, \ldots, h)$. The φ_i are not all linear; otherwise $f(K)$ would be unbounded. Assume thus $\varphi_0(y) = 0$ is of the form $\sum \mu_i y_i = 1$. Using this, one can make all other φ_i $(i = 1, \ldots, \ell)$ linear. Compactness of $f(K)$ implies it can be separated from $\sum y_i \geq M$, which implies (e.g., I.3, Ex. 1, p. 32) that adding some linear combination of the φ_j $(j \geq 1)$ to φ_0, one can assume $\mu_i > 0, i = 1, \ldots, k$. Since the f_i separate points, P can be rewritten as a polynomial Q in the $f_i(x)$: Q is a polynomial on $\mathbb{R}^k$, > 0 on $f(K)$. Adding a polynomial $L \sum_{i \geq 1} [\varphi_i(y)]^2$ for L sufficiently large will not affect the values on $f(K)$, but will make $Q > 0$ on $\{ y \in \mathbb{R}_+^k \mid \sum \mu_i y_i = 1 \}$. Apply now II.1, Ex. 4c.

e. Same statement as in II.1, Ex. 4d, but if K is a product of compact polyhedra K_j, one can use a sum with positive coefficients of all monomials. For each monomial, and for each j, the degree w.r.t. all f_i^j is d_j.

HINT. Remember from the proof of II.1, Ex. 4d, that for each K_j $(\#K_j > 1)$ we have a relation $\sum_i \mu_i^j f_i^j = 1$ with $\mu_i^j > 0$. Make sure that indeed all possible monomials have strictly positive coefficients.

Remark II.1.10. Observe that those results remain true in some sense for arbitrary finite dimensional compact convex sets: the polynomial function is still strictly positive in some neighborhood. One can squeeze a compact convex polyhedron (or a product of such polyhedra) that is in this neighborhood and that contains the given compact set in its interior. One obtains thus a similar representation, with a finite number of affine functionals that are strictly positive on the given compact convex set. Hence it also extends to compact convex sets in topological vector spaces, defining the polynomial functions as the algebra generated by the continuous affine functionals. In particular, if C is a compact convex set in a Hausdorff locally convex space E, then any linear functional on the polynomial functions on E that is non-negative on all finite products of continuous affine functionals that are positive on C is a non-negative Radon measure on C. (A little additional exercise has to be performed, for $E = \mathbb{R}^n$, to be sure to prove the result for polynomial functions on E and not just on C.)

Remark II.1.11. It would be interesting to know, even for applications like in II.1, Ex. 6, below, what polynomial functions have such a representation when asking only for non-negative coefficients.

5. Rational payoff functions

Consider a finite game, i.e., Ω, A and S are finite, with a privileged position ω_0, from where play remains in ω_0. Assume that, starting from any position, any pure strategy vector has a positive probability of eventually reaching ω_0.

a. Prove that the expected time for reaching ω_0 is uniformly bounded, over all behavioral (hence also general) strategies (and all possible starting points).

HINT. By finiteness, there exists $\varepsilon > 0$, and $n_0 < \infty$ such that for any pure strategy vector, and any starting point, ω_0 is reached before n_0 with probability $> \varepsilon$. Consider a behavioral strategy vector: by finiteness of the action space S, there is for each $a \in A$ an action with probability $\geq \#S^{-1}$. The probability that the corresponding pure strategy vector is played for the first n_0 stages is therefore $\geq \#S^{-n_0}$. Thus the probability of reaching ω_0 in that time is $\geq \varepsilon \#S^{-n_0} = \delta > 0$, whatever be the starting point and the behavioral strategy vector.

b. Assume a payoff function is given over Ω, zero at ω_0, and that the payoff of the game on Ω^∞ is obtained as the sum of the stage payoffs. Prove that the payoff is a rational function of the behavioral strategies, with a denominator that vanishes nowhere.

HINT. Denote by P the transition probability of the resulting Markov chain on Ω, by $u(\omega)$ the payoff function on Ω, and let V_ω denote the expected payoff starting from ω. Then $V = u + PV$ (u, V are column vectors). The equation and the column of P corresponding to ω_0 can be deleted, since $u(\omega_0) = V(\omega_0) = P_{\omega_0}(\{\omega_0\}^c) = 0$. II.1, Ex. 5a, implies then that the series $\sum P^n$ is summable, so $I - P$ has a non-zero determinant.

6. Rational payoff functions, the converse

Conversely, show that any normal form game, where each player i has a product of compact convex polyhedra $(K^i_a)_{a\in A^i}$ as pure strategy space, and where the payoff function F is rational with a non-vanishing denominator, arises from some game as in II.1, Ex. 5, where A^i is the set of i's signals, where his available actions at $a \in A^i$ are the extreme points v of K^i_a, and where the payoff to any behavioral strategy vector $\lambda^{i,a}_v$ ($\lambda^{i,a}_v \geq 0$, $\sum_v \lambda^{i,a}_v = 1$) is given by $F[(\sum_v \lambda^{i,a}_v \cdot v)_{a\in A^i, i\in \mathbf{I}}]$.

HINT. Assume w.l.o.g. that $\#K^i_a > 1$ for all (i, a), and that the corresponding set of affine constraints $f^{i,a}_c(x) \geq 0$ satisfies, multiplying each of them by the corresponding μ_c (cf. II.1, Ex. 4d), that $\sum_c f^{i,a}_c(x) = 1$ identically. Denote by $C^{i,a}$ the set of constraints $f^{i,a}_c$ of K^i_a, and by $V^{i,a}$ its set of extreme points.

Use a common denominator P for all players' payoff functions. Since it does not vanish, it can be assumed strictly positive, hence in the form in II.1, Ex. 4e, above. Further, multiplying it and the numerators by a positive constant, we can assume the coefficient of each term is strictly smaller than the coefficient of the corresponding term in the expansion of $[\prod_{a\in A^i, i\in\mathbf{I}}(\sum_{c\in C^{i,a}} f^{i,a}_c)]^d = Q(f)$. Thus this denominator can be written as $1 - (Q(f) - P(f)) = 1 - R(f)$, where $R(f) = \sum_m p_m m(f)$, m runs through all monomials of $Q(f)$, and $0 < p_m < 1$ for all m. Let $f^{i,a}_c(v) = q^{i,a}_v(c) : q^{i,a}_v(c) \geq 0$, and $\sum_{c\in C^{i,a}} q^{i,a}_v(c) = 1$. Then, for a mixed action $\lambda \in \Delta(V^{i,a})$ we have that $f^{i,a}(\lambda) = \sum_{v\in V^{i,a}} \lambda(v) q^{i,a}_v$ $(= q^{i,a}_\lambda)$ is a probability distribution on $C^{i,a}$, and any monomial m has the form $B_n \prod_{i,a,c}[q_\lambda(c)]^{n^{i,a}_c} = m_n(\lambda)$, where $n = (n^{i,a}_c)$ satisfies $n^{ia}_c \geq 0$, $\sum_{c\in C^{i,a}} n^{ia}_c = d$, and when $B_n = \prod_{i,a} B_{n^{ia}}$, $B_{n^{ia}}$ denotes the number of distinct orderings of a set containing $n^{i,a}_c$ objects of type c for all $c \in C^{i,a}$.

Represent also the numerators as $\sum_n u_m m(f)$, with $u_m \in \mathbb{R}^{\mathbf{I}}_n$; if necessary by increasing d. Fix an ordering on $\mathbf{I}$, and one on each A^i, obtaining thus an ordering on $A = \bigcup_{i\in\mathbf{I}} A^i$. Take the successive signals a in this order, repeating the whole sequence d times. Every choice of $v \in V^{i,a}$ is followed by a move of nature selecting $c \in C^{i,a}$ with probability $q_v^{i,a}(c)$. At the end of those $d \cdot \#A$ stages, count as an outcome the number of times n_c each c has occurred, to define a monomial m_n. It is clear that, with behavioral strategies $\lambda^{i,a}$, $\Pr(m_n) = m_n(\lambda)$. At outcome m_n, give u_{m_n} as a payoff (zero payoff at all previous positions) and use p_{m_n} as the probability of returning to the origin ω_1, $1 - p_{m_n}$ as the probability of going to the "cemetery" (absorbing state with payoff 0) ω_0.

Remark II.1.12. Observe that, since each period has a fixed number $d \cdot \#A$ of stages, and since $p_m < 1$ for all m, one could as well, correcting the p_m's, view this as a discounted game with a small discount factor.

Remark II.1.13. Observe also that behavioral strategies $\lambda^{i,a}$ have no influence on history except through their image in $K^{i,a}$.

Remark II.1.14. This provides an extensive form for the game in I.4, Ex. 9, p. 48.

7. Linear games

a. Consider a game like the one in II.1, Ex. 6, where every return is only to the origin ω_1, and where in addition every information set is met only once in between two returns. Then the payoff is a ratio of multilinear functions in the behavioral strategies. Conversely, every ratio of multilinear functions on a product of simplices, where the denominator never vanishes, is obtained in this way. (It is not clear whether this extends, as in II.1, Ex. 6, to compact convex polyhedra instead of simplices.)

b. Any game with compact convex strategy spaces and continuous payoff functions that are ratios of multilinear functions has a pure strategy equilibrium.

HINT. Prove quasi-concavity and use I.4, Ex. 20, p. 56.

c. The assumption in II.1, Ex. 7b, is much stronger than needed for the argument: it would suffice, e.g., if each player's payoff function were the ratio of a numerator that is concave in his own strategy and of a positive denominator that is linear in his own strategy, and even this linearity can be weakened to concavity (resp. convexity) if the numerator is ≤ 0 (resp. if this player's minmax value is ≥ 0).

d. The above yields "equilibria in behavioral strategies" for many games, even without the assumption of perfect recall. Observe, however, that this assumption is needed to conclude that those are indeed equilibria, via a short dynamic programming argument in each player's tree (cf. II.1, Ex. 8, below).

8. The natural tree structure.

a. One can define the sets of ("feasible") plays H_∞ (and hence histories H) such that, if the game has perfect recall for player i, his information sets have a natural tree structure (and such that the "a.s." clause in the definition of perfect recall becomes superfluous).

b. For an arbitrary game, define the tree of the game by adding an outside observer, a dummy player, who is told (and remembers) everything that happens in the game. Consider his tree. This is H, with its natural partial order.

9. Conditional probabilities.

Assume $(E, \mathscr{E})$, $(X, \mathscr{X})$, and $(Y, \mathscr{Y})$ are measurable spaces, with $\mathscr{Y}$ separable and separating, and with $(X, \mathscr{X})$ standard Borel (cf. Appendix A.6). Consider a transition probability P from E to X (denoted $P_e(dx)$), and a measurable function g from $E \times X$ to Y.

a. There exists a transition probability Q from $E \times Y$ to X (denoted $Q(dx \mid e, y)$) such that, for each $e \in E$, and for every positive measurable function f on X, $\int f(x)Q(dx \mid e, y)$ composed with g is a version of the conditional expectation $\mathsf{E}_{P_e}(f \mid \mathscr{F}_e)$ of f under P_e given the σ-field $\mathscr{F}_e$ spanned by $g(e, \cdot)$.

HINT. Show first that, for each bounded measurable function f on X, there exists a measurable function $\tilde{f}$ on $E \times Y$ such that $\tilde{f} \circ g(e, \cdot) = \mathsf{E}_{P_e}(f \mid \mathscr{F}_e)(.)$ P_e-a.e., $\forall e \in E$. To this effect, let $\mathscr{Y}_n$ be an increasing sequence of finite measurable partitions of Y that spans $\mathscr{Y}$, and let $\mathscr{F}_e^n$, $\tilde{f}^n(e, y)$ be associated with $\mathscr{Y}_n$ instead of $\mathscr{Y}$. Since $\mathscr{F}_e^n$ increases to $\mathscr{F}_e$, the martingale convergence theorem implies that $\tilde{f}(e, y) = \liminf_{n\to\infty} \tilde{f}^n(e, y)$ will do, provided we know the existence of the $\tilde{f}^n$: this reduces the problem to the case where $Y = \{y_1, \dots, y_k\}$ is finite, corresponding to a measurable partition $B_1, \dots, B_k$ of $E \times X$. Set then $\tilde{f}(e, y) = \sum_{i=1}^k \mathbb{1}_{y=y_i} \int_{B_i} f P_e(dx)/P_e(B_i)$ (with $0/0 = 0$). Measurability of $\tilde{f}$ will then follow (by composition) if we know that $\int h(e, x)P_e(dx)$ is measurable for any bounded measurable function h on $E \times X$; cf. (hint of) II.1, Ex. 9b, for this.

Identify now $(X, \mathscr{X})$ with $[0, 1]$ and the Borel sets, and select for each rational $r \in [0, 1]$, $\tilde{f}_r \geq 0$ as above, using $\mathbb{1}_{[0,r]}$ for f (and $\tilde{f}_1 = 1$). Let $F(x, e, y) = \inf_{r>x} \tilde{f}_r(e, y)$. Clearly F is measurable, $0 \leq F \leq 1$, and for each (e, y), F is monotone and right continuous in x: this defines then the transition probability $Q(dx \mid e, y)$. Show that $\int f(x)Q(dx \mid e, y)$ composed with g is indeed a version of $\mathsf{E}_{P_e}(f \mid \mathscr{F}_e)(y)$, first for $f = \mathbb{1}_{[0,\alpha]}$, then for indicators of finite unions of intervals, then by a monotone class argument for indicators of Borel sets, then for any positive Borel function.

b. For such a Q, and for a positive measurable function f on $X \times E \times Y$, $\int f(x, e, y)Q(dx \mid e, y)$ is well defined, and measurable on $E \times Y$, and one has

$$\int \left[\int f(x, e, y)Q(dx \mid e, y)\right] \left[(P_e \circ g_e^{-1})(dy)\right] = \int f(e, x, g(e, x))P_e(dx),$$

where $P_e \circ g_e^{-1}$ is the distribution of $g(e, x)$ on Y, where x is distributed according to P_e and is itself a transition probability.

HINT. Establish the result first for $f(e, x, y) = \mathbb{1}_{B(x)}\mathbb{1}_{C(e)}\mathbb{1}_{D(y)}$, then for finite unions of such rectangles, then (monotone class) for measurable indicator functions, then for all positive measurable functions.

c. $\{(e, y) \mid Q(\{x \mid g(e, x) = y\} \mid e, y) = 1\}$ is measurable and has for each e probability one under $P_e \circ g_e^{-1}$.

HINT. Show first that the graph G of g is measurable: with the same partitions $\mathscr{Y}_n$ as in II.1, Ex. 9a, the $G_n = \bigcup_{A \in \mathscr{Y}_n} A \times g^{-1}(A)$ are measurable and decrease to G (recall that $\mathscr{Y}$ is separating). Apply then II.1, Ex. 9b, to the indicator function f of G.

Remark II.1.15. We also proved along the way the following two lemmas, the first at the end of II.1, Ex. 9a, and the second as a restatement of II.1, Ex. 9b:

(1) If $F(e, x)$ is, for each $e \in E$, monotone and right continuous in x, with $0 \leq F(e, x) \leq F(e, 1) = 1$, then measurability of F on $(E, \mathscr{E})$ for each fixed x is equivalent to joint measurability of F and is still equivalent to F defining a transition probability from $(E, \mathscr{E})$ to $[0, 1]$.

(2) A transition probability P_e from $(E, \mathscr{E})$ to $(F, \mathscr{F})$ can equivalently be viewed as a transition probability from $(E, \mathscr{E})$ to $(E \times F, \mathscr{E} \otimes \mathscr{F})$. A measurable function induces a transition probability. The composition of transition probabilities is a transition probability. The composition of a transition probability with a measurable function equals its composition with the induced transition probability.

10. Sufficiency of mixed and behavioral strategies. (following Aumann, 1964) We want to prove Theorem II.1.6, p. 63.

a.

α. The perfect recall assumption allows us in particular to compute a measurable function $n(a)$, with $n(\iota) = 0$, $n(a) = 1 + n(\varphi(a))$: n is the "stage for player i."

Let $(S_n, \mathscr{S}_n)$ be the nth copy of i's action space S^i. Denote by $(A_k, \mathscr{A}_k)$ the subset of A^i where $n(a) = k$, and by $\varphi_n\colon A_n \to A_{n-1} \times S_{n-1}$ the restriction of φ. Allow i's behavioral strategies P_n, as probabilities on $(S_n, \mathscr{S}_n)$, to depend not only on $(A_n, \mathscr{A}_n)$, but also on the whole past $\prod_{t<n}(A_t \times S_t, \mathscr{A}_t \times \mathscr{S}_t)$, as well as on the auxiliary probability space $(X, \mathscr{X}, P)$ in the case of general strategies. At the end, one can always use the maps φ_n to rewrite them, if so desired, only as functions of A_n (with an arbitrary probability on S outside $\bigcup_n A_n$); but in this way, we can forget the maps φ_n.

This class of strategies of player i is not the most general one; there is no reason not to allow him to use an auxiliary probability space at every stage. Define thus a generalized strategy of player i as a sequence $(X_n, \mathscr{X}_n; P_{n-1})_{n=1}^{\infty}$, where $(X_n, \mathscr{X}_n)$ is a measurable space, and P_n a transition probability from $\prod_{1\le t\le n}[(S_{t-1}, \mathscr{S}_{t-1}) \times (X_t, \mathscr{X}_t) \times (A_t, \mathscr{A}_t)]$ to $(S_n, \mathscr{S}_n) \times (X_{n+1}, \mathscr{X}_{n+1})$ ($S_0 = \{0\}$).

Remark II.1.16. The general strategies correspond then to the case where $X_n = \{0\}$ for $n > 1$, behavioral strategies to $X_n = \{0\}$, $\forall n$; and mixed strategies by definition to general strategies where $(X_1, \mathscr{X}_1, P_0)$ is the unit interval with the Borel sets and Lebesgue measure, and where the transition probabilities become measurable functions σ_n from $(X_1, \mathscr{X}_1) \times \prod_{t\le n}(A_t, \mathscr{A}_t)$ to $(S_n, \mathscr{S}_n)$.

Remark II.1.17. The correspondence we will establish between general(ized) strategies, mixed strategies, and behavioral strategies will be completely independent of the surrounding game and depend only on the sequence of spaces A_t and S_t. Hence our freedom to modify the game below.

Remark II.1.18. Generalized strategies make sense only for games with perfect recall: they would turn any other game into a game with perfect recall (cf. also II.1, Ex. 14, p. 82).

β. There is no loss of generality in pooling all opponents of i together, including nature, as a single player, who is always informed of the whole past history and uses a behavioral strategy.

HINT. Denote by H_1 (resp. H_2, H_3) the sets of histories ending with an $\omega \in \Omega$ (resp. $a \in A$, $s \in S$). For the new game $\tilde{\Gamma}$, let $\tilde{\Omega} = H$, $\tilde{A}^i = A^i$. Note a (= last a) is a measurable function on H_2, let $\tilde{A}^{\text{opp}} = H \setminus \{\tilde{\omega} \in H_2 \mid a(\tilde{\omega}) \in A^i\}$, $\tilde{A} = \tilde{A}^i \cup \tilde{A}^{\text{opp}}$, and define $\tilde{a}$ by $\tilde{a}(\tilde{\omega}) = \tilde{\omega}$ for $\tilde{\omega} = \tilde{A}^{\text{opp}}$, and $\tilde{a}(\tilde{\omega}) = a(\tilde{\omega})$ otherwise. The set of actions $\tilde{S}^i$ of player i equals S, and let $\tilde{S}_1 = A$, $\tilde{S}_2 = S$ and $\tilde{S}_3 = \Omega$ be the sets of actions of the opponent corresponding to H_1, H_2, and H_3. The map $\tilde{q}$ is defined in the obvious way. Set $\tilde{S}^{\text{opp}} = \tilde{S}_1 \times \tilde{S}_2 \times \tilde{S}_3 \times \{1, 2, 3\}$ to have a single action space for the opponent; only the relevant component will be used. (One could similarly use now $\tilde{S} = \tilde{S}^i \times \tilde{S}^{\text{opp}}$, but we have to preserve the property that $\tilde{S}^i$ is standard Borel.) To make sure the opponent uses a behavioral strategy, include in the above construction the selection by any player $j \neq i$ of a point in one of his auxiliary spaces as a move in the game, if he uses a mixed (or a general) strategy, so all those choices appear in the space H of histories, hence in $\tilde{A}^{\text{opp}}$. Use the product of all auxiliary spaces, in order to stay with a single action space for the opponent. Observe finally there is a Borel map from the space of all such plays to plays of the original game: for legal plays, $\tilde{s}$ with index $i \in \{1, 2, 3\}$ can occur only at time equal to i mod 3, and s only at time 2 (mod 3). On this subset, keep s_t and replace $\tilde{s}_t$ by its coordinate i. Map the (measurable) remainder to some given play. This map is such that, if a strategy vector of the original game is transformed in the obvious way to a strategy pair in the new game, the map will transform correctly the induced probability distributions on histories.

Remark II.1.19. Note we did not change the sets A^i and S^i in the construction, hence also not the sets of strategies of player i. We can now view the set of histories as the set of sequences $(\tilde{s}_1, \tilde{s}_2, \ldots, \tilde{s}_t, s_{t+1}, \tilde{s}_{t+2}, \ldots)$, with a map α from the set H of all such finite sequences h to $A^i \cup \{\text{opp}\}$. If $\alpha(h) = \text{opp}$, the opponent picks the next point $\tilde{s}$ using a transition probability that depends on the whole h; otherwise player i picks the next s as a function of his own past history. α maps the empty sequence to "opp" and depends only on the last coordinate of the sequence since, if it is s, or if $\tilde{s}$ with index $\in \{2, 3\}$, it is mapped to "opp," while otherwise $\tilde{s}$ is already an element of A.

γ. Let $(T_n, \mathscr{T}_n)$ be the set of possible "histories between player i's stage $n-1$ and stage n." The opponent's strategy (and the rules of the game) yields a sequence of transition probabilities Q_n from $\prod_{t<n}(T_t \times A_t \times S_t, \mathscr{T}_t \otimes \mathscr{A}_t \otimes \mathscr{S}_t)$ to $(T_n \times A_n, \mathscr{T}_n \times \mathscr{A}_n)$. (Observe that Q_1 is just a probability on $T_1 \times A_1$.)

HINT. We have now a natural player partition (H^0, H^i) of H. We drop tildes. The opponents' strategy is now a transition probability R from H^0 to H, where the S^0 coordinate is just appended to the history. Complete R_1 in a transition probability $\overline{R}$ from H to H by sending all points in H^i to themselves. By Ionescu Tulcea's theorem, iterative use of $\overline{R}$ induces a transition probability $\tilde{R}$ from H to $(H)^\infty$, hence to the space $(T, \mathscr{T}) = H^i \cup H_\infty$. Take $(T_n, \mathscr{T}_n)$ to be a copy of $(T, \mathscr{T})$. Define Q_n, using the given map q from H^i to A^i, in the following way: if $t_{n-1} \in H_\infty$, $t_n = t_{n-1}$ and a_n is any given point in A^i; otherwise use $\tilde{R}$ from (t_{n-1}, s_{n-1}) (which belongs to H^0) to T_n. Q_1 is defined by applying $\tilde{R}$ to the empty sequence. Again, like at the end of II.1, Ex. 10aβ, note that the set of plays of the previous game is the set of all sequences in $[S^i \cup S^0]^\infty$, where every element of S^i has a predecessor in the subset S^{00} of S^0 where $\alpha \neq$ opp, and obtain an appropriate measurable map from the set of plays in our new game to that set. Since the set is measurable in $[S^0 \cup S^i]^\infty$, it suffices to get an appropriate measurable map to the latter. (Be careful again not to use conditions like "if t_n extends t_{n-1}," since such sets are not necessarily measurable given absence of separability and separateness.)

b. We keep the notations and definitions from II.1, Ex. 10a. Assume the spaces $(S_n, \mathscr{S}_n)$ are standard Borel. For every general(ized) strategy, there exists both a mixed strategy and a behavioral strategy such that, for every $(T_n, \mathscr{T}_n, Q_n)_{n=1}^\infty$, the induced probability on $\prod_n(T_n \times A_n \times S_n)$ is the same.

HINT.

(1) Set $(Y_n, \mathscr{Y}_n) = \prod_{t \le n}\left[(X_{t+1}, \mathscr{X}_{t+1}) \times (S_t, \mathscr{S}_t) \times (A_t, \mathscr{A}_t)\right]$, $Y_0 = \{0\}$, and f_n the projection from Y_n to S_n. Define the transition probability R_n from $(Y_{n-1}, \mathscr{Y}_{n-1}) \times (A_n, \mathscr{A}_n)$ to $(Y_n, \mathscr{Y}_n)$ from P_n (cf. Remark II.1.15, p. 69), R_1 is induced by P_0, P_1 and the identity on A_1.

(2) Denote by $\mathscr{Y}_n^0$ the trivial σ-field on Y_n, and by $\mathscr{Y}_n^k \supseteq \mathscr{Y}_n^{k-1}$ a separable sub σ-field of $\mathscr{Y}_n$ making $f_n : (Y_n, \mathscr{Y}_n^k) \to (S_n, \mathscr{S}_n)$ and $R_{n+1} : (Y_n, \mathscr{Y}_n^k) \times (A_{n+1}, \mathscr{A}_{n+1}) \to (Y_{n+1}, \mathscr{Y}_{n+1}^{k-1})$ measurable. Indeed, if R is a transition probability from $(E \times F, \mathscr{E} \times \mathscr{F})$ to $(G, \mathscr{G})$ and $\mathscr{G}$ is separable, there exists separable σ-fields $\mathscr{E}_0$ and $\mathscr{F}_0$ of $\mathscr{E}$ and $\mathscr{F}$ for which R is still a transition probability: denote by G_i a sequence generating $\mathscr{G}$, by $B_{ij} \in (\mathscr{E} \otimes \mathscr{F})$ the inverse images of the rational intervals I_j by $R(G_i \mid e, f)$, and by $E_{i,j,k} \times F_{i,j,k}$ a sequence of $(\mathscr{E} \times \mathscr{F})$-measurable rectangles generating a σ-field containing B_{ij}: span $\mathscr{E}_0$ (resp. $\mathscr{F}_0$) by the E_{ijk} (resp. F_{ijk}). It follows that the σ-fields $\mathscr{Y}_n^\infty$ spanned by the $\mathscr{Y}_n^k$ are separable, and for those the R_n are still transition probabilities and the f_n measurable.

(3) Let now $\tilde{Y}_n$ be the quotient of Y_n by the equivalence relation $y \sim y'$ if they belong to the same elements of $\mathscr{Y}_n^\infty$. The $\mathscr{Y}_n^\infty$ can still be viewed as a separable σ-field on $\tilde{Y}_n$, for which the atoms are the singletons. And R_n and f_n are already defined on the quotients $\tilde{Y}_n$. In short, we can now assume the σ-fields $\mathscr{Y}_n$ are separable, and separate points of Y_n. And similarly for the $(A_n, \mathscr{A}_n)$, we can construct a measurable map p_n to a space $(B_n, \mathscr{B}_n)$ that is separable and separating, and such that R_n is a transition probability from $(Y_{n-1}, \mathscr{Y}_{n-1}) \times (B_n, \mathscr{B}_n)$ to $(Y_n, \mathscr{Y}_n)$.

(4) If $\mathscr{Z}$ is a separable and separating σ-field on Z, then $(Z, \mathscr{Z})$ can be identified with a subset of the Cantor set $C = \{0, 1\}^\infty$, endowed with its Borel sets $\mathscr{C}$, a standard Borel space, by the map $z \mapsto (\mathbb{1}_{Z_i}(z))_{i=1}^\infty$, where Z_i denotes a sequence that generates $\mathscr{Z}$ (the subset being endowed with the trace σ-field). And any measurable map f from $(Z, \mathscr{Z})$ to $[0, 1]$ can be extended to C: indeed, this holds, by definition of the trace σ-field, for indicator functions; therefore it holds for their convex combinations, which are the step functions; hence if f_n is a sequence of step functions converging to f, with extensions $\overline{f}_n$, let $\overline{f} = \liminf_{n\to\infty} \overline{f}_n$.

(5) Using (4), we can view the Y_n and the B_n as subsets of $\overline{Y}_n$ and $\overline{B}_n$ which are copies of $([0, 1], \mathscr{B})$; the maps f_n have an extension to $\overline{Y}_n$, and the transition probabilities R_n can be viewed as transition probabilities from $Y_{n-1} \times B_n$ to $\overline{Y}_n$, assigning outer probability one to Y_n. Thus to show that the R_n too have an extension $\overline{R}_n$ as transition probabilities from $\overline{Y}_{n-1} \times \overline{B}_{n-1}$ to $\overline{Y}_n$, it suffices (by (4)) to show that the space $(M, \mathscr{M})$ of probability measures on $[0, 1]$ is a standard Borel space (in the weak*-topology), which is obvious (as a compact metric space), and to use Appendix A.9.e.

(6) We can thus think of all $(Y_n, \mathscr{Y}_n)$ and $(B_n, \mathscr{B}_n)$ as being copies of $([0, 1], \mathscr{B})$. Introduce for each n a copy $(U_n, \mathscr{U}_n, \lambda_n)$ of $([0, 1], \mathscr{B}, \lambda)$, λ being Lebesgue measure, and replace R_n by a measurable map h_n from $(Y_{n-1}, \mathscr{Y}_{n-1}) \times (B_n, \mathscr{B}_n) \times (U_n, \mathscr{U}_n)$ to $(Y_n, \mathscr{Y}_n)$ (cf. proof of Theorem II.1.6, p. 63). Composition of the h_t ($t \le n$) and of f_n yields a description of the strategy by Borel maps g_n from $\prod_{t\le n}[(B_t, \mathscr{B}_t) \times (U_t, \mathscr{U}_t)]$ to $(S_n, \mathscr{S}_n)$. Since $\prod_{n=1}^\infty (U_n, \mathscr{U}_n, \lambda_n)$ is itself Borel isomorphic to $([0, 1], \mathscr{B}, \lambda)$, we can as well think of g_n as Borel maps from $([0, 1], \mathscr{B}) \times \prod_{t\le n}(B_t, \mathscr{B}_t)$ to $(S_n, \mathscr{S}_n)$: this (together with the $p_n : A_n \to B_n$) is the mixed strategy.

(7) Check that, in each of the previous steps, the probability distribution induced on $\prod_n (T_n \times A_n \times S_n)$ did not change.

There only remains therefore to replace the mixed strategy by a behavioral strategy:

(8) Use now II.1, Ex. 9, p. 68, inductively for $n = 1, 2, 3, \ldots$; using $(A_n, \mathscr{A}_n) \times [\prod_{t<n}(A_t \times S_t, \mathscr{A}_t \times \mathscr{S}_t)] \times$ for $(E, \mathscr{E})(= (E_n, \mathscr{E}_n))$, $(S_n, \mathscr{S}_n)$ for $(Y, \mathscr{Y})$, the mixed strategy σ_n for g, $([0, 1], \mathscr{B})$ for $(X, \mathscr{X})$, P^n for P with $P^1 = \lambda$ and yielding $Q(B \mid e, y)$ for P^{n+1} and $P_e \circ g_e^{-1}$ as transition probability $\overline{P}^n$ from $(E_n, \mathscr{E}_n)$ to $(S_n, \mathscr{S}_n)$.

(9) The sequence $\overline{P}_n$ forms the required behavioral strategy. Check that here too the probability distributions induced on plays are unaffected.

Remark II.1.20. In particular, when games with perfect recall are presented in terms of incremental information (Remark II.1.4 after Theorem II.1.2), this proof shows that the correspondence between behavioral, mixed, and general(ized) strategies is completely independent of the game; it depends only on $(A_i, \mathscr{A}_i)$ and $(S_i, \mathscr{S}_i)$. It also shows that, in terms of mixed strategies, there is no need to remember past actions.

c. Show, without drastic modifications in the proof, that the above remains valid if the "set of dates for player i," instead of $\mathbb{N}$, is allowed to be any countable well-ordered set.

d. Consider a "countably linear" game for player i; i.e., there exists a countable measurable partition of $(A_i, \mathscr{A}_i)$ such that each partition element is met at most once along any play. Prove, like in (2) of II.1, Ex. 10b, p. 71, that general strategies for i can be replaced by mixed strategies.

e. If A^i is countable, and the game is linear for i, then every general strategy for i is equivalent to a probability distribution over pure strategies (without any standard Borel restriction on the action sets S_a^i).

HINT. Construct first a probability distribution over $X \times \sum^i = X \times (\prod_{a \in A^i} S_a^i)$, treating the different factors S_a^i as conditionally independent given X.

f. Show the above results remain valid with variable action sets, provided player i has a behavioral strategy (resp. pure strategy). (Apply the result with the embedding space S, then modify the obtained strategy where it is not carried by $\overline{S}$.)

g. Show that, without any assumption on the game, a generalized strategy can always be represented by $(X, \mathscr{X}, x_1, P, \sigma)$, where x_1 is the initial state in the auxiliary space $(X, \mathscr{X})$, P is a transition probability from $(X, \mathscr{X}) \times (A^i, \mathscr{A}^i)$ to $(X, \mathscr{X})$, and σ is a measurable map from $(X, \mathscr{X})$ to $(S^i, \mathscr{S}^i)$ (such that $\forall x, \forall a$, $P[\sigma^{-1}(\overline{S}_a^i) \mid x, a] = 1$).

11. Best replies.

a. Still in the context of II.1, Ex. 10a, p. 70, even the concept of a generalized strategy is not necessarily satisfactory as a concept of reply (say, in the definition of an equilibrium). Indeed, for a reply, the game and the strategies of the others, i.e., $(T_n, \mathscr{T}_n, Q_n)_{n=1}^{\infty}$, are given, so every time player i has to randomize according to P_n, the full probability measure on the conditioning space is known. It becomes then more natural to require the measurability of P_n only with respect to this measure and maybe also to require equalities to hold only a.e.

b. Assume Q is a "P-transition probability" from a probability space $(E, \mathscr{E}, P)$ to a standard Borel space $(F, \mathscr{F})$, i.e., $\forall A \in \mathscr{F}$, $Q_e(A)$ is P-measurable and P-a.e. $\in [0, 1]$, $Q_e(F) = 1$ P-a.e., and if $A_i \in \mathscr{F}$ is a disjoint sequence, then P-a.e. $\sum_i Q_e(A_i) = Q_e(\bigcup_i A_i)$. Show that there exists a unique probability $P \cdot Q$ on the product, satisfying $(P \cdot Q)(A \times B) = \int_A Q_e(B) P(de)$, $\forall A \in \mathscr{E}$, $\forall B \in \mathscr{F}$, and that there exists a transition probability $\overline{Q}$, with $P \cdot \overline{Q} = P \cdot Q$.

HINT. For example, fix a lifting (cf. II.1, Ex. 15, p. 84) ρ on $L_\infty(E, \mathscr{E}, P)$, view F as a compact metric space with its Borel sets, define $\overline{Q}_e(\varphi) = \rho[Q_e(\varphi)]$ for every continuous function φ on F, and use Riesz's theorem (cf. also II.1, Ex. 16, p. 86).

c. The above would, e.g., allow us to use, in "general replies," P-transition probabilities from the past to $(S_n, \mathscr{S}_n)$, but shows that it would not matter; the same probability distributions on histories will be generated as with true strategies.

d. Show that such probability distributions have the property that the conditional distribution on $T_n \times A_n$ given the past is given by Q_n and that the conditional distribution on S_n given {the past and $T_n \times A_n$} depends only on $A_n \times \prod_{t<n}(A_t \times S_t)$; i.e., S_n and $\prod_{t \leq n} T_t$ are conditionally independent given $A_n \times \prod_{t<n}(A_t \times S_t)$, and clearly any reasonable concept of reply of player i has to lead to distributions on histories having those two properties.

e. Conversely, show that any distribution on histories having those two properties can be generated by a behavioral strategy of player i (use II.1, Ex. 11b). There is thus no need to look for a concept of reply wider than the concept of strategy.

12. The definition of perfect recall.

a. Justifying the measurability assumption

α. The definition of a game with perfect recall for i given in Section II.1.c, p. 62, seems completely unsatisfactory. The conceptually correct definition is: for every feasible $a \in A^i$ (i.e., occurring along some feasible play), there exists a unique pair $\varphi(a) = (\beta(a), \sigma(a)) \in A^i \times S^i \cup \{\iota\}$ such that, for any feasible play where a occurs, either this is the first move of i along the play and then $(\beta(a), \sigma(a)) = \iota$ or the previous move of i was $\sigma(a)$ at $\beta(a)$. The maps β and σ are then completely defined by the model and are in no sense primitive data, hence their measurability should follow from assumptions on the primitive data of the model. To give a precise meaning to the above notion of "feasible play," reduce first, as in II.1, Ex. 1a, p. 64, the game to a deterministic one, by adding a player 0. Feasible plays are then all those compatible with the restrictions on action sets, and with the given initial state.

β. Denote by A_0^i the feasible part of A^i, and assume the game has perfect recall in the above sense; i.e., the map (α, σ) is well defined on A_0^i. If $(A_0^i, \mathscr{A}_0^i)$ is separable and separated, and $(S^i, \mathscr{S}^i)$ is standard Borel, then (α, σ) is measurable, and $(A_0^i, \mathscr{A}_0^i)$ is a Blackwell space, i.e., isomorphic to an analytic subset of [0, 1] (cf. Appendix A.6).

HINT.

(1) Show that one can always replace Ω by $X = \bigcup_{n\geq 0} S^n$, the measurable maps of the model induce the required measurable maps from $X \times S$ to X, from X to A, and from X to Ω, hence from $(X)^\infty$ to payoffs (which in fact factorizes through S^∞). Note X is standard Borel by our assumptions. Similarly, since $(A_0, \mathscr{A}_0)$ is separable and separated, it can be identified with a subset of $([0, 1], \mathscr{B})$, cf. (4) of II.1, Ex. 10b, p. 71, hence with $([0, 1], \mathscr{B})$ itself since the statement involves only A_0, which is unaffected. Extend the measurable partition $(A^i)_{i\in \mathbf{I}}$ to a measurable partition of [0, 1]. Assume thus $(A, \mathscr{A})$ is standard Borel.

(2) Let θ be the above map from X to A. Let $\psi\colon X \times S^\infty \to A^\infty$ be defined by $\psi(x, s_1, s_2, s_3, \ldots) = (\theta(x), \theta(x, s_1), \theta(x, s_1, s_2), \ldots)$: ψ is a measurable map between standard Borel spaces, so its graph $G \subseteq X \times (A \times S)^\infty$ is measurable, hence standard Borel.

(3) Given a Borel set B in $A^i \times S (\subseteq A \times S)$, $\tilde{B} = G \cap [X \times B \times (A \times S)_{n=1}^\infty]$ is Borel in the standard Borel space G. Let $T\colon G \to [\mathbb{N} \setminus \{0\}] \cup \{+\infty\}$: $T(g) = \min\{n \geq 1 \mid a_n \in A^i\}$, with $\min \emptyset = +\infty$, for $g = (x; a_0, s_0; a_1, s_1; \ldots)$. T is measurable. Thus $f(g) = a_{T(g)}$ for $T(g) < \infty$, $f(g) =$ "out" for $T(g) = +\infty$ is also measurable, as a composition: thus, $\overline{B} = f(\tilde{B}) \setminus \{\text{"out"}\}$ is analytic. And $\overline{B} = (\beta, \sigma)^{-1}(B)$.

(4) Thus the inverse image of any Borel set of $A^i \times S$ is analytic. The same holds for the inverse image of ι; just drop in the above argument the first factor $X \times A \times S$. Our map (β, σ) from A_0^i to $(A^i \times S) \cup \{\iota\}$ is such that the inverse image of any measurable set is analytic: A_0^i is analytic and, by the separation theorem for analytic sets (Appendix A.3.i), (β, σ) is measurable.

γ. The assumption in II.1, Ex. 12aβ, that $\mathscr{A}$ is separating is crucial: consider the one-person game with $A = X$ consisting of four points:

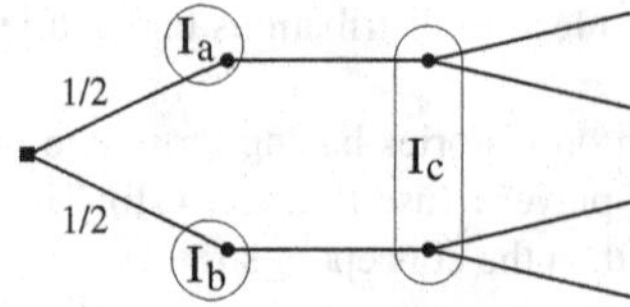

Figure II.2. The need for separating σ-fields.

δ. The separability assumption is also crucial: otherwise consider the same structure, but where initially nature picks a point in $[0, 1]$: in period 1 player Iobserves the Borel σ-field, and in period 2 he remembers only the σ-field generated by the singletons.

Remark II.1.21. It follows that the measurability assumption on (β, σ) is indeed a correct generalization of the definition to cases where $\mathscr{A}$ is possibly not separated or separating, while still remaining in a framework with an unambiguous set of feasible plays. (Possibly one has to reduce first A to some subset A^0, and similarly Ω to its feasible subset Ω^0 (with an appropriate separable σ-field), in such a way that, with A^0 and Ω^0, all assumptions of the model are still valid, that all strategies remain strategies, and that now A and Ω are Blackwell spaces, and each of their points is feasible.) Observe that, with this definition, we can not only, as in (1) of the hint in II.1, Ex. 12a, p. 74, above, identify Ω with X, but also A (or rather A^0) with $X - \mathscr{A}$ being a sub-σ-field. The canonical map φ from $(X, \mathscr{A}_i)$ to $(X, \mathscr{A}_i \otimes \mathscr{S})$ is then always well defined, whatever be the game, and the whole perfect recall assumption is about its measurability. Still equivalently, it could be phrased in terms of an increasing sequence of σ-fields of player i in H_∞.

We consider now how to extend the definition to the general model, with moves of nature, where, as mentioned before, there is no well defined set of feasible plays. We will therefore require the map φ to be defined a.e., and also only to be true a.e., in order not to have to reduce first A to some subset A^0 as above, and in order to have a definition independent of the set of feasible plays used.

Observe that, if there exists a strategy $\mathbf{I}^{\text{tuple}}$ or profile, there exists a behavioral strategy profile, and a set of plays that is negligible for every behavioral strategy profile is negligible for every strategy profile. So in the following, "a.s." will mean "a.s. for every (behavioral) strategy profile."

b. *The general case.*

α. For every separable σ-field $\mathscr{B}$ of $\mathscr{H}_\infty$, any given set of measurable maps $\varphi^i : A^i \to \overline{S}^i = [(A^i \times S) \cap \overline{S}] \cup \{\iota\}$, and every sequence of (general) strategies, there exist separable σ-fields $\tilde{\mathscr{A}}$ and $\tilde{\mathscr{O}}$ on A and Ω such that $\mathscr{B}$ is included in the corresponding product σ-field, such that all measurability assumptions of the model are still satisfied with the σ-fields $\tilde{\mathscr{A}}$ and $\tilde{\mathscr{O}}$, such that all given strategies are still strategies, and such that the φ^i are still measurable.

Hint. Observe that any element of a product σ-field belongs to a product of separable σ-fields. Start then with separable σ-fields $\mathscr{A}_0$ and $\mathscr{O}_0$ on A and Ω such that $\mathscr{B}$ is included in the corresponding product σ-field, such that the A^i are measurable, as well as the maps g^i and the set $\overline{S} \subseteq A \times S$. Define inductively $\mathscr{A}_{n+1} \supseteq \mathscr{A}_n$ and $\mathscr{O}_{n+1} \supseteq \mathscr{O}_n$ as separable σ-fields making all maps φ^i and all transition probabilities (those of nature and of the players) measurable when using $\mathscr{A}_n$ and $\mathscr{O}_n$ on the image. $\bigcup_n \mathscr{A}_n$ and $\bigcup_n \mathscr{O}_n$ answer the question.

β. Prove that the following conditions on a measurable map $\varphi^i : A^i \to \overline{S}^i$, defined a.e. on A^i (i.e., φ^i is well defined along a.e. play) are equivalent, letting, for $\omega \in H_\infty$, $T^i_n(\omega) = \inf\{ t > T^i_{n-1}(\omega) \mid a_t(\omega) \in A^i \}$ (and $T^i_0 = 0$, $\inf(\emptyset) = +\infty$):

- $\forall B \in \overline{\mathscr{S}}^i$, $\mathbb{1}_B \circ \varphi^i(a_{T^i_{n+1}}) = \mathbb{1}_B(s_{T^i_n})$ a.s. $\forall n \geq 1$ and $\varphi^i(a_{T^i_1}) = \{\iota\}$ a.s. s_t is the pair in $\overline{S}_t \subseteq (A \times S)_t$).
- $\forall C \in \overline{\mathscr{S}}^i \otimes \overline{\mathscr{S}}^i$ such that $(s_1, s_2) \in C \Longrightarrow s_1 \neq s_2$, $\mathbb{1}_C(s_{T^i_n}, \varphi^i(a_{T^i_{n+1}})) = 0$ a.s. $\forall n \geq 1$, and $\varphi^i(a_{T^i_1}) = \{\iota\}$.

Call such a function φ^i a recall function, and say then that player i has perfect recall. Prove also that, given a recall function for each player in $\mathbf{I}_0 \subseteq \mathbf{I}$, the set of plays where all those recall functions are well defined and exact has outer probability one for every strategy vector.

HINT. Observe that II.1, Ex. 12bα, remains valid if the φ^i are only defined a.e., except that then, for the separable σ-fields, φ^i will be defined a.e. only for the strategies in the prescribed sequence. Use this, and the fact that when $\mathscr{A}^i$ is separable and separating, $\{\,\omega \mid \varphi^i(a_{T^i_{n+1}}) = s_{T^i_n}\,\}$ is measurable, and has probability one by the first condition.

γ. Given an extensive form, for which there exists a strategy $\mathbf{I}^{\text{tuple}}$, assume $\omega_1 \in \tilde{\Omega} \subseteq \Omega$ and $\tilde{A} \subseteq A$ are such that the restriction to $\tilde{\Omega}$ and $\tilde{A}$ is also an extensive form; i.e., the outer probability of $\tilde{A}$ is one for every $\omega \in \tilde{\Omega}$ and the outer probability of $\tilde{\Omega}$ is one for every $(\omega, s) \in \tilde{\Omega} \times \tilde{\tilde{S}}$. Then if i has perfect recall in Γ, he also has it in $\tilde{\Gamma}$.

HINT. Show first that the behavioral strategy profile of $\tilde{\Gamma}$ are the restrictions of those in Γ, using that a behavioral strategy is a measurable map to the standard Borel space of probabilities on S, that measurable maps to a standard Borel space can always be extended, and that the set where such an extension is not a strategy is measurable, so that the extension can be replaced there by the given strategy profile of Γ. Show then that, for any strategy profile, the set of plays of $\tilde{\Gamma}$ is a subset with outer probability one of the set of plays of Γ, and define $\tilde{\varphi}^i$ as an appropriate restriction of φ^i.

δ. The converse of II.1, Ex. 12bγ, holds if $\tilde{A}$ is universally measurable (cf. Appendix A.4.d) in A, or if $(A, \mathscr{A})$ is standard Borel.

HINT. In the first case, there is no need to extend $\tilde{\varphi}$; in the second case, as noted in II.1, Ex. 12aγ, p. 74, $\tilde{\varphi}$ has an extension φ (with values in $\overline{S} \subseteq A \times S$) to some Borel subset of A containing $\tilde{A}$.

Remark II.1.22. II.1, Ex. 12bγ, and II.1, Ex. 12bδ, show thus that the definition of perfect recall is, as required, essentially independent of the surrounding space ("essentially" because of the small restrictions in the converse, which seem unavoidable). The definition is also flexible enough to include all cases studied in II.1, Ex. 12a, p. 74, without having first to restrict artificially the sets A and Ω to appropriate subsets A_0 and Ω_0.

13. A converse to II.1, Ex. 12a.

a.

α. Show that, under the assumptions of II.1, Ex. 12a, p. 74, one obtains a stronger form of perfect recall: the "a.s." qualifications hold not only for every strategy vector of the players, but also for every (pseudo-)strategy vector of players that would be fully informed about the whole past (i.e., in some sense, "whatever players do" instead of "whatever their strategies are").

Remark II.1.23. The purpose of the present exercise is to show that, in this form, the statement is an equivalence.

β. If $(A, \mathscr{A})$ is separable (and separated), and if a subset R of players has perfect recall in the strong a.s. sense as above, there exist measurable restrictions on the actions of nature, i.e., measurable subsets Ω^0 of Ω, C of $\Omega^0 \times A$ and K of $\Omega^0 \times A \times S \times \Omega^0$, such that $\omega_1 \in \Omega^0$, $\alpha(C_\omega) = 1$, $\forall \omega \in \Omega^0$, and such that $(\omega, a, s, \omega') \in K \Longrightarrow (\omega, a) \in C$, $(a, s) \in \overline{S}$, and $\forall (\omega, a, s) : (\omega, a) \in C, (a, s) \in \overline{S} \Longrightarrow q_{\omega,a,s}(K_{\omega,a,s}) = 1$, for which every feasible play (cf. II.1, Ex. 12aα, p. 74) exhibits perfect recall for all players in R (in the sense that, for some measurable functions φ^i $(i \in R)$ from a subset $\tilde{A}^i$ of A^i to

$\{(a, s) \in \overline{S} \mid a \in \tilde{A}^i\} \cup \{\iota\}$ (which coincide with the given functions on their common domain), $\varphi^i(a_t)$ is the previous pair (a, s) encountered by i along that play (or ι if none), for any $a_t \in A^i$ occurring along that play). (Outside Ω^0, one can use the original restrictions, if any.)

Actually, to avoid hiding any "perfect recall" type of assumptions, we will assume the strong "a.s." property only for "pseudo-strategy vectors," which are transition probabilities depending only on the current state and signal.

To make the definition of perfect recall non-vacuous, we also assume that there exists at least one (pseudo-)strategy vector σ_0 for the game, which can then be assumed to be behavioral.

The proof itself of the above statement is given in II.1, Ex. 13b, below.

γ. The following example shows the above strong form of perfect recall to be definitely stronger than the definition: nature picks x_1 in $[0, 1]$ with Lebesgue measure. Player II chooses x_2 in $[0, 1]$ after having observed x_1; then player I chooses x_3 after having observed $a = x_2 + \xi \pmod 1$, where the noise ξ is uniformly distributed on $[-\varepsilon, \varepsilon]$. Later player I has to move again, and will be reminded of (a, x_3), except if $x_3 = x_1$, in which case he gets a blank signal.

Clearly player I has perfect recall in this game, but not according to the strong variant of the definition. (The only purpose of player II's presence, instead of just letting player I move after nature, without information, is to prevent an objection that by interchanging the ordering of the moves (cf. II.1, Ex. 1c, p. 64) one would obtain perfect recall in the strong sense.)

δ. It follows that the only relaxation involved in our definition of perfect recall vis-à-vis the strong definition of II.1, Ex. 12a, lies in restricting (for the definition of "a.s.") the players to use only true strategies, which seems natural enough not to require further justification, and is indeed sufficient for the proof of Kuhn's theorem.

b. *General revision exercise, the "peeling method."*

We turn now to the proof of the statement in II.1, Ex. 13aβ. Actually, it is often more convenient to formulate a game already with restrictions on the moves of nature, in which case the transition probabilities only have to be defined on the relevant sets. We therefore allow those and require the sets Ω^0, C, and K to be co-analytic, and we construct smaller measurable sets Ω^0, C, and K for which every feasible play exhibits perfect recall.

In II.1, Ex. 13c, below, some required lemmas are given, and it is shown how to reduce the problem to the case where the spaces A and Ω are standard Borel, where φ is defined on the whole of A, and where the sets Ω^0, C, and K are Borel.

The central iteration of the proof is given in part II.1, Ex. 13d, and the final argument in II.1, Ex. 13e.

c. *Preliminaries.*

We first reduce (in II.1, Ex. 13cα, II.1, Ex. 13cβ, and II.1, Ex. 13cγ) to the standard Borel case.

α. If $\mathscr{A}$ is not separating, pass to the quotient, all assumptions remain valid, and measurable restrictions with the quotient induce these restrictions with the original.

β. Choose a separable sub-σ-field $\mathscr{O}_0$ on Ω such that:

- the payoff function is still measurable on the infinite product
- the sets Ω^0, C, and K are still co-analytic
- the transition probability α to $(A, \mathscr{A})$ is still measurable
- the given pseudo-strategy is still a transition probability from C to S.

HINT. Use that the transition probabilities are to separable spaces, that a measurable subset of a product is generated by countably many products of measurable sets, and that a Souslin scheme involves only countably many measurable sets.

Similarly, let now $\mathscr{O}_{n+1}$ be a separable sub-σ-field containing $\mathscr{O}_n$ and such that $q_{\omega,a,s}(A)$ is $\mathscr{O}_{n+1} \otimes \mathscr{A} \otimes \mathscr{S}$-measurable $\forall A \in \mathscr{O}_n$. The σ-field $\mathscr{O}_\infty$ spanned by $\bigcup_n \mathscr{O}_n$ is then a separable sub-σ-field on Ω for which all assumptions remain true. Conclude that we can also assume $(\Omega, \mathscr{O})$ to be separable and separated.

γ. A and Ω can now be viewed as subsets of standard Borel spaces $\tilde{A}$ and $\tilde{\Omega}$. Using Appendix A.9.a and Appendix A.9.e, select a measurable extension of the payoff function to $\tilde{\Omega}^\infty$; $\overline{\overline{S}}$, $\tilde{\Omega}^0$, $\tilde{C}$, and $\tilde{K}$ as measurable or co-analytic extensions of $\overline{S}$, Ω^0, C, and K in $\tilde{A} \times S$, $\tilde{\Omega}$, $\tilde{\Omega} \times \tilde{A}$, $\tilde{\Omega} \times \tilde{A} \times S \times \tilde{\Omega}$; $\tilde{\alpha}$ as a transition probability from $\tilde{\Omega}$ to $\tilde{A}$, $\tilde{q}$ as a transition probability from $\tilde{\Omega} \times \tilde{A} \times S$ to $\tilde{\Omega}$, $\tilde{\sigma}$ as a transition probability from $\tilde{\Omega} \times \tilde{A}$ to S, $(\tilde{A}^i)_{i \in I}$ as a measurable extension of the player partition, and finally $(\tilde{\varphi}^i)_{i \in R}$ as Borel maps from $\tilde{A}^i$ to $\overline{\overline{S}} \cap [\tilde{A}^i \times S] \cup \{\iota\}$.

δ. Before continuing we need four lemmas:

A. Let $D = \{(\omega, a) \in \tilde{\Omega} \times \tilde{A} \mid \tilde{\sigma}_{\omega,a}(\overline{\overline{S}}_a) = 1\}$. D is a Borel set containing C. We will define strategies in the enlarged game as transition probabilities from D to S, such that $\overline{\overline{S}}$ has probability 1.

- Note first that the restriction of any strategy in the enlarged game is a pseudo-strategy in the original; conversely, any strategy τ of the original game is such a restriction (consider any Borel extension $\tilde{\tau}$, and let $\overline{\tau}_{\omega,a} = \tilde{\tau}_{\omega,a}$ if $\tilde{\tau}_{\omega,a}(\overline{\overline{S}}_a) = 1$, $\overline{\tau}_{\omega,a} = \tilde{\sigma}_{\omega,a}$ otherwise).
- To construct (by Ionescu Tulcea's theorem) the probability distribution $P_{\tilde{\tau}}$ induced on plays ($\tilde{H}_\infty = (\tilde{\Omega} \times \tilde{A} \times S)^\infty$) in the enlarged game by a strategy $\tilde{\tau}$ in that game, extend first $\tilde{\tau}$ in an arbitrary Borel way on $(\tilde{\Omega} \times \tilde{A}) \setminus D$. Denote also by P_τ the probability distribution induced on $H_\infty = \{(\omega_t, a_t, s_t)_{t=1}^\infty \mid (\omega_t, a_t) \in C, (a_t, s_t) \in \overline{S}, \omega_1 = \omega_1\}$ by the restriction τ of $\tilde{\tau}$ to the original game, i.e., to C.

  Show that, for any measurable set B in $\tilde{H}_\infty$, $P_{\tilde{\tau}}(B) = P_\tau(B \cap H_\infty)$.

  HINT. Since the right-hand member is also a measure on $\tilde{H}_\infty$, it suffices to show equality on generators. Hence we can by induction assume that equality holds for all measurable B_1 in the product of the first n factors and prove that $P_{\tilde{\tau}}(B_1 \times B_2) = P_\tau(B_1 \times B_2 \cap H_\infty)$ for measurable B_2 in X_{n+1}; this is elementary.
- In particular $P_{\tilde{\tau}}$ depends only on τ, not on its extension.
- It follows also that the negligible subsets of H_∞ are the traces of the negligible subsets of $\tilde{H}_\infty$ (negligible: of probability zero for every P_τ, resp. $P_{\tilde{\tau}}$), and universally measurable, in particular analytic (Appendix A.4.d.1), subsets of $\tilde{H}_\infty$ are negligible iff their trace on H_∞ is negligible.
- Call a subset X of $\tilde{\Omega} \times \tilde{A} \times S \times \tilde{\Omega}$ negligible (and similarly for the original space), if for all n $\prod_{t<n}(\tilde{\Omega} \times \tilde{A} \times S)_t \times (X \times \tilde{A}_{n+1} \times S_{n+1}) \times \prod_{t>n+1}(\tilde{\Omega} \times \tilde{A} \times S)$ is negligible. It follows that such an analytic X is negligible iff its trace on $\Omega \times A \times S \times \Omega$ is negligible. The same holds for subsets of $\tilde{\Omega}$, of $\tilde{\Omega} \times \tilde{A}$, and of $\tilde{\Omega} \times \tilde{A} \times S$.

B. The set Π of probability distributions over plays $(\tilde{\Omega} \times \tilde{A} \times S)^\infty$ induced by (pseudo-) strategies is Borel. So the corresponding sets of feasible distributions on $\tilde{\Omega}$, $\tilde{\Omega} \times \tilde{A}$, $\tilde{\Omega} \times \tilde{A} \times S$, $\tilde{\Omega} \times \tilde{A} \times S \times \tilde{\Omega}$, which are the union over $t \geq 1$ of the marginals of Π on the relevant factor of the set of plays, are analytic. (Thus, the negligible subsets of one of those sets are those that are negligible for every feasible distribution.)

HINT. Like in II.1, Ex. 11d, and II.1, Ex. 11e, p. 73, and by II.1, Ex. 13cδA, p. 78, Π consists of those distributions on the standard Borel set of plays such that (α) the marginal on Ω_1 is the unit mass at ω_1 (a closed subset); (β) $(a_t, s_t) \in \tilde{\tilde{S}}\ \forall t$, a Borel condition; ($\gamma$) the conditional probabilities of nature are correct, i.e., given the factors $X_1, X_2, X_3, \ldots$, require that for every n and a countable generating family of Borel sets A in $\prod_1^n X_t$ and B in X_{n+1}, one has $\mu(A \times B) = \int_A r(B) d\mu$ (denoting by r the specified transition probability of nature), which is again a countable set of Borel conditions; (δ) the required conditional independence conditions hold for the ("pseudo-")players; i.e., s_t is independent of the past given (ω_t, a_t). Use II.1, Ex. 9, p. 68, to show that, if X, Y, and Z are standard Borel, the set of probability distributions on $X \times Y \times Z$ such that X and Y are conditionally independent given Z is a Borel set (take as parameter space E the space of all probabilities $X \times Y \times Z$). So this condition too determines a Borel subset. Finally, (ε) the conditional distribution σ of s_t given (ω_t, a_t) is the same for all t. For this it is sufficient to show that the set of pairs of distributions P, Q on $X \times Y$ (X, Y are standard Borel) that have the same conditional on Y given X is a Borel set. By II.1, Ex. 9, p. 68, there exists a conditional probability of Y given X for $\frac{1}{2}(P + Q)$, denoted by $R(dy \mid x, P + Q)$, which is jointly measurable in X and $(P + Q)$. The condition is then that, for measurable subsets X_1 of X and Y_1 of Y, $\int_{X_1} R(Y_1 \mid x, P + Q) P(dx) = P(X_1 \times Y_1)$, $\int_{X_1} R(Y_1 \mid x, P + Q) Q(dx) = Q(X_1 \times Y_1)$. For X_1 and Y_1 in countable generating sub-algebras, one gets in this way a countable family of equations, both members of which are Borel functions of (P, Q). Hence Lemma II.1, Ex. 13cδB.

C. An analytic subset X of $\tilde{\Omega} \times \tilde{A} \times S \times \tilde{\Omega}$ is negligible iff the analytic set $\{ (\omega, a, s) \mid \tilde{q}_{\omega,a,s}(X) > 0 \}$ is negligible.

HINT. Appendix A.9.f.

D. An analytic subset of $\tilde{\Omega} \times \tilde{\tilde{S}}$ is negligible iff its analytic projection on $\tilde{\Omega} \times \tilde{A}$ is negligible.

HINT. Clearly the projection is analytic, and the condition sufficient. Consider thus an analytic subset X of $\tilde{\Omega} \times \tilde{\tilde{S}}$, with analytic projection Y on $\tilde{\Omega} \times \tilde{A}$, and assume Y is not negligible: for some strategy $\tilde{\tau}$, and for some t, $P_{\tilde{\tau}}((\omega_t, a_t) \in Y) > 0$. By Appendix A.7.j, there exists a universally measurable map s from Y to S, with $(y, s(y)) \in X\ \forall y \in Y$. So there exists a Borel subset B of Y, such that the restriction of s to B is Borel measurable, and such that $P_{\tilde{\tau}}((\omega_t, a_t) \in B) > 0$. Let $\bar{s}(\omega, a)$ be the unit mass at $s(\omega, a)$ for $(\omega, a) \in B$, $\bar{s}(\omega, a) = \tilde{\sigma}(\omega, a)$ on $D \setminus B$ and consider the behavioral strategy $\tilde{s} = \frac{1}{2}\bar{s} + \frac{1}{2}\tilde{\tau}$: it has probability 2^{-t} of playing like $\tilde{\tau}$ before t and like $\bar{s}$ at t, so $P_{\tilde{s}}((\omega_t, a_t, s_t) \in X) \geq 2^{-t} P_{\tilde{\tau}}((\omega_t, a_t) \in B) > 0$: X is not negligible.

E. An analytic subset X of $\tilde{\Omega} \times \tilde{A}$ is negligible iff the analytic set $\{ \omega \mid \tilde{\alpha}_\omega(X) > 0 \}$ is negligible.

HINT. Appendix A.9.f.

F. Negligible analytic subsets of $\tilde{\Omega} \times \tilde{A} \times S \times \tilde{\Omega}$, etc., are contained in negligible Borel sets.

HINT. Use II.1, Ex. 13cδB, p. 78, and Appendix A.4.d.3.

G. For any negligible analytic subset N of $\tilde{\Omega} \times \tilde{A} \times S \times \tilde{\Omega}$, there exist Borel restrictions $\Omega^0 \subseteq \tilde{\Omega}^0, C^0 \subseteq \tilde{C}, K^0 \subseteq \tilde{K}$, such that $(\omega, a) \in C^0 \Longrightarrow \tilde{\sigma}_{\omega,a}(\tilde{\tilde{S}}_a) = 1$, and $K^0 \cap N = \emptyset$.

Remark II.1.24. It follows that, with those restrictions, the extended model (i.e., with $\sim$) is a true extensive form, with $S_a \neq \emptyset$ for every feasible a, and with $\tilde{\sigma}$ an everywhere defined pseudo-strategy.

HINT. Let $\tilde{C}_1 = \tilde{C} \cap D$, and add to N the complements of $\tilde{K}$, of $\tilde{C}_1 \times S \times \tilde{\Omega}$, and of $\tilde{\Omega}^0 \times \tilde{\tilde{S}} \times \tilde{\Omega}^0$, obtaining thus $\tilde{N}$. $\tilde{C}_1$ is still co-analytic, as a Borel subset of the co-analytic $\tilde{C}$, and all sets added are negligible by II.1, Ex. 13cδA, p. 78. So $\tilde{N}$ is a negligible analytic subset. Apply then II.1, Ex. 13cδF, p. 79, to get K_1 Borel disjoint from $\tilde{N}$ and with a negligible complement; apply then II.1, Ex. 13cδC, p. 79, to get that the Borel set $B_1 = \{ (\omega, a, s) \in \tilde{\Omega} \times \tilde{S} \mid \tilde{q}_{\omega,a,s}(K_1) < 1 \}$ is negligible, so its analytic projection P_1 on $\tilde{\Omega} \times \tilde{A}$ is (II.1, Ex. 13cδD, p. 79) also negligible; hence (II.1, Ex. 13cδF) disjoint from a Borel set $C_1 \subseteq \tilde{C}_1$ with a negligible complement, and, finally, by II.1, Ex. 13cδE, p. 79, $\Omega_1 = \{ \omega \mid \tilde{\alpha}_\omega(C_1) = 1 \}$ is a Borel set with a negligible complement, and clearly included in $\tilde{\Omega}_0$. Let now $K_2 = \{ (\omega, a, s, \omega') \in K_1 \mid \omega, \omega' \in \Omega_1, (\omega, a) \in C_1 \}$ and continue inductively, obtaining decreasing sequences of Borel sets K_n, C_n, Ω_n with $\tilde{\alpha}_\omega(C_n) = 1\ \forall \omega \in \Omega_n$, $(\omega, a) \in C_n \Longrightarrow [\tilde{\sigma}_{\omega,a}(\tilde{S}_a) = 1$ and $s \in \tilde{\tilde{S}}_a \Longrightarrow \tilde{q}_{\omega,a,s}(K_n) = 1]$, $(\omega, a, s, \omega') \in K_{n+1} \Longrightarrow \omega' \in \Omega_n$. Denote their intersection by K^0, C^0, Ω^0. Observe that $\omega_1 \in \Omega^0$ because Ω^0 has a negligible complement.

ε.

A. If we obtain a system of restrictions as in II.1, Ex. 13cδG, p. 79, where the perfect recall relations implied by the $\tilde{\varphi}^i$ are exact for every feasible path, the same will be true for the traces of Ω^0, C^0, and K^0 on the original spaces Ω and A, so the result will be proved (restricting also $\tilde{\varphi}^i$ to $(\tilde{\varphi}^i)_i^{-1}(S \cup \{\iota\})$).

B. Because such restrictions are measurable, it remains true (as in II.1, Ex. 13cδA, p. 78) that analytic subsets of K^0, C^0, etc., or the space of feasible paths, are negligible iff their trace on the original model is negligible. (And recall from II.1, Ex. 12, p. 74, that, when $\mathscr{A}$ is separable, $\varphi^i(a_{T_{n+1}}) = (a_{T_n}, s_{T_n})$ with probability one.)

C. Therefore, we can henceforth assume that II.1, Ex. 13cδG, p. 79, has been applied a first time, say, with $N = \emptyset$, so we are in a true extensive form model $(\Omega^0, C^0, K^0, \tilde{A}, (\tilde{A}^i)_{i \in \mathrm{I}}, S, \tilde{\tilde{S}}, \tilde{q}, \tilde{\alpha}, (\tilde{\varphi}^i)_{i \in R})$, which is fully standard Borel, and where (pseudo-)strategies are defined everywhere on C^0, in particular, $\overline{S}_a \neq \emptyset\ \forall (\omega, a) \in C^0$. Similarly $\tilde{\varphi}^i$ is now defined on the whole of $\tilde{A}^i$, $\tilde{\alpha}$ on Ω^0, and $\tilde{q}$ on $(C^0 \times S) \cap (\Omega^0 \times \tilde{\tilde{S}})$.

We can therefore henceforth drop the $\sim$ and the superscripts 0, and iteratively impose smaller and smaller restrictions, using each time without further reference II.1, Ex. 13cεB, above, and II.1, Ex. 13cδG, p. 79, without writing new superscripts.

D. Let $\Omega^i = \{ \omega \mid \alpha_\omega(A^i) = 0 \}$ and remove $\bigcup_i \Omega^i \times A^i$ from C. If $\Omega \times A^i$ is negligible, remove it also. For $i \in R$, let also $A_0^i = (\varphi^i)^{-1}(\iota)$, $A_{n+1}^i = (\varphi^i)^{-1}(A_n^i \times S)$, $A_\infty^i = A^i \setminus \bigcup_n A_n^i$. The A_n^i are Borel, the A_∞^i are negligible, and we remove $\Omega \times \bigcup_{i \in R} A_\infty^i$ from C: now $A^i = \bigcup_n A_n^i$. Define thus inductively the Borel map h^i on $S^i = (A^i \times S) \cap \overline{S}$ by $h^i(a, s) = (h^i(\varphi^i(a)), a, s)$, with $h^i(\iota) = \iota$ to initialize. And let $f^i(a) = h^i(\varphi^i(a))$.

d. *The main iteration.* The rest of the proof is to be done for all $i \in R$ in succession. So i is fixed henceforth.

α. Let $M = \bigcup_{n \geq 0} (S^i)^n$, where every sequence (including the empty one) is preceded by ι: h^i and f^i map S^i and A^i into the standard Borel space M.

Define first inductively the increasing sequences of analytic (Appendix A.9.f) subsets $D_1^n \subseteq \tilde{D}_1^n \subseteq \Omega$, $D_2^n \subseteq C$, $D_3^n \subseteq (\Omega \times \overline{S}) \cap (C \times S)$ with $D_j^0 = \tilde{D}_j^0 = \emptyset$, $D_2^n = \mathsf{Proj}(D_3^n)$, $D_1^n = \{ \omega \mid \alpha_\omega(D_2^n) > 0 \}$, $D_3^{n+1} = [(\Omega \times S^i) \cap (C \times S)] \cup \{ (\omega, a, s) \mid q_{\omega,a,s}(D_1^n) > 0 \}$, $\tilde{D}_j^n = \mathsf{Proj}(\{(\omega, a, s, \omega') \in K \mid \omega' \in D_1^n\})$; $(j = 1, 2, 3)$. Like in the proof of II.1, Ex. 13cδD, p. 79, observe that, by induction, for every initial probability distribution μ on D_j^n, there exists a pseudo-strategy vector τ such that, starting with μ and following τ, player i will have to play with positive probability before stage $n + 1$, and conversely, if μ assigns probability zero to D_j^n, then for any τ, player i will not have to play before stage $n + 1$.

$(*)$ In particular, by the same trick, for any non-negligible analytic subset of D_j^n, there exists a pseudo-strategy vector τ under which first this subset will be hit with positive probability, and next player i will with positive probability have to play at most n stages later.

It follows also that when stronger restrictions Ω, C, and K are imposed, the new D_j^n are just the restrictions of the old ones (while the $\tilde{D}_j^n$ may shrink).

β. Define now inductively Borel functions ψ_j from $\tilde{D}_j^n$ to M, with $\psi_3(\omega, a, s) = (f^i(a), a, s)$ on D_3^1, $\psi_2(\omega, a) = f^i(a)$ on D_2^1, $\psi_2(\omega, a) = \psi_3(\omega, a, s)$ if $a \notin A^i$ and $(\omega, a, s) \in \tilde{D}_3^n$, $\psi_1(\omega) = \psi_2(\omega, a)$ for $(\omega, a) \in \tilde{D}_2^n$, $\psi_3(\omega, a, s) = \psi_1(\omega')$ for $\omega' \in K_{\omega,a,s} \cap D_1^{n-1}$, all the while imposing further restrictions (Ω, C, K).

HINT. Assume by induction that the ψ_j are already defined with the above properties on the $\tilde{D}_j^n$. Consider $Q_{(\omega,a,s)}(B) = q_{\omega,a,s}[D_1^n \cap \psi_1^{-1}(B)]$ for any Borel set B in M, and prove that $N = \{(\omega, a, s) \mid Q_{\omega,a,s} \neq 0$ and $Q_{\omega,a,s}$ is not concentrated on a single point$\}$ is analytic. (D_1^n is the projection of a Borel set H in $\Omega \times [0, 1]$. The set of probabilities μ on $\Omega \times [0, 1]$ such that $\mu(H) > 0$, and such that the image of $\mu_{|H}$ by $\psi_1 \circ \pi$ (π being the projection) is not concentrated on a single point, is Borel, as the inverse image by a Borel map of the Borel set of positive measures on M that are not concentrated on a single point. Since it is standard Borel, it has an analytic projection in the space of probabilities on Ω (using Appendix A.7.j): N is the inverse image of this analytic set by the measurable Appendix A.9.e map q.) By $(*)$ and by the properties of ψ on the D_j^n, it follows that N is negligible, and so it can be neglected. Now $q_{\omega,a,s}(D_1^n) > 0 \Longrightarrow Q(\omega, a, s)$ is concentrated at a single point, say, $g(\omega, a, s)$. For any Borel set B in M, $g^{-1}(B) = \{(\omega, a, s) \mid q_{\omega,a,s}[D_1^n \cap \psi_1^{-1}(B)] > 0\}$ is analytic. Its complement $g^{-1}(B^c)$ is analytic too, so both are Borel in the analytic set $g^{-1}(M)$ (Appendix A.3.g). Thus g is a Borel function on its domain. Therefore $N = \{(\omega, a, s, \omega') \in (g^{-1}(M) \times D_1^n) \cap K \mid g(\omega, a, s) \neq \psi_1(\omega')\}$ is analytic as a Borel subset of an analytic set, and clearly negligible: we neglect it too. To obtain that g coincides with ψ_3 on D_3^n, it suffices now to obtain that $q_{\omega,a,s}(D_n^1) > 0$, $a \in A^i \Longrightarrow g(\omega, a, s) = (f^i(a), a, s)$. Let thus $N = \{(\omega, a, s) \in g^{-1}(M) \cap D_3^1 \mid g(\omega, a, s) \neq \psi_3(\omega, a, s)\}$: it is analytic as a Borel subset of an analytic set, and, by $(*)$ and the properties of ψ, negligible. Neglecting it, we can use g to extend ψ_3 to D_3^{n+1}. Consider now the analytic set $G = \{(\omega, a, m) \mid a \notin A^i, \exists s\colon (\omega, a, s) \in D_3^{n+1}, \psi_3(\omega, a, s) = m\}$; then $N = \{(\omega, a) \mid \#G_{\omega,a} > 1\}$ is analytic: viewing M as $[0, 1]$, one has $N = \bigcup_{r \in \mathbb{Q}} \{(\omega, a) \mid \exists m > r, (\omega, a, m) \in G\} \cap \{(\omega, a) \mid \exists m < r, (\omega, a, m) \in G\}$. For the same reason, there exist, using Appendix A.7.j, two universally measurable functions s_1 and s_2 defined on N, with $(\omega, a, s_i(\omega, a)) \in D_3^{n+1}$ and $\psi_3(\omega, a, s_1(\omega, a)) \neq \psi_3(\omega, a, s_2(\omega, a))$. As in $(*)$, construct now a strategy vector that reaches N with positive probability and in N plays Borel modifications of s_1 and s_2 with positive probability each, and afterwards reaches player i with positive probability in $n + 1$ steps: this is impossible, so N is negligible. Neglecting it, we obtain that G is the (analytic) graph of a function g from $\{(\omega, a) \in D_2^{n+1} \mid a \notin A^i\}$ to M, so g is Borel (Appendix A.3.g). This defines thus ψ_2 on the whole of D_2^{n+1}; there is clearly no problem of compatibility. To define now ψ_1 on D_1^{n+1}, use the same argument as used above for ψ_3 on D_3^{n+1}, but view, for the proof of analyticity, α as a transition probability from Ω to $\Omega \times A$ instead of to A; and notice also that there is no problem of compatibility. Finally, to extend the domains of definition to the $\tilde{D}_j^{n+1}$, notice that ψ_1 has a Borel extension to the whole of Ω (Appendix A.9.a). Then $\{(\omega, a) \in D_2^{n+1} \mid \psi_1(\omega) \neq \psi_2(\omega, a)\}$ is analytic as a Borel subset of an analytic set, and clearly negligible since for those ω, $\alpha_\omega(D_2^{n+1}) = 0$. Neglecting it, we have $\psi_1(\omega) = \psi_2(\omega, a)$ on $\operatorname{Proj} D_3^{n+1}$. Similarly, $\{(\omega, a, s, \omega') \in K \mid \omega' \in D_1^n, \psi_1(\omega') \neq \psi_1(\omega), a \notin A^i$ or $\psi_1(\omega') \neq (\psi_1(\omega), a, s), a \in A^i\}$ is analytic, and is now also negligible, since for those, $q_{\omega,a,s}(D_1^n) = 0$ (because if $q_{\omega,a,s}(D_1^n) > 0$, then both $\psi_1(\omega) = \psi_2(\omega, a)$ and $\psi_3(\omega, a, s) = \psi_1(\omega')$ for $\omega' \in K_{\omega,a,s} \cap D_1^n$). Neglecting it too completes the induction.

γ.

A. Once this induction is over, consider (with the new restrictions Ω, C, K) the increasing sequences of analytic sets D_j^n and $\tilde{D}_j^n$, and denote their union by D_j and $\tilde{D}_j$. The functions ψ_j are well defined on $\tilde{D}_j$ ($\supseteq D_j$); show that they are Borel.

HINT. Functions with an analytic graph on an analytic space are Borel.

B. We have now that $D_3 = [(\Omega \times S^i) \cap (C \times S)] \cup \{(\omega, a, s) \mid (\omega, a) \in C, (a, s) \in \overline{S}, q_{\omega,a,s}(D_1) > 0\}$, $D_2 = \mathsf{Proj}_C(D_3)$, $D_1 = \{\omega \mid \alpha_\omega(D_2) > 0\}$, and $\tilde{D}_j = \mathsf{Proj}\{(\omega, a, s, \omega') \in K \mid \omega' \in D_1\}$. And $\psi_1 \colon \tilde{D}_1 \to M$ is Borel such that, for $(\omega, a, s, \omega') \in K$, $\omega' \in D_1$, $\psi_1(\omega') = \psi_1(\omega)$ if $a \notin A^i$ and $\psi_1(\omega') = (\psi_1(\omega), a, s)$, $\psi_1(\omega) = f^i(a)$ if $a \in A^i$.

e. *End of the proof: last iteration.*

α. Using II.1, Ex. 13cεD, p. 80, show that $\mathsf{Proj}[(\Omega \times A^i) \cap C] \subseteq D_1$ and that if $D_1 \neq \emptyset$, $\omega_1 \in D_1$.

β. Show that, if $\omega_1 \in D_1$, $\psi_1(\omega_1) = \iota$, and that, along every feasible play, as long as ω_t remains in $\tilde{D}_1$, $\psi_1(\omega_t)$ is the correct sequence of past (a_n, s_n) $(n < t, a_n \in A^i)$. Thus player i can receive incorrect messages (from φ^i, or from ψ_1) only on feasible paths that have first left $\tilde{D}_1$, and next reentered D_1 (using II.1, Ex. 13eα), which they can do only by first passing through $\tilde{D}_1 \setminus D_1$.

γ. Denote by H_∞ the (standard Borel) space of feasible plays. Let $\eta \colon H_\infty \times \mathbb{N} \to M$, where $\eta(h, t)$ denotes the correct sequence of past (a_n, s_n) $(n < t, a_n \in A^i)$: η is Borel. Let $E = \{(h, t) \mid \eta(h, t) \neq \psi_1(\omega_t), \omega_t (= \omega_t(h)) \in \tilde{D}_1\}$: E is analytic as a Borel subset of an analytic set. Do now inductively for $t = 3, 4, 5, \ldots$, the following, under the inductive assumption that $\{(h, n) \in E \mid n < t\} = \emptyset$ (for $t = 3$, this follows from II.1, Ex. 13eβ).

δ. Let $N_t = \{\omega_t(h) \mid (h, t) \in E\}$: N_t is analytic (Appendix A.6) and, using II.1, Ex. 13eβ and the inductive assumption, $N_t \subseteq \tilde{D}_1 \setminus D_1$. Thus $L = \{(\omega, a, s, \omega') \in K \mid \omega \in N_t, \omega' \in D_1\}$ is analytic, and negligible (because $L = \{(\omega, a, s, \omega') \in L \mid q_{\omega,a,s}(D_1) = 0\} \cup \{(\omega, a, s, \omega') \in L \mid (\omega, a) \in D_2, \alpha_\omega(D_2) = 0\}$ since $N_t \cap D_1 = \emptyset$): therefore neglect it. The inductive assumption is now satisfied for $t + 1$.

ε. At the end of the iterations, $E = \emptyset$; since $\mathsf{Proj}[(\Omega \times A^i) \cap C] \subseteq D_1$, this implies that φ^i recalls the correct last information to player i along every feasible play.

14. Effectively perfect recall.

Assume player i has effectively perfect recall, and A^i is countable. Then every generalized strategy (cf. II.1, Ex. 10aα, p. 70) of player i is equivalent to a probability distribution over pure strategies.

Remark II.1.25. Since generalized strategies allow the player to recall all his past signals and moves, the statement is a strong way of expressing both that the terminology "effectively perfect recall" is justified, and that there is nothing more general than the usual mixed strategies for such games. Also, applied to pure strategies, it yields Theorem II.1.2, p. 61.

Remark II.1.26. Since player i is fixed, we will systematically drop the superscript i, and write, for instance, A for A^i.

a. *Equivalence of generalized strategies and distributions over policies.* Call policy a pure strategy of fictitious player i who would recall his past signals. Thus the space of policies is $\Theta = \prod_{n=1}^{\infty} \left(\prod_{a \in A_n} S_a\right)^{\prod_{t<n} A_t}$ (with the corresponding product σ-field), where A_n denotes the nth copy of A.

Prove the equivalence for A^i countable.

Hint. Given a generalized strategy $(X_n, \mathscr{X}_n, P_{n-1})_{n=1}^{\infty}$, where P_n is a transition probability from $\prod_{1 \le t \le n}(S_{t-1} \times X_t \times A_t)$ to $S_n \times X_{n+1}$, with $S_0 = \{0\}$, construct by induction probabilities

Q_n on $Y_n = X_1 \times \prod_{t=1}^{n} \left[\prod_{a \in k_t} (\overline{S}_{t,a} \times X_{t+1})\right]^{\prod_{s \le t} A_s}$ for $n = 0, \ldots, \infty$. (Use Q_{n-1}, P_n and the map $h_n \colon Y_{n-1} \times \prod_{t \le n} A_t \to \prod_{t \le n} (S_{t-1} \times X_t \times A_t)$. Treat the factors corresponding to different elements of $\prod_{t \le a} A_t$ as conditionally independent.) Use Ionescu Tulcea's theorem again to obtain Q_∞ on Y_∞. Take then the marginal distribution of Q_∞ on Θ, forgetting the factors X_t.

b. A "*μ-completely mixed*" *behavioral strategy of the opponents*. Given a probability distribution μ over Θ, there exists a behavioral strategy vector τ_μ of the opponents such that, for each general strategy τ of the opponents there is a μ-negligible subset N_τ of Θ such that $\forall \theta \notin N_\tau$, $\forall n$, $\forall (a_1, \ldots, a_n) \in A^n$, $P_{\theta,\tau}(a_1, \ldots, a_n) > 0 \Longrightarrow P_{\theta,\tau_\mu}(a_1, \ldots, a_n) > 0$. ($P(a_1, \ldots, a_n)$ is the probability that the n first signals received by i are $a_1, \ldots, a_n$, in this order.)

HINT. Let $\Theta^\tau_{a_1,\ldots,a_n} = \{\theta \mid P_{\theta,\tau}(a_1, \ldots, a_n) > 0\}$. If τ_k are behavioral strategies, and $\tau = \sum 2^{-k} \tau_k$, prove that $\Theta^\tau \supseteq \bigcup_k \Theta^{\tau_k}$. Deduce that there exists a behavioral strategy $\tau_{\mu,a_1,\ldots,a_n}$ such that $\Theta^{\tau_{\mu,a_1,\ldots,a_n}}_{a_1,\ldots,a_n} = \mu\text{-}\operatorname{ess\,sup}\{\Theta^\tau_{a_1,\ldots,a_n} \mid \tau \text{ behavioral strategy}\}$ and again that there exists τ_μ such that $\forall n$, $\forall (a_1, \ldots, a_n)$, $\forall \tau$ behavioral strategy, $\Theta^\tau_{a_1,\ldots,a_n} \subseteq \Theta^{\tau_\mu}_{a_1,\ldots,a_n}$ μ-a.e. Extend this conclusion to general strategy vectors τ using Fubini's theorem on the product of (Θ, μ) and the auxiliary spaces of the opponents. Let finally $N_\tau = \bigcup_{\{\alpha \in \bigcup_n A^n\}} \left[\Theta^\tau_\alpha \setminus \Theta^{\tau_\mu}_\alpha\right]$.

c. *A measurable recall function*. There exists a universally measurable function $\alpha \colon \Sigma \times A \to A \cup \{\iota\}$ such that, $\forall \sigma \in \Sigma$, P_{σ,τ_μ}-a.e., one has $\alpha(\sigma, a_1(\omega)) = \iota$ and $\alpha(\sigma, a_{n+1}(\omega)) = a_n(\omega)$ for $n \ge 1$. (Σ denotes the pure strategy space Σ^i of player i; thus $\prod_{a \in A} \overline{S}_a$. And $a_n(\omega)$ is the nth signal received by player i.)

HINT. Use von Neumann's selection theorem (Appendix A.7.j) on the measurable set:

$$G = \{(\sigma, f) \in \Sigma \times (A \cup \{\iota\})^A \mid P_{\sigma,\tau_\mu}\text{-a.s.:}$$
$$f(a_1(\omega)) = \iota,\ f(a_{n+1}(\omega)) = a_n(\omega)\ \forall n \ge 1\}.$$

(Show $G = \bigcap_{\substack{(a,a') \in A^2 \\ n \ge 1}} ([\{\sigma \mid P_{\sigma,\tau_\mu}(a_{n+1} = a \text{ and } a_n = a') = 0\} \times (A \cup \{\iota\})^A] \cup [\Sigma \times \{f \mid f(a) = a'\}])$, still intersected with a similar term for a_1.)

d. *End of the proof.*

α. Define inductively universally measurable maps $\alpha^n \colon \Sigma \times A \to (A \cup \{\iota\})^{n+1}$, using $\alpha(\sigma, \iota) = \iota$, by $\alpha^0(\sigma, a) = a$, $\alpha^{n+1}(\sigma, a) = \langle \alpha(\sigma, \alpha^n(\sigma, a)),\ \alpha^n(\sigma, a)\rangle$ (where $\langle\ ,\ \rangle$ stands for concatenation). Let $B_n = (\alpha^n)^{-1}(A^{n+1})$ universally measurable and define inductively universally measurable maps $\sigma_n \colon \Theta \to \Sigma$ with $[\sigma_{n+1}(\theta)](a) = \theta_{n+1}[\alpha^n(\sigma_n(\theta), a)]$ if $(\sigma_n(\theta), a) \in B_n$, $= [\sigma_n(\theta)](a)$ otherwise. Let finally $[\sigma_\infty(\theta)](a) = \lim_{n\to\infty} [\sigma_n(\theta)](a)$ if, for all sufficiently large n, $[\sigma_n(\theta)](a) \notin B_n$, $[\sigma_\infty(\theta)](a) = [\sigma_1(\theta)](a)$ otherwise. Show that σ_∞ is universally measurable too.

β. Show by induction over n that $\forall \tau$, $\forall \theta \notin N_\tau$, $\forall k \ge n-1$, $P_{\sigma_k(\theta),\tau}$, and $P_{\theta,\tau}$ coincide on histories up to a_n (the nth signal to i), including for $k = \infty$.

HINT. Assume the statement for n. Then $\forall a \in A^n$, $\forall \theta \notin N_\tau$, $\forall k \ge n-1$, $(P_{\theta,\tau}(a) =)$ $P_{\sigma_k(\theta),\tau}(a) > 0 \Longrightarrow \theta \in \Theta^{\tau_\mu}_a \Longrightarrow \alpha^{n-1}(\sigma_k(\theta), a_n) = a$, so $(\sigma_k(\theta), a_n) \in B_{n-1} \setminus \bigcup_{m \ge n} B_m$, and $[\sigma_k(\theta)](a_n) = \theta_n(a)$ $\forall k \ge n$. Conclude.

γ. The image distribution of μ by σ_∞ is the required distribution on Σ.

Remark II.1.27. Observe that the map we obtained from μ to $\sigma_\infty(\mu)$ is neither canonical nor linear: σ_∞ itself depends on μ, through α, and hence τ_μ.

Remark II.1.28. The proof shows that the apparently weaker definition of "effectively perfect recall" that for each pure strategy σ of i and every behavioral strategy vector

τ of the opponents, there exists a corresponding recall function $\alpha_{\sigma,\tau}$ of player i, is already sufficient: use τ_σ for τ (cf. II.1, Ex. 14b, p. 83) to obtain that α_σ can be selected independently of τ.

Remark II.1.29. What is the "right" definition of "effectively perfect recall" when A^i is standard Borel, i.e., one that would be equivalent to the present definition for A^i countable, and for which the present result would generalize for $(S^i, \mathscr{S}^i)$ standard Borel? (For part II.1, Ex. 14a, p. 82, one can use (7) of the hint to II.1, Ex. 10b, 72.)

Remark II.1.30. Because of this theorem, one can treat as (linear) games with countable A^i (and hence use Remarks II.1.6 and II.1.7, p. 63), a number of situations where the true signals do not fall in a countable set, e.g., because they are in fact the full past history of signals and moves, and S^i is not necessarily countable. This applies in particular to all games as modeled according to Remark II.1.4, p. 61.

In the next five exercises, we fix a complete probability space $(\Omega, \mathscr{A}, P)$.

15. Lifting

A **lifting** ρ is a homomorphism of rings with unit from $L_\infty(\Omega, \mathscr{A}, P)$ to $\mathscr{L}_\infty(\Omega, \mathscr{A}, P)$ such that $\rho(f) \in f$ (recall that the points of L_∞ are equivalence classes in $\mathscr{L}_\infty$).

a. There exists a lifting.

Hint. Call "linear lifting" a positive linear map from L_∞ to $\mathscr{L}_\infty$ such that $\rho(f) \in f$ and $\rho(1) = 1$. Clearly every lifting is linear. We first show the existence of a linear lifting. Consider the family of pairs formed by a sub-σ-field $\mathscr{B}$ (containing all null sets) and a linear lifting ρ on $L_\infty(\Omega, \mathscr{B}, P)$, ordered by $(\mathscr{B}_1, \rho_1) \le (\mathscr{B}_2, \rho_2)$ iff $\mathscr{B}_1 \subseteq \mathscr{B}_2$ and ρ_2 extends ρ_1. The family is non-empty (trivial σ-field), and the order is inductive; i.e., any totally ordered subfamily $(\mathscr{B}_\alpha, \rho_\alpha)$ is bounded from above: indeed, either there is no countable co-final set of indices, and then $\mathscr{B}_\infty = \bigcup_\alpha \mathscr{B}_\alpha$ is a σ-field, with an obvious linear lifting ρ_∞, or there is one, say, α_i; let then $\mathscr{B}_\infty$ be the σ-field spanned by $\bigcup_\alpha \mathscr{B}_\alpha$, and $\rho_\infty(f) = \lim_{\mathscr{U}} \rho_{\alpha_i}[\mathsf{E}(f \mid \mathscr{B}_{\alpha_i})]$, where $\mathscr{U}$ is an ultrafilter on the integers: ρ_∞ is again a linear lifting on $\mathscr{B}_\infty$, by the martingale convergence theorem. So, by Zorn's lemma, there exists a maximal pair $(\mathscr{B}, \rho)$. If $A \in \mathscr{A} \setminus \mathscr{B}$, construct a linear lifting extending ρ on the σ-field spanned by $\mathscr{B}$ and A. Hence the existence of a linear lifting ρ. Let then R denote the set of all linear liftings ρ' such that $[\rho(f)](\omega) = 1$ implies $[\rho'(f)](\omega) = 1$ for all ω and every indicator function f. R is clearly convex; to prove its compactness in $\mathbb{R}^{\Omega \times L_\infty}$ it suffices to show that for any limit point $\tilde{\rho}$, $\tilde{\rho}(f) \in f$ for all f. By linearity and positivity (which implies uniform continuity), it suffices to do this for indicator functions, say, $f = \mathbb{1}_A$. Then $\{\omega \mid [\rho(f)](\omega) = 1\} = A$ a.e., so $\tilde{\rho}(f) \ge f$ a.e., and similarly $\tilde{\rho}(1 - f) \ge 1 - f$ a.e., hence the result. So by Krein–Milman, R has an extreme point $\tilde{\rho}$. $\tilde{\rho}$ is then still extreme in the convex set of all linear liftings: if a convex combination of two linear liftings belongs to R, then each of them belongs to R. Hence $\tilde{\rho}$ is a lifting: for $f \in L_\infty, 0 \le f \le 1$, let $T_f : L_\infty \to \mathscr{L}_\infty : g \mapsto \tilde{\rho}(fg) - \tilde{\rho}(f)\tilde{\rho}(g)$, $T^1(g) = \tilde{\rho}(g) + T_f(g)$, $T^2(g) = \tilde{\rho}(g) - T_f(g)$. An immediate computation shows that the T^i are linear liftings, with $\tilde{\rho}$ as average. By extremality, $T_f = 0$, i.e., $\tilde{\rho}(fg) = \tilde{\rho}(f)\tilde{\rho}(g)$. By linearity, this extends then to all f.

b. L_∞ is a complete lattice: i.e., if $(f_\alpha)_{\alpha \in A}$ is a uniformly bounded decreasing net in L_∞, it has a greatest lower bound: $\operatorname{ess\,inf}_{\alpha \in A} f_\alpha$ in L_∞.

Hint. Consider $\inf_i f_{\alpha_i}$, where the sequence α_i is chosen such that $\inf_i \int f_{\alpha_i} dP = \inf_\alpha \int f_\alpha dP$.

c. For a lifting ρ, and for $f = \operatorname{ess\,inf}_{\alpha \in A} f_\alpha$, one has $[\inf_{\alpha \in A} \rho(f_\alpha)] \in f$.

Hint. The left-hand member is $\ge \rho(f)$ and $\le \inf_i \rho(f_{\alpha_i})$, and both those bounds are measurable with the same integral. Use again completeness.

Remark II.1.31. A lifting maps indicator functions to indicator functions, hence induces a map from subsets to subsets.

d. If Ω is a Hausdorff space, and P a regular probability, call a lifting strong if $\rho(f) \le \hat{f}$ on the support of P for all $f \in L_\infty$, where $\hat{f}(\omega) = \limsup_{V \in \mathscr{V}_\omega} \frac{1}{P(V)} \int_V f dP$, and where $\mathscr{V}_\omega$ denotes the decreasing net of all open neighborhoods of ω.

Observe (by regularity) that $\hat{f}$ is, outside the atoms of P, the smallest u.s.c. function greater than or equal to f a.e. on $\mathsf{Supp}\, P$, so it is equivalent to requiring that $\rho_\omega(f) \le f(\omega)$ for f u.s.c. and $\omega \in \mathsf{Supp}\, P$, or to requiring that $U \subseteq \rho(U)$ for every open subspace U of $\mathsf{Supp}\, P$.

Assume there is a sequence of compact metric subsets K_n such that $P(\bigcup_n K_n) = 1$. Then any (linear) lifting ρ is a.e. equal to a strong (linear) lifting $\overline{\rho}$.

Hint. Let $N = \bigcup_n N_n \cup (\bigcup_n K_n)^c$, where $N_n = \{\, \omega \mid \exists f \in C(K_n) : \rho_\omega(\overline{f}) \neq \overline{f}(\omega)$, where $\overline{f}(\omega) = f(\omega)$ for $\omega \in K_n$, $= 0$ otherwise $\}$. N_n, hence N, is negligible, by the separability of $C(K_n)$. For ω in $N \cap \mathsf{Supp}(P)$, let $\overline{p}_\omega$ be an extreme point (Krein–Milman) of the non-empty (Hahn–Banach) set of all positive linear functionals p on L_∞ satisfying $p(\mathbb{1}_O) = 1$ for every open set O containing ω. By the same argument as sub(1), $\overline{\rho}_\omega$ is multiplicative. Let $\overline{\rho}_\omega = \rho_\omega$ elsewhere: $\overline{\rho}$ is a lifting, a.e. equal to ρ. There remains to show that for O open, $\omega \in O \cap (K_n \setminus N_n)$, $\rho_\omega(O) = 1$: this follows from the definition of N_n, selecting $f \in C(K_n)$ with $0 \le f \le \mathbb{1}_O$ and $f(\omega) = 1$.

Remark II.1.32. Regular probabilities on most classical function spaces satisfy the above assumption (cf, e.g., Edwards, 1965), even when compact subsets are not metrizable.

e. A lifting ρ on (Ω, A, P) operates on a Baire-measurable map f with relatively compact values in a completely regular space E by $h(\rho(f)) = \rho(h \circ f)$ for every continuous function h on E. Prove the following:

α. Existence and uniqueness of $\rho(f)$.

β. $\rho(f)$ depends only on the equivalence class of f (i.e., all g such that $\forall h, h \circ g = h \circ f$ a.e.) and belongs to it.

γ. $\rho(f)$ is Borel-measurable, and the image measure on the Borel sets is regular.

Remark II.1.33. Thus, if E is a product (so f is a "stochastic process"), $\rho(f)$ is a "separable modification."

δ. If f_α are such maps to spaces E_α, and $f \colon \prod_\alpha E_\alpha \to E$ is continuous, $\rho(f \circ \prod_\alpha f_\alpha) = f \circ \prod_\alpha (\rho(f_\alpha))$.

One way to prove II.1, Ex. 15eγ, and II.1, Ex. 15eδ, is by the following two points:

ε. ρ defines a map from Ω into the (compact) space of characters S of L_∞. The map is by definition Baire-measurable. For the induced probability $\overline{P}$ on S, use II.1, Ex. 15b, p. 84, to show that any closed set with an empty interior is contained in a closed Baire set with measure zero and also that the closure of an open set is open (i.e., the space is hyperstonian). Deduce that $\overline{P}$ is "completion regular": the completion of $\overline{P}$ on the Baire σ-field is a regular probability on the Borel sets. Hence the map ρ is Borel measurable and induces a regular probability.

ζ. A map f as in II.1, Ex. 15e, induces an algebra-homomorphism from the space of continuous functions $C(E)$ into $C(S)$, hence by transposition a continuous map from S to E. $\rho(f)$ can equivalently be defined as the composition of this map with the map ρ from Ω to S.

16. Regular conditional probabilities

a.

α. Let u be a positive linear map from $C(K)$ to $L_\infty(\Omega, \mathscr{A}, P)$, where K is compact. Assume $u(1) = 1$. Then there exists a transition probability Q from $(\Omega, \mathscr{A}, P)$ to $(K, \mathscr{B})$, where $\mathscr{B}$ is the Borel σ-field on K, such that, for each ω, Q_ω is a regular Borel measure on K, and such that $Q(f) \in u(f)\,\forall f \in C(K)$.

HINT. Let $Q_\omega(f) = [\rho(u(f))](\omega)$ for $f \in C(K)$, and use Riesz's theorem. For C compact in K, denote by f_α the decreasing net of all continuous functions $\geq \mathbb{1}_C$, and use II.1, Ex. 15c, p. 84, to prove the measurability of $Q_\omega(C)$, so that Q_ω indeed has the required properties.

β. Those Q's have the additional property that, if f_α is a decreasing net of u.s.c. functions converging to f, then $Q(f) = \mathsf{ess\,inf}_\alpha\, Q(f_\alpha)$.

HINT. Observe that $Q(f_\alpha) \geq \rho(Q(f_\alpha))$.

γ. Using II.1, Ex. 15e, p. 85, one can even require Q to be a Borel-measurable map to $\Delta(K)$, inducing a regular image measure.

b. Conversely, it is clear that any such transition probability Q defines in this way a unique u, but it is more instructive to follow the longer route:

α. P and Q determine uniquely a probability distribution $P \otimes Q$ on $(\Omega, \mathscr{A}) \otimes (K, \mathscr{B})$, which has P as marginal.

β. For any probability distribution R on $(\Omega, \mathscr{A}) \otimes (K, \mathscr{B})$ having P as marginal, let $u(f) = \mathsf{E}_R(f \mid \mathscr{A})$ for any $f \in C(K)$: this is the required u.

γ. Although, given u, many Q's will satisfy the requirements of II.1, Ex. 16a, they will all induce the same R.

HINT. By II.1, Ex. 16aβ, for two such Q's, Q^1 and Q^2, one will have $Q^1(f) = Q^2(f)$ a.e. for any positive Borel function f on K.

II.1, Ex. 16aβ, yields also that:

δ. Those R's, being in one-to-one correspondence with their restriction to product sets, are exactly the positive measures on $(\Omega, \mathscr{A})$ with values in the space of regular Borel measures on $(K, \mathscr{B})$, such that $[R(A)](K) = P(A)$.

c. Conclude that, for any Hausdorff topological space K, with its Borel σ-field $\mathscr{B}$, and any measurable space $(\Omega, \mathscr{A})$, any probability R on the product whose marginal distribution on $(K, \mathscr{B})$ is regular can be decomposed into its marginal P on $(\Omega, \mathscr{A})$ and a regular conditional (in the sense of II.1, Ex. 16aγ) Q on $(K, \mathscr{B})$ given $(\Omega, \mathscr{A})$.

HINT. If $R(\Omega \times B)$ is regular, so is $R(A \times B)$ for each $A \in \mathscr{A}$. Consider first the case K compact; for arbitrary K, use the regularity of $R(\Omega \times B)$ to find a K_σ carrying this measure.

Remark II.1.34. In typical applications, Q becomes a behavioral strategy. The equivalent R is sometimes called a **distributional strategy**.

d. In the same setup, with K compact, conclude also that any probability measure on $\mathscr{A} \otimes \mathscr{B}_a$, where $\mathscr{B}_a$ denotes the Baire σ-field, spanned by the continuous functions, has a (clearly unique) regular extension to $\mathscr{A} \otimes \mathscr{B}$.

17. Convergence of transition probabilities.

a. Tychonoff's theorem yields that the pointwise convergence topology (with the weak* topology on L_∞) is compact on the set of u's defined in II.1, Ex. 16b.

b. Define, for regular transition probabilities Q from $(\Omega, \mathscr{A}, P)$ to $(K, \mathscr{B})$ (i.e., $\forall\omega$, Q_ω is a regular Borel probability, and $\forall B \in \mathscr{B}$, $Q_\omega(B)$ is measurable), the convergence concept $Q^\alpha \to Q$ iff $Q^\alpha_\omega(f) \to Q_\omega(f)$ $\sigma(L_\infty, L_1)$, $\forall f \in C(K)$, i.e., iff $\forall f \in C(K)$, $\forall A \in \mathscr{A}$, $\int_A Q^\alpha_\omega(f)P(d\omega) \to \int_A Q_\omega(f)P(d\omega)$. Conclude that this convergence concept derives from a compact Hausdorff topology on (equivalence classes of) Q's.

c. If K is metrizable, this topology is also strictly semi-compact (I.1, Ex. 7c, p. 14). If in addition $\mathscr{A}$ is separable, the topology is metrizable.

18. Operator interpretation of liftings.

a.

α. The assumptions in II.1, Ex. 16a, imply that $u \in \mathscr{L}(C(K), L_\infty)$, i.e., u is a (norm-)continuous linear map from $C(K)$ to L_∞.

β. For any such map u, there exists a kernel Q, i.e., $\forall\omega$, Q_ω is a regular Borel measure on K, and $\forall B \in \mathscr{B}$, $Q_\cdot(B)$ is measurable, such that $\|Q_\omega\| \leq \|u\|$ $\forall\omega$, $Q_\cdot(f) \in u(f)$ $\forall f \in C(K)$, and the marginal on K of $|P \otimes Q|$ is a regular Borel measure.

HINT. Proceed as in II.1, Ex. 16aα. For the last point, which corresponds to II.1, Ex. 16aβ, define $R^+ = [P \otimes Q]^+$, $R^- = [P \otimes Q]^-$, $u^+(f)$ as the Radon–Nikodym derivative of $\mu^+(B) = \int_{B\times K} f dR^+$ with respect to P and similarly for $u^-(f)$. u^+ and u^- are positive linear maps from $C(K)$ to L_∞, with $u = u^+ - u^-$. Hence we get Q^+ and Q^-, each one verifying II.1, Ex. 16aβ, and, by the linearity of the lifting, $Q = Q^+ - Q^-$, so $P \otimes Q^+ + P \otimes Q^- \geq |P \otimes Q|$.

γ. Since the converse to II.1, Ex. 18aβ, is obvious (cf. hint above), we get an isometry between $\mathscr{L}(C(K), L_\infty)$ and a space $L_\infty^{[C(K)]'}$ of equivalence classes of kernels satisfying the properties in II.1, Ex. 16aβ. We use this notation because the space of regular Borel measures can be seen as the dual $[C(K)]'$ of $C(K)$, and a kernel as a bounded ("scalarly") measurable map with values in this space (in fact, even Pettis-integrable when taking the space of bounded universally measurable functions on K as dual of the space of regular measures) (or again, using II.1, Ex. 15e, as a Borel map to $[C(K)]'$, with a regular image). The equivalence classes are derived from the norm, where $\|Q\| = \sup\{\, \|Q_\cdot(f)\|_\infty \mid f \in C(K),\ \|f\| \leq 1\,\}$.

b.

α. Any kernel Q_ω with $\sup_\omega \|Q_\omega\| < \infty$ defines a continuous linear functional φ_u on the space $L_1^{C(K)}$ of (equivalence classes of) Bochner-integrable functions with values in $C(K)$ — by $\varphi_u(f) = \int f d(P \otimes Q)$. And $\|\varphi_u\| \leq \sup_\omega \|Q_\omega\|$.

HINT. Bochner-integrable functions f are such that $\|f - f_n\| \to 0$, for measurable step functions f_n with values in $C(K)$, and where $\|g\| = \int^* \|g(\omega)\|\, P(d\omega)$ (where $\int^*$ denotes the upper integral). Deduce (Egorov), by selecting $\|f - f_n\|$ summable, that one can have in addition $\|f_n(\omega) - f(\omega)\| \to 0$ P-a.e., so in particular f is measurable on $\Omega \times K$, and similarly $Q_\omega(f(\omega))$ is measurable and $\|f(\omega)\|$ is even integrable since $\|f(\omega)\| \leq \|f_n(\omega)\| + \|f(\omega) - f_n(\omega)\|$. Since $\|Q_\omega\| \leq K < \infty$, we have then also $|Q_\omega(f(\omega))| \leq K\,\|f(\omega)\|$, so $Q_\omega(f(\omega))$ is integrable. Let then $\varphi_u(f) = \int Q_\omega(f(\omega))P(d\omega)$: linearity is obvious, and $|\varphi_u(f)| \leq \int K\,\|f(\omega)\|\, P(d\omega) = K\,\|f\|$, so $\|\varphi_u\| \leq K$. We have then also $\varphi_u(f_n) = \int f_n d(P \otimes Q)$ for all n; hence the f_n form a Cauchy sequence in $L_1(P \otimes Q)$, which converges pointwise to f: $f \in L_1(P \otimes Q)$, so $\varphi_u(f) = \int f d(P \otimes Q)$.

β. Any continuous linear functional φ on $L_1^{C(K)}$ defines a continuous linear map $u\colon C(K) \to L_\infty$, with $\|u\| \leq \|\varphi\|$.

HINT. $u(x) \in L_\infty\colon L_1 \to \mathbb{R}$, $f \mapsto \varphi(xf)$.

γ. The maps in II.1, Ex. 18bα and II.1, Ex. 18bβ (under the identification in II.1, Ex. 18a, above, of u and Q) define an isometry between $[L_1^{C(K)}]'$ and $\mathscr{L}(C(K), L_\infty)$.

HINT. $u \overset{(A)}{\mapsto} \varphi \overset{(B)}{\mapsto} u$ is obviously the identity. That $\varphi \overset{(B)}{\mapsto} u \overset{(A)}{\mapsto} \varphi$ is also the identity is sufficient to check on step functions, and hence on functions $\mathbb{1}_A \cdot x$ ($A \in \mathscr{A}$, $x \in C(K)$). The isometric aspect follows then because we have shown (using also II.1, Ex. 18aβ) that all maps decrease the norm.

δ. The isometries in II.1, Ex. 18aγ, and II.1, Ex. 18bγ, given II.1, Ex. 18aα, allow us to view (equivalence classes of) transition probabilities as a subset of the dual of $L_1^{C(K)}$. Show that the topology introduced in II.1, Ex. 17, p. 86, is the weak* topology.

c.

α. Any Banach space E can be viewed isometrically as a subspace of a space $C(K)$, taking for K the unit ball of the dual (Banach–Alaoglu).

β. Deduce from the above (and the Hahn–Banach theorem) the existence of (canonical) isometries between $(L_1^E)'$, $L_\infty^{E'}$ and $\mathscr{L}(E, L_\infty)$. [$L_\infty^{E'}$ is the set of equivalence classes of bounded maps f from Ω to E', which are scalarly measurable in the sense that $\forall x \in E$, $\langle f(\omega), x\rangle$ is measurable (or, which are Borel-measurable with a regular image), and with $\|f\| = \sup_{\|x\|\leq 1} \|\langle f(\omega), x\rangle\|_\infty$.]

HINT. Consider the barycenter of Q_ω.
A direct proof, from II.1, Ex. 15, p. 84, is just as easy, considering the embedding $L_1 \to (x \cdot L_1)$ of L_1 into L_1^E, for all $x \in E$.

Show that those spaces are also isometric to the space $B(L_1, E)$ of continuous bi-linear functionals on $L_1 \times E$.

γ. Show that L_1^E is isometric to the completed tensor product $L_1 \widehat{\otimes} E$ (for $z \in E \otimes F$, $\|z\| = \inf\{\sum_{i=1}^n \|x_i\| \cdot \|y_i\| \mid x_i \in E, y_i \in F, \sum_{i=1}^n x_i \otimes y_i = z\}$).

HINT. The "step functions" are dense in $L_1 \otimes E$. Also L_1^E is complete by the usual argument: if f_n is a Cauchy sequence, extract a subsequence with $\sum_n \|f_{n+1} - f_n\| < \infty$ (cf. hint in II.1, Ex. 18bα, p. 87). So both spaces can be viewed as a completion of the step functions: it suffices to prove there is an isometry on step functions.

δ. So the only additional information we got in the case of $E = C(K)$ is that $\forall \tilde{f} \in L_\infty^{E'}$, there exists $f \in \tilde{f}$ (with $\|f(\omega)\| \leq \|\tilde{f}\|$ $\forall\omega$ and) that is "scalarly well integrable" even when taking as a dual of E' all bounded universally measurable functions.

Show also (cf. II.1, Ex. 18aβ, p. 87) that when $E = C(K)$, our isometries are also isomorphisms of complete Banach lattices. And an additional isometry is obtained with the space of measures on $\Omega \times K$ whose absolute value has a regular projection on K and a projection on Ω bounded from above by $\lambda \cdot P$ for some $\lambda > 0$. Observe finally that if K is metrizable, $\|Q\| = \|(\|Q_\omega\|)\|_\infty$.

ε. Extend II.1, Ex. 18cβ, and II.1, Ex. 18cγ, above to the case where E is a locally convex space. (Then L_1^E is endowed with the semi-norms $\overline{p}(f) = \int^* p(f(\omega))P(d\omega)$, for every continuous semi-norm p on E. And the polars of the neighborhoods of zero in E are the equicontinuous subsets of E', which play therefore the role of the balls above.)

19. Strassen's theorem.

Assume (Ω, A, P) complete, and for each ω let p_ω be a sublinear functional (i.e., $p_\omega(\lambda x) = \lambda p_\omega(x)$ and $p_\omega(x + y) \leq p_\omega(x) + p_\omega(y)$ for $\lambda \geq 0$, $x, y \in E$) on a Banach space E, which is bounded, $\sup_\omega \sup_{\|x\|\leq 1} p_\omega(x) < \infty$, and weakly measurable, $p_\omega(x)$ is measurable $\forall x \in E$. Let also $\overline{p}(x) = \int p_\omega(x)P(d(\omega))$, and assume further that either

E is separable, or P is a regular Borel probability on the Hausdorff space Ω, such that $P(\bigcup_n K_n) = 1$ for appropriate compact metric subsets K_n, and $p_\omega(x)$ is upper semi-continuous $\forall x \in E$.

Then any linear functional $\overline{\varphi}$ on E that is bounded from above by $\overline{p}$ can be written as $\overline{\varphi}(x) = \int \varphi_\omega(x)P(d\omega)$, where φ is a bounded, Borel-measurable map to E' with the weak* topology, has a regular image measure, and satisfies $\varphi_\omega(x) \le p_\omega(x)$ everywhere.

HINT. Define $\tilde{p}$ on L_1^E (II.1, Ex. 18c, p. 88) by $\tilde{p}(f) = \int p_\omega(f(\omega))P(d\omega)$. Identifying E with the constant functions in L_1^E, $\tilde{p}$ extends $\overline{p}$. By the separation theorem (Proposition I.1.12, p. 9), take an extension $\tilde{\varphi}$ of $\overline{\varphi}$ with $\tilde{\varphi} \le \tilde{p}$: then (by II.1, Ex. 18c$\beta$, p. 88) $\tilde{\varphi}(f) = \int \varphi_\omega(f(\omega))P(d\omega)$. In particular, for $x \in E$ and $A \in \mathscr{A}$ we get, with $f = x\mathbb{1}_A$, $\int_A \varphi_\omega(x)P(d\omega) \le \int_A p_\omega(x)P(d\omega)$, hence $\varphi_\omega(x) \le p_\omega(x)$ a.e. If E is separable, use a dense sequence to find that, outside a negligible set, $\varphi_\omega(x) \le p_\omega(x)$ $\forall x \in E$, and use the separation theorem to redefine φ_ω on this negligible set such as to have the inequality everywhere. In the other case, assume by (II.1, Ex. 15d, p. 85) that φ was obtained by a strong lifting ρ: then we obtain $\forall x$, $\forall \omega$: $\varphi_\omega(x) = \rho(\varphi_\omega(x)) \le \rho(p_\omega(x)) \le p_\omega(x)$ (the last inequality follows since $p_\omega(x)$ is u.s.c. and the lifting is strong).

20. The Blackwell–Stein–Sherman–Cartier–Fell–Meyer–Ionescu-Tulcea Theorem. (Ionescu Tulcea and Ionescu Tulcea, 1969)

a. Let X and Y be two compact Hausdorff spaces, $\varphi\colon X \to Y$ a continuous map, $\mathscr{S} \subseteq C(Y)$ a convex cone such that $1 \in \mathscr{S}$ and $f, g \in \mathscr{S} \Longrightarrow \min(f, g) \in \mathscr{S}$. Let ν and $\mu \neq 0$ be regular non-negative measures on X and $\varphi(X)$, respectively, such that $\int_X (f \circ \varphi)d\nu \le \int_Y f d\mu$ $\forall f \in \mathscr{S}$. Assume $\mu(Y \setminus \bigcup_n K_n) = 0$ for appropriate compact metric subsets K_n. Then there is a Borel-measurable map $\lambda\colon y \mapsto \lambda_y$ from Y with the μ-measurable sets to the space $\mathscr{M}^+(X)$ of non-negative regular Borel measures on X with the weak* topology, such that μ has a regular image measure by λ with $\nu(B) = \int \lambda_y(B)\mu(dy)$ for every Borel set B, and $\lambda_y(f \circ \varphi) \le f(y)$, $\forall y \in \varphi(X)$, $\forall f \in \mathscr{S}$.

HINT. Letting $\lambda_y = 0$ for $y \notin \varphi(X)$ we can assume φ onto. Let then $p_y(f) = \inf\{\, h(y) \mid h \in \mathscr{S},\ h \circ \varphi \ge f \,\}$ for $f \in C(X)$, and $\overline{p}(f) = \int_Y p_y(f)\mu(dy)$. Observe (by regularity of μ) that $\overline{p}(f) \ge \nu(f)$, and apply Strassen's theorem ($\lambda_y \ge 0$ follows from $\lambda_y(f) \le p_y(f)$ for $f \le 0$).

b. For any Borel-measurable map $\lambda\colon \omega \mapsto \lambda_\omega$ from a complete probability space $(\Omega, \mathscr{A}, P)$ to $\Delta(X)$, where X is a Hausdorff K_σ, such that P has a regular image measure by λ, let $\overline{P}(B) = \int \lambda_\omega(B)P(d\omega)$ for every Borel set B. Then $\overline{P}$ is well defined, and $\overline{P} \in \Delta(X)$.

Remark II.1.35. The theorem is II.1, Ex. 20a, and II.1, Ex. 20b, is a comment on it; c.f., e.g., the proof of the claim in Theorem III.1.2, p. 127, below, for an example of its use.

Remark II.1.36. A classical case of this theorem is where φ is the identity and more specifically $X = Y$ is compact, convex in some locally convex space, and $\mathscr{S}$ is the cone of concave functions. This case is closely related to the concavification operators to be encountered later in Chapters V and VI.

Another is the following, which gives the "right form" (i.e., as in II.1, Ex. 9, p. 68, except for the parameterization by an auxiliary measurable space) of II.1, Ex. 16, p. 86.

21. Disintegration of measures.

Let $\varphi\colon X \to Y$ be a continuous map between Hausdorff spaces, $\nu \in \Delta(X)$, $\mu = \varphi(\nu)$ (Proposition I.1.8 part (1), p. 8). Assume that $\mu(\bigcup_n K_n) = 1$ for appropriate compact metric subsets K_n. Then there is a Borel measurable map $\lambda\colon y \mapsto \lambda_y$ from Y with the μ-measurable sets to $\mathcal{M}^+(X)$ with the weak* topology such that $\lambda_y \in \Delta(X)$ for $y \in \varphi(X)$, $\operatorname{Supp} \lambda_y \subseteq \varphi^{-1}(y)\ \forall y \in Y$, and μ has a regular image measure on $\Delta(X)$ by λ, with $\nu(B) = \int_Y \lambda_y(B)\mu(dy)$ for every Borel set B.

Hint. For X compact, this follows straight from II.1, Ex. 20, p. 89, with $\mathcal{S} = C(Y)$. The only problem here is to preserve the measurability properties of λ in the generalization. By regularity, there is no loss of generality in assuming the sequence K_n to be disjoint, and that $\forall n,\ K_n \subseteq \varphi(X)$, with $\mu(K_n) > 0$; λ_y can then be defined separately on each K_n, by selecting an arbitrary point mass in $\varphi^{-1}(y)$ for $y \in \varphi(X) \setminus \bigcup_n K_n$, and setting $\lambda_y = 0$ for $y \notin \varphi(X)$. After replacing X by $\varphi^{-1}(K_n)$ and renormalizing μ (cf. Appendix A.9.b.2, p. 521), this reduces the problem to the case where φ is onto and Y is compact metric.

Similarly, select a disjoint sequence of compact subsets X_n of X, with $\alpha_n \nu_n = \nu_{|X_n}$, $\nu_n \in \Delta(X_n)$, $\alpha_n > 0$, $\sum_n \alpha_n = 1$, $X_n = \operatorname{Supp} \nu_n$. Repeating the above argument, we can assume that $\varphi(\bigcup_n X_n) = Y$, and hence that X is the disjoint union of the X_n. Finally let $\mu_n = \varphi(\nu_n)$, $f_n = \alpha_n\, d\mu_n/d\mu$: $\sum_n f_n = 1$ a.e. Use Lusin's theorem to find disjoint compact subsets Y_k of Y, with $\mu(\bigcup_k Y_k) = 1$, and such that $f : y \mapsto (f_n(y))_{n=1}^{\infty}$ is continuous from Y_k to $\Delta(\mathbb{N})$. Repeating our first argument, it suffices to work on each Y_k separately; hence we can further assume $f : Y \to \Delta(\mathbb{N})$ is continuous. Fix now a strong lifting ρ on (Y, μ). Observe that $O_n = \{\, y \mid f_n(y) > 0 \,\}$ is open, and that μ_n and μ are mutually absolutely continuous on O_n, while μ_n vanishes outside. So ρ is still a strong lifting on (O_n, μ_n), and extends thus to a strong lifting ρ_n on $(\overline{O}_n, \mu_n)$. Since $\varphi(X_n) = \overline{O}_n$ (because $X_n = \operatorname{Supp} \nu_n$), use the compact case mentioned above to construct, with ρ_n, a regular conditional λ_n from $\overline{O}_n$ to $\Delta(X_n)$. Let $\overline{\lambda}_n(y) = \lambda_n(y)$ for $y \in O_n$, $\overline{\lambda}_n(y) = \nu_n$ for y outside O_n: now $\overline{\lambda}_n$ is μ-measurable from Y to $\Delta(X_n)$. Use II.1, Ex. 15e, p. 85, to let $\tilde{\lambda}_n = \rho(\overline{\lambda}_n)$; in particular, $\tilde{\lambda}_n(y) = \lambda_n(y)$ for $y \in O_n$. Since also $f = \rho(f)$, II.1, Ex. 15e, yields that the map $y \mapsto [f(y), (\tilde{\lambda}_n(y))_{n\in\mathbb{N}}]$ from (Y, μ) to $\Delta(\mathbb{N}) \times \prod_n \Delta(X_n)$ with the Borel sets is measurable, with a regular image measure. Since the map $\beta, (\mu_n)_{n\in\mathbb{N}} \mapsto \sum_n \beta_n \mu_n$ from $\Delta(\mathbb{N}) \times \prod_n \Delta(X_n)$ to $\Delta(X)$ is continuous, it follows that the composition $y \mapsto \lambda_y = \sum_n f_n(y)\tilde{\lambda}_n(y) = \sum_n f_n(y)\lambda_n(y)$ is measurable from (Y, μ) to $\Delta(X)$ with the Borel sets, with a regular image measure (and even satisfies $\lambda = \rho(\lambda)$). It clearly satisfies our requirements.

22. Games with almost perfect information. (Birch, 1955)
Consider a game where the position at each stage in a feasible play determines all the previous positions along the play, i.e., the history. A history h induces a **subgame** if for any feasible play consistent with h, any signal a_i to some player i on this play after (and including) h identifies h. A game has **almost perfect information** for player i if every history where he is playing induces a subgame, as well as the histories ending with one of his moves.

Show that a game with finitely many plays has an equilibrium where the players who have almost perfect information use pure strategies.

II.2. INFINITE GAMES

II.2.a. Infinite Games with Perfect Information

These games can be described as follows. We are given a set Ω (with discrete topology). Player I chooses a point ω_1 in Ω, and this choice is told to player II, who now selects some ω_2 in Ω. ω_2 is then announced to player I, who chooses ω_3, and so on. Hence both players play sequentially, knowing all previous moves. The game Γ corresponds thus to an infinite tree (with perfect information), which we identify with the set of histories or positions, $H = \bigcup_{n\geq 0} \Omega^n$, where $\Omega^0 = \{\emptyset\}$. $H_\infty = \Omega^\infty$ is the set of plays. We shall write

$\prec$ for the natural partial order on $H \cup H_\infty$, where $h \prec h'$ iff h' extends h, and a base of open sets in H_∞ (for the product topology) is given by the sets $\{ h' \in H_\infty \mid h \prec h' \}$, $h \in H$. As for the payoff, we are given a real-valued function g on H_∞. A pair of pure strategies (σ, τ) in $\Sigma \times \mathcal{T}$ (i.e., mappings from H to Ω) induces in a natural way ($h_1 = \sigma(\phi), h_{2n+1} = (h_{2n}, \sigma(h_{2n}))$, $h_{2n+2} = (h_{2n+1}, \tau(h_{2n+1}))$), a point $h_\infty = (\omega_1, \omega_2, \ldots, \omega_n, \ldots)$ in H_∞, and we define $\gamma(\sigma, \tau) = g(h_\infty)$. Given h in H, the **subgame** starting from h is played like Γ, player I (resp. II) moving first if h is of even (resp. odd) length and the play h_∞ induces the payoff $g(h, h_\infty)$ (where (h, h_∞) is h followed by h_∞). $H(\sigma)$ is the set of positions that can be reached if player I plays σ and $H_\infty(\sigma)$ is the corresponding set of plays. $H' \subseteq H$ is a I-sub-tree iff there exists σ of player I with $H(\sigma) \subseteq H'$. We then say that σ is compatible with H'.

The game Γ is open, closed, $G_\delta, \ldots$, Borel, when g is the indicator function of an open, closed, $G_\delta, \ldots$, Borel subset W of H_∞.

In this framework, the game is **determined** if one of the players has a **winning** pure strategy; i.e., either player I can force h_∞ to be in W (there exists σ such that $H_\infty(\sigma) \subseteq W$) or player II can force h_∞ to belong to its complement W^c.

The first result is:

Proposition II.2.1. *(Gale and Stewart, 1953) Open and closed games are determined.*

Proof. Assume first that W is open. Suppose that player I has no winning strategy in Γ. This implies that, for every ω_1, there exists ω_2 such that player I still has no winning strategy in the subgame starting from (ω_1, ω_2) (i.e., in which a play h_∞ induces a payoff $g(\omega_1, \omega_2, h_\infty)$). This defines inductively, for every n and every position $h_{2n+1} = (\omega_1, \ldots, \omega_{2n+1})$, a move ω_{2n+2} such that player I still has no winning in the subgame following $\omega_1, \ldots, \omega_{2n+2}$. Define τ to be a strategy of player II that makes the above choice of $\{\omega_{2n+2}\}_{n \geq 0}$. Then τ is winning. Otherwise, for some σ, (σ, τ) would generate a play h_∞ in W. Since W is open, there exists n in $\mathbb{N}$ such that (h_{2n+1}, h'_∞) belongs to W for every h'_∞ in H_∞, which contradicts the choice of ω_{2n+2}.

Similarly, if W is closed and player II has no winning strategy, there exists a first choice ω'_1 of player I such that player II still has no winning strategy in the subgame following ω'_1. Reversing the roles of the players implies that this subgame is open, hence determined, so that player I has a winning strategy σ' for it. It follows then that σ defined by (play ω'_1 then use σ') is a winning strategy for player I in the original game. ■

Remark II.2.1. The above result can be written in the following equivalent way: given W closed in H_∞, let $W^\prec = \{ h \in H \mid \exists h' \in W,\ h \prec h' \}$. Let $L^i(W)$, $i = \text{I}, \text{II}$, be the set of positions from where player i can force the set W. If $\emptyset \in L^i(W)$, then $L^i(W)$ is included in $W^\prec$ and is an i-winning sub-tree; i.e., every strategy compatible with $L^i(W)$ is winning.

Proposition II.2.2. *(Gale and Stewart, 1953) Under the Axiom of Choice, there exists an undetermined game.*

Proof. Take $\Omega = \{0, 1\}$. Note first that, for each σ of player I, the cardinality of the set $H_\infty(\sigma)$ is $\wp(\aleph_0)$. In fact, player II can follow on his stages any sequence of 0 and 1; on the other hand, one obviously has $\#\mathscr{T} \leq \wp(\aleph_0)$. Let us now construct a winning set W. Let α be the least ordinal such that there are $\wp(\aleph_0)$ ordinals less than α. We can thus index the players' strategies as σ_β, τ_β with $\beta \in \{\gamma \mid \gamma < \alpha\}$. Choose y in $H_\infty(\tau_0)$ and then x in $H_\infty(\sigma_0)$ with $x \neq y$. Inductively, if y_γ and x_γ have been chosen for $\gamma < \beta < \alpha$, the set $\{x_\gamma \mid \gamma < \beta\}$ has less than $\wp(\aleph_0)$ elements; hence $H_\infty(\tau_\beta) \setminus \{x_\gamma \mid \gamma < \beta\}$ is not empty. Choose y_β in it. Similarly, $H_\infty(\sigma_\beta) \setminus \{y_\gamma \mid \gamma \leq \beta\}$ is not empty, and we take x_β in it. We now claim that the sets $X = \{x_\beta \mid \beta < \alpha\}$ and $Y = \{y_\beta \mid \beta < \alpha\}$ are disjoint. Assume not and let $x_\beta = y_\gamma$. If $\gamma \leq \beta$ (resp. $\gamma > \beta$), we have a contradiction by the choice of x (resp. y). Choose finally W with $Y \subseteq W$ and $W \cap X = \phi$. Consider now σ in Σ. Then σ corresponds to some index, say, β. By construction, there exists a play x_β in $H_\infty(\sigma_\beta) \cap X$, hence a strategy τ of player II inducing against σ a play in X. Player I has no winning strategy; moreover, the maxmin (supinf) is 0. Similarly, player II has no winning strategy and the minmax is 1. ■

Proposition II.2.1 has been gradually extended to larger classes of games. The more general result is Martin (1975, 1985):

Theorem II.2.3. *Borel games are determined.*

We first introduce some notations and definitions.

Given a tree H, we denote also by $[H]$ the corresponding set of plays (that was also previously denoted H_∞).

$(H^\star, \pi, \phi)$ is a **covering** of the tree H if:

(1) $H^\star$ is a tree, π is a mapping from $[H^\star]$ to $[H]$, and ϕ a mapping from $\Sigma^\star$ (resp. $\mathscr{T}^\star$) to Σ (resp. $\mathscr{T}$), such that π and ϕ commute in the following sense: if $h \in [H(\phi(\sigma^\star))]$, there exists $h^\star \in [H^\star(\sigma^\star)]$ with $\pi(h^\star) = h$, and similarly for $\tau^\star$.

Lemma II.2.4. *Let $(H^\star, \pi, \phi)$ be a covering of H and $W \subseteq [H]$. If the game $(H^\star, \pi^{-1}(W))$ is determined, so is the game (H, W).*

Proof. In fact, let $\sigma^\star$ be a winning strategy in $(H^\star, \pi^{-1}(W))$ and let $\sigma = \phi(\sigma^\star)$. If h is a play in $[H]$ compatible with σ, there exists, by (1), a play $h^\star$ in $[H^\star]$ compatible with $\sigma^\star$ and with image h. Since $h^\star$ belongs to $\pi^{-1}(W)$, σ is winning. ■

The idea of the proof of the theorem is roughly to prove inductively that one can construct, for any Borel set W, a covering with $\pi^{-1}(W)$ closed. In fact, we need to work with more specific coverings. An ***n*-covering** is a covering that moreover satisfies:

(2) For all k, if $h_{|k}$ denotes the restriction of h to $\tilde{H}_k$ (histories of length at most k) and similarly for strategies, then $\pi(h^\star)_{|k}$ depends only on $h_{|k}$ and $\phi(\sigma^\star)_{|k}$ depends only on $\sigma^\star_{|k}$.
(3) $\tilde{H}_n = \tilde{H}^\star_n$ and $\phi(\sigma^\star)_{|n} = \sigma^*_{|n}$, and similarly for τ^*.

We can now define a projective limit of n-coverings by the following:

Lemma II.2.5. *Given H^0, assume that, for every integer k, $(H^{k+1}, \pi^{k+1}, \phi^{k+1})$ is an $(n+k)$-covering of H^k. Then there exists $H^\star$ and, for each k, a $(n+k)$-covering $(H^\star, \pi^{\star k}, \phi^{\star k})$ of H^k such that, for all k and all $h^\star$ in $[H^\star]$:*

$$\pi^{\star k}(h^\star) = \pi^{k+1} \circ \pi^{\star k+1}(h^\star).$$

Proof. By hypothesis, one has, for $\ell \geq k$, $\tilde{H}^\ell_{n+k} = \tilde{H}^k_{n+k}$. Define then $H^\star = \bigcup_k \tilde{H}^k_{n+k}$; hence $H^\star$ is also a tree. For $h^\star$ in $[H^\star]$, we define $\pi^{\star k}(h^\star)$ as follows: by composing the mappings π and ϕ, one has, for $\ell \geq k$, an n-covering $(H^\ell, \pi^{k\ell}, \phi^{k\ell})$ of H^k. Let us now choose h^ℓ in $[H^\ell]$ such that $h^\star_{|n+\ell} = h^\ell_{|n+\ell}$ and put $\pi^{\star k}(h^\star) = \lim_{\ell\to\infty} \pi^{k\ell}(h^\ell)$. Similarly, for $\sigma^\star$ in $\Sigma^\star$, choose, for each ℓ, σ^ℓ in Σ^ℓ that coincides with $\sigma^\star$ on $\tilde{H}^\ell_{n+\ell}$ and let $\phi^{\star k}(\sigma^\star) = \lim_{\ell\to\infty} \phi^{k\ell}(\sigma^\ell)$. It is easy to see that $(\pi^{\star k}, \phi^{\star k})$ are well defined and $(H^\star, \pi^{\star k}, \phi^{\star k})$ satisfies the requirements. ∎

Given a tree H, $W \subseteq [H]$ is **standard** if, for every integer n, there exists an n-covering $(H^\star, \pi, \phi)$ of H such that $H^{-1}(W)$ is clopen (open and closed) in $[H^\star]$. Theorem II.2.3 will then follow from Proposition II.2.1 and the following lemma.

Lemma II.2.6. *A closed set is standard.*

Proof of the Theorem. In fact, assuming this result, we first prove by induction that Borel sets are standard. Let $\mathbf{\Sigma}_1$ be the class of open sets and, for every countable ordinal α, let $\mathbf{\Pi}_\alpha = \{W \mid W^c \text{ is in } \mathbf{\Sigma}_\alpha\}$, $\mathbf{\Sigma}_\alpha = \{W \mid W \text{ is a countable union of sets in } \bigcup_{\beta<\alpha} \mathbf{\Pi}_\beta\}$. Assume that for all trees, all W in $\mathbf{\Pi}_\beta$, $\beta < \alpha$ are standard, and let $W = \cup W_k$ with W_k in $\mathbf{\Pi}_{\beta_k}$ with $\beta_k < \alpha$. Given n, let (T_1, π_1, ϕ_1) be an n-covering of H such that $H_1^{-1}(W_1)$ is clopen. Let now (T_2, π_2, ϕ_2) be an $(n+1)$-covering of T_1 such that $\pi_2^{-1} \circ \pi_1^{-1}(W_2)$ is clopen, and so on inductively. Using then Lemma II.2.5, one gets that $(H^\star, \pi^\star, \phi^\star)$ is an n-covering of H for which every $H^{\star-1}(W_k)$ is clopen and hence $\pi^{\star-1}(W)$ is open in $[H^\star]$. Just note that the complement of a standard set is standard; hence Borel sets are standard. Lemma II.2.4 proves then the theorem. ∎

Proof of the Lemma. Let W closed in $[H]$ and k an integer. A position $h^\star \in H^\star$ corresponds to a position h in H except at stages $2k+1$ and $2k+2$ where: $\omega^\star_{2k+1} = (\omega_{2k+1}, H_{\mathrm{I}})$, H_{I} being a I-sub-tree starting from $(\omega_1, \ldots, \omega_{2k+1})$. $\omega^\star_{2k+2}$ is either of the form $(\omega_{2k+2}, \langle 0, u\rangle)$, u being a history in H with even length extending $(\omega_1, \ldots, \omega_{2k+2})$ and belonging to $H_{\mathrm{I}} \setminus W^{\prec}$ (in this case, the moves after stage $2k+2$ have to extend u), or $(\omega_{2k+2}, \langle 1, H_{\mathrm{II}} \rangle)$, where H_{II} is a II-sub-tree of H_{I} contained in $W^{\prec}$ (the moves from $2k+2$ on then have to respect H_{II}). Note that since W is closed, this set of choices is non-empty (Proposition II.2.1). π is obviously the natural projection on H and, by definition, $h^{\star}$ belongs to $\pi^{-1}(W)$ if $(\omega_1, \ldots, \omega_n) \in W^{\prec}$ for all n, or, equivalently, if $\omega^{\star}_{2k+2}$ can be written as $(\cdot, \langle 1, \cdot \rangle)$, so that $H^{-1}(W)$ is clopen. It is easily seen that $H^{\star}$ is a tree; there thus remains to define ϕ.

(1) Consider first $\Sigma^{\star}$. On $\tilde{H}_{2k}$, σ coincides with $\sigma^{\star}$. Assume now $\sigma^{\star}(\omega_1, \ldots, \omega_{2k}) = (\omega_{2k+1}, H_{\mathrm{I}})$ and consider the H_{I} game starting from $(\omega_1, \ldots, \omega_{2k+1})$, where W^c is winning. This game, being open, is determined.
 (a) If player I has there a winning strategy, say, σ', let him use it until the (finite) stage where an even history h in $H_{\mathrm{I}} \setminus W^{\prec}$ is reached. Consider now the corresponding position $h^{\star}$ in $H^{\star}$ with $\pi(h^{\star}) = h$ and $\omega^{\star}_{2k+2} = (\omega_{2k+2}, \langle 0, h \rangle))$. This history is compatible with $\sigma^{\star}$, and I plays now in H (after h) by following $\sigma^{\star}$ in $H^{\star}$ after $h^{\star}$.
 (b) Otherwise, $(\omega_1, \ldots, \omega_{2k+1}) \in L^{\mathrm{II}}(W)$. At every history h in H, either there exists $h^{\star}$ in $H^{\star}$ with $\omega^{\star}_{2k+2} = (\omega_{2k+2}, \langle 1, L^{\mathrm{II}}(W) \rangle)$ and $\pi(h^{\star}) = h$, and then σ follows $\sigma^{\star}$ at $h^{\star}$; or, at some stage, the partial history h' is no longer in $L^{\mathrm{II}}(W)$. This implies that, after h', player I can force W^c, and we use the construction above (1a).

(2) For $\tau^{\star}$ in $\mathscr{T}^{\star}$, $\phi(\tau^{\star}) = \tau$ is defined as $\tau^{\star}$ on $\tilde{H}_{2k}$. Consider now, given $(\omega_1, \ldots, \omega_{2k+1})$, the game starting from this history where II is winning iff he reaches an even history h for which there exists a I-sub-tree, say, $H_{\mathrm{I}}(h)$, satisfying $\tau^{\star}(\omega_1, \ldots, \omega_{2k}, (\omega_{2k+1}, H_{\mathrm{I}}(h)) = (\omega_{2k+2}, \langle 0, h \rangle)$. Note that in this game, the set V of winning plays of I is closed. Consider again two cases:
 (a) If player II has a winning strategy in this game, he uses it to reach $h = (\omega_1, \ldots, \omega_{2\ell})$, then follows $\tau^{\star}$ from $(\omega_1, \ldots, (\omega_{2k+1}, H_{\mathrm{I}}(h)), (\omega_{2k+2}, \langle 0, h \rangle))$ on.
 (b) Else $(\omega_1, \ldots, \omega_{2k+1}) \in L^{\mathrm{I}}(V)$. Obviously $\tau^{\star}(\omega_1, \ldots, (\omega_{2k+1}, L^{\mathrm{I}}(V)))$ is of the form $(\omega_{2k+2}, \langle 1, H_{\mathrm{II}} \rangle)$ by the definition of the previous game. τ follows then $\tau^{\star}$ as long as h is the image of some possible $h^{\star}$. If not, this means that h is no longer in $L^{\mathrm{I}}(V)$ so that, after h, II has a winning strategy, and we are back to (2a).

It is now easy to check that ϕ is well defined and $(H^{\star}, \pi, \phi)$ is a k-covering of H. ■

Remark II.2.2. The theorem states that, if W is a "Borel property," the negation of the infinite sentence "$\exists\omega_1\ \forall\omega_2\ \exists\omega_3\ \forall\omega_4, \ldots$ such that W" is the sentence "$\forall\omega_1\ \exists\omega_2\ \forall\omega_3\ \exists\omega_4, \ldots$ such that [not W]." It yields thus an extension of the usual rule of negation to infinite sentences. Hence the interest of logicians in this question (cf., e.g., Moschovakis, 1980).

II.2.b. Remarks: Infinite Games without Perfect Information

Without the previous perfect information assumption the analysis is much harder, and only very partial results are available.

Γ is the game with perfect recall described as follows: S and T are finite sets, and both players choose at stage n independently moves s_n and t_n in S or T. $\omega_n = (s_n, t_n)$ in $\Omega = S \times T$ is then announced to both, and they proceed to the next stage. g is a real bounded measurable function on $(H_\infty, \mathscr{H}_\infty)$ (with the product σ-algebra induced by the discrete topology on each factor). Strategies are defined as mappings from H to $\Delta(S)$ or $\Delta(T)$, and the payoff is given by $\gamma(\sigma, \tau) = \mathsf{E}_{\sigma,\tau}(g)$. By the minmax theorem (e.g., Proposition I.1.9, p. 9) and Remark II.1.7, p. 64, we have immediately:

Lemma II.2.7. *If g is l.s.c., the game has a value, and player* II *has an optimal strategy.*

Remark II.2.3. This implies in particular that, if $g = \mathbb{1}_W$ with W open or closed, the game has a value (note however that one player may not have a winning strategy).

One can go one step further to obtain (Blackwell, 1969) (cf. also Orkin (1972b) for an extension to the Boolean algebra generated by the G_δ's):

Proposition II.2.8. *If W is a G_δ, the game has a value.*

Proof. Note first that W is a G_δ in H_∞ iff there exists a subset Y of H such that h_∞ belongs to W iff h_n belongs to Y for infinitely many n in $\mathbb{N}$ (i.e., h_∞ hits Y infinitely often). For any position x in H, denote by $\overline{v}(x)$ the minmax of the subgame $\Gamma(x)$ starting from x (and $\overline{v} = \overline{v}(\emptyset)$).

We now introduce $\Gamma'(x)$ as the subgame starting from x and with payoff $\overline{v}(y)$, where y is the entrance position in Y after x. Formally, let $\theta_x(h_\infty) = \min(\{n \mid 1 \le n < \infty,\ (x, h_n) \in Y\} \cup \{\infty\})$. Then the payoff of $\Gamma'(x)$ is f with $f(h_\infty) = \mathbb{1}_{n<\infty}\overline{v}(x, h_n)$, where $n = \theta_x(h_\infty)$. It is clear that f is l.s.c.; hence the previous lemma implies that $\Gamma'(x)$ has a value $v'(x)$ and player II has an optimal strategy $\tau'(x)$. Let us first remark that:

$$v'(x) \ge \overline{v}(x) \qquad \forall x \in H \tag{1}$$

(consider the following strategy for player II in $\Gamma(x)$: play according to $\tau'(x)$ until Y is reached; if Y is reached at position y, play then an ε-optimal strategy in $\Gamma(y)$).

Let us prove now that player I can guarantee $\overline{v}$, so that Γ has a value, namely, $\overline{v}$. Let $\varepsilon_m = \varepsilon/2^{m+1}$, and define inductively σ as follows: play ε_0-optimally in $\Gamma'(\phi)$ until Y is reached. If this happens at position y_1, play then ε_1-optimally in $\Gamma'(y_1)$ until Y is reached again. If this occurs at y_2, play ε_2-optimally in $\Gamma'(y_2)$, and so on. Given σ and any τ in $\mathscr{T}$, define a sequence of payoffs $\{\rho_m\}$ by: $\rho_0 = \overline{v}$ and $\rho_m = \overline{v}(y_m)$ if y_m is defined (i.e., if h_∞ hits Y at least m times) and 0 otherwise. Then we have:

$$\mathsf{E}_{\sigma,\tau}(\rho_{m+1} \mid \mathscr{H}_m) \geq \rho_m - \varepsilon_m, \tag{2}$$

where $\mathscr{H}_m$ is the σ-algebra generated by $(y_1, \ldots, y_m)$ on H_∞. This is clear if $\rho_m = 0$. Otherwise, after the position y_m, player I was playing ε_m optimally in $\Gamma'(y_m)$, meaning that his payoff, which is precisely ρ_{m+1}, has a conditional expectation greater than $v'(y_m) - \varepsilon_m$, hence the inequality (2), using (1). Taking expectation and summing in (2), we obtain:

$$\mathsf{E}_{\sigma,\tau}(\rho_m) \geq \rho_0 - (\varepsilon_1 + \cdots + \varepsilon_m) \geq \overline{v} - \varepsilon.$$

Since $0 \leq \rho_m \leq 1$ and ρ_m is 0 unless Y is hit m times, this implies that:

$$P_{\sigma,\tau}(Y \text{ is hit } m \text{ times}) \geq \overline{v} - \varepsilon,$$

and letting $m \to \infty$ yields:

$$P_{\sigma,\tau}(Y \text{ is hit infinitely often}) = P_{\sigma,\tau}(h_\infty \in W) \geq \overline{v} - \varepsilon. \tag{3}$$

■

EXERCISES

The games in II.2, Ex. 1–II.2, Ex. 3, are those described in Section II.2.b.

1. Counterexample in approximation. (Orkin, 1972a)
(Cf. also I.1, Ex. 4, p. 12 and I.1, Ex. 5, p. 12.)

Let $S, T = \{0, 1\}$, $\Omega = S \times T$. Define $Y'_n = \{\omega \in \Omega \mid \exists i \leq n \text{ with } \omega_i = (1, 1)\}$ and $Z = \{\omega \in \Omega \mid t_i = 0\ \forall i\}$. Show that the game with (closed) winning set $Y_n = Y'_n \cup Z$ is determined with value 0, and player II has a winning strategy. Prove that the game with winning set $Y = \bigcup_{n \geq 1} Y_n$ has value 1, and player I has a winning strategy. Y is the union of an open and a closed set, hence both a G_δ and an F_σ. (This shows that one can not use an approximation argument like in I.1, Ex. 2, p. 11, to prove the previous result by using open sets, or dually.)

2. (Orkin, 1972b)

Take $S, T = \{0, 1\}$, $\Omega = S \times T$. The winning set is $Z = X \cup Y$ with $X = \{\omega \mid \omega_n = (0, 0)$ for infinitely many n and $\omega_n = (1, 1)$ for infinitely many $n\}$ and $Y = \{\omega \mid \omega_n = (0, 0)$ for at most finitely many n and $\omega_n = (1, 1)$ for at most finitely many $n\}$. X is a G_δ and Y an F_σ. Show that the following is a winning strategy for I: he chooses 1 as long as II chooses 0, and reverses his behavior just after II does so.

3. A G_δ game. (Orkin, 1972b)

Let $\Omega = S \times T = \{0, 1\}^2$. As soon as I chooses 1, the game ends and player I wins if player II chooses 1 at that move and loses otherwise. If player I always plays 0, he wins iff player II chooses infinitely often 0 (cf. the related "Big Match," Chapter VII, VII.4, Ex. 4, p. 417). Show that the value of the game is 1 but player I has no optimal strategy.

HINT. An ε-optimal strategy (due to Blackwell) of player I is as follows: take $N > 1/\varepsilon$; let $N_j = 2^j N$, $j = 1, \ldots$, and divide the play into successive blocks of length N_j. On each block

j, player I selects a stage n_j uniformly distributed on this block and plays 1 at this stage iff the previous $n_j - 1$ moves of player II in this block were 1. Otherwise, he plays always 0 on this block.

4. Non-zero-sum Borel games (Mertens and Neyman). (cf. Mertens, 1987a)

We consider games with perfect information like in Section II.2.a, p. 90.

a. Prove that, if the payoff function g is Borel, the game has a value (consider the level sets).

b. Note that, if g takes finitely many values, the players have optimal strategies, and they can even be improved so as to remain still optimal at any position.

c. Assume now a set $\mathbf{I}$ of players (of whatever cardinality) and that each payoff function g^i satisfies II.2, Ex. 4a, and II.2, Ex. 4b. Define, for each i, $\{\sigma^j(i), j \in \mathbf{I}\}$ to be a strategy vector as improved in, II.2, Ex. 4b, in the two-person zero-sum game $(i, \{i\}^c)$ with payoff g^i. Let finally τ^i be defined as: play $\sigma^i(i)$ as long as the other players do so and switch to $\sigma^i(j)$ if player j deviates. This induces a pure equilibrium.

d. Deduce the existence of pure ε-equilibria for bounded Borel payoff functions.

5. The second separation theorem. (following Blackwell, 1967a)

(For notations and definitions below, cf. Appendix A.1 and Appendix A.2.a.)

Let $\mathscr{P}$ be a paving on a set X, with $\mathscr{P}_c \subseteq \mathscr{P}_s$. Given $C_n \in \mathscr{P}_{sc}$, there exists a sequence $B_n \in \mathscr{P}_{sc}$, $B_n \subseteq C_n$, which forms a partition of $\bigcup_n C_n$.

a. There is a loss of generality in assuming $\mathscr{P}$ to be a (σ-)field.

HINT. Use the stability of the Souslin operation ($\mathscr{P}_s = \mathscr{P}_{ss}$), which implies immediately $\mathscr{P}_s = \mathscr{P}_{s\sigma} = \mathscr{P}_{s\delta}$ since clearly $\mathscr{P}_\sigma \subseteq \mathscr{P}_s$, $\mathscr{P}_\delta \subseteq \mathscr{P}_s$: $\mathscr{B} = \mathscr{P} \cap \mathscr{P}_{sc}$ is thus a σ-field, with $\mathscr{P} \subseteq \mathscr{B}$ (assumption $\mathscr{P}_c \subseteq \mathscr{P}_s$), hence $\mathscr{P}_s \subseteq \mathscr{B}_s \subseteq \mathscr{P}_{ss} = \mathscr{P}_s$.

b. Let $A_n = C_n^c$ have the Souslin scheme $A_n = \bigcup_{\sigma \in \mathbb{N}^{\mathbb{N}}} \bigcap_{k \in \mathbb{N}} P^n_{\sigma_k}$ with $P^n_{\sigma_k}$ in the Boolean algebra $\mathscr{P}$, and where σ_k denotes the initial segment of length k of $\sigma \in \mathbb{N}^{\mathbb{N}}$. Set $P^n_{\sigma_0} = X$ ($\sigma_0 = \emptyset$). For $x \in X$, define the game Γ_x with players $n \in \mathbb{N}$ each picking an integer in the following order: 1,1,2,1,2,3,1,2,3,4,1,2,... At any stage t, denote by $h_t(n)$ the sequence of past choices of player n. The game continues until at some stage t, $x \notin P^n_{h_t(n)}$ for some player n, who is then declared the loser. The sets L_n of plays where player n loses are disjoint open sets in $\mathbb{N}^{\mathbb{N}}$. Let $L_0 = (\bigcup_{n \geq 1} L_n)^c$, and observe $L_0 = \emptyset$ for $x \notin A = \bigcap_n A_n$.

Let $A'_n = \{x \mid \text{player } n \text{ can avoid losing in } \Gamma_x\}$

$A''_n = \{x \mid \text{player } n \text{ cannot force a loss upon his opponents in } \Gamma_x\}$.

Show that:

(1) $A_n \subseteq A'_n$.
(2) $A'_n \cap A''_n = A$.
(3) $A'_n \cup A''_n = X$.
(4) $\bigcup_n A''_n = X$ (if everyone forces a loss upon his opponents, one will lose ...) (by 2 and 3, this is equivalent to $\bigcap_n A'_n = A$).
(5) A'_n and A''_n belong to $\mathscr{P}_s$.

HINT. For example, for A''_n, the set of x such that the opponents have a joint strategy τ that forces the closed set $L_0 \cup L_n$, i.e., such that, for any finite history h, either h is not compatible with τ, or no opponent has lost along h. Observe that the set of histories is countable; hence the set of strategies can be viewed as $\mathbb{N}^{\mathbb{N}}$: our condition on the pair (τ, x) is thus the intersection over countably many histories h of conditions "either τ belongs to some clopen set or x belongs to some set in the field $\mathscr{B}''$: $\{(\tau, x)\} = \bigcap \left[(K_i \times X) \cup (\mathbb{N}^{\mathbb{N}} \times B_i)\right]$ with K_i clopen, $B_i \in \mathscr{B}$. Use now the projection property, or, to keep the proof fully self-contained, write the corresponding Souslin scheme: $A_n'' = \bigcup_{\tau \in \mathbb{N}^{\mathbb{N}}} \bigcap_{k \in \mathbb{N}} Q_{\tau_k}^n$, with $Q_{\tau_k}^n = \bigcap \{B_i \mid i \leq k,\ \sigma \in K_i \Longrightarrow \sigma_k \neq \tau_k\} \in \mathscr{B}$.

c. Set now $B_n = (A_n')^c \cap \bigcap_{i<n} (A_i'')^c$ to finish the proof.

6. Borel sets via games. (Blackwell, 1981)

Let $H = \bigcup_{n \geq 0} \mathbb{N}^n$. $X \subseteq H$ is a stop rule if for all infinite sequences h_∞, there exists a unique x in X with $x \prec h_\infty$. Given a stop rule X, i.e., a function on X whose values are intervals of $\mathbb{R}$ and a real number u, consider the game $G(X, f, u)$ with perfect information on $\Omega = \mathbb{N}$, where I plays first and wins if $u \in f(\omega_1, \ldots, \omega_k)$, where $(\omega_1, \ldots, \omega_k)$ is in X. Let $B(X, f)$ be the set of u's for which I wins. Prove that the family $\mathscr{B}$ of all $B(X, f)$ is the σ-algebra of Borel sets on $\mathbb{R}$.

HINT. Note that $\mathscr{B}$ includes intervals. Prove that $\mathscr{B}$ is stable by countable unions and intersections. (Consider the extended game where I or II chooses first which game $G(X_n, f_n, u)$ to play.) For the converse note that $B(X, f)$ is analytic (as in II.2, Ex. 5) but $G(X, f, u)$ is clopen, hence by Proposition II.2.1, p. 91, $B(X, f)$ is coanalytic, and use Appendix A.3.i.

7. Analytic sets via games. (Dellacherie, 1980)

Let X be a compact metric space. $\mathscr{C} \subseteq \mathscr{P}(X)$ is a capacitance if:

(1) $A \in \mathscr{C}, A \subseteq B \Longrightarrow B \in \mathscr{C}$.
(2) $A_n \nearrow A$ and $A \in \mathscr{C} \Longrightarrow \exists n, A_n \in \mathscr{C}$.

Define a game G_A with perfect information as follows: I chooses $\mathscr{C}_1$ with $A \in \mathscr{C}_1$, II chooses $A_1 \subseteq A$, $A_1 \in \mathscr{C}_1$, I chooses $\mathscr{C}_2$ with $A_1 \in \mathscr{C}_2, \ldots$, and so on. II wins if $\bigcap_n \overline{A}_n \subseteq A$, where $\overline{A}_n$ is the closure of A_n. Let $\mathscr{D}$ be the family of sets A where II wins in G_A. Prove that $\mathscr{D}$ is the family $\mathscr{A}$ of analytic subsets of X.

HINT.

(1) $\mathscr{A} \subseteq \mathscr{D}$.
  (a) Let first $A = \bigcap_n \bigcup_m K_m^n$, where K_m^n is compact increasing in m for fixed n. Given $\mathscr{C}_1$ with $A \in \mathscr{C}_1$ there exists m_1 with $A \cap K_{m_1}^1 = \tau(\mathscr{C}_1)$ in $\mathscr{C}_1$. Given $\mathscr{C}_2$ with $\tau(\mathscr{C}_1) \in \mathscr{C}_2$, there exists m_2 with $\tau(\mathscr{C}_1) \cap K_{m_2}^2 = \tau(\mathscr{C}_1, \mathscr{C}_2) \in \mathscr{C}_2$. Since $\cap K_{m_i}^i \subseteq A$, τ is winning.
  (b) $\mathscr{D}$ is stable by continuous functions: let $\mathscr{C}' = \{B \mid f(B) \in \mathscr{C}\}$ and define, if τ' is winning for A', $f(A') = A$, $\tau(\mathscr{C}_1) = f(\tau'(\mathscr{C}_1'))$, $\tau(\mathscr{C}_1, \mathscr{C}_2) = f(\tau'(\mathscr{C}_1', \mathscr{C}_2'))$, and so on. Since $f(\cap K_n) = \cap f(K_n)$, K_n compact, τ is winning for A.
  (c) Any analytic set can be obtained since $f(A)$, f is continuous, and A is like in 1a, Appendix A.3.f.

(2) $\mathscr{D} \subseteq A$.
Let A be in $\mathscr{D}$ and τ a winning strategy for II. Note that the class of sets that cannot be written as $\bigcup_n B_n$, $B_n \subseteq \tau(\mathscr{C}_n)$, $\mathscr{C}_n$ capacitance containing A, is a capacitance, hence does not contain A. Thus $A = \bigcup_n \tau(\mathscr{C}_n)$ for some sequence $\mathscr{C}_n$. Similarly, for each ω_1 in $\mathbb{N}$, the family of sets that cannot be written as $\bigcup_n B_n$ with $B_n \subseteq \tau(\mathscr{C}_{\omega_1}, \mathscr{C}_n)$ for capacitances $\mathscr{C}_n$ containing $A_{\omega_1} = \tau(\mathscr{C}_{\omega_1})$ does not contain A_{ω_1}. Define then two mappings from finite sequences in $\mathbb{N}$ to capacitances and subsets of A such that, writing ω_k for the first k terms of some ω in $\mathbb{N}^{\mathbb{N}}$:
(a) $A_{\omega_k} = \tau(\mathscr{C}_{\omega_1}, \ldots, \mathscr{C}_{\omega_k})$.
(b) $A_{\omega_k} = \bigcup_n A_{\omega_k, n}$ with $A_\emptyset = A$.
Deduce that $\bigcap_k \overline{A}_{\omega_k} \subseteq A$ (τ is winning); hence, by 2b, $A = \bigcup_\omega \bigcap_k A_{\omega_k} = \bigcup_\omega \bigcap_k \overline{A}_{\omega_k}$. Hence A is analytic (Souslin scheme) (Appendix A.3.b).

8. Topological games and the Baire property (Choquet, Christensen, Saint Raymond). (Choquet, 1969; Saint-Raymond, 1983)

Given a topological space X consider the game with perfect information G where I chooses a non-empty open set U_1, then II chooses a non-empty open set $V_1 \subseteq U_1$, then I picks $U_2 \subseteq V_1$, and so on. II wins in G if $\bigcap_n V_n \neq \emptyset$. We say that X is of type B (resp. A) if I cannot win in G (resp. II wins).

Define similarly G' with moves U_n and (V_n, x_n), U_n, V_n open, x_n in X, $U_n \subseteq V_n \subseteq U_{n-1}$, where II wins if the sequence x_n has an accumulation point in $\bigcap_n V_n$, and G'' with moves (U_n, x_n) and V_n, U_n, V_n open, x_n in U_n, and $V_{n-1} \supseteq U_n \supseteq V_n \ni x_n$, where II wins if $\bigcap_n V_n \neq \emptyset$. We introduce similarly types $B', \ldots A''$.

Observe that property A (resp. A', A'') always implies property B (resp. B', B''), and that $A'' \Longrightarrow A' \Longrightarrow A$, $B'' \Longrightarrow B' \Longrightarrow B$.

a. The following spaces are of type A'': complete metric spaces, locally compact Hausdorff spaces, products of spaces of type A''.

b. Prove that X is of type B if and only if X is a Baire space.

HINT. If X is not Baire, let U be a non-empty open set $U \subseteq \bigcup_n F_n$, where F_n are closed sets with an empty interior. Let $\sigma(\phi) = U$, $\sigma(V_1, \ldots, V_n) = V_n \setminus F_n$; then σ is winning. If σ is winning, $\sigma(\phi) = U_1$ is of the first category. In fact, define $I_1 = \{1\}$, $U_1^1 = U_1$ and, recursively, a maximal family of non-empty open sets $(U_i^n, V_i^{n-1})_{i \in I_n}$ with:

(1) $(U_i^n)_{i \in I_n}$ are pairwise disjoint.
(2) $\forall i \in I_{n+1} \exists j \in I_n$, $V_i^{n+1} \subseteq U_j^n$.
(3) $U_{i_1}^1 \supseteq U_{i_2}^2 \supseteq \cdots \supseteq U_{i_n}^n$ implies $U_{i_n}^n = \sigma(V_{i_2}^1, \ldots, V_{i_n}^{n-1})$.
(4) $U_i^n \subseteq V_i^{n-1}$.

Let then $W_n = \bigcup_{i \in I_n} U_i^n$ and show inductively that W_n is dense in U_1: Assume it is true for n and let W be open and disjoint from W_{n+1}; let $i_n \in I_n$ with $W \cap U_{i_n}^n \neq \emptyset$. This determines a unique $(i_1, \ldots, i_n)$ by 3 and $V^n = W \cap U_{i_n}^n$, $U^{n+1} = \sigma(V_{i_2}^1, \ldots, V_{i_n}^{n-1})$ contradicts the maximality of the family. Finally, $\bigcap W_n = \emptyset$ since if it contains a, a is compatible with a play of σ and σ is winning.

c. A metrizable space is of type A'' iff it is topologically complete.

HINT. It suffices to show that if X is of type A'', X is a G_δ in its completion (E, d).

Show that there exists a family of indices $I_{\ldots}$ and open sets $O_{\ldots}$ in E constructed inductively by:

(1) $\omega_1 \in I, \ldots, \omega_{n+1} \in I_{\omega_1, \ldots, \omega_n}$.
(We shall write ω for such a compatible sequence and $\omega(n)$ for the first n terms.)
(2) $O_{\omega(n), \omega_{n+1}} \subseteq O_{\omega(n)}$, $X \cap (\bigcup_{\omega_{n+1}} O_{\omega(n), \omega_{n+1}}) = X \cap O_{\omega(n)}$, $d(O_{\omega(n)}) < 2^{-n}$.
(3) $\bigcap_n O_{\omega(n)}$ is a point of X.

Fix a well ordering on each I and define inductively $A_{\omega_1} = \bigcup_{\theta_1 < \omega_1} O_{\theta_1}$, $A_{\omega(n), \omega_{n+1}} = A_{\omega(n)} \cup (\bigcup_{\theta_{n+1} < \omega_{n+1}} O_{\omega(n), \theta_{n+1}})$; then $B_{\omega(n)} = O_{\omega(n)} \setminus A_{\omega(n)}$ and $X_n = \bigcup_\omega B_{\omega(n)}$, $Y = \bigcap_n X_n$. Note that $X \subseteq X_n$ hence $X \subseteq Y$. On the other hand, for every $\omega(n)$, the $B_{\omega(n), \omega_{n+1}}$ are included in $B_{\omega(n)}$ and disjoint, so that $Y = \bigcup_\omega \bigcap_n B_{\omega(n)} \subseteq \bigcup_\omega \bigcap_n O_{\omega(n)} \subseteq X$. It suffices to show that X_n is a G_δ in E. Since E is metric proceed by localization: $C \subseteq E$ is a G_δ iff for every open covering (F_i) of C, $C \cap F_i$ is a G_δ. (Use an open covering G_j of $\cup F_i$, finer than F_i and locally finite. Each $C \cap G_j$ is the intersection of a decreasing sequence $G_{j,n}$ of open subsets of G_j. Let $\Omega_n = \bigcup_j G_{j,n}$; since G_j is locally finite one has $\bigcap_n \Omega_n = \bigcup_j \bigcap_n G_{j,n} = \bigcup_j C \cap G_j = C$.)

The proof then follows by induction.

d. (Hausdorff) Deduce that: if X is topologically complete and f an open continuous mapping in a metrizable space, $f(X)$ is topologically complete.

e. If X separable is of type B, it is of type B'.

HINT. Let (a_n) be dense in X, and given σ' in G', let $\sigma(V_1, \dots, V_n) = \sigma'((V_1, a_1), \dots, (V_n, a_n))$. If τ wins against σ, $\cap V_n$ contains an accumulation point of (a_n); hence σ' is losing against (V_n, a_n).

f. A Hausdorff space X is a Namioka space if for all compact Y, all metrizable Z, and all f from $X \times Y$ to Z, separately continuous on X and Y, there exists a dense G_δ of X, A, such that f is continuous at each point of $A \times Y$.

Prove that if X is of type B', X is a Namioka space.

HINT. Else one can assume that $Z = [-1, 1]$ (consider the function $d(f(x, y_1), f(x, y_2))$ on $X \times (Y \times Y)$), and, using II.2, Ex. 8b, that on an open set W the oscillation of $F : x \mapsto f(x, \cdot)$ is $> \delta$. Let for each $k \geq 1$, $(P_j^k)_{j \geq 1}$ be a dense sequence in $\mathscr{P}^k$, the set of real continuous functions on $[-1, 1]^k$. Define σ by $\sigma(\phi) = W$ and $\sigma((V_1, x_1), \dots, (V_n, x_n)) = U_{n+1} = V_n \setminus \bigcup_{j+k \leq n} C_{k,j}$ with $C_{k,j} = \{x \mid \|F(x) - \varphi_{k,j}\| \leq \delta/3\}$ and $\varphi_{k,j}(y) = P_j^k(f(x_1, y), \dots, f(x_k, y))$. Since the diameter of $F(C_{k,j})$ is less than $2\delta/3$, $C_{k,j}$ has an empty interior in W, hence $U_{n+1} \neq \emptyset$. Let $(V_n, x_n)_{n \geq 1}$ be winning against σ. Write x_∞ for an accumulation point of (x_n) in $\bigcap_n V_n$. Let $\phi : Y \to [-1, 1]^{\mathbb{N}}$, $\phi(y) = (f(x_n, y))_n$. Since $\phi(y) = \phi(y')$ implies $f(x_\infty, y) = f(x_\infty, y')$ there exists φ continuous on the compact set $\phi(Y)$ with $F(x_\infty) = \varphi \circ \phi$, hence by Urysohn's theorem a continuous function ψ on $[-1, 1]^{\mathbb{N}}$ that coincides with φ on $\phi(Y)$. Let ψ_k on $[-1, 1]^k$ defined by $\psi_k(u_1, \dots, u_k) = \psi(u_1, \dots, u_k, 0, 0, \dots)$ and π_k the projection of $[-1, 1]^{\mathbb{N}}$ on $[-1, 1]^k$. By uniform continuity of ψ there exists k with $\|\psi - \psi_k \circ \pi_k\| \leq \delta/12$. Choose j with $\|\psi_k - P_j^k\| \leq \delta/4$; then $\|F(x_\infty) - \varphi_{k,j}\| \leq \delta/3$, hence $x_\infty \in C_{k,j}$, hence $x_\infty \notin \bigcap_n V_n$.

9. Games without value. (Davis, 1964)

Consider a game with perfect information where player I chooses a finite sequence in $\Omega = \{0, 1\}$, then II chooses a point in Ω, then I a finite sequence, and so on. Given W in Ω^∞, player I wins if the play belongs to W.

a. Prove that I wins iff W contains a perfect set.

HINT. If σ is winning, the set of plays consistent with σ is a perfect set in W.

Conversely, let P be perfect in W. Given h in $H = \bigcup_n \Omega^n$, $f(h) = \{x \in \Omega^\infty \mid h \prec x\}$ has an empty or perfect intersection with P. Deduce that $Q = \{h \in H \mid f(h, 0) \cap P$ and $f(h, 1) \cap P$ are perfect$\}$ is non-empty and induces a winning I-sub-tree.

b. Show that player II wins iff W is countable.

HINT. If W is countable $= \{w^n\}_{n \in \mathbb{N}}$, player II can force a play with $w^n \notin f(h_{2n})$, $\forall n$.

Show that if II has a winning strategy he has also a winning strategy that depends only on the position at stage n (and not on the history, i.e., the sequence of previous positions).

Thus, if τ is winning, for each w in W, there exists N such that $n \geq N$ implies $w \notin f(w_n, \tau(w_n))$. Denote by $N(w)$ the smallest such N, and let $W_k = \{w \in W \mid N(w) \leq k\}$. Note that for any h in Ω^k, $f(h) \cap W_k$ contains at most one point; hence W_k is finite.

10. An operator solution proof of Proposition II.2.8. (Blackwell, 1989)

For each function u in $\mathscr{U}$, i.e., defined on H with $0 \leq u \leq 1$ and each position x, let $\Gamma(u; x)$ be the game starting from x and with payoff $u(y)$, where y is the entrance position in Y after x. Note that $\Gamma(u; x)$ has a value, say, $Tu(x)$; this defines an operator T from $\mathscr{U}$ to itself.

Show T has a fixed point u^* and $u^*(\emptyset)$ is the value of the original G_δ game, say, $\Gamma(\emptyset)$.

HINT. For each countable ordinal α define u^α in $\mathscr{U}$ by:

$$u^0 \equiv 1, u^{\alpha+1} = Tu^\alpha, \text{ and if } \alpha \text{ is a limit ordinal } u^\alpha = \inf\{u^\beta \mid \beta < \alpha\}.$$

To prove that I can guarantee $u^*(\emptyset)$ let him play optimally in a sequence of games $\Gamma(u^*; y_m)$ (cf. the proof of Proposition II.2.8, p. 95). For II, prove inductively that for any countable ordinal α, any position x, and any $\varepsilon > 0$, he can obtain $u^\alpha(x) + \varepsilon$ in $\Gamma(x)$ (play first optimally in some $\Gamma(u^\beta; x)$; then obtain $u^\beta(y)$ in $\Gamma(y)$).

II.3. CORRELATED EQUILIBRIA AND EXTENSIONS

We follow here roughly the approach of Forges (1986a).

II.3.a. Correlated Equilibria

A **correlation device** c (for the player set $\mathbf{I}$) is a probability space $(E, \mathscr{E}, P)$ together with sub-σ-fields $(\mathscr{E}^i)_{i\in\mathbf{I}}$ of $\mathscr{E}$. The extension Γ_c of a game Γ by c is the game where first nature selects $e \in E$ according to P, next each player $i \in \mathbf{I}$ is informed of the events in $\mathscr{E}^i$ that contain e, then Γ is played (every player remembering all along his information about e).

A **correlated equilibrium** of Γ (Aumann, 1974) is a pair (c, equilibrium of Γ_c).

In such a correlated equilibrium, each player $i \in \mathbf{I}$ has a private probability space $(X^i, \mathscr{X}^i, Q^i)$ to do his own randomization (cf. Section II.1); one can replace E by its product with all X^i's, so as to reduce mixed (resp. general) strategy correlated equilibria to pure (resp. behavioral) strategy-correlated equilibria. Further, if the action sets are standard Borel and Γ is countably linear, then II.1, Ex. 10d, p. 72, allows us to reduce correlated equilibria in general strategies to the pure strategy case. Similarly, if the game is linear and A is countable, the method of II.1, Ex. 10e, p. 73 (with $(E, \mathscr{E}^i)$ instead of $(X, \mathscr{X})$), reduces behavioral strategy-correlated equilibria (hence, by the above, also general strategy-correlated equilibria) to the pure strategy case. (One cannot use directly the statement of II.1, Ex. 10e, since the set of signals of Γ_c is not countable.)

Henceforth we assume that Γ is a linear game with a countable signal space (recall II.1, Ex. 14, Remark II.1.30, p. 84).

Theorem II.3.1. *The correlated equilibria of* Γ *have distributions on the space* $(\Sigma, \mathscr{S}) = \prod_i (\Sigma^i, \mathscr{S}^i)$ *of pure strategy* **I**-tuples *of* Γ. *This set* C *of distributions is convex.*

PROOF. According to Remark II.1.6, p. 63, pure strategy-correlated equilibria can now also be seen as an $\mathbf{I}^{\text{tuple}}$ of measurable maps $\hat{\sigma}^i$ from $(E, \mathscr{E}^i, P)$ to i's pure strategy space $(\Sigma^i, \mathscr{S}^i)$ in Γ. Hence the first sentence.

Convexity follows from the fact that a lottery between two correlated equilibria yields again a correlated equilibrium, with device: ■

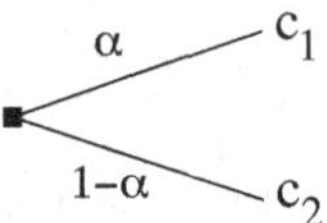

Figure II.3. Convexity of the correlated equilibria distributions.

Definition II.3.1. C is called the set of **correlated equilibrium distributions.** C_0 is the set of corresponding payoffs. A **canonical correlated equilibrium** is one where $c = ((\Sigma, \mathscr{S}), (\tilde{\mathscr{S}}^i)_{i \in \mathbf{I}}, P)$, where $(\Sigma, \mathscr{S}) = \prod_{i \in \mathbf{I}} (\Sigma^i, \mathscr{S}^i)$ and $\tilde{\mathscr{S}}^i$ is the σ-field on Σ spanned by $\mathscr{S}^i$, and where the equilibrium strategies are the projections from Σ to Σ^i $(i \in \mathbf{I})$. (The corresponding devices c are called canonical correlation devices.) Thus canonical correlated equilibria can be identified with their distributions.

Theorem II.3.2. *(Aumann, 1974) C is the set of canonical correlated equilibria.*

Proof. The maps $\hat{\sigma}_i$ of the previous proof allow us to take equivalently as the correlation device $(E \times \Sigma, \mathscr{E} \times \mathscr{S}, (\mathscr{E}^i \times \tilde{\mathscr{S}}^i)_{i \in \mathbf{I}})$ with the probability induced by P and the maps $\hat{\sigma}_i$, and the projections to Σ^i as equilibrium. Thus each player i is told by the device some $\sigma^i \in \Sigma^i$, plus some additional information about ω, and he uses the recommended σ^i. Hence a fortiori he would still be in equilibrium if he were told only σ^i; with less information, he has fewer strategies to deviate to. So the marginal on $(\Sigma, \mathscr{S}, (\tilde{\mathscr{S}}_i)_{i \in \mathbf{I}})$ is a canonical correlated equilibrium. ■

Theorem II.3.3. *C is weak***-closed if the action sets of* Γ *are separable metric, spaces, and each payoff function* $g^i(\sigma^i, \sigma^{-i})$ *is bounded and continuous on* Σ.

Proof. Σ is now also a separable metric space; the result follows then (cf. II.3, Ex. 1d, p. 111) from the fact that $P \in C$ can be equivalently characterized by $\int \Sigma \varphi(\sigma^i)[g^i(\sigma^i, \sigma^{-i}) - g^i(\tau^i, \sigma^{-i})] P(d\sigma) \geq 0$, $\forall \tau^i \in \Sigma^i$, $\forall i \in \mathbf{I}$, and for every bounded, positive continuous function φ on Σ^i. ■

Corollary II.3.4. *If* Σ *is finite, C is a compact, convex polyhedron.*

Proof. In that case, the above system of linear inequalities in P becomes finite, since any positive φ is a positive linear combination of the (finitely many) indicator functions of singletons. ■

Remark II.3.2. The correlated equilibrium concept is purely non-cooperative, it does not require any binding commitments, and players can build for themselves, during the pre-play communication stage, a device that makes the required randomization and signal to each player, once he leaves the room and the current stage is over, his recommended strategy.

Remark II.3.3. The assumption that the player remembers throughout the game his signal from the device, even in a game without perfect recall, fits completely with the standard interpretation for such games: it is the player (the "strategist") who is sitting in the room who gets the signal from the device. Afterwards he gives his instructions (including the signal if he wishes) to all his agents manning the different information sets. In the same spirit, and with the same motivation, is the classical assumption that each player knows what pure (or behavioral) strategy he uses; cf, e.g., the definition of effectively perfect recall.

Remark II.3.4. Under another interpretation, E stands for the set of all states of the world, including therefore the strategies $\sigma^i(e)$ that players are going to use in the game, and $\mathscr{E}^i$ stands for player i's private information (which includes $\sigma^i(e)$). The "Harsanyi doctrine" requires that each player's subjective probability on E be the conditional distribution derived from a common prior P given his private information $\mathscr{E}^i$. From individual decision theory, each player maximizes the expectation (with his subjective probability) of his utility function. It follows that $(E, (\mathscr{E}^i)_{i\in\mathbf{I}}, P, (s^i)_{i\in\mathbf{I}})$ is a correlated equilibrium (Aumann, 1987).

II.3.b. Multistage Games, Extensive Form Correlated Equilibria

Here we assume the game Γ under consideration is a **multistage game**. Intuitively, at each period, players play simultaneously, and they have effectively perfect recall. The easiest way to formalize this is to use a framework like that of Section II.1, except that now $A = \prod_{i\in\mathbf{I}} A^i$, $S = \prod_{i\in\mathbf{I}} S^i$. Thus, at position ω_n, a vector of signals $(a_n^i)_{i\in\mathbf{I}}$ is selected according to α_{ω_n}, each player i is told his signal a_n^i and selects then his action s_n^i, and then ω_{n+1} is selected according to q_{ω_n,a_n,s_n}.

Since the game has effectively perfect recall, we can use Remark II.1.4, p. 61, and assume that a^i contains just incremental information (it does not even have to contain the date, which the player knows by looking at the length of the sequence of past signals).

It is easy to see that to rewrite such a game in the general formalism of Section II.1, one subdivides each period into $\mathbf{I}$ sub-periods, where players play in turn (so all results and definitions of Section II.1 remain applicable). For the present problem, however, physical time is crucial (cf. II.3, Ex. 3, p. 111), and it is more convenient to handle it with the present formalism. For the need for effectively perfect recall, cf. II.3, Ex. 6, p. 113.

(In the context of correlation and communication, the differences between the general definitions of perfect recall in II.1, Ex. 12b, p. 75 and II.1, Ex. 13, p. 76, would conceivably matter, since the former apparently relies on players using independent strategies. And it is not clear what (intermediate?) form would be the "right" one. However, introducing as we do here effectively perfect recall as incremental information avoids such difficulties, and the sufficiency of mixed strategies in all extended games follows from II.1, Ex. 10a and II.1, Ex. 10b p. 70 (in the latter exercise one can stop at (7) of the hint to II.1, Ex. 10b, 72); cf. also the remark at the end of II.1, Ex. 10b, p. 71.)

An **autonomous device** a (for the player set $\mathbf{I}$) is a probability space $(E, \mathscr{E}, P)$ together with random variables m_n^i with values in a message space $(M^i, \mathscr{M}^i)$. The extension Γ_a of Γ by a is the game where first nature selects $e \in E$ according to P, then before each stage n each player i is informed of $m_n^i(e)$. Formally Γ_a is the multistage game with $(\tilde{\Omega}, \tilde{\mathscr{A}}) = (\Omega, \mathscr{A}) \otimes (E, \mathscr{E}) \otimes \mathbb{N}$, with an initial position $\tilde{\omega}_1$ added, from which nature selects (by $\tilde{\alpha}$) the point $(\omega_1, e, 1)$ (ω_1 deterministically, e according to P). The e coordinate is preserved throughout the game, while every selection by q of a new state ω is accompanied by a unit increment in the last coordinate. We have $(\tilde{A}^i, \tilde{\mathscr{A}}^i) = (A^i, \mathscr{A}^i) \otimes (M^i, \mathscr{M}^i) \otimes \mathbb{N}$, where at (ω, e, n), the first coordinate is selected according to α_ω, and the second is $(m_n^i(e), n)$.

An **extensive form correlated equilibrium** of Γ is a pair (a, equilibrium of Γ_a). In such an extensive form correlated equilibrium, each player $i \in \mathbf{I}$ has a private probability space $(X^i, \mathscr{X}^i, Q^i)$ to do his own randomization (cf. Section II.1); one can replace E by its product $\overline{E}$ with all X^i's, adding at every stage x^i to the current message m_n^i, so as to obtain an equivalent behavioral strategy equilibrium. Further, one can use II.1, Ex. 10d, p. 72, if the action set $(S^i, \mathscr{S}^i)$ is standard Borel, or the method of II.1, Ex. 10e, p. 73, if the set A^i is countable, to obtain an equivalent pure strategy equilibrium.

As in Section II.3.a, p. 101, we assume henceforth Γ has countably many signals, and obtain:

Theorem II.3.5. *The extensive form correlated equilibria have distributions on the space* $(\Sigma, \mathscr{S}) = \prod_{i \in \mathbf{I}} (\Sigma^i, \mathscr{S}^i)$ *of pure strategy* **I**-tuples *of* Γ. *This set* E *of distributions is convex. (*E_0 *will denote the set of payoffs corresponding to* E.*)*

Proof. Now there are also countably many finite sequences of signals, and recall from Section II.1 that pure strategies depend only on past signals, so one can still view the pure strategy space as a countable product of the action spaces. In particular, the pure strategy-correlated equilibrium yields measurable maps $\hat{\sigma}_n^i$ from $\overline{E}$ to $\Sigma_n^i = (S_n^i)^{\prod_{m \le n} A_m^i}$. The rest of the proof is the same as before. ∎

A **canonical extensive form correlated equilibrium** is one where the device $a = [\Sigma, \mathscr{S}, P; (\hat{\sigma}_n^i)_{n \in \mathbb{N}, i \in \mathbf{I}}, (\Sigma_n^i)_{n \in \mathbb{N}, i \in \mathbf{I}}]$, where $\hat{\sigma}_n^i$ are the projections, and where the equilibrium strategies are the identity maps from messages to Σ_n^i. They are identified with their distributions P.

Theorem II.3.6. *E is the set of canonical extensive form correlated equilibria.*

Proof. As for Theorem II.3.2, p. 102. ∎

Remark II.3.5. In fact, as with correlated equilibria, to get a truly canonical representation, without redundancies, one should still eliminate duplicate strategies from Σ; i.e., one should identify any two equivalent pure strategies of Σ^i; it is useless for the device to tell the player what to do in case he has deviated from a previous recommendation; this irrelevant (and potentially dangerous) information should be deleted for a canonical device.

Theorem II.3.7. *E is weak*-closed if the action sets of Γ are separable metric spaces, and each payoff function $g^i(\sigma^i, \sigma^{-i})$ is continuous on Σ and bounded.*

Proof. The proof of Theorem II.3.3, p. 102, has to be slightly modified: $P \in E$ can be equivalently characterized by the system of inequalities:

$$\int [g^i(\hat{\sigma}) - g^i(\overline{\sigma}^i(\hat{\sigma}^i), \hat{\sigma}^{-i})] P(d\hat{\sigma}) \geq 0,$$

where $\overline{\sigma}^i_n$ is a continuous map from $\hat{\sigma}^i_1 \cdots \hat{\sigma}^i_n$ to probabilities over a fixed (i.e., depending only on $\overline{\sigma}^i$) finite subset of Σ^i_n. Indeed, by Lebesgue's dominated convergence theorem, the same inequality will still hold if the $\overline{\sigma}^i_n$ are just Borel instead of continuous, because when stabilizing under pointwise limits the continuous maps from a separable metric space to a simplex one obtains all Borel maps. Hence the inequality is true whenever the $\overline{\sigma}^i_n$ are Borel maps from $\hat{\sigma}^i_1 \cdots \hat{\sigma}^i_n$ to Σ^i_n taking only finitely many values. Since any measurable map to a separable metric space is a pointwise limit of measurable maps taking only finitely many values, another use of Lebesgue's theorem yields the inequality whenever the $\overline{\sigma}^i_n$ are Borel maps from $\prod_{k \leq n} \Sigma^i_k$ to Σ^i_n. Then it expresses that, in the extended game Γ_a, player i has no profitable pure strategy deviation, i.e., $P \in E$. The result follows, since all our linear inequalities are obviously weak*-continuous. ■

Corollary II.3.8. *If Σ is finite, E is a compact, convex polyhedron.*

Proof. In this case, characterize E by the same set of inequalities as above, but where $\overline{\sigma}^i$ is an arbitrary map from $\prod_{k \leq n} \Sigma^i_k$ to Σ^i_n. ■

II.3.c. Communication Equilibria

We still assume Γ a multistage game. But here we want the device not only to send messages to the players before every stage ("sunspots"), but also to receive information from them, so as to embody the most general communication possibilities (e.g., letters given to a notary to be delivered at a later date, conditional on a specific event, to a specific subset of players). We still want the device to be completely outside the original game: it receives no direct information whatsoever about what is going on in the game, except through the players.

Thus, we think of the following scenario: at each stage n, first players receive their signal in Γ, then send some input to the device, then the device selects a vector of messages to the players, finally players choose an action in Γ (an illegal input by some player or an absence of input will be treated as a fixed input). Formally, we introduce the following:

Definition II.3.6. A tuple $d = \{E, \mathscr{E}, e_1, [(H_n^i, \mathscr{H}_n^i)_{i\in\mathbf{I}}, (M_n^i, \mathscr{M}_n^i)_{i\in\mathbf{I}}, P_n]_{n\in\mathbb{N}}\}$ is called a **communication device**. Here $e_1 \in E$ is the initial state of the device, H_n^i the space of inputs of player i at stage n, and M_n^i the space of messages to him, while P_n is a transition probability from $(E, \mathscr{E}) \otimes \bigotimes_{i\in\mathbf{I}}(H_n^i, \mathscr{H}_n^i)$ to $(E, \mathscr{E}) \otimes \bigotimes_i(M_n^i, \mathscr{M}_n^i)$ that selects, given the current state e_n and the current inputs h_n^i, the current messages m_n^i and the new state e_{n+1}.

Definition II.3.7. The extension Γ_d of Γ by d is the induced multistage game between players in **I**. Observe, however, that one can also consider it as a multistage game with $\mathbf{I}+1$ players, the added player being the device that has $\prod_{i\in\mathbf{I}}(H_n^i, \mathscr{H}_n^i)$ as the space of signals A_n^{dev} and $\prod_{i\in\mathbf{I}}(M_n^i, \mathscr{M}_n^i)$ as the action space S_n^{dev}, and that uses the generalized strategy (cf. II.1, Ex. 10aα, p. 70) $(E, \mathscr{E}, e_1, (P_n)_{n\in\mathbb{N}})$ (giving him zero payoff).

(It is easily seen that any generalized strategy can be written in the above form, where E is the space of all finite histories of internal choices, inputs, and messages.)

Definition II.3.8. A **communication equilibrium** of Γ is a pair (d, equilibrium of Γ_d).

Definition II.3.9. A communication device is **standard** if $(H_n^i, \mathscr{H}_n^i) = (A_n^i, \mathscr{A}_n^i)$, $(M_n^i, \mathscr{M}_n^i) = (S_n^i, \mathscr{S}_n^i)$.

Definition II.3.10. A **standard communication equilibrium** is one where the device is standard, and the equilibrium strategies are the identity maps. It is identified with the corresponding (generalized) strategy of the standard device.

Theorem II.3.9. *Every communication equilibrium is equivalent to (induces the same probability distribution on plays as) a standard communication equilibrium.*

Proof. Given the communication device, and the equilibrium strategies of the players, we describe the construction of the new (and "larger") standard device informally as follows (to avoid heavy notation, which would only obscure things). Think of the players' strategies as personal devices (which remember all their past choices, inputs, and outputs) that do all randomizations and computations for the player: the player just has to instruct it at each stage both of the signals he gets from the underlying game, to receive a recommended input to be sent to the central device, and of the message from the central device, to receive a recommended action to be taken in the underlying game. Certainly the player cannot deviate profitably, given such a setup, from being truthful to his own device and following its recommendations, since otherwise the composition of his deviation strategy and of his personal device would describe a profitable deviation from the given communication equilibrium. Assume now that he connects directly his personal device to the central device, such that the personal device sends inputs directly to the central device, without even informing him, and receives directly the messages from the central device, without informing him either. Then he has even fewer moves to deviate to (he can no longer act as a middleman between his personal device and the central device) and less information, so certainly he has no profitable deviation. The central device together with all connected personal devices can now be seen as one single big standard device, to which players report truthfully their signals, and whose recommended actions they follow. To construct formally the big device, just take care that the simultaneous randomizations in the different personal devices are done independently of each other; and take as state space the space of all finite histories of inputs, outputs, and internal choices of both the central device and all personal devices. ■

Remark II.3.11. Now we have really an $(\mathbf{I}+1)$-person multistage game, since the sets of signals and actions of all $(\mathbf{I}+1)$-players are fixed, and no longer variable as in the general definition. And the communication equilibria are the equilibria of this game, while the standard communication equilibria are those where the strategies of the original $\mathbf{I}$ players are the identity maps.

Remark II.3.12. To write the multistage game, however, we have to subdivide the stages of the original game: each stage has to be subdivided at least in 3. Actually, to define properly the relevant probabilities by Ionescu Tulcea's theorem, it is more convenient to subdivide stage t into $t_1 < t_2 < t_3 < t_4 < t_5$:

- At t_1, nature chooses the a_i and informs the players.
- At t_2, the players report to the device.
- At t_3, the device selects its new internal state and sends its messages to the players.
- At t_4, the players take an action in the game.
- At t_5, a new position is chosen by nature.

Corollary II.3.10. *If the spaces $(S^i, \mathscr{S}^i)$ are standard Borel, or if the sets A^i are countable, then:*

(1) *It suffices to consider pure strategy deviations by the players to determine the standard communication equilibria.*
(2) *Standard communication equilibria have a representation in the form of a mixed strategy (with auxiliary space $([0,1],\lambda)$) for the device, in the countable case ("first canonical representation"), in the form of a probability distribution over $\hat{\Sigma} = \prod_{n\in\mathbb{N}}(\prod_{a\in A_n} \overline{S}_{n,a}^{\prod_{t<n} A_t})$, the space of pure standard devices ("joint pure strategies" of the players).*

Proof. Use II.1, Ex. 10e, p. 73, in the countable case, and II.1, Ex. 10d, p. 72, in the standard Borel case, for the players to obtain (1), and for the device (the $(\mathbf{I}+1)$th player) for (2). ■

Corollary II.3.11. *If the spaces $(S^i, \mathscr{S}^i)$ are standard Borel, standard communication equilibria have a second canonical representation in the form of a* *behavioral strategy for the device, i.e., a sequence of transition probabilities P_n from $(\prod_{t<n} \overline{S}_t) \times A_n$ to S_n (carried by $\overline{S}_{n,a_n}$).*

Proof. Use II.1, Ex. 10a, and II.1, Ex. 10b, p. 70, for the device. ■

Standard communication equilibria in (first or second) canonical representation are called **canonical communication equilibria** (possibly with the qualifier "first" or "second").

Define D as the set of generalized strategies of the device in standard communication equilibria in the general case, use the second canonical representation in the standard Borel case, and use the first canonical representation in the countable case.

Denote by D_0 the set of corresponding payoff vectors.

Theorem II.3.12. *D is convex (but not in the second canonical representation).*

Proof. A random selection between two generalized strategies is again a generalized strategy. ■

Theorem II.3.13. *In the countable case, if the spaces $(S^i, \mathscr{S}^i)$ are separable metric spaces, D is weak*-closed, if each player's payoff function g^i is continuous and bounded over $\hat{\Sigma}$.*

Proof. Use Corollary II.3.10.1, p. 107, and argue as in Theorem II.3.7, p. 105. (Note the additional action sets A^i of the player, for his inputs to the device, are also separable metric.) ■

Corollary II.3.14. *If Σ is finite, D is a compact, convex polyhedron.*

Proof. Note that $\hat{\Sigma}$ is then also finite, as are the strategy sets of the players in the canonical Γ_d. Then as in Corollary II.3.8, p. 105. ■

II.3.d. Finite Games

Here we assume Σ finite, and use Corollaries II.3.4, II.3.8, and II.3.14. We now want to construct even nicer such finite devices that are in particular independent of the particular equilibrium selected.

Theorem II.3.15. *For each finite game there exists:*

1. *A universal autonomous device, whose output is, in period zero, a public integer and $\mathbf{I}$ private random variables uniform on a finite set A, all $(\mathbf{I}+1)$ of those independent; and in each of the following periods, a sequence of independent, public random variables, uniform on A. With this device, all extensive form correlated equilibria of the original game become feasible as pure strategy (Nash) equilibria of the extended game.*
2. *Similarly, a universal correlation device.*

(3) *A universal communication device, which is a finite automaton, all of whose signals are public, and with which all communication equilibria of the original game become feasible as Nash equilibria of the extended game; alternatively, one could use a randomizing automaton, and pure Nash equilibria. The first alternative may require the game to have rational payoffs.*

Remark II.3.13. In particular, there is no specific problem with those concepts of "bargaining about the device"; it is just the general problem of bargaining about (Nash) equilibria that one reencounters.

Proof. Since the set of possible signals from the device to the players is finite, one could select an independent random permutation of this finite set for each day and each player; the device could then announce publicly every day the whole vector of encoded signals, provided it informs each player privately before the start of play of his sequence of decoding keys. In this way, all devices give an independent and uniformly distributed sequence of public signals from the start of the game on; the only private information is, as in a correlated equilibrium, before the start of play.

The device could even select an independent set of such keys for each extreme point of the polyhedra of communication equilibria or of extensive form correlated equilibria, and simulate each of the extreme points in parallel independently, giving as a single output every period the whole vector indexed by the extreme points. In the case of extensive form correlated equilibria, the players can very well be told initially their keys for all extreme points, since the irrelevant keys will just give them information independent of the true game and of the extreme point they want to play. But in the case of communication equilibria, they should receive only the relevant decoding keys. In that case however, they can each be given an additional finite set of inputs to the device, to be used at stage 1, by which they inform the device of which extreme point they want to play. Each player receives the decoding key relative to the extreme point he announced; his inputs are transmitted as is to the sub-device simulating that extreme point, and for the other sub-devices the first input is always selected as a fictitious input for him. So, even if, in a game with incomplete information, all this communication happens after players know their true types, they have no incentive to deviate from announcing the right extreme point to the device, assuming all others do so. Once the device knows the extreme point, it gives to each one his decoding key (together with his stage 1 output). Those decoding keys can now themselves be encoded as before, with the key for this encoding being given before the start of the game, to preserve the property that from stage 1 on; all the device's announcements are public, independent and uniform.

For correlated equilibria, it suffices to simulate independently and in parallel the devices corresponding to each of the extreme points. All this can be realized by a fixed, finite automaton containing a fixed, finite lottery mechanism, and the required finite sets of input buttons and output signals for each player. With this universal (for the game in question) device, all extreme point equilibria can be realized.

Use now II.3, Ex. 2, p. 111, to add to it a coin-tossing mechanism, by which it will output publicly, at the start of the game, a sequence of ones, deciding each time independently with probability 2^{-n} to stop (2^n larger than the number of extreme points), which it signals by appending a zero: we still have a finite automaton, and now players can use the number of ones in the sequence to select an extreme point with whatever probability distribution they want. Thus, for each game, there is a fixed, finite automaton that is a universal communication device or autonomous device.

Finally, for the communication device, we can now use the possibility of inputs by the players to the device to assume all outputs of the device are public. Further, we can dispense with the need for a lottery mechanism in the device, by letting the players themselves input their decoding keys to the device and generate the required randomness by a jointly controlled lottery mechanism (II.3, Ex. 5), at least when the parameters of the game are rational. There is no problem for the sequence of zeros and ones needed to select the extreme point: players successively choose simultaneously at random a zero or a one, and the device just retransmits to each the sum mod 2: after a finite number of trials, players will know the corresponding integer, hence the corresponding extreme point, and will transmit this to the automaton. After that, players have to generate the finite lottery required by the device: if this is rational, it can be replaced by a finite lottery over a bigger number of events, say, n, with equal probability: the players pick to this effect a uniform number in $\mathbb{Z}_n$, and the machine uses the sum. ∎

EXERCISES

1. A direct proof of existence of correlated equilibrium (finite case). (Hart and Schmeidler, 1989)

Consider a two-person zero-sum game G where player I chooses a point s in $S = \prod S^i$, player II chooses a triple (i, r^i, t^i), $i \in \mathbf{I}$, $r^i, t^i \in S^i$, and the corresponding payoff is $h^i(s^{-i}, r^i) - h^i(s^{-i}, t^i)$ if $s^i = r^i$ and 0 otherwise.

a. Prove that, if $v(G) \geq 0$, an optimal strategy of I induces a correlated equilibrium.

b. Prove then that, given any mixed strategy $y = (y^i(r^i, t^i))$ of player II, player I can get 0.

HINT. By I.3, Ex. 9, p. 40, given non-negative numbers $a_{\ell m}$, $\ell, m \in M$, there exists $\alpha \in \Delta(M)$ such that, for any β in $\mathbb{R}^M$, $\phi(\alpha, \beta) = \sum_\ell \alpha_\ell \sum_m a_{\ell m}(\beta_\ell - \beta_m) = 0$. Take then, for i fixed, $a_{\ell m} = y^i(r^i, t^i)$, $\alpha_\ell = x^i(r^i)$, $\beta_\ell = h^i(s^{-i}, r^i)$, $\beta_m = h^i(s^{-i}, t^i)$ and deduce that x defined by $x(r) = \prod_i x^i(r^i)$ gives 0 in G.

c. (Peleg, 1969)

Consider now the following game Γ: the set of players is $\mathbb{N}$ and each player's strategy set is $\{0, 1\}$. The payoff function is given by:

$$g^i(s) = \begin{cases} s^i & \text{if } \sum_j s^j < \infty \text{ (finitely many ones),} \\ -s^i & \text{otherwise.} \end{cases}$$

Prove that there exists no Nash equilibrium.

HINT. Use the zero-one law.

Let $s(j)$ in S defined by $s^i(j) = 1$ iff $i \le j$. Define P_1 with support on the $s(j)$'s by $P_1(s(j)) = (1/j) - 1/(j+1)$ and P_0 product of its marginals on the S^i's with $P_0(s^i = 1) = 1/i$. Prove then that $(P_0 + P_1)/2$ is a correlated equilibrium.

d. The above method also yields the existence of correlated equilibria for continuous payoff functions on compact strategy spaces.

HINT. Either use a direct approximation, or let player II choose a triple of a player i, a strategy $s_0 \in S^i$, and a continuous non-negative function φ on S^i, with payoff $[h^i(s^{-i}, s^i) - h^i(s^{-i}, s_0)]\varphi(s^i)$. Note that in step a above, using Proposition I.1.9, p. 9, which requires strategies with finite support for player II, reduces the problem to one with finite strategy spaces. Continuity of the payoff function is used to pass from the non-profitability of step-function deviations to that of arbitrary deviations.

Remark II.3.14. In whatever way one uses such a method, one will need the upper semi-continuity of $h^i(s^{-i}, s^i) - h^i(s^{-i}, s_0)$ on S (player I's strategy space in the fictitious game), for each i and $s_0 \in S^i$. (Observe also that this is exactly what is needed for the upper semi-continuity of the best-reply correspondence.) This is equivalent to $h^i(s^{-i}, s^i) = f^i(s^{-i}, s^i) + g^i(s^{-i})$, where f^i is u.s.c. on S and continuous in s^{-i} for each s^i. g^i does not affect Nash equilibria or correlated equilibria, and we know the existence of Nash equilibria for f, I.4, Ex. 20, p. 56, at least in the compact metric case. (And note that the continuity assumption in II.3, Ex. 1d, implies that one can reduce the problem to the compact metric case, e.g., by Stone–Weierstrass.) Thus refinements of this method are unlikely to yield existence of correlated equilibria under much wider conditions than those known for the existence of equilibria.

2. (Blackwell, 1953)

a. Prove that, for $\lambda \le \frac{1}{n}$, $\lambda_m = \lambda(1-\lambda)^{m-1}$ and z in the simplex of $\mathbb{R}^n$, there exists a partition of $\{1, 2, \ldots, m, \ldots\}$, say, N_i, $i = 1, \ldots, n$ with $\sum_{m \in N_i} \lambda_m = z_i$.

b. Prove that if η_m is any other probability definition with the same property as λ_m above in a), and if $\lambda = \frac{1}{n}$, then $\sum_{n \le N} \eta_m \le \sum_{m \le N} \lambda_m$ for all N.

c. Prove that, if, along every play, player i moves at most once, with at most n actions, then any mixed (or behavioral) strategy of i is equivalent to a countable mixture of pure strategies with weights λ_m and $\lambda = \frac{1}{n}$.

3.

a. Prove in the following game that (2, 2) is an extensive form correlated equilibrium payoff but not a correlated equilibrium payoff.

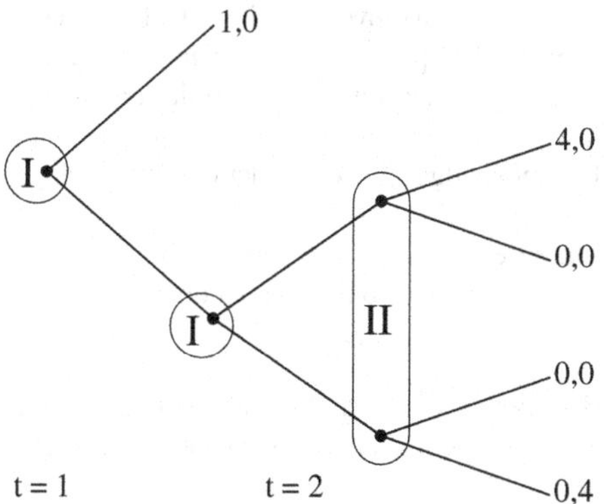

Figure II.4. Extensive form correlated equilibria are not correlated equilibria.

b. Consider the multistage game of Figure II.5.

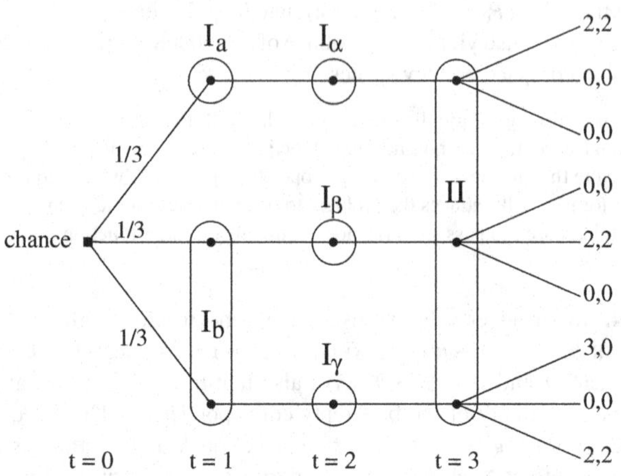

Figure II.5. Necessity of the timing structure.

Show that (2, 2) is a communication equilibrium. It is no longer so if the information is given at once at time $t = 1$. This shows that the additional structure of multistage games, i.e., the time function, is essential to this concept.

4. (Forges, 1990b)

a. In a correlated equilibrium of a two-person zero-sum game with finite strategy sets, the conditional probability over the opponent's actions given a pure strategy having positive probability is an optimal strategy of the opponent.

b. $\begin{pmatrix} \frac{1}{3} & \frac{1}{3} & 0 \\ \frac{1}{3} & 0 & 0 \\ 0 & 0 & 0 \end{pmatrix}$ is a correlated equilibrium of the game $\begin{pmatrix} 0 & 0 & 1 \\ 0 & 0 & -1 \\ -1 & 1 & 0 \end{pmatrix}$, while every convex combination of pairs of optimal strategies with $p(2, 2) = 0$ satisfies $p(1, 1) \geq \frac{1}{2}$.

c. The payoff to any communication equilibrium in a two-person zero-sum game is the value.

5. Define a general jointly controlled lottery over a finite set of alternatives A as a finite game, with elements of A instead of payoff vectors, together with an n-tuple of strategies such that no player can affect the resulting probability distribution on A by unilateral deviation.

a. Show that this implies that knowledge of his own action gives a player no information about the outcomes in A.

b. Show that general joint lotteries can only generate algebraic, hence countably many, distributions on A (and with two players only rational ones).

HINT. Use I.4, Ex. 21, p. 56.

c. Show that any rational distribution on A can be realized by an n-player lottery for any $n \geq 2$, which is fully symmetric in players and strategies, and where no proper coalition can affect the outcome.

HINT. Let k be the smallest common denominator of the probabilities: it suffices to select a uniform point in $\mathbb{Z}_k$. Each player does so and the results are added.

d. General joint lotteries that are stable against deviations by proper sub-coalitions (as like in II.3, Ex. 5c) yield rational probability distributions.

HINT. For $a_0 \in A$, use the minmax theorem for the games between one player and the opposing coalition with payoff 1 if a_0, and 0 otherwise.

6. Consider a multistage game:

At stage 1 players I and II play the game with the incomplete information given in Figure II.6 in which player I is informed about the state of nature (α or β).

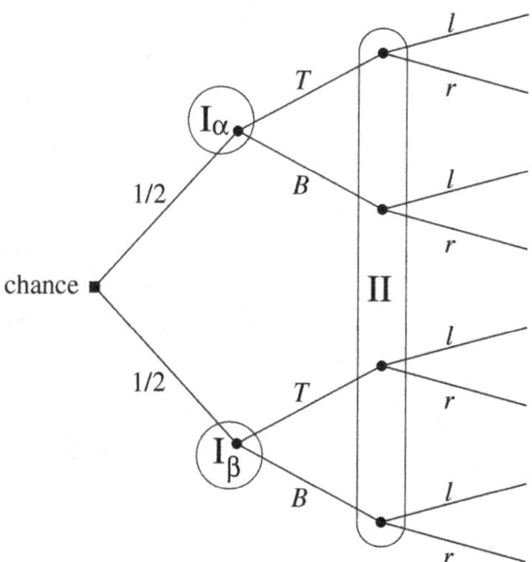

Figure II.6. Stage 1 of the multistage game.

At stage 2, while player I does not know the action of II in the first stage (and both players have perfect recall), the players play a 2×2 game whose payoff to I depends on the state of nature and the payoff of player II is identically 0. The complete multistage game is given in Figure II.7.

a. Show that the following distribution P on moves at time 1:

$$\begin{array}{c} \\ TT \\ TB \\ BT \\ BB \end{array} \begin{array}{c} \begin{array}{cc} \ell & r \end{array} \\ \begin{pmatrix} 1/9 & 2/9 \\ 5/9 & 5/18 \\ 2/9 & 4/9 \\ 1/9 & 1/18 \end{pmatrix} \end{array} \qquad (TB \text{ is } T \text{ if } \alpha,\ B \text{ if } \beta),$$

with player I choosing a at $t = 2$, defines an extensive form correlated equilibrium if the players do not recall their signal at stage 2 (but perfect recall of actions is still assumed).

b. Add a third player playing at stage 1, informed of the chance move. His payoffs are independent of a, b, c. Define 9 strategies as follows: strategy 0 corresponds to the above game and gives him payoff 0. Strategy $\alpha T \ell$ defines a payoff $x_{\alpha T \ell}$ for III if $(\alpha T \ell)$, -1 otherwise, with expectation zero under P and payoff 0 for I and II, and similarly for

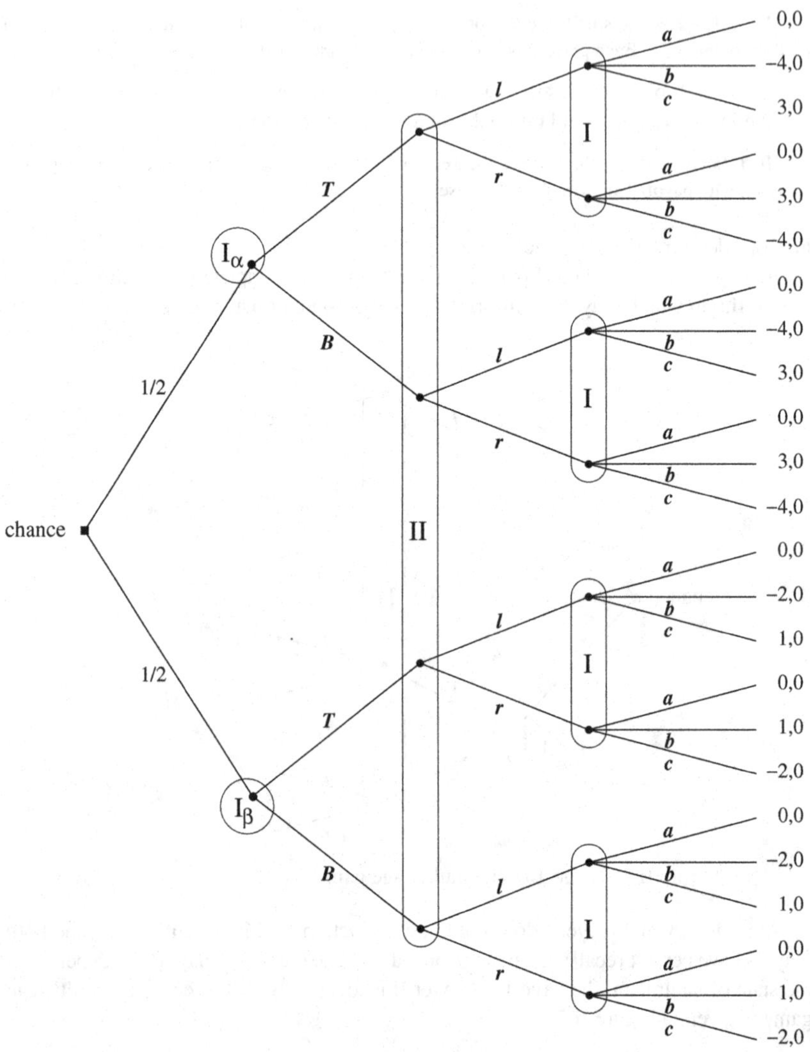

Figure II.7. The complete multistage game.

all seven other outcomes. Finally, add a dummy player with payoff 1 if I chooses a and III uses 0, and 0 otherwise. Show that no extensive form correlated equilibrium (with perfect recall) achieves the payoff obtained by P.

c. Prove the same result for communication equilibria.

HINT. Compute first the conditional distributions on $(T\ell, Tr, B\ell, Br)$ given α and β, and show that for any other conditional distributions, player III will deviate. Show that if the posteriors on ℓ computed by player I given his signals are requested to be in $[1/3, 2/3]$, P is the only correlated distribution compatible with the above conditionals. Check finally that with these conditional distributions player I will have an incentive to lie about his type.

Remark II.3.15. It is clear that any extensive form correlated equilibrium would still be one (in terms of the induced distribution of plays) if the players did not recall previous messages, but just let the device repeat them. So if this modification of the definition would not increase the set of equilibrium payoffs, for games with perfect recall, it might have given a plausible extension of the definition to games without perfect recall. The above example (which probably has generic variants) shows that this is definitely not so. Even in the most standard cases, it yields payoffs that are not even communication equilibrium payoffs: the most basic incentive constraints are violated. Hence the reason for sticking in the definition of multistage games to the perfect recall assumption: although technically one could do with much less, it is the only framework where we feel for the moment completely comfortable with the assumption of perfect recall of past signals: indeed, the justification in Remark II.3.3, p. 103, no longer applies; on the other hand, parallelism with the correlated equilibrium situation is an additional reason for maintaining perfect recall of past signals.

The example shows also that a variant applicable to any extensive form game, where the device would send a separate signal to every agent, i.e., correlated equilibria of the agent normal form, would a fortiori be too large. This is an additional reason (besides II.3, Ex. 3, p. 111) for sticking for the time being to the framework of multistage games.

7. Protocols and correlated equilibria. (Barany, 1992)

a. Let $\#\mathbf{I} = 4$, S^i be finite, $S = \prod S^i$, and E be a finite set endowed with a partition $\{E_s\}_{s \in S}$ and projections $\mathsf{Proj}_i : E \to S^i$ with $\mathsf{Proj}_i(e) = s_i$ if $e \in E_s$.

We describe here a procedure (protocol) of communication between the players according to which a point e in E will be chosen uniformly at random in E, each player being informed only of $\mathsf{Proj}_i(e)$. Moreover the probabilities are the same under non-detectable deviations.

(1) Recall that any subset of at least two players can generate in a non-manipulable way a discrete random variable X (say, the choice at random of a permutation of a finite set) that is common knowledge (II.3, Ex. 5, p. 112). (Note that with four players there exists a sequential procedure of binary communications where at the end only I and II know X: let players III and IV choose X_{III} and X_{IV}, respectively, and inform players I and II, who check that the signal is the same, and then use $X_{\text{III}} \circ X_{\text{IV}}$).

(2) For all i and all j, let α_i (resp. $\beta_{i,j}$, resp. γ) be a permutation of E chosen at random and known by $-i$ (i.e., $\mathbf{I} - \{i\}$) (resp. $\{i, j\}$, resp. $\{\text{I}, \text{II}\}$). Let also f be chosen at random in E and known by $\{\text{III}, \text{IV}\}$.

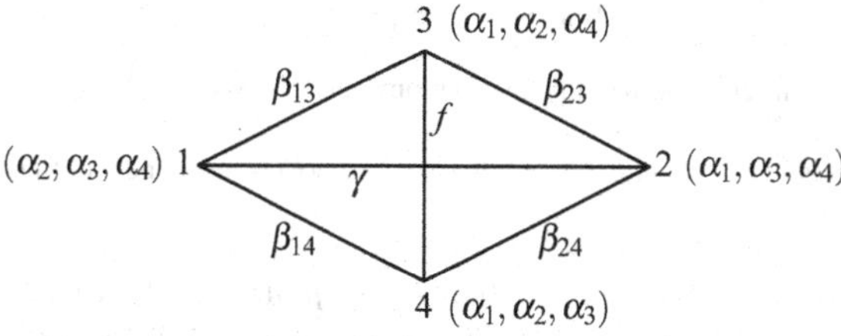

Figure II.8. The protocol.

At stage 1, I is informed of the following messages: $\beta_{\mathrm{II,III}} \circ \alpha_{\mathrm{I}}$ and $\beta_{\mathrm{II,IV}} \circ \alpha_{\mathrm{I}}$ from II, $\beta_{\mathrm{II,III}} \circ \alpha_{\mathrm{I}}$ from III, $\beta_{\mathrm{II,IV}} \circ \alpha_{\mathrm{I}}$ from IV. A similar procedure is applied to each player $i = \mathrm{II, III, IV}$.

At stage 2, III receives $\beta_{\mathrm{I,IV}} \circ \gamma$ from I and $\beta_{\mathrm{II,IV}} \circ \gamma$ from II (and symmetrically for IV).

At stage 3, I receives $\beta_{\mathrm{II,IV}} \circ \gamma(f)$ from III and $\beta_{\mathrm{II,III}} \circ \gamma(f)$ from IV (and dually for II).

At stage 4, I receives $\mathsf{Proj}_{\mathrm{I}} \circ \beta^{-1}_{\mathrm{II,III}}$ from II and III, II gets $\mathsf{Proj}_{\mathrm{II}} \circ \beta^{-1}_{\mathrm{I,IV}}$ from I and IV, III obtains $\mathsf{Proj}_{\mathrm{III}} \circ \beta^{-1}_{\mathrm{II,IV}}$ from II and IV, and IV is told $\mathsf{Proj}_{\mathrm{IV}} \circ \beta^{-1}_{\mathrm{I,II}}$ by I and II. The chosen point is $e = \gamma(f)$. Note that each player i knows $\mathsf{Proj}_i(e)$ and that at each stage the players can check detectable deviations (i.e., false messages). Show that the above procedure answers the question.

b. Deduce that in any game with *at least four players* and rational payoffs any correlated equilibrium distribution can be realized as a Nash equilibrium in the game extended by finite pre-play communication with a recording (i.e., each player has a move (STOP) that reveals all past events).

8. Communication equilibria and correlated equilibria in games of information transmission. (Forges, 1985)

Let G be a two-person game with incomplete information (cf. Section III.4, p. 153), with (finite) type set K for player I and (finite) action set S for player II. The type sets of player II and the action sets of player I are assumed to be singletons. The game G_M obtained by allowing player I to send a message in M to player II after the choice of nature is thus a "game of information transmission." Let q be a canonical communication equilibrium of G (described by a transition probability q from K to S).

There exists a correlated equilibrium of G_M (associated with a finite set M) that induces the same conditional distributions on S (given $k \in K$) as q.

HINT.

(1) Let P be the product probability distribution induced by q on S^K:

$$P(f) = \prod_k q(f(k) \mid k).$$

Let M_0 be a copy of $K \times A$. We first define a correlation device for G_{M_0}, which transmits $\sigma_0 \in M_0^K$ to player I and $\tau_0 \in S^{M_0}$ to player II. The device selects a permutation π_0 of M_0, uniformly and independently of f. Then let:

$$\begin{cases} \tilde{f}(k) &= (k, f(k)),\ k \in K, \\ \sigma_0 &= \pi_0 \circ \tilde{f}, \\ \tau_0 &= \mathsf{Proj}_S \circ \pi_0^{-1}. \end{cases}$$

Let Q_0 be the induced probability distribution over $K \times M_0^K \times S^{M_0}$. Q has the following properties:

(a) $\tau_0 \circ \sigma_0$ is independent of σ_0 and of τ_0; $\tau_0 \circ \sigma_0)(k)$ is independent of $(\tau_0 \circ \sigma_0)(\ell)$ if $k \neq \ell$.

(b) $Q_0((\tau_0 \circ \sigma_0)(k) = s) = q(s \mid k)\ \forall k \in K, \forall s \in S$.

(c) $Q_0(k \mid \sigma_0(k) = m, \tau_0) = p^k q(\tau_0(m) \mid k) / \sum_\ell p^\ell q(\tau_0(m) \mid \ell)$; i.e., the posterior probability distributions over K derived from the communication equilibrium and from the present scheme are the same.

(d) $Q_0(\tau_0(m) = s \mid \sigma_0) = q(s \mid k)$ if $m = \sigma(k)$, $k \in K$.

(2) The previous scheme can be completed so as to deter player I from sending $m \notin \sigma(K)$. Let M be a finite set (of at least $\#\{K \times A\}$ elements). Let the correlation device choose M_0 uniformly in M and $s \in S$ according to some $\rho \in \Delta(S)$, independently of all previous choices. Define $\sigma \in M^K$ by $\sigma(k) = \sigma_0(k)\ \forall k \in K$ and $\tau \in S^M$ by:

$$\begin{aligned} \tau(m) &= \tau_0(m) && \text{if } m \in M_0, \\ &= s && \text{if } m \notin M_0. \end{aligned}$$

The correlation device only transmits σ (resp. τ) to player I (resp. II). In particular, player I does not know M_0. Let Q denote the induced probability over $K \times M^K \times S^M$. Then:

- properties 1a–1d still hold with Q, σ, τ instead of Q_0, σ_0, τ_0
- π and the size of M can be chosen so that $Q(\tau(m) = s \mid \sigma) = \frac{1}{\#K} \sum_k q(s \mid k)$ if $m \notin \sigma(K)$: let $\rho(s) = \frac{1}{\#M - \#M_0}\left[\frac{\#M}{\#K} \sum_k q(s \mid k) - \#K\right]$ with $\#M \geq \max_s\left[\frac{\#K^2}{\sum_k q(s)k)}\right]$.

9. Universal mechanisms and communication equilibria. (Forges, 1992)

The previous result can be generalized to an $\#\mathbf{I}$-person game G with incomplete information ($\#\mathbf{I} \geq 4$). Let K^i (resp. S^i) be player i's finite set of types (resp. actions).

a. Let q be a canonical communication equilibrium in G (described by a transition probability from $K = \prod_i K^i$ to $S = \prod_i S^i$). Let us extend G by two stages of pre-play communication after the choice of nature:

> **Stage 1:** Every player i sends a public message in a copy L^i of K^i (let $L = \prod_i L^i$).
>
> **Stage 2:** Every player i sends a message in $M^j = L \times S^j$ to every player j in $\mathbf{I}^i = \{i+1, i+2, i+3\}$ (mod $\mathbf{I}$).

The correlation device first selects uniformly, independently of each other, the bijections $\gamma^i : L^i \to K^i$ ($i \in \mathbf{I}$) and, independently of this choice, $f \in S^K$ according to the probability distribution induced by q (cf. II.3, Ex. 8). Let $\gamma = (\gamma^i)_{i \in \mathbf{I}}$, let g be defined by $g \circ \gamma = f$, and let $g^i = \mathsf{Proj}_i \circ g$ (where Proj_i is the projection on S^i).

Given $g^i \in (S^i)^L$, the device chooses $\sigma^{ij} \in (M^j)^L$ and $\tau^i \in (A^i)^{M^i}$ ($i \in \mathbf{I}$, $j \in \mathbf{I}^i$) exactly as (σ_0, τ_0) were chosen, given f, in II.3, Ex. 8. The strategy for i, after receiving $(\gamma^i, \sigma^{ij}, \tau^i)$ (and k^i), is to announce $\gamma^i(k^i)$, and then to send $\sigma^{ij}(\ell)$ to $j \in \mathbf{I}^i$ if ℓ is the message at stage one. Finally, if at least two messages received by i coincide, say, to m^i, he plays $\tau^i(m^i)$.

Check that the above mechanism is in fact an equilibrium.

HINT. Note that the information during the pre-play communication phase is non-revealing, and that given $\tau^i(m^i) = s^i$ it is the same as in the initial communication scheme. Moreover, announcing $\overline{\ell}^i \neq \gamma^i(k^i)$ and playing $\overline{s}^i \neq s^i$ is the same as using $\overline{k}^i = (\gamma^i)^{-1}(\overline{\ell}^i)$ and $\overline{s}^i$ in the communication scheme.

Remark II.3.16. The above mechanism is universal (i.e., independent of the game G) and does not require recording (compare with the previous II.3, Ex. 7).

Remark II.3.17. Three players suffice if an alarm is allowed or messages in $[0, 1]$ can be used. (Inform player j of a code (in $[0, 1]$) on $L \times M^j$ while i knows only its restriction to the graph of σ^{ij}, $j \in \mathbf{I}_i$.)

b. Deduce that if the payoffs are rational in G, any communication equilibrium distribution can be obtained as a Nash equilibrium of the game extended by pre-play communication (after chance's move).

II.4. VECTOR PAYOFFS

In this section, we consider an analogue due to Blackwell (1956a) of the minmax theorem for matrix games with vector payoffs. Let (S, Σ) and $(T, \mathscr{T})$ be two measurable spaces, and ϕ a measurable mapping from $(S, \Sigma) \times (T, \mathscr{T})$ into the set of all probability distributions on Euclidian space $\mathbb{R}^k$ having finite first-order moments. At any stage n ($n = 1, \dots$), player I chooses a point s_n in S and II chooses simultaneously a point t_n in T; a point x_n in $\mathbb{R}^k$ is then chosen at random according to the distribution $\phi(s_n, t_n)$, independently of all other choices.

Both players may get, at every stage, some information, which, for I, includes at least x_n (and all x_i, $i \le n$). Let $\overline{x}_n = \frac{1}{n}\sum_1^n x_i$.

Definition II.4.1. A set C in $\mathbb{R}^k$ is **approachable** for a player if he has a strategy σ such that, for each $\varepsilon > 0$, there exists an integer N such that, for every strategy τ of his opponent,

$$\mathsf{Pr}_{\sigma,\tau}(\sup_{n\ge N} \delta_n \le \varepsilon) \ge 1 - \varepsilon \quad \text{and} \quad \sup_{n\ge N} \mathsf{E}_{\sigma\tau}(\delta_n) \le \varepsilon,$$

where $\delta_n = d(\overline{x}_n, C)$.

Definition II.4.2. A set C in $\mathbb{R}^k$ is **excludable** for a player if, for some $\varepsilon > 0$, the set $\overline{C}^{\varepsilon}$ is approachable for that player, where $\overline{C}^{\varepsilon} = \{x \mid d(x, C) \ge \varepsilon\}$.

Remark II.4.3. A set C is approachable iff its closure $\overline{C}$ is approachable.

Denote by $f(s, t)$ the barycenter (mean value) of $\phi(s, t)$, and assume that the $\phi(s, t)$ have second-order moments uniformly bounded by K. Denote also by P (resp. Q) the set of one-stage mixed strategies of I (resp. II) (i.e., probabilities on (S, Σ), resp. $(T, \mathscr{T})$). For any $p \in P$, denote by $R(p)$ the convex hull of $\{\int_S f(s, t)\,dp \mid t \in T\}$.

Theorem II.4.1. *Let C be any closed set in $\mathbb{R}^k$. Assume that, for every $x \notin C$, there is a p $(= p(x)) \in P$ such that the hyperplane through $y(x)$ (a closest point in C to x) and perpendicular to the line segment (x, y) separates x from $R(p)$. Then C is approachable by* I *with the strategy $f = (f_n)_{n\in\mathbb{N}}$, where:*

$$f_{n+1} = \begin{cases} p(\overline{x}_n) & \text{if } n > 0 \text{ and } \overline{x}_n \notin C, \\ \text{arbitrary} & \text{otherwise.} \end{cases}$$

With that strategy, one has:

$$\mathsf{E}(\delta_n^2) \le 4K/n \quad \text{and} \quad \mathsf{Pr}(\sup_{n\ge N} \delta_n \ge \varepsilon) \le 8K/\varepsilon^2 N.$$

Proof. Assume I uses the above-described strategy. Let $y_n = y(\overline{x}_n)$ and $u_n = \overline{x}_n - y_n$. The definition of f implies that (note that $u_n = 0$ if $\overline{x}_n \in C$):

$$\mathsf{E}(\langle u_n, x_{n+1}\rangle \mid x_1, \ldots, x_n) \leq \langle u_n, y_n\rangle \; ; \qquad \text{and} \tag{1}$$

$$\delta_{n+1}^2 \leq \|\overline{x}_{n+1} - y_n\|^2 = \|\overline{x}_n - y_n\|^2 + 2\langle \overline{x}_n - y_n, \overline{x}_{n+1} - \overline{x}_n\rangle + \|\overline{x}_{n+1} - \overline{x}_n\|^2 . \tag{2}$$

Inserting

$$\overline{x}_{n+1} - \overline{x}_n = (x_{n+1} - \overline{x}_n)/(n+1) = ((x_{n+1} - y_n) - (\overline{x}_n - y_n))/(n+1) ,$$

into (2), taking conditional expectations there, and using (1), we get

$$\mathsf{E}(\delta_{n+1}^2 \mid \mathscr{F}_n) \leq (1 - 2/(n+1))\, \delta_n^2 + w_n/(n+1)^2, \tag{3}$$

with $\mathscr{F}_n$ the σ-field spanned by $x_1, \ldots, x_n$, and $w_n = \mathsf{E}(\|x_{n+1} - \overline{x}_n\|^2 \mid \mathscr{F}_n)$. Note that

$$\mathsf{E}(w_n) \leq 2\,\mathsf{E}\,\|x_{n+1}\|^2 + 2\,\mathsf{E}\,\|\overline{x}_n\|^2 \leq 4K.$$

We claim that, for any sequence of random variables satisfying (3), where $w_n \geq 0$ and δ_n are $\mathscr{F}_n$-measurable and where $\mathsf{E}(w_n) \leq 4K$, one has:

$$\mathsf{E}(\delta_n^2) \leq \frac{4K}{n} \quad \text{and} \quad \mathsf{Pr}(\sup_{n\geq N} \delta_n \geq \varepsilon) \leq \frac{8K}{\varepsilon^2 N}.$$

Let first $e_n = \mathsf{E}(\delta_n^2/4K))$; from (3), $e_n \leq (1 - 2/n)e_{n-1} + 1/n^2$. It is readily checked that this implies, by induction for $n \geq 2$, that $e_n \leq 1/n$ (which, by the way, obviously holds for $n = 1$). So $\mathsf{E}(\delta_n^2) \leq 4K/n$. This implies in particular that δ_n converges in probability to zero. To show that it converges to zero with probability one, let $Z_n = \delta_n^2 + \mathsf{E}\left(\sum_n^\infty w_i/(i+1)^2 \mid \mathscr{F}_n\right)$. Replacing, in (3), $(1 - 2/(n+1))$ by 1, one sees that (3) implies $\mathsf{E}(Z_{n+1} \mid \mathscr{F}_n) \leq Z_n$; thus Z_n is a positive supermartingale, and

$$\mathsf{E}(Z_n) \leq \mathsf{E}(\delta_n^2) + 4K \sum_{n+1}^{\infty} 1/i^2 \leq 4K/n + 4K/n = 8K/n.$$

The supermartingale convergence theorem implies then that Z_n goes to zero with probability one, and a fortiori δ_n, since $0 \leq \delta_n^2 \leq Z_n$. More precisely, we get from Doob's maximal inequality for supermartingales (Neveu, 1970, Proposition IV.5.2) that

$$\mathsf{Pr}(\exists n \geq N : Z_n \geq \varepsilon) \leq \mathsf{E}(Z_N)/\varepsilon \leq \frac{8K}{\varepsilon N} ,$$

and thus the result follows. ■

Remark II.4.4. The approaching player has to know only $\overline{x}_n$ and not $x_1, \ldots, x_n$, at stage n.

Remark II.4.5. Theorem II.4.1 obviously remains true under the condition that, for any $x \notin C$, there is a sequence $p_i \in P$ such that:

$$\lim_{i\to\infty} \sup_{z\in R(p_i)} \langle z - y(x), x - y(x)\rangle \leq 0$$

(choosing, at stage n, a p_i such that this supremum is $\leq \delta/n^2$, where δ is some small positive number, and increasing K by δ).

Corollary II.4.2. *For any $p \in P$, $R(p)$ is approachable by* I *using the constant strategy $f_n = p$.*

For any $q \in Q$, denote by $T(q)$ the closed convex hull of $\{\int_T f(s,t)\,dq \mid s \in S\}$.

Theorem II.4.3. *Let C be a closed convex set in $\mathbb{R}^k$, and assume that the game with payoff function $\langle u, f(s,t)\rangle$ has a value $v(u)$ for all u in $\mathbb{R}^k$ such that $\inf_{x\in C}\langle u, x\rangle > -\infty$. Then:*

(1) *C is approachable by* I *iff, for all $q \in Q$, $T(q) \cap C \neq \phi$.*
(2) *If $T(q_0) \cap C = \phi$, then C is excludable by* II *(using the constant strategy q_0).*
(3) *The condition of Remark II.4.5 above is necessary and sufficient for approachability of C.*

Proof. The second statement follows right away from the previous corollary. There remains only to show that, if the condition of Remark II.4.5 is not satisfied, there exists a q_0 such that $T(q_0) \cap C = \phi$. Let $x_0 \notin C$ be such that the condition fails, and let $u = y(x_0) - x_0$. Then there exists $\varepsilon > 0$ such that, for each $p \in P$, $\inf_{x\in R(p)}\langle u, x\rangle < \min_{x\in C}\langle u, x\rangle - \varepsilon = M$. Thus $v(u) \leq M$ and therefore there exists $q_0 \in Q$ such that $\max_{x\in T(q_0)}\langle u, x\rangle \leq M + \varepsilon/2 = \min_{x\in C}\langle u, x\rangle - \varepsilon/2$. The result follows. ■

Remark II.4.6. The conditions for the existence of a value will be automatically satisfied, for instance, if S and T are compact and $f(s,t)$ is continuous in each variable (cf. remark after Theorem I.2.4, p. 21). If, for example, the u's such that $\inf_{x\in C}\langle u, x\rangle > -\infty$ have non-negative coordinates, one may even use Proposition I.2.2, p. 18, or Proposition I.2.5, p. 22, to establish the existence of a value.

Remark II.4.7. Theorem II.4.3 implies that any convex set is either approachable or excludable. This is analogous to the usual minmax theorem which in effect states the same thing for sets of the form $[a, +\infty[$ or $]-\infty, a]$ in $\mathbb{R}^1$.

Corollary II.4.4. *Under the hypotheses of Theorem II.4.3, a convex set C is approachable iff, for all u:*

$$v(u) \geq \inf_{x\in C}\langle u, x\rangle.$$

Even without those hypotheses, this condition is, for convex C, equivalent to the sufficient condition of approachability (Theorem II.4.1, p. 118) if $v(u)$ stands *for the* sup inf *value of the game, and its negation is equivalent to a sufficient condition for excludability if $v(u)$ stands for the* inf sup *value of the game.*

EXERCISES

1. (Blackwell, 1956a)

Assume that $f(s, t)$ is continuous in each variable, and that S and T are compact; then any closed set in $\mathbb{R}^1$ is either approachable or excludable.

HINT. Let v and v' be the values of the games with payoff functions $f(s, t)$ and $f(t, s)$, respectively. Prove that a closed set C is approachable iff $[v', v] \cap C \neq \phi$ in the case where $v' \leq v$ and $[v, v'] \subseteq C$ in the case where $v \leq v'$, and that C is excludable otherwise: in $\mathbb{R}$, any closed set is either approachable or excludable.

2. (Blackwell, 1956a)

In $\mathbb{R}^2$, there are sets that are neither approachable nor excludable.

HINT. Consider $A = \begin{pmatrix} (0,0) & (0,0) \\ (1,0) & (1,1) \end{pmatrix}$ and the set $C = \{(1/2, x_2) \mid 0 \leq x_2 \leq 1/4\} \cup \{(1, x_2) \mid 1/4 \leq x_2 \leq 1\}$.

(1) To show that C is not excludable, consider the strategy of I of playing row 2 for n stages and continuing for the next n stages with either row 1 or row 2 according to whether $(1/n)\sum_1^n x_2(i)$ is smaller or larger than $1/2$ (show that $\overline{x}(2n) \in C$).

(2) To show that C is not approachable, observe that II may play, at each stage i, column 1 or 2 according to whether $\overline{x}_1(i)$ is larger or smaller than $3/4$.

(3) Define a set to be weakly approachable (by I) if for each $\varepsilon > 0$, there exists an integer N and for all $n \geq N$ a strategy σ_n of I such that for all τ of II: $P_{\sigma_n,\tau}(\delta_n \leq \varepsilon) \geq 1 - \varepsilon$ and $\mathsf{E}_{\sigma_n,\tau}(\delta_n) \leq \varepsilon$. Prove that if a closed set D intersects the graph of any increasing function f from $[0, 1]$ to $[0, 1]$ with $f(x) - f(y) \leq x - y$, it is weakly approachable by I, and that otherwise the closure of its complement is weakly approachable by II.

3. Assume S and T are finite. Show that Theorem II.4.1, p. 118, remains valid if the $\phi(t)$ have only finite moments of order 1.

HINT. Use a truncation method.

4. A strong law of large numbers for martingales

Assume that $f(s, t) = 0$. Then any strategy pair approaches $\{0\}$. (Thus, if X_n is a martingale with $\mathsf{E}[(X_{n+1} - X_n)^2 \mid \mathscr{F}_n] \leq K$, then $X_n/n \to 0$ a.s.)

HINT. Let II choose both s and t and apply Theorem II.4.1, p. 118, or II.4, Ex. 3, if S and T are finite.

5. The same theorems hold if I, instead of being informed at each stage of x_n, is informed of $f(s_n, t_n)$, for instance, he is informed of the moves of both players in the extensive form.

HINT. Let I use the same strategy, with $f(s_n, t_n)$ replacing x_n, and use II.4, Ex. 4.

6. Under the assumptions of Theorem II.4.1, p. 118, $\mathsf{E}\left(\sup_{n \geq N} \delta_n\right) \leq 4\sqrt{2K/N}$.

HINT. Only the last inequality of the theorem is needed.

7. Bayes strategies. (Hannan, 1957; Blackwell, 1956b, cf. also Luce and Raiffa, 1957, App. A.8.6)

Let S and T be finite, $k = 1$, and let I be informed, after every stage, of II's pure strategy choice. If f_n denotes the frequency used by II in the first n stages, and if $\phi(q)$ denotes, for any probability q on T, the quantity $\max_s \int_t f(s,t)\,dq$, then define I's regret r_n at stage n to be the difference between $\phi(f_n)$ and his average actual payoff up to stage n. Then, I has a strategy in the infinitely repeated game such that, for any strategy of II, r_n goes to zero, more precisely, r_n is of the order of $1/\sqrt{n}$.

HINT. Take the actual payoff as first coordinate of a vector payoff, having $\#T$ additional coordinates that count the number of times every column is used.

8. (Mertens, 1980)

Consider a game in normal form. For any $T \subseteq \mathbf{I}$, let:

$$v_\alpha(T) = \left\{x \in \mathbb{R}^T \mid \exists \sigma \in \left(\prod_{i\in T} S_i\right) : \forall \tau \in \left(\prod_{i\notin T} S_i\right), \forall i \in T \int_{\prod_i S_i} F_i(s)\,d\sigma\,d\tau \geq x_i\right\},$$

$$v_\beta(T) = \left\{x \in \mathbb{R}^T \mid \forall \tau \in \left(\prod_{i\notin T} S_i\right), \exists \sigma \in \left(\prod_{i\in T} S_i\right) : \forall i \in T \int_{\prod_i S_i} F_i(s)\,d\sigma\,d\tau \geq x_i\right\}.$$

a. Show that always $v_\alpha \subseteq v_\beta$.

b. For any $\lambda \in \mathbb{R}^{\mathbf{I}}$, $\lambda \geq 0$, let $v_\lambda(T)$ be the value of the two-person zero-sum game having as players T and T^c and, as payoff function, $\sum_{i\in T} \lambda_i F_i$. Show that:

$$v_\beta(T) = \{x \in \mathbb{R}^T \mid \forall \lambda \in \mathbb{R}^{\mathbf{I}}, \lambda \geq 0 \ \sum_{i\in T} \lambda_i x_i \leq v_\lambda(T)\}.$$

c. Give an example where $v_\alpha \neq v_\beta$.

d. Consider the repeated game, where, after every stage, any coalition T is informed of the payoffs accruing to its members in that stage. Denote by v_α^n, v_β^n the corresponding "characteristic functions" v_α and v_β when the game is repeated n times, with the average payoff as payoff function, and similarly for v_α^∞ and v_β^∞. Show that $v_\beta^n = v_\beta^\infty = v_\alpha^\infty \supseteq v_\alpha^n$.

e. *Superadditivity.* (Aumann, 1961b)

Deduce from II.4, Ex. 8d, that, for any game, $v_\alpha(T)$ and $v_\beta(T)$ are convex and, if $T_1 \cap T_2 = \phi$, then

$$v_\alpha(T_1) \times v_\alpha(T_2) \subseteq v_\alpha(T_1 \cup T_2), \text{ and } v_\beta(T_1) \times v_\beta(T_2) \subseteq v_\beta(T_1 \cup T_2).$$

CHAPTER III

The Belief Space

In this chapter we give a formal treatment to the basic concepts of models with incomplete information, namely, beliefs, types, consistency of beliefs, common knowledge, etc. Given a parameter space K, we first construct the Universal Belief Space Ω. A point ω in Ω, which we call a state of the world, consists of (in addition to the value of the parameters) the specification of the "state of mind" of each of the players (i.e., the probabilities generated by beliefs on K, beliefs on these beliefs, and so on). We study the mathematical structure and properties of Ω, introducing the notion of belief subspace, which is closely related to the concept of common knowledge. We next define the concept of consistent beliefs as beliefs that can be derived as conditional probabilities from some common prior distribution, given each player's private information. We characterize the consistent states of the world (i.e., states of the world in which the players' beliefs are consistent). An approximation theorem is then presented stating roughly that any incomplete information situation can be approximated by one in which there are finitely many potential types of each player. In the last section we discuss models and strategic equilibria of games with incomplete information, based on the structure of the beliefs space developed in this chapter.

III.1. THE UNIVERSAL BELIEF SPACE

When considering a situation involving a finite player set **I** facing some uncertainty about a space K (which we refer to as the space of **states of nature**), one is naturally led to handle **infinite hierarchies of beliefs**: adopting a Bayesian approach, each player will base his decision on some subjective beliefs (i.e., probability measure) on K. Since the outcome is determined not only by the player's own actions but the other players' actions as well, and those are influenced by their beliefs on K, each player must also have beliefs on other players' beliefs on K. By the same argument he must have beliefs on other players' beliefs on his own beliefs on K, beliefs on other players' beliefs on his beliefs on their beliefs on K, etc. Thus it seems unavoidable to have an infinite hierarchy of beliefs for each player. These hierarchies are linked together by the fact that each belief of a player is also the subject of beliefs for the other players. The object of this section is to construct the space of these hierarchies.

III.1.a. States of the World and Types

Theorem III.1.1.

(1) *Given a Hausdorff space K and a player set* **I** *there exists a Hausdorff space $\Theta(K)$ and a homeomorphism δ_K from $\Theta(K)$ to $\Delta(K \times [\Theta(K)]^{\#\mathbf{I}-1})$ such that, letting Θ^i ($i \in \mathbf{I}$) denote a copy (cf. (4)) of $\Theta(K)$ and $\delta^i : \Theta^i \to \Delta(K \times \prod_{j \neq i} \Theta^j)$ the corresponding copy (cf. (4)) of δ_K, the following property holds:*

(P): Given topological spaces $(\Sigma^i)_{i \in \mathbf{I}}$ and $\tilde{K}$, and continuous maps σ^i from Σ^i to $\Delta(\tilde{K} \times \prod_{j \neq i} \Sigma^j)$ and $f : \tilde{K} \to K$, there exists a unique **I**-tuple *of (say, universally measurable) maps $\Theta^i(f)$ from Σ^i to Θ^i such that the following diagrams ($i \in \mathbf{I}$) commute, and those $\Theta^i(f)$ are continuous:*

$$
\begin{array}{ccc}
\Sigma^i & \xrightarrow{\ \sigma^i\ } & \Delta(\tilde{K} \times \prod_{j \neq i} \Sigma^j) \\
\Big\downarrow {\scriptstyle \Theta^i(f)} & & \Big\downarrow {\scriptstyle f} \qquad \Big\downarrow {\scriptstyle \Theta^j(f)} \\
\Theta^i & \xrightarrow{\ \delta^i\ } & \Delta(K \times \prod_{j \neq i} \Theta^j)
\end{array}
$$

(2) *Property (P) characterizes the spaces $\Theta(K)$ and maps δ_K: if satisfied by topological spaces $\tilde{\Theta}^i$ and continuous maps $\tilde{\delta}^i$, including that the right-hand arrow maps regular measures to regular measures (even just when the Σ^i are assumed Hausdorff, the σ^i and f homeomorphisms, and uniqueness is used only within the category of continuous maps), then the $\Theta^i(id_K)$: $\tilde{\Theta}^i \to \Theta^i$ are canonical homeomorphisms.*

(3) *Let $|\Theta^i_{-1}| = 1$, and define inductively maps p^i_n, q^i_n and spaces Θ^i_n by the commutativity of the following diagram (all $i \in \mathbf{I}$, and $n \geq -1$, but using the lower part of the diagram only for $n \geq 0$):*

$$
\begin{array}{ccc}
\Theta^i & \xrightarrow{\ \delta^i\ } & \Delta(K \times \prod_{j \neq i} \Theta^j\ ) \\
\Big\downarrow {\scriptstyle p^i_{n+1}} & & \Big\downarrow {\scriptstyle id_K} \qquad \Big\downarrow {\scriptstyle p^j_n} \\
\Theta^i_{n+1} & = & \Delta(K \times \prod_{j \neq i} \Theta^j_n\ ) \\
\Big\downarrow {\scriptstyle q^i_{n+1}} & & \Big\downarrow {\scriptstyle id_K} \qquad \Big\downarrow {\scriptstyle q^j_n} \\
\Theta^i_n & = & \Delta(K \times \prod_{j \neq i} \Theta^j_{n-1})
\end{array}
$$

Then the (Θ^i_n, q^i_n) form a projective system with limit Θ^i and $q^i_n \circ p^i_n = p^i_{n-1}$. Further the maps p^i_n are onto and have continuous selections r^i_n (i.e., $p^i_n \circ r^i_n = id_{\Theta^i_n}$). Defining inductively s^i_n by the commutative diagrams ($n \geq 0$, s^i_0 arbitrary):

$$\begin{array}{ccc} \Theta^i_{n+1} & = & \Delta(K \times \prod_{j\neq i} \Theta^j_n) \\ \uparrow{\scriptstyle s^i_{n+1}} & & \uparrow{\scriptstyle id_K} \qquad \uparrow{\scriptstyle s^j_n} \\ \Theta^i_n & = & \Delta(K \times \prod_{j\neq i} \Theta^j_{n-1}) \end{array},$$

one gets inductively $q^i_n \circ s^i_n = id_{\Theta^i_{n-1}}$, and one can then define r^i_n as the projective limit (i.e., $r^i_{n-1} = r^i_n \circ s^i_n$).

(4) *The "copies" in 1 are in the following sense: given bijections $\varphi_i : \{i\}^c \to \#\mathbf{I} - 1$, there exists a unique system of homeomorphisms $h_i : \Theta(K) \to \Theta^i$ such that the following diagrams:*

$$\begin{array}{ccc} \Theta(K) & \xrightarrow{\delta_K} & \Delta(K \times [\Theta(K)]^{\#\mathbf{I}-1}) \\ \downarrow{\scriptstyle h_i} & & \downarrow{\scriptstyle id_K} \qquad \downarrow{\scriptstyle \psi_i} \\ \Theta^i & \xrightarrow{\delta_i} & \Delta(K \times \prod_{j\neq i} \Theta^j) \end{array}$$

commute with $\psi_i(\theta_1, \ldots, \theta_{\#\mathbf{I}-1}) = (h_j(\theta_{\varphi_i(j)}))_{j\neq i}$, where the top line of the diagram is constructed by a projective limit as in part (3).

Proof. Recall that the space $\Delta(X)$ of regular probability measures with the weak* topology is Hausdorff if X is Hausdorff (Proposition I.1.4, p. 7), and that a product of Hausdorff spaces is also Hausdorff. One defines thus inductively a projective system of Hausdorff spaces Θ^i_n and continuous projections q^i_n by the lower part of the first diagram in (3), using part (1) of Proposition I.1.8, p. 8, to show that the maps are well defined and continuous. This defines a Hausdorff limit Θ^i, together with projections p^i_n to Θ^i_n. Hence the diagonal maps in the upper part of that diagram associate with every $\theta \in \Theta^i$ a projective system of regular probabilities on the spaces $X^i_n = K \times \prod_{j\neq i} \Theta^j_n$, and hence (by part (2) of Proposition I.1.8, p. 8), a regular probability $\delta^i(\theta)$ on the projective limit $X^i = K \times \prod_{j\neq i} \Theta^j$, such that the upper part of the diagram also commutes. To show the continuity of δ^i, observe that the topology on $\Delta(X^i)$ is the weakest topology for which the integrals of bounded l.s.c. functions f are l.s.c. Adding a constant, we can assume $f \geq 0$, and hence that f is the limit of an increasing sequence of positive linear combinations of indicators of open sets, which can further be approximated from inside by a finite union of basic open sets. Those are of the form $\{x \mid x_\ell \in U_\ell, \forall \ell \leq \ell_0\}$ with U_ℓ open in X^i_ℓ. By continuity of the projection maps from $X^i_{\ell_0}$ to X^i_ℓ, it suffices to take $\{x \mid x_{\ell_0} \in U_{\ell_0}\}$ as basic open sets. By the same argument, finite unions of such sets are again of this form. The result follows then from the definition of the topology on $\Delta(X^i_{\ell_0})$ and from the continuity of $p^i_{\ell_0+1}$.

To establish that δ^i is a homeomorphism, consider the map $g\colon \Delta(X^i) \to \Theta^i$: $g\colon \mu \mapsto [\mu \circ (\psi^i_n)^{-1}]_{n\geq 0}$, where $\psi^i_n\colon X^i \to X^i_n$ is the natural projection from X^i to X^i_n. The map g is well defined and continuous to $\prod_n \Delta(X^i_n) = \prod_n \Theta^i_n$ (by part (1) of Proposition I.1.8, p. 8). And commutativity of the diagram in (3) yields that $q^i_{n+1}([g(\mu)]_{n+1}) = [g(\mu)]_n$, so $g(\mu) \in \Theta^i$. There remains thus only to show that δ^i and g are inverse to each other: $g \circ \delta^i$ being the identity is obvious from the definitions, while for $\delta^i \circ g$: let $\theta = g(\mu)$ (i.e., $\theta_n = \mu \circ (\psi^i_n)^{-1}$), $\overline{\mu} = \delta^i(\theta)$. Then, by definition of δ^i, $\overline{\mu}$ is the only point in $\Delta(X^i)$ with $\overline{\mu} \circ (\psi^i_n)^{-1} = \theta_n$ $\forall n$. But μ is another such point, so $\mu = \overline{\mu}$: $\delta^i \circ g = id_{\Delta(X^i)}$.

We have constructed our spaces Θ^i and homeomorphisms δ^i, such that the first part of (3) holds, and the remaining part (from "Further ..." on) is now obvious, as well as (4). So there only remains to establish property (P), and then to prove part (2).

Define thus continuous maps φ^j_n inductively by the commutativity of the diagrams ($n \geq 0$) (using part (1) of Proposition I.1.8, p. 8):

$$\begin{array}{ccc}
\Sigma^i & \xrightarrow{\sigma^i} & \Delta(\tilde{K} \times \prod_{j\neq i} \Sigma^j\ ) \\
\downarrow \varphi^i_n & & \downarrow f \qquad \downarrow \varphi^j_{n-1} \\
\Theta^i_n & = & \Delta(K \times \prod_{j\neq i} \Theta^j_{n-1})
\end{array}$$

$q^i_n \circ \varphi^i_n = \varphi^i_{n-1}$ also follows inductively, so $(\varphi^i_n)_{n\geq -1} = \varphi^i = \Theta^i(f)\colon \Sigma^i \to \Theta^i$ is well defined and continuous. The required commutative diagram follows now by going to the limit in the above equalities. Finally, the uniqueness of $\Theta^i(f)$ follows by taking the composition of the diagram with the diagram in (3): by induction, all $p^i_n \circ (\Theta^i(f))$ are uniquely defined.

Part (2) is immediate: if φ^i and ψ^i denote, respectively, $\Theta^i(id_K)$ from $\tilde{\Theta}^i$ to Θ^i (using property (P) for the space Θ) and from Θ^i to $\tilde{\Theta}^i$ (using the property for $\tilde{\Theta}$), then $\varphi^i \circ \psi^i$ yields a commutative diagram:

$$\begin{array}{ccc}
\Theta^i & \xrightarrow{\delta^i} & \Delta(K \times \prod_{j\neq i} \Theta^j) \\
\downarrow \varphi^i\circ\psi^i & & \downarrow id_k \qquad \downarrow \varphi^j\circ\psi^j \\
\Theta^i & \xrightarrow{\delta^i} & \Delta(K \times \prod_{j\neq i} \Theta^j)
\end{array}$$

so $\varphi^i \circ \psi^i$ is the identity, by the uniqueness part of property (P), since the identity also makes the diagram commute. Similarly $\psi^i \circ \varphi^i$ is the identity, now using uniqueness for $\tilde{\Theta}^i$. So $\Theta^i(id_K)$ is a (canonical, uniqueness) homeomorphism. ■

Remark III.1.1. A reinterpretation of the result is the following: consider the category whose objects are systems $S = [(\Sigma^i, \delta^i)_{i\in\mathbf{I}}, K]$, where the Σ^i and K are topological spaces and $\delta^i : \Sigma^i \to \Delta(K \times \prod_{j\neq i} \Sigma^j)$ continuous maps, and where a morphism $\sigma : \tilde{S} \to S$ consists of continuous maps $\sigma^i : \tilde{\Sigma}^i \to \Sigma^i$ and $\overline{\sigma} : \tilde{K} \to K$ such that the following diagrams commute for all $i \in \mathbf{I}$:

$$\begin{array}{ccc} \tilde{\Sigma}^i & \xrightarrow{\tilde{\delta}^i} & \Delta(\tilde{K} \times \prod_{j\neq i} \tilde{\Sigma}^j) \\ \downarrow{\sigma^i} & & \downarrow{\overline{\sigma}} \quad \downarrow{\sigma^j} \\ \Sigma^i & \xrightarrow{\delta^i} & \Delta(K \times \prod_{j\neq i} \Sigma^j) \end{array}$$

which includes the requirement, if S is not Hausdorff, that the Borel measure $\mu \circ [\overline{\sigma} \times \prod_{j\neq i} \sigma^j]^{-1}$ is regular for every $\mu \in \Delta(\tilde{K} \times \prod_{j\neq i} \tilde{\Sigma}^j)$. The fact that this is a category is immediate. Then Θ is a covariant functor from the category of Hausdorff spaces and continuous maps to the category of systems. And the system Θ_K is characterized by the fact that, for any system $\tilde{S}$, any continuous map $\overline{\sigma} : \tilde{K} \to K$ extends to a unique morphism σ $(= [(\Theta^i(\overline{\sigma}))_{i\in\mathbf{I}}, \overline{\sigma}])$ from $\tilde{S}$ to Θ_K.

Remark III.1.2. In a similar vein, part (4) of the theorem leads us to study the functor Θ as a contravariant functor of player sets: a map $\varphi : \mathbf{I}_1 \to \mathbf{I}_2$ defines continuous maps $h_i : \Theta_2^{\varphi(i)} \to \Theta_1^i$ such that:

$$\begin{array}{ccc} \Theta_1^i & \xrightarrow{\delta_2^i} & \Delta(K \times \prod_{j\neq i} \Theta_1^j) \\ \uparrow{h_i} & & \uparrow{id_K} \quad \uparrow{\psi_i} \\ \Theta_2^{\varphi(i)} & \xrightarrow{(\delta_2^i, id_{\Theta_2}\varphi(i))} & \Delta(K \times \prod_{j\in\mathbf{I}_2} \Theta_2^j) \end{array}$$

commutes, with $\psi_i : (\theta_j)_{j\in\mathbf{I}_2} \mapsto [h_j(\theta_{\varphi(j)})]_{j\in\mathbf{I}_1\setminus\{i\}}$.

Theorem III.1.2.

(1) *If K is separable metric, compact, completely regular, K-analytic, K-Lusin, $\mathscr{Z}_{c\delta}$ in a compact, analytic, Lusin, Polish, quasi-Radon, τ-Radon, or countably Radon space, then so is $\Theta(K)$.*

(2) *In property (P), if the spaces Σ^i and $\tilde{K}$ are compact and non-empty, and the maps σ^i and f onto, then so is $\Theta^i(f)$.*

(3) (a) *If $f : K_1 \to K_2$ is one-to-one, or an inclusion (of a closed subset, of a $\mathscr{Z}$-subset, of a $\mathscr{Z}_{c\delta}$-subset), so is $\Theta(f) : \Theta(K_1) \to \Theta(K_2)$.*

(b) *If $K_1 \subseteq K_2$, then $\Theta(K_1) = \bigcap_n A_n$, with $A_{-1} = \Theta(K_2)$, and $A_{n+1} = \{\theta \in \Theta(K_2) \mid \delta(\theta)[K_1 \times (A_n)^{\#\mathbf{I}-1}] = 1\}$ (in the sense of inner measure, if necessary).*

(c) *If K_1 is K-analytic, and $f : K_1 \to K_2$ is onto, so is $\Theta(f)$.*

Remark III.1.3. For the definitions, cf. Appendix A.3, Appendix A.5, and Appendix A.9.

Proof. Part (1) follows from the fact that each of those categories of spaces is stable under countable products, closed subspaces, and the operation $X \to \Delta(X)$ (cf., e.g., Appendixes A.3.a, A.9.c, A.10.a, and A.10.b) and from Theorem III.1.1.3, p. 124.

For part (2): Assume first just that the spaces are K-analytic, and let $\overline{\Theta}^j = [\Theta^j(f)](\Sigma^j) \subseteq \Theta^j$: the $\overline{\Theta}^j$ are non-empty and K-analytic, δ^i maps $\overline{\Theta}^i$ into $\Delta(K \times \prod_{j\neq i} \overline{\Theta}^j) \subseteq \Delta(K \times \prod_{j\neq i} \Theta^j)$ (Appendix A.9.b.2), and the map is onto using Appendix A.9.b.3, hence it is a homeomorphism since δ^i itself is one (Theorem III.1.1, part (1), p. 124): we have reduced the problem to the case where f is the identity, the σ^i homeomorphisms, and the $\Theta^i(f)$ inclusions. It follows then, inductively using Appendix A.9.b.3 in the first diagram of Theorem III.1.1, part (3), p. 124, that $p^i_n(\overline{\Theta}^i) = \Theta^i_n$, which implies, in turn, by definition of the projective limit topology (Theorem III.1.1, part (3), p. 124), that $\overline{\Theta}^i$ is dense in Θ^i. Hence, in the compact case, $\overline{\Theta}_i$ is also compact, and being dense, equals Θ^i.

To prove part (3): Given $f\colon K_1 \to K_2$, observe from part (3) of Theorem III.1.1 that for inductively defined continuous maps φ^i_n, the following diagram commutes:

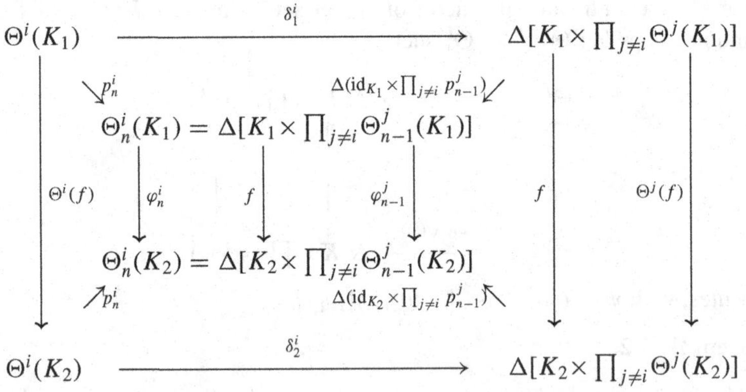

$$
\begin{array}{ccccc}
\Theta^i(K_1) & & \xrightarrow{\quad\delta^i_1\quad} & & \Delta[K_1\times \prod_{j\neq i}\Theta^j(K_1)] \\
 & \searrow^{p^i_n} & & \swarrow_{\Delta(\mathrm{id}_{K_1}\times\prod_{j\neq i} p^j_{n-1})} & \\
 & & \Theta^i_n(K_1) = \Delta[K_1\times \prod_{j\neq i}\Theta^j_{n-1}(K_1)] & & \\
\downarrow{\scriptstyle\Theta^i(f)} & & \downarrow{\scriptstyle\varphi^i_n} \qquad \downarrow{\scriptstyle f} \qquad \downarrow{\scriptstyle\varphi^j_{n-1}} & & \downarrow{\scriptstyle f} \qquad \downarrow{\scriptstyle\Theta^j(f)} \\
 & & \Theta^i_n(K_2) = \Delta[K_2\times \prod_{j\neq i}\Theta^j_{n-1}(K_2)] & & \\
 & \nearrow^{p^i_n} & & \nwarrow_{\Delta(\mathrm{id}_{K_2}\times\prod_{j\neq i} p^j_{n-1})} & \\
\Theta^i(K_2) & & \xrightarrow{\quad\delta^i_2\quad} & & \Delta[K_2\times \prod_{j\neq i}\Theta^j(K_2)]
\end{array}
$$

Indeed, induction in the central part of the diagram defines uniquely the (continuous) maps φ^i_n. By induction again, they yield commutativity of:

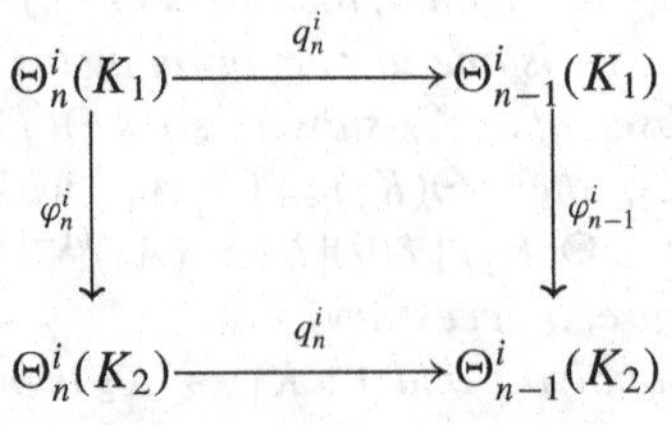

$$
\begin{array}{ccc}
\Theta^i_n(K_1) & \xrightarrow{\quad q^i_n\quad} & \Theta^i_{n-1}(K_1) \\
\downarrow{\scriptstyle\varphi^i_n} & & \downarrow{\scriptstyle\varphi^i_{n-1}} \\
\Theta^i_n(K_2) & \xrightarrow{\quad q^i_n\quad} & \Theta^i_{n-1}(K_2)
\end{array}
$$

Hence they define a unique, and continuous, map $\varphi^i : \Theta^i(K_1) \to \Theta^i(K_2)$ between the projective limits, such that $p^i_n \circ \varphi^i = \varphi^i_n \circ p^i_n$ for all n. So, using also part (3) of Theorem III.1.1, we get commutativity of:

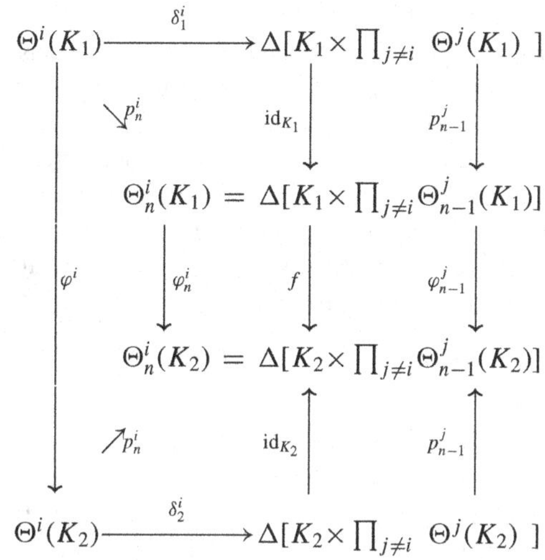

$$
\begin{array}{ccccc}
\Theta^i(K_1) & \xrightarrow{\delta^i_1} & \Delta[K_1 \times \prod_{j\neq i} & \Theta^j(K_1)\ ] \\
\Big\downarrow & \searrow p^i_n & \Big\downarrow \mathrm{id}_{K_1} & \Big\downarrow p^j_{n-1} \\
 & \Theta^i_n(K_1) = & \Delta[K_1 \times \prod_{j\neq i} & \Theta^j_{n-1}(K_1)] \\
\varphi^i & \Big\downarrow \varphi^i_n & \Big\downarrow f & \Big\downarrow \varphi^j_{n-1} \\
 & \Theta^i_n(K_2) = & \Delta[K_2 \times \prod_{j\neq i} & \Theta^j_{n-1}(K_2)] \\
\Big\downarrow & \nearrow p^i_n & \Big\uparrow \mathrm{id}_{K_2} & \Big\uparrow p^j_{n-1} \\
\Theta^i(K_2) & \xrightarrow{\delta^i_2} & \Delta[K_2 \times \prod_{j\neq i} & \Theta^j(K_2)\ ]
\end{array}
$$

This yields the commutativity of:

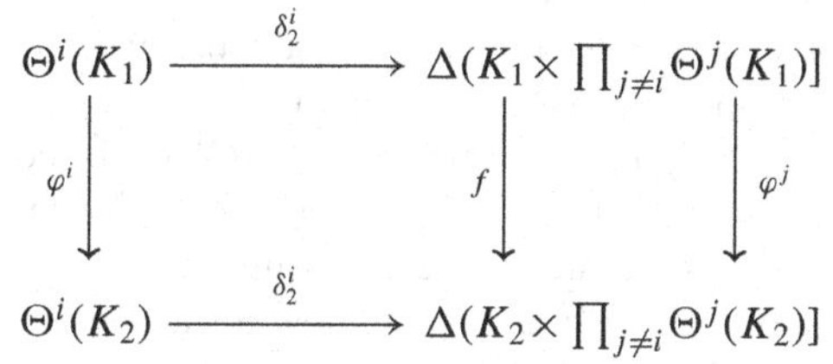

$$
\begin{array}{ccc}
\Theta^i(K_1) & \xrightarrow{\delta^i_2} & \Delta(K_1 \times \prod_{j\neq i} \Theta^j(K_1)] \\
\Big\downarrow \varphi^i & & \Big\downarrow f \qquad \Big\downarrow \varphi^j \\
\Theta^i(K_2) & \xrightarrow{\delta^i_2} & \Delta(K_2 \times \prod_{j\neq i} \Theta^j(K_2)]
\end{array}
$$

Indeed, if for some point in $\Theta^i(K_1)$, the two paths yielded two different measures on $K_2 \times \prod_{j\neq i} \Theta^j(K_2)$, the projections (by $id_{K_2} \times \prod_{j\neq i} p^j_n$) on $K_2 \times \prod_{j\neq i} \Theta^j_n(K_2)$ would already be different for some n (by uniqueness of projective limits for regular probability measures), contradicting the commutativity of the previous diagram. Hence, by the uniqueness part in property (P), we have $\varphi^i = \Theta^i(f)$, thus establishing our full diagram.

If now f is one-to-one, an inclusion (of a closed subset, or of a $\mathscr{K}_{c\delta}$-subset), or onto, the same induction that defines the φ^i_n shows, using Appendix A.9.b, that the φ^i_n have the same property. In the onto case, we use also the K-analyticity of the $\Theta^i_n(K_1)$, which follows, e.g., from that of $\Theta^i(K_1)$ (part (1) of Theorem III.1.1) and the onto character of p^i_n (part (3) of Theorem III.1.1) by Appendix A.3.a. Hence the conclusion for part (3a) follows from going to the projective limit (by our above diagrams) $\Theta^i(f)\colon \Theta^i(K_1) \to \Theta^i(K_2)$.

For part (3b), observe that, by part (3a) and Appendix A.2.b, $\Theta^i_1 \subseteq \Theta^i_2$ is such that δ^i induces a homeomorphism between Θ^i_1 and $\{\, \mu \in \Delta(K_2 \times \prod_{j\neq i} \Theta^j_2) \mid \mu(K_1 \times \prod_{j\neq i} \Theta^i_1) = 1 \,\}$. It follows then inductively that $\Theta^i_1 \subseteq A_n$, hence $\Theta^i_1 \subseteq A_\infty = \bigcap_n A_n$. On the other hand, it is by definition clear that δ^i maps

A_∞ onto $\Delta(K_1 \times (A_\infty)^{\#I-1})$ (hence homeomorphically). So by our diagram above, it follows inductively that $p_n^i(A_\infty) = \Theta_n^i(K_1)$: the image of some point in A_∞ by $[\Delta(id_{K_2} \times \prod_{j\neq i} p_{n-1}^j)] \circ \delta_n^i$ is by the induction hypothesis some element of $\Delta(K_1 \times \prod_{j\neq i} \Theta_{n-1}^j(K_1))$: recall that f and φ_{n-1}^j are inclusions, i.e., of $\Theta_n^i(K_1)$ (or rather its image by φ_n^i). Since the φ_n^i are inclusions, it follows that, for $\theta \in A_\infty$, the sequence $(p_n^i(\theta))_{n=-1}^\infty$ is a consistent sequence in the $\Theta_n^i(K_1)$, and hence stems from some point in $\Theta^i(K_1)$, so $A_\infty = \Theta^i(K_1)$.

It remains only to prove (3c). We start with some preliminaries. Given continuous maps $f_i\colon X_i \to Y$ ($i = 1, 2$; all spaces Hausdorff), the **fibered product** of f_1 and f_2 is the space $Z = \{ (x_1, x_2) \in X_1 \times X_2 \mid f_1(x_1) = f_2(x_2) \}$ (together with the projections p_1 and p_2 to X_1 and X_2). Let also $\Delta(f_i)$ denote the induced map between regular probabilities, etc. Then we claim:

The map $(\Delta(p_1), \Delta(p_2))$ from $\Delta(Z)$ to the fibered product of $\Delta(f_1)$ and $\Delta(f_2)$ is onto.

It is clearly into since $\Delta(f \circ g) = [\Delta(f)] \circ [\Delta(g)]$.

We first reduce the problem to the case of compact spaces. Assume thus this case solved, and fix $\mu_i \in \Delta(X_i)$ with $[\Delta(f_i)](\mu_i) = \nu$. Take K_i compact in X_i, with $\mu_i(K_i) \geq 1 - \varepsilon$; let ν_i be the image by f_i of $\mu_{i|K_i}$, with $h_i = d\nu_i/d\nu$: we have $\int h_i d\nu \geq 1 - \varepsilon$ with $0 \leq h_i \leq 1$, so with $h = \min(h_1, h_2)$ we have $\int h d\nu \geq 1 - 2\varepsilon$. Let then $g_i = (h/h_i) \circ f_i\colon X_i \to [0, 1]$, and $\sigma_i(B) = \int_{K_i \cap B} g_i(x)\mu_i(dx)$: then $\sigma_i \leq \mu_i$ has compact support, and $[\Delta(f_i)](\sigma_i) = h d\nu$. Continuing in the same way with the measures $\overline{\mu}_i = \mu_i - \sigma_i$, we see that we can write $\mu_i = \sum_{k=1}^\infty \alpha^k \mu_i^k$, where $\mu_i^k \in \Delta(X_i)$ has compact support, $[\Delta(f_i)](\mu_i^k) = \nu^k$, and $\alpha^k > 0$. Hence if we get $\lambda^k \in \Delta(Z)$ with $[\Delta(p_i)](\lambda^k) = \mu_i^k$, $\lambda = \sum_k \alpha^k \lambda^k$ will solve the problem. Assume thus $X_i = \mathrm{Supp}(\mu_i)$ and $Y = \mathrm{Supp}(\nu)$ are compact. We now show how to reduce the problem to the case where Y is in addition metrizable: denote by A the increasing filtering family of all separable closed sub-algebras of $C(Y)$ that contain the constants. For $\alpha \in A$, denote also by Y_α the corresponding (compact metric) quotient space, with $\varphi_\alpha\colon Y \to Y_\alpha$ as quotient mapping, and $Z_\alpha \subseteq X_1 \times X_2$ the fibered product of $\varphi_\alpha \circ f_1$ and $\varphi_\alpha \circ f_2$. Since Y_α is metrizable, there exists by assumption $\lambda_\alpha \in \Delta(Z_\alpha)$ with $[\Delta(p_i)](\lambda_\alpha) = \mu_i$. Since $(Z_\alpha)_{\alpha \in A}$ are a decreasing filtering family of compact sets, with Z as intersection, any limit point λ of the λ_α will belong to $\Delta(Z)$, and is mapped to μ_i by $\Delta(p_i)$.

So assume Y compact metric. By II.1, Ex. 21, p. 89, let λ_y^i be a measurable map from (Y, ν) to $\Delta(X_i)$ (observe f_i is onto) with the Borel sets, such that the image measure of ν on $\Delta(X_i)$ is regular, with $\mathrm{Supp}(\lambda_y^i) \subseteq f_i^{-1}(y)$ $\forall y$ and $\mu^i(B) = \int_Y \lambda_y^i(B)\nu(dy)$ for every Borel set B. λ^1 and λ^2 can be constructed with the same strong lifting ρ, hence $\lambda^i \rho = \rho(\lambda^i)$ yields (II.1, Ex. 15e, p. 85) that (λ^1, λ^2) is a measurable map from (Y, ν) to $\Delta(X_1) \times \Delta(X_2)$ with the Borel sets, such that the image measure of ν is regular. By the continuity of the product of two measures, from $\Delta(X_1) \times \Delta(X_2)$ to $\Delta(X_1 \times X_2)$ (Proposition I.1.7, p. 8), we obtain that, with $\lambda_y = \lambda_y^1 \otimes \lambda_y^2$, λ is a measurable map from (Y, ν) to $\Delta(X_1 \times X_2)$ with the Borel sets, inducing a regular image measure, in particular, by II.1, Ex. 20b, p. 89, $\lambda_y(B)$ is measurable for every Borel set B, and, with $\int \lambda_y(B)\nu(dy) = \sigma(B)$, $\sigma \in \Delta(X_1 \times X_2)$. Using Z for the Borel set B, we have $\lambda_y(Z) = 1 \;\; \forall y$, hence $\sigma(Z) = 1$, so $\sigma \in \Delta(Z)$. Finally, with $B = p_i^{-1}(\tilde{B})$, $\tilde{B}$ Borel in X_i, we obtain $\lambda_y(B) = \lambda_y^i(\tilde{B})$, hence $\sigma(B) = \int \lambda_y^i(\tilde{B})\nu(dy) = \mu^i(\tilde{B}) : [\Delta(p_i)](\sigma) = \mu^i$. This proves the claim.

For part (3c), consider the commutative diagram (cf. above):

$$\begin{array}{ccc} \Theta^i_{n+1}(K_1) & \xrightarrow{\;q^1_n\;} & \Theta^i_n(K_1) \\ \Big\downarrow{\scriptstyle \varphi^i_{n+1}} & & \Big\downarrow{\scriptstyle \varphi^i_n} \\ \Theta^i_{n+1}(K_2) & \xrightarrow{\;q^2_n\;} & \Theta^i_n(K_2) \end{array}$$

Such a diagram corresponds by definition to a continuous map $\psi_n = \varphi^i_{n+1} \times q^1_n$ from $\Theta^i_{n+1}(K_1)$ to the fibered product Z_n of q^2_n and φ^i_n. It suffices to prove that those maps ψ_n are onto: indeed, given then θ^2 in $\Theta^i(K_2)$, let $\theta^2_\ell = p^i_\ell(\theta^2)$ so $\theta^2_\ell = q^2_\ell(\theta^2_{\ell+1})$, and assume by induction we have already $\theta^1_\ell \in \Theta^i_\ell(K_1)$ for $\ell \leq n$, with $\varphi^i_\ell(\theta^1_\ell) = \theta^2_\ell$ and $q^1_{\ell-1}(\theta^1_\ell) = \theta^1_{\ell-1}$. Then $(\theta^2_{n+1}, \theta^1_n) \in Z_n$, hence the surjectivity of ψ_n will yield the existence of $\theta^1_{n+1} \in \Theta^i_{n+1}(K_1)$ with $\varphi^i_{n+1}(\theta^1_{n+1}) = \theta^2_{n+1}$ and $q^1_n(\theta^1_{n+1}) = \theta^1_n$: we obtain a full sequence $(\theta^1_n)_{n=-1}^{\infty}$, i.e., a point $\theta^1 \in \Theta^i(K_1)$ with, $\forall n$, $p^i_n(\theta^1) = \theta^1_n$, so $(\varphi^i_n \circ p^i_n)(\theta^1) = p^i_n(\theta^2) \;\; \forall n$, hence by our diagram in the beginning of the proof of part (3), $[\Theta^i(f)](\theta^1) = \theta^2$.

We will prove the surjectivity of ψ_n by induction. So assume $n \geq 0$, and ψ_{n-1} is onto. Let $X^i_n = K_i \times \prod_{j \neq i} \Theta^j_n(K_i)$, also $g_n = f \times \prod_{j \neq i} \varphi^j_n : X^1_n \to X^2_n$, and $h^i_n = id_{K_i} \times \prod_{j \neq i} q^j_n : X^i_{n+1} \to X^i_n$. In the commutative diagram:

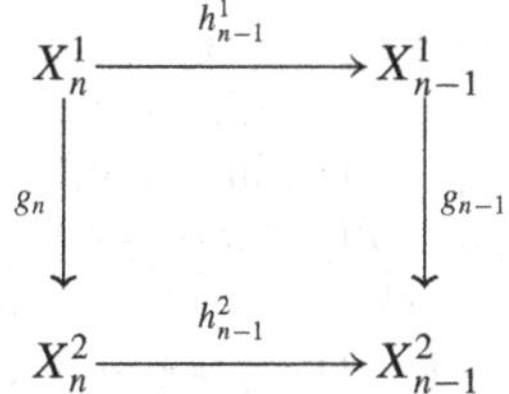

the surjectivity of ψ_{n-1} on each of the factors $\Theta^j (j \neq i)$ separately yields that of the induced map $\chi_n = g_n \times h^1_{n-1}$ from X^1_n to the fibered product P_n of h^2_{n-1} and g_{n-1}. And, by our diagram in the beginning of the proof of (3), proving the surjectivity of ψ_n amounts to prove that in the diagram:

$$\begin{array}{ccc} \Delta(X^1_n) & \xrightarrow{\;\Delta(h^1_{n-1})\;} & \Delta(X^1_{n-1}) \\ \Big\downarrow{\scriptstyle \Delta(g_n)} & & \Big\downarrow{\scriptstyle \Delta(g_{n-1})} \\ \Delta(X^2_n) & \xrightarrow{\;\Delta(h^2_{n-1})\;} & \Delta(X^2_{n-1}) \end{array}$$

the induced map from $\Delta(X_n^1)$ to the fibered product of $\Delta(h_{n-1}^2)$ and $\Delta(g_{n-1})$ is onto. But this is the composition of $\Delta(\chi_n)$ with the map from $\Delta(P_n)$ to the fibered product of $\Delta(h_{n-1}^2)$ and $\Delta(g_{n-1})$. The first is onto by Appendix A.9.b.3 (K-analyticity of X_n^1 follows from point 1 of the present theorem, the onto character of p_n^i, Theorem III.1.1 part 3, and Appendix A.3.a), and the second by our above claim. ■

Remark III.1.4. Compactness is clearly necessary in part (2); e.g., K-analyticity, to generalize at the same time Part (3c), would be insufficient. Consider, for example, any K-analytic set K, on which there exists a non-constant continuous function. Then there is a proper $\mathscr{Z}$-subset, say, Z, so by (3a) $\Theta^i(Z)$ is a $\mathscr{Z}$-subset of $\Theta^i(K)$: let $\overline{\Theta}_0^i = \Theta^i(K) \setminus \Theta^i(Z)$, $\overline{\Theta}_{n+1}^i = (\delta^i)^{-1}(\Delta(K \times \prod_{j\neq i} \overline{\Theta}_n^j))$. Observe that, using inductively Appendix A.9.b.2, the $\overline{\Theta}_n^i$ are $\mathscr{Z}_{c\delta}$-subsets of $\Theta^i(K)$. Further $\overline{\Theta}_1^i \subseteq \overline{\Theta}_0^i$, must clearly be disjoint from $\Theta^i(Z)$, so by induction the $\overline{\Theta}_n^i$ form a decreasing sequence. Let $\overline{\Theta}^i = \bigcap_n \overline{\Theta}_n^i$: clearly $\delta^i(\overline{\Theta}^i) = \Delta(K \times \prod_{j\neq i} \overline{\Theta}^j)$; further the $\overline{\Theta}^i$ are $\mathscr{Z}_{c\delta}$-subsets of $\Theta^i(K)$, strictly included in it, and non-empty, e.g., because they contain (by induction again) $\Theta^i(K \setminus Z)$.

Remark III.1.5. The previous remark implies in particular that the homeomorphism between $\overline{\Theta}^i$ and $\Delta(K \times \prod_{j\neq i} \overline{\Theta}^j)$ is far from sufficient to characterize the spaces $\Theta^i(K)$, even when the $\overline{\Theta}^i$ are restricted to be (nice, $\mathscr{Z}_{c\delta}$) subsets of $\Theta^i(K)$. There is a different sense in which it is insufficient as well, and this even with all spaces compact: one can have, with K compact, compact spaces $\overline{\Theta}^i$ and homeomorphisms σ_i from $\overline{\Theta}^i$ to $\Delta(K \times \prod_{j\neq i} \overline{\Theta}^j)$, without $\overline{\Theta}^i$ being in any sense homeomorphic to $\Theta^i(K)$. For instance, let $X_1 = [0, 1]$, $X_{n+1} = \Delta(X_n)$, $q_1 : X_2 \to X_1$ maps to the barycenter, $q_n = \Delta(q_{n-1})$: $X_{n+1} \to X_n$ for $n > 1$. Obviously the X_n are compact metric, and the q_n continuous and onto (induction). Let X be the projective limit (compact metric), with projections p_n onto X_n. For $x \in X$, the $p_{n+1}(x)$ define a projective system of probabilities on the $X_n (n \geq 1)$, hence a probability $\delta(x) \in \Delta(X)$. The map δ is clearly one-to-one, continuous, and onto, and so it is a homeomorphism from X to $\Delta(X)$ by compactness. Let then, for $\mathbf{I} = \{1, 2\}$, $\#K = 1$, $\overline{\Theta}^i = X$, with δ^i a copy of δ, $\delta^i : \overline{\Theta}^i \to \Delta(K \times \overline{\Theta}^j)$ $(i \neq j)$. So our $\overline{\Theta}^i$, δ^i have all required properties for the one-point space K, but still are in no sense homeomorphic to the one-point space $\Theta^i(K)$.

We prove now that property (P) still holds when the maps are only assumed measurable. Actually, our solution does not seem exactly right, since we have to restrict slightly the class of topological spaces considered: it would be more natural to investigate, for given spaces, for which class of maps the property still holds, rather than, for a given measurability concept, what class of spaces can be used.

Theorem III.1.3. *Assume that in property (P), the spaces Σ^i and $\tilde{K}$ are quasi-Radon (Appendix A.10.a), and the maps σ^i and f universally measurable.*

Then there exist unique maps $\Theta^i(f)$ making the diagram commutative in the sense that for every Borel set B in $K \times \prod_{j \neq i} \Theta^j$ such that $\tilde{B} = [f \times \prod_{j \neq i} \Theta^j(f)]^{-1}(B)$ is $\sigma^i(s_i)$ measurable, $[\sigma^i(s_i)](\tilde{B}) = [\delta^i[(\Theta^i(f))(s_i)]](B)$. Those $\Theta^i(f)$ are universally measurable, so the diagram is unrestrictedly commutative (even for all universally measurable B).

Proof. The proof is the same as in Theorem III.1.1, proving inductively that the φ_n^j are universally measurable (and uniquely defined), using Appendix A.10.a.6, Appendix A.9.d.1, Appendix A.10.a.5, and again Appendix A.9.d.1 at every step of the induction. Then by induction, we must have $p_n^i \circ \Theta^i(f) = \varphi_n^i$ for all n: $\Theta^i(f)$ is thereby uniquely defined, and its universal measurability follows by writing it as the composition (Appendix A.9.d.1) of the inclusion of Σ^i as the diagonal of $(\Sigma^i)^\infty$ and the universally measurable $\prod_n \varphi_n^i : (\Sigma^i)^\infty \to \prod_n \Theta_n^i$ (Appendix A.9.d.1), together with the remark that a universally measurable map is still universally measurable to every subspace of the image space that contains the range. Commutativity of the diagram follows now for every Borel set B of the form $(id_K \times \prod_{j \neq i} p_n^j)^{-1}(\tilde{B})$ with $\tilde{B}$ Borel, hence by a monotone class argument for all Borel sets (clearly any open set belongs to this monotone class, being a union of basic open sets). This extends then immediately to the universally measurable B's. ■

Remark III.1.6. In particular, if two quasi-Radon spaces are "universally measurably isomorphic," one obtains a similar isomorphism between their corresponding systems: thus, the $(\Theta^i(K), \delta^i)_{i \in \mathbf{I}}$ and their "universally measurable structure" (all universally measurable maps to and from all topological spaces) are uniquely determined by the universally measurable structure of K: in some sense, the solution is "purely" measure theoretic.

Also, one often encounters the variant of property (P) where the map f is replaced by a transition probability. Then:

Theorem III.1.4. *Assume in property (P) that K is quasi-Radon, f is a continuous map to $\Delta(K)$, and the maps σ^i are continuous. Then there are unique (in the same sense as in Theorem III.1.3) continuous maps $\Theta^i(f)$ making the diagram commutative, where the right-hand arrow is interpreted as $\beta \circ [\Delta(f \times \prod_{j \neq i} \mu^j \circ \Theta^j(f))]$, with the barycentric map β as in Appendix A.10.a and $\mu^j : \Theta^j \to \Delta(\Theta^j)$ mapping every point to the unit mass at this point.*

Proof. By the continuity of the product of probabilities (Proposition I.1.7, p. 8), and Appendix A.10.a.7 (the spaces are quasi-Radon as in Theorem III.1.2, part (1)), the proof is now as in Theorem III.1.1, p. 124, with the modified interpretation of the right-hand arrow. Only some more care is required to prove that $q_n^i \circ \varphi_n^i = \varphi_{n-1}^i$ also follows inductively. ■

Remark III.1.7. With $\tilde{K} = \Delta(K)$, $\Sigma^i = \Theta^i(\Delta(K))$, and f the identity, one obtains the canonical continuous map from $\Theta^i(\Delta(K))$ to $\Theta^i(K)$. So in the general case, when f has values in $\Delta(K)$ and all maps are universally measurable, one still obtains the result, assuming all spaces are quasi-Radon: $\Theta^i(f)$

is universally measurable from Σ^i to $\Theta^i(K)$, and obtained by composing the map from Σ^i to $\Theta^i(\Delta(K))$ obtained in Theorem III.1.3 with the canonical map above from $\Theta^i(\Delta(K))$ to $\Theta^i(K)$. Of course, a direct definition, like in Theorem III.1.4, is also possible.

Remark III.1.8. In the line of the remark after Theorem III.1.1, there is a category of quasi-Radon spaces, with universally measurable transition probabilities as morphisms; indeed, $f: X \to \Delta(Y)$ and $g: Y \to \Delta(Z)$ compose as $g * f = \beta \circ (\Delta(g)) \circ f$ (Appendix A.5.d and Appendix A.5.f). Remark III.1.7 shows then that Θ^i is a (covariant) functor from this category to the category of quasi-Radon systems with universally measurable morphisms.

Corollary III.1.5.

(1) *If K is countably Radon, or analytic, then for any other countably Radon or analytic topology on K with the same Borel σ-field or the same $\mathscr{B}_u$, one obtains another countably Radon or analytic topology on $\Theta(K)$, with the same map δ, and with the same Borel σ-field or same $\mathscr{B}_u$.*

(2) *Assume K is countably Radon, or analytic.*

Let $(\Sigma_i, \mathscr{S}_i)$ and $(\Omega, \mathscr{A})$ be measurable spaces, together with a transition probability Q from $(\Omega, \mathscr{A})$ to K with the Borel sets, and transition probabilities σ_i from $(\Sigma_i, \mathscr{S}_i)$ to $(\Omega, \mathscr{A}) \times \prod_{j \neq i}(\Sigma_j, \mathscr{S}_j)$. Then there exists a unique system of measurable maps $\Theta^i(Q)$ from $(\Sigma_i, \mathscr{S}_i)$ to $\Theta^i(K)$ with the Borel sets such that the diagrams of property (P) commute.

(3) *The measurable space $\Theta^i(K)$ with the Borel sets is uniquely characterized by the above property.*

Proof. Apply the above, and Appendix A.10.b, including Remark III.1.7, p. 133. ■

In view of Theorem III.1.1, p. 124, we refer to Θ as the **universal type space**. It is determined by K and $\mathbf{I}$ only. The space Θ^i is called the **type set** of player i.

We define now the space Ω by $\Omega = K \times \prod_{i \in \mathbf{I}} \Theta^i$. This space is called the **universal belief space**, and its elements are called **states of the world**.

The definition of Ω and the basic property of the type space, namely, that Θ^i is homeomorphic to $\Delta(K \times \prod_{j \neq i} \Theta^j)$, are the formal expression of Harsanyi's approach in modeling games with incomplete information; namely, a state of the world consists of a state of nature together with a list of types, one for each player. A type of a player defines a joint probability distribution on the states of nature and the types of the other players.

Note that our construction is based on some implicit assumptions on the players' beliefs: the subject of each player's beliefs is the states of nature and the beliefs of the others. He "knows" his own beliefs. Second, the definition of the projections φ_n^i implies that each level of player i's beliefs is compatible with his lower-level beliefs, and he believes that this is so for all players, and so on. An alternative approach is to make the player's beliefs be on the states of nature and all lower-level beliefs, including his own. If we do so, then the above-mentioned coherency conditions become explicit restrictions on the "admissible" beliefs. This is done in III.4, Ex. 2, p. 166.

Given $\theta \in \Theta^i$, let $\overline{\theta} = \delta^i(\theta) \times \varepsilon_\theta \in \Delta(\Omega)$, where ε_θ is the unit mass at θ. Recall that the product of regular probabilities is a continuous map (I.1.7, p. 8): the map $\theta \mapsto \overline{\theta}$ is continuous. So is the projection map $\theta^i : \Omega \to \Theta^i$, and hence also the map $\omega \mapsto \overline{\theta}^i_\omega$ from Ω to $\Delta(\Omega)$. $\theta^i(\omega)$ or $(\overline{\theta}^i_\omega)$ is referred to as **the type of player i at ω**. Note that if $\tilde{\omega} \in \mathsf{Supp}(\overline{\theta}^i_\omega)$ then $\overline{\theta}^i_{\tilde{\omega}} = \overline{\theta}^i_\omega$. In words: at any state of the world, each player knows his own type.

III.1.b. Belief Subspaces

The universal belief space Ω consists of all possible informational configurations regarding K. Any private or "public" information about K may restrict the conceivable states of the world to a subset of Ω containing all the beliefs of all players. This motivates the following definition.

Definition III.1.9. A **belief subspace** (BL-subspace) is a non-empty subset Y of Ω that satisfies:

$$\forall \omega \in Y \,,\; \overline{\theta}^i_\omega(Y) = 1 \quad \forall i \,.$$

A point of a BL-subspace Y can be written as $\omega = (k; \theta^1(\omega), \ldots, \theta^i(\omega), \ldots)$. The set $\theta^i(Y)$ is the **type set** of player i in the BL-subspace Y. Clearly Ω itself is a BL-subspace.

Examples of BL-subspaces

The following are examples of BL-subspaces corresponding to well-known classes of games.

(1) Games with complete information.
For fixed $k \in K$ let $Y = \{\omega\}$, where $\omega = (k; \varepsilon_\omega, \ldots, \varepsilon_\omega)$, and ε_ω is the measure on Y assigning unit mass to ω. This is a typical situation of complete information.

(2) Games with a random move to choose the state of nature.
For k_1 and k_2, two distinct elements in K, let:

$$Y = \{\omega_1, \omega_2\},$$

$$\omega_1 = (k_1; (p, 1-p), \ldots, (p, 1-p)),$$

$$\omega_2 = (k_2; (p, 1-p), \ldots, (p, 1-p)).$$

Here there is only one type of each player: $(p, 1-p)$, which assigns probability p to ω_1 and $(1-p)$ to ω_2. This is a situation in which a random move chooses the state of nature k_1 or k_2 with probabilities $(p, 1-p)$.

In the following examples there are two players, I and II, and the elements of K are "games" denoted by $G^1, G^2, \ldots$ or $G^{12}, G^{22}, \ldots$, etc.

(3) Games with incomplete information on one side:

$$Y = \{\omega_1, \ldots, \omega_K\} \text{ where for } k = 1, \ldots, K,$$

$$\omega_k = \left(G^k; \varepsilon_{\omega_k}, (p^1, \ldots, p^K)\right).$$

That is, the game $G^k \in \{G^1, \ldots, G^K\}$ is chosen according to the probability vector $p = (p^k)_{k \in K}$. Player I is informed which game was chosen and player II is not.

(4) Games with incomplete information "on $1\frac{1}{2}$ sides" (cf. VI.7, Ex. 8, p. 384).

$$Y = \{\omega_1, \omega_2, \omega_3\}, \text{ where:}$$

$$\omega_1 = \left(G^1; (1/3, 2/3, 0), (1, 0, 0)\right),$$

$$\omega_2 = \left(G^1; (1/3, 2/3, 0), (0, 1/2, 1/2)\right),$$

$$\omega_3 = \left(G^2; (0, 0, 1), (0, 1/2, 1/2)\right).$$

To see the main feature of this BL-subspace assume that the actual state of the world is ω_2. While player I knows that the game is G^1, he is uncertain about the "state of mind" of player II, i.e., whether he knows that it is G^1 (state ω_1) or his beliefs are $(1/2, 1/2)$ (state ω_2). Player I assigns to these two possibilities probabilities $1/3$ and $2/3$, respectively.

(5) Incomplete information on two sides: the independent case.

$$Y = \{\omega_{11}, \omega_{12}, \omega_{21}, \omega_{22}\}, \text{ where:}$$

$$\omega_{11} = \left(G^{11}; (1/2, 1/2, 0, 0), (1/3, 0, 2/3, 0)\right),$$

$$\omega_{12} = \left(G^{12}; (1/2, 1/2, 0, 0), (0, 1/3, 0, 2/3)\right),$$

$$\omega_{21} = \left(G^{21}; (0, 0, 1/2, 1/2), (1/3, 0, 2/3, 0)\right),$$

$$\omega_{22} = \left(G^{22}; (0, 0, 1/2, 1/2), (0, 1/3, 0, 2/3)\right).$$

Player I can be of two types: $\mathrm{I}_1 = (1/2, 1/2, 0, 0)$ or $\mathrm{I}_2 = (0, 0, 1/2, 1/2)$, while player II can be either of type $\mathrm{II}_1 = (1/3, 0, 2/3, 0)$ or $\mathrm{II}_2 = (0, 1/3, 0, 2/3)$. Note that each player knows his own type. An equivalent description of this informational structure is the following: chance chooses a pair of types from $\{\mathrm{I}_1, \mathrm{I}_2\} \times \{\mathrm{II}_1, \mathrm{II}_2\}$ according to the probability distribution:

$$\begin{array}{c} \\ \mathrm{I}_1 \\ \mathrm{I}_2 \end{array} \begin{array}{c} \begin{array}{cc} \mathrm{II}_1 & \mathrm{II}_2 \end{array} \\ \begin{pmatrix} 1/6 & 1/6 \\ 1/3 & 1/3 \end{pmatrix} \end{array}.$$

If the selected pair of types is $(\mathrm{I}_r, \mathrm{II}_s)$, each player is informed of his type (only), and then they proceed to play the game G^{rs}. Note that in this representation the types of the players are chosen independently.

(6) Incomplete information on two sides: the dependent case.

$$Y = \{\omega_{11}, \omega_{12}, \omega_{21}, \omega_{22}\}, \text{ where:}$$
$$\omega_{11} = \left(G^{11}; (1/2, 1/2, 0, 0), (1/3, 0, 2/3, 0)\right),$$
$$\omega_{12} = \left(G^{12}; (1/2, 1/2, 0, 0), (0, 1/7, 0, 6/7)\right),$$
$$\omega_{21} = \left(G^{21}; (0, 0, 1/4, 3/4), (1/3, 0, 2/3, 0)\right),$$
$$\omega_{22} = \left(G^{22}; (0, 0, 1/4, 3/4), (0, 1/7, 0, 6/7)\right).$$

This situation can be interpreted and represented in the same way as the previous example with the joint probability on types being:

$$\begin{array}{c} \\ \mathrm{I}_1 \\ \mathrm{I}_2 \end{array} \begin{array}{c} \begin{array}{cc} \mathrm{II}_1 & \mathrm{II}_2 \end{array} \\ \begin{pmatrix} 1/10 & 1/10 \\ 1/5 & 3/5 \end{pmatrix} \end{array}.$$

Thus, unlike in the previous example, the types of the two players are not independent.

(7) Incomplete information on two sides: the **inconsistent case**.

Consider a variant of the previous example in which the second type of player II is $\mathrm{II}_2 = (0, 1/5, 0, 4/5)$ instead of $(0, 1/7, 0, 6/7)$. With this modification the players' beliefs can no longer be viewed as conditional distributions, given each player's type, derived from some prior joint distribution on $\{\mathrm{I}_1, \mathrm{I}_2\} \times \{\mathrm{II}_1, \mathrm{II}_2\}$. Such situations of incomplete information are called inconsistent cases (cf. example in the next section).

The following are some general constructions of belief subspaces:

(1) Any union of belief subspaces is a belief subspace.
(2) In particular, the union Ω_f of all finite belief subspaces is a belief subspace.
(3) Any countable intersection of belief subspaces is a belief subspace.
(4) Any intersection of closed belief subspaces is a belief subspace.
(5) In particular, it follows that $\forall \omega \in \Omega$ there is a smallest closed belief subspace containing ω. It is obvious how to "construct" it directly (possibly by transfinite induction).
(6) (a) As a cautionary remark, observe that one could also use in (4) above "separately closed," in the sense that a subset is separately closed if the inverse image of every point in any factor Θ^i $(i \in \mathbf{I})$

is closed. One obtains thus also an analogous statement to (5), but associating with every $\omega \in \Omega$ a typically smaller BL-subspace.

(b) In the same vein, one could also define a concept of "topological BL-subspace" by requiring that $\forall \omega \in Y$, $\forall i \in \mathbf{I}$, $\mathsf{Supp}(\overline{\theta}^i_\omega) \subseteq Y$. Clearly, topological BL-subspaces are closed under arbitrary unions and intersections. In particular, for every $\omega \in \Omega$ there is a smallest topological BL-subspace containing it, which should be (typically) even smaller than the one obtained in (6a).

(7) Given $\Omega_0 \subseteq \Omega$, let $\Omega_{n+1} = \{\omega \in \Omega_n \mid \overline{\theta}^i_\omega(\Omega_n) = 1 \ \forall i \in \mathbf{I}\}$. Then $\Omega_\infty = \bigcap_n \Omega_n$ is a belief subspace. It is the subspace where Ω_0 is "common knowledge."

(a) Ω_∞ is the maximal (cf. (1)) belief subspace contained in Ω_0.

(b) When Ω_0 is closed, or a G_δ (or Borel, or universally measurable, or has any of the properties mentioned in Theorem III.1.2, part (1), p. 127, then so is Ω_∞.

(c) Observe that the above generalizes Theorem III.1.2, part (3b), p. 127. Cf. also III.4, Ex. 3, p. 166, for another application.

(8) Let $\Omega_0 = \{\omega \in \Omega \mid \omega \in \mathsf{Supp}(\overline{\theta}^i_\omega) \ \forall i \in \mathbf{I}\}$.

(a) If Ω is metrizable, then Ω_0 is a G_δ in Ω. Indeed, for a metric space E, the set $\{(e, \mu) \in E \times \Delta(E) \mid d(e, \mathsf{Supp}(\mu)) \geq \varepsilon\}$ is closed.

(b) In particular by 6b and Theorem III.1.2, part (1), p. 127, if K is separable metric, then Ω_∞ is a G_δ.

Remark III.1.10. It is the belief subspace where it is common knowledge that no player believes a neighborhood of the true state to be impossible. Consider an interpretation of Ω as a model for modal logic, where (Borel) subsets of Ω would correspond to propositions, and where $B_i(p)$, player i believes p, would be interpreted as θ^i_ω assigns probability one to the (Borel) set p. Observe that, when p is a closed set, $B_i(p)$ is one too. Restricting the model to Ω_∞ corresponds then to require the belief operators to be knowledge operators on closed sets. (One could also restrict propositions to the Boolean algebra generated by the closed sets.) (Thus, independently of the class of subsets to which one restricts propositions, there is a variant concept of $B_i(p)$ "behind the scenes," which is that player i assigns probability one to some closed subset of p.)

Other examples will be given in the next section.

III.2. CONSISTENCY AND COMMON KNOWLEDGE

The types of the players at a given state ω are probability distributions (beliefs) on Ω. A natural question is: Can these be conditional probability distributions derived from some prior probability on Ω, given the players' types?

Definition III.2.1. A probability distribution $Q \in \Delta(\Omega)$ is **consistent** if for all $i \in \mathbf{I}$ and every Borel set B of Ω:

$$Q(B) = \int_{\Omega} \overline{\theta}^{i}_{\omega}(B) Q(d\omega). \tag{1}$$

In words: Q is consistent if it equals the average (according to Q) of each of the beliefs $\overline{\theta}^{i}_{\omega}$. The following lemma proves that Definition III.2.1 indeed captures the intuitive meaning of consistency.

Lemma III.2.1. *If $Q \in \Delta(\Omega)$ is consistent then for all $i \in \mathbf{I}$, and for any Borel, or universally measurable subset A of Ω:*

$$\overline{\theta}^{i}_{\omega}(A) = Q(A \mid \mathscr{T}^{i})(\omega) \qquad Q\text{-a.e.}, \tag{2}$$

where $\mathscr{T}^{i}$ is the sub σ-field on Ω generated by θ^{i} and the Borel, or universally measurable, σ-field on Θ^{i}.

Proof. We have to prove that for any measurable set A in Ω and for any $B \in \mathscr{T}^{i}$:

$$\int_{B} \overline{\theta}^{i}_{\omega}(A) Q(d\omega) = \int_{B} \mathbb{1}_{A} Q(d\omega) .$$

The right-hand side is equal to $Q(A \cap B)$ so that the equation will follow from (1) (applied to the measurable set $A \cap B$) if we show that $\mathbb{1}_{B}(\omega)\overline{\theta}^{i}_{\omega}(A) = \overline{\theta}^{i}_{\omega}(A \cap B)$ for any $B \in \mathscr{T}^{i}$. This follows from the fact that $\overline{\theta}^{i}$ is constant on the support of $\overline{\theta}^{i}_{\omega}$, so that the full support is either in B or disjoint from B. ∎

Remark III.2.2. If K is completely regular, it suffices already that equation (1) be satisfied for bounded continuous functions instead of Borel sets. Indeed, since the completely regular spaces are the subspaces of compact spaces Θ^{i} and hence Ω are then completely regular too, so the equation passes from continuous functions to indicator functions of compact sets (by regularity of Q and $\overline{\theta}^{i}_{\omega}$), and then to Borel sets (by regularity of Q).

Remark III.2.3. Equation (1) remains valid with non-negative universally measurable functions instead of the Borel set B.

Denote by $\mathscr{P}$ the set of all consistent probabilities on Ω.

Theorem III.2.2. *The set $\mathscr{P}$ is closed and convex in $\Delta(\Omega)$.*

Proof. Convexity of $\mathscr{P}$ is obvious, and equation (1) is linear. Let thus $P_{\alpha} \in \mathscr{P}$ converge to $P \in \Delta(\Omega)$. Let $\mu(B) = \int \overline{\theta}^{i}_{\omega}(B) P(d\omega)$. Observe that, for any compact set C, $\mu(C) = \inf\{\, \mu(\overline{O}) \mid \overline{O}$ closure of an open set O containing $C\,\}$. Indeed, since Ω is T_2 and C compact, the intersection of those sets $\overline{O}$ equals C, so the $\overline{\theta}^{i}_{\omega}(\overline{O})$ form a decreasing net of u.s.c. functions converging to $\overline{\theta}^{i}_{\omega}(C)$ (by regularity of $\overline{\theta}^{i}_{\omega}$), hence, by the regularity of P, $\mu(\overline{O})$ decreases to $\mu(C)$.

By the upper semi-continuity of $\overline{\theta}^{i}_{\omega}(\overline{O})$, $\limsup_{\alpha} \int \overline{\theta}^{i}_{\omega}(\overline{O}) P_{\alpha}(d\omega) \leq \int \overline{\theta}^{i}_{\omega}(\overline{O}) P(d\omega)$, i.e., $\limsup_{\alpha} P_{\alpha}(\overline{O}) \leq \mu(\overline{O})$. But also $\liminf P_{\alpha}(O) \geq$

$P(O) \geq P(C)$. Hence $P(C) \leq \mu(\overline{O})$ for every $\overline{O}$, so $P(C) \leq \mu(C)$ for every compact set C. The regularity of P implies then that $P = \mu$. ■

Corollary III.2.3. *All topological properties of K mentioned in Theorem III.1.2.1, p. 127, are inherited by Ω and by $\mathscr{P}$.*

Proof. By Theorem III.1.2.1, they are inherited by Θ^i, and by $\Delta(K)$, by countable products and by closed subspaces. Therefore they are also inherited by $\Omega = K \times \prod_i \Theta^i$, hence by $\Delta(\Omega)$, hence by the closed subspace $\mathscr{P}$ of $\Delta(\Omega)$. ■

In general, a BL-subspace will fail to have a consistent distribution.

Example III.2.4. Consider a situation of two players, each of whom has two types. The BL-subspace Y has four points corresponding to the four possible couples of types:

$$Y = \begin{pmatrix} 11 & 12 \\ 21 & 22 \end{pmatrix}.$$

At each point of Y (an entry of the matrix), the first digit denotes the type of player I and the second that of player II. Similarly we denote the subjective probabilities of the players by:

$$\text{For I:} \quad \begin{matrix} & \text{II}_1 & \text{II}_2 \\ \text{I}_1 & p_1 & 1 - p_1 \\ \text{I}_2 & p_2 & 1 - p_2 \end{matrix}, \qquad \text{For II:} \quad \begin{matrix} & \text{II}_1 & \text{II}_2 \\ \text{I}_1 & q_1 & q_2 \\ \text{I}_2 & 1 - q_1 & 1 - q_2 \end{matrix}.$$

It is easily verified that there is a consistent distribution iff $q_1(1 - p_1)/[p_1(1 - q_1)] = q_2(1 - p_2)/[p_2(1 - q_2)]$.

Examples on BL-subspaces (continued).

(1) If K is a separable metric space, or is analytic, so is $\mathscr{P}$ (Corollary III.2.3). Hence $\mathscr{P}$ has a countable dense sequence $(P_n)_{n=1}^{\infty}$. By Theorem III.2.2, $P_\infty = \sum_1^\infty 2^{-n} P_n$ belongs to $\mathscr{P}$. Further $\mathsf{Supp}(P_n) \subseteq \mathsf{Supp}(P_\infty)$. Since the sequence P_n is dense, we obtain $\mathsf{Supp}(P) \subseteq \mathsf{Supp}(P_\infty) \forall P \in \mathscr{P}$: The set of supports of consistent probabilities has a maximal element ($\mathsf{Supp}(P_\infty)$), say, S. Even for general K, one can always define S as $\cup\{\mathsf{Supp}(P) \mid P \in \mathscr{P}\}$.

(2) For any $P \in \mathscr{P}$, $\mathsf{Supp}(P)$ is a (closed) BL-subspace. This can be combined with the constructions of Section III.1.b, like 2, 3, 4, or 8a, to yield other BL-subspaces.

(3) A variant of example (5) on p. 137 becomes now available, assuming K compact: for every decreasing net of supports of consistent probabilities, the intersection contains a minimal such set (using compactness of $\mathscr{P}$).

(4) Given Ω_0 as in example (7) on p. 138, and $P \in \mathscr{P}$, if $P(\Omega_0) = 1$, then $P(\Omega_\infty) = 1$.

(5) With Ω_0 as in example (8a) on p. 138, and $P \in \mathscr{P}$, one has $P(\Omega_0) = 1$.

(6) Combining all the above, let $S_0 = S \cap \Omega_\infty$, with Ω_∞ as in Example 8a, p. 138, and S as in Example 1 above. Then S_0 is a canonical BL-subspace, with $P(S_0) = 1$, $\forall P \in \mathscr{P}$, and expresses common knowledge of both consistency of beliefs and that nobody believes a neighborhood of the true state to be impossible.

(7) Assume K is standard Borel. So by Corollary III.1.5, p. 134, the Borel spaces Θ^i_K are uniquely determined, and are standard Borel too.

   (a) By II.1, Ex. 9, p. 68, there exists for every player i a Borel-measurable transition probability $q_i(dk \mid \theta)$ from $\prod_j \Theta^j$ to K, such that for every $\theta_i \in \Theta^i$, and every non-negative Borel function f on Ω, $\int_\Omega f(\omega)\overline{\theta}(d\omega) = \int[\int f(k, \theta_{-i}, \theta_i) q_i(dk \mid \theta_{-i}, \theta_i)]\overline{\theta}_i(d\theta_{-i})$, i.e., q_i is the conditional probability on K given θ, under the distribution $\overline{\theta}_i$. Indeed, use $E = \Theta^i$, $Y = \Theta^{-i} (= \prod_{j \neq i} \Theta^j)$, $X = Y \times K$, and g the projection. And since $g(e, x)$ is onto $\forall e \in E$, we can obtain in II.1, Ex. 9c, p. 69, that $Q(\{x \mid g(e, x) = y\} \mid e, y) = 1$ $\forall e, \forall y$, by modifying Q on the negligible set. Therefore Q can be viewed as a transition probability from $E \times Y$ to K.

   (b) It follows that $\forall P \in \mathscr{P}$, the q_i is also a version of the conditional probability on K given $\theta \in \prod_j \Theta^j$. In particular, $\Omega_0 = \{\theta \mid q_i = q_j \forall i, j\}$ is a Borel set with $P(\Omega_0) = 1$, $\forall P \in \mathscr{P}$.

   (c) Thus, the corresponding belief space Ω_∞ is a Borel subset of $\prod_i \Theta^i$, with $P(\Omega_\infty) = 1$ $\forall P \in \mathscr{P}$, and there is a Borel measurable transition probability q from Ω_∞ to K that is a version of the conditional probability on K given $\prod_i \Theta^i$ under every $P \in \mathscr{P}$, and under every $\overline{\theta}^i_\omega$, $\forall i \in \mathbf{I}$ and $\forall \omega \in \Omega_\infty$.

   (d) In the two-player case, one can do a bit better: Modify q^1 by setting it equal to q^2 on $\Theta^1_0 \times \Theta^2$, where $\Theta^1_0 = \{\theta^1 \mid \overline{\theta}^1(\Omega_0) = 1\}$. Doing then the same with q^2 and Θ^2_0 (instead of iterating the procedure, which may be transfinite), one can now choose for Ω_0 the set $\Theta^1_0 \times \Theta^2_0$, and obtain then a similar product set $\Theta^1_\infty \times \Theta^2_\infty$ for Ω_∞. Using Remark III.1.2, p. 127, one can now symmetrize the situation under permutations of the players, and obtain a single Borel set Θ_∞, which has probability one under any $\theta \in \Theta_\infty$, such that $\Theta_\infty \times \Theta_\infty$ has probability one under every $P \in \mathscr{P}$, and a single Borel transition $q(dk \mid \theta^1, \theta^2)$ on $(\Theta_\infty \times \Theta) \cup (\Theta \times \Theta_\infty)$, which is symmetric in (θ^1, θ^2), and is the conditional probability under any $P \in \mathscr{P}$ and under $\theta \in \Theta_\infty$. And when K is finite, one can further symmetrize under all permutations of K.

Remark III.2.5. Are there any canonical results in this vein? For example, does the union of such belief spaces cover the set S? Is there such a canonical belief space, even replacing Borel measurability by universal measurability, or by μ-measurability for every consistent prior and for each belief in the belief space?

Remark III.2.6. The above is frequently used, in the context of Section III.4 below. In that case, to every $k \in K$ there corresponds a game (payoff functions) g^k. Averaging them under such a common conditional q yields a model where one has a single game for every **I**-tuple of types. If further the (consistent) joint distribution is absolutely continuous on $\prod_{i \in \mathbf{I}} \Theta^i$ w.r.t. some product measure, then it is a.c. w.r.t. the product of its marginals, and one can, using $f(\theta)$ for its density with respect to the product of the marginals, replace every every game g^θ by $f(\theta) \cdot g^\theta$. In this way, one obtains a model (information scheme as below), where, furthermore, all players' private signals are independent. It would seem worthwhile to check what such transformations yield for the corresponding canonical consistent distributions (Theorem III.2.4 part 2, below).

Information Schemes

In games with incomplete information, the information structure is defined by an **information scheme**, $\mathscr{I}$, that consists of a probability space $\mathbf{E} = (E, \mathscr{E}, Q)$ and sub-σ-fields $\mathscr{E}^i$ (for each i in **I**), with a measurable mapping $\mathbf{k}_E$ from E to the space K of states of nature. The σ-field $\mathscr{E}^i$ describes the information of player i. The following theorem states that any information scheme has a canonical representation as a consistent probability measure on Ω. Denoting by $\mathbf{k}$ the canonical projection from Ω to K we have:

Theorem III.2.4. *Assume an information scheme $\mathscr{I}$ such that $\mathbf{k}_E$ is Borel-measurable and Q has a regular image measure μ.*

(1) *Then there exists a Q-measurable map φ from $(E, \mathscr{E})$ to Ω with the Borel sets such that:*
   (a) $(\mathbf{k} \circ \varphi)^{-1}(B) = (\mathbf{k}_E)^{-1}(B)$ *Q-a.e., for every Borel subset B of K.*
   (b) $Q \circ \varphi^{-1} \in \mathscr{P}$ *(or just: $\in \Delta(\Omega)$).*
   (c) $\overline{\theta}^i(\varphi(e))(B) = (Q[\varphi^{-1}(B) \mid \mathscr{E}_i])(e)$ *Q-a.e., for every Borel subset B of Ω and all $i \in \mathbf{I}$.*
(2) *If $\tilde{\varphi}$ is another such map, then $\varphi^{-1}(B) = \tilde{\varphi}^{-1}(B)$ Q-a.e., for every Borel set B of Ω. (In particular, $Q \circ \varphi^{-1}$ is uniquely defined.)*
(3) *Assume there exists $K_0 \subseteq K$ with $\mu(K_0) = 1$ such that points of K_0 are separated by some sequence of μ-measurable sets. Then:*
   (a) *Part (2) implies that $\tilde{\varphi} = \varphi$ Q-a.e.*
   (b) *In (1a) one can require $\mathbf{k} \circ \varphi = \mathbf{k}_E$.*
   (c) *One can further require that $\overline{\theta}^i(\varphi(e))$ be $\mathscr{E}^i$-measurable.*

Proof. During the proof of parts (1) and (2) we will assume $\mathscr{E}^i$ contains all negligible subsets of $(E, \mathscr{E}, Q)$. We start with the following:

Lemma III.2.5. *Let φ and $\tilde{\varphi}$ be two random variables on a probability space $(\Omega, \mathscr{B}, P)$ with values in a measurable space $(S, \mathscr{S})$.*

(1) *Assume that S is completely regular and $\mathscr{S}$ the Borel σ-field, that the distributions of φ and $\tilde{\varphi}$ are regular, or just τ-smooth (cf. Appendix A.10.a), and that for every real bounded continuous function f on S, $f \circ \varphi = f \circ \tilde{\varphi}$ a.e. Then the same holds true for any real Borel function f.*

(2) *Assume that $\mathscr{S}$ is separable and separating and that for every $T \in \mathscr{S}$, $\varphi^{-1}(T) = \tilde{\varphi}^{-1}(T)$ a.e.; then $\varphi = \tilde{\varphi}$ a.e. If $\mathscr{A} \subseteq \mathscr{B}$ is such that every element of $\mathscr{B}$ is a.e. equal to some element of $\mathscr{A}$, then there exists $\overline{\varphi}$ that is $\mathscr{A}$-measurable and is a.e. equal to φ.*

Proof. Part (1) Going to the Stone–Čech compactification, one can assume that the image space is compact. One obtains then first, by a monotone class argument, that $f \circ \varphi = f \circ \tilde{\varphi}$ a.e. for every Baire function f. So the distributions coincide on the Baire σ-field, hence (by regularity) on all compact sets, since those have a basis of open Baire neighborhoods, hence (by regularity) on all Borel sets. Let P be this distribution. For K compact, let O_n be, as just said, an open Baire set with $K \subseteq O_n$, $P(O_n \setminus K) \leq n^{-1}$; let $\hat{K} = \bigcap_n O_n$: $\hat{K}$ is a Baire set with $K \subseteq \hat{K}$, $P(\hat{K} \setminus K) = 0$. Hence $\varphi^{-1}(K) =_{a.e.} \varphi^{-1}(\hat{K}) =_{a.e} \tilde{\varphi}^{-1}(\hat{K}) =_{a.e.} \tilde{\varphi}^{-1}(K)$. So we still have $\varphi^{-1}(C) = \tilde{\varphi}^{-1}(C)$ a.e., for every K_σ-set C. The same conclusion follows now in the same way for Borel sets, since they can be approximated by regularity from inside by K_σ-sets. Hence the result.

Part (2) Let T_k be a sequence of generators of $\mathscr{S}$, and neglect the points where, for some k, $\varphi^{-1}(T_k) \neq \tilde{\varphi}^{-1}(T_k)$. Now $(\varphi, \tilde{\varphi})^{-1}(R_k) = \phi$ with $R_k = [T_k \times T_k^c] \cup [T_k^c \times T_k]$. Since $\bigcup_k R_k$ is the complement of the diagonal in $S \times S$, the first assertion follows. For the second assertion, reduce to the case where $(S, \mathscr{S})$ is a subset of [0, 1] with the Borel subsets and approximate φ uniformly by a sequence of step functions φ_n and let $\overline{\varphi} = \liminf \varphi_n$. ■

For the proof of the theorem, we first reduce the proof of parts (1) and (2) to the case where K is compact. Find a sequence C_n of disjoint compact subsets of K with $\mu(\bigcup_n C_n) = 1$. Denote by $\overline{K}$ the (locally compact) disjoint union of the C_n, and by $\hat{K}$ its one-point compactification. For part (2), observe first that φ (and $\tilde{\varphi}$) can be modified on a null set such as to have values in $\Omega_{\bigcup_n C_n} \subseteq \Omega_K$, by Theorem III.1.2, part (3b), p. 127. Indeed, assume that φ has already been modified such as to have values in $[(\bigcup_k C_k) \times (A_n)^{\mathbf{I}}]$; then, taking for B the latter subset in (1c), we get that $\overline{\theta}^i_{\varphi(e)}(B) = 1$ a.e., hence the induction step. Next, since $\overline{K}$ is a $\mathscr{K}_c$-set in $\hat{K}$, $\Omega_{\overline{K}}$ is a $\mathscr{K}_{c\delta}$ set (Theorem III.1.2, part (3a), p. 127) in the compact space (Theorem III.1.2, part (1), p. 127) $\Omega_{\hat{K}}$, hence K-Lusin (Appendix A.3.d, Appendix A.3.f). Hence the map from $\Omega_{\overline{K}}$ to $\Omega_{\bigcup_n C_n}$ is continuous, one-to-one, and onto (Theorem III.1.2, part (3a), p. 127, and part (3c)). Therefore φ and $\tilde{\varphi}$ still have the same properties when viewed as maps to $\Omega_{\overline{K}}$ by (Appendix A.9.b.4 and Appendix A.9.b.3). And clearly $\mathbf{k}_E$ can be viewed as $\overline{K}$-valued. Finally, Theorem III.1.2, part (3a), p. 127, allows us to assume that the values are in $\Omega_{\hat{K}}$ and in $\hat{K}$.

For part (1) of Theorem III.2.4, our assumptions are clearly still satisfied by $\hat{K}$ instead of K. Obtaining thus an appropriate $\Omega_{\hat{K}}$-valued φ, and letting $B_0 = \{\omega \in \Omega_{\hat{K}} \mid \mathbf{k}_\omega \in \overline{K}\}$, $B_{n+1} = \{\omega \in B_n \mid \overline{\theta}^i_\omega(B_n) = 1\ \forall i\}$; then, by Theorem III.2.4, parts (1a) and (1c), and inductively, we get $Q(\varphi^{-1}(B_n)) = 1\ \forall n$, and hence, after modifying φ on a null set, $\varphi\colon E \to \Omega_{\overline{K}} = \bigcap_n B_n$ (Theorem III.1.2, part (3b)). So, by Theorem III.1.2, part (3a), p. 127, composing φ with the continuous one-to-one map from $\Omega_{\overline{K}}$ to Ω_K will yield the desired result. Hence, for parts (1) and (2) of the theorem we can assume K compact.

We now start the proof of part (1). Let ρ be a lifting on $(E, \mathscr{E}, Q)$; and let $\overline{\mathbf{k}} = \rho(\mathbf{k}_E)$ (II.1, Ex. 15e, p. 85). Then, by the above lemma, we have $\mathbf{k}_E^{-1}(B) = \overline{\mathbf{k}}^{-1}(B)$ Q-a.e., for every Borel set B. So it suffices to prove part (1) with $\overline{\mathbf{k}}$ instead of $\mathbf{k}_E$; i.e., we can assume that $\mathbf{k}_E = \rho(\mathbf{k}_E)$. Assume, for $n \geq -1$, that $\varphi_n = (\mathbf{k}_E, (t^i_n)_{i\in\mathbf{I}})\colon E \to \Omega_n = K \times \prod_i \Theta^i_n$ is well defined, and Q-measurable, such that $\varphi_n = \rho(\varphi_n)$, hence φ_n is measurable to the Borel σ-field, with $Q \circ \varphi_n^{-1} \in \Delta(\Omega_n)$, by (II.1, Ex. 15e$\gamma$, p. 85), and such that $t^i_n(e)(B) = \mathsf{E}[(\varphi^i_{n-1})^{-1}(B) \mid \mathscr{E}_i](e)$ Q-a.e., for every Borel subset B of $X^i_{n-1} = K \times \prod_{j\neq i} \Theta^j_{n-1}$, where $\varphi^i_n = \mathsf{Proj}_{X^i_n} \circ \varphi_n$. Assume finally that $\varphi_{n-1} = \mathsf{Proj}_{\Omega_{n-1}} \circ \varphi_n$, where $\mathsf{Proj}_{\Omega_{n-1}} = \mathrm{id}_K \times \prod_i q^i_n$. Map then Q to its image on $(E, \mathscr{E}_i) \times X^i_n$ and apply II.1, Ex. 16c, to this image measure, yielding an $\mathscr{E}_i$-measurable map t^i_{n+1} to $\Theta^i_{n+1} = \Delta(X^i_n)$, such that $t^i_{n+1} = \rho(t^i_{n+1})$. Then $\varphi_{n+1} = (\mathbf{k}_E, (t^i_{n+1})_{i\in\mathbf{I}})\colon E \to \Omega_{n+1}$ satisfies $\varphi_{n+1} = \rho(\varphi_{n+1})$ by II.1, Ex. 15eδ, p. 85. By definition $t^i_{n+1}(e)(B) = \mathsf{E}[(\varphi^i_n)^{-1}(B) \mid \mathscr{E}_i](e)$ Q-a.e. for every Borel set B of X^i_n. In particular, for B Borel in X^i_{n-1}, and $h^i_n\colon X^i_n \to X^i_{n-1}$ the projection, we have:

$$
\begin{aligned}
[q^i_{n+1}(t^i_{n+1}(e))](B) &= t^i_{n+1}(e)[(h^i_n)^{-1}(B)] \\
&= \mathsf{E}[(h^i_n \circ \varphi^i_n)^{-1}(B) \mid \mathscr{E}_i](e) \\
&= \mathsf{E}[(\varphi^i_{n-1})^{-1}(B) \mid \mathscr{E}_i](e) = t^i_n(e)[B] \quad Q\text{-a.e.}
\end{aligned}
$$

So, as maps into $\Delta(X^i_{n-1})$, for every continuous linear functional ψ, we have $\psi \circ q^i_{n+1} \circ t^i_{n+1} = \psi \circ t^i_n$ Q-a.e. Hence, by the Stone–Weierstrass theorem, the same holds true for any continuous function ψ on $\Delta(X^i_{n-1})$. Therefore, by II.1, Ex. 15eα, and II.1, Ex. 15eβ, p. 85, $\rho[q^i_{n+1} \circ t^i_{n+1}] = \rho(t^i_n) = t^i_n$. But by II.1, Ex. 15e$\delta$, $\rho(q^i_{n+1} \circ t^i_{n+1}) = q^i_{n+1} \circ \rho(t^i_{n+1}) = q^i_{n+1} \circ t^i_{n+1}$. So $t^i_n = q^i_{n+1} \circ t^i_{n+1}$, and hence $\varphi_n = \mathsf{Proj}_{\Omega_n} \circ \varphi_{n+1}$. This finishes the induction step. So we have $\forall i$, $t^i(e) = (t^i_n(e))_{-1}^\infty$ an $\mathscr{E}^i$-measurable map to $(\Theta^i$, Borel sets), by the relation $t^i_{n-1} = q^i_n \circ t^i_n$ and because the Borel σ-field of Θ^i is generated by the projections p^i_n (since every closed set F equals $\bigcap_n p^i_n(F)$ by definition of the product topology). Also $t^i = \rho(t^i)$ by II.1, Ex. 15eδ, p. 85, and so similarly $\varphi = (\mathbf{k}_E, (t^i)_{i\in\mathbf{I}}) = \rho(\varphi)\colon E \to \Omega$. In particular, those maps are Borel measurable with $Q \circ \varphi^{-1} \in \Delta(\Omega)$. Further, for every Borel set B in X^i_n, with ψ^i_n the projection from X^i to X^i_n, we have $t^i(e)[(\psi^i_n)^{-1}(B)] = \mathsf{E}[(\varphi^i)^{-1}[(\psi^i_n)^{-1}(B)] \mid \mathscr{E}_i](e)$ Q-a.e. By our above remark concerning the Borel σ-field on a projective limit, we obtain thus by a monotone class argument that (since $t^i(e) = \delta^i(\theta^i_{\varphi(e)})$), for every Borel set B in X^i:

$$\delta^i(\theta^i_{\varphi(e)})[B] = \mathsf{E}[(\varphi^i)^{-1}(B) \mid \mathscr{E}_i](e)\ Q\text{-a.e.},$$

i.e., $\overline{\theta}^i_{\varphi(e)}(B) = \mathsf{E}[\varphi^{-1}(B) \mid \mathscr{E}_i](e)$ Q-a.e., for every set $B = \Theta^i \times \tilde{B}$, with $\tilde{B}$ Borel in X^i. Or, since $\theta^i_{\varphi(e)}$ is $\mathscr{E}_i$-measurable, we get, for any Borel sets B_1 in Θ^i and B_2 in X^i, that:

$$\begin{aligned}
\overline{\theta}^i_{\varphi(e)}(B_1 \times B_2) &= \mathbb{1}_{\theta^i_{\varphi(e)} \in B_1} \cdot \overline{\theta}^i_{\varphi(e)}(\Theta^i \times B_2) = \mathbb{1}_{\theta^i_{\varphi(e)} \in B_1}\, \mathsf{E}[\varphi^{-1}(\Theta^i \times B_2) \mid \mathscr{E}_i](e) \\
&= \mathsf{E}[\mathbb{1}_{\theta^i_{\varphi(e)} \in B_1} \cdot \mathbb{1}_{\varphi(e) \in \Theta^i \times B_2} \mid \mathscr{E}_i](e) \\
&= \mathsf{E}[\varphi^{-1}(B_1 \times B_2) \mid \mathscr{E}_i](e) \quad Q\text{-a.e.}
\end{aligned}$$

By additivity, the same formula remains then true for finite disjoint unions of sets $B_1 \times B_2$, and then by a monotone class argument we still get:

$$\overline{\theta}^i_{\varphi(e)}(B) = \mathsf{E}[\varphi^{-1}(B) \mid \mathscr{E}_i](e),$$

for every set B in the product of the Borel σ-fields on Θ^i and on X^i. Now, $\overline{\theta}^i_{\varphi(e)}$, as the composition of the continuous map $\omega \mapsto \overline{\theta}^i_\omega$ (cf. supra) and of the map φ satisfying $\varphi = \rho(\varphi)$ is a map from $(E, \mathscr{E}_i)$ to $\Delta(\Omega)$ with the Borel sets that satisfies $\overline{\theta}^i_{\varphi(e)} = \rho[\overline{\theta}^i_{\varphi(\cdot)}](e)$ and has a regular image measure (II.1, Ex. 15eγ, and II.1, Ex. 15eδ, p. 85). This one has a barycenter $\overline{P} \in \Delta(\Omega)$ since, by Appendix A.10.a.3, the compact space Ω is quasi-Radon; i.e., for every Borel set B in Ω, $\overline{\theta}^i_{\varphi(e)}(B)$ is measurable and $\int \overline{\theta}^i_{\varphi(e)}(B)Q(de) = \overline{P}(B)$. Also $Q \circ \varphi^{-1} = P \in \Delta(\Omega)$; i.e., for every Borel set B, $P(B) = \int \mathsf{E}(\varphi^{-1}(B) \mid \mathscr{E}_i)dQ$. Similarly, for $A \in \mathscr{E}$, let $\overline{P}_A(B) = \int_A \overline{\theta}^i_{\varphi(e)}(B)Q(de)$ and $P_A(B) = \int_A \mathsf{E}(\varphi^{-1}(B) \mid \mathscr{E}_i)dQ$: since $\overline{P}_A \leq \overline{P}$ and $P_A \leq P$, both are regular measures, which coincide by our previous formula on the product of the Borel σ-fields on Θ^i and on X^i. By regularity, this implies that they coincide on all compact sets, since those have a basis of open neighborhoods belonging to the product σ-field, and hence on all Borel sets. Thus, for every Borel set B in Ω, we have that:

$$\int_A \overline{\theta}^i_{\varphi(e)}(B)Q\,(de) = \int_A [\mathsf{E}(\varphi^{-1}(B) \mid \mathscr{E}_i)]\, dQ \quad \forall A \in \mathscr{E}.$$

This means the two measurable functions are equal a.e., proving part (1c) of the theorem. By part (1c) we have, for a Borel set B, $P(B) = Q(\varphi^{-1}(B)) = \int \mathsf{E}(\varphi^{-1}(B) \mid \mathscr{E}_i)dQ = \int \overline{\theta}^i_{\varphi(e)}(B)Q(de) = \int \overline{\theta}^i_\omega(B)P(dw)$. Since also $P \in \Delta(\Omega)$, this yields part (1b), completing the proof of part (1).

For part (2), denote by p_n the projection from Ω to Ω_n. Assume that $\varphi^{-1}[p_n^{-1}(B)] = \tilde{\varphi}^{-1}[p_n^{-1}(B)]$ Q-a.e., for every Borel set B in Ω_n. (By part (1a) of Theorem III.2.4, this inductive assumption holds for $n = -1$.) Then by part (1c) of Theorem III.2.4 we obtain that $\overline{\theta}^i_{\varphi(e)}(p_n^{-1}(B)) = \overline{\theta}^i_{\tilde{\varphi}(e)}(p_n^{-1}(B))$

Q-a.e., for every such B. Let thus $P_e = \overline{\theta}^i_{\varphi(e)} \circ p_n^{-1}$, $\tilde{P}_e = \overline{\theta}^i_{\tilde{\varphi}(e)} \circ p_n^{-1}$, both $\in \Delta(\Omega_n)$: then $P_e(B) = \tilde{P}_e(B)$ Q-a.e., $\forall B$ Borel. Hence for every continuous linear functional ψ on $\Delta(\Omega_n)$ we have $\psi \circ P_e = \psi \circ \tilde{P}_e$ Q-a.e., so, by Stone–Weierstrass, which remains true for every continuous function ψ on $\Delta(\Omega_n)$. Take now a continuous function F on $\Omega_{n+1} = K \times \prod_i \Theta^i_{n+1}$; it is, by Stone–Weierstrass again, approximated by linear combinations of functions $F = f_0 \times \prod_i \psi_i$, where $f_0 \in C(K)$ and ψ_i is continuous on $\Theta^i_{n+1} = \Delta(X^i_n)$. Hence $F \circ p_{n+1} \circ \varphi = f_0(\mathbf{k}_E \circ \varphi) \times \prod_i \psi_i\ (\mathsf{Proj}_{X^i_n}(P^i))$; here the argument of ψ_i equals $\mathsf{Proj}_{X^i_n}(P^i) = \mathsf{Proj}_{X^i_n}(\overline{\theta}^i_{\varphi(e)} \circ p_n^{-1}) = \theta^i_{n+1}(e)$. Since $\psi_i \circ \mathsf{Proj}_{X^i_n}$ is continuous on $\Delta(\Omega_n)$, we obtain equality a.e. when replacing φ by $\tilde{\varphi}$. So $F \circ p_{n+1} \circ \varphi = F \circ p_{n+1} \circ \tilde{\varphi}$ Q-a.e., for every $F \in C(\Omega_{n+1})$. Therefore, by the lemma, $\varphi^{-1}[p_{n+1}^{-1}(B)] = \tilde{\varphi}^{-1}(p_{n+1}^{-1}(B))$ Q-a.e., for every Borel set B in Ω_{n+1}. This completes the induction. It follows that, $\forall n, \forall F \in C(\Omega_n)$, $(F \circ p_n) \circ \varphi = (F \circ p_n) \circ \tilde{\varphi}$ Q-a.e. Since the functions $F \circ p_n$ are dense in $C(\Omega)$ (Stone–Weierstrass), the lemma yields finally that $\varphi^{-1}(B) = \tilde{\varphi}^{-1}(B)$ Q-a.e., for every Borel set B in Ω. This proves part (2).

As for part (3), we first prove the following claim:

Under the assumptions of part (3), there exists a sequence of disjoint compact metric subsets K_n of K such that $\mu(\bigcup_n K_n) = 1$.

Let C_k be a sequence of disjoint compact subsets of K_0, with $\mu(\bigcup_k C_k) = 1$; hence we can assume $K_0 = \bigcup_k C_k$. Let also M_n be the sequence of μ-measurable sets. Then $M_n \cap C_k$ differs from some Baire subset $B_{n,k}$ of C_k by a negligible set $N_{n,k}$. Let $f_{k,i}$ be a sequence of continuous functions on C_k that generates all $B_{n,k} (n = 1, 2, \dots)$. Let also $C_{k,j}$ be a sequence of disjoint compact subsets of $C_k \setminus (\bigcup_n N_{n,k})$ with $\mu(\bigcup_j C_{k,j}) = \mu(C_k)$. Then the points of $C_{k,j}$ are separated by the sequence of continuous functions $f_{k,i} (i = 1, 2, \dots)$, so $C_{k,j}$ is metrizable, and $\mu(\bigcup_{k,j} C_{k,j}) = 1$.

So let, $L = \bigcup_n K_n$. Then L is Lusin (e.g., Appendix A.5.f), so $\Omega_L \subseteq \Omega_K$ is Lusin too (parts (1) and (3) of Theorem III.1.2, p. 127). Further, as observed in the beginning of the proof of the theorem, φ (and $\tilde{\varphi}$) can be modified on a null set so as to have values in Ω_L, and similarly $\mathbf{k}_E$ can be assumed to have values in L. The result follows then from part (2) of Lemma III.2.5, p. 142 (separability is by definition, Appendix A.5). This completes the proof of Theorem III.2.4 ∎

Remark III.2.7. To facilitate the interpretation of parts (1a) and (2) of Theorem III.2.4, p. 142, if φ and $\tilde{\varphi}$ are two Borel measurable functions from a probability space to a Hausdorff space X, which have regular image measures and are such that, for every Borel set B, $\varphi^{-1}(B) = \tilde{\varphi}^{-1}(B)$ a.e., then the distribution of $(\varphi, \tilde{\varphi})$ on $X \times X$ endowed with the product of the Borel σ-fields is the restriction to this σ-field of some regular measure carried by the diagonal.

Remark III.2.8. If there exists a strong lifting for (K, μ) (II.1, Ex. 15d, p. 85), one can replace part (1a) of Theorem III.2.4, p. 142, by $\mathbf{k} \circ \varphi = \mathbf{k}_E$. Indeed, composing this lifting with the map $\mathbf{k}_E$ yields a lifting on a sub-σ-field of $(E, \mathscr{E})$, which can then be extended to a lifting ρ for $(E, \mathscr{E}, Q)$ (cf. (the proof of) II.1, Ex. 15a, p. 84). For this lifting, one will have $\rho(\mathbf{k}_E) = \mathbf{k}_E$ a.e.; they differ only on the negligible set where $\mathbf{k}_E$ takes values outside the support of μ. Hence one obtains, at the end of the construction, that $\mathbf{k} \circ \varphi = \mathbf{k}_E$ Q-a.e. Changing the K-coordinate of the map φ on the exceptional set yields then the result. But the condition in (II.1, Ex. 15d, p. 85) for the existence of a strong lifting is (cf. the above claim) equivalent to the condition in part (3) of Theorem III.2.4, p. 142, where our direct argument yields more.

Remark III.2.9. One can always, at the end of the construction, change the K-coordinate of φ and set it equal to $\mathbf{k}_E$, obtaining thus a map $\overline{\varphi}$. However, in the conclusions $\overline{\varphi}^{-1}$ is then restricted to the product of the Borel σ-field on K and to that on $\prod_{i \in \mathbf{I}} \Theta^i$.

Finite BL-subspaces

The notion of BL-subspaces is closely related to that of consistency and common knowledge. In the remainder of this section we study these relations for finite BL-subspaces: all beliefs $\overline{\theta}^i_\omega$ we use have finite support; i.e., we restrict ourselves to the space Ω_f of the construction (2) on p. 137.

Definition III.2.10. A BL-subspace Y is **consistent** if there is a consistent distribution P with $\operatorname{Supp}(P) = Y$.

Definition III.2.11. A state of the world $\omega \in \Omega$ is **consistent** if it belongs to some consistent BL-subspace, i.e., to $\Omega_f \cap S$.

Lemma III.2.6. *If ω is consistent then $\omega \in \operatorname{Supp}(\overline{\theta}^i_\omega)$ $\forall i \in \mathbf{I}$.*

Proof. Let $\omega \in Y$ and $P \in \mathscr{P}$ such that $\operatorname{Supp}(P) = Y$. Since $P(\omega) > 0$ and $\omega \in \mathscr{T}^i(\omega) = \{\tilde{\omega} \mid \theta^i(\tilde{\omega}) = \theta^i(\omega)\}$ it follows that $\overline{\theta}^i_\omega(\omega) = P(\omega \mid \mathscr{T}^i(\omega)) > 0$. ■

The term "common knowledge" is often used in game theory (including in this book) in an informal sense: something is common knowledge among the players if every player knows it, every player knows that every player knows it, every player knows that every player knows that every player knows it, etc. The most intuitive way to think of a common knowledge event is as an event that is announced (or shown) publicly. A formal definition of common knowledge was provided in Aumann (1976): a measurable space $(Y, \overline{\mathscr{Y}})$ of states of the world is given together with sub-σ-fields $\mathscr{Y}^i$ of $\overline{\mathscr{Y}}$, one for each player. An event A is common knowledge at ω if there exists $B \in \bigcap_{i \in \mathbf{I}} \mathscr{Y}^i$ with $\omega \in B \subseteq A$.

In our model, which is a model of beliefs, the natural analogue for "player i believes A" at ω is $\overline{\theta}^i_\omega(A) = 1$. And he would "know" A if further $\omega \in A$. In particular "player believes A" does not necessarily imply that A is true, and the "knowledge" operator as defined is somehow pathological, since when a player believes A, he has no way to know whether he actually knows it. This is because we did not impose any consistency conditions on the players' beliefs. To illustrate this consider the following BL-subspace.

Example III.2.12. In a two-player situation let $Y = \{\omega_1, \omega_2, \omega_3\}$, where:

$$\omega_1 = (k_1; (1,0,0)\ ,\ (0,1,0)),$$
$$\omega_2 = (k_2; (1,0,0)\ ,\ (0,1,0)),$$
$$\omega_3 = (k_3; (1,0,0)\ ,\ (0,1,0)).$$

If the true state of the world is ω_3, then player I "believes" that the state of nature is k_1, player II "believes" that it is k_2, while the true state of nature is k_3. This extremely inconsistent belief system, which can be found in the universal BL-space, does not make sense as a usual knowledge system. Nevertheless we can use this notion of "beliefs" to derive what each player i believes to be "common knowledge."

For $\omega \in Y$ and $i \in \mathbf{I}$ define: $C^i_{\omega,1} = \mathsf{Supp}(\overline{\theta}^i_{\omega})$, and inductively for $r = 1, 2, \dots$:

$$C^i_{\omega,r+1} = C^i_{\omega,r} \cup \Big(\bigcup_{\tilde{\omega} \in C^i_{\omega,r}} \bigcup_{j} \mathsf{Supp}(\overline{\theta}^j_{\tilde{\omega}}) \Big).$$

The interpretation of this sequence is straightforward: according to player i's beliefs at ω, any BL-subspace containing the state of the world (which he generally does not know) must contain all states that he believes are possible, i.e., $C^i_{\omega,1}$. Furthermore, it must contain all states considered possible by some player in any of the states in $C^i_{\omega,1}$. This is $C^i_{\omega,2}$, and so on. Denote the union of this sequence by C^i_{ω}. This is, according to player i's beliefs at ω, the minimal BL-subspace containing the real state of the world, but in fact it may not contain it. However, it is a BL-subspace, and if Y is a BL-subspace, then $C^i_{\omega} \subseteq Y$ for all i and for all ω in Y. For $\omega \in \Omega$, denote by $Y(\omega)$ the smallest BL-subspace containing ω.

Lemma III.2.7. *If ω is consistent then:*

(1) $\omega \in C^i_{\omega} = Y(\omega)$ *for all i.*
(2) *There exists a unique consistent probability P_{ω} with* $\mathsf{Supp}(P_{\omega}) = Y(\omega)$.

Proof. Part (1) is obvious: Since C^i_{ω} is a BL-subspace, and contains ω by Lemma III.2.6, it contains $Y(\omega)$. And, as observed above, $C^i_{\omega} \subseteq Y(\omega)$ always.

Part (2). For any ω, let $\mathscr{T}^i(\omega) = \{\, \tilde{\omega} \mid \theta^i(\tilde{\omega}) = \theta^i(\omega) \,\}$. For any $Q \in \mathscr{P}$, we have by consistency that for any j and any $\tilde{\omega} \in \mathsf{Supp}(\overline{\theta}^i_z)$, $Q(\tilde{\omega}) = \overline{\theta}^j_z(\tilde{\omega}) Q(\mathscr{T}^j(z))$; hence:

$$Q(z) > 0 \text{ and } \tilde{\omega} \in \mathsf{Supp}(\overline{\theta}^j_z) \Longrightarrow \frac{Q(\tilde{\omega})}{Q(z)} = \frac{\overline{\theta}^j_z(\tilde{\omega})}{\overline{\theta}^j_z(z)} > 0.$$

So by induction, if $Q(\omega) > 0$, then $Q(\tilde{\omega})$ is uniquely determined and > 0 $\forall \tilde{\omega} \in C^i_{\omega,r}$; hence $\forall \tilde{\omega} \in C^i_{\omega} = Y_{\omega}$. Take now any $Q \in \mathscr{P}$ that contains ω in its support; then $\text{Supp}(Q) \cap Y(\omega)$ is non-empty since it contains ω (by (1)); hence $Q(Y(\omega)) > 0$. The required consistent P_ω is:

$$P_\omega(\tilde{\omega}) = \begin{cases} 0 & \text{for } \tilde{\omega} \notin Y(\omega) \\ Q(\tilde{\omega})/Q(Y(\omega)) & \text{for } \tilde{\omega} \in Y(\omega). \end{cases} \tag{3}$$

■

Remark III.2.13. In view of the last lemma it makes sense to think of the consistent distribution P_ω on $Y(\omega)$ as a **prior distribution**, not only because it is so mathematically speaking, but also because it is considered "common knowledge" by all players: each player can first compute $Y(\omega)$, as C^i_ω, and then compute P_ω and test for consistency by checking whether P_ω is consistent and whether $Y_\omega = \text{Supp}(P_\omega)$, using just his own knowledge θ^i_ω. The key point in the proof of Lemma III.2.7, p. 148, is that a consistent state is in the support of each player's beliefs (Lemma III.2.6, p. 147). When this is not satisfied for a certain player, he may reach a wrong conclusion (in his test) that the current state is consistent, but his subjective probability of committing such a "type II" error is always zero. And he can never reach the wrong conclusion that the state is inconsistent when it is in fact consistent ("type I" error). The following examples show various types of ("objective") errors that may be committed by the players when $\omega \notin \text{Supp}(\overline{\theta}^i_\omega)$.

Example III.2.14. Consider a BL-subspace of two players, each of whom has the following two types:

$$Y = \begin{pmatrix} 11 & 12 \\ 21 & 22 \end{pmatrix}.$$

The subjective probability of each player on the types of the other player is given by:

$$\begin{matrix} & \text{II}_1 & \text{II}_2 \\ \begin{matrix} \text{I}_1 \\ \text{I}_2 \end{matrix} & \!\!\!\!\!\!\left(\begin{matrix} (1, 3/5) \\ (2/3, 2/5) \end{matrix}\right. & \left.\begin{matrix} (0, 0) \\ (1/3, 1) \end{matrix}\right) \end{matrix}.$$

This is to be read as follows: player II_1 assigns probability $3/5$ to the state 11 and $2/5$ to the state 21. Player I_2 assigns probability $2/3$ to the state 21 and $1/3$ to the state 22, etc. If the actual state of the world is $\omega = 12$, then $\text{Supp}(\overline{\theta}^{\text{I}}_\omega) = \{11\}$ and $\text{Supp}(\overline{\theta}^{\text{II}}_\omega) = \{22\}$. Both players will find the BL-subspace $\{11, 21, 22\}$ with the (only) consistent probability $(1/2, 1/3, 1/6)$. So both players will conclude that the state is consistent, committing a type II error. However, each player assigns to this event zero subjective probability. Note that in spite of its being inconsistent, the state $\omega = 12$ led both players to the same "consistent" space $Y(\omega) = \{11, 21, 22\}$. The next example shows that this is not guaranteed in an inconsistent state.

Example III.2.15. Consider the previous example with different subjective probabilities:

$$\begin{array}{c} \\ \mathrm{I}_1 \\ \mathrm{I}_2 \end{array} \begin{array}{c} \begin{array}{cc} \mathrm{II}_1 & \mathrm{II}_2 \end{array} \\ \begin{pmatrix} (1,1) & (0,0) \\ (0,0) & (1,1) \end{pmatrix} \end{array}.$$

If $\omega = 12$, player I will find the "consistent" $C^{\mathrm{I}}_{\omega} = \{11\}$ with probability $Q(11) = 1$, while player II will find $C^{\mathrm{II}}_{\omega} = \{22\}$ with $Q(22) = 1$.

Example III.2.16. A BL-subspace Y consists of 20 states with four types of player I and five types of player II. With the same notation as in the previous examples, Y is given by:

$$\begin{array}{c} \\ \mathrm{I}_1 \\ \mathrm{I}_2 \\ \mathrm{I}_3 \\ \mathrm{I}_4 \end{array} \begin{array}{c} \begin{array}{ccccc} \mathrm{II}_1 & \mathrm{II}_2 & \mathrm{II}_3 & \mathrm{II}_4 & \mathrm{II}_5 \end{array} \\ \begin{pmatrix} (0,0) & (1,3/5) & (0,0) & (0,0) & (0,0) \\ (1/3,1) & (2/3,2/5) & (0,0) & (0,0) & (0,0) \\ (0,0) & (0,0) & (0,1/2) & (1/4,1/2) & (3/4,1/3) \\ (0,0) & (0,0) & (0,1/2) & (1/4,1/2) & (3/4,2/3) \end{pmatrix} \end{array}.$$

If the actual state of the world is $\omega = 13$, player I finds $C^{\mathrm{I}}_{\omega} = \{21, 22, 12\}$ with the consistent probability distribution $Q = (1/6, 1/3, 1/2)$, and hence he will mistakenly conclude that the state is consistent. Player II, on the other hand, will find $C^{\mathrm{II}}_{\omega} = \{33, 34, 35, 43, 44, 45\}$ with no consistent Q on it. He will therefore correctly conclude that the state is inconsistent. Note that $\omega \notin \mathsf{Supp}(\overline{\theta}^{i}_{\omega})$. Unlike in previous examples player II reaches a correct negative conclusion despite $\omega \notin \mathsf{Supp}(\overline{\theta}^{\mathrm{II}}_{\omega})$, but this is just a coincidence.

Example III.2.17. Consider the following BL-subspace with 16 states and four types for each of the players I and II:

$$\begin{array}{c} \\ \mathrm{I}_1 \\ \mathrm{I}_2 \\ \mathrm{I}_3 \\ \mathrm{I}_4 \end{array} \begin{array}{c} \begin{array}{cccc} \mathrm{II}_1 & \mathrm{II}_2 & \mathrm{II}_3 & \mathrm{II}_4 \end{array} \\ \begin{pmatrix} (1,3/5) & (0,0) & (0,0) & (0,0) \\ (1/3,2/5) & (2/3,0) & (0,0) & (0,0) \\ (0,0) & (0,1/2) & (3/5,1/2) & (2/5,1/3) \\ (0,0) & (0,1/2) & (3/7,1/2) & (4/7,2/3) \end{pmatrix} \end{array}.$$

If the state of the world is $\omega = 13$, it is inconsistent and we expect player I to come to this conclusion. In fact, he will compute $C^{\mathrm{I}}_{\omega} = \{11, 21, 22, 32, 33, 34, 42, 43, 44\}$ but there will be no consistent distribution on it. (To see that: by Lemma III.2.1, p. 139, any consistent Q must have $Q(11) = 0$ since $\overline{\theta}^{\mathrm{II}}_{\omega}(11) = 0$ but also $Q(11) > 0$ since $\overline{\theta}^{\mathrm{I}}_{\omega}(11) > 0$.) So player I will in fact conclude that the state of the world is inconsistent. On the other hand, player II will compute $C^{\mathrm{II}}_{\omega} = \{33, 34, 43, 44\}$ with consistent distribution $Q = (1/4, 1/6, 1/4, 1/3)$ on it and mistakenly conclude that the state is consistent.

III.3. AN APPROXIMATION THEOREM

Most incomplete information models in the game theory literature, including most examples in this book, consist of **finite** BL-subspaces. In fact, any consistent BL-subspace can be approximated by a finite consistent BL-subspace. This is the content of the following theorem:

Theorem III.3.1. *The probabilities in $\mathscr{P}$ with finite support are dense in $\mathscr{P}$.*

Proof. We first consider the case in which K is a compact metric space.

(1) Let Q be a consistent probability on $\Omega = K \times \prod_i \Theta^i$. Let $\mathscr{K}_m$ and $\mathscr{C}^i_m$ be increasing sequences of measurable finite partitions of K and Θ^i, respectively, with the diameter of each partition element less than $1/m$. Let $\mathscr{E}_m$ be the following information scheme: ω is chosen according to Q, each player i is informed of the atom of $\mathscr{C}^i_m$ that contains $\theta^i(\omega)$, and the state of nature is some given element of the atom of $\mathscr{K}_m$ containing $k(\omega)$. Denote by Q_m the canonical consistent probability associated with this information scheme (Theorem III.2.4, p. 142). We shall prove that Q_m converges weakly to Q.

(2) We first need a preliminary lemma. Recall that given a random variable X from a probability space $(B, \mathscr{B}, P)$ to some compact metric space C with the Borel σ-field, we can consider the conditional distribution of X given a sub-σ-algebra $\mathscr{A} \subseteq \mathscr{B}$ as a transition probability from $(B, \mathscr{A})$ to C (cf. II.1, Ex. 16c, p. 86).

Lemma III.3.2. *Let X_m be a family of random variables from a probability space $(B, \mathscr{B}, P)$ to some compact metric space and let $\mathscr{B}_m$ be an increasing sequence of sub-σ-algebras converging to $\mathscr{B}_\infty$. Assume that X_m converges a.e. to some X_∞ and let P_m denote the conditional distribution of X_m given $\mathscr{B}_m$. Then a.e. P_m converges weakly to P_∞.*

Proof. Let $\mathscr{F}$ be a countable dense subset of continuous functions on C. For f in $\mathscr{F}$ let $Y_m = f(X_m)$, $\overline{Y}_m = \sup_{n \geq m} Y_n$, $\underline{Y}_m = \inf_{n \geq m} Y_n$. $\overline{Y}_m$ is a decreasing sequence converging a.e. to $Y_\infty = f(X_\infty)$. Let $\overline{Z}_m = \mathsf{E}(\overline{Y}_m \mid \mathscr{B}_m)$. $\overline{Z}_m$ is a bounded supermartingale that converges a.e. to some $\overline{Z}$. Note that $\overline{Z} \geq Y = \mathsf{E}(Y_\infty \mid \mathscr{B}_\infty)$ a.s. since $\mathsf{E}(\overline{Y}_m \mid \mathscr{B}_m) \geq \mathsf{E}(Y_\infty \mid \mathscr{B}_m)$ a.s. and this last term converges a.e. to Y. Similarly $\underline{Z} \leq Y$ a.e. But by the supermartingale property $\mathsf{E}(\overline{Z} - \underline{Z}) \leq \mathsf{E}(\overline{Z}_n - \underline{Z}_n) = \mathsf{E}(\overline{Y}_n - \underline{Y}_n)$, which tends to zero by the dominated convergence theorem. Hence $\overline{Z} = \underline{Z} = Y$ a.e. Hence $\mathsf{E}(f(X_m) \mid \mathscr{B}_m)$ converges a.e. to $\mathsf{E}(f(X_\infty) \mid \mathscr{B}_\infty)$, and the result follows. ∎

(3) Let φ^m be the map of Theorem 3.3, p. 142, corresponding to $\mathscr{E}_m$, from Ω to itself, and let φ^m_n be the composition of φ^m with the projection p_n from Ω to $\Omega_n = K \times \prod_i \Theta^i_n$. Note that φ^m_n converges (as $m \to \infty$) a.e. to p_n, inductively, since it is true on K, and by the previous lemma the conditional distribution of $\mathrm{Proj}_{X^i_n} \circ \varphi^m_n$ given $\mathscr{C}^i_m$ (i.e., the projection on Θ^i_{n+1}) converges a.e. to the conditional distribution of $\mathrm{Proj}_{X^i_n} \circ p_n$ given $\mathscr{C}^i_\infty$ (which is precisely $p^i_{n+1} \circ$

$\theta^i(\omega) = \theta^i_{n+1}(\omega)$; indeed, the σ-field $\mathscr{C}^i$ generated by all $\mathscr{C}^i_m$ is a separable sub-σ-field of the Borel σ-field on a compact metric space and has the points as atoms; hence it is the Borel σ-field on Θ^i (Appendix A.6)). It follows that φ^m converges Q-a.e. to the identity on Ω, and hence the claim.

(4) For a general compact K note first that for any continuous function f on Ω there exists a metrizable quotient space $\tilde{K}$ of K such that if p denotes the induced map from Ω to $\Omega_{\tilde{K}}$ (i.e., $p = [g_n \times \prod_i \Theta^i(g)]$ where g is the quotient map), then f factorizes through p (use that continuous functions on a product of compact sets can be approximated by polynomials in continuous functions on the factors and that continuous functions on the space of probabilities on a compact set S can be approximated by polynomials in the integrals of finitely many continuous functions on S). Next, given continuous functions $f_1, \ldots, f_n$ on Ω, construct such a metrizable quotient $\tilde{K}$ with the above property valid for all f_j, and use the previous case on $\tilde{K}$ to find a consistent approximation with finite support $\tilde{Q}_\varepsilon$ on $\Omega_{\tilde{K}}$ approximating the image $p(Q)$ up to ε w.r.t. the integral of each f_j. Finally, lift the $\tilde{K}$ coordinates in the support of $\tilde{Q}_\varepsilon$ back to K to get Q_ε ($= [\ell \times \prod_i \Theta^i(\ell)](\tilde{Q}_\varepsilon)$ where ℓ is the lifting map, i.e., any map having the right values and defined on the finitely many points in $\tilde{K}$ that have positive probability under $\tilde{Q}_\varepsilon$) on Ω.

(5) In the general case, let first K_n $(n = 1, \ldots \infty)$ be a sequence of disjoint compact subsets of K with $Q(L) = 1$ for $L = \bigcup_n K_n$. Observe that Ω together with Q can be viewed as an information scheme for L, by modifying the projection map to K on a null set, so Theorem III.2.4, p. 142, yields that it is represented by some consistent probability $\overline{Q}$ on $\Omega_L \subseteq \Omega_K$. $\overline{Q}$ is then also a good representation for this information scheme when viewed as having values in K; i.e., the map φ still satisfies conditions 1a, 1b, and 1a of Theorem III.2.4 if the range space is K. But Q itself with the identity map also satisfies them; hence by part (2) of the theorem we have $Q = \overline{Q}$, i.e., $Q(\Omega_L) = 1$. So we can assume $K = \bigcup_n K_n$. Denote by $\overline{K}$ the disjoint union of the K_n: then as observed in the proof of Theorem III.2.4, p. 142, $\Omega_{\overline{K}}$ and Ω_K are K-Lusin, and the induced map f from $\Omega_{\overline{K}}$ to Ω_K is continuous, one-to-one, onto, and a Borel isomorphism, so $\Delta(f)$ is also continuous and onto: Q can be viewed as a consistent probability on $\Omega_{\overline{K}}$ (formally, the one obtained from Theorem III.2.4, p. 142, by viewing the information scheme as having values in $\overline{K}$). And by the continuity of $\Delta(f)$, it suffices now to prove the result on $\Omega_{\overline{K}}$: we can assume K is a disjoint union of compact sets K_n, in particular locally compact, with one-point compactification $\hat{K}$. Since $\Omega_K \subseteq \Omega_{\hat{K}}$ (part (3a) of Theorem III.1.2, p. 127), Q can be viewed as a consistent probability for $\hat{K}$, which assigns probability zero to the point at infinity "∞." Then our previous construction yields indeed the desired result: taking care in part (4) to add to our sequence of continuous functions the indicators of the K_n yields that no point of K is identified with ∞ under the quotient mapping; if we further choose in (2) the singleton $\{\infty\}$ as an element of every partition $\mathscr{K}_m$, we indeed obtain that ∞ is not in the support of any of the approximating measures. ∎

Remark III.3.1. Cf. Mertens and Zamir (1985) for a proof that the set of finite belief subspaces is dense in the space of all closed belief subspaces, with the Hausdorff topology.

III.4. GAMES WITH INCOMPLETE INFORMATION

III.4.a. The Model

The objective of this chapter is to suggest a mathematical structure for the belief space in a situation of incomplete information involving several players. It is clear, however, that the main purpose of this structure is its application to games. Let us therefore conclude by showing briefly how this belief space is used in modeling **games with incomplete information**. To define a game we obviously have to add a few more ingredients to our model: each player i in $\mathbf{I}$ has an action set S^i (without loss of generality this may be assumed to be independent of player i's type. One can achieve this by taking as S^i the product of the type-dependent action set over all types). For i in $\mathbf{I}$ and ω in Ω there is a utility function u^i_ω that is a real-valued function defined in the product of the action sets $S = \prod_{i \in \mathbf{I}} S^i$. Given any finite BL-subspace Y, we first define a **vector payoff game** Γ_Y in which:

- The player set is $\mathbf{I}$.
- The strategy set Σ^i of player i is the set of mappings $\sigma^i : Y \to S^i$, which are θ^i-measurable.
- The payoff to player i resulting from the strategy profile $\sigma = (\sigma^i)_{i \in \mathbf{I}}$ is the vector payoff: $U_i(\sigma) = (U_{\theta^i}(\sigma))_{\theta^i \in \Theta^i}$ (i.e., a payoff for each type θ^i) where:

$$U_{\theta^i}(\sigma) = \int u^i_\omega(\sigma(\omega))\, d\overline{\theta}^i(\omega).$$

Note that U_{θ^i} is θ^i-measurable, as it should be. Although this is not a game in the usual sense, the concept of equilibrium can be defined in the usual way; namely:

Definition III.4.1. The strategy profile $\sigma = (\sigma^i)_{i \in \mathbf{I}}$ is an **equilibrium** in Γ_Y if for all ω in Y and for all i in $\mathbf{I}$:

$$U_{\theta^i(\omega)}(\sigma) \geq U_{\theta^i(\omega)}(\tilde{\sigma}^i, \sigma^{-i}) \text{ holds for all } \tilde{\sigma}^i \in \Sigma^i.$$

Remark III.4.2. Note that the above game is an $\mathbf{I}$-person game in which the payoff for player i is a vector with a number of coordinates equal to $\#\Theta^i$. It is easily seen that as far as equilibria are concerned, this game is equivalent to an ordinary $\prod_{i \in \mathbf{I}} \#\Theta^i$-person game in which each "player" $\theta^i \in \Theta^i$ selects an action in S^i and then nature selects his $\{i\}^c$ partners, one from each Θ^j, $j \neq i$, according to the distribution θ^i on Y. (This is a "Selten game"; cf. Harsanyi (1968b, Section 15, p. 496)). We can also define an $\mathbf{I}$-person game with the above strategy sets where the payoff function for player i is $\overline{U}^i = \Sigma_{\theta^i \in \Theta^i} \gamma_{\theta^i} U_{\theta^i}$, where for each $\theta^i \in \Theta^i$, γ_{θ^i} is a strictly positive constant. Clearly, independently of the constants γ_{θ^i} used, this game has the same equilibria as the vector payoff game (and hence the corresponding Selten game).

For a consistent BL-subspace one has the following theorem, which permits us, in looking for equilibria, to replace the normal form game by an equivalent extensive form game, called its **standard form** by Harsanyi.

Theorem III.4.1. *(Harsanyi, 1968b) Let Y be a consistent BL-subspace of Ω. Let Q be a consistent probability distribution whose support is Y. Then the game Γ_Y is equivalent to the following extensive form game:*

- *A chance move chooses $\omega \in Y$ according to Q; then each player $i \in \mathbf{I}$ is informed of his type $\theta^i(\omega)$.*
- *Each player $i \in \mathbf{I}$ chooses an action $s^i \in S^i$ and receives a payoff $U^i_{\theta^i(\omega)}(\sigma)$.*

Proof. Follows from the definitions and the fact that $\mathsf{Supp}(Q) = Y$. ■

The above theorem is especially appealing if one recalls that when Y is minimal consistent then there is a unique consistent probability distribution P on it.

III.4.b. Two-Person Zero-Sum Case

Now we start moving beyond considering the purely topological or even measure-theoretic aspects of beliefs to richer structures, more intimately tied to game-theoretic applications. Indeed, the canonical homeomorphism between Θ^i and $\Delta(K \times \prod_{j \neq i} \Theta^j)$ endows Θ with a canonical convex structure, which comes in addition to the canonical convex structure on $\mathscr{P}$. Further, given such a convex structure, one can consider various convex cones of continuous functions on spaces like $K \times \prod_j \Theta^j$, e.g., those functions that are jointly concave in the θ-vector, those that are separately convex, or one of the above with the further requirement of being independent of K. And, according to II.1, Ex. 20, p. 89, each such convex cone yields an ordering on the space of probability measures on this product, hence orderings on the spaces Θ and $\mathscr{P}$. In addition, given such orderings, one can define other cones, and hence other orderings, etc., by putting monotonicity requirements (possibly in addition to the concavity requirements) on the continuous functions.

The game-theoretic significance of some of those constructs appears already in (one-shot) games with incomplete information, which is our subject in this section, and much more seems to appear in the repeated case, which is the subject of Chapters V and VI. But all this is still clearly at a very exploratory stage: we will know (a first) part of what is to be understood only when it is developed fully in Chapter VI for general "entrance laws" (and in turn such general entrance laws in Chapter VI are needed for the simplest case in

Chapter IX). Although much remains to be clarified, even for one-shot zero-sum games with finite strategy sets, some insight can already be gained from what follows.

We assume here that the state space K and the strategy spaces S and T of players I and II respectively are compact, and that the payoff function $g^k(s,t)$ on $K \times S \times T$ is jointly continuous. (The reason for going beyond finite S and T is that in the next chapter we will want to apply those results to the discounted games.)

We first consider an auxiliary family of games, indexed by $\mathbf{P}$ in $\mathscr{P}$ and corresponding to the "canonical information scheme." For each $\mathbf{P}$ in $\mathscr{P}$ a (one-stage) zero-sum game $[g, \mathbf{P}]$ is now defined as follows: first a triple $(k, \theta^{\mathrm{I}}, \theta^{\mathrm{II}})$ is chosen in Ω according to $\mathbf{P}$. Next θ^i is told to player i, and finally each player selects simultaneously a move s in S (resp. t in T). The resulting payoff is then g^k_{st}. (The above description is known to both players.)

We shall prove here some properties of $[g, \mathbf{P}]$.

Proposition III.4.2. *$[g, \mathbf{P}]$ has a value $v_g(\mathbf{P})$, and both players have, for all $\varepsilon > 0$, ε-optimal strategies with a finite support consisting of pure strategies taking finitely many values. They also have ε-optimal strategies that are continuous behavioral strategies with support in a fixed, finite subset of their strategy space. Moreover, both players also have optimal strategies that are regular transition probabilities from Θ to S (resp. T).*

Note that the above statement indicates that $[g, \mathbf{P}]$ has a value in an unambiguous sense.

Proof. We still denote by $\mathbf{P}^i$ the marginal of $\mathbf{P}$ on Θ^i, the space of types of player i. As the mixed strategy space of the players we consider the compact (cf. II.1, Ex. 17, p. 86) space Σ (resp. $\mathscr{T}$) of regular transition probabilities from Θ^{I} (resp. Θ^{II}) to S (resp. T). The payoff is then in $L_\infty(\Omega \times S \times T, P \times \sigma \times \tau)$ and its expectation $\mathsf{E}_{\sigma,\tau,\mathbf{P}}(g) = \gamma(\sigma, \tau)$ is a bi-linear separately continuous function on $\Sigma \times \mathscr{T}$ (by II.1, Ex. 18b, p. 87, recall that a jointly continuous function on a product of two compact spaces can also be viewed as a continuous map from one of the factors into the Banach space of continuous functions on the other factor). Theorem I.1.1, p. 5, implies the existence of a value and of optimal strategies.

By the same property of jointly continuous maps, one can now find a finite subset S_0 of S and a Borel map $\varphi\colon S \to S_0$ such that $|g_k(s,t) - g_k(\varphi(s), t)| \le \varepsilon$ on $K \times S \times T$. The image by φ of player I's optimal strategy is then clearly ε-optimal and is carried by S_0.

For the second part consider $\sigma \mapsto \gamma(\sigma, \tau)$ as a mapping from S_0-valued transition probabilities, endowed with convergence in probability, to the space $\mathbb{R}^{\mathscr{T}}$, with uniform convergence (where $\mathscr{T}$ is the set of behavioral strategies of player II), and note that this mapping is continuous. It is then possible to obtain from our previous σ an ε-approximation in probability by a step function (resp., by a continuous function), say, σ_ε, which will be ε-optimal. Finally, note that

σ_ε can be written as a finite convex combination of pure strategies, hence the claim. ■

We now study $v_g(\mathbf{P})$ as a function of $\mathbf{P}$ on $\mathscr{P}$. Recall (Theorem III.2.2, p. 139, and Corollary III.2.3, p. 140) that this set of consistent probabilities is closed and convex.

Proposition III.4.3. *$v_g(\mathbf{P})$ is continuous and affine on $\mathscr{P}$.*

Proof. Let us first prove continuity. Denote by $\sigma = \{\sigma(\theta) \mid \sigma(\theta) \in \Delta(S), \theta \in \Theta\}$ an ε-optimal strategy of player I in $[g, \mathbf{P}]$, which we can assume, by Proposition III.4.2, to be continuous in θ. If player II is of type θ^{II} and uses the move t, his expected payoff against σ will be:

$$\int_{K\times\Theta^{\mathrm{I}}} \sigma(\theta^{\mathrm{I}}) g_t^k \, \theta^{\mathrm{II}}(dk, d\theta^{\mathrm{I}})$$

(with $\sigma(\theta^{\mathrm{I}}) g_t^k = \sum_s \sigma(\theta^{\mathrm{I}})(s) g_{s,t}^k$), which is a continuous linear function of θ^{II} by the above remarks. A best reply of player II is then obviously to choose, given θ^{II}, some t in T minimizing the above expression.

Let now $\mathbf{P}_\alpha$ converge to $\mathbf{P}$ in $\mathscr{P}$. It follows that σ guarantees to player I in $[g, \mathbf{P}_\alpha]$ an expected payoff of:

$$\int_{\Theta^{\mathrm{II}}} \{\min_{t\in T} \int_{K\times\Theta^{\mathrm{I}}} \sigma(\theta^{\mathrm{I}}) g_t^k \theta^{\mathrm{II}}(dk, d\theta^{\mathrm{I}})\} \mathbf{P}_\alpha^{\mathrm{II}}(d\theta^{\mathrm{II}}),$$

where $\mathbf{P}_\alpha^{\mathrm{II}}$ denotes the marginal of $\mathbf{P}_\alpha$ on Θ^{II} (recall that $\mathbf{P}_\alpha$ is consistent). Since the integrand is continuous, so is the integral. Note that this payoff is a lower bound for $v_g(\mathbf{P}_\alpha)_j$; hence by the choice of σ we obtain that v_g is lower semi-continuous at $\mathbf{P}$. Permuting the role of the players gives upper semi-continuity, hence the claim.

As for linearity, take $\mathbf{P}'$ and $\mathbf{P}''$ in $\mathscr{P}$ and let z in $(0, 1)$. Consider the "compound" game $[g; \mathscr{I}]$ corresponding to the following information scheme $\mathscr{I}$: first $\mathbf{P}'$ and $\mathbf{P}''$ are chosen with probabilities z and $1 - z$, next the players are informed of the result, and then the corresponding canonical information scheme is used. A map φ as in Theorem III.2.4, p. 142, is obviously constructed using the identity on both canonical information schemes, i.e., forgetting the first lottery. Since the conditions of Theorem III.2.4 are obviously satisfied, the canonical consistent probability associated with $\mathscr{I}$ is precisely $z\mathbf{P}' + (1 - z)\mathbf{P}''$. Now it is clear that the value of $[g; \mathscr{I}]$ is $\alpha v_g(\mathbf{P}') + (1 - \alpha) v_g(\mathbf{P}'')$; thus the following Proposition III.4.4 implies the linearity. ■

Recalling the description of the information structure before Proposition III.4.2, p. 155, note that we could also define the game by starting with an information scheme $\mathscr{I}$ consisting of some abstract probability space $\mathbf{E} = (E, \mathscr{E}, Q)$ equipped with a random variable $\tilde{k}$ with values in K and sub-σ-fields $\mathscr{E}^{\mathrm{I}}$ and $\mathscr{E}^{\mathrm{II}}$. Denote this game by $[g; \mathscr{I}]$ and its value by $v(g; \mathscr{I})$. Then we have the following equivalence lemma:

Proposition III.4.4. *Let $\widetilde{\mathbf{P}}$ denote the canonical consistent probability corresponding to the scheme $\mathscr{I}$ (Theorem III.2.4.1b, p. 142). Then:*

$$v(g;\mathscr{I}) = v_g(\widetilde{\mathbf{P}}).$$

Moreover, ε-optimal strategies in $[g, \widetilde{\mathbf{P}}]$ induce, by the projection mapping φ, ε-optimal strategies in $[g;\mathscr{I}]$.

Proof. Consider a strategy $\widetilde{\sigma}$ of player I in $[g, \widetilde{\mathbf{P}}]$. Denote by σ the strategy induced in $[g;\mathscr{I}]$ by the projection mapping φ. It will be sufficient to show that σ guarantees to player I as much in $[g;\mathscr{I}]$ as $\widetilde{\sigma}$ does in $[g, \widetilde{\mathbf{P}}]$.

Let us write the expected payoff for player II in $[g;\mathscr{I}]$ against σ, given his information $\mathscr{E}^{\mathrm{II}}$ and his move t. Using the structure of σ we obtain:

$$\int_C \widetilde{\sigma}(\theta^{\mathrm{I}} \circ \varphi(\cdot)) g_t^{\tilde{k}(\cdot)} Q(\cdot \mid \mathscr{E}^{\mathrm{II}}).$$

Now if θ^{II} denotes the image of e in player II's space of types, parts (1a) and (1c) of Theorem III.2.4, p. 142, imply that the above equals:

$$\int_{K\times\Theta} \widetilde{\sigma}(\theta^{\mathrm{I}}) g_t^k \overline{\theta}^{\mathrm{II}}(dk, d\theta^{\mathrm{I}}).$$

It follows that player's II best replies in $[g;\mathscr{I}]$ against σ at e are the same as his best replies to $\widetilde{\sigma}$ in $[g, \widetilde{\mathbf{P}}]$ at θ^{II} ($= \theta^{\mathrm{II}}(\varphi(e))$, and both lead to the same payoff. Finally this payoff is only a function of θ^{II}, and hence the average payoffs under Q and $\widetilde{\mathbf{P}}$ will also coincide. ■

It is now easy to compare two consistent probabilities when they come from comparable information schemes.

Definition III.4.3. Given $\mathbf{P}_1$ and $\mathbf{P}_2$ in $\mathscr{P}$, $\mathbf{P}_1$ is **more informative** to player I than $\mathbf{P}_2$, whenever there are two information schemes $\mathscr{I}_1$ and $\mathscr{I}_2$ of which they are canonical representations and such that $\mathscr{I}_1 = ((C), k, m_1^{\mathrm{I}}, m^{\mathrm{II}})$, $\mathscr{I}_2 = ((C), k, m_2^{\mathrm{I}}, m^{\mathrm{II}})$, with $m_2^{\mathrm{I}} = f(m_1^{\mathrm{I}})$ (i.e., player I has more information in $\mathscr{I}_1$).

Proposition III.4.5. *If $\mathbf{P}_1$ is more informative to player* I *than $\mathbf{P}_2$ then $v_g(\mathbf{P}_1) \geq v_g(\mathbf{P}_2)$.*

Proof. The result follows from Proposition III.4.4, p. 157, and the relation $v(g;\mathscr{I}_1) \geq v(g;\mathscr{I}_2)$, which is obvious since player I has more strategies in the first case and the payoffs are the same in both. ■

Remark III.4.4. It is clear that much sharper results are needed, basically analytic characterizations, along the lines of Blackwell's "comparison of experiments." Observe that there are two different sets of orderings one may be interested in characterizing: what is the transitive closure of the above? Call it $P_1 \succ_1 P_2$. Then define $P_1 R P_2$ as either $P_1 \succ_1 P_2$ or $P_2 \prec_2 P_1$ (P_2 is less informative to player II than P_1). What is the transitive closure of R? Call it $P_1 \succ P_2$. In addition to the analytic characterizations, does the latter order allow for a converse of Proposition III.4.5? (For example, is every continuous affine function on $\mathscr{P}$ that is monotone for $\succ$ a uniform limit of functions $v_g(P)$, where g varies over finite games?)

III.4.c. "Approachability" in One-Shot Games

We finally turn to a theorem that sharpens all the above. Henceforth g is fixed and will accordingly be dropped from the notation.

Definition III.4.5. $\mathbf{T} = \{\mathbf{t}\colon \Theta^{\mathrm{I}} \to \mathbb{R} \mid \exists$ a continuous behavioral strategy of player II as in Proposition III.4.2 such that $\mathbf{t} = \mathbf{t}_\tau : \theta^{\mathrm{I}} \mapsto \max_{s \in S} \int_{K \otimes \Theta^{\mathrm{II}}} g^k_{s,t} \tau(dt \mid \theta^{\mathrm{II}}) \theta^{\mathrm{I}}(dk, d\theta^{\mathrm{II}})\}$.

Definition III.4.6. For $\mu \in \Delta(\Theta^{\mathrm{I}})$, denote by P_μ the canonical consistent probability corresponding to the scheme $\mathscr{I}_\mu$ (Theorem III.2.4, part (1b), p. 142), where $\mathscr{I}_\mu = (\Theta^{\mathrm{I}} \times \Theta^{\mathrm{II}} \times K$, Borel sets, $\theta^{\mathrm{I}}(d\theta^{\mathrm{II}}, dk)\mu(d\theta^{\mathrm{I}})$, Θ^{I}, Θ^{II}, $\mathsf{Proj}_K)$.

Theorem III.4.6.

(1) $\int_{\Theta^{\mathrm{I}}} \mathbf{t}\, d\mu \geq v(P_\mu)\ \forall \mathbf{t} \in \mathbf{T}, \forall \mu \in \Delta(\Theta^{\mathrm{I}})$.
(2) *For every l.s.c., convex function F on $\Delta(\Theta^{\mathrm{I}})$, with $F(\mu) > v(P_\mu)\ \forall \mu$, $\exists \mathbf{t} \in \mathbf{T}$ with $\int \mathbf{t}\, d\mu < F(\mu) \forall \mu$.*

Proof. (1) A strategy τ of player II as in Proposition III.4.2, p. 155, guarantees that, $\forall \theta^{\mathrm{I}} \in \Delta(\Theta^{\mathrm{II}} \times K)$, player I's maximal expected payoff under θ^{I} equals $\mathbf{t}_\tau(\theta^{\mathrm{I}})$. Thus, under the scheme $\mathscr{I}$, the maximal expected payoff equals $\int \mathbf{t}_\tau(\theta^{\mathrm{I}})\mu(d\theta^{\mathrm{I}})$ (using a measurable selection theorem (Appendix A.7.j) to select μ-measurably for each θ^{I} an (ε)-optimal s), and hence the integral exceeds $v(g, \mathscr{I})$, and the result follows, by Proposition III.4.4, p. 157.

(2) Consider the game where player II chooses $\mathbf{t}_\tau \in \mathbf{T}$, player I chooses $\mu \in \Delta(\Theta^{\mathrm{I}})$, and the payoff equals $\int_{\Theta^{\mathrm{I}}} \mathbf{t}_\tau d\mu - F(\mu)$. Player I's strategy space is compact (by Theorem III.1.2, part (1), p. 127; remember our above assumption of compactness of K) and convex, and player II's set of τ's is convex. Further, the payoff is $< +\infty$, is concave and u.s.c. in μ, and is convex in τ since, for $\tau = \alpha\tau_1 + (1-\alpha)\tau_2$, $\mathbf{t}_\tau \leq \alpha\mathbf{t}_{\tau_1} + (1-\alpha)\mathbf{t}_{\tau_2}$, because it is always beneficial for player I to know the result of the coin toss with probabilities α and $1-\alpha$ rather than not. So all the assumptions of the minmax theorem (Proposition I.1.3, p. 6) are satisfied. Finally, by Proposition III.4.4, p. 157, $F(\mu) > v(P_\mu) = v(g, \mathscr{I})$. Hence approximating an ε-optimal τ in the game $[g, \mathscr{I}]$ by a continuous τ as in Proposition III.4.2, p. 155, which, as shown in (1) above, guarantees exactly $\int \mathbf{t}_\tau d\mu$, we obtain that the $\sup\inf$ of our game is negative. The result follows by the minmax theorem. ∎

We reformulate now the above result without using functions as general as F above.

Corollary III.4.7.

(1) *The function $v(P_\mu)$ is concave and u.s.c. on $\Delta(\Theta^{\mathrm{I}})$.*

(2) *For every continuous (or l.s.c.) function* f *on* Θ^{I}, *with* $\int f d\mu > v(P_\mu)\ \forall \mu, \exists \mathbf{t} \in \mathbf{T}$ *with* $\mathbf{t} < f$.
(3) $v(P_\mu) = \inf_{\mathbf{t}\in\mathbf{T}} \int \mathbf{t} d\mu$.

Proof. Let in Theorem III.4.6, part (2), $F(\nu) = +\infty$ for $\nu \neq \mu$, $F(\mu) = v(P_\mu) + \varepsilon$: we get $v(P_\mu) \geq \inf_{\mathbf{t}\in\mathbf{T}} \int \mathbf{t} d\mu$. By part (1) of Theorem III.4.6, we get then equality, i.e., (3), and hence (1). And (2) is obviously a particular case of part (2) of Theorem III.4.6. ■

Remark III.4.7. The corollary has the full force of the theorem, by the separation theorem (Propositions I.1.13 and I.1.15, p. 10). Therefore it also implies the following:

Corollary III.4.8. *Each player has continuous behavioral strategies (or strategies with finite support) as in Proposition III.4.2, p. 155, which are* ε*-optimal for all* $P \in \mathscr{P}$.

Proof. The maps from $\mathscr{P}$ to the corresponding marginals on Θ^{I} and on Θ^{II} are affine, continuous, and one to one, so they are affine homeomorphisms of compact (Corollary III.2.3, p. 140), convex sets. So when μ varies over this set of marginals, part (1) of Corollary III.4.7 yields that $v(P)$ is concave and u.s.c. on $\mathscr{P}$. Hence by duality it is affine and continuous. Define then $F(\mu) = v(P) + \varepsilon$ when μ is the projection of some $P \in \mathscr{P}$, $F(\mu) = +\infty$ otherwise: F is convex and l.s.c. Apply now part (2) of the theorem. ■

Remark III.4.8. The corollary "confirms" Remark III.2.13, p. 149: Lemma III.2.7 is restricted to finite *BL*-spaces, and states only that, under consistency, the minimal *BL*-subspace containing ω is common knowledge, so if players' beliefs satisfy the finiteness assumption and consistency, but especially if they believe that the true state of the world is always generated by the minimal consistent probability under which it has positive probability,[1] then they would be able to know the true game, and hence to play correctly, knowing just their own types. The corollary implies that knowing one's own type is sufficient to be able to play correctly, without any assumption beyond consistency.

Remark III.4.9. Further, the continuity of the behavioral strategies guarantees that it suffices for the player to know his own type approximately.

[1] Such an assumption would be quite inconsistent *in se* since there are quite obvious information schemes (like the one used in the proof of the second half of Proposition III.4.3, p. 156) that can generate ω without being minimal with this property. And when dispensing with the finiteness restriction, it becomes even formally nonsense, since for many states of the world, there may be so many consistent *BL*-subspaces containing it in their support (in whatever sense, cf., e.g., example 6 or 8a, p. 137) that there may very well even be no minimal one despite 3, p. 140, or that there may be several minimal ones.

Corollary III.4.9. *$v(P)$ is continuous and affine on $\mathscr{P}$.*

Proof. Was derived in the proof of Corollary III.4.8. Alternatively, $v(P)$ is the uniform limit (Corollary III.4.8) of the continuous affine functions $\int \mathbf{t}(\theta^{\mathrm{I}}_{\omega})P(d\omega)$. ∎

Remark III.4.10. The convexity of the functions $\mathbf{t} \in \mathbf{T}$ seems closely related to Proposition III.4.5, p. 157; cf. also Remark III.4.4, p. 157. But this relation remains to be elucidated.

Remark III.4.11. A (related) question to be elucidated is to state separate properties of the map $\mu \mapsto P_\mu$ and of the map $P \mapsto v(P)$, which ensure that the composition is concave and u.s.c. (part 1 of Corollary III.4.7).

Remark III.4.12. Is the composition continuous after all? Observe that modulo a proof that the set of functions $v_g(P)$, where g varies, separates points of $\mathscr{P}$, this would immediately imply the continuity of $\mu \mapsto P_\mu$, thus giving a first partial answer to Remark III.4.11. The continuity of this map would also be of great help whenever handling concavification and convexification operators (cf. below). Finally, the continuity of $v(P_\mu)$ would be a first step in showing that, with $\mathbf{T}_m$ being the set of minimal elements of $\{ f : \Theta^{\mathrm{I}} \to \mathbb{R} \mid f$ is convex and continuous, and $\int f\, d\mu \geq v(P_\mu)\, \forall \mu \}$, every $\mathbf{t} \in \mathbf{T}$ is bounded from below by some $f \in \mathbf{T}_m$, and $\mathbf{T}_m$ is equicontinuous. (It is a situation like this that we are going to encounter in Chapters V and VI, but in a more restrictive framework, where the μ's are restricted to being carried by those θ^{I}'s that assign probability one to a fixed, finite subset of Θ^{II}, and where the game is repeated, so those functions in $\mathbf{T}_m$ can be realized by some strategy of II (and the function guaranteed by any strategy of II is bounded from below by some $f \in \mathbf{T}_m$). Further there one tries to define those sets without using *any* topological restriction.)

Remark III.4.13. Observe that already now we could define some $\mathbf{T}_m$ by requiring only upper semi-continuity instead of continuity of the functions f, using, e.g., Zorn's lemma and the regularity of the measures. We would indeed have that any convex u.s.c. function f satisfying the inequalities, and thus a fortiori any l.s.c. f (convex or not) (part (2) of Corollary III.4.7), and a fortiori any $f \in \mathbf{T}$, is bounded from below by one in $\mathbf{T}_m$. But nothing more: even if we were to define $\tilde{\mathbf{T}}_m$ analogously while deleting the convexity restriction on the functions f, we do not know whether we would get the same set (cf. also I.3, Ex. 15c, p. 44, for how such a problem is handled in a finite dimensional case).

Remark III.4.14. The problem of equicontinuity in Remark III.4.13 provides an opportunity to mention two other such problems (conceivably somewhat related). Lipschitz properties are of crucial importance in Chapters V and VI.

(1) One expects a conditional expectation operator to be a smoothing operator, e.g., not to increase the Lipschitz constant for appropriate

distances. Assume thus a distance on K, or even take K finite, with distance 1 between any two distinct points. Consider the set E_0 of Lipschitz functions with Lipschitz constant 1 on K, viewed as functions on Ω, and then the smallest lattice E of functions on Ω that contains E_0 and contains the function $\omega \mapsto \overline{\theta}^i_\omega(f)\ \forall i \in \mathbf{I}, \forall f \in E$. Is E equicontinuous? (This is equivalent to the existence of a distance with the above-mentioned property.)

(2) For K finite, is the set of functions $v_g(P)$ on $\mathscr{P}$ equicontinuous? Here S and T vary over all finite sets, and g over all games with $|g^k_{s,t}| \leq 1$ $\forall k, \forall s, \forall t$. The answer is affirmative when P is restricted to those consistent probabilities that project to a point mass on one of the factors (cf. Mertens, 1987a).

III.4.d. Concavification and Convexification

We introduce here two types of definitions, motivated by part (1) of Corollary III.4.7, p. 158, that will be fundamental in the sequel.

Definition III.4.15. A real function f on $\mathscr{P}$ is *concave w.r.t.* I ($\mathsf{Cav}_{\mathrm{I}}$) (resp. *convex w.r.t.* II ($\mathsf{Vex}_{\mathrm{II}}$)) if $\mu \mapsto f(P_\mu)$ is concave on $\Delta(\Theta^{\mathrm{I}})$ (resp. convex on $\Delta(\Theta^{\mathrm{II}})$, with the obvious definition of P_μ).

Remark III.4.16. This is just a "template" definition: a number of variants of this definition are possible, e.g., concave and u.s.c. on $\Delta(\theta^I)$, or a minimum of integrals of convex continuous functions on θ^I, etc. When we extend the analysis of Chapter VI entirely to arbitrary entrance laws (after solving some of the open problems in this section), then we will also see which variant of concavity is the most useful.

With the same precautions, one can also define the following:

Definition III.4.17.

(1) For any $P \in \mathscr{P}$, denote by $\mathscr{I}_P$ the corresponding canonical information scheme (i.e., like $\mathscr{I}_\mu$ in Definition III.4.6, p. 158, but with P as the probability measure). For any information scheme $\mathscr{I}$, let $P_{\mathscr{I}}$ denote the corresponding canonical consistent probability as in Definition III.4.6, p. 158. Let also $\mathscr{I}_c$ denote the corresponding canonical information scheme.

(2) Given a function f on $\mathscr{P}$, and an information scheme $\mathscr{I}$, define $\overline{f}(\mathscr{I})$ as $f(P_{\mathscr{I}})$. With $\mathscr{I} = (E, \mathscr{E}, Q, (\mathscr{E}_i)_{i \in \mathbf{I}}, \tilde{k}_E)$ define also $\mathscr{I}_g$, $\forall g \in L_1(E, \mathscr{E}_1, Q)$ with $g \geq 0$, $\|g\|_1 = 1$ as the information scheme $(E, \mathscr{E}, g\,dQ, (\mathscr{E}_i)_{i \in \mathbf{I}}, \tilde{k}_E)$ (so $\mathscr{I} = \mathscr{I}_1$). Define finally $\hat{f}(\mathscr{I})$ as $\mathsf{sup}\{\sum \sigma_n \overline{f}(\mathscr{I}_{g_n}) \mid \sigma \in \Delta(N), \sum_n \sigma_n g_n = 1, N \text{ finite}\}$.

(3) Define now f on $\mathscr{P}$ as strongly concave (w.r.t. I) if $\overline{f}(\mathscr{I}) = \hat{f}(\mathscr{I})$ for every information scheme $\mathscr{I}$.

Remark III.4.18. Equivalently, $\hat{f}(\mathscr{I}_g)$ is the smallest concave function of g that is greater than or equal to $\overline{f}(\mathscr{I}_g)$. And f is strongly concave if $g \to \overline{f}(\mathscr{I}_g)$ is concave for every $\mathscr{I}$.

Definition III.4.19. A function f on $\mathscr{P}$ is monotone w.r.t. I, if for any information scheme $\mathscr{I}$, and any event $A \in \mathscr{E}_{\text{I}}$, the information scheme $\mathscr{I}_A$ obtained by adding $\forall i$, A to $\mathscr{E}_i$ satisfies $\overline{f}(\mathscr{I}) \geq \overline{f}(\mathscr{I}_A)$.

Remark III.4.20. In reference to our Remark III.4.4, p. 157, the above ordering corresponds (for two-person games) to a particular case of the monotonicity w.r.t. the ordering "$P \prec_2 P_A$." The particular case appears less natural than the general concept, since there is no good reason in general to restrict II's additional information to come from player I. However, this case will be sufficient for our purposes in this book. In particular, in Chapter V, player I is fully informed, so the distinction becomes immaterial, and in Chapter VI, "signaling matrices" are independent of the state of nature, so the only additional information a player can get must come from the other player. But again, the general meaning of those concepts, and their relation, remains to be elucidated.

Proposition III.4.10.

(1) *A strongly concave function w.r.t.* I *is concave w.r.t.* I.
(2) *The value function $v(P)$ of a game is strongly concave w.r.t.* I.
(3) *More precisely, if a concave real-valued function f on $\mathscr{P}$ is monotone w.r.t.* I, *it is strongly concave w.r.t.* I.
(4) *For every real-valued function f on $\mathscr{P}$, there is a smallest (strongly) concave function w.r.t.* I *that is greater than or equal to it, denoted by* $\mathsf{Cav}_{\text{I}}(f)$ *(resp.* $S\,\mathsf{Cav}_{\text{I}}(f)$*).*

Proof. (1) follows from the Radon–Nikodym theorem: if $\mu = \sum_n \sigma_n \mu_n$, let $g_n = d\mu_n/d\mu$, and apply Remark III.4.18 using $\mathscr{I}_\mu$ (Definition III.4.6) for the scheme $\mathscr{I}$.

(2) follows from (3) by Propositions III.4.3, p. 156, and III.4.5, p. 157, and Remark III.4.20.

(3) If $\mathscr{I}$ is an information scheme, with $g_n \in L_1^+(E, \mathscr{E}_{\text{I}}, Q)$ $\forall n \in N$, $\|g_n\|_1 = 1$, and $\sum_n \sigma_n g_n = 1$, define the information scheme $\mathscr{I}_{\sigma,g}$ as $[(E \times N, \mathscr{E} \times N, Q_{\sigma,g}), (\mathscr{E}_i \times N)_{i \in \text{I}}, \tilde{k}_E \circ \mathsf{Proj}_E]$ with $Q_{\sigma,g}$ defined by σ_n being the marginal probability of n, and $g_n(e)Q(de)$ the conditional probability on E given n. We first claim that, if f is monotone w.r.t. I, then $\overline{f}(\mathscr{I}) \geq \overline{f}(\mathscr{I}_{\sigma,g})$. Indeed, let $\overline{\mathscr{I}}_{\sigma,g}$ denote the same information scheme as $\mathscr{I}_{\sigma,g}$, except that players i different from I have only $\mathscr{E}_i$ (i.e., $(\mathsf{Proj}_E)^{-1}(\mathscr{E}_i)$) as private information. The monotonicity implies that $\overline{f}$ decreases whenever, starting from $\overline{\mathscr{I}}_{\sigma,g}$, one adds to all players' private information the events $n = 1$, then $n = 2$, etc.; so at the end $\overline{f}(\overline{\mathscr{I}}_{\sigma,g}) \geq \overline{f}(\mathscr{I}_{\sigma,g})$, and there remains only to show that $\overline{f}(\overline{\mathscr{I}}_{\sigma,g}) = \overline{f}(\mathscr{I})$. To prove that $\overline{\mathscr{I}}_{\sigma,g}$ and $\mathscr{I}$ have the same canonical distribution it suffices to show that:

Lemma III.4.11. *Let $\mathscr{I}$ be an information scheme $[(E, \mathscr{E}, Q), (\mathscr{E}_i)_{i\in\mathscr{I}}, \tilde{k}_E]$, and similarly for $\tilde{\mathscr{I}}$. Let $\psi\colon E \to \tilde{E}$ be a map, which is $(\mathscr{E}, \tilde{\mathscr{E}})$-measurable and also $(\mathscr{E}_i, \tilde{\mathscr{E}}_i)$-measurable $\forall i \in \mathbf{I}$, at least when all Q-negligible sets have been added to $\mathscr{E}$ and to all $\mathscr{E}_i$. Assume that $\tilde{Q} = Q \circ \psi^{-1}$, that for every Borel set B in K, $\tilde{k}_E^{-1}(B) = (\tilde{k}_{\tilde{E}} \circ \psi)^{-1}(B)$ Q-a.e., and that $\forall i \in \mathbf{I}$, $\mathscr{E}$ and $\mathscr{E}_i$ are conditionally independent given $\psi^{-1}(\tilde{\mathscr{E}}_i)$. Then $P_{\mathscr{I}} = P_{\tilde{\mathscr{I}}}$; more precisely, if one of the schemes satisfies the assumptions of Theorem III.2.4, p. 142, so does the other, and $\phi_{\tilde{\mathscr{I}}} \circ \psi$, where $\phi_{\tilde{\mathscr{I}}}$ is the map associated with $\tilde{\mathscr{I}}$ by part (1) of Theorem III.2.4, is such a map for $\mathscr{I}$.*

Remark III.4.21. The map ϕ itself from $\mathscr{I}$ to $\mathscr{I}_c$ has the above properties (part (1) of Theorem III.2.4, p. 142). It is thus a "maximal" map with those properties.

Proof. Obvious verification. ■

This lemma is indeed sufficient, because the $\mathscr{E}_{\mathrm{I}}$-measurability of g_n implies that, for $f \geq 0$, $\mathscr{E}$-measurable, $\mathsf{E}_Q(f \mid \mathscr{E}_{\mathrm{I}}) = \mathsf{E}_{g_n dQ}(f \mid \mathscr{E}_{\mathrm{I}})$, and hence the required conditional independence of $\mathscr{E}$ and $\mathscr{E}_{\mathrm{I}} \times N$ given $\mathscr{E}_{\mathrm{I}}$. Thus we have proved our claim that, under I-monotonicity, $\overline{f}(\mathscr{I}) \geq \overline{f}(\mathscr{I}_{\sigma,g})$.

There just remains to show that, under concavity, $\overline{f}(\mathscr{I}_{\sigma,g}) \geq \sum_n \sigma_n \overline{f}(\mathscr{I}_{g_n})$. This follows from the following lemma, which implies that $P_{\mathscr{I}_{\sigma,g}} = \sum_n \sigma_n P_{\mathscr{I}_{g_n}}$ (and which was already used implicitly in the proof of Proposition III.4.3, p. 156).

Lemma III.4.12. *Given an information scheme $\mathscr{I}$ satisfying the assumptions of Theorem III.2.4, p. 142, denote by $\overline{\mathscr{E}}_i$ the σ-field generated by $\mathscr{E}_i$ and all Q-null sets, and let $\mathscr{E}_{ck} = \bigcap_{i\in\mathbf{I}} \overline{\mathscr{E}}_i$. Given a countable $\mathscr{E}_{ck}$-measurable partition A_n, let $\sigma_n = Q(A_n)$, and, for $\sigma_n > 0$, $Q_n(B) = Q(B \mid A_n)$, and otherwise, e.g., $Q_n = Q$. Denote by $\mathscr{I}_{A_n}$ the same scheme with Q_n instead of Q. Then $P_{\mathscr{I}} = \sum_n \sigma_n P_{\mathscr{I}_{A_n}}$.*

Proof. Clearly $\mathscr{I}_{A_n}$ also satisfies the assumptions of Theorem III.2.4. Let ϕ_n be a map from $\mathscr{I}_{A_n}$ to Ω as in part (1) of Theorem III.2.4. Define ϕ by letting it equal ϕ_n on A_n. So $P_{\mathscr{I}_{A_n}} = \phi_n(Q_n) = \phi(Q_n) \in \mathscr{P}$, and thus (by closedness and convexity of $\mathscr{P}$) also $\sum_n \sigma_n P_{\mathscr{I}_{A_n}} \in \mathscr{P}$. But $\sum_n \sigma_n P_{\mathscr{I}_{A_n}} = \sum_n \sigma_n \phi(Q_n) = \phi(\sum \sigma_n Q_n) = \phi(Q)$. So $\phi(Q) \in \mathscr{P}$. The other two properties of the map ϕ required in part (1) of Theorem III.2.4 are also an obvious verification. The result follows then from part (2) of the same theorem. ■

This completes the proof of part (3).

For part (4), just observe that, using Remark III.4.18 for strong concavity, both concavity and strong concavity w.r.t. I are defined in terms of usual concavity of auxiliary functions, and that a lower bound of usually concave functions is usually concave.

This completes the proof of Proposition III.4.10. ■

Remark III.4.22. Observe thus that, given a real function f on $\mathscr{P}$, we can define the following "concavifications":

- $C_0(f)$ as the concavification over the convex set $\mathscr{P}$
- $C_4(f)$ as $\mathsf{Cav}_{\mathrm{I}}(f)$
- $C_5(f)$ as $S\,\mathsf{Cav}_{\mathrm{I}}(f)$
- $C_1(f)(P) = \hat{f}(\mathscr{I}_P)$
- $C_2(f)(P) = \mathsf{sup}\{\,\hat{f}(\mathscr{I}_\mu) \mid P_\mu = P\,\}$
- $C_3(f)(P) = \mathsf{sup}\{\,\hat{f}(\mathscr{I}) \mid P_{\mathscr{I}} = P\,\}$.

Remark III.4.23. All those functions are concave functions on the convex set $\mathscr{P}$. This is obvious for C_0, C_1, C_4, and C_5. For $C_2(f)$, let $\hat{f}(\mathscr{I}_{\mu_i}) \simeq C_2(f)(P_i)$, with $P = \alpha P_1 + (1-\alpha)P_2$, $P_i = P_{\mu_i}$. Choose Borel isomorphisms φ_1 and φ_2 of Θ^{II} with disjoint Borel subsets of Θ^{II}, and let, for $\theta \in \Theta^{\mathrm{I}} = \Delta(K \times \Theta^{\mathrm{II}})$, $\overline{\varphi}_i(\theta)$ be the image measure of θ under $id_K \times \varphi_i$, and let ν_i be the image measure of μ_i under $\overline{\varphi}_i$. Then $\mathscr{I}_{\nu_i}$ is Borel-isomorphic to $\mathscr{I}_{\mu_i}$, so (Lemma III.4.11, p. 162) $P_{\nu_i} = P_{\mu_i} = P_i$ and $\hat{f}(\mathscr{I}_{\nu_i}) = \hat{f}(\mathscr{I}_{\mu_i})$. Further, with $\nu = \alpha\nu_1 + (1-\alpha)\nu_2$, Lemma III.4.12, p. 163, yields that $P_\nu = \alpha P_{\nu_1} + (1-\alpha)P_{\nu_2} = P$. Thus $\hat{f}(\mathscr{I}_\nu) \geq \alpha\hat{f}(\mathscr{I}_{\nu_1}) + (1-\alpha)\hat{f}(\mathscr{I}_{\nu_2}) = \alpha\hat{f}(\mathscr{I}_{\mu_1}) + (1-\alpha)\hat{f}(\mathscr{I}_{\mu_2}) \simeq \alpha[C_2(f)](P_1) + (1-\alpha)[(C_2(f)](P_2)$, hence the result. Finally, for $C_3(f)$, the argument is similar: there is no need for the Borel isomorphisms; just construct the obvious larger information scheme $\mathscr{I}$ where $\mathscr{I}_1$ or $\mathscr{I}_2$ is selected at random with probability α or $(1-\alpha)$, and the choice is told to both players.

Remark III.4.24. We have the following obvious relations between the C_i: $C_0(f) \leq C_1(f) \leq C_2(f) \leq C_3(f) \leq C_5(f)$, and $C_2(f) \leq C_4(f) \leq C_5(f)$. There is obviously a reasonable hope that $C_2 = C_3$ (remember the Borel isomorphisms: there might be a similar trick that produces, for any $\mathscr{I}$, some $\mathscr{I}_\mu$ that is "sufficiently isomorphic"). A fortiori one "should" have $C_3 \leq C_4$. Also the obvious reason for having defined C_2 and C_3 is that they were the natural candidates for being equal resp. to C_4 and C_5. By our above inequalities, either of those equalities would imply $C_4 \leq C_3$. Finally, the reason to have introduced C_1 is that, in all our applications in Chapters V and VI, $C_1(f) = C_5(f)$. But this might depend on some monotonicity properties of the functions f considered; in particular the "u"-functions used there are monotone. Since we also use iterated operators like $\mathsf{Vex}_{\mathrm{II}}\,\mathsf{Cav}_{\mathrm{I}}(f)$, it would be important to know what monotonicity properties of f are preserved by what concavification operators.

Remark III.4.25. Consider the following cautionary example, where there may be difficulties even when everything is finite. Let $K = \{A, B\}$, fix $\theta^\alpha \neq \theta^\beta$ in Θ^{II}, let $\theta^1 = \frac{1}{2}\delta_{(A,\theta^\alpha)} + \frac{1}{2}\delta_{(B,\theta^\beta)} \in \Theta^{\mathrm{I}}$ and $\theta^2 = \frac{1}{2}\delta_{(B,\theta^\alpha)} + \frac{1}{2}\delta_{(A,\theta^\beta)} \in \Theta^{\mathrm{I}}$, and let $\mu = \frac{1}{2}\delta_{\theta^1} + \frac{1}{2}\delta_{\theta^2} \in \Delta(\Theta^{\mathrm{I}})$. Then $P = P_\mu$ is (e.g., by Lemma III.4.11, p. 162) the canonical distribution of the information scheme where it is common knowledge that A and B are selected with equal probability, i.e., $P = \frac{1}{2}\delta_{\omega_A} + \frac{1}{2}\delta_{\omega_B}$, with $\omega_A = (\theta^{\mathrm{I}}, \theta^{\mathrm{II}}, A)$, $\omega_B = (\theta^{\mathrm{I}}, \theta^{\mathrm{II}}, B)$, $\overline{\theta}^{\mathrm{I}} = \overline{\theta}^{\mathrm{II}} = P$. So, since P projects as a unit mass on Θ^{I}, we have, for any function f, $C_0(f)(P) = C_1(f)(P) = f(P)$.

Let also Q be the canonical distribution of the information scheme where A and B are selected with equal probability, while player II is informed of this choice and player I is not, i.e., $Q = \frac{1}{2}\delta_{\omega_a} + \frac{1}{2}\delta\omega_b$, with $\omega_a = (\theta, \theta_a, A)$, $\omega_b = (\theta, \theta_b, B)$, $\theta = Q$, $\theta_a = \delta_{\omega_a}$, $\theta_b = \delta_{\omega_b}$.

Consider now, for the scheme $\mathscr{I}_\mu$, the functions $g_1 = 2\cdot\mathbb{1}_{\{\theta^1\}}$, $g_2 = 2\cdot\mathbb{1}_{\{\theta^2\}}$, and $\sigma_1 = \sigma_2 = \frac{1}{2}$. Then $P_{(\mathscr{I}_\mu)_{g_1}} = P_{(\mathscr{I}_\mu)_{g_2}} = Q$, so $\hat{f}(\mathscr{I}_\mu) \geq f(Q)$. Hence if $f(Q) > f(P)$, we have $C_2(f) \neq C_1(f)$.

Remark III.4.26. Observe that the above example relies on a non-monotonicity of f: $f(Q) > f(P)$. To finish confusing this issue, consider now a variant of the above where $\mu_\varepsilon = \frac{1}{2}(1+\varepsilon)\delta_{\theta^1} + \frac{1}{2}(1-\varepsilon)\delta_{\theta^2}$. Then $P_\varepsilon = P_{\mu^\varepsilon}$ is the unique consistent probability on (dropping superscripts ε on all ω's and θ's) $\{\omega_{11}, \omega_{12}, \omega_{21}, \omega_{22}\}$ with $\omega_{11} = (A, \theta^1, \theta^\alpha)$, $\omega_{12} = (B, \theta^1, \theta^\beta)$, $\omega_{21} = (B, \theta^1, \theta^\beta)$, $\omega_{22} = (A, \theta^2, \theta^\beta)$, $\theta^1 = \frac{1}{2}\delta_{\omega_{11}} + \frac{1}{2}\delta_{\omega_{12}}$, $\theta^2 = \frac{1}{2}\delta_{\omega_{21}} + \frac{1}{2}\delta_{\omega_{22}}$, $\theta^\alpha = \frac{1}{2}(1+\varepsilon)\delta_{\omega_{11}} + \frac{1}{2}(1-\varepsilon)\delta_{\omega_{21}}$, and $\theta^\beta = \frac{1}{2}(1+\varepsilon)\delta_{\omega_{12}} + \frac{1}{2}(1-\varepsilon)\delta_{\omega_{22}}$. (And $\theta^1 \neq \theta^2$, $\theta^\alpha \neq \theta^\beta$.)

We claim that $\omega_{ij}^\varepsilon \to \omega_{ij}^\infty$, and $P_\varepsilon \to P_\infty = P$, where $\omega_{11}^\infty = \omega_{22}^\infty = \omega_A$, $\omega_{12}^\infty = \omega_{21}^\infty = \omega_B$. Otherwise, extract ($\Omega$ and $\mathscr{P}$ are compact metric) a subsequence along which ω_{ij}^ε converges and P_ε converges, but the limits are not the above. By this convergence, our relations between the ω_{ij}^ε and the $\theta^{*,\varepsilon}$ pass to the limit, yielding that P_∞ is a consistent probability on $\{\omega_{11}^\infty, \omega_{12}^\infty, \omega_{21}^\infty, \omega_{22}^\infty\}$ with $\omega_{11} = (A, \theta^{1,\infty}, \theta^{\alpha,\infty})$, etc., $\theta^{1,\infty} = \frac{1}{2}\delta_{\omega_{11}^\infty} + \frac{1}{2}\delta_{\omega_{12}^\infty}$, $\theta^{2,\infty} = \cdots$, $\theta^{\alpha,\infty} = \frac{1}{2}\delta_{\omega_{11}^\infty} + \frac{1}{2}\delta_{\omega_{21}^\infty}$, $\theta^{\beta,\infty} = \cdots$. If either $\theta^{1,\infty} \neq \theta^{2,\infty}$ or $\theta^{\alpha,\infty} \neq \theta^{\beta,\infty}$, the four points ω_{ij}^∞ are different, so the canonical information scheme associated with P_∞ is isomorphic to our original $\mathscr{I}_\mu$ (of Remark III.4.25), so they have the same consistent distribution P. Since $P_\infty \in \mathscr{P}$, it equals its own consistent distribution, so $P_\infty = P$. However, if both $\theta^{1,\infty} = \theta^{2,\infty}$ and $\theta^{\alpha,\infty} = \theta^{\beta,\infty}$, then $\omega_{11}^\infty = \omega_{22}^\infty$ and $\omega_{12}^\infty = \omega_{21}^\infty$, and the canonical information scheme associated with P_∞ is isomorphic to that of P, hence again $P_\infty = P$, by the same argument. So, either way, $P_\infty = P$. It follows then that $\omega_{11}^\infty = \omega_{22}^\infty$, being in the support of P and being mapped to A, must equal ω_A, and similarly $\omega_{12}^\infty = \omega_{21}^\infty = \omega_B$. Hence our convergence; so $\theta^{\alpha,\varepsilon} \to \theta^{\mathrm{II}}$, $\theta^{\beta,\varepsilon} \to \theta^{\mathrm{II}}$, $\theta^{1,\varepsilon} \to \theta^{\mathrm{I}}$, $\theta^{2,\varepsilon} \to \theta^{\mathrm{I}}$.

For the canonical scheme $\mathscr{I}_{P_\varepsilon}$, let $g_1^\varepsilon = \frac{2}{1+\varepsilon}\mathbb{1}_{\theta^{1,\varepsilon}}$, $g_2^\varepsilon = \frac{2}{1-\varepsilon}\mathbb{1}_{\theta^{2,\varepsilon}}$, $\sigma_1^\varepsilon = \frac{1+\varepsilon}{2}$, $\sigma_2^\varepsilon = \frac{1-\varepsilon}{2}$. Then, as above, $P_{(\mathscr{I}_{P_\varepsilon})_{g_1^\varepsilon}} = P_{(\mathscr{I}_{P_\varepsilon})_{g_2^\varepsilon}} = Q$, so $\hat{f}(\mathscr{I}_{P_\varepsilon}) \geq f(Q)$, hence $[C_1(f)](P_\varepsilon) \geq f(Q)$.

Since $P_\varepsilon \to P$, any u.s.c. function φ on $\mathscr{P}$ with $\varphi \geq C_1(f)$, in particular $C_1(f)$ itself when u.s.c., satisfies $\varphi(P) \geq f(Q)$. So it appears that the relations between the different $C_i(f)$'s may be substantially strengthened, not only under monotonicity assumptions of f, but also possibly under topological assumptions, either on f, or on $C_i(f)$, or as a variant of the concavification operators (cf. Remark III.4.16, and recall also the u.s.c. in part (1) of Corollary III.4.7, p. 158, and that all "u"-functions are continuous on $\mathscr{P}$).

EXERCISES

1. If $f: K_1 \to K_2$ is Borel and surjective between analytic spaces, so is $\Theta(f)$.

HINT. Appendix A.7.j.

2. An alternative construction of the belief space (Mertens and Zamir, 1985)

If we take the beliefs of a player to be a joint probability distribution on K and the beliefs of all players (including his own) we make the belief spaces be the same for all players. The coherency of the beliefs are imposed as restrictions on these larger dimensional probabilities. This can be done as follows:

a. Define the sequence $\{Y_r\}_{r=0}^{\infty}$ of belief spaces by: $Y_0 = K$ and for $r = 1, 2, \ldots$,

$$Y_r = \{\omega_r \in Y_{r-1} \times [\Delta(Y_{r-1})]^{\mathbf{I}} \mid \text{the two conditions below are satisfied}\}.$$

(1) For all $i \in \mathbf{I}$, the marginal distribution of $\theta_r^i(\omega_r)$ on the ith copy of $\Delta(Y_{r-1})$ is the Dirac mass at $\theta_{r-1}^i(\rho_{r-1}(\omega_r))$.

(2) For all $i \in \mathbf{I}$, the marginal distribution of $\theta_r^i(\omega_r)$ on Y_{r-2} is $\theta_{r-2}^i(\rho_{r-1}(\omega_r))$. Here ρ_{r-1} and θ_r^i are the projections from Y_r to Y_{r-1} and the ith copy of $\Delta(Y_{r-1})$, respectively.

Note that (1) imposes the condition that each player "knows" his own beliefs while (2) is the condition that each level of beliefs is compatible with the lower levels. The fact that θ_r^i is a mapping to $\Delta(Y_{r-1})$ implies that it is common knowledge that (1) and (2) are satisfied.

b. Define the universal belief space Ω to be the projective limit of $\{Y_r\}_{r=0}^{\infty}$ with respect to the projections $\rho_{r-1}\colon Y_r \to Y_{r-1}$.

c. Prove that $\rho_r(Y_{r+1}) = Y_r$ for all $r = 0, 1, 2, \ldots$. Hence $\rho_r(\Omega) = Y_r$ for all $r = 0, 1, 2, \ldots$, and in particular $\Omega \neq \emptyset$.

d. Prove that each $\omega \in \Omega$ and $i \in \mathbf{I}$ uniquely determine a probability measure $\overline{\theta}^i_{\omega}$ in $\Delta(\Omega)$ and the mapping $\overline{\theta}^i : \Omega \to \Delta(\Omega)$ is continuous.

e. Prove that as a consequence of conditions (1) and (2), for any $\omega \in \Omega$ and any $i \in \mathbf{I}$:

$$\text{if } \tilde{\omega} \in \mathsf{Supp}(\overline{\theta}^i_{\omega}) \text{ then } \overline{\theta}^i_{\tilde{\omega}} = \overline{\theta}^i_{\omega}.$$

f. Let $\Theta^i = \overline{\theta}^i(\Omega) \subseteq \Delta(\Omega)$ and prove that:

(1) The space Ω is homeomorphic to $K \times \prod_{i \in \mathbf{I}} \Theta^i$.

(2) The space Θ^i is homeomorphic to $\Delta(K \times \prod_{j \neq i} \Theta^j)$.

(3) Property (P) of Theorem III.1.1, p. 124, is satisfied.

3. Universal *BL*-space in games with private information.

a. Show that the formalism introduced in Section III.1, p. 123, can also be used in situations in which players have some exogenous private information (i.e., a σ-field $\mathscr{K}^i$ on K).

HINT. Construct Ω as in Section III.1 and define Ω_0 as follows:

$$\Omega_0 = \{\omega \mid \overline{\theta}^i_{\omega}[X] = 1 \; \forall X\colon k(\omega) \in X \in \mathscr{K}^i, \; \forall i \in \mathbf{I}\}.$$

Use Example 7, p. 138, to obtain Ω_{∞} as the universal *BL*-space for this game with private information.

Remark III.4.27. The above is just a definition. To be useful, it should be accompanied by theorems, and, in particular, representation theorems like Theorem III.2.4,. And those may require some additional assumptions (e.g., universal measurability of $\mathscr{K}^i$, topological assumptions, etc.).

b. (Böge and Eisele, 1979), (Aumann, 1974), (Aumann, 1985) Consider the situation in which $K = K_0 \times U \times S$ (where K_0 is the space of states, S is the action space, and U is the set of utility functions, **I**-tuples of real-valued functions on $K_0 \times S$). For each player let $\mathscr{K}^i$ be the partition of K generated by the projection on his own utility and action space (and their Borel σ-field). One can then apply the above construction to obtain the appropriate universal BL-space.

Next consider only BL-subspaces where each player maximizes his expected utility and apply again a procedure like that in III.4, Ex. 3a, to construct a universal such BL-subspace. Every BL-subspace of this universal space then describes a game with incomplete information together with one of its equilibria. If K_0 and U are singletons, one obtains Aumann's Bayesian interpretation of correlated equilibria (cf. Remark II.3.4, p. 103).

4. Lower semi-continuity of payoff in terms of information (Forges, 1988a)

The following illustrates the decision-theoretic relevance of the weak* topology on information that was used in this chapter (cf. also, in this vein, Proposition III.4.3, p. 156):

Let K be a finite set, U a separable metric space, and $f : U \times \Delta(K) \to \overline{\mathbb{R}}_+$ be lower semi-continuous, and convex on $\Delta(K)$ for each $u \in U$.

Let $\phi(P) = \int_U f(u, [P(k \mid u)]_{k \in K}) P(du)$ for $P \in \Delta(K \times U)$.

Then ϕ is convex and lower semi-continuous, and $\{ (P, \phi(P)) \mid P$ has finite support$\}$ is dense in the graph of ϕ.

Remark III.4.28. Regularity of P plays no role; the theorem remains true over the set of all Borel probability measures.

Remark III.4.29. A decision maker who observes u before making a decision d, whose payoff $\alpha_d^k(u)$ depends on the unknown state of nature (k, u), will obtain $f(u, P(k \mid u)) = \sup_d \sum_k P(k \mid u) \alpha_d^k(u)$, a convex, continuous function f of $P(k \mid u)$, depending also on u. Hence his (ex ante) expected payoff is $\phi(P)$. Lower semi-continuity expresses the fact that there can be a loss of information (and never a gain) in going to the limit on an observed random variable; e.g., let $u_n(\omega) = [u_1(\omega)]/n$: u_∞ is zero, and loses all the information. An application will be found in Chapter IX, Section IX.3, p. 495.

Remark III.4.30. Assume the function f is extended by homogeneity of degree 1 from $\Delta(K)$ to $\mathbb{R}_+^K$. Then:

$$\phi(P) = \int_U f(u, (P(k, du))_{k \in K}),$$

in the sense that for any measure λ on U such that all measures $P_k(du) = P(k, du)$ $(k \in K)$ are absolutely continuous w.r.t. λ:

$$\phi(P) = \int_U f[u, (h_k(u))_{k \in K}] \lambda\, (du),$$

where $h_k(u)$ is the Radon–Nikodym derivative of $P(k, du)$ w.r.t. λ, thus justifying the notation $\phi(P) = \int_U f[u, (h_k(u)\lambda\,(du))_{k\in K}] = \int_U f[u, (P(k, du))_{k\in K}]$ (cf., e.g., Edwards, 1965, IV.15.11).

HINT. Prove first that the integral does not depend on λ (g_u also is positively homogeneous of degree 1). Next set λ equal to the marginal distribution of u.

a. *Reduction to the case where U is compact metric, and f is independent of u and is a maximum of finitely many linear functions on $\mathbb{R}_+^K$*

HINT. Let $(\overline{U}, d)$ be a compact metric space containing U. For fixed $\tilde{u} \in U$, the separation theorem yields that $f(\tilde{u}, \cdot)$ is the supremum of the linear functions on $\Delta(K)$ that are strictly smaller, and those can further be chosen with rational coefficients. Let φ be such a linear function, and use the compactness of $\Delta(K)$ and the lower semi-continuity of f to show that, for some $\varepsilon_0 > 0$, one still has $f(u, x) > \varphi(x)\,\forall x \in \Delta(K)$ whenever $d(u, \tilde{u}) < \varepsilon_0$. If u_n is a dense sequence in U, and ε is rational with $\frac{1}{2}\varepsilon_0 < \varepsilon < \varepsilon_0$, and one chooses n_0 such that $d(u_{n_0}, \tilde{u}) < \frac{\varepsilon}{k+1}$, then $[1 - \frac{k+1}{k\varepsilon} d(u, u_{n_0})]^+[\varphi(x)]^+ = F_{k,n_0,\varepsilon,\varphi}(u, x)$ is everywhere $\le f$, and at $\tilde{u}$ it is $\ge (1 - \frac{1}{k})[\varphi(x)]^+$. Hence f is the supremum of the set of all functions $F_{k,n,\varepsilon,\varphi}$ (k and n integers, ε rational, φ with rational coefficients) that lie everywhere below. Let F_i enumerate this set of functions: the sequence $f_j = \max_{i\le j} F_i$ increases to f, and consists of bounded Lipschitz functions on $\overline{U} \times \Delta(K)$ that are, for every $u \in \overline{U}$, piecewise linear and convex on $\Delta(K)$. Hence (by the monotone convergence theorem) it suffices to prove the property for such functions. In particular we can henceforth assume U is compact metric.

Fix now $\varepsilon > 0$, and for $u \in U$ let O_u be an open neighborhood such that $u' \in O_u \Longrightarrow \left|f(u', x) - f(u, x)\right| < \varepsilon\ \forall x \in \Delta(K)$. Let u_i $(i = 1, \ldots n)$ be a finite subset such that the O_{u_i} cover U, and let g be a corresponding continuous partition of unity, i.e., g_i is continuous, with values in [0, 1], vanishes outside of O_i, and $\sum_{i=1}^n g_i(u) = 1, \forall_u \in U$.

Then $h(u, x) = \sum_{i=1}^n g_i(u) f(u_i, x)$ is uniformly ε-close to f, so it suffices to prove the result for h. Hence it suffices to prove it for one function $g_i(u)f(u_i, x)$: we can assume our function has the form $g(u)h(x)$, where $g\colon U \to \mathbb{R}_+$ is continuous, and $h\colon \Delta(K) \to \mathbb{R}_+$ is a maximum of finitely many linear functions.

Define now a map $P \mapsto \tilde{P}$ from $\Delta(K \times U)$ to the space M of non-negative, bounded measures on $K \times U$, by $\tilde{P}(k \times B) = \int_B g(u)P(k, du)$ for every Borel set B in U. The map is clearly linear and continuous. Further $\tilde{P}(k \mid u) = P(k \mid u)$ a.e., so we get $\phi(P) = \int h([\tilde{P}(k \mid u)]_{k\in K})\tilde{P}(du)$. Since $P \mapsto \tilde{P}$ is linear and continuous, it suffices therefore to prove lower semi-continuity and convexity on M of the map $P \mapsto \int h([P(k \mid u)]_{k\in K})P(du)$. Since the map is positively homogeneous of degree one, it suffices to prove lower semi-continuity and convexity on $\Delta(K \times U)$.

b. *Lower semi-continuity: reduction to the case where furthermore the marginal of P on K is fixed*

HINT. Since $\Delta(K \times U)$ is metrizable, consider a sequence $P_n \to P$. We want to show that $\liminf \phi(P_n) \ge \phi(P)$. Let $p(k)$ (resp. $p_n(k)$) be the marginals on K: then $p_n \to p$. So, for $\varepsilon > 0$, choose n_0 such that $(1 + \varepsilon)p_n(k) \ge p(k)\ \forall k, \forall n \ge n_0$. Extracting a subsequence, we can assume this holds for all n, and also that $\{k \mid p_n(k) > 0\}$ is independent of n, hence we can assume it is the whole of K: $p_n(k) > 0\ \forall n, \forall k$. Then $P_n(k, du)$ can be written as $p_n(k)g_{n,k}(u)P_n(du)$. If $p(k) > 0$, then $g_{n,k}(u)P_n(du) \to P(du \mid k)$ weakly. Assume that everywhere $g_{n,k} \ge 0$, $\sum_k p_n(k)g_{n,k}(u) = 1$, so $P_n(k \mid u) = p_n(k)g_{n,k}(u)$ and $\phi(P_n) = \int f[(p_n(k)g_{n,k}(u))_{k\in K}]P_n(du)$. Let $\overline{P}_n(k, du) = p(k)g_{n,k}(u)P_n(du)$: $\overline{P}_n \to P$ weakly, and $\overline{P}_n(du) = h_n(u)P_n(du)$ with $h_n(u) = \sum_k p_k g_{n,k}(u)$, so $\overline{P}_n(k \mid u) = p_k \overline{g}_{n,k}(u)$ with $\overline{g}_{n,k}(u) = g_{n,k}(u)/h_n(u)$. Thus $\phi(\overline{P}_n) = \int f[(p(k)\overline{g}_{n,k}(u))_{k\in K}]h_n(u)P_n(du)$.

Now $(1 + \varepsilon)p_n \ge p$ yields $h_n(u) \le 1 + \varepsilon$. Since $\int h_n(u)P_n(du) = 1$, this yields that $h_n(u) \ge 1 - \sqrt{\varepsilon}$ with $P_n(du)$-probability at least $1 - \sqrt{\varepsilon}$. In that case, we get $(1 + \varepsilon)p_n(k)g_{n,k}(u) \ge p(k)g_{n,k}(u) \ge (1 - \sqrt{\varepsilon})p(k)\overline{g}_{n,k}(u)$. Since both points belong to $\Delta(K)$, the arguments of f in the expressions of $\phi(P_n)$ and $\phi(\overline{P}_n)$ differ by less than $2\sqrt{\varepsilon}$ in norm. Using the Lipschitz character (with constant L) of f, and again that $h_n \leq 1+\varepsilon$, we obtain that $(1+\varepsilon)[\phi(P_n)+2L\sqrt{\varepsilon}] \geq \phi(\overline{P}_n)$. So it suffices to prove that $\liminf \phi(\overline{P}_n) \geq \phi(P)$.

c. *Use of the Dudley–Skohorod theorem*

HINT. Since the marginal $p(k)$ on K is fixed, and can be assumed strictly positive, we know that $P_n(du \mid k) \to P(du \mid k)$ weakly, for each k. Apply thus the Dudley–Skohorod theorem for each of those conditional distributions to construct a probability space (Ω, A, Q) together with a random variable $k(\omega)$ to K and a sequence $u_n(\omega)$ converging a.e. to $u(\omega)$ such that P_n is the distribution of $(k(\omega), u_n(\omega))$ and P that of $(k(\omega), u(\omega))$. Let $J_k = \{\,\omega \mid k(\omega) = k\,\}$.

Thus we want to show that, if $u_n(\omega) \to u_\infty(\omega)$ a.s., and J_k is a finite measurable partition, then:

$$\liminf_{n\to\infty} \mathsf{E}\, f([Q(J_k \mid u_n(\omega))]_{k\in K}) \geq \mathsf{E}\, f([Q(J_k \mid u_\infty(\omega))]_{k\in K}).$$

d. *Lemma* Let $(\Omega, \mathscr{A}, Q)$ be a probability space, with a finite measurable partition $(J_k)_{k\in K}$, and a sequence of random variables $u_n(\omega) \to u_\infty(\omega)$ with values in a separable metric space U. Let $q_n^k = Q(\mathbf{I}_k \mid u_n)$. Then:

(1) Weak* limits q of the q_n exist and satisfy $\mathsf{E}(q \mid u_\infty) = q_\infty$.
(2) For any weak* limit q of the q_n there exists a sequence of convex combinations $r_i = \sum_n \alpha_n^i q_n$, with $\alpha_n^i = 0$ for i sufficiently large, and $r_i \to q$ a.e., hence $\mathsf{E}(r_i \mid u_\infty) \to \mathsf{E}(q \mid u_\infty) = q_\infty$ a.s.

HINT. The existence follows from Banach–Alaoglu. For (2): use I.2, Ex. 12, p. 28, Egorov's theorem, and Kelley et al. (1963, p. 212). For part (1), consider $f \in C(U)$, then $f(u_n)$ is uniformly bounded and converges a.e. to $f(u_\infty)$, so the convergence is uniform on weakly compact subsets of L_1; in particular, extract first a weakly (or weak*)-convergent subsequence from the q_n, $\mathsf{E}(q^k f(u_\infty)) = \lim_{n\to\infty} \mathsf{E}(q_n^k f(u_n)) = \lim_{n\to\infty} \mathsf{E}[\mathbb{1}_{J_k} f(u_n)] = \mathsf{E}(\mathbb{1}_{J_k} f(u_\infty))$. Extend this equation to positive Borel f, and conclude.

e. *Lower semi-continuity*

HINT. By III.4, Ex. 4a, III.4, Ex. 4b, III.4, Ex. 4c, and the notations of III.4, Ex. 4d, it suffices (taking a subsequence) to show that:

$$\begin{aligned}\mathsf{E}\, f(q_\infty) &= \lim_{i\to\infty} \mathsf{E}\, f[\mathsf{E}(r_i \mid u_\infty)]\\ &\leq \limsup_{n\to\infty} \mathsf{E}\, f(E(q_n \mid u_\infty))\\ &\leq \limsup_{n\to\infty} \mathsf{E}\, f(q_n),\end{aligned}$$

which follows from III.4, Ex. 4d, and the convexity of f (I.3, Ex. 14, p. 43).

f. *Density*

HINT. Make a Borel partition of $U \times \Delta(K)$ into finitely many Borel sets of diameter $< \varepsilon$ each, map this partition back into U, and map the whole mass of each partition element to some point of that element. This yields measures with finite support P_ε that converge weak* to P and such that $\phi(P_\varepsilon) \to \phi(P)$.

g. *Convexity*

HINT. Prove first (using Remark III.4.30, p. 167) convexity over the set of probabilities with finite support: this boils down to the convexity of f. Consider now P (and similarly Q) arbitrary. Apply then III.4, Ex. 4f, and use the lower semi-continuity.

Remark III.4.31. We shall later use the following result in the specific case where U is the set of continuous convex functions from $\Delta(K)$ to $\mathbb{R}_+$, with $f(u, \cdot) = u(\cdot)$.

5. Lower semi-continuity (continued)

In the same situation as above, decompose measures P on $K \times U$ into their marginal p on K and a conditional $\tau_k(du)$ on U given K. Let $\psi(\tau)\colon p \mapsto \phi(p \otimes \tau)$.

Then ψ is a convex, l.s.c. map with values in the set $\tilde{C}$ of l.s.c. convex maps from $\Delta(K)$ to $\overline{\mathbb{R}}_+$ (l.s.c. of ψ means: $\forall g$ continuous on $\Delta(K)$, $\{\, \tau \mid \psi(\tau) > g \,\}$ is weak*-open).

HINT. Convexity follows from III.4, Ex. 4. For the lower semi-continuity, use compactness of $\Delta(K)$.

CHAPTER IV

General Model of Repeated Games

IV.1. THE MODEL

In this chapter we introduce formally the general model of repeated games.

We start with a non-cooperative game G and define a new game Γ_∞, a play of which is an infinite sequence of plays of G.

In fact, it appears in many applications that current moves not only influence the current payoff but also the future play, hence some state variable of the model. This is the reason why stochastic games appear in a natural way.

Moreover we have to describe the information available to the players. There may be some differences between their initial knowledge of the characteristics: initial state, preferences, even transition law. This is taken into account in the framework of games with incomplete information.

Finally it is necessary for a full description of the game to specify what additional information is transmitted to the players after each stage of the play. It is easy to see that assuming the knowledge of the other players' strategies is unrealistic. A more plausible weaker assumption may be that only the actual moves are observed. An even weaker assumption is that only the individual player's payoff is known to him. Even more generally, we may consider a model without full monitoring of previous moves, or of the outcomes, or even of the players' own payoffs. This leads to the notion of signals that may depend in a random way on the actual moves and state.

To integrate all such effects it is sufficient to define a state- and move-dependent lottery that selects at every stage the signals for the players, their payoffs, and the next state of nature. If one wants in addition to incorporate the effect of information lags, this transition may also depend on the past events. In fact, we will see that this quite huge construction can be reduced to a simple and convenient form (cf. Proposition IV.2.3, p. 183).

It follows from the above presentation that this model is an adequate description of a stationary multistage game in the sense that its formulation is time-shift invariant (which may require adding new states and payoffs, if necessary) and needs only some counter to let the stage of the game be known to the players.

We will give more formally a first model of the game and introduce explicitly the main definitions.

Definition IV.1.1. A **repeated game** is a finite multistage game, where for $\omega \in \Omega^\infty$, $g^i(\omega) = \lim_{n\to\infty} \frac{1}{n} \sum_{k\leq n} h^i(\omega_k)$, for some function h^i from Ω to $\mathbb{R}$ (cf. Sections II.1.a, p. 58, and II.3.b, p. 103).

Here "finite" means all sets (Ω, A, S) are finite. The assumption on the payoff function also gives a finite description for the latter, the set Ω being finite. There only remains the need to be a bit more explicit about the solution concepts, since the payoff function g^i is not always everywhere defined.

In fact, we will consider here an equivalent and more convenient model where q is independent of A (II.1.a.4, p. 59) and h is defined on $\Omega \times S$. Other equivalent representations will be studied in Section IV.2, p. 178.

IV.1.a. States, Signals, and Transitions

We are given a finite set of **states** K and a finite set of players $\mathbf{I}$ (there will be no confusion in using $\mathbf{I}$ to denote both the set and its cardinality). For each player i in $\mathbf{I}$, let S^i be its finite set of **moves** (or **actions**) and A^i its finite set of **signals**. (K being finite, both sets can be assumed to be independent of the state k in K, duplicating eventually moves or signals.) Denote as usual by S and A the products of the S^i and A^i, resp., over $\mathbf{I}$.

P is an (initial) probability on $K \times A$ and Q is a transition probability from $K \times S$ to $W \times K \times A$, where W is some compact set in $\mathbb{R}^{\mathbf{I}}$ (payoffs are uniformly bounded). Let G be the marginal distribution induced by Q on W so that $G^k(s^1, \ldots, s^{\mathbf{I}})$ denotes the distribution of the vector payoff in state k given the vector of moves s. Similarly the marginal distribution of Q on K corresponds to the transition on the state space, and the marginal distribution of Q on A determines the distribution of the signals.

The **repeated game** Γ_∞ is played as follows:

- At stage 0 a point (k_1, a_1) is chosen in $K \times A$ according to P, and a_1^i is announced to player i, for each i.
- At each stage n, $n \geq 1$, each player i chooses independently a move s_n^i in S^i. The distribution $Q(k_n, s_n)$ is used to choose a point (g_n, k_{n+1}, a_{n+1}) in $W \times K \times A$. The new state is k_{n+1}. The signal a_{n+1}^i is announced to player i and g_n^i is his payoff, for all i in $\mathbf{I}$. (Note that the payoff is not explicitly observed; it may be deduced from the signal.)

The above description is known to the players. To complete explicitly the information structure of the game we still have to assume that each player remembers all the information he received in the past (effectively perfect recall). Γ_∞ is thus a game in extensive form as defined in Chapter II, p. 58. (To obtain explicitly the same description, divide each stage into $\mathbf{I}$ substages and let the players play in order, extending the transition on states, signals, and payoffs in the obvious way.) The specificity of this game is its stationary aspect, both of the transitions and of the payoffs (cf. Section II.1.b, p. 60).

A **play** of Γ_∞ is then identified with an infinite sequence $(k_1, a_1, s_1, g_1, k_2, a_2, \dots, s_n, g_n, k_{n+1}, a_{n+1}, \dots)$. As before we denote by H_∞ the set of plays. An initial sequence of length n of a play, i.e., ending with $(\dots, k_n, a_n)$, will be called an n-history, and H_n will denote the corresponding set. The set of all **histories** (or positions) is $H = \bigcup_{n\geq 1} H_n$.

If on some play and for some n the sequence $\ell^i = (a_1^i, \dots, a_n^i)$ determines the sequence $m^{-i} = (a_1^{-i}, s_1^{-i}, \dots, s_{n-1}^{-i}, a_n^{-i})$, for all i, we define the **subgame** from position $\ell = (a_1, \dots, a_n)$ with the same moves, signals, transitions, and payoffs as the game F_∞, but starting with an initial distribution on $K \times A^n$ defined by ℓ and the law of k_n given ℓ (which is known to all players). Finally given h_∞ in H_∞, we write h_n for its projection on H_n, $\mathscr{H}_n$ is the σ-algebra on H_∞ generated by H_n and $\mathscr{H}_\infty = \bigvee_{n\geq 1} \mathscr{H}_n$ (product σ-algebra). $\mathscr{H}$ will denote the induced σ-algebra on H.

We will also write g for the stream of payoffs $(g_1, \dots, g_n, \dots)$.

IV.1.b. Strategies and Payoffs

By the above description the information of player i before stage n is a vector $(a_1^i, \dots, a_n^i)$ in $\prod_{m=1}^n (A^i)_m$.

Denote by $\mathscr{H}_n^i$ the σ-field induced by this set on H_∞. The restriction to each H_n defines a measurable structure on H, written $\mathscr{H}^i$, that describes i's **information partition** on H.

A **pure strategy** s^i is thus a measurable mapping from $(H, \mathscr{H}^i)$ into S^i. (Note that the pure strategy set of player i is a product of finite sets.)

A **mixed strategy** σ^i is then as usual a probability on this compact set (with the product topology induced by the discrete topology on each factor), and the corresponding set will be denoted by Σ^i.

One can always add player i's last move to his signal (Theorem II.1.2, p. 61) and then perfect recall implies (Theorem II.1.6, p. 63) that we can equivalently view σ^i as a mapping from $(H, \mathscr{H}^i)$ into $\Delta(S^i) = X^i$. According to this interpretation it is also useful to think of σ^i as a sequence $(\sigma_n^i)_{n\geq 1}$, where σ_n^i is the restriction of σ^i to H_n and corresponds to the "strategy at stage n." One can as well consider each σ_n^i as being defined on H_∞ with $\sigma_n^i(h_\infty) = \sigma^i(h_n)$.

As payoff function for the game we will consider the Cesàro limit of the sequence of stage payoffs g_n. This may not be defined for every feasible play (i.e., the game is not a well-specified game in normal form), but we will take care of this fact when defining the solutions and show that this specification of the payoffs is unambiguous and sufficient.

Note that this model can also be used to study two other important classes of games, namely:

Discounted games: Γ_λ has payoff function $\overline{g}_\lambda = \lambda \sum_{n=1}^\infty (1 - \lambda)^{n-1} g_n$ with $\lambda \in (0, 1]$.

In order to reduce this game to the previous model, add for each point in $K \times S$ a new absorbing state with payoff $\mathsf{E}(G^k(s))$ forever. Now the new transition will operate in two stages, the first one being like the old transition, and the second one choosing with probability λ the absorbing state corresponding to (k, s) and with probability $(1 - \lambda)$ keeping the same state and giving a zero payoff. Note that one could also work with different discount rates for each player.

Finitely repeated games: Γ_N has payoff function $\overline{g}_N = 1/N \sum_{n=1}^{N} g_n$, $N \in \mathbb{N}$.

In this case a reduction similar to the previous one can be done, after replacing K by its product by $\{1, \dots N\}$ and using "time-dependent parameters" $\lambda_n = 1/(N - n + 1)$.

Basically the reason for using these averages is that they preserve the stationary character of the game (cf. IV.1, Ex. 1, p. 178).

IV.1.c. Zero-Sum Case

For solution concepts in the two-person zero-sum case, an unambiguous solution is provided by the value and a corresponding pair of ε-optimal strategies.

Before defining these concepts in our framework, let us introduce some notational principles. In general, in the two-person case we will write: s, σ, a (resp. t, τ, b,) for the moves, strategies, and signals of player I (the maximizer) (resp. player II), and S, Σ, A (resp. $T, \mathscr{T}, B$,) for the corresponding sets.

Given σ and τ, $P_{\sigma,\tau}$ is the probability induced on $(H_\infty, \mathscr{H}_\infty)$ by P, Q, σ, τ (cf. Proposition II.1.5, p. 63), and $\mathsf{E}_{\sigma,\tau}$ is the corresponding expectation.

Definition IV.1.2.
Player I **can guarantee** d if:

$$\forall \varepsilon > 0, \exists \sigma_\varepsilon, \exists N, \text{ such that}: \quad \mathsf{E}_{\sigma_\varepsilon,\tau}(\overline{g}_n) \geq d - \varepsilon, \quad \forall \tau, \forall n \geq N. \tag{1}$$

Player II **can defend** d if:

$$\forall \varepsilon > 0, \forall \sigma, \exists \tau, \exists N, \text{ such that}: \quad \mathsf{E}_{\sigma,\tau}(\overline{g}_n) \leq d + \varepsilon, \quad \forall n \geq N. \tag{2}$$

$\underline{v}$ is the **maxmin** of Γ_∞ if player I can guarantee $\underline{v}$ and player II can defend $\underline{v}$.

In this case a strategy σ_ε associated to $\underline{v}$ is **ε-optimal**. A strategy is **optimal** if it is ε-optimal for all ε.

The **minmax** $\overline{v}$ and (ε-) optimal strategies for player II are defined in a dual way.

The game has a **value**, denoted by v_∞, iff $\underline{v} = \overline{v}$, and then $v_\infty = \underline{v} = \overline{v}$.

Remark IV.1.3. Whenever possible, for example, in stochastic games (cf. Chapter VII, p. 392), one may also require (1) and its dual for $N = \infty$, namely:

$$\mathsf{E}_{\sigma_\varepsilon,\tau}(\liminf_{n\to\infty} \overline{g}_n) \geq \underline{v} - \varepsilon, \forall\tau, \tag{3}$$

$$\mathsf{E}_{\sigma,\tau_\varepsilon}(\limsup_{n\to\infty} \overline{g}_n) \leq \underline{v} + \varepsilon, \forall\sigma. \tag{4}$$

Remark IV.1.4. Note that with the above definitions the existence of $\underline{v}$ and $\overline{v}$ has to be proved. Note also that the definitions provide insights into the study of the long but finite games Γ_n or of the games with small discount factor Γ_λ. For the first class it is clear that σ_ε guarantees a payoff $\underline{v} - \varepsilon$ in any Γ_n with $n \geq N$. As for the second it follows clearly from (1) that for any discount factor λ smaller than some $\overline{\lambda}$, function of N, and the payoff range W only, one has $\forall\tau$, $\mathsf{E}_{\sigma_\varepsilon,\tau}(\overline{g}_\lambda) \geq \underline{v} - \varepsilon$ as well. Hence σ_ε also guarantees $\underline{v} - \varepsilon$ in any Γ_λ with $\lambda \leq \overline{\lambda}$. Moreover, in both cases, by (2), $\underline{v}$ is the best that can be achieved by strategies that do not depend on the exact specification of the duration or of the discount factor of the game.

Remark IV.1.5. Condition (1) is a uniform (in τ) property on the liminf of the average expected payoff. On the other hand (3) corresponds to a payoff function defined on plays and would be a desirable property.

The following game shows that it may not hold.

Example IV.1.6. Consider a zero-sum game with two states and payoff matrices $G^1 = (1, 0)$, $G^2 = (0, 1)$ (player I is a dummy player). Assume $\mathsf{Pr}\{k_n = 1, \forall n\} = \mathsf{Pr}\{k_n = 2, \forall n\} = 1/2$. Obviously $\mathsf{E}_{\sigma,\tau}(\overline{g}_n) = 1/2$, for all σ, τ, but if player II plays left and right in alternating blocks of size L_m with $L_m/L_{m-1} \to \infty$, then $\mathsf{E}_{\sigma,\tau}(\liminf \overline{g}_n) = 0$.

Another approach would then be to define a payoff for pure strategy pairs (i.e., taking expectation with respect to all random parameters of the game or all corresponding plays), by associating to the sequence of stage payoffs some limit, say, liminf (hence obtaining $1/2$ in the previous example). In this case, too, the normal form game may have no value satisfying (1) to (4):

Example IV.1.7. Consider the same model as above with the following payoff matrices:

$$G^1 = \begin{pmatrix} 2 & 0 \end{pmatrix} \qquad G^2 = \begin{pmatrix} 0 & 1 \\ -1 & 2 \end{pmatrix},$$

and player I knows the state. The moves of player II are not announced to I, and the signals to II are a or b according to the following probability distributions:

$$Q^1 = \big((1/3, 2/3) \quad (1/3, 2/3)\big) \qquad Q^2 = \begin{pmatrix} (0, 1) & (0, 1) \\ (2/3, 1/3) & (2/3, 1/3) \end{pmatrix}$$

(e.g., if $k = 2$, I plays B and II L, and a will be announced to II with probability $2/3$). Note that by playing $\sigma_0 = (1/2, 1/2)$ i.i.d. if $k = 2$, player I obtains a constant expected payoff $3/4$, and this is the only way "not to reveal information" about the state.

Considering the measure μ_σ induced by any strategy σ of I on $\mathscr{H}^{\text{II}}$ (σ-field of information of II), one then obtains that: if σ guarantees $3/4 - \delta$, then $\|\mu_\sigma - \mu_{\sigma_0}\| \le (16/3)\delta$ (cf. V.5, Ex. 13, p. 312). Assume now δ small.

Let $N_n = 2^{2^n}$ and define a strategy τ of II as follows:

Play arbitrarily at stage 1. If the first signal is a, play N_1 times R, then N_2 times L, and so on, and do the reverse if b is announced at stage 1.

Since the frequency of the signal a under μ_σ is near $1/3$ (being near the one under μ_{σ_0}), the frequency of B under σ, if $k = 2$, is near $1/2$; hence denoting by f_m^1 and f_m^2 the frequencies of L until the end of block m, and by φ_m the corresponding average expected payoff, one obtains that φ_m is near $3/4 + \mathsf{E}(f_m^1 - f_m^2)$ for m large enough and almost all pure strategies in the support of σ.

Note that $\mathsf{E}(f_m^1)$ is near $2/3$ if m is odd and near $1/3$ if m is even. As for the expectation of f_m^2 we obtain: when the first move is T, this expectation is 1 if m is odd and 0 if m is even. Similarly, when the first move is B this expectation is $1/3$ if m is odd and $2/3$ if m is even. It follows that in each case $\liminf \varphi_m$ is $3/4 - 1/3$, hence $\mathsf{E}_{\sigma,\tau}(\liminf \overline{g}_n)$ is near $5/12$ for such strategies. (See V.5, Ex. 13, p. 312, for precise computations.)

Remaining with the finite games Γ_n or the discounted games Γ_λ, it is clear by Proposition I.2.4, p. 21, that they possess a value, denoted by v_n or v_λ, since our finiteness assumptions imply that the payoffs $\overline{\gamma}_n(\sigma, \tau) = \mathsf{E}_{\sigma,\tau}(\overline{g}_n)$ and $\overline{\gamma}_\lambda(\sigma, \tau) = \mathsf{E}_{\sigma,\tau}(\overline{g}_\lambda)$ are continuous on the product of the compact pure strategy spaces.

It follows from the previous definitions that the existence of v_∞ also implies that both $\lim_{n\to\infty} v_n$ and $\lim_{\lambda\to 0} v_\lambda$ exist and satisfy: $v_\infty = \lim_{n\to\infty} v_n = \lim_{\lambda\to 0} v_\lambda$. In this situation, ε-optimal strategies are also ε-optimal in any sufficiently long game as well as in any game with a sufficiently small discount factor.

Now when $\underline{v} < \overline{v}$ (recall that the definitions clearly imply $\underline{v} \le \overline{v}$), another main question of research will be the study of the nets v_n and v_λ (as $n \to \infty$ and $\lambda \to 0$) and of the asymptotic behavior of the corresponding optimal strategies.

Before going to the non-zero-sum case, let us recall that the study of $\overline{v}$ is also of primary interest in this case because it defines the individually rational level, i.e., what player I can obtain in the worst situation where the other players are considered as a single player trying to minimize his payoff (cf. Section IV.4, p. 190).

IV.1.d. Non-Zero-Sum Case

In the non-zero-sum case we will be mainly interested in equilibria and correlated or communication equilibria (cf. Section I.I.4, p. 45, and II.II.3, p. 101).

Recall that the latter form a larger set but present some conceptual advantages and have a much nicer mathematical structure. Furthermore their natural extensions to repeated games seem ideally suited to take into account the relation between the initial information of the players and the information they obtain through the correlation device. (The equilibria of a one-stage game Γ_1 with state-independent payoffs are correlated equilibria in the underlying game with no signals.) Both those concepts have been criticized and several refinements have been proposed, but many further complications arise because we are considering infinite games.

To define equilibria and equilibrium payoffs we proceed as follows: first, we ask for the analogue of the uniformity condition for the value.

Definition IV.1.8. σ is a **uniform equilibrium** if $\overline{\gamma}_n^i(\sigma)$ converges to some $\overline{\gamma}^i(\sigma)$ and, for all $\varepsilon > 0$, there exists N such that $n \geq N$ implies $\overline{\gamma}_n^i(\sigma_{-i}, \tau^i) \leq \overline{\gamma}^i(\sigma) + \varepsilon$, for all i and all τ^i.

To avoid the difficulties arising from the lack of a well-specified payoff, one also introduces a family of games: for each Banach limit $\mathscr{L}$ (cf. I.2, Ex. 10, p. 27) we define a normal form game $\Gamma_{\mathscr{L}}$ by the strategy sets Σ^i and the payoff $\mathscr{L}(\mathsf{E}_\sigma(\overline{g}_n^i))$, $i \in \mathbf{I}$.

Definition IV.1.9. If the set of equilibrium payoffs of $\Gamma_{\mathscr{L}}$ does not depend on $\mathscr{L}$ and each of these payoffs can moreover be realized by a uniform equilibrium, we define it as the set E_∞ of **equilibrium payoffs** in Γ_∞. Similarly C_∞ and D_∞ correspond to correlated and communication equilibrium payoffs (cf. Section II.3, p. 101).

Note that the concept of uniform equilibrium is rather strong: it corresponds to a strategy independent of ε in (1), p. 174. It implies in particular that any equilibrium payoff can be sustained by a strategy vector that is in equilibrium in every $\Gamma_{\mathscr{L}}$.

Weaker conditions, which are needed for stochastic games and related to E_0, are payoffs ε-close to ε-equilibrium payoffs, for all $\varepsilon > 0$ (cf. Section VII.4, p. 410).

Finally, since strategies in Γ_∞ induce strategies in any subgame of it, we can define a **subgame perfect equilibrium** as strategies inducing an equilibrium in any subgame.

The above arguments (interest of the zero-sum case, use of it for the non-zero-sum setup, conceptual and mathematical complications in the latter) indicate why we will largely concentrate in this chapter as well as in this book on the zero-sum case (cf., however, Section II.4, p. 118, IV.2, p. 178, and IV.4, p. 190, Chapter VII, p. 392, and Chapter IX, p. 481).

IV.1.e. Stochastic Games and Games with Incomplete Information

These two classes of repeated games will be extensively studied, and a first presentation follows, according to our general formulation.

In a **stochastic game**, the current state and the stage payoff are known to all players: for all i and all n, the signal a^i_{n+1} differs on two histories where k_{n+1} or g_n are not the same. The main case is obtained when the signal is the same for all players and consists of (s_n, k_{n+1}) at stage $n+1$; cf. Chapter VII, p. 392.

In a **game with incomplete information** the state is constant along the play: $k_n = k_1$, for all n, but unknown to at least one player; cf. Chapter V, p. 215, and Chapter VI, p. 326.

It follows that in the first case the main goal is to control the transitions on the state space, while in the second the decisive aspects concern the transmission of information. Nevertheless we will see that the two fields are deeply related and are better understood when studied in parallel.

EXERCISES

1. Recursive utilities. Cf., e.g., references in Kreps and Porteus (1979) and Becker et al. (1989).

a. If x_n denotes the outcome at stage n, "recursive utilities" are defined recursively by $U_n(x_n, x_{n+1}, \dots) = \Phi_n(x_n, U_{n+1}(x_{n+1}, \dots))$, where Φ_n is non-decreasing in the second variable. Show that, for the U_n to be von Neumann–Morgenstern utilities, one needs:

$$\Phi_n(x, U) = \alpha_n(x) + \beta_n(x)U, \quad \beta_n \geq 0.$$

b. Consider a repeated game with payoffs defined recursively by $U_n = \alpha_n + \beta_n . U_{n+1}$, where α_n and β_n are stationary functions of $(a_{n-m}, k_{n-m}, s_{n-m}, \dots, a_n, k_n, s_n, a_{n+1}, k_{n+1})$ and $\beta_n \leq 1$. Show how to obtain an equivalent game with enlarged space $\widetilde{K}$ where the payoff is $\sum_n g(\widetilde{k}_n)$ (or $\lim(1/n) \sum_n g(\widetilde{k}_n)$).

IV.2. EQUIVALENT REPRESENTATIONS

We will describe here different variants in the formalization that may make the model more tractable in analyzing some of its properties.

IV.2.a. Simple Transformations

(1) Let us first remark that information lags are easily incorporated in our model; more precisely, consider a stationary bounded recall transition, namely, Q defined on H, where for some fixed m, any n, and any h_n in H_n (resp. h_m in H_m), if h_{n+m} denotes (h_n, h_m), then $Q(h_{n+m})$ is only a function of h_m. It is then enough to redefine a new set of states, say, as $K \times H_m$, and to extend in an obvious way P and Q to remain in the same class. One can similarly deal with non-stationary transitions with finite memory.

(2) To dispense with the initial lottery and the initial information of the players, it is enough to add a new initial state from where, whatever the actions of the players are, the payoff is 0 and the new state as

well as the signals to the players are selected according to the initial distribution. (This will shift one stage further all the payoffs but does not influence the long-term average.)

(3) As for the payoffs one can first assume that W is included in $\{g \in \mathbb{R}^{\mathbf{I}} \mid g_i \geq 0, \forall i \in \mathbf{I}, \sum_i g_i \leq 1\}$ by adding some constant and then rescaling.

One can now replace the distribution on the payoffs by any other distribution having the same expectation: for example, take a deterministic payoff, or a probability with support on the extreme points of the simplex $\Delta(\mathbf{I})$ and the zero vector in $\mathbb{R}^{\mathbf{I}}$. In fact, this change has no information effect on the game, and hence does not influence the strategies. Moreover the expected payoff at each stage remains the same. It now follows from II.4, Ex. 4, p. 121, that for any choice of σ the difference of the average payoffs $\overline{g}_n$ in both formulations will converge to zero a.s. Hence the asymptotic properties of the game are not affected by this change.

(4) Taking the second variant above we have now a finite set of payoffs. Redefine then the set of states as to include the old states, the vector payoffs, and the vector of signals, namely, $K \times W \times A$, and extend the transition on the new K in the natural way. We obtain then a model where the game starts at some initial state and, after each stage, a new state is chosen at random as a function of the old stage and the actions of the players at that stage. Signals to the players and payoffs are now functions of the new state.

One can also, without affecting the asymptotic behavior, shift the payoffs one stage further and assume that the payoff is only a function of the current state. Note now that the players' signals can be viewed as a partition of K such that before each stage each player is told the element of his partition that contains the true state.

The game is thus described by the following elements:

- a finite set of states K with an initial state k_0
- a finite set of moves S^i for each player i in $\mathbf{I}$
- a transition probability P from $K \times S$ to K
- a partition $\mathbf{K}^i$ of K, for each i in $\mathbf{I}$
- a partition $\mathbf{W} = \{W^0, W^1, \ldots, W^{\mathbf{I}}\}$ of K

(where W^0 corresponds to the set of states with zero payoff and W^i to those with payoff 1 to player i).

Before each stage, every player i is told in which element of $\mathbf{K}^i$ the current state k is. He then chooses an action in S^i and receives a payoff 1 iff k belongs to W^i. Then P selects a new state, and the game proceeds to the next stage. Note that W^i is the set of winning states for player i, W^0 corresponds to a draw, and each player maximizes his expected winning frequency. In the zero-sum case one can scale player I's payoff to lie between 0 and 1, and then obtain a partition of K in $W^{\mathrm{I}} \cup W^{\mathrm{II}}$: there is no draw.

We have thus proved:

Proposition IV.2.1. *The games described in Section IV.1.a, p. 172, and IV.2.a, p. 178, have the same asymptotic properties.*

IV.2.b. A Deterministic Framework

We will assume here that all the coefficients defining the previous transition probability P are rational, and we will reduce the model to deterministic P. The construction will be done here for the two-person zero-sum case (for the general case, cf. Mertens (1987a)). The purpose of this transformation is to have a better feeling of the essential structure of the problem while adding a mild assumption.

So let m be a common denominator to all rational coefficients that appear in P. Let $\mathbb{Z}_m = \mathbb{Z}/m\mathbb{Z}$. If $(X_n)_{n\geq 0}$ is a sequence of i.i.d. random variables uniformly distributed on $\mathbb{Z}_m$, then P can be represented as a function from $K \times S \times T \times \mathbb{Z}_m$ to K such that $k_{n+1} = P(k_n, s_n, t_n, x_n)$. In fact, we will show that the players can generate themselves such a sequence (cf. also II.3, Ex. 5, p. 112).

Assume that each player i chooses at each stage n, besides his action, an element z_n^i in $\mathbb{Z}_m$, and take as random variables the sum in $\mathbb{Z}_m$ of these two choices. Formally we have a new game $\widetilde{\Gamma}$ where $\widetilde{S} = S \times \mathbb{Z}_m$, $\widetilde{T} = T \times \mathbb{Z}_m$ and $k_{n+1} = \widetilde{P}(k_n, \widetilde{s}_n, \widetilde{t}_n) = P(k_n, s_n, t_n, z_n^{\mathrm{I}} + z_n^{\mathrm{II}})$. (We keep the same signaling structure: no player is ever informed of any of the past auxiliary choices of his opponent.)

Proposition IV.2.2. Γ *and* $\widetilde{\Gamma}$ *have the same asymptotic properties.*

Proof. Let us prove this first for $\underline{v}$: existence, value, and ε-optimal strategies.

We denote by $\mathbb{Z}_m^\infty$ the compact group $\prod_1^\infty (\mathbb{Z}_m)_n$, by z a generic element in it, and by μ the Haar measure on it.

Given $\widetilde{\sigma}$ in $\widetilde{\Sigma}$ (strategy set of player I in $\widetilde{\Gamma}$) and z in $\mathbb{Z}_m^\infty$ define $\widetilde{\sigma}_z$ by $(s_n, z_n^{\mathrm{I}} + z_n)$ at each stage n ($\widetilde{\tau}_z$ is defined similarly). Considering $\widetilde{\sigma}_z$ as a transition probability from $\mathbb{Z}_m^\infty$ to pure strategies in $\widetilde{\Gamma}$ one can introduce $\underline{\widetilde{\sigma}} = \int \widetilde{\sigma}_z \mu(dz)$, which is a mixed strategy in $\widetilde{\Gamma}$, and denote by $\underline{\sigma}$ its projection (marginal distribution) in Γ.

Now for any $\underline{\sigma}$ in Σ we can define $\mu \otimes \underline{\sigma}$ in $\widetilde{\Sigma}$, and it follows from the previous construction that $\underline{\widetilde{\sigma}}$ and $\mu \otimes \underline{\sigma}$ induce the same behavioral strategies, and hence by Kuhn's theorem (Theorem II.1.3, p. 62) the same distribution on histories in $\widetilde{\Gamma}$ for every $\widetilde{\tau}$.

Note finally that the map $\widetilde{\sigma} \mapsto \widetilde{\sigma}_z$ is a permutation of $\widetilde{\Sigma}$, the map $\widetilde{\sigma} \mapsto \underline{\sigma}$ from $\widetilde{\Sigma}$ to Σ is onto, and that $(\widetilde{\sigma}_z, \widetilde{\tau}_{-z})$ induces the same distribution on histories as $(\widetilde{\sigma}, \widetilde{\tau})$.

Given any bounded measurable function f on $(H_\infty, \mathscr{H}_\infty)$ (as $\overline{g}_n$ or $\liminf \overline{g}_n$) we therefore have, for any $\widetilde{\sigma}$:

$$f_{\widetilde{\sigma}} \equiv \inf_{\widetilde{\tau}} \mathsf{E}_{\widetilde{\sigma},\widetilde{\tau}}(f) = \inf_{\widetilde{\tau}} \mathsf{E}_{\widetilde{\sigma}_z,\widetilde{\tau}_{-z}}(f) = \inf_{\widetilde{\tau}} \mathsf{E}_{\widetilde{\sigma}_z,\widetilde{\tau}}(f) = f_{\widetilde{\sigma}_z}.$$

Hence:

$$\mathsf{E}_{\underline{\widetilde{\sigma}},\widetilde{\tau}}(f) = \int \mu(dz)\, \mathsf{E}_{\widetilde{\sigma}_z,\widetilde{\tau}}(f) \geq f_{\widetilde{\sigma}},$$

and thus also:

$$\mathsf{E}_{\mu\otimes\underline{\sigma},\widetilde{\tau}}(f) \geq f_{\widetilde{\sigma}}$$

and:

$$f_{\mu} \otimes \underline{\sigma} \geq f_{\widetilde{\sigma}}.$$

Defining similarly in Γ, $f_\sigma \equiv \inf_\tau \mathsf{E}_{\sigma,\tau}(f)$, we claim that $f_{\underline{\sigma}} = f_\mu \otimes \underline{\sigma}$.

In fact, using the properties of the Haar measure:

$$\begin{aligned}\mathsf{E}_{\mu\otimes\underline{\sigma},\widetilde{\tau}}(f) = \mathsf{E}_{(\mu\otimes\underline{\sigma})_{-z},\widetilde{\tau}_z}(f) = \mathsf{E}_{\mu\otimes\underline{\sigma},\widetilde{\tau}_z}(f) &= \int \mu(dz)\, \mathsf{E}_{\mu\otimes\underline{\sigma},\widetilde{\tau}_z}(f)\\ &= \mathsf{E}_{\mu\otimes\underline{\sigma},\underline{\widetilde{\tau}}}(f) = \mathsf{E}_{\mu\otimes\underline{\sigma},\mu\otimes\underline{\tau}}(f).\end{aligned}$$

Now, under $\mu \otimes \underline{\sigma}$ and $\mu \otimes \underline{\tau}$ the random variables z^{I} and z^{II} are independent and their marginals uniform on $\mathbb{Z}_m$, and hence $\mathsf{E}_{\mu\otimes\underline{\sigma},\mu\otimes\underline{\tau}} = \mathsf{E}_{\underline{\sigma},\underline{\tau}}$.

We obtain thus:

$$\mathsf{E}_{\mu\otimes\underline{\sigma},\widetilde{\tau}}(f) = \mathsf{E}_{\underline{\sigma},\underline{\tau}}(f), \tag{1}$$

and also:

$$\mathsf{E}_{\underline{\sigma},\underline{\tau}}(f) = \mathsf{E}_{\widetilde{\sigma},\mu\otimes\underline{\tau}}(f), \tag{2}$$

hence the claim.

Coming back to Definition IV.1.2, p. 174, it follows from $f_{\underline{\sigma}} \geq f_{\widetilde{\sigma}}$ and $f_{\underline{\sigma}} = f_\mu \otimes \underline{\sigma}$ that $(\widetilde{\sigma}, w)$ satisfies (1), p. 174, in $\widetilde{\Gamma}$ only if $(\underline{\sigma}, w)$ satisfies it in Γ, and the latter holds iff $(\mu \otimes \underline{\sigma}, w)$ satisfies (1) in $\widetilde{\Gamma}$.

Similarly (2) implies that if w satisfies (2), p. 174, in Γ, then it also does in $\widetilde{\Gamma}$. Finally (1) shows the reverse inequality since $\mu \otimes \Sigma$ is included in $\widetilde{\Sigma}$. This implies that the maxmin will exist in Γ iff it exists in $\widetilde{\Gamma}$. In this case its value will be the same, and ε-optimal strategies can be mapped through $\underline{\sigma} \mapsto \mu \otimes \underline{\sigma}$.

It is easy to see that analogous results for v_λ or v_n follow from the same arguments. ■

IV.2.c. A Combinatorial Form

The aim of this last transformation is to push one step further toward a simple sequential combinatorial form.

We first rank the players in cyclical order (identifying **I** and $\mathbb{Z}_{\mathbf{I}}$) and subdivide each stage into **I** substages, player i being the only one to choose an action at each stage $n \equiv i$ (mod **I**). The new set of states F is partitioned into subsets $F^1, \ldots, F^{\mathbf{I}}$ and an element in F^i is a point in E together with the last actions of players j, $1 \leq j \leq i-1$.

After each substage **I**, P is used to compute an element of F (in fact, of $F^1 = E$), as a function of the old element in $E = F^1$ and the vector of actions, or equivalently as a function of the element in $F^{\mathbf{I}}$ and the last action of player **I**.

Since all players' payoffs are functions only of the point in F^1, included in F^i for all i, one can delay them so that player i's winning set W^i will be a subset of F^i.

Each player's action set S^i can now be considered as a subset of the set of functions from F^i to F^{i+1}. In fact, to model his information one can replace S^i by the set of $\mathbf{K}^i$, measurable functions from F^i to S^i , hence to F^{i+1}, and give him his private information in $\mathbf{K}^i$ about the true state only after his move.

We thus obtain the following combinatorial form:

- a finite set of states F with an initial state f_0 and a partition $F^1, \ldots, F^{\mathbf{I}}$ of F.
- for each F^i a partition $\mathscr{F}^i$ and a set Y^i of functions from F^i to F^{i+1}.
- a subset W of F.

The play of the game is as follows, starting from f_0. At the current state f in F^i, player i selects a function y^i in Y^i. He then gets a payoff 1 iff f is in W, zero otherwise, and is told the element of $\mathscr{F}^i$ that contains f. The new state is now $y^i(f)$ in F^{i+1}. The players want to maximize their expected winning frequencies.

Replacing now Y^i by $Y = \prod_{i \in \mathbf{I}} Y^i$, and letting $\mathscr{F}$ be the partition $\bigcup_{i \in \mathbf{I}} \mathscr{F}^i$ of F, we reach the following description, coming back to our standard notations: K is the state space, S is a set of functions from K to K, A is a partition on K, and $a(k)$ is the point in A containing k. Players play in cyclical order, choosing an element s_n of S at each time n, and then being informed of $a(k_n)$. The new state is $k_{n+1} = s_n(k_n)$, and the player who moved receives 1 if $k_n \in W$, and zero otherwise. In the two-person zero-sum case, he receives 1 from his opponent if $k_n \in W$, and pays him 1 otherwise.

We finally show how to reduce this description further (by enlarging K) to the case where $\#S = \#A = 2$. Fix a two-element set $\{f, g\}$ and a map from $\{f, g\}^l$ onto S. Fix also a map from A into $\{a_1, a_2\}^h$. Replace every stage of the above game by a block of $l \cdot \mathbf{I}$ substages followed by a block of $h \cdot \mathbf{I}$ substages. If this was a stage for player i, at every substage corresponding to a player $j \neq i$ this player's choice in $\{f, g\}$ has no effect, and this player is told a_1. On the first l substages corresponding to player i, this player is told a_1, and his sequence of choices in $\{f, g\}$ gives a point in $\{f, g\}^l$, and hence determines that the map $s \in S$ is to be used. The signal in A that he has to hear is then encoded in $\{a_1, a_2\}^h$ and told to him over the last h substages, where his choices in $\{f, g\}$ have no effect. As for payoffs, all substages except the last substage of player i are outside W, and on the last substage the correct set W is used. Thus we now have a model where $S = \{f, g\} \subseteq K^K$, and where $A = \{a_1, a_2\}$, i.e., it corresponds also to a subset of K.

We thus have proved:

Proposition IV.2.3. *If P (as obtained in IV.2.a, p. 178) is rational, the games described in Section IV.1.a, p. 172, and IV.2.c, p. 182, have the same asymptotic properties.*

IV.3. RECURSIVE STRUCTURE

In this section we will study what is the natural space in which one can model the information obtained during the game while keeping the stationary aspects.

Basically we are looking for entrance laws that allow us to start the study at any stage of the game: we will see that a basic structure like common knowledge of a prior on the state space and private partitions is not enough.

In this part again, we will concentrate on two-person zero-sum games, but the analysis can be extended to more general cases (cf. Chapter III and Mertens (1987a)).

IV.3.a. A Canonical Representation

Consider a pair of strategies in Γ. Together with the description of the game, including the initial conditions, they determine a probability distribution on $(H_\infty, \mathscr{H}_\infty)$, i.e., the space of plays, that both players can compute. By the previous reductions, at stage n, the future play of the game depends only on the current state k_n. Each player i, $i = \text{I}, \text{II}$, has in addition accumulated some signals that can be modeled by means of some set M^i. More precisely k_n is a random variable from $(H_\infty, \mathscr{H}_\infty)$ to K, and the information of player i is a random variable m^i from $(H_\infty, \mathscr{H}_\infty)$ to M^i. In our framework, there exists moreover an underlying probability Q on $(H_\infty, \mathscr{H}_\infty)$, defined by P and the strategies. If we let $(E, \mathscr{E}) = (H_\infty, \mathscr{H}_\infty)$ and $\mathscr{E}^i$ be the sub-σ-field generated by m^i, we obtain an information scheme; hence by Theorem III.2.4, p. 142, there exists a canonical representation on Ω with $\mathbf{P}_n$ in $\mathscr{P}$. Note that this probability contains all relevant information about the past; more precisely, the future aspects of the game should be the same if it was starting at stage n using $\mathbf{P}_n$ to choose the state and the information to the players (we use here the zero-sum assumption).

It is clear that typically these $\mathbf{P}_n$ will have specific properties, basically finite support in our finite framework, but one sees easily that generically their size cannot be bounded, hence the advantage of working directly with the closure $\mathscr{P}$ in order to have a stationary set of "state variables," which are the **entrance laws** $\mathbf{P}_n$. Before seeing in the next paragraph the merits of such an approach, let us remark at this point that $\mathbf{P}_{n+1}$ is easily constructed using $\mathbf{P}_n$ and the behavioral strategies at stage n (i.e., the restriction of σ and τ to H_n), and that similarly, according to Section IV.2.b, p. 180, the payoff at stage n for player i is simply $\mathsf{E}_{\sigma,\tau}(g_n^i) = \mathbf{P}_n(W^i)$.

IV.3.b. The Recursive Formula

We first want to be able to apply the results of Section III.4.b, p. 154, to the finite game Γ_n and the discounted game Γ_λ.

Proposition IV.3.1. *The results of Section III.4.b, p. 154, apply to v_n and v_λ, since these strategies are behavioral strategies.*

Proof. Indeed, both Γ_n and Γ_λ have K finite, and S and T compact metric, with $g_k(s,t)$ continuous. It remains to show that the results are still true with behavioral strategies. This follows from II.1, Ex. 10, except possibly for the continuity. For this aspect, let the finite subset S_0 of S consist, for Γ_n of the whole of S, and for Γ_λ, of all pure strategies that from a certain stage n_0 on play always the first pure strategy (n_0 is fixed). There is no problem in requiring further in Section III.4.b that every pure strategy in S_0 have strictly positive probability. Then the map from mixed strategies to behavioral strategies is continuous (with the above set S_0). ∎

We are now going to use fully the structure of "entrance laws" that we introduced in Section IV.3.a, p. 183. To obtain a nice recursive formula it will be convenient to keep with the framework of Section IV.2, p. 178, where the current payoff is only a function of the state at this stage and where the information is given at the end of each stage.

Assume then some entrance law $\mathbf{P}$ and behavioral strategies x and y of the players for the first stage, namely, measurable mappings from Θ to $\Delta(S)$ or $\Delta(T)$.

We define $\mathscr{I}(\mathbf{P}, x, y)$ as the following information scheme: first a triple $(k, \theta^{\mathrm{I}}, \theta^{\mathrm{II}})$ in Ω is selected according to $\mathbf{P}$ and player i is informed of θ^i. Both players then independently select moves according to $x(\theta^{\mathrm{I}})$ or $y(\theta^{\mathrm{II}})$. Finally a new state and random signals $(\widetilde{k}, a^{\mathrm{I}}, a^{\mathrm{II}})$ are selected in the game as usual as a function of the old state and the pair of moves. Formally:

$$\mathscr{I}(\mathbf{P}, x, y) = (\Omega; \mathbf{P}_{x,y}; \widetilde{k}; (\theta^{\mathrm{I}}, s, a^{\mathrm{I}}); (\theta^{\mathrm{II}}, t, a^{\mathrm{II}})).$$

Finally $\mathbf{P}[x, y]$ in $\mathscr{P}$ will denote the corresponding canonical probability.

We can now justify the well-foundedness of the previous point of view by stating our main result:

Theorem IV.3.2 (Recursive Formula).

(1) *Let $v(\mathbf{P})$ stand for either $v_\lambda(\mathbf{P})$ or $v_n(\mathbf{P})$. Then both* $\max_x \min_y v(\mathbf{P}[x, y])$ *and* $\min_y \max_x v(\mathbf{P}[x, y])$ *exist and are equal.*
(2) *Denoting by $V(v[\mathbf{P}])$ this saddle point value we have:*

$$v_\lambda(\mathbf{P}) = \lambda\, \mathsf{E}_\mathbf{P}(g_1) + (1-\lambda)V(v_\lambda[\mathbf{P}]),$$

$$nv_n(\mathbf{P}) = \mathsf{E}_\mathbf{P}(g_1) + (n-1)V(v_{n-1}[\mathbf{P}]).$$

(3) *In the space of all bounded functions on $\mathscr{P}$, v_λ and v_n are uniquely determined by the above formulae.*

Proof. Let $\sigma = (\sigma_n)_{n\geq 1}$ and $\tau = (\tau_n)_{n\geq 1}$ be behavioral strategies of players I and II in Γ_λ and assume σ optimal. Let us write σ_+ or τ_+ for the sequences $(\sigma_n)_{n\geq 2}$ or $(\tau_n)_{n\geq 2}$ and note that both σ_+ and τ_+ are behavioral strategies in $[\Gamma_\lambda; \mathscr{I}(\mathbf{P}, \sigma_1, \tau_1))]$. Denoting the corresponding expected payoff by $\overline{g}_\lambda(\mathscr{I}(\mathbf{P}, \sigma_1, \tau_1); \sigma_+, \tau_+)$, we thus obtain, writing the total payoff in Γ_λ as the sum of the first-stage payoff and the remaining one:

$$\begin{aligned} v_\lambda(\mathbf{P}) &\leq \overline{g}_\lambda(\mathbf{P}; \sigma, \tau) \\ &= \lambda\, \mathsf{E}_\mathbf{P}(g_1) + (1-\lambda)\overline{g}_\lambda(\mathscr{I}(\mathbf{P}, \sigma_1, \tau_1); \sigma_+, \tau_+). \end{aligned}$$

Taking the infimum in τ_+ on the right-hand side, then the maximum in σ_+, we also obtain:

$$v_\lambda(\mathbf{P}) \leq \lambda\, \mathsf{E}_\mathbf{P}(g_1) + (1-\lambda) \sup_{\sigma_+} \inf_{\tau_+} \overline{g}_\lambda(\mathscr{I}(\mathbf{P}, \sigma_1, \tau_1); \sigma_+, \tau_+).$$

Using Propositions III.4.4, p. 157, and the above IV.3.1, the $\sup\inf$ is precisely $v_\lambda[\mathscr{I}(\mathbf{P}, \sigma_1, \tau_1)]$, i.e., $v_\lambda(\mathbf{P}[\sigma_1, \tau_1])$. Thus:

$$v_\lambda(\mathbf{P}) \leq \lambda\, \mathsf{E}_\mathbf{P}(g_1) + (1-\lambda)v_\lambda(\mathbf{P}[\sigma_1, \tau_1]).$$

Then, since τ_1 is arbitrary:

$$v_\lambda(\mathbf{P}) \leq \lambda\, \mathsf{E}_\mathbf{P}(g_1) + (1-\lambda) \inf_{\tau_1} v_\lambda(\mathbf{P}[\sigma_1, \tau_1]).$$

It remains to prove that we can actually replace the inf by a min.

For this purpose consider now the λ-discounted game where player I is restricted to use σ_1 in the first stage. Redefining the state space it is easily seen that this game belongs to the same family; hence, by Proposition IV.3.1, p. 184, it has a value and optimal strategies. It follows that even if player I were informed about the first stage strategy τ_1 of player II, the value would be the same and the optimal strategy still optimal. But the value of this variant is precisely the previous right-hand member where now player II has an optimal strategy; hence:

$$v_\lambda(\mathbf{P}) \leq \lambda\, \mathsf{E}_\mathbf{P}(g_1) + (1-\lambda) \min_{\tau_1} v_\lambda(\mathbf{P}[\sigma_1, \tau_1]).$$

Denote by σ_1^* and τ_1^* the first stage components of optimal strategies of both players in Γ_λ. We have shown that, for all σ_1^*, $\min_{\tau_1} v_\lambda(\mathbf{P}[\sigma_1^*, \tau_1])$ exists and:

$$v_\lambda(\mathbf{P}) \leq \lambda\, \mathsf{E}_{\mathbf{P}}(g_1) + (1-\lambda) \min_{\tau_1} v_\lambda(\mathbf{P}[\sigma_1^*, \tau_1]).$$

Since the dual result holds, we obtain finally:

$$\max_{\sigma_1} v_\lambda(\mathbf{P}[\sigma_1, \tau_1^*]) \leq \min_{\tau_1} v_\lambda(\mathbf{P}[\sigma_1^*, \tau_1]),$$

so that σ_1^*, τ_1^* is a saddle point of $v_\lambda(\mathbf{P}[\cdot,\cdot])$; hence $V(v_\lambda[\mathbf{P}])$ exists and satisfies:

$$v_\lambda(\mathbf{P}) = \lambda\, \mathsf{E}_{\mathbf{P}}(g_1) + (1-\lambda) V(v_\lambda[\mathbf{P}]).$$

The results concerning $v_n(\mathbf{P})$ are obtained in the same way.

To prove part (3), p. 185, note first that v_n is uniquely determined given v_{n-1} and that v_1 is well defined.

For v_λ replace V by the previous $\sup\inf$ in the equation. Note that the operator involved is contracting; hence use Picard's contraction principle in the space of all bounded functions on $\mathscr{P}$ (Lemma VII.1.1, p. 393) to get a unique solution. This completes the proof of the theorem. ∎

Define thus an operator Ψ on bounded functions on $\mathscr{P}$ by:

$$[\Psi(f)](\mathbf{P}) = \mathsf{E}_{\mathbf{P}}(g_1) + V[f(\mathbf{P})]$$

(where to avoid ambiguity V is chosen to be the $\inf\sup$), and note that Ψ is non-expansive.

Denoting $V_\lambda = (1/\lambda) v_\lambda$ and $V_n = n v_n$ one has:

$$V_\lambda = \Psi[(1-\lambda)V_\lambda] \text{ and } V_n = \Psi[V_{n-1}].$$

This recursive formula (or rather its particular incarnations) will play a fundamental role in the next chapters, in proving asymptotic properties of Γ_n or Γ_λ. It will also allow us to get precise bounds on the speed of convergence of v_n and v_λ to their limits.

Another use of this formula is to show that we have reduced the problem of studying Γ_n or Γ_λ to the same problem for a class of stochastic games. Indeed, denote by Y^{I} and Y^{II} the set of Borel functions from Θ^{I} or Θ^{II} to $\Delta(S)$ or $\Delta(T)$. Let us define Γ^* as the stochastic game with continuous state and actions spaces $\mathscr{P}, Y^{\mathrm{I}}, Y^{\mathrm{II}}$, played as follows: if $\mathbf{P}$ is the current state and $y^{\mathrm{I}}, y^{\mathrm{II}}$ the actions selected by the players, the current payoff is $\mathsf{E}_{\mathbf{P}}(g_1)$ and the new state is $\mathbf{P}[y^{\mathrm{I}}, y^{\mathrm{II}}]$.

Γ^* is thus a "deterministic stochastic" game where the current payoff is solely a function of the current state. Write $\Gamma_n^*(\mathbf{P})$ and $\Gamma_\lambda^*(\mathbf{P})$ for the finite and discounted versions of Γ^* starting at state $\mathbf{P}$. Then we have:

Proposition IV.3.3. *$\Gamma_n^*(\mathbf{P})$ and $\Gamma_\lambda^*(\mathbf{P})$ have values $v_n^*(\mathbf{P})$ and $v_\lambda^*(\mathbf{P})$ and optimal strategies. Moreover:*

$$v_\lambda^* = v_\lambda \quad v_n^* = v_n.$$

Proof. We will prove that there exist optimal Borel pure strategies that are at each stage versions of the corresponding component of optimal strategies in Γ_λ, resp. Γ_n.

For Γ_n^* the proof follows immediately by induction on n.

For Γ_λ^* assume that both players use the above-described strategies. The recursive formula implies obviously that the payoff will be v_λ. Assume now that player II is allowed to choose arbitrarily his strategy during the first n stages, but has to play the above strategy thereafter. At stage n, using the recursive formula his optimal choice is again to use an optimal strategy in $\Gamma_\lambda(\mathbf{P}_n)$. By induction his optimal play will always have this property: he cannot get below $v_\lambda(\mathbf{P})$ within this class of strategies. Finally, since the payoff depends only up to ε on the play of the game after stage n, for n large enough, it follows that the prescribed strategy of player I guarantees him $v_\lambda(\mathbf{P})$. A dual statement for player II now implies the result. ∎

The purpose of the two next sections will be to present some classes of games belonging to this general model while having a very specific structure (other examples will be found in the exercises). The hope is that this will help the reader to get a better feeling for the basic aspects of repeated games and to see how different presentations can be handled in the general framework.

EXERCISES

1. Gleason's game.

Three positions, say, A, B, C, with corresponding payoffs $1, 2, -3$, are arranged in cyclic order, and alternatively each player tells the referee whether he wants to move clockwise or counterclockwise, after which the referee tells him his position.

a. Prove that there exists a sequence w_n with $|v_n(p) - w_n| \leq K/n$, for some $K > 0$, where $v_n(p)$ is the value of an n-stage game with initial probability p on the states and any kind of initial signals. Moreover each player can guarantee w_n up to $O(1/n)$ by a strategy independent of his initial information.

HINT. Consider the least favorable situation for I: II knows the initial position, and p is public knowledge. Write $v_n(p^A, p^B, p^C)$ for the corresponding value and let $u_A(q) = v_n(0, q, 1-q)$, $u_B(q) = v_n(1-q, 0, q)$, $u_C(q) = v_n(q, 1-q, 0)$, $u(q)$ is the median of those three numbers, and $w_n = \min_q u(q) = u(q_0)$. Given the strategy of player II and his own last position, say, D, player I can compute the last mixed action q of player II. Let him play $(1/2, 1/2)$ i.i.d. until the first stage where $u_D(q) \geq u(q)$ and from then on optimally in the remaining game.

Similarly, in the most favorable situation for player I, player II can play alternatively and independently $(1/2, 1/2)$ and $(q_0, 1-q_0)$ until being informed, after a random choice $(q_0, 1-q_0)$, of a last position B or C (assuming $u_A(q_0) > u(q_0)$) and from then on play optimally.

Finally remark that the payoff guaranteed by a strategy of player I in the first situation is linear in p and consider an optimal strategy for some interior point p.

b. Deduce from IV.3, Ex. 1a, that player I can guarantee $\limsup w_n$.

c. Conclude that Γ has a value v and both players have optimal strategies independent of the initial information.

Remark IV.3.1. The value of v and the existence of optimal stationary strategies are still open problems.

2. A game with two-move information lag. (Dubins, 1957), (Karlin, 1957), (Ferguson, 1967)

We consider the following game Γ. Player II moves on the integers by choosing at each time n an element $t_n \in \{-1, +1\}$. His position after time n is $x_n = \sum_{i=1}^{n} t_i$, and y_n is the corresponding history: $\{x_1, \ldots, x_n\}$. The information of player I at time n is y_{n-2}, and his aim is to guess the actual position of player II, i.e., x_n.

Formally let θ be the time where player I tries to guess the position of player II by choosing some x. The corresponding payoff is then $\mathbb{1}_{\theta<\infty} \times \mathbb{1}_{x_\theta = x}$.

a. Let Γ_n be the n-stage game (where the payoff is identically 0 after stage n) and denote by v_n its value.

Prove that Γ has a value v with $v = \lim \uparrow v_n$ and that player II has an optimal strategy τ^* in Γ (use I.1, Ex. 2b, p. 11).

We want now to compute explicitly v and to describe ε-optimal strategies. In IV.3, Ex. 2b, and IV.3, Ex. 2c, two alternative approaches are used to obtain v and τ^*. In IV.3, Ex. 2d, it is proved that player I has no optimal strategy. In IV.3, Ex. 2e, a more general model is analyzed, and an ε-optimal strategy of player I is obtained.

b.

α. Given a history y of length n we introduce the positions that can occur at time $n+2$, namely: $x^0(y) = x_n, x^1(y) = x_n + 2, x^{-1}(y) = x_n - 2$.

Let τ be a strategy of player II and $Y(\tau)$ the set of paths having positive probability under τ. For y in $Y(\tau)$, $Q^i(\tau, y)$ is the conditional probability, given τ and y such that $\{x_{n+2} = x^i(y)\}$, $i = -1, 0, 1$. Show the following:

There is no τ such that for all y in $Y(\tau)$, $Q^i(\tau, y) \leq 1/3$.
τ is optimal iff for all y in $Y(\tau)$, $Q^i(\tau, y) \leq v$, i=-1,0,1.

β. Given τ and y of length n, let $\tau(y)$ denote the probability that $t_{n+1} = 1$. Define τ' by $\tau'(\emptyset) = 1/2$ and, for y of length n, by $\tau'(y) = \rho$ if $t_n = 1, \tau'(y) = 1 - \rho$ if $t_n = -1$. Prove that there exists ρ such that the corresponding $\tau' (= \tau'(\rho))$ guarantees $u = (3 - \sqrt{5})/2$ to player II. Deduce that player II has no Markov ε-optimal strategy (cf. Section IV.5, p. 205).

γ. Take now some optimal τ and assume $\tau(y) = \alpha_1 > \rho$ for some $y \in Y(\tau)$. Define $\alpha_2 = 1 - \tau(y, -1)$, where $(y, x, x', \ldots)$ is the path y followed by x then x', and so on. Let $\beta_1 = \alpha_1$, $\beta_2 = (1 - 2v)/(1 - \beta_1)$. Prove that $\alpha_2 \geq \beta_2$ and construct inductively α_n, β_n with $1 \geq \alpha_n \geq \beta_n = (1 - 2v)/(1 - \beta_{n-1})$ and β_n increasing. Deduce a contradiction by going to the limit.

δ. Prove that τ is optimal iff $\tau(\emptyset) \in [1 - \rho, \rho]$ and τ coincides with τ' thereafter. Deduce that $v = u$.

c. Let $w_n(\alpha)$ be the value of the game Γ_n, where, moreover, player II is restricted to using strategies τ satisfying $\tau(\emptyset) = \alpha$. (Put $w_1 \equiv 0$.)

α. Prove that (by a recursive formula):

$$w_n(\alpha) = T w_{n-1}(\alpha) \equiv \min_{0 \leq \beta, \gamma \leq 1} \max \begin{cases} \beta\alpha \\ (1-\beta)\alpha + \gamma(1-\alpha) \\ (1-\alpha)(1-\gamma) \\ \alpha w_{n-1}(\beta) + (1-\alpha) w_{n-1}(\gamma) \end{cases}$$

and that:

$$v_n = \min_{0 \leq \alpha \leq 1} w_n(\alpha) = w_n(1/2).$$

β. Prove that w_n converges uniformly to some continuous function w satisfying $w = Tw$ and that $v = \min_{0 \le \alpha \le 1} w(\alpha)$.

γ. Let $\delta = \max\{\alpha \mid w(\alpha) = v\}$ and let (β, γ) be the corresponding values achieving the minimum in $Tw(\delta)$. Show that (β, γ) belongs to $[1-\delta, \delta]$ and that $v \ge 1-\delta$. Prove then that $v > 1-\delta$ implies $v > u$ and use IV.3, Ex. 2bβ, to get finally $\beta = 1-\gamma = \delta$ and $v = u$. Deduce that τ' is optimal.

d.

α. Assume that σ is optimal and let y_{n-2} be a minimal history such that $P_\sigma(\theta = n \mid y_{n-2}) = a > 0$. Prove then that player I has to choose $x = x_{n-2}$.

β. Show now that if there exists α such that $a(1-\alpha) + (1-a)w(\alpha) < v$, then σ is not optimal. Prove then inductively on n that there exists $L > 0$ and for every n, $\varepsilon_n > 0$ such that for $\varepsilon < \varepsilon_n$:

$$w(\rho + \varepsilon) - w(\rho) \le L\rho^n \varepsilon.$$

Deduce finally the above inequality.

γ. Alternative approach: Let b be the probability, given $y_{n-1} = (y_{n-2}, 1)$, that $\theta = n+1$ and $x = x^1_{n-1}$ and similarly c for $y_{n-1} = (y_{n-2}, -1)$ and $x = x^{-1}_{n-1}$. Prove, by letting player II play some $\tau'(\rho + \varepsilon)$, that b and c are greater than a/ρ and deduce inductively a contradiction.

e. We consider now an extension of Γ where player II is moving on a graph satisfying the following conditions:

- No edge joins a vertex to itself.
- Each vertex is joined to $k+1$ vertices.
- There are no four-sided figures.

α. Define a strategy τ^* of player II as follows: $\tau^*(\emptyset)$ is uniform on the $(k+1)$ adjacent vertices. Given y of length n, τ goes to x_{n-1} with probability $1-kp$ and to each other's vertices with probability p. (Note that condition (c) above implies that the positions after two stages differ if the first move is not the same, unless they are both the initial one.) Show that there exists p such that the corresponding τ^* guarantees $u_k = (k^2 + 2 - k\sqrt{k^2+4})/2$.

Let $\theta < u_k$. We want to construct σ that guarantees θ to player I.

β. Define first inductively a sequence $\{q_n\}$ by:

- $q_0 = 1$, $q_1/(q_0 + (k^2+1)q_1) = \theta$. Then q_n satisfies:
- $(q_0 + \cdots + q_{n-2} + q_n)/(q_0 + (k^2+1)(q_0 + \cdots + q_{n-1} + q_n)) = \theta$.

Let $R = (1 - (k^2+1)\theta)^{-1}$ and prove that:

- $q_n = D[(R + \sqrt{R^2 - 4R})/2]^n + (1-D)[(R - \sqrt{R^2-4R})/2]^n$ with
- $2D = 1 - ((k^2-1)R + 2)/((k^2+1)\sqrt{R^2-4R})$, and that $1 < R < 4$ for θ sufficiently close to u_k.

Show then that there exists a first n, say N, with $q_n \le q_{n-1}$. Define now $q = \sum_{n=0}^N q_n$ and $p_n = q_n/q$.

γ. Define finally σ by:

- Initial procedure: $P_\sigma(\theta = 2, x = 0) = p_0$, and given x_1, $P_\sigma(\theta = 3, x) = p_1$ for all x such that there exists a feasible path $y_3 = (x_1, x_2, x_3)$ with $x_2 \ne 0$ and $x_3 = x$.
- If $x_2 \ne 0$, start the initial procedure at stage 2 from x_2.

- Else let $P_\sigma(\theta = 4, x) = p_2$, for all $(k^2 + 1)$ positions x such that there exists $y_4 = (x_1, 0, x_3, x_4)$ with $x_3 \neq x_1$ and $x_4 = x$ (i.e., a history leading to x without passing by x_1 again.
- If $x_3 \neq x_1$, start the initial procedure at stage 3 from x_3.
- Else let $P_\sigma(\theta = 5, x) = p_3$ for all x such that there exists $y_5 = (x_1, 0, x_1, x_4, x_5)$ with $x_4 \neq 0$, and $x_5 = x$, and so on.

Prove that for all τ: $P_\sigma(\theta < \infty) = 1$ and that σ guarantees θ.

IV.4. SUPERGAMES

We will consider in this section a particular version of the general model where there is only one state. In this case the repeated game is called the **supergame** associated with the one-shot game.

The simplest framework corresponds to standard signaling (all the players are told the previous moves): we obtain a game with **complete information** and **full monitoring**.

IV.4.a. Standard Signaling

We first introduce some notations:

D is the set of **feasible payoffs** (with correlated strategies in Γ_1), i.e., the convex hull of the set of payoffs attainable with pure strategies in the one-shot game. (Recall that the payoffs are uniformly bounded by some constant C.)

The **minmax level** for player i is defined by $v^i = \min_{X^{-i}} \max_{X^i} \gamma_1^i(x^i, x^{-i})$. $x^{-i}(i)$ denotes a point in X^{-i} realizing the above minimum. v with component v^i is the **threat point**.

The set of **feasible and individually rational** (i.r.) payoffs is defined by:

$$E = \{d \in D \mid d^i \geq v^i \ \forall i \in \mathbf{I}\}.$$

We denote by E_∞, E_λ, E_n the set of equilibrium payoffs in Γ_∞, Γ_λ, Γ_n, respectively.

The following basic result, known as the folk theorem, is the starting point of the theory of supergames. It states that the set of equilibrium payoffs in the infinitely repeated game coincides with the set of feasible and i.r. payoffs of the one-shot version.

Theorem IV.4.1. $E_\infty = E$.

Proof. The inclusion $E_\infty \subseteq E$ is easy. First notice that each stage payoff g_n is in D (closed and convex); hence also the average, expectation, and limits of g_n are in D; thus any equilibrium payoff (in fact, any feasible payoff in Γ_∞, Γ_λ, or Γ_n) is in D. To prove that the payoff is necessarily i.r., recall that full monitoring is assumed. Hence, given any history h and the vector of mixed strategies of his opponents σ^{-i}, player i has a reply to the corresponding vector of mixed moves $\sigma^{-i}(h)$ that gives him at that stage a payoff greater than v^i.

The proof that any point in E corresponds to an equilibrium payoff relies on two basic tools: **plan** and **punishment**.

A plan is a play, h, that leads to a specified payoff.

A punishment is a strategy that dictates to play $x^{-i}(i)$ i.i.d. as soon as player i deviates: a **deviation** means that the actual history h' is not an initial part of the play h and, by denoting by n the first stage where this holds, player i is the first (in some order) among the players whose moves at that stage do not coincide with the one defined by h.

It is now clear how to define through a plan and punishments an **I**-tuple of strategies: the players are requested to follow h and to punish the first deviator (if any). It follows that every play leading to an i.r. payoff will correspond to an equilibrium since by the above description any potential deviation of i (leading to a one-shot bounded gain) would induce a future expected stage payoff at most v^i, hence a limiting average payoff less than or equal to v^i.

It remains thus to note that the repetition of the game allows us to convexify the set of feasible payoffs: in fact, given d in D, there exist actions $\{s_t^i\}$, $i = 1, \dots, \mathbf{I}$, $t = 1, \dots, \mathbf{I}+1$ and barycentric coefficients μ_t such that $d = \sum_t \mu_t \gamma_1(s_t)$. Let p_t^n/q^n be rational approximations of μ_t converging, as $n \to \infty$, to μ_t (in the simplex of dimension $\mathbf{I}+1$). The plan is now defined by a sequence of blocks indexed by n. On the nth block (of length q^n) the play consists of p_1^n times s_1, then p_2^n times $s_2, \dots,$ and so on. The payoff associated with h is clearly d. This proves the theorem. ■

Note that one can just as well define the plan by choosing at each stage n, the (first in some order) vector of pure moves that minimizes the distance from the new average payoff $\overline{g}_n$ to d. This yields a Borel map from E to equilibria.

Remark IV.4.1. We prove the above result by using the expected stage payoff. It is worthwhile to notice that it still holds if one considers the payoff on the play, namely, the random variables $\overline{g}_n$, and ask for non-profitable deviation and $\overline{g}_\infty = d$ a.e. (Use II.4, Ex. 4, p. 121.)

We now turn to similar properties for Γ_λ and Γ_n.

Concerning the discounted game, the asymptotic set of equilibria may differ from E (Forges et al., 1986), as shown by the following three-person game where player III is a dummy:

$$\begin{pmatrix} (1,0,0) & (0,1,0) \\ (0,1,0) & (1,0,1) \end{pmatrix}.$$

Since this is basically a zero-sum game between players I and II, the only equilibrium (optimal) strategies are $(1/2, 1/2)$ i.i.d. in Γ_λ as well as in Γ_n; hence the only equilibrium payoff is $(1/2, 1/2, 1/4)$. On the other hand E contains the point $(1/2, 1/2, 1/2)$.

Nevertheless the following generic result holds:

Theorem IV.4.2. *Assume that there exists some d in E with $d^i > v^i$ for all i. Then E_λ converges (in the Hausdorff topology) to E as λ goes to 0.*

Proof. By the hypothesis and the convexity of E, it is enough to prove that any point d in E with $d^i > v^i$ belongs to E_λ for λ small enough. The idea of the proof is then very similar to the previous one.

We first construct a play leading to d. Decompose d according to the extreme points of D (attainable through pure moves) to get $d = \sum_{t=1}^{\mathbf{I}+1} \mu_t d_t$. (Note that an approximation of d for λ small is easy to obtain, as in the previous proof, but we will obtain here an exact representation, for the use of this result; cf. IV.4, Ex. 7, p. 202; cf. also II.3, Ex. 2, p. 111).

Assume $\lambda \le 1/(\mathbf{I}+1)$; then one of the μ_t, say, μ_1, is larger than λ, and we can write $d = \lambda d_1 + (1-\lambda)d(2)$ with $d(2)$ in D, or, more precisely, in $\{d_t\}$. Doing the same decomposition with $d(2)$ we obtain inductively a sequence d^n in $\{d_t\}$ with $d = \sum_{n=1}^{\infty} \lambda(1-\lambda)^{n-1} d^n$. h is then defined at stage n by the moves in S leading to d^n, and $\overline{\gamma}_\lambda(h) = \sum_n \lambda(1-\lambda)^{n-1} d^n = d$.

Moreover, if in the previous construction we use a greedy algorithm choosing at each stage a vector of moves such that $d(n+1)$ is the closest to d, we obtain that the sequence $\{d^n\}_{n \ge m}$ is still a good approximation of d. Formally: $\forall d \in D, \forall \varepsilon > 0, \exists \overline{\lambda}, \forall \lambda \le \overline{\lambda}, \exists h$, such that $\gamma_\lambda(h) = d$ and for any decomposition $h = (h', h'')$ with h' in H, $\|d - \overline{\gamma}_\lambda(h'')\| \le \varepsilon$ (h is ε-**adapted** to d). To complete the proof let $2\varepsilon = \min_i \|d^i - v^i\|$, and let λ be small enough so that the one-shot gain by deviation, at most $2\lambda C$, is less than the loss due to the punishment, at least $(1-\lambda)\varepsilon$. ∎

Remark IV.4.2. One can show that $\overline{\gamma}_\lambda(\Sigma) = D$ as soon as $\lambda \le 1/\mathbf{I}$ (cf. IV.4, Ex. 1, p. 201).

Remark IV.4.3. It is also easy to see that the result holds without restriction for $\mathbf{I} = 2$, or, more generally, if $\exists d \in D$, $d^i > v^i$ for all but one player i (IV.4, Ex. 6, p. 202).

We finally consider the finitely repeated games, where no similar generic result holds, the classical counterexample being the Prisoner's Dilemma described by the following payoff matrix:

$$\begin{pmatrix} (3,3) & (0,4) \\ (0,4) & (1,1) \end{pmatrix}$$

and where $E_n = (\{1, 1\})$ for all n.

In fact we have (recall that v is the threat point):

Proposition IV.4.3. *Assume* $E_1 = \{v\}$; *then* $E_n = \{v\}$ *for all* n.

Proof. Given an equilibrium σ, let m be the smallest integer such that after each history of length m compatible with σ, σ induces the payoff v at each of the remaining stages. By the hypothesis $m \le n-1$. If $m > 0$, consider a history of length $m-1$ compatible with σ and where at stage $(m-1)$, σ does not lead to v. Clearly one of the players then has a profitable deviation at that stage and cannot be punished later. ∎

A sufficient condition for convergence to E is given by the following:

Theorem IV.4.4. *(Benoît and Krishna, 1987) Assume that for all i there exists $e(i)$ in E_1 with $e^i(i) > v^i$. Then E_n converges in the Hausdorff topology to E_n as n goes to infinity.*

Proof. The idea is to avoid backward-induction effects by ending the play by a phase of rewarding or punishment consisting of a fixed number of stages: the influence on the total payoff will be negligible as n goes to infinity.

Given a play h this phase will be a sequence of R cycles of mixed moves leading to the payoffs $(e(1), \ldots, e(\mathbf{I}))$ if the previous history follows h and a sequence of i.i.d. punishments $x^{-i}(i)$ in the case of a previous deviation of i.

Now given d in E, let $\delta = \min_i(e^i(i) - v^i)$ and $\varepsilon \leq \delta/2$. Choose an ε-rational approximation d in E as in the proof of the folk theorem, corresponding to a history h' of length N. Let $R > 2C/\delta$; then for $n \geq 2C(R\mathbf{I} + N)/\varepsilon$, the strategies defined by a play h consisting of a cycle of histories h' (until stage $n - R\mathbf{I}$) followed by the last phase defined above clearly induce an equilibrium with a payoff within 2ε of d. In fact, any deviation where some h' is played will be observed, hence punished. On the other hand, if h is followed during the first phase the second one consists of a sequence of one-shot equilibria where no deviation is profitable. ∎

Remark IV.4.4. It is clear that a sufficient condition for the previous result to hold is $\forall i, \exists n_i, \exists e(i) \in E_{n_i}$ with $e^i(i) > v^i$.

More precise results can be obtained for $\mathbf{I} = 2$ (cf. Benoît and Krishna, 1987). For related results with subgame perfect equilibria, cf. IV.4, Ex. 3–IV.4, Ex. 8.

IV.4.b. Partial Monitoring

Most of the results of this section are due to Lehrer (1990, 1991, 1992a, 1992b).

IV.4.b.1. Notations and Definitions

Coming back to the general model we assume still here that there is only one state but after each stage n each player i is told $Q^i(s_n)$, where Q^i is a mapping from S to A^i. Note that equivalently $Q^i(s^i, \cdot)$ can be viewed as a partition of S^{-i}, $Q^i(s^i, s^{-i})$ being the partition element containing s^{-i}.

Let us first provide a general characterization of uniform equilibria in supergames:

Proposition IV.4.5. *d is a uniform equilibrium payoff iff there exists a sequence ε_m decreasing to 0, N_m, and σ_m, such that σ_m is an ε_m equilibrium in Γ_{N_m} leading to a payoff within ε_m of d.*

Proof. The condition is obviously necessary.

For the sufficiency define superblocks M_m as a sequence of l_m blocks of size N_m and let σ be: play σ_m on M_m (i.e., starting with an empty history after each cycle of N_m moves). Choose l_m such that $2CN_{m+1}/(\ell_m \times N_m) \leq \varepsilon_m$. It follows easily that if $n \in M_{m+1}$, σ is a $2(\sum_{k\leq m} \varepsilon_k \ell_k N_k / \sum_{k\leq m} \ell_k N_k)$ equilibrium in Γ_n, hence the result.

For correlated equilibria define the auxiliary space as $\Omega = \prod_m (\Omega_m)^{l_m}$ with the product probability induced by the correlation device on each factor. Due to the independence it is easily verified that announcing the signals at the beginning of the game or at the beginning of each block gives the same result. ■

Remark IV.4.5. The same requirement in a general repeated game would lead to E_0 (cf. VII).

We first consider the two-person case and assume **a non-trivial signaling structure**; hence for each player $i = \text{I}, \text{II}$ and $j \neq i$ there exists s^i in S^i and s^j, t^j in S^j satisfying:

$$Q^i(s^i, s^j) \neq Q^i(s^i, t^j) \tag{$\star$}$$

so that the players can communicate through their moves (the other case is much simpler to analyze (cf. IV.4, Ex. 9, p. 203)).

Since in general the signals are not common knowledge, equilibrium strategies σ, given an atom of the σ-algebra of common knowledge events (finest σ-algebra containing all $\mathscr{H}^i$) having positive probability under σ, do not induce an equilibrium, but rather a correlated equilibrium. In fact, those are much easier to deal with.

Definition IV.4.6. We define two relations between moves by:

$$s^i \sim t^i \iff Q^j(s^i, s^j) = Q^j(t^i, s^j) \text{ for all } s^j \text{ in } S^j$$

(this means that after one stage, player j has no possibility to distinguish whether i was playing s^i or t^i) and:

$$s^i \succ t^i \iff [(s^i \sim t^i) \text{ and } (Q^i(t^i, s^j) \neq Q^i(t^i, t^j) \text{ implies } Q^i(s^i, s^j) \neq Q^i(s^i, t^j) \text{ for all } s^j, t^j \text{ in } S^j)]$$

(player i is always getting more information on j's move by playing s^i rather than t^i).

Then we have:

Lemma IV.4.6. *Given a pure strategy σ^i, at each history h player i can use any action t^i rather than $\sigma^i(h) = s^i$ with $t^i \succ s^i$, while still inducing the same probability distribution on $\mathscr{H}^j$.*

Proof. By playing t^i the signal to player j will be the same. Now for the next stage since the partition on player j's moves is finer with t^i than with s^i, player

i can deduce what would have been his signal if he had played s^i and plays accordingly in the future. ∎

Let $\Delta(S)$ be the set of probabilities on S (correlated moves) and extend the payoff to $\Delta(S)$ by integration. The sets of equilibrium payoffs will be characterized through the following sets:

$$\mathbf{A}^i = \{P \in \Delta(S) \mid t^i \succ s^i \Longrightarrow \sum_{s^j} P(s^i, s^j) G^i(s^i, s^j) \geq \sum_{s^j} P(s^i, s^j) G^i(t^i, s^j)\},$$

$$\mathbf{B}^i = \mathbf{A}^i \cap X = \{x \in X \mid t^i \succ s^i \Longrightarrow x^i(s^i) G^i(s^i, x^j) \geq x^i(s^i) G^i(t^i, x^j)\}.$$

Remark IV.4.7. Let $\mathbf{A}^i = \mathrm{Co}(\mathbf{B}^i)$ be the convex hull $\mathbf{B}^i$. In fact $\mathbf{A}^i$ is convex and contains $\mathbf{B}^i$. Now given P in A^i, for any s^i with $\rho(s^i) = \sum_{s^j} P(s^i, s^j) > 0$, $(s^i, y^j) \in \mathbf{B}^i$ with $y^j(s^j) = P(s^i, s^j)/\rho(s^i)$.

Remark IV.4.8. Note that like in the folk theorem these sets are defined through the one-shot game only.

Remark IV.4.9. It turns out that the sets of equilibrium payoffs for our rather strong definition in Section IV.1.d, p. 176, exist: E_∞ for equilibria and C_∞, D_∞ for correlated and communication equilibria. (For liminf payoffs, cf. IV.4, Ex. 8, p. 202.)

IV.4.b.2. Correlated and Communication Equilibria

Let us characterize correlated and communication equilibrium payoffs. We write *IR* for the set of individually rational payoffs; it will obviously contain any equilibrium payoff.

Theorem IV.4.7. $D_\infty = C_\infty = G(\bigcap_i \mathbf{A}^i) \cap IR$.

Proof. We first prove inclusion of D_∞ in the right-hand set. Assume that $d = (d^{\mathrm{I}}, d^{\mathrm{II}})$ is an $\mathscr{L}$-equilibrium payoff not in $G(\bigcap_i \mathbf{A}^i)$ (the inclusion in *IR* is standard; cf. Theorem IV.4.1, p. 190, above).

Denoting by P_n the correlated distribution on S induced by the equilibrium strategies at stage n and $\overline{P}_n = (1/n)\sum_1^n P_m$, one has $d = G(\widetilde{P})$, with $\widetilde{P} = \mathscr{L}(\overline{P}_n)$.

Given any P in $\Delta(S)$ let us define P^i in $\mathbf{A}^i$ as follows. First introduce a map ϕ^i from S^i to S^i such that $\sum_{s^j} P(s^i, s^j) G^i(\phi(s^i), s^j)$ maximizes $\sum_{s^j} P(s^i, s^j) G^i(t^i, s^j)$ on the set $\{t^i \succ s^i\}$ and then let $P^i(t^i, s^j) = \sum_{s^i, \phi(s^i) = t^i} P(s^i, s^j)$.

In words, we replace any action s^i of i in the support of P by a best reply t^i of i against P, from among the moves that are more informative than s^i.

Assuming $\widetilde{P} \notin \mathbf{A}^{\mathrm{I}}$, define an alternative strategy of player I as follows. At each stage use $\phi^{\mathrm{I}}(s^{\mathrm{I}})$ (computed for $\widetilde{P}$) rather than s^{I} and keep for the following stages the signal that would have been obtained by using s^{I}.

We obtain thus (using Lemma IV.4.6, p. 194):

$$\mathscr{L}\left(\overline{\gamma}_n^{\mathrm{I}}(\tau^{\mathrm{I}}, \sigma^{\mathrm{II}})\right) = G^{\mathrm{I}}(\widetilde{P}^{\mathrm{I}}) > G^{\mathrm{I}}(\widetilde{P}),$$

hence the contradiction and the required inclusion.

(Note that the same inclusion holds for more than two players with the appropriate extension of $\succ$.)

Consider now P in $\bigcap_i \mathbf{A}^i$ with $G(P)$ in IR. By the previous Proposition IV.4.5, p. 193, it is enough to construct, for any $\varepsilon_0 > 0$, an ε_0-equilibrium in a finite game with a payoff within ε_0 of $G(P)$. Let $\varepsilon_0 = 8\varepsilon$.

Using the hypothesis of non-trivial signaling structure we can define an injective mapping from A^i to finite sequences of signals for j (for example, a finite sequence of elements in $\{Q^j(s^i, t^j), Q^j(t^i, t^j)\}$ satisfying ($\star$)), so that both players have a code to report their signal at some stage in a bounded (say, by B) number of stages.

The strategies will be defined on blocks of stages as follows. Let $\eta < \varepsilon/4C, n$ such that $(2n + 2B)/2^n \leq \eta$ and define $N_1 = 2^n + 2n + 2B$. We now describe the behavior on a block of size N_1.

During the first 2^n stages the players are requested to play according to some correlation device $\overline{R}$. Define first a probability R on $\Omega^{\mathrm{I}} \times \Omega^{\mathrm{II}} = S^{\mathrm{I}} \cup (S^{\mathrm{I}} \times S^{\mathrm{II}})) \times (S^{\mathrm{II}} \cup (S^{\mathrm{II}} \times S^{\mathrm{I}}))$ by the following procedure: take the convex combination of the uniform distribution on S (with coefficient η) and P (coefficient $(1 - \eta)$) and independently announce with probability η to one of the players the move of his opponent, namely:

$$R(s) = (\eta/\#S + (1 - \eta)P(s))/(1 + 2\eta),$$
$$R(s^i, \{s^i, s^j\}) = \eta R(s).$$

Then $\overline{R}$ is the product of 2^n independent copies of R, a signal is selected in $(\Omega^{\mathrm{I}} \times \Omega^{\mathrm{II}})^{2^n}$ according to it, and its component on $(\Omega^i)^{2^n}$ is transmitted to i who is supposed to follow the projection on $(S^i)^{2^n}$. Note that with positive probability at each stage every move is played, and every move that player i has to play is announced with positive probability to player j.

During the next n stages player I plays an i.i.d. mixture $(1/2, 1/2)$ on the moves $(s^{\mathrm{I}}, t^{\mathrm{I}})$, and player II uses s^{II} with $Q^{\mathrm{II}}(s^{\mathrm{I}}, s^{\mathrm{II}}) \neq Q^{\mathrm{II}}(t^{\mathrm{I}}, s^{\mathrm{II}})$, and symmetrically for the next n stages. These random moves are used to generate random times, say, θ^{II} and θ^{I}, that are independent and uniformly distributed on the previous 2^n stages and public knowledge.

Finally during the last B stages the previously defined code is alternatively used by each player i to report the signal he got at stage θ^i.

This ends the description of the strategies "on the equilibrium path" on these N^1 stages, and note that the corresponding payoff is within $4\eta C$ (hence less than ε) of $G(P)$.

Consider now a collection of M blocks of size N_1, call it a superblock N_2, and finally define N as a family of M' superblocks N_2.

Define strategies in Γ_N as independent sequences of strategies as above on each block of size N_1. Namely, the signals are chosen according to the product of independent probabilities and announced at the beginning of the game. On each block of size N_1 the players play according to the corresponding component of their sequence of signals during the first 2^n stages, and then as described above. We say that a deviation τ^i for player i is ε-profitable in Γ_N if $\gamma_N^i(\tau^i, \sigma^j) > G^i(P) + \varepsilon$ and prove, by specifying the strategies "in case of detected deviation," that for N large enough there are no 6ε-profitable strategies, and hence σ is an ε_0-equilibrium.

We first show that on blocks of size N_1 any 3ε-profitable deviation has a strictly positive probability π of being detected. Note, in fact, that on each such block, a deviation near the end (i.e., during the last $2n + 2B$ stages) modifies the payoff on this block by less than $\varepsilon/2$. Hence we only consider deviation at other stages. Note that on these stages the move of each player is independent of the past; hence it is sufficient to consider history-independent deviation. Now by the choice of R if τ^i gives 2ε more than σ^i against R, the gain is at least ε against P. Recall that by playing t^i rather than s^i and $t^i \succ s^i$, the payoff is not increased since P belongs to A^i. On the other hand, if $t^i \not\succ s^i$, there is a positive probability that player j is told i's recommendation, i.e., s^i, and is using at this stage a revealing move, namely, t^j with either (a) $Q^j(s^i, t^j) \neq Q^j(t^i, t^j)$, or (b) $Q^i(s^i, t^j) \neq Q^i(t^i, t^j)$. In case (a) j observes i's deviation at that stage; in case (b), there is a positive (and independent) probability that player i will be asked to report his signal at that stage and will give a wrong answer observable by j.

Obviously the strategy of each player in case of a wrong signal is to punish forever, hence to reduce the payoff to at most $\gamma^i(P)$ (recall that $\gamma(P)$ is *IR*).

Define now M (the number of blocks N_1 in N_2) such that $(1 - \pi)^{\varepsilon M/C} \leq \varepsilon/2C$. It follows then from the above computations that if τ^i is 4ε-profitable on a superblock N_2, a deviation will be detected with probability at least $1 - \varepsilon/2C$.

Define finally M' so that the relative size of a superblock N_2 in games of length $N = M'N_2$ is at most $\varepsilon/2C$. We obtain:

$$\gamma_N^i(\tau^i, \sigma^j) \leq \varepsilon + (1 - \varepsilon/2C)(\gamma^i(P) + 4\varepsilon + 2C/M') \leq \gamma^i(P) + 6\varepsilon,$$

hence the result. ∎

The main difficulties in trying to extend the previous result to equilibria are:

- The lack of common knowledge events on which to condition the analysis, while remaining in an equilibrium framework, i.e., without being led to correlated equilibria.
- The fact that one cannot restrict the players to using pure actions and the right equivalence classes of mixed moves are hard to define.

A simple and useful result uses the following set:

$$\mathbf{C}^i = \{x \in X \mid y^i \in X^i \; Q^j(y^i, \cdot) = Q^j(x^i, \cdot) \Longrightarrow G^i(y^i, x^{-i}) \leq G^i(x^i, x^{-i})\}.$$

($Q^j(x^i, \cdot)$ is a mapping from S^j to probabilities on j's signals.)

Note that $\mathbf{C}^i \subseteq \mathbf{B}^i$.

Proposition IV.4.8. *All points of* $\operatorname{Co} G(\bigcap_i \mathbf{C}^i) \cap IR$ *are uniform equilibrium payoffs.*

Proof. We first prove that d in $G(\bigcap_i \mathbf{C}^i) \cap IR$ is a uniform equilibrium payoff. So fix x in $\bigcap_i \mathbf{C}^i$ with $G(x) = d$. Each player is required to play x^i_ε i.i.d. where x^i_ε is $(1-\varepsilon)x^i + \varepsilon\overline{y}^i$ ($\overline{y}^i$ uniform on S^i). The checking is done at the end of blocks of increasing sizes, say, $N_\ell = 2^\ell$. Player i is punished for $N_\ell C/\varepsilon$ stages if the empirical distribution of player j's signals on block ℓ differs by more than ε from what it should be according to $Q^j(x^i_\varepsilon, \cdot)$, namely, if $\max_{t^j} \max_{a^j} \mid Q^j(x^i_\varepsilon, t^j)(a^j) - |\{1 \le m \le 2^\ell; a^j_m = a^j; t^j_m = t^j\}|/|\{1 \le m \le 2^\ell; t^j_m = t^j\}| \mid \ge \varepsilon$. After the punishment phase one plays on block $\ell + 1$.

Let $\varepsilon_0 = 6C\varepsilon$. It is easy to check that the strategies described above induce an ε_0-equilibrium with payoff within ε_0 of d in a sufficiently long game, hence the result by Proposition IV.4.5, p. 193. (See Section V.3.c, p. 230, for similar computations made in more detail.)

If $d \in \operatorname{Co} G(\bigcap_i \mathbf{C}_i) \cap IR$, just alternate between plays defined as above, corresponding to different points in $G(\bigcap_i \mathbf{C}_i)$. ■

We will now study specific cases.

IV.4.b.3. Observable Payoffs

We still consider two players, but we assume here that the signal reveals the payoff, namely:

$$G^i(s^i, s^j) \neq G^i(s^i, t^j) \implies Q^i(s^i, s^j) \neq Q^i(s^i, t^j) \text{ for all } i, s^i, s^j, t^j.$$

This signaling structure implies specific properties on the payoffs like the following:

Lemma IV.4.9. $\forall x \in X$, *(resp.* $\mathbf{C}^i, \mathbf{B}^i$*),* $\exists y^j$ *such that* $(x^i, y^j) \in X \cap \mathbf{C}^j$*, (resp.* $\mathbf{C}^i \cap \mathbf{C}^j$, $\mathbf{B}^i \cap \mathbf{C}^j$*) and* $G^i(\cdot, x^j) = G^i(\cdot, y^j)$.

Proof. Given x^j, let y^j satisfying $Q^i(x^j, \cdot) = Q^i(y^j, \cdot)$ and $(x^i, y^j) \in \mathbf{C}^j$. The previous equality implies that i's payoff against x^j or y^j is the same whatever his strategy is. Hence if $(x^i, x^j) \in \mathbf{C}^i$ (resp. $\mathbf{B}^i$) we still have $(x^i, y^j) \in \mathbf{C}^i$ (resp. $\mathbf{B}^i$). ■

Recall that v^i is the minmax for i and that $x^{-i}(i)$ realizes it.

Lemma IV.4.10. *There exists a point* d_0 *in* $G(\bigcap_i \mathbf{C}^i)$ *with* $d^i_0 \le v^i, i = \mathrm{I}, \mathrm{II}$.

Proof. Start with x defined by the punishing strategy $x^i(j), i = \mathrm{I}, \mathrm{II}$ and use Lemma IV.4.9 for both. ■

Lemma IV.4.11. $\operatorname{Co} G(\bigcap_i \mathbf{B}^i) \cap IR = \bigcap_i \operatorname{Co} G(\mathbf{B}^i) \cap IR$.

Proof. Consider d in $\bigcap_i \operatorname{Co} G(\mathbf{B}^i)$ with d^j maximal among the points in this set with the same d^i. Present then d as a barycenter of payoffs from points in $\mathbf{B}^i$, say, $d = \sum_k \lambda_k G(x_k)$. We now prove that x_k is in $\mathbf{B}^j$ for all k. In fact, as in Lemma IV.4.9 above, one could otherwise define y_k in $\mathbf{B}^i$, which induces the same payoff to i and a strictly better one to j. Averaging over the λ's would give a point in $\operatorname{Co} G(\bigcap_i \mathbf{B}^i)$ with a higher d^j.

Now any point d in $\bigcap_i \operatorname{Co} G(\mathbf{B}^i) \cap IR$ is in the convex hull of $\overline{d}$ (the same d^i and d^j maximal on $\bigcap_i \operatorname{Co} G(\mathbf{B}^i)$), $\underline{d}$ (defined dually), and d_0 (introduced in Lemma IV.4.10). Since these three points are in $G(\bigcap_i \mathbf{B}^i)$, the result follows. ■

Given a set $D \subseteq \mathbb{R}^n$, its admissible points are those $x \in D$, such that $y \geq x$, $y \in D$ implies $y = x$.

Lemma IV.4.12. *The set Ad of admissible points of* $G(\bigcap_i \mathbf{B}^i)$ *is included in* $G(\bigcap_i \mathbf{C}^i)$.

Proof. Use again, as in Lemma IV.4.9, the fact that if x is not in $\mathbf{C}^i$ one can modify x^i to y^i such that $(y^i, x^j) \in \mathbf{C}^i \cap \mathbf{B}^j$, player i's payoff is increased, and player j's payoff is the same. ■

Theorem IV.4.13.

$$E_\infty = C_\infty = D_\infty = \operatorname{Co} G\Big(\bigcap_i \mathbf{B}^i\Big) \cap IR$$
$$= \bigcap_i \operatorname{Co} G(\mathbf{B}^i) \cap IR.$$

Proof. The inclusion is clear from Theorem IV.4.7 since $\operatorname{Co} G(\mathbf{B}^i)$ equals $G(\mathbf{A}^i)$.

We represent all points in $\operatorname{Co} G(\bigcap_i \mathbf{B}^i) \cap IR$ as barycenters of points where "simple" strategies are used. We already have two components: d_0 (Lemma IV.4.10) and the admissible part Ad (Lemma IV.4.12).

Consider now payoffs on the other part of the boundary:

Lemma IV.4.14. *Let d be an extreme point of* $\operatorname{Co} G(\bigcap_i \mathbf{B}_i) \setminus Ad$ *such that d^i is maximal among the points having in this set the same d^j. Then $d = G(x)$ for some x with:*

(1) *$x^j = s^j$ is a pure move.*
(2) *x^i is a best reply to s^j among the set of y^i satisfying:*

$$Q^j(y^i, s^j) = Q^j(x^i, s^j).$$

(3) *$t^j \succ s^j$ implies that t^j is a duplicate of s^j (i.e., same signals and payoffs to both players).*

Proof. Let $d = G(y)$ with $y \in \bigcap_i \mathbf{B}^i$. Note first that $y \in \mathbf{C}^i$ (otherwise, as in Lemma IV.4.9, p. 198, one could find y' in $\mathbf{C}^i \cap \mathbf{B}^j$ with the same payoff for j and a higher payoff for i. Let us now prove that one can take y^j pure. Otherwise, for each t^j in the support of y^j, $(y^i, t^j) \in \mathbf{B}^j$. By Lemma IV.4.9

there again exists $x^i(t^j)$ such that $(x^i(t^j), t^j) \in \mathbf{C}^i \cap \mathbf{B}^j$, keeping the same payoff for j and increasing i's payoff. Hence, if $y^j = \sum \alpha(t^j)t^j$, one obtains $d^j = \sum \alpha(t^j)G^j(x^i(t^j), t^j)$ and $d^i \leq \sum \alpha(t^j)G^i(x^i(t^j), t^j)$. and since d is a point of $\mathrm{Co}\, G(\bigcap_i \mathbf{B}^i)$ with maximal d^i on the d^j line, this implies that the second relation is an equality, hence $(y^i, t^j) \in \mathbf{B}^i \cap \mathbf{B}^j$ for all t^j; finally, since d is an extreme point, this finally implies $d = G(y^i, t^j)$.

We can moreover assume that no s^j satisfies $s^j \succ t^j$ and $t^j \not\succ s^j$. Otherwise denote again here by s^j a maximal point of this preorder, among the maximizers of $G^j(y^i, \cdot)$. If $G^j(y^i, s^j) = G^j(y^i, t^j)$, take (y^i, s^j) as a new initial point (obviously in $\mathbf{C}^i \cap \mathbf{B}^j$). If not, then $G^j(y^i, s^j) < G^j(y^i, t^j)$ (recall that (y^i, t^j) belongs to $\mathbf{B}^j$), and (y^i, s^j) in $\mathbf{C}^i \cap \mathbf{B}^j$ induces a payoff d' with $d_i = d_i'$ and $d_j > d_j'$ contradicting the choice of d ($d \notin Ad$ and is extreme).

Coming back to our pair (y^i, t^j), assume that there exists x^i with $Q^j(x^i, t^j) = Q^j(y^i, t^j)$ and $G^i(x^i, t^j) > G^i(y^i, t^j)$. One can then even assume $(x^i, t^j) \in \mathbf{C}^i$ (as in Lemma IV.4.9). The choice of d implies then $(x^i, t^j) \notin \mathbf{B}^j$.

By the above remark on t^j letting $(x^i, s^j) \in \mathbf{B}^j$ with $s^j \succ t^j$, one has also $t^j \succ s^j$, so that: $Q^j(x^i, t^j) = Q^j(y^i, t^j)$ implies $Q^j(x^i, s^j) = Q^j(y^i, s^j)$. Now $Q^j(x^i, u^j) = Q^j(y^i, u^j)$ implies $G^j(x^i, u^j) = G^j(y^i, u^j)$ for all u^j, hence $G^j(x^i, t^j) < G^j(x^i, s^j)$ implies $G^j(y^i, t^j) < G^j(y^i, s^j)$, and this again contradicts the fact that (y^i, t^j) is in $\mathbf{B}^j$. ∎

We can now describe the equilibrium strategies: decompose an *IR* payoff d as a (finite) convex combination of payoffs induced by elements in $\mathbf{C}^i \cap \mathbf{C}^j$ or extreme points of $\mathrm{Co}\, G(\bigcap_i \mathbf{B}^i) \setminus Ad$, say, $d = \sum_k \alpha(k)d(k)$. A play corresponding to the payoff $d(k)$ will be used on a fraction $\alpha(k)$ of the stages (using as usual rational approximation). It is thus sufficient to describe these plays: for points in $G(\bigcap_i \mathbf{C}^i)$ use Proposition IV.4.8, p. 198; for the other points we use the previous Lemma IV.4.14: let $d = G(x^i, s^j)$ satisfy the corresponding properties. Player j will be asked to play always s^j and player I to play i.i.d. some perturbation x_ε^i of x^i with strictly positive probability on each move.

It follows then easily from the properties of (x^i, s^j) that player i has no profitable non-detectable deviations (as in the previous theorem, j uses $x^j(i)$ for finitely many stages if the empirical distribution of signals differs too much from $Q^j(x^i, s^j)$).

On the other hand, to check that j does not deviate, since i is playing completely mixed, the arguments in the proof of the previous Theorem IV.4.7, p. 195, still apply: player j will be repeatedly asked to report his signal at some random move, and in the case of profitable deviation with positive probability his answer will be wrong. ∎

IV.4.b.4. "Semi-Standard" Information

We end now this section by presenting a result concerning the case with **I** players where the signal received by each player is public and independent of his own move.

The action sets S^i are equipped with a partition $\tilde{S}^i$, and after each stage every player is only informed of the element of the product partition that contains the vector of moves. Denote by $\tilde{x}^i$ the probability induced by x^i on $\tilde{S}^i$; then the previous sets $\mathbf{B}^i$ are:

$$\mathbf{D}^i = \{x \in X \mid G^i(x) \geq G^i(y^i, x^{-i}) \text{ for all } y^i \text{ with } \tilde{y}^i = \tilde{x}^i\},$$

and they coincide with the previous $\mathbf{C}^i$.

Proposition IV.4.15. $E_\infty = \operatorname{Co} G(\bigcap_i \mathbf{D}^i) \cap IR$.

Proof. The proof that any payoff in the right-hand side set can be achieved as an equilibrium payoff is obtained as in Proposition IV.4.8, p. 198, above, but with a simpler proof. (Note that the statistics on the signals sent by i are common knowledge, and there is no need for x_ε.)

To get the other inclusion we explicitly use the fact that there exists a "common knowledge" σ-algebra, conditional on which moves of the players are still independent. Indeed, the initial strategy σ can be replaced by $\tilde{\sigma}$ where at each stage n and for each player i, $\sigma^i_n(h_n)$ is modified to $\tilde{\sigma}^i_n(h_n) = \mathsf{E}(s^i_n \mid \tilde{h}_n)$ with h_n in $\tilde{h}_n$, without changing the payoff or the equilibrium condition.

On the corresponding events $\tilde{h}_n$, if $\tilde{\sigma}$ is not in $\mathbf{D}^i$, player i can profitably deviate, without being detected (as in Lemma IV.4.6, p. 194). Denoting by $\mathbf{D}^i_\varepsilon$ an ε-neighborhood of $\mathbf{D}^i$ the equilibrium condition leads to $\mathscr{L}(\Pr(\widetilde{\sigma}_n \notin \mathbf{D}^i_\varepsilon)) = 0$, for all i and all positive ε, so that $\mathscr{L}(\Pr(\widetilde{\sigma}_n \notin \bigcap_i \mathbf{D}^i_\varepsilon)) = 0$, hence also $\mathscr{L}(\Pr(\widetilde{\sigma}_n \notin (\bigcap_i \mathbf{D}^i)_\varepsilon)) = 0$, for all positive ε.

Letting σ^* be such that: $\sigma^*(h)$ is in $\mathbf{D}^i$ and is a closest point to $\widetilde{\sigma}(h)$, for all h, one obtains: $\mathscr{L}(\gamma_n(\sigma^*)) = \mathscr{L}(\gamma_n(\widetilde{\sigma}))$, hence the result since the first term is in $\operatorname{Co} G(\bigcap_i \mathbf{D}^i)$ (by I.2, Ex. 13, p. 28, and I.3, Ex. 10d, p. 40). ■

Remark IV.4.10. As the partitions become finer the equilibrium set increases (basically the set of non-detectable deviations is smaller): one goes from the convex hull of E_1 (equilibrium payoff set of Γ_1) to the set of feasible i.r. payoffs (Theorem IV.4.1, p. 190).

Remark IV.4.11. Note that E_∞ may differ from C_∞ (take a game where $\operatorname{Co} E_1 \neq C_1$ and let $\widetilde{S}^i = \{S^i\}$).

EXERCISES

Full monitoring is assumed in IV.4, Ex. 1–IV.4, Ex. 7.

1. Use the fact that $\gamma_1(X)$ is connected and I.3, Ex. 10, p. 40, to prove that $D_\lambda = D$ for $\lambda \leq 1/\#\mathbf{I}$. Show that it is the best bound.

2. Prove Theorem IV.4.2, p. 191, in the general case for $\#\mathbf{I} = 2$.

In the following exercises on subgame perfect equilibria we will denote by E'_∞, E'_n, E'_λ the set of subgame perfect equilibrium payoffs in Γ_∞, Γ_n, Γ_λ, respectively.

3. Perfect folk theorem. (Aumann and Shapley, 1994), (Rubinstein, 1994).
Prove that $E'_\infty = E_\infty = E$.

HINT. In the proof of Theorem IV.4.1, p. 190, it suffices to punish the last deviator (say, at stage n) during n stages, then revert to the original plan (ignoring deviations during punishment phases).

4. A property of subgame perfect equilibria in discounted multi-move games
Say that τ^i is a **one-stage deviation** from σ^i if τ^i coincides with σ^i except at some history h_n.

Prove that an n-tuple σ is a subgame perfect equilibrium in Γ_λ iff there is no profitable one-stage deviation in the subgame starting at that stage.

HINT. No stationary structure is required: we only need the total payoff to be the discounted sum of the uniformly bounded stage payoff, in fact, simply continuous.

Use the continuity to reduce to the case where σ is always played from some stage on and look at the last stage where a deviation is still profitable.

5. A recursive formula for subgame perfect equilibria in discounted games.
Given a bounded set F of $\mathbb{R}^{\mathbf{I}}$, let $\phi_\lambda(F)$ be the set of equilibrium payoffs of the one-shot games with payoff $\lambda\gamma_1 + (1-\lambda)f$, where f is a mapping from S (histories at stage 2) to F. Prove that E'_λ is the largest (for inclusion) bounded fixed point of ϕ_λ.

HINT. Assume $F \subseteq \phi_\lambda(F)$ and construct inductively a sequence of future expected payoffs and adapted equilibria. Prove that the strategies defined by this sequence induce the same future expected payoff so that $F \subseteq E'_\lambda$ by using the previous exercise.

6. Prove Theorem IV.4.2, p. 191, under the assumption: $\exists d \in D, d^i > v^i$, for all $i \neq 1$.

HINT. Show that either the condition of Theorem IV.4.2 holds or there exists no feasible payoff with $d^1 > v^1$.

7. (Fudenberg and Maskin, 1986)
Consider the following three person game (player I chooses the row, player II the column, player III the matrix):

$$\begin{pmatrix}(1,1,1) & (0,0,0)\\(0,0,0) & (0,0,0)\end{pmatrix} \quad \begin{pmatrix}(0,0,0) & (0,0,0)\\(0,0,0) & (1,1,1)\end{pmatrix}.$$

Prove that any point (z,z,z) in E'_λ (or in E'_n) satisfies $z \geq 1/4$, for all $\lambda \in (0,1)$ (and all $n \geq 1$). Compute E and compare with Theorem IV.4.2, p. 191.

8. Perfect equilibria in discounted games (Fudenberg and Maskin, 1986)
Assume E with non-empty interior. Prove that E'_λ converges to E.

HINT. Consider d in D such that the ball centered at d with radius 3ε is included in E, and, let $h(\varepsilon,\lambda)$ be ε-adapted to d (i.e., such that $\gamma_\lambda(h) = d$ and $\left|\gamma_\lambda(h'') - d\right| \leq \varepsilon$ for any decomposition $h = (h', h'')$). Define R such that $2C < R\varepsilon$, and, for each i and every history ℓ of length R, let $d(\ell, i)$ be defined by $d^j = \sum_{n=1}^{R} \lambda(1-\lambda)^{n-1}\gamma_n^j(\ell_n) + (1-(1-\lambda)^R)d^j(\ell, i)$ for $j \neq i$, and $d^i(\ell, i) = d^i - 2\varepsilon$. Observe that for λ small enough one has $d(\ell, i) \in E$ and $\left|d^j(\ell, i) - d^j\right| \leq \varepsilon$, and prove that for λ small enough, there exists $\tilde{h}(\ell, i) (= \tilde{h})$ ε-adapted to $d(\ell, i)$ with moreover $\overline{\gamma}^i_\lambda(\tilde{h}'') \geq d^i(\ell, i)$ for all decompositions $\tilde{h} = (\tilde{h}', \tilde{h}'')$.

Consider now the following strategies σ: play h, and if i deviates, use R times $x^{-i}(i)$, then if ℓ have been achieved, follow $\tilde{h}(\ell, i)$. Inductively, if $\tilde{h}(\ell', j)$ is played and player k deviates, use

R times $x^{-k}(k)$, then if ℓ'' results, follow $\tilde{h}(\ell'', k)$. Deviations during the R stages where some punishment strategy is used are ignored.

9. Lower equilibrium payoffs (Nontrivial signaling) (Lehrer, 1989)

Say that σ is a lower equilibrium if: $\overline{\gamma}_n(\sigma)$ converges to some $\gamma(\sigma)$ and for all i and all τ^i, $\liminf \overline{\gamma}^i_n(\tau^i, \sigma^{-i}) \geq \gamma^i(\sigma)$. Denote by lE_∞ and lC_∞ the corresponding sets of equilibrium and correlated equilibrium payoffs.

a. Prove that $lC_\infty \subseteq G(\mathbf{A}^i)$.

HINT. Prove as in Theorem IV.4.7 that otherwise player i has profitable deviations on a set of stages with positive lower density.

b. Prove that $\bigcap_i \operatorname{Co} G(\mathbf{B}^i) \cap IR \subseteq lE_\infty$.

HINT. Define a sequence of blocks of length ℓ_n with $\ell_n / \sum_{k \leq n} \ell_k \to \infty$. On odd blocks approximate d in $\bigcap_i \operatorname{Co} G(\mathbf{B}^i)$ by a rational combination of points in $g(\mathbf{B}^i)$, where moreover player I uses a pure move. Let then player II use an i.i.d. sequence of perturbations with full support of his previous mixed move. Player I is thus checked on odd blocks (deviations where $t^i \not\sim s^i$ will be detected with high probability and punished during a large finite number of stages). For the other deviations he is asked to report, using the usual code, at stage n^2 the signal he got at stage n. A similar construction holds for II on even blocks, and punishments are forever.

c. Deduce that $lE_\infty = lC_\infty = \bigcap_i G(\mathbf{A}^i) \cap IR$

d. Show that $\bigcap_i G(\mathbf{A}^i) \cap IR \neq G(\bigcap_i \mathbf{A}^i) \cap IR$ and similarly for $\mathbf{B}^i$.

HINT. Take $\begin{pmatrix} (2,2) & (1,1) \\ (1,1) & (0,0) \end{pmatrix}$ and white signals (duplicating strategies if necessary).

10. Trivial signaling

Prove that if player I has trivial information (i.e., $Q^{\mathrm{I}}(s^{\mathrm{I}}, \cdot)$ constant on S^{II} for all s^{I}) the previous results (Theorem IV.4.7, p. 195, Theorem IV.4.13, p. 199, and IV.4, Ex. 9, p. 203) hold with $\mathbf{A}^i$ replaced by:

$$\tilde{\mathbf{A}}^i = \{P \in \Delta(S) \mid \sum_{s^j} P(s^i, s^j) G^i(s^i, s^j) \geq \sum_{s^j} P(s^i, s^j) G^i(t^i, s^j)$$
$$\text{for all } s^i, t^i \text{ with } t^i \sim s^i\},$$

and $\mathbf{B}^i$ by $\mathbf{C}^i$.

11. Correlated equilibria with semi-standard information (Naudé, 1991)

Prove that, in the framework of Section IV.4.b.4, p. 200, $C_\infty = D_\infty = G(\bigcap_i \mathbf{A}^i) \cap IR$.

12. A constructive approach to E_∞ (Lehrer, 1992c)

Given $\varepsilon > 0$, define:

$$C^i_\varepsilon = \{x \in X \mid G^i(x^i, x^j) \geq G^i(y^i, x^j)$$
$$- \varepsilon \text{ for all } y^i \in X^i \text{ with } Q^j(x^i, \cdot) = Q^j(y^i, \cdot)\}$$

and let $C_\varepsilon = \bigcap_i C^i_\varepsilon$.

Define similarly $C^{(n)}_\varepsilon$ for the n-stage game G_n viewed as a one-shot game in normal form with the natural extension of the signaling function Q.

Prove that: $E_\infty = \bigcap_\varepsilon \overline{\left(\bigcup_n G_n(C^{(n)}_\varepsilon)\right)}$.

HINT. Use the ideas of the proof of Proposition IV.4.8, p. 198.

13. Internal correlation. (Lehrer, 1991)

a. Assume that two players can communicate through the following public signaling matrix $Q = \begin{pmatrix} a & b \\ b & b \end{pmatrix}$, where a and b are two arbitrary signals.

Consider now any $S \times T$ correlation matrix M corresponding to a canonical correlation device and with rational entries, say, r_{st}/r. We will describe a procedure and strategies (σ, τ) of both players that will generate M and such that unilateral deviations σ' satisfying $\sigma' \sim \sigma$ (with respect to the distribution on signals induced by Q) will still mimic M in terms of probabilities and information.

(1) Let R be the l.c.m. of the r_{st}. We define a $(S \times R) \times (T \times R)$ matrix Φ of zeros and ones as follows: the "block" (s, t) is a $R \times R$ matrix of the form:

$$\begin{pmatrix} \text{“1”} & \text{“0”} & \cdots & \text{“0”} \\ \text{“0”} & \text{“1”} & \cdots & \text{“0”} \\ \vdots & \vdots & \ddots & \vdots \\ \text{“0”} & \text{“0”} & \cdots & \text{“1”}, \end{pmatrix},$$

where "1" (resp. "0") stands for a $r_{st} \times r_{st}$ matrix of ones (resp. zeros).

Denote by (α, β) an entry of Φ and note that if $\alpha \in s$ (i.e., α is a line in the block s); then $\sum_{\beta \in t} \Phi(\alpha, \beta) = r_{st}$. Assume now that α and β are chosen at random uniformly. Then one has $P(\alpha \in s, \beta \in t \mid \Phi(\alpha, \beta) = 1) = r_{st}/r$ and $P(\beta \in t \mid \alpha, \Phi(\alpha, \beta) = 1) = \frac{r_{st}}{\sum_k r_{sk}}$.

The matrix Q is now used to check whether $(\alpha, \beta) \in Z = \{(\alpha, \beta) \mid \Phi(\alpha, \beta) = 0\}$: Top (resp. Left) meaning "yes, I uses α" (resp. II uses β), Bottom (resp. Right) meaning "no," and recall that a "no" answer is not informative.

(2) The strategy σ (τ is similar) is now formally defined as follows:
Step 1: Choose α uniformly among the $S \times R$ lines of Φ.
Step 2: Given an enumeration of the elements of Z, answer "yes" each time an element (α', β') is checked, with $\alpha = \alpha'$.
Step 3: Finally report: "I chose α," by using a code as usual (cf. the proof of Theorem IV.4.7, p. 195).
A pure strategy for I, say, ω, is thus defined by a couple $(f_\omega, \theta_\omega)$, where f_ω is a mapping from Z to {yes, no} and θ_ω is a line of Φ. An alternative strategy σ' is thus a probability, say, P', on such ω's.

(3) The procedure works as follows: there is first a checking phase corresponding to answers to an enumeration of Z. As soon as the entry a of Q appears (corresponding under σ and τ to a double "yes"), the procedure starts again. If this occurs at a stage where (α, β) is checked, we call this event: a failure at (α, β). If the previous phase generates a sequence of b's, called a success, one proceeds to the report phase.

Clearly, under σ and τ, the procedure will produce an outcome (α, β) after a random time with finite expectation. Prove that if $\sigma' \sim \sigma$, it will induce the same distribution on outcomes, given τ.

HINT. Show that $\forall \beta$: $P'\{\omega \mid f_\omega(\cdot, \beta) \text{ leads to failure at } \alpha\} = \frac{1}{S \times R}$, $\forall \alpha$: $(\alpha, \beta) \in Z$; and that $P'\{\omega \mid \theta_\omega = \alpha,\ f_\omega(\cdot, \beta) \text{ yields success}\} = \frac{\mathbb{1}_{(\alpha,\beta) \notin Z}}{|\{\alpha \mid \Phi(\alpha,\beta)=1\}|}$, which in turn implies $P'\{\omega \mid \theta_\omega = \alpha\} = \frac{1}{S \times R}$.

Finally, given $\theta_\omega = \alpha$, prove that: $\{\beta \mid \Phi(\alpha, \beta) = 1\} = \{\beta \mid f_\omega(\cdot, \beta) \text{ induces a success}\}$ and conclude.

b. Consider a two-person game with the following signaling structure: given any pair of moves (s, t), the signal is public and is either (s, t) or a constant, say, ζ.

Say that s is non-revealing if the corresponding line of signals contains only ζ, and revealing otherwise. In case of only non-revealing moves, E_∞ is obviously the convex hull of E_1. We now assume the existence of revealing moves.

Then $E_\infty = C_\infty = D_\infty = G(\bigcap_i \mathbf{A}^i) \cap IR$.

HINT. Prove the result directly if one player has only revealing strategies.

Otherwise note that there exists a submatrix of signals like the Q described in part IV.4, Ex. 13a, By IV.4, Ex. 12, it is then enough to show that for any payoff d in $G(\bigcap_i \mathbf{A}^i)$ and any $\varepsilon > 0$ there exists n and $(\widetilde{\sigma}, \widetilde{\tau})$ in G_n inducing d' in $C_\varepsilon^{(n)}$, ε-close to d.

Given M in $\bigcap_i \mathbf{A}^i$, use the strategies (σ, τ) defined in part IV.4, Ex. 13a, adding between step 2 and step 3 a large (compared to the expected length of the checking and report phases) number of stages, say, L, during which (s, t) is played if $(\alpha \in s, \beta \in t)$.

(Note that if $\widetilde{\sigma}' \sim \widetilde{\sigma}$ and $\widetilde{\sigma}'$ produces some $\alpha \in s$, there is no gain in playing $s' \neq s$ during the above L stages: in fact, either player I's signal is ζ or his move is revealed.)

IV.5. RECURSIVE GAMES

Recursive games were first defined and studied by Everett (1957). They are two-person zero-sum stochastic games where the payoff is either 0 or absorbing. More precisely we are given a finite set $J \cup K$ of states, sets of actions S, T, a transition probability Q from $K \times S \times T$ to $J \cup K$, and some real function G on J. The game Γ is now played as follows: given some state k_n in K at stage n, both players choose simultaneously their moves (s_n, t_n) and a new state k_{n+1} is selected according to Q, the current stage payoff being 0. If k_n is in J, the payoff is $g_n = G(k_n)$ for each following stage. It follows that given any play h_∞ we can associate to the stream of payoffs g its Cesàro limit $\overline{g}$; i.e., $\lim_{n\to\infty} \overline{g}_n$ exists. Γ is thus a "well-defined" game in normal form with vector payoff function $\gamma(\sigma, \tau) = E_{\sigma,\tau}(\overline{g})$, where $\gamma^k(\sigma, \tau)$ is the payoff in Γ^k, i.e., Γ where the initial state is k. Obviously we are interested only in Γ^k for k in K, and we will consider just those.

Note now that if we define the stopping time θ on H_∞ by $\theta(h) = \min(\{n \mid k_n \in J\} \cup \{\infty\})$, the payoff is given by $\overline{g}(h) = \mathbb{1}_{\theta(h)<\infty} G(k_{\theta(h)})$.

The analysis is somehow easier if we use another representation. First we will shift the payoffs one stage backwards, so that at stage n, given (k_n, s_n, t_n) in $K \times S \times T$, the payoff is $\sum_{j \in J} Q(j; k_n, s_n, t_n) G(j) \equiv E(f_n)$, where $f_n = G(k_{n+1}) \mathbb{1}_J(k_{n+1})$.

We can now let f_n be 0 if k_n is in J and define the payoff up to stage n $\tilde{f}_n$ as the sum of the previous payoffs, $\tilde{f}_n = \sum_{m=1}^n f_m$. It is then clear that $\tilde{f}_n$ converges to some $\tilde{f}$ and that starting from k in K, $\overline{g}$ and $\tilde{f}$ coincide.

We will also write P for the restriction of Q to K; hence for all s, t, $P(s, t)$ is a positive kernel on K with mass less or equal to 1.

Given α in $\mathbb{R}^K$, let $G^k(\alpha)$ be the one-stage game obtained through Γ starting from k and with an absorbing payoff of α^ℓ if ℓ in K is the state at stage 2. If this game has a value, we denote it by $U^k(\alpha)$.

Note that the recursive formula in Theorem IV.3.2, p. 184, says that if Γ has a value w, it verifies $w = U(w)$.

A strategy is Markov (resp. stationary) if it depends only on the current state and stage (resp. state). We can now state the main result due to Everett (1957) (cf. also Orkin, 1972c):

Theorem IV.5.1. *If U exists on $K \times \mathbb{R}^K$, the recursive game has a value. Moreover both players have ε-optimal Markov strategies. (In particular, if S and T are finite, then the above strategies are stationary.)*

Proof. We first prove two lemmas, the first being straightforward.

Lemma IV.5.2.

(1) $\|U(\alpha) - U(\beta)\| \leq \|\alpha - \beta\|$.
(2) *If* $\alpha \geq \beta$ *in* $\mathbb{R}^K$, *then* $U(\alpha) \geq U(\beta)$ *in* $\mathbb{R}^K$.

We define now the following sets:

$$C_1 = \{\alpha \in \mathbb{R}^K \mid U^k(\alpha) \geq \alpha^k \text{ and } U^k(\alpha) > \alpha^k \text{ if } \alpha^k > 0\},$$

$$C_2 = \{\alpha \in \mathbb{R}^K \mid U^k(\alpha) \leq \alpha^k \text{ and } U^k(\alpha) < \alpha^k \text{ if } \alpha^k < 0\}.$$

The vectors in C_1 consist of lower bounds of the maxmin of Γ since we have:

Lemma IV.5.3. *Player* I *can guarantee any α in C_1 with Markov strategies.*

Proof. Given α in C_1, define $K(\alpha) = \{k \in K \mid \alpha^k > 0\}$. Let $\delta = \min\{U^k(\alpha) - \alpha^k \mid k \in K(\alpha)\}$, hence $\delta > 0$, and finally let $e = \mathbb{1}_{K(\alpha)}$ in $\mathbb{R}^K$. Given $\varepsilon > 0$, denote by x_n^k an $(\varepsilon/2^n)$ optimal strategy of player I in $G^k(\alpha)$ and define σ as: play according to x_n^k in state k, at stage n. For any strategy τ of player II, one has (using the definition of σ and the choice of α):

$$\mathsf{E}_{\sigma,\tau}\Big(\sum_{m=1}^{n} f_m + \alpha^{k_{n+1}} \mid \mathscr{H}_n\Big) \geq \sum_{m=1}^{n-1} f_m + \alpha^{k_n} + \delta e^{k_n} - \varepsilon/2^n.$$

Hence by recursion:

$$\mathsf{E}_{\sigma,\tau}\Big(\sum_{m=1}^{n} f_m + \alpha^{k_{n+1}}\Big) \geq \alpha^{k_1} + \delta\, \mathsf{E}\Big(\sum_{m=1}^{n} e^{k_m}\Big) - \varepsilon.$$

Now, since $\alpha \leq \delta M e$ for M large enough we obtain first:

$$\varphi_n(\sigma, \tau) = \mathsf{E}_{\sigma,\tau}(\widetilde{f}_n) \geq \alpha^{k_1} + \delta\, \mathsf{E}\Big(\sum_{m=1}^{n} e^{k_m} - e^{k_{n+1}}\Big) - \varepsilon.$$

Thus $\mathsf{E}(\sum e^{k_m})$ converges, so $\mathsf{E}(e^{k_{n+1}})$ goes to 0. Hence:

$$\gamma(\sigma, \tau) = \lim \varphi_n(\sigma, \tau) \geq \alpha - \varepsilon, \tag{3}$$

■

completing the proof of the proof of Lemma IV.5.3.

So it will thus suffice to show by induction on $\#K$, the number of active states, that $\overline{C}_1 \cap \overline{C}_2 \neq \emptyset$, where $\overline{C}_i$ denotes the closure of C_i.

Assume first $\#K = 1$ and consider $G^1(\alpha)$. By Lemma IV.5.2.1, p. 206, U^1 is a non-expansive mapping from $[-C, C]$ to itself, where as usual C is a uniform bound on the payoffs. It follows that U^1 has a non-empty closed interval of fixed points, and we will write α^* for one of its elements with smallest norm. α^* belongs to $\overline{C}_1$: if $\alpha^* \leq 0$, because it is a fixed point of U^1; while if $\alpha^* > 0$, let $\alpha < \alpha^*$; then $U^1(\alpha) > \alpha$, implying α is in C_1; hence $\alpha^* \in \overline{C}_1$. Dually $\alpha^* \in \overline{C}_2$.

Assume now that $\overline{C}_1 \cap \overline{C}_2 \neq \emptyset$ for all games with strictly less than $\#K$ active states. Obviously this set is then reduced to the value vector.

For each real α, define the game $\Gamma_1(\alpha)$ as a recursive game with $\#K - 1$ active states deduced from Γ by adding to J state 1 with an absorbing payoff α. By induction it has a value for all initial k. Write $\Phi_1(\alpha)$ for the vector in $\mathbb{R}^K$ of its components in K. Consider now $G^1(\Phi_1(\alpha))$ and write $u(\alpha) = U^1(\Phi_1(\alpha))$ for its value. Obviously u is a non-expansive mapping from $[-C, C]$ to itself, and we choose again α^* to be a fixed point with minimum norm.

We claim that $\Phi_1(\alpha^*)$ belongs to $\overline{C}_1$. Consider the following two cases:

If $\alpha^* > 0$, we can choose as above for every positive and small enough ε, $\alpha = \alpha^* - \varepsilon > 0$, such that $u(\alpha) > \alpha$. By induction there exists, for all $\delta > 0$, a $(\#K - 1)$-dimensional vector β such that $\left|\beta^k - \Phi_1^k(\alpha)\right| \leq \delta$ and β belongs to the set C_1 of the reduced game $\{\Gamma_1^k(\alpha) \mid k \in K, k \neq 1\}$. Using Lemma IV.5.2 we obtain by continuity that $U^1(\alpha, \beta) > \alpha$ for δ small enough. Note that for $k \neq 1$, $U^k(\alpha, \beta)$ is also the value of $G'(\beta)$, where G' is the one-shot game related to $\{\Gamma_1^k(\alpha) \mid k \in K, k \neq 1\}$. Thus (α, β) belongs to the set C_1 for the original game, hence the claim.

If $\alpha^* \leq 0$, let L be the set of states k in K for which $\Phi_1^k(\alpha^*) = \alpha^*$ and denote by M its complement in K. Consider the recursive game $\Gamma_L(\alpha)$ with active states set M, where the states in L are now absorbing with the same payoff α, and write $\Phi_L(\alpha)$ for its vector of values on K. Note that $U(\Phi_1(\alpha^*)) = \Phi_1(\alpha^*) = \Phi_L(\alpha^*)$, for all k in K (by recursive formula IV.3.2).

Then we have $\Phi_L^k(\alpha^*) - \Phi_L^k(\alpha) < \alpha^* - \alpha$ for all $\alpha < \alpha^*$ and all k in M. Indeed, given σ^* (resp. τ) ε-optimal for player I (resp. player II) in $\Phi^k(\alpha^*)$ (resp. $\Phi^k(\alpha)$), let $\pi = \mathsf{Pr}_{\sigma^*,\tau}(\exists n; k_n \in L)$. The payoff corresponding to (σ^*, τ) in $\Phi_L^k(\alpha^*)$ (resp. $\Phi_L^k(\alpha)$) can be written as $\pi\alpha^* + (1 - \pi)c$ (resp. $\pi\alpha + (1 - \pi)c$); hence we obtain: $\pi(\alpha^* - \alpha) \geq \Phi_L^k(\alpha^*) - \Phi_L^k(\alpha) - 2\varepsilon$. Letting $\varepsilon \to 0$, this implies first the weak inequality above, and that equality would yield $\pi \to 1$, so $\Phi_L^k(\alpha^*) = \alpha^*$, contradicting the definition of M.

It follows that for all $\varepsilon > 0$, there exists $\delta > 0$ such that $\Phi_L^k(\alpha) - \delta \geq \Phi_L^k(\alpha^*) - \varepsilon$ for $\alpha = \alpha^* - \varepsilon$ and all k in M. Let now ξ in $\mathbb{R}^M$ be such that:

$$\left|\xi^k - \Phi_L^k(\alpha)\right| < \delta \qquad k \in M. \tag{4}$$

$$\xi \text{ belongs to the set } C_1 \text{ of the reduced game } \{\Gamma_L^k(\alpha) \mid k \in M\}. \tag{5}$$

One has $U^k(\Phi_L(\alpha^*) - \varepsilon) \geq \alpha^* - \varepsilon$ for all k in L. By monotonicity this implies $U^k((\Phi_L(\alpha) - \delta)\mathbb{1}_M, \alpha\mathbb{1}_L) \geq \alpha$ for all k in L; hence using (4) we obtain:

$$U^k(\xi, \alpha\mathbb{1}_L) \geq \alpha \qquad \text{for all } k \text{ in } L. \tag{6}$$

Since $\alpha \leq 0$, (5) and (6) just imply that $(\xi, \alpha\mathbb{1}_L)$ is in the set C_1 for the original game. Using the continuity (Lemma IV.5.2 again) we finally get that $\Phi_1(\alpha^*)$ belongs to the closure of C_1, and this proves the theorem. ■

EXERCISES

1. Applications of recursive games. (Orkin, 1972c)

a. Consider the games defined in II.2.b, p. 95. Let $T_1, \ldots, T_n$ be disjoint sets of positions of length k with corresponding payoffs $c_1, \ldots, c_n$. Let $T = \bigcup_{1 \leq i \leq n} T_i$, θ be the entrance time in T after any position: $\theta = \min(\{n \mid (\omega_{n-k+1}, \ldots, \omega_n) \in T\} \cup \{\infty\})$, and define the payoff as $g(h_\infty) = \mathbb{1}_{\theta<\infty} . c_i \mathbb{1}_{h_\infty \in T_i}$.

Prove that the game has a value.

b. Consider a finite (i.e., S, T, K, finite) two-person zero-sum discounted stochastic game Γ_λ (at each stage both players know the previous history). Using Theorem IV.5.1, p. 206, prove that v_λ exists.

2. Ruin games. (Milnor and Shapley, 1957)

Let G be an $S \times T$ real matrix, and $0 \leq r \leq R$. The associated ruin game, $\Gamma(r)$, is a repeated game where both players choose moves (s_n, t_n) at stage n inducing a new fortune $r_n = r_{n-1} + G_{s_n t_n}$ with $r_0 = r$. The payoff is 1 (resp. 0) on every play where $[R, +\infty)$ (resp.$(-\infty, 0]$) is hit first, and some function Q on H_∞ otherwise, with $0 \leq Q \leq 1$.

a. *Preliminary results.* Given a real function $f : \mathbb{R} \to \mathbb{R}$ we introduce $W_f : \mathbb{R} \to \mathbb{R}$ where $W_f(r)$ is the value of the $S \times T$matrix $B_f(r)$ with coefficients $f(r + G_{st})$.

α. Let:

$$(Tf)(r) = \begin{cases} 1 & r \geq R \\ W(r) \quad \text{and} & R > r > 0 \\ 0 & 0 \geq r. \end{cases}$$

Prove that if player I can guarantee $f(r)$ in $\Gamma(r)$, for all $r \in \mathbb{R}$, he can also guarantee $(Tf)(r)$.

β. Let $f_0(r) = \mathbb{1}_{[R,+\infty[}(r)$ and $f_n = Tf_{n-1}$. Prove that $f_n \uparrow \underline{f}$, that $\underline{f}$ is increasing, and that player I can guarantee it. Define similarly $f^0(r) = \mathbb{1}_{]0,+\infty[}$ and $\overline{f} = \lim \downarrow T^n f^0$.

γ. Prove that if $\Gamma(r)$ has a value $v(r)$, then v satisfies:

$$v = Tv \text{ and } \underline{f} \leq v \leq \overline{f}. \tag{$\star$}$$

Deduce from IV.5, Ex. 2aβ, that if ($\star$) has a unique solution, w, then w is the value of Γ and it is independent of Q.

b. *Special case: coefficients in $\mathbb{Z}$.*

α. Let $G = \begin{pmatrix} rr1 & -b \\ -c & d \end{pmatrix}$ with $b, c, d \in \mathbb{N}^*$. Prove that $\underline{f}$ is strictly monotone on the integers in $(0, R)$.

HINT. Let w be another solution of ($\star$) and $k = \max\{n \mid\mid w(n) - \underline{f}(n) \mid = \delta = \max_m \mid w(m) - \underline{f}(m) \mid\}$. Assume $w(k) > \underline{f}(k)$. Let x (resp. y) be an optimal strategy for player I (resp. II) in $B_w(k)$ (resp. $B_{\underline{f}}(k)$). Compute the payoff associated to (x, y) to prove $\delta = 0$ and conclude.

β. Assume Q constant and prove directly that Γ has a value by using Theorem IV.5.1.

c. *Further results.*

α. Given the w bounded solution of ($\star$) define a w-local strategy of player I as follows: given the fortune $r_n \in (0, 1)$ at stage n, play at stage $n + 1$ an optimal strategy in $B_w(r_n)$. Let σ be a w-local strategy. Prove that, for every τ, $W_w(r_n)$ is a bounded submartingale and $P_{\sigma,\tau}(r_n > 0, \forall n) \geq w(r_0)$.

Deduce that: if $Q \equiv 1$ (resp. $Q \equiv 0$), Γ has a value $\overline{f}$ (resp. $\underline{f}$); moreover, if w is strictly monotone and $G_{st} \neq 0$, $\forall(s, t)$, the game has a value, independent of Q.

β. Properties of $\overline{f}$. Prove that the following conditions are equivalent:

(1) $\overline{f}$ is continuous at R.
(2) $\overline{f}(r) = 1$ on $(0, +\infty)$.
(3) G has a non-negative row.

γ. Properties of $\underline{f}$. Prove that the following conditions are equivalent:

(1) $\underline{f}$ is continuous at R.
(2) $\overline{f}(r) = 1$ on $(0, +\infty)$.
(3) Every subset of columns of G has a non-zero, non-negative row.

HINT. To prove (3) $\Longrightarrow$ (2), let q be the smallest non-zero $|G_{st}|$ and r such that $\underline{f}(r) < \underline{f}(r + q)$. Consider then an optimal strategy of player I in $B_{\underline{f}}(r)$.

d. *A special case: if G is zero-free, then Γ has a value, independent of Q.*

HINT. We can assume that the value of G is positive and by IV.5, Ex. 2cγ, that $\underline{f}$ is discontinuous at R. We are going to construct a strictly monotone solution of some approximation T_ε of T. Let $C = \max|G_{st}|$ and define:

$$w_0(r) = \begin{cases} \varepsilon(r - R - C) & r < R \\ 1 + \varepsilon(r - R - C) & r \geq R \end{cases} \quad \text{and}$$

$$w_n(r) = \begin{cases} \varepsilon(r - R - C) & r \leq 0 \\ Bw_{n-1}(r) & r \in (0, R) \\ 1 + \varepsilon(r - R - C) & r \geq R. \end{cases}$$

(1) Prove that $w_n(r) \uparrow$ to some $w(r)$.
(2) Prove that for ε small enough $w_n(r) - \varepsilon r$ is monotone for all n. (For the case $0 < r < R \leq s$, prove that $w_n \leq \underline{f}$ and choose ε such that $\varepsilon C \leq 1 - \underline{f}(R^-)$).
(3) Deduce then the result.

For the existence of optimal strategies, cf. Milnor and Shapley (1957).

e. *General case.* We assume here the following restriction on Q: whenever r_n converges, say, to $r \in (0, R)$, then the value of Q on the corresponding history is only a function, say, P^*, of r. We extend now P^* to $\mathbb{R}$ by putting $P^* = 0$ on $(-\infty, 0]$ and $= 1$ on $[R, +\infty)$, and we define Q^* as the restriction of Q to non-convergent payoffs.

If P^* is increasing, then Γ has a value, independent of Q^*.

HINT.

(1) Consider the following auxiliary game $\Gamma^*_w(r)$, for w bounded and $r \in (0, R)$. If $G_{st} \neq 0$, the payoff is $w(r + G_{st})$ and the game ends. If $G_{st} = 0$, the game is repeated. The payoff corresponding to a non-terminating play is $P^*(r)$. Use Theorem IV.5.1, p. 206, to prove that $\Gamma^*_w(r)$ has a value $V^*_w(r)$.

(2) Define a new operator T^* by $T^*w(r) = \begin{cases} V^*_w(r) & r \in (0, R) \\ P^*(r) & r \notin (0, R) \end{cases}$ and introduce $\underline{f}^*$ as in IV.5, Ex. 2aβ. Prove that there exists a monotone solution to:

$$T^*w = w. \qquad (\star\star)$$

(3) Assume that $(\star\star)$ has a strictly monotone solution w. Prove that w is the value of Γ. (Let $\varepsilon_m = \varepsilon/2^{m+1}$, $n_m = \min\{l \geq n_{m-1} \mid r_l \neq r_{n_{m-1}}\}$; player I plays an ε_m-optimal strategy in $\Gamma^*_w(r_{n_m})$ between stages n_m and $n_{m+1} - 1$.)

(4) Define now, as in IV.5, Ex. 2d), P^*_ε as being equal to P^* on $(0, R)$ and

$$P^*_\varepsilon(r) = \begin{cases} \varepsilon(r - R - C) & r \leq 0 \\ 1 + \varepsilon(r - R - C) & r \geq R \end{cases}.$$

Prove then that the corresponding equation $(\star\star)$ possesses, if the value of G is positive and $\underline{f}_*$ is discontinuous at R, a strictly monotone solution.

(5) Prove finally that if $\underline{f}$ and P^* have jumps at R, so does $\underline{f}^*$, and conclude by approximating P^*.

3. A game with no value (Zamir, 1971–1972)

a. Consider the game with incomplete information, where $k \in K = \{1, 2\}$ is chosen according to $p = (1/2, 1/2)$ and remains fixed, no player being informed of it:

$$G^1 = \begin{pmatrix} 0 & 8 \\ 0 & 8 \end{pmatrix}, \quad A^1 = \begin{pmatrix} a & a \\ b & c \end{pmatrix}, \quad G^2 = \begin{pmatrix} 8 & 0 \\ 8 & 0 \end{pmatrix}, \quad A^2 = \begin{pmatrix} a & a \\ d & c \end{pmatrix}.$$

After each move (s, t), A^k_{st} is announced to both players. Prove that $\lim v_n = v_\infty = 4$.

b. Consider now Γ, played as in IV.5, Ex. 3a, with $K = \{1, 2, 3\}$, $p = (1/4, 1/4, 1/2)$, G^k, A^k, $k = 1, 2$ as above and

$$G^3 = \begin{pmatrix} 0 & -4 \\ 0 & 0 \end{pmatrix}, \qquad A^3 = \begin{pmatrix} a & a \\ e & f \end{pmatrix}.$$

α. Prove that $\overline{v} = \lim v_n = 1$.

HINT. Let II play (1/2,1/2) as long as a is announced and optimally thereafter. For player I take $s_n = 1$ if $P_\tau(t_n = 1) \geq 1/2$, and $s_n = 2$ otherwise.

β. Prove that $\underline{v} = 0$.

HINT. Let $q_n = P_\sigma(s_n = 1 \mid a_m = a, \forall m = 1, \ldots, n-1)$ and $q = \prod_1^\infty q_n$. If $q = 0$, player II plays $t_n = 1$ as long as only a appears. If $q > 0$, player II plays $t_n = 1$ up to some large stage N and t_n thereafter.

4. Duels.

We consider here a noisy duel (cf. I.2, Ex. 9, p. 26) between time 0 and 1, with symmetric accuracy function $Q(t) = t$, and where player I (resp. II) has m bullets (resp. n). Let $v(m, n)$ be the corresponding value.

a. Prove that $v(1, 1) = 1/2$ and that both players have optimal strategies.

b. Prove by induction (recursive formula) that $v(m, n) = (m - n)/(m + n)$, that player I has an optimal strategy when $m > n$ (shoot at time $1/m + n$ if player II did not shoot before) and only an ε-optimal strategy otherwise (shoot at random on a small interval around $1/m + n$, if player II did not shoot before).

PART B

THE CENTRAL RESULTS

CHAPTER V

Full Information on One Side

We now start to study repeated games with incomplete information. In the present chapter we consider the simplest class of those games, namely, two-person zero-sum games in which one player, say, player I, is fully informed about the state of nature, while the other player, player II, knows only the prior distribution according to which the state is chosen.

V.1. GENERAL PROPERTIES

In this section we prove some general properties of a one-shot game with incomplete information, which later will be applied to various versions of the game: finitely or infinitely repeated games or discounted games. The game considered here is a two-person zero-sum game of the following form: chance chooses a state k from a finite set K of states (games) according to some probability $p \in \Pi = \Delta(K)$. Player I (the maximizer) is informed which k was chosen but player II is not. Players I and II then choose simultaneously $\sigma^k \in \Sigma$ and $\tau \in \mathscr{T}$, respectively, and finally $G^k(\sigma^k, \tau)$ is paid to player I by player II. The sets Σ and $\mathscr{T}$ are some convex sets of strategies, and the payoff functions $G^k(\sigma^k, \tau)$ are bi-linear and uniformly bounded on $\Sigma \times \mathscr{T}$.

In normal form this is a game in which the strategies are $\sigma \in \Sigma^K$ and $\tau \in \mathscr{T}$, respectively, and the payoff function is $G^p(\sigma, \tau) = \sum_k p^k G^k(\sigma^k, \tau)$. Denote this game by $\Gamma(p)$.

Theorem V.1.1. $\overline{w}(p) = \inf_\tau \sup_\sigma G^p(\sigma, \tau)$ *and* $\underline{w}(p) = \sup_\sigma \inf_\tau G^p(\sigma, \tau)$ *are concave.*

Proof. The proof is the same for both functions. We write it for $\overline{w}(p)$. Let $(p_e)_{e\in E}$ be finitely many points in $\Delta(K)$, and let $\alpha = (\alpha_e)_{e\in E}$ be a point in $\Delta(E)$ such that $\sum_{e\in E} \alpha_e p_e = p$; we claim that $\overline{w}(p) \geq \sum_{e\in E} \alpha_e \overline{w}(p_e)$. To see that, consider the following two-stage game: a chance move chooses $e \in E$ according to the probability distribution $(\alpha_e)_{e\in E}$, then $k \in K$ is chosen according to p_e, the players choose $\sigma^k \in \Sigma$ and $\tau \in \mathscr{T}$, respectively, and the payoff is $G^k(\sigma^k, \tau)$. We consider two versions in both of which player I is informed of everything (both e and k) while player II may or may not be informed of the value of e (but in any case he is not informed of the value of k).

Now if player II is informed of the outcome e, the situation following the first lottery is equivalent to $\Gamma(p_e)$. Thus, the $\inf_\tau \sup_\sigma$ for the game in which player II is informed of the outcome of the first stage is $\sum_{e\in E} \alpha_e \overline{w}(p_e)$. This game is more favorable to II than the game in which he is not informed of the value of e, which is equivalent to $\Gamma(\sum_e \alpha_e p_e) = \Gamma(p)$. Therefore we have:

$$\overline{w}(p) \geq \sum_{e\in E} \alpha_e \overline{w}(p_e). \tag{1}$$

■

Remark V.1.1. Since player II's strategy space and the payoff function are completely general, nothing prevents the game from being a normal form game in which player II first observes the result of a k-dependent lottery, i.e., his own "type," and then chooses his action. We obtain thus the concavity of $\overline{w}(p)$ and $\underline{w}(p)$ in games with incomplete information on both sides, when p is restricted to the subset of the simplex where player I's conditional probability on the state k, given his own type, is fixed.

Remark V.1.2. The concavity of $\underline{w}(p)$ can also be proved constructively. For this let us first prove the following proposition, which we shall refer to as the **splitting procedure**.

Proposition V.1.2. *Let $(p_e)_{e\in E}$ be finitely many points in $\Delta(K)$, and let $\alpha = (\alpha_e)_{e\in E}$ be a point in $\Delta(E)$ with $\sum_{e\in E} \alpha_e p_e = p$; then there are vectors $(\mu^k)_{k\in K}$ in $\Delta(E)$ such that the probability distribution P on $K \times E$ obtained by the composition of p and $(\mu^k)_{k\in K}$ (i.e., $k \in K$ is chosen according to p and then $e \in E$ is chosen according to μ^k) satisfies: for all $e \in E$:*

$$P(\cdot \mid e) = p_e \qquad \text{and} \qquad P(e) = \alpha_e.$$

Proof. If $p^k = 0$, μ^k can be chosen arbitrarily in $\Delta(E)$. If $p^k > 0$, μ^k is given by $\mu^k(e) = \alpha_e p_e^k / p^k$. Using Bayes' formula the required properties are directly verified. ■

Corollary V.1.3. *The function $\underline{w}(p)$ is concave.*

Proof. Let $p = \sum_e \alpha_e p_e$. Let player I use the above-described lottery and then use an ε-optimal strategy in $\Gamma(p_e)$. In this way he obtains at least $\sum_e \alpha_e \underline{w}(p_e) - \varepsilon$, even if player II is informed of the outcome of the lottery. So $\underline{w}(p)$ is certainly larger than that. ■

Proposition V.1.4. *For any $\tau \in \mathscr{T}$, the function $\sup_\sigma G^p(\sigma, \tau)$ is linear in p.*

Proof. Indeed, player I just optimizes, given k (and τ), yielding:

$$\sup_\sigma G^p(\sigma, \tau) = \sum_k p^k \sup_{\sigma^k} G^k(\sigma^k, \tau). \tag{2}$$

■

Remark V.1.3. The last proposition provides another proof of the concavity of $\overline{w}(p)$.

Corollary V.1.5. *If $\Sigma = \Delta(S)$ and $\mathscr{T} = \Delta(T)$ where S and T are finite, then the function $\overline{w}(p)$ is piecewise linear.*

Proof. Knowing already that $\overline{w}(p)$ is concave, we have to show that the set

$$A = \{\alpha = (\alpha_k)_{k\in K} \in \mathbb{R}^K \mid \exists \tau \text{ such that } G^k(s^k, \tau) \le \alpha_k \,; \forall s^k \in S\ \forall k\}$$

is a convex polyhedron. This is true since it is written as the projection of the polyhedron (in $(\alpha, \tau) \in \mathbb{R}^K \times \mathbb{R}^T$):

$$\{(\alpha, \tau) \mid \sum_{t\in T} \tau_t G^k(s^k, t) - \alpha_k \le 0 \,; \forall s^k \in S\ \forall k\}.$$

Indeed, since obviously $A \subseteq \{\alpha \in \mathbb{R}^K \mid \alpha_k \ge -C\ \forall k\}$, for sufficiently large constant C, any point in A is bounded from below by a convex combination of extreme points. Hence we have $\overline{w}(p) = \min_\alpha \sum_k \alpha_k p_k$, where α varies over the finitely many extreme points. ■

Another general property worth mentioning is the Lipschitz property of all functions of interest, in particular $\overline{w}(p)$. This follows just from the uniform boundedness of the payoffs, and hence it is valid for any repeated game as defined in Chapter IV, p. 171.

Theorem V.1.6. *The function $\overline{w}(p)$ is Lipschitz with constant C (the bound on the absolute value of payoffs).*

Proof. Indeed, the payoff functions of two games $\Gamma(p_1)$ and $\Gamma(p_2)$ differ by at most $C\,\|p_1 - p_2\|_1$. ■

Definition V.1.4. Given any real-valued function f on $\Pi = \Delta(K)$, we denote by $\mathsf{Cav}\, f$ the (pointwise) minimal function g, concave and greater than f on Π.

V.2. ELEMENTARY TOOLS AND THE FULL MONITORING CASE

In this section we introduce some elementary tools frequently used in repeated games with incomplete information. We do this by studying first the relatively simple special case of **full monitoring**. This is the case in which the moves (and only the moves) of the players at each stage are observed by both of them, and hence they serve as the (only) device for transmitting information about the state of nature. This important special case will serve to show the results and the main ideas in a simpler framework. The more complex general case will be treated in later sections.

The game considered here is a special case of the general model introduced in Chapter IV, p. 171: there are two players, I and II, with finite action sets S and T, respectively. The state space is a finite set K on which the prior probability distribution is $p \in \Delta(K)$. The payoff in state $k \in K$ is given by the $(S \times T)$ matrix G^k with elements G^k_{st}. Let $C = \max_{k,s,t} |G^k_{st}|$.

The repeated game $\Gamma(p)$ is played as follows:

- At stage 0 a chance move chooses $k \in K$ with probability distribution $p \in \Delta(K)$. The result is told to player I, the row chooser, but not to player II, who knows only the initial probability distribution p.
- At stage m; $m = 1, 2, \ldots$, player I chooses $s_m \in S$, and II chooses $t_m \in T$, and (s_m, t_m) is announced. The payoff g_m, for player I, is $G^k_{s_m t_m}$.

Denote the n-stage game by $\Gamma_n(p)$ and its value by $v_n(p)$ (cf. Section IV.1.b, p. 173). The infinite λ-discounted game is denoted by $\Gamma_\lambda(p)$ and its value by $v_\lambda(p)$. We also consider the infinitely repeated game $\Gamma_\infty(p)$ without specifying the payoff function and with the usual definitions of minmax, maxmin, and value $v_\infty(p)$ (cf. Section IV.1.c, p. 174).

For illustration, think of the following example:

Example V.2.1. Consider a game with two states $K = \{1, 2\}$ in which the payoffs and the probability are given by:

$$G^1 = \begin{pmatrix} 1 & 0 \\ 0 & 0 \end{pmatrix}, \quad G^2 = \begin{pmatrix} 0 & 0 \\ 0 & 1 \end{pmatrix}, \quad p = (1/2, 1/2).$$

The main feature of this game is that the informed player's moves will typically depend (among other things) on his information (i.e., on the value of k). Since these moves are observed by the uninformed player, they serve as a channel that can transfer information about the actual state k. This must be taken into account by player I when choosing his strategy. In our example, for instance, playing at some stage the move $s = 1$ if $k = 1$ and $s = 2$ if $k = 2$ is a dominant strategy as far as the payoffs at that stage are concerned. However, such behavior will reveal the value of k to player II and by that enable him to reduce the payoffs to 0 in all subsequent stages. This is, of course, very disadvantageous in the long run, and player I would be better off even by simply ignoring his information: playing the mixed move $(1/2, 1/2)$ at each stage independently of the value of k guarantees an expected payoff of at least $1/4$ per stage. We shall see that this is in fact the best he can do in the long run in this game.

V.2.a. Posterior Probabilities and Non-Revealing Strategies

For $n = 1, 2, \ldots$, let $H^{\text{II}}_n = [S \times T]^{n-1}$ be the set of histories for player II, or II-histories, at stage n. (An element $h_n \in H^{\text{II}}_n$ is a sequence $(s_1, t_1; s_2, t_2; \ldots; s_{n-1}, t_{n-1})$ of moves of both players in the first $n-1$ stages of the game; it is known by both players at stage n.) Compared with the similar notations in IV.1.a, a II-history does not contain the state k, and the set of plays is $H_\infty = K \times (S \times T)^\infty$, with the usual σ-algebra $\mathscr{H}_\infty$. Let $\mathscr{H}^{\text{II}}_n$ be the σ-algebra on H_∞ generated by the cylinders above H^{II}_n and corresponding to II's information partition (Section IV.1.b, p. 173).

Any strategies σ and τ, of players I and II, respectively, and $p \in \Delta(K)$ induce a probability distribution $P^p_{\sigma,\tau}$ on the measurable space of plays. This will be our basic probability space, and we will simply write P or E for probability or expectation when no confusion can arise. We denote by p_n the conditional probability on K given $\mathscr{H}^{\mathrm{II}}_n$, i.e.:

$$p^k_n = P(k \mid \mathscr{H}^{\mathrm{II}}_n), \forall k \in K.$$

This random variable on $\mathscr{H}^{\mathrm{II}}_n$ has a clear interpretation: this is player II's **posterior probability distribution** on K at stage n given the history up to that stage. Let $p_1 \equiv p$ by definition. These posterior probabilities turn out to be the natural **state variable** of the game and therefore play a central role in our analysis.

First observe that the sequence $(p_n)^\infty_{n=1}$ is a $(\mathscr{H}^{\mathrm{II}}_n)^\infty_{n=1}$ martingale, being a sequence of conditional probabilities with respect to an increasing sequence of σ-fields, i.e.:

$$\mathsf{E}(p_{n+1} \mid \mathscr{H}^{\mathrm{II}}_n) = p_n, \forall n = 1, 2, \ldots.$$

In particular this implies $\mathsf{E}(p_n) = p$, $\forall n$. Furthermore, since this martingale is uniformly bounded, we have the following bound on its variation in the L_1-norm $\|\cdot\|$:

Lemma V.2.1. $$\frac{1}{n}\sum_{m=1}^{n} \mathsf{E}\,\|p_{m+1} - p_m\| \leq \sum_k \sqrt{\frac{p^k(1-p^k)}{n}}.$$

Proof. Note that for a martingale $(p_m)^n_{m=1}$ and for any $k \in K$, and $m = 1, \ldots, n$:

$$\begin{aligned}
\mathsf{E}(p^k_{m+1} - p^k_m)^2 &= \mathsf{E}(\mathsf{E}[(p^k_{m+1} - p^k_m)^2 \mid \mathscr{H}^{\mathrm{II}}_m]) \\
&= \mathsf{E}(\mathsf{E}[(p^k_{m+1})^2 \mid \mathscr{H}^{\mathrm{II}}_m] - 2p^k_m\,\mathsf{E}[p^k_{m+1} \mid \mathscr{H}^{\mathrm{II}}_m] + (p^k_m)^2) \\
&= \mathsf{E}(\mathsf{E}[(p^k_{m+1})^2 \mid \mathscr{H}^{\mathrm{II}}_m] - (p^k_m)^2) \\
&= \mathsf{E}((p^k_{m+1})^2 - (p^k_m)^2).
\end{aligned}$$

Hence:

$$\mathsf{E}\sum_{m=1}^{n}(p^k_{m+1} - p^k_m)^2 = \mathsf{E}((p^k_{m+1})^2 - (p^k_1)^2) \leq p^k_1(1 - p^k_1).$$

Use now the fact that $\|x\|_1 \leq \|x\|_2$ on the probability space in which m is chosen, independently of h_n in H^{II}_n, uniformly between 1 and n, to obtain:

$$\mathsf{E}\frac{1}{n}\sum_{m=1}^{n}\left|p^k_{m+1} - p^k_m\right| \leq \sqrt{\frac{1}{n}\mathsf{E}\sum_{m=1}^{n}(p^k_{m+1} - p^k_m)^2} \leq \sqrt{\frac{p^k(1-p^k)}{n}}.$$

The proof is concluded by summing on $k \in K$. ∎

Remark V.2.2. Note that $\sum_k \sqrt{p^k(1-p^k)} \leq \sqrt{\#K - 1}$ since the left-hand side is maximized by $p^k = 1/\#K$ for all k. Intuitively, Lemma V.2.1 above means that at "most of the stages" p_{m+1} cannot be very different from p_m.

By induction one can compute explicitly p_m: given a strategy σ of player I, a stage n, and a II-history $h_n \in H_n^{\mathrm{II}}$ let $\sigma(h_n) = (x_n^k)_{k\in K}$, denote the vector of mixed moves of player I at that stage. Namely, he uses the mixed move $x_n^k = (x_n^k(s))_{s\in S} \in X = \Delta(S)$ in the game G^k. Given $p_n(h_n) = p_n$, let $\overline{x}_n = \sum_{k\in K} p_n^k x_n^k$ be the (conditional) average mixed move of player I at stage n. The (conditional) probability distribution of p_{n+1} can now be written by Bayes' formula: $\forall s \in S$ such that $\overline{x}_n(s) > 0$ and $\forall k \in K$:

$$p_{n+1}^k(s) = P(k \mid h_n, s_n = s) = \frac{p_n^k x_n^k(s)}{\overline{x}_n(s)}. \tag{1}$$

It follows that if $x_n^k = \overline{x}_n$ whenever $p_n^k > 0$, then $p_{n+1} = p_n$; hence:

Proposition V.2.2. *Given any II-history h_n, the posterior probabilities do not change at stage n if player I's mixed move at that stage is independent of the state k over all values of k for which $p_n^k > 0$.*

In such a case we shall say that player I plays **non-revealing** at stage n, and we define the corresponding set:

Definition V.2.3. $\mathrm{NR} = \{x \in X^K \mid x^k = x^{k'} \ \forall k, k' \in K\}$.

Due to the full monitoring assumption, not revealing the information is equivalent to not using the information. But then the outcome of the initial chance move (choosing k) is not needed during the game: this lottery can just as well be made at the end, just to compute the payoff.

Definition V.2.4. For p in $\Delta(K)$, the non-revealing game at p, denoted by $D(p)$, is the (one-shot) two-person zero-sum game with payoff matrix:

$$D(p) = \langle p, G\rangle = \sum_{k\in K} p^k G^k.$$

Let $u(p)$ denote the value of $D(p)$.

Remark V.2.5. Clearly u is a continuous function on $\Delta(K)$ (and Lipschitz with constant C).

Coming back to the martingale generated by player I's strategy, we shall now see that at the stages m in which p_{m+1} is close to p_m, player I is not playing "very revealingly," and player II can keep his maximal payoff close to u.

Given a strategy σ of player I, let $\sigma_n = (\sigma_n^k)_{k\in K}$ be "the strategy at stage n" (cf. Section IV.1.b, p. 173). Its average (over K) is the random variable $\overline{\sigma}_n = \mathsf{E}(\sigma_n \mid \mathscr{H}_n^{\mathrm{II}}) = \sum_k p_n^k \sigma_n^k$. Note that $\overline{\sigma}_n$, like σ_n, is a function on H_n and that it has values in NR.

A very crucial element in the theory is the following property: it is intuitively clear that if the σ_n^k are close (i.e., all near $\overline{\sigma}_n$), p_{n+1} will be close to p_n. In fact, a much more precise relation is valid; namely, these two distances are equal.

Lemma V.2.3. *For any strategies σ and τ of the two players:*

$$\mathsf{E}(\|\sigma_n - \overline{\sigma}_n\| \mid \mathscr{H}_n^{\mathrm{II}}) = \mathsf{E}(\|p_{n+1} - p_n\| \mid \mathscr{H}_n^{\mathrm{II}}).$$

Proof. Let ζ denote a generic point in H_n^{II}. In accordance with our previous notation we write x_n for $\sigma_n(\zeta)$ and hence $\overline{x}_n$ for $\overline{\sigma}_n(\zeta)$. For $s \in S$, the s coordinates of these vectors are denoted by $x_n(s)$ and $\overline{x}_n(s)$, respectively. Evaluating the above left-hand-side expectation at ζ we have:

$$\mathsf{E}(\|\sigma_n - \overline{\sigma}_n\| \mid \zeta) = \sum_k p_n^k(\zeta) \left\|x_n^k - \overline{x}_n\right\| = \sum_k p_n^k(\zeta) \sum_s \left|x_n^k(s) - \overline{x}_n(s)\right|.$$

On the other hand, by the definition of p_n:

$$\mathsf{E}(\|p_{n+1} - p_n\| \mid \zeta) = \sum_s P(s \mid \zeta) \, \|p_{n+1}(\zeta, s) - p_n(\zeta)\|,$$

where by (1), p. 220:

$$P(s \mid \zeta) = \overline{x}_n(s) \text{ and } p_{n+1}^k(\zeta, s) = \frac{p_n^k(\zeta) x_n^k(s)}{\overline{x}_n(s)} \text{ if } \overline{x}_n(s) > 0.$$

So we obtain:

$$\begin{aligned}\mathsf{E}(\|p_{n+1} - p_n\| \mid \zeta) &= \sum_s \overline{x}_n(s) \sum_k \left| \frac{p_n^k(\zeta) x_n^k(s)}{\overline{x}_n(s)} - p_n^k(\zeta) \right| \\ &= \sum_k p_n^k(\zeta) \sum_s \left|x_n^k(s) - \overline{x}_n(s)\right| \\ &= \mathsf{E}(\|\sigma_n - \overline{\sigma}_n\| \mid \zeta).\end{aligned}$$

■

We observe now that the distance between payoffs is bounded by the distance between the corresponding strategies. In fact, given σ and τ, let $\rho_n(\sigma, \tau) = \mathsf{E}(g_n \mid \mathscr{H}_n^{\mathrm{II}})$, and define $\tilde{\sigma}(n)$ to be the same as the strategy σ except for stage n where $\tilde{\sigma}_n(n) = \overline{\sigma}_n$; then we have:

Lemma V.2.4. *For any σ and τ:*

$$|\rho_n(\sigma, \tau) - \rho_n(\tilde{\sigma}(n), \tau)| \le C\, \mathsf{E}(\|\sigma_n - \overline{\sigma}_n\| \mid \mathscr{H}_n^{\mathrm{II}}).$$

Proof. Note that p_n is the same under σ and under $\tilde{\sigma}(n)$. Again let $\zeta \in H_n^{\mathrm{II}}$ and write $\tau_n(\zeta) = y_n$. We have:

$$\rho_n(\sigma, \tau)(\zeta) = \sum_k p_n^k(\zeta) x_n^k G^k y_n$$

and

$$\rho_n(\tilde{\sigma}(n), \tau_n)(\zeta) = \sum_k p_n^k(\zeta) \overline{x}_n G^k y_n.$$

So we get:

$$|\rho_n(\sigma, \tau) - \rho_n(\tilde{\sigma}(n), \tau)|(\zeta) \le C \sum_k p_n^k(\zeta) \left\|x_n^k - \overline{x}_n\right\|$$

$$= C \; \mathsf{E}(\|\sigma_n - \overline{\sigma}_n\| \mid \zeta).$$

■

V.2.b. $\lim v_n(p)$ and $v_\infty(p)$

We state first a property valid for the general case (Section V.3, p. 225):

Proposition V.2.5. *In any version of the repeated game ($\Gamma_n(p)$, $\Gamma_\lambda(p)$, or $\Gamma_\infty(p)$), if player* I *can guarantee $f(p)$, then he can also guarantee* Cav $f(p)$.

Proof. The proof is similar to that of Corollary V.1.3, p. 216: given $\varepsilon > 0$ and p, choose $(p_e)_{e\in E}$ in $\Delta(K)$ with $\#E \le \#K + 1$ and $\alpha \in \Delta(E)$, such that $p = \sum \alpha_e p_e$, $\mathsf{Cav}\, f(p) \le \sum \alpha_e f(p_e) + \varepsilon$ (Carathéodory). Then player I performs the lottery described in Proposition V.1.2, p. 216, and guarantees $f(p_e)$ in $\Gamma(p_e)$. This gives the proof for $\Gamma_n(p)$ and $\Gamma_\lambda(p)$. As for $\Gamma_\infty(p)$ note that if the strategy that $\varepsilon/\#E$-guarantees $f(p)$ in $\Gamma_\infty(p_e)$ corresponds to N_e, then the above-described strategy 2ε-guarantees $\mathsf{Cav}\, f(p)$ with the corresponding $N = \max N_e$. ■

Proposition V.2.6. *Player* I *can guarantee* $\mathsf{Cav}\, u(p)$ *in* $\Gamma_\infty(p)$. *Moreover,* $v_n(p)$ *and* $v_\lambda(p)$ *are both at least* $\mathsf{Cav}\, u(p)$ *(for all n and all $\lambda > 0$).*

Proof. If player I uses NR moves at all stages, the posterior probabilities remain constant. Hence the (conditional) payoff at each stage can be computed from the NR game $D(p)$. In particular by playing an optimal strategy in $D(p)$ player I can obtain an expected payoff of at least $u(p)$ at each stage, hence $v_n(p) \ge u(p)$ and $v_\lambda(p) \ge u(p)$, and player I can guarantee $u(p)$ also in $\Gamma_\infty(p)$. The result follows now from Proposition V.2.5, p. 222. ■

Proposition V.2.7. *For all p in $\Delta(K)$ and all n:*

$$v_n(p) \le \mathsf{Cav}\, u(p) + \frac{C}{\sqrt{n}} \sum_k \sqrt{p^k(1-p^k)}.$$

Proof. Making use of the minmax theorem it is enough to prove that for any strategy σ of player I in $\Gamma_n(p)$, there exists a strategy τ of player II such that:

$$\overline{\gamma}_n(\sigma, \tau) \le \mathsf{Cav}\, u(p) + \frac{C}{\sqrt{n}} \sum_k \sqrt{p^k(1-p^k)}.$$

Given σ, let τ be the following strategy of player II: at stage m, given $h_m = \zeta$, compute $p_m(\zeta)$ and play a mixed action $\tau_m(\zeta)$, which is optimal in $D(p_m(\zeta))$.

By Lemma V.2.4, p. 221, and Lemma V.2.3, p. 221, for $m = 1, \ldots, n$:

$$\rho_m(\sigma, \tau) \le \rho_m(\tilde{\sigma}(m), \tau) + C\, \mathsf{E}(\|p_{m+1} - p_m\| \mid \mathscr{H}_m^{\mathrm{II}}).$$

Now:

$$\rho_m(\tilde{\sigma}(m), \tau) = \sum_k p_m^k \overline{\sigma}_m G^k \tau_m,$$

with $\overline{\sigma}_m \in \mathrm{NR}$ and τ_m optimal in $D(p_m)$, hence:

$$\rho_m(\tilde{\sigma}(m), \tau) \leq u(p_m) \leq \operatorname{Cav} u(p_m),$$

which yields:

$$\mathsf{E}(g_m \mid \mathscr{H}_m^{\mathrm{II}}) = \rho_m(\sigma, \tau) \leq \operatorname{Cav} u(p_m) + C\,\mathsf{E}(\|p_{m+1} - p_m\| \mid \mathscr{H}_m^{\mathrm{II}}).$$

Averaging on $m = 1, \ldots, n$ and over all possible histories $\zeta \in H_m^{\mathrm{II}}$ we obtain (using $\mathsf{E}\operatorname{Cav} u(p_m) \leq \operatorname{Cav} u(p)$, by Jensen's inequality):

$$\overline{\gamma}_n(\sigma, \tau) \leq \operatorname{Cav} u(p) + \frac{C}{n} \sum_{m=1}^{n} \mathsf{E}\,\|p_{m+1} - p_m\|.$$

The claimed inequality now follows from Lemma V.2.1, p. 219. ∎

The main result of this section can thus be written as:

Theorem V.2.8. *For all $p \in \Delta(K)$, $\lim_{n\to\infty} v_n(p)$ exists and equals $\operatorname{Cav} u(p)$. Furthermore the speed of convergence is bounded by:*

$$0 \leq v_n(p) - \operatorname{Cav} u(p) \leq \frac{C}{\sqrt{n}} \sum_k \sqrt{p^k(1-p^k)}.$$

Proof. Follows from Proposition V.2.6, p. 222, and Proposition V.2.7, p. 222. ∎

Corollary V.2.9. *$\lim_{\lambda\to 0} v_\lambda(p)$ exists and equals $\operatorname{Cav} u(p)$, and the speed of convergence satisfies:*

$$0 \leq v_\lambda(p) - \operatorname{Cav} u(p) \leq C\sqrt{\frac{\lambda}{2-\lambda}} \sum_k \sqrt{p^k(1-p^k)}.$$

Proof. The bound in this case follows also from the strategy in Proposition V.2.7, p. 222, since:

$$\begin{aligned}
&\sum_1^\infty \lambda(1-\lambda)^{m-1}\,\mathsf{E}\,\|p_{m+1}^k - p_m^k\| \\
&\quad \leq \mathsf{E}\Big[\Big(\sum_1^\infty \lambda^2(1-\lambda)^{2(m-1)} \cdot \sum_1^\infty (p_{m+1}^k - p_m^k)^2\Big)^{1/2}\Big] \\
&\quad \leq \Big(\frac{\lambda^2}{1-(1-\lambda)^2}\Big)^{1/2} \Big(\mathsf{E}\sum_{m=1}^\infty (p_{m+1}^k - p_m^k)^2\Big)^{1/2} \\
&\quad \leq \sqrt{\frac{\lambda}{2-\lambda}}\sqrt{p^k(1-p^k)}.
\end{aligned}$$

∎

Having proved the existence of the asymptotic value we are now in a position to establish the value of the infinite game $\Gamma_\infty(p)$.

Theorem V.2.10. *For all $p \in \Delta(K)$ the value $v_\infty(p)$ of $\Gamma_\infty(p)$ exists and equals* $\mathsf{Cav}\, u(p)$.

Proof. Use Proposition V.2.6, p. 222, Theorem V.2.8, p. 223, and Theorem V.3.1, p. 226. ■

A proof for the general case is given in Theorem V.3.3, p. 230, below. For the full monitoring case we provide now an alternative proof by constructing optimal strategies for both players. In fact, Proposition V.2.6, p. 222 (through Proposition V.2.5, p. 222) provides an optimal strategy for player I. An optimal strategy for player II is given in the next section. It is based on the notion of approachability (cf. Section II.4, p. 118), which plays a very central role in repeated games with incomplete information.

V.2.c. Approachability Strategy

Let $\ell = (\ell^k)_{k\in K}$ be a supporting hyperplane to $\mathsf{Cav}\, u(p)$ at p (recall that u is continuous), i.e.:

$$\mathsf{Cav}\, u(p) = \langle \ell, p\rangle = \sum_k \ell^k p^k$$

and

$$u(q) \le \langle \ell, q\rangle, \quad \forall q \in \Delta(K).$$

Consider now $\Gamma_\infty(p)$ as a game with vector payoffs in $\mathbb{R}^K$ (cf. Section II.4, p. 118). The kth coordinate is the payoff according to G^k.

Proposition V.2.11. *The set*

$$M = \{m \in \mathbb{R}^K \mid m^k \le \ell^k,\ \forall k \in K\}$$

is approachable by player II.

Proof. Since M is convex, using Corollary II.4.4, p. 120, it suffices to prove that for all $z \in \mathbb{R}^K$:

$$w(z) \ge \inf_{m\in M} \langle m, z\rangle,$$

where $w(z)$ is the value of the game with payoff $\sum_k z^k G^k$ in which player II is the maximizer. The above inequality is obviously satisfied if $z^k > 0$ for some $k \in K$ or if $z = 0$. Otherwise let $q \in \Delta(K)$ be the normalization (to a unit vector) of $-z$.

Since $-w(-q) = u(q)$ the condition becomes:

$$u(q) \le \langle \ell, q\rangle \quad \text{for all } q \in \Delta(K),$$

and follows from the property of ℓ as a supporting hyperplane. This completes the proof. ■

Note that the corresponding approachability strategy is then an optimal strategy of player II, since for every n the average expected payoff up to stage n satisfies (cf. Section II.4, p. 118):

$$\overline{\gamma}_n = \langle p, \overline{g}_n \rangle \leq \langle p, \ell \rangle + \frac{K}{\sqrt{n}} = \operatorname{Cav} u(p) + \frac{K}{\sqrt{n}},$$

hence completing the proof of Theorem V.2.10, p. 224. This proof leads to an explicit optimal strategy for the uninformed player using the sufficient condition for the approachability of convex sets (cf. V.5, Ex. 2, p. 302).

Example V.2.1, p. 218, revisited.

In this example $D(p)$ is the matrix game:

$$p\begin{pmatrix} 1 & 0 \\ 0 & 0 \end{pmatrix} + (1-p)\begin{pmatrix} 0 & 0 \\ 0 & 1 \end{pmatrix} = \begin{pmatrix} p & 0 \\ 0 & 1-p \end{pmatrix},$$

and its value is $u(p) = p(1-p)$. Since this is a concave function of p, $\operatorname{Cav} u(p) = u(p) = p(1-p)$, and we have:

$$\lim_{n\to\infty} v_n(p) = v_\infty(p) = p(1-p).$$

(Thus $v_\infty(1/2) = 1/4$.) So asymptotically the value is that of the game in which none of the players is informed about the value of k. In other words the informed player has an advantage only in games of finite length. This advantage can be measured by $v_n(p) - v_\infty(p)$. By Theorem V.2.8, p. 223, this is bounded by:

$$v_n(p) - p(1-p) \leq \frac{2\sqrt{p(1-p)}}{\sqrt{n}} \leq \frac{1}{\sqrt{n}}.$$

Later (cf. Proposition V.5.7, p. 300) we shall see that for this specific game this bound can be improved and that in fact:

$$v_n(p) - p(1-p) = O\left(\frac{\ln n}{n}\right).$$

V.3. THE GENERAL CASE

We proceed now to generalize the model by dropping the assumption of full monitoring: we no longer assume that the moves are announced after each stage but rather some individual message is transmitted to each player. We will prove that our main result so far, namely, the existence of v_∞, extends to this case. However, several significantly new ideas will be required.

The model we consider here is the same as that defined in the previous section but with no restrictions on the signaling. The model is described by two finite sets of signals A (for player I), B (for player II), and transition probability Q from $K \times S \times T$ to $A \times B$. We denote by $Q^k_{s,t}$ the probability distribution at (k, s, t).

The repeated game $\Gamma(p)$ is played as in the full monitoring case except that at each stage n, $(n \geq 1)$, as player I chooses s_n and player II chooses t_n, the distribution $Q^k_{s_n t_n}$ is used to choose (a_n, b_n) in $A \times B$. The signal a_n is announced to player I and b_n is announced to player II. The games $\Gamma_n(p)$, $\Gamma_\infty(p)$, and $\Gamma_\lambda(p)$ are defined as usually based on the payoff sequence $(g_n)_{n=1}^\infty$. Occasionally we write Γ or $\Gamma(p)$ just for the data of the game (excluding or including p).

V.3.a. $\lim v_n(p)$ and $v_\infty(p)$

The first result for all repeated games with incomplete information on one side is the convergence of v_n and v_λ:

Theorem V.3.1. *v_n and v_λ converge uniformly (as $n \to \infty$ and $\lambda \to 0$, respectively) to the same limit which can moreover be guaranteed by player* II.

Proof. Let τ_n be an n^{-1}-optimal strategy of player II in $\Gamma_n(p)$, let $v_{n_i}(p)$ converge to $\liminf_{n\to\infty} v_n(p)$ and let τ be the following strategy of player II: for $i = 1, 2 \ldots$, play n_{i+1} times τ_{n_i} (thus during $n_i n_{i+1}$ stages) before increasing i by 1.

Let us prove that this strategy τ guarantees player II $\liminf_{n\to\infty} v_n(p)$. It is sufficient to show that on each block where (according to τ) player II has to play τ_{n_i}, the average payoff per stage is at most $v_{n_i}(p)$. This follows by first computing the conditional expectation (of the average payoff) with respect to player I's σ-field of information $\mathscr{H}^{\mathrm{I}}_{n_i}$ and then taking expectation.

It follows that $v_n(p)$ converges (uniformly, by Theorem V.1.6, p. 217).

As to the convergence of v_λ, the above-described strategy of player II proves that:

$$\limsup_{\lambda\to 0} v_\lambda(p) \leq \lim_{n\to\infty} v_n(p).$$

To complete the proof we shall prove that $\lim_{n\to\infty} v_n(p) \leq \liminf_{\lambda\to 0} v_\lambda(p)$ by showing that $\lim_{n\to\infty} v_n(p) \leq v_\lambda(p)$, for any $\lambda > 0$. In fact, given $\lambda > 0$, let τ_λ be an optimal strategy of player II in the λ-discounted game and consider the following strategy (for player II): start playing τ_λ and at each stage restart τ_λ with probability λ, and with probability $(1 - \lambda)$ continue playing the previously started τ_λ. With this strategy, for any $\varepsilon > 0$, we have $\mathsf{E}(\overline{g}_n) \leq v_\lambda + \varepsilon$ for all n sufficiently large (compared to $1/\lambda$). It follows that $\lim_{n\to\infty} v_n(p) \leq v_\lambda(p)$. ∎

Remark V.3.1. The argument used here for the convergence of v_n is even more general and will be used later in a different context (cf. Gleason's game, IV.5, Ex. 1, p. 208). It does not require, for instance, that the state remain fixed throughout the game but just that player II can "almost" control it (in particular this is the case in irreducible stochastic games).

Remark V.3.2. If we interpret the discounted game as a repeated game with probability λ of stopping after each stage, then the convergence of v_λ can be generalized as follows: let $a = \{a_n\}_{n=1}^{\infty}$ be a probability distribution on the positive integers with $a_n \geq a_{n+1}$. Let Γ_a have $\sum_n a_n g_n$ as payoff function, and $v_a(p)$ as value. If $\{a^\ell\}_{\ell=1}^{\infty}$ is a sequence of such distributions with a_1^ℓ going to zero, then $\lim_{\ell\to\infty} v_{a^\ell}(p) = \lim_{n\to\infty} v_n(p)$.

V.3.b. The Non-Revealing Game

With the concavity properties proved in Section V.1, the next step is to get lower bounds for the various values, i.e., to get the results of Proposition V.2.6, p. 222, for the general case. To do that we need to extend the notion of the non-revealing game.

The main feature of repeated games with incomplete information is the possibility of a player to collect information about the state of nature along the play of the game. This information he deduces from the sequence of signals he receives. In the games considered in this chapter, the uninformed player, player II, tries to learn about k from the signals $(b_1, b_2, \dots)$, which he receives in stages $1, 2, \dots$, respectively. In the full monitoring case b_n is just (s_n, t_n), the (pure) moves of the players at stage n. In the general case b_n is a random variable whose distribution is the marginal distribution on B of $Q^k_{s_n,t_n}$ where k is the state chosen at stage 0. Since player I knows k and his moves typically depend on this knowledge, his moves may be revealing to player II; i.e., they may enable him to learn something about k via the signals. This motivates the following definition. As usual, $x = (x^k)_{k\in K} \in X^K$ denotes a strategy of player I in the one-stage game $\Gamma_1(p)$, where $X = \Delta(S)$ is the set of his mixed moves.

Definition V.3.3. $x \in X^K$ is called **non-revealing** at $p \in \Delta(K)$ if

$$\text{For any } t \in T: \quad P^p_{x,t}(b) > 0 \Longrightarrow P^p_{x,t}(k \mid b) = p^k \;\; \forall k \in K, \forall b \in B. \qquad (1)$$

Denote by $\mathrm{NR}(p)$ the set of non-revealing strategies p.

To obtain an operational expression for $\mathrm{NR}(p)$, let $Q^{\mathrm{II},k}$ be the $S \times T$ matrix whose st element, denoted by $Q^{\mathrm{II},k}_{st}$ is the marginal distribution on B of Q^k_{st}. The elements $Q^{\mathrm{II},k}_{st}$ are probability vectors in the simplex $\Delta(B)$. If in $\Gamma_1(p)$ player I uses $x = (x^k)_{k\in K}$ and player II uses $y \in \Delta(T)$, then if the state is k, the probability distribution of the signal b received by II is $x^k Q^{\mathrm{II},k} y$ (x^k is thought of as a row vector and y as a column vector).

Lemma V.3.2.

$$\mathrm{NR}(p) = \{x \in X^K \mid x^k Q^{\mathrm{II},k} = x^{k'} Q^{\mathrm{II},k'} \textit{ whenever } p^k > 0 \textit{ and } p^{k'} > 0\}.$$

(For any move $t \in T$ of player II, the distribution of b (induced by t and x^k) in the kth state is the same for all k for which $p^k > 0$.)

Proof. $x \in \mathrm{NR}(p)$ means that $\forall b \in B$:

$$p^k > 0,\; p^{k'} > 0 \Longrightarrow P_{p,x,t}(k \mid b) = P_{p,x,t}(k' \mid b).$$

But since:

$$P_{p,x,t}(k \mid b) = \frac{p^k(x^k Q_t^{\mathrm{II},k})(b)}{\sum_{k' \in K} p^{k'}(x^{k'} Q_t^{\mathrm{II},k'})(b)},$$

$P_{p,x,t}(k \mid b) = P_{p,x,t}(k' \mid b)$ is equivalent to $P_{p,x,t}(b \mid k) = P_{p,x,t}(b \mid k')$. ■

Remark V.3.4. Note that if p_0 is an extreme point of $\Delta(K)$, then $\mathrm{NR}(p_0) = X^K$. This follows readily from the definition of $\mathrm{NR}(p)$ and is intuitively obvious: an extreme point of $\Delta(K)$ corresponds to a situation of complete information, where k is known to both players; hence every strategy of I is non-revealing since there is nothing to reveal. Note also that by Definition V.3.3 above, the posterior probabilities remain constant as a result of any sequence of moves in $\mathrm{NR}(p)$. This will be intensively used in the sequel. Finally, note that $\mathrm{NR}(p)$ depends only on the support $K(p)$ of p.

Definition V.3.5. Given Γ and p, the **non-revealing game** (NR-game), denoted by $D(p)$, is the one-stage game in which player I's strategy set is restricted to $\mathrm{NR}(p)$.

We denote by $u(p)$ the value of $D(p)$ and refer to it as the NR-value. If $\mathrm{NR}(p) = \emptyset$ we define $u(p) = -\infty$.

Remark V.3.6. $\operatorname{Cav} u$ is Lipschitz with constant C.

In the following examples (for $x \in [0, 1]$ we abbreviate $(1 - x)$ by x'):

$$K = \{1, 2\} \qquad B = \{a, b, c, \dots\} \qquad (p, p') \in \Delta(K).$$

It will be convenient to denote elements of $\Delta(B)$ by a (meaning: signal a with probability 1), $b, c, \dots$, or by $\frac{1}{2}b \overset{*}{+} \frac{1}{2}c$ (meaning signals b or c with probability 1/2 each), etc.

Example V.3.7. The first important example is that of games with full monitoring treated in the previous section. This is the special case in which for all k, s, and t, Q_{st}^k is a unit mass at the signal $b = (s, t)$. It is worth recalling the main properties of this case for future reference:

(1) The projection of $\mathrm{NR}(p)$ on the support of p lies on the diagonal of X^K; i.e., player I plays independently of his information about k.
(2) The signals received by player II are independent of his own moves, and therefore player II has no "information incentive" to play a certain action.
(3) The information that player II can get on k is only through the moves of player I (since the signals are state independent).

As we will see later, dropping some of the above properties implies adding substantial difficulty and complexity to the analysis.

Example V.3.8. Consider the game with $K = \{1, 2\}$, payoff matrices:

$$G^1 = \begin{pmatrix} 1 & 0 \\ 0 & 0 \end{pmatrix} \qquad G^2 = \begin{pmatrix} 0 & 0 \\ 0 & 1 \end{pmatrix},$$

and with signaling matrices:

$$Q^1 = \begin{pmatrix} a & b \\ c & d \end{pmatrix} \qquad Q^2 = \begin{pmatrix} c & d \\ a & b \end{pmatrix}.$$

For $0 < p < 1$, $x \in \mathrm{NR}(p)$ has to satisfy:

$$x_1 a \overset{*}{+} x_1' c = x_2 c \overset{*}{+} x_2' a,$$

$$x_1 b \overset{*}{+} x_1' d = x_2 d \overset{*}{+} x_2' b,$$

which implies $x_1 = x_2'$ and so for $0 < p < 1$,

$$\mathrm{NR}(p) = \big\{\big((\alpha, \alpha'), (\alpha', \alpha)\big) \bigm| 0 \le \alpha \le 1\big\}$$

and

$$\begin{pmatrix} p & p' \\ 0 & 0 \end{pmatrix}, \quad \text{with value } u(p) = \min(p, p').$$

The equation for $u(p)$ is valid for all $p \in [0, 1]$ since $u(1) = u(0) = 0$.

Note that unlike in the full monitoring case where non-revealing strategies were strategies that did not use the information about k, in this example, in order to play non-revealingly, player I has to use his information about the state k: he has to play differently in the two games. For example, the optimal strategy in $D(p)$ for $0 < p < 1$ is to play the top row if $k = 1$ and the bottom row if $k = 2$.

Example V.3.9. The same game as in the previous example with:

$$Q^1 = \begin{pmatrix} a & b \\ c & d \end{pmatrix} \qquad Q^2 = \begin{pmatrix} a & e \\ f & d \end{pmatrix}.$$

For $0 < p < 1$, a strategy $x \in \mathrm{NR}(p)$ has to satisfy:

$$x_1 a \overset{*}{+} x_1' c = x_2 a \overset{*}{+} x_2' f,$$

$$x_1 b \overset{*}{+} x_1' d = x_2 e \overset{*}{+} x_2' d,$$

which is impossible; hence $\mathrm{NR}(p) = \emptyset$ for $0 < p < 1$ and therefore:

$$u(p) = \begin{cases} 0 & \text{if } pp' = 0 \\ -\infty & \text{if } pp' > 0. \end{cases}$$

Example V.3.10. Let $K = \{1, 2, 3\}$ and let the signaling matrices for both players be:

$$Q^1 = Q^2 = \begin{pmatrix} a & b \\ c & d \end{pmatrix} \qquad Q^3 = \begin{pmatrix} a' & b' \\ c' & d' \end{pmatrix}.$$

The signals following the first stage are **partially revealing**: if the signals are in $\{a', b', c', d'\}$ it will become common knowledge that $k = 3$ and the game is reduced to a complete information game in which G^3 is played repeatedly. If, on the other hand, the signals are in $\{a, b, c, d\}$, the game will be reduced to $\hat{\Gamma}(\hat{p})$, in which:

$$\hat{K} = \{1, 2\}, \qquad \hat{p} = (p^1, p^2)/(p^1 + p^2),$$

and the payoff matrices are G^1, G^2. In either case, the game resulting after the first stage is one with full monitoring.

V.3.c. Study of $v_\infty(p)$

We intend to prove here:

Theorem V.3.3. $v_\infty(p) = \mathsf{Cav}\, u(p)$ *for all* p *in* Π.

Proof. By Theorem V.3.1, p. 226, we know that $\lim v_n(p)$ (and similarly $\lim_{\lambda \to 0} v_\lambda$) exist and player II can guarantee this limit in $\Gamma_\infty(p)$. As for player I, observe first that in the general case also player I can guarantee $u(p)$ in $\Gamma_n(p)$ (as well as in $\Gamma_\infty(p)$ and $\Gamma_\lambda(p)$). This is obvious if $\mathrm{NR}(p) = \emptyset$ (since then $u(p) = -\infty$), otherwise it is achieved by playing i.i.d. at each stage a fixed optimal strategy in $D(p)$. Combined with Proposition V.2.5, p. 222, this yields the analogue of Proposition V.2.6, p. 222, namely:

Proposition V.3.4. *For all* $p \in \Delta(K)$ *player* I *can guarantee* $\mathsf{Cav}\, u(p)$ *in* $\Gamma_\infty(p)$. *Moreover,* $v_n(p)$ *and* $v_\lambda(p)$ *are both at least* $\mathsf{Cav}\, u(p)$ *(for all* n *and all* $\lambda > 0$*).*

It follows from the above that the existence of $v_\infty(p)$ will be established by the following:

Proposition V.3.5. $\limsup v_n(p) \leq \mathsf{Cav}\, u(p)$.

Proof. In proving this inequality, we need the posterior probabilities p_n^k to be known by both players. To achieve this we modify the game so that after each stage, both the signal of player II and the pair of moves are communicated also to player I (in addition to his own signal). With this new signaling structure $\mathscr{H}^{\mathrm{II}} \subseteq \mathscr{H}^{\mathrm{I}}$, and hence $\mathscr{H}^{\mathrm{II}}$ is public knowledge. Since, being in favor of player I, this modification can only increase v_n it is sufficient to prove the above inequality for the modified game.

Let ζ denote a II-history in H^{II}, i.e., a sequence of signals to II where the signal includes II's move. As in the previous section we denote by p_n the conditional probability on K given II's information up to stage n (i.e., $p_n^k = P(k \mid \mathscr{H}_n^{\mathrm{II}})\ \forall k \in K$). For the evaluation at ζ we write $p_n(\zeta)$ (if $n = 1$, as the history ω consists of one signal b, we simply write $p(b)$).

As we already observed, the key object in measuring the amount of information revealed by player I at stage n is $\mathsf{E}\{\|p_{n+1} - p_n\| \mid \mathscr{H}_n^{\mathrm{II}}\}$. This quantity depends not only on the mixed move of player I at that stage but also on p_n.

Intuitively, he may play "very differently" at state k with very small p^k and still reveal "very little." This indicates that the appropriate space to work with is the space of probabilities on the product space $K \times S$. So let $Z = \Delta(K \times S)$. Given $z \in Z$, denote its marginal on K by $p_z = (p_z^k)_{k \in K} \in \Delta(K)$, and its conditional on S given K by $x_z \in X^K$, where, for $k \in K$ with $p_z^k > 0$ and $s \in S$, $x_z^k(s) = z(k, s)/p_z^k$. Hence any pair (p, x) with $p \in \Delta(K)$ and $x \in X^K$ determines uniquely a point $z(p, x) \in Z$.

Consider the following subset of Z:

$$Z_0 = \{z \in Z \mid x_z \in \mathrm{NR}(p_z)\}.$$

For $z \in Z$ denote by $d(z, Z_0)$ its (Euclidian) distance from Z_0. For $z \in Z$ and $y \in Y$ define:

$$e(z, y) = \mathsf{E}_{x_z, y}(\|p_z(b)\|^2 - \|p_z\|^2),$$

which can also be written as:

$$e(z, y) = \mathsf{E}(\|p_z(b) - p_z\|^2) = \mathsf{E}\sum_k (p_z^k(b) - p_z^k)^2.$$

Lemma V.3.6. *Given a completely mixed y, then $\forall \xi > 0$, $\exists \eta > 0$, such that:*

$$e(z, y) < \eta \Longrightarrow d(z, Z_0)) < \xi\,.$$

Proof. If the lemma is false, then there exist $(\eta_j > 0)_{j=1}^{\infty}$ satisfying $\lim_{j \to \infty} \eta_j = 0$ and $(z_j)_{j=1}^{\infty}$ such that $\forall j$:

$$e(z_j, y) < \eta_j \quad \text{and} \quad d(z_j, Z_0) > \xi.$$

We may assume without loss of generality that (z_j) converges, say, to z, which (by continuity of $e(\cdot, y)$ and $d(\cdot, Z_0)$) will then satisfy:

$$e(z, y) = 0 \quad \text{and} \quad d(z, Z_0) \geq \xi,$$

in contradiction with Lemma V.3.3, p. 227, since if y is completely mixed (i.e., $y(t) > 0$ for all $t \in T$), then $e(z, y) = 0$ if and only if $z \in Z_0$. ■

We need a version of the last lemma in which η does not depend on y provided it is in $Y_\varepsilon = \{y \in Y \mid y(t) \geq \varepsilon\}$.

Corollary V.3.7. *Given $\xi > 0$ and $\varepsilon > 0$, $\exists \eta > 0$ such that $\forall y \in Y_\varepsilon$:*

$$e(z, y) < \eta \Longrightarrow d(z, Z_0) < \xi\,.$$

Proof. Note that $e(z, y)$ is linear in y, so if y^0 is the uniform distribution on T we have:

$$y \in Y_\varepsilon \Longrightarrow e(z, y) \geq \varepsilon e(z, y^0)\,.$$

For ξ and y^0, let $\tilde{\eta}$ be determined by Lemma V.3.6, p. 231, and take $\eta = \varepsilon\tilde{\eta}$. ■

Given $t \in T$ and z, we consider $G_t = (G_{st}^k)_{s \in S}^{k \in K}$ as a point in $\mathbb{R}^{K \times S}$. The expected payoff can then be written as $\langle z, G_t \rangle = \sum_k p^k x^k G_t^k$. For $y \in Y$ and

$\varepsilon < 1/\#T$ define the ε-perturbation of y (denoted by y^ε) as follows: $y^\varepsilon(t) = (1 - \#T\varepsilon)y(t) + \varepsilon$, $\forall t \in T$. We say that $y \in Y$ is a best reply to z if:

$$\langle z, G_t \rangle < \langle z, G_{t'} \rangle \Longrightarrow y(t') = 0 .$$

Lemma V.3.8. *There exists a constant $\tilde{C}$ such that $\forall \varepsilon > 0$, $\exists \eta > 0$ such that if y is a best reply to z and $e(z, y^\varepsilon) < \eta$, then:*

$$\gamma(z, y^\varepsilon) = \langle z, G y^\varepsilon \rangle \leq \operatorname{Cav} u(p) + \tilde{C}\varepsilon.$$

Proof. Recall that C is an upper bound for all payoffs' absolute values and take $\tilde{C} = 1 + C(1 + \#S)$. Let:

$$f(z) = \min_{t \in T} \gamma(z, t) = \min_{t \in T} \langle z, G_t \rangle.$$

This is a continuous function on Z_0 as the minimum of finitely many such functions. By definition of Z_0:

$$z \in Z_0 \Longrightarrow x_z \in \mathrm{NR}(p_z) \Longrightarrow f(z) \leq u(p_z) .$$

On the other hand, since y is a best reply to z, $\gamma(z, y) = f(z)$. But $\gamma(z, y)$ is linear in y and hence Lipschitz with constant C, and so we have:

$$\gamma(z, y^\varepsilon) \leq f(z) + C\varepsilon.$$

Let $\psi(\varepsilon)$ be the modulus of the uniform continuity of f. For $\varepsilon > 0$ apply Corollary V.3.7, p. 231, with $\xi = \min(\psi(\varepsilon), \varepsilon)$ and ε to obtain $\eta > 0$. To see that it has the required property, since $e(z(p, x), y^\varepsilon) < \eta$, it follows from Corollary V.3.7 that $\exists z_0 \in Z_0$ such that $\|z(p, x) - z_0\| < \psi(\varepsilon)$ and hence $|f(z(p, x)) - f(z_0)| < \varepsilon$. So we obtain:

$$\gamma(x, y^\varepsilon) \leq f(z(p, x)) + C\varepsilon \leq f(z_0) + \varepsilon + C\varepsilon \leq u(p_{z_0}) + (1 + C)\varepsilon.$$

Finally note that, if $z_0 = (p_0, x_0)$, then $\|p - p_0\| \leq \#S \, \|z(p, x) - z_0\| < \#S\varepsilon$. Also, since $\operatorname{Cav} u(p)$ is Lipschitz with constant C, we have:

$$\operatorname{Cav} u(p_0) \leq \operatorname{Cav} u(p) + C \, \|p - p_0\| \leq \operatorname{Cav} u(p) + C\#S\varepsilon.$$

We conclude that:

$$\gamma(x, y^\varepsilon) \leq \operatorname{Cav} u(p) + C\#S\varepsilon + (1 + C)\varepsilon = \operatorname{Cav} u(p) + \tilde{C}\varepsilon. \qquad (2)$$

■

Given any strategy σ of player I and any $\varepsilon > 0$, we construct now the following reply $\tau = \tau(\sigma, \varepsilon)$ for player II: at any stage m, given a II-history ζ, play a mixed move $y_m(\zeta)$ that is an ε-perturbation of a best reply to $(p_m(\zeta), x_m(\zeta))$. By Lemma V.3.8, p. 232, $\exists \eta > 0$ such that for any stage m:

$$e_m(\zeta) \stackrel{\text{def}}{=} e(p_m(\zeta), x_m(\zeta), y_m(\zeta)) < \eta \Longrightarrow g_m(\zeta) \leq \operatorname{Cav} u(p_m(\zeta)) + 2\tilde{C}\varepsilon.$$

Now for any n:

$$\#K \geq \mathsf{E}(\|p_{n+1}(\zeta)\|^2 - \|p\|^2) = \sum_{m=1}^{n} \mathsf{E}(\|p_{m+1}(\zeta)\|^2 - \|p_m(\zeta)\|^2)$$
$$= \sum_{m=1}^{n} \mathsf{E}(e_m(\zeta)).$$

It follows that $\mathsf{E}(e_m(\zeta)) \leq \varepsilon\eta$ for at least $[n - \#K/(\varepsilon\eta)]$ stages, and on these stages $P^p_{\sigma,\tau}\{e_m(\zeta) \geq \eta\} < \varepsilon$. On this last event we have (note that $C \leq \tilde{C}$):

$$g_m(\zeta) \leq \mathsf{Cav}\, u(p_m(\zeta)) + 2\tilde{C},$$

while on the complement (by Lemma V.3.8, p. 232):

$$g_m(\zeta) \leq \mathsf{Cav}\, u(p_m(\zeta)) + 2\tilde{C}\varepsilon.$$

Thus, for stages m such that $\mathsf{E}(e_m(\zeta)) \leq \varepsilon\eta$ we get:

$$\gamma_m \leq \mathsf{E}(\mathsf{Cav}\, u(p_m(\zeta)) + 4\tilde{C}\varepsilon) \leq \mathsf{Cav}\, u(p) + 4\tilde{C}\varepsilon.$$

On the other stages the expected payoff is bounded from above by $\gamma_m \leq 2\tilde{C}$. Taking the average on n stages we have:

$$\overline{\gamma}_n \leq \mathsf{Cav}\, u(p) + 4\tilde{C}\varepsilon + 2C\frac{\#K}{n\varepsilon\eta}.$$

For $n \geq N > \#K/(\varepsilon^2\eta)$ the last term is less than $2\tilde{C}\varepsilon$; hence we conclude:

For any strategy of player I and for any $\varepsilon > 0$, there is a reply strategy of player II and N such that for $n \geq N$:

$$\overline{\gamma}_n \leq \mathsf{Cav}\, u(p) + 6\tilde{C}\varepsilon.$$

Hence for $n \geq N$:

$$v_n(p) \leq \mathsf{Cav}\, u(p) + 6\tilde{C}\varepsilon,$$

implying $\limsup_{n\to\infty} v_n(p) \leq \mathsf{Cav}\, u(p)$, and therefore $\lim_{n\to\infty} v_n(p) = \mathsf{Cav}\, u(p)$. This completes the proof of Proposition V.3.5, p. 230, and with it the proof of Theorem V.3.3, p. 230. ■

V.3.d. Optimal Strategy for the Uninformed Player

We shall now provide an approachability strategy for player II that guarantees $\mathsf{Cav}\, u(p)$. This generalizes the (full monitoring) strategy in Section V.2.c, p. 224.

The main feature of the optimal strategy for player II in the full monitoring case (cf. the proof of Theorem V.2.10, p. 224) is that it is based on the statistics $\overline{g}_n = \frac{1}{n}\sum_{m=1}^{n} g_m$, viewed as a vector payoff function on histories. This is the average of the stage vector payoffs $(G^k_{s_m t_m})_{k\in K}$, which are observable by player II in the full monitoring case since he observes the moves (s_m, t_m) for

$m = 1, \ldots, n$. In the general case, since $\overline{g}_n$ is no longer observable by player II, another optimal strategy is to be provided that is based only on the II-history $(b_1, \ldots, b_n)$ available to him at each stage. Before defining formally this strategy let us discuss first the principal ideas involved.

For any signal $b \in B$, any move $t \in T$, and any stage n, let β_n^{tb} be the proportion of stages, up to stage n, in which b was obtained by player II following a move t, out of all stages in which move t was played, i.e.:

$$\beta_n^{tb} = \frac{|\{m \mid m \leq n, b_m = b, t_m = t\}|}{|\{m \mid m \leq n, t_m = t\}|}.$$

The vector $\beta_n = (\beta_n^{tb})_{t \in T, b \in B}$, which is observable by player II after each stage n, is the basis for his strategy. The vector payoff ξ_n, which plays the role of the non-observable g_n, is, roughly speaking, the worst vector payoff that is compatible (up to a small deviation δ) with the observed vectors $\beta_1, \ldots, \beta_n$ and with the assumption that player I was playing i.i.d. To this vector payoff we shall apply Blackwell's approachability theorem. The definition of ξ_n and the strategy of player II will be such that:

- The ξ-payoff will be as close as we wish to $\operatorname{Cav} u(p)$.
- The actual unobserved payoff will not exceed the observed ξ-payoff by more than arbitrarily small ε.

V.3.d.1. The strategy construction

Let us start by some notations that will be used in the construction of the strategy.

Let $\mathscr{B} = [\Delta(B)]^T$. This is the set that contains all possible β_n vectors.

For $y \in \Delta(T)$ let $\tilde{y}$ be the strategy (in Γ_n or Γ_∞) that plays the mixed move y repeatedly and independently at each stage.

For $(s, t) \in S \times T$ we denote by f_n^s and φ_n^{st}, respectively, the frequencies of s and (s, t) up to stage n:

$$f_n^s = \frac{1}{n}\#\{m \mid m \leq n, s_m = s\}, \qquad f_n = (f_n^s)_{s \in S},$$

$$\varphi_n^{st} = \frac{1}{n}\#\{m \mid m \leq n, s_m = s, t_m = t\}.$$

Lemma V.3.9. *Given $\tilde{y}$ and σ in $\Gamma_\infty(p)$, then $\forall (s, t) \in S \times T$:*

$$P_{\sigma\tilde{y}}\Big(\lim_{n\to\infty} (\varphi_n^{st} - f_n^s y_t) = 0\Big) = 1.$$

Proof. For fixed $(s_0, t_0) \in S \times T$, consider the game in which at each stage m player I chooses $s_m \in S$ and the payoff is $R(s_m)$, where $R(s) = \mathbb{1}_{s=s_0, t=t_0} - \mathbb{1}_{s=s_0} y_{t_0}$, and t is a random variable with distribution y (thus player II is dummy.) Since:

$$\mathsf{E}(\mathbb{1}_{s=s_0,t=t_0}) = P(s = s_0)P(t = t_0 \mid s = s_0) = \mathsf{E}(\mathbb{1}_{s=s_0}) y_{t_0},$$

we have $\mathsf{E}(R(s)) = 0 \; \forall s \in S$.

It follows from II.4, Ex. 4, p. 121, that the set $\{0\}$ is approachable by any strategy σ of player I. The approachability in this case amounts to:

$$P_{\sigma,\tilde{y}}\Big(\lim_{n\to\infty}\frac{1}{n}\sum_{m=1}^{n}R(s_m)=0\Big)=1,$$

which is equivalent to:

$$P_{\sigma,\tilde{y}}\left(\lim_{n\to\infty}(\varphi_n^{s_0 t_0}-f_n^{s_0}y_{t_0})=0\right)=1. \tag{3}$$

■

Remark V.3.11. As noted in II.4, Ex. 4, p. 121, we applied here a version of a strong law of large numbers. The one-player auxiliary game that we defined is actually a situation in which a gambler (player I) is to choose a betting system (cf., e.g., Feller, 1966, vol. I, p. 199): at each stage m, based on his past gamble experience at stages $1,\ldots,m-1$ only, he decides either not to participate in the gamble (he chooses $s\neq s_0$) or to participate (he chooses $s=s_0$), in which case he either wins $1-y_{t_0}$ (if $t=t_0$) or loses y_{t_0} (if $t\neq t_0$). The form of the strong law of large numbers states that whatever betting system he chooses, his average net profit tends to zero with probability 1 exactly as it does if he participates in all stages (by the usual strong law of large numbers).

Lemma V.3.10. *Let $\tilde{y}$ be a stationary strategy of player* II *such that $y(t)>0\ \forall t\in T$; then for any strategy σ of player* I *and for all $k\in K$:*

$$P^k_{\sigma^k,\tilde{y}}\left(\lim_{n\to\infty}(\overline{g}_n-f_nGy)=0\right)=1, \tag{4}$$

$$P^k_{\sigma^k,\tilde{y}}\left(\lim_{n\to\infty}(\beta_n-f_nQ)=0\right)=1. \tag{5}$$

Proof. By Definition $\overline{g}_n^k=\sum_{s\in S}\sum_{t\in T}\varphi_n^{st}G_{st}^k$, so (4) follows from Lemma V.3.9, p. 234. Now when the state is k and moves (s,t) are played, the random signal b to player II has the distribution Q_{st}^k. So

$$(f_nQ^k)^{tb}=\sum_{s\in S}f_n^sQ_{st}^k(b)\ \forall n,\forall t\in T,\forall b\in B.$$

On the other hand, β_n^{tb} can be written as:

$$\beta_n^{tb}=\sum_{s\in S}\left(\varphi_n^{st}\frac{\#\{m\mid m\le n\,,\ s_m=s\,,\ t_m=t\,,\ b_n=b\}}{\#\{m\mid m\le n\,,\ s_m=s\,,\ t_m=t\}}\right)\Big/\frac{\#\{m\mid m\le n\,,\ t_m=t\}}{n}.$$

Since player II is playing $\tilde{y}$, by the strong law of large numbers:

$$\lim_{n\to\infty}\frac{\#\{m\mid m\le n,\ t_m=t\}}{n}=y_t>0\ \text{a.s.},$$

and given k:

$$\lim_{n\to\infty} \varphi_n^{st} \left[\frac{\#\{m \mid m \le n, s_m = s, t_m = t, b_n = b\}}{\#\{m \mid m \le n, s_m = s, t_m = t\}} - Q^k_{st}(b) \right] = 0 \text{ a.s.}$$

It follows that with probability 1 and $\forall k, \forall b$:

$$\lim_{n\to\infty} (\beta_n^{tb} - (f_n Q^k)^{tb}) = \lim_{n\to\infty} \sum_{s\in S} (\varphi_n^{st}/y_t - f_n^s) Q^k_{st}(b),$$

and this limit is 0 with probability 1 by Lemma V.3.9, p. 234. ■

Remark V.3.12. The meaning of Lemma V.3.10 is that when player II uses for a long period a stationary strategy that assigns positive probability to all pure moves, then, up to an arbitrarily small error, he may assume, both for payoff considerations and for information considerations, that player I has also been using a stationary strategy, namely, the stationary strategy $f_n = (f_n^s)_{s\in S}$. Note furthermore that if we use the version of the law of large numbers derived from Blackwell's approachability theorem (II.4.1, p. 118, and II.4, Ex. 4, p. 121) we obtain an exact bound for the speed of convergence which can be used to compute the length of the period required for a given level of error. This bound does not depend on y in the first formula and depends on $1/y_t$ in the second one.

For the rest of the construction of an optimal strategy for player II it will be convenient to have the following modifications of the game. Consider the game $\Gamma_\infty(p_0)$. Let $\ell \in \mathbb{R}^K$ be a supporting hyperplane to $\mathsf{Cav}\, u$ at p_0, i.e., $\langle \ell, p_0\rangle = \mathsf{Cav}\, u(p_0)$ and $\mathsf{Cav}\, u(p) \le \langle \ell, p\rangle, \quad \forall p \in \Delta(K)$. By subtracting ℓ^k from all entries of G^k, we get a new game for which $\mathsf{Cav}\, u(p_0) = 0$ and $u(p) \le 0, \forall p \in \Delta(K)$. Clearly any strategy that guarantees 0 in the new game guarantees $\mathsf{Cav}\, u(p_0)$ in the original game. Next, by dividing all payoffs in the (modified) game by an appropriate positive number we may assume without loss of generality that $\left|G^k_{st}\right| \le 1$, for all k, s, and t.

In view of Lemma V.3.10, p. 235, let us define the following functions: for $\delta > 0$, $\beta \in \mathscr{B}$, and $y \in \Delta(T)$ let:

$$F(k, \beta, \delta) = \{f \in \Delta(S) \mid \|f Q^k - \beta\| \le \delta\},$$

$$\xi^k(\beta, y, \delta) = \max\{f G^k y \mid f \in F(k, \beta, \delta)\}.$$

Here $\|\cdot\|$ is the ℓ_1 norm in $\mathbb{R}^{T\times B}$. If $F(k, \beta, \delta) = \emptyset$, we define $\xi^k(\beta, y, \delta) = -\infty$. The meaning of these functions is quite straightforward: if β is the observed vector of frequencies of signals to player II, then $F(k, \beta, \delta)$ is the set of all stationary strategies f in $\Delta(S)$ of player I that could have yielded in state k a frequency vector that is δ-close to the observed β. Consequently, when it is finite, $\xi^k(\beta, y, \delta)$ is the worst payoff that player II might have paid in state k while playing $\tilde{y}$. The following proposition formalizes this interpretation:

Lemma V.3.11. *Given y with $y(t) > 0$ for all $t \in T$, and given $\eta > 0$ and $\delta > 0$, there exists an $M = M(\eta, \delta)$ such that for any strategy σ of player* I *and any $k \in K$, $m \geq M$ implies:*

$$P_{\sigma^k, \tilde{y}}\{\overline{g}_m^k > \xi^k(\beta_m, y, \delta) + \eta\} < \eta.$$

Proof. Since convergence with probability 1 implies convergence in probability, by Lemma V.3.10, p. 235, there is an $M = M(\eta, \delta)$ such that for any strategy σ of player I, $m \geq M$ implies:

$$P_{\sigma^k, \tilde{y}}\{f_m \notin F(k, \beta_m, \delta)\} < \eta/2,$$

$$P_{\sigma^k, \tilde{y}}\{\overline{g}_m^k > f_m G^k y + \eta\} < \eta/2.$$

Since in the intersection of the complements of the above two events $\xi^k(\beta_m, y, \delta) \geq f_m G^k y$ and $\overline{g}_m^k \leq f_m G^k y + \eta$, which imply $\overline{g}_m^k \leq \xi^k(\beta_m, y, \delta) + \eta$, it follows that:

$$P_{\sigma^k, \tilde{y}}\{\overline{g}_m^k > \xi^k(\beta_m, y, \delta) + \eta\} < \eta. \tag{6}$$

■

Note that by the remark following Lemma V.3.10, p. 235, the dependence of the constant M on y is through $1/y_t$; therefore if for $\varepsilon > 0$ we let:

$$\Delta_\varepsilon(T) = \{y \in \Delta(T) \mid y_t \geq \frac{\varepsilon}{\#T}; \quad \forall t \in T\},$$

we have:

Corollary V.3.12. *In Lemma V.3.11 there is an M satisfying the statement uniformly for all $y \in \Delta_\varepsilon(T)$.*

We denote now:

$$X(k, \beta, \delta) = \{x \in X^K \mid x^k \in F(k, \beta, \delta)\},$$

$$\delta\mathrm{NR}(p) = \bigcup_{\beta \in \mathscr{B}} \bigcap_{k:\, p^k > 0} X(k, \beta, \delta).$$

The set $\delta\mathrm{NR}(p)$ is compact since it is the projection on X^K of the compact set

$$\left\{(x, \beta) \in X^K \times \mathscr{B} \;\middle|\; \|x^k Q^k - \beta\| \leq \delta \;\forall k \in K(p)\right\},$$

and by definition $\bigcap_{\delta > 0} \delta\mathrm{NR}(p) = \mathrm{NR}(p)$.

It follows that $\max_{x \in \delta\mathrm{NR}(p)} \langle c, x\rangle$ converges uniformly to $\max_{x \in \mathrm{NR}(p)} \langle c, x\rangle$ as δ goes to 0, for any c in the unit ball of $\mathbb{R}^{K \times S}$. Since there are finitely many distinct sets $\mathrm{NR}(p)$ we obtain the following:

Lemma V.3.13. *For every $\varepsilon > 0$ there exists $\overline{\delta} = \overline{\delta}(\varepsilon)$ such that $\delta \in (0, \overline{\delta}]$ implies:*

$$\max_{x \in \delta\mathrm{NR}(p)} \langle c, x\rangle \leq \max_{x \in \mathrm{NR}(p)} \langle c, x\rangle + \varepsilon,$$

for all $c \in \mathbb{R}^{K \times S}$ with $\|c\| \leq 1$ and for all p.

For $p \in \Delta(K)$ let $Y(p) = \{y \in \Delta(T) \mid y \text{ is optimal for player II in } D(p)\}$.

Lemma V.3.14. *For each $\varepsilon > 0$ there exists $\overline{\delta} = \overline{\delta}(\varepsilon)$ such that $\forall \beta \in \mathscr{B}$:*

$$y \in Y(p) \Longrightarrow \langle p, \xi(\beta, y, \delta)\rangle \leq \varepsilon \; \forall \delta \in (0, \overline{\delta}] .$$

Proof.

$$\langle p, \xi(\beta, y, \delta)\rangle = \sum_{k \in K} p^k \max_{f \in F(k,\beta,\delta)} f G^k y$$

$$= \max_{x \in \bigcap_{k:p^k>0} X(k,\beta,\delta)} \sum_{k \in K} p^k x^k G^k y.$$

So by definition of $\delta\mathrm{NR}(p)$:

$$\langle p, \xi(\beta, y, \delta)\rangle \leq \max_{x \in \delta\mathrm{NR}(p)} \sum_{k \in K} p^k x^k G^k y.$$

The proof then follows from Lemma V.3.13, p. 237, and from the optimality of y in $D(p)$. ■

We will use now the approachability theorem to prove that player II can decrease $\overline{g}_n$ down to 0 or, in view of the last lemma, to decrease $\xi(\beta, y, \delta)$ down to ε. Since ξ is an upper bound to the real vector payoff $\overline{g}_n$ only if player II uses a strictly mixed and stationary strategy, we divide the stages of the game $\Gamma_\infty(p)$ into blocks consisting of a large number of stages each. Within the mth block, player II plays a certain, strictly mixed, stationary strategy $\tilde{y}^m$. Our approximation of the average vector payoff in the mth block will be $\xi_m = \xi(\beta_m, y^m, \delta)$, for a certain δ. The strategies y^m will be chosen so as to decrease $\langle p_0, \xi_m\rangle$ to zero.

For any given $\delta > 0$ consider the game with vector payoffs where, at each stage, player I chooses $\beta \in \mathscr{B}$, player II chooses $y \in \Delta_\varepsilon(T)$, and the payoff is $\xi(\beta, y, \delta)$:

Proposition V.3.15. *For every $\varepsilon > 0$ there exists $\overline{\delta} = \overline{\delta}(\varepsilon)$ and $N = N(\varepsilon)$ such that for any sequence β_m there is a sequence $y^m = y^m(\xi_1, \ldots, \xi_m)$ in $\Delta_\varepsilon(T)$ such that:*

$$n \geq N(\varepsilon) \Longrightarrow \mathsf{E}(\overline{\xi}^k_n) \leq 3\varepsilon \; \forall k \in K \,, \text{ where } \overline{\xi}^k_n = \frac{1}{n}\sum_{m=1}^{n} \xi^k_m \,.$$

Proof. We prove that the set $M_{2\varepsilon} = \{x \in \mathbb{R}^K \mid x^k \leq 2\varepsilon \; \forall k\}$ is approachable in the auxiliary game for player II using strategies in $\Delta_\varepsilon(T)$ only. Since $\left|G^k_{st}\right| \leq 1$, it is enough to prove that the set M_ε is approachable using any strategy in $\Delta(T)$. Since M_ε is convex, using Corollary II.4.4, p. 120, it is enough to prove that for all $z \in \mathbb{R}^K$:

$$w(z) \geq \inf_{m \in M\varepsilon} \langle m, z\rangle,$$

where $w(z)$ is the value of the game with payoff $\sum_k z^k \xi^k$ in which player II is the maximizer. The above inequality is obviously satisfied if $z^k > 0$ for some $k \in K$ or if $z = 0$. Otherwise let $q \in \Delta(K)$ be the normalization (to a unit vector) of $-z$. Since $-w(-q) = u(q)$ and since for $z > 0$ the right-hand-side minimizer in M_ε is at $m = (\varepsilon, \dots, \varepsilon)$, the condition becomes:

$$\max_\beta \min_{y \in \Delta_\varepsilon(T)} \langle q, \xi(\beta, y, \delta) \rangle \leq \varepsilon,$$

which is true by Lemma V.3.14, p. 238. ■

We shall now use the above result to provide an optimal strategy for the uninformed player. Given $\varepsilon > 0$, let $\overline{\delta}$, N be determined by Proposition V.3.15, p. 238. Let M be determined by Corollary V.3.12, p. 237, for $\delta = \overline{\delta}$ and $\eta = \varepsilon / N$.

Consider the following strategy τ_ε: player II plays in blocks of length M each. In all the stages of the mth block he plays i.i.d. the same mixed move $y^m \in \Delta_\varepsilon(T)$, which is determined as follows: y^1 is arbitrary. At the beginning of the mth block ($m \geq 1$), player II computes ξ_{m-1} for the last block and plays $y^m(\xi_1, \dots, \xi_{m-1})$, determined also by Proposition V.3.15, p. 238, i.i.d. in that block.

By our construction, on a segment of N blocks (with duration $n_\varepsilon = N \cdot M$), the expected average payoff per stage is $\leq 4\varepsilon$, whatever k may be.

Using this for a sequence ε_i decreasing to 0 (with the corresponding n_{ε_i}) and repeating the argument in the proof of Proposition IV.4.5, p. 193, we can construct a single strategy τ such that for any ε there exists $N(\varepsilon)$ satisfying $\overline{\gamma}_n^k \leq \varepsilon$ for all σ, k, and $n \geq N(\varepsilon)$. This is an optimal strategy of player II.

Summing up, the main results so far are the existence of $\lim v_n(p)$, $\lim v_\lambda(p)$, and $v_\infty(p)$, which are given explicitly and depend on the signaling matrices of player II only (and not on those of player I). By V.5, Ex. 3, p. 302, this value, as a function of p, is semi-algebraic.

V.3.e. Approachability

The section is independent of the rest of the chapter, except for (a particular case of) Proposition V.3.5, p. 230.

In the next theorem, we use B as a short notation for $B \times T$ (when the signals do not inform player II of his move).

Theorem V.3.16. *Let φ be a convex function $\geq u$ on Π. For any sequence $\varepsilon_n > 0$ converging to zero there is a strategy τ of player II in Γ_∞ and a map $\mathbf{l}\colon \bigcup_n B^n \to \mathbb{R}^K$ for which:*

(1) $\varphi_n(p) = \max_{b \in B^n} \langle \mathbf{l}(b), p \rangle$ *is decreasing, with* $\lim_{n\to\infty} \varphi_n(p) \leq \varphi(p)$. $\varphi_n(p) \leq 2C$ *and* $\forall b \in B^n$, *there exists p strictly positive with* $\langle \mathbf{l}(b), p \rangle = \varphi_n(p)$.

(2) *Given a play* ω, *define* $\mathbf{l}_n(\omega) = \mathbf{l}^k(b_1, \ldots, b_n)$. *Let* $E_n = \overline{g}_n - \mathbf{l}_n$, *and* $N = \sup\{n \mid E_n > 0\}$ $(\sup \emptyset = 0)$. *Then* $\sup_{\sigma,k} P^k_{\sigma,\tau}(N \geq n) \leq \exp(-n\varepsilon_n)$, $\forall n \geq 0$.

(3) *Let* $M_n = \sup_{\substack{\sigma,k \\ m \leq n}} \|E_m\|_{L_\infty(\sigma,\tau,k)}$. *Then* $\varepsilon_n(M_n - 3C) \leq 1$.

Remark V.3.13. We will be interested in sequences converging slowly to 0: $n\varepsilon_n \to \infty$; cf. (2), and (3) means that one can select bounds for M_n that increase arbitrarily slowly to $+\infty$ (cf. above V.3.c, p. 230).

Remark V.3.14. The geometric meaning of (1) is that $\mathbf{l}(B^n)$ is the efficient frontier of its convex comprehensive hull, and the sequence of those sets is decreasing. The point $p = p_b \in \operatorname{int}(\Delta(K))$ is such that $\langle \mathbf{l}(b), p\rangle \geq \langle \mathbf{l}(b'), p\rangle\ \forall b' \in \bigcup_{m \geq n} B^m$. It might be interpreted therefore as a kind of "objective" posterior of player II on the states of nature (i.e., independent of any prior on σ).

Remark V.3.15. When the signals do not inform player II of his moves, and $\mathbf{l}$ is thus a map on $\bigcup_n (B \times T)^n$, we have a game of essentially perfect recall, where (II.1, p. 58) one has to think of τ as a mixed strategy of II, i.e., a probability distribution over pure strategies. Every pure strategy $\tilde{t}$ selected by τ allows us then to compute player II's moves in terms of his past signals, and generates thus from $\mathbf{l}$ the map $\mathbf{l}_{\tilde{t}}$ from $\bigcup_n B^n$ to $\mathbb{R}^K$. Hence τ can be viewed as a probability distribution over pairs $(\tilde{t}, \mathbf{l}_{\tilde{t}})$, and $\mathbf{l}_{\tilde{t}}$ yields indeed an estimated vector payoff to player II solely on the basis of his signals.

Proof. The proof is subdivided in three parts.

Part A. The building blocks

Proposition V.3.17. *Let* φ *be a continuous convex function,* $\varphi > u$, *on* Π. *Then there exists* N, *a strategy* τ *of player* II *in* Γ_N, *and a map* $\mathbf{l}\colon B^N \to \mathbf{L}_\varphi = \{x \in \mathbb{R}^K \mid \langle p, x\rangle \leq \varphi(p)\ \forall p \in \Delta(K)\}$ *such that for every strategy* σ *of player* I *in* Γ_N *and for all* $k \in K$, $\mathsf{E}^k_{\sigma,\tau}(E_N) \leq 0$.

Proof.

Step 1. *Simplification of the game.*

Replace first the game Γ by a game Γ' more favorable to player I, replacing S by $K \times S$: an action in Γ' is the choice of a type and of an action of that type in Γ, with the corresponding payoffs and signals, except that the payoff equals $-M$ whenever player I "lies" about his type. Since u', as a function of M, decreases to u, we can find M sufficiently large such that still $u' < \varphi$ everywhere, by compactness. In Γ', Q is independent of the state of nature k, and by Theorem II.1.2, p. 61, we can assume that Q informs each player of his own pure action in Γ'.

Replace now Γ' by its δ-modification Γ'', even more favorable to player I, where II's choice of t results in t with probability $1 - \delta$, in which case his only signal is (t, blank), and player I's is selected according to Q, and results with probability δ in a uniform distribution over T choosing t', in which case his signal is (t, b) and player I's is a, where (a, b) is selected according to $Q_{s,t'}$ (recall that b includes t' and a includes s). For δ sufficiently small, we still have $u'' < \varphi$ everywhere, and now Q^{II} is independent of t.

Consider now Γ''', with $u''' = u'' < \varphi$, even more favorable to I, obtained by informing player I at each stage of player II's signal. Then every information player I gets in addition to player II's signal and his own pure action choice is irrelevant; he can simulate it by doing some additional randomization himself. Discarding it, we obtain a model Γ^4 where $Q_s(b)$ selects a signal b just as a function of player I's pure action choice, and player II is informed of (t, b) and player I of (s, t, b).

In this game, let $\mathrm{NR} = \bigcap_p \mathrm{NR}(p) = \mathrm{NR}(p_0)$ for any interior point p_0. Then for all p, $\mathrm{NR}(p)$ and NR have the same projection on $\{k \mid p_k > 0\}$; in particular $u(p)$ can be computed by restricting player I to the compact convex polyhedron NR. Replace now player I's pure strategy set by the set of extreme points e of NR (this includes all former strategies): by definition of NR, $Q_e(b)$ is well defined and independent of $k \in K$. And player II's message will be of the form (t, b) and player I's of the form $(e, s, t, b,)$, but repeating our previous argument leading from Γ''' to Γ^4 we can assume player I just hears (e, t, b). Now, in Γ^5, we have in addition the property that $\forall x \in \mathrm{NR}, \exists \sigma_x \in \Delta(S)$ such that, for all $k \in K$, $Q_{\sigma_x}(b) = Q_{x^k}(b)\ \forall b \in B$ and $\sigma_x G^k = x^k G^k$. In particular $u(p) = \mathrm{Val}\langle p, G\rangle$.

Step 2. *Construction of (N_0, τ) (τ mixed strategy of player II in Γ_{N_0}) such that $(\overline{\gamma}^k_{N_0}(\sigma, \tau))_{k\in K} \in \mathbf{L}_{\varphi-\varepsilon}$ for all non-revealing strategies σ of I in Γ'_{N_0}.*

We first argue in the game Γ^5. Since $\varphi > u$, one can find $\varepsilon > 0$ and φ', with $u < \varphi' < \varphi - \varepsilon$ and φ' a maximum of finitely many linear functions; i.e., it is the convexification of a function with values φ_i at p_i ($i \in I$, I finite), and $(+\infty)$ elsewhere.

Consider then the game $\overline{\Gamma}$ where player I is initially informed of $i \in I$ (chosen with probability λ_i), next $G^i = \langle p_i, G\rangle$ is to be played, with the same Q as above: we have $\overline{u}(\lambda) = u(\sum \lambda_i p_i) < \varphi'(\sum \lambda_i p_i) \leq \sum \lambda_i \varphi_i$, for all λ (using $u(p) = \mathrm{Val}\langle p, G\rangle$).

Hence, by Proposition V.3.5, p. 230 (in the game $\overline{\Gamma}$), there exists N_0 such that $\mathrm{Val}(\overline{\Gamma}_{N_0}(\lambda)) < \sum \lambda_i \varphi_i$ for all λ. Apply the minmax theorem in the finite game $\tilde{\Gamma}$ where player I chooses his type i and a pure strategy in $\overline{\Gamma}_{N_0}$, player II chooses a pure strategy in $\overline{\Gamma}_{N_0}$, and the payoff equals $-\varphi_i$ plus the payoff in $\overline{\Gamma}^i_{N_0}$: there exists a strategy τ of II in $\overline{\Gamma}_{N_0}$, i.e., in $\Gamma^5_{N_0}$, that guarantees him zero in this game. This means that, for any $i \in I$, and every strategy σ of player I in $\Gamma^5_{N_0}$ that is independent of k, $\mathsf{E}^{p_i}_{\sigma,\tau}(\overline{g}_{N_0}) \leq \varphi_i$. Since, for fixed (σ, τ), $\mathsf{E}^{p}_{\sigma,\tau}(\overline{g}_{N_0})$ is linear in p: this means therefore that $(\overline{\gamma}^k_{N_0}(\sigma, \tau))_{k\in K} \in \mathbf{L}_{\varphi-\varepsilon}$ for all strategies σ in $\Gamma^5_{N_0}$ that are independent of k.

τ is also a strategy in Γ'' (player II's action sets and information are the same), and it is clear what is the corresponding ("generalized"; cf. II.1, Ex. 10aα, p. 70) strategy in Γ'_{N_0}, which, by II.1, Ex. 14, p. 82, can be assumed to be also a mixed strategy in the original game Γ_{N_0}, i.e., depending only on his signals in that game.

Consider a non-revealing strategy σ of player I in Γ'_{N_0}. It is still a strategy, and non-revealing, in Γ'''_{N_0}.

To go to $\Gamma^4_{N_0}$, change it by letting player I do his own randomizations, on an auxiliary probability space: we still have a non-revealing (generalized) strategy in $\Gamma^4_{N_0}$. Write it as a behavioral strategy σ^k_n. Modify it now in the following way: after stage 1, player I uses the conditional probability on s_1 given k and b_1 to average his "strategy for the future" w.r.t. s_1; rewrite this new strategy for the future as a behavioral strategy, which now depends no longer on s_1. The joint distribution of $(k, s_2, t_2, b_2, \dots)$ is the same as before, hence the expected payoff from stage 2 on is not affected, and clearly the expected payoff in stage 1 is also the same, so the modification does not affect expected payoffs in the game (here we use crucially the additive separability of payoffs). For the same reason, the new strategy is still non-revealing. Do now the same with this new "strategy for the future" and s_2, and so on: we obtain a non-revealing σ of player I such that σ^k_n depends only on the past signals of II, which yields the same payoffs as the previous one.

Since σ is non-revealing in Γ^4, this implies now that every history h of signals of II that has positive probability under σ for some $k \in K$ (and some τ) has positive probability under σ for every $k \in K$, and that for every such h of length n, $\sigma_n(h) \in \text{NR}$. There is no problem in modifying σ for the other histories; thus σ is a map from the histories of player II to NR. Hence, in Γ^5, we can find an equivalent map from the histories of player II to $\Delta(S)$: in particular, this is independent of $k \in K$.

Step 3. *End of the proof.*

Write now Γ'_{N_0} as a one-shot game, with a single strategy, τ, for player II, and where every pure strategy s of player I yields a joint distribution of payoffs and signals that is the joint distribution of the average payoff up to stage N_0 and the sequence of N_0 pairs of signals it induces by τ in Γ'_{N_0}. In this game, by step 2, every non-revealing strategy of player I yields a payoff in $\mathbf{L}_{\varphi-\varepsilon}$; i.e., the new u-function is still $\leq \varphi - \varepsilon$. Further, there is no loss in adding again to player I's signal knowledge of his own pure strategy choice and of player II's signals. Denote this game by $\tilde{\Gamma}$ and the corresponding alphabet for player II (resp. I) by $\tilde{B}$ (resp. $\tilde{A}$).

Denote by $D \subseteq \Delta(\tilde{B})$ the (compact) convex hull of the points $(\tilde{Q}^{\text{II}}_s)_{s\in\tilde{S}}$, where $\tilde{Q}^{\text{II}}_s$ is the marginal distribution on $\tilde{B}$ of $\tilde{Q}_s$. For every $\pi \in \Delta(\tilde{B})$, denote by $\overline{\pi}$ the closest point in D, and let $\hat{\mathbf{I}}^k(\pi) = \max\{\sum_{s\in\tilde{S}} x_s \tilde{g}^k_s \mid x \in \Delta(\tilde{S}), \sum_{s\in\tilde{S}} x_s q^{\text{II}}_s(b) = \overline{\pi}(b)\ \forall b \in \tilde{B}\}$ ($\tilde{g}^k_s$ is the expected payoff in $\tilde{\Gamma}^k$ induced by action $s \in \tilde{S}$).

Observe that, for all π, $\hat{\mathbf{I}}(\pi)$ is the payoff to a non-revealing strategy (x^k induces for all k the same distribution of signals $\overline{\pi}$); hence $\hat{\mathbf{I}}\colon \Delta(\tilde{B}) \to \mathbf{L}_{\varphi-\varepsilon}$. Further, $\hat{\mathbf{I}}$ is clearly Lipschitz, by I.3, Ex. 4q, p. 35.

Fix now $k \in K$, and consider $\tilde{\Gamma}^k$ as a game with vector payoffs in $\mathbb{R} \times \Delta(\tilde{A} \times \tilde{B})$, action s yielding $\tilde{g}_s^k$, and the random pair of signals generated by $\tilde{Q}_s$. The set $C = \{(r, \pi) \in \mathbb{R} \times D \mid r \leq \hat{\mathbf{l}}^k(\pi)\}$ (i.e., one neglects the coordinate in $\tilde{A}$, which was kept only in order that player I's strategy set remain the same in $\tilde{\Gamma}$) is closed and convex, as the (comprehensive hull of the) linear image of $\Delta(\tilde{S})$, and is, by II.4.2, p. 120, approachable by player II: i.e., there exist constants M_k such that for all n, all σ, and all k, $\mathsf{E}_{\sigma^k} d[(\overline{\tilde{g}}_n^k, f_n), C] \leq \frac{M_k}{\sqrt{n}}$ (II.4.1, p. 118), where f_n denotes the empirical frequency on $\tilde{B}$ until stage n. The Lipschitz character of $\hat{\mathbf{l}}$ implies therefore that there exists $M > 0$ such that for all σ, k, and n, $\mathsf{E}_{\sigma^k}(\overline{\tilde{g}}_n^k - \hat{\mathbf{l}}^k(f_n))^+ \leq M/\sqrt{n}$. In particular, let $N_1 \geq (M/\varepsilon)^2$ and define $\tilde{\mathbf{l}}$: $\tilde{B}^{N_1} \to \mathbf{L}_\varphi$ as $(\hat{\mathbf{l}}^k(f_{N_1}) + \varepsilon)_{k \in K}$; then $\mathsf{E}_{\sigma^k}(\overline{\tilde{g}}_{N_1}^k - \tilde{\mathbf{l}}_{N_1}^k) \leq 0$ for all σ and k.

Revert now to Γ', with $N = N_0 \cdot N_1$, so $B^N = \tilde{B}^{N_1}$: we have a strategy τ in Γ'_N, and $\mathbf{l}$: $B^N \to \mathbf{L}_\varphi$ such that, for all σ and k, $\mathsf{E}_{\sigma,\tau}^k(\overline{g}_N - \mathbf{l}_N) \leq 0$. This remains then true in the original game Γ, which differs from Γ' only by the fact that player I has fewer strategies σ (as mentioned, if in Γ player II's signal does not inform him of his move, $\mathbf{l}$ becomes a map from $(B \times T)^N$ to $\mathbf{L}_\varphi$).

This completes the proof of Proposition V.3.17, p. 240. ■

Part B. Construction of the strategy, and parts (1) and (3) of the theorem

Denote, for any $p_0 \in \Delta(K)$, by ψ_{p_0} the convexification of the function having value $u(p_0)$ at p_0, $C^k = \max_{s,t} G_{s,t}^k$ at the kth extreme point, and $+\infty$ elsewhere. Observe that $\psi_{p_0} \geq u$ everywhere: player II guarantees it in $D(p)$ by playing an optimal strategy in $D(p_0)$ (any strategy if $\mathrm{NR}(p_0) = \emptyset$). It follows that, for any convex function $\varphi \geq u$, denoting by $\tilde{\varphi}$ the function equal to C^k at the kth extreme point and equal to φ elsewhere, the function $\overline{\varphi} = \min(\varphi, \mathsf{Vex}\,\tilde{\varphi})$ is convex, with $u \leq \overline{\varphi} \leq \varphi$, and has value $\leq C^k$ at the kth extreme point. It suffices therefore to prove the result for functions φ that have value $\leq C^k$ at the kth extreme point. In particular such functions have values in $[-\infty, C]$ and are thus upper semi-continuous. Therefore, if f_ℓ is a decreasing sequence of continuous functions converging to φ, and $\psi_\ell = \ell^{-1} + \mathsf{Vex}(f_\ell)$, the ψ_ℓ are continuous convex functions $> u$ and decreasing to φ.

Hence we have, by Proposition V.3.17, for each ℓ, an integer N_ℓ, a strategy τ_ℓ of player II in Γ_{N_ℓ}, and a function $\hat{\mathbf{l}}_\ell$ from B^{N_ℓ} to $\mathbf{L}_{\psi_\ell}$ such that, for all strategies σ of player I in Γ_{N_ℓ} and all $k \in K$:

$$\mathsf{E}_{\sigma,\tau_\ell}^k(\overline{g}_{N_\ell} - \hat{\mathbf{l}}_\ell) \leq 0$$

(with the slight abuse of notation that $\hat{\mathbf{l}}_\ell(\omega) = \hat{\mathbf{l}}_\ell^{k(\omega)}(b_1(\omega), \ldots, b_{N_\ell}(\omega))$). There is no loss of generality in assuming $N_\ell > N_{\ell-1}$.

We show first that, if necessary by extracting a subsequence, we can further assume that $\varphi_\ell(p) = \max_{b \in B^{N_\ell}} \langle \hat{\mathbf{l}}_\ell(b), p \rangle$ decreases to φ. For this, observe first (e.g., by Zorn's lemma, but this is not needed: since $\varphi < +\infty$, it suffices to minimize on rational points) that $\varphi \geq \overline{\varphi} \geq u$, where $\overline{\varphi}$ is a minimal element of the set of convex functions $\geq u$. So we can assume φ itself is minimal. Next, observe that φ_ℓ is a convex function $\geq u$: our inequality implies that $\mathsf{E}_{\sigma,\tau_\ell}(\overline{g}_{N_\ell}) \leq \mathsf{E}_{\sigma,\tau_\ell}[\mathsf{E}_{\sigma,\tau_\ell}(\hat{\mathbf{l}}_\ell \mid \mathscr{H}^{\mathrm{II}}_{N_\ell})] = \mathsf{E}_{\sigma,\tau_\ell}(\sum_k p^k_{N_\ell} \hat{\mathbf{l}}^k_\ell) \leq \mathsf{E}_{\sigma,\tau_\ell}\, \varphi_\ell(p_{N_\ell})$, and so, if σ is an optimal strategy in $D(p)$, repeated independently stage after stage, then $p_{N_\ell} = p$, and $\mathsf{E}_{\sigma,\tau_\ell}(\overline{g}_{N_\ell}) \geq u(p)$, and hence $u(p) \leq \varphi_\ell(p)$. Since $\varphi_\ell \leq \psi_\ell$ and ψ_ℓ converges to φ, we obtain that $\limsup \varphi_\ell \leq \varphi$. But $\limsup \varphi_\ell$ is convex and $\geq u$, and so by the minimality of φ we have $\limsup \varphi_\ell = \varphi$. Since the same argument applies along any subsequence, we obtain $\lim_{\ell\to\infty} \varphi_\ell = \varphi$. This implies that $\varepsilon_\ell = \max_p[\varphi(p) - \varphi_\ell(p)]$ converges to zero by I.3, Ex. 15c, p. 44. Let us thus add $\eta_\ell = \sup_{i\geq \ell} \varepsilon_i + \ell^{-1}$ to the function $\hat{\mathbf{l}}_\ell$; we obtain now that $\varphi_\ell > \varphi$, and the other properties are still valid. Define finally a subsequence ℓ_i inductively by $\ell_1 = \min\{\ell \mid \psi_\ell + \eta_\ell \leq 2C\}$, $\ell_{i+1} = \min\{\ell \mid \psi_\ell + \eta_\ell < \varphi_{\ell_i}\}$ (this exists, by compactness and by continuity of the ψ_ℓ and φ_{ℓ_i}, since $\varphi_{\ell_i} > \varphi$ and $\psi_\ell + \eta_\ell$ decreases to φ). Now $\varphi_{\ell_i} > \varphi_{\ell_{i+1}}$. Assume thus the original sequence satisfies this. So we can henceforth replace the original sequence ψ_ℓ by $\psi_\ell(p) = \max_{b\in B^{N_\ell}} \langle \hat{\mathbf{l}}_\ell(b), p\rangle$: this one also decreases to φ. Replace finally $\hat{\mathbf{l}}_1$ by the constant function $2C$. Choose also $C_\ell = \max(C_{\ell-1}, C + \max_{b\in B^{N_\ell}, k\in K} |\hat{\mathbf{l}}^k_\ell(b)|)$, $(C_0 = 0)$.

Denote then by S^k_ℓ the pure strategy set of player I in $\Gamma^k_{N_\ell}$, and by $P^k_{\ell,s}$ the joint distribution (on $\mathbb{R} \times A^{N_\ell}$, given τ_ℓ, $k \in K$ and $s \in S^k_\ell$) of $\overline{g}^k_{N_\ell} - \hat{\mathbf{l}}^k_\ell$ and of the signals of player I (in A^{N_ℓ}). Denote also by $\mu^k_{\ell,s}$ the marginal of $P^k_{\ell,s}$ on $\mathbb{R}$. Each $\mu^k_{\ell,s}$ has support in $[-C_\ell, C_\ell]$ and barycenter $e^k_{\ell,s} \leq 0$.

Define now the strategy τ of player II in Γ_∞ as follows: for an appropriate sequence of positive integers R_ℓ, play for R_1 successive blocks of length N_1 the strategy τ_1, then for R_2 blocks τ_2, etc. Define also, at any stage n, given a decreasing sequence η_n converging to zero to be specified later, $\mathbf{l}_n(b_1, \ldots, b_n)$ as η_n plus n^{-1} times the sum over all previous blocks of the corresponding value of $\hat{a}$ multiplied by the corresponding block length, plus C times the number of stages in the last, incomplete block.

Let $n = \sum_{j=1}^{i-1} R_j N_j + m N_i + r$, with $0 \leq m < R_i$ and $0 \leq r < N_i$. Then $\langle \mathbf{l}_n, p\rangle - \eta_n \leq \frac{1}{n}[\sum_{j=1}^{i-1} R_j N_j \psi_j(p) + m N_i \psi_i(p) + rC] = \varphi_n(p)$.

Denote by $f_n(p)$ the same function, but where C is replaced by $\psi_i(p)$. Since $\psi_\ell(p)$ decreases to $\varphi(p)$, $f_n(p)$ are a decreasing sequence of convex Lipschitz functions converging to φ, and $\varphi_n(p) \leq \frac{r}{n}[C - \psi_i(p)] + f_n(p)$. Now $C_i \geq \max_p |C - \psi_i(p)|$, so let $\delta_m = \sup_{n\geq m}(\frac{r}{n} C_i)$ (recall r and the index i vary with n).

For $\frac{r}{n} C_i$ to converge to zero, it suffices to consider values of n where $r = N_i - 1$, and then where $m = 0$: thus one needs $N_\ell C_\ell / (\sum_{i=1}^{\ell-1} N_i R_i + N_\ell)$ to converge to zero. For this it suffices that $R_{\ell-1} \geq N_\ell C_\ell$ (since $N_{\ell-1} \to +\infty$). Assume the sequence R_ℓ satisfies this condition. Then δ_n converges to zero. Let then $\overline{\varphi}_n(p) = f_n(p) + \delta_n + \eta_n$: $\overline{\varphi}_n$ is a decreasing sequence of convex Lipschitz functions converging to φ, and for all n, $\mathbf{l}_n : B^n \to \mathbf{L}_{\overline{\varphi}_n}$.

We show now how to modify this function $\mathbf{l}$ so as to satisfy also 1. With the above notation, let $n_0 = \sum_{j=1}^{i-1} R_j N_j + m N_i$. Observe $\varphi_{n_0}(p) = f_{n_0}(p) = \max_{b\in B^{n_0}} \langle \mathbf{l}_{n_0}(b), p\rangle - \eta_{n_0}$: since over each block there exists such a maximizing string of signals, it suffices to put those together. Define now $\bar{\mathbf{l}}_n$ as $\mathbf{l}_n$, but replacing the term C in the last incomplete block by a repetition of the last $\hat{\mathbf{l}}_i$ estimated ($\hat{\mathbf{l}}_{i-1}$ if $m = 0$): the same argument shows that $g_n(p) = \max_{b \in B^n} \langle \bar{\mathbf{l}}_n(b), p \rangle - \eta_n = \frac{1}{n}[\sum_{j=1}^{i-1} R_j N_j \psi_j(p) + (mN_i + r)\psi_i(p)]$ (here again, $\psi_{i-1}(p)$ if $m = 0$), and as before the functions g_n decrease to φ. So by adding δ_n to $\bar{\mathbf{l}}_n$ and to g_n, those properties are preserved and now $\bar{\mathbf{l}} \geq \mathbf{l}$, so all our estimates in part C for $\mathbf{l}$ will a fortiori apply to $\bar{\mathbf{l}}$.

Finally, to have all properties of 1, increase still, for each $b \in B^n$, the coordinates of $\bar{\mathbf{l}}_n(b)$ so as to obtain $\langle \bar{\mathbf{l}}_n(b), p \rangle = g_n(p) + \eta_n$ for some interior p. Finally, for the inequality $\varphi_n(p) \leq 2C$, replace $\bar{\mathbf{l}}$ by the identical zero function if $C = 0$, otherwise, since $\max_{b \in B^n} \langle \bar{\mathbf{l}}_n(b), p \rangle$ decreases to $\varphi(p)$, and since by minimality $\varphi(p) \leq C$ for all p as seen above, there exists n_0 with $\bar{\mathbf{l}}_{n_0}(b) < 2C$ for all $b \in B^{n_0}$. Just set $\bar{\mathbf{l}}_n = 2C$ for $n < n_0$; this preserves all other properties. This yields the function of the theorem; for part C, however, it will be sufficient to deal with the original function $\mathbf{l}$.

For part (3), observe that now for all n, $E_n \geq -3C$, and $M_1 \leq 3C$. Choose each R_ℓ sufficiently large such that $\varepsilon_{R_\ell N_\ell}(C_{\ell+1} - 3C) \leq 1$. Then (3) follows immediately for the original function $\mathbf{l}$. Since the true function $\bar{\mathbf{l}}$ is greater than or equal to $\mathbf{l}$, part (3) follows a fortiori for $\bar{\mathbf{l}}$ (the true E_n being anyway $\geq -3C$).

We also proved along the way:

Corollary V.3.18. *Every convex function $\varphi \geq u$ is bounded from below by a minimal such function, which has value $\leq \max_{s,t} G^k_{s,t}$ at the kth extreme point.*

Part C. Part (2) of the theorem

Step 1. *Given $F(x)$ convex increasing with $\frac{F(x)}{x} \to \infty$, $\frac{F(x)}{x^2} \to 0$, one can select R_ℓ so as to have for X standard normal, $\mathsf{E}^k_{\sigma,\tau} f(E_n) \leq \mathsf{E} f(\frac{\sqrt{F(n)}}{n} X - \eta_n)$ for all σ, k, n, and for all increasing convex f.*

Let $W_i = \sum_{j=1}^{i} N_{\ell_j} X_{s_j}$, $T_i = \sum_{j=1}^{i} N_{\ell_j}$, where $s_j \in S^k_{\ell_j}$ denotes the pure strategy choice of player I in block j of length N_{ℓ_j}, and X_{s_j} is selected according to $\mu^k_{\ell_j,s_j}$. Then, during block $i+1$, i.e., for $T_i \leq n < T_{i+1}$, we have $\overline{g}^k_n - \mathbf{l}^k(b_1, \ldots, b_n) \leq \frac{W_i}{n} - \eta_{T_i}$. We first try to replace W_i by random variables $\tilde{W}_i$ such that $\mathsf{E} f(W_i) \leq \mathsf{E} f(\tilde{W}_i)$ for any convex increasing f.

Thus, by monotonicity of f, we can replace each X_{s_j} by $X_{s_j} - e^k_{\ell_j,s_j}$, since $e^k_{\ell_j,s_j} \leq 0$; i.e., we are reduced to the case where each $\mu^k_{\ell,s}$ has barycenter zero and a support included in $[-2C_\ell, 2C_\ell]$. Consider now random variables Y'_j, whose conditional distribution given all other variables in the problem, including the other Y's, is carried by $\{-2C_{\ell_j}, 2C_{\ell_j}\}$ and has expectation X_{s_j}: by the convexity of f, and Jensen's inequality, we can replace the X_{s_j} by Y'_j; i.e., we can assume that each $\mu^k_{\ell,s}$ not only has expectation zero, but also is carried by $\{-2C_\ell, 2C_\ell\}$. Thus it assigns probability $\frac{1}{2}$ to each of those points. In particular, all strategies of player I and all $k \in K$ reduce now to the same problem; if we let $Y'_j = 2C_{\ell_j} Y_j$, then the Y_j are an i.i.d. sequence, uniform on $\{-1, 1\}$. Let now V_j be an i.i.d. sequence of standard normal random variables (i.e., with mean zero and variance one), independent of all others. Since $\mathsf{E}(|V_j|) = \sqrt{\frac{2}{\pi}}$, the $V'_j = Y_j\,|V_j|\,\sqrt{\frac{\pi}{2}}$ have Y_j as conditional expectation given all other variables, so we can replace the Y_j by those, and they are i.i.d. normal with standard deviation $\sqrt{\frac{\pi}{2}}$. To sum up, we can define $\tilde{W}_i$ by replacing X_{s_j} by $\sqrt{2\pi}C_{\ell_j}X_j$, where the X_j are an i.i.d. sequence of standard normal variables.

Let $D_\ell = \sqrt{2\pi}C_\ell$. The variance of $\tilde{W}_i$ equals: $V(T_i) = \sum_{j=1}^{i}(D_{\ell_j}N_{\ell_j})^2$. During superblock ℓ, the function V therefore has slope $N_\ell D_\ell^2$, which increases to $+\infty$.

Fix now a convex increasing function F from $\mathbb{R}_+$ to itself such that $\lim_{x\to\infty} F(x)/x = +\infty$ and $\lim_{x\to\infty} F(x)/x^2 = 0$, and define the successive R_ℓ as follows: continue superblock ℓ as long as needed so that from the end-point of the graph of $(V(T), T)$ reached at the end of superblock ℓ, the straight line with slope $N_{\ell+1}D_{\ell+1}^2$ will lie everywhere below the graph of $F(T)$. (And increase R_ℓ if necessary still some more to satisfy also our previous condition $R_\ell \geq N_{\ell+1}C_{\ell+1}$.) This defines now fully the strategy τ, given the function F. And by construction, we have now $V(T) \leq F(T)$ for all $T \geq R_1N_1$.

Hence, for all $i \geq R_1$, we can still add (by Jensen's inequality again) to $\tilde{W}_i$ an independent normal variable with mean zero and variance $F(T) - V(T)$, so the $\tilde{W}_i$ become normal with mean zero and variance $F(T_i)$.

Finally, since for $T_i \leq n < T_{i+1}$ we have $E_n \leq \frac{W_i}{n} - \eta_{T_i}$, since $\eta_n \leq \eta_{T_i}$, and since $F(n) \geq F(T_i)$ we can conclude, by a last use of Jensen's inequality, that for all $n \geq R_1N_1$, and all convex increasing functions f, $\mathsf{E}[f(E_n)] \leq \mathsf{E}[f(\frac{W_n}{n} - \eta_n)]$, where W_n is normal $(0, F(n))$, i.e., $\mathsf{E}\,f(E_n) \leq \mathsf{E}\,f(\frac{\sqrt{F(n)}}{n}X - \eta_n)$, where X is standard normal: this completes step (1).

Step 2. *Two lemmas.*

Lemma V.3.19. *Consider a couple of random variables (X, Y), where Y is standard normal. Assume $\mathsf{E}\,f(X) \leq \mathsf{E}\,f(Y)$ for all convex increasing functions f (f is Lipschitz and bounded from below). Then $\Pr(X \geq \lambda) < \mathrm{Erf}(\lambda - \frac{1}{\lambda})$ for all $\lambda > 0$ (with $\mathrm{Erf}(\mu) = \Pr(Y \geq \mu)$).*

Proof. Let $f(x) = (x - r)^+$: $f(\lambda)\Pr\big(f(X) \geq f(\lambda)\big) \leq f(X)$. So for $r < \lambda$:

$$\Pr(X \geq \lambda) \leq \frac{1}{\lambda - r}\int_r^\infty (y - r)\frac{1}{\sqrt{2\pi}}e^{-y^2/2}dy$$

$$= \frac{1}{\lambda - r}\left[\frac{1}{\sqrt{2\pi}}e^{-r^2/2} - r\mathrm{Erf}(r)\right].$$

The derivative of the right-hand member w.r.t. r equals:

$$\frac{1}{(\lambda - r)^2}\left[\frac{1}{\sqrt{2\pi}}e^{-r^2/2} - \lambda\mathrm{Erf}(r)\right].$$

So choose r such that $\lambda = e^{-r^2/2}/(\sqrt{2\pi}\,\mathrm{Erf}(r)) = F(r)$.

(There always exists a unique such r, because the right-hand member is strictly increasing from 0 ($r = -\infty$) to $+\infty$ ($r = +\infty$). This follows from the inequality $\mathrm{Erf}(r) < e^{-r^2/2}/(r\sqrt{2\pi})$ for $r > 0$, which ensures both that the derivative of the right-hand member is positive for $r > 0$, and it is obviously so for $r \leq 0$, and that the right-hand member tends to $+\infty$ with r. The zero limit at $r = -\infty$ is obvious. The inequality $r\mathrm{Erf}(r) < \frac{1}{\sqrt{2\pi}}e^{-r^2/2}$ follows in turn by expressing $\mathsf{E}(Y - r)^+ > 0$, and also implies that the chosen r is $< \lambda$.)

Substituting thus $\lambda\mathrm{Erf}(r)$ for $\frac{1}{\sqrt{2\pi}}e^{-r^2/2}$ in our upper bound yields:

$$P(X \geq \lambda) \leq \mathrm{Erf}(r).$$

There only remains to show that $r > \lambda - 1/\lambda$, i.e., by the previously checked strict monotonicity of F, that $\lambda > F(\lambda - 1/\lambda)$, or, letting $x = \lambda - 1/\lambda$ and hence ($\lambda > 0$) $\lambda = \frac{x+\sqrt{x^2+4}}{2}$, that $\frac{x+\sqrt{x^2+4}}{2} > F(x)$, or $\sqrt{2\pi}\mathrm{Erf}(x) - \frac{2e^{-x^2/2}}{x+\sqrt{x^2+4}}$ is positive. Since the limit at $+\infty$ is clearly zero, it suffices to check that the function is decreasing. Taking the derivative, this amounts to $x\sqrt{x^2+4} < x^2 + 2$, which is obvious. ■

Lemma V.3.20. *For every sequence ε_n converging to zero there exists a sequence δ_n converging to zero such that $\forall n \geq 1$:*

$$\sum_{m=n}^{\infty} \mathrm{Erf}\sqrt{m\delta_m} \leq \mathsf{exp}(-n\varepsilon_n).$$

Proof. By the bound $\mathrm{Erf}(x) \leq \frac{1}{\sqrt{2\pi x}}e^{-x^2/2}$ (e.g., Lemma V.3.19), it suffices to get $n\delta_n \geq 1/(2\pi)$ and $\sum_{m=n}^{\infty} e^{-m\delta_m/2} \leq \mathsf{exp}(-f(n))$, with $f(n) \geq n\varepsilon_n$. For the latter inequality, it suffices to have:

$$e^{-n\delta_n/2} \leq e^{-f(n)} - e^{-f(n+1)} \text{ (so } f(n) < f(n+1)\text{), i.e.,}$$

$$\frac{\delta_n}{2} \geq \frac{-1}{n}\,\mathsf{ln}\left(e^{-f(n)} - e^{-f(n+1)}\right) = \frac{f(n+1)}{n} - \frac{1}{n}\,\mathsf{ln}\left(e^{f(n+1)-f(n)} - 1\right).$$

Hence for such $\delta_n \to 0$ to exist it suffices that $\frac{f(n)}{n} \to 0$ (so also $\frac{f(n+1)}{n} \to 0$) and $\mathsf{lim\,inf}_{n\to\infty} \frac{1}{n}\,\mathsf{ln}(f(n+1) - f(n)) \geq 0$ (since $e^x - 1 \geq x$). So it suffices that $f(n+1) - f(n) \geq 1/[n(n+1)]$. Hence $f(n) = 1 - n^{-1} + \mathsf{max}_{i\leq n}\, i\varepsilon_i$ will do. ■

Step 3. *End of the proof.*

From step 1, let $f(\frac{\sqrt{F(n)}}{n}X - \eta_n) = g(X)$, so $f(E_n) = g[\frac{n}{\sqrt{F(n)}}(E_n + \eta_n)]$, and $\mathsf{E}\,g(\frac{n}{\sqrt{F(n)}}(E_n + \eta_n)) \leq \mathsf{E}\,g(X)$ for all n and all convex increasing g. Hence, by Lemma V.3.19:

$$\mathsf{Pr}\left[\frac{n}{\sqrt{F(n)}}(E_n + \eta_n) \geq \lambda\right] \leq \mathrm{Erf}\left(\lambda - \frac{1}{\lambda}\right) \quad \text{for all } \lambda > 0,$$

i.e., for $\lambda' = \frac{\sqrt{F(n)}}{n}\lambda - \eta_n$:

$$\mathsf{Pr}(E_n \geq \lambda') \leq \operatorname{Erf}\left[\frac{n}{\sqrt{F(n)}}(\lambda' + \eta_n) - \frac{\sqrt{F(n)}}{n(\lambda' + \eta_n)}\right] \text{ for all } \lambda' \geq 0.$$

For a sequence δ_n decreasing to zero, choose now η_n and F such that:

$$\frac{n}{\sqrt{F(n)}}(\lambda + \eta_n) - \frac{\sqrt{F(n)}}{n(\lambda + \eta_n)} \geq \sqrt{n\delta_n}(\lambda + 1) \text{ for all } \lambda \geq 0, \text{ i.e. for } \lambda = 0.$$

For example, take $\eta_n = \left(\frac{2}{n} + \delta_n\right)^{\frac{1}{3}}$, and F to be the convexification of n/η_n. Those satisfy all our requirements, so, for all $n \geq R_1 N_1$, we have $\mathsf{Pr}(E_n \geq \lambda) \leq \operatorname{Erf}\left[\sqrt{n\delta_n}(\lambda + 1)\right]$ for all $\lambda \geq 0$. To obtain this also for the other values of n, just increase η_n for those such as to have $\mathbf{l}_n^k(b) > C \; \forall b \in B^n, \forall n \leq R_1 N_1, \forall k \in K$; then $\mathsf{Pr}(E_n \geq 0) = 0$.

Now, $\mathsf{Pr}(N \geq n) \leq \sum_{m=n}^{\infty} \mathsf{Pr}(E_n > 0) \leq \sum_{m=n}^{\infty} \operatorname{Erf}\sqrt{m\delta_m}$, and so part (2) of the theorem follows from Lemma V.3.20.

This completes the proof of Theorem V.3.16. ∎

V.3.f. The Errors E_n^+ in the Approachability Theorem

Lemma V.3.21. *Let $\Psi = \{\psi : \mathbb{N} \times \mathbb{R}_+ \to \mathbb{R}_+ \mid \forall n, \psi(n, x)$ is non-decreasing in x and $\forall x, \lim_{n\to+\infty} \frac{\psi(n,x)}{n} = 0\}$. And let $\Psi_0 = \{\psi \in \Psi \mid \psi(0, x) = 0\}$.*

(1) *Every sequence $\psi_i \in \Psi$ is bounded from above by an additively separable one:*

$$\psi_i(n, x) \leq K_i + g(x) + f(n)$$

(i.e., $g : \mathbb{R}_+ \to \mathbb{R}_+$ is non-decreasing and $\lim_{n\to\infty} \frac{f(n)}{n} = 0$). (Hence by adding, e.g., $\sqrt{x}$ to g and $\sqrt{n}$ to f we will have $\psi_i(n, x) \leq f(n) + g(x)$ except in a bounded region.)

(2) *$\forall \psi \in \Psi_0, \exists f, h : f(nh(x)) \in \Psi_0$ and $\psi(n, x) \leq f(nh(x))$.*

Proof. (1) Let j enumerate the set of pairs (i, m), with $f_j(n) = \psi_i(n, m)$, and let $f(n) = \max\{f_j(n) \mid \forall k \leq j, \forall \ell \geq n, f_k(\ell) \leq \ell/j\}$: then $f_j(n) \leq f(n)$ for n large enough, so there exists $\varphi(i, m)$ with $\psi_i(n, m) \leq \varphi(i, m) + f(n)$. Let $g_0(m) = \max_{i\leq m} \varphi(i, m)$: $\varphi(i, m) \leq g_0(m), \forall m \geq i$, so $\varphi(i, m) \leq g_0(m) + K_i$; hence with $g(x) = \max_{m<x+1} g_0(m)$ we obtain (1).

(2) By (1), we assume that $\psi(n, x) = f(n) + g(x)$ for $n \geq 1$. Replace $f(n)$ by $\max_{i\leq n} f(i) + \ln n$, so $f(kn) \geq f(n) + \ln k$, and extend f by linear interpolation to $\mathbb{R}_+$, with $f(0) = 0$. Now $h(x) = \sup_{n\geq 1} \frac{1}{n} f^{-1}(f(n) + g(x))$ is finite ($\leq 1 + \exp g(x)$) and monotone, and $f(n) + g(x) \leq f(nh(x))$ for all x and all $n \geq 1$. This completes the proof since $\psi(0, x) = 0$. ∎

Remark V.3.16. We will be basically interested in Ψ or Ψ_0, which is a convex cone and lattice, etc. The lemma gives us convenient co-final sets to work with.

Remark V.3.17. Non-decreasing functions g from $\mathbb{R}_+$ to itself can always be bounded from above by very "nice" ones, e.g., that have an everywhere convergent power expansion with all positive coefficients. Similarly, f with $\lim_{x\to\infty}\frac{f(x)}{x}=0$ can be replaced by its concavification, and a number of further conditions can be imposed.

Corollary V.3.22. ***Main Corollary***

(1) *For every $\psi\in\Psi_0$, $(\tau,\mathbf{l})$ can be chosen in Theorem V.3.16, p. 239, such that $\forall k,\sigma,\lambda\geq 0$:*

$$P^k_{\sigma,\tau}\big[\psi(N,M_N)\geq\lambda\big]\leq e^{-\lambda}.$$

(2) *Equivalently (Lemma V.3.21, p. 248), for every pair of non-decreasing functions h and f from $\mathbb{R}_+$ to itself such that $\lim_{x\to\infty}\frac{f(x)}{x}=0$ there exists $(\tau,\mathbf{l})$ such that $\forall k,\sigma,\lambda\geq 0$:*

$$P^k_{\sigma,\tau}\big(Nh(M_N)>\lambda\big)\leq \exp -f(\lambda).$$

Proof. Assume by Lemma V.3.21 $\psi(n,x)\leq f(n)+g(x)$. By part (3) of the theorem, we can select M_n to increase as slowly to $+\infty$ as desired, in particular such that $g(M_n)\leq Af(n)$; then $K(n)=\psi(n,M_n)$ still satisfies $\frac{K(n)}{n}\to 0$. We have then to show that we can find $(\tau,\mathbf{l})$ such that $P(N\geq n)$ $(=P(K(N)\geq K(n))\leq \exp -K(n)$ $\forall n\geq 1$. This is part (2) of the theorem. ∎

Corollary V.3.23.

(1) $\forall\psi\in\Psi_0$ *there exists $(\tau,\mathbf{l})$ such that in addition the Laplace transform $\mathcal{L}^k_{\tau,\mathbf{l},\psi}(\alpha)=\sup_\sigma \mathsf{E}^k_{\sigma,\tau}\exp[\alpha\psi(N,M_N)]$ is finite.*

(2) *Given a sequence $\psi_i\in\Psi_0$, choose ψ_0 such that $\psi_i\leq\psi_0+K_i$ (cf. Lemma V.3.21, p. 248). Let ψ in Ψ_0 be such that $\psi(n,x)\geq\psi_0(n,x)+\ell(n)$ with $\ell(n)\to\infty$. For any $(\tau,\mathbf{l})$ as in Theorem V.3.16, p. 239, which further satisfies, for each k where possible, that $\forall\sigma$, $P^k_{\sigma,\tau}(N=0)=1$, $\exists L_i$ such that:*

$$\mathcal{L}^k_{\tau,\mathbf{l},\psi_i}(\alpha)\leq L_i\mathcal{L}^k_{\tau,\mathbf{l},\psi}(\alpha)\ \textit{for all}\ \alpha,i,\textit{and}\ k$$

(and the same inequality holds with $L_i=1$ for all α sufficiently large).

Proof. (1) Apply Lemma V.3.21.1, p. 248, to the sequence $i\psi\in\Psi_0$, so $i\psi\leq\psi'+K_i$ with $\psi'\in\Psi$; apply then the main corollary to ψ' to conclude that $\sup_{\sigma,k}\mathsf{E}\,e^{\frac{1}{2}\psi'(N,M_N)}<+\infty$; hence $\mathcal{L}^k(\alpha)<\infty$ since for $i\geq 2\alpha$, $\alpha\psi\leq\frac{1}{2}\psi'+\frac{1}{2}K_i$.

(2) We first show that the full statement follows from the parenthesis. It suffices to show that the inequality holds for $\alpha\leq 0$, since it also holds for α sufficiently large, and increasing L_i will make it hold everywhere. For $\alpha\leq 0$, we have $\mathcal{L}^k_{\tau,\mathbf{l},\psi_i}(\alpha)\leq 1$, and $\mathcal{L}^k_{\tau,\mathbf{l},\psi}(\alpha)\geq\inf_\sigma P^k_{\sigma,\tau}(N=0)>0$ (since $\varepsilon_1>0$ in the theorem). Hence the claim.

For the parenthesis, there is something to prove only if $\mathcal{L}^k_{\tau,\mathbf{l},\psi}(\alpha)<\infty$ everywhere (in particular, $P^k_{\sigma,\tau}(N<\infty)=1$ for all σ). Fix thus such $(k,\tau,\mathbf{l})$.

Observe that $\mathscr{L}^k_{\tau,\mathbf{l},\psi_i}(\alpha) \le e^{K_i\alpha}\mathscr{L}^k_{\tau,\mathbf{l},\psi_0}(\alpha)$ (for $\alpha \ge 0$), so it suffices to show that $\frac{1}{\alpha}[\ln \mathscr{L}^k_{\tau,\mathbf{l},\psi}(\alpha) - \ln \mathscr{L}^k_{\tau,\mathbf{l},\psi_0}(\alpha)] \to +\infty$. $(\tau, \mathbf{l})$ determines the sequence M_n; let thus $G(n) = \exp \psi_0(n, M_n)$, $H(n) = \exp \psi(n, M_n)$: we have $G(n) \ge 1$, $\frac{H(n)}{G(n)} \ge e_n = \exp(\ell_n) \to +\infty$, and we want to show that $\frac{\sup_\sigma \|H(N)\|_\alpha}{\sup_\sigma \|G(N)\|_\alpha}$ goes to $+\infty$ with α.

Observe first that we can assume there exists some σ_1 under which the distribution p_1 of N has infinite support. Otherwise $\exists n_0 : P^k_{\sigma,\tau}(N \le n_0) = 1$ $\forall\sigma$ (if $P^k_{\sigma_n,\tau}(N \ge n) > 0\ \forall n$; then $\sigma = \sum 2^{-n}\sigma_n$ would give infinite support to N), so that setting $\mathbf{l}_n = 2C$ for $n \le n_0$ would show that one can have $P^k_{\sigma,\tau}(N = 0) = 1\ \forall\sigma$, which implies that $\mathscr{L}^k_{\tau,\mathbf{l},\psi}$ is identically one for any $\psi \in \Psi_0$, so the conclusion is obvious.

It suffices to prove the convergence along any subsequence α_i with $\alpha_i \ge 2^i$ ($i \ge 2$). Let thus p_i be the distribution of N induced (under k, τ, $\mathbf{l}$) by some σ that (approximately) maximizes $\|G(N)\|_{\alpha_i}$, and let $p = \sum_{i\ge1} 2^{-i} p_i$.

p is induced by some strategy (by convexity). Also $p \ge 2^{-i} p_i$ yields $\|G\|_{L_{\alpha_i}(p)} \ge (2^{-i})^{1/\alpha_i}\, \|G\|_{L_{\alpha_i}(p_i)}$; since $(2^{-i})^{1/\alpha_i} \to 1$, it follows that it suffices to show that $\frac{\|H\|_\alpha}{\|G\|_\alpha} \to +\infty$ for the probability distribution p with infinite support on $\mathbb{N}$.

If $\|G\|_\alpha$ is bounded, the proof is completed, because $H(n) \ge G(n) \cdot e_n \ge e_n$ converges to $+\infty$, and so $\|H\|_\alpha$ converges to $+\infty$ because p has infinite support (recall $\|X\|_\alpha$ is monotone and converges to $\|X\|_\infty$), and $\|G\|_\alpha \ge 1$. Otherwise (by the same monotonicity) $\|G\|_\alpha$ converges to $+\infty$, which means that, letting, for $\lambda > 0$, $N_\lambda = \{n \mid G(n) \ge \lambda\}$ and $e_\lambda = \min\{e_n \mid n \in N_\lambda\}$, we have $p(N_\lambda) > 0$ and $e_\lambda \to +\infty$. Then:

$$\frac{\|H\|_\alpha}{\|G\|_\alpha} \ge \frac{e_\lambda \left\|G\mathbb{1}_{N_\lambda}\right\|_\alpha}{\left\|G\mathbb{1}_{N_\lambda}\right\|_\alpha [1 + \frac{1}{p(N_\lambda)}]^{1/\alpha}}.$$

Since the bracket converges to 1 as $\alpha \to +\infty$, we obtain $\liminf_{\alpha\to\infty} \frac{\|H\|_\alpha}{\|G\|_\alpha} \ge e_\lambda$, and since $e_\lambda \to \infty$ this completes the proof. ∎

Remark V.3.18. $f(\alpha) = \exp(\alpha x)$ is log-convex (has a convex logarithm). Check that an average of two log-convex functions still has the same property (reduce first to the case where the two are exponential functions, next to the verification that $\ln(1 + e^x)$ is convex). Going to the limit, conclude that a Laplace transform $\mathsf{E}\exp(\alpha X)$ is log-convex, and since the supremum of a log-convex function is log-convex, it follows that $\mathscr{L}^k_{\tau,\alpha,\psi}(\alpha)$ is log-convex.

Remark V.3.19. Part (1) of the corollary has the same force as the main corollary: fix such a $(\tau, \mathbf{l})$, and fix also k. Let $\varphi(n) = \psi(n, M_n)$, $F_\sigma(\alpha) = \mathsf{E}_\sigma \exp(\alpha\varphi(N))$, $F(\alpha) = \sup_\sigma F_\sigma(\alpha) < \infty$. Then, for $\alpha > 0$, $e^{\alpha\lambda} P_\sigma(\varphi(N) \ge \lambda) \le F_\sigma(\alpha)$, so $\sup_\sigma P_\sigma(\psi(N, M_N) \ge \lambda) \le \exp[\ln F(\alpha) - \alpha\lambda]$ for all $\alpha \ge 0$. By the convexity of the bracket (Remark V.3.18), the minimum over α of the right-hand member is easily obtained as being $\exp[-\int_{\lambda_0}^{\lambda} G(s)ds]$ for $\lambda \ge \lambda_0$, where the function $G(\lambda)$ gives the root of the derivative of the bracket w.r.t. α

(make a picture!). G could have horizontal and vertical segments, and could take the value $+\infty$, but is monotone and converges to $+\infty$. λ_0 is (any) root of $G(\lambda_0) = 0$, i.e., $\lambda_0 = \mathsf{E}_\sigma \varphi(N)$ for some strategy σ. So $H(\lambda) = \int_{\lambda_0}^{\lambda} G(s)ds$ is convex (with minimum $H(\lambda_0) = 0$) and satisfies $H(\lambda)/\lambda \to +\infty$, in particular $H(\lambda) \geq \lambda$ for $\lambda \geq \lambda_1$, hence $\sup_\sigma P_\sigma\big(\psi(N, M_N) \geq \lambda\big) \leq e^{-\lambda}$ for $\lambda \geq \lambda_1$. This bounds correctly the probability for all $N \geq n_1$, and it is trivial to remember that one can always increase $\mathbf{l}$ to $2C$ for $1 \leq n \leq n_1$ such as to give zero probability to those values of N.

Remark V.3.20. The main corollary, or (cf. Remark V.3.19) the above, imply our Gaussian bound (on E_n) proved during the proof of the theorem. Indeed, given ε_n, let $h(x) = (x+1)^4 \mathbb{1}_{x>0}$, and $f(x) = \frac{1}{2} + \frac{1}{2}(\sqrt{x}\delta(x) + 1)^2$, where $\delta(x) \to 0$ is such that $x\delta(x^4)$ is non-decreasing and $\delta(n) \geq \sqrt{\varepsilon_n}$ (thus $\delta(x) = x^{-1/4} \max_{n \leq x} n^{1/4}\sqrt{\varepsilon_n}$). Then $\forall M_n \geq 0$, $n^{1/4}(M_n + 1)\delta(n(M_n + 1)^4) \geq n^{1/4}\sqrt{\varepsilon_n}$, so $f(nh(M_n)) \geq \frac{1}{2} + \frac{1}{2}\left[\sqrt{n\varepsilon_n}(M_n + 1) + 1\right]^2$, hence $\exp\big(-f(nh(M_n))\big) \leq \operatorname{Erf}\big(\sqrt{n\varepsilon_n}(M_n + 1)\big)$ (using $\operatorname{Erf}(x) \geq \frac{2}{\sqrt{2\pi}} \frac{e^{-x^2/2}}{x+\sqrt{x^2+4}} \geq \frac{1}{\sqrt{2\pi}} \frac{e^{-x^2/2}}{x+1} \geq \frac{1}{\sqrt{2\pi}} e^{-\frac{x^2}{2} - x} \geq \exp -(\frac{1}{2}x^2 + x + 1)$; cf. proof of Lemma V.3.9). $\delta(x) \to 0$ yields $\frac{f(x)}{x} \to 0$, so let, by the main corollary, $(\tau, \mathbf{l})$ be such that $\Pr(Nh(M_N) \geq x) \leq \exp -f(x)$ for all $x > 0$ and all σ, k. Then, for $\lambda \geq M_n$, we have $\Pr(E_n > \lambda) = 0 \leq \operatorname{Erf}\sqrt{n\varepsilon_n}(\lambda + 1)$, and for $0 \leq \lambda \leq M_n$ we have $\Pr(E_n > \lambda) \leq \Pr(N \geq n) = \Pr(Nh(M_N) \geq nh(M_n)) \leq \exp -f(nh(M_n)) \leq \operatorname{Erf}(\sqrt{n\varepsilon_n}(M_n + 1)) \leq \operatorname{Erf}(\sqrt{n\varepsilon_n}(\lambda + 1))$.

(It is therefore clear such a Gaussian bound applies not only to E_n, but also to any function $h(E_n)$.)

Remark V.3.21. In typical applications, $\psi(n, M_n)$ will take the form $f(nh(M_n))$, where the random variable $Nh(M_N)$ bounds random variables like $\sum_n h(E_n)$ ($h(x) = 0$ for $x \leq 0$: recall E_n is the error at stage n), or like $\sup_n nE_n$, the maximum non-normalized error (for $h(x) = x^+$), or N itself.

Remark V.3.22. The above results are sharp; even for repeated coin tosses (a single state of nature, and both players use their optimal strategy i.i.d., i.e., "matching pennies") the above results cannot be improved, and would not be true for $f(nh(x))$ with f the identity, and thus for $\psi(N, M_N) = N$ itself.

Indeed, denote by $\overline{g}_n$ the frequency of successes, and $T_\eta = |\{n \mid \overline{g}_n > \eta\}|$ for $1/2 < \eta < 1$ (i.e., we do not even ask that $\eta_n \to \frac{1}{2}$, and T_η is much smaller that N). Even in this most favorable case it is not true that T_η has a finite Laplace transform; the region where it is finite shrinks to zero as $\eta \to \frac{1}{2}$, so one cannot relax the requirement that $\frac{f(x)}{x} \to 0$. To see this, apply first Theorem 2, p. 399, in Feller (1966), and next Lemma 1, p. 398 (Feller, 1966), to the random walk $n(\overline{g}_n - \eta)$, to conclude, letting $n \to \infty$, that $\Pr(T_\eta = k) = q_\infty p_k$; hence $\mathsf{E}\, s^{T_\eta} = q_\infty p(s)$ will be finite if $p(s)$ is so; i.e., by Formulae 7.13 and 7.2 (ibid.), if $\tau(s) < 1$ with $\tau(s) = \sum_n s^n P(\overline{g}_1 \leq \eta, \overline{g}_2 \leq \eta, \ldots, \overline{g}_{n-1} \leq \eta, \overline{g}_n > \eta)$. The probability in the right-hand member is $\geq P(\overline{g}_k \leq \eta\ \forall k)$. $P(\overline{g}_n > \eta \mid \overline{g}_{n-1} \leq \eta) \geq \frac{1}{2} P(T_\eta = 0)$ $P(\overline{g}_{n-1}$ takes its largest possible value $\leq \eta)$.

Evaluating this last probability by Stirling's formula we get $1 \geq \left[2\sqrt{2\pi\eta(1-\eta)}\right]^{-1} P(T_\eta = 0)\sum_n \frac{1}{\sqrt{n}}\left(\frac{s}{2\eta^\eta(1-\eta)^{1-\eta}}\right)^n$, so this convergence requires that $s \leq 2\eta^\eta(1-\eta)^{1-\eta}$, which converges to 1 as $\eta \to \frac{1}{2}$. The result becomes even stronger: let $S_\eta = \min\{n \geq 1 \mid \overline{g}_n \leq \eta\}$; the same conclusions apply even to S_η. Indeed, using Formula 7.15, p. 397 (Feller, 1966), we obtain $\Pr(T_\eta = k) = q_\infty \Pr(S_\eta > k)$, hence $q_\infty E \exp(\alpha S_\eta) = \Pr(T_\eta = 0) + (e^\alpha - 1)\,\mathsf{E}\exp(\alpha T_\eta) = +\infty$ for $\alpha \geq \varphi(\eta) = \ln(2\eta^\eta(1-\eta)^{1-\eta})$.

Let us show that, if $\eta_n \to \frac{1}{2}$, the above implies that, even in our "typical applications" of the previous remark, the Laplace transform will be infinite for all $\alpha > 0$ if we let $f(x) = x$. There is no loss in assuming η_n to be decreasing. Consider first the random variable N, or just T, the total number of errors. Given $\alpha > 0$, let $n_0 = \min\{n \mid \varphi(\eta_n) \leq \alpha\}$.

To prove that $\mathsf{E}\exp(\alpha T) = \infty$, it suffices to show that $\mathsf{E}[\exp \alpha T \mid \overline{g}_{n_0} = 1] = \infty$, since the condition has positive probability. But the conditional distribution of T, given $\overline{g}_{n_0} = 1$, is clearly (stochastically) larger than $S_{\eta_{n_0}}$, hence the result. Consider now the random variable $X = \sum_n h(E_n)$, with $E_n = (\overline{g}_n - \eta_n)^+$ and $h\colon [0, \frac{1}{2}[\to \mathbb{R}_+$ non-decreasing and not identically zero. Let $x_0 < \frac{1}{2}$ be such that $h(x_0) > 0$, and choose n_0 large such that $\eta_{n_0} < \frac{1}{2} - x_0$. Then $\sum_n h(E_n) \geq h(x_0)|\{n \geq n_0 \mid \overline{g}_n \geq x_0 + \eta_{n_0} + \frac{1}{2}\}|$. Hence, by the same conditional bound as above, $\mathsf{E}\exp(\alpha X) = +\infty$ for $\alpha \geq \varphi(x_0 + \eta_{n_0} + \frac{1}{2})$, i.e., letting $n_0 \to \infty$, for $\alpha > \varphi(x_0 + \frac{1}{2})$. Thus here also the Laplace transform of X is never finite for $\alpha \geq \ln(2)$ and is infinite for all $\alpha > 0$ if $x > 0$ implies $h(x) > 0$.

Consider finally $Y = \sup_n n(\overline{g}_n - \eta_n)^+$. For $1 > \eta > \eta_{n_0}$, we have, conditional on $\overline{g}_{n_0} = 1$, $Y \geq (\eta - \eta_{n_0})S_\eta$, hence $\mathsf{E}\exp(\alpha Y) = \infty$ if $\mathsf{E}\exp[\alpha(\eta - \eta_{n_0})S_\eta] = \infty$, hence if $\alpha(\eta - \eta_{n_0}) \geq f(\eta)$. That is, for $\eta_{n_0} = \frac{1}{2} + \frac{1}{4}\varepsilon < \frac{3}{4}$ and $\eta = 2\eta_{n_0} - \frac{1}{2}$, if $\alpha \geq \frac{2}{\varepsilon}\left[(1+\varepsilon)\ln(1+\varepsilon) + (1-\varepsilon)\ln(1-\varepsilon)\right]$, hence for all $\alpha > 0$ by letting $n_0 \to \infty$ and thus $\varepsilon \to 0$.

Remark V.3.23. The main corollary is essentially equivalent to the theorem: it obviously implies part (2) (with $h(x) = \mathbb{1}_{x>0}$), but also (with any h converging to $+\infty$) part (3), as soon as in at least one state of nature some randomness is present like in "matching pennies."

Indeed, it can be written $P(N \geq n) \leq \exp - f(nh(M_n))$, but if the "matching pennies" aspect is present, we obtain a lower bound as in Remark V.3.22: for $n \geq n_0$, $P(N \geq n) \geq \Pr(\overline{g}_n$ is the first value exceeding $\eta_{n_0}) \sim \frac{K(\eta_{n_0})}{\sqrt{n}} \exp(-n\delta(\eta_{n_0}))$, where η_n decreases to $\frac{1}{2}$, so $\delta(\eta_n) = \ln[2\eta_n^{\eta_n}(1-\eta_n)^{1-\eta_n}]$ decreases to zero. Hence for $n \geq n_0'$ we have $f(nh(M_n)) \leq 2n\delta(\eta_{n_0})$, so $\limsup \frac{1}{n} f(nh(M_n)) \leq 2\delta(\eta_{n_0})$, hence $\frac{1}{n} f(nh(M_n)) \to 0$. In particular, for $n \geq n_0$, $h(M_n) \leq \frac{1}{n} f^{-1}(n)$. Since, given an arbitrary sequence ρ_n converging to $+\infty$, $h(\rho_n)$ converges to $+\infty$, and having bounded h from below by a strictly (for $x \geq x_0$) monotone one converging to $+\infty$, we can then choose f such that $\frac{1}{n} f^{-1}(n) \leq h(\rho_n)$, and so conclude that $M_n \leq \rho_n$ for n sufficiently large. To obtain the inequality also for $n \leq n_0$ it suffices to set $\mathbf{l}_n = 2C$ for $n \leq n_0$.

Remark V.3.24. The same proof as in Corollary V.3.23, p. 249, yields even an improved result: let $\overline{\psi}(n,x) = 2[\psi(n,x) + \ell_n]$. The proof shows that there exists a single strategy σ such that $\mathsf{E}_{\sigma,\tau} \exp[2^i \overline{\psi}(N, M_N)] \geq 2^{-i} \mathscr{L}^k_{\tau,\mathbf{l},\overline{\psi}}(2^i) \geq 2^{-i} \mathscr{L}^k_{\tau,\mathbf{l},\psi+\ell}(\alpha)$ for $2^i \leq \alpha \leq 2^{i+1}$, so $\mathsf{E}_{\sigma,\tau} \exp[\alpha \overline{\psi}(N, M_N)] \geq \frac{1}{\alpha} \mathscr{L}^k_{\tau,\mathbf{l},\psi+\ell}(\alpha)$ ($\alpha \geq 4$). But it also shows that $\frac{1}{\alpha}[\ln \mathscr{L}^k_{\tau,\mathbf{l},\psi+\ell}(\alpha) - \ln \mathscr{L}^k_{\tau,\mathbf{l},\psi}(\alpha)] \to +\infty$, and since $\frac{1}{\alpha} \ln \alpha \to 0$, it follows that, for $\alpha \geq \alpha_0$, $\frac{1}{\alpha} \mathscr{L}^k_{\tau,\mathbf{l},\psi+\ell}(\alpha) \geq \mathscr{L}^k_{\tau,\mathbf{l},\psi}(\alpha)$. Using again the fact that $\mathsf{E}_{\sigma,\tau} \exp[\alpha \overline{\psi}(N, M_N)]$ is bounded away from zero, we obtain that $\mathscr{L}^k_{\tau,\mathbf{l},\psi}(\alpha) \leq L\, \mathsf{E}^k_{\sigma,\tau} \exp[\alpha \overline{\psi}(N, M_N)]$. And therefore, for all i, $\mathscr{L}^k_{\tau,\mathbf{l},\psi_i}(\alpha) \leq L_i\, \mathsf{E}^k_{\sigma,\tau} \exp[\alpha \overline{\psi}(N, M_N)]$: now the right-hand member is a true Laplace transform, for a fixed distribution induced by a single strategy σ.

Remark V.3.25. The fact that the expectation of a random variable X under $\mathsf{E}^k_{\sigma,\tau}$ is uniformly bounded over σ does not a priori imply that the dominated convergence theorem for variables $\leq X$ holds uniformly in σ. Still it is this type of result that we need, e.g., to conclude that $\sup_\sigma \|\sup_{m \geq n} m E^+_m\|_{L_p(\sigma)}$ (cf. Remark V.3.20, p. 251) converges to zero when $n \to \infty$, since all our concepts in this book are based on errors converging to zero uniformly over σ.

However, in the present case this implication holds: if $X_i(e_1, e_2, \dots)$ converges pointwise to zero, then for all n, since there are only finitely many histories of length n, there are only finitely many possible sequences $(e_1, e_2, \dots, e_n, 0, 0, 0, \dots)$, hence X_i converges to zero uniformly on them, so that, for i sufficiently large, $\{X_i \geq \varepsilon\}$ is included in $\{N \geq n\}$. Our results (main corollary, or Remark V.3.19, p. 250) imply that $\sup_\sigma \int_{\{N \geq n\}} X$ converges to zero (say, for $X \in \Psi$, and $(\tau, \mathbf{l})$ as in the main corollary).

Further, for a given pointwise convergent sequence X_i, our results yield an easy criterion for the existence of such an X and $(\tau, \mathbf{l})$ (we assume X_i are just functions of the errors $e_1, \dots, e_n, \dots$): let $Y = \sup_i X_i$ (Y is finite since X_i is convergent), and $\varphi(n,m) = \max\{Y(e_1, \dots, e_n, 0, 0, 0, \dots) \mid e_i \leq m\ \forall i\}$: we need $\frac{1}{n} \ln \varphi(n,m) \to 0$ for all m.

Now we turn to another estimate, relative to the norm-summability of the errors in L_p (cf. Remark V.3.28 below).

Lemma V.3.24.

(1) *Let $f_i \colon \mathbb{R}_+ \to \mathbb{R}$ be such that $f_i(x)/x$ is bounded and converges to zero at ∞. Then there exists $f \colon \mathbb{R}_+ \to \mathbb{R}$ concave, Lipschitz, with $f(0) = 0 = \lim_{x\to\infty} f(x)/x$ such that, for some function $r \colon \mathbb{R}_+ \to \mathbb{R}$ satisfying $r(x) \geq 1$ and $\lim_{x\to\infty} r(x) = +\infty$, one has $f(\prod_{i=1}^n x_i) \geq r(\sum_i^n x_i) \prod_{i=1}^n f_i(x_i)$.*

(2) *Let also $\ell \colon \mathbb{R}_+ \to \mathbb{R}$ be locally bounded, with $\lim_{x\to\infty} \ell(x)/x = 0$ and $\lim_{x\to 0} \ell(x) = -\infty$. Fix $\underline{r} \geq 1$ and assume $f_1(x) \geq 0$.*

Then the function f can moreover satisfy $f(x_1 x_2) \geq f_1(x_1)[\tilde{r}(x_1 + x_2) + \ell(x_2)]$ with $\lim_{x\to+\infty} \tilde{r}(x) = +\infty$ and $\tilde{r}(x) \geq \underline{r}$.

Proof. Part (1) Let $g = \mathsf{Cav}(\max_i |f_i|)$: g is Lipschitz, with $g(0) = 0 = \lim_{x\to\infty} g(x)/x$, and we can assume $f_i = g$. Let $\overline{r}(x) = \sqrt{x/g(x)}$, $\overline{g}(x) = \overline{r}(x)g(x)$: $\overline{g}$ is like g, and $\overline{r}$ is monotone, strictly positive, and converges to $+\infty$. Let $f_0(u) = \sup_{\prod x_i = u} \prod_{i=1}^n \overline{g}(x_i)$: if L is the Lipschitz constant of $\overline{g}$, we have $\frac{1}{u} f_0(u) = \sup \prod_{i=1}^n \frac{\overline{g}(x_i)}{x_i} \le L^n$, and if $u_k = \prod_{i=1}^n x_k^i \to \infty$, then at least one coordinate, say, x_k^1, converges to ∞ (along a subsequence), so $\frac{1}{u_k} f_0(u_k) \le \frac{\overline{g}(x_k^1)}{x_k^1} L^{n-1}$ converges to zero. So $\frac{1}{u} f_0(u)$ is bounded and converges to zero, and $f_0(\prod_i x_i) \ge \prod_{i=1}^n \overline{r}(x_i) \prod_{i=1}^n g(x_i)$. Thus $f = (\frac{1}{\overline{r}(0)})^n \mathsf{Cav}\, f_0$ satisfies our requirements, with $r(s) = (\frac{1}{\overline{r}(0)})^n \min_{\sum x_i = s} \prod \overline{r}(x_i)$.

Part (2) Replace ℓ by $\mathsf{Cav}(\ell)$, and add $\sqrt{x}$ to be sure that $\ell(x) \to +\infty$. Let $f_2(\cdot) = \mathsf{Cav}([\underline{r} + \ell(\cdot)]^+)$; $f(x_1 x_2) \ge \overline{r}(x_1 + x_2) f_1(x_1) f_2(x_2)$ with $\overline{r}(x) \ge 1$ converging to ∞. Let $\tilde{r}(u) = \min_{x \le u}(\overline{r}(u) f_2(x) - \ell(x))$: it suffices to show that $\tilde{r}(x) \ge \underline{r}$ and converges to $+\infty$ as x goes to $+\infty$. The first point is immediate, so there remains to show that $\overline{r}(u_i) f_2(x_i) - \ell(x_i) \le K$ for $0 \le x_i \le u_i$ implies u_i is bounded. Observe first that $x_i \ge \underline{x} > 0$ (with $\ell(\underline{x}) = -K$). If $x_i \ge \ell^{-1}(0)$, then $K \ge \overline{r}(u_i) f_2(x_i) - \ell(x_i) \ge [\overline{r}(u_i) - 1]\ell(x_i) + \overline{r}(u_i)$ implies $\overline{r}(u_i) \le K$. And if $-K \le \ell(x_i) \le 0$, then $\overline{r}(u_i) \le K / f_2(\underline{x})$. ■

Corollary V.3.25. *Let $h\colon \mathbb{R}_+ \to \mathbb{R}_+$ be monotone, with $h(0) = 0$. Assume $p_n/n \to 0$, $p_n \ge 0$. Let also, by the above Lemma (2), $f\colon \mathbb{R}_+ \to \mathbb{R}_+$ be concave, Lipschitz, with $f(0) = 0 = \lim_{x\to\infty} f(x)/x$, and such that $f(nx) > p_n[\ln(x) + r_n]$ for some sequence $r_n \ge \underline{r}$ converging to $+\infty$. For any such f, and for $(\tau, \mathbf{l})$ satisfying the main corollary with (f, h), one has $\sup_{\sigma,k} \|h(E_n)\|_{p_n} \le e^{-r_n}$; hence the sequence converges to zero, and its maximum can be made arbitrarily small. In particular, $\sum_n \sup_{\sigma,k} \|h(E_n)\|_{p_n}^{\ln(n)} < +\infty$.*

Proof. For such $(\tau, \mathbf{l})$ and all σ, k, we have:

$$\begin{aligned}\|h(E_n)\|_{p_n} &\le h(M_n)[\Pr(E_n > 0)]^{1/p_n} \le h(M_n)[\Pr(N \ge n)]^{1/p_n} \\ &\le h(M_n)\exp[-f(nh(M_n))/p_n]\end{aligned}$$

(the last inequality because f is increasing (if p_n is identically zero, the conclusion is obvious), and noting that, if $h(M_n) = 0$, there is nothing to prove). So $\|h(E_n)\|_{p_n} \le e^{-r_n}$. The "in particular" clause is obvious. ■

Remark V.3.26. A direct proof that some $(\tau, \mathbf{l})$ guarantees $\sup_{\sigma,k} \|h(E_n)\|_{p_n} \to 0$ is also immediate (i.e., without the lemma) from the theorem. The only additional point here is that it follows already from the main corollary alone, and just by the choice of an appropriate f.

Remark V.3.27. Since one can always assume $h(x) \ge 1$ for $x > 0$, the apparently more general statement with $\left[\mathsf{E}(h(E_n))^{q_n}\right]^{1/p_n}$ where $q_n/n \to 0$ and $p_n/n \to 0$ is equivalent to the present one: indeed, if $h(x) \ne 0 \Longrightarrow h(x) \ge 1$, the terms increase only if q_n is increased, so we can assume $q_n \ge p_n$; next, if a sequence converges to zero (or is summable), all but finitely many terms are increased if p_n is increased, so $q_n = p_n$.

Remark V.3.28. In particular, for all $p > 0$, $q > 0$, $(\sup_{\sigma,k} \|h(E_n)\|_p)_{n=1}^{\infty} \in \ell_q$. (Take $q_n = p$, $p_n = \frac{p}{q}\ln(n)$ in Remark V.3.27; thus it follows from the summability in Corollary V.3.25 with $\frac{p_n}{\ln(n)} \to +\infty$.)

Remark V.3.29. Even for matching pennies (cf. Remark V.3.22), with $h\colon [0, \frac{1}{2}[\to \mathbb{R}_+$ not identically zero, one needs $p_n/n \to 0$: indeed, for fixed δ ($\frac{1}{2} < \delta < 1$), the probability in n fair coin tosses of obtaining the smallest possible frequency $\geq \delta$ is, by Stirling's formula (cf. Remark V.3.22 above), $\frac{K(\delta)}{\sqrt{n}} e^{-n\varphi(\delta)}$, with $K(\delta) = [2\pi\delta(1-\delta)]^{-1/2} > 0$ and $\varphi(\delta) = \ln[2\delta^{\delta}(1-\delta)^{1-\delta}] > 0$. Hence if $h(x_0) > 0$, $x_0 < \frac{1}{2}$ we have, for $\eta_{n_0} < \frac{1}{2} - x_0$ and letting $\delta\frac{1}{2} + x_0 + \eta_{n_0}$, that, for all $n \geq n_0$, $\mathsf{E}[h(E_n)]^{p_n} \geq [h(x_0)]^{p_n} \frac{K(\delta)}{\sqrt{n}} e^{-n\varphi(\delta)}$, so for $p_{n_i} \geq \varepsilon n_i$, $\|h(E_n)\|_{p_{n_i}} \geq h(x_0)(\frac{K(\delta)}{\sqrt{n_i}})^{1/\varepsilon n_i} \exp \frac{-\varphi(\delta)}{\varepsilon}$ for all i sufficiently large, and the limit $h(x_0) \exp \frac{-\varphi(\delta)}{\varepsilon}$ of the lower bound is > 0.

Remark V.3.30. For h such that $h(x) \neq 0 \Longrightarrow h(x) \geq 1$ one obtains again part (2) of the theorem: say, $\underline{r} = 1$; then $\|h(E_n)\|_{p_n} \leq e^{-1}$ implies that $\Pr(E_n > 0) \leq e^{-p_n}$, and so Lemma V.3.20, p. 247, yields the conclusion.

Corollary V.3.26. *One can further require in the theorem that, for all n, σ, and k:*

$$\mathsf{E}^k_{\sigma,\tau}(E_n) \leq 0.$$

Proof. Since (Corollary V.3.25), $\mathsf{E}^k_{\sigma,\tau}(E_n^+) \leq \delta_n$ where δ_n decreases to zero, it suffices to add δ_n to the function $\mathbf{l}_n$ (and again replace $\mathbf{l}_n$ by $2C$ if $\mathbf{l}_n^k(b) > 2C$ for some $b \in B^n$ and $k \in K$). ■

Remark V.3.31. In the present setup, bounding the error E_n^+ is the only game in town: the other side of the coin, the speed of convergence of φ_n to φ, seems much more difficult to access with the present methods of proof; it would probably require a direct proof, like in Section II.4, p. 118, and is even hard to formulate in the present framework, since when φ is not continuous the convergence is not uniform, and φ may even take at some points the value $-\infty$.

One can study this other aspect only under some constraints on the errors E_n^+, and so the present subsection investigating what can be achieved in this respect seems a necessary first step. Another clear prerequisite, even for the case of linear functions φ, is to have some improvements on the results of Section V.5.b, p. 296, and to know exactly what speed of convergence of $v_n(p)$ to $v_\infty(p)$ can be achieved.

Remark V.3.32. But when the function u is continuous, as happens, for instance, when the distribution of player II's signals is independent of the state of nature, one sees at least how to formulate precisely this other aspect.

Observe first that each minimal φ is then continuous, so (e.g., by Dini's theorem) the convergence of $\varphi_n(p)$ to $\varphi(p)$ is uniform: $\varphi_n(p) \le \varphi(p) + \delta_n$, where the corresponding speed of convergence δ_n is a positive sequence decreasing to zero.

In this framework, it may be more natural to lower the function $\mathbf{l}$ to a map $\hat{\mathbf{l}}$ from $\bigcup_n B^n$ to (the efficient frontier of) $\mathbf{L}_\varphi = \{x \in \mathbb{R}^K \mid \langle p, x\rangle \le \varphi(p)\ \forall p \in \Delta(K)\}$, and let $\mathbf{l}_n = \hat{\mathbf{l}}_n + \delta_n$. The problem becomes then the optimal tradeoff between the speed of convergence δ_n and the size of the estimation errors E_n^+. (From Proposition V.5.1, p. 295, below, it is clear that in general we will not be able to get δ_n better than $n^{-1/3}$; in a "matching pennies"-like case this yields $\mathsf{Pr}(E_n > 0) \sim \exp(-2n^{1/3})$; hence sharp bounds (of the same order) can still be obtained (by summing) for $\mathsf{Pr}(N \ge n)$.)

Further, observe that this error term δ_n can be selected independently of φ: the minimal φ are all Lipschitz with constant C, and $\le C$ in absolute value. Hence select, by compactness, for each $\varepsilon = 3^{-\ell}$, a finite subset $\varphi_1, \ldots, \varphi_{k_\varepsilon}$ such that every minimal φ has thus one of those φ_i's with $\varphi + 3^{-\ell} \le \varphi_i \le \varphi + 3.3^{-\ell}$; hence if such a φ is selected for each ℓ, they will indeed form a sequence decreasing to φ. And since for each ℓ, we have a finite number of them, we can take, in the proof of the theorem, for N_ℓ the maximum of the corresponding quantities (and $C_\ell = 2C$), and so all quantities in the proof of the theorem, and hence the corresponding final estimates, will be independent of the particular φ: all φ will be approximated with the same speed of convergence δ_n and the same bounds on errors E_n^+.

(If one wants to make sure to obtain the same monotonicity (part (1) in the theorem), just replace "3" by "4" in the definition of ε and φ_i above, and use the slack to make sure, by increasing N_ℓ if necessary (apply the present theorem to approximating φ_i), that $\mathsf{max}_{b \in B^{N_\ell}} \langle \mathbf{l}(b), p\rangle$ is between φ_i and $\varphi_i - 4^{-\ell}$.)

Remark V.3.33. Another case, which could be investigated separately, and which would lead to weakening the above bounds, is that where the payoffs are random (and selected by the same lottery as the one selecting the signals) and have finite first (or second) moments. In such a case, one could presumably use a similar method as in the present theorem: use the present theorem for the game where the random payoffs have been replaced by their conditional expectation given the state of nature, the pair of moves, and the pair of signals (the present theorem applies even with random payoffs as long as they have bounded support). Then imagine, as in the present proof, that one is only interested in convex functions of the errors, and make a dilatation (or a "spread," i.e., a replacement of a value x in the support by a probability measure with mean x) of each of the conditional distributions of payoffs (given state, actions, and signals) to some common distribution (still with a zero mean): then the differences between the actual payoffs and the fictitious payoffs used in the application of the theorem are an i.i.d. sequence X_n with zero expectation. Hence, this reduces the problem to that of such a sequence X_n: finding bounds on the errors $\overline{X}_n - \eta_n$, for an appropriate η_n, using then a similar technique as in Lemma V.3.19, p. 246, to dispense with the restriction to convex functions by increasing η_n, so that one gets bounds for the differences between the original actual payoffs and the fictitious payoff, and finally adding η_n to $\mathbf{l}_n$.

V.3.g. Implications of the Approachability Theorem

Corollary V.3.27. *Given $(\tau, \mathbf{l})$, define for every strategy σ of player* I, $N_\sigma (= N_{\sigma,\tau,\mathbf{l}})$ *on* II*-histories by:*

$$N_\sigma(\zeta) = \sup\{n \mid \exists k\colon\ \mathsf{E}^k_{\sigma,\tau}(\overline{g}_n \mid \mathscr{H}^{\mathrm{II}}_n)(\zeta) \geq \mathbf{l}^k(b_1, \ldots, b_n)\}.$$

(Recall $\mathscr{H}^{\mathrm{II}}_n$ is the σ-field spanned by $\prod_1^n(B \times T)$).

(1) *For $n > N_\sigma$, $\mathsf{E}_{\sigma,\tau}(\overline{g}_n \mid \mathscr{H}^{\mathrm{II}}_n) \leq \varphi_n(p_n)$.*
(2) *In Theorem V.3.16, p. 239 (and in its corollaries), one can further require of $(\tau, \mathbf{l})$ that:*

$$\sup_{\sigma,k} P^k_{\sigma,\tau}(N_\sigma \geq n) \leq \exp(-n\varepsilon_n)\ \forall n \geq 0.$$

(3) *As a consequence, one has then, for every weak*($\sigma(L_\infty, L_1)$)–limit point $\overline{g}_\infty$ of $\overline{g}_n$, and every σ:*

$$\mathsf{E}_{\sigma,\tau}(\overline{g}_\infty \mid \mathscr{H}^{\mathrm{II}}_\infty) \leq \limsup_{n\to\infty} \mathsf{E}_{\sigma,\tau}(\overline{g}_n \mid \mathscr{H}^{\mathrm{II}}_n) \leq \varphi(p_\infty).$$

Proof.

(1) follows by averaging over k (part (1) of Theorem V.3.16, p. 239), recalling that $p_n(k) = P(k \mid \mathscr{H}^{\mathrm{II}}_n)$, and that $\{\mathsf{E}^k(\overline{g}^k_n \mid \mathscr{H}^{\mathrm{II}}_n)(\zeta) < \mathbf{l}^k_n(b_1, \ldots, b_n)\ \forall k \in K\}$ is $\mathscr{H}^{\mathrm{II}}_n$-measurable and contains $\{N_\sigma < n\}$.
(2) From $P^k_{\sigma,\tau}(E_n > 0) \leq e^{-f(n)}$ and $E_n \leq M_n$ we obtain:

$$P^k_{\sigma,\tau}[\mathsf{E}(E_n^+ \mid \mathscr{H}^{\mathrm{II}}_n) \geq \lambda_n] \leq \frac{1}{\lambda_n} M_n e^{-f(n)} \leq e^{-n\delta_n},$$

where $\delta_n \geq \frac{f(n)}{n} + \frac{1}{n}\ln\lambda_n - \frac{1}{n}\ln M_n$ is an arbitrary sequence converging to zero provided one chooses (part (3) of the theorem) $\ln M_n \leq n\delta_n$, (part (2)) $f(n) = 3n\delta_n$, and $\ln\lambda_n \geq -n\delta_n$, λ_n decreasing to zero. (All this is completely independent of σ and k.) Hence by adding now λ_n to $\mathbf{l}_n$ one obtains:

$$\mathsf{Pr}^k_{\sigma,\tau}(\mathsf{E}(\overline{g}_n \mid \mathscr{H}^{\mathrm{II}}_n) \geq \mathbf{l}^k_n) \leq e^{-n\delta_n},$$

and so $\mathsf{Pr}^k_{\sigma,\tau}(N_\sigma \geq n) \leq \sum_n^\infty e^{-\ell\delta_\ell}$: use of the proof of Lemma V.3.20, p. 247, completes the proof.
(3) Part (1) yields that $\mathsf{E}(\overline{g}_n \mid \mathscr{H}^{\mathrm{II}}_n) \leq \varphi_{n_0}(p_n)$ for $n \geq n_0 \vee N_\sigma$ (part (1) of Theorem V.3.16), and so (by the martingale convergence theorem for p_n and continuity of φ_{n_0}) $X = \limsup_{n\to\infty} \mathsf{E}(\overline{g}_n \mid \mathscr{H}^{\mathrm{II}}_n) \leq \varphi_{n_0}(p_\infty)$,

hence the second inequality when $n_0 \to +\infty$. And, by Fatou's lemma:

$$\mathsf{E}(X \mid \mathscr{H}^{\mathrm{II}}_{n_0}) \geq \limsup_{n\to\infty} \mathsf{E}(\overline{g}_n \mid \mathscr{H}^{\mathrm{II}}_{n_0}) \geq \mathsf{E}(\overline{g}_\infty \mid \mathscr{H}^{\mathrm{II}}_{n_0})$$

(finiteness of $\mathscr{H}^{\mathrm{II}}_{n_0}$), and so letting $n_0 \to \infty$ yields the first inequality. ■

There is obviously also a converse to Theorem V.3.16, p. 239, namely:

Definition V.3.34. For any strategy τ of player II, and any Banach limit $\mathscr{L}$ (I.2, Ex. 13, p. 28), let $h_{\tau,\mathscr{L},\sigma}(p) = \mathscr{L}(\overline{\gamma}_n(p,\sigma,\tau))$, and $\varphi_{\tau,\mathscr{L}}(p) = \sup_{\sigma\in[\mathrm{NR}(p)]^\infty} h_{\tau,\mathscr{L},\sigma}(p)$ (where $\sigma \in [\mathrm{NR}(p)]^\infty$ means σ is the i.i.d. repetition of some element of $\mathrm{NR}(p)$).

Proposition V.3.28.

(1) *$h_{\tau,\mathscr{L},\sigma}$ is linear, and $\varphi_{\tau,\mathscr{L}}$ is convex and $\geq u$.*
(2) *If τ corresponds by Theorem V.3.16 to some convex $\varphi \geq u$, $\varphi_{\tau,\mathscr{L}} \leq \varphi$ for every $\mathscr{L}$; more precisely: $\limsup_{n\to\infty} \sup_{\sigma\in\mathrm{NR}^n(p)} \overline{\gamma}_n(p,\sigma,\tau) \leq \varphi(p)$ (where $\mathrm{NR}^n(p)$ is the set of non-revealing strategies of player I in $\Gamma_n(p)$).*

Proof.

(1) The linearity of h is obvious. For each face F of $\Delta(K)$, let $\sum_F = [\mathrm{NR}(p)]^\infty$ for p interior in F, and for $\sigma \in \sum_F$, let $\underline{h}_{\tau,\mathscr{L},\sigma,F}(p) = h_{\tau,\mathscr{L},\sigma}(p)$ for $p \in F$, $\underline{h}_{\tau,\mathscr{L},\sigma,F}(p) = -\infty$ for $p \notin F$. Then $\underline{h}$ is convex, and $\varphi_{\tau,\mathscr{L}} = \sup_{\sigma,F} \underline{h}_{\tau,\mathscr{L},\sigma,F}$ is thus also convex. Finally $\varphi_{\tau,\mathscr{L}}(p) \geq u(p)$ is obvious, taking σ optimal in $D(p)$.
(2) The better inequality follows directly from part (2) of Corollary V.3.27, p. 257, since $p_n = p$ for $\sigma \in \mathrm{NR}^n(p)$. ■

In the particular case of linear functions, our results yield the following.

Definition V.3.35. Let $\overline{Z} = \{z \in \mathbb{R}^K \mid \exists\tau\colon \forall\sigma,\ \forall k, \limsup_{n\to\infty} \overline{\gamma}^k_n(\sigma,\tau) \leq z^k\}$ and $\underline{Z} = \{z \in \mathbb{R}^K \mid \exists\tau\colon \forall\sigma\exists\mathscr{L}\colon \forall k\ \mathscr{L}(\overline{\gamma}^k_n(\sigma,\tau)) \leq z^k\}$.

Remark V.3.36. The existence of $\mathscr{L}$ just means that the convex hull of the limit points intersects $z - \mathbb{R}^K_+$.

Corollary V.3.29.

(1) $\overline{Z} = \underline{Z} = Z = \{z \in \mathbb{R}^K \mid \langle p, z\rangle \geq u(p)\ \forall p \in \Delta(K)\}$.
In particular the set is closed, convex, compactly generated (by $Z \cap [-C, C]^K$), and has $v_\infty(p) = \mathrm{Cav}\, u(p)$ as support function.
*Z is therefore called the set of **approachable vectors**.*
(2) *The strategies $(\tau, \mathbf{l})$ of Theorem V.3.16, p. 239, corresponding to $z \in Z$ can be taken of the form $\mathbf{l}_n = z + \varepsilon_n$, where the sequence $\varepsilon_n \in \mathbb{R}_+$ decreasing to zero is independent of $z \in Z$.*

Remark V.3.37. In a game with vector payoffs, as in Section II.4, p. 118, the signals are the moves, and players use a single strategy, independent of the coordinate. In our context, this is equivalent to saying that player I uses a non-revealing strategy. So our results (including Remark V.3.32, p. 255) include those of Section II.4, p. 118 (at least for convex sets C satisfying $C - D = C$, where D is the positive orthant for some ordering on $\mathbb{R}^n$, i.e., D is a closed convex cone with non-empty interior), except of course for the explicit $\sqrt{n}$ rate of convergence.

In general, however, the result is easier to formulate, as done here, in terms of approaching convex functions than in terms of approaching convex sets, since when the convex function is discontinuous there is no clear corresponding convex set.

Remark V.3.38. A caricatural example of later applications (chiefly to correlated equilibria in non-zero-sum games) is the following. Imagine player I is not initially informed about the true state of nature, but receives some private information about it. Imagine also the signals are the moves. Then player I's initial information is characterized by some $p \in \Delta(K)$, while player II's is by some probability distribution μ over $\Delta(K)$, and, in the game, μ is first used to select p, I is told of p, then p is used to select $k \in K$, no player being informed. To model this as in this chapter, we would need to introduce each p as a different state of nature, with the corresponding average game, and then compute the u-function and concavify it over this infinite dimensional simplex.

But by Theorem V.3.16, p. 239 (and Proposition V.3.28, p. 258), the best player II can do is to select some convex function φ on $\Delta(K)$ with φ greater than or equal to the usual u-function, and guarantee that player I will not get more than $\varphi(p)$ whatever his type p is. Thus the optimal φ (and hence the optimal strategy) will be the one minimizing $\int_{\Delta(K)} \varphi(p)\mu(dp)$ over all convex $\varphi \geq u$. (See also Remark V.3.48, p. 268.)

V.3.h. A Continuum of Types

We extend here (by Theorem V.3.35, p. 266) Theorem V.3.16, p. 239, to the case of a continuum of types of player I or, equivalently, as in next chapter, to the case where for each of his types there are several different payoff matrices, and where player II wants to guarantee some vector payoff in those.

Assume a repeated game with incomplete information Γ described as follows. Player II has no initial private information. Nature first chooses $i \in I$ (I finite), which determines the pure strategy set S_i of player I, and sets Ω_i of types of I and K_i of $S_i \times T$ payoff matrices. K_i is finite, and Ω_i is a measurable space. The $S_i \times T$ signaling matrix Q_ω of probability distributions on $A \times B$ depends only on $\omega \in \Omega_i$, and the set B is finite, while A may be any measurable space. The marginal distribution Q^{II}_ω of Q_ω on B is independent of $\omega \in \Omega_i$, and hence will be denoted Q^{II}_i. Given $i \in I$ nature selects $(\omega, k) \in \Omega_i \times K_i$, and informs player I of ω. The game is then played forever as usually.

More generally, the payoff functions in K_i could be functions on $S_i \times T \times B$ or, if Q_ω is independent of $\omega \in \Omega_i$ (so: Q_i) and A is finite, on $S_i \times T \times A \times B$: we only need that every history in $S_i \times T \times A \times B$ determines a history of vector payoffs in $\mathbb{R}^{K_i}$.

We will also write Ω for the (disjoint) union $\bigcup_{i\in I} \Omega_i$. The above can be viewed as the extension of our standard model with incomplete information on one side to the case of a continuum of types of player I but sticking to the assumption of finitely many signaling matrices Q_i^{II}. Indeed, finiteness of K_i is no real restriction (as long as payoffs are uniformly bounded), since the space of $S_i \times T$ payoff matrices is finite dimensional anyway.

The function u is the same as usual; however, since Ω may be infinite, it is more convenient to view u as being defined on $M = \Delta(P)$ with $P = \bigcup_{i\in I} \Delta(K_i)$, the point in P being player I's probability distribution over the payoff matrices. For $\mu \in M$ let $I_\mu = \{i \in I \mid \mu(\Delta(K_i)) > 0\}$.

Proposition V.3.30.

(1) (a) *u is u.s.c. and has a Lipschitz restriction to each open face $M_{I_0} = \{\mu \in M \mid I_\mu = I_0\}$. u is continuous if the S_i and the Q_i^{II} are independent of $i \in I$.*

(b) *u is monotone: define $\mu_1 \le \mu_2$ iff $\int f(p)\mu_1(dp) \le \int f(p)\mu_2(dp)$ for every real-valued function f whose restriction to every $\Delta(K_i)$ is convex. Then $\mu_1 \le \mu_2$ implies $u(\mu_1) \le u(\mu_2)$.*

(2) *By adding finitely many convex combinations (depending just on the Q_i^{II}, thus independently of the sets K_i or the corresponding payoff matrices) to the pure action sets S_i one obtains that, $\forall \mu \in M$, both best replies and optimal strategies in* NR(μ) *are given by mixtures of pure strategies in* NR(μ).

(3) *Assume the actions mentioned in (2) have been added. For every $i \in I$, let $V_i = \{(Q_i^{\mathrm{II}}(s,t))_{t\in T} \mid s \in S_i\}$. For every vector $v = (v_t)_{t\in T}$ of probability distributions on B, every $\tau \in \Delta(T)$, and $p \in \Delta(K_i)$ let, with* $\max \emptyset = -\infty$:

$$F_v(p,\tau) = \max\left\{ \sum_{t\in T, k\in K_i} p^k G^k_{s,t} \tau(t) \;\middle|\; s \in S_i : Q_i^{\mathrm{II}}(s,t) = v_t \;\; \forall t \in T \right\}.$$

Let also $f_v(\tau) = \int_P F_v(p,\tau)\mu(dp)$, and $f(\tau) = \max_v f_v(\tau) = \max\{f_v(\tau) \mid v \in \bigcap_{I_\mu} V_i\}$: then $u(\mu) = \min_\tau f(\tau)$.

Remark V.3.39. Thus $u(\mu)$ is the value of a game, depending linearly on μ, where player I has finitely many strategies (say, $\bigcup_{i\in I} V_i$), and the payoff function is convex and continuous (even Lipschitz) on the strategy space $\Delta(T)$ of player II.

Remark V.3.40. For the order in Proposition V.3.30.1b, cf. Remark II.1.35, p. 89.

Proof. We start with parts (2) and (3). For $i \in I$, let W_i be the convex hull of V_i. Take $\mu \in M_{I_0}$. A behavioral strategy$[x_i(p)]_{i\in I}$ belongs to NR(μ) iff

$\exists v \in \bigcap_{I_0} W_i$ such that $\sum_{s\in S_i} x_i(p)(s)Q_i^{\mathrm{II}}(s,t) = v_t$, μ-a.e. $\forall t \in T$. Modifying it on a null set, we can assume $\sum_{s\in S_i} x_i(p)(s)Q_i^{\mathrm{II}}(s,t) = v_t$ $\forall t \in T, \forall p \in K_i$, $\forall i \in I_0$. Note that $\mathrm{NR}(\mu)$ is a (weak*) closed, hence compact, convex subset of the strategy space of player I (e.g., II.1, Ex. 19, p. 88), and so the minmax Theorem I.1.1, p. 5, applies and $u(\mu)$ is well defined. Therefore:

$$u(\mu) = \min_{\tau\in\Delta(T)} \max_{v\in\bigcap_{I_0} W_i} \int_P \mu(dp) G_v(h(p,\tau)),$$

where, for $p \in \Delta(K_i)$, $[h(p,\tau)]_s = \sum_{\substack{t\in T\\ k\in K_i}} p^k G^k_{s,t}\tau(t)$ for $s \in S_i$, $= 0$ otherwise, and $G_v(h) = \max\{\sum_{\bigcup_{I_0} S_i} x(s)h(s) \mid \forall i \in I_0, (x_s)_{s\in S_i} \in \Delta(S_i)$ and $\sum_{s\in S_i} x(s)Q_i^{\mathrm{II}}(s,t) = v_t \ \forall t \in T\}$. (The measurable selection is trivial.)

By I.3, Ex. 11h, p. 42, the function $G_v(h)$ is, still for fixed $i \in I_0$, concave in v, convex in h, and piecewise bi-linear in (v, h); i.e., there exists a triangulation of the polyhedron $\bigcap_{i\in I_0} W_i$ such that, whatever h vanishing outside $\bigcup_{I_0} S$ is, $G_v(h)$ is linear in v on each simplex of this triangulation. Hence for each $\tau \in \Delta(T)$, a best reply $x(p) \in \mathrm{NR}(\mu)$, which determines some $v \in \bigcap_{I_0} W_i$, can be viewed equivalently as the random selection of some vertices v_α of the sub-polyhedron containing v (and with v as expectation), followed by the use of a maximizer in the definition of $G_{v_\alpha}[h(p,\tau)]$, which (for $p \in \Delta(K_i)$) can be selected as one of the finitely many extreme points of the polyhedron $X^i_{v_\alpha} = \{x \in \Delta(S_i) \mid \sum_{s\in S_i} x(s)Q_i^{\mathrm{II}}(s,t) = v_{\alpha,t} \ \forall t \in T\}$. Add, therefore, for all $i \in I_0$, to S_i all extreme points of all $X^i_{v_\alpha}$, for every vertex v_α of our subdivision of $\bigcap_{I_0} W_i$, and repeat the same thing for each of the finitely many subsets I_0 of I. Now, $\forall\mu \in M$ and $\forall\tau \in \Delta(T)$, player I has a pure strategy best reply in $\mathrm{NR}(\mu)$. Hence $G_v(h(p,\tau)) = F_v(p,\tau)$, and part (3) follows.

For part (2), let us still show that, $\forall\mu \in M$, player I has optimal strategies that are mixtures of pure strategies in $\mathrm{NR}(\mu)$. Since he has best replies in this set, it suffices to show that the minmax theorem applies with this strategy set. For each v, denote by Σ_v the set of behavioral strategies $x(p)$ of player I whose support is compatible with v, i.e., such that, $\forall i \in I_0, \forall p \in K_i, \forall s \in S_i : [x(p)](s) > 0$ one has $(Q_i^{\mathrm{II}}(s,t))_{t\in T} = v$. Since Σ_v is the set of behavioral strategies of player I in a game with finite action sets, it is compact and convex (II.1, Ex. 19, p. 88). Denote by Σ_{I_0} the convex hull of $\bigcup \sum_v$: since only finitely many of them are non-empty, Σ_{I_0} is still compact and convex, and every strategy in Σ_{I_0} is a (finite) mixture of behavioral strategies. Hence the minmax theorem (Theorem I.1.1, p. 5) applies with Σ_{I_0} as strategy space, showing that player I can guarantee $u(\mu)$ with a strategy in Σ_{I_0}. To prove our claim, it suffices therefore to show that every behavioral strategy in Σ_v can be replaced by a mixture of pure strategies in Σ_v, which follows from II.1, Ex. 10, p. 70.

Part (1) follows now immediately from part (3). ■

Remark V.3.41. If $W_{i_1} = W_{i_2}$ (recall W_i is the convex hull of V_i), one can add convex combinations of pure strategies to the sets S_{i_1} and S_{i_2}, such that, after this addition, one obtains $V_{i_1} = V_{i_2}$. By duplicating then pure strategies if necessary, one can get that in addition each point v in $V_{i_1} = V_{i_2}$ is generated by as many pure strategies in S_{i_1} as in S_{i_2}. Hence, renumbering now the strategies will yield $Q^{\text{II}}_{i_1} = Q^{\text{II}}_{i_2}$: one can now pool the two indices i_1 and i_2 into one, with the disjoint union of K_{i_1} and K_{i_2} as set of games.

Remark V.3.42. Extending the strategy sets as in the above proposition, one sees that the restriction of u to an open face M_{I_0} has a Lipschitz extension u_{I_0} to its closure $\overline{M}_{I_0} = \{\mu \in M \mid I_\mu \subseteq I_0\}$: $\min_\tau \max_{\bigcap_{i\in I_0} V_i} f_v(\tau)$.

This is itself the u-function of some game in our class, where in addition S_i and Q^{II}_i are independent of i: the formula shows that it suffices to delete all $i \notin I_0$ and all $s \in S_i$ that do not lead to some $v \in \bigcap_{i\in I_0} V_i$. As shown in Remark V.3.41, we obtain then after duplicating strategies that Q^{II}_i is independent of $i \in I$ $(= I_0)$.

We now extend Proposition V.3.17, p. 240.

Proposition V.3.31. *Let φ be a l.s.c. convex function on M, $\varphi > u$. Then there exists N, a strategy τ of II in Γ_N, and a map $\mathbf{l}\colon B^N \to C(P)$ ($C(P)$ denoting the set of continuous functions on P with a convex (piecewise linear) restriction to each $\Delta(K_i)$) such that:*

(1) $\forall b \in B^N, \forall \mu \in M, \langle \mu, \mathbf{l}(b)\rangle \le \varphi(\mu)$.
(2) *On a history in Γ_N starting with $p \in \Delta(K_i)$, and where the choice of $k \in K_i$ happens at the end of history, and so $(\overline{g}^k_N)_{k\in K_i}$ is a random vector, define the random variable:*

$$(E_N =)\ E = \max_{q\in\Delta(K_i)} [\sum_{k\in K_i} q^k \overline{g}^k_N - [\mathbf{l}(b)](q)].$$

Then:

$$\mathsf{E}^p_{\sigma,\tau}(E) \le 0 \textit{ for all } \sigma \textit{ and } p.$$

Proof. We just mention the differences with the proof of Proposition V.3.17, p. 240. First increase player II's information by informing him in addition after each stage of his move; next increase player I's information by informing him in addition of player II's signal and of his own move. At this stage, player I's old signal is uncorrelated (given player I's other information) with anything in the game; it thus serves just to describe a generalized strategy of player I, which can equivalently be described as a (behavioral or mixed) strategy (II.1, Ex. 10, p. 70) that uses just player II's past signals, player I's past moves, and his own type. The old signals can therefore be discarded (except in the case where the payoff depends on them).

Thus, at this stage the signaling matrices Q_i select a message for player II that, in particular, informs him of his last move, and player I's message contains player II's message together with his own past move; Q_i depends only on i, not on the type of player I.

Then, one can replace Γ by Γ' by replacing each S_i by $\bigcup_j S_j$. u' still decreases to u: there is something to prove only if the lower bound v of the $u'_M(\mu)$ is $> -\infty$; in that case, following the proof in the previous proposition that the minmax theorem holds for those games, the sets Σ_M of behavioral strategies of player I in NR(μ) that guarantee him at least v are a decreasing sequence of non-empty compact sets; by the monotone convergence theorem, any strategy in the intersection guarantees v with $M = \infty$, and hence is a non-revealing strategy in the original game that guarantees v. Hence the convergence. Since φ is l.s.c. $> u$, and u'_M are, by the previous proposition, u.s.c. and decrease to u, there will be M sufficiently large such that $\varphi > u'_M$ (compactness). It suffices to prove the proposition for this game Γ'.

As in Remark V.3.41 above, since Q_i is now independent of i, one can pool all K_i's together into their disjoint union K, and set $\varphi(\mu) = +\infty$ for every μ on $\Delta(K)$ that is not carried by $\bigcup_i \Delta(K_i)$. This preserves convexity and lower semi-continuity, and so if we prove the result on $\Delta(K)$, it will suffice at the end to replace the maps $\mathbf{l}(b)$ on $\Delta(K)$ by their restriction to $\bigcup_i \Delta(K_i)$.

We have thus reduced the problem to that of a single i, i.e., a single set S, a single K, and a single Q. Now the function u is, by the previous proposition, continuous, and even Lipschitz.

Consider now an increasing sequence L_n of finite Borel partitions of $\Delta(K)$ such that the maximum diameter δ_n of the partition elements tends to zero. For each n, and every μ on $\Delta(K)$, denote by $\overline{\mu}_n$ the corresponding point in $\Delta(L_n)$; also for every $\ell \in L_n$ let $\overline{G}^{\ell}_{s,t} = \sup_{p\in\ell} \sum_k p^k G^k_{s,t}$. This game $\overline{\Gamma}^n$ can be viewed as a game covered by Theorem V.3.16, p. 239, i.e., with finite set of types L_n. But it can equivalently be viewed as the original game Γ, but where the payoff function $\langle p, G\rangle$ has been increased to $\overline{G}^{\ell(p)}$. By our assumptions on the sequence L_n, this implies that $\overline{u}^n(\overline{\mu}_n)$ decreases uniformly to $u(\mu)$. Let also $\overline{\varphi}^n(\overline{\mu}_n) = \inf\{\varphi(\mu) \mid \mu(\ell) = \overline{\mu}_n(\ell)\ \forall \ell \in L_n\}$: since the map $\mu \to \overline{\mu}_n$ is linear, $\overline{\varphi}^n$ is convex on $\Delta(L_n)$; since L_n is increasing, so is $\overline{\varphi}^n(\overline{\mu}_n)$; finally $\varphi > u$, together with l.s.c. of φ, u.s.c. of u, and compactness of M imply that there exists $\varepsilon > 0$ such that $d(\mu_1, \mu_2) \leq \varepsilon$ implies $\varphi(\mu_1) \geq u(\mu_2) + \varepsilon$. Choose, e.g., as distance $d(\mu_1, \mu_2) = \sup\{\langle \mu_1 - \mu_2, f\rangle \mid f$ has Lipschitz constant 1 on $\Delta(K)\}$. Then $\overline{\mu}_n = \overline{\nu}_n$ implies $d(\mu, \nu) \leq \delta_n$, so choosing ν_n with $\varphi(\nu_n)$ approximating $\overline{\varphi}^n(\mu_n)$ and $\nu_n(\ell) = \overline{\mu}_n(\ell)\ \ \forall \ell \in L_n$ yields that $\overline{\varphi}^n(\overline{\mu}_n) \geq u(\mu) + \varepsilon$ for all μ and all $n \geq n_0$ (with $\delta_{n_0} \leq \varepsilon$). Uniform convergence of $\overline{u}^n(\overline{\mu}_n)$ to $u(\mu)$ implies thus that, for all $n \geq n_1$, $\overline{\varphi}^n \geq \overline{u}^n + \frac{1}{2}\varepsilon$ on $\Delta(L_n)$. Hence, even if $\overline{\varphi}^n$ was not l.s.c., the same inequality would, by continuity of $\overline{u}^n$, still hold for the l.s.c. regularization of $\overline{\varphi}^{n_1}$. Therefore, to those two we can apply Proposition V.3.17, p. 240, and obtain the existence of N and of a strategy τ of player II in the N-stage repetition of $\overline{\Gamma}^{n_1}$ such that, for all non-revealing strategies σ of I in this game, $\sum_{\ell\in L_{n_1}} q_\ell \overline{\gamma}^{\ell}_N(\sigma, \tau) \leq \overline{\varphi}^{n_1}(q) - \varepsilon/4$ for all $q \in \Delta(L_{n_1})$.

Since $\overline{\Gamma}^{n_1}$ differs from Γ' only by having a larger payoff function, and since $\overline{\varphi}^{n_1}(\overline{\mu}^{n_1}) \leq \varphi(\mu)$ for all $\mu \in \Delta(M)$, we obtain a fortiori that $\overline{\gamma}^{\mu}_N(\sigma, \tau) = \int \overline{\gamma}^{p}_N(\sigma, \tau)\mu(dp) \leq \varphi(\mu) - \varepsilon/4$ for all μ, and every non-revealing strategy σ of player I in Γ'_N.

This completes the analogue of step (2) in the proof of Proposition V.3.17.

For step (3), consider now Γ'_N as a one-shot game $\tilde{\Gamma}$, with a single strategy τ for player II. The u-function $\tilde{u}(\mu)$ of $\tilde{\Gamma}$ is thus convex, continuous, and strictly smaller than φ. But $\tilde{\Gamma}$ can also be viewed as a game with (random) vector payoffs, in $\mathbb{R}^K \times \Delta(\tilde{B})$, where every history in Γ'_N is mapped to the corresponding payoff in $\mathbb{R}^K$ and the corresponding string of messages ($\in B^N = \tilde{B}$, identified with the extreme points of $\Delta(\tilde{B})$), and where therefore pure strategy $\tilde{s}$ yields a random outcome in $\mathbb{R}^K \times \Delta(\tilde{B})$ whose distribution $\pi_{\tilde{s}}$ is induced by the distribution of histories under $\tilde{s}$ and τ. Denote the barycenter of $\pi_{\tilde{s}}$ by $(f_{\tilde{s}}, \beta_{\tilde{s}}) \in \mathbb{R}^K \times \Delta(\tilde{B})$, and let D be the convex hull of those points. By Theorem V.4.1, p. 281, D is approachable in $\tilde{\Gamma}$; i.e., for some constant M, and every strategy σ of player I (as before, there is no loss of generality in assuming that, in $\tilde{\Gamma}$, player I is informed after each stage of the full vector payoff and of his pure strategy $\tilde{s}$), $\mathsf{E}_\sigma[d[(f_n, \beta_n), D]] \le M/\sqrt{n}$, where (f_n, β_n) denotes the random average payoff after n repetitions of $\tilde{\Gamma}$. Denote by D' the projection of D on $\Delta(\tilde{B})$; for $\beta \in \Delta(\tilde{B})$ denote by $\overline{\beta}$ its projection on P; and for $\beta \in P$ let $D_\beta = \{f \in \mathbb{R}^K \mid (f, \beta) \in D\}$. Then the map $\beta \to D_\beta$ is Lipschitz by I.3, Ex. 4q, p. 35, say, with constant L, and $\beta \to \overline{\beta}$ is clearly also Lipschitz with constant 1. So $d[f_n, D_{\overline{\beta}_n}] \le (L+1)d[(f_n, \beta_n), D]$; hence with $M' = M(L+1)$ we have $\mathsf{E}_\sigma\, d(f_n, D_{\overline{\beta}_n}) \le M'/\sqrt{n}$ for all n and σ.

Denote by C' the maximum absolute value of payoffs in Γ', i.e., $C' = \max_{k,s,t}|G^k_{s,t}|$ (G being the expected payoff matrix of Γ' now). Let also $[\mathbf{l}(\beta_n)](p) = \max\{\sum_k p^k \varphi_k \mid \varphi \in D_{\overline{\beta}_n}\}$. Clearly $\mathbf{l}(\beta_n)$ is a convex function on $\Delta(K)$, piecewise linear since $D_{\overline{\beta}_n}$ is a polyhedron, and with Lipschitz constant and uniform norm $\le C'$. Further, using $\tilde{G}^p$ for $\sum_k p^k \tilde{G}^k$, $[(\mathbf{l}(\beta_n)](p) = \sum_{\tilde{s} \in \tilde{S}} x(p)(\tilde{s})\tilde{G}^p_{\tilde{s}} = \max\{\sum_{\tilde{s}} x(\tilde{s})\tilde{G}^p_{\tilde{s}} \mid x \in \Delta(\tilde{S}),\ \sum x(\tilde{s})\tilde{Q}^{\mathrm{II}}_{\tilde{s}}(b) = \overline{\beta}_n(b)\ \forall b \in \tilde{B}\}$, the existence of a measurable selection $x(p)$ is trivial. Hence $x(p)$ is a non-revealing strategy of player I in $\tilde{\Gamma}$, since it yields, for every type p, the same distribution $\overline{\beta}$ on the signals of II. Therefore $\int [\mathbf{l}(\beta_n)](p)\mu(dp) \le \tilde{u}(\mu)$ for all μ and all β_n. Finally $\max_{p \in \Delta(K)}[\overline{g}^p_n - [\mathbf{l}(\beta_n)](p)] \le C'' d(f_n, D_{\overline{\beta}_n})$, and so for $\tilde{M} = C'' \cdot M'$, $\mathsf{E}_\sigma \max_{p \in \Delta(K)}[\overline{g}^p_n - [\mathbf{l}(\beta_n)](p)] \le \tilde{M}/\sqrt{n}$ for all n and σ. Thus, choosing $0 < \delta < \min_\mu(\varphi(\mu) - \tilde{u}(\mu))$, adding δ to every function $\mathbf{l}(\beta_n)$, and choosing $N_1 > [\tilde{M}/\delta]^2$ we obtain that in $\tilde{\Gamma}_{N_1}$, $\mathsf{E}_\sigma \max_{p \in \Delta(K)}[\overline{g}^p_{N_1} - [\mathbf{l}(\beta_{N_1})](p)] \le 0\ \forall \sigma$ and $\int [\mathbf{l}(\beta_{N_1})](p)\mu(dp) < \varphi(\mu)\ \forall \mu, \forall \beta_{N_1}$.

Reverting now to the original game completes the proof of the proposition. ∎

Remark V.3.43. The proof also shows that, if in Γ all S_i and Q^{II}_i are identical, then $\mathbf{l}(b)$ has, for all $b \in B^N$, Lipschitz constant and uniform norm $\le C$.

Lemma V.3.32. *Denote by M the space of all probability measures on a separable metric space P. Endow M with the metric (for fixed positive constants C_u, C_ℓ) $d(\mu, \nu) = \sup\{\langle \mu - \nu, f\rangle \mid f$ is Lipschitz with constant C_ℓ and $\sup_x f(x) - \inf_x f(x) \le C_u\}$:*

(1) *All those metrics, when C_u and C_ℓ vary, or when the distance on P is changed to an equivalent distance, are equivalent and induce the*

weak**-topology. In particular they admit the same class of Lipschitz functions.*

(2) *For any extended real-valued function* u *on a convex set* C*, any convex function* $\varphi \geq u$ *is bounded from below by a minimal such function.*

(3) *If* $u\colon M \to \mathbb{R}$ *is Lipschitz with constant* C*, any minimal convex function* $\geq u$ *has the same Lipschitz constant.*

Proof. Part (1) is obvious, except perhaps that the metric induces the weak*-topology. If a sequence μ_n converges to μ according to the metric, this implies $\int f d\mu_n \to \int f d\mu$ for all bounded Lipschitz functions, hence for every bounded continuous function, since this is the limit both of an increasing and of a decreasing net (or even sequence) of bounded Lipschitz functions. Conversely, such a set of Lipschitz functions is compact in the uniform topology, i.e., the topology of uniform convergence on the unit ball of the dual of the bounded continuous functions. So, by Ascoli's theorem, it is equicontinuous on this unit ball. This yields the converse.

Part (2) follows straight from Zorn's lemma.

For part (3), let φ be a function $\geq u$. Define the Lipschitz regularization $\hat{\varphi}$ of φ as the largest function with Lipschitz constant C, which is $\leq \varphi$; this is well defined, because u is such a function, and the supremum of a family of functions with Lipschitz constant C has the same constant. Assume φ was convex: we claim $\hat{\varphi}$ is convex. Indeed, $\hat{\varphi}(\mu) = \inf_\nu[\varphi(\nu) + Cd(\mu, \nu)]$, so it suffices to prove convexity of $\varphi(\nu)$, which is assumed, and of $d(\mu, \nu)$, which is obvious from its definition as a supremum of continuous linear functionals $\int f d(\mu - \nu)$.

Thus if φ is minimal convex, $\varphi = \hat{\varphi}$: it has Lipschitz constant C. ∎

Corollary V.3.33.

(1) *Every minimal convex function* $\varphi \geq u$ *is the limit of a decreasing sequence of convex continuous functions.*

(2) *Its restriction to every open face has Lipschitz constant* C.

Proof. For each open face I_0, in the sense of Remark V.3.42, we can by part (2) find a minimal convex function φ_{I_0} that is $\leq \varphi$ everywhere and that is, on $\overline{M}_{I_0}$, $\geq u_{I_0}$ (thus, $\varphi_{I_0} = -\infty$ outside $\overline{M}_{I_0}$). This is because, by upper semi-continuity of u (Proposition V.3.30, p. 260), $u_{I_0} \leq u \leq \varphi$ on $\overline{M}_{I_0}$. Since u_{I_0} is Lipschitz with constant C, φ_{I_0} has the same Lipschitz constant (Lemma V.3.32, p. 264) on $\overline{M}_{I_0}$. In particular, φ_{I_0} is convex and u.s.c., so $\psi = \max_{I_0} \varphi_{I_0}$ is convex and $u \leq \psi \leq \varphi : \varphi = \max_{I_0} \varphi_{I_0}$ by minimality. Hence part (2). For part (1), it suffices to construct such a decreasing sequence for each φ_{I_0}: taking term by term maxima will then yield the result. Let thus, e.g., $\overline{\varphi}_{I_0} = +\infty$ outside $\overline{M}_{I_0}$, $= \varphi_{I_0}$ on $\overline{M}_{I_0}$, and consider its Lipschitz regularization $\widehat{\overline{\varphi}}_{I_0}$, as in the proof of Lemma V.3.32, p. 264: $\hat{\overline{\varphi}}_{I_0}$ is convex, Lipschitz, and coincides with φ_{I_0} on $\overline{M}_{I_0}$. Thus $\varphi_n(\mu) = n^{-1} + \hat{\overline{\varphi}}_{I_0}(\mu) - n\mu(\bigcup_{i \notin I_0} \Delta(K_i))$ satisfies our requirements. ∎

Corollary V.3.34. *Assume φ is a minimal convex function $\geq u$, and that the convex functions $\varphi_n \geq u$ are such that* $\limsup \varphi_n \leq \varphi$. *Then* $e_n = \sup_\mu[\varphi(\mu) - \varphi_n(\mu)]$ *converges to zero.*

Proof. Since $\limsup \varphi_n$ is convex and $\geq u$, minimality of φ implies $\limsup \varphi_n = \varphi$. Since this remains true for any subsequence, $\varphi_n \to \varphi$ pointwise. In particular (without even taking sup), $\liminf e_n \geq 0$. In the other direction, if we bound from below each φ_n by a minimal convex function $\geq u$ using part (2, p. 265) of Lemma V.3.32, our assumption remains valid. So we can assume the φ_n are minimal convex $\geq u$. By part (2) of Corollary V.3.33, their restrictions to every open face M_{I_0} have Lipschitz constant C. Since they converge pointwise to φ, this convergence is uniform on every M_{I_0}, hence on M. ■

We are now ready for the generalization of Theorem V.3.16, p. 239.

Theorem V.3.35. *In the above-described game, given a convex function $\varphi \geq u$, and a sequence $\varepsilon_n > 0$ converging to zero, there exists a strategy τ of player* II *and a map* $\mathbf{l}\colon \bigcup_n B^n \to C(P)$ *such that:*

(1) $\varphi_n(\mu) = \max_{b \in B^n} \langle \mu, \mathbf{l}(b) \rangle$ *is decreasing, with* $\lim_{n\to\infty} \varphi_n(\mu) \leq \varphi(\mu)$, $\varphi_n \leq 2C$, *and* $\forall n, \forall b \in B^n$, $\mathbf{l}(b)$ *is a maximal (measurable) function such that* $\langle \mu, \mathbf{l}(b) \rangle \leq \varphi_n(\mu)$.

(2) *Define for each n, E_n as in V.3.31: this is on a space of histories that includes the initial choice of $i \in I$, but not the choice of the type of player* I *or of the payoff matrix. Let* $N = \sup\{n \mid E_n > 0\}$, *with* $\sup(\emptyset) = 0$.
Then $\sup_{i, p \in \Delta(K_i), \sigma} P^{i,p}_{\sigma,\tau}(N \geq n) \leq \exp(-n\varepsilon_n)\ \forall n \geq 0$.

(3) *Let* $M_n = \sup_{\substack{i,p,\sigma \\ m \leq n}} \|E_m\|_{L_\infty(\sigma^p,\tau,i)}$. *Then* $\varepsilon_n(M_n - 3C) \leq 1$.

Remark V.3.44. The interpretation of the theorem is the same as for Theorem V.3.16, p. 239. But now N becomes the last stage where the vector payoff does not belong to the convex set having $\mathbf{l}_n(b)$ as support function.

Proof. There remains to do the analogue of part (B) of the proof of Theorem V.3.16 (part (C) will be the same). Reduce first, as in the beginning of the proof of Proposition V.3.31, p. 262, to the case where Q_i depends only on i. Now the suprema, in parts (2) and (3) of the theorem, can be taken just over σ^p instead of over ω and σ.

Use part (2, p. 265), of Lemma V.3.32 to replace φ by a minimal convex function, then part (1) of Corollary V.3.33, p. 265, to obtain a strictly decreasing sequence ψ_ℓ of convex continuous functions converging to φ, then Proposition V.3.31, for each ℓ, to obtain corresponding τ_ℓ, N_ℓ, and $\hat{\mathbf{l}}_\ell\colon B^{N_\ell} \to C(P)$. Without loss of generality, we can assume $N_\ell > N_{\ell-1}$. Then $\varphi_\ell(\mu) = \max_{b \in B^{N_\ell}} \langle \mu, \hat{\mathbf{l}}_\ell(b) \rangle$ is convex and $\leq \psi_\ell$ by Proposition V.3.31. Also $\varphi_\ell \geq u$, as already argued in the beginning of part (B) of Theorem V.3.16, p. 239 (by letting player I play independently stage after stage some fixed optimal strategy in $D(\mu)$, the non-revealing aspect of this strategy is used in that, in $\int [\mathsf{E}_{\sigma^p}([\hat{\mathbf{I}}_\ell(b)](p))]\mu(dp)$, the distribution of $b \in B^{N_\ell}$ is independent of p). Thus, let $\delta_\ell = \ell^{-1} + \mathsf{sup}_{\ell' \geq \ell} \mathsf{sup}_\mu [\varphi(\mu) - \varphi_\ell(\mu)]$: by Corollary V.3.34, p. 266, δ_ℓ converges to zero. Hence, adding the constant δ_ℓ to the function $\mathbf{I}(b)$ for each $b \in B^{N_\ell}$, and to ψ_ℓ, we still have ψ_ℓ decreasing to φ, and all conclusions of Proposition V.3.31, but now $\varphi_\ell > \varphi\ \forall \ell$. Hence, by compactness, we can extract a subsequence ℓ_i such that φ_{ℓ_i} is decreasing to φ, and such that further $\varphi_{\ell_1} \leq 2C$. (If $C = 0$, the theorem is obvious; otherwise, choosing ℓ_1 such that $\delta_{\ell_1} \leq C$ does the job, since before the addition $\varphi_\ell \leq C$. Next, since the ψ_ℓ are continuous and decreasing to φ, and since φ_{ℓ_i} is continuous and $> \varphi$, define inductively $\ell_{i+1} = \mathsf{min}\{\ell > \ell_i \mid \psi_\ell < \varphi_{\ell_i}\}$.) Thus, we can assume that, for our original sequence, $2C \geq \psi_\ell(p) = \mathsf{max}_{b \in B^{N_\ell}} \langle \mu, \hat{\mathbf{I}}_\ell(b) \rangle$. Replace now also $\hat{\mathbf{I}}_1$ by the constant function $2C$, and let $C_\ell = \mathsf{max}(C_{\ell-1}, C + \mathsf{max}_{b \in B^{N_\ell}} \mathsf{max}_{p \in P} |[\hat{\mathbf{I}}_\ell(b)](p)|)$, $C_0 = 0$.

Denote then by S^i_ℓ the pure strategy set of player I in $\Gamma^i_{N_\ell}$, where he is not informed of the choice of $p \in \Delta(K_i)$; let $P^i_{\ell,s}$ be the joint distribution (on $\mathbb{R} \times A^{N_\ell}$, given τ_ℓ, $i \in I$ and $s \in S^i_\ell$) of E_{N_ℓ} and of the signals of player I (in A^{N_ℓ}).

The rest of part (B) is now as before, with the obvious changes in notation, like $p \to \mu$. As for the matter of increasing the "coordinates" of $\bar{\mathbf{I}}_n(b)$ so as to obtain equality with $g_n + \eta_n$, observe that, when increasing them thus in a maximal way, one obtains a convex combination of other functions $\bar{\mathbf{I}}_n(b')$, and thus still a function in $C(P)$. Indeed, B^{N_ℓ} is finite, and so we are as in a polyhedral case.

Part (C) is identical to the previous case, except that in the beginning the inequality $E_n \leq \frac{W_i}{n} - \eta_{T_i}$ is justified by the fact that the maximum of a sum is less than or equal to the sum of the maxima. ∎

Remark V.3.45. Some work is required to be able to deal with any convex function $\varphi \geq u$, and to get the sequence φ_n to be decreasing, but the prize is worthwhile: not only does it yield the strongest possible form of convergence for the φ_n, and the weakest possible assumptions on φ, but, more importantly, it makes the statement completely "non-topological": no weak⋆ or other topology on M appears explicitly or implicitly in the statement, which remains therefore just as valid on Ω as on P, when one replaces M by an arbitrary convex set of probability measures on Ω. Make first the reduction to the case Q_i depending only on $i \in I$, then let $p_\omega \in P$ be a version of the conditional probability on $\bigcup_{i \in I} K_i$ given ω, and use it to map all $\mu \in M$ to their images $\tilde{\mu}$ in $\Delta(P)$. Observe that $\tilde{\mu}_1 = \tilde{\mu}_2 \Longrightarrow u(\mu_1) = u(\mu_2)$, and that since $\mu \to \tilde{\mu}$ is linear, $\tilde{\varphi}(\nu) = \mathsf{inf}\{\varphi(\mu) \mid \tilde{\mu} = \nu\}$ (with $\mathsf{inf}\, \emptyset = +\infty$) is a convex function on $\Delta(P)$, $\geq u$. Apply the theorem to that function. Transform finally the function $\mathbf{I}(b) \in C(P)$ to the function $[\mathbf{I}(b)](p_\omega)$ on Ω. Then $\mathsf{sup}_{i, p \in \Delta(K_i), \sigma}$ is $\mathsf{sup}_{\omega, \sigma}$, $P^{i,p}_{\sigma,\tau}$ is $P^\omega_{\sigma,\tau}$, and $L_\infty(\sigma^p, \tau, i)$ becomes $L_\infty(\sigma^\omega, \tau)$.

Remark V.3.46. In the same vein, the sets K_i are often a nuisance, and it is sometimes more convenient to argue directly in a standard model with incomplete information on one side, with one payoff matrix G_ω $(S_i \times T)$ for each $\omega \in \Omega_i$ (i.e., the matrix $\sum_{K_i} p^k_\omega G^k$). As long as payoffs are uniformly bounded, this model is perfectly equivalent, since one can then always include all possible $S_i \times T$ matrices G_ω in a large simplex and take its set of vertices for K_i.

In such a framework, the functions $\mathbf{l}(b) \in C(P)$ become piecewise affine convex functions of G_ω. It seems one should be able to do somewhat better and obtain them as piecewise linear functions minus a constant, with other properties like monotonicity, invariance under addition of constants, etc.

Still in this framework, a more canonical representation is possible, in which μ is a probability measure over payoff matrices, or more generally a bounded positive measure, extending everything by homogeneity of degree 1. In addition to the previously found properties, like the above-mentioned invariance under addition of constants, monotonicity w.r.t. the usual order, the monotonicity of Proposition V.3.30, p. 260, etc., one obtains now that two measures determine the same model if they differ only by rescaling some matrices G_ω, and rescaling in a compensatory way the mass attached to them (i.e., if the vector measures $G^1_\omega \mu^1(d\omega)$ and $G^2_\omega \mu^2(d\omega)$ are the same). This can be used to rescale all matrices $G \neq 0$ onto the unit sphere (for some norm), and hence to get rid of the assumption of uniformly bounded payoffs.

Remark V.3.47. Could the theorem in some sense be "decomposed," e.g., into:

- an intrinsic characterization (independent of payoffs ... but this may be a fallacy, since payoff matrices are the linear functionals on $\Delta(S \times T)$) of "approachable" sets, for instance, in $\prod_i \Delta(S^i \times T)$ or $\Delta(B)$
- a proof that, for given payoff matrices:
  - the above "approachable" sets are characterized by convex functions $\geq u$
  - the corresponding "approach strategies" yield also the function $\mathbf{l}(b)$.

Remark V.3.48. Statistically perfect monitoring

A particular case where things simplify, and that may give a better feel for the theorem, is that where, for each i and $k \in K_i$, every column of G^k is a linear combination of the columns $Q^i_t(b)$ $(t \in T, b \in B)$. (This is substantially more general than asking that the $S^i \times (T \times B)$-matrix $Q^i_{s,t}(b)$ be of full row rank, since whenever the game arises from some extensive form where several mixed strategies of player I correspond to the same behavioral strategies, those several mixed strategies will induce the same distribution on B for each $t \in T$, and so there is no full row rank, but will also induce the same payoffs for each $t \in T$.)

Indeed, in such a case, if we expand the pure strategy sets S_i as in Proposition V.3.30, p. 260, our assumption implies that all pure strategies corresponding to some $v \in V_i$ are duplicates (induce the same payoffs): thus, after identification, one can think of V_i itself as the pure strategy set S_i. But then the "max" in

$F_v(p,\tau)$ disappears, and so F_v is bi-linear in (p,τ); hence f_v is linear in τ and depends only on the "barycenter" $\overline{\mu} \in \Delta(K)$ of μ, i.e., the induced probability distribution $K = \bigcup_i K_i$. So u becomes a function on $\Delta(K)$, which is the value of an "average game." Further, since $\mu \to \overline{\mu}$ is linear, if φ is a convex function on M with $\varphi(\mu) \geq u(\overline{\mu})$, then $\overline{\varphi}\colon \Delta(K) \to \mathbb{R}$ defined by $\overline{\varphi}(\pi) = \inf\{\varphi(\mu) \mid \overline{\mu} = \pi\}$ is convex on $\Delta(K)$ and $\geq u$. Thus we can limit attention to those convex functions φ on M that arise from some convex function $\overline{\varphi} \geq u$ on $\Delta(K)$ by $\varphi(\mu) = \overline{\varphi}(\overline{\mu})$. For each $b \in \bigcup_n B^n$, let then $\bar{\mathbf{l}}(b)$ denote the (linear) concavification of $\mathbf{l}(b)$ (thus, $\bar{\mathbf{l}}(b) \in \mathbb{R}^K$). Denote also, for $\mu \in P$ or for $\overline{\mu} \in \Delta(K)$, by $\tilde{\mu} \in M$ the corresponding measure carried by the extreme points of the $\Delta(K_i)$. Then for each μ, $\langle \mu, \bar{\mathbf{l}}(b)\rangle = \langle \overline{\mu}, \bar{\mathbf{l}}(b)\rangle = \langle \tilde{\mu}, \mathbf{l}(b)\rangle \leq \varphi_n(\tilde{\mu})$ $= \overline{\varphi}_n(\overline{\mu})$ by definition. So part (1) of Theorem V.3.35, p. 266, used for $\tilde{\mu}$, yields that $\overline{\varphi}_n(\overline{\mu}) = \max_{b \in B^n} \langle \overline{\mu}, \bar{\mathbf{l}}(b)\rangle$; hence the $\overline{\varphi}_n$ are piecewise linear and convex on $\Delta(K)$. It also yields that $\overline{\varphi}_n(\overline{\mu})$ decreases and has limit $\leq \overline{\varphi}(\overline{\mu}) = \varphi(\mu)$. Finally, $\overline{\varphi}_n \leq 2C$ and the maximality of $\bar{\mathbf{l}}$ also follow immediately from the corresponding properties of φ_n and $\mathbf{l}$. For parts (2) and (3) of that theorem, note that by increasing thus $\mathbf{l}$ to $\overline{a}$, we have only decreased E_n, and so our bounds are a fortiori valid. And now N is simply the last time where $\bar{\mathbf{l}}_n(b)$ is not an upper bound for the vector payoff in $\mathbb{R}^{K_i}$. Thus, the theorem implies that, under our assumptions, the maps $\mathbf{l}(b)$ can all be taken linear on each $\Delta(K_i)$. The φ_n become then convex functions on $\Delta(K)$, and the theorem becomes an approachability theorem of the convex sets in $\mathbb{R}^K$ having the φ_n as support functions.

Remark V.3.49. Still under the same assumptions as in the previous remark, it is clear that, faced with such a strategy τ, the best player I can obtain, when constrained by such an approachable set, if he is of type $p \in \Delta(K_i)$, is the amount $\varphi_n(p)$ in the n-stage game (here $\Delta(K_i)$ is identified with the corresponding face of $\Delta(K)$). Hence, player II will guarantee himself in the n-stage game the amount $\int \varphi_n(p)\mu(dp)$, hence in the infinite game $\int \varphi_\infty(p)\mu(dp)$ by monotone convergence, i.e., $\int \overline{\varphi}(p)\mu(dp)$ if he has chosen $\overline{\varphi}$ minimal convex above u on $\Delta(K)$. So an optimal strategy of player II is to minimize $\int \overline{\varphi}(p)\mu(dp)$ among all minimal convex functions on $\Delta(K)$ that are $\geq u$, and next to approach this $\overline{\varphi}$ as in the theorem (cf. also Remark V.3.54, p. 274).

Remark V.3.50. Part (2) of Corollary V.3.33, p. 265, or Corollary V.3.34, p. 266, provides a compact T_1-topology (with countable basis) on the space of minimal convex functions φ (or $\overline{\varphi}$ as in the above remark) that are $\geq u$: take as the basis of neighborhoods of φ all φ' that are uniformly $> \varphi - \varepsilon$ (cf. I.3, Ex. 15c, p. 44). In this topology, expressions like $\int \varphi(p)\mu(dp)$ above are l.s.c; hence the relevant minima are achieved. Thus the theorem can be viewed as providing compact spaces of "sufficient" strategies for the infinite game. (Recall from Section I.1, p. 4, that the minmax theorem does not require the T_2-assumption on strategy spaces.)

V.3.i. Implications of the Approachability Theorem (continued)

We extend here the results of Section V.3.g to the setup of Section V.3.h.

Corollary V.3.36. *Corollary V.3.27, p. 257, remains word for word true in the present setup, when replacing $k \in K$ by $p \in P$, and the posterior probability p_n on $\Delta(K)$ (including $n = \infty$) by the posterior probability μ_n on $\Delta(P)$.*

Proof. Use the same proof. Observe that the martingale convergence theorem holds for probability distributions on a compact metric space, using the weak* topology (reduce to the scalar case by considering a countable dense set of continuous functions). ■

Definition V.3.51. Replace p by μ in Definition V.3.34, p. 258.

Proposition V.3.37. *Proposition V.3.28, p. 258, remains word for word true replacing $p \in \Delta(K)$ by $\mu \in \Delta(P)$. In part (2) we have further that $\varphi_\tau = \varphi_{\tau,\mathscr{L}}$ is independent of $\mathscr{L}$, and is a minimal convex function $\geq u$ having all properties of Corollary V.3.33, p. 265. And we have both $\limsup_{n\to\infty} \sup_{\sigma \in \mathrm{NR}^n(\mu)} \overline{\gamma}_n(\mu, \sigma, \tau) \leq \varphi_\tau(\mu)$ and the existence of $\sigma \in \mathrm{NR}^\infty(\mu)$ (in fact, $\sigma \in \Delta([\mathrm{NR}(\mu)]^\infty)$) such that $\overline{\gamma}_n(\mu, \sigma, \tau) \to \varphi_\tau(\mu)$.*

Proof. For the faces F of $\Delta(K)$, use the $\overline{M}_{I_0}$ of Remark V.3.40, p. 260. Since τ is in fact derived from φ_0, some minimal convex function $\leq \varphi$ and $\geq u$, we obtain $\varphi_{\tau,\mathscr{L}} \leq \varphi_0$, hence by minimality of φ_0, $\varphi_{\tau,\mathscr{L}} = \varphi_0\ \forall \mathscr{L}$: there remains only to construct $\sigma \in NR^\infty(\mu)$. Consider the game ($\mu$ and τ fixed) when I chooses $\sigma \in [\mathrm{NR}(\mu)]^\infty$ and II chooses $\mathscr{L}$, with payoff $h_{\tau,\mathscr{L},\sigma}(\mu) = f(\sigma, \mathscr{L})$. We have just shown that $\max_\sigma f(\sigma, \mathscr{L}) = \varphi_\tau(\mu)\ \forall \mathscr{L}$. Further, player II has a compact convex strategy set (in ℓ'_∞, $\sigma(\ell'_\infty, \ell_\infty)$), such that, $\forall \sigma$, $f(\sigma, \mathscr{L})$ is affine and continuous in $\mathscr{L}$. So, by the minmax Theorem I.1.3, p. 6, there exist convex combinations σ_k of strategies in $[\mathrm{NR}(\mu)]^\infty$ such that:

$$\min_{\mathscr{L}} f(\sigma_k, \mathscr{L}) > \varphi_\tau(\mu) - 1/k, \quad \text{i.e. } \liminf_{n\to\infty} \overline{\gamma}_n(\mu, \sigma_k, \tau) > \varphi_\tau(\mu) - 1/k.$$

Choose thus $n_k > n_{k-1}$ such that for $n \geq n_k$ $\sup_{\sigma \in \mathrm{NR}^n(\mu)} \overline{\gamma}_n(\mu, \sigma, \tau) \leq \varphi_\tau(\mu) + k^{-1}$, and $\overline{\gamma}_n(\mu, \sigma_k, \tau) \geq \varphi_\tau(\mu) - k^{-1}$.

Select now $N_0 = 0$, $N_k \geq n_{k+1}$, $\frac{N_{k+1}}{k+1} \geq 3\frac{N_k}{k}$, such that the N_k are "end of block"-dates for the strategy τ of player II, i.e., such that his strategy after N_k is independent of the history up to N_k. And define $\sigma \in \mathrm{NR}^\infty(\mu)$ as using σ_k at all dates n with $N_{k-1} < n \leq N_k$ (using, e.g., independent realizations of all σ_k).

Assume, by induction, that $\overline{\gamma}_{N_k}(\mu, \sigma, \tau) \geq \varphi_\tau(\mu) - 2k^{-1}$; so for $N_k \leq n \leq N_{k+1}$:

$$\begin{aligned}\overline{\gamma}_n(\mu, \sigma, \tau) &\geq \overline{\gamma}_n(\mu, \sigma_{k+1}, \tau) - \frac{N_k}{n}(\overline{\gamma}_{N_k}(\mu, \sigma_{k+1}, \tau) - \overline{\gamma}_{N_k}(\mu, \sigma, \tau)) \\ &\geq \overline{\gamma}_n(\mu, \sigma_{k+1}, \tau) - \frac{3N_k}{kn},\end{aligned}$$

using our induction assumption and the first inequality determining $n_k(\le N_k)$. Letting thus $n = N_{k+1}$ and using $\frac{N_{k+1}}{k+1} \ge \frac{3N_k}{k}$ and the second inequality determining $n_{k+1}(\le N_{k+1})$ we obtain $\overline{\gamma}_{N_{k+1}}(\mu,\sigma,\tau) \ge [\varphi_\tau(\mu) - (k+1)^{-1}] - (k+1)^{-1}$: this is the induction step. Since for $k = 1$ the inequality follows from $N_1 \ge n_1$, our induction is proved for all k. Our formula yields then $\overline{\gamma}_n(\mu,\sigma,\tau) \ge \varphi_\tau(\mu) - \frac{1}{k+1} - \frac{3N_k}{kn}$, for $N_k \le n \le N_{k+1}$. Since $N_k \ge n_{k+1}$, it follows that $\overline{\gamma}_n(\mu,\sigma,\tau) \ge \varphi_\tau(\mu) - \frac{4}{k}$: thus $\liminf_{n\to\infty} \overline{\gamma}_n(\mu,\sigma,\tau) \ge \varphi_\tau(\mu)$. ■

Remark V.3.52. Since our existence proof of $\sigma \in \mathrm{NR}^\infty(\mu)$ depends explicitly on the form of the τ's constructed in Theorem V.3.35, p. 266, it would be better, instead of the last part of the statement, to have that $\sup_{\sigma\in\mathrm{Co}[\mathrm{NR}(\mu)]^\infty} \liminf_{n\to\infty} \overline{\gamma}_n(\mu,\sigma,\tau) = \varphi(\mu)$ whenever φ is minimal convex $\ge u$, and for every strategy τ of player II such that $\varphi_{\tau,\mathscr{L}} \le \varphi\ \forall \mathscr{L}$. (Here $\sigma \in \mathrm{Co}[\mathrm{NR}(\mu)]^\infty$ means σ is a convex combination of strategies in $[\mathrm{NR}(\mu)]^\infty$, in particular $\sigma \in \mathrm{NR}^\infty(\mu)$.)

We turn now to affine functions $\ge u$, and the value of the game.

Proposition V.3.38. *Let* $\mathbf{H} = \{h\colon P \to [-C, C] \mid h_{|\Delta(K_i)}$ *be convex* $\forall i$, h *have Lipschitz constant* $\le C$, $\int_P h(p)\mu(dp) \ge u(\mu)\ \forall \mu \in \Delta(P)\}$, *and let* $\mathbf{H}_0$ *denote the minimal elements of* $\mathbf{H}$. *Then:*

(1) *Every (extended real-valued) affine function* $\ge u$ *is bounded from below by a minimal such function.*
(2) *The minimal such functions are the functions* $\int_P h(p)\mu(dp)$, *for* $h \in \mathbf{H}_0$.
(3) $\mathbf{H}$ *is compact and convex in the uniform norm, and* $\mathbf{H}_0$ *is compact in the* T_1 *topology with a countable basis where the sets* $\{h \in \mathbf{H}_0 \mid h > h_0 - \varepsilon\}$ *form a basis of neighborhoods of* $h_0 \in \mathbf{H}_0$.
(4) $\mathbf{H}_0$ *is a* G_δ *in* $\mathbf{H}$, *and the inclusion map is a Borel isomorphism. Further, there exists a Borel map* $r\colon \mathbf{H} \to \mathbf{H}_0$ *such that* $r(h) \le h\ \forall h$.

Proof. Part (1) follows from Zorn's lemma.

For part (2), assume φ is minimal affine; construct by Lemma V.3.32, p. 264, a minimal convex ψ with $u \le \psi \le \varphi$. By Corollary V.3.33, p. 265, ψ is u.s.c., and its restriction to every open face M_{I_0} has Lipschitz constant C. And φ is minimal affine $\ge \psi$. Let then $(B_1, \ldots, B_n)$ be a Borel partition of P into subsets of diameter $\le \varepsilon$, and, in particular, every B_j is contained in a single $\Delta(K_i)$. For $\mu \in \Delta(P)$, let $\alpha_j = \mu(B_j)$, $\mu_j(B) = \big(\mu(B \cap B_j)\big)/\alpha_j$ if $\alpha_j > 0$, and μ_j is an arbitrary probability on B_j otherwise. Then $\varphi(\mu) = \sum_j \alpha_j \varphi(\mu_j) \ge \sum_j \alpha_j \psi(\mu_j)$. And since μ_j and every unit mass δ_p for $p \in B_j$ are contained in the same open face, and are ε-distant from each other, we have $\left|\psi(\mu_j) - \int \psi(\delta_p)\mu_j(dp)\right| \le C\varepsilon$, thus $\varphi(\mu) \ge \int \psi(\delta_p)\mu(dp) - C\varepsilon$, hence $\varphi(\mu) \ge \int \psi(\delta_p)\mu(dp)$. Let $h(p) = \psi(\delta_p)$. By part (2) of Corollary V.3.33, h has Lipschitz constant C. Further, by convexity of ψ, $\psi(\mu) \le \sum \alpha_j \psi(\mu_j) \le \sum \alpha_j \int \psi(\delta_p)\mu_j(dp) + C\varepsilon = \int h(p)\mu(dp) + C\varepsilon$ by the same inequality as above, hence $\psi(\mu) \le \int h(p)\mu(dp)$. So by minimality of φ

we obtain $\varphi(\mu) = \int h(p)\mu(dp)$. Further, by Theorem V.3.35, p. 266, let $\psi^n(\mu) = \max_{b \in B^n} \int_P a_b(p)\mu(dp)$: we have that ψ^n decreases to ψ. In particular, $h^n(p) = \psi^n(\delta_p) = \max_{b \in B^n} a_b(p)$ decreases to $h(p)$. So the convexity of $a_b(p)$ implies that of h^n and hence of h. This proves part (2).

The compactness and convexity of $\mathbf{H}$ are obvious. Let $V_\varepsilon(h_0) = \{h \in \mathbf{H}_0 \mid h > h_0 - \varepsilon\}$: obviously $h \in V_\varepsilon(h_0) \Longrightarrow \exists \eta > 0$: $V_\eta(h) \subseteq V_\varepsilon(h_0)$, and so the $V_\varepsilon(h)$ form the basis of a topology on $\mathbf{H}_0$, which is equivalent to the specified basis of neighborhoods. This topology is compact because, for any ultrafilter $\mathscr{U}$ on $\mathbf{H}_0$, if h denotes the limit of $\mathscr{U}$ in the (compact) space $\mathbf{H}$, and $h_0 \leq h$, $h_0 \in \mathbf{H}_0$, then obviously h_0 is a limit point of $\mathscr{U}$ in $\mathbf{H}_0$. It is T_1 because for $h_i \in \mathbf{H}_0$ $(i = 1, 2)$, if $h_1 \neq h_2$, there exists $\varepsilon > 0$ such that $h_2 \notin V_\varepsilon(h_1)$ by minimality of h_2. Finally, it is second countable: since $\mathbf{H}_0 \subseteq \mathbf{H}$, we can find a sequence $h_i \in \mathbf{H}_0$ that is dense in $\mathbf{H}_0$ in the uniform topology. Consider the sequence of open sets $U_{k,i} = V_{k^{-1}}(h_i)$: we have to show that, given $h \in \mathbf{H}_0$ and $\varepsilon > 0$, $\exists (k, i)$ with $h \in U_{k,i} \subseteq V_\varepsilon(h)$: choose $0 < d < k^{-1}$, $d + k^{-1} < \varepsilon$, and h_i d-close to h in the uniform distance. This proves part (3).

For $f, h \in \mathbf{H}$, let $S_f(h)$ denote the convexification of $f \wedge h$. Thus $S_f(h)$ is convex, has Lipschitz constant C, and is $\leq h$, and so, if $\int [S_f(h)](p)\mu(dp) \geq u(\mu)$ $\forall \mu$, we will have $S_f(h) \in \mathbf{H}$. But, since $S_f : h \to S_f(h)$ is continuous (Lipschitz constant 1 in the uniform topology), $\mathbf{H}_f = \{h \in \mathbf{H} \mid S_f(h) \in \mathbf{H}\}$ is closed (compactness of $\mathbf{H}$). Let thus $T_f(h) = S_f(h)$ for $h \in \mathbf{H}_f$, $T_f(h) = h$ otherwise: we have $T_f : \mathbf{H} \to \mathbf{H}$ is Borel, with $T_f(h) \leq h$ $\forall h$, and $T_f(h) \leq f$ if $\exists h_0 \in \mathbf{H}$: $h_0 \leq h \wedge f$. Let now f_i denote a dense sequence in $\mathbf{H}$, and add to it all $S_C(f_n + \varepsilon)$ for $\varepsilon \geq 0$ rational. Define Borel maps $R_n : \mathbf{H} \to \mathbf{H}$ by $R_0(h) = h$, $R_n = T_{f_n} \circ R_{n-1}$. Observe that $R_n(h)$ is decreasing in $\mathbf{H}$; compactness of $\mathbf{H}$ yields thus $R_n(h) \to R_\infty(h)$ pointwise, so R_∞ is Borel also. Clearly $R_\infty(h) \leq h$: further either $R_n(h) \leq f_n$, so $R_\infty(h) \leq f_n$, or there is no $h_0 \in \mathbf{H}$ with $h_0 \leq R_n(h)$, $h_0 \leq f_n$, so certainly not with $h_0 \leq R_\infty(h)$, $h_0 \leq f_n$. Thus, for all n, $T_{f_n}(h_0) = h_0$ for $h_0 = R_\infty(h)$. This means $h_0 \leq f_n$ if there exists $h_1 \in \mathbf{H}$ with $h_1 \leq h_0 \wedge f_n$. So assume $g \in \mathbf{H}$, $g \leq h_0$, $g \neq h_0$. Since the sequence f_n is dense, we can extract from it a subsequence n_i with $\| f_{n_i} - g \| < \varepsilon_{n_i}$. Choose ε_{n_i} rational; since $f_{n_i} + \varepsilon_{n_i} > g$ we can extract a further subsequence so as to make them decrease to g. Then also $S_C(f_{n_i} + \varepsilon_{n_i})$ decreases to g: there exists a subsequence of the f_n that decreases to g. In particular, there is $f_{n_0} \geq g$ such that f_{n_0} is not $\geq h_0$. But since $g \in \mathbf{H}$, $g \leq f_{n_0} \wedge h_0$, this means $T_{f_{n_0}}(h_0) \neq h_0$: a contradiction. Thus h_0 is minimal in $\mathbf{H}$: $R_\infty(\mathbf{H}) \subseteq \mathbf{H}_0$. Since $R_\infty(h) \leq h$ it follows that $R_\infty(\mathbf{H}) = \mathbf{H}_0$, and R_∞ is the identity on $\mathbf{H}_0$. This establishes the existence of our Borel map r, which, as we have further shown, is Borel even as a map from $\mathbf{H}$ to itself. On the other hand, let $B = \{(h_1, h_2) \in \mathbf{H} \times \mathbf{H} \mid h_2 \leq h_1, h_2 \neq h_1\}$: B is a K_σ in a compact metric space, as a difference of two closed sets, and $\mathbf{H}_0^c$, being the projection of B on the first factor, is therefore also a K_σ. Thus $\mathbf{H}_0$ is a G_δ in $\mathbf{H}$.

Thus, to complete the proof, there remains to show that the two measurable structures on $\mathbf{H}_0$ coincide, i.e., that the inclusion map $\mathbf{H}_0 \subseteq \mathbf{H}$ is Borel (because clearly the subspace topology on $\mathbf{H}_0$ is stronger than the topology on $\mathbf{H}_0$). Since $\mathbf{H}$ is compact metric, its Borel sets are generated by the evaluation maps $h \to h(p)$ $(p \in P)$ (using either the first separation theorem, or Stone–Weierstrass). Thus it suffices to show that $h \to h(p)$ is Borel-measurable on $\mathbf{H}_0$, which is obvious since $\{h \mid h(p) > \alpha\}$ is clearly open. ■

Remark V.3.53. Parts (3) and (4) of the last proposition imply that every probability measure on the Borel sets of $\mathbf{H}_0$ is regular (cf. Section I.1.d, p. 6): the Borel set is also Borel in $\mathbf{H}$, and the measure a (regular) measure on $\mathbf{H}$, and so the Borel set can be approximated from inside by a compact subset of $\mathbf{H}$; being contained in $\mathbf{H}_0$, this subset is closed (and clearly compact) in $\mathbf{H}_0$.

Proposition V.3.39.

(1) *Define* $(\mathsf{Cav}\, u)(\mu) = \mathsf{sup}\{\sum_{i=1}^n \alpha_i u(\mu_i) \mid \alpha_i \geq 0,\ \sum \alpha_i = 1,\ \sum \alpha_i \mu_i = \mu\}$ *(i.e., it is the smallest concave function that is* $\geq u$*). Then* $(\mathsf{Cav}\, u)(\mu) = \mathsf{max}\{\int u(\nu)\rho(d\nu) \mid \rho$ *probability measure,* $\int \nu\rho(d\nu) = \mu\}$*, and has Lipschitz constant* C.

(2) $\int h(p)\mu(dp)$ *is ("uniformly") l.s.c. on* $\mathbf{H}_0 \times M$.

(3) $(\mathsf{Cav}\, u)(\mu) = \mathsf{min}_{h \in \mathbf{H}_0} \int h(p)\mu(dp)$.

(4) *Every convex function* $\geq \mathsf{Cav}\, u$ *is bounded from below by some function* $\int h(p)\mu(dp)$ *with* $h \in \mathbf{H}_0$.

Proof. Part (1). Since $\{\rho \mid \int \nu\rho(d\nu) = \mu\}$ is compact, and since u is u.s.c. (Corollary V.3.33, p. 265, part (1)), it is clear that the maximum is achieved and is $\geq (\mathsf{Cav}\, u)(\mu)$. Conversely, given ρ, consider for every $I_0 \subseteq I$, $I_0 \neq \phi$, the restriction ρ_{I_0} of ρ to the open face M_{I_0}, and some measure $\tilde{\rho}_{I_0}$ with finite support on M_{I_0}, such that $\tilde{\rho}_{I_0}$ has the same mass and the same barycenter as ρ_{I_0} and is ε-close to ρ_{I_0}. (For example, find for every $\mu \in \overline{M}_{I_0}$ a closed neighborhood of diameter $\leq \varepsilon$ of the form $\{\nu \in \overline{M}_{I_0} \mid \nu(f_i) \geq 0\}$, where the f_i are finitely many continuous functions on P. Extract a finite open covering by the interiors of those sets, and let $(g_j)_{j=1}^k$ enumerate the finitely many continuous functions on P thus obtained. Let $g\colon M_{I_0} \to \{-1, 0, 1\}^k$, $g(\nu) = (\mathsf{sign}(\nu(g_j)))_{j=1}^k$, and let $B_\ell = g^{-1}(\ell)$ for $\ell \in \{-1, 0, 1\}^k$. The B_ℓ are a Borel partition of M_{I_0} into convex sets of diameter $\leq \varepsilon$; define $\tilde{\rho}_{I_0}$ by assigning mass $\rho_{I_0}(B_\ell)$ to the barycenter of the normalized restriction of ρ_{I_0} to B_ℓ.) Let also $\tilde{\rho} = \sum_{I_0} \tilde{\rho}_{I_0}$. Then, since u has Lipschitz constant C on every M_{I_0} (part (1) of Corollary V.3.30, p. 260), we have $\left|\int u(\nu)\rho(d\nu) - \int u(\nu)\tilde{\rho}(d\nu)\right| \leq C\varepsilon$. Since $\tilde{\rho}$ has finite support and has barycenter μ, this proves our second formula for $\mathsf{Cav}\, u$. Observe that, with the u.s.c. of u, this implies immediately that $\mathsf{Cav}\, u$ is u.s.c. since the set of probability measures ρ on M is compact. The Lipschitz aspect will follow from part (3) of Corollary V.3.39 since a Lipschitz constant is preserved when taking minima.

Part (2). Obviously we have $\int h d\tilde{\mu} > \int h_0 d\mu - 2\varepsilon$ for $h \in V_\varepsilon(h_0)$ $(h, h_0 \in \mathbf{H}_0)$, if $d(\tilde{\mu}, \mu) < \frac{\varepsilon}{C}$, using the Lipschitz property of h_0.

Part (3). The minimum is achieved by part (2) and compactness of $\mathbf{H}_0$ (part (3) of Corollary V.3.38, p. 271). It is obviously $\geq (\mathsf{Cav}\, u)(\mu)$. So to prove equality, consider the locally convex space $F = E \times \mathbb{R}$, where E is the set of all bounded measures on P with the weak* topology. Let $K = \{(\mu, x) \mid \mu \in M, (\mathsf{Cav}\, u)(\mu) \geq x \geq -C\} \subseteq F$. By the compactness of M in E and $\mathsf{Cav}\, u$ being u.s.c. (cf. supra), K is compact, and clearly convex, in F. Consider $x_0 > (\mathsf{Cav}\, u)(\mu_0) : (\mu_0, x_0) \notin K$, so it can be (strictly) separated from K by a continuous linear functional on F (cf. Section I.1.13, p. 10), which takes the form $\langle \mu, f\rangle + \alpha x$, for some continuous function f on P; i.e., we have $\langle \mu_0, f\rangle + \alpha x_0 > \max\{\langle \mu, f\rangle + \alpha x \mid (\mu, x) \in K\}$. Let $x_1 = (\mathsf{Cav}\, u)(\mu_0)$: we have $x_0 > x_1$, and $\langle \mu_0, f\rangle + \alpha x_0 > \langle \mu_0, f\rangle + \alpha x_1$, hence $\alpha > 0$, and so we can divide f by α, and obtain $\langle \mu_0, f\rangle + x_0 > \max\{\langle \mu, f\rangle + (\mathsf{Cav}\, u)(\mu) \mid \mu \in M\} = \beta$. Let thus $g = \beta - f$: we have $(\mathsf{Cav}\, u)(\mu) \leq \int g\, d\mu$, and $\int g\, d\mu_0 < x_0$. By Proposition V.3.38, p. 271, it follows that $\inf_{h \in \mathbf{H}_0} \int h\, d\mu_0 < x_0$. Since $x_0 > (\mathsf{Cav}\, u)(\mu_0)$ was arbitrary, the conclusion follows.

Part (4). By Lemma V.3.32, p. 264, assume φ minimal, hence Lipschitz, $\mathsf{Cav}\, u$ being Lipschitz. Separate then, as above, K from $\{\mu, x) \mid x \geq \varphi(\mu) + n^{-1}\}$, yielding an affine function ψ_n between $\mathsf{Cav}\, u$ and $\varphi + n^{-1}$. Take a limit ψ following some ultrafilter: it is affine, and $\mathsf{Cav}\, u \leq \psi \leq \varphi$. Conclude by Proposition V.3.38, p. 271. ∎

Remark V.3.54. In the situation of Remarks V.3.48 and V.3.49 after Theorem V.3.35, p. 266, we claim that viewing u as a function on $\Delta(K)$, $(\mathsf{Cav}\, u)(\mu) = \max\{\int_{\Delta(K)} u\, d\nu \mid \nu \preceq \mu\}$, where the order $\nu \preceq \mu$ means $\int \psi d\nu \leq \int \psi d\mu$ for all convex real-valued ψ on $\Delta(K)$.

Indeed, observe first the maximum in the right-hand member is achieved: since every ψ is the limit of a decreasing sequence of ψ's that are furthermore continuous, the definition of the order would remain the same if one required in addition continuity of ψ. Therefore, $\{\nu \mid \nu \preceq \mu\}$ is closed, and the maximum is achieved.

Next, observe that the functions $h \in \mathbf{H}_0$ are those convex functions such that $\int_P h(p)\mu(dp) \geq u(\overline{\mu})$ for every μ on P with barycenter $\overline{\mu}$. Let $p_i \in \Delta(K_i)$ be the barycenter of the restriction of μ to $\Delta(K_i)$: by convexity, it suffices that $\sum_i \alpha_i h(p_i) \geq u(\sum_i \alpha_i p_i)$ whenever $p_i \in \Delta(K_i), \alpha_i \geq 0, \sum_i \alpha_i = 1$. This means that, denoting by $\overline{h}$ the convexification of h (i.e., the largest convex function on $\Delta(K)$ that coincides with h on each $\Delta(K_i)$), $\overline{h}(q) \geq u(q)\ \ \forall q \in \Delta(K)$: $\mathbf{H}_0$ can be identified with the set of minimal convex functions on $\Delta(K)$ that bound u from above; i.e., it coincides with the minimal functions $\overline{\varphi}$ of Remark V.3.48 (but the functions h apply to measures $\mu \in M$ through $\int h(q)\mu(dq)$, while for φ it is $\varphi(\overline{\mu})$, $\overline{\mu}$ being the barycenter of μ).

Assume now $\nu \preceq \mu$: then for $h \in \mathbf{H}_0$, we have $\int u d\nu \leq \int h d\nu \leq \int h d\mu$, so by part (3) of Proposition V.3.39, p. 273, we have $\int u d\nu \leq (\mathsf{Cav}\, u)(\mu)$. So the maximum is less or equal to $(\mathsf{Cav}\, u)(\mu)$. Conversely, choose by Proposition 1 $\sum_i \alpha_i \mu_i = \mu, \sum_i \alpha_i u(\overline{\mu}_i) \geq (\mathsf{Cav}\, u)(\mu) - \varepsilon$. Let $\nu = \sum \alpha_i \delta_{\overline{\mu}_i}$; we have

$\int u d\nu \geq (\mathsf{Cav}\, u)(\mu) - \varepsilon$, and clearly, by Jensen's inequality, $\int \psi d\nu \leq \int \psi d\mu$ for any convex ψ, i.e., $\nu \preceq \mu$.

Proposition V.3.40.

(1) *There exists a Borel map $\mu \mapsto \overline{Q}_\mu$ from M to $\Delta(M)$ such that, for every μ, $\mu = \int \nu \overline{Q}_\mu(d\nu)$; i.e., μ is the barycenter of $\overline{Q}_\mu$, and $\int u(\nu)\overline{Q}_\mu(d\nu) = (\mathsf{Cav}\, u)(\mu)$.*

(2) *For every such map $\overline{Q}_\mu$, there exists $Q_\mu(d\nu \mid p)$, s.t. $(\mu, p) \mapsto Q_\mu(\cdot \mid p)$ is Borel from $M \times P$ to $\Delta(M)$ and is, for every μ, a version of the conditional distribution of ν given p under $\nu(dp)\overline{Q}_\mu(d\nu)$, i.e., $\int f(p,\nu)\nu(dp)\overline{Q}_\mu(d\nu) = \int f(p,\nu)Q_\mu(d\nu \mid p)\mu(dp)$ for every non-negative Borel function f on $P \times M$. In other words, $\forall \nu$, ν in $\Delta(P)$ is the posterior on P given that $\nu \in M$ was observed, when $\nu \in M$ was selected according to $Q_\mu(d\nu \mid p)$ and the true state $p \in P$ according to $\mu(dp)$.*

(3) *There exists a Borel map $\sigma(\mu, p)$ on $M \times P$ such that, for $p \in \Delta(K_i)$, $\sigma(\mu, p) \in \Delta(S_i)$, and such that, $\forall \mu$, $\sigma(\mu, \cdot)$ is an optimal strategy in* NR(μ).

(4) *$\forall \mu$, the strategy of player* I *consisting in selecting, given his observation $p \in P$, $\nu \in M$ according to $Q_\mu(d\nu \mid p)$, then using $\sigma(\nu, p)$ independently at each stage, is an optimal strategy in $\Gamma^\infty(\mu)$ (written as a generalized strategy; cf. II.1, Ex. 10, p. 70); i.e., it guarantees him $(\mathsf{Cav}\, u)(\mu)$ at every stage n: $\mathsf{E}_{\mu,\sigma,\tau}(\gamma_n) \geq (\mathsf{Cav}\, u)(\mu)$ $\forall n$, $\forall \tau$. (Thus, this strategy (or the corresponding mixed strategy) depends in a Borel way on the parameter μ.)*

Proof. Part (1). The set E of pairs $(\mu, \overline{Q})$ satisfying the requirements is a closed subset of $M \times \Delta(M)$ by part (1) of Proposition V.3.39, p. 273, and non-empty above every μ by part (1) of Lemma V.3.33, p. 265. Use thus Appendix A.7.i.

Part (2) follows from II.1, Ex. 9, p. 68.

Part (3). It suffices to define σ on each open face M_{I_0} separately. By Remark V.3.42, p. 262, this reduces the problem to that of a single i; thus $\#I = 1$. So one can take NR independent of μ. Further, by part (2) of Proposition V.3.30, p. 260, we can reduce NR to the mixtures of pure strategies in NR: the set S is partitioned into subsets $(S_v)_{v \in V}$, and $Q^{\mathrm{II}}_{s,t}$ depends only on v: we can write $Q^{\mathrm{II}}_{v,t}$, i.e., optimal strategies in NR can be written as $\alpha_v \in \Delta(V)$, together with, for each $v \in V$, a type-dependent selection of $s \in S_v$, i.e., $\forall v \in V$, a Borel map σ_v from $\Delta(K)$ to $\Delta(S_v)$. Let us first view $\overline{\sigma}$ as the measure $\mu(dp)\alpha(v)\sigma_{v,p}(ds)$ on $\Delta(K) \times S$. As we said, v and $\Delta(K)$ must be independent; i.e., we need $\overline{\sigma}(A \cap S_v) = \mu(A)\overline{\sigma}(S_v)$ for every Borel set A in $\Delta(K)$ and $v \in V$. This set of pairs $(\mu, \overline{\sigma})$ is clearly weak*-compact: the Borel sets A can be replaced by continuous functions, and an optimal strategy is one that maximizes $\min_{t \in T} \int \overline{\sigma}(dp, ds) G^p_{s,t}$, which is weak*-continuous. An u.s.c. correspondence like that from μ to the set of compatible $\overline{\sigma}$ is a Borel map to compact subsets with the Hausdorff topology (Appendix A.7.b). But again the correspondence from compact subsets with the Hausdorff topology to the corresponding set of maximizers of some continuous function is u.s.c., hence Borel, so the composite map, from μ to the set of optimal $\overline{\sigma}$ at μ, is a Borel map to compact sets, and hence admits a Borel selection $\overline{\sigma}_\mu$ (Appendix A.7.i). Apply now, e.g., II.1, Ex. 9, p. 68, to obtain non-negative Borel functions $(\sigma_s(\mu, p))_{s\in S}$ with $\sum_s \sigma_s = 1$ such that $\sigma_s(\mu, \cdot)$ is a Radon–Nikodym derivative of $\overline{\sigma}(A \times \{s\})$ w.r.t. $\mu = \overline{\sigma}(A \times S)$.

Part (4) is obvious. ∎

Remark V.3.55. Non-revealing strategies have also a basically finite dimensional representation: the payoff $\gamma(\overline{\sigma}, \tau)$ resulting from $\overline{\sigma}$ and τ equals, as seen above, $\int \overline{\sigma}(dp, ds)G^p_{s,\tau}$. Since G^p is linear in p, this means only the barycenter $\overline{p}_s$ of the distribution $\nu_s(dp)$ of p given s matters, together with $\lambda_v(s)$, the probability of s given S_v, and α_v. Our above condition on $\overline{\sigma}$ becomes: $\forall v, \sum_{S_v} \lambda_v(s)\nu_s = \mu$. The condition that there exist such ν_s with barycenter $\overline{p}_s$ is that μ is obtained by dilatation of the measure $\sum_{S_v} \lambda_v(s)\delta_{\overline{p}_s}$; i.e., by Strassen's theorem (II.1, Ex. 20, p. 89), it follows that $\sum_{S_v} \lambda_v(s)\varphi(\overline{p}_s) \le \int \varphi(p)\mu(dp)$ for every convex (continuous) function φ on $\Delta(K)$ and $v \in V$.

So this is the system of inequalities describing the constraints on the λ_v and the $\overline{p}_s$, and in terms of those variables, letting $\lambda(s) = \alpha_v\lambda_v(s)$ for $s \in S_v$, we have $\gamma(\lambda, \overline{p}; \tau) = \sum_s \lambda(s)G^{\overline{p}_s}_{s,\tau}$.

We turn now to the optimal strategies of player II.

Proposition V.3.41.

(1) *There exists a Borel map* $h\colon \mu \mapsto h_\mu$ *from* M *to* $\mathbf{H}_0$ *such that* $(\operatorname{Cav} u)(\mu) = \int h_\mu(p)\mu(dp)$.

(2) *For every sequence* ε_n *converging to zero there exists a sequence* δ_n *with* $2 \ge \delta_n \ge \delta_{n+1}$ *converging to zero and a continuous map* $\tau\colon h \mapsto \tau_h$ *from* $\mathbf{H}$ *to behavioral strategies of player* II *in* Γ_∞ *(or to mixed strategies, with the weak* topology), such that* $\forall h \in \mathbf{H}$, $\forall n \ge 0$, $\forall i \in I$, $\forall p \in \Delta(K_i)$, $\forall \sigma$, $P^{i,p}_{\sigma,\tau_h}(N \ge n) \le \exp(-n\varepsilon_n)$, *where* $N = \sup\{n \mid E_n > C\delta_n\}$ *(and* $\sup(\emptyset) = 0$*), and where* $E_n = \max_{q\in\Delta(K_i)} \left[\sum_{k\in K_i} q^k \overline{g}^k_n - h(q)\right]$.
Further, δ_n *can be chosen to depend only on the sequence* ε_n *and on the* $Q^i_{s,t}(b)(b \in B, s \in S_i, t \in T, i \in I)$*, provided one sets* $E_n = d(\overline{g}_n, \mathbf{L}_h)$*, with* $\mathbf{L}_h = \{x \in \mathbb{R}^{K_i} \mid \langle q, x\rangle \le h(q),\ \forall q \in \Delta(K_i)\}$*, and with* d *being the Euclidian distance, and provided one interprets the constant* C *as* $\max_{i,s,t} d[(G^k_{s,t})_{k\in K_i}, 0]$.

Remark V.3.56. It seems plausible one might be able to select τ_h independently of the sequence ε_n. This would be equivalent to requiring $\limsup_{n\to\infty}[F_n(y))]^{1/n} < 1\ \forall y > 0$, where $F_n(y) = \sup_{i,p,\sigma} P^{i,p}_{\sigma,\tau_h}(E_n > y)$. It would thus lead at the same time to a much simpler and a much sharper statement. It would, however, probably require a completely different proof, where the strategy is not built up from longer and longer blocks. (Even with a single state of nature, assume we have for each block of length n a strategy τ_n such that $E_n = +1$ or -1 with probability $\frac{1}{2}$ each (thus no "error term"). If we use successively such longer and longer blocks, this will force $\limsup_{n\to\infty}[F_n(y)]^{1/n} = 1$.)

Remark V.3.57. The reinterpretation with the Euclidian distances in the "further" clause is in order to obtain a sequence δ_n independent of the dimensions $\#K_i$ of the space of vector payoffs.

Proof. Part (1). Let $\mathbf{H}(\mu) = \{h \in \mathbf{H} \mid \int h\, d_\mu = (\mathsf{Cav}\, u)(\mu)\}$, $\mathbf{H}_0(\mu) = \mathbf{H}(\mu) \cap \mathbf{H}_0$. By part (2) of Proposition V.3.39, p. 273, $\mathbf{H}_0(\mu) \neq \emptyset$. By the (joint) continuity of $\int h d\mu$ and the continuity of $\mathsf{Cav}\, u$ (1, p. 273), the correspondence $\mathbf{H}(\mu)$ is u.s.c. Hence, by Appendix A.7.i, there is a measurable selection; composing this with the map r of part (4) of Proposition V.3.38, p. 271, yields the result.

Part (2). Fix $h \in \mathbf{H}$, and apply Theorem V.3.35, p. 266, to get a corresponding (τ, a). Observe that $\varphi_n(\mu) = \max_{b\in B^n} \int [\mathbf{l}(b)](p)\mu(dp)$ are a decreasing sequence of continuous functions, with a limit less than or equal to the continuous function $\varphi(\mu) = \int h(p)\mu(dp)$. So, by Dini's theorem, $\delta_n = \max_\mu(\varphi_n(\mu) - \varphi(\mu))$ decreases to zero. So $\forall n$, $\forall b \in B^n$, $\forall \mu \in M$, we have $\int [\mathbf{l}(b)](p)\mu(dp) \le \int h(p)\mu(dp) + \delta_n$, thus $[\mathbf{l}(b)](p) \le h(p) + \delta_n$: we can assume without loss of generality that $[\mathbf{l}(b)](p) = h(p) + \delta_n$, since $h \in C(P)$. By part (2) of Theorem V.3.35, p. 266, we have thus $P^{i,p}_{\sigma,\tau}(E_n > \delta_n) \le \exp(-n\varepsilon_n)$ $\forall i \in I$, $\forall p \in \Delta(K_i)$, $\forall n$, $\forall \sigma$. Since $|E_n| \le 2C$ we obtain $\mathsf{E}^{i,p}_{\sigma,\tau}(E_n) \le \delta_n + 2C \exp(-n\varepsilon_n) = \delta'_n(h)$.

Let $f(n, \tau, h) = \sup_{i,p,\sigma} \mathsf{E}^{i,p}_{\sigma,\tau}(E_n)$, where $h \in \mathbf{H}$ appears in E_n, and τ varies over all strategies of player II. Clearly f has Lipschitz constant 1 with respect to h. Let $g(n, h) = \inf_\tau f(n, \tau, h)$: g also has Lipschitz constant 1, and we have just seen that $\forall h$, $g(n, h) \le \delta'_n(h)$, and so $\limsup_{n\to\infty} g(n, h) \le 0$. By compactness of $\mathbf{H}$, we have uniform convergence: there exists a sequence δ''_n decreasing to zero such that $\forall n$, $\forall h \in \mathbf{H}$, $\exists \tau_{n,h}$: $f(n, \tau_{n,h}, h) < \delta''_n$. Further, we can assume $\tau_{n,h}$ completely mixed since player II has a finite pure strategy set in Γ_n. By the Lipschitz property of f, there is an open neighborhood U_h of h such that $f(n, \tau_{n,h}, h') < \delta''_n$ $\forall h' \in U_h$. Extract a finite covering $(U_{h_j})_{j\in J}$ from this open covering, and consider a corresponding continuous partition of unity (φ: $\mathbf{H} \to \Delta(J)$ such that $\varphi_j(h) > 0 \Longrightarrow h \in U_{h_j}$). Let $\tau_n(h) = \sum_{j\in J} \varphi_j(h)\tau_{n,h_j}$ (the convex structure here being that of mixed strategies). Since f is a supremum of linear functions of τ, $\{\tau \mid f(n, \tau, h) < \delta''_n\}$ is convex, and since $\forall h$, $\varphi_j(h) > 0 \Longrightarrow f(n, \tau_{n,h_j}, h) < \delta''_n$, we obtain $f(n, \tau_n(h), h) < \delta''_n$ $\forall n, \forall h$. Clearly $\tau_n(h)$ depends continuously on h; since it is completely mixed for all h, the corresponding behavioral strategy is also a continuous function of h. And $\forall h \in \mathbf{H}$, $\forall i \in I$, $\forall p \in \Delta(K_i)$, $\forall n > 0$, $\forall \sigma$ $\mathsf{E}^{i,p}_{\sigma,\tau_n(h)}(E_n) \le \delta''_n$.

There only remains to repeat, with this sequence of strategies $\tau_n(h)$ (and with $[\mathbf{l}(b)](p) = h(p) + \delta''_n$ $\forall b \in B^n$), the last part of the proof of Theorem V.3.35, p. 266, i.e., of Theorem V.3.16, p. 239.

To obtain also the "further" clause, consider first the case where the payoffs $G^k_{s,t}$ are non-random, i.e., depend only on the action pair (s,t). Note that it suffices to obtain a single sequence δ_n valid for all games (and all sets K_i) with $C = 1$. Fix then a subset L_i of $\mathbb{R}^{S_i \times T}$ with $\#L_i = \#\{S_i \times T\} + 1$ such that the simplex spanned by L_i contains the unit ball (for the maximum norm) and is contained in a ball of minimal diameter, say, $\zeta(\#\{S_i \times T\})$. Let $\overline{C} = \max_{i \in I} \zeta(\#\{S_i \times T\})$.

Construct as above a sequence δ_n and a map τ_h for the game with the sets L_i instead of K_i: we claim this is the required sequence; there only remains to construct a corresponding map $\overline{\tau}$ for the game with sets K_i.

By construction we have, for each $k \in K_i$, a probability distribution π_k over L_i such that $G^k = \sum_{\ell \in L_i} \pi_{k\ell} G^\ell$. This induces an affine map φ from $P = \bigcup_i \Delta(K_i)$ to $Q = \bigcup_i \Delta(L_i)$, with $\varphi(p) = \sum_{k \in K_i} p^k \pi_{k\ell}$ for $p \in \Delta(K_i)$, $\ell \in L_i$. Denote the u-functions of the games with K_i and L_i by u and v, respectively, and observe that $u(\mu) = v(\varphi(\mu))\ \forall \mu \in \Delta(P)$.

Indeed, best replies in Γ_{NR} can be chosen to be $\varphi(p)$-measurable, and so the result follows using the minmax theorem with this σ-field. Given $h\colon P \to \mathbb{R}$ in $\mathbf{H}$ $(= \mathbf{H}_K)$, let $\overline{h}(q) = \min\{h(p) \mid \varphi(p) = q\}$ (with $\min \phi = +\infty$). Then $\overline{h}\colon Q \to \mathbb{R}$ is convex and l.s.c., and for every $\nu \in \Delta(Q)$ for which $\int \overline{h}(q)\nu(dq) < \infty$ there exists (by the measurable selection theorem) $\mu \in \Delta(P)$ with $\varphi(\mu) = \nu$ and with $\int \overline{h}(q)\nu(dq) = \int h(p)\mu(dp) \geq u(\mu) = v(\nu)$. So $\int \overline{h}(q)\nu(dq)$ is an affine function $\geq v$. Denote by $\varphi^*(h)\colon Q \to \mathbb{R}$ the Lipschitz regularization with constant $\overline{C}$ (as in the proof of (3) in Lemma V.3.32, p. 264) of $\mathrm{Vex}\min(\overline{h}, \overline{C})$: by parts (1) and (2) of Proposition V.3.38, p. 271, we also have that $\int [\varphi^*(h)](q)\nu(dq)$ is an affine function $\geq v$, and so $\varphi^*(h)$ belongs to $\mathbf{H}_L$ (for the game with L_i). The map φ^* is clearly continuous (from $\mathbf{H}_K$ to $\mathbf{H}_L$), with $h(p) \geq [\varphi^*(h)](\varphi(p))\ \forall p \in P, \forall h \in \mathbf{H}_K$. Define then $\overline{\tau}_h$ as $\tau_{\varphi*(h)}$: the result is now clear, since the random variables E_n (with K) are less than or equal to the corresponding E_n with L.

Finally, we turn to the general case. Consider the auxiliary game $\tilde{\Gamma}$ where the random payoffs $G^k_{s,t,a,b}$ have been replaced by their barycenter $G^k_{s,t}$, and on every history, consider, besides the actual average vector payoff $\overline{g}_n$, its analogue $\overline{\tilde{g}}_n$ that would arise from $\tilde{\Gamma}$. Observe that $\max_{k,s,t} \left|G^k_{s,t}\right| \leq C$; so let τ and δ_n be those constructed above for the game $\tilde{\Gamma}$: now (2) holds, with $E_n = \max_{q \in \Delta(K_i)} [\sum_{k \in K_i} q^k \overline{\tilde{g}}^k_n - h(q)]$. Then $d(\overline{\tilde{g}}_n, \mathbf{L}_h) \leq E_n \sqrt{\mathrm{dim}}$, dim being the dimension of the space. But, as seen above, this dimension is in fact bounded by $\#\{S_i \times T\}$ instead of $\#K_i$. Hence, after multiplying the sequence δ_n by $\max_{i \in I} \sqrt{\#\{S_i \times T\}}$, we obtain indeed the desired statement, but still with $\overline{\tilde{g}}_n$ instead of $\overline{g}_n$. Observe now that, by II.4, Ex. 6, p. 121 (in the game with vector payoffs $G^k_{s,t,a,b} - G^k_{s,t}$), $\mathsf{E}\sup_{m \geq n} d(\overline{g}_n, \overline{\tilde{g}}_n) \leq 4\sqrt{2}\frac{C}{\sqrt{n}}$.

Let thus $E_n = d(\overline{g}_n, \mathbf{L}_h)$, $\tilde{E}_n = d(\overline{\tilde{g}}_n, \mathbf{L}_h)$: we have $\mathsf{E}_{\tau,\sigma}(E_n) \leq \mathsf{E}(\tilde{E}_n) + 4\sqrt{2}\frac{C}{\sqrt{n}} \leq 4\sqrt{2}\frac{C}{\sqrt{n}} + C\delta_n + C\exp(-n\varepsilon_n) = C\eta_n$, where the sequence η_n converges to zero and depends only on the $Q^i_{s,t}(b)$. Since also $0 \leq E_n \leq C$, it suffices now again to repeat part (3) of the proof of Theorem V.3.16, p. 239, with $N_\ell = \ell$, τ_ℓ the restriction of τ to the first ℓ stages, and the variables $\frac{E_\ell}{C}$. ■

Remark V.3.58. Given the above results, Definition V.3.35 and Corollary V.3.29, p. 258, generalize now directly, by interpreting this time $\overline{Z}$ and $\underline{Z}$ as sets of affine functions on M, and Z as compactly generated by $\mathbf{H}_0$.

Remark V.3.59. If one thinks of $\Delta(K_i)$ as a neighborhood of zero in the space of all $S_i \times T$ matrices, then, for $h \in \mathbf{H}_0$, $h_{|\Delta(K_i)}$ becomes a convex function on this neighborhood. Its minimality implies immediately that it is positively homogeneous of degree one, so extends to the whole space; similarly it is monotone and invariant under addition of constants. (The latter two properties imply the Lipschitz property and uniform norm with constant C.)

Remark V.3.60. When $\#I = 1$, Proposition V.3.41.2, p. 276, becomes an extension of the approachability theorem of Section II.4, p. 118, to the case where the game with vector payoffs has signals; i.e., the game is described by having, for every pure strategy pair s, t, a probability distribution over triplets formed of a signal of player I, a signal of player II, and a vector payoff in the ball of radius C. The sets S, T, and B must be finite.

Indeed, one can always assume that II's signals inform him of his own action; the worst case is then when player I's signal consists of his own move, player II's signal, and the actual vector payoff, and any additional information is irrelevant. Formally the previous treatment requires player I's set of signals to be finite, but one sees that the above argument still applies in this case.

Also, at first sight this concerns only approachability of convex sets A such that $A - \mathbb{R}^K_+ \subseteq A$, but this yields immediately the general result by mapping $\mathbb{R}^K$ into $\mathbb{R}^{2K}$ by the map $\varphi_{2i-1}(x) = x_i$, $\varphi_{2i}(x) = -x_i$: for any arbitrary convex set A and point x in $\mathbb{R}^K$, let $\tilde{x} = \varphi(x)$, $\tilde{A} = \varphi(A) - \mathbb{R}^{2K}_+$: then $d(x, A) \leq d(\tilde{x}, \tilde{A}) \leq \sqrt{2}d(x, A)$, and so our approachability theorem for the set $\tilde{A}$ immediately implies the corresponding result for the general compact convex set A (and consequently for any closed convex A, by replacing it by its intersection with the ball of radius C).

Remark V.3.61. The corresponding excludability criterion is obvious (e.g., from part (4) of Proposition V.3.40, p. 275): for any other convex set C, the corresponding function h_C is such that $\int h_C(p)\mu(dp) < u(\mu)$ for some $\mu \in \Delta(P)$, which (by continuity of u) can be assumed to have finite support. That is, there exists $\varepsilon > 0$, $(p_j)_{j \in J}$ in $\Delta(K)$ with J finite, and $\sigma_j \in \Delta(S)$ such that, for any one-stage strategy of player II, all σ_j induce the same probability distribution on signals for player II, and such that, for any strategy τ of player II in Γ_∞, if $z_n(j)$ denotes the expected vector payoff generated by τ and by the i.i.d. play of σ_j in Γ_n, then $\max_J[\langle p_j, z_n(j)\rangle - \sup_{z \in C}\langle p_j, z\rangle] \geq \varepsilon$ for all n.

V.4. THE ROLE OF THE NORMAL DISTRIBUTION

The appearance of $1/\sqrt{n}$ in the speed of convergence may have the following probabilistic interpretation: consider a game with $K = \{1, 2\}$ and both G^1 and G^2 are 2×2 games. Suppose that $\operatorname{Cav} u(p) = u(p)$. So $\lim_{n\to\infty} v_n(p) = u(p)$, which means that in the limit as $n \to \infty$ player I can obtain no more than $u(p)$, which is what he can guarantee by ignoring his additional information and playing identically in both games. Nevertheless player I can generally obtain more than $u(p)$ in $\Gamma_n(p)$ for any finite n. In order to do this he has to play differently in the two possible games. In other words, he has to deviate from this non-revealing strategy. How much can he deviate, and how much can he gain by this deviation? Let $(s, 1-s)$ be player I's optimal mixed move in $D(p)$ (i.e., play the first pure move with probability s and the second with probability $1-s$ $(0 \le s \le 1)$.) By definition, if player I plays this mixed move repeatedly in all n stages of $\Gamma_n(p)$, he guarantees $u(p)$. If player I in fact does this, the actual choice of pure move made by him can be regarded as a Bernoulli trial with probabilities $(s, 1-s)$. By the Central Limit Theorem, the proportion of times that the first pure move is played in n such trials is approximately normally distributed around the mean s with a standard deviation of the order of $1/\sqrt{n}$. Therefore if player I wishes to "cheat" player II by making use of his additional information (i.e., playing different mixed moves in the two possible games) without enabling him to detect it, he has to do this in such a way that this proportion will fall within the limits of a few standard deviations, i.e., $\alpha/\sqrt{n}$ from s. Using again the minmax theorem, any deviation of a higher order will be detected and used by player II to hold the payoff to a number smaller than $u(p)$. Clearly a deviation of an order not higher than $1/\sqrt{n}$ from $(s, 1-s)$ will make a deviation in the payoff that is also of an order not higher than $1/\sqrt{n}$. The existence of games with **error term** $\delta_n(p) = v_n(p) - v_\infty(p) \approx (1/\sqrt{n})$ implies that there are games in which player I can exhaust the whole probabilistic deviation mentioned above. In other games he may be able to exhaust only a small part of it, such as $\approx (\frac{\ln n}{n})$ or $\approx (1/n)$.

In this section we shall see that the connection of the error term to the Central Limit Theorem is even much closer than what is outlined above. The normal distribution appears explicitly in the asymptotic behavior of $v_n(p)$. In the next section we prove some more results about the speed of convergence of $v_n(p)$.

Example V.4.1. Consider the following game with $K = \{1, 2\}$, full monitoring, and payoff matrices:

$$G^1 = \begin{pmatrix} 3 & -1 \\ -3 & 1 \end{pmatrix}, \quad G^2 = \begin{pmatrix} 2 & -2 \\ -2 & 2 \end{pmatrix},$$

and the prior probability distribution on K is $(p, 1-p)$.

We know that $v_n(p)$, which equals in this case the error term $\delta_n(p) = v_n(p) - v_\infty(p)$, is bounded by (by Theorem V.2.8, p. 223):

$$0 \le v_n(p) \le \frac{6\sqrt{pp'}}{\sqrt{n}}.$$

For this specific game sharper bounds can be obtained: $v_n(p) \leq \frac{\sqrt{pp'}}{\sqrt{n}}$ (see V.5, Ex. 10a, p. 307) and $v_n(p) \geq \frac{pp'}{\sqrt{n}}$, cf. Zamir (1971–1972). It turns out, however, that a much stronger result can be proved, namely:

Theorem V.4.1. *For all $p \in [0, 1]$:*

$$\lim_{n\to\infty} \sqrt{n}\, v_n(p) = \phi(p),$$

where

$$\phi(p) = \frac{1}{\sqrt{2\pi}} e^{-\frac{1}{2}x_p^2} \text{ and } \frac{1}{\sqrt{2\pi}} \int_{-\infty}^{x_p} e^{-\frac{1}{2}x^2} dx = p.$$

In words: The limit of $\sqrt{n}v_n(p)$ is the standard normal density function evaluated at its p-quantile.

Another way to state this theorem is: The coefficient of the leading term (i.e., of $1/\sqrt{n}$) in the expansion of $v_n(p)$ is $\phi(p)$. Before proving this puzzling result it may be helpful to outline the heuristic arguments that lead to it. For this we shall need the following recursive formula for v_n, which will be useful also in later sections.

Lemma V.4.2. ***(Recursive Formula)*** *For any two-person zero-sum game with incomplete information on one side (player II is uninformed) and with full monitoring, the following holds for all $p \in \Delta(K)$ and for all $n \geq 1$:*

$$v_{n+1}(p) = \frac{1}{n+1} \max_{x\in X^K}\Big(\min_{t\in T} \sum_{k\in K} p^k x^k G_t^k + n \sum_s \overline{x}_s v_n(p_s)\Big), \tag{1}$$

where $\overline{x} = \sum_{k\in K} p^k x^k$, and the probabilities $p_s = (p_s^k)_{k\in K} \in \Delta(K)$ are given by $p_s^k = p^k x_s^k / \overline{x}_s$ for all s such that $\overline{x}_s > 0$, and G_t^k is the t-th column of G^k.

Proof. This is clearly a special case of the general recursive formula given in Theorem IV.3.2 (cf. V.5, Ex. 6, p. 305): nevertheless we give here an elementary proof that is available in this case: a strategy of player I in $\Gamma_{n+1}(p)$ includes an element $x = (x^k)_{k\in K}$ of X^K where if the state is k, player I plays in the first-stage the mixed move $x^k = (x_s^k)_{s\in S}$ in $\Delta(S)$. If player II plays at first-stage his pure move $t \in T$, the expected first-stage payoff is $\sum_{k\in K} p^k x^k G_t^k$. Given x and given $s_1 = s$, the conditional probability distribution on K is $p_s = P(\cdot \mid s)$. By playing optimally in $\Gamma_n(p_s)$, player I can guarantee a conditional expected cumulative payoff of at least $nv_n(p_s)$ for the last n stages. Since the probability of s is $\overline{x}_s = \sum_{k\in K} p^k x^k$ we conclude that x followed by an optimal strategy in the resulting $\Gamma_n(p_s)$ guarantees player I at least:

$$\frac{1}{n+1} \min_{t\in T}\Big(\sum_{k\in K} p^k x^k G_t^k + n \sum_s \overline{x}_s v_n(p_s)\Big),$$

which, since the p_s are independent of t, equals:

$$\frac{1}{n+1}\Big(\min_{t\in T}\sum_{k\in K} p^k x^k G_t^k + n\sum_s \overline{x}_s v_n(p_s)\Big).$$

Taking the maximum over X^K it follows that $v_{n+1}(p)$ is greater than or equal to the right-hand side of equation (1). The other direction of the inequality is obtained using the minmax theorem: given σ (and hence x), player II can minimize his expected payoff at the first stage and then, following a move s, compute p_s and play optimally in $\Gamma_n(p_s)$. In doing so he guarantees the maximand $(\cdots)$ in the right-hand side of equation (1). This proves the inequality: $v_{n+1} \leq \cdots$ and completes the proof of the lemma. ∎

V.4.a. The Heuristics of the Result

Our departure point is the recursive formula (1), which for this game reads:

$$\begin{aligned} v_{n+1}(p) &\\ = \frac{1}{n+1} \max_{0\leq x,y\leq 1} &\{\min[3p(x-x')+2p'(y-y'), p(x'-x)+2p'(y'-y)] \\ &+n(\overline{x}v_n(p_T)+\overline{x}'v_n(p_B))\}, \end{aligned} \tag{2}$$

where (x, x'), (y, y') are the mixed strategies of player I in G^1 and G^2, respectively:

$$(\overline{x}, \overline{x}') = (px + p'y, px' + p'y') \tag{3}$$

and

$$p_T = \frac{px}{\overline{x}} \qquad p_B = \frac{px'}{\overline{x}'}. \tag{4}$$

Assume (as often turns out to be the case in our proofs) that the $\max_{0\leq x,y\leq 1}$ in that formula is achieved when x and y equalize player II's expected payoff for a left first move and a right first move, i.e.:

$$3p(x-x')+2p'(y-y') = p(x'-x)+2p'(y'-y),$$

which is $y = 1/2 - p(x-x')/(2p')$. Changing the variable to $\xi = p(x-x')$ and denoting $U_n(p) = \sqrt{n}v_n(p)$ we obtain (using the notation $a\wedge b = \min(a,b)$):

$$U_{n+1}(p) = \frac{1}{\sqrt{n+1}} \max_{0\leq\xi\leq p\wedge p'} \Big\{\xi + \frac{\sqrt{n}}{2}(U_n(p+\xi)+U_n(p-\xi))\Big\}. \tag{5}$$

Suppose now that $\lim_{n\to\infty} U_n(p)$ exists and equals $\varphi(p)$. Letting $\xi = \alpha_n/\sqrt{n}$ we then have:

$$\begin{aligned}\sqrt{1+\frac{1}{n}}\,\varphi(p) &\simeq \max_{\alpha_n}\Big\{\frac{\alpha_n}{n} + \frac{1}{2}[\varphi(p+\frac{\alpha_n}{\sqrt{n}}) + \varphi(p-\frac{\alpha_n}{\sqrt{n}})]\Big\}\\ &\simeq \max_{\alpha_n}\Big\{\frac{\alpha_n}{n} + \varphi(p) + \frac{\alpha_n^2}{2n}\varphi''(p)\Big\}\\ &= \varphi(p) + \frac{1}{n}\max_{\alpha_n}\Big\{\alpha_n + \frac{\alpha_n^2}{2}\varphi''(p)\Big\}\\ &= \varphi(p) - \frac{1}{2n\varphi''(p)}.\end{aligned}$$

On the other hand, $(\sqrt{1+1/n})\varphi \simeq \varphi + \varphi/(2n)$, thus $\varphi = -1/\varphi''$. We conclude that if $\sqrt{n}v_n(p)$ converges, the limit is a solution of the differential equation:

$$\varphi(p)\varphi''(p) + 1 = 0. \tag{6}$$

To solve equation (6) we first have:

$$\varphi'(p) = -\int_{1/2}^{p} \frac{1}{\varphi(p)}dp.$$

Here we have chosen $1/2$ as the lower bound of the integration so as to have $\varphi'(p) = 0$, which is implied by the symmetry of $\varphi(p)$ about $p = 1/2$. (This is a property of all $U_n(p)$ and can be easily proved by inducting using (5) and the symmetry of the arbitrary $U_0(p)$.) Now let:

$$z(p) = -\varphi'(p) = \int_{1/2}^{p} \frac{1}{\varphi(p)}dp.$$

We have $z'(p) = 1/\varphi(p)$, and thus $\varphi = dp/dz$. Replacing the variable p by z we get:

$$\varphi_z' = \varphi_p'\frac{dp}{dz} = \varphi_p'\varphi = -z\varphi,$$

and thus $\ln\varphi = K - z^2/2$, or:

$$\varphi = \frac{A}{\sqrt{2\pi}}e^{-\frac{1}{2}z^2}, \tag{7}$$

for some constant A. Since $\varphi = dp/dz$:

$$p = B + \int_{-\infty}^{z(p)} \frac{A}{\sqrt{2\pi}}e^{-\frac{1}{2}x^2}dx, \tag{8}$$

for some constant B. Denoting by $F(x)$ the cumulative standard normal distribution we have therefore:

$$\varphi(z) = AF'(z),$$
$$p = B + AF(z).$$

Now $\varphi \geq 0$ and $\varphi \not\equiv 0$ imply $A > 0$, from which it follows by (8) that $z(p)$ is increasing in p. Since $\varphi(0) = \varphi(1) = 0$ we have by (7): $z(0) = -\infty$ and $z(1) = +\infty$, and therefore by (8) we have:

$$0 = B, \qquad 1 = B + A.$$

So $\varphi(p) = F'(z)$ and $p = F(z)$; i.e., $\varphi(p)$ is the standard normal density evaluated at its p-quantile, i.e., $\phi(p)$.

Remark V.4.2. Note that the above heuristic has nothing to do with the intuitive argument in the beginning of this section. In other words the normal distribution appeared not through the Central Limit Theorem but rather as the solution of a certain differential equation. As we shall see later in this section, this is not an isolated result for only this specific example, but rather a general one. At least for 2×2 games we know so far the following: whenever the leading term in the expansion of the error term is $1/\sqrt{n}$, the coefficient is an appropriately scaled ϕ function.

V.4.b. Proof of Theorem V.4.1

For the formal proof of Theorem V.4.1, p. 281, we need the following general result about martingales in [0, 1]. Let $\mathscr{X}_p^n = \{X_m\}_{m=1}^n$ denote an n-martingale bounded in [0, 1] with $\mathsf{E}(X_1) = p$, and let $V(\mathscr{X}_p^n)$ denote its L_1 variation, i.e.:

$$V(\mathscr{X}_p^n) = \sum_{m=1}^{n-1} \mathsf{E}(|X_{m+1} - X_m|).$$

Then we have:

Theorem V.4.3. *(The L_1 variation of a bounded martingale.)*

$$\limsup_{n\to\infty} \sup_{\mathscr{X}_p^n} \left[\frac{1}{\sqrt{n}} V(\mathscr{X}_p^n)\right] = \phi(p).$$

Proof. The proof uses several lemmas (two of which are proved in the appendix to this chapter), and it is concluded after Lemma V.4.10, p. 288.

For $p \in [0, 1]$ let $S(p) = \{(\xi, \eta) \mid 0 \leq \xi \leq p';\ 0 \leq \eta \leq p\}$ and define two sequences of functions on [0, 1], $\{\varphi_n\}$ and $\{\psi_n\}$ by $\varphi_1 \equiv \psi_1 \equiv 0$, and for

$n = 1, 2, \ldots$:

$$\sqrt{n+1}\varphi_{n+1}(p) = \max_{(\xi,\eta)\in S(p)} \left[\sqrt{n}\Big(\frac{\eta}{\xi+\eta}\psi_n(p+\xi) + \frac{\xi}{\xi+\eta}\psi_n(p-\eta)\Big) + \frac{2\xi\eta}{\xi+\eta}\right], \tag{9}$$

$$\psi_{n+1} = \mathsf{Cav}\,\varphi_{n+1}. \tag{10}$$

In the recursive formula (9) the expression in the square brackets is defined to be $\sqrt{n}\psi_n(p)$ for $\xi = \eta = 0$. We first observe that:

$$\varphi_n(0) = \psi_n(0) = \varphi_n(1) = \psi_n(1) = 0 \ \text{ for all } n.$$

It also follows readily from the definitions that:

$$\varphi_2(p) = \psi_2(p) = 2p(1-p) \ \text{ for } p \in [0, 1]. \tag{11}$$

Remark V.4.3. All functions $\{\varphi_n\}_{n=1}^{\infty}$ and $\{\psi_n\}_{n=1}^{\infty}$ are symmetric about $p = 1/2$. This is easily proved by induction using (9) and (10) and observing that the Cav operator preserves symmetry about $p = 1/2$.

Lemma V.4.4.

$$\sup_{\mathscr{X}_p^2} V(\mathscr{X}_p^2) = \psi_2(p) = 2p(1-p).$$

Proof. Follows readily by Jensen's inequality since $|x - p|$ is convex. ∎

Lemma V.4.5. *For all n and for all* $p \in [0, 1]$*:*

$$\sup_{\mathscr{X}_p^n} \left[\frac{1}{\sqrt{n}} V(\mathscr{X}_p^n)\right] \le \psi_n(p).$$

Proof. For $n = 1$ both sides are 0, and for $n = 2$ the inequality follows from Lemma V.4.7, p. 287, and equation (11). Proceeding by induction, assume it is true for $n \le m - 1$, and let us prove it for $n = m$. Since $\psi_m = \mathsf{Cav}\,\varphi_m$ it is enough to prove that for $p \in [0, 1]$:

$$\sup_{\mathscr{X}_p^m} \left[\frac{1}{\sqrt{m}} V(\mathscr{X}_p^m)\right] \le \varphi_m(p).$$

To prove this, let $\Omega_L = \{X_2 \le p\}$, $\Omega_R = \{X_2 > p\}$, $\lambda = P(\Omega_R)$. For any $\mathscr{X}_p^m$ we have:

$$\begin{aligned} V(\mathscr{X}_p^m) &= \sum_2^m \mathsf{E}(|X_i - X_{i-1}|) \\ &= \mathsf{E}(|X_2 - p|) + \lambda \sum_3^m \mathsf{E}(|X_i - X_{i-1}| \mid \Omega_R) \\ &\quad + (1-\lambda) \sum_3^m \mathsf{E}(|X_i - X_{i-1}| \mid \Omega_L), \end{aligned}$$

which is, by induction hypothesis, with $X_L = \mathsf{E}(X_2 \mid \Omega_L)$ and $X_R = \mathsf{E}(X_2 \mid \Omega_R)$ is less than or equal to:

$$\lambda(X_R - p) + (1-\lambda)(p - X_L) + \sqrt{m-1}\,[\lambda\psi_{m-1}(X_R) + (1-\lambda)\psi_{m-1}(X_L)]\,.$$

Let $X_R = p + \xi$, $X_L = p - \eta$: then $\xi \geq 0$, $\eta \geq 0$, $\lambda = \eta/(\xi+\eta)$, and the last inequality becomes:

$$V(\mathscr{X}_p^m) \leq \sqrt{m-1}\left[\frac{\eta}{\xi+\eta}\psi_{m-1}(p+\xi) + \frac{\xi}{\xi+\eta}\psi_{m-1}(p-\eta)\right] + \frac{2\xi\eta}{\xi+\eta}.$$

Hence by definition $V(\mathscr{X}_p^m) \leq \sqrt{m}\varphi_m(p)$, concluding the proof of Lemma V.4.5. ∎

Proceeding in the proof of Theorem V.4.3, p. 284, define the sequence $\{(\tilde{\phi}_n\})_{n=1}^{\infty}$ of functions on $[0, 1]$ by $\tilde{\phi}_1 \equiv 0$ and for $n = 1, 2, \ldots$:

$$\sqrt{n+1}\tilde{\phi}_{n+1}(p)$$
$$= \max_{(\xi,\eta)\in S(p)}\left[\sqrt{n}\left(\frac{\eta}{\xi+\eta}\tilde{\phi}_n(p+\xi) + \frac{\xi}{\xi+\eta}\tilde{\phi}_n(p-\eta)\right) + \frac{2\xi\eta}{\xi+\eta}\right]. \quad (12)$$

Here again the expression in the square brackets is defined to be $\sqrt{n}\tilde{\phi}_n(p)$ if $\xi = \eta = 0$. It follows readily from the definitions that for all p and all n, $\psi_n(p) \geq \tilde{\phi}_n(p)$:

Lemma V.4.6. *For all n and all $p \in [0, 1]$:*

$$\sup_{\mathscr{X}_p^n} \frac{1}{\sqrt{n}} V(\mathscr{X}_p^n) \geq \tilde{\phi}_n(p).$$

Proof. For each $n = 2, 3, \ldots$ and $p \in [0, 1]$ we construct a martingale $\mathscr{X}_p^n$ s.t.:

$$\frac{1}{\sqrt{n}} V(\mathscr{X}_p^n) = \tilde{\phi}_n(p). \quad (13)$$

We do the construction inductively on n: For $n = 2$ let $P\{X_2 = 0\} = p'$, $P\{X_2 = 1\} = p$; then $V(\mathscr{X}_p^2) = 2pp' = \tilde{\phi}_2(p)$. Assume that for each $m \leq n$, we constructed $\mathscr{X}_p^m = \{X_i(p)\}_{i=1}^m$ having the right variation, and let us construct $\mathscr{X}_p^{n+1}$. Let (ξ_n, η_n) be a point at which the maximum is attained in (12). Define the martingale $\mathscr{X}_p^{n+1} = \{Z_i(p)\}_{i=1}^{n+1}$ as follows:

$$Z_1(p) \equiv p,$$

$$P\{Z_2(p) = p + \xi_n\} = \frac{\eta_n}{\xi_n + \eta_n}\ ;\ P\{Z_2(p) = p - \eta_n\} = \frac{\xi_n}{\xi_n + \eta_n}, \quad (14)$$

and for $i = 2, \ldots, n$:

$$(Z_{i+1}(p) \mid Z_2(p) = p + \xi_n) = X_i(p + \xi_n),$$
$$(Z_{i+1}(p) \mid Z_2(p) = p - \eta_n) = X_i(p - \eta_n).$$

It follows from (12) and (14) that:

$$\begin{aligned}
&\frac{1}{\sqrt{n+1}} V(\mathscr{X}_p^{n+1}) \\
&= \frac{1}{\sqrt{n+1}} \left[2\xi_n\eta_n + \eta_n V(\mathscr{X}_{p+\xi_n}^n) + \xi_n V(\mathscr{X}_{p-\eta_n}^n)\right] / (\xi_n + \eta_n) \\
&= \frac{1}{\sqrt{n+1}} \left[2\xi_n\eta_n + \sqrt{n}\left(\eta_n\tilde{\phi}_n(p+\xi_n) + \xi_n\tilde{\phi}_n(p-\eta_n)\right)\right] / (\xi_n + \eta_n) \\
&= \tilde{\phi}_{n+1}(p).
\end{aligned}$$

This completes the proof of Lemma V.4.6. ■

To proceed we need the following two properties of the normal distribution $\phi(p)$:

Lemma V.4.7. *There exists a constant $c > 0$ such that for $p \in [0, 1]$ and for all $n \geq 1$:*

$$\frac{1}{\sqrt{n+1}} \max_{0 \leq x \leq p \wedge p'} \left[\frac{\sqrt{n}}{2}(\phi(p+x) + \phi(p-x)) + x\right] \geq \phi(p) - \frac{c}{\sqrt{n^2}}. \tag{15}$$

Here $p \wedge p' = \min(p, p')$.

Lemma V.4.8. *There exists a constant $K > 0$ such that for $p \in [0, 1]$ and for all $n \geq 1$:*

$$\begin{aligned}
&\frac{1}{\sqrt{n+1}} \max_{(\xi,\eta) \in S(p)} \left[\sqrt{n}\left(\frac{\eta}{\xi+\eta}\phi(p+\xi) + \frac{\xi}{\xi+\eta}\phi(p-\eta)\right) + \frac{2\xi\eta}{\xi+\eta}\right] \\
&\leq \phi(p) + \frac{K}{n^2}.
\end{aligned} \tag{16}$$

The rather lengthy and technical proofs to these lemmas are given in the appendix to this chapter.

Lemma V.4.9. *There exists $\alpha > 0$ such that for all $n \geq 1$ and for all $p \in [0, 1]$:*

$$\tilde{\phi}_n(p) \geq \phi(p) - \frac{\alpha}{\sqrt{n}}. \tag{17}$$

Proof. We first prove by induction on k that for $n \geq 1$:

$$\tilde{\phi}_{n+k}(p) \geq \phi(p) - \frac{1}{\sqrt{n+k}}\left[\frac{\sqrt{n}}{2} + \sum_{i=n}^{n+k} \frac{4c}{i\sqrt{i}}\right], \tag{18}$$

for $k = 0, 1, \ldots$, where c is the constant in Lemma V.4.7. In fact, for $k = 0$, $\tilde{\phi}_n(p) \geq 0 \geq \phi(p) - 1/2$. For the next step notice that in Lemma V.4.7 we may replace c/n^2 by $4c/(n+1)^2$. Assume that (18) holds for k; then, by

Lemma V.4.7:

$$\tilde{\phi}_{n+k+1}(p)$$

$$= \frac{1}{\sqrt{n+k+1}} \max_{(\xi,\eta)\in S(p)} \left[\sqrt{n+k}\left(\eta\tilde{\phi}_{n+k}(p+\xi) + \xi\tilde{\phi}_{n+k}(p-\eta)\right) + 2\xi\eta\right] / (\xi+\eta)$$

$$\geq \frac{1}{\sqrt{n+k+1}} \max_{0\leq x\leq p\wedge p'} \left[\frac{\sqrt{n+k}}{2}\left(\tilde{\phi}_{n+k}(p+x) + \tilde{\phi}_{n+k}(p-x)\right) + x\right]$$

$$\geq \frac{1}{\sqrt{n+k+1}} \max_{0\leq x\leq p\wedge p'} \left[\frac{\sqrt{n+k}}{2}(\phi(p+x) + \phi(p-x)) + x - \left(\frac{\sqrt{n}}{2} + \sum_{i=n}^{n+k}\frac{4c}{i\sqrt{i}}\right)\right]$$

$$\geq \phi(p) - \frac{4c}{(n+k+1)^2} - \frac{1}{\sqrt{n+k+1}}\left(\frac{\sqrt{n}}{2} + \sum_{i=n}^{n+k}\frac{4c}{i\sqrt{i}}\right)$$

$$= \phi(p) - \frac{1}{\sqrt{n+k+1}}\left(\frac{\sqrt{n}}{2} + \sum_{i=n}^{n+k+1}\frac{4c}{i\sqrt{i}}\right),$$

completing the proof of (18), from which we obtain for $n = 1$:

$$\tilde{\phi}_{k+1}(p) \geq \phi(p) - \frac{1}{\sqrt{k+1}}\left(\frac{1}{2} + \sum_{i=1}^{\infty}\frac{4c}{i\sqrt{i}}\right) = \phi(p) - \frac{\alpha}{\sqrt{k+1}},$$

where $\alpha = 1/2 + 4c\sum_{i=1}^{\infty} i^{-3/2}$. Since this holds for all k, the proof of Lemma V.4.9 is completed. ∎

Lemma V.4.10. *There exists $\beta > 0$ such that for all $n \geq 1$ and for all $p \in [0,1]$:*

$$\psi_n(p) \leq \phi(p) + \frac{\beta}{\sqrt{n}}. \tag{19}$$

Proof. The proof is almost identical to that of the previous lemma. First $\psi_2(p) = 2pp' \leq \phi(p) + 1/2$. Next use Lemma V.4.8 and (9), p. 285, to prove that:

$$\psi_{k+1}(p) \leq \phi(p) + \frac{1}{\sqrt{k+1}}\left(\frac{1}{2} + \sum_{i=1}^{k+1}\frac{K}{i\sqrt{i}}\right) \tag{20}$$

implies:

$$\varphi_{k+2}(p) \leq \phi(p) + \frac{1}{\sqrt{k+2}}\left(\frac{1}{2} + \sum_{i=1}^{k+2}\frac{K}{i\sqrt{i}}\right), \tag{21}$$

where K is the constant in Lemma V.4.8. Observing that the right-hand side of the last inequality is a concave function of p, it implies:

$$\psi_{k+1} \leq \operatorname{Cav}\varphi_{k+2}(p) \leq \phi(p) + \frac{1}{\sqrt{k+2}}\left(\frac{1}{2} + \sum_{i=1}^{k+2}\frac{K}{i\sqrt{i}}\right), \tag{22}$$

proving that (20) holds for all k, and hence the lemma, with $\beta = 1/2 + K\sum_{i=1}^{\infty} i^{-3/2}$. ■

We are now ready to conclude the proof of Theorem V.4.3, p. 284: by Lemmas V.4.6, p. 286, and V.4.9, p. 287, we have:

$$\liminf_{n\to\infty} \sup_{\mathscr{X}_p^n} \left[\frac{1}{\sqrt{n}} V(\mathscr{X}_p^n)\right] \geq \liminf_{n\to\infty} \tilde{\phi}_n(p) \geq \phi(p),$$

and by Lemma V.4.5, p. 285, and Lemma V.4.10:

$$\limsup_{n\to\infty} \sup_{\mathscr{X}_p^n} \left[\frac{1}{\sqrt{n}} V(\mathscr{X}_p^n)\right] \leq \limsup_{n\to\infty} \psi_n(p) \leq \phi(p). \tag{23}$$

■

Corollary V.4.11. *The martingale $\mathscr{X}_p^n$ constructed in the proof of Lemma V.4.6, p. 286, satisfies:*

$$\lim_{n\to\infty} \left[\frac{1}{\sqrt{n}} V(\mathscr{X}_p^n)\right] = \phi(p) \text{ for } p \in [0,1],$$

with speed of convergence of the order of $1/\sqrt{n}$.

Proof. By Lemmas V.4.9 and V.4.10 we get:

$$\phi(p) - \frac{\alpha}{\sqrt{n}} \leq \tilde{\phi}_n(p) \leq \psi_n(p) \leq \phi(p) + \frac{\beta}{\sqrt{n}}. \tag{24}$$

■

Proof of Theorem V.4.1, p. 281. Given any strategy σ of player I in $\Gamma_n(p)$ let τ_σ be the reply of player II consisting of playing optimally in $D(p_m)$ at stage m for $m = 1, 2, \ldots$. Then the conditional expected payoff at stage m satisfies:

$$\rho_m(\sigma, \tau_\sigma) \leq \mathsf{E}(|p_{m+1} - p_m| \mid \mathscr{H}_m^{\mathrm{II}}). \tag{25}$$

This is a somewhat stronger inequality than the general one derived in the proof of Proposition V.2.7, p. 222, the difference being that in the specific game we are dealing with, the constant $2C = 2\max_{k,s,t} \left|G_{st}^k\right|$ can be replaced by 1 (just by estimating errors more tightly; cf. V.5, Ex. 10a, p. 307).

From (25), taking the average over m and expectation over histories we have:

$$\overline{\gamma}_n(\sigma, \tau_\sigma) \leq \frac{1}{n}\sum_{m=1}^{n} \mathsf{E}(|p_{m+1} - p_m|),$$

(where $p_1 = p$) and hence:

$$v_n(p) \leq \max_\sigma \frac{1}{n}\sum_{m=1}^{n} \mathsf{E}(|p_{m+1} - p_m|). \tag{26}$$

Since the sequence $\{p_m\}_{m=1}^{\infty}$ is such a martingale, we combine Theorem V.4.3, p. 284, with inequality (26) to obtain:

$$\limsup_{n\to\infty} \sqrt{n}v_n(p) \leq \phi(p). \tag{27}$$

Next we shall find a lower bound for $\liminf_{n\to\infty} \sqrt{n}v_n(p)$. To do this we denote $w_n(p) = \sqrt{n}v_n(p)$ and proceed, as we did for the heuristic argument (i.e., use the recursive formula (2), p. 282, restrict the first-stage strategy by $y = 1/2 - p(x - x')/(2p')$, and let $\xi = p(x - x')$), to obtain the recursive inequality:

$$w_{n+1}(p) \geq \frac{1}{\sqrt{n+1}} \max_{0\leq\xi\leq p\wedge p'} \{\xi + \frac{\sqrt{n}}{2}(w_n(p+\xi) + w_n(p-\xi))\}. \tag{28}$$

Define now the sequence of functions $\{U_n(p)\}_{m=0}^{\infty}$ by $U_0(p) \equiv 0$ and the recursive relation (5), p. 282; then clearly $U_n(p) \leq w_n(p)$ for all $p \in [0, 1]$ and for all n. Therefore to complete the proof of the theorem it suffices to prove:

$$\liminf_{n\to\infty} U_n(p) \geq \phi(p). \tag{29}$$

First we claim that for any n the inequality

$$U_{n+m}(p) \geq \phi(p) - \frac{\sqrt{n}}{2\sqrt{n+m}} - \sum_{i=n}^{n+m} \frac{c}{i^2} \tag{30}$$

holds for $m = 0, 1, 2, \ldots$, where c is a constant in Lemma V.4.7, p. 287. This is proved by induction on m; it is clearly true for $m = 0$ since $U_n(p) \geq 0 \geq \phi(p) - 1/2$. Assume it holds for m; using (5), p. 282, we have:

$$\begin{aligned}
U_{n+m+1}(p) &= \frac{1}{\sqrt{n+m+1}} \max_{0\leq\xi\leq p\wedge p'} \{\xi + \frac{\sqrt{n+m}}{2}(U_{n+m}(p+\xi) \\
&\quad + U_{n+m}(p-\xi))\} \\
&\geq \frac{1}{\sqrt{n+m+1}} \max_{0\leq\xi\leq p\wedge p'} \{\xi + \frac{\sqrt{n+m}}{2}(\phi(p+\xi) - \frac{\sqrt{n}}{2\sqrt{n+m}} \\
&\quad - \sum_{i=n}^{n+m} \frac{c}{i^2} + \phi(p-\xi) - \frac{\sqrt{n}}{2\sqrt{n+m}} - \sum_{i=n}^{n+m} \frac{c}{i^2})\} \\
&\geq \frac{1}{\sqrt{n+m+1}} \max_{0\leq\xi\leq p\wedge p'} \{\xi + \frac{\sqrt{n+m}}{2}(\phi(p+\xi) + \phi(p-\xi))\} \\
&\quad - \frac{\sqrt{n}}{2\sqrt{n+m+1}} - \sum_{i=n}^{n+m} \frac{c}{i^2}.
\end{aligned}$$

So by (15), p. 287, we get:

$$U_{n+m+1}(p) \geq \phi(p) - \frac{c}{(n+m+1)^2} - \frac{\sqrt{n}}{2\sqrt{n+m+1}} - \sum_{i=n}^{n+m} \frac{c}{i^2}$$

$$= \phi(p) - \frac{\sqrt{n}}{2\sqrt{n+m+1}} - \sum_{i=n}^{n+m+1} \frac{c}{i^2},$$

which establishes (30), from which we get:

$$\liminf_{n\to\infty} U_n(p) = \liminf_{m\to\infty} U_{n+m}(p) \geq \phi(p) - \sum_{i=n}^{\infty} \frac{c}{i^2}.$$

Since the last inequality must hold for every n and since $c\sum_{i=n}^{\infty} i^{-2} < \infty$, this completes the proof of (29) and hence the proof of Theorem V.4.1. ■

V.4.c. More General Results

In this section we present results showing that the appearance of the normal distribution in the asymptotic value of the game in Example V.4.1, p. 280, is not an isolated incident but rather part of a general phenomenon. Unfortunately the proofs of these results are technically quite involved and lengthy, which makes them unaffordable in the framework of this book. They can be found in Mertens and Zamir (1995). (See also De Meyer, 1996a; De Meyer, 1996b.)

We consider here any two 2×2 payoff matrices G^1 and G^2. To state the results we need some notations. Let $G^k = (G^k_{st})$ for $k = 1, 2$, $s = 1, 2$, $t = 1, 2$, and denote:

- For $k = 1, 2$, $\Delta_k = G^k_{11} + G^k_{22} - G^k_{12} - G^k_{21}$.
- Define $\delta(G^1, G^2)$ by:

$$\delta(G^1, G^2) = \begin{cases} 1 & \text{If player I has a strategy that is optimal in } D(p)\ \forall p \in [0,1], \\ 0 & \text{otherwise.} \end{cases}$$

- For $p \in [0, 1]$ let (t_p, t'_p) be an optimal strategy of player II in $D(p)$ (we use t_2 for t_0 since it is optimal in G^2).
- For $p \in [0, 1]$ (given t_1, t_2 and t_p) let $q = q(p)$ be defined by $t_p = qt_1 + q't_2$.
- Finally we define:

$$K(G^1, G^2, p) = \delta(G^1, G^2)\,|t_1 - t_2|\,\sqrt{ss'}\,\left|p\Delta_1 + p'\Delta_2\right|,$$

where s is the uniformly optimal move of player I in $D(p)$ (relevant only if it exists and is unique, i.e., when $\delta(G^1, G^2) \neq 0$).

Our result can be now stated as follows:

Theorem V.4.12. *In any game with incomplete information on one side with full monitoring, $K = \{1, 2\}$, and payoff matrices G^1 and G^2, there exists $A > 0$ such that for all n and for all $p \in [0, 1]$:*

$$\left| v_n(p) - \mathsf{Cav}\, u(p) - K(G^1, G^2, p)\phi(q(p))\frac{1}{\sqrt{n}} \right| \le \frac{A}{n^{2/3}}, \tag{31}$$

where ϕ is the normal density function defined in Theorem V.4.1, p. 281.

Remark V.4.4. The theorem provides the highest-order term (in n) in the expansion of the error term $v_n(p) - \mathsf{Cav}\, u(p)$, namely, that of order $1/\sqrt{n}$: the coefficient of this term is a multiple of an appropriately scaled ϕ function.

Remark V.4.5. Both the constant $K(G^1, G^2, p)$ and the argument $q(p)$ are, as they should be, invariant under addition of a constant to all payoffs.

Remark V.4.6. Inequality (31) states that the error term is of order $1/\sqrt{n}$ (i.e., $K(G^1, G^2, p) \neq 0$) if and only if player I has the same strictly mixed optimal strategy in G^1 and in G^2 (and therefore in $D(p)$ for all $p \in [0, 1]$), while player II's optimal strategies are different in G^1 and in G^2.

Remark V.4.7. A priori t_1, t_2, and s may not be unique, which would mean that $K(G^1, G^2, p)$ is not well defined. However, observe that in a (non-constant) 2×2 game player I has a strictly mixed uniformly optimal move s in $D(p)$ only when player II has a unique optimal move in each game. If s is (mixed and) not unique, player II must have the same optimal pure move in both games and hence $(t_1 - t_2) = 0$. This means that whenever $|t_1 - t_2| \neq 0$, s is unique and if $\delta(G^1, G^2)\sqrt{ss'} \neq 0$, then t_1 and t_2 are unique. Hence K is always well defined.

Remark V.4.8. The existence of a (unique) $q = q(p)$ satisfying $t_p = qt_1 + q't_2$ is part of the statement of the theorem, i.e., whenever $K(G^1, G^2, p) \neq 0$, $q(p)$ is well defined.

Remark V.4.9. Note finally that in the example in the previous section we have:

$$\delta(G^1, G^2) = 1, s = 1/2, t_1 = 1/4, t_2 = 1/2, \Delta_1 = \Delta_2 = 8$$

and hence $K(G^1, G^2, p) = 1$. Also since:

$$t_p = \frac{p + 2p'}{4} = pt_1 + p't_2,$$

we have $q(p) = p$ for all $p \in [0, 1]$, and therefore $K(G^1, G^2, p)\phi(q(p)) = \phi(p)$.

Let us indicate now the main steps in the proof in order to see how the special example in Theorem V.4.1, p. 281, evolves to the general result in Theorem V.4.12, p. 292.

Step 1. *If the payoff matrices are:*

$$G^1 = \begin{pmatrix} \theta' a & -\theta' a' \\ \theta a & \theta a' \end{pmatrix} \text{ and } G^2 = \begin{pmatrix} \theta' b & -\theta' b' \\ \theta b & \theta b' \end{pmatrix},$$

where a, b and θ are in $[0, 1]$, then there exists $A > 0$ such that for all n and for all $p \in [0, 1]$:

$$\left| \sqrt{n} v_n(p) - |a-b| \sqrt{\theta\theta'} \phi(p) \right| \leq C \frac{\ln n}{n}. \tag{32}$$

- In these games:

  $u(p) \equiv 0, \delta(G^1, G^2) = 1, s = \theta, t_1 = a', t_2 = b', \Delta_1 = \Delta_2 = 1,$

  and so $K(G^1, G^2, p) = |a-b| \sqrt{\theta\theta'}$. Also the optimal move of player II in $D(p)$ is $t_p = pa' + p'b' = pt_1 + p't_2$, which implies that $q(p) = p$. So inequality (32) is in fact a special case of (31).
- This is a first step in generalizing Example V.4.1, p. 280. In that example $a = 3/4$, $b = 1/2$, $\theta = 1/2$, and all payoffs are multiplied by 8.
- The proof of Step 1 is basically the same as the first part of the proof of Theorem V.4.1, p. 281, namely, the proof of inequality (27), p. 290.

Step 2. *Extend the result in Step 1 by applying two standard transformations to the payoff matrices; adding a constant to all payoffs (this adds the same constant to all value functions of the games) and multiplying each matrix by a positive constant adds the same constant to all value functions of the games: for $\alpha > 0$, $\beta > 0$, if $\tilde{G}^1 = \alpha G^1$ and $\tilde{G}^2 = \beta G^2$, then $\forall p \in [0, 1]$ and $\forall n$:*

$$\tilde{u}(p) = (p\alpha + p'\beta) u \left(\frac{p\alpha}{p\alpha + p'\beta} \right), \tag{33}$$

and similar transformations hold for $\operatorname{Cav} u(p)$ and $v_n(p)$.

The proof of (33) is straightforward. The consequence of this step is that if a game satisfies (31), then so does any game obtainable from it by standard transformations. In particular: all games obtainable from the games considered in Step 1 satisfy (31).

Step 3. *If $u(p) = pv(G^1) + p'v(G^2)$, then:*

- *If $K(G^1, G^2, p) \neq 0$ for some p, $0 < p < 1$, then the game is obtainable from the class of games in Step 1 by standard transformations. Hence it satisfies* (31).
- *If $K(G^1, G^2, p) = 0$ for all $p \in [0, 1]$, then there exists $A > 0$ such that*

$$v_n(p) - u(p) \leq \frac{A}{n} \min(p, p').$$

Step 4. *If $K(G^1, G^2, p) \neq 0$ for some $p \in [0, 1]$, then u is linear.*

By Step 3 all games with linear u satisfy (31), and by Step 4, whenever u is not linear, then $K(G^1, G^2, p) \equiv 0$, and so the last step is:

Step 5. *If u is not linear in* $[0, 1]$, *then:*

$$\exists A > 0 \text{ such that } \forall n \text{ and } \forall p \in [0,1] \quad v_n(p) - \operatorname{Cav} u(p) \le \frac{A}{n^{2/3}}.$$

The proof of this step is rather lengthy and involves some non-trivial arguments. However, all these arguments concern terms of order lower than $1/\sqrt{n}$. As far as the $1/\sqrt{n}$ term and the normal function ϕ are concerned, these are completely covered by Steps 1 to 4.

V.5. THE SPEED OF CONVERGENCE OF v_n

In this section we study more closely the nature of the uniform convergence of the values $v_n(p)$ of the finite games $\Gamma_n(p)$ to $v_\infty(p)$, which is the value of $\Gamma_\infty(p)$. For the case of full monitoring, by Theorem V.2.8, p. 223, the speed of this convergence is bounded from above by $O(1/\sqrt{n})$. (As we shall prove in Theorem VI.6.2, p. 365, this is also true for the case of incomplete information on two sides.) This is the least upper bound for that case since in Theorem V.4.1, p. 281, we provided a game with $v(p) \equiv 0$ and $\lim_{n\to\infty} \sqrt{n} v_n(p) = \phi(p)$.

V.5.a. State-Independent Signaling

Without the full monitoring assumption, $O(1/\sqrt{n})$ is no longer an upper bound for the speed of convergence of $v_n(p)$. The next level of generality is the case of state-independent signals; i.e., the signaling matrices Q^k are the same for all $k \in K$. For this case it will be proved (VI.6, p. 365) that even for incomplete information on two sides the speed of convergence is bounded above by $O(1/\sqrt[3]{n})$. We shall now prove that this is in fact the least upper bound.

Example V.5.1. Let $K = \{1, 2\}$. The payoff matrices G^1, G^2 and the signaling matrices Q^1, Q^2 (to player II) are given by:

$$G^1 = \begin{pmatrix} 1 & 3 & -1 \\ 1 & -3 & 1 \end{pmatrix}, \quad G^2 = \begin{pmatrix} 1 & 2 & -2 \\ 1 & -2 & 2 \end{pmatrix}, \quad Q^1 = Q^2 = \begin{pmatrix} a & c & d \\ b & c & d \end{pmatrix}.$$

Observe that deleting the left strategy of player II and changing the signaling matrices so as to provide full monitoring we obtain the game in Example V.4.1, p. 280, for which we have just proved $\delta_n(p) \approx (1/\sqrt{n})$. However, in our present example player II is not informed of the last move of his opponent unless he chooses his left strategy, which is strictly dominated in terms of payoffs. In other words, player II has to pay one unit whenever he wants to observe his opponent's move. Since observing the moves of the informed player is his only way to collect information about the state k, it is not surprising that his learning process will be slower and/or more costly than in Example V.4.1, p. 280. This means a slower rate of convergence of v_n to v_∞.

Keeping the same notations as in Example V.4.1, p. 280, the set of non-revealing moves is readily seen to be the set:

$$\mathrm{NR}(p) = \{(x, y) \mid x = y \,;\, 0 \le x \le 1\} \text{ if } 0 < p < 1,$$

and the non-revealing game is therefore:

$$D(p) = \begin{pmatrix} 1 & 3p + 2p' & -p - 2p' \\ 1 & -3p - 2p' & p + 2p' \end{pmatrix}$$

with value $u(p) = 0$ for $0 < p < 1$. Since also $v(G^1) = v(G^2) = 0$, we conclude that u, and therefore v_∞, are the same as in Example V.4.1, p. 280, namely:

$$v(p) = \operatorname{Cav} u(p) = u(p) = 0 \qquad \forall p \in [0, 1].$$

Proposition V.5.1. *For the game in Example V.5.1 the following holds:*

$$\forall n \ge 1 \textit{ and } \forall p \in [0, 1]: \quad v_n(p) \ge \frac{p(1-p)}{\sqrt[3]{n}}.$$

Proof. The recursive formula from Lemma V.4.2, p. 281, yields here:

$$\begin{aligned} v_{n+1} = \frac{1}{n+1} \max_{0 \le x, y \le 1} \min_{0 \le \varepsilon \le 1} \{ & \varepsilon \\ & + (1-\varepsilon) \min[3p(x - x') + 2p'(y - y'), p(x' - x) + 2p'(y' - y)] \\ & + n(1-\varepsilon) v_n(p) + n\varepsilon[\overline{x} v_n(p_T) + \overline{x}' v_n(p_B)]\}, \end{aligned} \tag{1}$$

where $\overline{x}$ is given by (3), p. 282, and p_T, p_B are given by (4), p. 282.

For $n = 1$, $v_1(p) = \min(p, p') \ge pp'$ in accordance with the proposition. We proceed by induction on n: assume the inequality holds for n and for all $p \in [0, 1]$. In the recursive formula, restrict x and y by $p(x - x') = p'(y' - y) \stackrel{\text{def}}{=} \delta$ to obtain, by the induction hypothesis:

$$v_{n+1}(p) \ge \max_{|\delta| \le \min(p, p')} \min_{0 \le \varepsilon \le 1} \frac{1}{n+1} [\varepsilon + pp' n^{2/3} + (1-\varepsilon)\delta - \varepsilon n^{2/3} \delta^2]. \tag{2}$$

Since the function $[\ldots]$ is concave in δ (and linear in ε) we apply the minmax theorem to first maximize on δ. The maximum is at $\delta = \min[pp', (1-\varepsilon)/(2\varepsilon n^{2/3})]$. Letting $A = pp'$ and noticing that $(n+1)^{2/3} - n^{2/3} \le 2/(3n^{1/3})$, it then suffices to prove that:

$$n \ge 1, 0 \le \varepsilon \le 1, 0 \le A \le \frac{1}{4}, \text{ and } \delta = \min[A, \frac{1-\varepsilon}{2\varepsilon n^{2/3}}] \text{ imply:}$$

$$\varepsilon + (1-\varepsilon)\delta - \varepsilon n^{2/3} \delta^2 \ge \frac{2A}{3n^{1/3}}.$$

If $\delta = A$, the left-hand side is linear (and increasing) in ε, and the inequality obviously holds for $\varepsilon = 0$. So it suffices to check it at the maximum value of ε, where $\delta = (1-\varepsilon)/(2\varepsilon n^{2/3})$. Thus we may assume that $\delta = (1-\varepsilon)/(2\varepsilon n^{2/3}) \leq A$, and we have then to show that $0 < \varepsilon$ and $A \leq 1/4$, imply:

$$\varepsilon + \frac{(1-\varepsilon)^2}{4\varepsilon n^{2/3}} \geq \frac{2A}{3n^{1/3}},$$

and it is clearly enough to prove this for $A = 1/4$. Thus letting $\xi = 1/n^{1/3}$, we have to prove that $\xi \leq 1, 0 < \varepsilon \leq 1$, imply $\frac{(1-\varepsilon)^2}{\varepsilon}\xi^2 - \frac{2}{3}\xi + 4\varepsilon \geq 0$. The unconstrained minimum in ξ is at $\xi_0 = \frac{\varepsilon}{3(1-\varepsilon)^2}$, where the value of the function is $\varepsilon(4 - \frac{1}{9(1-\varepsilon)^2})$. Thus the inequality is proved for $\varepsilon \leq 5/6$. For $5/6 < \varepsilon \leq 1$ the minimum is at $\xi = 1$, where the inequality is obviously satisfied for these values of ε. This completes the proof of the proposition. ∎

Combining the previous proposition with the result of Theorem VI.6.1, p. 365, we conclude (again since $v_n(p) = \delta_n(p)$):

Corollary V.5.2. *For the game in Example V.5.1, p. 294, the speed of convergence of v_n is $(1/\sqrt[3]{n})$.*

V.5.b. State-Dependent Signaling

In the previous sections we were able to determine the least upper bound for the speed of convergence of $v_n(p)$ for the full monitoring case and for the case of state-independent signaling. The results are much less complete for games with state-dependent signaling. Here we have only partial results for the case of two states and common signals to both players. So from here on in this section we assume $K = \{1, 2\}$.

Recall that $\mathrm{NR}(p)$ depends only on the support of p. So it is the same for $0 < p < 1$. Denote this set simply by NR.

Theorem V.5.3. *If* $\mathrm{NR} = \emptyset$, *then for some* $C_1 > 0$*:*

$$v_n(p) \leq \operatorname{Cav} u(p) + C_1\sqrt[4]{pp'/n},$$

for all $p \in [0,1]$ *and for all* n.

Proof. In establishing upper bounds for v_n we first modify the game in favor of player I so as to have $\mathscr{H}_n^{\mathrm{II}} \subseteq \mathscr{H}_n^{\mathrm{I}}$ (cf. Section V.3.c, p. 230), and hence the posterior probabilities p_n (given $\mathscr{H}_n^{\mathrm{II}}$) are common knowledge. The proof is carried out in four steps, some of which will be used also in the next theorem.

Step 1. $v_1(p) \leq \operatorname{Cav} u(p) + 2Cpp'$.

This is a consequence of the Lipschitz property of $v_1(p)$:

$$\begin{aligned} v_1(p) &\leq \min[v_1(0) + Cp, v_1(1) + Cp'] \leq pv_1(1) + p'v_1(0) + 2Cpp' \\ &= pu_1(1) + p'u_1(0) + 2Cpp' \leq \operatorname{Cav} u(p) + 2Cpp'. \end{aligned} \tag{3}$$

Step 2. *For any strategy σ of player* I, *if at stage m player* II *plays his uniformly mixed move y^0 (i.e., $y^0(t) = 1/\#T$, $\forall t \in T$), then:*

$$\mathsf{E}(|p_{m+1} - p_m| \mid \mathscr{H}_m^{\mathrm{II}}) = p_m p'_m d(x), \tag{4}$$

where

$$d(x) = \frac{1}{\#T} \sum_t \sum_b \left| x^1 Q_t^1(b) - x^2 Q_t^2(b) \right|.$$

Here $x = (x^1, x^2)$ is the strategy of player I *at stage m and Q_t^k is the t-th column of Q^k. Note that $d(x) = 0$ if and only if $x \in$* NR.

To see this observe that when x and $t \in T$ are played, the probability of a signal $b \in B$ is:

$$P(b) = p_m x^1 Q_t^1(b) + p'_m x^2 Q_t^2(b).$$

In this event, the new conditional probability of $\{k = 1\}$ will be:

$$p_{m+1}(b) = \frac{p_m x^1 Q_t^1(b)}{p_m x^1 Q_t^1(b) + p'_m x^2 Q_t^2(b)}.$$

Step 3. *If* NR $= \emptyset$, *then there exists a constant $\eta > 0$ such that $d(x) \geq \eta$; $\forall\, x \in X^2$.*

In fact, $d(x)$ is a non-negative continuous function of x on the compact set X^2 and therefore attains its minimum there. This minimum cannot be 0 since this would imply NR $\neq \emptyset$.

Step 4. In $\Gamma_n(p)$, given any strategy σ of player I, at each stage m let player II play y^0 with probability ε_n (to be determined later), and with probability $1 - \varepsilon_n$ play the strategy that guarantees (Step 1) $\mathsf{E}(g_m \mid \mathscr{H}_m^{\mathrm{II}}) \leq \operatorname{Cav} u(p_m) + 2C p_m p'_m$. By Steps 2 and 3 we get:

$$\mathsf{E}(|p_{m+1} - p_m| \mid \mathscr{H}_m^{\mathrm{II}}) \geq \eta \varepsilon_n p_m p'_m.$$

Hence we have for all m:

$$\begin{aligned}
\mathsf{E}(g_m \mid \mathscr{H}_m^{\mathrm{II}}) &\leq \operatorname{Cav} u(p_m) + \varepsilon_n C + 2(1 - \varepsilon_n) C p_m p'_m \\
&\leq \operatorname{Cav} u(p_m) + \varepsilon_n C + \frac{2C}{\eta \varepsilon_n} \mathsf{E}(|p_{m+1} - p_m| \mid \mathscr{H}_m^{\mathrm{II}}).
\end{aligned}$$

Taking the average over the n stages and the expectation on $\mathscr{H}_m^{\mathrm{II}}$ we obtain (using Lemma V.2.1, p. 219):

$$\overline{\gamma}_n \leq \operatorname{Cav} u(p) + \varepsilon_n C + \frac{2C}{\eta \varepsilon_n} \sqrt{\frac{pp'}{n}}.$$

Choosing $\varepsilon_n = \sqrt{2/\eta}\sqrt[4]{pp'/n}$, using $C_1 = C\sqrt{8/\eta}$, we conclude that:

$$v_n(p) \leq \operatorname{Cav} u(p) + C_1 \sqrt[4]{pp'/n}. \tag{5}$$

∎

To bound the error term for the case in which NR $\neq \emptyset$ we need the following:

Lemma V.5.4. *Let Δ be a non-empty polyhedron in $\mathbb{R}^m$ and let L_i with $i = 1, \ldots, d$ be linear functionals. Define:*

$$\text{NR} = \{x \in \Delta \mid L_i x = 0\,;\; i = 1, \ldots, d\}.$$

If NR $\neq \emptyset$*, then there exists a constant $\beta > 0$ such that for all $x \in \Delta$:*

$$\max_i |L_i x| \geq \beta \, \|x - \text{NR}\| \,.$$

(Here $\|x - \text{NR}\| = \min_{x' \in \text{NR}} \|x - x'\|$, $\|\cdot\|$ being a norm in $\mathbb{R}^m$.)

Proof. This is a consequence of I.3, Ex. 4q, p. 35, which states that if L is an affine map from Δ to $\mathbb{R}^d$, then $L^{-1}(x)$ is a Lipschitz function (in the Hausdorff distance) of $x \in L(\Delta)$ (where distance is derived from the given norms). ∎

Theorem V.5.5. *For any $\Gamma_n(p)$ there exists a constant C_2 such that for all n and for all $p \in [0, 1]$:*

$$v_n(p) \leq \mathsf{Cav}\, u(p) + C_2 \sqrt[6]{pp'/n}.$$

Proof. If NR $= \emptyset$ the claimed inequality follows from Theorem V.5.3, p. 296. Assume therefore that NR $\neq \emptyset$; then by Lemma V.5.4, p. 298, there exists $\beta > 0$ such that for all $x \in X^2$:

$$d(x) \geq \beta \, \|x - \text{NR}\| \,. \tag{6}$$

Notice that, given any strategy of player I, player II, by playing at stage m an optimal move in $D(p_m)$, guarantees:

$$\mathsf{E}(g_m \mid \mathscr{H}_m^{\text{II}}) \leq \mathsf{Cav}\, u(p) + C \, \|x - \text{NR}\| \leq \mathsf{Cav}\, u(p) + C d(x)/\beta.$$

Combined with Step 1 of Theorem V.5.3 this yields: given σ, player II can guarantee at each stage m:

$$\begin{aligned} \mathsf{E}(g_m \mid \mathscr{H}_m^{\text{II}}) &\leq \mathsf{Cav}\, u(p_m) + C \min(2 p_m p_m', d(x)/\beta) \\ &\leq \mathsf{Cav}\, u(p_m) + C \sqrt{2 p_m p_m' d(x)/\beta}. \end{aligned}$$

The proof now proceeds as in the previous theorem: at each stage m player II plays with probability ε_n the uniform move y^0, and with probability $(1 - \varepsilon_n)$ he plays the above move. This guarantees (using Step 2):

$$\begin{aligned} \mathsf{E}(g_m \mid \mathscr{H}_m^{\text{II}}) &\leq \mathsf{Cav}\, u(p_m) + C\varepsilon_n + (1 - \varepsilon_n) C \sqrt{2 p_m p_m' d(x)/\beta} \\ &\leq \mathsf{Cav}\, u(p_m) + C\varepsilon_n + C \sqrt{\frac{2}{\beta \varepsilon_n}} \sqrt{\mathsf{E}(|p_{m+1} - p_m| \mid \mathscr{H}_m^{\text{II}})}. \end{aligned}$$

Taking averages over all n stages and expectation on $\mathscr{H}_m^{\text{II}}$ we get (using the Cauchy–Schwartz inequality and Theorem V.2.8, p. 223):

$$\overline{\gamma}_n \leq \operatorname{Cav} u(p) + C\varepsilon_n + \frac{C}{\sqrt{n}}\sqrt{\frac{2}{\beta\varepsilon_n}}\sqrt{\sum_1^n \mathsf{E}(|p_{m+1} - p_m| \mid \mathscr{H}^{\text{II}})}$$

$$\leq \operatorname{Cav} u(p) + C\varepsilon_n + \sqrt{\frac{2C}{\beta\varepsilon_n}}\sqrt[4]{\frac{pp'}{n}}.$$

Choosing $\varepsilon_n = \sqrt[3]{4/\beta}\sqrt[6]{pp'/n}$ we conclude:

$$v_n(p) \leq \operatorname{Cav} u(p) + C_2\sqrt[6]{pp'/n},$$

where $C_2 = 4C/\sqrt[3]{2\beta}$, completing the proof. ∎

V.5.c. Games with Error Term $\approx (\ln n)/n$

We start by proving a lemma that provides a sufficient condition for the error term to be bounded by $(\ln n)/n$. For the sake of simplicity only, the lemma is stated and proved for two states. It can be done for any finite set of states K (cf. V.5, Ex. 10c, p. 308).

Lemma V.5.6. *Let $\Gamma(p)$ be a game with full monitoring and two states. If $u(p)$ is twice differentiable and $\exists\eta > 0$ such that $\forall p \in [0, 1]$, $u''(p) < -\eta$, then for some constant $A > 0$, $\delta_n(p) \leq A(\ln n)/n$ for all $p \in [0, 1]$.*

Proof. Note first that if player II plays an optimal strategy in $D(p)$ he guarantees a first-stage payoff of at most $u(p) + 2C\,\mathsf{E}\,|p_2 - p|$ (where p_2 is the conditional probability of $\{k = 1\}$ after the first stage). This follows from Lemma V.2.4, p. 221, and Lemma V.2.3, p. 221 (and can be easily verified directly for this simple case). In particular this implies that $\forall x \in X^2$:

$$\min_{t\in T}(px^1G_t^1 + p'x^2G_t^2) \leq u(p) + 2C\,\mathsf{E}\,|p_2 - p|. \tag{7}$$

For any (finite) distribution of p_2 (with $\mathsf{E}(p_2) = p$) we have:

$$v_\infty(p) - \mathsf{E}\,v_\infty(p_2) \geq \frac{\eta}{2}\,\mathsf{E}\,|p_2 - p|^2. \tag{8}$$

This follows by using Taylor's expansion of $v_\infty(q)$ for each value q of p_2:

$$v_\infty(q) = v_\infty(p) + (q - p)v'_\infty(p) + \frac{1}{2}(q - p)^2 v''_\infty(\xi)$$

$$\leq v_\infty(p) + (q - p)v'_\infty(p) - \frac{\eta}{2}(q - p)^2,$$

where $\xi = p + \theta(q - p)$, $0 \leq \theta \leq 1$. Taking expectation on p_2 we obtain inequality (8).

Since $\sum_{r=1}^n \frac{1}{r} = O(\ln n)$, the proof of the lemma will follow if we prove the existence of $A > 0$ such that for all $p \in [0, 1]$ and all n, the functions

$V_n(p) = nv_n(p)$ satisfy:

$$V_n(p) \le nv_\infty(p) + A\sum_{r<n} r^{-1}. \tag{9}$$

We prove this by induction on n: choose A_1 large enough to make (9) true for $n = 1$ and let $A = \max(A_1, C^2/(2\eta))$. By the recursive formula (1), p. 281, inequality (7), p. 299, and the induction hypothesis, we have:

$$\begin{aligned}
V_{n+1}(p) &\le \max_{x\in X^2}\{u(p) + 2C\,\mathsf{E}\,|p_2 - p| + \mathsf{E}\,V_n(p_2)\} \\
&\le \max_{x\in X^2}\{v_\infty(p) + 2C\,\mathsf{E}\,|p_2 - p| + n\,\mathsf{E}(v_\infty(p_2)) + A\sum_{r<n} r^{-1}\} \\
&= \max_{x\in X^2}\{(n+1)v_\infty(p) + A\sum_{r<n} r^{-1} + 2C\,\mathsf{E}\,|p_2 - p| \\
&\quad - n\big(v_\infty(p) - \mathsf{E}\,v_\infty(p_2)\big)\},
\end{aligned}$$

and by (8):

$$\begin{aligned}
V_{n+1}(p) &\le (n+1)v_\infty(p) + A\sum_{r<n} r^{-1} \\
&\quad + \max_{x\in X^2}\{2C\,\mathsf{E}\,|p_2 - p| - \frac{n\eta}{2}\,\mathsf{E}\,|p_2 - p|^2\} \\
&\le (n+1)v_\infty(p) + A\sum_{r<n} r^{-1} \\
&\quad + \max_{x\in X^2}\{2C\,\mathsf{E}\,|p_2 - p| - \frac{n\eta}{2}(\mathsf{E}\,|p_2 - p|)^2\}.
\end{aligned}$$

Since on the right-hand side only p_2 depends on x, maximization with respect to $\mathsf{E}\,|p_2 - p|$ yields:

$$\begin{aligned}
V_{n+1}(p) &\le (n+1)v_\infty(p) + A\sum_{r<n} r^{-1} + \frac{2C^2}{\eta n} \\
&\le (n+1)v_\infty(p) + A\sum_{r<n} r^{-1},
\end{aligned}$$

completing the proof of Lemma V.5.6. ■

For instance, in Example V.2.1, p. 218, observe that $v_\infty(p) = u(p) = pp'$, which implies that $v''(p) = -2 \;\; \forall p \in [0, 1]$. Consequently, the error term of this game is bounded by $(O(\ln n)/n)$. We shall now prove that $(O(\ln n)/n)$ is also a lower bound.

Proposition V.5.7. *In the game in Example V.2.1, p. 218:*

$$\delta_n(p) = v_n(p) - v_\infty(p) \approx \Big(\frac{\ln n}{n}\Big).$$

Proof. Let (α, α') (β, β') be the first-stage mixed moves in G^1 and G^2, respectively. The recursive formula (1), p. 281, gives for this game:

$$v_{n+1}(p) = \max_{\substack{0\le\alpha\le 1\\ 0\le\beta\le 1}} \frac{1}{n+1}\left\{ \min(\alpha p, \beta' p') + n\left[(\alpha p+\beta p')v_n\left(\frac{\alpha p}{\alpha p+\beta p'}\right)\right.\right.$$

$$\left.\left. + (\alpha' p+\beta' p')v_n\left(\frac{\alpha' p}{\alpha' p+\beta' p'}\right)\right]\right\}.$$

Letting $V_n(p) = nv_n(p)$, $x = \alpha p$, $y = \beta' p'$, we rewrite this as:

$$V_{n+1}(p) = \max_{\substack{0\le x\le p\\ 0\le y\le p'}} \left\{ \min(x, y) + (p' + x - y)V_n\left(\frac{x}{p' + x - y}\right)\right.$$

$$\left. + (p - x + y)V_n\left(\frac{p-x}{p-x+y}\right)\right\}.$$

We shall prove that for some large N, the inequality:

$$V_n(p) \ge C_n pp' - D_n \stackrel{\text{def}}{=} F_n(p)$$

is satisfied for all $n \ge N$ with $C_n = n + \frac{1}{4}\ln n$ and $B_n \stackrel{\text{def}}{=} D_{n+1} - D_n = (\ln n)/(8n)^2$. Since B_n is summable, this will imply $V_n(p) \ge C_n pp' - D$ for some constant D for $n \ge N$ and hence for all n, by choosing D sufficiently large. This will establish the required lower bound $v_n(p) - v_\infty(p) \ge (pp'/4)(\ln n)/n - D/n$.

Using the recursive formula, the induction step is to prove that for $n \ge N$ and p with $0 \le p \le 1/2$ (by the symmetry of u and v_n about $p = 1/2$):

$$F_{n+1}(p) = \max_{\substack{0\le x\le p\\ 0\le y\le p'}} \left\{ \min(x, y) + (p' + x - y)F_n\left(\frac{x}{p' + x - y}\right)\right.$$

$$\left. + (p - x + y)F_n\left(\frac{p-x}{p-x+y}\right)\right\}.$$

Replacing F by its formula and setting $x = y = pp'(1+\delta)$ with $\delta = \min(\frac{p}{p'}, \frac{1}{2C_n})$, we want to prove:

$$C_{n+1}pp' - D_{n+1} \le C_n pp' - D_n + pp'(1 + \delta - C_n\delta^2).$$

Using $\ln(1 + \frac{1}{n}) \le \frac{1}{n}$ and $C_n \ge n$ it is enough to prove (setting $z = p/p'$):

$$\frac{1}{4n} - \frac{B_n}{pp'} \le \begin{cases} z - C_n z^2 & \text{if } z \le (2C_n)^{-1}1 \\ (4C_n)^{-1} & \text{if } z \ge (2C_n)^{-1}. \end{cases}$$

- For the first case it will suffice to have $\frac{1}{4n} + C_n z^2 \le \frac{B_n}{z}$, and by the monotonicity it is enough if it is satisfied for $z = 1/(2C_n)$, i.e., if $1 + C_n/n \le 8B_nC_n^2$. This is clearly true for n sufficiently large since the left-hand side is bounded and the right-hand side tends to infinity.

- For the second case it is enough to check for $p = 1/2$, i.e., $16B_n \geq 1/n - 1/C_n$. In fact:

$$\frac{1}{n} - \frac{1}{C_n} = \frac{\ln n}{4nC_n} \leq \frac{\ln n}{4n^2} = 16B_n.$$

This completes the proof of the proposition. ■

EXERCISES

1. Subadditivity of $V_n = nv_n$.

a. Using the argument in the proof of Theorem V.3.1, p. 226, prove that for any n and m:

$$V_{n+m} \leq V_n + V_m.$$

In particular $v_{2n} \leq v_n$.

b. Deduce that v_n converges.

2. Optimal strategy for player II: Explicit construction.

In the case of full monitoring, prove that the following is an optimal strategy for player II in $\Gamma_\infty(p_0)$. Let $c \in \mathbb{R}^K$ be a supporting hyperplane to the graph of $\operatorname{Cav} u$ at p_0, and $D = \{x \in \mathbb{R}^K \mid x \leq c\}$. At stage $n+1$, $n = 1, 2, \ldots$, compute the average vector payoff $\overline{g}_n$ up to that stage. If $\overline{g}_n \in D$, play arbitrarily. If $\overline{g}_n \notin D$, let $\xi \in D$ be the closest point to $\overline{g}_n$ in D, compute $q = (\overline{g}_n - \xi)/\left\|\overline{g}_n - \xi\right\| \in \Delta(K)$, and play an optimal mixed move in $D(q)$.

HINT. Use Section II.4, p. 118.

3. Semi-algebraicity of v_∞.

Prove that $v_\infty(p)$ is semi-algebraic.

HINT. $u(p)$ is piecewise rational, $v_\infty(p)$ is linear on $\{p \mid \operatorname{Cav} u(p) > u(p)\}$, and the boundary of $\{p \mid \operatorname{Cav} u(p) = u(p)\}$ is determined by polynomial equations.

4. Non-existence of a Markovian equilibrium in $\Gamma_n(p)$.

Consider the game with two states, full monitoring, and payoff matrices:

$$G^1 = \begin{pmatrix} 2 & 0 \\ 0 & -1 \end{pmatrix} \quad G^2 = \begin{pmatrix} -1 & 0 \\ 0 & 2 \end{pmatrix}.$$

a. Prove that:

$$V_1(p) = 2\min(p, p') = 2(p \wedge p'),$$

$$V_2(p) = \min\{3(p \wedge p'), 1 + (p \wedge p')/2\},$$

$$V_3(p) = \begin{cases} \frac{1}{2} + \frac{9}{4}p & \text{for } \frac{2}{5} \leq p \leq \frac{6}{13} \\ \frac{4}{5}(1 + 2p) & \text{for } \frac{6}{13} \leq p \leq \frac{1}{2}, \end{cases}$$

where (p, p') is the probability distribution on the states and $V_n(p) = nv_n(p)$.

b. Prove that for any optimal strategy of player I in $\Gamma_2(\frac{1}{2})$ the posterior probability after stage 1 equals $\frac{1}{2}$ a.s. Conclude that (for any optimal strategy of player I) any

Markovian strategy of player II (i.e., a strategy in which each stage behavior is the same for two histories leading to the same posterior probability) is history-independent.

HINT. In any of his optimal strategies, player I plays $(\frac{1}{2}, \frac{1}{2})$ at the first stage in both states.

c. Prove that with history-independent strategies, player II can guarantee not more than $2V_1(1/2) = 2$, which is worse than $V_2(1/2)$. Conclude that for any optimal strategy of player I, no Markovian strategy of player II is a best reply. Consequently there does not exist a pair of Markovian optimal strategies in $\Gamma_2(\frac{1}{2})$.

d. Prove that the same negative conclusion is valid also for $\Gamma_3(p)$ for the whole interval $\frac{2}{5} < p < \frac{6}{13}$.

HINT. Any optimal strategy of player I leads with positive probability, after stage 1, to the posterior probability $\frac{1}{2}$.

5. Proving $\lim v_n(p) = \operatorname{Cav} u(p)$ by the recursive formula.

The recursive formula (Lemma V.4.2, p. 281), which we used mainly to study the speed of convergence of v_n, can be used also to prove the convergence itself, namely, to prove $\lim_{n\to\infty} v_n(p) = \operatorname{Cav} u(p)$. In the proof outlined here we make use of the following result (Kohlberg and Neyman, 1981):

Let X be a Banach space with norm $\|\cdot\|$ and denote its dual by X^*. Let $\Psi: X \to X$ be a non-expansive mapping, i.e.:

$$\|\Psi x - \Psi y\| \le \|x - y\| \quad \textit{for all } x \textit{ and } y \textit{ in } X. \tag{10}$$

Let $\rho = \inf_{x\in X} \|\Psi x - x\|$, then:

$$\forall x \in X,\ \lim_{n\to\infty} \left\| \frac{\Psi^n x}{n} \right\| = \rho, \tag{11}$$

$$\forall x \in X \exists f_x \in X^*:\ \|f_x\| = 1 \textit{ and } f_x(\Psi^n x - x) \ge n\rho,\ \ \forall n. \tag{12}$$

To use this result let X be the set of continuous functions on $\Delta(K)$ endowed with the maximum norm, and let Ψ be the mapping defined (cf. Section IV.3.b, p. 184) by the recursive formula (Lemma V.4.2, p. 281) (without the factor $1/(n+1)$), i.e., for $w \in X$:

$$(\Psi w)(p) = \max_{x\in X^K}\Big(\min_t \sum_k p^k x^k G_t^k + \mathsf{E}_\sigma\, w(p_s)\Big), \tag{13}$$

where X^K and p_s are as in Lemma V.4.2.

a. Prove that $\lim v_n(p)$ exists by proving the following:

α. If we let $v_0 = \mathbf{0}$ (the 0-function in X), then $\forall n \ge 0$, $\Psi^n \mathbf{0} = n v_n$.

β. The mapping Ψ is non-expansive.

γ. By (11), $\max_p |v_n(p)|$ converges as $n \to \infty$. By adding the same constant to all G^k we may assume w.l.o.g. that $v_n(p) \ge 0\ \forall p \in \Delta(K)$, and hence $\lim_{n\to\infty} \max_p v_n(p)$ exists.

δ. Adding a constant $-\alpha^k$ to all entries of G^k we have that:

$$\lim_{n\to\infty} \max_p (v_n(p) - \langle \alpha, p\rangle) \text{ exists } \forall \alpha \in \mathbb{R}^K.$$

So if we denote:

$$\phi_n(\alpha) = \max_p (v_n(p) - \langle \alpha, p\rangle),$$

then, for all α, the sequence $\phi_n(\alpha)$ converges to, say, $\phi(\alpha)$. However, $\phi_n(\alpha)$ are all Lipschitz with constant 1, and hence the convergence $\phi_n(\alpha) \to \phi(\alpha)$ is uniform and $\phi(\alpha)$ is continuous.

ε. Show that $v_n(p) = \min_\alpha(\phi_n(\alpha) - \langle \alpha, p \rangle)$.

HINT. The inequality $\leq$ follows from the definition of $\phi_n(\alpha)$. As for the other direction, since v_n is concave, let α_0 be a supporting hyperplane to v_n at p_0; then $\phi_n(\alpha_0) = 0$ and:

$$v_n(p_0) = \langle \alpha_0, p_0 \rangle = \phi_n(\alpha_0) + \langle \alpha_0, p_0 \rangle \geq \min_\alpha(\phi_n(\alpha) + \langle \alpha, p_0 \rangle).$$

ζ. Conclude that:

$$\lim_{n\to\infty} v_n(p) = \min_\alpha(\phi(\alpha) - \langle \alpha, p \rangle) \stackrel{\text{def}}{=} v_\infty(p).$$

Since v_n are all Lipschitz with the same constant, the convergence is uniform and $v_\infty(p)$ is concave.

b. Prove that $v_\infty(p) = \operatorname{Cav} u(p)$ by showing that:

α. Since v_∞ is concave and $v_\infty(p) \geq u(p)$ (this holds for all v_n), we have $v_\infty(p) \geq \operatorname{Cav} u(p)$. Therefore to complete the proof it is enough to show that $v_\infty(p) = u(p)$ at each point p of strict concavity of v_∞ (i.e., at the extreme points of the epigraph of v_∞, $\{(p, x) \mid x \leq v_\infty(p)\}$).

β. At each point p_0 of strict concavity of v_∞ there is a supporting hyperplane α such that the maximum of $v_\infty(p) + \langle \alpha, p \rangle$ is attained only at p_0. Adding α^k to all entries of G^k, the u function becomes $u(p) + \langle \alpha, p \rangle$, the v_∞ function becomes $v_\infty(p) + \langle \alpha, p \rangle$, and p_0 is the only maximum of the new v_∞.

γ. Take $x = \mathbf{0}$ in (12) and let μ be a regular Borel measure of norm 1 on $\Delta(K)$ representing $f_\mathbf{0}$, i.e.:

$$f_\mathbf{0}(w) = \int w(p)\, \mu(dp) \quad \forall w \in X.$$

So by (12) and V.5, Ex. 5aα:

$$f_\mathbf{0}(\Psi^n \mathbf{0} - \mathbf{0}) = \int n v_n(p)\, \mu(dp) \geq n\rho.$$

Hence:

$$\int v_\infty(p)\, \mu(dp) \geq \rho. \tag{14}$$

But by (11) and V.5, Ex. 5aα and V.5, Ex. 5bβ, we get:

$$\rho = \lim_{n\to\infty} \left\| \frac{1}{n} \Psi^n \mathbf{0} \right\| = \|v_\infty\| = v(p_0).$$

Since p_0 is the unique maximum of v_∞, inequality (14) implies that $\mu = \delta_{p_0}$ (unit mass at p_0).

δ. $\lim_{n\to\infty} \left\| \frac{1}{n} \Psi^n w - v_\infty \right\| = 0$ for all w.

HINT. Since $\lim_{n\to\infty} \|v_n - v_\infty\| = 0$, and (by non-expansiveness) $\|\Psi^n w - \Psi^n \mathbf{0}\| \leq \|w\|$.

ε. For any w and its f_w (according to (12)):

$$f_w\left(\frac{\Psi^n w}{n} - v_\infty\right) + f_w\left(v_\infty - \frac{w}{n}\right) = f_w\left(\frac{\Psi^n w}{n} - \frac{w}{n}\right) \geq \rho.$$

So by V.5, Ex. 5bδ (since $f_w(\mathbf{0}) = 0$), $f_w(v_\infty) \geq \rho$; therefore if f_w is represented by the measure μ_w, then $\mu_w = \delta_{p_0}$ for every w.

ζ. From the definitions of Ψ and u, it follows that $\Psi w \geq u + w$ for all w. Hence $\rho \geq \|u\|$ and by V.5, Ex. 5bε:

$$(\Psi w - w)(p_0) \geq \rho \geq \|u\| . \tag{15}$$

η. Choose $w \in X$ such that $w(p) \in [0, 1]$, $\forall p$, $w(p_0) = 1$, and $w(p) = 0 \ \forall p$ such that $\|p - p_0\| > \varepsilon$. Since:

$$\mathsf{E}_x \|p - p_s\| = \mathsf{E}_p \|x - \overline{x}\| \quad \text{where } \overline{x}^k = \sum_k p^k x^k, \ \forall k,$$

we have from (13), p. 303, that:

$$\Psi w(p_0) \leq u(p_0) + w(p_0) + c\varepsilon.$$

Hence by (15):

$$u(p_0) + c\varepsilon \geq (\Psi w - w)(p_0) \geq \rho \geq \|u\| .$$

Since this must hold for all $\varepsilon > 0$, we conclude that $u(p_0) = \|u\| = \rho = v_\infty(p_0)$, completing the proof.

6. Recursive formula.

a. Prove that in a game in which the signals to player I are **more informative** than those to player II (i.e., $\mathscr{H}^{\mathrm{I}} \supseteq \mathscr{H}^{\mathrm{II}}$), the following generalization of the recursive formula of Lemma V.4.2, p. 281, holds:

$$v_{n+1}(p) = \frac{1}{n+1} \max_{x \in X^K} \min_{t \in T} \{ \sum_{k \in K} p^k x^k G_t^k + n \sum_{b \in B} q_{bt} v_n(p_{bt}) \},$$

where if $\tilde{Q}_t$ is the probability distribution on $K \times S \times A \times B$ induced by p and x, and given that player II uses move $t \in T$, then $q_{bt} = \tilde{Q}_t(b)$ (i.e., $q_{bt} = \sum_k \sum_a p^k x^k Q_t^k(a, b)$), and p_{bt} is the conditional probability distribution on K given b (and t). In terms of the functions $V_n = n v_n$, made positively homogeneous of degree 1, and the variable $z \in \Delta(K \times S)$, this formula can be rewritten as:

$$V_{n+1}(p) = \max_{\overline{z}^k = p^k} \min_{t \in T} \{ z G_t + \sum_{b \in B} V_n[(z^k Q_t^k(b))_{k \in K}] \}.$$

Here $\overline{z}^k = \sum_{s \in S} z_s^k$ is the marginal probability of k according to z.

b. Prove that this formula is a special case of the general recursive formula (Theorem IV.3.2, p. 184).

Hint. A game with incomplete information on one side with a finite state space K corresponds to a finite BL-subspace Y_p with a consistent probability $p \in \mathscr{P}$ that is also an element of $\Delta(K)$ (cf. Example 3, p. 136).

Given a pair of strategies (x, y) of the two players in the first stage, any $p \in \Delta(K)$ is mapped into a probability distribution $P[x, y] \in \Delta(\Delta(K))$ that is the distribution on Ω of the posterior probability distribution on K given the signal to the uninformed player. Hence in this special case the state space Ω in Theorem IV.3.2, p. 184, may be restricted to a much smaller space, namely, $\Delta(K)$.

Note that, unlike in the more special Lemma V.4.2, p. 281, the operation $\min_{t \in T}$ cannot be applied to the first-stage term only, since now q_{bt} and p_{bt} also depend on t.

7. Monotonicity of v_n.

Assuming $\mathscr{H}^{\mathrm{I}} \supseteq \mathscr{H}^{\mathrm{II}}$, use the recursive formula of V.5, Ex. 6, to prove that the sequence of value functions v_n is decreasing, i.e.:

$$v_{n+1}(p) \leq v_n(p) \qquad \forall n \geq 1, \forall p \in [0,1].$$

HINT. The proof is by induction on n. For $n = 1$ it follows from V.5, Ex. 1, p. 302. Make use of the concavity of v_n and the fact that p_{bt} is a martingale.

8. Non-monotonicity of v_n. (Lehrer, 1987)

An intuitive argument supporting the monotonicity of v_n is the following: player I has, at the beginning of the game, some information not available to player II. This advantage can only diminish as the game progresses since player II (and only he) can gain more information about the state. The following example shows this intuitive argument to be false unless player I always knows whatever player II knows.

Consider the game in which $K = \{1, 2, 3\}$, $p = (1/3, 1/3, 1/3)$. The moves of player I are $S = \{\alpha, \beta\}$ and of player II are: $T = \{t_1, t_2, t_3, t_4, t_5\}$. The payoff matrices are:

$$G^1 = \begin{pmatrix} 100 & 4 & 0 & 4 & 4 \\ 100 & 0 & 4 & 4 & 4 \end{pmatrix}, \quad G^2 = \begin{pmatrix} 0 & 100 & 4 & 4 & 4 \\ 4 & 100 & 0 & 4 & 4 \end{pmatrix},$$

$$G^3 = \begin{pmatrix} 4 & 0 & 100 & 4 & 4 \\ 0 & 4 & 100 & 4 & 4 \end{pmatrix}.$$

The signaling matrices for player I:

$$A^1 = A^2 = A^3 = \begin{pmatrix} 1 & 2 & 3 & \theta & \theta \\ 1 & 2 & 3 & \theta & \theta \end{pmatrix}.$$

The signaling matrices for player II:

$$B^1 = \begin{pmatrix} \theta & \theta & \theta & a & b \\ \theta & \theta & \theta & c & d \end{pmatrix}, \quad B^2 = \begin{pmatrix} \theta & \theta & \theta & c & e \\ \theta & \theta & \theta & f & b \end{pmatrix},$$

$$B^3 = \begin{pmatrix} \theta & \theta & \theta & f & d \\ \theta & \theta & \theta & a & e \end{pmatrix}.$$

Recall that in addition to his signal each player knows his own move. In words, the signaling structure is as follows: player I gets to know the move of player II except for moves t_4 and t_5, between which he cannot distinguish. Player II gets no information about either k or the move of player I whenever he chooses t_1, t_2 or t_3. When he plays t_4 or t_5, he gets a signal that enables him to exclude one of the states.

Prove that $v_1 \geq v_2 < v_3$.

HINT.

(1) Clearly $v_1 \leq 4$.

(2) The following strategy for player II in Γ_2 shows that $v_2 \leq 3$:

At the first stage play $\frac{1}{2}t_4 \overset{*}{+} \frac{1}{2}t_5$, and at the second stage:

- Play t_1 if received signal e or f.
- Play t_2 if received signal a or d.
- Play t_3 if received signal c or b.

(3) The following strategy of player I in Γ_3 shows that $v_3 \geq 10/3$:

At the first two stages play $(1/2, 1/2)$ (i.e., $\frac{1}{2}\alpha \overset{*}{+} \frac{1}{2}\beta$.) If both signals received were θ, play $(1/2, 1/2)$ at the third stage as well. Otherwise let t be the first signal different from θ (i.e., 1, 2, or 3). At the third stage:

- When $k = 1$ play $(1/2, 1/2)$ if $t = 1$, α if $t = 2$, and β if $t = 3$.
- When $k = 2$ play α if $t = 1$, $(1/2, 1/2)$ if $t = 2$, and β if $t = 3$.
- When $k = 3$ play α if $t = 1$, β if $t = 2$, and $(1/2, 1/2)$ if $t = 3$.

Conclude that the game under consideration does not have a recursive formula as in V.5, Ex. 6, p. 305. How do the conditions for that formula fail in this example?

9. The impact of the signals on the value.

In Section V.5.b, p. 296, we saw that the signaling structure may affect the speed of convergence of v_n. Work out the details of the following example (due to Ponssard and Sorin) to show that the effect of the signaling may occur already in v_2.

Let $K = \{1, 2\}$. The payoff matrices are:

$$G^1 = \begin{pmatrix} 0 & 2 & 2 \\ 0 & 2 & -3 \end{pmatrix}, \qquad G^2 = \begin{pmatrix} 2 & 0 & -3 \\ 2 & 0 & 2 \end{pmatrix},$$

and consider the two cases where the signaling matrices to player II are:

$$Q^1 = Q^2 = \begin{pmatrix} a & b & c \\ a & b & f \end{pmatrix}, \qquad \text{(Case 1)}$$

$$\tilde{Q}^1 = \tilde{Q}^2 = \begin{pmatrix} a & b & c \\ d & e & f \end{pmatrix}. \qquad \text{(Case 2)}$$

In both cases player I is informed of the moves of both players. Show that:

a. In both cases NR(p) (for $0 < p < 1$) is the set of moves independent of k.

b. In both cases:

$$u(p) = \begin{cases} 2p & \text{if } p \in [0,\ 2/7] \\ 2 - 5p & \text{if } p \in [2/7,\ 1/2] \\ u(1-p) & \text{if } p \in [1/2,\ 1]. \end{cases}$$

c. In both cases:

$$v_\infty(p) = \lim v_n(p) = 2\min(p,\ \frac{2}{7},\ 1-p).$$

d. In both cases $v_1(p) = 2\min(p, 1-p)$ for $p \in [0, 1]$.

e. For $p \notin [2/7, 5/7]$, $v_n(p) = v_1(p)\ \forall n$ (use the monotonicity of v_n).

f. Using the recursive formula show that in Case 1:

$$v_2(p) = v_1(p) = 2\min(p, 1-p) \quad \text{for } p \in [0, 1],$$

while in Case 2:

$$v_2(p) = (3p+2)/5 \quad \text{for } p \in [2/7, 5/7].$$

Remark V.5.2. The last point provides an example of the fact that $v_1 = v_2$ does not imply that v_n is constant in n: in Case 1, $v_1 = v_2$ but $\lim v_n(p) \neq v_1(p)$ for $p \in [2/7, 5/7]$.

10. On the speed of convergence of v_n.

a. For the game in Example V.4.1, p. 280, bound from above more carefully to reduce the Lipschitz constant to half of the maximum difference between payoffs. Conclude that for this game $v_n(p) \leq \sqrt{pp'/n}$.

b. For the game in Example V.5.1, p. 294, prove directly (by induction using the recursive formula) that for all n and for all $p \in [0, 1]$:

$$v_n(p) \leq \frac{\alpha\sqrt{pp'}}{\sqrt[3]{n}} \quad \text{with } \alpha = \sqrt[3]{192}.$$

c. Prove Lemma V.5.6, p. 299 for any finite state set K of size k: if $u(p)$ is twice differentiable, let $u''(p)$ be the $(k-1) \times (k-1)$ matrix with elements:

$$(u''(p))_{ij} = \frac{\partial^2 u(p)}{\partial p^i \partial p^j} \quad \text{for } 1 \leq i \leq k-1 \,;\, 1 \leq j \leq k-1.$$

If $\exists \eta > 0$ such that $eu''(p)\tilde{e} \leq -\eta$, for all $p \in \Delta(K)$ and for any unit vector $e \in \mathbb{R}^{k-1}$ ($\tilde{e}$ is the transposition of e), then for some constant $A > 0$, $\delta_n(p) \leq A\frac{\ln n}{n}$ for all $p \in \Delta(K)$.

d.

α. Show that for the game of Example V.2.1, p. 218:

$$V_n(p) \leq \left(n + 1 + \frac{1}{4}\ln(n+1)\right)pp'.$$

HINT. Cf. the proof of Proposition V.5.7, p. 300. Let:
$F(\alpha) = \max_{\substack{0 \leq x \leq p \\ 0 \leq y \leq p'}} \frac{1}{pp'}\{\min(x, y) + \alpha\left[\phi(x, p' - y) + \phi(p - x, y) - \phi(p, p')\right]\}$ with $\phi(p, q) = \frac{pq}{p+q}$. Show that $F(\alpha) = 2 - \alpha$ for $\alpha \leq 1/2$ and $F(\alpha) = 1 + \frac{1}{4\alpha}$ for $\alpha \geq 1/2$, and that if $C_0 \geq 0$ and $C_{n+1} - C_n \geq F(C_n)$, then $V_n(p) \leq C_n pp'$.

β. In Proposition V.5.7, p. 300, it was shown that $V_n(p) \geq (n + 1 + \frac{1}{4}\ln(n+1))pp' - D$ for some D.

Show there is no $\tilde{D}$ such that $V_n(p) \geq \left[n + 1 + \frac{1}{4}\ln(n+1))pp' - \tilde{D}\right]pp'$.

HINT. Use Theorem V.1.6, p. 217.

Remark V.5.3. One should be able, even in general, to get by analytic means (i.e., without having to care about the combinatorial end effect) the expansion of v_n up to terms of the order of Kpp' (i.e., an expression $\phi_n(p)$ with $|V_n(p) - \phi_n(p)| \leq Kpp'$), and one needs to do so if the expansion is to be useful also for small values of p. V.5, Ex. 10dβ shows therefore that even for this specific game we still need some improvement.

γ. Deduce from the above that for this game no separable expression of the form $\phi_n(p) = \alpha_n\phi(p)$ will satisfy $|V_n(p) - \phi_n(p)| \leq Kpp'$.

e. Prove the following sufficient condition for the error term to be of the order $0(1/n)$. Such an error term means that the cumulative excess of payoff to $\mathsf{Cav}\,u$ is bounded.

In a game with $K = \{1, 2\}$, if $\exists \alpha > 0$ such that for all $p \in [0, 1]$ and for all $n \geq 1$:

$$v_\infty(p) - u(p) \geq \alpha pp',$$

then:

$$v_n(p) \leq v_\infty(p) + A\frac{\sqrt{pp'}}{n},$$

for some constant $A > 0$.

This result can also be proved for any finite K (cf. Zamir, 1971–1972).

HINT.

- For $x = (x^1, x^2) \in X^2$ let $\|x^1 - x^2\| = \sum_{s\in S} |x_s^1 - x_s^2|$ and prove:

$$\min_{t\in T}(px^1 G_t^1 + p'x^2 G_t^2) \le u(p) + Cpp' \left\|x^1 - x^2\right\|_1 .$$

- Given $x \in X^2$, if p_s is the conditional probability of $\{k = 1\}$ resulting from move s then $\mathsf{E}\sqrt{p_s p_s'} = \sqrt{pp'}\sum_s \sqrt{x_s^1 x_s^2}$, and, since $\sqrt{z^1 z^2} \le \overline{z} - (z^1 - z^2)^2/(8\overline{z})$ with $\overline{z} = (z_1 + z_2)/2$:

$$\mathsf{E}\sqrt{p_s p_s'} \le (1 - \tfrac{1}{8}\left\|x^1 - x^2\right\|_2^2)\sqrt{pp'}.$$

- Use the recursive formula to prove the result, with $A = \#SC^2/\alpha$, by induction on n. The main inductive step, where $E_n(p) = n(v_n(p) - v_\infty(p))$ is assumed to be less than or equal to $A\sqrt{pp'}$, is:

$$E_{n+1}(p) \le \max_{\delta\ge 0}\bigl[-\alpha pp' + \sqrt{\#S}Cpp'\delta + A\sqrt{pp'}(1 - \tfrac{\delta^2}{8})\bigr],$$

using δ for $\left\|x^1 - x^2\right\|_2$.

Remark V.5.4. For the game

$$G^1 = \begin{pmatrix} 1 & -1 \\ -1 & 1 \end{pmatrix}, \qquad G^2 = \begin{pmatrix} -2 & 0 \\ 0 & 2 \end{pmatrix},$$

$u(p) = \max(-p, -q^2/p)$, with $q = 1 - p$, and hence $v_\infty(p) = 0$. So, part V.5, Ex. 10e, is not applicable. In fact, it was proved in Mertens and Zamir (1995) that for this game (and whenever $\min(\#S, \#T) \le 2 = \#K$, and $u(p) < v_\infty(p)$ for $0 < p < 1$):

$$v_n(p) - v_\infty(p) \le (K \ln n)/n.$$

f. To show that this cannot be improved, show that, for this game, $v_n(p) \ge \frac{K}{n} W_n(q)$ with $W_n(q) = g_n(q) - qg_n(1)$, $g_n(x) = \ln(1 + n^{\frac{1}{3}}x)$ (and, e.g., $K = \frac{1}{3}$).

HINT.

(1) It suffices by the recursive formula to show that:

$$W_{n+1}(q) \le \max_{\substack{0\le u\le p\\ 0\le v\le q}}\left[\frac{2v - 2u + p - 2q}{K} + (u+v)W_n\left(\frac{v}{u+v}\right)\right.$$
$$\left. + (1-u-v)W_n\left(\frac{q-v}{1-u-v}\right)\right],$$

i.e., that

$$\min_{\substack{0\le u\le v+\frac{1}{2}p-q\\ 0\le v\le q}} \frac{W_{n+1}(q) - (u+v)W_n\bigl(\frac{v}{u+v}\bigr) - (1-u-v)W_n\bigl(\frac{q-v}{1-u-v}\bigr)}{2v - 2u + p - 2q} \le K^{-1}.$$

Now $W_{n+1}(q) - W_n(q) = f_n(q) - qf_n(1)$, with $f_n(x) = \ln\bigl(1 + \frac{[(1+n^{-1})^{1/3}-1]q}{n^{-1/3}+q}\bigr)$. Since f_n is monotone, we have:

$$\frac{f_n(q) - qf_n(1)}{1-q} \le f_n(q) \le \frac{[(1+n^{-1})^{1/3} - 1]q}{n^{-1/3}+q} \le \frac{q}{3n(n^{-1/3}+q)},$$

so

$$W_{n+1}(q) - W_n(q) \le \frac{1-q}{3n\left(1+\frac{1}{n^{1/3}q}\right)}.$$

Thus we have to show that:

$$\min_{\substack{0\le u\le v+\frac{1}{2}p-q\\ 0\le v\le q}} \frac{\varphi_n(p,q)+g_n(q)-(u+v)g_n\left(\frac{v}{u+v}\right)-(1-u-v)g_n\left(\frac{q-v}{1-u-v}\right)}{2v-2u+p-2q} \le K^{-1}$$

with $\varphi_n(p,q) = p/[3n(1+1/qn^{1/3})]$.

(2) Case $q \le \dfrac{1}{2}$.

Let $u = \frac{1}{2} - q$, $v = q - \frac{1}{2}z$. Our problem becomes, with $\psi_n(q,z) = 2g_n(q) - (1-z)g_n\left(\frac{2q-z}{1-z}\right) - (1+z)g_n\left(\frac{z}{1+z}\right)$, to show that $F_n(q) = \min_{0\le z\le q} \dfrac{\varphi_n(p,q)+\frac{1}{2}\psi_n(q,z)}{q-z} \le K^{-1}$.

Now:

$$\begin{aligned}
\psi_n(q,z) &= \ln\left[1+\frac{1}{\left(\frac{q+n^{-1/3}}{q-z(1+n^{-1/3})}\right)^2-1}\right] + z\ln\left[1+2\frac{qn^{1/3}-z(1+n^{1/3})}{1+z(1+n^{1/3})}\right]\\
&\quad + (1-z)\ln(1-z) + (1+z)\ln(1+z)\\
&\le \ln\left[1+\frac{1}{\left(\frac{q+n^{-1/3}}{q-z}\right)^2-1}\right] + z\ln\left[1+2\frac{q-z}{n^{-1/3}+z}\right] + (2\ln 2)z^2\\
&\le \frac{1}{\left(\frac{q+n^{-1/3}}{q-z}\right)^2-1} + \frac{2z(q-z)}{z+n^{-1/3}} + (2\ln 2)z^2\\
&\le \frac{1}{\left(\frac{q+n^{-1/3}}{q-z}\right)^2-1} + 2(q-z) + (2\ln 2)q^2.
\end{aligned}$$

So, with $B = q + n^{-1/3}$, $A = q^2\ln 2 + pq/(3nB)$, $w = (q-z)/B$:

$$F_n(q) \le 1 + \frac{1}{B}\min_{0\le w\le q/B}\left[\frac{A}{w} + \frac{1}{2}\frac{w}{1-u^2}\right].$$

Now $w = \sqrt{2A}/(\sqrt{2A}+1)$ (whenever $\le q/B = \delta$, i.e., whenever $2A \le \left(\frac{\delta}{1-\delta}\right)^2$) yields a minimum $\le \sqrt{2A} + A$, and $w = \delta$ yields $A/\delta + \frac{1}{2}\frac{\delta}{1-\delta^2}$ whenever $\left(\frac{\delta}{1-\delta}\right)^2 \le 2A$, and hence $\frac{1}{2}\frac{\delta}{1-\delta^2} \le A/\delta$. So $F_n(q) \le 1 + \frac{1}{B}\max(2AB/q, \sqrt{2A}+A)$.

Now $A = q^2\ln 2 + \frac{1}{3n}pq/(q+n^{-1/3}) \le q^2\ln 2 + \frac{1}{3}pq/(q+1) \le \frac{1}{4}\left[\ln 2 + \frac{1}{3}\frac{2}{3}\right] \le \frac{1}{4}$. So $\sqrt{2A} + A \le \frac{5}{2}\sqrt{A}$, and we get $F_n(q) \le 1 + \max(2A/q, 5\sqrt{A}/2B)$.

Further $2A/q \le (2\ln 2)q + \frac{4}{3}/(q+1) - \frac{2}{3} \le \ln 2 + \frac{2}{9} < 2$.

Also, $\frac{5}{2}\frac{\sqrt{A}}{B} \le \frac{5}{4}\sqrt{\frac{\ln 2}{(\varepsilon+1/2)^2} + \frac{\varepsilon^3/3}{(\varepsilon+1/2)^3}} \le \frac{5}{2}\sqrt{\ln 2} < 2$, so: $F_n(q) \le 3\ \forall q \le \frac{1}{2}$, $\forall n$.

(3) Case $q \ge \dfrac{1}{2}$.

Let then $u = 0$, and $v = 1 - \frac{5}{4}p$. Then we get $F_n(q) = \left[\varphi_n(p,q) + \chi_n(p,q)\right]/(p/2)$ with:

$$\chi_n(p,q) = \ln\frac{1+n^{1/3}q}{1+n^{1/3}} + \frac{5}{4}p\ln\frac{1+n^{1/3}}{1+n^{1/3}/5}$$
$$\le \frac{p/q}{1+n^{1/3}} - p + \frac{5p}{4}\ln 5 - \frac{5p}{n^{1/3}+5}.$$

Hence:

$$F_n(q) \le \frac{2}{3n\left(1+1/(qn^{1/3})\right)} + \frac{2}{q(1+n^{1/3})} - \frac{10}{5+n^{1/3}} - 2 + \frac{5}{2}\ln 5$$
$$\le \frac{2}{3n+6n^{2/3}} + \frac{4}{1+n^{1/3}} - \frac{10}{5+n^{1/3}} - 2 + \frac{5}{2}\ln 5$$
$$\le \frac{5}{2}\ln 5 - \frac{13}{9} \le 3,$$

$\forall q \ge \frac{1}{2}, \forall n \ge 1.$

(4) $K = \frac{1}{3}$ also satisfies the inequality for $n = 1$.

11. A game with incomplete information played by "non-Bayesian players." (Megiddo, 1980); cf. also VII.5, Ex. 6, p. 427.

Consider a game with incomplete information on one side in which the uninformed player II is told his payoff at each stage.

a. Prove that $u(p)$ is linear.

HINT. NR(p) is the set of strategies of player I that yield, against any strategy of player II, the same expected payoff in all games in the support of p.

b. Prove that if $\operatorname{Cav} u$ is linear, then every optimal strategy of player II at an interior point of $\Delta(K)$ is optimal for all p.

HINT. Use Proposition V.1.4, p. 216.

c. *Extension to countable K*. Prove that for countable K player II still has a strategy that guarantees $v(G^k)$ for all k, by playing optimally in a sequence of finite games.

d. Consider now a situation in which the payoff is according to some matrix G, and player II knows only the set of his moves (columns) and is told his payoff at each stage. Prove that for this situation V.5, Ex. 11c, still holds.

HINT. Observe that in V.5, Ex. 11c, a strategy is still optimal if it responds to an unexpected payoff as to a closest possible payoff.

12. Discounted repeated games with incomplete information. (Mayberry, 1967)

Consider the game $\Gamma_\lambda(p)$ with value $v_\lambda(p)$.

a. Prove that:

$$v_\lambda(p) = \max_x\left\{\lambda \min_t \sum_k p^k x^k G_t^k + (1-\lambda)\sum_s \overline{x}_s v_\lambda(p_s)\right\}. \tag{1}$$

b. For game in Example V.2.1, p. 218, prove that:

$$v_\lambda(p) = \max_{s,t}\left\{\lambda \min(ps, p't') + (1-\lambda)(\overline{s}v_\lambda(ps/\overline{s}) + \overline{s}'v_\lambda(ps'/\overline{s}'))\right\}. \tag{2}$$

Here $(s,t) \in X^2$ is the pair of mixed moves used by player I in the first stage and $\overline{s} = ps + p't$.

c. Using the concavity of v_λ, prove that the maximum in (2) is obtained at $ps = p't'$; hence, denoting ps by x and using the symmetry of v_λ, obtain:

$$v_\lambda(p) = \begin{cases} \max_{0 \le x \le p}\{\lambda x + (1-\lambda)(p v_\lambda((p-x)/p) + p' v_\lambda(x/p'))\} & \text{for } 0 \le p \le \frac{1}{2} \\ v_\lambda(p') & \text{for } \frac{1}{2} \le p \le 1. \end{cases} \tag{3}$$

d. For $2/3 \le \lambda \le 1$, use the concavity and the Lipschitz property of v_λ to simplify (3) further to:

$$v_\lambda(p) = \begin{cases} \lambda p + (1-\lambda) p' v_\lambda(p/p') & \text{for } 0 \le p \le \frac{1}{2} \\ v_\lambda(p') & \text{for } \frac{1}{2} \le p \le 1. \end{cases} \tag{4}$$

e. Observe that equation (4) reduces the problem of computing v_λ at any rational $p = n/m \le 1/2$ to the problem of computing v_λ at some other rational q with a smaller denominator. Use (4) to compute $v_\lambda(p)$ at some rational values of p:

$$\begin{aligned} v_\lambda(1/2) &= \lambda/2, \\ v_\lambda(1/3) &= \lambda(2-\lambda)/3, \\ v_\lambda(1/4) &= \lambda(3 - 3\lambda + \lambda^2)/4, \\ v_\lambda(1/5) &= \lambda(4 - 6\lambda + 4\lambda^2 - \lambda^3)/5, \\ v_\lambda(2/5) &= 2/5 - (2 - 4\lambda + 4\lambda^2 - \lambda^3)/5. \end{aligned}$$

f. By differentiating (4) obtain (letting $v'_\lambda = \frac{dv_\lambda}{dp}$):

$$v'_\lambda(p) = (1-\lambda)(1 - p/p')v'_\lambda(p/p') - (1-\lambda)v_\lambda(p/p'). \tag{5}$$

From this conclude (using the symmetry of v_λ) that for $2/3 < \lambda < 1$, and at $p = 1/2$, the function has a left derivative and a right derivative, *but they are not equal.*

g. Prove by induction on the denominator that for any rational p, the sequence of derivatives obtained by repeated use of equation (5) leads to $v'_\lambda(1/2)$.

h. Combining the last two results conclude that for $2/3 < \lambda < 1$: although v_λ is concave, it has discontinuous derivatives at every rational point.

13. On the notion of guaranteeing.

Consider the game in Example IV.1.7, p. 175: $K = \{1,2\}$, $p = (1/2, 1/2)$, and the payoff matrices are:

$$G^1 = \begin{pmatrix} 2 & 0 \end{pmatrix}, \qquad G^2 = \begin{pmatrix} 0 & 1 \\ -1 & 2 \end{pmatrix}.$$

The moves of player II are not announced to player I, and the signals to player II are a or b according to the distributions:

$$Q^1 = \begin{pmatrix} (\frac{1}{3}, \frac{2}{3}) & (\frac{1}{3}, \frac{2}{3}) \end{pmatrix}, \qquad Q^2 = \begin{pmatrix} (0,1) & (0,1) \\ (\frac{2}{3}, \frac{1}{3}) & (\frac{2}{3}, \frac{1}{3}) \end{pmatrix}.$$

a. Prove that: $\operatorname{Cav} u(p) = \frac{3}{4} - \frac{3}{2}\left|p - \frac{1}{2}\right|$ (hence $\operatorname{Cav} u(1/2) = 3/4$).

b. Assume from now on that $p = 1/2$. Denote by σ the strategy of player I if $k = 2$ and by σ_0 the strategy consisting of playing $(1/2, 1/2)$ i.i.d. in all stages.

Prove that given σ, the probability distribution of p_n is independent of player II's strategy. Denote by μ_σ the measure induced by σ on $(H_\infty, \mathscr{H}_\infty^{\mathrm{II}})$. Use Fubini's Theorem on $K \times H_\infty$ to obtain: $\frac{1}{2}\|\mu_\sigma - \mu_{\sigma_0}\| = 2\,\mathsf{E}\,\|p_\infty - \frac{1}{2}\|$.

Deduce that if $\|\mu_\sigma - \mu_{\sigma_0}\| > \delta > 0$, there exists a τ such that $\limsup \mathsf{E}_{\sigma,\tau}(\overline{g}_n) \leq \frac{3}{4} - \frac{3}{16}\delta$.

c. Consider now the following strategy τ of player II. If the first signal is a, play N_1 times Right, then N_2 times Left, and so on, with $N_n = 2^{2^n}$; $n = 1, 2, \ldots$. If the first signal is b, start with N_1 times Left, etc.

d. Prove that if $\varphi_{B,m}$ denotes the relative frequency of the times in which B (bottom row) is played in the mth block when $k = 2$, then for all large enough m:

$$\left\|\mu_\sigma - \mu_{\sigma_0}\right\| < \varepsilon \Longrightarrow \left|\mathsf{E}(\varphi_{B,m}) - 1/2\right| \leq \frac{9}{2}\varepsilon\,.$$

e. Denote by f_m^1 and f_m^2 the relative frequency of Left in games G^1 and G^2, respectively, up to stage N_m (the end of the mth block.) Prove that for any play of the game that results from σ and τ the expected payoff up to stage N_m is:

$$\frac{3}{4} + \mathsf{E}\left(f_m^1 - f_m^2\right) \pm 9\varepsilon.$$

f. Conditioning on the first move of player I in G^2 prove that $\mathsf{E}(f_m^1)$ is near $1/3$ if m is even and near $2/3$ if m is odd. Also show that:

$$\mathsf{E}\left(f_{2n}^2 \mid T\right) = 0, \qquad \mathsf{E}\left(f_{2n}^2 \mid B\right) \simeq 2/3 = \Pr(b_1 = a \mid B),$$
$$\mathsf{E}\left(f_{2n+1}^2 \mid T\right), \simeq 1, \qquad \mathsf{E}\left(f_{2n+1}^2 \mid B\right) \simeq 1/3.$$

g. Conclude that in all cases (whether the first move in G^2 is T or B):

$$\mathsf{E}_{\sigma,\tau}(\liminf \overline{g}_n) = 5/12 \pm 9\varepsilon < 3/4.$$

h. Prove a similar result for the following game with full monitoring and payoff matrices:

$$G^1 = \begin{pmatrix} 1 & 0 \\ 0 & 0 \end{pmatrix} \qquad G^2 = \begin{pmatrix} -1 & 1 \\ 0 & 0 \end{pmatrix}$$

at $p = 1/2$.

14. The conjugate recursive formula. (De Meyer, 1996a,b)

Consider a game Γ_n with full monitoring so that Lemma V.4.2, p. 281, holds. Denote by v_n^* (defined on $\mathbb{R}^K$) the conjugate function of v_n (extended to $-\infty$ outside $\Pi = \Delta(K)$):

$$v_n^*(\alpha) = \min_{p \in \Pi}\{\langle \alpha, p\rangle - v_n(p)\}.$$

a. Prove that $v_n^*(\alpha)$ is the value of a game $\Gamma_n^*(\alpha)$ played as follows: at stage 0, I (in this case the minimizer) chooses k in K, II being uninformed. Then the play is as in Γ_n (after the chance move), and the payoff is $\alpha^k - \overline{g}_n^k$.

b. Show that v_n^* satisfies:

$$v_{n+1}^*(\alpha) = \max_{y\in\Delta(T)} \min_{s\in S} \frac{n}{n+1} v_n^*\Big(\frac{n+1}{n}\alpha - \frac{1}{n}\sum_t g_{st} y_t\Big).$$

HINT. Deduce from Lemma V.4.2, p. 281, that:

$$v_{n+1}^*(\alpha)$$
$$= \frac{1}{n+1} \min_{\theta\in\Theta} \max_{y\in\Delta(T)} \Big\{(n+1)\langle\alpha,\theta_K\rangle - \sum_{s,t,k} g_{st}^k y_t \theta(k,s) - n\sum_s \theta(s) v_n\left(\theta(\cdot \mid s)\right)\Big\},$$

where $\Theta = \Delta(K \times S)$, θ_K denotes the marginal of θ on K, and $\theta(\cdot \mid s)$ is the conditional on K given s. Apply then a minmax theorem.

c. Show that I and II have optimal strategies in Γ^* that do not depend on the previous moves of II. Call $\widetilde{\Sigma}_n^*$ and $\widetilde{\mathscr{T}}_n^*$ the corresponding sets, in particular $\widetilde{\Sigma}_n^* = \Delta(K \times S^n)$.

Deduce that:

$$v_n^*(\alpha) = \max_{\tau\in\widetilde{\mathscr{T}}_n^*} \min_{\sigma\in\widetilde{\Sigma}_n^*} \Big(\sum_{a\in I^n} \sigma(a) \min_k(\alpha^k - \mathsf{E}_{a,\tau}\, \overline{g}_n^k)\Big).$$

15. Optimal strategies in finite games.

Assume standard signaling so that Lemma V.4.2, p. 281, holds.

a. Show that player I has an optimal strategy that depends only on his own past moves, or, more precisely, on the stage m and the state variable p_m computed by II (cf. V.5, Ex. 6, p. 305).

b. Given τ strategy of II in Γ_n, let $\beta^k(\tau) = \max_\sigma \mathsf{E}_{\sigma,\tau}^k \overline{g}_n$.

α. Recall that $v_n(p) = \min_\tau \langle\beta(\tau), p\rangle$ and that $\forall\beta \in B_n = \{\beta \in \mathbb{R}^K \mid \langle\beta, q\rangle \geq v_n(q) \text{ on } \Pi\}$, $\exists\tau$ such that $\beta \geq \beta(\tau)$ (cf. Corollary V.1.5, p. 217).

β. An optimal strategy of II in $\Gamma_n(p)$ is thus defined by a sequence of vectors β and mixed moves y s.t. $\beta_n \in B_n$, $\langle\beta_n, p\rangle \leq v_n(p)$, and inductively, at stage $n-m+1$, given $\beta_m \in B_m$, $y_{n-m+1} = y$ and $(\beta_{m-1,s})_{s\in S}$ satisfy: $\beta_{m-1,s} \in B_{m-1}, \forall s$ and $m\beta_m^k = (m-1)\beta_{m-1,s}^k + \sum_t G_{st}^k y_t, \forall k, \forall s$.

Hence at stage $n-m+1$, player II uses y_{n-m+1}, and if I's move is s, the next reference vector is $\beta_{n-m,s}$. (See also VI.7, Ex. 6, p. 382, and VI.7, Ex. 7, p. 383.)

16. An alternative proof of Theorem V.4.1. (Heuer, 1991a)

We again consider the following two-state game (Example V.4.1, p. 280, above):

$$G^1 = \begin{pmatrix} 3 & -1 \\ -3 & 1 \end{pmatrix} \quad \text{and} \quad G^2 = \begin{pmatrix} 2 & -2 \\ -2 & 2 \end{pmatrix}$$

with $p = P(k = 1)$.

Define $b(k,n) = \binom{n}{k}2^{-n}$, $B(k,n) = \sum_{m\leq k} b(m,n)$, for $0 \leq k \leq n$, and $B(-1,n) = 0$.

a. Let $p_{k,n} = B(k-1,n)$, $k = 0,\dots,n+1$, and prove that v_n is linear on each interval $[p_{k,n}, p_{k+1,n}]$ with values $v_n(p_{k,n}) = \frac{1}{2}b(k-1,n-1)$.

So $v_n(p) = \min_{k=0,\dots,n+1}\langle\beta_{k,n}, p\rangle, \forall p$, with $\beta_{k,n}^2 = \frac{1}{2}b(k,n-1) - (1-\frac{2k}{n})B(k,n)$ and $\beta_{k,n}^1 = \beta_{k,n}^2 + (1-\frac{2k}{n})$.

HINT. For player II, use V.5, Ex. 15, to obtain $\beta_{k,n+1}$ by playing Left with probability $\frac{1}{2} - \frac{1}{4}B(k-1,n)$, and then approaching $\beta_{k,n}$ (resp. $\beta_{k-1,n}$) if Top (resp. Bottom).

For player I it is enough to show that he can obtain v_n at each $p_{k,n}$. Note that:

$$v_{n+1}(p_{k,n+1}) = \frac{1}{2}\left(v_n(p_{k-1,n}) + v_n(p_{k,n})\right),$$

and use at $p_{k,n}$ the splitting defined by:

$$x^1(T) = \frac{B(k-1,n-1)}{2B(k-1,n)} \quad \text{and} \quad x^2(T) = \frac{1-B(k-1,n-1)}{2(1-B(k-1,n))}.$$

b. Deduce Theorem V.4.1, p. 281.

HINT. Let $\zeta(m,p) = \min\{k \mid B(k,n) \geq p\}$. Show that $\left(2\zeta(m,p)-n\right)/\sqrt{n}$ converges to x_p and use Stirling's formula.

17. Exhausting information.

Consider the model of Section V.3, and fix a strategy σ of player I. This defines the sequence of posterior probabilities p_n of player II everywhere on the set B_σ of histories in $\bigcup_n B^n$ that are reachable under σ. Let $D_n = \sum_k \sum_{m \geq n} [p_{m+1}(k) - p_m(k)]^2$.

For any behavioral strategy τ of player II (thus defined everywhere on $\bigcup_n B^n$), let (cf. proof of Lemma V.2.1, p. 219):

$$X_n^\tau = \mathsf{E}_\tau\Big[\sum_k (p_\infty^2(k) - p_n^2(k)) \;\Big|\; \mathscr{H}_n^{\mathrm{II}}\Big] = \mathsf{E}_\tau\big[D_n \mid \mathscr{H}_n^{\mathrm{II}}\big]$$

$$= \mathsf{E}_\tau\Big[\sum_k (p_\infty(k) - p_n(k))^2 \;\Big|\; \mathscr{H}_n^{\mathrm{II}}\Big].$$

Let $V_n = \sup_\tau X_n^\tau$. Then:

(1) X^τ and V are well defined on B_σ.
(2) V is a supermartingale (with values in [0, 1]) under $P_{\sigma,\tau}$ for all τ, and conditional on every $h \in B_\sigma$.
(3) There exists a strategy τ_σ such that, $\forall h \in B_\sigma$, $V_n \to 0$, $P_{\sigma,\tau_\sigma}(\cdot \mid h)$ a.s.
(4) $\forall h \in B_\sigma, \forall \tau, \sum_k p(k \mid h)\, \| P_\tau(\cdot \mid k,h) - P_\tau(\cdot \mid h)\| \leq \sqrt{\#K\, V(h)}$, where $\|\cdot\|$ is the norm of measures on B_∞.

HINT. For (2), prove first that X^τ is a $P_{\sigma,\tau}$ supermartingale; next construct an approximately optimal, or just sufficient, τ for $h \in B^n$, given approximately optimal ones in B^{n+1}. Observe that this argument shows also that the X_n^τ are a lattice. For the bound, use the first formula for X^τ.

For (3), let $n_0 = 0$, and given $n_1, \ldots, n_k$ ($n_i < n_{i+1}$) and strategies τ_k for the histories of length n ($n_{k-1} \leq n < n_k$), consider, for $h \in B_\sigma$ of length n_k, a strategy τ^h for the future such that $X_{n_k}^{\tau^h}(h) > V_{n_k}(h) - k^{-1}$, next $n_{k+1} = \min\{n > n_k \mid \forall h \in B_\sigma \cap B^{n_k}, \mathsf{E}_{\tau^h}[D_{n_k} - D_n \mid h] > V_{n_k}(h) - k^{-1}\}$, and let τ_{k+1} consist of using τ^h after h until stage n_{k+1}. The τ_k's taken together form a strategy τ_σ. And for $h \in B_\sigma \cap B^{n_k}$, and any strategy τ that coincides with τ_σ between n_k and n_{k+1}, $V_{n_k}(h) \geq \mathsf{E}_\tau(D_{n_k} \mid h) = \mathsf{E}_{\tau_\sigma}[D_{n_k} - D_{n_{k+1}} \mid h] + \mathsf{E}_{\tau_\sigma}[X_{n_{k+1}}^\tau \mid h] > V_{n_k}(h) - k^{-1} + \mathsf{E}_{\tau_\sigma}[X_{n_{k+1}}^\tau \mid h]$ yields that $\mathsf{E}_{\tau_\sigma}[X_{n_{k+1}}^\tau \mid h] \leq k^{-1}$. Since τ is arbitrary, and the X_n^τ are directed, this yields $\mathsf{E}_{\tau_\sigma}[V_{n_{k+1}} \mid h] \leq k^{-1}$, hence $\mathsf{E}_{\tau_\sigma}[V_{n_\ell} \mid h] \leq \ell^{-1}, \forall \ell > k$. So conditional on h, V_n is a positive supermartingale with expectation converging to 0. Conclude.

For (4), apply first (conditionally) Fubini's theorem (cf. VI.2.1, p. 328), and then Hölder's inequality to get a bound $\sqrt{\#K\, X^\tau(h)}$.

Remark V.5.5. This is, in fact, an exercise on (non-stationary) dynamic programming, or statistics.

Remark V.5.6. One could have used the strict inequality in the definition of τ_k to make this strategy in addition completely mixed, hence τ_σ also, in this way dispensing with the complication of the conditional statement in (3) (and similarly in (2)).

But it is in this form that the statement will be used (cf., e.g., Section IX.3, p. 495, of also Section VI.3.a) in the sense that it implies that if one were to change τ_σ to another arbitrary strategy for the first n stages (n arbitrary), it would still have the same property.

V.6. APPENDIX

In this appendix we shall prove Lemmas V.4.7, p. 287, and V.4.8, p. 287, concerning two properties of the normal density function $\phi(p)$ defined in Theorem V.4.1, p. 281. We start by examining the derivatives of the functions $\phi(p)$ and x_p.

Proposition V.6.1. *The functions $\phi(p)$ and x_p satisfy:*

(1) $\phi'(p) = -x_p$
(2) $x'_p = 1/\phi(p)$
(3) $\phi''(p) = -1/\phi(p) = -x'_p$
(4) $\phi^{(3)}(p) = -x_p/\phi^2(p)$
(5) $\phi^{(4)}(p) = -(1 + 2x_p^2)/\phi^3(p)$
(6) $\phi^{(5)}(p) = -x_p(7 + 6x_p^2)/\phi^4(p)$
(7) $\phi^{(6)}(p) = -(4x_p^2 + 7)(1 + 6x_p^2)/\phi^5(p)$
(8) $\phi^{(2n)}(p) \le 0;\ \ n = 1, 2, \ldots.$

Proof. Parts (1) to (7) are results of straightforward differentiation. Part (8) will follow if we prove that:

$$\phi^{(2n)}(p) = \frac{-1}{\phi^{2n-1}(p)} \sum_{j=0}^{n-1} a_j x_p^{2j},$$

where $a_j \ge 0$ for $j = 1, \ldots, n-1$.

We prove this by induction. By (3) it is true for $n = 1$. Assume it is true for n; then:

$$\begin{aligned}
&\phi^{(2n+1)}(p)\\
&= \frac{-1}{\phi^{2n}(p)} \left\{ \sum_{j=0}^{n-1} [(2n-1)a_j + 2(j+1)a_{j+1}] x_p^{2j+1} + (2n-1)a_{n-1}x_p^{2n-1} \right\}\\
&= \frac{-1}{\phi^{2n+1}(p)} \sum_{j=0}^{n-1} \beta_j x_p^{2j+1},
\end{aligned}$$

where $\beta_j \geq 0$, $j = 0, \ldots, n-1$. Consequently:

$$\phi^{(2n+2)}(p) = \frac{-1}{\phi^{2n+1}(p)} \left[2n \sum_{j=0}^{n-1} \beta_j x_p^{2j+2} + \sum_{j=0}^{n-1} (2j+1)\beta_j x_p^{2j} \right]$$

$$= \frac{-1}{\phi^{2n+1}(p)} \sum_{j=0}^{n+1} \gamma_j x_p^{2j},$$

where $\gamma_j \geq 0$, $j = 0, 1, \ldots, n+1$, which concludes the proof of the proposition. ■

Proposition V.6.2. *Define the sequence* $\{p_n\}_1^\infty$ *by:*

$$\exp(-\frac{1}{2}x_{p_n}^2) = \frac{1}{n} \qquad \textit{and} \qquad p_n \leq \frac{1}{2};$$

then there exists n_0 *such that for any* $n \geq n_0$*:*

$$p_n \leq p \leq p_n' \Longrightarrow \phi(p)/\sqrt{n} \leq \min(p, p'). \tag{1}$$

Proof. First by definition $p = (1/\sqrt{2\pi}) \int_{-\infty}^{x_p} e^{-\frac{1}{2}x^2} dx$, from which we have:

$$p_n \leq p \leq p_n' \iff x_p^2 \leq x_{p_n}^2 \iff \exp(-\frac{1}{2}x_p^2) \geq \exp(-\frac{1}{2}x_{p_n}^2),$$

hence $p_n \leq p \leq p_n' \iff \exp(-\frac{1}{2}x_p^2) \geq 1/n$, and the statement (1) may now be written as:

$$\exp\left(-\frac{1}{2}x_p^2\right) \geq \frac{1}{n} \Longrightarrow \frac{1}{\sqrt{n}} \frac{1}{\sqrt{2\pi}} e^{-\frac{1}{2}x_p^2}$$

$$\leq \min\Big(\frac{1}{\sqrt{2\pi}} \int_{-\infty}^{x_p} e^{-\frac{1}{2}x^2} dx, \frac{1}{\sqrt{2\pi}} \int_{x_p}^{\infty} e^{-\frac{1}{2}x^2} dx\Big).$$

The statement on the right-hand side is:

$$\frac{1}{\sqrt{n}} \frac{1}{\sqrt{2\pi}} e^{-\frac{1}{2}x_p^2} \leq \frac{1}{\sqrt{2\pi}} \int_{-\infty}^{-|x_p|} e^{-\frac{1}{2}x^2} dx.$$

We may therefore consider just, say, $x_p \leq 0$, and prove (by replacing x_p by y) that:

$$\frac{1}{\sqrt{n}} \frac{1}{\sqrt{2\pi}} e^{-\frac{1}{2}y^2} \leq \frac{1}{\sqrt{2\pi}} \int_{-\infty}^{y} e^{-\frac{1}{2}x^2} dx \tag{2}$$

holds whenever $e^{-\frac{1}{2}y^2} \geq 1/n$ and $y \leq 0$.

Now (2) is true (for all $n \geq 3$) whenever $-1 \leq y \leq 0$. This is because it is true for $y = -1$ (by direct computation) and the left-hand side is concave on $-1 \leq y \leq 0$ and has a smaller slope than the right-hand side, which is convex on $-1 \leq y \leq 0$ (cf. Figure V.1).

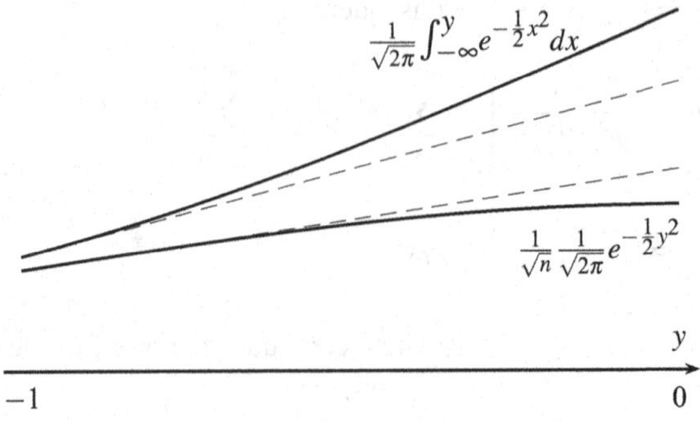

Figure V.1. An inequality.

For $x < -1$, $de^{-\frac{1}{2}x^2}/dx$ is positive and increasing. Hence at any point $y < -1$, the part of the tangent to the left of y lies below the line $e^{-\frac{1}{2}x^2}$. It intersects the x-axis at $y + 1/y$ (cf. Figure V.2). Thus the integral on the right-hand side of (2), p. 317, can be bounded by:

$$\int_{-\infty}^{y} e^{-\frac{1}{2}x^2}dx \geq -\frac{1}{2y}e^{-\frac{1}{2}y^2},$$

and it suffices to prove that:

$$e^{-\frac{1}{2}y^2} \geq \frac{1}{n} \Longrightarrow -\frac{1}{2y} \geq \frac{1}{\sqrt{n}}.$$

In fact:

$$e^{-\frac{1}{2}y^2} \geq \frac{1}{n} \Longrightarrow |y| = -y \leq \sqrt{2\ln n} \Longrightarrow -\frac{1}{2y} \geq \frac{1}{2\sqrt{2\ln n}},$$

and since $(\ln n)/n \to 0$, let n_0 be such that $n \geq n_0$ implies $-1/(2y) \geq 1/\sqrt{n}$, and we have thus proved (2), p. 317, for $n \geq n_0$, which completes the proof of Proposition V.6.2, p. 317. ■

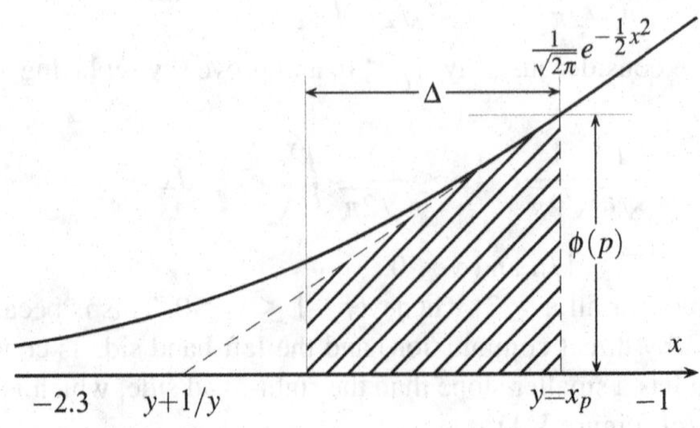

Figure V.2. A tangent to the error curve.

Proof of Lemma V.4.7, p. 287. Using Proposition V.6.1, p. 316, we expand the first term on the left-hand side of equation (15) in Section V.4 (Lemma V.4.7, p. 287) as follows: for some $0 \le \delta \le x$:

$$\frac{1}{2}[\phi(p+x)+\phi(p-x)]$$

$$= \phi(p) + \frac{x^2}{2}\phi''(p) + \frac{x^4}{4!}\frac{1}{2}[\phi^{(4)}(p+\delta)+\phi^{(4)}(p-\delta)] \tag{3}$$

$$= \phi(p) - \frac{x^2}{2\phi(p)} - \frac{x^4}{4!}\frac{1}{2}\left(\frac{1+2x^2_{p+\delta}}{\phi^3(p+\delta)} + \frac{1+2x^2_{p-\delta}}{\phi^3(p-\delta)}\right). \tag{4}$$

Clearly it is enough to prove equation (15), p. 287, for $n \ge n_0$ for any fixed n_0, and then to modify the constant c so as to make equation (15) hold for all n.

Define p_n by $\exp(-\frac{1}{2}x^2_{p_n}) = 1/n$ and $p_n \le 1/2$; then by Proposition V.6.2, p. 317, $x = \phi(p)/\sqrt{n}$ is in the domain of maximization in (15), p. 287, for $n \ge n_0$; hence, denoting the left-hand side of equation (15) by A, we get, using equation (4) for $x = \phi(p)/\sqrt{n}$:

$$A - \phi(p) \ge \frac{\phi(p)}{\sqrt{n+1}}\left[\sqrt{n} + \frac{1}{2\sqrt{n}} - \sqrt{n+1}\right]$$

$$-\frac{1}{2}\left(\frac{1+2x^2_{p+\delta}}{\phi^3(p+\delta)} + \frac{1+2x^2_{p-\delta}}{\phi^3(p-\delta)}\right)\frac{\phi^4(p)}{4!n^2\sqrt{n+1}}\sqrt{n},$$

which implies (since the bracket is positive):

$$A - \phi(p) \ge -\frac{1}{2}\left(\frac{1+2x^2_{p+\delta}}{\phi^3(p+\delta)} + \frac{1+2x^2_{p-\delta}}{\phi^3(p-\delta)}\right)\frac{\phi^4(p)}{4!n^2}, \tag{5}$$

where $0 \le \delta \le \phi(p)/\sqrt{n}$.

Notice that $\phi^{(4)}(p) = -(1+2x_p^2)/\phi^3(p)$ is symmetric about $p = 1/2$ since $\phi(p)$ is symmetric about $p = 1/2$ and since $x_{p'} = -x_p$. It follows from (5) that for $p \le 1/2$:

$$A - \phi(p) \ge -\frac{1+2x^2_{p-\delta}}{\phi^3(p-\delta)}\frac{\phi^4(p)}{4!n^2},$$

which is:

$$A - \phi(p) \ge -(1+2x^2_{p-\delta})\frac{1}{\sqrt{2\pi}}\exp\left(\frac{3}{2}x^2_{p-\delta} - 2x_p^2\right)\frac{1}{4!n^2}. \tag{6}$$

Now $1 + 2x^2 \le 8\exp(x^2/4)$ for all x; hence:

$$A - \phi(p) \ge \frac{-8}{4!n^2\sqrt{2\pi}}\exp\left(\frac{7}{4}x^2_{p-\delta} - 2x_p^2\right). \tag{7}$$

We now establish the existence of a constant $\tilde{K}$ such that $x_p - x_{p-\delta} \le \tilde{K}/\sqrt{n}$ holds for $p_n \le p \le p_n'$, $p \le 1/2$, and n sufficiently large. Since $0 \le \delta \le \phi(p)/\sqrt{n}$ and since $x_p - x_{p-\delta}$ is monotonically increasing in δ, we have to show that $\Delta \le \tilde{K}/\sqrt{n}$, where $\Delta = x_p - x_{p-\phi(p)/\sqrt{n}}$. Letting $y = x_p \le 0$ we claim in other words that:

$$\frac{\phi(p)}{\sqrt{n}} = \frac{1}{\sqrt{2\pi}} \int_{y-\Delta}^{y} e^{-\frac{1}{2}x^2} dx \text{ implies } \Delta \le \frac{\tilde{K}}{\sqrt{n}}.$$

In fact for $-1 \le y \le 0$ we have:

$$\frac{1}{\sqrt{2\pi n}} \ge \frac{\phi(p)}{\sqrt{n}} = \frac{1}{\sqrt{2\pi}} \int_{y-\Delta}^{y} e^{-\frac{1}{2}x^2} dx \ge \frac{\Delta}{\sqrt{2\pi e}},$$

which implies $\Delta \le \sqrt{e}/\sqrt{n}$.

For $y \le -1$ the tangent to $(1/\sqrt{2\pi}) \exp(-\frac{1}{2}x^2)$ at $x = y$ lies below the function and intersects the x axis at $y + 1/y$ (cf. Figure V.2 for the argument here) forming a triangular area $(-1/2y)(1/\sqrt{2\pi}) \exp(-\frac{1}{2}y^2) = \phi(p)/(2\,|y|)$. Now $p \ge p_n$ implies $|y| = |x_p| \le |x_{p_n}| = \sqrt{2 \ln n} \le 1/2\sqrt{n}$ for n sufficiently large, hence the triangular area is $\ge \phi(p)/\sqrt{n}$, which implies $\Delta \le 1/|y|$. The area of the shaded trapezoid is $\phi(p)(2 - |y|\,\Delta)\Delta/2$, and so:

$$\frac{\phi(p)}{\sqrt{n}} = \frac{1}{\sqrt{2\pi}} \int_{y-\Delta}^{y} e^{-\frac{1}{2}x^2} dx \ge \phi(p)(2 - |y|\,\Delta)\frac{\Delta}{2} \ge \phi(p)\frac{\Delta}{2}.$$

This completes the proof that $\Delta \le \frac{\tilde{K}}{\sqrt{n}}$ for a suitable $\tilde{K}$ and n sufficiently large. From this we get:

$$x_{p-\delta}^2 = (x_p - \Delta)^2 \le \left(x_p - \frac{\tilde{K}}{\sqrt{n}}\right)^2 = x_p^2 - \frac{2\tilde{K}x_p}{\sqrt{n}} + \frac{\tilde{K}^2}{n}$$

and

$$\frac{7}{4}x_{p-\delta}^2 - 2x_p^2 = -\frac{1}{4}x_p^2 - \frac{7\tilde{K}x_p}{2\sqrt{n}} + \frac{7\tilde{K}^2}{4n}. \tag{8}$$

Since $x_p < 0$, the right-hand side has a maximum (with respect to n) at some n_0; hence:

$$\frac{7}{4}x_{p-\delta}^2 - 2x_p^2 \le -\frac{1}{4}x_p^2 - \frac{7\tilde{K}x_p}{2\sqrt{n_0}} + \frac{7\tilde{K}^2}{4n_0} \le K, \tag{9}$$

where K is the maximum of the parabola (in x_p) on the right-hand side. Combining (7) and (9) we finally obtain the existence of a constant $C_1 > 0$ such that:

$$A \ge \phi(p) - C_1/n^2 \text{ for } n \ge n_0 \text{ and } p_n \le p \le p_n'. \tag{10}$$

It remains to establish (10) also for $p \le p_n$ or $p \ge p'_n$. In this case, by the definition of p_n: $\exp(-\frac{1}{2}x^2) \le 1/n$ and therefore $\phi(p) \le 1/(n\sqrt{2\pi})$. So (choosing $x = 0$):

$$\frac{1}{\sqrt{n+1}} \max_{0 \le x \le p \wedge p'} \left[\frac{\sqrt{n}}{2}(\phi(p+x) + \phi(p-x)) + x \right] \ge \frac{\sqrt{n}}{\sqrt{n+1}} \phi(p)$$
$$\ge \phi(p) - \frac{\phi(p)}{2n+1} \ge \phi(p) - \frac{1}{n(2n+1)\sqrt{2\pi}} \ge \phi(p) - \frac{C_2}{n^2}$$

for some constant C_2. Choose now C_3 such that $A \ge \phi(p) - C_3/n^2$ for $1 \le n \le n_0$, and finally choose $c = \max(C_1, C_2, C_3)$. This completes the proof of Lemma V.4.7, p. 287. ■

Proof of Lemma V.4.8. We have to prove the existence of a constant $K > 0$ such that for $0 \le p \le 1$:

$$\frac{1}{\sqrt{n+1}} \max_{(\xi,\eta) \in S(p)} \left[\sqrt{n} \left(\frac{\eta}{\xi+\eta} \phi(p+\xi) + \frac{\xi}{\xi+\eta} \phi(p-\eta) \right) + \frac{2\xi\eta}{\xi+\eta} \right] \le \phi(p) + \frac{K}{n^2}, \tag{11}$$

where $S(p) = \{(\xi, \eta) \mid 0 \le \xi \le p' \,;\, 0 \le \eta \le p\}$.

Since ϕ is continuous and $S(p)$ is compact, the maximum in (11) is achieved, say, at (ξ_0, η_0). Since $(d\phi/dp)_{1-} = -\infty$, $(d\phi/dp)_{0+} = +\infty$ it follows that $\xi_0 \ne p'$ and $\eta_0 \ne p$. Furthermore we claim that if $pp' \ne 0$ then $\xi_0 \ne 0$ and $\eta_0 \ne 0$. In fact, denote the function to be maximized in (11) by $F(\xi, \eta)$; then $F(0, \eta) = F(\xi, 0) = \sqrt{n}\phi(p)$, while:

$$\max_{(\xi,\eta) \in S(p)} F(\xi, \eta) \ge \max_{0 \le x \le p \wedge p'} F(x, x)$$
$$= \sqrt{n}\phi(p) + \max_{0 \le x \le p \wedge p'} ([O(x^2) + x]) > \sqrt{n}\phi(p).$$

We conclude that (ξ_0, η_0) is a local maximum of $F(\xi, \eta)$ in $S(p)$. Equating first partial derivatives to 0 yields:

$$\sqrt{n} \frac{\eta_0}{(\xi_0+\eta_0)^2} \left[\phi(p-\eta_0) - \phi(p+\xi_0) \right] + \sqrt{n} \frac{\eta_0}{\xi_0+\eta_0} \phi'(p+\xi_0) + \frac{2\eta_0^2}{(\xi_0+\eta_0)^2} = 0 \tag{12}$$

and

$$\sqrt{n} \frac{\xi_0}{(\xi_0+\eta_0)^2} \left[\phi(p+\xi_0) - \phi(p-\eta_0) \right] - \sqrt{n} \frac{\xi_0}{\xi_0+\eta_0} \phi'(p-\eta_0) + \frac{2\xi_0^2}{(\xi_0+\eta_0)^2} = 0. \tag{13}$$

Dividing (12) by $\eta_0/(\xi_0+\eta_0)$, (13) by $\xi_0/(\xi_0+\eta_0)$, and adding the results we get:

$$\sqrt{n}\left[\phi'(p+\xi_0) - \phi'(p-\eta_0)\right] + 2 = 0\,.$$

Recalling that $\phi'(p) = -x_p$ we have:

$$x_{p+\xi_0} - x_{p-\eta_0} = 2/\sqrt{n}. \tag{14}$$

By the mean value theorem:

$$x_{p+\xi_0} - x_{p-\eta_0} = \big[(p+\xi_0) - (p-\eta_0)\big]x'_{\theta(p+\xi_0)+(1-\theta)(p-\eta_0)}$$

for some $0 \le \theta \le 1$.

Using (14) and recalling that $x'_p = 1/\phi(p)$ we get:

$$\xi_0 + \eta_0 = (2/\sqrt{n})\phi(\theta(p+\xi_0) + (1-\theta)(p-\eta_0)). \tag{15}$$

Now

$$\begin{aligned}
&\frac{\phi(\theta(p+\xi_0) + (1-\theta)(p-\eta_0))}{\phi(p)} \\
&= \exp\left\{\frac{1}{2}\big[x_p^2 - x^2_{p+\theta\xi_0-(1-\theta)\eta_0}\big]\right\} \\
&= \exp\left\{\frac{1}{2}\big[x_p + x_{p+\theta\xi_0-(1-\theta)\eta_0}\big]\big[x_p - x_{p+\theta\xi_0-(1-\theta)\eta_0}\big]\right\}.
\end{aligned} \tag{16}$$

Since x_p is monotonically increasing in p we get from (16):

$$[x_p + x_{p+\theta\xi_0-(1-\theta)\eta_0}][x_p - x_{p+\theta\xi_0-(1-\theta)\eta_0}] \le (2/\sqrt{n})(2\left|x_p\right| + 2/\sqrt{n}),$$

and by (15) and (16) therefore:

$$\xi_0 + \eta_0 = (2/\sqrt{n})\phi(p)\exp\big(2\left|x_p\right|/\sqrt{n}\big)\exp(2/n). \tag{17}$$

Denote

$$G(\xi,\eta) = \frac{\eta}{\xi+\eta}\phi(p+\xi) + \frac{\xi}{\xi+\eta}\phi(p-\eta).$$

Expanding $\phi(p+\xi)$ and $\phi(p-\eta)$ yields:

$$\begin{aligned}
G(\xi,\eta) &= \phi(p) + \frac{1}{2}\xi\eta\phi''(p) + \frac{1}{6}\xi\eta(\xi-\eta)\phi'''(p) \\
&\quad + \frac{1}{24}\xi\eta(\xi^2 - \xi\eta + \eta^2)\phi^{(4)}(p) \\
&\quad + \frac{1}{120}\left[\frac{\eta\xi^5}{\xi+\eta}\phi^{(5)}(p+\sigma_1\xi) - \frac{\xi\eta^5}{\xi+\eta}\phi^{(5)}(p-\sigma_2\eta)\right],
\end{aligned} \tag{18}$$

where $0 \le \sigma_1 \le 1$ and $0 \le \sigma_2 \le 1$.

Consider the last term in (18) which we denote by $K(p;\xi,\eta)$. Since $\phi^{(5)}$ is decreasing we have by Proposition V.6.1, p. 316:

$$K(p;\xi,\eta) \le -\frac{1}{120}\xi\eta(\xi^2+\eta^2)(\xi-\eta)x_p(7+6x_p^2)/\phi^4(p).$$

By (17), since $\max(\xi\eta, \xi^2+\eta^2) \le (\xi+\eta)^2$ and $\xi - \eta \le \xi + \eta$, we have:

$$K(p;\xi_0,\eta_0) \le -\frac{1}{120}\left[\frac{2}{\sqrt{n}}\phi(p)\exp\left(\frac{2|x_p|}{\sqrt{n}}+\frac{2}{n}\right)\right]^5 \frac{x_p(7+6x_p^2)}{\phi^{(4)}(p)} \tag{19}$$

$$= \frac{4}{15\sqrt{n^5}}\left[\phi(p)x_p(7+6x_p^2)\exp\left(\frac{10|x_p|}{\sqrt{n}}+\frac{10}{n}\right)\right] \tag{20}$$

$$= \frac{4}{15\sqrt{2\pi n^5}}\left[x_p(7+6x_p^2)\exp\left(\frac{10|x_p|}{\sqrt{n}}+\frac{10}{n}-\frac{1}{2}x_p^2\right)\right]. \tag{21}$$

The last expression is clearly a bounded function of x_p and hence:

$$K(p;\xi_0,\eta_0) \le \frac{K_1}{n^2} \tag{22}$$

for some constant K_1.

By (18) and (22), using Proposition V.6.1, p. 316, we obtain:

$$G(\xi_0,\eta_0) \le \phi(p) - \frac{\xi_0\eta_0}{2\phi(p)} - \frac{\xi_0\eta_0(\xi_0-\eta_0)x_p}{6\phi^2(p)} - \frac{\xi_0\eta_0(\xi_0^2-\xi_0\eta_0+\eta_0^2)(1+2x_p^2)}{24\phi^3(p)} + \frac{K_1}{n^2}. \tag{23}$$

Therefore:

$$\max_{(\xi,\eta)\in S(p)}\left[G(\xi,\eta)+\frac{1}{\sqrt{n}}\frac{2\xi\eta}{\xi+\eta}\right] \le \phi(p) + \frac{K_1}{n^2} + \max_{(\xi,\eta)\in S(p)} D(\xi,\eta), \tag{24}$$

where

$$D(\xi,\eta) = \frac{1}{\sqrt{n}}\frac{2\xi\eta}{\xi+\eta} - \frac{\xi\eta}{2\phi(p)} - \frac{\xi\eta(\xi-\eta)x_p}{6\phi^2(p)} - \frac{\xi\eta(\xi^2-\xi\eta+\eta^2)(1+2x_p^2)}{24\phi^3(p)}. \tag{25}$$

Observe that $D(0,\eta) = D(\xi,0) = 0$ and $D(\varepsilon,\varepsilon) > 0$ for $\varepsilon > 0$ sufficiently small. Also $D(\xi,\eta) \to -\infty$ as $\xi \to \infty$ or $\eta \to \infty$. It follows that D restricted to the non-negative orthant has a global maximum, which is also a local maximum. Equating first derivatives of $D(\xi,\eta)$ to 0 and adding $\frac{1}{\eta}\frac{\partial D}{\partial \xi} + \frac{1}{\xi}\frac{\partial D}{\partial \eta}$ we get:

$$\frac{2}{\sqrt{n}(\xi+\eta)} - \frac{1}{\phi(p)} + \frac{(\xi-\eta)x_p}{2\phi^2(p)} - \frac{(\xi^2-\xi\eta+\eta^2)(1+2x_p^2)}{6\phi^3(p)} = 0. \tag{26}$$

Subtracting $\frac{1}{\eta}\frac{\partial D}{\partial \xi} - \frac{1}{\xi}\frac{\partial D}{\partial \eta}$ we get:

$$-\frac{2(\xi-\eta)}{\sqrt{n}(\xi+\eta)^2} - \frac{(\xi+\eta)x_p}{6\phi^2(p)} - \frac{(\xi^2-\eta^2)(1+2x_p^2)}{12\phi^3(p)} = 0. \tag{27}$$

Dividing (27) by $(\xi^2 - \eta^2)$ and eliminating $(\eta - \xi)$ yields:

$$\eta - \xi = \frac{\frac{x_p}{\phi^2(p)}}{\frac{12}{\sqrt{n}(\xi+\eta)^3} + \frac{\frac{1}{2}+x_p^2}{\phi^3(p)}}. \tag{28}$$

Replacing $(\xi^2 - \xi\eta + \eta^2)$ in (26) by $\frac{1}{4}(\xi+\eta)^2 + \frac{3}{4}(\xi-\eta)^2$ and $(\xi - \eta)$ by its value according to (28) results in:

$$\frac{2}{\sqrt{n}(\xi+\eta)} - \frac{1}{\phi(p)} + \frac{\frac{x_p^2}{\phi^4(p)}}{\frac{24}{\sqrt{n}(\xi+\eta)^3} + \frac{1+2x_p^2}{\phi^3(p)}}$$

$$- \frac{1+2x_p^2}{24\phi^3(p)}\left[(\xi+\eta)^2 + \frac{3\frac{x_p}{\phi^2(p)}}{\frac{12}{\sqrt{n}(\xi+\eta)^3} + \frac{\frac{1}{2}+x_p^2}{\phi^3(p)}}\right]^2 = 0.$$

The first term in the last equation tends to $+\infty$ as $(\xi+\eta) \to 0$; the last term is always negative, and the third is bounded from above by $[1/\phi(p)]\{\max_x[x/(1+2x^2)]\}$, which is $1/(2\sqrt{2}\phi(p))$. So if we denote the left-hand side by $L(\xi, \eta)$ we can bound it by

$$L(\xi, \eta) \le \frac{2}{\sqrt{n}(\xi+\eta)} - \frac{1}{\phi(p)} + \frac{1}{2\sqrt{2}\phi(p)}. \tag{29}$$

The right-hand side of (29) is non-negative if and only if $\xi + \eta \le \alpha\phi(p)/\sqrt{n}$ where $\alpha = 2/(1 - 1/(2\sqrt{2})) \simeq 3.1$. It follows therefore that any solution (ξ, η) of (26) and (28) must satisfy:

$$\xi + \eta \le \frac{\alpha\phi(p)}{\sqrt{n}}. \tag{30}$$

By (28) we get that at the maximum (ξ, η):

$$|\eta - \xi| \le \frac{|x_p|\,\phi(p)}{\frac{12n}{\alpha^3} + \frac{1}{2} + x_p^2} < \frac{|x_p|\,\phi(p)\alpha^3}{12n}. \tag{31}$$

Being interested in obtaining an upper bound for the global maximum of D we replace its two terms by an upper bound at the maximum. The resulting function will have a maximum that is greater than or equal that of D. Now, the last term of D (in (25)) is not positive, and as for the third term, by (30) and (31):

$$\xi\eta(\xi - \eta)\frac{x_p}{6\phi^2(p)} \le \frac{|x_p|\,\phi(p)\alpha^5}{72n^2} \le \frac{\alpha^5}{72n^2}\max_x \frac{1}{\sqrt{2\pi}}|x|\exp(-\frac{1}{2}x^2) \le \frac{K_2}{n^2}.$$

We conclude that:

$$\max_{\xi,\eta} D(\xi, \eta) \le \frac{K_2}{n^2} + \max_{\xi,\eta} D_1(\xi, \eta), \tag{32}$$

where K_2 is a constant and

$$D_1(\xi,\eta) = \frac{2\xi\eta}{\sqrt{n}(\xi+\eta)} - \frac{\xi\eta}{2\phi(p)}. \tag{33}$$

Equating first partial derivatives of D_1 to 0 we get:

$$\frac{1}{\eta}\frac{\partial D_1}{\partial \xi} = \frac{2\eta}{\sqrt{n}(\xi+\eta)^2} - \frac{1}{2\phi(p)} = 0,$$

$$\frac{1}{\xi}\frac{\partial D_1}{\partial \eta} = \frac{2\xi}{\sqrt{n}(\xi+\eta)^2} - \frac{1}{2\phi(p)} = 0,$$

which imply $\xi = \eta = \phi(p)/\sqrt{n}$ and hence:

$$\max_{\xi,\eta} D_1(\xi,\eta) \le \frac{\phi(p)}{2n}. \tag{34}$$

By (24), (32), and (34):

$$\max_{(\xi,\eta)\in S(p)} \left[G(\xi,\eta) + \frac{2\xi\eta}{\sqrt{n}(\xi+\eta)} \right] \le \phi(p)\left(1+\frac{1}{2n}\right) + \frac{K_1+K_2}{n^2}. \tag{35}$$

Combining with (11), p. 321, we have now by (35):

$$\frac{1}{\sqrt{n+1}} \max_{(\xi,\eta)\in S(p)} \left[\sqrt{n}\frac{\eta}{\xi+\eta}\phi(p+\xi) + \sqrt{n}\frac{\xi}{\xi+\eta}\phi(p-\eta) + \frac{2\xi\eta}{\xi+\eta} \right]$$

$$= \frac{\sqrt{n}}{\sqrt{n+1}} \max_{(\xi,\eta)\in S(p)} \left[G(\xi,\eta) + \frac{2\xi\eta}{\sqrt{n}(\xi+\eta)} \right]$$

$$\le \phi(p)\left(1+\frac{1}{2n}\right)\frac{\sqrt{n}}{\sqrt{n+1}} + \frac{K_1+K_2}{n^2}. \tag{36}$$

Now notice that $\sqrt{1+\frac{1}{n}} \ge 1 + \frac{1}{2n} - \frac{1}{8n^2}$; therefore:

$$\left(1+\frac{1}{2n}\right)\frac{\sqrt{n}}{\sqrt{n+1}} - 1 \le \frac{\frac{1}{8n^2}}{1+\frac{1}{2n}-\frac{1}{8n^2}} \le \frac{K_3}{n^2},$$

where K_3 is a constant. It follows that:

$$\phi(p)\left(1+\frac{1}{2n}\right)\frac{\sqrt{n}}{\sqrt{n+1}} + \frac{K_1+K_2}{n^2} \le \phi(p) + \phi(p)\frac{K_3}{n^2}$$

$$+ \frac{K_1+K_2}{n^2} \le \phi(p) + \frac{K}{n^2},$$

where K is a constant. Combined with (36) this concludes the proof of Lemma V.4.8. ■

CHAPTER VI

Incomplete Information on Two Sides

VI.1. INTRODUCTION

The case of incomplete information on both sides is where neither player knows completely the state of nature. We can assume w.l.o.g. that the initial signals are chosen according to some probability P on $K \times A \times B$ satisfying: for each k, there exists one and only one pair (a, b) with $P(k, a, b) > 0$. Just take $K' = K \times A \times B$ as a new state space and extend payoff and signaling matrices on K' in the obvious way. It follows that the initial signals of I (resp. II) define a partition K^{I} (resp. K^{II}) of K. The case in which one of the two partitions K^{I} and K^{II} of K is $\{\{1\}, \{2\}, \dots, \{\#K\}\}$ was treated in the last chapter.

No general results are yet available for the whole class of such games. This chapter will be devoted to the sub-case in which Q^k is **independent of** k; i.e., the information gained at each stage does not depend on the state of nature and is determined completely by the players' moves at that stage. Omitting the index k for the state of nature, the transition probability on signals will therefore be denoted by Q from $S \times T$ to $A \times B$.

We shall in a first part compute the minmax and maxmin of the infinitely repeated game. In the second part, we study the asymptotic value $\lim v_n$ of the finitely repeated games, which will be proved to exist always. A formula for $\lim v_n$ will be proved with a few remarks on the speed of convergence.

We shall give some procedures to solve the functional equations determining $\lim v_n$ and illustrate them by examples.

VI.2. GENERAL PREPARATIONS

In this section, we prove some lemmas that will be needed later in this chapter.

VI.2.a. Definitions and Notations

VI.2.a.1. Non-Revealing Strategies

$\mathscr{K}^{\mathrm{I}}$ (resp. $\mathscr{K}^{\mathrm{II}}$) is the σ-field generated by K^{I} (resp. K^{II}) on K.

A one-stage strategy of I is called **non-revealing** if for each column of Q, the marginal probability distribution on B induced on the letters of that column is independent of the state of nature $k \in K$. Formally $x = (x^k)_{k \in K}$ in $\Delta(S)^K$ is non-revealing if it is $\mathscr{K}^{\mathrm{I}}$ measurable and $\sum_{s \in S} x^k(s) Q_{s,t}(b)$ is independent of k for all t in T, b in B.

The set of non-revealing one-stage strategies of I is denoted by NR^{I}. Similarly $\mathrm{NR}^{\mathrm{II}}$ is the set of non-revealing one-stage strategies of II, i.e., strategies such that for each row of Q, the marginal probability distribution on A on the letters of that row does not depend on $k \in K$. NR^{I} and $\mathrm{NR}^{\mathrm{II}}$ are closed convex polyhedra, obviously non-empty as they contain, e.g., the strategies constant on K.

$D_{\mathrm{NR}}(p) = D(p)$ is the one-stage game in which I and II are restricted to strategies in NR^{I} and $\mathrm{NR}^{\mathrm{II}}$, respectively. The value of $D(p)$ is denoted by $u(p)$.

Remark VI.2.1. Note that the definition of non-revealing one-stage strategies given above differs slightly from the usual general definition of that concept, which is: a one-stage strategy of I is non-revealing if the marginal probability distribution on B induced on the letters of any column in Q is constant a.e. on K (i.e., it is the same for every k s.t. $p^k > 0$). With this definition, the set of non-revealing strategies depends (even discontinuously) on p and has to be denoted by $\mathrm{NR}^{\mathrm{I}}(p)$ and $\mathrm{NR}^{\mathrm{II}}(p)$. However, it is easily seen that the modified $D_{\mathrm{NR}(p)}(p)$, though formally different from $D(p)$, will have the same value $u(p)$ (the projections of NR^{I} and $\mathrm{NR}^{\mathrm{I}}(p)$ on $K(p)$ are the same). Since all results will be formulated in terms of $u(p)$ we conclude that the two definitions of non-revealing are equivalent. For obvious reasons we prefer the above definition which makes NR^{I} and $\mathrm{NR}^{\mathrm{II}}$ independent of p.

Remark VI.2.2. Note that to define non-revealing strategies in terms of posterior probabilities (as in Chapter III, p. 123) one has to consider the game where player II has no initial information.

Remark VI.2.3. Note that $u(p)$ is continuous in p on the simplex $\Pi = \Delta(K)$ of prior probabilities.

VI.2.a.2. Concavification

Definition VI.2.4. A function on the simplex Π of probabilities is said to be **concave with respect to I** (w.r.t. I, for short) if for every $p = (p^k)_{k \in K}$ in Π it has concave restriction on the subset $\Pi^{\mathrm{I}}(p)$ of Π, where:

$$\Pi^{\mathrm{I}}(p) = \Big\{ (\alpha^k p^k)_{k \in K} \mid \alpha^k \geq 0,\ \forall k \in K, \sum_k \alpha^k p^k = 1, \\ \text{and } (\alpha^k)_{k \in K} \text{ is } \mathscr{K}^{\mathrm{I}}\text{-measurable} \Big\}.$$

A function on Π is said to be **convex with respect to II** if for every $p = (p^k)_{k\in K}$ in Π, it has a convex restriction to the subset $\Pi^{\mathrm{II}}(p)$ of Π, where:

$$\Pi^{\mathrm{II}}(p) = \Big\{ (\beta^k p^k)_{k\in K} \mid \beta^k \geq 0,\ \forall k \in K; \sum_k \beta^k p^k = 1, \\ \text{and } (\beta^k)_{k\in K} \text{ is } \mathscr{K}^{\mathrm{II}}\text{-measurable} \Big\}.$$

Remark VI.2.5. For any $p \in \Pi$ both $\Pi^{\mathrm{I}}(p)$ and $\Pi^{\mathrm{II}}(p)$ are convex and compact subsets of Π containing p, thus justifying the definition.

Definition VI.2.6. Given any function g on Π, denote by $\mathsf{Cav}_{\mathrm{I}}\, g$ the (pointwise) minimal function $f \geq g$, which is concave w.r.t. I. Similarly denote by $\mathsf{Vex}_{\mathrm{II}}\, g$ the (pointwise) maximal function $f \leq g$, which is convex w.r.t. II. $\mathsf{Cav}_{\mathrm{I}}\, g$ is called the **concavification** of g w.r.t. I, and $\mathsf{Vex}_{\mathrm{II}}\, g$ is called the **convexification** of g w.r.t. II.

Remark VI.2.7. Note that if $K^{\mathrm{I}} = \{\{k\}_{k\in K}\}$ and $K^{\mathrm{II}} = \{K\}$, $\mathsf{Cav}_{\mathrm{I}}\, g$ is the usual $\mathsf{Cav}\, g$ on Π and $\mathsf{Vex}_{\mathrm{II}}\, g$ is g.

VI.2.b. Preliminary Results

Lemma VI.2.1. *Let P be a positive measure on the product of two measurable spaces $(X, \mathscr{X}) \otimes (Y, \mathscr{Y})$ that has a density with respect to the product of its marginals. Then:*

$$\mathsf{E}(\|P(dy \mid x) - P(dy)\|) = \mathsf{E}(\|P(dx \mid y) - P(dx)\|).$$

Proof. Write $P(dx, dy) = f(x, y)P(dx)P(dy)$:

$$\mathsf{E}(\|P(dy \mid x) - P(dy)\|) = \int_X \int_Y |f(x, y)P(dy) - P(dy)|\, P(dx)$$

hence by Fubini's theorem equals:

$$\int_{X\times Y} |f(x, y)P(dy)P(dx) - P(dy)P(dx)|\,. \tag{1}$$

■

Remark VI.2.8. The quantity appearing in Lemma VI.2.1 is therefore a natural measure of independence between X and Y.

Recall that a random variable X with values in a Banach space B is **Bochner integrable** if there exists a sequence X_n of measurable step functions with values in B such that $\mathsf{E}\, \|X - X_n\| \to 0$ (Dunford and Schwartz, 1958, III.2).

Lemma VI.2.2. *For any (Bochner-) integrable random variable X with values in a Banach space B, and any $y \in B$:*

$$\mathsf{E}(\|X - \mathsf{E}(X)\|) \leq 2\,\mathsf{E}(\|X - y\|).$$

Proof. $\mathsf{E}(\|X - \mathsf{E}(X)\|) \leq \mathsf{E}(\|X - y\| + \|\mathsf{E}(X) - y\|) \leq 2\,\mathsf{E}(\|X - y\|)$ by the triangle inequality and Jensen's inequality (using convexity of the norm). ■

Lemma VI.2.3. *Let E^{I} be any finite set, and $p = \sum_{e\in E^{\mathrm{I}}} \lambda_e p_e$ where $p_e \in \Pi^{\mathrm{I}}(p)$, $\lambda \in \Delta(E^{\mathrm{I}})$; then player* I *has a $\mathscr{K}^{\mathrm{I}}$-measurable transition probability* *from K to E^{I} such that the resulting compound probability on $K \times E^{\mathrm{I}}$ satisfies:*

- *The (marginal) probability of e is λ_e, $\forall e \in E^{\mathrm{I}}$*
- *The conditional probability on K given $e \in E^{\mathrm{I}}$ is p_e.*

Remark VI.2.9. This is a K^{I} measurable version of Proposition V.1.2, p. 216.

Proof. For $e \in E^{\mathrm{I}}$, let $p_e = (\alpha_e^k p^k)_{k \in K}$; then the required transition probability is defined by $P(e \mid k) = \lambda_e \alpha_e^k$ for $e \in E^{\mathrm{I}}, k \in K$. ■

Lemma VI.2.4. *Let $f(p)$ and $g(p)$ be functions on Π such that $g(p) \leq \mathsf{Cav}_{\mathrm{I}} f(p)$ and let $\#E^{\mathrm{I}} = \#K^{\mathrm{I}}$; then for any $p_0 \in \Pi$ and $\varepsilon > 0$ there are $p_e \in \Pi^{\mathrm{I}}(p_0)$, $e \in E^{\mathrm{I}}$, and $\lambda_e \geq 0$ with $\sum_e \lambda_e = 1$ such that $\sum_e \lambda_e p_e = p_0$ and $\sum_e \lambda_e f(p_e) \geq g(p_0) - \varepsilon$.*

If $f(p)$ is continuous, this is also true for $\varepsilon = 0$.

Proof. The proof is an application of Carathéodory's theorem, since $\Pi^{\mathrm{I}}(p_0)$ is $(\#K^{\mathrm{I}} - 1)$ (equal to $(\#E^{\mathrm{I}} - 1)$) dimensional. ■

Remark VI.2.10. The two functional equations $g(p) \leq \mathsf{Cav}_{\mathrm{I}} \min\{u(p), g(p)\}$ and $g(p) \geq \mathsf{Vex}_{\mathrm{II}} \max\{u(p), g(p)\}$ will play a very important role in this chapter.

Proposition VI.2.5. *Let $P = (P_\theta)$ be a transition probability from a probability space $(\Theta, \mathscr{C}, \mu)$ to a finite measurable space $(\Omega, \mathscr{A})$ on which a finite collection $\mathscr{F}$ of measurable functions with values in $[0, 1]$ is given; then:*

$$\inf_{P' \in \mathrm{NR}} \mathsf{E}(\| P_\theta - P'_\theta \|_1) \leq R \max_{f \in \mathscr{F}} \mathsf{E}(|P_\theta(f) - \mathsf{E}(P_\theta(f))|)$$

for some constant R depending only on Ω and $\mathscr{F}$.

Remark VI.2.11. Here $P' \in \mathrm{NR}$ means that P' is a transition probability satisfying $P'_\theta(f) = \int f(\omega) P'_\theta(d\omega)$, that it is constant on Θ for any f in $\mathscr{F}$, and that $\|\cdot\|_1$ stands for L_1 norm on Ω.

Remark VI.2.12. Lemma V.2.3 of Chapter V consists of a weaker version of this proposition and could in fact be derived from it.

In order to prove the proposition, we are going to prove the following stronger result, of which part 2 implies Proposition VI.2.5.

Proposition VI.2.6.

(1) *For any pair of probabilities P_1 and P_2 on $(\Omega, \mathscr{A})$:*

$$\min_{\tilde{P}_2 \sim P_2} \| P_1 - \tilde{P}_2 \|_1 \leq R \max_{f \in \mathscr{F}} |P_1(f) - P_2(f)|,$$

where $\tilde{P}_2 \sim P_2$ means $\tilde{P}_2(f) = P_2(f), \forall f \in \mathscr{F}$.

(2) $\min_{P'_\theta \sim_{\mathsf{E}} P_\theta} \mathsf{E}(\| P_\theta - P'_\theta \|_1) \leq \tilde{R} \max_f \min_z \mathsf{E}(|P_\theta(f) - z|)$.

Further, the constants R and $\tilde{R}$ can be chosen to depend only on Ω and $\mathscr{F}$.

Proof. We apply I.3, Ex. 4q, p. 35, in the following setup: the closed convex polyhedron is the simplex Δ of all probability measures on Ω. E^n is the appropriate Euclidian space containing it. φ is the affine transformation defined (on the simplex of probabilities) by $\varphi(P) = (P(f))_{f\in\mathscr{F}}$. Take the maximum norm in the range space of φ. Part (1) of the proposition follows now from the Lipschitz property of φ^{-1}. (Notice that the left-hand side in part (1) is less than $d(G(P_1), G(P_2))$.)

To prove the second part of the proposition we use the first part for $P_1 = P_\theta$ and $P_2 = \mathsf{E}(P_\theta)$ to establish (using, e.g., Appendix A.7.j, p. 519) the existence of $P'_\theta \sim \mathsf{E}(P_\theta)$ such that:

$$\left\| P_\theta - P'_\theta \right\|_1 \leq R \max_f |P_\theta(f) - \mathsf{E}(P_\theta(f))| .$$

Taking expectation with respect to θ and using Lemma VI.2.2 we obtain:

$$\begin{aligned}\mathsf{E}(\left\| P_\theta - P'_\theta \right\|_1) &\leq R(\#\mathscr{F}) \max_f \mathsf{E}(|P_\theta(f) - \mathsf{E}(P_\theta(f))|) \\ &\leq \tilde{R} \max_f \min_z \mathsf{E}(|P_\theta(f) - z|),\end{aligned}$$

where $\tilde{R} = 2R(\#\mathscr{F})$ is again a constant depending on Ω and $\mathscr{F}$ only. This completes the proof of the proposition. ■

Remark VI.2.13. Part 2 can in fact be improved (Mertens, 1973) by requiring further that $\mathsf{E}\, P'_\theta = \mathsf{E}\, P_\theta$.

VI.2.c. An Auxiliary Game

By virtue of Dalkey's theorem (Theorem II.1.2, p. 61), we can assume from now on, without loss of generality, that no letter of B appears with positive probability in two different rows of Q (resp. no letter of A in two different columns). This situation can be achieved, for instance, by replacing a letter a in the sth row of Q by a_s. This modification of Q does not change NR^{I}, $\mathrm{NR}^{\mathrm{II}}$, $D(p)$, or $u(p)$ (by their definitions) and does not change $v_n(p)$, $\underline{v}(p)$, or $\overline{v}(p)$ (by Dalkey's theorem). However, it will enable us to identify rows of Q with random variables on T with values in A. To analyze the game it will be useful to introduce a "lower game" (and dually an "upper game") having a simpler structure:

Define $\underline{\Gamma}(p)$ as the repeated game obtained from our original $\Gamma(p)$ by putting:

(1) $\underline{S} = S \cup S'$ (where S' is a copy of S) is the action set of player I.
(2) $\underline{G}^k \binom{G^k}{-|C|}$, $k \in K$, where $|C|$ is a $S' \times T$ matrix having the constant entry $C = \left(\max\{\left|G^k_{st}\right| \mid s \in S, t \in T, k \in K\}\right)$.
(3) $\underline{Q}$ is a $\underline{S} \times T$ matrix in which the entries are probability distributions on $\underline{A} \times \underline{B} = (A \times \{a_0\}) \times (B \cup \tilde{B})$, where $a_0 \notin A$ and $\tilde{B}$ is a (large enough) set of signals disjoint from B, such that the following is satisfied:
   - $\forall s \in S,\ \forall t \in T,\ \forall b \in B,\ \underline{Q}_{s,t}(a, b) = \mathbb{1}_{a=a_0} Q_{s,t}(b)$.
   - $\forall s \in S',\ \forall t \in T,\ \underline{Q}_{s,t}(a, b) = \mathbb{1}_{b=b(s,t,a)} Q_{s,t}(a)$, where $b(s, t, a) \in \tilde{B}$ and $s' \neq s$ or $t' \neq t$ or $a' \neq a$ implies $b(s, t, a) \neq b(s', t', a')$.

(4) I is restricted to play each of his additional pure strategies (i.e., those in S' numbered from $(\#S+1)$ to $2\#S$ with probability $\delta/\#S$ for some $\delta > 0$ to be specified later.

In words, $\underline{\Gamma}(p)$ differs from $\Gamma(p)$ by the fact that I has to pay an amount C for hearing the signals in A induced by Q. Furthermore he is restricted to use this option of buying information exactly with probability δ, while with probability $(1-\delta)$ he gets no information whatsoever. Whenever he does receive non-trivial information, his signal is completely known to II. Clearly this modification introduces asymmetry between the players (i.e., gives advantages to II). We introduce this modification in order to prove that player I can guarantee what we claim to be the maxmin of the game, despite the disadvantageous modifications. Interchanging the roles of the players in an obvious way would provide the dual statements that establish minmax.

We will still use letters a, $a \in \underline{A}$ (resp. b, $b \in \underline{B}$) for the signals to player I (resp. II) appearing in the support of $\underline{Q}$.

VI.2.d. The Probabilistic Structure

From here on, let E^{I} be an index set of the same cardinality as K^{I}. An element of E^{I} will be denoted by e. As we shall see soon we will consider a special representation of the behavioral strategies of I in which, in each stage n, he performs a lottery to choose an element in E^{I}. The probability distribution on E^{I} may of course depend on all the information available to him. Then he will use a strategy in NR^{I} that may depend only on the outcome of the lottery (i.e., the element of E^{I} that was chosen) and the history of the game *not including his type* (the element of K^{I}). This representation of the behavioral strategies of I plays a very crucial role in this chapter. In what follows we write formally the probabilistic structure of the game under such a strategy (and a strategy of II).

Let $\Omega = K \times [E^{\mathrm{I}} \times \underline{S} \times T \times \underline{A} \times \underline{B}]^{\mathbb{N}}$. The nth factor spaces E^{I}, $\underline{S}$, etc., of Ω will be denoted by E^{I}_n, $\underline{S}_n$, etc., respectively.

Unless otherwise specified, any set Z will be assumed to be endowed with its discrete σ-field $\mathscr{P}(Z)$. Let $\mathscr{K} = \mathscr{P}(K)$. The nth factor space $E^{\mathrm{I}} \times \underline{S} \times T \times \underline{A} \times \underline{B}$ of Ω represents therefore the five outcomes of stage n, namely, the result of the lottery performed by I before the stage (E^{I}), the pair of actions chosen by the two players ($\underline{S} \times T$), and the pair of signals received at the end of the stage ($\underline{A} \times \underline{B}$).

In what follows we introduce a certain number of σ-fields on Ω. Any σ-field on a factor of Ω will be identified with the corresponding σ-field on Ω. For two σ-fields $\mathscr{A}$ and $\mathscr{B}$, $\mathscr{A} \vee \mathscr{B}$ denotes the σ-field generated by $\mathscr{A}$ and $\mathscr{B}$, and similarly, for a notation like $\bigvee_{i=1}^{n} \mathscr{A}_i$. If $\mathscr{A}$ and $\mathscr{B}$ are defined on two different spaces A and B, then $\mathscr{A} \otimes \mathscr{B}$ denotes the product σ-field on $A \times B$.

As a general guide and motivation for the definitions to come we adopt the following notational conventions:

- σ-fields generated (among other things) by the signals from $\underline{A}$ and $\underline{B}$ will be denoted by the letter $\mathscr{H}$.

- A superscript I or II (or both) indicates that the announced signals of $\underline{A}$ or $\underline{B}$ (or both), respectively, are among the generators of the σ-field under consideration. Including $\underline{A}$ here will also imply including $\mathscr{P}(E^{\mathrm{I}})$.
- A subscript I or II indicates that the initial information $\mathscr{K}^{\mathrm{I}}$ (of I) or $\mathscr{K}^{\mathrm{II}}$ (of II), respectively, is among the generators of the σ-field under consideration.
- An index n indicates as usual that the σ-field under consideration corresponds to the situation before the nth move in the game.
- Adding a $\sim$ on top of a σ-field of index n indicates that we add $\mathscr{P}(E^{\mathrm{I}}_{n+1})$ to the generators of the given σ-field. In other words, adding a $\sim$ corresponds to adding the outcome of the lottery of the next stage as an additional information.

Let us now define formally the σ-fields on Ω that we shall need.

Denote by $\underline{\mathscr{H}}^{\mathrm{I}}_n$ and $\underline{\mathscr{H}}^{\mathrm{II}}_n$ the σ-fields generated by $\underline{A}$ and $\underline{B}$, respectively, on the nth factor space $\underline{A}_n \times \underline{B}_n$. Note that by definition $\underline{\mathscr{H}}^{\mathrm{I}}_n \subseteq \underline{\mathscr{H}}^{\mathrm{II}}_n$. From these we construct the following σ-fields:

$\mathscr{H}^{\mathrm{I}}_n := \vee_{i=1}^{n-1}(\underline{\mathscr{H}}^{\mathrm{I}}_i \otimes \mathscr{P}(E^{\mathrm{I}}_i))$: All information collected by I before stage n, excluding the information about his own type.

$\mathscr{H}^{\mathrm{II}}_n := \vee_{i=1}^{n-1}\underline{\mathscr{H}}^{\mathrm{II}}_i$: All information collected by II before stage n, excluding the information about his own type.

$\mathscr{H}^{\mathrm{I}}_{\mathrm{I},n} := \mathscr{H}^{\mathrm{I}}_n \vee \mathscr{K}^{\mathrm{I}}$: All information collected by I before stage n, including the information about his own type.

$\mathscr{H}^{\mathrm{II}}_{\mathrm{II},n} := \mathscr{H}^{\mathrm{II}}_n \vee \mathscr{K}^{\mathrm{II}}$: All information collected by II before stage n, including the information about his own type.

$\tilde{\mathscr{H}}^{\mathrm{I}}_n := \mathscr{H}^{\mathrm{I}}_n \vee \mathscr{P}(E^{\mathrm{I}}_n)$: All information available to I before move n, excluding the information about his own type, but including the outcome of the lottery at that stage.

$\tilde{\mathscr{H}}^{\mathrm{I}}_{\mathrm{I},n} := \mathscr{H}^{\mathrm{I}}_{\mathrm{I},n} \vee \mathscr{P}(E^{\mathrm{I}}_n) = \tilde{\mathscr{H}}^{\mathrm{I}}_n \vee \mathscr{K}^{\mathrm{I}}$: All information available to I before move n, including the information about his type and the outcome of the lottery.

$\tilde{\mathscr{H}}^{\mathrm{I}}_{\mathrm{II},n} := \tilde{\mathscr{H}}^{\mathrm{I}}_n \vee \mathscr{K}^{\mathrm{II}}$: All the information in $\tilde{\mathscr{H}}^{\mathrm{I}}_n$ plus the information about the type of II.

$\mathscr{H}^{\mathrm{I,II}}_n := \mathscr{H}^{\mathrm{I}}_n \vee \mathscr{H}^{\mathrm{II}}_n$: All information received by both players not including the information about their types.

$\mathscr{H}^{\mathrm{I,II}}_{\mathrm{II},n} := \mathscr{H}^{\mathrm{II}}_{\mathrm{II},n} \vee \mathscr{H}^{\mathrm{I}}_n$: All information received by both players plus the information about the type of II.

Finally, let $\mathscr{G}$ be the σ-field generated by the moves and the outcomes of the lotteries before stage n, i.e.:

$$\mathscr{G}_n = \left[\vee_{i=1}^{n-1}\mathscr{P}(\underline{S}_i \times T_i \times E^{\mathrm{I}}_i \times \underline{A}_i \times \underline{B}_i)\right] \vee \mathscr{K}; \quad \tilde{\mathscr{G}}_n = \mathscr{G}_n \vee \mathscr{P}(E^{\mathrm{I}}_n).$$

By virtue of Dalkey's theorem we may assume that II uses a behavioral strategy; i.e., at every stage n he uses a transition probability τ^n from $(\Omega, \mathscr{H}^{\mathrm{II}}_{\mathrm{II},n})$ to the

nth factor space T_n. As for I, the only strategies we will consider for him will be of the following type: at each stage n he uses first a transition probability from $(\Omega, \mathscr{H}^{\mathrm{I}}_{\mathrm{I},n})$ to E^{I}_n, and then he uses a $\tilde{\mathscr{H}}^{\mathrm{I}}_n$-measurable function from Ω to NR^{I} that selects a point in $\underline{S}_n$.

Given such a pair of strategies σ and τ for the two players and the probability distribution $p = (p^k)$ on $\mathscr{K}$ of the initial choice of nature, the probability $P_{\sigma,\tau}$ on $(\Omega, \mathscr{G}_\infty)$ is completely defined by the following requirements:

(1) The conditional distribution on E^{I}_n given $\mathscr{G}_n$ is $\mathscr{H}^{\mathrm{I}}_{\mathrm{I},n}$-measurable and is given by I's strategy (thus, E^{I}_n and $\mathscr{G}_n$ are conditionally independent given $\mathscr{H}^{\mathrm{I}}_{\mathrm{I},n}$).

(2) $\underline{S}_n$ and T_n are conditionally independent given $\tilde{\mathscr{H}}_n$.

(3) The conditional distribution on T_n given $\tilde{\mathscr{G}}_n$ is $\mathscr{H}^{\mathrm{II}}_{\mathrm{II},n}$-measurable and is given by II's strategy (thus, T_n and $\tilde{\mathscr{H}}_n$ are conditionally independent given $\mathscr{H}^{\mathrm{II}}_{\mathrm{II},n}$).

(4) The conditional distribution on $\underline{S}_n$ given $\tilde{\mathscr{G}}_n$ is $\tilde{\mathscr{H}}^{\mathrm{I}}_{\mathrm{I},n}$-measurable and is given by I's strategy (thus, $\underline{S}_n$ and $\tilde{\mathscr{G}}_n$ are conditionally independent given $\tilde{\mathscr{H}}^{\mathrm{I}}_{\mathrm{I},n}$).

(5) For any column of Q, the signal of player II, considered as a random variable on $\underline{S}_n$, is conditionally independent of $\tilde{\mathscr{G}}_n$ given $\tilde{\mathscr{H}}^{\mathrm{I}}_n$ (i.e., the conditional probability of b given $\tilde{\mathscr{G}}_n$ is $\tilde{\mathscr{H}}^{\mathrm{I}}_n$-measurable).

(6) The distribution of the pair of signals, given the whole past, including stage 0 and including the last pair of moves (s,t), is given by the transition probability $\underline{Q}_{s,t}$ (as a function of those moves only).

When it is understood which are the underlying strategies σ and τ, we shall omit the subscripts in $P_{\sigma,\tau}$ and write $(\Omega, \mathscr{G}_\infty, P)$ for the probability space generated by the strategies σ and τ via the above six conditions.

Lemma VI.2.7. *For any pair of strategies σ and τ of the above-specified types, there exists one and only one probability on $(\Omega, \mathscr{G}_\infty)$ satisfying (1) to (6). And conversely, to every such probability there corresponds a pair of strategies of the specified type. This is no longer true if any one of the conditions is omitted.*

Proof. See VI.7, Ex. 1, p. 379. ■

Given an increasing sequence of σ-fields $(\mathscr{A}_n)_{n\in\overline{\mathbb{N}}}$ (with $\mathscr{A}_\infty = \vee_n \mathscr{A}_n$) on $(\Omega, \mathscr{A})$ and a stopping time θ w.r.t. $(\mathscr{A}_n)_{n\in\overline{\mathbb{N}}}$ and with values in $\overline{\mathbb{N}}$, we define the σ-field $\mathscr{A}_\theta$ by:

$$A_\theta = \{\, A \mid A \in \mathscr{A},\, A \cap \{\theta \le n\} \in \mathscr{A}_n \;\forall n \in \overline{\mathbb{N}}\, \}.$$

Remark VI.2.14. Note that $\{\theta = n\} \in \mathscr{A}_n \cap \mathscr{A}_\theta$.

Define also for any $(\tilde{\mathscr{H}}^{\mathrm{I}}_{\mathrm{II},n})$-stopping time θ, $\tilde{\mathscr{H}}^{\mathrm{I}}_{\mathrm{II},\theta-}$ as the σ-field generated by $\mathscr{K}^{\mathrm{II}}$ and the sets $A \cap \{n < \theta\}\ \forall A \in \tilde{\mathscr{H}}^{\mathrm{I}}_{\mathrm{II},n}\ \forall n \in \overline{\mathbb{N}}$. It should be thought of as the σ-fields of $(\tilde{\mathscr{H}}^{\mathrm{I}}_{\mathrm{II}})$-events strictly before θ.

Remark VI.2.15. Note that θ is $(\tilde{\mathscr{H}}^{\mathrm{I}}_{\mathrm{II},\theta-})$-measurable, that $\tilde{\mathscr{H}}^{\mathrm{I}}_{\mathrm{II},n-} = \tilde{\mathscr{H}}^{\mathrm{I}}_{\mathrm{II},n-1}$ for $n \geq 1$ and $\tilde{\mathscr{H}}^{\mathrm{I}}_{\mathrm{II},1-} = \mathscr{K}^{\mathrm{II}}$, and that the restrictions of $\tilde{\mathscr{H}}^{\mathrm{I}}_{\mathrm{II},\theta-}$ and $\tilde{\mathscr{H}}^{\mathrm{I}}_{\mathrm{II},n-}$ to $\{\theta = n\}$ coincide.

We shall prove now an essential property of the probability space $(\Omega, \mathscr{G}_\infty, P)$ generated by any pair of strategies σ and τ of the above-mentioned type.

From here on we will write $p_n(k)$ for $P(k \mid \mathscr{H}^{\mathrm{I}}_n)$ and $\tilde{p}_n(k)$ for $P(k \mid \tilde{\mathscr{H}}^{\mathrm{I}}_n)$. The initial probability is thus p_1.

Proposition VI.2.8. *For any probability satisfying conditions (1)–(6) and for any $(\mathscr{H}^{\mathrm{I}}_{\mathrm{II},n})$-stopping time θ, $\mathscr{H}^{\mathrm{I,II}}_{\mathrm{II},\theta}$ and $\mathscr{K}$ are conditionally independent given $\tilde{\mathscr{H}}^{\mathrm{I}}_{\mathrm{II},\theta-}$.*

Corollary VI.2.9. *For any n, any $k \in K$, and any $\omega \in \Omega$:*

$$\begin{aligned}
p_{n+1}(k \mid \mathscr{K}^{\mathrm{II}})(\omega) &= P(k \mid a_1, \ldots, a_n, e_1, \ldots, e_n, \kappa^{\mathrm{II}}) \\
&= P(k \mid b_1, \ldots, b_n, e_1, \ldots, e_n, \kappa^{\mathrm{II}}) \\
&= P(k \mid b_1, \ldots, b_{n-1}, e_1, \ldots, e_n, \kappa^{\mathrm{II}}) \\
&= P(k \mid a_1, \ldots, a_{n-1}, e_1, \ldots, e_n, \kappa^{\mathrm{II}}) \\
&= \tilde{p}_n(k \mid \mathscr{K}^{\mathrm{II}})(\omega),
\end{aligned}$$

where $\kappa^{\mathrm{II}} \in K^{\mathrm{II}}$ and $e_i \in E^{\mathrm{I}}_i = 1, \ldots, n$.

Proof of the Corollary.

- The first and last equalities are definitions.
- The equality of the third and next-to-last terms is the statement of Proposition VI.2.8 for $\theta \equiv n + 1$, remembering that, in $\underline{\Gamma}$, "given b_i" also implies "given a_i," $i = 1, 2, \ldots, n$ (i.e., the letters a may be considered as forming a partition of the letters b).
- The conditioning σ-fields in the second and fourth terms are intermediate between those in the third and next-to-last terms. ■

Proof of Proposition VI.2.8. Let us first prove the proposition for a stopping time θ that is constant: $\theta \equiv n < +\infty$. We do this by induction on n. We make again use of the fact that the letters a in $\underline{A}$ form a partition of the letters b in $\underline{B}$. By the induction hypothesis we have (cf. Corollary VI.2.9):

$$P(k \mid b_1, \ldots, b_n, e_1, \ldots, e_n, \kappa^{\mathrm{II}}) = P(k \mid a_1, \ldots, a_n, e_1, \ldots, e_n, \kappa^{\mathrm{II}}),$$

and this holds obviously also for $n = 1$. On the other hand by condition (1) above:

$$P(e_{n+1} \mid b_1, \ldots, b_n, e_1, \ldots, e_n, k) = P(e_{n+1} \mid a_1, \ldots, a_n, e_1, \ldots, e_n, k).$$

These two relations imply:

$$P(e_{n+1},k\mid b_1,\dots,b_n,e_1,\dots,e_n,\kappa^{\mathrm{II}})$$
$$=P(e_{n+1},k\mid a_1,\dots,a_n,e_1,\dots,e_n,\kappa^{\mathrm{II}}),$$

and thus $P(k\mid b_1,\dots,b_n,e_1,\dots,e_{n+1},\kappa^{\mathrm{II}})=P(k\mid a_1,\dots,a_n,e_1,\dots,e_{n+1},\kappa^{\mathrm{II}})$, which is the conditional independence of $\mathscr{H}^{\mathrm{I,II}}_{\mathrm{II},n+1}$ and $\mathscr{K}$ given $\tilde{\mathscr{H}}^{\mathrm{I}}_{\mathrm{II},n+1}$, or, in other words:

$$P(b_1,\dots,b_n\mid a_1,\dots,a_n,e_1,\dots,e_{n+1},k)$$
$$=P(b_1,\dots,b_n\mid a_1,\dots,a_n,e_1,\dots,e_{n+1},\kappa^{\mathrm{II}}).\qquad(*)$$

For any b in $\underline{B}$ (resp. a in A), denote by $t(b)$ (resp. $s(a)$) the column (resp. the row) of $\underline{Q}$ where the signal b (resp. a) has a positive probability. Then:

$$P\left(b_{n+1}\mid\tilde{\mathscr{G}}_{n+1}\right)=\mathsf{E}\left(\underline{Q}_{s_{n+1},t_{n+1}}(b_{n+1})\mid\tilde{\mathscr{G}}_{n+1}\right)$$
$$=P\left(t_{n+1}=t(b_{n+1})\mid\tilde{\mathscr{G}}_{n+1}\right)\mathsf{E}\left(\underline{Q}_{s_{n+1},t(b_{n+1})}(b_{n+1})\mid\tilde{\mathscr{G}}_{n+1}\right)$$
$$=P\left(t_{n+1}=t(b_{n+1})\mid\mathscr{H}^{\mathrm{II}}_{\mathrm{II},n+1}\right)\mathsf{E}\left(\underline{Q}_{s_{n+1},t(b_{n+1})}(b_{n+1})\mid\tilde{\mathscr{H}}^{\mathrm{I}}_{n+1}\right)\quad\text{(by (2) and (6))}$$
$$=P\left(b_{n+1}\mid\mathscr{H}^{\mathrm{I,II}}_{\mathrm{II},n+2}\right).\qquad\text{(by (3), (4), and (5))}$$

Together with (*) this implies:

$$P(b_1,\dots,b_{n+1}\mid a_1,\dots a_n,e_1,\dots,e_{n+1},k)$$
$$=P(b_1,\dots b_{n+1}\mid a_1,\dots,a_n,e_1,\dots,e_{n+1},\kappa^{\mathrm{II}}),$$

which is the conditional independence of $\mathscr{H}^{\mathrm{I,II}}_{\mathrm{II},n+2}$ and $\mathscr{K}$ given $\tilde{\mathscr{H}}^{\mathrm{I}}_{\mathrm{II},n+1}$.

This completes the proof of the proposition for a constant stopping time $\theta\equiv n+1$. Let now θ be any $(\mathscr{H}^{\mathrm{I}}_{\mathrm{II},n})$-stopping time. We want to show that $P(k\mid\mathscr{H}^{\mathrm{I,II}}_{\mathrm{II},\theta})$ is $(\tilde{\mathscr{H}}^{\mathrm{I}}_{\mathrm{II},\theta-})$-measurable.

Let $Z_n=P(k\mid\mathscr{H}^{\mathrm{I,II}}_{\mathrm{II},n})$, $X_n=P(k\mid\tilde{\mathscr{H}}^{\mathrm{I}}_{\mathrm{II},n})$: we have just shown that $Z_n=X_{n-1}$. Since θ is a $(\mathscr{H}^{\mathrm{I,II}}_{\mathrm{II},n})$-stopping time as well, we have $P(k\mid\mathscr{H}^{\mathrm{I,II}}_{\mathrm{II},\theta})=Z_\theta$, and hence equals $X_{\theta-1}$.

Thus we only have to show that, if X_n is an $\mathscr{A}_n$-adapted process (for $\mathscr{A}_n=\tilde{\mathscr{H}}^{\mathrm{I}}_{\mathrm{II},n}$), converging a.e. to X_∞ (martingale convergence theorem), and if θ is an $\mathscr{A}_n$-stopping time, then $X_{\theta-1}$ is $(\mathscr{A}_{\theta-})$-measurable: indeed, this will imply that $P(k\mid\mathscr{H}^{\mathrm{I,II}}_{\mathrm{II},\theta})$ is $(\mathscr{H}^{\mathrm{I}}_{\mathrm{II},\theta-})$-measurable, and since one checks immediately (on generators) that $\tilde{\mathscr{H}}^{\mathrm{I}}_{\mathrm{II},\theta-}\subseteq\mathscr{H}^{\mathrm{I,II}}_{\mathrm{II},\theta}$, it will indeed follow that $P(k\mid\mathscr{H}^{\mathrm{I,II}}_{\mathrm{II},\theta})=P(k\mid\tilde{\mathscr{H}}^{\mathrm{I}}_{\mathrm{II},\theta-})$, hence the result.

Consider thus our adapted process X_n and let $Y_n=X_{n-1}\mathbb{1}_{\theta=n}$. Since $X_{\theta-1}=\sum_{n\in\overline{\mathbb{N}}}Y_n$, it suffices to show that Y_n is $(\mathscr{A}_{\theta-})$-measurable. From the characterization in terms of generators, we know that $X_{n-1}\mathbb{1}_{\theta\geq n}$ is $(\mathscr{A}_{\theta-})$-measurable, and hence, letting $n\to\infty$, $Y_\infty=X_\infty\mathbb{1}_{\theta=\infty}$ is also $(\mathscr{A}_{\theta-})$-measurable, and also, for $X\equiv 1$, we obtain the $\mathscr{A}_{\theta-}$-measurability of θ, and hence of $\mathbb{1}_{\theta=n}$, and therefore of $Y_n = (X_{n-1}\mathbb{1}_{\theta \geq n})\mathbb{1}_{\theta = n}$. This completes the proof of Proposition VI.2.8. ■

Let now θ be a $\mathscr{H}_n^{\mathrm{I}}$-stopping time, let ω stand for a typical point in $\tilde{\mathscr{H}}_\theta^{\mathrm{I}}$ (i.e., a mapping from Ω to $\tilde{\mathscr{H}}_\theta^{\mathrm{I}}$ associating to a point in Ω the atom of $\tilde{\mathscr{H}}_\theta^{\mathrm{I}}$ containing it), and for each $k \in K$, $t \in T$, let $\overline{\tau}^k(\omega)(t) = P(t_{\theta+1} = t \mid \omega, k)$.

Proposition VI.2.10. *$\overline{\tau}^k(\omega)(t)$ is $\mathscr{K}^{\mathrm{II}}$-measurable in k and $\mathscr{H}_\theta^{\mathrm{I}}$-measurable in ω.*

Proof. $P\left(t_{\theta+1} = t \middle| \tilde{\mathscr{H}}_\theta^{\mathrm{I}} \vee \mathscr{K}\right) = \mathsf{E}\left[P(t_{\theta+1} = t | \tilde{\mathscr{G}}_\theta) \middle| \tilde{\mathscr{H}}_\theta^{\mathrm{I}} \vee \mathscr{K}\right]$.

Now by condition (3) of the probability $P_{\sigma,\tau}$ (p. 333), extended to stopping times, $P(t_{\theta+1} = t \mid \tilde{\mathscr{G}}_\theta)$ is $(\mathscr{H}_{\mathrm{II},\theta}^{\mathrm{II}})$-measurable. Therefore, by condition (1) there, extended to stopping times, we get that:

$$\overline{\tau}^k(\omega)(t) = \mathsf{E}\left[P(t_{\theta+1} = t | \mathscr{H}_{\mathrm{II},\theta}^{\mathrm{II}}) \middle| \tilde{\mathscr{H}}_\theta^{\mathrm{I}} \vee \mathscr{K}\right]$$

is $(\mathscr{H}_\theta^{\mathrm{I}} \vee \mathscr{K})$-measurable:

$$\overline{\tau}^k(\omega)(t) = \mathsf{E}\left[P(t_{\theta+1} = t | \mathscr{H}_{\mathrm{II},\theta}^{\mathrm{II}}) \middle| \mathscr{H}_\theta^{\mathrm{I}} \vee \mathscr{K}\right].$$

Note that $\tilde{\mathscr{H}}_{\mathrm{II},\theta^-}^{\mathrm{I}} \subseteq \mathscr{H}_{\mathrm{II},\theta}^{\mathrm{I}} \subseteq \mathscr{H}_{\mathrm{II},\theta}^{\mathrm{I,II}}$, as seen in the proof of Proposition VI.2.8. Hence the corresponding result, in the form "$P(k \mid \mathscr{H}_{\mathrm{II},\theta}^{\mathrm{I,II}})$ is $(\tilde{\mathscr{H}}_{\mathrm{II},\theta^-}^{\mathrm{I}})$-measurable," remains a fortiori true when replacing $\tilde{\mathscr{H}}_{\mathrm{II},\theta^-}^{\mathrm{I}}$ by $\mathscr{H}_{\mathrm{II},\theta}^{\mathrm{I}}$: $\mathscr{H}_{\mathrm{II},\theta}^{\mathrm{I,II}}$ and $(\mathscr{K} \vee \mathscr{H}_\theta^{\mathrm{I}})$ are conditionally independent given $\mathscr{H}_{\mathrm{II},\theta}^{\mathrm{I}}$. Since the inner conditional expectation in our last formula for $\overline{\tau}$ is $(\mathscr{H}_{\mathrm{II},\theta}^{\mathrm{I,II}})$-measurable, it follows that $\overline{\tau}(w)(t)$ is $(\mathscr{H}_{\mathrm{II},\theta}^{\mathrm{I}})$-measurable. In particular, for each ω, $\overline{\tau}^k$ is $\mathscr{K}^{\mathrm{II}}$-measurable w.r.t. k: hence $\overline{\tau}$ defines a $\mathscr{H}_\theta^{\mathrm{I}}$-measurable map from Ω to strategies of player II in the one-shot game. ■

Remark VI.2.16. The interpretation of Proposition VI.2.10 is that, if we imagine that I announces the outcomes of his lotteries to II, and that II uses $\overline{\tau}$ as "strategy," everything will be as if both players had the same signaling matrices.

Let ω stand for a typical point in $\tilde{\mathscr{H}}_n^{\mathrm{I}}$.

Lemma VI.2.11. *For any pair of strategies σ and τ and for any $n = 1, 2, \ldots$, and $k \in K$:*

$$\mathsf{E}\left(|p_{n+1}(k) - \tilde{p}_n(k)| \mid \tilde{\mathscr{H}}_n^{\mathrm{I}}\right)(\omega) = \tilde{p}_n(k)\frac{\delta}{\#S}\sum_{a \in A}\left|q_\tau^k(\omega, a) - \sum_{\ell \in K}\tilde{p}_n(\ell)q_\tau^\ell(\omega, a)\right|,$$

where for each a in A: $q_\tau^k(\omega, a) = \sum_{t \in T}\overline{\tau}^k(\omega)(t) \cdot \underline{Q}_{s(a),t}(a)$.

Proof. Recall that by definition $p_n(k) = P(k \mid \mathscr{H}_n^{\mathrm{I}})$ and $\tilde{p}_n(k) = P(k \mid \tilde{\mathscr{H}}_n^{\mathrm{I}})$. Thus:

$$p_{n+1}(k)(\omega, a_n) = \frac{\tilde{p}_n(k)P(a_n \mid \omega, k)}{\sum_{\ell \in K}\tilde{p}_n(\ell)P(a_n \mid \omega, \ell)}.$$

But:

$$P(a_n = a \mid \omega, k) = 1 - \delta \quad \text{if} \quad a = a^0.$$

For a in A we obtain:

$$\begin{aligned} P(a_n = a \mid \omega, k) &= \sum_{s \in \underline{S}, t \in T} P(s_n = s, t_n = t, a_n = a \mid \omega, k) \\ &= \sum_{\underline{S} \times T} \underline{Q}_{s,t}(a) \,\mathsf{E}(P(s_n = s, t_n = t \mid \tilde{G}_n) \mid \omega, k) \\ &= \sum_{T} \underline{Q}_{s(a),t}(a) \,\mathsf{E}(P(s_n = s(a) \mid \tilde{G}_n) P(t_n = t \mid \tilde{G}_n) \mid \omega, k) \\ &= (\delta/\#S) \sum_{T} \underline{Q}_{s(a),t}(a) \overline{\tau}^k(\omega)(t) = (\delta/\#S) q_\tau^k(\omega, a). \end{aligned}$$

Thus:

$$P(a_n = a \mid \omega) = \begin{cases} 1 - \delta & \text{if } a = a^0 \\ (\delta/\#S) \sum_\ell \tilde{p}_n(\ell) q_\tau^\ell(\omega, a) & \text{if } a \neq a^0. \end{cases}$$

Taking the expectation over all possible values of a_n concludes the proof of the lemma. ■

Lemma VI.2.12. *For any strategy τ of II and any n:*

$$\inf_{\tilde{\tau} \in \mathrm{NR}^{\mathrm{II}}} \sum_{k \in K} \tilde{p}_n(k) \left\| \overline{\tau}^k(\omega) - \tilde{\tau}^k(\omega) \right\|_1 \leq R(|S|/\delta) \,\mathsf{E}\left(\sum_{k \in K} |p_{n+1}(k) - \tilde{p}_n(k)| \middle| \tilde{\mathscr{H}}_n^{\mathrm{I}} \right)(\omega),$$

where R is a constant that depends only on Q.

Proof. Given ω in $\tilde{\mathscr{H}}_n^{\mathrm{I}}$, each of "strategies" $\overline{\tau}^k(\omega)$ and $\tilde{\tau}^k(\omega)$ is a transition probability from $(K, \mathscr{H}^{\mathrm{II}}, \tilde{p}_n)$ to $\mathscr{P}(T \times A^S)$. We can thus rewrite the left-hand side of the inequality of the lemma as:

$$\inf_{\tilde{\tau} \in \mathrm{NR}^{\mathrm{II}}} \mathsf{E} \left\| \overline{\tau}^k(\omega) - \tilde{\tau}^k(\omega) \right\|_1 \stackrel{\text{def}}{=} (L)$$

and use Proposition VI.2.5 with $\Theta = K$, $Q = \tilde{p}_n$, $\Omega = T$, and with each f being the probability of a signal a, i.e., $f(t) = \underline{Q}_{s(a),t}(a)$. We obtain:

$$\begin{aligned} (L) &\leq R \max_{a \in A} \mathsf{E} \left| q_\tau^k(\omega, a) - \mathsf{E}\, q_\tau^k(\omega, a) \right| \\ &\leq R \sum_{k \in K} \sum_{a \in A} \tilde{p}_n(k) \left| q_\tau^k(\omega, a) - \sum_{\ell \in K} \tilde{p}_n(\ell) q_\tau^\ell(\omega, a) \right|, \end{aligned}$$

and the result follows from Lemma VI.2.11. ■

Let ρ_n denote the conditional expectation of the payoff of stage n, given $\tilde{\mathscr{H}}_n^{\mathrm{I}}$, in the game Γ.

Lemma VI.2.13. *If at some stage n, player* I *uses after his lottery an optimal strategy in $D(q_n)$, q_n being $\tilde{\mathscr{H}}_n^{\mathrm{I}}$-measurable, then:*

$$\rho_n \geq u(q_n) - \frac{CR\#S}{\delta} \sum_{k \in K} \mathsf{E}\Big(|p_{n+1}(k) - \tilde{p}_n(k)| \;\Big|\; \tilde{\mathscr{H}}_n^{\mathrm{I}}\Big) - 2\delta C - C \sum_{k \in K} \big|\tilde{p}_n(k) - q_n^k\big|$$

(recall that $C = \max_{s,t,k} \big|G_{s,t}^k\big|$ and R is the constant from Lemma VI.2.12.)

Proof. Let $\underline{\sigma} = \underline{\sigma}^k(\omega)$ be a strategy of I that is optimal in $D(q_n)$ and let τ be the strategy of II, then, since $\underline{\sigma}\,\underline{G}\tau$ is the conditional expected payoff given $\tilde{\mathscr{G}}_n$ (i.e., for η in $\tilde{\mathscr{G}}_n$, equal to $\underline{\sigma}^{k(\eta)}(\eta)\underline{G}^{k(\eta)}\tau^{k(\eta)}(\eta)$):

$$\rho_n = \mathsf{E}\Big[\mathsf{E}\left(\underline{\sigma}\,\underline{G}\tau \mid \tilde{\mathscr{H}}_n^{\mathrm{I}} \vee \mathscr{K}\right) \;\Big|\; \tilde{\mathscr{H}}_n^{\mathrm{I}}\Big] = \mathsf{E}\Big[\underline{\sigma}\,\underline{G}\overline{\tau} \;\Big|\; \tilde{\mathscr{H}}_n^{\mathrm{I}}\Big]$$

or:

$$\rho_n(\omega) = \sum_{k \in K} \tilde{p}_n(k)\underline{\sigma}^k(\omega)\underline{G}^k\overline{\tau}^k(\omega).$$

Recall (Proposition VI.2.10) that $\overline{\tau}^k$ is $\mathscr{K}^{\mathrm{II}}$-measurable in k, and that by definition of $\underline{\Gamma}_n(p)$, $\underline{\sigma}^k$ consists of playing with probability $(\delta/\#S)$ each of the additional rows, and with probability $(1-\delta)$ some strategy σ^k in the upper $\#S$ rows. Let $\tilde{\tau}^k(\omega) \in \mathrm{NR}^{\mathrm{II}}$:

$$\begin{aligned}
\rho_n(\omega) &\geq (1-\delta)\sum_k \tilde{p}_n(k)\sigma^k(\omega)G^k\tilde{\tau}^k(\omega) \\
&\quad - (1-\delta)C\sum_k \tilde{p}_n(k)\sum_{t \in T}\big|\overline{\tau}^k(\omega)(t) - \tilde{\tau}^k(\omega)(t)\big| - \delta C \\
&\geq (1-\delta)\sum_k q_n^k\sigma^k(\omega)G^k\tilde{\tau}^k(\omega) - C\sum_k\big|\tilde{p}_n(k) - q_n^k\big| \\
&\quad - C\sum_k \tilde{p}_n(k)\left\|\overline{\tau}^k(\omega) - \tilde{\tau}^k(\omega)\right\|_1 - \delta C,
\end{aligned}$$

and therefore since $\sigma^k(\omega)$ is optimal in $D(q_n)$:

$$\begin{aligned}
\rho_n(\omega) &\geq u(q_n) - C\sum_k \tilde{p}_n(k)\left\|\overline{\tau}^k(\omega) - \tilde{\tau}^k(\omega)\right\|_1 \\
&\quad - 2\delta C - C\sum_k\big|\tilde{p}_n(k) - q_n^k\big|.
\end{aligned}$$

Applying Lemma VI.2.12 we obtain the required inequality. ∎

Lemma VI.2.14. *For any real-valued function f on Π that is convex w.r.t.* II*:*

$$\mathsf{E}(f(p_{n+1}) \mid \tilde{\mathscr{H}}_n^{\mathrm{I}}) \geq f(\tilde{p}_n), \quad \forall n.$$

Proof. Since by definition $\mathsf{E}(p_{n+1} \mid \tilde{\mathscr{H}}_n^{\mathrm{I}}) = \tilde{p}_n$, the proof is just an application of Jensen's inequality to the convex function $f(p)$ provided we prove that $p_{n+1} \in \Pi^{\mathrm{II}}(\tilde{p}_n)$. (For example, I.3, Ex. 14bγ, p. 43, the required measurability of f follows since the distribution of $(\tilde{p}_n, p_{n+1})$ is discrete.) We have thus to show that $p_{n+1}(k) = g(k)\tilde{p}_n(k)$ with $g(k)$ $(\mathscr{K}^{\mathrm{II}} \vee \tilde{\mathscr{H}}_n^{\mathrm{I}})$-measurable.

Now this follows from the explicit expression of $p_{n+1}(k)$ as given in the proof of Lemma VI.2.11, recalling that $\overline{\tau}^k(\omega)$ is $\mathscr{K}^{\mathrm{II}}$-measurable (Proposition VI.2.10). ∎

VI.3. THE INFINITE GAME

VI.3.a. Minmax and Maxmin

We are now ready for the first of the two main results of this chapter, namely, to prove the existence and to characterize the minmax and the maxmin of the infinite game $\Gamma_\infty(p)$.

For any pair of strategies σ and τ in $\Gamma_\infty(p)$ and for any positive integer n we denote as usual by $\overline{\gamma}_n(\sigma, \tau)$ the expected average payoff for the first n stages, i.e., $\overline{\gamma}_n(\sigma, \tau) = \mathsf{E}\left(\frac{1}{n}\sum_{m=1}^{n} G^k_{s_m,t_m}\right)$, where E is the expectation with respect to the probability measure induced by σ, τ, and p.

Theorem VI.3.1. *The minmax of Γ_∞ exists and is given by:*

$$\overline{v}(p) = \underset{\mathrm{II}}{\mathsf{Vex}}\,\underset{\mathrm{I}}{\mathsf{Cav}}\, u(p).$$

Obviously a dual result interchanging the roles of the players establishes that $\mathsf{Cav}_{\mathrm{I}}\,\mathsf{Vex}_{\mathrm{II}}\, u$ is the maxmin of Γ_∞.

Proof. The proof is split into three parts. We first prove some results on strategies in Γ_∞; then we show that I can defend $\mathsf{Vex}_{\mathrm{II}}\,\mathsf{Cav}_{\mathrm{I}}\, u$ and, finally, that II can guarantee the same amount (cf. Definition IV.1.2, p. 174).

Part A. Preliminary Results

For any strategy σ of I, for any time n, and for any $e \in E^{\mathrm{I}}$, denote by $\sigma_{n,e}$ the strategy (i.e., the set of transition probabilities) of I that coincides with σ except at time n, where $P(e_n = e) = 1$. In other words, $\sigma_{n,e}$ is the same as σ except that in the lottery at stage n, e is chosen deterministically independently of the history.

Lemma VI.3.2. *For any strategies σ of I and τ of II, for any time n, and $e \in E^{\mathrm{I}}$, the conditional probability distribution given $\tilde{\mathscr{H}}^{\mathrm{I}}_{\mathrm{I},n}$ induced by $P_{\sigma,\tau}$ and $P_{\sigma_{n,e},\tau}$ on $\mathscr{G}_\infty$ coincide on $\{e_n = e\}$.*

Proof. Let $k \in \kappa^{\mathrm{I}} \in K^{\mathrm{I}}$; we have to show that for any $m \geq n$ the probability:

$$P(k; e_1, s_1, t_1, a_1, b_1, \ldots, e_m, s_m, t_m, a_m, b_m, e_{m+1} \mid$$
$$\kappa^{\mathrm{I}}; e_1, a_1, e_2, a_2, \ldots, e_{n-1}, a_{n-1}, e_n)$$

does not depend on whether P stands for $P_{\sigma,\tau}$ or $P_{\sigma_{n,e}\tau}$ (since this means coincidence of the two conditional probabilities on $\tilde{\mathscr{G}}_m$ for all m, and hence on $\mathcal{G}_\infty$). Using inductively conditions (1)–(4), p. 333, this statement can be reduced to the case where $m = n$, i.e., to:

$$P(k; e_1, s_1, t_1, a_1, b_1, \ldots, e_{n-1}, s_{n-1}, t_{n-1}, a_{n-1}, b_{n-1}, e_n \mid \kappa^{\mathrm{I}}; a_1, e_2, a_2, \ldots, e_{n-1}, a_{n-1}, e_n),$$

which equals:

$$P(k; e_1, s_1, t_1, a_1, b_1, \ldots, e_{n-1}, s_{n-1}, t_{n-1}, a_{n-1}, b_{n-1} \mid \kappa^{\mathrm{I}}; a_1, e_2, a_2, \ldots, e_{n-1}, a_{n-1}, e_n),$$

and by condition (1) equals:

$$P(k; e_1, s_1, t_1, a_1, t_1, \ldots, e_{n-1}, s_{n-1}, t_{n-1}, a_{n-1}, b_{n-1} \mid \kappa^{\mathrm{I}}; e_1, a_1, \ldots, e_{n-1}, a_{n-1}).$$

The result now follows from the fact that $P_{\sigma,\tau}$ and $P_{\sigma_{n,e}\tau}$ coincide on $\mathcal{G}_n$. ■

Define now $\mathrm{NR}^{\mathrm{I}}_\infty$ to be the set of strategies of I such that for every n and every $e \in E^{\mathrm{I}}$, $P(e_n = e) \in \{0, 1\}$.

Given a strategy τ of II and $\eta > 0$, define also $\sigma_0 \in \mathrm{NR}^{\mathrm{I}}_\infty$ and N by:

$$\mathsf{E}_{\sigma_0,\tau}\left[\sum_K \sum_{n<N} (p_{n+1}(k) - p_n(k))^2\right] > \sup_{\sigma \in \mathrm{NR}^{\mathrm{I}}_\infty} \mathsf{E}_{\sigma,\tau}\left[\sum_K \sum_n (p_{n+1}(k) - p_n(k))^2\right] - \eta.$$

Note that for any σ, τ, and p, $\{p_n\}_{n=1}^\infty$ is a martingale bounded in the simplex Π, which implies that the sum of squares $\sum_K \sum_{n=1}^\infty (p_{n+1}(k) - p_n(k))^2$ has expectation ≤ 1, and hence σ_0 is well defined.

In words, $\mathrm{NR}^{\mathrm{I}}_\infty$ is the set of strategies of I that actually use no lotteries and hence is a sequence of one-stage non-revealing strategies (i.e., in NR^{I}). Interpreting $(p_{n+1}(k) - p_n(k))^2$ as a measure of the information revealed at stage n, we may interpret σ_0 as the non-revealing strategy that exhausts the largest (up to η) amount of information that can be exhausted from τ by I without revealing anything itself.

It follows from Hölder's inequality and the definition of $\mathrm{NR}^{\mathrm{I}}_\infty$ (which implies that $\tilde{p}_n = p_n$ a.s.), σ_0, and N that:

Lemma VI.3.3. *For any strategy σ in $\mathrm{NR}^{\mathrm{I}}_\infty$ that coincides with σ_0 up to stage $N - 1$ and for any $n \geq N$:*

$$\mathsf{E}\left[\sum_{k \in K} \left|P(k \mid \mathscr{H}^{\mathrm{I}}_n) - P(k \mid \mathscr{H}^{\mathrm{I}}_N)\right|\right] \leq \sqrt{\eta \# K}.$$

Lemma VI.3.4. *Let σ be any strategy of* I *that coincides with σ_0 up to stage $N - 1$ and such that for all τ, for all $e \in E^{\mathrm{I}}$, and for all $n \neq N$, $P(e_n = e) \in \{0, 1\}$. Then for any $n \geq N$:*

$$\mathsf{E}\left(\sum_{k \in K} |\tilde{p}_n(k) - \tilde{p}_N(k)|\right) \leq 2\# K^{\mathrm{I}} \sqrt{\eta \# K}.$$

Proof. As usual let P be the probability distribution determined by σ, τ, and p. By Lemma VI.2.1, p. 328, applied conditionally to $\mathscr{H}_N^{\mathrm{I}}$ (as $\mathscr{K}$ plays the role of $\mathscr{Y}$ and $\tilde{\mathscr{H}}_n^{\mathrm{I}}$ plays the role of $\mathscr{X}$) we have, denoting $\|\cdot\|_{\tilde{\mathscr{H}}_n^{\mathrm{I}}}$ simply as $\|\cdot\|_n$:

$$\begin{aligned}&\mathsf{E}\left(\sum_k \|P(k \mid \tilde{\mathscr{H}}_n^{\mathrm{I}}) - P(k \mid \tilde{\mathscr{H}}_N^{\mathrm{I}})\| \mid \tilde{\mathscr{H}}_N^{\mathrm{I}}\right)\\ &\quad = \sum_k P(k \mid \tilde{\mathscr{H}}_N^{\mathrm{I}}) \left\|P(\cdot \mid \tilde{\mathscr{H}}_N^{\mathrm{I}}, k) - P(\cdot \mid \tilde{\mathscr{H}}_N^{\mathrm{I}})\right\|_n\\ &\quad = \sum_k P(k \mid \tilde{\mathscr{H}}_N^{\mathrm{I}}) \left\|P(\cdot \mid \tilde{\mathscr{H}}_N^{\mathrm{I}}, k) - \sum_{\ell \in K} P(\ell \mid \tilde{\mathscr{H}}_N^{\mathrm{I}}) P(\cdot \mid \tilde{\mathscr{H}}_N^{\mathrm{I}}, \ell)\right\|_n .\end{aligned}$$

By Lemma VI.2.2, p. 328, applied conditionally to $\mathscr{H}_N^{\mathrm{I}}$, we get therefore:

$$\begin{aligned}&\mathsf{E}\Big(\sum_k \|P(k \mid \tilde{\mathscr{H}}_n^{\mathrm{I}}) - P(k \mid \tilde{\mathscr{H}}_N^{\mathrm{I}})\| \;\Big|\; \tilde{\mathscr{H}}_N^{\mathrm{I}}\Big)\\ &\quad \le 2 \sum_k P(k \mid \tilde{\mathscr{H}}_N^{\mathrm{I}}) \Big\|P(\cdot \mid \tilde{\mathscr{H}}_N^{\mathrm{I}}, k) - \sum_{\ell \in K} P(\ell \mid \mathscr{H}_N^{\mathrm{I}}) P(\cdot \mid \tilde{\mathscr{H}}_N^{\mathrm{I}}, \ell)\Big\|_n . \qquad (1)\end{aligned}$$

Let now (ω, e) stand for a typical element in $\mathscr{H}_N^{\mathrm{I}} \times E^{\mathrm{I}} = \tilde{\mathscr{H}}_N^{\mathrm{I}}$ and define:

$$X(k, \omega, e) = \Big\|P(\cdot \mid \omega, e, k) - \sum_\ell P(\ell \mid \omega) P(\cdot \mid \omega, e, \ell)\Big\|_n .$$

From the given strategy σ we derive the strategies $\sigma_e = \sigma_{N,e}$, $e \in E^{\mathrm{I}}$. Note that $\sigma_e \in \mathrm{NR}_\infty^{\mathrm{I}}$ for all $e \in E^{\mathrm{I}}$. Using Lemma VI.3.2 we have also that, if P' denotes $P_{\sigma_e,\tau}$:

$$X(k, \omega, e) = \Big\|P'(\cdot \mid \omega, e, k) - \sum_\ell P'(\ell \mid \omega) P'(\cdot \mid \omega, e, \ell)\Big\|_n ,$$

and by definition of σ_e:

$$X(k, \omega, e) = \Big\|P'(\cdot \mid \omega, k) - \sum_\ell P'(\ell \mid \omega) P'(\cdot \mid \omega, \ell)\Big\|_n . \qquad (2)$$

Note that in σ_e, the lottery before move N is eliminated, therefore conditioning on $\mathscr{H}_N^{\mathrm{I}}$ or $\tilde{\mathscr{H}}_N^{\mathrm{I}}$ is equivalent.

Let now:

$$Y(\omega, e) = \sum_k P'(k \mid \omega) X(k, \omega, e).$$

But $P' = P_{\sigma_{N,e},\tau}$ and $P = P_{\sigma,\tau}$ coincide on $\mathscr{G}_n$; therefore:

$$Y = \sum_k P(k \mid \omega) X(k, \omega, e).$$

Rewrite now (1) as:

$$\mathsf{E}\left(\sum_k |\tilde{p}_n(k) - \tilde{p}_N(k)| \;\Big|\; \omega, e\right) \leq 2\sum_k P(k \mid \omega, e) X(k, \omega, e).$$

Taking conditional expectation over e given $\omega \in \mathscr{H}_N^{\mathrm{I}}$ we get:

$$\begin{aligned}\mathsf{E}\left(\sum_k |\tilde{p}_n(k) - \tilde{p}_N(k)| \;\Big|\; \omega\right) &\leq 2\sum_e \sum_k P(k, e \mid \omega) X(k, \omega, e)\\ &\leq 2\sum_k P(k \mid \omega)\sum_e X(k, \omega, e) = 2\sum_e Y(\omega, e).\end{aligned}$$

But by the definition of $Y(\omega, e)$ and (2):

$$Y(\omega, e) = \sum_k P'(k \mid \omega)\left\| P'(\cdot \mid \omega, k) - \sum_\ell P'(\ell \mid \omega) P'(\cdot \mid \omega, \ell)\right\|_n.$$

Applying Lemma VI.2.1, p. 328, conditionally to $\mathscr{H}_N^{\mathrm{I}}$ with $\mathscr{K}$ in the role of $\mathscr{Y}$ and $\tilde{\mathscr{H}}_N^{\mathrm{I}}$ in the role of $\mathscr{X}$, we obtain:

$$\begin{aligned}Y(\omega, e) &= \mathsf{E}\left(\sum_k \left|P'(k \mid \tilde{\mathscr{H}}_n^{\mathrm{I}}) - P'(k \mid \omega)\right| \;\Big|\; \omega\right)\\ &= \mathsf{E}\left(\sum_k \left|\tilde{p}'_n(k) - \tilde{p}'_N(k)\right| \;\Big|\; \omega\right),\end{aligned}$$

where $\tilde{p}'_n$ and $\tilde{p}'_N$ are the probabilities derived from the strategy σ_e, which is a strategy in $\mathrm{NR}_\infty^{\mathrm{I}}$ that coincides with σ_0 up to state $N - 1$; therefore by Lemma VI.3.3:

$$\mathsf{E}(Y(\omega, e)) \leq \sqrt{\eta \# K} \quad \forall e \in E^{\mathrm{I}},$$

and finally by taking expectations over $\mathscr{H}_n^{\mathrm{I}}$ in (2) we get:

$$\mathsf{E}\left(\sum_k |\tilde{p}_n(k) - \tilde{p}_N(k)|\right) \leq 2\sum_e \sqrt{\eta \# K} = 2\# K^{\mathrm{I}}\sqrt{\eta \# K},$$

which concludes the proof of Lemma VI.3.4. ■

Part B. Player I can defend Vex Cav *u*

For any given strategy τ of II and $\eta > 0$, let σ_0 and N be defined as in Lemma VI.3.3, p. 340, and consider the following strategy σ of I:

- Play σ_0 up to stage $N - 1$.
- Use the transition probability described in Lemma VI.2.4, p. 329, with $p = p_N$, $g(p) = \mathsf{Cav}_{\mathrm{I}}\, u$ and $\varepsilon = 0$, to choose $e_N \in E_N^{\mathrm{I}}$.
- After stage N play at every stage independently an optimal strategy in $D(\tilde{p}_N)$.

For $n \geq N$ denote as usual by ρ_n the conditional expected payoff at stage n given $\tilde{\mathscr{H}}_n^{\mathrm{I}}$. By Lemma VI.2.13, p. 338, we have:

$$\rho_n \geq u(\tilde{p}_N) - \frac{CR\#S}{\delta} \sum_k \mathsf{E}\left(|p_{n+1}(k) - \tilde{p}_n(k)| \mid \tilde{\mathscr{H}}_n^{\mathrm{I}}\right) - C \sum_k |\tilde{p}_N(k) - \tilde{p}_n(k)| - 2\delta C.$$

Note that for any pair of strategies $\{p_1, \tilde{p}_1, p_2, \tilde{p}_2, \dots, p_n, \tilde{p}_n, \dots\}$ is a martingale in Π. By construction of σ, $\tilde{p}_n = p_n$ for $n \neq N$, and for $n = N$ we have by Lemma VI.2.4, p. 329:

$$\mathsf{E}(u(\tilde{p}_N) \mid \mathscr{H}_N^{\mathrm{I}}) \geq (\underset{\mathrm{I}}{\mathsf{Cav}}\, u)(p_N) \geq (\underset{\mathrm{II}}{\mathsf{Vex}}\, \underset{\mathrm{I}}{\mathsf{Cav}}\, u)(p_N). \tag{3}$$

Now by Lemma VI.2.14, p. 338, applied to $f(p) = (\mathsf{Vex}_{\mathrm{II}}\, \mathsf{Cav}_{\mathrm{I}}\, u)(p)$, we have that for all n:

$$\mathsf{E}\left((\underset{\mathrm{II}}{\mathsf{Vex}}\, \underset{\mathrm{I}}{\mathsf{Cav}}\, u)(p_{n+1}) \mid \tilde{\mathscr{H}}_n^{\mathrm{I}}\right) \geq (\underset{\mathrm{II}}{\mathsf{Vex}}\, \underset{\mathrm{I}}{\mathsf{Cav}}\, u)(\tilde{p}_n).$$

It follows that $(\mathsf{Vex}\,\mathsf{Cav}\, u)(p), (\mathsf{Vex}\,\mathsf{Cav}\, u)(\tilde{p}_1), \dots, (\mathsf{Vex}\,\mathsf{Cav}\, u)(p_m), (\mathsf{Vex}\,\mathsf{Cav}\, u)(\tilde{p}_m), \dots, (\mathsf{Vex}\,\mathsf{Cav}\, u)(p_N)$ is a submartingale, and hence (3) yields:

$$\mathsf{E}(u(\tilde{p}_N)) \geq (\underset{\mathrm{II}}{\mathsf{Vex}}\, \underset{\mathrm{I}}{\mathsf{Cav}}\, u)(p).$$

Therefore (using Lemma VI.3.4, p. 340):

$$\mathsf{E}(\rho_n) \geq (\underset{\mathrm{II}}{\mathsf{Vex}}\, \underset{\mathrm{I}}{\mathsf{Cav}}\, u)(p) - \frac{CR\#S}{\delta} \sum_K \mathsf{E}\, |p_{n+1}(k) - \tilde{p}_n(k)| - 2C\#K^{\mathrm{I}}\sqrt{\eta\#K} - 2C\delta.$$

Summing on n from N to $N+m$, dividing by $N+m$, and recalling that (cf. Lemma V.2.1, p. 219) $\sum_{k\in K} \frac{1}{m} \sum_{n=N}^{m+N} \mathsf{E}(|p_{n+1}(k) - \tilde{p}_n(k)|) \leq \sqrt{\frac{\#K-1}{m}}$, we get:

$$\overline{\gamma}_{N+m}(\sigma, \tau) \geq \frac{-2CN}{N+m} + (\underset{\mathrm{II}}{\mathsf{Vex}}\, \underset{\mathrm{I}}{\mathsf{Cav}}\, u)(p) - 2C\delta - 2C\#K^{\mathrm{I}}\sqrt{\eta\#K} - \frac{CR\#S}{\delta}\sqrt{\frac{\#K}{m}}.$$

Finally, for each ε we may choose η and δ small enough and then N_0 big enough so as to have:

$$\overline{\gamma}_n(\sigma, \tau) > (\underset{\mathrm{II}}{\mathsf{Vex}}\, \underset{\mathrm{I}}{\mathsf{Cav}}\, u)(p) - \varepsilon, \quad \forall n > N_0.$$

This completes the second part of the proof of the theorem.

Part C. Player II can guarantee Vex Cav *u*

The proof of this part is derived from the results on the value of games with lack of information on one side (Theorem V.3.3, p. 230).

Observe first that if we add as additional columns in T all extreme points of $\mathrm{NR}^{\mathrm{II}}$, and we define the corresponding columns of payoffs and signals in the obvious way, the game $\Gamma_\infty(p)$ is actually unchanged. However, by doing so, the new set $\mathrm{NR}^{\mathrm{II}}$ becomes essentially the set of constant strategies (independent of k).

Now we make the game less favorable to player II by replacing his signals on these additional columns by a constant letter. In the new game, the distribution on signals is still independent of the state of nature.

Thus, if II ignores his private information (i.e., κ^{II}) and if for each $\kappa^{\mathrm{I}} \in K^{\mathrm{I}}$ we let $q^{\kappa^{\mathrm{I}}} = \sum_{k \in \kappa^{\mathrm{I}}} p^k$ and take as payoffs $A^{\kappa^{\mathrm{I}}} = \frac{1}{q^{\kappa^{\mathrm{I}}}} \sum_{k \in \kappa^{\mathrm{I}}} p^k G^k$ (and keep the same distribution on signals), we obtain a game Γ^* with incomplete information on one side, where K^{I} is the set of states of nature, q is the initial probability distribution on it, and player I is informed. In this game consider the set $\mathrm{NR}(q)$ of non-revealing strategies of player I (as defined in Chapter V) and note that its projection on the support of q equals the corresponding projection of NR^{I} (as defined in VI.2.a.1, p. 326). Indeed, this is true even if the additional columns are deleted. Letting $w'(q)$ (resp. $w(q)$) be the value of the one-shot game where player I plays in $\mathrm{NR}(q)$, resp. NR^{I}, we thus have $w'(q) = w(q)$ for all q. By Theorem V.3.3, p. 230, the value of the game Γ is $\mathsf{Cav}\, w'$.

Now by our construction $w(q) = u(p)$ and $\mathsf{Cav}\, w'(q) = \mathsf{Cav}_{\mathrm{I}}\, u(p)$, and so by Theorem V.3.3, for each p, II has a strategy $\tau(p)$, and for each $\varepsilon > 0$ there is N s.t. $\overline{\gamma}_n(\sigma, \tau(p)) < (\mathsf{Cav}_{\mathrm{I}}\, u)(p) + \varepsilon$, for all $n > N$ and for all σ of I.

By Lemma VI.2.4, p. 329 (or rather its dual for II with $\mathsf{Cav}_{\mathrm{I}}\, u$ in the place of g and f), II has a transition probability from K^{II} to E^{II} (of the same cardinality as K^{II}) such that if p_e is the conditional probability on K given the outcome $e \in E^{\mathrm{II}}$, then:

$$\mathsf{E}(\tilde{p}_e) = p \qquad \text{and} \qquad \mathsf{E}\left((\underset{\mathrm{I}}{\mathsf{Cav}}\, u)(p_e)\right) = (\underset{\mathrm{II}}{\mathsf{Vex}}\,\underset{\mathrm{I}}{\mathsf{Cav}}\, u)(p).$$

The desired strategy τ of II can now be described as follows: use the above-described transition probability to choose $e \in E^{\mathrm{II}}$. If the outcome is e, play from there on the strategy $\tau(p_e)$ (to guarantee $(\mathsf{Cav}_{\mathrm{I}}\, u)(p_e)$). It follows that for each $\varepsilon > 0$ we have with $N = \max N(p_e)$:

$$\overline{\gamma}(\sigma, \tau) < (\underset{\mathrm{II}}{\mathsf{Vex}}\,\underset{\mathrm{I}}{\mathsf{Cav}}\, u)(p) + \varepsilon, \ \forall n > N \ \forall \sigma.$$

This completes the proof of C and hence of Theorem VI.3.1. ■

An immediate consequence of the theorem is:

Corollary VI.3.5. $\Gamma_\infty(p)$ *has a value if and only if:*

$$\underset{\mathrm{I}}{\mathsf{Cav}}\,\underset{\mathrm{II}}{\mathsf{Vex}}\, u = \underset{\mathrm{II}}{\mathsf{Vex}}\,\underset{\mathrm{I}}{\mathsf{Cav}}\, u,$$

and then this (either side of the equation) is the value.

VI.7, Ex. 3 p. 379 and VI.7, Ex. 4, p. 379, will illustrate that Γ_∞ generally has no value.

VI.3.b. Approachability

VI.3.b.1. The finite case

Another consequence of Theorem VI.3.1, p. 339, and a sharpening, needed in Chapter IX, is the following characterization of approachable vectors. For $\kappa \in K^{\mathrm{I}}$, let $\overline{\gamma}_n(\sigma, \tau, \kappa) = \mathsf{E}_{p,\sigma,\tau}(\overline{g}_n \mid \kappa)$, where $\overline{g}_n$ is the average payoff over the first n stages.

Definition VI.3.1. Let $\overline{Z}_p = \left\{ z \in \mathbb{R}^{K^I} \mid \exists \tau : \forall \sigma, \forall \kappa, \ \limsup_{n\to\infty} \overline{\gamma}_n(\sigma, \tau, \kappa) \leq z^\kappa \right\}$, and $\underline{Z}_p = \left\{ z \in \mathbb{R}^{K^I} \mid \exists \tau : \forall \sigma, \exists \mathscr{L} \text{ (Banach limit)} : \forall \kappa, \mathscr{L}(\overline{\gamma}_n(\sigma, \tau, \kappa)) \leq z^\kappa \right\}$.

Remark VI.3.2. We will shortly show that $\overline{Z}_p = \underline{Z}_p$, which will justify the notation Z_p and the name **approachable vectors** for its elements. Also, the existence of $\mathscr{L}$ (I.2, Ex. 13, p. 28) just means that the convex hull of the limit points of $\overline{\gamma}_n(\sigma, \tau, \cdot)$ intersects $\underline{Z}_p - \mathbb{R}_+^{K^I}$, while for the definition of $\overline{Z}_p$ one requires inclusion. That is, $\overline{Z}_p$ can be defined in the same way as $\underline{Z}_p$, but with "$\forall \mathscr{L}$" instead of "$\exists \mathscr{L}$."

Definition VI.3.3. $W_p = \{ w \in \mathbb{R}^{K^I} \mid \langle \lambda, w \rangle \geq u(\lambda \cdot p) \ \forall \lambda \in \Delta(K^{\mathrm{I}}) \}$ with the notation $(\lambda \cdot p)(k) = \sum_{\kappa \in K^{\mathrm{I}}} \lambda_\kappa p(k \mid \kappa)$.

Proposition VI.3.6.

(1) *$\underline{Z}_p = \overline{Z}_p = Z_p$ is closed and convex; more precisely,* $Z_p = \{ z \in \mathbb{R}^{K^I} \mid \langle \lambda, z \rangle \geq (\mathsf{Vex}_{\mathrm{II}} \mathsf{Cav}_{\mathrm{I}}\, u)(\lambda \cdot p) \quad \forall \lambda \in \Delta(K^{\mathrm{I}}) \}$.

(2) *Z_p (and W_p) are compactly generated:* $Z_p = (Z_p \cap [-C, C]^{K^{\mathrm{I}}}) + \mathbb{R}_+^{K^I}$.

(3) $Z_p = \{ [\frac{1}{p(\kappa)} \sum_{e \in E} \pi(e) p_e(\kappa) w_e^\kappa]_{\kappa \in K^{\mathrm{I}}} | \pi \in \Delta(E); \forall e \in E, (w_e \in W_{p_e}$ *and* $p_e \in \Pi^{\mathrm{II}}(p)); \sum_{e \in E} \pi(e) p_e = p \}$ *where E is a set with cardinality* $\# K^{\mathrm{I}} + \# K^{\mathrm{II}}$.

(4) $\min_{z \in Z_p} \langle \lambda, z \rangle = (\mathsf{Vex}_{\mathrm{II}} \mathsf{Cav}_{\mathrm{I}}\, u)(\lambda \cdot p) \quad \forall \lambda \in \Delta(K^{\mathrm{I}})$.

Remark VI.3.4. Part (3) says in particular that any approachable vector $z \in Z_p$ can be approached by a "standard strategy" where player II first makes a type-dependent lottery on the set E, and then, given $e \in E$ and the corresponding posterior p_e, approaches $w_e \in W_{p_e}$ with an approachability strategy as in Section V.3.g, p. 257 (independent of his type).

Proof. Let the right-hand member in (3) be denoted by Y_p. By the arguments at the end of the proof of part C, we have $Y_p \subseteq \overline{Z}_p \subseteq \underline{Z}_p$. Further, denoting the right-hand member in (1) by X_p, we have $\underline{Z}_p \subseteq X_p$, by part B, p. 342 (used at $p' = \lambda \cdot p$ where there would be strict inequality). So to prove (1) and (3), it suffices to show that $X_p \subseteq Y_p$. Finally, the proof of part C, p. 343, also shows that player II can guarantee the minmax with standard strategies (and with $\#E \leq \#K^{\mathrm{I}} + \#K^{\mathrm{II}}$), and hence (4) follows: $\min_{z \in Y_p} \langle \lambda, z \rangle = (\mathsf{Vex}_{\mathrm{II}} \mathsf{Cav}_{\mathrm{I}}\, u)(\lambda \cdot p)$ (which equals $\varphi(\lambda)$, the support function of X_p). So if we show that Y_p is closed and convex, $X_p \subseteq Y_p$ will follow by Proposition I.1.13, p. 10. For the convexity, observe first that Y_p would be convex if the cardinality of E was arbitrary and allowed to vary with the point $y \in Y_p$ considered: indeed, in that case to obtain a convex combination $\sum \alpha_i y_i$, it would suffice for player II to make first a lottery (even type-independent) with weights α_i to select some y_i, then to make the correspondent type-dependent lottery to choose $e \in E_i$, etc.: but the whole procedure is clearly equivalent to one single type-dependent lottery on $\bigcup_i E_i$ (disjoint union). But with $\#E$ arbitrary, the conditions just express that (given $p_e \in \Pi^{\mathrm{II}}(p)$ and $w_e \in W_{p_e}$):

$$\sum_e \pi(e)[p_e(\kappa) w_e^\kappa] = p(\kappa) y^\kappa \qquad \forall \kappa \in K^{\mathrm{I}} \qquad \text{and}$$

$$\sum_e \pi(e) p_e(\kappa) = p(\kappa) \qquad \forall \kappa \in K^{\mathrm{II}}.$$

The second set of equations also implies $\sum \pi(e) = 1$, and so we have the right-hand member, as a vector in $\mathbb{R}^{\#K^{\mathrm{I}} + \#K^{\mathrm{II}} - 1}$, expressed as a convex combination of similar vectors in the left-hand member: by Carathéodory (I.3, Ex. 10, p. 40), it suffices to have $\pi(e) > 0$ for $\#K^{\mathrm{I}} + \#K^{\mathrm{II}}$ values of e (Fenchel's theorem would yield a better result). Hence the convexity.

Thus there remains to prove (2), and the closure of Y_p. But if we prove (2) for W_p it will immediately follow that $Y_p = \overline{Y}_p + \mathbb{R}_+^{K^I}$, when $\overline{Y}_p$ is defined as Y_p but with, instead of W_{p_e}, $W_{p_e} \cap [-C, C]^{K^{\mathrm{I}}}$. $\overline{Y}_p$ is then clearly compact, hence Y_p is closed (and compactly generated), hence (1) and (3) hold, hence $Z_p (= Y_p)$ is also compactly generated: it remains only to establish (2) for W_p. This also follows from the proof of Theorem VI.3.1, part C, where we have shown that $(\mathsf{Cav}_{\mathrm{I}}\, u)(\lambda \cdot p) = \psi(\lambda)$ was the value $(\mathsf{Cav}\, w)(\lambda)$ of a repeated game Γ with incomplete information on one side $(A^\kappa)_{\kappa \in K^{\mathrm{I}}}$, where all payoffs are $\leq C$ in absolute value: hence, in order to deduce this from the above results, without additional argument, note that $W_p \subseteq Y_p \subseteq \overline{Z}_p \subseteq X_p$, for Γ, but for Γ, $X_p = W_p$ obviously (the $\mathsf{Vex}_{\mathrm{II}}$ operation is the identity), and so it suffices to establish (b) for $\overline{Z}_p$ and Γ, which is a trivial consequence of the definition. ■

Remark VI.3.5. In the above proof it was apparently assumed that $p(\kappa) > 0$, $\forall \kappa \in K^{\mathrm{I}}$. However, the definitions of $\overline{Z}_p$, $\underline{Z}_p$, and W_p depend only on $[p(k \mid \kappa)]_{\kappa \in K^{\mathrm{I}}}$. So the subscripts p should be interpreted as standing for such a conditional probability on K given $\mathscr{K}^{\mathrm{I}}$. To make the proposition fully correct in those terms, just reinterpret the quantity $\frac{1}{p(\kappa)} \pi(e) p_e(\kappa)$ in 3 as $\sum_{k \in K} p(k \mid \kappa) q_k(e)$, with $q_k \in \Delta(E)$ $\forall k \in K$ and $q_k(e)$ $\mathscr{K}^{\mathrm{II}}$-measurable $\forall e \in E$. (In the proof (convexity of Y_p) there is obviously no problem in assuming that we have in addition some strictly positive probability on K^{I}.)

Corollary VI.3.7. *If $z \notin Z_p$, there exists a compact convex set C disjoint from $z - \mathbb{R}_+^{K^I}$, such that $\forall \tau, \exists \sigma, \exists N > 0$: $\forall n \geq N, \overline{\gamma}_n(\sigma, \tau) \in C$.*

Proof. Choose $\lambda \in \Delta(K^{\mathrm{I}})$ with $\langle \lambda, z \rangle + 2\varepsilon < (\mathsf{Vex}_{\mathrm{II}}\,\mathsf{Cav}_{\mathrm{I}}\,u)(\lambda \cdot p)$, take as convex set $\{\, x \in [-C, C]^{K^{\mathrm{I}}} \mid \langle \lambda, x \rangle \geq \langle \lambda, z \rangle + \varepsilon \,\}$, and use the proof of B. ■

Corollary VI.3.8. $\mathsf{Vex}_{\mathrm{II}}\,\mathsf{Cav}_{\mathrm{I}}\,u$ *is concave w.r.t.* I.

Proof. By Proposition VI.3.6.4. ■

VI.3.b.2. More intrinsically: NR*–strategies*

We look now for a different characterization of W_p, by a set, with corresponding strategies, that are independent of p. This leads, at the same time, to extending the previous results to the case of a continuum of types of player I.

We consider thus the case where the set of states of nature is $K \times I \times J$, with a probability distribution π on it, and where the sets K and J are finite, while I can be an arbitrary measurable space. The payoff matrix depends on K, while I (resp. J) is the initial information of player I (resp. II).

Actually, we can therefore, as in the previous chapter, identify I with $\Delta(K \times J)$ and use p for elements of $\Delta(K \times J)$, and π will become a probability distribution on $P = \Delta(K \times J)$. u becomes then a function on $\Delta(P)$.

Theorem VI.3.9.

(1) *In the above framework, Propositions V.3.38 up to V.3.41, p. 271, remain word for word true (with $\#I = 1$, $\Delta(K_i) = P$), if in Propositions V.3.40, part (4), p. 275, and V.3.41, part (2), p. 276, the strategies of player* II *are understood as non-revealing strategies in Γ_∞ and if the conclusion of Proposition V.3.41, part (2), is weakened as in part (2) below.*

(2) *Assume here for notational simplicity that* I*'s signals inform him of his last move.*
   (a) *For every non-revealing strategy τ_h of player* II*, there exist random variables $X_{h,n} \colon A^n \to \mathbb{R}^{K \times J}$ such that for all $n > 0$, all $p \in \Delta(K \times J) = P$, and all strategies σ of player* I*:*
   $$\mathsf{E}^p_{\sigma,\tau_h}\big(\overline{g}_n \mid \mathscr{H}^{\mathrm{I}}_{\mathrm{I},n}\big) = \langle p, X_{h,n} \rangle.$$
   Note thus that $X^{k,j}_{h,n} = \mathsf{E}_{\sigma,\tau^j_h}\big(\overline{g}^k_n \mid \mathscr{H}^{\mathrm{I}}_{\mathrm{I},n}\big) = \mathsf{E}_{\tau^j_h}\big(\overline{g}^k_n \mid A^n\big)$ is independent of p and σ^p.
   (b) *For every $h \in \mathbf{H}$, let $\mathbf{L}_h = \{\, x \in \mathbb{R}^{K \times J} \mid \langle p, x \rangle \leq h(p)\ \forall p \in P \,\}$. Then, for some sequence η_n decreasing to zero and that depends only on Q and on $\#J$, we have, for all $h \in \mathbf{H}$, all n, all strategies σ of player* I*, all $p \in P$, and all $j \in J$, that $\mathsf{E}_{\sigma^p,\tau_h}\big[\mathsf{sup}_{m \geq n}\, d(X_{h,m}, \mathbf{L}_h)\big] \leq C\eta_n$.*

Remark VI.3.6. τ_h being non-revealing, the distribution of X_h under σ^p and τ^j_h is independent of $j \in J$, hence the notation $\mathsf{E}_{\sigma^p,\tau_h}$ instead of $\mathsf{E}_{\sigma^p,\tau^j_h}$ or of $\mathsf{E}^{p,j}_{\sigma,\tau_h}$.

Proof. Part (1). Use the reduction in the beginning of C. It is clear that the optimal strategy of player II obtained in Proposition V.3.41.2 after this reduction is non-revealing in Γ_∞. As for V.3.40.4, it is easiest to give a direct proof, either by using the techniques of the present chapter (Proposition VI.2.10, p. 336, yields that $\overline{\tau}(\omega)$ is in NR if τ is in NR_∞; cf. also Lemma VI.2.13, p. 338), or, in order to use the statements themselves, by discretizing P, e.g., as in the proof of Proposition V.3.31, p. 262, while making sure that σ_p does not vary by more than δ_n for $p \in \ell \in L_n$ (where σ is a given NR-strategy of I).

Part (2a). Since τ_h is non-revealing, we have $P^q_{\sigma,\tau_h}(k, j \mid \mathscr{H}^{\mathrm{I}}_{\mathrm{I},n}) = q^{k,j}$, and hence $\mathsf{E}^q_{\sigma,\tau_h}(\overline{g}_n \mid \mathscr{H}^{\mathrm{I}}_{\mathrm{I},n}) = \sum_{k,j} q^{kj}\, \mathsf{E}_{\sigma^q,\tau_h^j}(\overline{g}^k_n \mid A^n)$. Let thus $\sigma_0 = \sigma^q$, $\tau_0 = \tau^j_h$. Since $\overline{g}^k_n$ is a function of (η_1, η_2) it remains to show that $P_{\sigma_0,\tau_0}((\eta_1, \eta_2) \mid \eta_1)$ is independent of σ_0, for all $\eta_1 \in A^n$, $\eta_2 \in (T \times B)^n$, and $n > 0$. Assume thus by induction that the statement is proved for all smaller values of n, and let $\eta_1 = (\xi_1, s, \alpha, \eta_2 = (\xi_2, t, \beta)$. Then:

$$
\begin{aligned}
&P_{\sigma_0,\tau_0}((\eta_1, \eta_2) \mid \eta_1)\\
&\quad = P_{\sigma_0,\tau_0}(\xi_2, s, t, \alpha, \beta \mid \xi_1) \Big/ \sum_{\xi_2,t,\beta} P_{\sigma_0,\tau_0}(\xi_2, s, t, \alpha, \beta \mid \xi_1)\\
&\quad = P_{\tau_0}((\xi_1, \xi_2) \mid \xi_1) P_{\sigma_0}(s \mid \xi_1) P_{\tau_0}(t \mid \xi_2) P((\alpha, \beta) \mid (s, t)) \Big/ \sum_{\xi_2,t,b} \cdots,
\end{aligned}
$$

and, after dividing numerator and denominator by the common factor $P_{\sigma_0}(s \mid \xi_1)$ one sees that σ_0 no longer appears in the expression.

(Recall from the proof of Proposition V.3.41.2, p. 276, that the τ_h are completely mixed, and so the $X^{k,j}_{h,n}$ are indeed well defined over the whole of A^n. Observe further that, for fixed $\omega \in \bigcup_n A^n$, the $X^{k,j}_{h,n}$ take the form $X^{k,j}_h(\omega) = \sum_{s,t} F^\omega_{s,t}(\tau^j_h) G^k_{s,t}$, where $F^\omega(\tau)$ is a probability distribution over $S \times T$ varying continuously with τ.)

Part (2b). Fix a sequence ε_n, take the corresponding map τ_h from Proposition V.3.41.2, p. 276, in the auxiliary game Γ^* of C, together with the corresponding sequence δ_n. Observe the matrix Q^* of Γ^*, and hence the sequence δ_n depends only on Q and on $\#J$. Fix $h \in \mathbf{H}$, and a type-independent strategy σ of player I (the strategy σ^p of the statement, for some fixed p). Thus, σ is a transition probability from $\bigcup_n A^n$ to S. It clearly suffices to consider such σ. Write τ for τ_h for short, and similarly X for X_h. By definition of the auxiliary game, writing T_e for the set of extreme NR-strategies, τ is a transition probability from $\bigcup_n [B \cup T_e]^n$ to $(T \cup T_e)$, assuming for simplicity that in the original game player II's signal informs him of his action.

σ, τ, and p determine a probability distribution on the space $\Omega_0 = [A \times (B \cup T_e)]^\infty$; in this representation we use explicitly that both players' signals in the original game inform them of their actions; in fact, every step consists first of a transition probability from the past to $S \times (T \cup T_e)$, and then of using Q to go from $S \times T$ to $A \times B$ and Q^* to go from $S \times T_e$ to $A \times T_e$ (with the identity on the factor T_e).

Consider now the induced probability distribution on $\Omega_1 = [A \times (B \cup T_e) \times T^J]^\infty = \Omega_0 \times (T^J)^\infty$, where all factors T are conditionally independent given Ω_0 and depend only on the same dated factor $A \times (B \cup T_e)$, with $\mathsf{Pr}(t_j = t \mid a, b) = 1$ if t is the column where "b" appears, and $\mathsf{Pr}(t_j = t \mid a, t_e) = t_e^j(t) Q_{st}(a)/v_{e,s}(a)$. Here t_e^j is the behavioral strategy in state $j \in J$ induced by the extreme point t_e, s is the row containing "a," and $v_{e,s}(a) = \sum_t t_e^j(t) Q_{st}(a)$ is independent of j since t_e is non-revealing. Define on Ω_1 the sequence of random variables $f_n^{k,j}(\omega) = G^k(s_n(\omega), t_n^j(\omega))$, where $t_n^j(\omega)$ is the projection of ω on the factor $j (\in J)$ of the nth factor T^J of Ω, and $s_n(\omega)$ is the row containing the projection $a_n(\omega)$ of ω on the nth factor A of Ω. And, as usual, $\overline{f}_n = \frac{1}{n} \sum_{m \le n} f_m$.

Observe now that, on this probability space, the distribution on A^∞ is the distribution induced in the true game by the strategies σ and τ^j, whatever $j \in J$ is; i.e., it is the distribution used in the statement. Also, for every $j \in J$, the distribution of the sequence $(a_n(\omega), t_n^j(\omega))$ is the distribution induced in the true game by σ and τ^j, since we have essentially generated t_j by its correct conditional distribution, so that $X_n^{kj} = \mathsf{E}(\overline{f}_n^{kj} \mid \mathscr{A}^n)$ (by part (1)).

Observe finally that the distribution on Ω_1 and the sequence $f_n(\omega)$ in $(\mathbb{R}^{K \times J})^\infty$ are the distributions of the sequence of pairs of signals and of vector payoffs generated by the strategies σ and τ in the auxiliary game $\tilde{\Gamma}^*$, defined as Γ^* but having a random vector payoff in $\mathbb{R}^{K \times J}$, where the joint distribution of the vector payoff and the pair of signals, given the pair of moves, is defined as follows: first use the signaling matrix Q^* of Γ^* to select the pair of signals in $A \times (B \cup T_e)$; use then our above-defined $\mathsf{Pr}(t_j = t \mid A \times B \cup T_e))$, independently for each $j \in J$, to select t_j's at random, and let the vector payoff in $\mathbb{R}^{K \times J}$ be $G^k_{s(a), t_j}$, where $s(a)$ is the row containing $a \in A$. Note that Γ^* is obtained from $\tilde{\Gamma}^*$ by replacing the random payoffs by their expectations.

Define now $\overline{\Gamma}$ from $\tilde{\Gamma}^*$ by replacing the random payoffs by their conditional expectations given the pair of signals in $A \times (B \cup T_e)$; i.e., $\overline{\Gamma}$ is described by the same signaling matrix as Γ^*, and by a vector payoff function $\overline{G}^{k,j}_{a,t}$ defined on $A \times \overline{T}$ (with $\overline{T} = T \cup T_e$, or on $A \times (B \cup T_e)$, by recalling that $b \in B$ determines $t \in T$ and that $a \in A$ determines $s \in S$). Note that it depends only on $t \in \overline{T}$, and not on $b \in B$, because when $b \in B$ appears, the $t \in T$ is determined, and the corresponding vector payoff is the constant $G^k_{s,t}$. Thus $u_n^{kj} = \overline{G}^{k,j}_{a_n, t_n} = \mathsf{E}(g_n^{kj} \mid \Omega_0)$, and therefore we still have $X_n = \mathsf{E}(\overline{u}_n \mid \mathscr{A}^n)$, where $\overline{u}_n = \frac{1}{n} \sum_{m \le n} u_n$.

Observe that all random variables are now defined on Ω_0, and we no longer need the bigger and more artificial space Ω_1, which was just used to establish the above formula.

We can now analyze this game with vector payoffs $\overline{\Gamma}$ as a game with incomplete information on one side, with state space $\overline{K} = K \times J$, strategy sets S and $\overline{T}$, the signaling matrix Q^*, and, for each state $k \in \overline{K}$, the payoff function $\overline{G}^k$ defined on $A \times \overline{T}$. A point $p \in \Delta(\overline{K})$ is initially selected at random, told to player I, and then the true state in $\overline{K}$ is selected according to p.

Proposition V.3.41, part (2), p. 276, yields then the result, with $\eta_n = \exp(-n\varepsilon_n) + \delta_n$. (Equivalently, one could apply Remark V.3.60, p. 279, immediately to the above game with vector payoffs.)

Observe that we used above, for convenience, the fact that the strategy τ and the sequence δ_n of Proposition V.3.41.2 are the same for Γ^* and for $\overline{\Gamma}$, as follows from the proof of that proposition. Otherwise, we should have started this proof immediately with $\overline{\Gamma}$ instead of Γ^*. ■

Remark VI.3.7. The reason for weakening the conclusion of Proposition V.3.41.2 is that in the present setup we have no natural probability distribution over the payoff $\overline{f}_n^{kj}$. Even if we assume that complete mixed strategies are given for both players (instead of behavioral strategies: thus we have a probability distribution over player I's action and player II's J-tuple of actions after every history), the randomness of the signals prevents us from obtaining the joint distribution: this would require us to know for every J-tuple of n-histories (or at least for every J-tuple of pairs of moves) the probability distribution over the corresponding J-tuple of pairs of signals (i.e., the "mixed strategy of nature").

Remark VI.3.8. One could, however, now use the present result, together with the techniques of the last chapter for building blocks, to construct another strategy τ_h, consisting of longer and longer "superblocks," each of which is a finite repetition of the same basic block, such that the statement of Proposition V.3.41, part (2), would hold (for vectors in $\mathbb{R}^{K \times J}$) uniformly over all "mixed strategies of nature" as above and over all mixed strategies of player II that are compatible with τ_h (and, e.g., preserve the independence between successive blocks). But this does not seem to be the right way of doing it; there should be a simpler statement, not involving such "mixed strategies of nature," that implies the above. We are probably still missing part of the structure of the problem.

VI.3.b.3. Convexification again

Definition VI.3.9. Given a function v on $\Delta(P)$, define the convexification $(\mathrm{Vex}\, v)(\pi)$ as follows: let $\overline{\pi}$ be the probability measure on $P \times K \times J$ induced by π; decompose it into its marginal λ^π on J and a conditional distribution $\nu_j^\pi(k, dp)$ on $K \times P$ given J. For every $\lambda \in \Delta(J)$, let $\pi(\lambda) \in \Delta(P)$ be the distribution under $\lambda \otimes \nu^\pi$ of the conditional distribution (under $\lambda \otimes \nu^\pi$) of (k, j) given $p \in P$. Then $(\mathrm{Vex}\, v)(\pi)$ is the value at λ^π of the convexification of $v[\pi(\lambda)]$ over $\Delta(J)$.

Remark VI.3.10. The definition is unambiguous, because for all j where $\lambda^\pi(j) > 0$, ν_j is uniquely defined, and so the function $v[\pi(\lambda)]$ is uniquely defined on the face of $\Delta(J)$ spanned by λ^π, and hence its convexification is uniquely defined at λ^π.

Remark VI.3.11. $\pi(\lambda)$ is a (weak*-) continuous function of λ; in particular, if v is (lower semi-) continuous, the convexification is then achieved by convex combinations ("splitting") of $\#J$ points (I.3, Ex. 10, p. 40).

Remark VI.3.12. The function $\mathsf{Cav}\, u$ being well defined (and continuous) by Theorem VI.3.9, the above applies in particular to $\mathsf{Vex}\,\mathsf{Cav}\, u$.

Remark VI.3.13. The definition translates analytically as follows. Assume v has been extended by homogeneity of degree 1 to all bounded non-negative measures on P. For $\alpha \in \mathbb{R}_+^J$ ($\alpha_j = \lambda_j/\lambda_j^\pi$; cf. Remark VI.3.10 for the case $\lambda_j^\pi = 0$), define $\phi_\alpha \colon P \to P$ by $[\phi_\alpha(p)]_{k,j} = \alpha^j p^{k,j}/(\sum_{k',j'} \alpha^{j'} p^{k',j'})$. Observe that ϕ_α maps convex sets to convex sets and, if $\alpha \gg 0$, has $\phi_{\alpha^{-1}}$ as inverse (with $(\alpha^{-1})_j = (\alpha_j)^{-1}$). Then $\pi(\alpha)$ is the image by ϕ_α of the measure having $\sum_{k,j} \alpha^j p^{kj}$ as density with respect to π (or equivalently, if $\alpha \gg 0$, it is the measure having $1/\sum_{k,j}(p^{k,j}/\alpha^j)$ as density with respect to the image $\phi_\alpha(\pi)$ of π). And, with $g_\pi : \mathbb{R}_+^J \to \mathbb{R}$ defined by $g_\pi(\alpha) = v[\pi(\alpha)]$, one has $(\mathsf{Vex}\, v)(\pi) = (\mathsf{Vex}\, g_\pi)(1, 1, \ldots, 1)$. Observe that ϕ_α is well defined only on $\{\, p \in P \mid \sum_{k,j} \alpha^j p^{kj} > 0\}$, but that the density $\sum_{k,j} \alpha^j p^{kj}$ vanishes on the complement, and so the image $\pi(\alpha)$ is always well defined, $\forall \alpha \in \mathbb{R}_+^J$. Also, in the line of Remark VI.3.10, $\pi(\alpha)$ does not depend on the coordinates α_j of α for which $\lambda_j^\pi = 0$.

VI.3.b.4. More intrinsically: Approachability

Recall the definition of the lower topology (I.3, Ex. 15, p. 44) on the cone $C(P)$ (cf. Proposition V.3.31, p. 262) of continuous convex functions on a compact convex set P and of the "weak*"-topology on the set of regular probability measures on a compact space C (Definition I.1.11, p. 6).

Theorem VI.3.10. *Denote by* $\mathbf{T}$ *(resp.* $\mathbf{T}_0$*) the space of transition probabilities* $\mathbf{t}$ *from* J *to* $\mathbf{H}$ *with the uniform topology (resp.* $\mathbf{H}_0$ *with the lower topology). Endow* $\mathbf{T}$ *and* $\mathbf{T}_0$ *with the weak* topology (cf. remark after Proposition V.3.38, p. 271). For every* $\mathbf{t} \in \mathbf{T}$*, let* $\forall p \in P$*:*

$$z_{\mathbf{t}}(p) = \mathsf{E}_{p\otimes \mathbf{t}}\, h[(p \otimes \mathbf{t})(K \times J \mid h)]$$
$$= \int h\big([p_{k,j}\mathbf{t}_j(dh)]_{(k,j)\in K\times J}\big),$$

assuming in the latter the functions $h \in \mathbf{H}$ *are extended by homogeneity of degree one to* $\mathbb{R}_+^{K\times J}$ *(cf. III.4, Ex. 5, p. 170).*

(1) $\mathbf{T}$ *is compact metric, and the space* $\mathbf{T}_0$ *is compact,* T_1*, with a countable basis, and the inclusion map in* $\mathbf{T}$ *has a* G_δ*-image and is a Borel isomorphism with its image.*
(2) *The topology of* $\mathbf{T}_0$ *is the weakest topology such that,* $\forall j \in J$*,* $\int F(h)\mathbf{t}_j(dh)$ *is lower semi-continuous whenever* $F(h) = \phi(h(p_1), \ldots, h(p_n))$*, where* ϕ *is an increasing continuous function on* $\mathbb{R}^n$*.*
(3) • *z is convex in* $p \otimes \mathbf{t}$*;*
 • $\forall \mathbf{t} \in \mathbf{T}$*,* $z_{\mathbf{t}}$ *has Lipschitz constant* $3C$ *and uniform bound* C*;*

- $z\colon \mathbf{t} \mapsto z_{\mathbf{t}}$ *from* $\mathbf{T}$ *or* $\mathbf{T}_0$ *to* $C(P)$ *with the lower topology has a compact graph (in the case of* $\mathbf{T}$*, this is equivalent to the continuity of the map).*

(4) $\forall \mathbf{t} \in \mathbf{T}$, *the strategy* τ *of player* II *generated by* $\mathbf{t}$ *(via Proposition V.3.41, part (2), p. 276 (Theorem VI.3.9, p. 347)) is such that,* $\forall \sigma, \forall n, \forall p, \mathsf{E}^p_{\sigma,\tau}(\overline{g}_n) \leq z_{\mathbf{t}}(p) + \eta_n$ *(e.g., with* $\eta_n = \delta_n + C\exp(-n\varepsilon_n)$*).*

(5) $\forall \pi, (\mathsf{Vex}\,\mathsf{Cav}\,u)(\pi) = \min_{\mathbf{t}} \int z_{\mathbf{t}}(p)\pi(dp)$.

(6) *Every convex function* $\varphi(\pi)$ *on* $\Delta(P)$ *with* $\varphi \geq \mathsf{Vex}\,\mathsf{Cav}\,u$ *is bounded from below by some* $\int z_{\mathbf{t}}(p)\,\pi(dp)$.

(7) *The minmax of* $\Gamma(\pi)$ *exists and equals* $(\mathsf{Vex}\,\mathsf{Cav}\,u)(\pi)$.

Proof.

(1) Since $\mathbf{H}_0$ has a countable base (Proposition V.3.38, part (2), p. 271), the weak* topology on $\mathbf{T}_0$ also has: let O_n be a basis of $\mathbf{H}_0$, which can be made stable under finite unions. Then the functions $r_0 + \sum_{i=1\cdots k} r_i \mathbb{1}_{O_{n_i}}$, where the r_i are rational ($r_i > 0$ for $i > 0$) form a sequence of lower semi-continuous functions, such that every bounded lower semi-continuous function is the limit of an increasing subsequence. This shows that the topology is also the coarsest topology for which the functions $\mu(O_n)$ are lower semi-continuous. Observe also that this topology is T_1: if μ_2 belongs to the closure of μ_1, we would have that $\mu_2(F) \geq \mu_1(F)$ for every closed set F; but every subset D of $\mathbf{H}_0$ that is compact in the $\mathbf{H}$-topology is closed (since if $f \in \overline{D}$, any ultrafilter that refines the trace on D of the filter of neighborhoods of f has some limit $\tilde{f}$ in D in the $\mathbf{H}$-topology, and so $f \leq \tilde{f}$, hence $f = \tilde{f} \in D$, since $\tilde{f} \in \mathbf{H}_0$ is minimal). Thus $\mu_2(K) \geq \mu_1(K)$, hence $\mu_2(B) \geq \mu_1(B)$ for any Borel set B, since $\mathbf{H}_0$ is a G_δ in the compact metric space $\mathbf{H}$ (Proposition V.3.38, part (4), p. 271), and therefore $\mu_1 = \mu_2$ since both are probability measures. To prove compactness of $\mathbf{T}$, use, e.g., that it has a countable base, extract for any sequence a subsequence that converges, say, to μ, in the weak* topology on $\mathbf{H}$, and consider the image of μ by the map r of Proposition V.3.38, part (4) (and use the Dudley–Skohorod theorem if desired). The fact that the image of the inclusion map is a G_δ follows immediately from Proposition V.3.38, part (4), while the measurability of the map is shown as follows: there is no loss of generality (e.g., by adding a constant to all payoffs), in assuming that all functions $f \in \mathbf{H}$ are positive. By the Stone–Weierstrass theorem, the functions $f \mapsto f(p_1)f(p_2)\cdots f(p_n)$ span all continuous functions on $\mathbf{H}$. Therefore, since $\mathbf{H}$ is compact metric, the Borel structure on $\Delta(\mathbf{H})$ is generated by the functions $\mu \mapsto \int[f(p_1)f(p_2)\cdots f(p_n)]\mu(df)$. So it suffices to show that such a function is lower semi-continuous on $\Delta(\mathbf{H}_0)$, hence that $f \mapsto f(p_1)f(p_2)\cdots f(p_n)$ is lower semi-continuous on $\mathbf{H}_0$, hence, f being positive, that the evaluation maps $f \mapsto f(p)$ are lower semi-continuous on $\mathbf{H}_0$, which follows immediately from the definition of the topology.

(2) Clearly $F(h)$ is a real-valued lower semi-continuous function on $\mathbf{H}_0$, and hence its integral is lower semi-continuous on $\mathbf{T}_0$. Conversely, we have to

show that then $\mathbf{t}_j(O)$ is lower semi-continuous for every open set O. It suffices to prove this for finite unions $\bigcup_i O_i$ of basic open sets and for intersections $O_i = \bigcap_j U_{ij}$, where the U_{ij} belong to some sub-base of open sets. By the Lipschitz character of $h \in \mathbf{H}_0$, the topology of $\mathbf{H}_0$ has as sub-base the sets $\{ h \mid h(p) > \alpha \}$ for $p \in P, \alpha \in \mathbb{R}$. Let thus $U_{ij} = \{ h \in \mathbf{H}_0 \mid h(p_{ij}) > \alpha_{ij} \}$, and let $F(h) = \max_i \min_j \min[1, (h(p_{ij}) - \alpha_{ij})^+/\varepsilon]$: F has the required properties and increases to $\mathbb{1}_O$ when $\varepsilon \downarrow 0$ (the function ϕ is only weakly increasing on $\mathbb{R}^n$, but could be made strictly increasing while preserving all properties by subtracting, e.g., $\varepsilon[1 + \exp \sum_1^n x_i]^{-1}$).

(3) III.4, Ex. 4, p. 167, yields the convexity of z in $p \otimes \mathbf{t}$ and its lower semi-continuity. Further, since $\|h\| \le C$ for $h \in \mathbf{H}$ (Theorem VI.3.9, p. 347, and Proposition V.3.38, p. 271), we have clearly $\|z_{\mathbf{t}}\| \le C$. In particular, for each $\mathbf{t}$, $z_{\mathbf{t}}$ is a lower semi-continuous real-valued convex function on $\Delta(P)$, hence continuous. Further, III.4, Ex. 4, p. 167, shows that, to prove that $z_{\mathbf{t}}$ has Lipschitz constant $3C$, it suffices to consider the case where $\mathbf{t}$ has finite support. In such a case, it follows immediately from the second formula for $z_{\mathbf{t}}$, and from an elementary computation showing that if h on $\Delta(P)$ has Lipschitz constant C, its extension by homogeneity to $\mathbb{R}_+^{K \times J}$ has Lipschitz constant $3C$. Finally, the lower semi-continuity obtained from III.4, Ex. 5, p. 170, yields the compactness of the graph of $z\colon \mathbf{T} \to C(P)$, i.e., continuity of z since $\mathbf{T}$ is compact Hausdorff. There remains to show that it still holds with $\mathbf{T}_0$ and its weaker topology. Consider an ultrafilter on this graph. It converges, say, to $(\mathbf{t}_\infty, z_{\mathbf{t}_\infty})$ in $\mathbf{T} \times C(P)$ by the previous point. Let $\underline{\mathbf{t}}$ be the image of $\mathbf{t}_\infty$ under the map r of Proposition V.3.38, part (4): clearly $\underline{\mathbf{t}} \in \mathbf{T}_0$ (cf. also the remark after Proposition V.3.38, p. 271), and the ultrafilter converges to $\underline{\mathbf{t}}$ in $\mathbf{T}_0$ by part (2) since $\int F(h)\underline{\mathbf{t}}_j(dh) \le \int F(h)\mathbf{t}_{\infty,j}(dh) = \lim_{\mathscr{U}} \int F(h)\mathbf{t}_j(dh)$, using first the monotonicity and then the continuity properties of F. Since also $\lim_{\mathscr{U}} z_{\mathbf{t}} = z_{\mathbf{t}_\infty}$ uniformly, it follows that $(\underline{\mathbf{t}}, z_{\underline{\mathbf{t}}})$ will be a limit point of $\mathscr{U}$ in $\mathbf{T}_0 \times C(P)$ if we prove that $z_{\underline{\mathbf{t}}} \le z_{\mathbf{t}_\infty}$. Now, using I.3, Ex. 14bα, p. 43, with $\Omega = \mathbf{H}$, $X(\omega) = (p \otimes \mathbf{t}_\infty)(K \times J \mid h)$, $\mathscr{B}$ the σ-field spanned by $r(h)$, $g(\omega, x) = [r(h)](x)$, we get $z_{\underline{\mathbf{t}}}(p) = \mathsf{E}_{p \otimes \mathbf{t}_\infty}([r(h)][(p \times \mathbf{t}_\infty)(K \times J \mid r(h))]) \le \mathsf{E}_{p \otimes \mathbf{t}_\infty}([r(h)][(p \otimes \mathbf{t}_\infty)(K \times J \mid h)]) \le z_{\mathbf{t}_\infty}(p)$. This proves part (3).

(4) This is clear after Theorem VI.3.9, even if we assume player I is in addition informed before his first move of the choice of h by player II.

(5) and (7) We first show that $\int z_{\mathbf{t}}(p)\pi(dp) \ge (\mathsf{Vex}\,\mathsf{Cav}\,u)(\pi)\ \forall \pi, \forall \mathbf{t}$. By (4), it suffices therefore to show that, against any strategy $\mathbf{t}$ of player II, player I has a reply yielding him $(\mathsf{Vex}\,\mathsf{Cav}\,u)(\pi) - \varepsilon$, i.e., to prove the other half of (7) (the first half will then follow from (4) and (5)). For every finite Borel partition α of P, define $\Gamma_\alpha(\pi)$ to be the same game, but where player I is initially informed only of the element of α containing the true p instead of the value itself of p. Clearly it suffices to exhibit, for an appropriate α, a reply in $\Gamma_\alpha(\pi)$ yielding $(\mathsf{Vex}\,\mathsf{Cav}\,u)(\pi) - \varepsilon$. Since $\Gamma_\alpha(\pi)$ is a game with finitely many types for both players, it suffices therefore by Theorem VI.3.1 to show that $F_\alpha(\pi)$ converges to $(\mathsf{Vex}\,\mathsf{Cav}\,u)(\pi)$, where $F_\alpha(\pi) = (\mathsf{Vex}_{\mathrm{II}}\,\mathsf{Cav}_{\mathrm{I}}\,u_\alpha)(\pi)$, u_α being the u-function of Γ_α. Further $F_\alpha(\pi)$ (and u_α, and $\mathsf{Cav}_{\mathrm{I}}\,u_\alpha$) is clearly

increasing, since a finer partition yields a game more favorable to I. Let $\delta(\alpha)$ be the maximum diameter of the elements of α. Clearly $\delta(\alpha)$ tends to zero. For every α, denote also by $\overline{\alpha}$ the same partition, together with the specification of some point P_ρ in every element ρ of α, and denote by $\Gamma_{\overline{\alpha}}(\pi)$ the same game as above, except that, after an element of $\overline{\alpha}$ has been selected according to π, the pair in $K \times J$ is selected according to the specified point in that element of $\overline{\alpha}$. Clearly the difference between the payoff functions of Γ_α and of $\Gamma_{\overline{\alpha}}$ is $\leq \delta(\alpha)$, hence $\|u_\alpha - u_{\overline{\alpha}}\| \leq \delta(\alpha)$, and thus also $\left\| F_\alpha(\pi) - \mathsf{Vex}_{\mathrm{II}} \mathsf{Cav}_{\mathrm{I}} u_{\overline{\alpha}}(\pi) \right\| \leq \delta(\alpha)$. But $\Gamma_{\overline{\alpha}}(\pi)$ can also be interpreted as the game where $p \in P$ is selected according to π, and told to player I, and then the pair in $K \times J$ is selected according to the specified point in the partition element containing p. In this version, it has the same strategy sets as $\Gamma(\pi)$ and payoff functions that differ by less than $\delta(\alpha)$, hence also $\|u - u_{\overline{\alpha}}\| \leq \delta(\alpha)$. Now the $\mathsf{Cav}_{\mathrm{I}}$ operation, for $\Gamma_{\overline{\alpha}}$, is just the concavification over π, since the map from π to the marginal on player I's types is affine, and everything else is independent of π. Thus we obtain that $\left\| \mathsf{Cav}\, u - \mathsf{Cav}_{\mathrm{I}} u_{\overline{\alpha}} \right\| \leq \delta(\alpha)$.

Let now $f(\pi) = \mathsf{Cav}_{\mathrm{I}} u_{\overline{\alpha}}(\pi)$. It follows from the above that there only remains to show that $\left|(\mathsf{Vex}\,\mathsf{Cav}\, u)(\pi) - (\mathsf{Vex}_{\mathrm{II}} f)(\pi)\right| \leq 3\delta(\alpha)$. But since $\left\|\mathsf{Cav}\, u - f\right\| \leq \delta(\alpha)$, we have also $\left\|\mathsf{Vex}\,\mathsf{Cav}\, u - \mathsf{Vex}\, f\right\| \leq \delta(\alpha)$, and so it suffices to show that $\|\mathsf{Vex}\, f - \mathsf{Vex}_{\mathrm{II}} f\| \leq 2\delta(\alpha)$.

$(\mathsf{Vex}_{\mathrm{II}} f)(\pi)$ is to be computed in the finite game generated by $\overline{\alpha}$; this is the game having as "canonical measure" $\pi_{\overline{\alpha}} = \sum_{\rho \in \alpha} \pi(\rho)\delta_{P_\rho}$. Hence (by Remark VI.3.13 above) $(\mathsf{Vex}_{\mathrm{II}} f)(\pi) = (\mathsf{Vex}\, f)(\pi_{\overline{\alpha}})$. Thus we are concerned with the difference $|(\mathsf{Vex}\, f)(\pi) - (\mathsf{Vex}\, f)(\pi_{\overline{\alpha}})|$; up to an additional error of at most $2\delta(\alpha)$, we can now set f equal to the concave Lipschitz function $\mathsf{Cav}\, u$. Hence, by Remark VI.3.13 above, we want, letting $g_\alpha(\lambda) = f[\pi_\alpha(\lambda)]$ for $\lambda \in \mathbb{R}^J_+$, that g_α converge to g_∞ uniformly on compact sets; given the homogeneity of degree 1, this ensures convergence of the convexifications. Thus we need, by the uniform continuity of f, that $\pi_\alpha(\lambda) \to \pi_\infty(\lambda)$ weak*, uniformly over compact sets of $\mathbb{R}^J_+$. To make this uniformity more precise, observe that f can be uniformly approximated by $\mathsf{min}_i \int h_i(p)\pi(dp)$ (Proposition V.3.39.3, p. 273), where the h_i are convex and Lipschitz. Thus we need that, for every convex Lipschitz function h on P, $\int h(p)[\pi_\alpha(\lambda)](dp) \to \int h(p)[\pi_\infty(\lambda)](dp)$ uniformly over compact sets of $\mathbb{R}^J_+$, i.e. (cf. Remark VI.3.13 above), $\int (h[\phi_\lambda(p)])(\sum_{k,j} \lambda^j p^{kj})\pi_\alpha(dp) \to \int (h[\phi_\lambda(p)])(\sum_{kj} \lambda^j p^{kj})\pi_\infty(dp)$. We can w.l.o.g. also assume that h is extended by homogeneity of degree 1; this becomes then $\int h[(\lambda^j p^{kj})_{j,k \in J \times K}]\pi_\alpha(dp) \to \int h[(\lambda^j p^{kj})_{j,k \in J \times K}]\pi_\infty(dp)$. (Observe that where $\phi_\lambda(p)$ is not defined, and the density is equal to zero, the new integrand $h[\ldots]$ is also zero.) Since now the integrand is clearly jointly continuous in λ and p, the result follows immediately, e.g., by Ascoli's theorem.

Observe that we obtain the further conclusions that $\mathsf{Vex}\,\mathsf{Cav}\, u$ is weak*-continuous in π, that $(\mathsf{Vex}\,\mathsf{Cav}\, u)(\pi) = \mathsf{Vex}_{\lambda=(1,1,\ldots,1)} \left[\mathsf{min}_{h \in \mathbf{H}_0} \int h(\lambda \cdot p)\pi(dp)\right]$, and that player I can defend $\mathsf{Vex}\,\mathsf{Cav}\, u$ against any strategy $\mathbf{t}$.

Since (cf. Remark VI.3.11, p. 350) the convexification is achieved by convex combinations (splitting) of a finite set E of points, with $\#E = \#J$, we obtain $(\mathsf{Vex\,Cav}\,u)(\pi) = \sum_{e\in E} \alpha_e \int h_e(\lambda_e \cdot p)\pi(dp)$, with $\alpha_e \geq 0$, $\sum_e \alpha_e = 1$, $\sum \alpha_e \lambda_e = (1, 1, 1, \dots, 1)$. Let now $\xi_{je} = \alpha_e \lambda_{ej}$, and use the homogeneity of h_e: we have $(\mathsf{Vex\,Cav}\,u)(\pi) = \int \left\{\sum_{e\in E} h_e \left[(\xi_{je} p_{jk})_{j,k\in J\times K}\right]\right\} \pi(dp)$: interpreting ξ_{je} as $\mathbf{t}_j(\{h_e\})$, we see that our integrand is exactly equal to $z_{\mathbf{t}}(p)$ (cf. the second formula in the definition).

Thus we obtain also the other direction of (5), and with the additional information that one can choose a minimizing $\mathbf{t}$ with support $\leq \#J$. In particular, $(\mathsf{Vex\,Cav}\,u)$ is concave, and Lipschitz with constant $3C$.

(6) Take a minimal such φ (by Zorn's lemma). By Lemma V.3.32, part (3), p. 265, φ is Lipschitz. Consider now the two-person zero-sum game where player II's strategy set is $\mathbf{T}$, player I's is $\Delta(P)$, and the payoff function equals $\int z_{\mathbf{t}}(p)\pi(dp) - \varphi(\pi)$: $\mathbf{T}$ and $\Delta(P)$ are compact and convex, and the payoff is concave and continuous (Lipschitz) w.r.t. π (by the Lipschitz property of $z_{\mathbf{t}}$ (part (3)) and of φ (above)), and convex and l.s.c. w.r.t. $\mathbf{t}$ (part (3) again). Further, by part (5), the maxmin is less than or equal to zero ($\varphi \leq \mathsf{Vex\,Cav}\,u$). The conclusion follows then from the minmax theorem (e.g., I.1.1, p. 5). ∎

Remark VI.3.14. The set $\mathbf{H}$ of "approachable functions" are those functions of I's type that II can approach in a NR way. This restriction is lifted for the "approachable payoffs" $z_{\mathbf{t}}$ for $\mathbf{t} \in \mathbf{T}$.

Remark VI.3.15. The end of the proof of part (3) shows that in part (6) one can in addition require $\mathbf{t} \in \mathbf{T}_0$. Further, denote by $\mathbf{H}_e$ the set of extreme points of $\mathbf{H}_0$ (i.e., the set of extreme points of $\mathbf{H}$ that belong to $\mathbf{H}_0$). Then, by a standard argument, $\mathbf{H}_e$ is a G_δ in $\mathbf{H}$ (using Proposition V.3.38, part (4), p. 271, and the fact that the extreme points of $\mathbf{H}$ form a G_δ, since $\{ (x + y)/2 \mid x \in \mathbf{H}, y \in \mathbf{H}, d(x, y) \geq n^{-1} \}$ is closed). So (still using Proposition V.3.38, part (4)) $\mathbf{H}_e$ is also Borel in $\mathbf{H}_0$, and $\mathbf{H}_0$ and $\mathbf{H}$ induce the same (standard) Borel structure on $\mathbf{H}_e$. It follows then from part (1) that $\mathbf{T}_e$, the set of transition probabilities from J to $\mathbf{H}_e$, is a well-defined subset of $\mathbf{T}$ and of $\mathbf{T}_0$, and a G_δ in $\mathbf{T}$, and a Borel subset of $\mathbf{T}_0$, with $\mathbf{T}$ and $\mathbf{T}_0$ inducing the same Borel structure on $\mathbf{T}_e$. We claim that one can in part (6) in addition require $\mathbf{t} \in \mathbf{T}_e$.

Indeed, use Choquet's integral representation theorem together with Appendix A.7.j, p. 519, to construct a (universally measurable) transition probability Q_h from $\mathbf{H}$ to its set of extreme points, such that every $h \in \mathbf{H}$ is the barycenter of Q_h. Observe that this implies that, for $h \in \mathbf{H}_0$, Q_h is carried by $\mathbf{H}_0$ (Proposition V.3.38, part (4) again), and hence by $\mathbf{H}_e$. Hence, for our above $\mathbf{t} \in \mathbf{T}_0$, $\underline{\mathbf{t}}$ defined as $\underline{\mathbf{t}}_j(B) = \int_{\mathbf{H}_0} Q_h(B)\mathbf{t}_j(dh)$ belongs to $\mathbf{T}_e$. There only remains to show that $z_{\underline{\mathbf{t}}} \leq z_{\mathbf{t}}$.

Let h_1 be chosen according to $\mathbf{t}$, and h_2 according to Q_{h_1}. Observe that h_2 is conditionally independent of $K \times J$ given h_1, and so $(p \otimes \mathbf{t})(K \times J \mid h_1) = (p \otimes \mathbf{t})(K \times J \mid h_1, h_2) = X(h_1)$. Then $z_{\mathbf{t}}(p) = \mathsf{E}[h_1(X(h_1))] = \mathsf{E}[h_2(X(h_1))] \geq \mathsf{E}[h_2(\mathsf{E}(X(h_1) \mid h_2))]$, by I.3, Ex. 14b$\alpha$, p. 43. Since $X(h_1) =$

$(p \otimes \mathbf{t})(K \times J \mid h_1, h_2)$, we have $\mathsf{E}(X(h_1) \mid h_2) = (p \otimes \mathbf{t})(K \times J \mid h_2)$, and thus our right-hand member equals $z_{\mathbf{t}}(p)$.

Remark VI.3.16. $\mathbf{H}_e$ is better (more directly) characterized as the set of extreme points of the convex set of all affine (resp. convex) functions that bound u (resp. $\mathsf{Cav}\, u$) from above.

Indeed, $\mathbf{H}_e$ is clearly contained in the set of affine functions that bound u from above; and this set is contained in the set of convex functions that bound $\mathsf{Cav}\, u$ from above by the definition in Proposition V.3.39.1, p. 273. Now any $h \in \mathbf{H}_e$ is extreme in the latter set (and therefore in the former): otherwise we would have $h = \frac{1}{2}(h_1 + h_2)$, with $h_1 \neq h_2$, convex, and hence both are affine since their sum is affine and hence $h_1 \geq \underline{h}_1$, $h_2 \geq \underline{h}_2$ with $\underline{h}_i \in \mathbf{H}_0$ by Proposition V.3.38, parts (1) and (2), p. 271. Minimality of h yields then that both inequalities are equalities, contradicting that h is an extreme point of $\mathbf{H}$. Conversely, let h be an extreme point of our convex set. By Proposition V.3.38, parts (1) and (2) (Proposition V.3.39, part (4)) it suffices to show that h is minimal in the set; otherwise, by the same property, we have some affine h_0 in the set, with $h_0 \leq h$, $h_0 \neq h$. Then $h_1 = 2h - h_0$ also belongs to the set, and hence $h = \frac{1}{2}(h_0 + h_1)$ would not be extreme.

Corollary VI.3.11. $\mathbf{t}$ *in parts (5) and (6) can be assumed to vary over* $\mathbf{T}_e$*, and in part (5) to have in addition a support of cardinality* $\leq \# J$.

Proof. We just proved this for part (6). For part (5), this follows from the end of the proof of part (5), by observing that $\min_{h \in \mathbf{H}_0} \int (\lambda \cdot p) \pi(dp) = \min_{h \in \mathbf{H}_e} \int h(\lambda \cdot p) \pi(dp)$ (using, e.g., our above Q_h, or just the Krein–Milman theorem). ∎

Corollary VI.3.12. *Any co-final subset of the* $z_{\mathbf{t}}$ $(\mathbf{t} \in \mathbf{T})$*, like* $\{ z_{\mathbf{t}} \mid \mathbf{t} \in \mathbf{T}_0 \}$ *or* $\{ z_{\mathbf{t}} \mid \mathbf{t} \in \mathbf{T}_e \}$*, is compact in the lower topology.*

Proof. Continuity of $z \colon \mathbf{T} \to C(P)$ (part (3)) and compactness of $\mathbf{T}$ yield compactness of $\{ z_{\mathbf{t}} \mid \mathbf{t} \in \mathbf{T} \}$. For co-final subsets, the result follows then by definition of the lower topology. $\mathbf{T}_0$ and $\mathbf{T}_e$ generate co-final subsets by Corollary VI.3.11. ∎

Corollary VI.3.13. *In the framework of Definition VI.3.3 and Proposition VI.3.6, p. 345 (thus where* J *is a partition of* K*, so that* $p \in P = \Delta(K)$ *completely determines* $\overline{p} \in \Delta(K \times J)$*, and where the* $p(\cdot \mid \kappa)$ *for* $\kappa \in K^{\mathrm{I}}$ *are mutually singular measures on* K*)* $\left\{ \left(h[p(\cdot \mid \kappa)]\right)_{\kappa \in K^{\mathrm{I}}} \in \mathbb{R}^{K^{\mathrm{I}}} \;\middle|\; h \in \mathbf{H}_0 \right\}$ *is co-final in* W_p *and similarly for the* $z_{\mathbf{t}}$ $(\mathbf{t} \in \mathbf{T}_0)$ *and the sets* Z_p.

Proof. Given $w \in W_p$, let $\varphi \colon \Delta(K) \to \mathbb{R}$ be defined by $\varphi[p(\cdot \mid \kappa)] = w^\kappa$ for $\kappa \in K^{\mathrm{I}}$, $\varphi = +\infty$ elsewhere. For $\lambda \in \Delta(P)$ we have thus that $\int \varphi(q) \lambda(dq)$ is affine; we claim it is $\geq u(\lambda)$. Indeed, this is obvious if $\lambda\{\varphi = \infty\} > 0$; else λ corresponds to $\overline{\lambda} \in \Delta(K^{\mathrm{I}})$, and $\int \varphi(q) \lambda(dq) = \langle \overline{\lambda}, w \rangle \geq u(\overline{\lambda} \cdot p) = u(\lambda)$.

Hence one direction of the proof follows from Proposition V.3.38, part (1) and part (2), p. 271.

There only remains to show that, for $h \in \mathbf{H}_0$, $w = (h[p(\cdot \mid \kappa)])_{\kappa \in K^{\mathrm{I}}} \in W_p$. This again follows from $\langle \overline{\lambda}, w \rangle = \int h(q)\lambda(dq) \geq u(\lambda) = u(\overline{\lambda} \cdot p)$.

The proof of the second statement is completely similar. ■

Remark VI.3.17. Given this "translation" in Corollary VI.3.13, it is now clear that Theorem VI.3.10 to Corollary VI.3.12 fully contain Proposition VI.3.6.

Remark VI.3.18. In the case of statistically perfect monitoring of player I by player II (cf. Remarks V.3.48 and V.3.49 after Theorem V.3.35, p. 266, and the Remark V.3.39, p. 273), those remarks show that u becomes then a function on $\Delta(K \times J)$, mapping a probability distribution on this simplex to its barycenter, that $(\mathsf{Cav}\, u)(\mu) = \mathsf{max}_{\nu \preceq \mu} \int_{\Delta(K \times J)} u d\nu$, and that $\mathbf{H}_0$ consists now of the minimal convex functions on $\Delta(K \times J)$ that are (pointwise) greater than or equal to u.

Remark VI.3.19. In the case of statistically perfect monitoring of player II by player I, u becomes a function on $\Delta(\Delta(K))$, by mapping a measure μ on $\Delta(K \times J)$ to its image measure on $\Delta(K)$ by the map from $\Delta(K \times J)$ to $\Delta(K)$ that maps every probability measure on $K \times J$ to its marginal on K. Indeed, the non-revealing strategies of player II are then payoff equivalent to strategies that are independent of his type $j \in J$, and so this type becomes irrelevant in the non-revealing game. $\mathbf{H}_0$ consists then of the minimal convex functions on $\Delta(K)$ such that $\int h(p)\mu(dp) \geq u(\mu)\ \forall \mu \in \Delta(\Delta(K))$, and so $\mathsf{Cav}\, u$ is also a function on $\Delta(\Delta(K))$.

Remark VI.3.20. When there is statistically perfect monitoring on both sides, the previous remark yields that the results of Remark VI.3.18 then become valid with $\Delta(K)$ instead of $\Delta(K \times J)$.

VI.4. THE LIMIT OF $v_n(p)$

In this section we prove that $\lim_{n\to\infty} v_n(p)$ always exists, where $v_n(p)$ is the value of the n-stage game $\Gamma_n(p)$. We will also give a formula for $\lim_{n\to\infty} v_n(p)$.

Recall that $\underline{\Gamma}(p)$ is the δ-perturbation of the game that is to the disadvantage of I (cf. VI.2.c, p. 330). Let $\underline{v}_{n,\delta}(p)$ be the maxmin of the δ-perturbed $\underline{\Gamma}_n(p)$.

Let $\underline{w}_\delta(p) = \liminf_{n\to\infty} \underline{v}_{n,\delta}(p)$. Let also $\underline{w} = \liminf_{\delta\to 0} \underline{w}_\delta$. Notice that $\underline{w}_\delta(p)$ and $\underline{w}(p)$ have the Lipschitz property since $u(p)$ and $v_n(p)$ are uniformly Lipschitz. Moreover:

Proposition VI.4.1. $\underline{w}(p)$ *is concave w.r.t.* I.

Proof. By Theorem V.1.1, p. 215, the $\underline{v}_n(p)$ $\forall n$ are all concave w.r.t. I. The proposition then follows from the fact that the minimum of two concave functions is concave. ■

Lemma VI.4.2. *Given any strategy τ of II in $\underline{\Gamma}_n(p)$ there is a strategy σ of I such that the probability $P_{\sigma,\tau}$ on $(\Omega, \mathscr{G}_n)$ satisfies: if $\theta = \min\{ m \mid u(p_m) \leq \underline{w}_\delta(p_m) \}$, then:*

(1) *For $m \leq \theta$, I uses at stage m an optimal strategy in $D(p_m)$.*
(2) *After stage θ, I uses $\sigma_{p_{\theta+1},n-\theta}$, where $\sigma_{p,m}$ is an optimal behavioral strategy in $\underline{\Gamma}_m(p)$ represented in such a way that conditions (1)–(6) of p. 333 hold.*

Proof. The proof is a straightforward construction of the strategy outlined above which consists of computing at each stage m, $p_n(k) = \tilde{p}_m(k)$, playing optimally in $D(p_m)$ as long as $u(p_m) > \underline{w}_\delta(p_m)$, and playing in the last $(n - \theta)$ stages an optimal behavioral strategy in $\underline{\Gamma}_{n-\theta}(p_{\theta+1})$ where $\theta = \min\{ m \mid u(p_m) \leq \underline{w}_\delta(p_m) \}$, for instance, by making all lotteries a one-to-one mapping between K^{I} and E^{I}_m. ■

Lemma VI.4.3. *For any strategy τ of II and the corresponding strategy σ of I described in Lemma VI.4.2:*

$$\mathsf{E}\left(\frac{1}{n-\theta}\sum_{m=\theta+1}^{n} G^k_{s_m,t_m} \;\middle|\; \tilde{\mathscr{H}}^{\mathrm{I}}_\theta\right) \geq \underline{v}_{n-\theta}(p_{\theta+1}).$$

Proof. The claim of this lemma is that the expected average payoff from time θ to n is at least the value of $\underline{\Gamma}_{n-\theta}(p_{\theta+1})$. Intuitively this is so since I plays optimally in that game. The formal proof is the following.

Let ω stand for a typical point in $\mathscr{H}^{\mathrm{I}}_\theta$ and for any m let F^k_m be the matrix of $\underline{\Gamma}_m(p)$ if the true state of nature is k and let $\sigma^k_{p,m}$ be an optimal strategy of I in this matrix game. Let $(\tau^k)_{k\in K}$ be a strategy of II in $\underline{\Gamma}_{n-\theta}(p_\theta)$; $(\tau^k)_{k\in K}$ is therefore $\mathscr{K}^{\mathrm{II}}$-measurable in k and may depend on the information $(b_1, \ldots, b_\theta)$.

Now:

$$\mathsf{E}\left(\frac{1}{n-\theta}\sum_{m=\theta+1}^{n} G^k_{s_m,t_m} \;\middle|\; \mathscr{G}_\theta\right) = \sigma^k_{p_{\theta+1},n-\theta} F^k_{n-\theta} \tau^k,$$

which implies:

$$\mathsf{E}\left(\frac{1}{n-\theta}\sum_{m=\theta+1}^{n} G^k_{s_m,t_m} \;\middle|\; \mathscr{H}^{\mathrm{I}}_\theta \vee \mathscr{K}\right) = \sigma^k_{p_{\theta(\omega)+1},n-\theta(\omega)} F^k_{n-\theta(\omega)} \overline{\tau}^k(\omega),$$

where $\overline{\tau}^k(\omega) = \mathsf{E}(\tau^k(b_1, \ldots, b_\theta) \mid \mathscr{H}^{\mathrm{I}}_\theta \vee \mathscr{K})$. So:

$$\mathsf{E}\left(\frac{1}{n-\theta}\sum_{m=\theta+1}^{n} G^k_{s_m,t_m} \;\middle|\; \mathscr{H}^{\mathrm{I}}_\theta\right) = \sum_k p_{\theta+1}(k \mid \omega) \sigma^k_{p_{\theta(\omega)+1},n-\theta(\omega)} F^k_{n-\theta(\omega)} \overline{\tau}^k(\omega).$$

This is the payoff in $\underline{\Gamma}_{n-\theta(\omega)}(p_{\theta(\omega)+1})$ resulting from the optimal strategy $\sigma_{p_{\theta(\omega)+1},n-\theta(\omega)}$ of I in that game and from $(\overline{\tau}^k(\omega))_{k\in K}$. Since θ is a $\mathscr{H}^{\mathrm{I}}_n$-stopping time, by Proposition VI.2.10, $\overline{\tau}^k(\omega)$ is $\mathscr{K}^{\mathrm{II}}$-measurable in K and hence also a strategy in the game. The above expectation is thus at least the value of that game, i.e., $\underline{v}_{n-\theta}(p_{\theta+1})$. ■

Proposition VI.4.4. $\underline{w} \geq \mathrm{Vex}_{\mathrm{II}} \max(u, \underline{w})$.

Proof. Define $\Delta(p, n) = (\underline{w}_\delta(p) - \underline{v}_{n,\delta}(p))^+$. Since $\underline{w}_\delta$ and $\underline{v}_{n,\delta}$ are uniformly Lipschitz, $\Delta(p, n)$ converges to 0 uniformly in p.

Take now a game $\underline{\Gamma}_n(p)$ and for any optimal strategy τ of II, let I play the strategy described in Lemma VI.4.2; then, if $\rho = \frac{1}{n}\sum_{m=1}^n \rho_m$, we have, using Lemma VI.2.13 (with $q_m = \tilde{p}_m = p_m$) and Lemma VI.4.3:

$$\begin{aligned}\mathsf{E}\big(\mathsf{E}(\rho \mid \mathscr{H}_\theta^{\mathrm{I}})\big) \geq \frac{1}{n}\mathsf{E}\Bigg\{&\sum_{m=1}^{\theta}\Big[u(p_m) - \frac{CR\#S}{\delta}\sum_k \mathsf{E}\big(|p_{m+1}(k) - p_m(k)| \mid \mathscr{H}_m^{\mathrm{I}}\big)\Big] \\ &+ \frac{n-\theta}{n}\underline{v}_{n-\theta}(p_{\theta+1}) - 2\delta C\Bigg\} \\ = \frac{1}{n}\mathsf{E}\Bigg\{&\sum_{m=1}^{\theta} u(p_m) + (n-\theta)\underline{w}_\delta(p_{\theta+1}) - (n-\theta)\Delta(p_{\theta+1}, n-\theta) - 2\delta C \\ &- \frac{CR\#S}{\delta}\sum_{m=1}^{\theta}\Big[\sum_k \mathsf{E}\big(|p_{m+1}(k) - p_m(k)| \mid \mathscr{H}_m^{\mathrm{I}}\big)\Big]\Bigg\}.\end{aligned}$$

Since up to stage θ, I uses strategies in NR^{I}, $p_m \in \Pi^{\mathrm{II}}(p)$ for $m = 0, 1, \ldots, \theta$, and since, by the definition of θ, $u(p_m) = \max\{u(p_m), \underline{w}_\delta(p_m)\}$, we have for the expectation (over $\mathscr{H}_\theta^{\mathrm{I}}$) of the first term:

$$\frac{1}{n}\mathsf{E}\left(\sum_{m=1}^{\theta} u(p_m) + (n-\theta)\underline{w}_\delta(p_\tau)\right) \geq \operatorname*{Vex}_{\mathrm{II}} \max(u, \underline{w}_\delta)(p).$$

By Lemma V.2.1, p. 219:

$$\frac{1}{n}\sum_{m=1}^{\theta}\sum_k \mathsf{E}\big|p_{m+1}(k) - p_m(k)\big| \leq \sqrt{\frac{\#K - 1}{n}}.$$

For any $0 < N \leq n$:

$$\begin{aligned}\mathsf{E}\left(\frac{n-\theta}{n}\Delta(p_{\theta+1}, n-\theta)\right) &\leq \sum_{m=1}^{n-N}\big[\max_p \Delta(p, n-m)\big]P(\theta = m) \\ &\quad + \frac{N}{n}\sum_{m=n-N+1}^{n}\big[\max_p \Delta(p, n-m)\big]P(\theta = m) \\ &\leq \max_p \sup_{\ell \geq N} \Delta(p, \ell) + 2C\frac{N}{n};\end{aligned}$$

therefore:

$$\underline{v}_{n,\delta}(p) \geq \mathsf{E}(\rho) \geq \operatorname*{Vex}_{\mathrm{II}} \max(u, \underline{w}_\delta)(p) - \frac{CR\#S}{\delta}\sqrt{\frac{\#K}{n}} - \max_p \sup_{\ell \geq N} \Delta(p,\ell) - 2C\frac{N}{n} - 2C\delta.$$

Choosing $N = \sqrt{n}$ and letting n go to infinity we get $\underline{w}_\delta(p) \geq \mathsf{Vex}_{\mathrm{II}} \max(u, \underline{w}_\delta)(p) - 2C\delta$, and from this, our result follows using the Lipschitz property of the $\underline{w}_\delta$. ∎

Lemma VI.4.5. *The set of functions g satisfying $g \geq \mathsf{Cav}_{\mathrm{I}} \mathsf{Vex}_{\mathrm{II}} \max(u, g)$ has a smallest element g_0 satisfying $g_0 = \mathsf{Cav}_{\mathrm{I}} \mathsf{Vex}_{\mathrm{II}} \max(u, g_0)$.*

Proof. The proof follows from the following simply verified observations:

- $g \equiv \max_{p \in \Pi} u(p)$ is a solution, and so the set is non-empty.
- The pointwise $\inf$ of all solutions is still one.
- If, for a solution g, $g(p_0) = \big(\mathsf{Cav}_{\mathrm{I}} \mathsf{Vex}_{\mathrm{II}} \max(u, g)\big)(p_0) + \varepsilon$ for some $p_0 \in \Pi$ and $\varepsilon > 0$, then the function

$$\tilde{g}(p) = \begin{cases} g(p) & \text{if } p \neq p_0 \\ g(p) - \varepsilon & \text{if } p = p_0 \end{cases}$$

is also a solution, and strictly smaller. ∎

Lemma VI.4.6.

$$\sum_{m=1}^{n} \sum_{k \in K} \mathsf{E}\left|p_m(k) - \tilde{p}_{m-1}(k)\right| \leq \sqrt{n\delta}\,\psi(p) \ \ \textit{with}\ \ \psi(p) = \sum_{k \in K} \sqrt{p^k(1-p^k)}.$$

Proof. Consider the measure space $\Omega \times \mathbb{N}$, with measure $\lambda = P \times \mu$, where μ is the counting measure on $\mathbb{N}$. Consider some fixed k.

Let $X(\omega, m) = \left|p_{m+1}(k) - \tilde{p}_m(k)\right|$, $m = 1, \ldots, n$, and $X(\omega, m) = 0$ otherwise. Let $Y(\omega, m) = \mathbb{1}_{s_m(\omega) \in \underline{S} \setminus S}$, $m = 1, \ldots, n$, and $Y(\omega, m) = 0$ otherwise. Then $X = XY$, and the left-hand member is equal to $\int X\, d\lambda = \int XY\, d\lambda \leq \|X\|_2 \|Y\|_2$ by the Cauchy–Schwartz inequality. Since:

$$\begin{aligned} \|X\|_2^2 &= \mathsf{E}\sum_1^n \big(p_{m+1}(k) - \tilde{p}_m(k)\big)^2 \\ &\leq \mathsf{E}\left(\sum_{m=1}^n \big(p_{m+1}(k) - \tilde{p}_m(k)\big)^2 + \sum_{m=1}^n \big(\tilde{p}_m(k) - p_m(k)\big)^2\right) \\ &= \mathsf{E}\big(p_{n+1}(k) - p_1(k)\big)^2 \leq p^k(1-p^k) \end{aligned}$$

and

$$\|Y\|_2^2 = \sum_{m=1}^n P\big(s_m(\omega) \in \underline{S} \setminus S\big) = n\delta,$$

the result follows. ∎

Proposition VI.4.7. *Let $f(p)$ be any function on Π satisfying $f \le \operatorname{Vex}_{\mathrm{II}} \operatorname{Cav}_{\mathrm{I}} \min(u, f)$ and define $d(p,n) = (f(p) - \underline{v}_n(p))^+$; then:*

$$d(p,n) \le C\left[\frac{\#SR\psi(p)}{\sqrt{n\delta}} + 2\delta\right].$$

In particular (letting $n \to \infty$ and then $\delta \to 0$), we have $f \le \underline{w}$.

Proof. It is clearly sufficient to prove the proposition for the sup of all such functions f, and in view of Lemma VI.4.5 we may therefore assume without loss of generality that $f(p) = \operatorname{Vex}_{\mathrm{II}} \operatorname{Cav}_{\mathrm{I}} \min(u, f)$. In particular we may assume that f is convex w.r.t. II.

By Lemma VI.2.4, for each p_n, I has a transition probability from $\mathscr{H}^{\mathrm{I}}_{\mathrm{I},n}$ to E^{I}_{n+1} such that if $\tilde{p}_n(k) = P(k \mid \tilde{H}^{\mathrm{I}}_n)$, then $f(p_n) \le \mathsf{E}(\min(u(\tilde{p}_n), f(\tilde{p}_n))) + \varepsilon 2^{-n}$.

For any τ of II in $\underline{\Gamma}_n(p)$, consider the strategy of I that after each stage $n (n = 1, \ldots, m)$ uses the above-mentioned transition probability and then an optimal strategy in $D(\tilde{p}_n)$. By Lemma VI.2.13, the payoff at stage n satisfies:

$$\rho_n \ge u(\tilde{p}_n) - \frac{CR\#S}{\delta} \sum_{k \in K} \mathsf{E}\big(|p_{n+1}(k) - \tilde{p}_n(k)| \bigm| \tilde{\mathscr{H}}^{\mathrm{I}}_n\big) - 2\delta C,$$

$$\mathsf{E}\big(\rho_n \bigm| \mathscr{H}^{\mathrm{I}}_n\big) \ge f(p_n) - \frac{CR\#S}{\delta} \sum_{k \in K} \mathsf{E}\big(|p_{n+1}(k) - \tilde{p}_n(k)| \bigm| \mathscr{H}^{\mathrm{I}}_n\big) - 2\delta C - \varepsilon 2^{-n}.$$

Since f is convex w.r.t. II we have by Lemma VI.2.14 that $\mathsf{E}(f(p_{n+1}) \mid \tilde{\mathscr{H}}^{\mathrm{I}}_n) \ge f(\tilde{p}_n)$ and also $\mathsf{E}(f(\tilde{p}_n) \mid \mathscr{H}^{\mathrm{I}}_n) \ge f(p_n) - \varepsilon 2^{-n}$, and hence $\mathsf{E}(f(p_n)) \ge f(p) - \varepsilon$.

By Lemma VI.4.6, we obtain thus:

$$\underline{v}_n(p) \ge \mathsf{E}\left(\frac{1}{n}\sum_{m=1}^{n} \rho_m\right) \ge f(p) - C\left[\frac{\#SR\psi(p)}{\sqrt{n\delta}} + 2\delta\right] - 2\varepsilon.$$

ε being arbitrary can be set equal to zero. ∎

Corollary VI.4.8. $v = \lim v_n$ *exists and is equal to both $\overline{w}$ and $\underline{w}$. It satisfies:*

$$\operatorname*{Cav}_{\mathrm{I}} \operatorname*{Vex}_{\mathrm{II}} \max(u, v) \le v \le \operatorname*{Vex}_{\mathrm{II}} \operatorname*{Cav}_{\mathrm{I}} \min(u, v).$$

Proof. By the dual of Proposition VI.4.4, $\overline{w} \le \operatorname{Cav}_{\mathrm{I}} \min(u, \overline{w})$, and so, by Proposition VI.4.1, $\overline{w} \le \operatorname{Vex}_{\mathrm{II}} \operatorname{Cav}_{\mathrm{I}} \min(u, \overline{w})$, and thus, by Proposition VI.4.7, $\overline{w} \le \underline{w}$. Since clearly $\underline{v}_{n,\delta} \le v_n \le \overline{v}_{n,\delta}$ for any $\delta > 0$, the corollary follows. ∎

Corollary VI.4.9.

$$v_n(p) \ge v(p) - 3C\sqrt[3]{\frac{[\#SR\psi(p)]^2}{2n}},$$

$$v_n(p) \le v(p) + 3C\sqrt[3]{\frac{[\#TR'\psi(p)]^2}{2n}}.$$

Remark VI.4.1. Remember that the constant R (Proposition VI.2.5) depends only on the information structure of the game.

Proof. By Corollary VI.4.8, we can apply Proposition VI.4.7 with $f = v$; since $v_n \geq \underline{v}_n$, we get $v - v_n \leq C\left[2\delta + \frac{\#SR\psi(p)}{\sqrt{n\delta}}\right]$ for any $\delta > 0$.

Letting now $\delta = [\#SR\psi(p)]^{\frac{2}{3}}/(2(2n)^{\frac{1}{3}})$ yields the first inequality. The second is dual. ■

Proposition VI.4.10.

(1) *Consider the functional inequalities:*
  (a) $f \geq \mathsf{Cav}_{\mathrm{I}}\, \mathsf{Vex}_{\mathrm{II}} \max(u, f)$.
  (b) $f \leq \mathsf{Vex}_{\mathrm{II}}\, \mathsf{Cav}_{\mathrm{I}} \min(u, f)$.
  Then v is the smallest solution of 1a and the largest solution of 1b. In particular v is the only solution of the system (1a, 1b).

(2) *v is the only solution of the system (2a, 2b):*
  (a) $g = \mathsf{Vex}_{\mathrm{II}} \max(u, g)$.
  (b) $g = \mathsf{Cav}_{\mathrm{I}} \min(u, g)$.

Remark VI.4.2. It follows that if $\mathsf{Cav}_{\mathrm{I}}\, \mathsf{Vex}_{\mathrm{II}}\, u = \mathsf{Vex}_{\mathrm{II}}\, \mathsf{Cav}_{\mathrm{I}}\, u$, then this is also $v = \lim v_n$ (as it should be, knowing that this is the value of $\Gamma_\infty(p)$). In fact, since v satisfies (2a, 2b) we have:

$$v = \underset{\mathrm{I}}{\mathsf{Cav}}\, \underset{\mathrm{II}}{\mathsf{Vex}} \max(u, v) \geq \underset{\mathrm{I}}{\mathsf{Cav}}\, \underset{\mathrm{II}}{\mathsf{Vex}}\, u = \underset{\mathrm{II}}{\mathsf{Vex}}\, \underset{\mathrm{I}}{\mathsf{Cav}}\, u \geq \underset{\mathrm{II}}{\mathsf{Vex}}\, \underset{\mathrm{I}}{\mathsf{Cav}} \min(u, v) = v.$$

Proof. By Corollary VI.4.8, v is a solution of 1b. By Proposition VI.4.7, any solution f of 1b satisfies $f \leq \underline{w} = v$, i.e., v, is the largest solution of 1b, and dually it is the smallest solution of 1a. This proves (1).

To prove (2), observe that since v is convex w.r.t. II, $v \leq \mathsf{Vex}_{\mathrm{II}} \max(u, v)$, but by (1) v satisfies $v \geq \mathsf{Cav}_{\mathrm{I}}\, \mathsf{Vex}_{\mathrm{II}} \max(u, v) \geq \mathsf{Vex}_{\mathrm{II}} \max(u, v)$; hence v is a solution of 2a (and similarly of 2b). To prove that it is the only solution, note that any solution of (2a, 2b) is both concave w.r.t. I and convex w.r.t. II and therefore it is also a solution to (1a,1b). Since by (1) v is the only solution of (1a, 1b), the result follows. ■

VI.5. THE FUNCTIONAL EQUATIONS: EXISTENCE AND UNIQUENESS

Denote by $\mathscr{C}(\Pi)$ the space of all continuous functions on the simplex Π, and by U the subset of $\mathscr{C}(\Pi)$ consisting of those functions that are "u-functions," i.e., values of $D(p)$, for some two-person zero-sum game with incomplete information $\Gamma(p)$ with full monitoring. Denote by φ the mapping from U to $\mathscr{C}(\Pi)$ defined by $\varphi(u) = v = \lim v_n$ (whatever the game $\Gamma(p)$ is, such that u is the value of $D(p)$, using Proposition VI.4.10). For the rest of this section, $\mathscr{C}(\Pi)$ is assumed to be endowed with the topology of uniform convergence.

Recall that a vector lattice is an ordered vector space V such that the maximum and the minimum of two elements of V exist (in V).

Proposition VI.5.1.

(1) *U is a vector lattice containing the affine functions.*
(2) *U is dense in $\mathscr{C}(\Pi)$.*

Proof. We proceed by the following assertions:

(α) U contains the affine functions, obviously.

(β) $u \in U \Longrightarrow -u \in U$.

If u arises from the game with matrices $(G^k)_{k\in K}$, then $-u$ arises from the game with matrices $[-(G^k)']_{k\in K}$, where the prime denotes transposition.

(γ) $u \in U, \lambda \geq 0 \Longrightarrow \lambda u \in U$.

If u arises from $(G^k)_{k\in K}$, then λu arises from $(\lambda G^k)_{k\in K}$.

(δ) $u_1 \in U$ and $u_2 \in U$ imply $u_1 + u_2 \in U$.

Let u_i arise from $(G^{k,i})_{k\in K}$ with pure strategy sets S_i for I and T_i for II; $i = 1, 2$. Then $u_1 + u_2$ arises from $(D^k)_{k\in K}$, where D^k with index set $S_1 \times S_2$ for rows and $T_1 \times T_2$ for columns is defined by:

$$D^k_{(s_1,s_2),(t_1,t_2)} = G^{k,1}_{s_1,t_1} + G^{k,2}_{s_2,t_2}, \quad (s_1, s_2) \in S_1 \times S_2; \quad (t_1, t_2) \in T_1 \times T_2.$$

Assertions α to δ prove that U is a vector space containing the affine functions. The lattice property follows from:

(ϵ) $u \in U \Longrightarrow u^+ \in U$.

If u arises from $(G^k)_{k\in K}$, then u^+ arises from the same matrices, each with an additional row of zeroes.

This completes the proof of part (1). Part (2) follows from part (1) by the Stone–Weierstrass theorem, since the affine functions are clearly separating. ∎

Proposition VI.5.2. *The map $\varphi\colon U \to \mathscr{C}(\Pi)$ has a unique continuous extension $\varphi\colon \mathscr{C}(\Pi) \to \mathscr{C}(\Pi)$: this extension is monotone and Lipschitz with constant 1 (or non-expansive, i.e, $\|\varphi(f) - \varphi(g)\| \leq \|f - g\|$).*

Proof. The mapping φ is monotone and non-expansive. Indeed, monotonicity follows from Proposition VI.4.10.1a. It also follows from the same proposition that for any constant ε, $\varphi(u + \varepsilon) = \varphi(u) + \varepsilon$ (since clearly $\varphi(u) + \varepsilon$ is a solution for 1a and 1b, and hence it is the only solution). This together with monotonicity implies that φ is non-expansive. Since by Proposition VI.5.1.2 U is dense in $\mathscr{C}(\Pi)$, it follows that there is a unique continuous extension $\varphi\colon \mathscr{C}(\Pi) \to \mathscr{C}(\Pi)$, which is monotone and non-expansive. ∎

Theorem VI.5.3. *Consider the functional inequalities u, f, and g denoting arbitrary functions on the simplex:*

$$f \geq \underset{\text{I}}{\operatorname{Cav}}\, \underset{\text{II}}{\operatorname{Vex}} \max(u, f), \tag{α}$$

$$f \leq \underset{\text{II}}{\operatorname{Vex}}\, \underset{\text{I}}{\operatorname{Cav}} \min(u, f), \tag{β}$$

$$g = \underset{\text{II}}{\operatorname{Vex}} \max(u, g), \tag{α'}$$

$$g = \underset{\text{I}}{\operatorname{Cav}} \min(u, g). \tag{β'}$$

There exists a monotone non-expansive mapping $\varphi\colon \mathscr{C}(\Pi) \to \mathscr{C}(\Pi)$, *such that, for any* $u \in \mathscr{C}(\Pi)$, $\varphi(u)$ *is the smallest* f *satisfying* (α) *and the largest* f *satisfying* (β), *and thus in particular the only solution* f *of the system* (α), (β).

$\varphi(u)$ *is also the only solution* g *of the system* (α'), (β').

Proof. The operators max, min, $\mathrm{Cav}_{\mathrm{I}}$, and $\mathrm{Vex}_{\mathrm{II}}$ being monotone and non-expansive, Propositions VI.4.10 and VI.5.2 imply immediately that $\varphi(u)$ satisfies (α), (β), (α'), and (β').

If we prove that $\varphi(u)$ is the smallest solution of (α) (and the largest of (β)), the proof will be completed in the same way as in Proposition VI.4.10.

In fact, let f be any solution of (α), and let $\{u_n\}_{n=1}^{\infty}$ be an increasing sequence in U converging uniformly to u (such a sequence exists by Proposition VI.5.1). By monotonicity of the operators involved, since f is a solution of (α), it is a fortiori a solution of $f \geq \mathrm{Cav}_{\mathrm{I}}\,\mathrm{Vex}_{\mathrm{II}}\max(u_n, f)$, and so by Proposition VI.4.10.1a, $f \geq \varphi(u_n)$ for $n = 1, 2, \ldots$. But by continuity $\varphi(u_n) \to_{n\to\infty} \varphi(u)$ and so $f \geq \varphi(u)$, i.e., $\varphi(u)$ is indeed the smallest solution of (α) (and similarly the largest solution of (β)), which completes the proof of the theorem. ■

Remark VI.5.1. Theorem VI.5.3 is of a purely functional theoretic nature and involves no game theory at all. So it should be provable independently of our game-theoretical context (cf. VI.7, Ex. 9, p. 385).

Theorem VI.5.4 (An approximation procedure for $\varphi(u)$). *Define* $\underline{v}_0 = -\infty$, $\overline{v}_0 = +\infty$, $\underline{v}_{n+1} = \mathrm{Cav}_{\mathrm{I}}\,\mathrm{Vex}_{\mathrm{II}}\max(u, \underline{v}_n)$, $\overline{v}_{n+1} = \mathrm{Vex}_{\mathrm{II}}\,\mathrm{Cav}_{\mathrm{I}}\min(u, \overline{v}_n)$; $n = 0, 1, 2, \ldots$. *Then:* $\{\underline{v}_n\}_{n=1}^{\infty}$ *is monotonically increasing,* $\{\overline{v}_n\}_{n=1}^{\infty}$ *is monotonically decreasing, and both sequences converge uniformly to* $\varphi(u)$.

Remark VI.5.2. $\underline{v}_1$ (resp. $\overline{v}_1$) is the sup inf (resp. inf sup) of Γ_∞ if $u(p)$ is the value of $D(p)$.

Proof. Since u is continuous on a compact set, it is uniformly continuous, and it is easily checked that the operators max, min, $\mathrm{Cav}_{\mathrm{I}}$, and $\mathrm{Vex}_{\mathrm{II}}$ preserve the modulus of uniform continuity. It follows that both sequences $\{\underline{v}_n\}_{n=1}^{\infty}$ and $\{\overline{v}_n\}_{n=1}^{\infty}$ are equicontinuous and obviously bounded.

Let us prove inductively that $\underline{v}_n \leq \underline{v}_{n+1}$. It is clearly true for $n = 0$. If $\underline{v}_{n-1} \leq \underline{v}_n$, then $\underline{v}_n = \mathrm{Cav}_{\mathrm{I}}\,\mathrm{Vex}_{\mathrm{II}}\max(u, \underline{v}_{n-1}) \leq \mathrm{Cav}_{\mathrm{I}}\,\mathrm{Vex}_{\mathrm{II}}\max(u, \underline{v}_n) = \underline{v}_{n+1}$.

Let us prove inductively that $\underline{v}_n \leq \varphi(u)$. It is clearly true for $n = 0$. If $\underline{v}_{n-1} \leq \varphi(u)$, then $\underline{v}_n = \mathrm{Cav}_{\mathrm{I}}\,\mathrm{Vex}_{\mathrm{II}}\max(u, \underline{v}_{n-1}) \leq \mathrm{Cav}_{\mathrm{I}}\,\mathrm{Vex}_{\mathrm{II}}\max(u, \varphi(u)) \leq \varphi(u)$ (by Theorem VI.5.3).

Let $\underline{v} = \lim_{n\to\infty} \underline{v}_n$. This limit is uniform by the equicontinuity of the sequence. Then $\underline{v} = \mathrm{Cav}_{\mathrm{I}}\,\mathrm{Vex}_{\mathrm{II}}\max(u, \underline{v})$ and $\underline{v} \leq \varphi(u)$. But Theorem VI.5.3 implies $\underline{v} \geq \varphi(u)$, hence $\underline{v} = \varphi(u)$, i.e., $\{\underline{v}_n\}_{n=1}^{\infty}$ converges uniformly to $\varphi(u)$. The same arguments apply to the sequence $\overline{v}_n$. ■

Corollary VI.5.5. *If* u *is a continuous function on the simplex* Π, *both* $\mathrm{Cav}_{\mathrm{I}}\,\mathrm{Vex}_{\mathrm{II}}\,u$ *and* $\mathrm{Vex}_{\mathrm{II}}\,\mathrm{Cav}_{\mathrm{I}}\,u$ *are concave w.r.t.* I *and convex w.r.t.* II.

Proof. Apply Corollary VI.3.8 and Proposition VI.5.1. ■

VI.6. ON THE SPEED OF CONVERGENCE OF v_n

Corollaries VI.4.8 and VI.4.9 yield now immediately:

Theorem VI.6.1. *For any game as described in Section VI.1, the sequence v_n of values of the n-stage games converges, and since the function u is defined in the beginning of Section VI.2 and the operator φ according to Theorem VI.5.3, we have that:*

$$\lim_{n\to\infty} v_n(p) = \varphi(u)(p),$$

or, more precisely:

$$v_n - \varphi(u) \le 3C\sqrt[3]{\frac{[\#TR\psi(p)]^2}{2n}}$$

$$\varphi(u) - v_n \le 3C\sqrt[3]{\frac{[\#SR\psi(p)]^2}{2n}}.$$

Remark VI.6.1. Corollary V.5.2, p. 296, yields an example satisfying our assumptions and where $|v - v_n|$ is of the order $1/\sqrt[3]{n}$, and hence the bound for the speed of convergence given in Theorem VI.6.1 is the best possible.

A special case for which a smaller error term is valid is the case of "full monitoring." This is the case in which the information revealed to both players at each stage is just the pair (s, t) of pure moves chosen, also called **standard signaling**.

Theorem VI.6.2. *For games with full monitoring, $|v_n - v|$ is at most of the order $1/\sqrt{n}$. More precisely:*

$$\left|v_n(p) - v(p)\right| \le \frac{C\sum_k \sqrt{p^k(1-p^k)}}{\sqrt{n}},$$

and there are games in which $v_n(p) - v(p) = O\left(\frac{1}{\sqrt{n}}\right)$.

Proof. This result is obtained in exactly the same manner as that in Theorem VI.6.1 with the simplification that we do not have to do the modification of the games Γ_n to $\underline{\Gamma}_n$ and can work directly with $\Gamma_n(p)$ and $v_n(p)$.

The main changes in the proofs are:

- In Lemma VI.2.11, the right-hand side reduces to:

$$\tilde{p}_n(k)\sum_{t\in T}\left|\overline{\tau}^k(\omega_n)(t) - \sum_{k\in K}\tilde{p}_n(k)\overline{\tau}^k(\omega_n)(t)\right|.$$

  Lemma VI.2.12 becomes superfluous.
- Consequently, in Lemma VI.2.13, $\#SR/\delta$ is replaced by 1, and the term $2\delta C$ is replaced by zero.
- From this point a proposition similar to Proposition VI.4.4 can be proved with the same strategy described in the proof there, but this

time in view of the changes in Lemmas VI.2.11, VI.2.12, and VI.2.13, we get:

$$v_n = \mathsf{E}\left(\frac{1}{n}\sum_{m=1}^{n}\rho_m\right) \geq f(p) - \frac{C\sum_k \sqrt{p^k(1-p^k)}}{\sqrt{n}}.$$

As for the second part of the theorem, the game (with incomplete information on one side described in Chapter V) belongs to the family of games under consideration and has $|v_n - v| = O\left(\frac{1}{\sqrt{n}}\right)$. ■

VI.7. EXAMPLES

The examples that we shall treat here belong to a special subclass of the general class of games we treated in this chapter. This subclass is special in two respects:

- We assume *full monitoring*.
- The set of states of nature K can be arranged in a matrix such that the elements of K^{I} are the rows and those of K^{II} are the columns, thus $K = K^{\mathrm{I}} \times K^{\mathrm{II}}$. Moreover, the probability distribution p on K is such that $p(i, j) = q_{\mathrm{I}}^i q_{\mathrm{II}}^j$ for $i \in K^{\mathrm{I}}$, $j \in K^{\mathrm{II}}$, where $q_{\mathrm{I}} = (q_{\mathrm{I}}^i)_{i\in K^{\mathrm{I}}}$ and $q_{\mathrm{II}} = (q_{\mathrm{II}}^j)_{j\in K^{\mathrm{II}}}$ are two probability vectors on K^{I} and K^{II}, respectively. We will call such a probability p a product probability and denote it by $p = q_{\mathrm{I}} \times q_{\mathrm{II}}$. We denote by P the set of product probabilities. P is therefore a subset of the simplex Π of all probability distributions on $K = K^{\mathrm{I}} \times K^{\mathrm{II}}$.

The significance of the subclass of games satisfying the second assumption is the following: think of the elements of K^{I} (resp. K^{II}) as the possible types of I (resp. II). Thus a state of nature $(i, j) \in K$ consists of a pair of types $i \in K^{\mathrm{I}}$ and $j \in K^{\mathrm{II}}$, and after the actual choice of types (i.e., the state of nature) each player knows his own type. The meaning of $p \in P$ is then that the two types are chosen independently; $i \in K^{\mathrm{I}}$ is chosen according to q_{I}, and $j \in K^{\mathrm{II}}$ is chosen independently according to q_{II}. Or equivalently: I's conditional probability on the types of II is independent of his own type (and vice versa for II). Due to this interpretation, the case $K = K^{\mathrm{I}} \times K^{\mathrm{II}}$ and $p \in P$ is often referred to as the **independent case**. It is easily seen that if $p = q_{\mathrm{I}} \times q_{\mathrm{II}} \in P$, then:

$$\Pi^{\mathrm{I}}(p) = \{\, q_{\mathrm{I}} \times q'_{\mathrm{II}} \mid q'_{\mathrm{II}} \text{ is any probability vector on } K^{\mathrm{II}} \,\} \subseteq P,$$

$$\Pi^{\mathrm{II}}(p) = \{\, q'_{\mathrm{I}} \times q_{\mathrm{II}} \mid q'_{\mathrm{I}} \text{ is any probability vector on } K^{\mathrm{I}} \,\} \subseteq P.$$

It follows that the operators $\mathsf{Cav}_{\mathrm{I}}$ and $\mathsf{Vex}_{\mathrm{II}}$ can be carried within the subset P of product probabilities without our having to evaluate the function under consideration (such as $u(p)$) outside P. (Note, however, that P is not a convex set.)

If we write $P = Q_{\mathrm{I}} \times Q_{\mathrm{II}}$, where Q_{I} and Q_{II} are the simplices of probability vectors on K^{I} and K^{II}, respectively, then our concepts for this case become:

- u, the value of the game $\sum_{(i,j)\in K^{\mathrm{I}}\times K^{\mathrm{II}}} q_{\mathrm{I}}(i)q_{\mathrm{II}}(j)G^{i,j}$, is a function $u(q_{\mathrm{I}}, q_{\mathrm{II}})$ on $Q_{\mathrm{I}} \times Q_{\mathrm{II}}$;
- $\mathsf{Cav}_{\mathrm{I}}\, f$ is the concavification of f w.r.t. the variable q_{I} keeping q_{II} constant, and $\mathsf{Vex}_{\mathrm{II}}\, f$ is the convexification of f w.r.t. the variable q_{II}; hence also $\mathsf{Cav}_{q_{\mathrm{I}}}$ and $\mathsf{Vex}_{q_{\mathrm{II}}}$.
- $v(q_{\mathrm{I}}, q_{\mathrm{II}}) = \lim_{n\to\infty} v_n(q_{\mathrm{I}}, q_{\mathrm{II}})$.

The equations determining v (i.e., equations (2a and 2b) of Proposition VI.4.10) become now:

$$v = \mathsf{Vex}_{q_{\mathrm{II}}} \max(u, v), \tag{1}$$

$$v = \mathsf{Cav}_{q_{\mathrm{I}}} \min(u, v). \tag{2}$$

In the first set of examples, there are two types of each player, i.e., $\#K^{\mathrm{I}} = \#K^{\mathrm{II}} = 2$. We denote by $q_{\mathrm{I}} = (x, x')$; $q_{\mathrm{II}} = (y, y')$ the probability distribution on $\mathscr{K}^{\mathrm{I}}$ and $\mathscr{K}^{\mathrm{II}}$, respectively (as usual $x' = 1 - x$, $y' = 1 - y$). All functions involved in the solution such as u, v, $\mathsf{Cav}\, u$, $\mathsf{Vex}\, u$, etc., will be described as functions of (x, y) defined on the unit square $[0, 1] \times [0, 1]$.

Even in this very special case we do not have in general an explicit solution of equations (1) and (2). However, it turns out that the most useful result for solving these equations is the following observation (arising from the fact that in dimension 1, $\mathsf{Cav}\, f(p) > f(p)$ implies that f is linear at p):

(1) At points (x, y) where $u(x, y) > v(x, y)$, the operation Vex_q is non-trivial at that point; hence v is linear in the y direction.
(2) At points (x, y) where $u(x, y) < v(x, y)$, v is linear in the x direction.

In view of the continuity of u and v it suffices therefore to find the locus of points (x, y) at which $v(x, y) = u(x, y)$.

Before starting with our examples let us first prove some general properties of the limit function v that are very useful for computing it. Recall that $v(x, y)$ is Lipschitz both in x and in y. Together with the property that v is convex in x and concave in y, this will imply the existence of directional derivatives for v at any point in all directions.

Proposition VI.7.1. *Let D be a closed polyhedral subset of $R_x \times R_y$, where R_x and R_y are two finite dimensional vector spaces. Assume that D has a convex section at any $x \in R_x$ and at any $y \in R_y$ (i.e., $(\{x\} \times R_y) \cap D$ and $(R_x \times \{y\}) \cap D$ are convex sets for each $(x, y) \in R_x \times R_y$). Let $f : D \to \mathbb{R}$ satisfy:*

- *f is Lipschitz.*
- *f is concave on $(R_x, y) \cap D$ $\forall y \in R_y$ and convex on $(x, R_y) \cap D$ $\forall x \in R_x$.*

Denote by $F_x(x_0, y_0)$ (and similarly F_y) the tangent cone to $f(x, y_0)$ at x_0, i.e.:

$$F_x(x_0, y_0)(h) = \lim_{\tau \to 0^+} \frac{f(x_0 + \tau h, y_0) - f(x_0, y_0)}{\tau}, \quad \text{for all } h \in R_x,$$

for which $f(x_0 + \tau h, y_0)$ is defined for sufficiently small $\tau > 0$. Then for any $(x_0, y_0) \in D$:

$$\big|[f(x_0 + a, y_0 + b) - f(x_0, y_0)] - [F_x(x_0, y_0)(a) + F_y(x_0, y_0)(b)]\big| = o\big(\|a, b\|\big) \tag{3}$$

holds $\forall (a, b) \in R_x \times R_y$ for which all terms are defined.

Proof. Choose $\|a, b\|$ sufficiently small so that in addition $f(x_0 + a, y_0)$ and $f(x_0, y_0 + b)$ are defined. Let $\mathscr{S}(\xi, \eta) = [f(x_0 + \xi a, y_0 + \eta b) - f(x_0, y_0)] - [\xi F_x(x_0, y_0)(a) + \eta F_y(x_0, y_0)(b)]$; then $\mathscr{S}$ is defined on the vertices of $[0, 1]^2$, and therefore (by convexity of the sections) on the whole $[0, 1]^2$. Also $\mathscr{S}$ is concave in ξ (for each η) and convex in η (for each ξ), and $(\frac{d\mathscr{S}(\theta,0)}{d\theta})_{\theta=0^+} = (\frac{d\mathscr{S}(0,\theta)}{d\theta})_{\theta=0^+} = 0$; so by the concavity and convexity of $\mathscr{S}$ we have:

$$\mathscr{S}(0, \theta) \geq 0 \text{ and } \mathscr{S}(\theta, 0) \leq 0, \quad \forall \theta \geq 0.$$

We shall first prove that:

$$\lim_{\theta \to 0^+} \frac{\mathscr{S}(\theta, \theta)}{\theta} = 0. \tag{4}$$

Let $\{\theta_i\}_{i=1}^{\infty}, \theta_i \geq 0, \theta_i \to 0$ be s.t. $\lim_{i \to \infty} \frac{\mathscr{S}(\theta_i, \theta_i)}{\theta_i} = d \in \mathbb{R}$. We must show that $d = 0$.

For any $\underline{d} < d$ take N large enough s.t. $i \geq N \Longrightarrow \frac{\mathscr{S}(\theta_i, \theta_i)}{\theta_i} \geq \underline{d}$. Considering the cut of $\mathscr{S}$ at $\xi = \theta_i$, the straight line ℓ through $[(\theta_i, \theta_i), \mathscr{S}(\theta_i, \theta_i)]$ and $[(\theta_i, 0), 0]$ is below $\mathscr{S}$ for $\eta > \theta_i$ (cf. Figure VI.1), i.e., $\mathscr{S}(\theta_i; \eta) \geq \frac{\mathscr{S}(\theta_i, \theta_i)}{\theta_i}\eta$ for $\eta \geq \theta_i$, which for $i \geq N$ is $\mathscr{S}(\theta_i, \eta) \geq \underline{d}\eta$. Letting $i \to \infty$ we get $\mathscr{S}(0, \eta) \geq \underline{d}\eta$. Dividing both sides by η and letting $\eta \to 0_+$ we get $0 \geq \underline{d}$. Since this is true for any $\underline{d} < d$, we have $d \leq 0$. Dually, using the concavity in ξ of $\mathscr{S}(\xi, \theta)$ we get $d \geq 0$, which concludes the proof of equation (4).

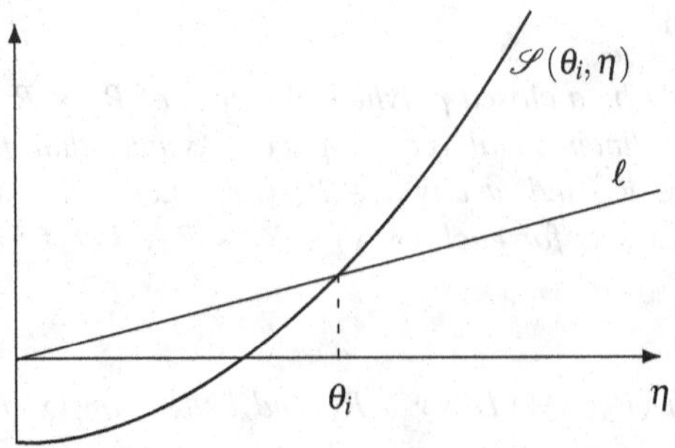

Figure VI.1. An implication of convexity.

Now recalling the definition of $\mathscr{S}$ we rewrite (4) as:

$$\left|f(x_0+\theta a, y_0+\theta b) - f(x_0, y_0) - [F_x(x_0, y_0)(\theta a) + F_y(x_0, y_0)(\theta b)]\right| = o(\theta), \tag{5}$$

which holds for any $(a, b) \in R_x \times R_y$ and $\theta \geq 0$ for which all terms are defined. Finally (3) follows from (5) in a standard way using f Lipschitz and D closed, polyhedral. ∎

For the case $R_x = R_y = \mathbb{R}$, i.e., when f is a function on the real plane, we have:

Corollary VI.7.2. *Any function f on $\mathbb{R}^2$ that is concave in x (for each y) and convex in y (for each x) and has the Lipschitz property has at each point at most four supporting hyperplanes, one on each orthant (with the origin at the point under consideration).*

This corollary applies in particular to the limit value function $v = \lim_{n\to\infty} v_n$ in the independent case. However, for this function more differentiability properties can be proved by using the additional properties of v, namely, that it is the solution of (1) and (2). For the sake of simplicity we shall state and prove these properties for the case we are presently interested in, namely, when u and v are functions on the plane. Similar results might be obtained for more general cases by replacing partial derivatives by tangent cones.

Proposition VI.7.3. *At any point (x, y) where $u(x, y) = v(x, y)$ and $\frac{\partial u}{\partial x}$ and $\frac{\partial u}{\partial y}$ exist:*

(1) *v is differentiable, except for the following cases:*
  (a) *$\frac{\partial v}{\partial x}$ exists and equals $\frac{\partial u}{\partial x}$, in which case $\frac{\partial v}{\partial y}$ may fail to exist.*
  (b) *$\frac{\partial v}{\partial y}$ exists and equals $\frac{\partial u}{\partial y}$, in which case $\frac{\partial v}{\partial x}$ may fail to exist.*

(2) *If in addition u is differentiable at (x, y), then:*

$$\frac{\partial u}{\partial x}\Delta x + \frac{\partial u}{\partial y}\Delta y = \frac{\partial v}{\partial x}\Delta x + \frac{\partial v}{\partial y}\Delta y + o(\|\Delta x, \Delta y\|) \tag{6}$$

for all $(\Delta x, \Delta y)$ for which $v(x+\Delta x, y+\Delta y) = u(x+\Delta x, y+\Delta y)$. When $\frac{\partial v}{\partial x}$ does not exist, it can be replaced in (6) by any of the directional partial derivatives $\frac{\partial v}{\partial x^+}$ or $\frac{\partial v}{\partial x^-}$ $\left(\frac{\partial v}{\partial y^+}\text{ or }\frac{\partial v}{\partial y^-}\right)$. However, if either $\frac{\partial v}{\partial x^+}$ or $\frac{\partial v}{\partial x^-}$ equals $\frac{\partial u}{\partial x}$, this one has to be used in (6) (similarly for the y direction).

Remark VI.7.1. Equation (6) provides a differential equation determining the "line" where $u = v$ when such a "line" exists:

$$\frac{\partial u}{\partial x}dx + \frac{\partial u}{\partial y}dy = \frac{\partial v}{\partial x}dx + \frac{\partial v}{\partial y}dy. \tag{7}$$

Remark VI.7.2. Note that VI.7.3.1 implies that a partial derivative in the "direction of linearity" can be always substituted for the corresponding partial derivative in (6); i.e., for instance, in the x direction, where v is convex, we can always take $\frac{\partial v}{\partial x^+}$ when $\frac{\partial v}{\partial x^+} \leq \frac{\partial u}{\partial x}$ and $\frac{\partial v}{\partial x^-}$ when $\frac{\partial v}{\partial x^-} \geq \frac{\partial u}{\partial x}$.

Proof. (1) If either $\frac{\partial v}{\partial x^+} \neq \frac{\partial u}{\partial x}$ or $\frac{\partial v}{\partial x^-} \neq \frac{\partial u}{\partial x}$, then either $\frac{\partial v}{\partial x^+} < \frac{\partial u}{\partial x}$ or $\frac{\partial v}{\partial x^-} > \frac{\partial u}{\partial x}$ (since v is concave in x). Consider, for instance, the first case, i.e., $\frac{\partial v}{\partial x^+} < \frac{\partial u}{\partial x}$. Since v and u have the Lipschitz property, there exists $\varepsilon > 0$ such that:

$$0 < \xi < \varepsilon \text{ and } \eta \leq \varepsilon\xi \text{ imply } v(x+\xi, y+\eta) < u(x+\xi, y+\eta).$$

Therefore v is linear in y in this region (cf. property (1) above), and so:

$$v(x+\xi, y+\varepsilon\xi) + v(x+\xi, y-\varepsilon\xi) - 2v(x+\xi, y) = 0,$$

and applying Proposition VI.7.1, p. 367, to the left-hand side we obtain:

$$\varepsilon\xi\frac{\partial v}{\partial y^+} - \varepsilon\xi\frac{\partial v}{\partial y^-} + o(\xi) = 0,$$

which implies the existence of $\frac{\partial v}{\partial y}$, and hence proves (1) for the first case. The second case is treated in the same way.

(2) By Proposition VI.7.1 applied to v and the differentiability of u we have:

$$\frac{\partial u}{\partial x}\Delta x + \frac{\partial u}{\partial y}\Delta y = \alpha\Delta x + \beta\Delta y + o(\|\Delta x, \Delta y\|), \tag{8}$$

where $\alpha = \frac{\partial v}{\partial x^+}$ if $\Delta x \geq 0$; similarly for β. When v is differentiable this is just what is claimed in (2), so assume that v is not differentiable. Then by (1) we may assume that $\frac{\partial v}{\partial x^+} = \frac{\partial v}{\partial x^-} = \frac{\partial u}{\partial x}$, and so (8) becomes:

$$\frac{\partial u}{\partial y}\Delta y = \beta\Delta y + o(\|\Delta x, \Delta y\|).$$

Clearly the two possible choices of β are equivalent, provided one takes $\beta = \frac{\partial u}{\partial y}$ if possible. This completes the proof of Proposition VI.7.3. ∎

We are now ready to present some numerical examples.

Example VI.7.3. *(Aumann and Maschler, 1967)*

$$K = \{(1,1), (1,2), (2,1), (2,2)\},$$

$$K^{\mathrm{I}} = \{(1,1), (1,2)\}, \{(2,1), (2,2)\},$$

$$K^{\mathrm{II}} = \{(1,1), (2,1)\}, \{(1,2), (2,2)\}.$$

When K is arranged in a matrix with K^{I} as the set of rows and K^{II} as the set of columns, the corresponding payoff matrices G^{ij} ($i = 1, 2; j = 1, 2$) are:

$$\begin{array}{cc} & y \qquad\qquad\qquad y' \\ x & \begin{pmatrix} 1 & 2 & 0 \\ -1 & 2 & 0 \\ 1 & 2 & 0 \\ -1 & 2 & 0 \end{pmatrix} \begin{pmatrix} -1 & 0 & 2 \\ 1 & 0 & 2 \\ 1 & 0 & 2 \\ -1 & 0 & 2 \end{pmatrix}, \\ x' & \begin{pmatrix} 1 & 0 & 2 \\ -1 & 0 & 2 \\ -1 & 0 & 2 \\ 1 & 0 & 2 \end{pmatrix} \begin{pmatrix} -1 & 2 & 0 \\ 1 & 2 & 0 \\ -1 & 2 & 0 \\ 1 & 2 & 0 \end{pmatrix}. \end{array}$$

The probability distribution on the rows (K^{I}) is $q_{\mathrm{I}} = (x, x')$ and the probability distribution on the columns (K^{II}) is $q_{\mathrm{II}} = (y, y')$. The non-revealing game $D(x, y)$ is:

$$D(x, y) = xyG^{11} + xy'G^{12} + x'yG^{21} + x'y'G^{22},$$

which is:

$$\begin{pmatrix} xy - xy' + x'y - x'y' & 2xy + 2x'y' & 2xy' + 2x'y \\ -xy + xy' - x'y + x'y' & 2xy + 2x'y' & 2xy' + 2x'y \\ xy + xy' - x'y - x'y' & 2xy + 2x'y' & 2xy' + 2x'y \\ -xy - xy' + x'y + x'y' & 2xy + 2x'y' & 2xy' + 2x'y \end{pmatrix}.$$

The value $u(x, y)$ of this game is given in Figure VI.2.

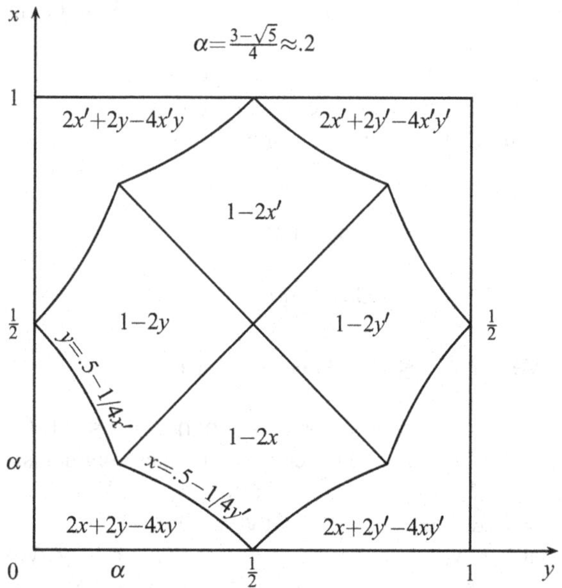

Figure VI.2. $u(x, y)$ of Example VI.7.3.

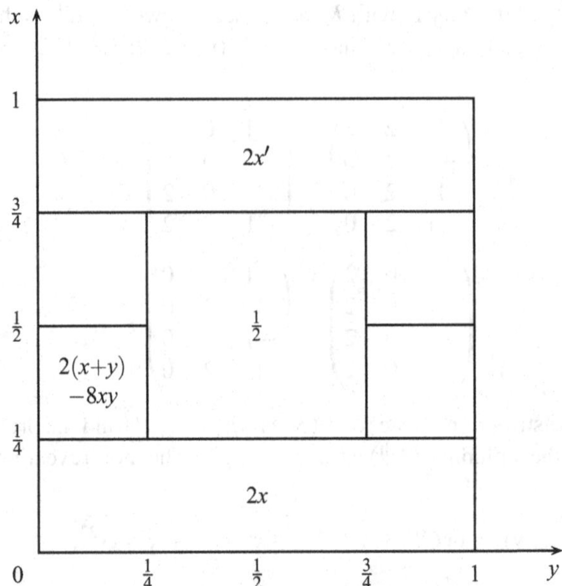

Figure VI.3. $\underline{v} = \mathsf{Cav}_x \mathsf{Vex}_y u$ for Example VI.7.3.

Note that according to our notation the value of u at the corners of the square are the values of the corresponding matrices. Note also that u is symmetric with respect to $x = \frac{1}{2}$ and with respect to $y = \frac{1}{2}$.

Convexifying in the y direction and then concavifying in the x direction (all by brute force) yields $\underline{v} = \mathsf{Cav}_x \mathsf{Vex}_y u$ in Figure VI.3, and similarly for $\overline{v} = \mathsf{Vex}_y \mathsf{Cav}_x u$ in Figure VI.4.

It is readily seen that for about half the points (x, y) in the square, $\mathsf{Cav}_x \mathsf{Vex}_y u \neq \mathsf{Vex}_y \mathsf{Cav}_x u$, and hence v_∞ does not exist.

Let us compute now the asymptotic value $v = \lim_{n\to\infty} v_n$ by solving the equations:

$$v = \operatorname*{Vex}_y \max(u, v)$$

$$v = \operatorname*{Cav}_x \min(u, v).$$

Recall that $\mathsf{Cav}_x \mathsf{Vex}_y u \leq v \leq \mathsf{Vex}_y \mathsf{Cav}_x u$, so that:

(1) On $\{(x, y) \mid y = 0 \text{ or } y = 1 \text{ or } x = \frac{1}{2}, \min(y, y') \leq \alpha\}$ $\mathsf{Cav}_x \mathsf{Vex}_y u = \mathsf{Vex}_y \mathsf{Cav}_x u = u$, and hence $v = u$ on these segments.
(2) On $\{(x, y) \mid x \leq \frac{1}{4} \text{ or } x' \leq \frac{1}{4}\}$, $\mathsf{Cav}_x \mathsf{Vex}_y u = \mathsf{Vex}_y \mathsf{Cav}_x u$, and hence $v = \mathsf{Cav}_x \mathsf{Vex}_y u = \mathsf{Vex}_y \mathsf{Cav}_x u$ there.
(3) On the set $\{(x, y) \mid \frac{1}{4} < x < \frac{3}{4}, \frac{1}{4} < y < \frac{3}{4}\}$, $u < \mathsf{Cav}_x \mathsf{Vex}_y u$, and hence $u < v$ on this set and hence v is linear in x there. Since at the

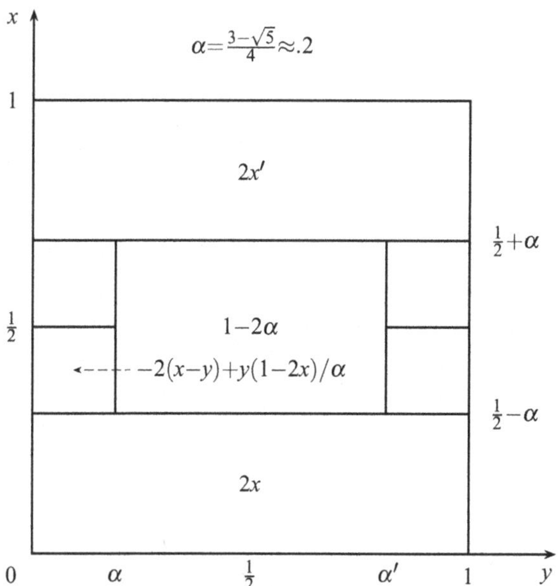

Figure VI.4. $\overline{v} = \mathsf{Vex}_y\, \mathsf{Cav}_x\, u$ for Example VI.7.3.

boundaries $x = \frac{1}{4}$ and $x = \frac{3}{4}$, $v = \frac{1}{2}$ (cf. (2)), we conclude that $v = \frac{1}{2}$ on this set.

(4) Consider now the function v on $x = \frac{1}{2}$. From (2) and (3) it follows that (cf. Figure VI.5):

$$v(\tfrac{1}{2}, y) = \begin{cases} 1 - 2y & 0 \le y \le \alpha \\ \text{not yet determined} & \alpha < y < \frac{1}{4} \\ \frac{1}{2} & \frac{1}{4} \le y \le \frac{1}{2} \\ \text{not yet determined} & \frac{1}{4} < y < \alpha' \\ 1 - 2y' & \alpha' \le y \le 1. \end{cases}$$

Since $v(\frac{1}{2}, y)$ is convex in y we get:

$$v(\tfrac{1}{2}, y) = \begin{cases} 1 - 2y & 0 \le y \le \frac{1}{4} \\ \frac{1}{2} & \frac{1}{4} \le y \le \frac{1}{2} \\ 1 - 2y' & \frac{1}{2} \le y \le 1. \end{cases}$$

In view of the symmetries of v w.r.t. $x = \frac{1}{2}$ and w.r.t. $y = \frac{1}{2}$, it remains now to determine $v(x, y)$ on the set $\{\, (x, y) \mid \frac{1}{4} < x < \frac{1}{2},\ 0 < y < \frac{1}{4} \,\}$. Take a point (x_0, y_0) in this set and consider first the section $v(x_0, y)$. Since $y_0 = (4y_0)\cdot\frac{1}{4} + (1 - 4y_0)\cdot 0$ and $v(x_0, y)$ is convex, it follows that (cf. Figure VI.6) $v(x_0, y_0) \le (4y_0)v(x_0, \frac{1}{4}) + (1 - 4y_0)v(x_0, 0)$, which is $v(x_0, y_0) \le 2x_0 + 2y_0 - 8x_0 y_0$.

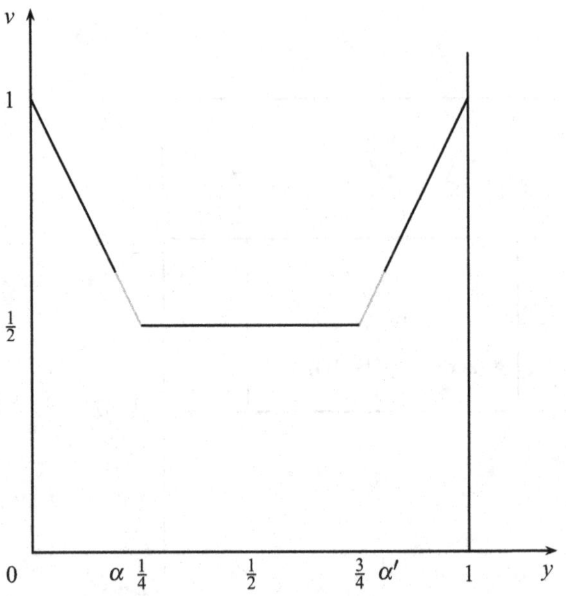

Figure VI.5. $v(\frac{1}{2}, y)$ for Example VI.7.3.

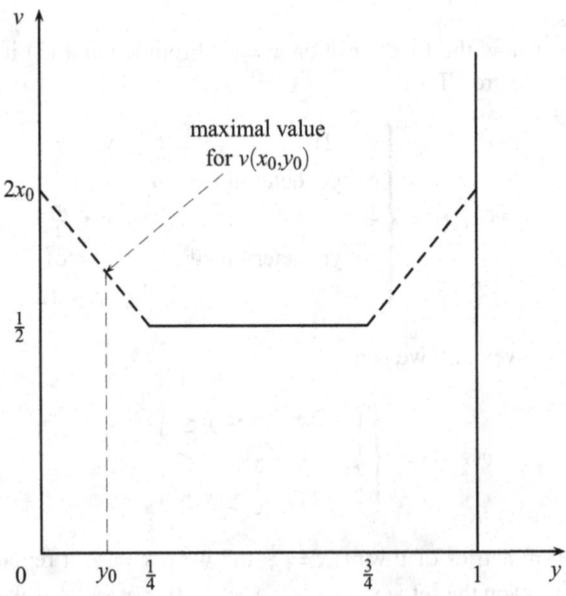

Figure VI.6. $v(x_0, y)$, with $\frac{1}{4} < x_0 < \frac{1}{2}$.

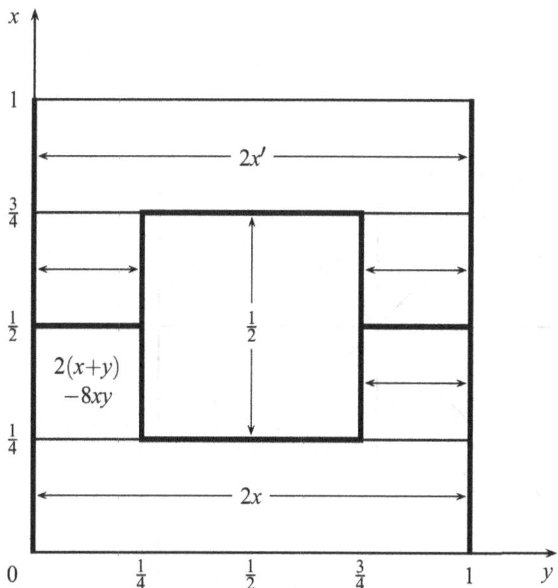

Figure VI.7. $v = \lim v_n$ for Example VI.7.3.

Similarly, using the concavity of $v(x, y_0)$ we get $v(x_0, y_0) \geq 2x_0 + 2y_0 - 8x_0y_0$; hence in the region under consideration $v(x, y) = 2x + 2y - 8xy$, and it is obtained as a linear interpolation in the y direction between $v(0, y)$ and $v(\frac{1}{4}, y)$.

Summing up our construction this function $v = \lim v_n$ is given by Figure VI.7. The thick lines in this figure are the locus of the points $\{(x, y) \mid v(x, y) = u(x, y)\}$. The values of v on the square are obtained by linear interpolation between thick lines in the directions indicated by the arrows.

Note that one can check v, once it is obtained, by verifying the equations (1) and (2), p. 367, since v is the unique solution of these equations.

We see that in this first example $\lim v_n$ coincides with one of its bounds, namely, with $\underline{v} = \operatorname{Cav}_x \operatorname{Vex}_y u$. In our second example we no longer have such a coincidence.

Example VI.7.4. Our second example has the payoff matrices G^{ij} ($i = 1, 2$; $j = 1, 2$):

$$
\begin{array}{ccc}
 & y & y' \\
x & \begin{pmatrix} 0 & 0 & 0 & 0 \\ -1 & 1 & +1 & -1 \end{pmatrix} & \begin{pmatrix} 1 & -1 & +1 & -1 \\ 0 & 0 & 0 & 0 \end{pmatrix}, \\
x' & \begin{pmatrix} -1 & 1 & -1 & +1 \\ 0 & 0 & 0 & 0 \end{pmatrix} & \begin{pmatrix} 0 & 0 & 0 & 0 \\ 1 & -1 & -1 & +1 \end{pmatrix}.
\end{array}
$$

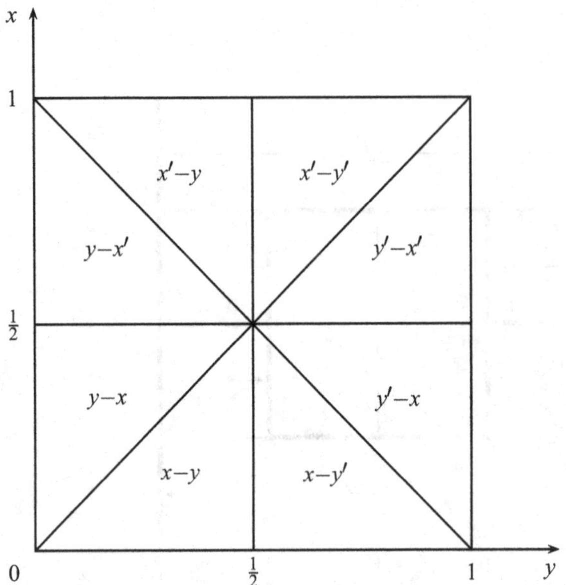

Figure VI.8. $u(x, y)$ of Example VI.7.4.

The non-revealing game $D(x, y)$ is given by the matrix game:

$$\begin{pmatrix} x - y & y - x & x - y & y - x \\ y' - x & x - y' & x - y' & y' - x \end{pmatrix}.$$

Its value u, the maxmin $\mathsf{Cav}_x \mathsf{Vex}_y u$, and the minmax $\mathsf{Vex}_y \mathsf{Cav}_x u$ are given in Figures VI.8, VI.9, and VI.10 and may be verified by the reader as an exercise.

Note that this game, like the previous one, is symmetric w.r.t. $x = \frac{1}{2}$ and w.r.t. $y = \frac{1}{2}$. So it suffices to find v on $\{ (x, y) \mid x \le \frac{1}{2}, y \le \frac{1}{2} \}$. To do this we proceed through the following steps:

(1) On the segment $\{ (x, \frac{1}{2}) \mid x \le \frac{1}{4} \}$, $\mathsf{Cav}_x \mathsf{Vex}_y u = \mathsf{Vex}_y \mathsf{Cav}_x u = u$. So $v = u$ there.

(2) At $(0, 0)$, $\mathsf{Cav}_x \mathsf{Vex}_y u = \mathsf{Vex}_y \mathsf{Cav}_x u = u$ so $v(0, 0) = u(0, 0)$. (This is true for any game and any point-mass on K.)

(3) On the triangle $\{ (x, y) \mid 0 < x \le y < \frac{1}{2} \}$, $u > \mathsf{Vex}\,\mathsf{Cav}_x u$, and so $u > v$ and consequently v is linear in y in this region.

(4) Since $\mathsf{Cav}_x \mathsf{Vex}_y = \mathsf{Vex}_y \mathsf{Cav}_x$ on the boundary of the square, $v(\cdot, 0) = \mathsf{Cav}_x u(\cdot, 0) = 0$, and so $v(x, 0) > u(x, 0)$ for $0 < x < 1$.

From (3) and (4), it follows that a "curve" on which $v = u$ starts at $(0, 0)$ and lies between $y = 0$ and the diagonal $y = x$.

(5) From (4), $v(\frac{1}{2}, \varepsilon) < u(\frac{1}{2}, \varepsilon)$ for $\varepsilon > 0$ sufficiently small. Hence $v(\frac{1}{2}, \varepsilon)$ is obtained by linear interpolation in the x direction, say (using symmetry), $v(\frac{1}{2}, \varepsilon) = \frac{1}{2} v(x, \varepsilon) + \frac{1}{2} v(x', \varepsilon)$. But $v(x, \varepsilon) < 0$ since $\mathsf{Vex}_y \mathsf{Cav}_x u < 0$ at (x, ε) for $x \neq \frac{1}{2}$. It follows that $v(\frac{1}{2}, \varepsilon) < 0$

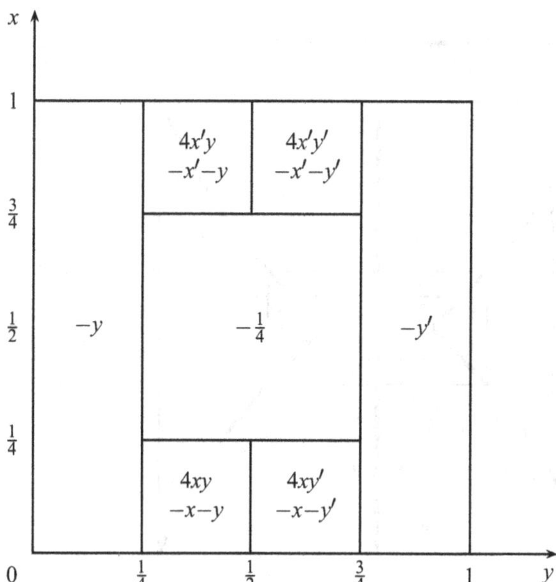

Figure VI.9. $\underline{v} = \mathsf{Cav}_x \mathsf{Vex}_y\, u$ of Example VI.7.4.

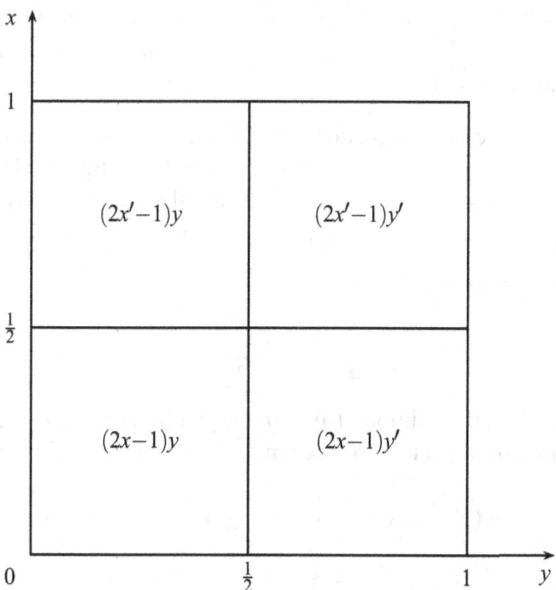

Figure VI.10. $\overline{v} = \mathsf{Vex}_y \mathsf{Cav}_x\, u$ of Example VI.7.4.

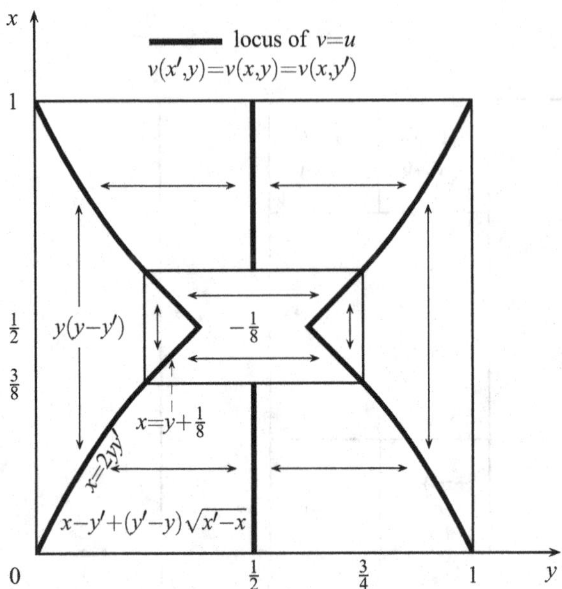

Figure VI.11. $v = \lim v_n$ for Example VI.7.4.

and by symmetry $v(\frac{1}{2}, \varepsilon') < 0$. From the convexity of $v(\frac{1}{2}, y)$ it follows that $v(\frac{1}{2}, \frac{1}{2}) < 0 = u(\frac{1}{2}, \frac{1}{2})$. This implies that if we denote $\{(x, \frac{1}{2}) \mid x \le \xi\}$ the segment on which $v = u$ and that contains the segment in 1, then $\xi < \frac{1}{2}$.

We apply now the differential equation part (7), p. 369, to determine the curve where $v = u$ between $y = 0$ and the line $y = x$ (cf. Figure VI.11). By the symmetry of v w.r.t. $x = \frac{1}{2}$, $\frac{\partial v}{\partial x} = 0$; also $\frac{\partial v}{\partial y}$ is the slope of v, say from (x, y) to $(x, \frac{1}{2})$ (where $v(x, \frac{1}{2}) = x - \frac{1}{2}$); so, since $u(x, y) = y - x$, (7) yields $dy - dx = \frac{(x-\frac{1}{2})-(y-x)}{\frac{1}{2}-y} \cdot dy$ for $x \le \xi$, i.e.:

$$\frac{dx}{2-4x} = \frac{dy}{1-2y}$$

Together with the initial condition $x(0) = 0$ this yields the curve $x = 2yy'$. By linear interpolation between this and the curves $y = \frac{1}{2}$ and $x' = 2yy'$ we have:

$$v(x, y) = x - y' + (y' - y)\sqrt{x' - x} \text{ for } 0 \le x \le \xi\,,\; x \le 2yy'\,,\; y \le \frac{1}{2}$$

$$= y(y - y') \text{ for } 2yy' \le x \le (2yy')',\; 0 \le y \le \eta\,,$$

$$\text{where } \eta \le \frac{1}{2},\; \xi = 2\eta\eta'$$

To determine the point ξ, η we note that above ξ, u is strictly greater than v on $y = \frac{1}{2}$. Hence v is linear (in y from the first line to its symmetric w.r.t.

$y = \frac{1}{2}$). This implies that $v(x, \cdot)$ is constant for $x \geq \xi$, and hence $\left(\frac{\partial v}{\partial y}\right)_\xi = 0$. This yields:

$$\frac{\partial}{\partial y}(x - y' + (y' - y)\sqrt{x' - x}) = 0,$$

i.e., $1 - 2\sqrt{\xi' - \xi} = 0$ or $\xi = \frac{3}{8}$, $\eta = \frac{1}{4}$. Beyond the point (ξ, η), v is linear between the curve $v = u$ and is symmetric w.r.t. $x = \frac{1}{2}$ and $y = \frac{1}{2}$, in the indicated directions. The equation $x = x(y)$ of this curve is again obtained by equation (7), which is:

$$dy - dx = 0.$$

Together with the initial condition (ξ, η) this gives $x = \frac{1}{8} + y$.

Finally, linear interpolation in the indicated directions gives $v(x, y) = -\frac{1}{8}$ for $\frac{3}{8} \leq x \leq \frac{5}{8}$, $\frac{1}{4} \leq y \leq \frac{3}{4}$. Summing up, the resulting $v = \lim v_n$ of Example VI.7.4 is given in Figure VI.11.

EXERCISES

1. Prove Lemma VI.2.7, p. 333.

HINT. Define by induction a unique probability on $(\Omega, \mathscr{G}_n)$, and then let $n \to \infty$ using Ionescu Tulcea's theorem (Neveu, 1970); cf. Proposition II.1.5, p. 63.

2. Prove that if $u(p)$ is either concave w.r.t. I or convex w.r.t. II then Γ_∞ has a value.

3. Consider u on $[0, 1]^2$ with $u(\cdot, y)$ and $u(x, \cdot)$ piecewise linear satisfying:

$$\begin{array}{lll} u(0,0) = 0, & u(\frac{1}{2}, 0) = 1, & u(1,0) = 0, \\ u(0, \frac{1}{2}) = 1, & u(\frac{1}{2}, \frac{1}{2}) = 0, & u(1, \frac{1}{2}) = 1, \\ u(0,1) = 0, & u(\frac{1}{2}, 1) = 1, & u(1,1) = 0, \end{array}$$

and prove that $\operatorname{Vex}\operatorname{Cav}_x u(\frac{1}{2}, \frac{1}{2}) = 1$, $\operatorname{Cav}_x \operatorname{Vex}_y u(\frac{1}{2}, \frac{1}{2}) = 0$.

4. Prove that $\{ u \in \mathscr{C}(\Pi) \mid \operatorname{Cav}_{\mathrm{I}} \operatorname{Vex}_{\mathrm{II}} u \neq \operatorname{Vex}_{\mathrm{II}} \operatorname{Cav}_{\mathrm{I}} u \}$ is open and dense in $\mathscr{C}(\Pi)$.

5. Another example.

This example again has the same structure as the two examples in Section VI.7. It differs from them only by the payoff matrices G^{ij}, which are now:

$$\begin{array}{cc} & \quad y \qquad\qquad\quad y' \\ x & \begin{pmatrix} 0 & 0 \\ -1 & -1 \end{pmatrix} \begin{pmatrix} +1 & -1 \\ 0 & 0 \end{pmatrix}, \\ x' & \begin{pmatrix} -1 & +1 \\ 0 & 0 \end{pmatrix} \begin{pmatrix} 0 & 0 \\ -1 & -1 \end{pmatrix}. \end{array}$$

HINT. The non-revealing game $D(x, y)$ is the matrix game:

$$\begin{pmatrix} x - y & y - x \\ -xy - x'y' & -xy - x'y' \end{pmatrix}.$$

Verify that the functions $u(x, y)$, $\overline{v}_\infty$ and $\underline{v}_\infty$, are as in Figures VI.12, VI.13, and VI.14.

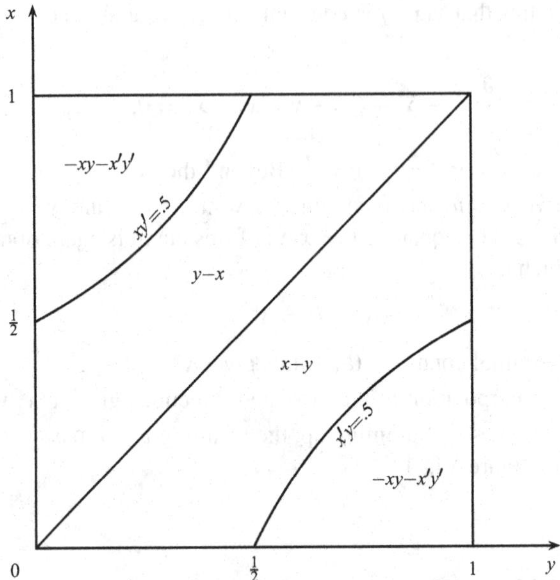

Figure VI.12. $u(x, y)$ in VI.7, Ex. 5.

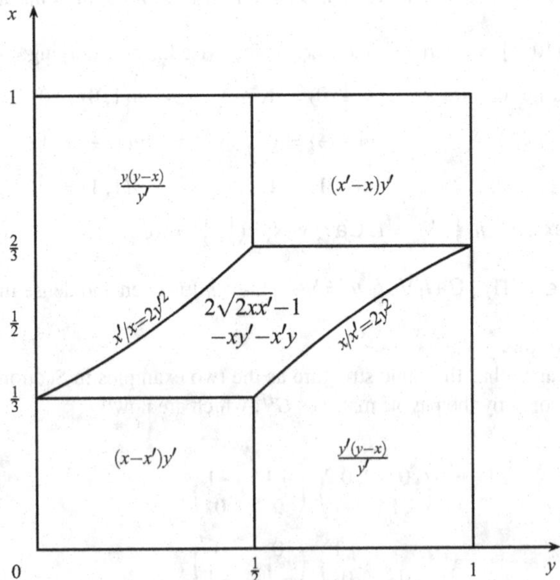

Figure VI.13. $\text{Vex}_y \, \text{Cav}_x \, u$ in VI.7, Ex. 5.

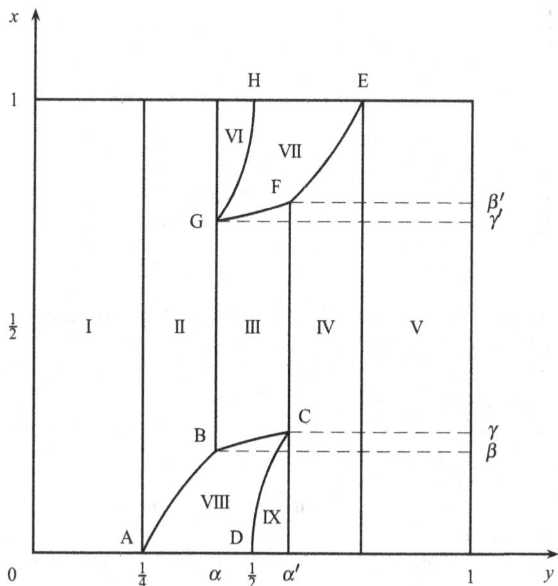

Figure VI.14. $\underline{v}_\infty = \mathsf{Cav}_x \mathsf{Vex}_y u$ in VI.7, Ex. 5.

The equations of the curves and the values of $\mathsf{Cav}_x \mathsf{Vex}_y u$ in the various regions of Figure VI.14 are given in Figure VI.15. The values of α, β, and γ are found by intersecting the corresponding lines and approximately $\alpha = .416$, $\beta = .225$, $\gamma = .268$. Note that although u is symmetric with respect to the main diagonal: $u(x, y) = u(y, x)$, the functions $\mathsf{Cav\,Vex}\, u$ and $\mathsf{Vex\,Cav}\, u$ do not have this symmetry because of the difference between the operations Cav_x and Vex_y. However, the game and hence all the functions u, $\mathsf{Cav\,Vex}\, u$, $\mathsf{Vex\,Cav}\, u$, and v have the symmetry $f(x, y) = f(x', y')$.

To find $v = \lim v_n$, proceed by the following steps:

(1) $u = \overline{v}_\infty = \underline{v}_\infty$, and hence $v = u$ on the segments $[(0, \frac{1}{2}), (0, 1)]$ and $[(1, 0), (1, \frac{1}{2})]$.
(2) $u < \mathsf{Cav\,Vex}\, u$ and hence $u < v$ on the lines $x'y = \frac{1}{2}$ and $y'x = \frac{1}{2}$.

Region	$\mathsf{Cav}_x \mathsf{Vex}_y u$	Curve	Equation
I	$-y$	AB	$2x'\sqrt{y} = 1$
II	$(4y - 4\sqrt{y} + 1)x' - y$	EF	$2x\sqrt{y'} = 1$
III	$\frac{1}{4(\sqrt{y}+\sqrt{y'})^2} - \frac{x\sqrt{y'}+x'\sqrt{y}}{\sqrt{y}+\sqrt{y'}}$	BC	$x = \frac{1}{2} - \frac{1}{4}(y + \sqrt{yy'})^{-1}$
IV	$(4y' - 4\sqrt{y'} + 1)x - y'$	FG	$x = \frac{1}{2} + \frac{1}{4}(y' + \sqrt{yy'})^{-1}$
V	$-y'$	GH	$x' = \frac{1}{2}\sqrt{1 - y/y'}$
VI	$[(4y' - 1) - 4\sqrt{y'(y' - y)}]x' - y$		
VII	$(4xx' - 1)y' - x'$	CD	$x = \frac{1}{2}\sqrt{1 - y'/y}$
VIII	$(4xx' - 1)y - x$		
IX	$[(4y - 1) - 4\sqrt{y(y - y')}]x - y'$		

Figure VI.15. The equations of Figure VI.14.

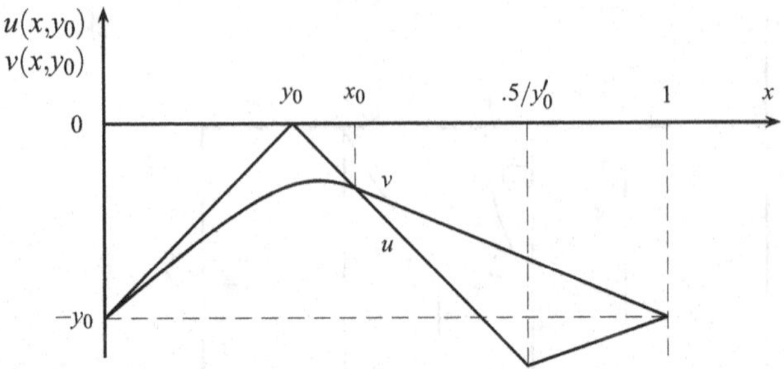

Figure VI.16. $u(x, y_0)$ and $v(x, y_0)$, $0 < y_0 < \frac{1}{2}$, for the example in VI.7, Ex. 5.

(3) $u > \operatorname{Vex}\operatorname{Cav} u$ and hence $u > v$ on $x = y, 0 < x < 1$.
(4) $u > \operatorname{Vex}\operatorname{Cav} u$ and hence $u > v$ on $\{(x, \frac{1}{2} - \varepsilon) \mid 0 \le x \le \frac{1}{2}\}$ for any small $\varepsilon > 0$, and similarly on $\{(x, \frac{1}{2} + \varepsilon) \mid \frac{1}{2} \le x \le 1\}$.
(5) $u = v$ for $x = y = 0$ and for $x = y = 1$.
(6) For any $y_0 < \frac{1}{2}$, $u(x, y_0)$ is piecewise linear, and from (1) to (5) it follows that it has the following structure:
   - $u(0, y_0) = v(0, y_0)$ and $u(x, y_0)$ is linearly increasing from $x = 0$ to $x = y_0$ and $u(x, y_0) > v(x, y_0)$ for $0 < x \le y_0$.
   - $u(x, y_0)$ decreases linearly from $x = y_0$ to $x = \frac{1}{2y'_0}$ where $u\left(\frac{1}{2y'_0}, y_0\right) < v\left(\frac{1}{2y'_0}, y_0\right)$.
   - $u(x, y_0)$ increases linearly from $x = \frac{1}{2y'_0}$ to $x = 1$, $u(x, y_0) \le v(x, y_0)$ for $\frac{1}{2y'_0} \le x \le 1$, and equality holds only for $x = 1$.

Since $v(x, y_0)$ is concave and continuous on $0 \le x \le 1$, the relation between $u(x, y_0)$ and $v(x, y_0)$ must be of the form given by Figure VI.16. Conclude that for each $0 < y_0 < \frac{1}{2}$ there is a *unique* x_0 for which $u(x_0, y_0) = v(x_0, y_0)$, and hence there is a unique interior line of $u = v$ from $(0, 0)$ to $(1, \frac{1}{2})$ and of course its image by the transformation $x \mapsto x'$, $y \mapsto y'$. The resulting $\lim v_n$ function is thus given in Figure VI.17, without specifying the equation of the lines. For that, cf. Mertens and Zamir (1971).

6. Bilinearity.

a. Consider an n-stage repeated game $\Gamma_n(p, q)$ with lack of information on both sides in the independent case with $K = L \times M$, p probability on L and q on M. By taking the normal form, one gets finite sets of moves, say, I (resp. J) for player I (resp. II) and a corresponding payoff depending on the state, say, $c_{ij}^{\ell m}$. A strategy for player I is thus defined by some vector $x = (x_i^\ell, \ell \in L)$, where $x_i^\ell = \Pr(\text{move } i \mid \text{I's type is } \ell)$, and similarly for player II. Prove that $V_n(p, q)$ is the value of the following dual linear programming problems:

$$\max \sum_m q^m u^m \qquad\qquad \min \sum_\ell p^\ell u^\ell$$

$$\sum_{i,\ell} \alpha_i^\ell c_{ij}^{\ell m} \ge u^m \quad \forall j, \forall m \qquad\qquad \sum_{j,m} \beta_j^m c_{ij}^{\ell m} \le u^\ell \quad \forall i, \forall \ell$$

$$\sum_i \alpha_i^\ell = p^\ell \quad \forall \ell \qquad\qquad \sum_j \beta_j^m = q^m \quad \forall m$$

$$\alpha_i^\ell \ge 0 \quad \forall i, \forall \ell \qquad\qquad \beta_j^m \ge 0 \quad \forall j, \forall m,$$

and deduce that $V_n(p, q)$ is concave in p and convex in q.

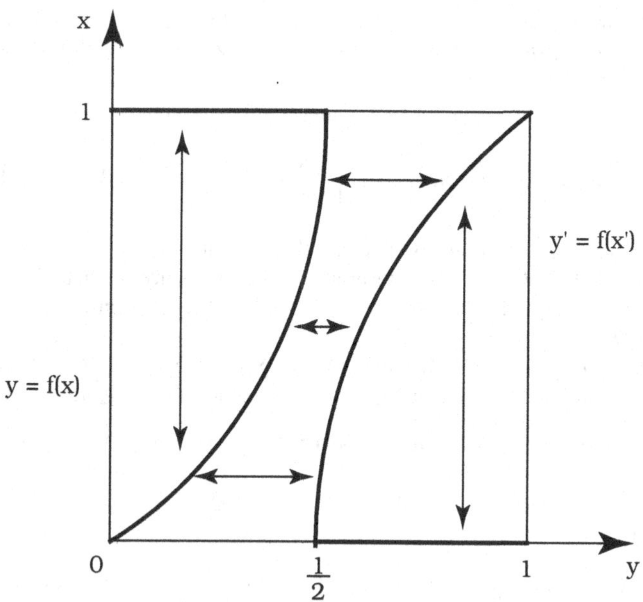

Figure VI.17. $v = \lim v_n$ for the example in VI.7, Ex. 5.

b. Recall from I.3, Ex. 11eγ, p. 41, that a real function f defined on the product $C \times D$ of two convex polyhedra is "piecewise bi-linear" if there exists a finite partition of C (resp. D) into convex polyhedra C_m (resp. D_n) such that the restriction of f to each product $C_m \times D_n$ is bi-linear. Deduce from the above L.P. formulation in VI.7, Ex. 6a, that $V_n(p, q)$ is piecewise bi-linear (cf. I.3, Ex. 11h, p. 42).

c. Prove then that in order to compute $V_n(p, q)$ one can use the following finite algorithm:

Compute first $V_n(0, q)$ and $V_n(p, 0)$.

Given q_m that corresponds to a peak of $V_n(0, q)$ compute $V_n(p, q_m)$ and so on (and similarly in the other direction).

When no new peaks are reached extend $V_n(p, q)$ by bi-linearity.

d. Consider now the dependent case with state space K and initial probability and partitions p, K^{I}, K^{II}. Say that a function f on P is I-linear if for all p its restriction to $\Pi^{\mathrm{I}}(p)$ is linear and similarly for II-linear. Write $V_n(p)$ as the value of a linear programming problem as in VI.7, Ex. 6a, to prove that it is I-concave and II-convex. Let $Q(p) = \{q \in P \mid q^k = \delta\alpha^k\beta^k p^k$, where $p_\alpha = (\alpha^k p^k) \in \Pi^{\mathrm{I}}(p)$ and $p_\beta = (\beta^k p^k) \in \Pi^{\mathrm{II}}(p)\}$, and prove that $V_n(p)$ is piecewise I-II bi-linear on $Q(p)$ for each p.

7. Sequential games.

a. *A recursive formula.* Consider $\Gamma_n(p, q)$ as above (VI.7, Ex. 6a), but where the players are choosing their moves sequentially, being informed of the previous choice of their opponents. Consider first the reduced game where player I is restricted to use the move s at stage one (for all states) and let $V_n^s(p, q)$ be its value. Prove then that $V_n(p, q) = \mathrm{Cav}_p \max_s V_n^s(p, q)$.

HINT. Prove that against each first-stage strategy x_s^ℓ of player I, player II can decrease the payoff to $\sum_s \lambda(s) V_n^s(p^\ell(s), q)$ with $p^\ell(s) = \mathsf{Pr}_x(\ell \mid s)$ and $\lambda(s) = \mathsf{Pr}_x(s)$. Then use the minmax theorem.

Then deduce by induction that the recursive formula can be rewritten as:

$$nV_n(p,q) = \operatorname*{Cav}_p \max_s \operatorname*{Vex}_q \min_t \Big\{ \sum_{\ell,m} p^\ell q^m G_{st}^{\ell m} + (n-1)V_{n-1}(p,q) \Big\}.$$

b. *Monotonicity of the values.* Use then the fact that $\mathsf{Vex}(f+g) \ge \mathsf{Vex}\, f + \mathsf{Vex}\, g$ and $\mathsf{Cav}(f + \mathsf{Cav}\, f) = 2\,\mathsf{Cav}\, f$ to prove that the sequence $V_n(p,q)$ is increasing. Deduce that if player II is uninformed, the sequence $V_n(p)$ is constant (Ponssard and Zamir, 1973).

c. *Speed of convergence.* Let $f(p,q) = -(\sum_s \min_t \sum_{\ell m} p^\ell q^m G_{st}^{\ell m} + R_0)$, where R_0 is a constant such that $v_1 \ge v + f$. Assume by induction $nv_n \ge nv + f$ to get:

$$(n+1)v_{n+1}(p,q) \ge (n+1)\operatorname*{Cav}_p(\min\{u(p,q), v(p,q)\}) + f(p,q)$$

and use VI.7, Ex. 7b, and Proposition VI.4.10, p. 362, to get finally $|v - v_n| \le \frac{R}{n}$ for some constant R.

HINT. Take $\#L = 1$, $\#M = 2$, $G^1 = \begin{pmatrix} 0 & 1 \\ 1 & -2 \end{pmatrix}$, $G^2 = \begin{pmatrix} 1 & -2 \\ 0 & 1 \end{pmatrix}$ to prove that it is the best bound.

d. *Extend the previous results VI.7, Ex. 7a, VI.7, Ex. 7b, and VI.7, Ex. 7c to the dependent case.*

e. *Construction of optimal strategies.* (The length of the game being fixed, we drop the index n.) For each history h let V^h be the value of the "restricted game starting from h" and define:

$$A^h(p) = \{\alpha \in \mathbb{R}^L \mid \langle \alpha, q \rangle \le V^h(p,q) \text{ on } Q\},$$
$$A^h(p,q) = \{\alpha \in A^h(p) \mid \langle \alpha, q \rangle = V^h(p,q)\},$$

and similarly $B^h(q)$, $B^h(p,q)$. Prove, using VI.7, Ex. 7a, and VI.7, Ex. 6b, that for any $\ell \in L(p,q)$ there exists $(\lambda_s, p(s), \alpha_s)$ for $s \in S$ such that:

1. $\sum \lambda_s p(s) = p$, $\lambda_s \ge 0$, $\sum \lambda_s = 1$, $V(p,q) = \sum \lambda V^s(p(s), q)$.
2. $\alpha_s \in A^s(p(s))$.
3. $\langle (\sum \lambda_s \alpha_s - \alpha), q' \rangle \ge 0$ for all q' in Q.

Deduce that an optimal strategy for player I is to generate $p(s)$ at stage 1 and to take the corresponding α_s as the new parameter α_s for his future choice. (Note that this strategy will even be optimal after each history if after each odd history h, followed by some move t of player II, one chooses a maximal element in the set $\alpha' \in A^{ht}(p)$ with $\alpha' \ge \alpha^h$ as the new state parameter.)

8. Lack of information on $1\frac{1}{2}$ sides.

Consider the following game $\Gamma(\lambda, r, s)$ with λ, r, s in $[0,1]$: first, $t \in \{r, s\}$ is chosen, with $\mathsf{Pr}(t = r) = \lambda$, and this choice is told to player II; then a game with a lack of information on one side is played: there are two states of nature, say, two payoff matrices A and B, the choice is according to t, and only player I is informed.

a. Write this game as a game with incomplete information on both sides (dependent case) with four states of the world (cf. Chapter V) and $K_{\mathrm{I}} = \{(1,3),(2,4)\}$,

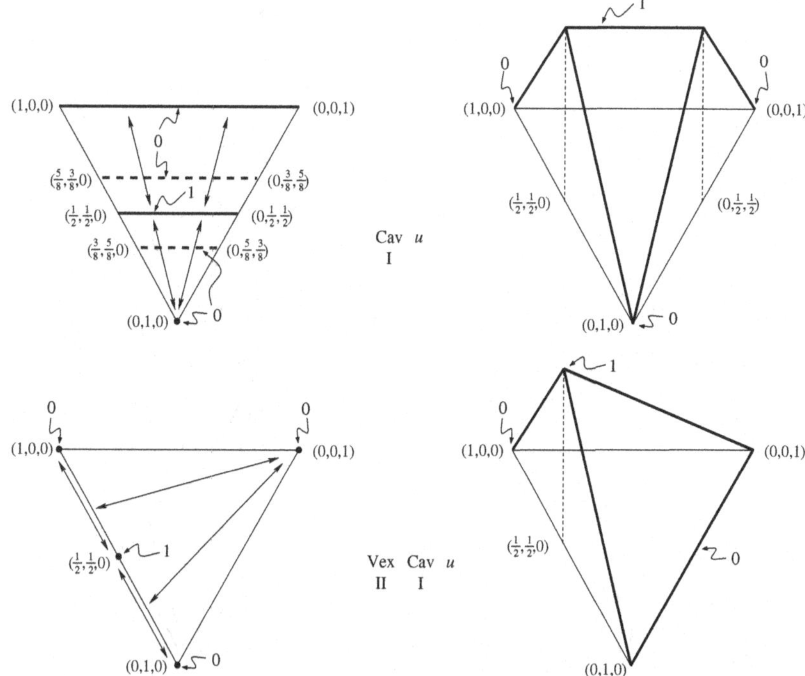

Figure VI.18. The functions $\mathsf{Cav}_{\mathrm{I}}\, u$ and $\mathsf{Vex}_{\mathrm{II}}\, \mathsf{Cav}_{\mathrm{I}}\, u$ in Ex. 8c.

$K_{\mathrm{II}} = \{(1,2)(3,4)\}$, $G^1 = G^3 = A$, $G^2 = G^4 = B$, and $p = (\lambda r, \lambda r', \lambda' s, \lambda' s')$. (Note that player I knows the true payoff matrix (state of nature) but not the beliefs of II (state of the world).)

b. Define w on $[0,1]$ by $w(q) = \operatorname{val}(qA + q'B)$, $\pi(p) = p_1/(p_1+p_2)$, $\rho(p) = p_3/(p_3+p_4)$, and $\mathsf{Vex}_{|a,b|}$ to be the Vex operator on the interval with end points a and b. Prove that:

- $\mathsf{Cav}_{\mathrm{I}}\, u(p) = \mathsf{Cav}\, w(p_1 + p_3)$
- $\mathsf{Vex}_{\mathrm{II}}\, u(p) = \mathsf{Vex}_{|\pi(p),\rho(p)|}\, w(p_1 + p_3)$
- $\mathsf{Vex}_{\mathrm{II}}\, \mathsf{Cav}_{\mathrm{I}}\, u(p) = \lambda\, \mathsf{Cav}\, w(r) + \lambda'\, \mathsf{Cav}\, w(s)$
- $\mathsf{Cav}_{\mathrm{I}}\, \mathsf{Vex}_{\mathrm{II}}\, u(p) =$ $\sup_{t,p^1,p^2}\{ t\, \mathsf{Vex}_{|\pi(p^1),\rho(p^1)|}\, w(p_1^1 + p_3^1) + t'\, \mathsf{Vex}_{|\pi(p^2),\rho(p^2)|}\, w(p_1^2 + p_3^2) \mid t \in [0,1],\ tp^1 + t'p^2 = p,\ p^i \in \Pi^{\mathrm{I}}(p) \quad i = 1,2 \}$

c. Example: Let $A = \begin{pmatrix} 5 & -3 \\ 0 & 0 \end{pmatrix}$, $B = \begin{pmatrix} -3 & 5 \\ 0 & 0 \end{pmatrix}$, and take $s = 1$. Verify that $\overline{v}$, v, and $\underline{v}$ have the shapes given in Figures VI.18, VI.19, and VI.20, and hence that there exists a game $\Gamma(\lambda, r, s)$ with $\underline{v} < v < \overline{v}$.

9. An analytic proof of Theorem VI.5.3.

Let $F = \{ f \mid f \text{ satisfies } (\alpha) \}$.

a. Prove that $F \neq \emptyset$, $\underline{w} = \inf\{ f \mid f \in F \}$ belongs to F and $\underline{w} = \mathsf{Cav}_{\mathrm{I}}\, \mathsf{Vex}_{\mathrm{II}} \max(u, \underline{w})$.

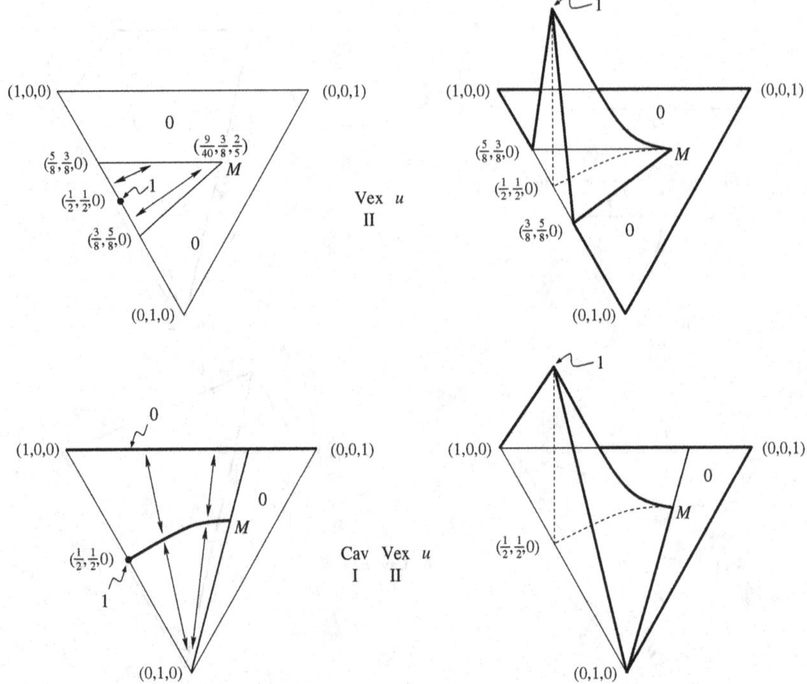

Figure VI.19. The functions $\mathsf{Vex}_{\mathrm{II}}\, u$ and $\mathsf{Cav}_{\mathrm{I}}\, \mathsf{Vex}_{\mathrm{II}}\, u$ in Ex. 8c.

b. Prove that for any real function f on Π, $\mathsf{Cav}_{\mathrm{I}}\, \mathsf{Vex}_{\mathrm{II}}\, f$ is II-convex.

Hint. Assume that g is II-convex. To show that $\mathsf{Cav}_{\mathrm{I}}\, g$ is II-convex, prove that $\mathsf{Cav}_{\mathrm{I}}\, g = T^n g$ for n large enough, with:

$$Tg(p) = \sup_{\mu, p^1, p^2} \{\mu g(p^1) + \mu' g(p^2) \mid p^i \in \pi_{\mathrm{I}}(p), \mu \in [0,1], \mu p^1 + \mu' p^2 = p\},$$

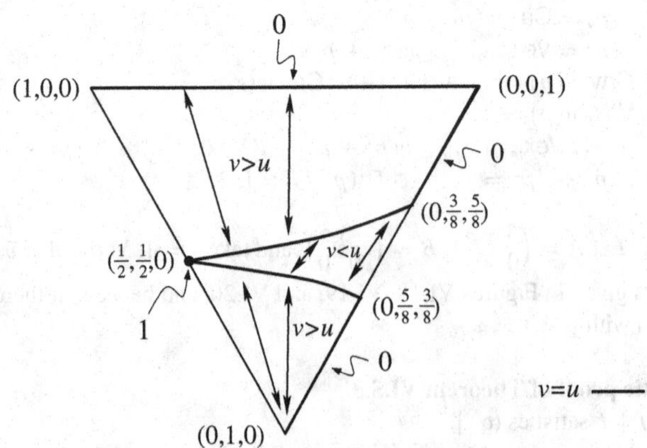

Figure VI.20. The functions u and $v = \lim_{n\to\infty} v_n$ in Ex. 8c.

and that T preserves II-convexity. For this last point, to each triple (μ, p^1, p^2) as above and its dual triple (λ, q^1, q^2) (i.e., with $q^i \in \Pi^{\mathrm{II}}(p)$, $\lambda \in [0,1]$ and $\lambda q^1 + \lambda' q^2 = p$) associate new variables $\pi_{ij}, \alpha_i, \beta_j$, for $i = 1,2$, $j = 1,2$, with:

$$\pi_{ij} \in \Pi^{\mathrm{II}}(p^i), \qquad \alpha_i \pi_{i1} + \alpha_i' \pi_{i2} = p^i, \qquad \alpha_i \in [0,1] \quad i = 1,2$$

$$\pi_{ij} \in \Pi^{\mathrm{I}}(p^j), \qquad \beta_j \pi_{1j} + \beta_j' \pi_{2j} = q^j, \qquad \beta_j \in [0,1] \quad j = 1,2$$

and $\mu\alpha_1 = \lambda\beta_1$, $(1-\mu)\alpha_2 = \lambda(1-\beta_2)$, $\mu(1-\alpha_1) = (1-\lambda)\beta_2$, $(1-\mu)(1-\alpha_1) = (1-\lambda)(1-\beta_2)$.

c. Deduce that $\underline{w} = \mathrm{Vex}_{\mathrm{II}} \max(u, \underline{w})$. Define $\{\underline{u}_n\}$ by $\underline{u}_{n+1} = \mathrm{Cav}_{\mathrm{I}} \mathrm{Vex}_{\mathrm{II}} \max(u, \underline{u}_n)$ with $\underline{u}_0 = -\infty$, and prove that $\underline{u}_n$ increases uniformly to $\underline{w}$. Introduce similarly $\overline{w}$ and $\overline{u}_n$.

d. Let $\mathscr{U} = \{u \mid u$ can be written as $u(p) = \max_{i \in I} \min_{j \in J} \sum_k a_{ij}^k p^k$, I, J finite sets$\}$. Prove that, for all u in $\mathscr{U}$, $\overline{w} \leq \underline{w}$.

HINT. Define $v_0 \equiv 0$ and $n v_n(p) = \mathrm{Cav}_{\mathrm{I}} \max_i \mathrm{Vex}_{\mathrm{II}} \min_j (\sum_k a_{ij}^k p^k + (n-1) v_{n-1}(p))$ and prove: $v_n \leq \underline{u}_n$, $v_n \geq \overline{u}_n + R/n$ for some constant R. Compare VI.7, Ex. 7c.

e. Prove that $\underline{w} \leq \overline{w}$.

HINT. Show that one obtains the same $\underline{w}, \overline{w}$ when starting with $u' = \max(u, \underline{u}_1)$ and deduce inductively that $\overline{w} \geq \underline{u}_n$, and the result for $u \in \mathscr{U}$.

f. Show finally that $\mathscr{U}$ is dense in $C(\Pi)$ (compare Proposition VI.5.1, p. 363) and use Proposition VI.5.2, p. 363.

10. Consider a game Γ as defined in Chapter V, with corresponding v_n and u. Define a game Γ_L' where the set of moves of player I is now $S \times K$, the signaling matrices are $H'^{\mathrm{I}}, H'^{\mathrm{II}}$ with

$$H'^{\mathrm{I}}((s,k),t) = H^{\mathrm{I},k}(s,t),$$

and similarly for H'^{II}, with the same initial information, and with payoff matrices:

$$G^k((s,k),t) = \begin{cases} -L & \text{if } k' \neq k, \text{ for all } s, t \\ G^k(s,t) & \text{if } k = k'. \end{cases}$$

a. Prove that Γ_L' belongs to the class of Chapter VI with associated $v_{n,L}'$ and u_L', hence $\lim_{n\to\infty} v_{n,L}' = \mathrm{Cav}\, u_L'$.

b. Show that $v_{n,L}' \geq v_n$ and that $\mathrm{Cav}\, u_L' \searrow \mathrm{Cav}\, u$ as $L \to +\infty$.

c. Deduce Theorem V.3.3, p. 230.

HINT. To avoid circular reasoning, since Theorem V.3.3 is apparently used in part C of VI.3.1, p. 339, proceed as follows: first the convergence of v_n is established. This yields that $\lim v_n = \mathrm{Cav}\, u$ for the games of Chapter V, as seen above. This implies immediately $v_\infty = \mathrm{Cav}\, u$ for those games; hence Theorem V.3.3 follows, and finally VI.3.1.

11. Asymptotically optimal strategies in finite games. (Heuer, 1991b)

Assuming Theorem VI.5.3, p. 363 (cf. also VI.7, Ex. 9, p. 385) we construct strategies that guarantee $v + O(1/\sqrt{n})$ in Γ_n for the case of standard signaling, hence implying Corollary VI.4.9, p. 361, for the limit of v_n and the speed of convergence.

The basic idea is reminiscent of Blackwell's approachability strategy (say, for II, cf. V.5, Ex. 2, p. 302), starting with a vector β supporting v, but then aiming at stage

r to reach β_r (in the remaining $n - r + 1$-stage game) so that, given the past payoffs, the average would be β. We will consider the independent case (cf. examples in Section VI.7, p. 366, and VI.7, Ex. 6–VI.7, Ex. 7 p. 382). Hence $K = L \times M$, $p \in \Delta(L)$, $q \in \Delta(M)$, and $v = \mathsf{Cav}_p \min(u, v) = \mathsf{Vex}_q \max(u, v)$. Let $B(q) = \{\beta \in \mathbb{R}^K \mid \langle \beta, p \rangle \geq v(p, q), \forall p \in \Delta(L)\}$, and $B(p, q) = \{\beta \in B(q) \mid \langle \beta, p \rangle = v(p, q)\}$ is the supergradient of v at the point (p, q), in the direction of p.

a. Note that if $q = \sum_j \lambda_j q_j$, with $q_j \in \Delta(M)$ and $\lambda \in \Delta(J)$, then $\sum_j \lambda_j B(q_j) \subseteq B(q)$.

Prove that if moreover $v(p, q) = \sum_j \lambda_j v(p, q_j)$, with $v(p, q_j) = u(p, q_j)$ and $v(p, \cdot) < u(p, \cdot)$ on the interior of the convex hull of the q_j's, then $\sum_j \lambda_j B(q_j) = B(q)$. (Use the continuity of u and v and the Remarks in Section VI.7, p. 366.)

b. Recall that $\overline{\gamma}_n(\sigma, \tau) = \mathsf{E}^{p,q}_{\sigma,\tau}(\frac{1}{n}\sum_{r=1}^n g_r)$, where g_r is the payoff at stage r. Define $p_r^\ell = P(\ell \mid \mathscr{H}_r)$, $q_r^m = P(m \mid \mathscr{H}_r)$, and $\rho_r^\ell = \mathsf{E}^{\ell,q}_{\sigma,\tau}(g_r \mid \mathscr{H}_r)$ (recall standard signaling). Hence $\overline{\gamma}_n(\sigma, \tau)$ can also be written as $\mathsf{E}_{\sigma,\tau}(\frac{1}{n}\langle p_n, \sum_r \rho_r \rangle)$.

c. We now define a strategy for II inductively. Given (p, q) and $\beta \in B(p, q)$, let $\pi_1 = p$, $q_1 = q$, $\xi_1 = \widetilde{\beta}_1 = \beta_1 = \widetilde{\xi}_1 = \beta$. At stage 1 player II plays optimally in $D(p_1, q_1)$. Then define ξ_2 by $n\widetilde{\xi}_1 = (n-1)\xi_2 + \rho_1$. Similarly at stage r, given ξ_r, we consider the following cases:

(1) If $\xi_r \in B(q_{r-1})$, τ is arbitrary at this stage. One puts $\pi_r = \pi_{r-1}$, $q_r = q_{r-1}$, $\widetilde{\xi}_r = \xi_r = \widetilde{\beta}_r = \beta_r$.

(2) If $\xi_r \notin B(q_{r-1})$, let β_r denote its projection on $B(q_{r-1})$; this defines $\pi_r \in \Delta(L)$, π_r proportional to $\beta_r - \xi_r$, such that $\beta_r \in B(\pi_r, q_{r-1})$.
- If $v(\pi_r, q_{r-1}) \geq u(\pi_r, q_{r-1})$, τ consists of playing optimally in $D(\pi_r, q_r)$ at that stage, with $q_r = q_{r-1}$. Then $\widetilde{\beta}_r = \beta_r$ and $\widetilde{\xi}_r = \xi_r$.
- If $v(\pi_r, q_{r-1}) < u(\pi_r, q_{r-1})$, use VI.7, Ex. 11b, to decompose β_r as $\sum_j \beta_{r,j}$ with $\beta_{r,j} \in B(\pi_r, q_{r-1,j})$. In this case τ consists of first doing a splitting (Proposition V.1.2, p. 216) to generate the $q_{r-1,j}$'s, and then if j is chosen, playing optimally in $D(\pi_r, q_r)$ with, obviously, $q_r = q_{r-1,j}$. Then let $\widetilde{\beta}_r = \beta_{r,j}$ and $\widetilde{\xi}_r = \xi_r - \beta_r + \widetilde{\beta}_r$ and note that $\mathsf{E}(\widetilde{\xi}_r \mid \xi_r) = \xi_r$.

Finally let us define ξ_{r+1} through the following equation: $(n - r + 1)\widetilde{\xi}_r = (n - r)\xi_{r+1} + \rho_r$.

Show that given any non-revealing $\overline{\sigma}$ one has $\mathsf{E}_{\overline{\sigma},\tau}[\langle\langle \xi_r - \beta_r \rangle, (\widetilde{\beta}_r - \rho_r)\rangle] \leq 0$.

d. Show that:

$$\overline{\gamma}_n(\sigma, \tau) - v(p, q) = \frac{1}{n}\mathsf{E}_{\sigma,\tau}(\langle p_n, \rho_n - \xi_n \rangle) \leq \frac{2C}{n} + \frac{1}{n}\mathsf{E}_{\sigma,\tau}(\langle p_n, \beta_n - \xi_n \rangle),$$

and note also that there exists $\overline{\sigma}$ non-revealing such that:

$$\left|\mathsf{E}_{\sigma,\tau}(\langle p_n, \beta_n - \xi_n \rangle)\right| \leq \left(\mathsf{E}_{\overline{\sigma},\tau}(\|\beta_n - \xi_n\|_2^2)\right)^{1/2}.$$

Then prove inductively:

$$\mathsf{E}[\|\xi_r - \beta_r\|^2] \leq 4\#LC^2 r/(n + 1 - r)^2,$$

and conclude.

HINT. $\mathsf{E}[\|\xi_{r+1} - \beta_{r+1}\|^2] \leq \mathsf{E}[\|\xi_{r+1} - \widetilde{\beta}_r\|^2]$; then use the equality $\widetilde{\xi}_r - \widetilde{\beta}_r = \xi_r - \beta_r$ and VI.7, Ex. 11e).

e. Extend the result to the dependent case.

12. A continuum of types on both sides. (Following Forges, 1988a)

Remark VI.7.5. In this chapter, notably in Section V.3.b, we could not treat the case of a continuum of types of both sides; only the "approached player" could have a continuum of types. As underscored repeatedly in Chapter III, the inability to study the general case at this stage seems at least in part to be due to a lack of study of the fundamental concepts in Chapter III; cf., e.g., the introduction to Section III.4.b, many remarks thereafter, and most of Section III.4.d, in particular Remark III.4.16 and the final remarks. In particular, the first natural step toward a generalization would be to reformulate the known results (in particular Theorem VI.3.10, p. 351) in the canonical framework of Chapter III, and it was shown there (final remarks) that even the basic concept of concavification is not clear.

Yet we need such results in Chapter IX, in order to study communication equilibria of games with a *finite* set of types, for the case where the approaching player has a continuum of types (even though there the approached player could have a finite set of types). Another reason for studying the general case is the basic problem underlying this book: to obtain maxmin, minmax, and lim v_n for all two-person zero-sum repeated games (Chapter IV), or at least, to begin with, for all two-person zero-sum repeated games with incomplete information (i.e., to generalize this chapter to the case where the signaling function Q is state dependent). Indeed, as shown in Chapter VIII (Section VIII.2), the general case leads to situations where the number of points in the support of the current posterior consistent probability (Chapter IV, Section IV.3) grows to infinity, and so conceivably one might as well study them from the outset without restricting the support to being finite, and anyway a number of concepts and tools will presumably be required to work directly on $\mathscr{P}$: the chief candidates for those will be the ones already needed in the particular case of this chapter.

It is thus clear that a satisfactory treatment of the present chapter would require the framework of a continuum of types on both sides.

In a first stage, one could restrict the prior to being absolutely continuous w.r.t. some product measure (i.e., w.r.t. the product of its marginals). This restriction, which is preserved when going from an information scheme to its canonical representation, would keep the complete symmetry between both players in the assumptions of this chapter (hence allowing one by duality to cut the number of statements and proofs in half) and would still be sufficiently general to encompass all known cases and to lead to the elucidation of the right concepts, while at the same time being technically quite helpful, e.g., in arguments like the one below, or possibly in proving that player I can defend Vex Cav.

We present next a very first result in this direction: not only is it extremely partial, but chiefly it involves the additional restriction of statistically perfect monitoring of player II by player I. But it will suffice for our applications in Chapter IX.

a. Consider a game with statistically perfect monitoring of player II by player I. Describe the initial information of the players in the following way:

- The space of types of player II is a measurable space $(J, \mathscr{J})$.
- The space of types of player I is a measurable space $(I, \mathscr{I})$ together with a transition probability θ ($= \theta_i(k, dj)$) from $(I, \mathscr{I})$ to $(J, \mathscr{J}) \times K$, and an initial probability measure γ on $(I, \mathscr{I})$.

As usual (cf. Remark VI.3.19, p. 357), let $\mathbf{H} = \{h\colon \mathbb{R}_+^K \to \mathbb{R} \mid h$ is convex, positively homogeneous of degree 1, $h_{|\Delta(K)}$ has Lipschitz constant C and is $\leq C$, $\int_{\Delta(K)} h(\pi)\mu(d\pi) \geq u(\mu)\ \forall \mu \in \Delta(\Delta(K))\}$, and let (Theorem VI.3.10) $\mathbf{T}$ be the set of transition probabilities $\mathbf{t}$ from $(J, \mathscr{J})$ to $\mathbf{H}$.

Given $\mathbf{t} \in \mathbf{T}$, let $z_{\mathbf{t}}(\theta) = \int_{\mathbf{H}} h\left[\left(\int_J \mathbf{t}(dh|j)\theta(k, dj)\right)_{k \in K}\right] \quad \forall \theta \in \Delta(K \times J)$.

(1) • Player II's strategy induced by $\mathbf{t}$ guarantee that type i's payoff is $\leq z_{\mathbf{t}}(\theta_i)$.
• $z_{\mathbf{t}}(\theta_i)$ is measurable on $(I, \mathscr{I})$ and convex in θ.

(2) Assume that the measures θ_i $(i \in I)$ are dominated, i.e., $\exists \overline{\theta} \in \Delta(J)$, such that $\forall i \in I$, θ_i is absolutely continuous w.r.t. $\overline{\theta}$. Then $\forall \mathscr{L}$ Banach limit, $\forall \tau_0$ strategy of player II, $\exists \mathbf{t} \in \mathbf{T}$ s.t.:

$$\forall \lambda \in \Delta(I) \quad \sup_\sigma \mathscr{L}\,\mathsf{E}^{\lambda}_{\sigma,\tau_0}(\overline{g}_m) \geq \int z_{\mathbf{t}}(\theta_i)\lambda(d_i).$$

Hint. The first point of (1) is as in the text; measurability is standard (observe first that $i \mapsto \int_J \mathbf{t}(dh|j)\theta_i(k, dj)$ is a transition probability from $(I, \mathscr{I})$ to $K \times H$, hence a measurable map to $\Delta(K \times H)$ (Appendix A.9.e), and use the lower semi-continuity of ϕ in III.4, Ex. 4, p. 167). Similarly convexity follows from that of ϕ.

As for part (2): let $F_\sigma(\lambda) = \mathscr{L}\,\mathsf{E}^{\lambda}_{\sigma,\tau_0}(\overline{g}_m)$, $F(\lambda) = \sup_\sigma F_\sigma(\lambda)$; clearly F_σ is affine, and so F is convex. There is no loss of generality in assuming $\mathscr{J}$ separable, by reducing it first to the σ-field generated by τ_0. Fix then an increasing sequence of measurable partitions Π_n that generates $\mathscr{J}$. For any Π, define Γ^Π as the same game, but where player II's σ-field $\mathscr{J}$ is reduced to $\mathscr{J}^\Pi$, which is the (finite) σ-field spanned by Π. Viewing τ_0 as a transition probability from $(J, \mathscr{J})$ to the pure strategy space in Γ_∞, define also τ_0^Π, the strategy in Γ^Π corresponding to τ_0 in Γ, as $\mathsf{E}_{\overline{\theta}}(\tau_0(j) \mid \mathscr{J}^\Pi)$. Let finally F^n_σ and F^n be the functions corresponding to F_σ and F in Γ^{Π_n} with $\tau_0^{\Pi_n}$.

Observe that, since $\mathscr{J}^{\Pi_n} \subseteq \mathscr{J}$, $\tau_0^{\Pi_n}$ is also a strategy in Γ; and clearly, for all λ, σ, and m, $\mathsf{E}^{\lambda}_{\sigma,\tau_0^{\Pi_n}}(\overline{g}_m)$ is the same, say, $F^n_{\sigma,m}(\lambda)$, whether computed in Γ or in Γ^{Π_n}.

• Let $f^n_k(i, j) = \sum_{B \in \Pi_n} \mathbb{1}_B(j)\theta_i(B \times k)/\overline{\theta}(B \times k)$, and $f_k = \liminf_{m \to \infty} f^n_k$. f^n and f are measurable on $I \times J$, and by the martingale convergence theorem f^n converges to f a.e. and in L_1 under $\overline{\theta}(dj)\lambda(di)$, $\forall \lambda$. And f is a Radon–Nikodym density of $\theta_i(k, dj)\lambda(di)$ w.r.t. $\overline{\theta}(dj)\lambda(di)$. Now, since $|\overline{g}_m| \leq C$ uniformly, computation in Γ shows that:

$$\begin{aligned}&\left|F^n_{\sigma,m}(\lambda) - F_{\sigma,m}(\lambda)\right|\\ &\quad \leq C\int \sum_k \left|f^n_k(i, j) - f_k(i, j)\right|\overline{\theta}(dj)\lambda(di) \stackrel{\text{def}}{=} CG^n(\lambda),\end{aligned}$$

with $G^n(\lambda)$ converging to zero as seen above. Hence $|F^n_\sigma(\lambda) - F_\sigma(\lambda)| \leq CG^n(\lambda)$, and thus also:

$$F^n(\lambda) \to F(\lambda). \tag{9}$$

• Observe that Γ^Π is a game with a finite set of types for player II; hence Theorem VI.3.10 is applicable. Denote by $\pi(\lambda)$ the image measure of λ in $\Delta(K \times \Pi)$; since τ_0^Π is still a strategy in the "semi-canonical" game of Theorem VI.3.10, $F^\Pi(\lambda)$ is a function φ of $\pi(\lambda)$. Define φ as $+\infty$ outside the range of the map π. By part (7), we have $\varphi \geq \operatorname{Vex}\operatorname{Cav}$ on $\Delta(\Delta(K \times \Pi))$, and the convexity of φ follows immediately from that of F^Π and from the linearity of $\lambda \mapsto \pi(\lambda)$. Hence by part (6) there exists $\forall n$ $\mathbf{t}^n \in \mathbf{T}$ ($\mathscr{J}^{\Pi_n}$-measurable) such that:

$$\int z_{\mathbf{t}^n}(\theta^n_i)\lambda(di) \leq F^n(\lambda) \quad \forall \lambda, \tag{10}$$

where $\theta^n_i = f^n_k(i, j)\overline{\theta}(dj)$.

• $\mathbf{T}$ is compact metric since $\mathbf{H}$ is so and $\mathscr{J}$ is separable (II.1, Ex. 17c, p. 87). Extract thus if necessary a subsequence such that $\mathbf{t}^n$ converges, say, to $\mathbf{t}$. Consider now

$P_i^n = \int_J \mathbf{t}^n(dh|j)\, f_k^n(i,j)\overline{\theta}(dj) \in \Delta(K \times H)$. Since f^n converges in L_1 to f and $\mathbf{t}^n$ converges weak* to $\mathbf{t}$, we get that P_i^n converges weakly to P_i for all i. So, by III.4, Ex. 4, p. 167, using the function $f(h,p) = h(p)$, $\liminf_{n\to\infty} \int_H h\left[\{\int_J P_i^n(k,dh)\}_{k\in K}\right] \geq \int_H h\left[\{\int_J P_i(k,dh)\}_{k\in K}\right]$, i.e., $\liminf_{n\to\infty} z_{\mathbf{t}^n}(\theta_i^n) \geq z_{\mathbf{t}}(\theta_i)$. Hence, by Fatou's lemma, (9) and (10) yield the result.

b. *Particular cases.*

α. Cf. Remark VI.3.20, p. 357.

β. If player I's information includes the knowledge of the true state of nature (as in VI.7, Ex. 8), then his posteriors are, whatever $\mathbf{t}$ is used, concentrated on the true state, and so only the values of h at the vertices of $\Delta(K)$ matter. Thus any h can be taken affine (replaced by its concavification). Further randomizing over different h's serves no purpose, since the posteriors are not affected: one can as well use the average h. So in this case, a "strategy" $\mathbf{t}$ of player II is simply a measurable map from $(J, \mathscr{J})$ to $\{h \in \mathbb{R}^K \mid \forall p \in \Delta(K), \langle h, p\rangle \geq u(\mu)\ \forall \mu \in \Delta(\Delta(K)) \text{ with } \overline{\mu} = p\}$.

(In case there is statistically perfect monitoring on both sides (cf. VI.7, Ex. 12bα above), this last condition clearly reduces to $\langle h, p\rangle \geq u(p)\ \forall p \in \Delta(K)$.)

γ. Observe how the case in VI.7, Ex. 12bβ, above, yields a direct generalization of the approachability results in Chapter V.

CHAPTER VII

Stochastic Games

A stochastic game is a repeated game where the players are at each stage informed of the current state and the previous moves. According to the general model of Chapter IV, this means that the signal transmitted to each player i according to the transition probability Q includes the new state and the previous moves. It follows that the game is equivalently described by the action sets S^i, $i \in \mathbf{I}$, the state space K, a transition probability P from $S \times K$ to K, and a payoff mapping g from $S \times K$ to $\mathbb{R}^{\mathbf{I}}$.

VII.1. DISCOUNTED CASE

It appears that in this framework our finiteness assumptions are not really used and that we can work with the following more general setup:

- The state space is a measurable space $(\Omega, \mathscr{A})$.
- The action space of player i is a measurable space $(S^i, \mathscr{S}^i)$ (with $S = \prod_i S^i$).
- P is a transition probability from $\Omega \times S$ to Ω; hence for A in $\mathscr{A}$, $P(A \mid \omega, s)$ is the probability that tomorrow's state belongs to A given today's state ω and actions s.

A strategy for a player is again a transition probability from histories of the form $(\omega_1, s_1, \ldots, s_{n-1}, \omega_n)$ to actions. A **Markov** strategy depends only, at stage n, on the current state ω_n. A **stationary** strategy is a time-invariant function of the infinite past, accompanied by a fictitious history before time zero. To force the influence of the remote past to vanish, one may in addition impose the condition that the function be continuous, say, in the product topology.

The main tool when dealing with the discounted case is the following class of one-shot games: given a vector $f(= (f^i)_{i \in \mathbf{I}})$ of bounded real-valued measurable functions on $(\Omega, \mathscr{A})$, define the single-stage game $\Gamma(f)_\omega$, $\omega \in \Omega$, with action sets S^i and (vector) payoff:

$$\phi(f)_\omega(s) = g(\omega, s) + \int f(\tilde{\omega}) P(d\tilde{\omega} \mid \omega, s).$$

VII.1.a. Zero-Sum Case

Here the basic technique for establishing the existence of a value is based on the "contraction mapping principle."

Lemma VII.1.1. *Let (E, d) be a complete metric space, $\varepsilon > 0$, and $f : E \to E$, such that $d(f(x), f(y)) \leq (1-\varepsilon)d(x, y)$ for all (x, y). Then f has a unique fixed point $\overline{x} \in E$, and for any $x \in E$, the sequence $f^n(x)$ converges to $\overline{x}$.*

Proof. $d(f^{n+1}(x), f^n(x)) \leq (1-\varepsilon)d(f^n(x), f^{n-1}(x))$, and hence by induction $d(f^{n+1}(x), f^n(x)) \leq (1-\varepsilon)^n d(f(x), x)$; thus by the triangle inequality:

$$d\big(f^{n+k}(x), f^n(x)\big) \leq \Big(\sum_{i=n}^{\infty}(1-\varepsilon)^i\Big)d\big(f(x), x\big) = \frac{(1-\varepsilon)^n}{\varepsilon}d\big(f(x), x\big).$$

Since the right-hand member goes to zero with n, the sequence $f^n(x)$ is a Cauchy sequence; hence there is convergence (by completeness), say, to $\overline{x}$. But $d(f^{n+1}(y), f(\overline{x})) \leq (1-\varepsilon)d(f^n(y), \overline{x})$, and hence going to the limit yields $d(\overline{y}, f(\overline{x})) \leq (1-\varepsilon)d(\overline{y}, \overline{x})$: setting $y = x$ (hence $\overline{y} = \overline{x}$) yields $d(\overline{x}, f(\overline{x})) = 0$; i.e., $\overline{x}$ is a fixed point; then setting $y = \overline{y}$ to be any other fixed point yields $d(\overline{y}, \overline{x}) \leq (1-\varepsilon)d(\overline{y}, \overline{x})$, hence $\overline{y} = \overline{x} : \overline{x}$ is the unique fixed point. ■

The idea about use of the contraction principle in proving the existence of a value of Γ_λ is that any uncertainty about tomorrow's payoff is reduced by a factor of $(1-\lambda)$, λ being the discount factor, when evaluated in today's terms. So if one can solve "today's" game for any given payoffs for the future, one will get a contraction mapping.

The basic requirement is thus that "today's game" has a value for any choice of a "payoff for the future" in an appropriate complete metric space and yields a payoff in the same metric space. So, for any given f in (B, d), which is a complete metric space of bounded measurable functions on $(\Omega, \mathscr{A})$, with d the uniform distance, our aim is to show that (with the notation of Section IV.3.b, p. 184):

(1) For each ω in Ω the game $\Gamma(f)_\omega$ has a value, say, $\Psi(f)(\omega)$.
(2) $\Psi(f)$ belongs to B.
(3) The games $\Gamma(f)$ have ε-optimal strategies (i.e., strategies that are ε-optimal for any $\omega \in \Omega$).

Lemma VII.1.2. *Assume that the distance on B is $d(f_1, f_2) = \sup_\Omega |f_1(\omega) - f_2(\omega)|$; then under (1) and (2), there exists a solution $V_\lambda \in B$ of $f = \Psi[(1-\lambda)f]$.*

Proof. Ψ maps B into B and is clearly monotone. Since $\Psi(f + c) = c + \Psi(f)$ for any constant function c, we have:

$$d(\Psi(f_1), \Psi(f_2)) \leq d(f_1, f_2).$$

Thus $f \mapsto \Psi[(1-\lambda)f]$ satisfies Lemma VII.1.1. ■

Lemma VII.1.3. *Under (1), (2), and (3), Γ_λ has a value λV_λ. If μ is an ε-optimal strategy in $\Gamma((1-\lambda)V_\lambda)$, then the corresponding stationary strategy $\overline{\mu}$ is ε-optimal in Γ_λ.*

Proof. For any f in B and any strategies σ and τ in Γ_λ, the expectation

$$\mathsf{E}_{\sigma,\tau}\Big(\sum_{m\leq n}(1-\lambda)^{m-1}g_m + (1-\lambda)^n f(\omega_{n+1})\Big)$$

converges (uniformly) to $\overline{\gamma}_\lambda(\sigma,\tau)/\lambda$ as n goes to ∞.

Conditional on $\mathscr{H}_m$ (generated by $(\omega_1, s_1, \ldots, s_{m-1}, \omega_m)$), one has by the definition of $\overline{\mu}$:

$$\mathsf{E}_{\overline{\mu},\tau}\big(g_m + (1-\lambda)(V_\lambda(\omega_{m+1}) - \delta)\,\big|\,\mathscr{H}_m\big) \geq V_\lambda(\omega_m) - \varepsilon - (1-\lambda)\delta.$$

So taking $\delta = \varepsilon/\lambda$ one obtains:

$$\mathsf{E}_{\overline{\mu},\tau}\Big(\sum_{m\leq n}(1-\lambda)^{m-1}g_m + (1-\lambda)^n\big(V_\lambda(\omega_{n+1}) - \frac{\varepsilon}{\lambda}\big)\Big) \geq V_\lambda - \frac{\varepsilon}{\lambda};$$

hence $\overline{\gamma}_\lambda(\overline{\mu},\tau) \geq \lambda V_\lambda - \varepsilon$. ∎

Remark VII.1.1. Using similarly V_n for the non-normalized value nv_n of Γ_n, one obtains in the same way $V_{n+1} = \Psi(V_n)$, with $V_0 = 0$.

The following two examples are meant merely to illustrate the method; they do not strive for the utmost generality (cf., e.g., VII.4, Ex. 18, for the more general form of the following proposition).

Proposition VII.1.4. *The state space is a standard Borel (cf. Appendix A.6, p.517) space $(\Omega, \mathscr{A})$, the action sets are compact metric spaces S and T, and the payoff function $g(\omega, s, t)$ and the transition probability $P(A \mid \omega, s, t)$ are, for each given $A \in \mathscr{A}$, measurable on $(\Omega \times S \times T)$ and are, for fixed ω, separately continuous in s and in t. Further, g is bounded. Then the discounted game has a value and $\mathscr{A}$-measurable optimal stationary Markov strategies.*

Proof. Consider the Banach space B of bounded measurable functions on $(\Omega, \mathscr{A})$. For $f \in B$ (representing the future (non-normalized) payoff), today's payoff is $h(\omega, s, t) = \phi((1-\lambda)f)_\omega(s,t)$. The assumptions guarantee that this is, like g, measurable on $\Omega \times S \times T$ and, for each ω, separately continuous in s and t. We know from Theorem I.2.4, p. 21, that, for each ω, such a game has a value $V(\omega)$. Clearly $\phi((1-\lambda)f)$ is bounded, and hence V also. It remains to show the measurability of V.

For μ in $\Delta(S)$, let $H(\omega, \mu, t) = \int h(\omega, s, t)\mu(ds)$: the measurability of H is easy and well known (e.g., just approximate the integrand by a linear combination of indicator functions of sets $A \times X \times Y$, with $A \in \mathscr{A}$, and $X \in \mathscr{S}$, $Y \in \mathscr{T}$), its linearity and (weak) continuity in μ is obvious, and the continuity in t follows immediately from Lebesgue's bounded convergence theorem. Hence $F(\omega, \mu) = \min_t H(\omega, \mu, t)$ is measurable (because by continuity it is sufficient to take the infimum over a countable dense set) and upper semi-continuous and concave in μ. Similarly for ν in $\Delta(T)$, we have a lower semi-continuous, convex measurable function $G(\omega, \nu)$ defined by $G(\omega, \nu) = \max_s \int h(\omega, s, t)\nu(dt)$. Hence the graph $\{(\omega, \mu, \nu) \mid F(\omega, \mu) \geq G(\omega, \nu)\}$ is measurable and has, for each ω, compact non-empty values, which are the corresponding optimal strategy pairs. Such a graph has a measurable selection (Appendix A.7.i, p. 519, and Appendix A.8.b, p. 519), thus yielding measurable optimal strategy selections (μ_ω, ν_ω), and also the measurability of $V(\omega) = F(\omega, \mu_\omega)$ (by composition).

The result follows now from Lemma VII.1.3. ■

In the next proposition, we relax the very strong continuity assumption on the transition probabilities as a function of the actions, at the expense of stronger assumptions on the dependence on the state.

Proposition VII.1.5. *Assume the state space Ω is metrizable and the action sets S and T are compact metric, and that $g(\omega, s, t)$ and $\int f(\tilde{\omega})P(\tilde{\omega} \mid \omega, s, t)$ are, for each bounded continuous f, continuous on $\Omega \times S$ for fixed t and on $\Omega \times T$ for fixed s. Further, g is bounded. Then the discounted game has a value (which is continuous as a function of the initial state) and Borel-measurable optimal stationary Markov strategies.*

Proof. We show that, under those assumptions, we get a contracting operator on the space B of bounded continuous functions on Ω. We use the notation of the previous proof. h is separately continuous in (ω, s) and (ω, t). Hence $V(\omega)$ exists. It follows that H is continuous in (ω, t) (by Lebesgue's dominated convergence theorem, as before). Hence $F(\omega, \mu)$ is, for fixed μ, continuous in ω (by continuity of $H(\cdot, \mu, \cdot)$ and compactness of T). Hence $V(\omega) = \sup_\mu F(\omega, \mu)$ is lower semi-continuous. Dually V is upper semi-continuous, hence continuous, i.e., $V \in B$: we have our contracting operator; the rest of the proof is similar to Proposition VII.1.4, using this time that the optimal strategy correspondence is upper semi-continuous. ■

Remark VII.1.2. In some sense Proposition VII.1.5 is much better than Proposition VII.1.4: at least, if one were to strengthen the separate continuity property in Proposition VII.1.4 to a joint continuity property, one could immediately construct a separable metrizable topology on Ω such that the assumptions of Proposition VII.1.5 would also hold (with joint continuity). So Proposition VII.1.5 "essentially" includes Proposition VII.1.4; but it allows complete flexibility in the transitions; e.g., the next state is a continuous function of current state and actions, while in Proposition VII.1.4 one is, for example, constrained to a dominated set of probabilities when a player's action varies.

VII.1.b. Non-Zero-Sum Case (Finite)

We assume here again that the basic spaces (S and Ω) are finite. Recall that a subgame perfect equilibrium is an **I**-tuple σ such that after any history h, $h = (\omega_1, s_1, \ldots, \omega_n, s_n)$, σ_h is an equilibrium in Γ_λ, where σ_h is defined on $h' = (\omega'_1, s'_1, \ldots, \omega'_m)$ by $\sigma_h(h') = \sigma(\omega_1, s_1, \ldots, \omega_n, s_n, \omega'_1, s'_1, \ldots, \omega'_m)$.

Lemma VII.1.6. *Assume that* $x = (x(\cdot \mid \omega))_{\omega \in \Omega}$ *with* $x(\cdot \mid \omega) \in X (= \prod_i \Delta(S^i))$ *form, for each* ω*, a Nash equilibrium of* $\Gamma((1-\lambda)f)_\omega$ *with payoff* $f(\omega)$*; then the corresponding stationary strategies* $\overline{x}$ *define a subgame perfect equilibrium of* Γ_λ *with payoff* λf*.*

Proof. As in Lemma VII.1.3, p. 394, for any σ and bounded h, $\mathsf{E}_\sigma(\sum_{m\leq n}(1-\lambda)^{m-1}g_m + (1-\lambda)^n h(\omega_{n+1}))$ converges to $\overline{\gamma}_\lambda(\sigma)/\lambda$. By the definition of $\overline{x}$ one has:

$$\mathsf{E}_{\overline{x}}(g_m + (1-\lambda)f(\omega_{m+1}) \mid \mathscr{H}_m) = f(\omega_m),$$

and hence $\overline{\gamma}_\lambda(\overline{x}) = \lambda f$. Similarly, after each history the future payoff in Γ_λ if $\overline{x}$ is used is λf. Hence, if $\sigma'(h)$, say, is a profitable one-stage deviation at h, against $\overline{x}$, then the corresponding first component is a profitable deviation, against x, in the one-shot game with payoff $\lambda\phi((1-\lambda)f)$, a contradiction since x is a Nash equilibrium of $\Gamma((1-\lambda)f)$. The result now follows from the fact that σ is a subgame perfect equilibrium in Γ_λ iff there is no profitable one-stage deviation, after any history (IV.4, Ex. 4, p. 202). ∎

Proposition VII.1.7. *The discounted game* Γ_λ *has a subgame perfect equilibrium in stationary Markov strategies.*

Proof. Define a correspondence ψ from $X^\Omega \times [-C, C]^{\mathrm{I}\times\Omega} = Z$ to itself by: $\psi(x, f) = \{ (y, h) \in Z \mid$ for each i and each ω, $y^i(\cdot \mid \omega)$ is a best reply against x in $\Gamma((1-\lambda)f)_\omega$, which yields payoff $h^i(\omega)$ to player i $\}$. ψ is clearly u.s.c. and convex compact-valued; hence Kakutani's fixed point theorem (Kakutani, 1941) (e.g., proof of Theorem I.4.1, p. 45) leads to the existence of fixed points. Now Lemma VII.1.6 applies. ∎

Remark VII.1.3. The proof of Proposition VII.1.7 extends clearly to more general setups, e.g., immediately to the case of compact action sets, with payoffs and transitions depending continuously on the vector of actions.

VII.1.c. Non-Zero-Sum Case (General)

In fact, one can similarly get the existence of subgame perfect equilibria (i.e., measurable strategies that form, for every initial state ω, a subgame perfect equilibrium) even under assumptions hardly stronger than in Proposition VII.1.4.

- The restriction to a standard Borel space $(\Omega, \mathscr{A})$ is superfluous; an arbitrary measurable space will do.
- One can also allow for compact action sets $S^i(\omega)$ that vary measurably with ω, in the following sense: $S^i(\omega) \subseteq \overline{S}^i$, $(\overline{S}^i, \mathscr{S}^i)$ is a separable and separating measurable space, each subset $S^i(\omega)$ is endowed with some compact topology, the σ-field $\mathscr{S}^i$ is generated by the real-valued measurable functions that have a continuous restriction to each set $S^i(\omega)$, and $\{\omega \mid S^i(\omega) \cap O \neq \emptyset\}$ is measurable for each $O \in \mathscr{S}^i$ whose trace on each set $S^i(\omega)$ is open.

- The uniformly bounded payoff functions $g^i(\omega, s)$ and the transition probability $P(A \mid \omega, s)$ are measurable (for each $A \in \mathscr{A}$) on the graph of $S(\omega) = \prod_i S^i(\omega)$; and, for each $\omega \in \Omega$, $g^i(\omega, s)$ and $P(\cdot \mid \omega, s)$ are continuous functions on $S(\omega)$, in the norm topology for P, i.e., $s_n \to s$ implies that $\sup_A |P(A \mid \omega, s_n) - P(A \mid \omega, s)|$ converges to zero.

The basic idea of the proof is somewhat reminiscent of what we did in the zero-sum case; i.e., start with a "large" compact-valued measurable correspondence from state space to payoff space, K_0, e.g., the set of all feasible payoffs. Given a measurable map to compact-valued subsets K, define $[\Psi(K)]_\omega$ as the set of all Nash equilibrium payoffs for the uniform closure of all games $\Gamma((1-\lambda)f)_\omega$, letting f vary through all measurable selections from K. Prove that $\Psi(K)$ is a measurable map to compact subsets. Get in this way inductively a decreasing sequence of measurable maps to compact subsets $K_n = \Psi^n(K_0)$, with $K = \bigcap_n K_n$: K is then also measurable; further $K_{n+1} = \Psi(K_n)$ goes to the limit and yields $K = \Psi(K)$. Observe that, at each point $s \in S(\omega)$, the set of payoffs $\Gamma((1-\lambda)f)_{\omega,s}$ is already closed, when f varies through all measurable selections from K. Thus one can choose, first for each $(\omega, p) \in K$, a continuous payoff function $\gamma_{\omega,p}(s)$ on $S(\omega)$ that is a uniform limit of functions $\Gamma[(1-\lambda)f]_{\omega,s}$ (f measurable selection from K), and a Nash equilibrium $\sigma_{\omega,p}$ of $\gamma_{\omega,p}$ with payoff p, and next for each $s \in S(\omega)$, a measurable selection $f_{\omega,p,s}$ from K with $\Gamma[(1-\lambda)f_{\omega,p,s}]_{\omega,s} = \gamma_{\omega,p}(s)$. Doing all this in a measurable way yields a strategy: if the next state is $\tilde{\omega}$, just repeat the same thing with $f_{\omega,p,s}(\tilde{\omega})$ instead of p.

One can see the close analogy with the previous method, only in the zero-sum case the contracting aspect, i.e., the minmax theorem, ensured that the correspondences K_n would decrease at a rate $(1-\lambda)$, and hence converge to a single point.

The proof is, however, technically more involved; so we refer the reader to Mertens and Parthasarathy (2003) for it. There the reader will also find how the above assumptions can be further relaxed; e.g., the functions g^i do not need to be uniformly bounded, and the discount factor can be allowed to depend a.o. on the player, on the stage, and on the past sequence of states.

In fact, a much simpler proof (one page) is possible under the following additional assumptions (Mertens and Parthasarathy, 1991):

- The state space $(\Omega, \mathscr{A})$ is separable.
- The action sets $S^i(\omega)$ are finite and independent of ω.
- The transition probabilities are dominated by a single measure μ on $(\Omega, \mathscr{A})$.
- The payoff function is bounded, and a fixed discount rate is used.

In the general case, the strategies obtained are neither Markov nor stationary; they only have the very weak stationarity property that strategies are stationary functions of the current state and the currently expected payoff vector for the future (the "current expectations"). In the particular case above, one obtains strategies somewhat closer to Markov: the behavioral strategies can be chosen so as to be a function only of the current and the previous state. And if in addition the transition probability is non-atomic, one can further obtain stationarity (cf. Mertens and Parthasarathy, 1991): the function is the same at every period. We give the proof, since it is so simple and already contains in a nutshell several ideas of the general case.

Theorem VII.1.8. *Under the above assumptions, there exists a subgame perfect stationary equilibrium.*

Proof. Let $|g^i(\omega, s)| \leq c$, and $F_0 = \{ f \in [L_\infty(\mu)]^{\mathbf{I}} \mid \|f_i\|_\infty \leq c \, \forall i \in \mathbf{I} \}$. For $f \in F_0$, let $N_f(\omega) = \{$Nash equilibrium payoffs of $G_{f,\omega} = \Gamma((1-\lambda)f)_\omega \}$. $\emptyset \neq N_f(\omega) \subseteq [-c/\lambda, c/\lambda]^{\mathbf{I}}$. Denote by $\mathscr{N}_f$ the set of all μ-measurable selections from the convex hull of $N_f(\omega)$. Note that $\mathscr{N}_f \neq \emptyset$ using a selection theorem (Appendix A.7, p. 518). Observe also that the correspondence $f \mapsto \mathscr{N}_f$ from F_0 to itself is convex-valued, and weak*-upper semi-continuous: if $f_n \xrightarrow{w^*} f$, then $G_{f_n,\omega} \to G_{f,\omega}$ pointwise, and so $\limsup N_{f_n}(\omega) \subseteq N_f(\omega)$. Thus if $\varphi_n \in \mathscr{N}_{f_n}$ converges weak* to φ, then φ is the a.e. limit of a sequence of convex combinations of the φ_n, hence $\varphi \in \mathscr{N}_f$. It follows then from Fan's fixed point theorem (Fan, 1952) that $\mathscr{N}$ has a fixed point: $f_0 \in \mathscr{N}_{f_0}$, i.e. (by Lyapunov's theorem) $\int f_0(\tilde{\omega}) P(d\tilde{\omega} \mid \omega, s)$ is a measurable selection from the graph of $(\omega, s) \mapsto \int N_{f_0}(\tilde{\omega}) P(d\tilde{\omega} \mid \omega, s)$. And $\omega \mapsto N_{f_0}(\omega)$ is a measurable map to compact subsets of $\mathbb{R}^{\mathbf{I}}$ as the composition of the measurable map $\omega \mapsto G_{f_0,\omega}$ with the equilibrium correspondence, which is by upper semi-continuity a Borel map from games to compact sets. By the measurable choice theorem in Mertens (2003), it follows thus that there exists a measurable selection $\psi(\omega, \tilde{\omega}) \in N_{f_0}(\tilde{\omega})$ such that $G_{f_0(\cdot),\omega} = G_{\psi(\omega,\cdot),\omega}$. Denote by $\sigma(p, G)$ a Borel selection of an equilibrium with payoff p of the game G. The stationary equilibrium is now to play $\sigma[\psi(\omega, \tilde{\omega}), G_{f_0,\tilde{\omega}}]$ at state $\tilde{\omega}$, denoting by ω the previous state. ∎

Remark VII.1.4. Observe that all the trouble w.r.t. the Markovian character of the strategies stems from the non-atomic part of the transitions: under the same assumptions as in the general case above, if one assumes the transition probabilities to be purely atomic, one obtains immediately the existence of subgame perfect equilibria in stationary Markov strategies, e.g., by going to the limit with the result of the remark after Proposition VII.1.7, following an ultrafilter on the increasing net of all finite subsets of Ω. (To truncate the game to a finite subset, add, e.g., an absorbing state with payoff zero, which replaces the complement of this finite subset. The argument assumes $\mathscr{A}$ is the class of all subsets; if $\mathscr{A}$ is separable, one can always replace it by the class of all subsets on the corresponding quotient space while preserving all assumptions; and it is shown in Mertens and Parthasarathy (2003) how to reduce the general problem to the case where $\mathscr{A}$ is separable. Measurability of the strategies is anyway almost immaterial here, since the assumptions imply that, for any initial state, only countably many states are reachable.)

Remark VII.1.5. The above remark is well illustrated by the previous proof: one has to convexify the set of Nash equilibrium payoffs, because a weak*-limit belongs pointwise only to the convex hull of the pointwise limits (it is not because of the fixed-point argument, which is not used in the other proofs). So $f_0(\omega)$ is only a convex combination of equilibrium payoffs of $G_{f_0,\omega}$, and one will play equilibria. So one must select the equilibria, as a function of tomorrow's state $\tilde{\omega}$, so as to get today the same game $G_{f_0,\omega}$. This uses basically a measurable version of Lyapunov's theorem, because (by finiteness of action sets) at ω only finitely many measures on $\tilde{\omega}$ have to be considered. But it is clear that the solution to such a problem depends on the vector measure, i.e., on ω: the equilibrium played tomorrow at $\tilde{\omega}$ will depend on ω.

Remark VII.1.6. To illustrate this in still another way, under the same assumptions, there exist stationary Markov sunspot equilibria (extensive form correlated equilibria (cf. Section II.3.b, p. 103) with public signals): if one convexifies the set of Nash equilibria, there is no problem; cf. VII.4, Ex. 11, p. 419.

Remark VII.1.7. The assumption of norm-continuity of the transitions as a function of the actions is quite strong. Typically, one needs some form of noise in the model to ensure it. The best-behaved model where it is not satisfied, and where existence of equilibria is not known, is the following. Take as action sets for each player the one-point compactification of the integers, and take the Cantor set as state space. Assume the reward function, and the probability for each Borel subset of the state space, are jointly continuous in state and actions, and use standard discounting. (And assume even further that the transitions are non-atomic; they are then all dominated by a fixed non-atomic probability.)

VII.2. ASYMPTOTIC ANALYSIS, FINITE CASE: THE ALGEBRAIC ASPECT

As seen above, we need to find the stationary Markov equilibria looking for fixed points V of the operator Ψ of the previous paragraph, i.e., by solving $V = \Psi((1-\lambda)V)$ (Lemma VII.1.2, p. 393) or by finding an f Nash equilibrium payoff in $\Gamma((1-\lambda)f)$ (Lemma VII.1.6, p. 396).

When state and action sets are finite, this becomes a system of finitely many polynomial equations and inequalities in finitely many variables as defined by the correspondence ψ (Proposition VII.1.7, p. 396). The system is also polynomial (affine) in λ.

We have thus shown:

Proposition VII.2.1. *The set* $E = \{(\lambda; g_1, \sigma^1; g_2, \sigma^2; \dots) \mid 0 < \lambda \le 1,$ *the* σ^i *form a stationary Markov equilibrium with payoff vector* g^i *for the* λ*-discounted game*$\}$ *is, for each fixed* λ*, compact, non-empty, and semi-algebraic (i.e., the set of solutions of a system of polynomial equations and inequalities).*

Moreover one has:

Lemma VII.2.2. *Any set as in Proposition VII.2.1 contains a subset with the same properties consisting of a singleton, for each fixed λ (i.e., the equilibrium is a semi-algebraic function of λ).*

Proof. Denote by C the given set as a subset of some Euclidian space $\mathbb{R}^k$. Let $C_0 = \{ (\lambda, x) \in C \mid d(x, 0) \text{ is minimal} \}$, and $C_\ell = \{ (\lambda, x) \in C_{\ell-1} \mid d(x, e_\ell) \text{ is minimal} \}$ for $1 \leq \ell \leq k$, where the e_ℓ are the basis vectors of $\mathbb{R}^k$, and d is the Euclidian distance. If both (λ, x) and (λ, y) belong to C_k, then x and y are the same distance to zero and to all basis vectors, hence $x = y$. Since clearly C_ℓ is non-empty and compact for each λ (induction), C_k is indeed the graph of a function. Also the semi-algebraicity of C_ℓ follows by induction, using Corollary I.3.2, p. 31. ∎

Theorem VII.2.3. *For any (finite) stochastic game, there exist $\lambda_0 > 0$, a positive integer M, and Puiseux series expansions (g denotes the normalized payoff):*

$$g^i_\omega(\lambda) = \sum_{k \geq 0} h^{i,\omega}_k \lambda^{k/M}$$

$$\sigma^i_\omega(s)(\lambda) = \sum_{k \geq 0} \alpha^{i,\omega,s}_k \lambda^{k/M}, \quad \forall i \in \mathbf{I}, \forall s \in S_i,$$

such that, for all $\lambda \in]0, \lambda_0]$, the $\sigma^i(\lambda)$ form a stationary Markov equilibrium, with payoff vector $g(\lambda)$, of the λ-discounted game. (And those functions $\sigma^i(\lambda)$, $g(\lambda)$ are semi-algebraic on $[0, \lambda_0]$.)

Proof. Apply Lemma VII.2.2 to select a semi-algebraic function $(g(\lambda), \sigma(\lambda))$ from the graph E of stationary Markov equilibria. Each coordinate of this function is then a real-valued semi-algebraic function on $[0, 1]$ (by projection): such functions $f(\lambda)$ have a Puiseux-series expansion (Ahlfors, 1953) in the neighborhood of zero, i.e., $f(\lambda) = \sum_{k \geq k_0} \varphi_k \lambda^{k/M}$ for some $k_0 \in \mathbb{Z}$, $M \in \mathbb{N} \setminus \{0\}$, such that the series is absolutely convergent to $f(\lambda)$ on some interval $]0, \lambda_0]$ ($\lambda_0 > 0$). Now each of our coordinates $f(\lambda)$ is bounded (remember we use normalized payoffs), hence one has $k_0 \geq 0$, and thus we can set $\varphi_k = 0$ for $0 \leq k < k_0$ and use $k_0 = 0$.

Replace now all different M's by their least common multiple over the different coordinates, and replace the different λ_0's by their minimum, to obtain the result. ∎

Corollary VII.2.4. *For such a solution and any $\lambda_1 < \lambda_0$, $\|(dg/d\lambda, d\sigma/d\lambda)\| \leq A\lambda^{-(M-1)/M}$ for some $A > 0$ and any $\lambda \leq \lambda_1$.*

Proof. Such an absolutely convergent series can be differentiated term by term in the interior of its radius of convergence. ∎

Remark VII.2.1. Every value of M in the above results can indeed occur: cf. VII.4, Ex. 3.

VII.3. ε-OPTIMAL STRATEGIES IN THE UNDISCOUNTED GAME

VII.3.a. The Theorem

We consider here two-person zero-sum games. No finiteness or other conditions are imposed, but we assume the payoffs to be uniformly bounded and the values $v_\lambda(\omega)$ of the discounted games to exist. We will exhibit sufficient conditions for the existence of strategies that guarantee in a strong sense (cf. Section IV.1.c, p. 174) some function $v_\infty(\omega)$ (up to ε). The theorem requires the announcement only of the payoffs, not of the moves.

Theorem VII.3.1. *Assume a stochastic game where:*

(1) *payoffs are uniformly bounded;*
(2) *the values $v_\lambda(\omega)$ of the λ-discounted games exist, as well as ε-optimal strategies in the sense of* (3), *p. 393;*
(3) $\forall\alpha < 1$ *there exists a sequence λ_i $(0 < \lambda_i \leq 1)$ such that, denoting by $\|\cdot\|$ the supremum norm over the state space: $\lambda_{i+1} \geq \alpha\lambda_i, \lim_{i\to\infty}\lambda_i = 0$ and $\sum_i \left\|v_{\lambda_i} - v_{\lambda_{i+1}}\right\| < +\infty$.*

Then the game has a value v_∞. More precisely, $\forall\varepsilon > 0$, $\exists\sigma_\varepsilon$, $\exists N_0$ such that:

$$\forall n \geq N_0, \forall\omega \in \Omega, \forall\tau, \mathsf{E}^\omega_{\sigma_\varepsilon\tau}(\overline{g}_n) \geq v_\infty(\omega) - \varepsilon \quad \textit{and} \quad \mathsf{E}^\omega_{\sigma_\varepsilon\tau}\liminf_{n\to\infty}(\overline{g}_n) \geq v_\infty(\omega) - \varepsilon$$

and dually for player II.

Proof. Denote by A the largest absolute value of the payoffs times four, and let w.l.o.g. $0 < \varepsilon \leq A$, $\delta = \varepsilon/(12A)$.

Take two functions $L(s)$ and $\lambda(s)$ of a real variable s, such that $0 < \lambda(s) \leq 1$ and $L(s) > 0$. Assume $\exists M > 0$, such that, for $s \geq M$, $|\theta| \leq A$, and every ω:

$$|v(\omega, \lambda(s)) - v_\infty(\omega)| \leq \delta A, \tag{1}$$

$$AL(s) \leq \delta s, \tag{2}$$

$$|\lambda(s + \theta L(s)) - \lambda(s)| \leq \delta\lambda(s), \tag{3}$$

$$|v(\omega, \lambda(s + \theta L(s))) - v(\omega, \lambda(s))| \leq \delta AL(s)\lambda(s), \tag{4}$$

$$\int_M^\infty \lambda(s)\,ds \leq \delta A, \tag{5}$$

$$\lambda \text{ is strictly decreasing and } L \text{ is integer-valued.} \tag{6}$$

Call the above set of conditions $H(L, \lambda, A, \delta)$.

VII.3.b. Proof of the Theorem under $H(L, \lambda, A, \delta)$

Define now inductively, using g_i and ω_i for payoff and state at stage i ($i = 1, 2, \ldots$), starting with $s_0 \geq M$:

$$\lambda_k = \lambda(s_k),\ L_k = L(s_k),\ B_0 = 1,\ B_{k+1} = B_k + L_k,$$

$$s_{k+1} = \max[M, s_k + \sum_{B_k \leq i < B_{k+1}} (g_i - v_\infty(\omega_{B_{k+1}}) + \varepsilon/2)].$$

Observe that:

$$|s_{k+1} - s_k| \leq AL_k, \tag{7}$$

and that, by (5) and (6), $\lim_{s\to\infty} s\lambda(s) = 0$, hence by (2) $\lim_{s\to\infty} \lambda(s)L(s) = 0$, hence

$$\lambda(s)L(s) \leq \delta \quad \text{for} \quad s \geq M \quad \text{by choosing } M \text{ sufficiently large.} \tag{8}$$

Let also $\ell_k = v(\omega_{B_k}, \lambda_k)$, $\tilde{\ell}_k = v(\omega_{B_{k+1}}, \lambda_k)$, and note that by (4):

$$\left|\tilde{\ell}_k - \ell_{k+1}\right| \leq \delta AL_k\lambda_k. \tag{9}$$

Player I's strategy σ consists in playing for $B_k \leq i < B_{k+1}$ a $(\delta AL_k\lambda_k)$-optimal strategy in the λ_k-discounted game. The following computations are for an arbitrary strategy τ of player II, and E stands for $\mathsf{E}_{\sigma,\tau}$.

Hence, denoting by $\mathscr{H}_k$ the σ-field of all past events at stage B_k, up to and including the choice of ω_{B_k}:

$$\ell_k \leq \mathsf{E}\big[\lambda_k \sum_{0\leq i<L_k} (1-\lambda_k)^i g_{B_k+i} + (1-\lambda_k)^{L_k}\tilde{\ell}_k \mid \mathscr{H}_k\big] + \delta AL_k\lambda_k,$$

or, as $1 - \lambda \sum_{i<L}(1-\lambda)^i = (1-\lambda)^L$:

$$\mathsf{E}\big[\tilde{\ell}_k - \ell_k + \lambda_k \sum_{i<L_k}(1-\lambda_k)^i(g_{B_k+i} - \tilde{\ell}_k) \mid \mathscr{H}_k\big] \geq -\delta AL_k\lambda_k.$$

Using (9), $1 - \lambda L \leq (1-\lambda)^i \leq 1$ for $i < L$, (8), and (1), we get:

$$\mathsf{E}\big[\ell_{k+1} - \ell_k + \lambda_k \sum_{B_k\leq i<B_{k+1}} \big(g_i - v_\infty(\omega_{B_{k+1}})\big) \mid \mathscr{H}_k\big] \geq -4\delta AL_k\lambda_k,$$

and hence, since $s_{k+1} - s_k \geq \sum_{B_k\leq i<B_{k+1}} : \big(g_i - v_\infty(\omega_{B_{k+1}}) + 6A\delta\big)$:

$$\mathsf{E}\big[\ell_{k+1} - \ell_k + \lambda_k(s_{k+1} - s_k) \mid \mathscr{H}_k\big] \geq 2\delta AL_k\lambda_k.$$

Now, using (3) and (7), we get:

$$\lambda_k(s_{k+1} - s_k) - \delta AL_k\lambda_k \leq \int_{s_k}^{s_{k+1}} \lambda(s)ds = t_k - t_{k+1}$$

(letting $t_k = \int_{s_k}^{\infty} \lambda(x)dx$ – note that by (5), $t_k \leq \delta A$). Thus $\mathsf{E}[Y_{k+1} \mid \mathscr{H}_k] \geq Y_k + \delta AL_k\lambda_k$, for $Y_k = \ell_k - t_k$, note that $|Y_k| \leq A/2$. Thus $A \geq \mathsf{E}(Y_k - Y_0) \geq$

$\delta A\, \mathsf{E}(\sum_{\ell<k} L_\ell \lambda_\ell)$, and hence, by monotone convergence, $\mathsf{E}\big(\sum_k L_k\lambda_k\big) \le 1/\delta$, so that:

$$\mathsf{E}\Big(\sum_k \mathbb{1}_{s_k=M}\Big) \le \frac{1}{\delta\lambda(M)}\,. \tag{10}$$

Also, Y is a bounded submartingale, hence converges a.e. to Y_∞, and by the optional stopping theorem $\mathsf{E}(Y_T) \ge Y_0 = \ell_0 - t_0 \ge \ell_0 - \delta A$ for any stopping time T (including ∞).

Let $k(i)$ denote the stopping time $\min\{\, k \mid B_k > i\,\}$, $k(\infty) = \infty$; and let $\overline{\ell}_i = v_\infty(\omega_{B_{k(i)}})$. It follows, using that (by (1)) $\overline{\ell}_i \ge \ell_{k(i)} - \delta A \ge Y_{k(i)} - \delta A$, that:

$$\mathsf{E}(\overline{\ell}_i) \ge \overline{\ell}_0 - 3\delta A \quad \text{for all } \ i = 1,\dots,\infty \ \text{ (letting } \ \overline{\ell}_\infty = \liminf_{i\to\infty} \overline{\ell}_i). \tag{11}$$

The definition of s_k yields:

$$s_{k+1} - s_k \le \sum_{B_k \le i < B_{k+1}} (g_i - \overline{\ell}_i) + 6\delta A L_k + \mathbb{1}_{s_{k+1}=M} A L_k/2.$$

By (2) and (7), when $s_{k+1} = M$, $AL_k \le \delta M/(1-\delta)$; thus, by summing:

$$s_k - s_0 \le \sum_{i<B_k} (g_i - \overline{\ell}_i) + 6\delta A B_k + \delta M \sum_1^k \mathbb{1}_{s_\ell = M};$$

hence:

$$\sum_1^n g_i \ge s_{k(n)} - s_0 + \sum_0^n \overline{\ell}_i - 6\delta A n - A(B_{k(n)} - n) - \delta M \sum_0^\infty \mathbb{1}_{s_k=M}.$$

But:

$$B_{k(n)} - n \le L(s_{k(n)-1}) \le A^{-1}\delta s_{k(n)-1} \le \delta(A^{-1}s_0 + n)$$

(using a.o. (2)); hence:

$$\sum_1^n g_i \ge \sum_1^n \overline{\ell}_i - 7A\delta n - (1+\delta)s_0 - \delta M \sum_1^\infty \mathbb{1}_{s_k=M}.$$

It follows now from (10) and (11) that, for all n:

$$\mathsf{E}(\overline{g}_n) \ge \overline{\ell}_0 - 10A\delta - \frac{K}{n}, \quad \text{with} \quad K = 2s_0 + \frac{M}{\lambda(M)},$$

and hence:

$$\mathsf{E}(\overline{g}_n) \ge v_\infty(\omega) - \varepsilon \quad \text{for} \quad n = N_0, N_0+1, \dots, +\infty, \quad \text{with} \quad N_0 \ge \frac{6K}{\varepsilon},$$

and the strategy described is ε-optimal. ■

Remark VII.3.1. Further, those ε-optimal strategies are still ε-optimal, in the same sense, in any subgame, and they consist in playing in successive blocks k of length L_k whichever $(\delta A L_k \lambda_k)$-optimal strategy in the modification $\Gamma(\lambda_k, L_k)$ of the λ_k discounted game, where from stage L_k on, the payoff $v_{\lambda_k}(\omega_{L_k})$ is received forever. (One sees immediately that only $(\delta A L_k \lambda_k)$-optimality in $\Gamma(\lambda_k, L_k)$ was used in the proof under $H(L, \lambda, A, \delta)$.) The subgame property follows from the fact that in every subgame, one uses (with the right proviso for the first block) a strategy (M, s_n) of the same ε-optimal type as (M, s_0) of the full game.

Remark VII.3.2. We can already solve the finite case. By Corollary VII.2.4, p. 400, $\|dv_\lambda/d\lambda\|$ is an integrable function (in the neighborhood of 0, but part (1) of the proposition below implies it is bounded elsewhere), and so the conditions $H(L, \lambda, A, \delta)$ immediately yield that any functions L (integer-valued) and λ (integrable) that satisfy $\delta ds/d\,|\ln \lambda| \geq \|dv_\lambda/d\lambda\|$ (cf. (4)) and $\delta ds/d\,|\ln \lambda| \geq AL(s)$ (cf. (3)) will typically work (indeed, for sufficiently smooth functions $\lambda(s)$ (or $s(\lambda)$), e.g., for power functions, the last condition, (2), will typically follow from the others). The cited corollary immediately yields a multitude of such functions. One such particularly simple choice is to take $\lambda(s) = 1/[s \ln^2 s]$; $L(s) = 1$ (or any choice s.t. $L(s)/s \to 0$); this yields an extremely simple strategy working for all finite games, the only game-dependent parameter being the link between ε and $M(\varepsilon)$.

VII.3.c. End of the Proof

The theorem will now follow from the next proposition:

Proposition VII.3.2.

(1) *Under assumptions (1) and (2) of the theorem, v_λ/λ is a Lipschitz function of $1/\lambda$ (with the maximum absolute value of payoffs C as Lipschitz constant); in particular v_λ is a Lipschitz function of $\ln \lambda$.*

In (2), (3), and (4) below, v_λ is an arbitrary function with values in a metric space.

(2) *If v_λ is a Lipschitz function of $\ln(\lambda)$, then assumption (3) of Theorem VII.3.1 is equivalent to assumption* (c*):

$$\exists \lambda_i : \lim \lambda_i = 0, \lim \lambda_{i+1}/\lambda_i = 1 = \lambda_0, \sum_i d(v_{\lambda_{i+1}}, v_{\lambda_i}) < +\infty. \tag{c*}$$

(3) *If v_λ is a Lipschitz function of $\ln(\lambda)$, then assumption* (c*) *implies the existence of functions L and λ such that, for any $A > 0$ and $\delta > 0$, $H(L, \lambda, A, \delta)$ holds.*

(4) *Conversely, if for every $\delta > 0$ there exists L and λ such that, for some $A > 0$, $H(L, \lambda, A, \delta)$ holds (where conditions* (1), (2), *and* (6) *can be deleted), then v_λ satisfies assumption (3) of the theorem.*

Proof. (1) v_λ/λ is the value of the game with payoff function $\sum_0^\infty (1-\lambda)^i x_i$ ($|x_i| < C$). Thus the payoff functions corresponding to v_λ/λ and v_μ/μ differ by at most $A|1/\lambda - 1/\mu|$. Hence the conclusion. It is clear that this Lipschitz condition implies both the boundedness of v_λ and the Lipschitz character of v_λ as a function of $\ln\lambda$.

(2) It suffices to show that () $\Longrightarrow$ (c*). Add first finitely many values α^k ($k = 0, 1, 2, \dots k_0$) in the beginning of the sequence λ_i (with $k_0 = \max\{\, j \mid \alpha^j > \lambda_0 \,\}$): we have now in addition $\lambda_0 = 1$. Let now $i_0 = 0$, $i_{k+1} = \min\{\, i \mid \lambda_i < \lambda_{i_k} \,\}$, and $\tilde\lambda_k = \lambda_{i_k}$: the inequality $\tilde\lambda_{k+1} \ge \alpha\tilde\lambda_k$ is still true, and by the triangle inequality $\sum \|v_{\tilde\lambda_{k+1}} - v_{\|}\tilde\lambda_k < \infty$: we have now in addition that the sequence λ_i is strictly decreasing. Let thus, for $n \ge 1$, $(x_i^n)_{i=0}^\infty$ satisfy $x_0^n = 1$, $0 < \ln(x_i^n/x_{i+n}^n) \le 2^{-n}$, $x_i^n \to 0$, and $\sum_i d(v(x_{i+1}^n), v(x_i^n)) < +\infty$. Choose then $(a_n)_{n=1}^\infty$ such that $a_1 = 1$, $\ln(a_N/a_{n+1}) > 1$, and $\sum_{n,i} \mathbb{1}_{x_i^n \le a_n} d(v(x_{i+1}^n), v(x_i^n)) < +\infty$. Let λ_i be the enumeration in decreasing order of $\{\, x_i^n \mid a_{n+1} < x_i^n \le a_n,\ n \ge 1, i \ge 0 \,\}$: obviously $\lambda_0 = 1$, $\lambda_i \to 0$. To verify the other conditions on λ_i, let $\overline{a}_n = \min\{\, x_i^{n-1} \mid x_i^{n-1} > a_n \,\}$, $\underline{a}_n = \max\{\, x_i^n \mid x_i^n \le a_n \,\}$. As $\ln(\overline{a}_n/\underline{a}_n) = \ln(\overline{a}_n/a_n) + \ln(a_n/\underline{a}_n) \le 2^{-n+1} + 2^{-n}$, $\lambda_{i+1}/\lambda_i \to 1$, and also $d(v(\overline{a}_n), v(\underline{a}_n)) \le K(2^{-n+1} + 2^{-n})$ (Lipschitz property), which is summable; therefore:

$$\sum_i d(v(\lambda_{i+1}), v(\lambda_i)) \le \sum_{n=1}^\infty \sum_{x_i^n \le a_n} d(v(x_{i+1}^n), v(x_i^n)) + \sum_{n=1}^\infty d(v(\overline{a}_n), v(\underline{a}_n)) < +\infty.$$

(3) We will do a more general construction but of the same type as the one suggested in Remark VII.3.5 below. To see the ideas of the following proof in a more transparent framework it may be useful to check this case first.

Let $f(\lambda) = \sum_{\lambda_i \ge \lambda} d(v(\lambda_i), v(\lambda_{i-1}))$, $\Delta[a,b] = f(a) - f(b)$, and $\ell_i = \Delta[y_n^{i+1}, y_n^i]$, where $y_n = n/(n+1), n \ge 1$. Then $\sum_{-\infty}^{+\infty} \ell_i \le \sum_k d(v(\lambda_k), v(\lambda_{k-1})) < +\infty$. Let also $\overline{\ell}_i = \sum_{|j| \le 2} \ell_{i+j}$, $g_n(x) = 2n[\mathbb{1}_{x \le 1} + \overline{\ell}_i y_n^{-i}]$ for $y_n^{i+1} < x \le y_n^i$, and define h_n by linear interpolation from the values $h_n(y_n^i) = n\sum_{j<i}[g_n(y_n^{j+1}) + g_n(y_n^j) + g_n(y_n^{j-1})]$. Then $g_n \ge n$ on [0,1] and h_n is continuous, decreasing, $\ge ng_n$ and integrable (e.g., $\int_0^\infty h_n(x)dx \le \sum_i h_n(y_n^i)(y_n^{i-1} - y_n^i) = n(y_n^{-1} - 1)\sum_{j<i} y_n^i[g_n(y_n^{j+1}) + g_n(y_n^j) + g_n(y_n^{j-1})] = n\sum_j y_n^j[g_n(y_n^{j+1}) + g_n(y_n^j) + g_n(y_n^{j-1})] \le 3ny_n^{-1}\sum_j y_n^j g_n(y_n^j) = 6n(n+1)$ $[1/(1-y_n) + \sum_i \overline{\ell}_i] < +\infty$). Further, for $y_n^{i+1} < x \le y_n^i$, $\Delta[xy_n^2, xy_n^{-2}] \le \Delta[y_n^{i+3}, y_n^{i-2}] \le \overline{\ell}_i \le y_n^i g_n(x)/(2n) \le xg_n(x)/n$. Moreover, by the linearity on those intervals of $g_n(x)$ and $h_n(xy_n^k)$, $h_n(y_n^{i+1}) = h_n(y_n^i) + n[g_n(y_n^{i+1}) + g_n(y_n^i) + g_n(y_n^{i-1})]$ implies that $h_n(x) + ng_n(x) \le h_n(xy_n)$ and $h_n(x) - ng_n(x) \ge h_n(xy_n^{-1})$. Choose $(a_n)_{n=1}^\infty$ such that $\frac{1}{2} \ge a_n > a_{n+1} > 0$, $\inf\{\, \lambda_i/\lambda_{i-1} \mid \lambda_i \le 2a_n \,\} \ge y_n$ and $\sum_n \int_0^{a_n} h_n(x)dx < +\infty$. Set $\overline{h}_n(x) = h_n(x)(2 - x/a_n)^+$. Then $\overline{h}(x) = \sum_1^\infty \overline{h}_n(x)$ is continuous, decreasing (strictly on $[0, 2a_1]$), and integrable. Hence so is $\overline{h}^{-1}(s)$ ($s > 0$). Let $n(x) = |\{\, n \mid a_n \ge x \,\}|$, $g_0(x) = 1$, $\overline{g}(x) = g_{n(x)}(x)$, $y_0 = 1/2$; $x_i = xy_{n(x)}^i$:

then $\overline{g}(x) \geq n(x) \underset{x\to 0}{\longrightarrow} \infty$, $\Delta[x_2, x_{-2}] \leq x\overline{g}(x)/n(x)$, and $\overline{h}(x) - \overline{h}(x_{-1}) \geq \overline{h}_{n(x)}(x) - \overline{h}_{n(x)}(x_{-1}) \geq h_{n(x)}(x) - h_{n(x)}(xy^{-1}_{n(x)}) \geq n(x)g_{n(x)}(x) = n(x)\overline{g}(x)$, and thus $\overline{h}(x)/\overline{g}(x) \geq n(x) \underset{x\to 0}{\longrightarrow} \infty$. Similarly $\overline{h}(x_{+1}) - \overline{h}(x) \geq n(x)\overline{g}(x)$. Thus $|\overline{h}(z) - \overline{h}(x)| \leq n(x)\overline{g}(x)$ implies $x_1 \leq z \leq x_{-1}$; so if further $\lambda_{i+1} \leq z \leq \lambda_i$, then $x_2 \leq \lambda_{i+1} < \lambda_i \leq x_{-2}$, because $\lambda_{i+1} \leq xy^{-1}_{n(x)} \leq a_{n(x)}y^{-1}_{n(x)} \leq 2a_{n(x)}$, so that $\lambda_{i+1}/\lambda_i \geq y_{n(x)}$ (assume $n(x) \geq 1$). Therefore if $\lambda(s)$ is the closest λ_i to $x = \overline{h}^{-1}(s)$, and $L(s) = \overline{g}(x)$, $N(s) = n(x)$, then $\lambda(s + \theta L(s)) \in [x_2, x_{-2}]$ for $|\theta| \leq N(s)$, and hence:

$$d[v(\lambda(s + \theta L(s)), v(\lambda(s))] \leq \Delta[x_2, x_{-2}] \leq 2\lambda(s)L(s)/N(s),$$

and:

$$\left| \ln \frac{\lambda(s + \theta L(s))}{\lambda(s)} \right| \leq \ln y^{-4}_{N(s)} \leq \frac{4}{N(s)}.$$

Further:

$$\frac{L(s)}{s} \leq \frac{\overline{g}(x)}{\overline{h}(x)} \leq \frac{1}{N(s)},$$

and $s \to \infty \Longrightarrow x \to 0 \Longrightarrow N(s) = n(x) \to \infty$. So, the above inequalities will give (4), (3), and (2), respectively. Clearly λ is decreasing and integrable, and $0 < \lambda \leq 1$, hence (5). Perturb λ slightly so as to make it strictly decreasing (by continuity of v_λ), and replace L by its integer part (recall $L(s) \geq N(s) \to \infty$), hence (6). Condition (c*) implies that the sequence v_{λ_i} is a Cauchy sequence, hence convergent, say, to v_∞. By the choice of λ this implies (1): $H(L, \lambda, A, \delta)$ obtains for all $A > 0$, $\delta > 0$.

(4) Let $s_0 = M$, $L_i = AL(s_i)$, $s_{i+1} = s_i + L_i$, $\lambda = \lambda(s_i)$. Then by (4) $\sum_i \|v(\lambda_{i+1}) - v(\lambda_i)\| \leq \delta \sum_i \lambda_i L_i = \delta \sum_i \lambda_i(s_{i+1} - s_i) \leq \delta(1-\delta)^{-1} \sum_i \int_{s_i}^{s_{i+1}} \lambda(s)ds < +\infty$ (by (3) and (5)). Hence $\lambda_i \to 0 (L_i \gg 0)$, and (by (3)) $\lambda_{i+1} \geq (1-\delta)\lambda_i$. ■

Remark VII.3.3. Thus one can always use the same functions λ and L for any given game, i.e., independently of ε; taking also $s_0 = M$ then yields a family of ε-optimal strategies where only the parameter M changes with ε. (The arbitrary s_0 was just needed for the subgame property.)

Remark VII.3.4. Condition (3) of the theorem is always satisfied when v_λ is of bounded variation or when (for some function v_∞) $\|v_\lambda - v_\infty\|/\lambda$ is integrable. Indeed, this implies the integrability of $\|v_\lambda - v_\infty\|$ as a function of $\ln \lambda$; let then λ_i denote the minimizer of $\|v_\lambda - v_\infty\|$ in $[\beta^{i+1}, \beta^i]$ to satisfy condition (3).

Remark VII.3.5. When v_λ is of bounded variation, a much simpler construction of L and λ is possible than in the proposition: just set $L = 1$, $\varphi(x) = \int_0^x \|dv_\lambda\|$ (i.e., the total variation of v_λ between 0 and x), $s(\lambda) = \int_\lambda^1 x^{-1} d\sqrt{\varphi(x)} + 1/\sqrt{\lambda}$, and $\lambda(s)$ the inverse function (cf. VII.4, Ex. 14, p. 421).

Remark VII.3.6. Under the assumptions of the theorem, v_λ converges uniformly to v_∞: recall that (c*) implies the uniform convergence of v_{λ_i} to v_∞, and the Lipschitz character of v_λ as a function of $\ln \lambda$ implies that, for $\lambda_{i+1} \leq \lambda \leq \lambda_i$, $d(v_\lambda, v_{\lambda_i}) \leq K \ln(\lambda_i/\lambda_{i+1}) \to 0$. Thus the conclusion, by part (2) of the proposition. In fact the statement itself of the theorem, with N_0 independent of the initial state, implies immediately the uniform convergence of v_n and of v_λ.

Remark VII.3.7. The function $\lambda(s)$ constructed in Proposition VII.3.2, p. 404, was strictly decreasing, and thus with a continuous inverse $s(\lambda)$; but it cannot be made continuous. Indeed, the same proof shows that:

Proposition VII.3.3. *The following conditions on v_λ are equivalent:*

(1) *For some $A > 0$ and δ $(0 < \delta < 1)$ there exist L and λ that satisfy $H(L, \lambda, A, \delta)$ (without* (1), (2), *and* (6)), *where λ is continuous.*
(2) *There exist L and λ (continuous) that satisfy $H(L, \lambda, A, \delta)$ for any $A > 0$ and $\delta > 0$.*
(3) $\exists(\lambda_i)_{i=0}^\infty : \inf_i \lambda_{i+1}/\lambda_i > 0 = \lim_i \lambda_i, \sum_i \Delta[\lambda_{i+1}, \lambda_i] < +\infty$.
(4) $\forall(\lambda_i)_{i=0}^\infty : \sup_i \lambda_{i+1}/\lambda_i < 1, \lambda_i > 0 \Longrightarrow \sum_i \Delta[\lambda_{i+1}, \lambda_i] < +\infty$.

Here $\Delta[\lambda, \mu] = \max_{\lambda \leq \lambda_1 \leq \lambda_2 \leq \mu} d(v_{\lambda_1}, v_{\lambda_2})$.

Proof. Show, as in Proposition VII.3.2, that (1) $\Longrightarrow$ (3) $\Longrightarrow$ (4) $\Longrightarrow$ (2). In (3) $\Longrightarrow$ (4), just note that the sequence of (4) has only a bounded number of terms between two successive terms in the sequence of (3). In (4) $\Longrightarrow$ (2), work directly with the present function Δ, do not use the sequence λ_i, and set $\lambda(s) = \overline{h}^{-1}(s)$. ■

Remark VII.3.8. Condition (3) or (4) are not implied by the Lipschitz property and (c*).

VII.3.d. Particular Cases (Finite Games, Two-Person Zero-Sum)

VII.3.d.1. When the stochastic game is a normalized form of a game with perfect information, then the games $\Gamma_\omega((1-\lambda)v)_\omega$ are also normal forms of games with perfect information, and hence have pure strategy solutions, which form a closed, semi-algebraic subset of the set of all solutions: applying Theorem VII.2.3 to those yields that, for some $\lambda_0 > 0$, there exists a pure strategy vector such that the corresponding stationary strategies are optimal in the λ-discounted game for all $\lambda \leq \lambda_0$. Such strategy vectors (pure or not) are also called "uniformly discount optimal" (Blackwell, 1962).

Observe that the perfect-information case in particular includes the situation where one player is a dummy, which corresponds to Markov decision processes or dynamic programming (cf. Section VII.5, p. 424).

VII.3.d.2. Whenever there exist uniformly discount optimal strategies, the expansion of v_λ is in integer powers of λ: v_λ is in fact a rational function of λ, being the solution of the linear system $v_\lambda = \lambda g + (1-\lambda)Pv_\lambda$, where g and P are the single-stage expected payoff and the transition probability generated by the strategy pair.

VII.3.d.3. Whenever there exists a strategy σ in the one-shot game that is $o(\lambda)$-optimal in $\Gamma(\lambda, 1)$, then for each $\varepsilon > 0$, one ε-optimal strategy of the theorem will consist in playing this all the time: the corresponding stationary strategy is optimal (in the strong sense of the theorem) in the infinite game. (Recall Remark VII.3.1, p. 404.)

VII.3.d.4. Since the value exists in such a strong sense, it follows in particular that applying the theorem to the one-person case, the payoff $\underline{v}(\sigma)$ guaranteed by a stationary Markov strategy σ is also completely unambiguous. Further, the preceding points imply the existence of a pure, stationary Markov best reply, which is best for all $\lambda \leq \lambda_0$, and that $\underline{v}_\lambda(\sigma) \geq \underline{v}(\sigma) - K\lambda$. One checks similarly that $\underline{v}_n(\sigma) \geq \underline{v}(\sigma) - K/n$ (cf. VII.4, Ex. 6, p. 418).

It follows in particular that if both players have stationary Markov optimal strategies in Γ_∞, then $\|v_\lambda - v_\infty\| \leq K\lambda$, $\|v_n - v_\infty\| \leq K/n$ (and those strategies guarantee such bounds) (and in particular $\left\|v_\lambda - \underline{v}_\lambda(\sigma)\right\| \leq K'\lambda$, so that the corresponding one-shot strategies are $O(\lambda)$-optimal in $\Gamma(\lambda, 1)$).

VII.3.d.5. It follows that VII.3.d.3 can be improved to: whenever there exists a stationary Markov strategy σ which is $o(1)$ optimal in $\Gamma(\lambda)$ (i.e., $\left\|\underline{v}_\lambda(\sigma) - v_\lambda\right\| \to 0$ as $\lambda \to 0$), then σ is optimal in the infinite game. This is an improvement because an easy induction yields that the $\varepsilon[1-(1-\lambda)^L]$-optimality of σ in $\Gamma(\lambda, L)$ implies its $\varepsilon[1-(1-\lambda)^{KL}]$-optimality in $\Gamma(\lambda, KL)$, hence its ε-optimality in $\Gamma(\lambda)$.

VII.3.d.6. Apply the above in the N-person case for each player, considering all others together as nature: a stationary Markov strategy vector that is, $\forall\varepsilon > 0$, an ε-equilibrium of $\Gamma(\lambda)$ for all sufficiently small λ, is also an equilibrium of Γ_∞.

VII.3.d.7. The perfect information case can always be rewritten (extending the state space and adjusting the discount factor) as a stochastic game where in each state only one player moves. Actually the same conclusions hold (in the two-person case) if we assume only that, in each state, the transition probability depends on only one player's action ("switching control" (Vrieze et al., 1983)): assume, e.g., player I controls the transitions at state ω; by Theorem VII.2.3, p. 400, we can assume that the sets S_0 and T_0 of best replies at ω for the stationary Markov equilibria $(\sigma_\lambda, \tau_\lambda)$ are independent of λ for $\lambda \leq \lambda_0$.

The equilibrium condition of Proposition VII.1.7, p. 396, takes then the following form at ω (σ and τ being probabilities on S_0 and T_0):

$$\sum_s \sigma_{\lambda,\omega}(s)[g^2_\omega(s,t) - g^2_\omega(s,\tilde{t})] \geq 0 \qquad \forall t \in T_0,\ \forall \tilde{t},$$

$$V^2_{\lambda,\omega} = \sum_s \sigma_{\lambda,\omega}(s)[g^2_\omega(s,t) + w^2_{\lambda,\omega}(s)] \qquad \text{for some } t \in T_0,$$

$$w_{\lambda,\omega}(s) = (1-\lambda)\sum_{\tilde{\omega}} p(\tilde{\omega} \mid \omega, s) V_{\lambda,\tilde{\omega}},$$

$$V^1_{\lambda,\omega} = \sum_t \tau_{\lambda,\omega}(t) g^1_\omega(s,t) + w^1_{\lambda,\omega}(s)\ \forall s \in S_0, \quad \text{with inequalities for } s \notin S_0.$$

The first set of inequalities describes a polyhedron of probabilities on S_0, independent of λ, with extreme points $\sigma^1_\omega \dots \sigma^k_\omega$. So $\sigma_{\lambda,\omega} = \sum_{i=1}^k \mu^\lambda_\omega(i)\sigma^i_\omega$, with $\mu^\lambda_\omega(i) \geq 0$. The second inequality takes then the form: $V^2_{\lambda,\omega} = \sum_{i=1}^k \mu^\lambda_\omega(i)[G_i(\omega) + (1-\lambda)\sum_{\tilde{\omega}} q_{i,\omega}(\tilde{\omega})V^2_{\lambda,\tilde{\omega}}]$.

Hence, by semi-algebraicity again, there exist, for each ω, indices i_0 and i_1 such that $G_{i_0}(\omega) + (1-\lambda)\sum_{\tilde{\omega}} q_{i_0,\omega}(\tilde{\omega})V^2_{\lambda,\tilde{\omega}} \leq V^2_{\lambda,\omega} \leq G_{i_1}(\omega) + (1-\lambda)\sum_{\tilde{\omega}} q_{i_1,\omega}(\tilde{\omega})V^2_{\lambda,\tilde{\omega}}$ for all sufficiently small λ, say, $\lambda \leq \lambda_0$. And conversely, for any solution v^2_λ of this pair of inequalities, one obtains the corresponding σ, by a rational computation. Similarly, the last system of inequalities, by eliminating τ, yields a system of linear inequalities in the variables $V^1_{\lambda,\omega} - (1-\lambda)\sum_{\tilde{\omega}} p(\tilde{\omega} \mid \omega, s)V^1_{\lambda,\tilde{\omega}}$. Putting those inequalities together, for all states, yields a system of linear inequalities in V^1_λ and a similar system in V^2_λ: those systems have a solution for all $\lambda \leq \lambda_0$, and any such solution can be extended by a rational computation to a solution in $\sigma_\lambda, \tau_\lambda$. Finally, since such a system of linear inequalities has only finitely many possible bases, and each such base is valid in a semi-algebraic subset of λ's, i.e., a finite union of intervals, it follows that one such basis is valid in a whole neighborhood of zero: inverting it, one obtains solutions V^1_λ and V^2_λ in the field $K(\lambda)$ of rational fractions in λ, with coefficients in the field K generated by the data of the game, and thus there exists a stationary Markov equilibrium (σ, τ) in $K(\lambda)$, for all $\lambda \leq \lambda_1, \lambda_1 > 0$. Further, the above describes a finite algorithm for computing it.

Now, observe there are two cases where we can in addition assume that σ_λ is independent of λ, hence equal to its limit σ_0:

(1) In the zero-sum case, since every extreme point σ^i_ω is a best reply of player I, they all yield the same expected payoff to I, and hence, by the zero-sum assumption, also to player II: hence $V^2_{\lambda,\omega} = G_i(\omega) + (1-\lambda)\sum_{\tilde{\omega}} q_{i,\omega}(\tilde{\omega})V^2_{\lambda,\tilde{\omega}}$ for all i, and thus any weights $\mu^\lambda_i(\omega)$ are satisfactory, in particular constant weights.

(2) If it is the same player who controls the transitions in all states, then varying μ will only vary player II's expected payoffs in all states, and those do not affect any other inequality in the system.

In each of those cases, then, it is obvious that, if one were to replace in all states the passive player's $\tau(\lambda)$ by its limit $\tau(0)$, which differs from it (rational fractions . . .) by at most $K\lambda$, the expected payoffs, under whatever strategies σ of the controlling agents, would vary by at most $CK\lambda$, where C is the maximum absolute value of all payoffs: indeed, transitions are not affected at all, so the probability distribution on the sequence of states remains unaffected, and in every state, the current payoff varies by at most $CK\lambda$. Hence by VII.3.d.6 above, (σ_0, τ_0) is a stationary Markov equilibrium of Γ_∞.

So, in those two cases, the rational fraction solutions can be chosen to be constant in λ ("uniformly discount optimal") for the controlling player and are also solutions for $\lambda = 0$; in particular, our finite algorithm computes rationally an equilibrium of the undiscounted game.

VII.4. THE TWO-PERSON NON-ZERO-SUM UNDISCOUNTED CASE

Note first that there may be no uniform equilibrium; hence E_∞ may be empty. In fact, already in the zero-sum case there exist no optimal strategies (cf. VII.4, Ex. 4). Thus we define a set E_0 of equilibrium payoffs as $\bigcap_{\varepsilon>0} E_\varepsilon$, where

$$E_\varepsilon = \{ d \in \mathbb{R}^{\mathbf{I}} \mid \exists \sigma, \tau \text{ and } N \text{ such that: } \forall n \geq N \quad \overline{\gamma}_n^i(\sigma, \tau) \geq d^i - \varepsilon \quad (i = 1, 2),$$
$$\text{and} \quad \forall \sigma', \forall \tau' \quad \overline{\gamma}_n^1(\sigma', \tau) \leq d^1 + \varepsilon, \quad \overline{\gamma}_n^2(\sigma, \tau') \leq d^2 + \varepsilon \}.$$

Note that obviously $E_\infty \subseteq E_0$ and that they coincide for supergames (cf. IV.4, p. 190).

VII.4.a. An Example

At first sight Sections VII.2 and VII.3 may lead to the idea that a proof of existence of equilibria in the undiscounted game could be obtained along the following lines: by Theorem VII.2.3, p. 400, choose a semi-algebraic, stationary Markov equilibrium $\sigma(\lambda)$ of the discounted game Γ_λ, for $\lambda \in (0, 1]$. Prove then that the limit as λ goes to 0 of the corresponding payoff belongs to E_0 by constructing equilibrium strategies of the kind: at stage n use $\sigma(\lambda_n)$, where λ_n is some function of the past history h_n.

We prove now that this conjecture is false by studying a game where E_0 is non-empty and disjoint from the set of equilibrium payoffs, E_λ, of any discounted game Γ_λ.

Definition VII.4.1. A stochastic game is called a game with **absorbing states** if all states except one are absorbing, i.e., such that $P(\omega'; \omega, s) = 0$ if $\omega' \neq \omega$.

Obviously we consider then only the game starting from the non-absorbing state, ω_0, and the state changes at most once during a play (compare with recursive games (Section IV.5, p. 205)).

The example is as follows: we consider a two-person game with absorbing states with two strategies for each player and the following payoff matrix:

$$\begin{pmatrix} (1,0)^* & (0,2)^* \\ (0,1) & (1,0) \end{pmatrix},$$

where a * denotes an absorbing payoff (i.e., the constant payoff corresponding to an absorbing state) and no * means that the state is unchanged. Basically as soon as I plays Top the game is over; otherwise the game is repeated.

It is clear that the sets of feasible payoffs in Γ_n, Γ_λ, or Γ_∞ coincide with the convex hull of $\{(1,0); (0,1); (0,2)\}$. Moreover, player I (resp. II) can guarantee 1/2 (resp. 2/3) (cf. VII.4, Ex. 8, p. 418).

Let us write $V = \{1/2, 2/3\}$ for the threat point and note that the set of feasible individually rational admissible payoffs is $P = \{(\alpha, 2(1-\alpha)) \mid 1/2 \le \alpha \le 2/3\}$ (cf. Section IV.4, p. 190). Write E_λ (resp. E_n) for the set of equilibrium payoffs in Γ_λ (resp. Γ_n).

Proposition VII.4.1. *E_λ is reduced to $\{V\}$ for all λ in* $(0, 1]$.

Remark VII.4.2. The same result holds for the finitely repeated game, namely, $E_n = \{V\}$ for all n (cf. VII.4, Ex. 8, p. 418).

Proof. Given an equilibrium pair (σ, τ) of strategies in Γ_λ, denote by (x, y) the corresponding mixed move at stage 1, where x (resp. y) stands for the probability of Top (resp. Left). Remark first that $x = 1$ is impossible (the only best reply would be $y = 0$ inducing a non-individually rational payoff for player I). Similarly we have $y \neq 1$. Since λ is fixed, let us write w for the maximal equilibrium payoff of II in Γ_λ (compactness) and write again (σ, τ) for corresponding equilibrium strategies. Define also w' (resp. w'') as the normalized payoff for player II from stage 2 on, induced by (σ, τ) after the first stage history Bottom Left (resp. Bottom Right) and note that by the previous Remark w'' is also an equilibrium payoff. Assume first that $x = 0$. $y \neq 1$ implies $w = (1-\lambda)w''$ which contradicts the choice of w. On the other hand, $y = 0$ implies that the only best reply is $x = 0$. We are thus left with the case $x, y \in (0, 1)$. Hence w' is also an equilibrium payoff, and the equilibrium conditions imply:

$$w = \lambda(1-x) + (1-\lambda)(1-x)w' = 2x + (1-\lambda)(1-x)w''.$$

Hence:

$$(1-x)(\lambda + (1-\lambda)w) \ge w \quad \text{and} \quad (1-x)(2 - (1-\lambda)w) \le 2 - w,$$

which implies:

$$(2-w)(\lambda + (1-\lambda)w) \ge w(2 - (1-\lambda)w),$$

and finally:

$$2\lambda \geq 3\lambda w.$$

Thus E_λ is included in the set $\{ g \in \mathbb{R}^2 \mid g_2 = 2/3 \}$ for all $\lambda \in (0, 1]$. Consider now an equilibrium pair inducing the maximal payoff for player I, say u. Define as above u' and u'' and write the equilibrium conditions: $u = y = y(1-\lambda)u' + (1-y)(\lambda + (1-\lambda)u'')$.

Using the definition of u this leads to $u \leq u^2(1-\lambda) + (1-u)(\lambda + (1-\lambda))u)$, which gives $2u\lambda \leq \lambda$. Hence $u = 1/2$ and $E_\lambda = \{V\}$. ∎

We now study E_0.

Lemma VII.4.2. $E_0 \subseteq P$.

Proof. Since any equilibrium payoff is feasible and individually rational it is actually sufficient to prove that E_0 is included in the segment $[(1,0);(0,2)]$. But in fact, if the probability of reaching an absorbing payoff on the equilibrium path is less than one, player I is essentially playing Bottom after some finite stage. Note that the corresponding feasible payoffs after this stage are no longer individually rational, hence the contradiction. Formally let θ stand for the stopping time corresponding to the first Top and let (σ, τ) be an equilibrium. Assume that $\rho = \mathsf{Pr}_{\sigma,\tau}(\theta = +\infty) > 0$. Given $\eta > 0$, define N such that $\mathsf{Pr}_{\sigma,\tau}(\theta < +\infty \mid \theta \geq N) < \eta$. The sum of the expected payoffs after N conditional on $\theta \geq N$ is thus at most $(1-\eta) + 2\eta$. Thus, for $\eta < 1/18$, one player can increase his payoff by 1/18 by deviating. The total expected gain is at least $\rho/18$; hence for any ε equilibrium $\rho \leq 18\varepsilon$, and $2g^{\mathrm{I}} + g^{\mathrm{II}} \geq 2 - 18\varepsilon$. ∎

Moreover, one can obtain explicitly the set of equilibrium payoffs.

Proposition VII.4.3. $E_0 = P$.

Proof. Take $g = (\alpha; 2(1-\alpha))$ in P with $1/2 \leq \alpha \leq 2/3$. We define the equilibrium strategies as follows:

- τ for player II is to play i.i.d. with $\mathsf{Pr}(\mathrm{L}) = \alpha$.
- σ for player I is to use an ε^2-optimal strategy in the zero-sum game $\tilde{\Gamma}$ with payoff matrix:

$$\begin{pmatrix} (1-\alpha_\varepsilon)^* & -\alpha_\varepsilon^* \\ -(1-\alpha_\varepsilon)/\varepsilon & \alpha_\varepsilon/\varepsilon \end{pmatrix}$$

with $\alpha_\varepsilon = \alpha - \varepsilon$.

Hence, if $\tilde{\gamma}$ is the payoff for player I in $\tilde{\Gamma}$, then for n large enough and any τ', we have $\tilde{\gamma}_n(\sigma, \tau') \geq -\varepsilon^2$, with $\rho_{\sigma,\tau}(\theta < +\infty) \geq 1 - \varepsilon$ and so σ is an ε-best reply to τ, since $\alpha \geq 1/2$.

On the other hand, we have for n sufficiently large and any τ':

$$\tilde{\gamma}_n(\sigma, \tau') = \rho\big((1-\alpha_\varepsilon)\overline{y} - \alpha_\varepsilon(1-\overline{y})\big) + (1-\rho)\big(-(1-\alpha_\varepsilon)\tilde{y} + \alpha_\varepsilon(1-\tilde{y})\big)/\varepsilon \geq -\varepsilon^2 \tag{1}$$

and

$$\rho\big((1-\alpha_\varepsilon)\overline{y} - \alpha_\varepsilon(1-\overline{y})\big) \geq -\varepsilon^2, \tag{2}$$

where $\rho = \frac{1}{n}\,\mathsf{E}[(n-\theta)^+]$, $\rho\overline{y} = \frac{1}{n}\,\mathsf{E}\left[(n-\theta)^+\mathbb{1}_{t_\theta = L}\right]$, $\tilde{y}(1-\rho) = \frac{1}{n}\sum_1^n \mathsf{E}\{t_m = \mathrm{L}, \theta > m\}$. Since $\gamma_n^{\mathrm{II}}(\sigma,\tau') = \rho(2(1-\overline{y})) + (1-\rho)\tilde{y}$ we obtain:

$$\begin{aligned}
\gamma_n^{\mathrm{II}}(\sigma,\tau') &\leq 2\rho - (2-\varepsilon)\rho\overline{y} + \varepsilon^3 + (1-\rho)\alpha_\varepsilon - \varepsilon\rho\alpha_\varepsilon && \text{by (1)}\\
&\leq 2\rho + (2-\varepsilon)(\varepsilon^2 - \rho\alpha_\varepsilon) + \varepsilon^3 + (1-\rho)\alpha_\varepsilon - \varepsilon\rho\alpha_\varepsilon && \text{by (2)}\\
&= \rho(2 - 3\alpha_\varepsilon) + \alpha_\varepsilon + 2\varepsilon^2\\
&\leq 2(1-\alpha_\varepsilon) + 2\varepsilon^2 && \text{since } \alpha \leq 2/3\\
&\leq 2(1-\alpha) + 2\varepsilon + 2\varepsilon^2,
\end{aligned}$$

and hence the inclusion $E_0 \supseteq P$ and the result by the previous Lemma VII.4.2. ■

Remark VII.4.3. The two previous propositions show a clear discontinuity in the set of equilibrium payoffs between E_λ and E_0 as λ goes to 0 (compare the zero-sum case, e.g., VII.3.6, p. 407). Recall that the above ε-equilibria are also ε-equilibria in all sufficiently long finite games, and hence also in all Γ_λ for λ sufficiently small. One is thus led to wonder whether E_0 is not a more appropriate concept when analyzing long games than $\lim_{\lambda\to 0} E_\lambda$: does the latter not rely too much on common knowledge of each other's exact discount factor, and on exact maximization?

VII.4.b. Games with Absorbing States

This section shows the existence of equilibria for two-person games with absorbing states (Vrieze and Thuijsman, 1989).

By selecting an equilibrium payoff for each potential new state and taking expectation w.r.t. the transition probability, we are reduced to the case where the game is described by an $S \times T$ matrix where the (s,t) entry consists of a payoff vector $G_{s,t}$ in $\mathbb{R}^2$, a number $P_{s,t}$ in $[0,1]$ (probability of reaching the set of absorbing states), and a corresponding absorbing payoff, say, $A_{s,t}$ in $\mathbb{R}^2$. Given a non-absorbing past, if (s,t) is the pair of choices at stage n the payoff at that stage is $g_n = G_{s,t}$. With probability $P_{s,t}$ the payoff for all future stages will be $A_{s,t}$, and with probability $(1-P_{s,t})$ stage $n+1$ will be like stage n.

We shall write X, Y for the set of stationary Markov strategies in Γ_∞ that we identify with the set of mixed actions. By Theorem VII.2.3, for λ small enough there exist equilibrium strategies (x_λ, y_λ) in Γ_λ, with payoff $w_\lambda = \overline{\gamma}_\lambda(x_\lambda, y_\lambda)$ in $\mathbb{R}^2$, such that (x_λ, y_λ) converges to (x_∞, y_∞) and w_λ to w_∞ as $\lambda \to 0$. Let v_λ^{I} (resp. v_∞^{I}) be the value of the zero-sum game obtained through Γ_λ (resp. Γ_∞) when player II minimizes player I's payoff and similarly $v_\lambda^{\mathrm{II}}, v_\infty^{\mathrm{II}}$. Finally $v_\infty = (v_\infty^{\mathrm{I}}, v_\infty^{\mathrm{II}})$.

Lemma VII.4.4. $w^i_\infty \geq v^i_\infty$, $i = \text{I}, \text{II}$.

Proof. The equilibrium condition implies that $w^i_\lambda \geq v^i_\lambda$, and Theorem VII.3.1 shows that $\lim_{\lambda\to 0} v^i_\lambda = v^i_\infty$. ■

Lemma VII.4.5. $w^{\text{I}}_\infty = \lim_{\lambda\to 0} \overline{\gamma}^{\text{I}}_\lambda(x_\infty, y_\lambda)$.

Proof. The equilibrium condition implies that $\overline{\gamma}^{\text{I}}_\lambda(x_\infty, y_\lambda) \leq w^{\text{I}}_\lambda$. Now for λ small enough the support $S(x_\infty)$ of x_∞ in S is included in $S(x_\lambda)$, hence the result. ■

Note that for any pair of stationary Markov strategies (x, y) the payoff in Γ_∞ is well defined (as $\lim_{\lambda\to 0} \overline{\gamma}_\lambda(x, y)$ or $\lim_{n\to\infty} \overline{\gamma}_n(x, y)$) and will simply be denoted by $\gamma(x, y)$. The vector $\gamma(x_\infty, y_\infty)$ will play a crucial role in the proof: it corresponds to the non-discounted payoff of the limit of the discounted (optimal) strategies (as opposed to the w_∞ limit of the discounted payoff of the discounted strategies).

Definition VII.4.4. Let $R \subseteq S \times T$ be the set of absorbing entries, i.e., such that $P_{s,t} > 0$. Define $B(x, y) = \sum x_s A_{st} P_{s,t} y_t$, $P(x, y) = \sum x_s P_{s,t} y_t$. A couple (x, y) in $X \times Y$ is **absorbing** if $(S(x) \times T(y)) \cap R \neq \emptyset$ or equivalently $P(x, y) > 0$. In this case let $A(x, y) = B(x, y)/P(x, y)$.

Since:

$$\overline{\gamma}_\lambda(x, y) = \lambda x G y + (1-\lambda)[B(x, y) + (1 - P(x, y))\overline{\gamma}_\lambda(x, y)], \tag{3}$$

we obtain that if $\lim_{\lambda\to 0} \tilde{x}_\lambda = x$ and $\lim_{\lambda\to 0} \tilde{y}_\lambda = y$ with (x, y) absorbing, then:

$$\lim_{\lambda\to 0} \overline{\gamma}_\lambda(\tilde{x}_\lambda, \tilde{y}_\lambda) = \gamma(x, y) = A(x, y). \tag{4}$$

In particular the equilibrium condition implies that:

$$\text{if} \quad (x_\infty, y) \quad \text{is absorbing,} \quad \gamma^{\text{II}}(x_\infty, y) \leq w^{\text{II}}_\infty, \tag{5}$$

and, using Lemma VII.4.5, that:

$$\text{if} \quad (x_\infty, y_\lambda) \quad \text{is non-absorbing for} \quad \lambda \in (0, \overline{\lambda}], \quad \text{then} \quad \gamma^{\text{I}}(x_\infty, y_\infty) = w^{\text{I}}_\infty. \tag{6}$$

It follows that either:

Case A

- (x_∞, y_∞) is absorbing and $\gamma(x_\infty, y_\infty) = w_\infty$ by (4).
- or (x_∞, y_λ) and (x_λ, y_∞) are non-absorbing for $\lambda \in (0, \overline{\lambda}]$ and again $\gamma(x_\infty, y_\infty) = w_\infty$ by (6); or

Case B (x_∞, y_∞) is non-absorbing and (x_∞, y_λ) or (x_λ, y_∞) is absorbing for λ sufficiently small.

Assume, for example, that (x_∞, y_λ) is absorbing and define y''_λ as the restriction of y_λ on $\{\, t \mid (x_\infty, t) \text{ is absorbing} \,\}$ and $y_\lambda = y'_\lambda + y''_\lambda$. Obviously $y'_\lambda \to y_\infty$. Let then z be a limit point in Y of $z_\lambda = y''_\lambda / \|y''_\lambda\|$ as $\lambda \to 0$. Since $\overline{\gamma}^{\text{II}}_\lambda(x_\lambda, z_\lambda) =$

$\overline{\gamma}^{\mathrm{II}}_\lambda(x_\lambda, y_\lambda)$ and (x_∞, z) is absorbing we obtain by (4) $\gamma^{\mathrm{II}}(x_\infty, z) = w^{\mathrm{II}}_\infty$. Using (3) we get:

$$\overline{\gamma}^{\mathrm{I}}_\lambda(x_\infty, y_\lambda) = \frac{\lambda}{\lambda + (1-\lambda)P(x_\infty, y_\lambda)} x_\infty G y_\lambda + \left(1 - \frac{\lambda}{\lambda + (1-\lambda)P(x_\infty, y_\lambda)}\right) \frac{B(x_\infty, y_\lambda)}{P(x_\infty, y_\lambda)}.$$

Note that $B(x_\infty, y_\lambda) = B(x_\infty, y''_\lambda)$ and $P(x_\infty, y_\lambda) = P(x_\infty, y''_\lambda)$. Thus $A(x_\infty, y_\lambda) = A(x_\infty, y''_\lambda) = A(x_\infty, z_\lambda)$. Hence if μ is a limit point of $\lambda/\big(\lambda + (1+\lambda)P(x_\infty, y_\lambda)\big)$ we obtain, using Lemma VII.4.5 and (4), that:

$$w^{\mathrm{I}}_\infty = \mu\gamma^{\mathrm{I}}(x_\infty, y_\infty) + (1-\mu)\gamma^{\mathrm{I}}(x_\infty, z). \tag{7}$$

We can now prove the following:

Theorem VII.4.6. $E_0 \neq \emptyset$.

Proof.

(1) Assume first that $\gamma^i(x_\infty, y_\infty) \geq w^i_\infty$, $i = \mathrm{I}, \mathrm{II}$. By Lemma VII.4.4 $\gamma^i(x_\infty, y_\infty) \geq v^i_\infty$, $i = \mathrm{I}, \mathrm{II}$. The equilibrium strategies consist first of playing (x_∞, y_∞) until some large stage N and then to punish, i.e., to reduce the payoff to v^{I}_∞, say, as soon as $\|\overline{x}_n - x_\infty\| \geq \varepsilon$ for $n \geq N$ where $\overline{x}_n$ is the empirical distribution of moves of player I up to stage n, and similarly for II. To prove the equilibrium condition, note that non-absorbing deviations will be observed and punished and by (5) absorbing deviations are not profitable since by stationarity the future expected payoff, before an absorbing state, is still $\gamma(x_\infty, y_\infty)$. Hence $\gamma(x_\infty, y_\infty) \in E_0$.

(2) If $\gamma^{\mathrm{I}}(x_\infty, y_\infty) < w^{\mathrm{I}}_\infty$, then by the above analysis we are in case B where (x_∞, y_λ) is absorbing for λ small. Then (7) implies that $\gamma^{\mathrm{I}}(x_\infty, z) > w^{\mathrm{I}}_\infty$ and $\gamma(x_\infty, z)$ belongs to E_0. In fact, $\gamma^{\mathrm{II}}(x_\infty, z) = w^{\mathrm{II}}_\infty$, hence by Lemma VII.4.4 $\gamma(x_\infty, z) \geq v_\infty$, and we now describe the equilibrium strategies:

- Player I uses x_∞, until some large stage N_1 and then reduces player II's payoff to v^{II}_∞;
- Player II plays y_∞ with probability $(1-\delta)$ and z with probability δ as long as $\overline{x}_n$ is near x_∞ for $n \geq N_2$, and reduces I's payoff to v^{I}_∞ otherwise.

Given $\varepsilon > 0$, N_2, δ, and N_1 are chosen such that: $P_{x_\infty}(|\overline{x}_n - x_\infty| \geq \varepsilon) \leq \varepsilon$ for $n \geq N_2$, $(1-\delta)^{N_2} \leq \varepsilon$, $N_1 \geq N_2$, and $(1-\delta)^{N_1} \geq \varepsilon$, so that $n \geq N_1/\varepsilon$ implies $\overline{\gamma}_n(\sigma, \tau) \geq \gamma(x_\infty, z) - 4\varepsilon$. If player II deviates, a non-absorbing payoff will not be profitable, and by (5) the same will be true for an absorbing payoff.

As for player I, let θ be the first stage, if any, where $|\overline{x}_n - x_\infty| \geq \varepsilon$. For $n \geq N_1/\varepsilon$, if $\theta \geq n$, then the payoff against z is near $\gamma^{\mathrm{I}}(x_\infty, z)$ and the payoff against y_∞, if (x_∞, y_∞) is absorbing, is less than w^{I}

(by (5)). Similarly, if $N_2 < \theta < n$, then the absorbing payoff up to θ is near $\gamma^{\mathrm{I}}(x_\infty, z)$ or less than it and the payoff after θ is less than w^{I}. Finally, if $\theta \leq N_2$, the payoff up to θ is with probability $\geq 1 - \varepsilon$ obtained against y_∞, hence less than w^{I} if absorbing. ■

EXERCISES

1. Properties of the operator Ψ.

a. Consider a zero-sum stochastic game with finite state space K. For $x \in \mathbb{R}^K$, we want the value $\Psi(x)$ of $\Gamma(x)$ to exist: assume thus that S and T are compact, that $g^k(s,t)$ are separately u.s.c.-ℓ.s.c., and that $p(k \mid \ell; s, t)$ are separately continuous (even if one were interested only in $x \geq 0$, where an u.s.c.-ℓ.s.c. assumption would suffice, this assumption would imply separate continuity because probabilities sum to one). Then $\Psi \colon \mathbb{R}^K \to \mathbb{R}^K$ is a well-defined operator.

α. Ψ is monotone and $\Psi(x + c) = \Psi(x) + c$ for any constant vector c (cf. I.1, Ex. 1, p. 11). To obtain additional properties of Ψ, assume that g is bounded, and so:

β. $\|\lambda\Psi(x) - \mu\Psi(y)\| \leq M\,|\lambda - \mu| + \|\lambda x - \mu y\|$

(using systematically the maximum norm on $\mathbb{R}^K$) and that either S and T are metrizable (I.1, Ex. 7b, p. 14) or g is separately continuous (I.2, Ex. 1, p. 24), and so I.1, Ex. 6, p. 12, and I.1, Ex. 8, p. 14, are applicable to the functions $f(\lambda, x) = \lambda\Psi^k(x/\lambda)$ $(\lambda \geq 0)$ defined on $\mathbb{R}_+ \times \mathbb{R}^K$. Taking thus derivatives at $(0, x)$ yields:

γ. $\|\Psi(x + y) - A(x) - \Psi_x(y)\| \leq (1 + \|y\|)F[x/(1 + \|y\|)]$,

where $\Psi_x = \Psi_{\lambda x}$ $(\lambda > 0)$, A is positively homogeneous of degree 1, $F \leq M$, and $\lim_{\lambda \to \infty} F(\lambda x) = 0$.

Also the formula for the derivatives yields that:

δ. Ψ_x has the same properties as $\Psi = \Psi_0$, with the same constant M, and associated A_x, F_x, Ψ_{xy}, etc. (and $\Psi_x = \Psi_{x0} = \Psi_{xx}$).

(More precisely, for some universal constant c, Exercises 1aα–1aδ in Section VII.4 hold for $M = c \cdot \sup_{k,s,t} \left|g^k(s,t)\right|$.)

b. A number of other properties follow from the above:

α. $\|\Psi(y)\| \leq M + \|y\|$ (cf. VII.4, Ex. 1aβ)).

β. $\|\Psi(x) - A(x)\| \leq 2M$.

HINT. Use VII.4, Ex. 1bα, for Ψ_x (cf. VII.4, Ex. 1aδ) and $y = 0$, then VII.4, Ex. 1aγ, for $y = 0$; actually, a direct proof yields $\|\Psi(x) - A(x)\| \leq M$).

γ. $A(x) = \lim_{\lambda \to 0} \lambda^{-1}\Psi(\lambda x)$ (from VII.4, Ex. 1bβ, and homogeneity).

δ. A is monotone, $A(x + c) = A(x) + c$ (from VII.4, Ex. 1bγ, and VII.4, Ex. 1aα).

ε. $\|A(x + y) - A(x) - A_x(y)\| \leq \|y\|\,F(x/\|y\|)$ (from VII.4, Ex. 1aγ, using VII.4, Ex. 1bγ, and VII.4, Ex. 1aδ).

ζ. $\Psi_x(y) = \lim_{\lambda \to \infty}[\Psi(\lambda x + y) - \lambda A(x)]$ (from VII.4, Ex. 1aγ).

η. $A_x(y) = \lim_{\lambda \to \infty}[A(\lambda x + y) - \lambda A(x)]$ (from VII.4, Ex. 1bε (and VII.4, Ex. 1aγ), and the formula implied by VII.4, Ex. 1bγ, using VII.4, Ex. 1aδ).

θ. ("Euler's formula") $A_x(x) = A(x)$.

In particular, VII.4, Ex. 1aα–VII.4, Ex. 1aδ, determine uniquely A (cf. VII.4, Ex. 1bγ) and Ψ_x (cf. VII.4, Ex. 1bζ).

2. $\lim v_n$ for games with absorbing states. (Kohlberg, 1974)

Give a direct proof of existence of $\lim v_n$ for games with absorbing states.

HINT. Let $\overline{u}(\omega) = g(\omega)$ for $\omega \neq \omega_0$, $\overline{u}(\omega_0) = u$. Prove that $D(u) = \lim_{\lambda\to\infty}[\Psi^{\omega_0}(\lambda\overline{u}) - (\lambda + 1)u]$ exists for all u (cf. VII.4, Ex. 1 above) and is strictly monotone. Letting u_0 be such that $(u - u_0)D(u) < 0$ for all $u \neq u_0$, prove first that for every $\varepsilon > 0$, $\limsup v_n > u_0 - \varepsilon$, and then that $\liminf v_n > u_0 - \varepsilon$; conclude that $\lim v_n = u_0$.

3. Consider the following $(n \times n)$ game with absorbing states (recall that a * denotes an absorbing payoff and no * means that the state is unchanged):

$$\begin{pmatrix} 1^* & 0^* & 0^* & \cdots & \cdots & \cdots & 0^* \\ 0 & 1^* & 0^* & \cdots & \cdots & \cdots & 0^* \\ \vdots & \ddots & \ddots & \ddots & & & \vdots \\ 0 & \cdots & 0 & 1^* & 0^* & \cdots & 0^* \\ \vdots & & & \ddots & \ddots & \ddots & \vdots \\ 0 & \cdots & \cdots & \cdots & 0 & 1^* & 0^* \\ 0 & \cdots & \cdots & \cdots & 0 & 0 & 1^* \end{pmatrix},$$

and prove that $v(\lambda) = (1 - \lambda^{1/n})/(1 - \lambda)$.

4. Big match. (Blackwell and Ferguson, 1968)

Consider the following game with absorbing states: $\begin{pmatrix} 1^* & 0^* \\ 0 & 1 \end{pmatrix}$.

a. Prove that $v_n = v_\lambda \equiv 1/2 \quad \forall n, \forall \lambda$.
b. Prove that player I has no optimal strategies in Γ_∞.
c. Prove that player II can guarantee 1/2.
d. Prove that player I cannot guarantee more than 0 with Markov strategies.
e. A strategy φ with **finite memory** (say, for I) is defined by an internal (finite) state space, say, K, and two functions: q from $K \times T$ to $\Delta(K)$ that determines the new internal state as a function of the old one and of the move of the opponent, and f from K to $\Delta(S)$ that determines the move as a function of the current internal state. Prove that by adding new states one can assume f to be S-valued. Note that φ and a stationary strategy y of player II define a Markov chain on K, and that we can identify the internal states that induce through f the action Top. Use then the fact that the ergodic classes depend only on the support of y to deduce that I cannot guarantee more than 0 with such strategies.
f. Verify that if we modify the original proof of existence of v_∞ (Blackwell and Ferguson, 1968) (where $\lambda(s) = 1/s^2$, $N(s) = 1$, $\varepsilon = 0$, $M = 0$, and s_0 is large) by letting, at stage k, $\overline{\lambda}_k = \inf_{i\leq k}\lambda_i$ and playing $\sigma_{\overline{\lambda}_k}$ we obtain $E(g_\infty) = 0$ and $\liminf E(g_n) < 1/2$.
g. Verify in the following variant that a lower bound M is needed for the optimal strategy (i.e., there is an upper bound on λ_k):

$$\begin{pmatrix} 1^* & 0^* & 0^* \\ 0 & 1 & 1/2^* \end{pmatrix}.$$

h. Show that, for a game where the absorbing boxes of the matrix are all those belonging to a fixed subset of rows, v_n and v_λ are constant.

5. Need for uniform convergence. Consider the following one-person game: $\Omega = \mathbb{N} \cup \{\delta\}, S = \mathbb{N}$.

$P(n; n+1, s) = 1 \quad \forall n \geq 0, \forall s; \qquad P(0; 0, s) = 1 \quad \forall s; \qquad P(n; \delta, s) = 1$ iff $n = s$.

$\forall s \quad g(\omega, s) = \begin{cases} -1 & \text{if } \omega = 0 \\ 0 & \text{otherwise.} \end{cases}$

Prove that $\lim v_\lambda(\omega) = \lim v_n(\omega) = v_\infty(\omega) = -1$, for all $\omega \neq \delta$; and that $v_\lambda(\delta) = v_n(\delta) = 0$. Note that, on every history starting from δ, $\liminf \overline{x}_n$ is -1, but if v_∞ exists in our strong sense, it should equal $\lim v_\lambda$.

Prove that $\| v_\lambda - \lim v_\lambda \| = 1$.

Note that if we consider this game as a recursive game (cf. Section IV.5, p. 205) it has a well-defined value, being everywhere -1.

6. Study of $\lim v_n$. (Bewley and Kohlberg, 1976b)

a. Let λV_λ be the value of Γ_λ (Lemma VII.1.2). $V_\lambda = \Psi((1-\lambda)V_\lambda)$ (Lemma VII.1.2). Assume Ω finite. Then there exists $M > 0$ and vectors $a_\ell \in \mathbb{R}^\Omega$, $\ell = 0, \ldots, M-1$ such that $V_\lambda = v_\infty/\lambda + \sum_{\ell=0}^{M-1} a_\ell \lambda^{-\ell/M} + O\left(\lambda^{1/M}\right)$.

Deduce that $\Psi\left(v_\infty(\lambda^{-1} - 1) + \sum_{\ell=0}^{M-1} a_\ell \lambda^{-\ell/M}\right) = v_\infty/\lambda + \sum_{\ell=0}^{M-1} a_\ell \lambda^{-\ell/M} + O(\lambda^{1/M})$ and that for n large enough:

$$\Psi\left(v_\infty(n-1) + \sum_{\ell=0}^{M-1} a_\ell n^{\ell/M}\right) = v_\infty n + \sum_{\ell=0}^{M-1} a_\ell n^{\ell/M} + O(n^{-1/M}). \tag{8}$$

Prove then that if $V_n = n v_n$ is the non-normalized value of Γ_n, one has:

$$\left| V_n - v_\infty n - \sum_{\ell=0}^{M-1} a_\ell n^{\ell/M} \right| \leq \left| V_{n-1} - v_\infty(n-1) - \sum_{\ell=0}^{M-1} a_\ell n^{\ell/M} \right| + O(n^{-1/M}),$$

and hence that $\lim v_n = v_\infty$.

Remark VII.4.5. Bewley and Kohlberg prove, in fact, there is a similar expansion for the value of the n-stage game: $v_n = v_\infty + \sum_{k=1}^{M-1} a_k n^{-k/M} + n^{-1} \cdot O(\log n)$.

The expansion has to stop at that stage: cf. VII.4, Ex. 7, below.

b. Consider now the perfect information case so that $M = 1$. Prove that (8) can be strengthened to:

$$\Psi(v_\infty(n-1) + a_0) = v_\infty n + a_0.$$

Deduce that $|V_n - v_\infty n|$ is uniformly bounded.

7. (Bewley and Kohlberg, 1976b)

Consider the game $\begin{pmatrix} -1^* & 1 \\ 1 & 0 \end{pmatrix}$. Let $x_1 = 1/3$, $x_{n+1} = x_n + 1/(n+3)$. Prove that $V_n \leq x_n$ and $x_{n+1} - V_{n+1} \leq x_n - V_n + \beta_n$, where (β_n) is a convergent series. Deduce that $V_n \sim \log n$, and so has no asymptotic expansion in fractional powers of n; cf. VII.4, Ex. 6a, above.

8.

a. Prove that in the example in Section VII.4.a the minmax is $1/2$ for player I and $2/3$ for player II (use VII.4, Ex. 4).

b. Prove by induction that $E_n = \{V\}$.

9. Feasible payoffs. Denote by F_λ (resp. F_∞) the set of feasible payoffs in Γ_λ (resp. Γ_∞). (Note that they depend on the initial state ω.) Prove that $\mathsf{Co}\, F_\lambda$ and $\mathsf{Co}\, F_\infty$ have finitely many extreme points and that $\mathsf{Co}\, F_\lambda$ converges to $\mathsf{Co}\, F_\infty$.

HINT. Consider the one-person dynamic programming problem whose payoff is the scalar product $\langle u, g\rangle$ and let u vary in $\mathbb{R}^{\mathbf{I}}$.

10. Irreducible games. A stochastic game is irreducible if for any vector of (pure) stationary Markov strategies the induced Markov chain on states is irreducible.

a. *Zero-Sum Case.* Prove that $\lim v_n$ exists and is independent of the initial state. Deduce that v_∞ exists.

b. *Non-Zero-Sum Case.* Prove that F_∞ is convex and independent of the initial state. Prove that F_λ converges to F_∞. Deduce results analogous to Theorems IV.4.1, p. 190, IV.4.2, p. 191, IV.4, Ex. 3, p. 202, and IV.4, Ex. 8, p. 202.

11. Correlated equilibrium.

a. (Nowak and Raghavan, 1992) Consider a game as in Section VII.1.c, p. 396 with moreover $(\Omega, \mathscr{A})$ separable, and $P(\cdot \mid \omega, s)$ dominated by μ. Prove the existence of a stationary public extensive form correlated equilibrium (i.e., generated by a sequence of public i.i.d. random variables).

HINT. Consider the proof of Theorem VII.1.8, p. 398. To prove the measurability of $\omega \mapsto N_f(\omega)$ (closed subsets of compact metric spaces being endowed with the Hausdorff topology), identify $G_f(\omega)$ with its graph in $\overline{S} \times [-c/\lambda, c/\lambda]^{\mathbf{I}}$, and show that:

(1) $\omega \mapsto G_f(\omega)$ is measurable;
(2) the map from the space of all such graphs to the corresponding set of Nash equilibria is upper semi-continuous, hence Borel; and
(3) the continuity of the map from (graph, Nash equilibrium) to payoffs.

Note that $f \mapsto \mathscr{N}_f$ is still weak upper semi-continuous; hence there exists a fixed point $f_0 \in \mathscr{N}_{f_0}$. Use then a measurable version of Carathéodory's theorem (Castaing and Valadier, 1977, Th. IV.11 or Mertens, 2003) to represent f_0 as $\sum_{i=1}^{\mathbf{I}+1} \lambda_i(\cdot) f_i(\cdot)$ with $f_i \in N_{f_0}$. If x_n is uniform on $[0, 1)$, play at stage n, if the state is ω, a measurable equilibrium leading to $f_i(\omega)$ in $\Gamma((1-\lambda) f_0)\omega$ (using the inverse image of the continuous projection (graph, Nash Equilibrium) $\to$ (graph, payoffs)) if $x_n \in [\sum_{j=1}^{i-1} \lambda_j(\omega), \sum_{j=1}^{i} \lambda_j(\omega))$.

b. (Duffie et al., 1994)

α. Let S be a complete separable metric space and G a correspondence from S to $\Delta(S)$, convex-valued, and with a closed graph. J measurable in S is self-justified if $G(s) \cap \Delta(J) \neq \emptyset$ for all $s \in J$. For J self-justified, μ is invariant for J (under π) if π is a measurable selection from G and μ in $\Delta(J)$ satisfies:

$$\int \pi(s)(B)\mu(ds) = \mu(B)$$

for all B measurable $\subseteq J$. Prove that if J is compact and self-justified the set of invariant measures is non-empty compact convex: hence there exists an ergodic measure for π (extreme point). Consider the restriction of G to J and $\Delta(J)$ that we still denote by G. Let $\overline{G}$ be the graph and $m_1^{(\nu)}, m_2^{(\nu)}$ the two marginals of $\nu \in \Delta(\overline{G})$ on G and $\Delta(G)$. If $\eta \in \Delta(\Delta(J))$ let $\mathsf{E}(\eta)$ denote its mean. Show that $\mathsf{E} \circ m_2 \circ m_1^{-1}$ has a fixed point μ: there exists some ν such that $\mathsf{E}\, m_2(\nu) = m_1(\nu) = \mu$. Thus there exists a transition probability P from J to $\Delta(\Delta(J))$ with $\mu \otimes P = \nu$. Show that $E P(s) \in G(s)$ μ-a.s.

HINT. Given f real continuous on J and c real, let $A_2 = \{ \rho \in \Delta(J) \mid \int f d\rho > c \}$ and suppose that $\mu\{ s \mid G(s) \cap A_2 = \emptyset, (EP(s)) \in A_2 \} > 0$. Then $A_1 = \{ s \mid G(s) \cap A_2 = \emptyset, P(s)(A_2) > 0 \}$ satisfies $\mu(A_1) > 0$ and $0 = \nu(\overline{G} \cap A_1 \times A_2) = \int_{A_1} P(s)(A_2)\mu(ds) > 0$.

Deduce that there exists a measurable selection Π of G with $\mu \circ \Pi = \mu$. Observe that the set of ν satisfying $Em_2(\nu) = m_1(\nu)$ is compact convex and that every invariant measure μ is obtained from some solution $(\mu \otimes \Pi)$.

β. Consider a discounted stochastic game where Ω, S^i are metric compact, g^i is continuous on $\Omega \times S$, and the transition satisfies:

- norm continuity on $\Omega \times S$
- joint mutual absolute continuity, i.e., $q(\cdot; \omega, s) \ll q(\cdot; \omega', s')$.

Let $c = \|g\| / \lambda$ and $Z = [-c, +c]^{\mathbf{I}}$. Define $W = \Omega \times Y$, $Y = \prod_i \Delta(S^i) \times Z$ and a correspondence G from W to $\Delta(W)$ by: for $\overline{w} = (\overline{\omega}, \overline{x}, \overline{z})$, $G(\overline{w}) = \{ \nu \in \Delta(W) \mid \nu = \nu_\Omega \otimes \nu^Y$ (marginal on Ω, conditional on Y given ω) such that:

- $\nu_\Omega = q(\cdot \mid \overline{\omega}, \overline{x}) \equiv \int q(\cdot \mid \overline{\omega}, s)\overline{x}(ds)$
- $\overline{x}$ is an equilibrium with payoff $\overline{z}$ in the game:

$$f^i(x, \overline{\omega}) = g^i(x, \overline{\omega}) + (1 - \lambda) \int z^i d[q(\cdot \mid \overline{\omega}, x) \otimes \nu^Y] \}.$$

Show that G is convex-valued with a closed graph. (Use VII.4, Ex. 11bα, to get the norm continuity of $q(\cdot \mid \omega, s)$, and note that for $\nu_n \in \Delta(A \times B)$, $\rho_n \in \Delta(A)$, A, B compact metric, $\nu_n \to \nu$ (weak), $\nu_{n_A} \to \nu_A$ (norm), $\rho_n \to \rho$ (norm), $\rho \ll \nu_A$ imply $\rho_n \otimes \nu_n^B \to \rho \otimes \nu^B$ (weak).)

Deduce the existence of a justified set $W^* \subseteq W$ for G. (Consider the sequence of compact $W = W_0$, $W_{n+1} = \{ w \in W \mid \exists \nu \in G(w), \nu(W_n) = 1 \}$.) (Prove inductively that $\mathsf{Proj}_\Omega(W_n) = \Omega$ (Theorem I.4.1, p. 45).)

γ. Deduce the existence of a stationary equilibrium with an ergodic measure in the extended game with state space W^* and transition from $W^* \times S$ to $\Delta(W^*)$ given by:

$$q^*(\cdot \mid \omega, x, z; s) = q(\cdot \mid \omega, s) \otimes \Pi(\omega, x, z)$$

(where Π is the selection from G). (Let $\sigma^*(\omega, x, z) = x$.)

12. (Federgruen, 1978)

In the following stochastic game with perfect information there are no pure stationary Markov equilibria (the first two coordinates indicate payoffs, the other two coordinates indicate the corresponding transition probabilities):

$$\begin{pmatrix} (0, 1; 2/3, 1/3) \\ (0, -1; 1/3, 2/3) \end{pmatrix} \qquad ((1, 0; 2/3, 1/3) \ (-1, 0; 1/3, 2/3))$$

State 1 — State 2

Player I plays — Player II plays.

13. (Nowak and Raghavan, 1991)

Consider the following game with countable state space $\mathbb{N}$. The payoff is always 0 except in state 1 where it is 1. States 0 and 1 are absorbing. Given state $\omega = n$ the transition probabilities are deterministic and given by the following $S \times T$ matrix:

$$\begin{pmatrix} 1 & 0 \\ n+1 & n-1 \end{pmatrix}.$$

a. Prove that v_∞ exists and player II has an optimal stationary Markov strategy. Deduce that $v_\infty(n)$ decreases to $1/2$.

HINT. Consider the largest state ω where $v(\omega) \geq \frac{1}{2}$. Prove that there exists $\delta > \frac{1}{2}$ such that the probability $y(\cdot)$ of II playing Left satisfies $y(\omega') \geq \delta$ for $\omega' \geq \omega$.

b. Prove that with stationary Markov strategies player I cannot guarantee more than 0, as the initial state goes to infinity.

HINT. Let $x(\cdot)$ be the probability of Top. If $\sum_\omega x(\omega) < \infty$, II plays Left, and Right otherwise.

Remark VII.4.6. This game can be viewed as a recursive game or as a "positive" game, i.e., with the payoff being the sum of the (positive) stage payoffs. Compare with Section IV.5, p. 205, and (Ornstein, 1969); cf. VII.5, Ex. 4a, p. 426; cf. also Nowak (1985a).

14. Prove Remark VII.3.5, p. 406 (use Remark VII.3.2, p. 404).

15. Games with no signals on moves.

a. In a stochastic game with finite state and action sets, v_n and v_λ remain unchanged if the moves are not announced, but v_∞ may no longer exist.

b. (Coulomb, 1992)

Consider a game with absorbing states: G (resp. A) corresponds to the non-absorbing (resp. absorbing) payoffs and P is the absorbing transition. Define φ on $\Delta(S) \times \Delta(T)$ by:

$$\varphi(x, y) = \begin{cases} xGy & \text{if } (x, y) \text{ is non-absorbing } (xPy = 0), \\ \left(\sum x_s y_t A_{st} P_{st}\right)/xPy & \text{otherwise.} \end{cases}$$

Prove that the maxmin $\underline{v}$ of the game exists and equals $\max_x \min_y \varphi(x, y)$.

HINT. To prove that player I cannot get more consider a stage-by-stage best reply of player II to the conditional strategy of I given a non-absorbing past and use the following property:

$$\forall \delta > 0, \exists \varepsilon_0, \exists N : \forall \varepsilon \leq \varepsilon_0, \forall x : \left[\varphi(x, t') \leq \underline{v} + \delta \Longrightarrow xP_{t'} \leq \varepsilon\right]$$
$$\Longrightarrow \exists t : \left[xP_t \leq N\varepsilon \text{ and } xA_t \leq \underline{v} + 2\delta\right]. \qquad (9)$$

16. Let $\Omega = [0, 1]^{\mathbb{N}}$, X_n the nth projection, and $\mathscr{F}_n = \sigma(X_1, \ldots, X_{n-1})$. Prove that for all t in $[0, 1]$ and all $\varepsilon > 0$ there exists N and a randomized stopping time θ on $(\Omega, (\mathscr{F}_n))$ (i.e., $A_n(\omega) = \Pr(\theta(\omega) \leq n)$ is $\mathscr{F}_n$-measurable and $0 \leq A_n \leq A_{n+1} \leq 1$) satisfying:

1. $\forall n, \sum_{m \leq n}(A_m - A_{m-1})(X_m - t) \geq -\varepsilon$.
2. $\forall n \geq N, \frac{1}{n}\sum_{m=1}^n X_m \geq t + \varepsilon \Longrightarrow A_n \geq 1 - \varepsilon$.

HINT. Obtain θ as an ε-optimal strategy in a stochastic game.

17. Stochastic games as normal forms for general repeated games. Show that Sections IV.2, p. 178, and IV.3, p. 183, reduce in effect the asymptotic analysis of a general repeated game to that of a "deterministic stochastic" game, i.e., a stochastic game with perfect information and no moves of nature.

18. Upper analytic payoff functions. (Nowak, 1985a)

We use the notations of Section VII.1 and of Appendix A. Assume Ω, S, T, $\overline{S} \subseteq \Omega \times S$, $\overline{T} \subseteq \Omega \times T$, and $C = \{(\omega, s, t) \mid \omega \in \Omega,\ (\omega, s) \in \overline{S},\ (\omega, t) \in \overline{T}\}$ are Borel subsets of Polish spaces. g and $P(A \mid \cdot)$ are measurable on C and g is bounded.

Moreover $\overline{T}_\omega = \{t \mid (\omega, t) \in \overline{T}\}$ is compact; $g(\omega, s, \cdot)$ is l.s.c., and $P(A \mid \omega, s, \cdot)$ is continuous on $\overline{T}_\omega$, for all ω. Let $B = \{f : \Omega \to \mathbb{R} \mid f \text{ bounded and } \forall x \in \mathbb{R}\ \{f > x\} \in \mathscr{A}\}$ denote the set of bounded upper analytic functions on Ω; we write $\mathscr{A}$ for analytic sets and $\mathscr{B}$ for Borel sets.

Then the discounted game has a value (which belongs to B); player I has an ε-optimal $\mathscr{A}_{(\sigma,c)}$-measurable strategy and player II an optimal $\mathscr{A}_{(\sigma,c),s,(\sigma,c)}$-measurable strategy.

a. Show that, given f in B, $\Gamma(f)_\omega$ has a value $\Psi(f)_\omega$ and that $\Psi(f) \in B$.

HINT.

- Proposition I.1.9, p. 9, applied to $h(\omega, s, t)$ on $\overline{S}_\omega \times \overline{T}_\omega$ implies the existence of a value $V(\omega)$.
- Let:

$$\mathscr{M} = \{(\omega, \mu) \mid \omega \in \Omega,\ \mu \in \Delta(\overline{S}_\omega)\}$$

$$\mathscr{N} = \{(\omega, \nu) \mid \omega \in \Omega,\ \nu \in \Delta(\overline{T}_\omega)\} \quad \text{and}$$

$$\mathscr{C} = \{(\omega, \mu, \nu) \mid \omega \in \Omega,\ \mu \in \mathscr{M}_\omega, \nu \in \mathscr{N}_\omega\}.$$

Note that these sets are Borel subsets of Polish spaces too (Appendix A.9.c, p. 521), and that $\mathscr{N}_\omega$ is compact for all ω. Also $H(\omega, \mu, \nu)$ is upper analytic on $\mathscr{C}$ (Appendix A.9.f, p. 522) and $H(\omega, \mu, \cdot)$ l.s.c. on $\mathscr{N}_\omega$. Recall that $F(\omega, \mu) = \inf_{t \in \overline{T}_\omega} H(\omega, \mu, t)$ and $V(\omega) = \sup_{\mu \in \mathscr{M}_\omega} F(\omega, \mu)$. Hence to obtain $V \in B$ and the existence of ε-optimal $\mathscr{A}_{(\sigma,c)}$-measurable strategies for I it is enough to show that F is upper analytic on $\mathscr{M}$. Let $g_n(\omega, s, t) = \inf_{t' \in \overline{T}_\omega}[g(\omega, s, t') + nd(t, t')]$, where d is the metric on T. g_n is Borel measurable on C (Appendix A.8.a, p. 519), and, continuous in t. g_n increases to g, hence H_n (defined as H but with g_n) increases to H, and, by compactness of $\overline{T}_\omega$, F_n increases to F. It remains to prove the property for F_n. Let ζ_k be a dense family of Borel selections of $\overline{T}$ (Appendix A.8.b, p. 519). Then $F_n(\omega, \mu) = \inf_k H_n(\omega, \mu, \zeta_k(\omega))$ and the result follows (Appendix A.7.j, p. 519).
- Finally for II's strategy, it suffices to show that $G(\omega, \nu)$ is $\mathscr{A}^{\Omega}_{(\sigma,c)} \otimes \mathscr{B}^{\Delta(T)}$-measurable. In fact, then $\{(\omega, \nu) \mid G(\omega, \nu) = V(\omega)\}$ is also $\mathscr{A}^{\Omega}_{(\sigma,c)} \otimes \mathscr{B}^{\Delta(T)}$-measurable. Apply then Appendix A.7.j, p. 519. Using g_n as above, it is enough to prove the property for G_n, which is upper analytic. Let then ν_k be a dense family of Borel selection of $\mathscr{N}$; hence $f_k(\omega) = G_n(\omega, \nu_k(\omega))$ is upper analytic and thus $\mathscr{A}_{(\sigma,c)}$-measurable. Finally, since G_n is n-Lipschitz, $G_n(\omega, \nu) = \sup_k[f_k(\omega) - (n+1)d'(\nu_k, \nu)]$ is $\mathscr{A}^{\Omega}_{(\sigma,c)} \otimes \mathscr{B}^{\Delta(T)}$-measurable ($d'$ being the distance on $\Delta(T)$ defining the weak topology).

b. Then use Lemmas VII.1.2 and VII.1.3 (p. 393) on B.

19. An operator solution for stochastic games with limsup payoff. (Maitra and Sudderth, 1992) Consider a two-person zero-sum stochastic game with Ω countable, S and T finite, and $0 \le g \le 1$. The payoff of the infinitely repeated game is defined on each history by $g^* = \limsup \overline{g}_n$.

Then the game has a value.

a. Reduce the problem to the case where first g_n depends only on ω_n and moreover $g^* = \limsup g_n$. It will be convenient to start from $n = 0$; hence let $H_n = (\Omega \times S \times T)^n \times \Omega$.

b. A stopping rule θ is a stopping time on $(H_\infty, \mathscr{H}_\infty)$ that is everywhere finite. To every stopping rule θ is associated an ordinal number called the index, $\alpha(\theta)$, and defined inductively by: $\alpha(0) = 0$ and for $\theta \not\equiv 0$ $\alpha(\theta) = \sup\{\alpha(\theta[h_1]) + 1 \mid h_1 \in H_1\}$, where $\theta[h_1]$ is θ after h_1, i.e., $\theta[h_1](h_\infty) = \theta(h_1, h_\infty) - 1$. Show that for any probability P on $(H_\infty, \mathscr{H}_\infty)$ and any function $u \in \mathscr{U} = \{u \colon \Omega \to [0,1]\}$, one has:

$$\int u^* dP = \inf_\theta \sup_{\zeta \geq \theta} \int u(\omega_\zeta) dP. \qquad (\star)$$

c. For every u and n we define an auxiliary game $\Gamma^n(u)$ in which player I has the option to "leave" the game after move n; i.e., in addition to σ, player I chooses a stopping rule $\theta \geq n$ and the payoff is $g_\theta = g(\omega_\theta)$. This game is often called *leavable* for player I after move n.

Define an operator Φ on $\mathscr{U}$ by: $\Phi u(\omega_0) = \text{val}\,(\mathsf{E}_{\sigma,\tau}\, u(\omega_1))$ (corresponding to the value of the one-shot game $\mathscr{G}u$, i.e., where $\theta \equiv 1$) and a sequence:

$$U_0 = u\ ,\ U_{n+1} = u \vee \Phi U_n\ ,\ U = \sup U_n.$$

Deduce that U is the least function in $\mathscr{U}$ with $U \geq u \vee \Phi U$ and that $U = u \vee \Phi U$. Prove that the value of $\Gamma^0(u)$ is U.

HINT. For player II, prove by induction on $\alpha(\theta)$ that $\mathsf{E}^\omega_{\sigma,\tau}\, u(\omega_\theta) \leq U(\omega)$, by letting him play at each stage n optimally in $\mathscr{G}u$ starting from ω_n. Deduce that the value Ψu of $\Gamma^1(u)$ is ΦU.

d. The idea is now to approximate in some sense the original game Γ by leavable games Γ^n, with $n \to \infty$, using $(\star)$. Define $Q_0 = \Psi g$ and for each countable ordinal ξ, $Q_\xi = \Psi(g \wedge \inf_{\eta<\xi} Q_\eta)$; then $Q = \inf Q_\xi$ and show that $Q = \Psi(g \wedge Q)$.

e. Prove that player I can guarantee any $w \in \mathscr{U}$ satisfying $w \leq \Psi(g \wedge w)$.

HINT. Let him play a sequence of ε_n strategies in $\Gamma^1(g \wedge w)$ that induces a strictly increasing sequence θ_n of stopping rules with $\mathsf{E}_{\sigma,\tau}((g \wedge w)(\omega_{\theta_n}) \geq w(\omega_0) - \varepsilon$.

f. Deduce finally that Q is the value of Γ by showing by induction that player II can guarantee any Q_ξ. In particular Q is the largest solution of $w = \Psi(g \wedge w)$.

HINT. Assume that he can guarantee $\widetilde{Q} = \inf_{\eta<\xi} Q_\eta$ with some $\widetilde{\tau}$. Let τ^* be optimal in $\Gamma^1(g \wedge \widetilde{Q})$ and $m = \inf\{n \mid g(\omega_n) > \widetilde{Q}(\omega_n)\}$. Player II plays τ^* up to m and then $\widetilde{\tau}$. Show that for any $\varepsilon > 0$ there exists a stopping rule ζ such that $\theta \geq \zeta$ implies $\mathsf{E}_{\sigma,\tau}\, g(\omega_\theta) \leq \mathsf{E}_{\sigma,\tau^*}((g \wedge \widetilde{Q})(\omega_{\theta\wedge m})) + \varepsilon$.

g. The proof of the preceding point could be adapted to show that the minmax of Γ, say $\overline{V}$, satisfies $\overline{V} \leq \Psi(g \wedge \overline{V})$, hence an alternative proof, without using Q. (Compare Proposition II.2.8, p. 95, and II.2, Ex. 10, p. 100.)

h. (Maitra and Sudderth, 1993)

The result (assuming the reduction in VII.4, Ex. 19a, done) extends to a much more general setup: Ω, S, T are Borel subsets of Polish spaces (the last two can even vary in a measurable way with ω). T is compact, the transition is continuous in t, and g is bounded and upper analytic.

HINT. The idea of VII.4, Ex. 19g, cannot be used since measurability conditions on $\overline{V}$ are not present. The proof basically follows VII.4, Ex. 19d, VII.4, Ex. 19e, VII.4, Ex. 19f, but is much more delicate. First prove that U is upper analytic (VII.4, Ex. 18). Let $B = \{(\omega, x) \mid g(\omega) > x\}$, and for any real function w on Ω denote by $E(w)$ its epigraph $= \{(\omega, x) \mid w(\omega) \leq x\}$. Given $C \subseteq \Omega \times [0,1]$, define a function χ_C on Ω by $\chi_C(\omega) = \sup\{x \in [0,1] \mid (\omega, x) \in C^c \cap B\}$ so that $\chi_{E(w)} = u \wedge w$. One defines now Θ from subsets of $\Omega \times [0,1]$ to subsets of $\Omega \times [0,1]$ by:

$$\Theta(C) = \{ (\omega, x) \in \Omega \times [0,1] \mid [\Psi(\chi_C)](\omega) \le x \}.$$

Show that Θ preserves coanalytic sets and that $\Theta(E(w)) = E(\Psi(u \wedge v))$. Moschovakis' theorem (Appendix A.8.c, p. 520) or rather its dual then implies, letting $\Theta^0 = \Theta(\emptyset)$, that $\Theta^\infty = \bigcup_{\xi<\omega_1} \Theta^\xi = E(Q) = E(\Psi(u \wedge Q))$ and that Q is upper analytic. Prove then that Q is the value and that both players have universally measurable ε-optimal strategies.

20. Solvable states. (Vieille, 1993)

Consider a finite two-person non-zero-sum stochastic game. Define a subset R of states to be solvable if there exist $(x, y) \in \Delta(S) \times \Delta(T)$ such that:

- R is ergodic with respect to P and (x, y)
- $\forall \omega \in R, \forall t \in T, \mathsf{E}^{\omega}_{x,t}(v^{\mathrm{II}}_\infty) \le \gamma^{\mathrm{II}}_R(x, y)$ (and similarly for player I), where $\gamma_R(x, y)$ is the asymptotic average payoff on R.

a. Prove the existence of solvable states, i.e., non-empty solvable subsets.

HINT. Let x be a limit of optimal strategies of player I for v^{I}_λ and let y be a best reply. Show that there exists an ergodic class R with $\gamma^{\mathrm{I}}_R(x, y) \ge v^{\mathrm{I}}_\infty$, where moreover R is included in the subset of states where v^{I}_∞ is maximal.

b. Show that, if the initial state is solvable, an equilibrium exists.

c. Show that if $\#\Omega \le 3$, the game has an equilibrium.

VII.5. REMINDER ABOUT DYNAMIC PROGRAMMING

A dynamic programming problem is a one-player stochastic game specified by a state space Ω, an action space S, a set of constraints $A \subseteq \Omega \times S$, and a transition p from $\Omega \times S$ to Ω. Ω and S are standard Borel (Appendix A.6, p. 517), A is a Blackwell space (*ibid.*) with $\mathsf{Proj}_\Omega A = \Omega$, and p is a Borel transition probability. Let $H_n = (\Omega \times S)^{n-1} \times \Omega$, $H = \bigcup_{n\ge1} H_n$. Strategies are $\mathscr{U}$-measurable transitions from H to S with $\sigma(\omega_1, s_1, \dots, s_{n-1}, \omega_n)\,(A_{\omega_n}) = 1$, where $A_{\omega_n} = \{ s \mid (\omega_n, s) \in A \}$ and $\mathscr{U}$ is either the σ-field $\mathscr{B}_u$ (Appendix A.4.d.1, p. 515) of universally measurable sets ($\mathscr{B}$ are the Borel sets on H) or $\mathscr{B}_{(s,c)}$ (Appendix A.1, p. 511). M^* (resp. M, resp. SM) is the set of Markovian (resp. pure Markovian, resp. pure stationary Markovian) strategies, i.e., satisfying $\sigma(\omega_1, \dots, \omega_n) = \sigma_n(\omega_n)$ (resp. σ_n pure, resp. $\sigma_n (= x)$ pure and independent of n). It follows that given a $\mathscr{U}$-measurable mapping f (bounded above or below) defined on plays ($= H_\infty = (\Omega \times S)^{\mathbb{N}}$), for any strategy σ and initial probability $q \in \Delta(\Omega)$, $\int f d(\sigma \otimes q) = \varphi^q(\sigma)$ is well defined and $\omega \mapsto \varphi^\omega(\sigma)$ is $\mathscr{U}$-measurable. In particular, if f stands for the payoff $\widetilde{g}$ on plays, we obtain a payoff function γ on $\Omega \times \Sigma$. The value is then $V^\omega = \mathsf{sup}_\sigma \gamma^\omega(\sigma)$, and, given $\varepsilon \ge 0$, σ is ε-optimal at ω if:

$$\gamma^\omega(\sigma) \ge \begin{cases} (V^\omega - \varepsilon) & \text{if } V^\omega < \infty \\ \quad 1/\varepsilon & \text{if } V^\omega = +\infty, \end{cases}$$

and σ is ε-optimal if it is ε-optimal at every ω.

We will consider the case where $\widetilde{g} = \lim g_n$ with g_n defined on $(\Omega \times S)^n$ and upper analytic (i.e., $\{g_n > t\}$ or $\{g_n \geq t\}$ is a Blackwell space for all t). More precisely let g be an upper analytic bounded function on $(\Omega \times S)$ and consider the following cases:[1]

(D) Discounted Case: $g_n(\omega_1, \dots, s_n) = \sum_{i=1}^{n} g(\omega_i, s_i)(1-\lambda)^{i-1}$ (Blackwell, 1965),

(P) Positive Case: $g \geq 0$ and $g_n(\omega_1, \dots, s_n) = \sum_{i=1}^{n} g(\omega_i, s_i)$ (Blackwell, 1967b),

(N) Negative Case: $g \leq 0$ and $g_n(\omega_1, \dots, s_n) = \sum_{i=1}^{n} g(\omega_i, s_i)$ (Strauch, 1966).

EXERCISES

1. General properties

a. Prove that for any ω in Ω and σ in Σ, there exists τ in M^* with $\gamma^\omega(\sigma) = \gamma^\omega(\tau)$.

Hint. Denote by $\rho_n^\omega(\sigma)$ and $\zeta_n^\omega(\sigma)$ the probabilities induced by σ starting from ω on the nth-factor Ω and $\Omega \times S$. Use the von Neumann selection theorem (Appendix A.7.j, p. 519) to define τ in M^* such that for all B Borel in $\Omega \times S$:

$$\zeta_n^\omega(\sigma)(B) = \int \tau_n(\widetilde{\omega})(B_{\widetilde{\omega}})\rho_n^\omega(\sigma)(d\widetilde{\omega}).$$

b. Given π in $\Delta(\Omega \times S)$ let $\widehat{\pi}$ be the marginal on Ω and define $C \subseteq \Delta(\Omega) \times \Delta(\Omega \times S)$ by $C = \{(q, \pi) \mid \widehat{\pi} = q, \pi(A) = 1\}$. Let $\mathscr{M}$ be the family of sequences $\{\mu_n\}$, $\mu_n \colon \Delta(\Omega) \to \Delta(\Omega \times S)$ with a graph in C and define $\theta \colon \Delta(\Omega \times S) \to \Delta(\Omega)$ by $\theta(\pi)(K) = \int p(K \mid \omega, s)\pi(d\omega, ds)$ for all Borel K in Ω. Thus, given an initial q on $\Delta(\Omega)$, μ in $\mathscr{M}$ defines (through θ) a distribution on plays. Prove that, given σ in M^*, there exists μ in $\mathscr{M}$ inducing the same ζ_n^ω (for all ω); given q in $\Delta(\Omega)$ and μ in $\mathscr{M}$, there exists σ in M^* inducing the same ζ_n^q.

c. Deduce that $V^\omega = \sup_{\mu \in \mathscr{M}} \gamma^\omega(\mu)$. Denote by Π the set of probabilities on plays that are generated by some q in $\Delta(\Omega)$ and μ in $\mathscr{M}$. Show that Π is Blackwell.

Hint. $\{\pi \in \Delta(\Omega \times S) \mid \pi(A) = 1\}$ is Blackwell.

Deduce that $(q, \mu) \mapsto \gamma^q(\mu)$ is upper analytic. Use the von Neumann selection theorem to show that $\omega \mapsto V^\omega$ is upper analytic (thus $\mathscr{U}$-measurable).

d. Given a $\mathscr{U}$-transition y from Ω to S, define Φ_y on bounded or positive $\mathscr{U}$-measurable mappings f on Ω by:

$$\Phi_y f^\omega = \int (g(\omega, s) + \int f(\widetilde{\omega})p(d\widetilde{\omega} \mid \omega, s))y(\omega)(ds)$$

and

$$\Psi f^\omega = \sup_{s \in A_\omega} \{g(\omega, s) + \int f(\widetilde{\omega})p(d\widetilde{\omega} \mid \omega, s)\}.$$

[1] Other sources include Blackwell (1970), Dubins and Savage (1965), and Shreve and Bertsekas (1979).

Show that:

$$\text{(D)} \qquad \Psi(1-\lambda)V = V \tag{1}$$

$$\text{(N), (P)} \qquad \Psi V = V. \tag{2}$$

2. Existence of ε-optimal strategies.

a. (D) Prove that (1) has a unique solution.
(P) $W \geq 0$ and $\mathscr{U}$-measurable and $W \geq \Psi W \Longrightarrow W \geq V$.
(N) $W \leq 0$ and $\mathscr{U}$-measurable and $W \leq \Psi W \Longrightarrow W \leq V$.

HINT. Let $\varepsilon = \sum \varepsilon_i$ and y_i a $\mathscr{U}$-measurable mapping from Ω to S with:

$$W - \sum_{j \leq i} \varepsilon_j \leq \Phi_{y_i}(\prod\nolimits_{j<i} \Phi_{y_j})W.$$

b. (D) (N) Given σ in M^*, there exists τ in M with $\gamma(\sigma) = \gamma(\tau)$.

HINT. Purify inductively on histories with increasing length.

There exists ε-optimal σ in M.

HINT. Use (1) or (2) and VII.5, Ex. 2a.

If there exists σ optimal, then there exists τ in SM optimal.
(D) If σ is ε-optimal, there exists ε/λ-optimal τ in SM (cf. Lemma VII.1.3, p. 394).
c. x in SM is optimal implies that $V = \Phi_x V$ and $\gamma(x) = \Psi\gamma(x)$.
(D) (N) $V = \Phi_x V \Longrightarrow x$ optimal.
(D) (P) $\gamma(x) = \Psi\gamma(x) \Longrightarrow x$ optimal.
d. Let $\Psi^\infty(0) = \lim_n \Psi^n(0)$.
(P) (D) $\Psi^\infty(0) = V$,
(N) $\Psi^\infty(0) \geq V$ and $\Psi^\infty(0) = V \iff \Psi(\Psi^\infty(0)) = \Psi^\infty(0)$.
e. (P) There exists ε-optimal σ.

HINT. Use VII.5, Ex. 2d.

3. Special cases.

a. *S finite.* (D) (N) There exists σ in SM optimal.

b. (N) No ε-optimality in SM (compare VII.5, Ex. 2, and VII.5, Ex. 2b): take $\Omega = \{0, 1\}$, $S = \mathbb{N}$. State 0 is absorbing with (total) payoff -1. In state 1 the payoff is 0 and move n leads to state 0 with probability $1/n$.

$\Psi^\infty(0) \neq V$ (compare VII.5, Ex. 2d): take $\Omega = S = \mathbb{N}$. The transition is deterministic from state n to $n-1$ with payoff 0 until state 1 absorbing with (total) payoff -1. In state 0 the payoff is -1 and move n leads to state n.

4. (P) ; Ω countable and $V < +\infty$.

a. *ε-optimality.* (Ornstein, 1969) Prove that: $\forall \varepsilon > 0$, $\exists x \in SM$ with $\gamma(x) \geq (1-\varepsilon)V$.

HINT.

- Prove the result for Ω finite, using case (D).
- Given $K \subseteq \Omega$ denote by γ_K the payoff in the model where all states in K^c are absorbing with zero payoff. Prove that given ω and $\eta > 0$ there exist x in SM and K finite with $\gamma_K^\omega(x) > (1-\eta)V^\omega$.

- Let $\delta > 0$ and $L = \{\omega' \in K \mid V^{\omega'} \geq (1+\delta)\gamma^{\omega'}(x)\}$. Prove that $\gamma^{\omega}_{K\setminus L}(x) \geq (1 - \eta - 2\eta/\delta)V^{\omega}$ (decompose the payoff induced by x at ω before and after the entrance in L).
- Given $\varepsilon > 0$ let δ and η satisfy $1/(1+\delta) \leq 1 - \varepsilon/2$ and $\eta + 2\eta/\delta \leq \varepsilon$. Let $\mathscr{S}$ be the set of strategies that coincide with x when the current state is in $K \setminus L$. Show that $\sup_{\sigma \in \mathscr{S}} \gamma^{\omega}(\sigma) \geq (1-\varepsilon)V^{\omega}$.
- Modify the initial model by imposing the transition induced by x on $K \setminus L$. The new value is at least $(1-\varepsilon)$ the old one, and any strategy in SM will give $(1-\varepsilon)$ when starting from ω.
- Enumerate the elements in Ω and repeat the same procedure.

b. *Need for V finite in VII.5, Ex. 4a.* Let $\Omega = \mathbb{Z} \cup \{\delta\}$, $S = \mathbb{N}$. At state 0 move n leads to state n; then there is a deterministic translation to $n-1$ with payoff 1. On the states in $-\mathbb{N}$, the payoff is 0, and one goes from $-n$ to 0 with probability $1/n$, and to the absorbing state δ (with payoff 0) with probability $1 - 1/n$. Obviously $V^{\omega} = +\infty$ on $\mathbb{N}$, hence on $\mathbb{Z}$, but $\gamma^n(x) \xrightarrow[n \to -\infty]{} 0$ for all x in SM.

c. *No additive error term in VII.5, Ex. 4a.* Let $\Omega = L \cup M$, let L and M be countable, and let $S = \{1, 2\}$. From l_n move 1 leads to l_{n+1} (with a probability 1/2) or m_0 (probability 1/2) with payoff 0. Move 2 leads to m_{2^n-1}. The payoff is 1 on M with a deterministic transition from m_n to m_{n-1} until m_0 absorbing with payoff 0. Show that $V^{l_n} \geq 2^n$ and that for any x in SM there exists ω in L with $\gamma^{\omega}(x) \leq V^{\omega} - 1$.

d. *Optimality in VII.5, Ex. 4a.* In the framework of VII.5, Ex. 4a, prove that if there exists an optimal σ, there exists one in SM.

HINT. Show that if x satisfies $V = \Phi_x V$ and there exists $t > 0$ with $\gamma(x) > tV$, then x is optimal. Use then VII.5, Ex. 4a.

e. *No optimality in VII.5, Ex. 4a.* When S is finite and there is no x in SM that is optimal: let $\Omega = \mathbb{N}$. 0 is absorbing with payoff 0. In state n move 1 leads to state $n+1$ with payoff 0 and move 2 leads to state 0 with payoff $1 - 1/n$.

5. Average case. Let now $\gamma^{\omega}(\sigma) = \liminf \mathsf{E}^{\omega}_{\sigma}(\sum_{i=1}^{n} g(\omega_i, s_i)/n)$.

a. *S finite and Ω countable.*

α. Move 1 leads from n to $n+1$ with payoff 0. Move 2 leads from n to n with payoff $1 - 1/n$. There exists an optimal strategy and no optimal strategy in SM.

β. Move 1 leads from n to $n+1$ with payoff 0. Move 2 leads from n to δ absorbing with payoff 0 with probability α_n and to $-n$ with probability $1 - \alpha_n$. The payoff is 1 on $-\mathbb{N}$ with a deterministic transition from $-n$ to $-(n-1)$. Let $\alpha = \prod_n (1 - \alpha_n) > 0$. Then $V^0 \geq \alpha/2$ and for all x in SM, $\gamma^0(x) = 0$.

b. *Ω finite and S countable.* 0 is absorbing with payoff 0. From 1 move n leads to 0 with probability $1/n$ and to 1 with payoff 1 otherwise. There is no ε-optimal strategy in SM.

6. Adaptive competitive decision. (Rosenfeld, 1964)

Consider the following game Γ: a finite set of $S \times T$ matrices G^k, $k \in K$, is given. At stage 0 one element k^* is selected according to some probability p known to the players. At each stage n both players select moves s_n, t_n and are told the corresponding payoff $g_n = G^{k^*}_{s_n t_n}$ and the moves. This is a very special kind of game with incomplete information (cf. V.5, Ex. 11, p. 311, and Section VI.1, p. 326, for related results). Denote by v^k the value of G^k and by v its expectation: $v = \sum_{k \in K} p^k v^k$. We consider the infinite game with a payoff function up to stage n $R_n = n(\overline{g}_n - v^{k^*})$. Take as state set the set of subsets of K.

Then there exists a constant R such that both players can guarantee R with stationary Markovian (SM^*) strategies.

(In particular this implies that $\overline{\gamma}_n$ converges to v with a speed of convergence of $O(1/n)$.)

a. Show that if σ is in SM^* for each τ there exists τ' in SM^* with $\mathsf{E}_{\sigma,\tau}(R_n) \le \mathsf{E}_{\sigma,\tau'}(R_n)$.

b. For any non-expansive increasing map $f\colon \mathbb{R} \to \mathbb{R}$ let:

$$S(f) = \begin{cases} -\infty & \text{if } f(x) < x, \forall x \\ +\infty & \text{if } f(x) > x, \forall x \\ x^* \text{ s.t. } f(x^*) = x^*,\ |x^*| = \min\{\,|x| \mid f(x) = x\,\} & \text{otherwise.} \end{cases}$$

Prove that $\lim f^n(0) = S(f)$. Let $D_1(f) = \{\,x \mid x < f(x) \text{ or } x = f(x) \le 0\,\}$. Let $D_2(f) = \{\,x \mid x > f(x) \text{ or } x = f(x) \ge 0\,\}$. Show that if $x \in D_1(f)$, $\exists N,\ n \ge N \Longrightarrow f^n(0) \ge x$.

c. Assume first that only one outcome is unknown. This means that $G^k_{st} = G^{k'}_{st}$ for all k, k' and $(s,t) \ne (1,1)$ (these (s,t) are non-revealing). Consider the auxiliary one-shot matrix game $G(x)$ where x is real, with payoff:

$$G_{11}(x) = \sum_k p^k G^k_{11} - v, \qquad G_{st}(x) = G_{st} - v + x \quad \text{for } (s,t) \ne (1,1),$$

and denote by $w(x)$ its value.

α. Prove that if $x \in D_1(w)$, there exists a SM^* strategy σ of player I and N such that $n \ge N \Longrightarrow \mathsf{E}_{\sigma,\tau}(R_n) \ge x$, for all τ.

β. Show that $\overline{D}_1(w) \cap \overline{D}_2(w) \ne \emptyset$ (in particular $D_1 \ne \emptyset$).

d. Prove the result by induction on the number of unknown outcomes. Given a revealing payoff entry (s,t) let $\overline{R}(s,t) = \sum_k R(\Gamma \text{ given } G^k_{st})p^k$, and define a matrix by:

$$G_{st}(x) = \begin{cases} \sum_k p^k G^k_{st} - v + x & \text{if } (s,t) \text{ is non-revealing,} \\ \sum_k p^k G^k_{st} - v + \overline{R}(s,t) & \text{otherwise.} \end{cases}$$

Conclude by following the proof in VII.5, Ex. 6a.

e. Consider a finite family of games with the same strategy spaces, each of which has a value, and extend the result with Markovian strategies.

PART C

FURTHER DEVELOPMENTS

CHAPTER VIII

Extensions and Further Results

We study here extensions of the models of Chapters VI and VII.

The first three sections deal with games with lack of information on both sides where signals and states are correlated: a first class is the symmetric case, a second one corresponds to games with no signals, and a third one leads to a first approach to the full monitoring case.

The last section is devoted to a study of specific classes of stochastic games with incomplete information.

VIII.1. INCOMPLETE INFORMATION: THE SYMMETRIC CASE

In this section we consider games with incomplete information where the signaling pattern is symmetric so that at each stage both players get the same signals.

Formally we are given a finite collection of $S \times T$ matrices G^k, $k \in K$, with initial probability p in $\Pi = \Delta(K)$, and the players have no initial information on the true state k except p. We denote by A the common finite set of signals (the extension to a measurable setup is easy) and by A^k the corresponding signaling matrices.

Given k and a couple of moves (s, t), a signal a is announced to both players according to the probability distribution $A^k_{s,t}$ on A. Assuming perfect recall means in this framework that for all k, k' in K, $s \neq s'$ or $t \neq t'$ implies that $A^k_{s,t}$ and $A^{k'}_{s',t'}$ have disjoint support.

Denoting by $\Gamma(p)$ this game we have the following:

Theorem VIII.1.1. *$\Gamma(p)$ has a value.*

Proof. Define first the set of non-revealing moves, or more precisely non-revealing entries, at p by $\mathrm{NR}(p) = \{(s,t) \in S \times T \mid p_1 = p\}$ where p_1 is the posterior probability on K if (s,t) is played, i.e., for all a such that $\mathsf{Pr}_{s,t,p}(a) \equiv A^p_{st}(a) = \sum_k p^k A^k_{st}(a) > 0$, $p_1(a) = p^k A^k_{st}(a)/A^p_{st}(a)$. Given w, a bounded real function on Π and p in Π, we define a stochastic game with absorbing states $\Gamma^*(w, p)$ (cf. Section VII.4.a, p. 410) by the matrix:

$$G_{st}(w,p) = \begin{cases} \sum_k p^k G^k_{s,t} & \text{if } (s,t) \in \mathrm{NR}(p) \\ \left[\mathsf{E}_{s,t,p}(w(p_1))\right]^* \equiv \left[\sum_a A^p_{st}(a) w(p_1(a))\right]^* & \text{otherwise,} \end{cases}$$

where as usual a star * denotes an absorbing entry. By Theorem VII.3.1, p. 401, $\Gamma^*(w, p)$ has a value, say, $Vw(p)$.

Note that if Γ is a value v on Π, then v is a solution of the recursive equation (cf. Section IV.3.2, p. 184):

$$w = Vw. \tag{1}$$

The proof that Γ has a value will be done by induction on the number of states in K. We therefore assume that for all games with strictly less than $\#K$ states the value exists (and is a solution of the corresponding equation (1)), this being clearly true for $\#K = 1$. Note then that v is defined and continuous (in fact, even Lipschitz) on $\partial\Pi$. Let us now prove some properties of the operator V.

We first remark that $u \le w$ on Π implies:

$$\forall p \in \Pi, \quad 0 \le Vw(p) - Vu(p) \le \max_{(s,t)\notin \mathrm{NR}(p)} \{G_{st}(w,p) - G_{st}(u,p)\}, \tag{2}$$

and that V is continuous (for the uniform norm). Then we have:

Lemma VIII.1.2. *Let u be a real continuous function on Π with $u_{|\partial\Pi} = v$. Then Vu is continuous on Π and coincides with v on $\partial\Pi$.*

Proof. It is clear that $p \in \partial\Pi$ implies $p_1 \in \partial\Pi$, and hence $G(u, p)$ and $G(v, p)$ coincide on $\partial\Pi$ so that $Vu(p) = v(p)$ on $\partial\Pi$. In particular $Vu(p)$ is continuous there.

Now on $\Pi \setminus \partial\Pi$, $\mathrm{NR}(p)$ is constant, equal, say, to NR, and hence Vu is again continuous.

Finally, if $p \in \partial\Pi$ with $\mathrm{NR} \subsetneq \mathrm{NR}(p)$, note first that if $p^m \to p$, with $p^m \in \Pi \setminus \partial\Pi$, then $p^m_1(s,t) \to p_1(s,t) = p$ for (s,t) in $\mathrm{NR}(p) \setminus \mathrm{NR}$. Hence $G_{st}(u, p^m) \to \mathsf{E}_{s,t,p}(u(p_1)) = u(p) = v(p)$. Note now that in a game with an absorbing payoff replacing a non-absorbing entry by an absorbing one, equal to the value, does not change the value. Hence the value of the new game $\Gamma'(u, p)$, where the payoff is $v(p)$ for (s,t) in $\mathrm{NR}(p) \setminus \mathrm{NR}$, is still $v(p)$, hence the continuity. ∎

Lemma VIII.1.3. *If player I can guarantee u in Γ, he can also guarantee Vu.*

Proof. Let player I use in $\Gamma(p)$ an ε-optimal strategy in $\Gamma^*(u, p)$ and switch to a strategy that ε-guarantees u in Γ, at the current posterior probability, as soon as one absorbing entry is reached.

Formally, denote by g^* the payoff in $\Gamma^*(u)$; then there exist σ^* and N_0 such that:

$$\mathsf{E}_{\sigma,\tau,p}(\overline{g}^*_n) \ge Vu(p) - \varepsilon, \qquad \forall \tau, \forall n \ge N_0.$$

But for every p there exist $\sigma(p)$ and $N(p)$ such that:

$$\mathsf{E}_{\sigma(p),\tau,p}(\overline{g}_n) \geq u(p) - \varepsilon, \qquad \forall \tau, \forall n \geq N(p).$$

We define now θ as the entrance time to an absorbing payoff in Γ^* and σ as: σ^* until θ and $\sigma(p_\theta)$ thereafter. Then:

$$\overline{g}_n = \frac{1}{n}\left\{\left[\sum_{m=1}^{\theta\wedge n} g_m^* + (n - \theta \wedge n)u(p_\theta)\right] + \left[\sum_{m=\theta\wedge n+1}^{n} g_m - (n - \theta \wedge n)u(p_\theta)\right]\right\}.$$

Let N_1 be an upper bound for $N(p_1)$. Then for $n \geq N_0 + (C/\varepsilon)N_1$, we obtain:

$$\mathsf{E}_{\sigma,\tau,p}(\overline{g}_n) \geq Vu(p) - \varepsilon - \varepsilon. \tag{3}$$

■

We can now prove the theorem.

Player I can obviously guarantee $u_0(p) = \mathsf{sup}_{q\in\partial\Pi}\{v(q) - C\,\|p - q\|_1\}$, which is Lipschitz on Π. Hence by Lemma VIII.1.3, p. 432, he can guarantee any u_n, $n \geq 0$, with $u_{n+1} = \mathsf{max}\{u_n, Vu_n\}$. u_n is continuous by Lemma VIII.1.2, p. 432; hence $u \equiv \lim\uparrow u_n$ is l.s.c. Player I can guarantee u that coincides with v on $\partial\Pi$ and satisfies $u \geq Vu$. Define similarly w_0, w_n, and w. Obviously $w \geq u$ on Π. Let us prove the equality, and hence the result. Assume $w > u$ and let:

$$D = \{p \in \Pi \mid w(p) - u(p) = d = \sup_{q\in P}(w(q) - u(q)) > 0\},$$

and note that D is compact. Consider now some extreme point p^* of its convex hull. We have then: $Vw(p^*) - Vu(p^*) \geq d$. Note that $p^* \notin \partial\Pi$ and that NR $=$ $S \times T$ implies $d = 0$ by (2). Hence let $(s,t) \notin$ NR and note that the support of the corresponding p_1^* is not included in D. Obviously then $\mathsf{E}\{w(p_1) - u(p_1)\} < d$, hence a contradiction (by (2) again). ■

The same proof shows uniqueness:

Corollary VIII.1.4. *Let u' and u'' be two continuous solutions of* (1). *Then they coincide.*

Proof. By induction both functions coincide on $\partial\Pi$. Let $u_1 = \mathsf{min}(u', u'')$, $u_2 = \mathsf{max}(u', u'')$. Then $u_1 \geq Vu_1$ and $u_2 \leq Vu_2$. u_1 and u_2 are continuous and coincide on $\partial\Pi$, and hence everywhere by the previous proof. ■

VIII.2. GAMES WITH NO SIGNALS

VIII.2.a. Presentation

These games were introduced in Mertens and Zamir (1976a) under the name "repeated games without a recursive structure." According to our analysis in Chapter IV, the meaning is that the support of the associated consistent probabilities cannot be bounded, and hence no analysis based on finite dimensional state variables, as in Chapters V and VI or in the previous section, can be achieved.

The description of the game consists again of a finite collection of $S \times T$ payoff matrices G^k, k in K, with some initial probability p on Π, and none of the players is informed of the initial state. The transition probability on the signals is again defined by a family of matrices A^k, but where for all (s,t) in $S \times T$, A^k_{st} is deterministic, with support in $\{0, k\}$ (the extension to random signals is simple): either both players receive a "blank" signal ("0") or the state is completely revealed. We can thus assume in the second case that the payoff is equal to the value of the revealed game and absorbing from this time on. It is then sufficient to define the strategies on the "blank" histories, hence the name "game with no signals."

It will be convenient to assume the value of each G^k to be zero (we subtract the expectation of the value of G^k from the payoffs) and to multiply G^k by p^k, so that the expected payoff will be the sum of the conditional expected payoff, given k in K. Since p is fixed, we will write Γ_∞ for $\Gamma_\infty(p)$.

The analysis of the game will be done as follows:

- We first construct an auxiliary one-shot game $\overline{G}$ in normal form; basically we consider a class of strategies that mimic some strategies in Γ_∞, and we define the payoff in $\overline{G}$ as the corresponding asymptotic payoff in Γ_∞. We prove that $\overline{G}$ has a value $v(\overline{G})$.
- Then we show that the minmax in Γ_∞ exists and equals $v(\overline{G})$: in fact, the class chosen above is sufficient in the sense that none of the players can do better, for the minmax, than using a strategy in this class.
- Since there are games with no value we consider finally v_n and v_λ and prove that they converge.

VIII.2.b. An Auxiliary Game

We define the one-shot game $\overline{G}$ by the following strategy sets $\overline{X}_1$, $\overline{Y}$ and payoff function F:

$$\overline{X}_1 = \oplus_{S' \subseteq S} \Delta(S') \times \mathbb{N}^{S \setminus S'} \times S', \ \overline{Y} = \oplus_{T' \subseteq T} \Delta(T') \times \mathbb{N}^{T \setminus T'}.$$

Given x in $\overline{X}_1$ (resp. y in $\overline{Y}$) we denote the corresponding subset S' (resp. T') by S^x (resp. T^y), the first component by α^x (resp. β^y), the second by c^x (resp. d^y), and the third by s^x. We will also consider α^x and c^x as defined on S with $\alpha^x_s = 0$ for $s \notin S^x$ and $c^x_{s'} = 0$ for $s' \in S^x$. Let us denote by B^k be the subset of non-revealing entries, given k:

$$B^k = \{(s,t) \in S \times T \mid A^k(s,t) = 0\},$$

and by B^k_s (resp. B^k_t) the corresponding sections:

$$B^k_s = \{t \in T \mid (s,t) \in B^k\}, \ B^k_t = \{s \in S \mid (s,t) \in B^k\}.$$

We can now introduce the payoff $F(x, y) = \sum_k F^k(x, y)$, with:

$$F^k(x, y) = \mathbb{1}_{S^x \times T^y \subseteq B^k} \prod_t \alpha^x(B_t^k)^{d_t^y} \prod_s \beta^y(B_s^k)^{c_s^x} (s^x G^k \beta^y).$$

The interpretation of the strategies in $\overline{G}$ is given by the following strategies in Γ. For y in $\overline{Y}$: play β^y i.i.d. except for $d(y) = \sum_t d_t^y$ exceptional moves uniformly distributed before some large stage N_0. On d_t^y of these stages player II plays the move t. For x in $\overline{X}_1$, α^x and c^x have similar meanings, but player I uses s^x after stage N_0. Note that $F^k(x, y)$ can be expressed as:

$$F^k = \rho^k(x, y) f^k(x, y),$$

where:

$$\rho^k(x, y) = \mathbb{1}_{S^x \times T^y \subseteq B^k} \prod_t \alpha^x(B_t^k)^{d_t^y} \prod_s \beta^y(B_s^k)^{c_s^x}$$

stands for the asymptotic probability that the game is not revealed, given k, and:

$$f^k(x, y) = s^x G^k \beta^y$$

is the asymptotic payoff given this event. We also define:

$$X_1 = \{x \in \overline{X}_1 \mid \alpha_s^x > 0, \forall s \in S^x\}, \; Y = \{y \in \overline{Y} \mid \beta_t^y > 0, \forall t \in T^y\}.$$

We begin by proving that $\overline{G}$ has a value:

Proposition VIII.2.1. *The game $\overline{G}$ has a value $v(\overline{G})$, and both players have ε-optimal strategies with finite support on X_1 and Y.*

Proof. We first define a topology on $\overline{X}_1$ and $\overline{Y}$ for which these sets are compact. Let $X_1^* = \oplus_{S' \subseteq S} \Delta(S') \times \overline{\mathbb{N}}^{S \setminus S'} \times S'$, where $\overline{\mathbb{N}} = \mathbb{N} \cup \{\infty\}$, and define a mapping ι from X_1^* to $\overline{X}_1$ by:

$$\iota(x^*) = x \quad \text{with} \quad \begin{cases} S^x = S^{x^*} \cup \{s \mid c_s^{x^*} = \infty\} & \\ \alpha_s^x = \alpha_s^{x^*} & \text{for } s \in S^{x^*} \\ \alpha_s^x = 0 & \text{for } s \in S^x \setminus S^{x^*} \\ c_s^x = c_s^{x^*} & \text{for } s \notin S^x \\ s^x = s^{x^*}. & \end{cases}$$

Note that $F(x^*, y) = F(\iota(x^*), y)$ for all y in $\overline{Y}$. Endow now $\overline{X}_1$ with the strongest topology for which ι is continuous. Since X_1^* is compact, so is $\overline{X}_1$. A similar construction is done for $\overline{Y}$.

F is now uniformly bounded and measurable for any product measure on the product of compacts $\overline{X}_1 \times \overline{Y}$. Note that F is continuous on $\overline{X}_1$ for each y in Y and similarly on $\overline{Y}$ for each x in X_1. Moreover, for each x in $\overline{X}_1$ there exists a sequence x_m in X_1 such that $F(x_m, y)$ converges to $F(x, y)$ for all y in $\overline{Y}$; and similarly for y in $\overline{Y}$.

Apply now Proposition I.2.3, p. 19, to get the result. ■

VIII.2.c. Minmax and Maxmin

Theorem VIII.2.2.

- *$\overline{v}$ exists and equals $v(\overline{G})$.*
- *Player II has an ε-optimal strategy that is a finite mixture of i.i.d. sequences, each one associated with a finite number of exceptional moves, uniformly distributed before some stage N_0.*
- *Dual results hold for $\underline{v}$.*

Proof. The proof is divided into two parts corresponding to conditions (1) and (2) of Definition IV.1.2, p. 174.

Part A. Player I can defend $v(\overline{G})$

Before starting the proof let us present the main ideas. Since we are looking for a best reply, player I can wait long enough to decompose player II's strategy into moves played finitely or infinitely many times. Using then an optimal strategy in $\overline{G}$, he can also give a best reply to the behavior of II "at infinity." Finally this "asymptotic measure" can be approximated by a distribution on finite times and will describe, with the initial strategy in $\overline{G}$, the reply of I in Γ_∞.

Given $\varepsilon > 0$, assume $C \geq 1$ and define $\eta = \varepsilon/9C$. Let τ be a strategy of player II in Γ_∞. With our conventions in Section VIII.2.a, τ can be viewed as a probability on T^∞. We will denote in this section this set by Ω, with generic element $\omega = (t_1, \dots, t_n, \dots)$ or $\omega \colon \mathbb{N} \to T$.

We first introduce some notations:

- Given $T' \subseteq T$, let us denote by $\Omega_{T'}$ the elements ω with "support" in T', namely:

$$\Omega_{T'} = \{\omega \in \Omega \mid T(\omega) \equiv \{t \in T \mid \#\omega^{-1}(t) = \infty\} = T'\}.$$

  $\{\Omega_{T'}\}_{T' \subseteq T}$ is clearly a partition of Ω. Let $d_t(\omega)$ be the number of exceptional moves: $d_t(\omega) = \#\omega^{-1}(t)$ for $t \notin T(\omega)$, and $d_t(\omega) = 0$ for $t \in T(\omega)$.
- Given χ, the η-optimal strategy of player I in $\overline{G}$ with finite support on X_1 (cf. Proposition VIII.2.1, p. 435), we define:

$$\delta = \min\{\alpha_s^x \mid \chi(x) > 0, s \in S^x\}, \qquad \text{thus} \quad \delta > 0, \qquad \text{and}$$
$$\overline{c}_s = \max(\{0\} \cup \{c_s^x \mid \chi(x) > 0\}), \qquad \overline{c} = \sum_s \overline{c}_s.$$

- Given $N_1 \geq N_0$ in $\mathbb{N}$ and $T' \subseteq T$ let:

  $\Omega^1_{T'} = \{\omega \in \Omega_{T'} \mid \forall t \notin T',\ \omega^{-1}(t) \cap [N_0, +\infty) = \emptyset\}$,

  $\Omega^2_{T'} = \{\omega \in \Omega_{T'} \mid \forall t \in T', \#\{\omega^{-1}(t) \cap [1, N_0]\} > \ln(\eta)/\ln(1-\delta)\}$,

  $\Omega^3_{T'} = \{\omega \in \Omega_{T'} \mid \forall t \in T', \#\{\omega^{-1}(t) \cap [N_0, N_1]\} > \overline{c}\}$, and

  $\Omega^*_{T'} = \bigcap_i \Omega^i_{T'}$.

  We now choose N_0 and N_1 such that for all $T' \subseteq T$ with $\tau(\Omega_{T'}) > 0$: $\tau(\Omega^i_{T'} \mid \Omega_{T'}) > 1 - \eta, i = 1, 2, 3$, hence $\tau(\Omega^*_{T'} \mid \Omega_{T'}) > 1 - 3\eta$. This means that with high probability there will be no exceptional move after N_0 and that each element in the support of ω will appear a large number of times before N_0 and between N_0 and N_1.
- Given χ and any array Θ in $(N_0, +\infty)^{\overline{c}}$ with components $\{\theta_{sc} \mid s \in S, 1 \leq c \leq \overline{c}_s\}$ we define the strategy $\sigma(\Theta)$ of player I in Γ as first choosing $x \in X_1$ with χ, then using $\sigma[x](\Theta)$: play α^x i.i.d. before N_0, and afterwards play s^x at each stage, except, $\forall s \notin S^x$, c^x_s additional moves s, played at times θ_{sc} $(1 \leq c \leq c^x_s)$.
- Let finally $N_2 = N_1 \vee \max_\Theta \theta_{sc}$.

In the next two lemmas Θ is fixed, and we will write $\sigma[x]$ for $\sigma[x](\Theta)$.

Lemma VIII.2.3. *Let* $\pi^k_1(\sigma[x], \omega) = \mathbb{1}_{S^x \times T(\omega) \subseteq B^k} \prod_t \alpha^x(B^k_t)^{d_t(\omega)}$ *and* $P^k_1(\sigma[x], \omega) = \Pr\{k$ *is not announced before* $N_0 \mid k, \sigma, \omega\}$. *Then:*

$$\left|\pi^k_1(\sigma[x], \omega) - P^k_1(\sigma[x], \omega)\right| \leq \eta,\ \textit{for all } \omega \textit{ in } \Omega^*_{T(\omega)}.$$

Proof. Let $T(\omega) = T'$. Since ω is in $\Omega^1_{T'}$ one has:

$$P^k_1(\sigma[x], \omega) = \prod_{t \in T'} \alpha^x(B^k_t)^{\#\{\omega^{-1}(t) \cap [1, N_0)\}} \prod_t \alpha^x(B^k_t)^{d_t(\omega)}.$$

Now if $S^x \times T' \nsubseteq B^k$, let t in T' with $S^x \nsubseteq B^k_t$. Since $\omega \in \Omega^2_{T'}$ this implies:

$$\alpha^x(B^k_t)^{\#\{\omega^{-1}(t) \cap [1, N_0)\}} < (1-\delta)^{\ln \eta / \ln(1-\delta)} = \eta,$$

hence the result. ■

Lemma VIII.2.4. *Let* $\pi^k_2(\sigma[x], \omega) = \mathbb{1}_{T(\omega) \subseteq B^k_{s^x}} \prod_s \prod_{c=1}^{c^x_s} \mathbb{1}_{\omega(\theta_{sc}) \in B^k_s}$, *and let* $P^k_2(\sigma[x], \omega, n) = \Pr\{k$ *is not announced between* N_0 *and* $n \mid k, \sigma, \omega$, *and* k *is not announced before* $N_0\}$. *Assume* $n > N_2$; *then:*

$$\pi^k_2(\sigma[x], \omega) = P^k_2(\sigma[x], \omega, n), \quad \textit{for all } \omega \textit{ in } \Omega^*_{T(\omega)}.$$

Proof. Let again $T' = T(\omega)$ and recall first that $\omega \in \Omega^1_{T'}$ implies $\omega(m) \in T'$ for $m \geq N_0$. Note also that the moves of player I before and after N_0 are independent, and hence:

$$P_2^k(\sigma[x],\omega,n) = \mathsf{Pr}\{\omega(n)\in B^k_{s_m}\ \forall m\colon N_0\le m\le n \mid k,\sigma,\omega\}$$
$$= \prod_s \prod_{c=1}^{c_s^x} \mathbb{1}_{\omega(\theta_{sc})\in B_s^k} \prod_{N_0\le m\le n, n\notin\Theta} \mathbb{1}_{\omega(m)\in B^k_{s^x}}.$$

Since $\omega\in\Omega^3_{T'}$, the last product is precisely $\mathbb{1}_{T(\omega)\subseteq B^k_{s^x}}$. ■

We obtain thus, writing the payoff as: $\gamma_n(\sigma,\tau) = \mathsf{E}_{\chi,\tau}\{\sum_k \mathsf{Pr}(k \text{ not revealed before } n \mid k,\sigma[x],\omega)\,\mathsf{E}(G^k_{s_n t_n} \mid k \text{ is not revealed before } n,\sigma[x],\omega)\}$, the following majorization: $|\gamma_n(\sigma,\tau) - \mathsf{E}_{\chi,\tau}(\sum_k \pi_1^k(\sigma[x],\omega)\pi_2^k(\sigma[x],\omega,n)\sum_{t\in T(\omega)} G^k_{s^x t}\mathbb{1}_{\omega(n)=t})| \le C\eta + C\tau\{\bigcup_\omega(\Omega_{T(\omega)}\setminus\Omega^*_{T(\omega)})\} \le 4C\eta$. Reintroducing explicitly Θ, we obtain a minorization of the payoff:

$$\gamma_n(\sigma,\tau) \ge \mathsf{E}_\tau[\varphi\{(\omega(\theta))_{\theta\in\Theta},\omega(n),\omega\}] - 4C\eta,$$

where:

$$\varphi\{(\omega(\theta))_{\theta\in\Theta},\omega(n),\omega\} =$$
$$\mathsf{E}_\chi\Big[\sum_k \mathbb{1}_{S^x\times T(\omega)\subseteq B^k} \prod_t \alpha^x(B^k_t)^{d_t(\omega)} \prod_s\prod_{c=1}^{c_s^x} \mathbb{1}_{\omega(\theta_{sc})\in B^k_s\cap T(\omega)} G^k_{s^x\omega(n)}\mathbb{1}_{\omega(n)\in T(\omega)}\Big].$$

Let $\tilde\omega(n)\in L_\infty(\Omega;\tau)^{\#T}$ describe the random move of player II at each stage n and define $\Phi\colon L_\infty(\Omega;\tau)^{\#T(\#\Theta+1)}\to\mathbb{R}$ by $\Phi\{(\tilde\omega(\theta))_{\theta\in\Theta},\tilde\omega(n))\} = \mathsf{E}_\tau[\varphi\{(\omega(\theta))_{\theta\in\Theta},\omega(n),\omega\}]$. Then:

$$\gamma_n(\sigma,\tau) \ge \Phi\{(\widetilde\omega(\theta))_{\theta\in\Theta},\widetilde\omega(n))\} - 4C\eta. \tag{1}$$

We are now going to study Φ. Let D be the set of limit points of $\{\tilde\omega(n)\}$ in $L_\infty(\Omega;\tau)^{\#T}$ for $\sigma(L_\infty,L_1)$ and denote by F its closed convex hull. Define finally Φ^* from $F\times F$ to $\mathbb{R}$ by: $\Phi^*(f,g) = \Phi\{(f),g\}$ where (f) is the Θ-vector f. Remark first that:

$$\Phi^*(f,f) = \Phi\{(f),f\} \ge v(\overline{G}) - \eta, \qquad \text{for all } f \text{ in } F. \tag{2}$$

Indeed, note that if $\tilde\omega(\theta) = \tilde\omega(n) = f$, then $\varphi\{(f(\omega)),f(\omega),\omega\}$ is the payoff in $\overline{G}$ induced by χ and the pure strategy $\{T(\omega),f(\omega),d(\omega)\}$ of player II (recall that the support of $f(\omega)$ is included in $T(\omega)$), thus greater than $v(\overline{G})-\eta$, hence the claim by taking the expectation w.r.t. τ.

Now F is compact convex, and Φ^* is continuous, and hence by Theorem I.2.4, p. 21, Φ^* has a value, say, w. Player I has an η-optimal strategy ν with finite support on F and Φ^* being affine w.r.t. g, while player II has a pure optimal strategy, say, g^*. Hence, by using (2):

$$\forall g \in F, \quad \eta + \int_F \Phi^*(f, g)\nu(df) \geq w \geq \sup_{f \in F} \Phi^*(f, g^*) \tag{3}$$

$$\geq \Phi^*(g^*, g^*) \tag{4}$$

$$\geq v(\overline{G}) - \eta. \tag{5}$$

By convexity, F is also the closed convex hull of D in the Mackey topology; hence, since on bounded sets of L_∞ this topology coincides with the topology of convergence in probability (cf. I.2, Ex. 16, p. 30), we obtain that every f in F is a limit in probability of some sequence of convex combination of elements in the sequence $\{\widetilde{\omega}(n)\}$. More precisely, for all $f \in F$, all n, and all $j = 1, 2, \ldots$, there exists μ with finite support on $[n, +\infty)$ such that:

$$\Pr\Big(\big\| f - \sum_i \mu(i)\tilde{\omega}(i)\big\| > \eta\Big) < \eta^j.$$

Define inductively, for $j = 1, 2, \ldots$, a sequence of η^j approximations μ_j, with disjoint supports, starting from $N_0 = n$. Let $J > \overline{c}^2/2\varepsilon$ and $\overline{\mu} = 1/J \sum_{j=1}^{J} \mu_j$. Now we have:

$$\Pr\Big(\big\| f - \sum_i \overline{\mu}(i)\tilde{\omega}(i)\big\| > \eta\Big) < \eta/(1-\eta). \tag{6}$$

We then use $\overline{\mu}$ to select independently the $\overline{c}$ points of Θ in $[N_0, +\infty)$. Note that the probability of twice selecting the same i is smaller than $\sum_i \binom{\overline{c}}{2}\overline{\mu}^2(i) < \overline{c}^2/2 \max_i \overline{\mu}(i) < \eta$ by the choice of J. Given f in F, let us write σ^f for the strategy using $\overline{\mu}$ $(= \overline{\mu}^f)$ to choose Θ and then playing $\sigma(\Theta)$. Let $N^f > N_2$ with $\overline{\mu}\{(N^f, +\infty)\} = 0$. Then for $n > N^f$ we obtain the following, using (1):

$$\gamma_n(\sigma^f, \tau) \geq \mathsf{E}_{\overline{\mu}^f}\, \Phi\{(\tilde{\omega}(\theta))_{\theta \in \Theta}, \tilde{\omega}(n))\} - 5C\eta.$$

Since Φ is linear in each $\tilde{\omega}(\theta)$ and θ is i.i.d., (6) implies that for η small enough:

$$\gamma_n(\sigma^f, \tau) \geq \Phi\{(f), \tilde{\omega}(n)\} - 7C\eta. \tag{7}$$

Let N_j be a sequence along which γ_n converges to $\liminf \gamma_n$, and we still denote by N_j a subsequence on which $\tilde{\omega}(n)$ converges $\sigma(L_\infty, L_1)$ to some $g \in D \subseteq F$. We obtain:

$$\begin{aligned} \liminf \gamma_n(\sigma^f, \tau) &= \lim \gamma_{N_j}(\sigma^f, \tau) \geq \lim \Phi\{(f), \tilde{\omega}(N_j)\} - 7C\eta \\ &= \Phi^*(f, g) - 7C\eta. \end{aligned}$$

Let finally σ^ν denote the strategy of player I that chooses first f according to ν and then plays σ^f. Then:

$$\begin{aligned}\liminf \gamma_n(\sigma^\nu, \tau) &= \liminf \int_F \gamma_n(\sigma^f, \tau)\nu(df)\\ &\geq \int_F \liminf \gamma_n(\sigma^f, \tau)\nu(df)\\ &\geq \int_F \Phi^*(f, g)\nu(df) - 7C\eta\\ &\geq v(\overline{G}) - 9C\eta \qquad \text{using (3).}\end{aligned}$$

We have thus proved that, for all $\varepsilon > 0$, and for all τ, there exists σ with:

$$\liminf \gamma_n(\sigma, \tau) \geq v(\overline{G}) - \varepsilon.$$

Obviously the same lower bound for $\overline{\gamma}_n$ follows, which completes the proof of A.

Part B. Player II can guarantee $v(\overline{G})$

This part is much easier to explain: a pure strategy of player II in $\overline{G}$ induces a strategy in Γ_∞ by playing β i.i.d. except at finitely many stages where the exceptional moves are used. We will show that if these moves are uniformly spread over a large number of stages, player I's behavior can be approximated by a strategy in $\overline{G}$, so that the payoffs in both games will be close. The result will then follow by letting player II make an initial choice according to an optimal strategy in $\overline{G}$.

Let $\varepsilon > 0$ and ψ be an ε-optimal strategy for player II in $\overline{G}$ with finite support in Y. Define: $\overline{d} = \max\{d(y) = \sum_t d_t^y \mid y \in Y, \psi(y) > 0\} + 1$, and $\delta = \min\{\beta_t^y \mid y \in Y, t \in T^y \text{ and } \psi(y) > 0\}$. Choose finally $N_0 > (|\ln \varepsilon| \cdot \#S\overline{d}(\overline{d} + 1))/\varepsilon^{\overline{d}+1}\delta$ and define a strategy $\tau = \tau(N_0)$ of player II in Γ as:

- Use first ψ to select y in Y and then play the following $\tau[y; N_0]$.
- Generate random times $\{\theta_{td} \mid t \notin T^y, 1 \leq d \leq d_t^y\}$, by choosing independently and uniformly stages in $[1, N_0]$ (with new choices if some of these stages coincide). Let us write $\Theta = \{\theta_{td}\}$.
- Play now β^y i.i.d. except at stages θ_{td} where t is played.

Let ω in S^∞ be a pure strategy of player I in Γ, and let us compute the payoff induced by ω and τ. For this purpose, we will represent ω as a strategy in $\overline{G}$; given ω, N_0, and some $r \in \mathbb{N}$, define $x[\omega; r; N_0]$ as follows: let $n_s = \#\{\omega^{-1}(s) \cap [1, N_0]\}$, then $S^x = \{s \mid n_s \geq r\}$; $\alpha_s^x = n_s / \sum_{i \in S^x} n_i, s \in S^x$; $c_s^x = n_s, s \notin S^x$.

We first approximate the probability $Q^k(\omega, \tau)$ that the game is not revealed before stage N_0, given k, ω, τ.

Lemma VIII.2.5. *Let* $N_0 > (|\ln \varepsilon| .\#S\overline{d}(\overline{d}+1))/\varepsilon^{\overline{d}+1}\delta$ *and* $r = ((\overline{d}+1)|\ln \varepsilon|)/\ln(1-\delta)$*; then:*

$$\left|Q^k(\omega, \tau[y; N_0]) - \rho^k(x[\omega; r; N_0], y)\right| \leq 7\varepsilon.$$

Proof. Since ω, hence x, is fixed, we will write S' for S^x and α (resp. c) for α^x (resp.c^x); we will also use $\zeta(td)$ for $\omega(\theta_{td})$, Q for $Q^k(\omega, \tau[y; N_0])$, and E for $\mathsf{E}_{\tau[y;N_0]}$. Then we have:

$$Q = \mathsf{E}[\mathbb{1}_{\{\forall t, d,\, \zeta(td) \in B_t^k\}} \mathbb{1}_{\{\forall n \notin \Theta, 1 \leq n \leq N_0,\, j_n \in B^k_{\omega(n)}\}}].$$

This can be written as:

$$Q = \mathsf{E}\left[\prod_t \prod_{d=1}^{d_t^y} \mathbb{1}_{t \in B^k_{\zeta(td)}} \prod_{\substack{n \notin \Theta \\ 1 \leq n < N_0}} \beta^y(B^k_{\omega(n)})\right]$$

$$= \prod_{n=1}^{N_0} \beta^y(B^k_{\omega(n)}) \mathsf{E}\left[\prod_t \prod_{d=1}^{d_t^y} \mathbb{1}_{t \in B^k_{\zeta(td)}} / \beta^y(B^k_{\zeta(td)})\right].$$

Let us remark that, with $\mathbb{I} = \mathbb{1}_{\{\forall s,\, n_s = 0 \text{ or } \beta^y(B_s^k) \geq \varepsilon\}}$:

$$\left\| Q - \mathbb{I} \prod_s \beta^y(B_s^k)^{n_s} \mathsf{E}\left[\prod_t \prod_{d=1}^{d_t^y} \sum_{s \in B_t^k} \mathbb{1}_{\zeta(td)=s} / \beta^y(B_s^k)\right]\right\| \leq 2\varepsilon. \tag{8}$$

In fact, if at some stage n, $\omega(n) = s$ with $\beta^y(B_s^k) \leq \varepsilon$, then $Q \leq 2\varepsilon$ since $\Pr(n \in \Theta) \leq \overline{d}/N_0 < \varepsilon$. Now the probability that the random times θ_{td} differ from the original i.i.d. choices θ^*_{td} is:

$$\Pr\{\exists (t, d) \neq (t', d'), \theta^*_{td} = \theta^*_{t'd'}\} \leq 1 - \prod_{c=1}^{\overline{c}} (1 - c/N_0) \leq 1 - \exp(-\overline{c}^2/N_0) \leq \varepsilon^{\overline{c}+1}. \tag{9}$$

Otherwise the θ_{td} are i.i.d. and uniformly distributed, and hence:

$$\mathsf{E}\left[\prod_t \prod_{d=1}^{d_t^y} \sum_{s \in B_t^k} \mathbb{1}_{\zeta(td)=s} / \beta^y(B_s^k)\right] = \prod_t \sum_{s \in B_t^k} \left(\frac{n_s/N_0}{\beta^y(B_s^k)}\right)^{d_t^y}. \tag{10}$$

Recall that $\beta^y(B_s^k) < 1$ implies $\beta^y(B_s^k) \leq 1 - \delta$, and hence $n_s \geq r$ implies:

$$\left|\beta^y(B_s^k)^{n_s} - \mathbb{1}_{T^y \subseteq B_s^k}\right| \leq \varepsilon^{\overline{d}+1}. \tag{11}$$

Note finally that by the choice of N_0, $s \notin S^x$ implies $n_s/N_0 \leq (\varepsilon^{\overline{d}+1})/\#S\overline{d}$, and that the function $\prod_t z_t^{d_t^y}$ has Lipschitz constant $\overline{d}\varepsilon^{-\overline{d}+1}$ on $0 \leq z_t \leq 1/\varepsilon$, so that:

$$\mathbb{I}\left|\prod_t \sum_{s \in B_t^k} \left(\frac{n_s/N_0}{\beta^y(B_s^k)}\right)^{d_t^y} - \prod_t \sum_{s \in S^x \cap B_t^k} \left(\frac{n_s/N_0}{\beta^y(B_s^k)}\right)^{d_t^y}\right| \leq \varepsilon. \tag{12}$$

Obviously we have:

$$\square \prod_t \sum_{s \in S^x \cap B_t^k} \left(\frac{n_s/N_0}{\beta^y(B_s^k)}\right)^{d_t^y} \leq \varepsilon^{-\overline{d}}. \tag{13}$$

We use now (9)–(13) to get in (8):

$$\left| Q - \square \prod_{s \notin S^x} \beta^y(B_s^k)^{n_s} \mathbb{1}_{S^x \times T^y \subseteq B^k} \prod_t \sum_{s \in S^x \cap B_t^k} \left(\frac{n_s/N_0}{\beta^y(B_s^k)}\right)^{d_t^y} \right| \leq 5\varepsilon.$$

Finally, for $s \notin S^x$, with $n_s \neq 0$ and $\beta^y(B_s^k) < \varepsilon$, the second part above is smaller than ε, and hence we obtain:

$$\left| Q - \mathbb{1}_{S^x \times T^y \subseteq B^k} \prod_s \beta^y(B_s^k)^{c_s} \prod_t \sum_{s \in S^x \cap B_t^k} (n_s/N_0)^{d_t^y} \right| \leq 6\varepsilon. \tag{14}$$

It remains to replace n_s/N_0 by $\alpha_s = n_s/\sum_{s \in S^x} n_s$, but $\sum_{s \in S^x} n_s/N_0 \geq 1 - (\#S/N_0)r > 1 - \varepsilon^{\overline{d}+1}/\overline{d}$ so that $(\sum_{s \in S^x} n_s/N_0)^{-\overline{d}} < 1 + 2\varepsilon$ for ε small enough. Coming back to (14), we finally get: $|Q - \mathbb{1}_{S^x \times T^y \subseteq B^k} \prod_s \beta^y(B_s^k)^{c_s} \prod_t \alpha(B_t^k)^{d_t^y}| \leq 7\varepsilon$. ∎

Returning to the proof of B, let us now compute the average payoff in Γ at some stage $n > N_0/\varepsilon$. Define for $s \in S$ and $j > N_0$: $m_s^j = \#\{\omega^{-1}(s) \cap]N_0, j]\}$ and $n_s^j = \#\{\omega^{-1}(s) \cap [1, j]\}$. Then we have:

$$n\overline{\gamma}_n(\omega, \tau) \leq CN_0 + \sum_s \sum_{j=N_0}^{n-1} \mathbb{1}_{\omega_{j+1}=s} \mathsf{E}_\tau \sum_k Q^k$$
$$\left[\prod_{s' \neq s} (\beta^y(B_{s'}^k))^{m_{s'}^j}\right] \mathbb{1}_{T^y \subseteq B_s^k} sG^k \beta^y + \frac{C}{\delta},$$

where the last term comes from the fact that if $T^y \not\subseteq B_s^k$, then the average number of times s is played before k is revealed is less than $1/\delta$. Using the evaluation of Q^k in the previous Lemma VIII.2.5 we obtain:

$$\overline{\gamma}_n(\omega, \tau) \leq (1/n)\Big(\sum_{j=N_0}^{n-1} \sum_s \mathbb{1}_{\omega_{j+1}=s} \mathsf{E}_\tau \sum_k \mathbb{1}_{S^x \times T^y \subseteq B^k} \prod_y (\alpha^x(B_t^k))^{c_t^y}$$
$$\left[\prod_{\substack{s' \notin S^x \\ s' \neq s}} (\beta^y(B_{s'}^k))^{n_{s'}^j}\right] \mathbb{1}_{T^y \subseteq B_s^k} sG^k \beta^y + 10C\varepsilon\Big).$$

It remains to remark that the term $\mathsf{E}_\tau(\dots)$ equals precisely the payoff F in $\overline{G}$, corresponding to ψ, and the pure strategy x' defined by $S^{x'} = S^x \cup S$; $\alpha^{x'} = \alpha^x$ on S^x, and $\alpha^s = 0$; $c_s^{x'} = n_s^j$ on $S^{x'}$; $s^{x'} = s$. By the choice of ψ, $F(x', \psi) \leq v(\overline{G}) + C\varepsilon$, implying $\overline{\gamma}_n(\omega, \tau) \leq \frac{1}{n}((n - N_0)(v(\overline{G}) + C\varepsilon)) + 10C\varepsilon \leq v(\overline{G}) + 12C\varepsilon$.

This completes the proof of B, and hence of Theorem VIII.2.2. ■

For examples where $v(\overline{G}) \neq v(\underline{G})$ ($\underline{G}$ being obviously defined in a dual way); cf. VIII.4, Ex. 2, p. 475. We are thus led to study $\lim v_n$ and $\lim v_\lambda$.

VIII.2.d. $\lim v_n$ and $\lim v_\lambda$

As in the previous section, the analysis will be done through comparison with an auxiliary game. Note however that we cannot use an asymptotic approximation of the payoffs since the game is basically finite. What we will do is use a sequence of "approximating games." (Compare Section VIII.4.a below, where a single "limit" game can be constructed.)

For each L in $\mathbb{N}$ we construct a game G_L. The heuristic interpretation of G_L is Γ_n played in L large blocks, on each of which both players are using stationary strategies, except for some singular moves. The strategy sets in G_L are $\overline{X}^L$ and $\overline{Y}^L$, where, as before:

$$\overline{X} = \oplus_{S' \subseteq S} \Delta(S') \times \mathbb{N}^{S \setminus S'},$$

$$\overline{Y} = \oplus_{T' \subseteq T} \Delta(T') \times \mathbb{N}^{T \setminus T'}.$$

As in Section VIII.2.b we will write $x = (S^x, \alpha^x, c^x)$ and similarly for y. The probability of getting the signal 0, under x and y and given k, is again:

$$\rho^k(x, y) = \mathbb{1}_{S^x \times T^y \subseteq B^k} \prod_t \alpha^x(B_t^k)^{d_t^y} \prod_s \beta^y(B_s^k)^{c_s^x},$$

and the payoff is $f^k(x, y) = \alpha^x G^k \beta^y$. Given $x = \{x(l)\}$ (resp. $y = \{y(l)\}$) in $\overline{X}^L$ (resp. $\overline{Y}^L$), we define F_L by:

$$F_L(x, y) = \sum_k \frac{1}{L} \sum_{l=1}^{L} \Big(\prod_{m=0}^{l-1} \rho^k\{x(m), y(m)\} \Big) f^k(x(l) y(l)),$$

with $\rho^k\{x(0), y(0)\} = 1$. We introduce also $X = \{x \in \overline{X} \mid \alpha^x > 0 \text{ on } S^x\}$ and similarly Y.

Then we have the following result, the proof of which is similar to Proposition VIII.2.1:

Proposition VIII.2.6. *G_L has a value w_L and both players have ε-optimal strategies with finite support in X^L and Y^L.*

We can now state:

Theorem VIII.2.7. *$\lim_{n\to\infty} v_n$ and $\lim_{L\to\infty} w_L$ exist and coincide.*

Proof.

Part A. Sketch of the proof

Obviously it will be sufficient to show that $\liminf v_n \geq \limsup w_L$.

Denote then $\limsup w_L$ by w. Given $\varepsilon > 0$ and L_0 large enough we shall choose $L \geq L_0$ with $w_L \geq w - \varepsilon$ and χ_L an ε-optimal strategy of player I in G^L with finite support in X^L. Each x in the support of χ_L will induce a strategy $\sigma[x]$ of player I in Γ_n for n large enough. On the other hand, each pure strategy τ of player II in Γ_n will be represented as a strategy $y[\tau]$ in Y^L. We shall then prove that there exists $N(\varepsilon, L)$ such that $n \geq N(\varepsilon, L)$ implies:

$$\overline{\gamma}_n\big(\sigma[x], \tau\big) \geq F_L\big(x, y[\tau]\big) - 8\varepsilon \tag{15}$$

for all $x \in \operatorname{Supp} \chi_L$ and all $\tau \in \mathcal{T}$. Integrating will give:

$$\mathsf{E}_{\chi_L}\big(\overline{\gamma}_n(\sigma[x], \tau)\big) \geq F_L\big(\chi_L, y[\tau]\big) - 8\varepsilon.$$

Thus, defining σ in Γ_n as: select x according to χ_L and then play $\sigma[x]$, we obtain:

$$v_n \geq w_L - 9\varepsilon \geq w - 10\varepsilon.$$

Part B. Preliminary results

Given $x \in X$ we construct a strategy σ in Γ_n for n large enough. Let $c^x = \sum_s c_s^x$. σ will consist of playing α^x i.i.d. at each stage except on c^x stages. These exceptional stages are obtained by using c^x independent random variables θ_{sc}^*, $s \in S$, $1 \leq c \leq c_s^x$, uniformly distributed on $[1, n]$ (adding new trials if some choices coincide so that the final choices are θ_{sc}). At stage θ_{sc}, σ consists of playing s. Denote this strategy by $\sigma[x; n]$.

Given τ, a pure strategy of player II in Γ_n, we construct now y in Y. Let $d_t = \#\{j \mid \tau_j = t, 1 \leq j \leq n\}$ and given some r in $\mathbb{N}$, let $T' = \{t \in T \mid d_t \geq r\}$. Define y by $T^y = T'$; $\beta_t^y = d_t / \sum_{t \in T'} d_t$ for $t \in T'$; $d_t^y = d_t$ for $t \notin T'$. We denote this strategy by $y[\tau; r; n]$. Let $\mathscr{A}_m$ be the event $\{a_j = 0 \mid 1 \leq j \leq m\}$, where as usual a_j is the signal at stage j.

Then we rewrite Lemma VIII.2.5, p. 441, as:

Lemma VIII.2.8. *Let x in X and $\delta_x = \min\{\alpha_s^x \mid s \in S^x\}$. Choose $1/4 > \varepsilon_1 > 0$ and $r = (c^x + 1)\,|\ln \varepsilon_1| / \ln(1 - \delta_x)$. Then $n \geq |\ln \varepsilon_1| \cdot \# T c^x (c^x + 1)/\varepsilon_1^{c^x + 1} \delta_x$ implies:*

$$\big|\rho^k\{x, y[\tau; r; n]\} - P_{\sigma[x;n],\tau,k}(\mathscr{A}_n)\big| < 7\varepsilon_1.$$

Part C. Construction of σ in Σ and y in Y^L

Given $\varepsilon > 0$, let $\varepsilon' = \varepsilon / K$ and choose L_0 such that:

$$(1 - \varepsilon')^{\lfloor L_0^{1/2} \rfloor} \leq \varepsilon' \text{ and } \lfloor L_0^{1/2} \rfloor^{-1} \leq \varepsilon', \tag{16}$$

where $\lfloor \dots \rfloor$ denotes the integral part. Take $L \geq L_0$ and χ_L as in part A. Let $\delta = \min\{\delta_{x(l)} \mid 1 \leq l \leq L, x = \{x(l)\} \in \operatorname{Supp} \chi_L\}$, let $\overline{c} = \max\{c^{x(l)} \mid 1 \leq l \leq L$, and let $x = \{x(l)\} \in \operatorname{Supp} \chi_L\}$. Assume $\varepsilon_1 < \varepsilon'/7L$, $r = (\overline{c} + 1)\,|\ln \varepsilon_1|\, \ln(1 - \delta)$, and $N_0 \geq |\ln \varepsilon_1| \cdot \# T \overline{c}(\overline{c} + 1)/\varepsilon_1^{\overline{c}+1} \delta$. For $n = NL + n_1$ with $n_1 \leq L$ and $N \geq N_0$, we construct σ in Γ_n by specifying this strategy on each block l of length N, $l = 1, \dots, L$, (the lth block consists of the stages $m \in N(l) \equiv \{(l - 1)N + 1, \dots, lN\}$) to be $\sigma(l) \equiv \sigma[x(l); N]$. Similarly, given a pure strategy τ

of player II in Γ_n, we consider the restriction $\tau(l)$ of τ on each block l and define $y = \{y(l)\}$ by $y(l) = y[\tau(l); r; N]$, where (cf. B) $d_t(l) = \#\{m \in N(l) \mid \tau_m = t\}$, and so on.

Part D. Comparison of the payoffs

We are going to compare the payoffs in G_L for x and y and in Γ_n for σ and τ. Note that it is sufficient to approximate on each block and that we can work conditionally on the state being k, since the mappings $x \mapsto \sigma$ and $\tau \mapsto y$ do not depend on k. Accordingly, we shall drop the index k until (18). In G_L the payoff on block l is:

$$F_l(x, y) = \prod_{m=0}^{l-1} \rho\{x(m), y(m)\} f(x(l)y(l)),$$

and in Γ_n the payoff on the corresponding block can be written as:

$$\Phi_l(\sigma, \tau) \equiv \prod_{m=0}^{l-1} Q_m(\sigma, \tau)\varphi_l(\sigma, \tau),$$

where $Q_m(\sigma, \tau) = P_{\sigma,\tau}\{\mathscr{A}_{mN} \mid \mathscr{A}_{(m-1)N}\}$ and $\varphi_l(\sigma, \tau)$ is the average expected payoff on the stages in $N(l)$ conditional on $\mathscr{A}_{(l-1)N}$. By the choice of r and N_0 it follows from Lemma VIII.2.5, p. 441, that:

$$\left|\rho\{x(m), y(m)\} - Q_m(\sigma, \tau)\right| \leq 7\varepsilon_1,$$

hence:

$$\left|\prod_{m=0}^{l} \rho\{x(m), y(m)\} - \prod_{m=0}^{l} Q_m(\sigma, \tau)\right| \leq 7L\varepsilon_1 \leq \varepsilon', \quad \text{for all } l. \tag{17}$$

It remains then to compare $f_l (= f(x(l)y(l)))$ to φ_l. We shall first ignore the blocks where Q_m is small; in fact, after many such blocks the game will be revealed with high probability, and both F_l and Φ_l become approximately 0. Now on the blocks where Q_m is large, the expected average payoff given $\mathscr{A}_{(m-1)N}$ is near the Cesàro mean; hence f_m is near φ_m. Formally let $M_l = \{m \mid 1 \leq m \leq l,\ Q_m(\sigma, \tau) \leq 1 - \varepsilon'\}$, and let $m_l = \#M_l$. Define $l' = \min\{\{l \mid m_l \geq \lfloor L^{1/2} \rfloor\} \cup \{L + 1\}\}$. It follows from (16) that on $\{l' \leq L\}$, $\prod_{m=0}^{l'} Q_m \leq \varepsilon'$; hence using (17), we have for $l > l'$:

$$|F_l - \Phi_l| \leq 3\varepsilon' C.$$

The number of blocks in $M_{l'}$ is at most $\varepsilon' L$ by (16); hence it remains to consider $l \in \{1, \ldots, l'\} \setminus M_{l'}$. We have:

$$\varphi_l(\sigma, \tau) = \frac{1}{N} \sum_{m \in N(l)} \lambda_m \, \mathsf{E}_{\sigma,\tau}(G_{s_m t_m}),$$

where $\lambda_m = \Pr(\mathscr{A}_{m-1} \mid \mathscr{A}_{(l-1)N})$; hence $\lambda_m \geq 1 - \varepsilon', \forall m$, implying:

$$\Big|\varphi_l(\sigma, \tau) - \mathsf{E}_{\sigma,\tau} \frac{1}{N}(\sum_m G_{s_m t_m})\Big| < C\varepsilon'.$$

Using (9) we obtain that $\{\theta_{sc}\}$ will coincide with $\{\theta^*_{sc}\}$ with probability greater than $(1 - \varepsilon')$. On this event, they define a random subset of $\overline{c}$ stages in $N(l)$ such that on its complement:

- Player I plays $\alpha(l)$ i.i.d.
- The expected empirical distribution of τ is as on $N(l)$, say, $\tau^*(l) = \frac{1}{N}\sum_{m\in N(l)} \tau_m$.

It follows from the choice of r and N_0 that:

$$\big|\tau^*(l) - \beta(l)\big| \leq \varepsilon',$$

and hence:

$$\Big|\frac{1}{N}\mathsf{E}_{\sigma,\tau}(\sum_m G_{s_m t_m}) - \alpha(l)G\beta(l)\Big| \leq 3\varepsilon'.$$

Thus, for all $l \notin M_{l'}$, one has:

$$|F_l - \Phi_l| \leq 5\varepsilon'.$$

This implies:

$$\Big|\sum_{k\in K}\sum_{l\in L}(F^k_l - \Phi^k_l)\Big| \leq (5\varepsilon' L + \lfloor L^{1/2}\rfloor)K, \tag{18}$$

and finally:

$$\big|\overline{\gamma}_n(\sigma, \tau) - F_L(x, y)\big| \leq (5\varepsilon' L + \lfloor L^{1/2}\rfloor)K + 2L/n,$$

which implies (15). ∎

Basically the same construction will give:

Theorem VIII.2.9. $\lim v_\lambda$ *exists and* $\lim_{\lambda\to 0} v_\lambda = \lim_{L\to\infty} w_L$.

Proof. Given L and λ small enough, define $\{n_l\}, l = 1, \dots L$, by requiring $\sum_{n_l+1}^{n_{l+1}} \lambda(1-\lambda)^{m-1}$ to be near $1/L$. Now x induces σ with $\sigma(l) = \sigma[x(l); n_l]$. Given τ, denote by $\tau(l)$ its restriction to the lth block of length n_l and define $y(l)$ as $y[\tau(l); r; n_l]$. The approximations are then very similar to those in the previous section. ∎

VIII.3. A GAME WITH STATE-DEPENDENT SIGNALING MATRICES

VIII.3.a. Introduction and Notation

We consider here (not symmetrical) games with lack of information on both sides but where the signaling matrices do depend on the state (compare Chapter VI).

The simplest case is given by the following data: $K = \{0, 1\}^2 = L \times M$; we write $k = (l, m)$. The probability on K is the product $p \otimes q$ of its marginals, and we denote by P and Q the corresponding simplices. At stage 0, player I is informed about l and player II about m. The payoffs are defined by 2×2 payoff matrices G^{lm}, and the signaling matrices are the same for both players and given by:

$$A^{11} = \begin{pmatrix} T & L \\ c & d \end{pmatrix} \qquad A^{10} = \begin{pmatrix} T & R \\ c & d \end{pmatrix}$$

$$A^{01} = \begin{pmatrix} B & L \\ c & d \end{pmatrix} \qquad A^{00} = \begin{pmatrix} B & R \\ c & d \end{pmatrix}.$$

Remark VIII.3.1. The signals include the moves.

Remark VIII.3.2. As soon as player I plays Top some "type" is revealed: l if player II played Left at this stage, or m if he played Right.

Remark VIII.3.3. The previous game $\Gamma(p, q)$ has a value, $v(p, q)$, as soon as $p^1 p^0 q^1 q^0 = 0$, by the results of Chapter V.

Notation

- We write NS for the set of non-separating strategies (i.e., strategies that do not depend on the announced type). As in Chapter V, and this is one of the main differences with Chapter VI, NS is not included in the set NR of non-revealing strategies.
- θ is the stopping time corresponding to the first time I plays Top.
- We denote by $G(p, q)$ the average of the matrices G^k, and we will also write $\gamma^{pq}(\sigma, \tau)$ as $\sum_{lm} p^l q^m \gamma^{lm}(\sigma^l, \tau^m)$ for the payoff, where σ^l is σ given l and similarly for τ.

VIII.3.b. Minmax

We prove in this section the existence of the minmax and give an explicit formula for it. As in Section VIII.2 the construction relies on an auxiliary game.

Let $G(p)$ be the infinitely repeated stochastic game with lack of information on one side described by:

$$p^1 \qquad G^1 = \begin{pmatrix} g_{11}^{1*} & g_{12}^{1*} \\ g_{21}^{1} & g_{22}^{1} \end{pmatrix}$$

$$p^0 \qquad G^0 = \begin{pmatrix} g_{11}^{0*} & g_{12}^{0*} \\ g_{21}^{0} & g_{22}^{0} \end{pmatrix},$$

where a star (*) denotes an absorbing payoff (cf. Section VII.4.a, p. 410). Player I is informed, and we assume full monitoring. Denote by $w_1(p)$ the value of the one-shot $G_1(p)$.

Proposition VIII.3.1. *minmax $G(p)$ exists and equals $w_1(p)$.*

Proof. As usual we split the proof into two parts.

Part A. Player II can guarantee $w_1(p)$

In fact, let y be an optimal strategy of player II in $G(p)$ and define τ as: play y i.i.d. Given σ, the strategy of player I, and τ, let $z^l(n) = \mathsf{Pr}_{\sigma^l,\tau}(\theta \le n)$ and $x^l(n)$ be the vector in $\Delta(S)$ with first component $z^l(n)$. Since the play of player II is independent of σ, we easily obtain for the expected payoff ρ_n in $G(p)$ at stage n:

$$\rho_n(\sigma,\tau) = \sum_l p^l x^l(n) G^l y,$$

and hence, by the choice of y, $\overline{\rho}_n(\sigma,\tau) \le w_1(p)$, for all n and all σ.

Part B. Player II cannot get less than $w_1(p)$

Given τ, the strategy of player II in $G(p)$, note first that it is enough to define τ at stage n conditional on $\{\theta \ge n\}$, and hence τ is independent of the moves of player I. We can thus introduce $y_n = \mathsf{E}_\tau(t_n) \in \Delta(T)$. Given x, the optimal strategy of player I in $G_1(p)$, and y in $\Delta(T)$, define $\rho'(x,y)$ (resp. $\rho''(x,y)$) to be the absorbing (resp. non-absorbing) component of the payoff that they induce in $G_1(p)$. Formally:

$$\rho'(x,y) = \sum_l p^l x_1^l (G^l y)_1 \qquad \rho''(x,y) = \sum_l p^l x_2^l (G^l y)_2.$$

Let $\varepsilon > 0$ and choose N such that:

$$\rho'(x,y_N) \ge \sup_n \rho'(x,y_n) - \varepsilon.$$

Define σ as: play always Bottom except at stage N where x is used. For $n \ge N$ we get:

$$\begin{aligned}\rho_n(\sigma,\tau) &= \rho'(x,y_N) + \rho''(x,y_n)\\ &\ge \rho'(x,y_n) + \rho''(x,y_n) - \varepsilon\\ &\ge w_1(p) - \varepsilon,\end{aligned}$$

and hence $n \ge CN/\varepsilon$ implies $\overline{\rho}_n(\sigma,\tau) \ge w_1(p) - 2\varepsilon$. ■

Given $\alpha = (\alpha^1,\alpha^0)$ and $\beta = (\beta^1,\beta^0)$ in $\mathbb{R}^2$, $G(p,q;\alpha,\beta)$ is a game of the previous class with:

$$G^1 = \begin{pmatrix} v(1,q)^* & (q^1\alpha^1 + q^0\beta^1)^* \\ G_{21}(1,q) & G_{22}(1,q)\end{pmatrix}, \quad G^0 = \begin{pmatrix} v(0,q)^* & (q^1\alpha^0 + q^0\beta^0)^* \\ G_{21}(0,q) & G_{22}(0,q)\end{pmatrix}.$$

Let $w_1(p,q;\alpha,\beta)$ be the value of $G_1(p,q;\alpha,\beta)$, and hence, by Proposition VIII.3.1, the minmax of $G(p,q;\alpha,\beta)$.

We introduce two closed convex sets of vector payoffs in $\mathbb{R}^2$:

$$\mathscr{A} = \{\alpha \mid \alpha^1 r^1 + \alpha^0 r^0 \geq v(r, 1) \text{ for all } r \text{ in } P\},$$

$$\mathscr{B} = \{\beta \mid \beta^1 r^1 + \beta^0 r^0 \geq v(r, 0) \text{ for all } r \text{ in } P\}.$$

Remark VIII.3.4. $\mathscr{A}$ (resp. $\mathscr{B}$) corresponds to the affine upper bounds of $v(\cdot, 1)$ (resp. $v(\cdot, 0)$).

Theorem VIII.3.2. *$\overline{v}(p, q)$ exists on $P \times Q$ and is given by:*

$$\overline{v}(p, q) = \operatorname{Vex}_q \min_{\substack{\alpha \in \mathscr{A} \\ \beta \in \mathscr{B}}} w_1(p, q; \alpha, \beta).$$

Proof. The proof is again divided in two parts corresponding to conditions (1) and (2) of the definition of the minmax (Section IV.1.c, p. 174).

Part C. Player II can guarantee this payoff

Since player II knows m, it is enough by Theorem V.1.1, p. 215, to prove that given any (α, β) in $\mathscr{A} \times \mathscr{B}$, he can guarantee $w_1(p, q; \alpha, \beta)$. Consider now the following class $\mathscr{T}^*$ of strategies of player II:

1. Play NS up to stage θ.
2. If $a_\theta = \mathrm{T}$ (resp. B) play from this stage on optimally in $\Gamma(1, q)$ (resp. $\Gamma(0, q)$) (cf. Section V.3, p. 225).
3. If $a_\theta = \mathrm{L}$ (resp. R) play from this stage on a strategy that approaches the vector payoff α (resp. β) (cf. Section V.3 again).

Note that this construction is consistent: for (2), since player II was playing NS until θ, the posterior on M after this stage is still q; as for (3), $\mathscr{A}$ is precisely the set of vector payoffs that player II can approach in the game with lack of information on one side defined for $m = 1$.

It is now quite clear that, if player II is playing in $\mathscr{T}^*$, the original game $\Gamma(p, q)$ is equivalent to the auxiliary game G so that by playing an optimal strategy in $\mathscr{T}^*$ for G, player II can obtain in Γ minmax G. In fact, let y be an optimal strategy of player II in $G_1(p, q; \alpha, \beta)$ and given $\varepsilon > 0$, let $\tau(1)$ and $N(1)$ such that:

$$\overline{\gamma}_n^{l1}(\sigma, \tau) \leq \alpha^l + \varepsilon, \; l = 0, 1, \quad \text{for all } n \geq N(1) \text{ and all } \sigma,$$

and define similarly $\tau(0)$ and $N(0)$. Let $N = \max\{N(1), N(0)\}$ and τ be the corresponding strategy in $\mathscr{T}^*$ where 1 consists of playing y i.i.d., and 3 is to play $\tau(1)$ or $\tau(0)$.

Given a strategy σ of player I in Γ, let us consider the payoff $\overline{\gamma}_n^{pq}(\sigma, \tau)$. It suffices to bound $\overline{\gamma}_n^{1,q}(\sigma^1, \tau)$ from above, but by definition of τ and θ one has:

$$P_{\sigma^1, \tau}\{t_n = \mathrm{L} \mid n \leq \theta\} = y,$$

hence:

$$\mathsf{E}_{q,\sigma^1,\tau}[g_n \mid n \le \theta] = (G(1,q)y)_2.$$

Moreover, under (σ^1,τ), a_θ will take the values T, L, R with the respective probabilities y_1, y_2q^1, y_2q^0. Finally we have:

$$\mathsf{E}_{q,\sigma^1,t}[g_n \mid n > \theta \text{ and } a_\theta = \mathrm{T}] \le v(1,q),$$

and if $n \ge \theta + N$:

$$\mathsf{E}_{q,\sigma^1,\tau}\Big[(n-\theta)^{-1}\sum_{i=\theta}^{n} g_i \;\Big|\; a_\theta = \mathrm{L}\Big] \le \alpha^1 + \varepsilon.$$

From the previous evaluations we deduce that $n\overline{\gamma}_n^{1q}(\sigma^1,\tau)$ is bounded by:

$$\begin{aligned}\mathsf{E}_{\sigma^1,\tau}[(\theta\wedge n)(G(1,q)y)_2 + (n-(\theta\wedge n))\{y_1v(1,q)\\ + y_2(q^1\alpha^1+q^0\beta^1)\}] + n\varepsilon + 2CN.\end{aligned}$$

Let now $F(x,y) \equiv F(x,y;p,q;\alpha,\beta)$ be the payoff in $G_1(p,q;\alpha,\beta)$ when (x,y) is played. Then we have:

$$\overline{\gamma}_n(\sigma,\tau) \le F(\xi,y) + \varepsilon + 2CN/n,$$

where $\xi^l \in \Delta(S)$ with $\xi_2^l = (1/n)\,\mathsf{E}_{\sigma^l,\tau}(\theta\wedge n), l = 1,0$. So finally by the choice of y we get that $n \ge 2CN/\varepsilon$ implies:

$$\overline{\gamma}_n(\sigma,\tau) \le w_1(p,q;\alpha,\beta) + 2\varepsilon, \quad \text{for all } \sigma.$$

Part D. Player II cannot get less than $\overline{v}$

We want here to exhibit good replies of player I. A priori such a strategy, i.e., mainly a distribution of the stopping time θ given l, should depend on the posterior behavior of player II, which in turn could also be a function of θ. We are thus led to use a fixed point, or minmax, argument. Given (p,q) fixed, let us denote by $\varphi(\alpha,\beta)$ the set of optimal strategies of player I in $G_1(p,q;\alpha,\beta)$ defined as above by $x^l, l = 1,0$. Denote by $\psi(x)$ the set of vectors (α,β) in $\mathscr{A}\times\mathscr{B}$ that minimize $p^1x_1^1(q^1\alpha^1+q^0\beta^1)+p^0x_1^0(q^1\alpha^0+q^0\beta^0)$ or equivalently that minimize the absorbing payoff given x in G_1. Remark that $(\alpha,\beta)\in\psi(x)$ iff α is a supporting hyperplane to $v(.,1)$ at the posterior probability π with $\pi^1(x) = \mathsf{Pr}\{l = 1 \mid T, x\}$. Since the correspondences φ and ψ are u.s.c. and compact convex-valued, it follows that $\varphi\circ\psi$ has a fixed point, say, $\overline{x}(=\{\overline{x}^l(p,q)\})$. The construction of σ can now be explained: given τ, the strategy of player II, player I first plays Bottom until some stage N after which the martingale q_n of posterior probabilities on M is essentially constant. Player I now uses $\overline{x}(p,q_N)$ to compute the stage where his non-absorbing against τ is minimal and plays then once $\overline{x}$. Assuming this strategy for player I, a best reply of player II would be to use (α,β) in $\psi(\overline{x})$; hence the corresponding payoff is some $w_1(p,q_N;\alpha,\beta)$.

The formal proof follows. Denote by b the strategy of player I: "play always Bottom," and given τ, define N such that:

$$\mathsf{E}_{q,b,\tau}\big[\|q_n - q_N\|\big] \le \varepsilon, \ \forall n \ge N. \tag{1}$$

Use $\zeta(N)$ for the random variable $\overline{x}(p, q_N)$, π^N for $\pi(\overline{x}(p, q_N))$; and for $n \ge N$ define:

$$y_1(n) = P_{q,b,\tau}\{t_n = \mathrm{L} \mid \mathscr{H}_N\} \quad \text{and} \quad y_1^m(n) = P_{q,b,\tau^m}\{t_n = \mathrm{L} \mid \mathscr{H}_N\}.$$

Hence:

$$\mathsf{E}_{q,b,\tau}\big[\|y(n) - y^m(n)\| \mid \mathscr{H}_N\big] \le \mathsf{E}\big[\|q_{n+1} - q_N\| \mid \mathscr{H}_N\big] \stackrel{\text{def}}{=} \delta(n+1, N). \tag{2}$$

Denote finally by $\rho''(p, q; x, y)$ the non-absorbing payoff in $G_1(p, q)$, given x and y. For $\varepsilon > 0$, define $N^* \ge N$ such that:

$$\rho''\big(p, q_N; \zeta(N), y(N^*)\big) \le \rho''\big(p, q_N; \zeta(N), y(n)\big) + \varepsilon, \forall n \ge N. \tag{3}$$

σ is played as follows:

- Play b up to stage $N^* - 1$.
- Use $\zeta(N)$ at stage N^*.
  - If $s_n = \mathrm{B}$, keep playing b.
  - If $s_n = \mathrm{T}$, use an optimal strategy in the revealed game, namely:
    * If $a_{N^*} = \mathrm{L}$, use a strategy that gives at least $v(\pi_N, 1)$ at each further stage, and similarly if $a_{N^*} = \mathrm{R}$. (Recall that since player I was playing b up to stage $N^* - 1$ the posterior probability p_{N^*} is precisely π_N.)
    * If $a_{N^*} = \mathrm{T}$: given $\varepsilon > 0$, choose a strategy and some $\overline{N}$ such that $n \ge \overline{N}$ implies:

$$\mathsf{E}\left(\sum_{N^*+1}^{N^*+n} g_i \mid \mathscr{H}_{N^*}\right) \ge v(1, q_{N^*}) - \varepsilon, \forall \tau.$$

(Since $v(p, .)$ is Lipschitz, $\overline{N}$ can be chosen uniformly w.r.t. q_{N^*}.)

Before evaluating the payoff let us compute the probabilities of the different signals. We have:

$$\begin{aligned}
&\Pr\big(s_{N^*} = \mathrm{B} \mid \mathscr{H}_N\big) = p^1\zeta_2^1(N) + p^0\zeta_2^0(N),\\
&\Pr\big(a_{N^*} = \mathrm{T} \mid \mathscr{H}_N\big) = p^1\zeta_1^1(N) y_1(N^*),\\
&\Pr\big(a_{N^*} = \mathrm{L} \mid \mathscr{H}_N\big) = (p^1\zeta_1^1(N) + p^0\zeta_1^0(N)) q_N^1 y_2^1(N^*),
\end{aligned}$$

and analogous formulae for B and R.

It follows, using (2), that for $n \geq \overline{N}$:

$$\mathsf{E}\left(\sum_{N^*+1}^{N^*+n} g_i \middle| \mathscr{H}_N\right) \geq \sum_{i=N^*+1}^{N^*+n} \left(\rho''(p, q_N; \zeta(N), y(i)) - C\delta(i, N)\right)$$

$$+ n\big[p^1\zeta_1^1(N)y_1(N^*)v(1, q_{N^*}) + p^0\zeta_1^0(N)y_1(N^*)v(0, q_{N^*})$$

$$- \varepsilon + \left(p^1\zeta_2^1(N) + p^0\zeta_2^0(N)\right)y_2(N_*)\left(q_N^1 v(\pi_N, 1)\right.$$

$$\left. + q_N^0 v(\pi_N, 0)\right) - C\delta(N^*, N)\big].$$

Using (1) and (3) and the choice of ζ imply that the right-hand side can be bounded from below by the payoff in G_1:

$$\mathsf{E}\left(\sum_{N^*+1}^{N^*+n} g_i \mid \mathscr{H}_N\right) \geq F\left(\zeta(N), y(N^*); p, q_N; \alpha, \beta\right) - 2nC\varepsilon - 2n\varepsilon$$

for all (α, β) in $\mathscr{A} \times \mathscr{B}$. Since $\zeta(N)$ is optimal in G_1 at (p, q_N), we obtain, taking expectation and using Jensen's inequality:

$$\mathsf{E}\left(\sum_{N^*+1}^{N^*+n} g_i\right) \geq n \operatorname{Vex} \min_{\alpha\beta} w_1(p, q; \alpha, \beta) - 2n\varepsilon - 2nC\varepsilon.$$

Thus $n \geq N^* + \overline{N}$ implies $\overline{\gamma}_n(\sigma, \tau) \geq \operatorname{Vex} \min_{\alpha\beta} w_1(p, q; \alpha, \beta) - 5\varepsilon(C \vee 1)$. ∎

VIII.3.c. Maxmin

We prove in this section the existence of the maxmin and give an expression for it.

As in Section VIII.3.b we introduce the sets of vector payoffs that player I can obtain, namely:

$$\mathscr{C} = \{\gamma = (\gamma^1, \gamma^0) \mid \gamma^1 r^1 + \gamma^0 r^0 \leq v(1, r), \text{ for all } r \text{ in } Q\},$$

$$\mathscr{D} = \{\delta = (\delta^1, \delta^0) \mid \delta^1 r^1 + \delta^0 r^0 \leq v(0, r), \text{ for all } r \text{ in } Q\}.$$

Note that, since $v(., q)$ is concave, we obviously have:

$$p^1\gamma^m + p^0\delta^m \leq v(p, m), \quad m = 1, 0, \quad \text{for all } p \in P \text{ and all } (\gamma, \delta) \in \mathscr{C} \times \mathscr{D}. \quad (4)$$

VIII.3.c.1. Sketch of the Proof

Here player I can do better than using NS strategies and then concavifying, because player II does not have a reply that could allow him to observe the moves and to play non-revealingly until the convergence of the posterior probabilities on L. Basically a strategy of player I will be described by the distribution of the stopping time θ and by the behavior after θ. The second aspect is similar to Section VIII.3.b, namely, play in the game on P, at the posterior probability induced by his strategy if m is revealed, or approach some vector payoff in $\mathscr{C} \times \mathscr{D}$, if l is revealed. Since this last choice is history-dependent, some minmax argument will also be needed. As for the first part, as long as he is playing Bottom, player I observes the moves of his opponent. Because of (4), we can restrict ourselves to monotone behavior of the kind: play Top iff the frequency of Right exceeds some number, say, z, like in the "Big Match" (cf. VII.4, Ex. 4, p. 417). It remains to choose this number, and this can be done at random in a type-dependent way. A best reply of player II will then be to evaluate these distributions and to play an increasing frequency of Right up to some type-dependent level, say, u, that can also be random.

VIII.3.c.2. Preparations for the Proof

We are thus led to define U as the set of positive measures μ with finite support on [0, 1] and total mass less than 1 and V as the set of probability distributions ν on [0, 1]. $\overline{\mathscr{C}}$ (resp. $\overline{\mathscr{D}}$) is the set of measurable mappings from [0, 1] to $\mathscr{C}$ (resp. $\mathscr{D}$). Given μ^1 and μ^0 in U let π^l be a Radon–Nikodym derivative of $p^l\mu^l$ w.r.t. $\mu^* \equiv p^1\mu^1 + p^0\mu^0$ and $\rho^l(z) = p^l\mu^l(]z, 1])/\mu^*(]z, 1])$. Note that if $\mu^1(dz)$ is interpreted as the probability of "playing Top at level z" given $l = 1$, then $\pi(z)$ is the posterior probability on P if θ arises at z and $\rho(z)$ is the posterior probability, given Bottom up to this level z. Define also a payoff function on $P \times Q \times U^2 \times \overline{\mathscr{C}} \times \overline{\mathscr{D}} \times V^2$ by:

$$\varphi(p, q; \mu^1, \mu^0; \overline{\gamma}, \overline{\delta}; \nu^1, \nu^0) = \sum_m q^m \varphi^m(p; \mu^1, \mu^0; \overline{\gamma}, \overline{\delta}; \nu^m)$$

with:

$$\begin{aligned}
&\varphi^m(p; \mu^1, \mu^0; \overline{\gamma}, \overline{\delta}; \nu^m)\\
&= \int_0^1 \nu^m([z, 1])\big\{zv\big(\pi(z), m\big) + (1 - z)\big(\pi^1(z)\overline{\gamma}^m(z) + \pi^0(z)\overline{\delta}^m(z)\big)\big\}\mu^*(dz)\\
&\quad + \int_0^1 \mu^*(]z, 1])J(z, m)\nu^m(dz)
\end{aligned}$$

and where $J(z, m) = \min_{o \le u \le z}\{ug_{22}(\rho(z), m) + (1 - u)g_{21}(\rho(z), m)\}$.

In order to state the result, it remains to introduce:

$$\underline{\Phi}(p, q; \mu^1, \mu^0) = \sup_{\overline{\mathscr{C}} \times \overline{\mathscr{D}}} \inf_{V^2} \varphi(p, q; \mu^1, \mu^0; \overline{\gamma}, \overline{\delta}; \nu^1, \nu^0),$$

$$\overline{\Phi}(p, q; \mu^1, \mu^0) = \inf_{V^2} \sup_{\overline{\mathscr{C}} \times \overline{\mathscr{D}}} \varphi(p, q; \mu^1, \mu^0; \overline{\gamma}, \overline{\delta}; \nu^1, \nu^0).$$

Then we have:

Proposition VIII.3.3. $\underline{\Phi}(p, q; \mu^1, \mu^0) = \overline{\Phi}(p, q; \mu^1, \mu^0)$ *on* $P \times Q \times U^2$.

Proof. Remark first that φ depends upon $\overline{\gamma}$ and $\overline{\delta}$ only through their values at the finitely many points $\{z_i\}$, $i = 1, \ldots, R$ in the union of the supports of μ^0 and μ^1. Hence we can replace $\overline{\mathscr{C}}$ by the convex compact set $(\mathscr{C} \cap [-C, C])^R$ and similarly for $\overline{\mathscr{D}}$. Note now that V is convex and φ affine with respect to $(\overline{\gamma}, \overline{\delta})$. We can then apply Theorem I.1.1, p. 5, to get $\overline{\Phi} = \underline{\Phi}$. ■

Remark VIII.3.5. We shall use later the fact that a best reply to ν minimizes:

$$\overline{\gamma}^1(z)q^1\nu^1([z,1]) + \overline{\gamma}^0(z)q^0\nu^0([z,1]) \tag{5}$$

with $\overline{\gamma}(z) \in \mathscr{C}$. It follows that $\overline{\gamma}(z)$ is a supporting hyperplane for $v(1, .)$ at the point $q(z)$ with: $q^1(z) = q^1\nu^1([z,1])/\{q^1\nu^1([z,1]) + q^0\nu^0([z,1])\}$. According to the previous interpretation this corresponds to the posterior probability that player I computes given θ and z (i.e., the conditional on M, given the event $\{u \geq z\}$).

Theorem VIII.3.4. *$\underline{v}$ exists on $P \times Q$ and is given by:*

$$\underline{v}(p,q) = \sup_{U^2} \underline{\Phi}(p,q;\mu^1,\mu^0).$$

Proof.

Part A. Player II can defend $\underline{v}$

Given $\varepsilon > 0$ and σ strategy of player I, let $R = 1/\varepsilon$, $z_r = r/R$, $r = 0, \ldots, R$ and define:

- $\tau(0) =$ play always L,
- $Q^l(0) = P_{\sigma^l,\tau(0)}(\theta < \infty)$, $\quad l = 1, 0$;

then $n(0)$ and $P^l(0)$ such that:

- $P^l(0) = P_{\sigma^l,\tau(0)}\big(\theta \leq n(0)\big) \geq Q^l(0) - \varepsilon, \quad l = 1, 0.$

Introduce now inductively on r, given $\tau(r-1)$ and $n(r-1)$:

- $\mathscr{T}(r)$: the set of strategies that coincide with $\tau(r-1)$ up to stage $n(r-1)$ and such that $P_\tau(t_n = \mathrm{R}) \leq z_r, \forall n$,
- $Q^l(r) = \sup_{\tau \in \mathscr{T}(r)} P_{\sigma^l,\tau}(\theta < \infty), \quad l = 1, 0$;

then $\tau(r) \in \mathscr{T}(r)$, $n(r) \geq n(r-1)$ and $P^l(r)$ such that:

- $P^l(r) = P_{\sigma^l,\tau(r)}(\theta \leq n(r)) \geq Q^l(r) - \varepsilon/2^r, \quad l = 1, 0.$

Let μ^l be the measure in U with mass $P^l(r) - P^l(r-1)$ at point z_r, $l = 0, 1$, and let $\overline{\nu}$ in V^2 be an εC-optimal strategy for player II for the payoff $\overline{\Phi}(p,q;\mu^1,\mu^0)$. We finally introduce ν as an atomic approximation of $\overline{\nu}$: ν^m has a mass $\overline{\nu}(]z_{r-1}, z_r])$ at point z_r.

The strategy τ of player II is now described as:

- Choose z_r according to ν^m, given $m = 0, 1$.
- Play $\tau(r)$ up to stage θ and optimally thereafter in the revealed game.

In order to compute the expected payoff at some stage $n \geq n(R)$ we first study the different events induced by a_θ. Recall first that by construction the event $\{\exists r, \tau(r)$ is played and $n \geq \theta > n(r)\}$ has a probability less than 2ε, so that we will work on its complement. Since $P_{\sigma^l,\tau(r)}(\theta > n(r)) = \mu^l(]z_r, 1])$, we can compute the posterior probabilities on L and get:

$$P_{\sigma,\tau(r)}\bigl(l = 1 \bigm| \theta > n(r)\bigr) = \rho^1(z_r).$$

Now for $j \geq r$ $P_{\sigma^l,\tau(j)}\{n(r-1) < \theta \leq n(r)\} = \mu^l(]z_{r-1}, z_r])$, and so $P_{\sigma,\tau(j)}$ $\{l = 1 \mid n(r-1) < \theta \leq n(r)\} = \pi^1(z_r)$. Similarly for the posteriors on M induced by ν:

$$\begin{aligned}\Pr\{m = 1 \mid n(r-1) < \theta \leq n(r)\} &= \Pr\{m = 1 \mid \tau(j) \\ &\text{is played, with } j \geq r\} = q^1(z_r).\end{aligned}$$

Define still $u_r = \Pr\{t_\theta = \mathrm{R} \mid n(r-1) < \theta \leq n(r)\}$ and recall that:

$$u_r \leq z_r \quad \text{a.s.} \tag{6}$$

One obtains thus the following description:

- If $\theta > n$ and player II plays $\tau(r)$, his posterior probability on L is $\rho(z_r)$, and he can minimize in $J(z_r, m)$.
- If $n(r-1) < \theta \leq n(r)$, $P(t_\theta = \mathrm{R}) = u_r$. Given T, the posterior probabilities at stage θ on $L \times M$ are: $(1, q(z_r))$, and given L, they are: $(\pi(z_r), 1)$.

It follows that for n large enough:

$$\begin{aligned}
&n \sum_{n(R)}^{n(R)+n} \gamma_n(\sigma, \tau) \\
&\quad \leq \sum_{r=0}^{R} \Biggl(u_r \Bigl\{ \sum_m q^m \nu^m([z_r, 1]) v(\pi(z_r), m) \Bigr\} \Bigl\{ \sum_l p^l \mu^l([z_{r-1}, z_r]) \Bigr\} \\
&\qquad + (1 - u_r) \Bigl\{ \sum_m q^m \nu^m([z_r, 1]) \Bigr\} \Bigl\{ \sum_l p^l \mu^l([z_{r-1}, z_r]) v(l, q(z_r)) \Bigr\} \\
&\qquad + \mu^*([z_r, 1]) \Bigl\{ \sum_m J(z_r, m) q^m \nu^m([z_{r-1}, z_r]) \Bigr\} \Biggr) + 4C\varepsilon.
\end{aligned}$$

Using (4), (5), and (6), there exists $(\overline{\gamma}, \overline{\delta}) \in \overline{\mathscr{C}} \times \overline{\mathscr{D}}$ such that:

$$n \sum_{n(R)}^{n(R)+n} \gamma_n(\sigma, \tau) \leq \varphi(p, q; \mu^1, \mu^0; \overline{\gamma}, \overline{\delta}; \nu^1, \nu^0) + 4C\varepsilon.$$

By the choice of ν and $\overline{\nu}$ it follows that:

$$n\sum_{n(R)}^{n(R)+n}\gamma_n(\sigma,\tau)\le\varphi(p,q;\mu^1,\mu^0;\overline{\gamma},\overline{\delta};\overline{\nu}^1,\overline{\nu}^0)+4C\varepsilon+C\varepsilon$$

$$\le\overline{\Phi}(p,q;\mu^1,\mu^0)+6C\varepsilon.$$

Finally there exists $\overline{N}$ such that $n\ge\overline{N}$ implies:

$$\overline{\gamma}_n(\sigma,\tau)\le\overline{\Phi}(p,q;\mu^1,\mu^0)+7C\varepsilon,$$

and hence claim A.

Part B. Player I can guarantee $\underline{v}$

Let us first choose μ that realizes $\sup_{U^2}\underline{\Phi}(p,q;\cdot,\cdot)$ up to ε and $\overline{\gamma},\overline{\delta}$, ε-optimal in the corresponding $\underline{\Phi}(p,q;\mu^1,\mu^0)$. We shall write Z for a finite set $\{z_r\mid r=0,\dots,R\}$ that contains the support of $\mu^l, l=1,0$ (we assume $\varepsilon\ge(z_r-z_{r-1})\ge 0$), ζ_r^l for $\mu^l(z_r)$, and γ_r (resp. δ_r) for $\overline{\gamma}(z_r)$ (resp. $\overline{\delta}(z_r)$).

Let us consider a family of stochastic games $\Gamma^*(z)$ described by:

$$\begin{pmatrix}-z^* & (1-z)^*\\ z & -(1-z)\end{pmatrix},$$

and write $\sigma(z)$ for an ε-optimal strategy of player I in it, i.e., such that for all $n\ge N(z)$ and all τ:

$$\overline{\gamma}_n^*(\sigma,\tau)\ge-\varepsilon. \tag{7}$$

Let $N_0=\max\{N(z_r)\}$. We first define a family of stopping times by: $\theta(0)=1$, and inductively $\theta(r)$ is θ induced by $\sigma(z_r)$ from stage $\theta(r-1)$ on. Let also $\theta(R+1)=\infty$. The strategy σ of player I is now as follows: given l, choose $r\in Z$ with probability ζ_r^l or $R+1$ with probability $1-\mu^l(Z)$. Play then Bottom up to stage $\theta(r), 0\le r\le R+1$, and Top at stage $\theta(r)$. Obviously, after time θ, player I plays optimally in the revealed game if $a_\theta=$ L or R, and approaches γ^r (resp. δ_r) if $a_\theta=$ T (resp. B), using an (N_1,ε)-strategy. Let $N=\max\{N_0,N_1\}$.

We shall now prove that player I can guarantee, for each m, $\inf_z\varphi^m(p;\mu^1,\mu^0;\overline{\gamma},\overline{\delta};\omega_z)$, where ω_z is the Dirac mass at z. By the properties of μ and $(\overline{\gamma},\overline{\delta})$ and the definition of $\underline{v}$ the result will follow. Given n and τ, the strategy of player II, we define:

$$I(r)=\{j\mid\theta(r-1)\wedge n<j\le\theta(r)\wedge n\}\qquad I_r=\#I(r)$$

$$u_r=\mathbb{1}_{t_{\theta(r)}=\mathrm{R}}\qquad\overline{u}_r=(1/I_r)\sum_{I(r)}\mathbb{1}_{t_j=\mathrm{R}}.$$

Hence player I is using $\sigma(z_r)$ during I_r stages on the block $I(r)$, where $(u_r,\overline{u}_r)$ describe the behavior of player II. Note also that if $\{\theta=\theta(r)\}$ with $a_\theta=$ L, the posterior on L is $\pi(z_r)$ (defined through μ) and $\rho(z_r)$ if $\{\theta > \theta(r)\}$. We obtain thus that:

$$n\overline{\gamma}_n^{p1}(\sigma,\tau^1) \geq \mathsf{E}_{s,\tau}\left[\sum_{r=0}^{R+1} I_r\left(\sum_{j=0}^{r-1}\{u_j(p^1\zeta_j^1 + p^0\zeta_j^0)v(\pi(z_j),1)\right.\right.$$

$$\left. + (1-u_j)(p^1\zeta_j^1\gamma_j^1 + p^0\zeta_j^0\delta_j^1)\}\mathbb{1}_{I_r\geq N}\right)$$

$$+\left[p^1\left(1-\sum_1^{r-1}\zeta_j^1\right)+p^0\left(1-\sum_1^{r-1}\zeta_j^0\right)\right]\left[g_{22}(\overline{u}_r\rho(z_{r-1},1)\right.$$

$$\left.\left. + (1-\overline{u}_r)g_{21}(\rho(z_{r-1},1)\right]\right] - C\varepsilon.$$

By the choice of $\sigma(z_r)$ we obtain on $I(r)$ that $\mathsf{E}\{I_r.\overline{u}_r\} \leq N + \mathsf{E}(I_r)(z_r+\varepsilon)$, and hence the expectation of the last term in (8) is bounded from below by $J(z_{r-1},1) - ((R+1)N + 2\varepsilon)C$. Using again (4), we obtain:

$$n\overline{\gamma}_n^{p1}(\sigma,\tau^1) \geq \mathsf{E}\sum_{r=1}^{R+1} I_r U^1(z_r) + D.C - \big((R+1)N + 2\varepsilon\big)C, \tag{8}$$

where $U^1(z)$ stands for $\varphi^m(p;\mu^1,\mu^0;\overline{\gamma},\overline{\delta};\omega_z)$ and $D = \mathsf{E}\{\sum_r I_r \sum_{j=0}^{r-1} \zeta_j(u_j - z_j)\}$. Note that $u_j - z_j = u_j(1-z_j) + (1-u_j)(-z_j)$ is the absorbing payoff in $\Gamma^*(z_j)$, and that this payoff occurs at stage $\theta(j)$ and lasts for $\sum_{j+1}^{R+1} I_r$ stages. By the choice of $\sigma(z_j)$ we thus have:

$$\mathsf{E}\sum_j I_j(u_j - z_j) \geq -\varepsilon N, \quad \text{so that } D \geq -\varepsilon N(R+1).$$

We get now from (8): $n\overline{\gamma}_n^{p1}(\sigma,\tau^1) \geq \min_r U^1(z_r) - C(R+1)N - n(R+3)\varepsilon$.

A similar result for $\overline{\gamma}_n^{p0}$ implies finally that for all $\varepsilon > 0$, there exists N^* and σ such that, for all $n \geq N^*$, $\overline{\gamma}_n(\sigma,\tau) \geq \inf_{\mathcal{V}^2}\varphi(p,q;\mu^1,\mu^0;\overline{\gamma},\overline{\delta};\nu^1,\nu^0) - \varepsilon_0$, hence the result. ■

VIII.4. STOCHASTIC GAMES WITH INCOMPLETE INFORMATION

We will consider in this section a family of two-person zero-sum stochastic games with incomplete information on one side and full monitoring, described by a set of states K, a probability p on K, and for each k a matrix G^k with absorbing payoffs where moreover the set of absorbing entries is independent of k. One can view the set of states as $K \times L$, with incomplete information on one side on K and complete information on L; the first component is chosen at the beginning of the game and kept fixed, and the transition on L is independent of it.

VIII.4.a. A First Class

Here the game is described by matrices G^k with $\#S = 2$ where the first line is absorbing.

VIII.4.a.1. Minmax

As we already saw in Section VIII.3 when considering games with state-dependent signaling matrices, the minmax of the infinitely repeated game equals the value of the one-shot game (Proposition VIII.3.1).

Proposition VIII.4.1. $\overline{v}(p) = v_1(p)$.

Before looking at the maxmin let us consider the n-stage game Γ_n.

VIII.4.a.2. Lim v_n

We first remark that the recursive formula (IV.3.2, p. 184) can be written as:

$$(n+1)v_{n+1}(p) = \max_x \min_y \Big\{(n+1)\sum_k p^k x_1^k G_1^k y + \sum_k p^k x_2^k G_2^k y + n\overline{x}_2 v_n(p_2)\Big\},$$

where G_s^k is row s of the matrix G^k, $y \in Y = \Delta(T)$, $x = \{x^k\}$ with x^k in $X = \Delta(S)$, $\overline{x}_2 = \sum_k p^k x_2^k$, and p_2 is the conditional probability on K, given p, x, and the move $s = 2$.

It follows that the value of Γ_n is the same if both players use strategies independent of the histories: from the above formula player I can compute inductively an optimal strategy that depends only on the posterior on K (i.e., on his previous random choice in X^K and move in S), and hence is independent of the moves of II; now against such a strategy, player II cannot do better than conditioning on his own previous moves; and finally as soon as player I plays $s = 1$, the game is over. It suffices thus to define the strategies at each stage, conditional on a sequence of $s = 2$ up to that stage. This remark allows us to approximate Γ_n for n large by a game in continuous time on [0, 1] (we do not need a family as in Section VIII.2.d).

More precisely, since a strategy of player II is a sequence $(y_1, \dots, y_n)$ in Y, it will be represented by a measurable mapping f from [0, 1] to Y: $f_t(\omega)$ is the probability of move t at time ω. Similarly, a strategy of player I being a K-vector of sequences in X will be described by a family of K positive Borel measures of mass less than one on [0, 1], say, ρ^k, where $\rho^k([0, \omega])$, denoted by $\underline{\rho}^k(\omega)$, is the probability of playing move 1 before time ω in game k. Given f and ρ^k, the payoff in game k will be absorbing from time ω on, with probability $\rho^k(d\omega)$ and value $G_1^k f(\omega)$, and non-absorbing at that time with probability $1 - \underline{\rho}^k(\omega)$ and value $G_2^k f(\omega)$. Denoting by F and Q the corresponding sets for f and each ρ^k, we now can define a game $\Gamma(p)$ on $F \times Q^K$ with payoff: $\varphi(f, \{\rho^k\}) = \sum_k p^k \varphi^k(f, \rho^k)$, where:

$$\varphi^k(f, \rho^k) = \int_0^1 \Big[(1-\omega)G_1^k f(\omega)\rho^k(d\omega) + G_2^k f(\omega)(1 - \underline{\rho}^k(\omega))\ell(d\omega)\Big],$$

and ℓ stands for the Lebesgue measure on $[0, 1]$.

Lemma VIII.4.2. *$\Gamma(p)$ has a value $v(p)$.*

Proof. Denote by $\underline{v}(p)$ and $\overline{v}(p)$ the maxmin and minmax of $\Gamma(p)$, and similarly by $\underline{v}'(p)$ and $\overline{v}'(p)$ when player II's strategy set is reduced to F', which denotes the set of continuous functions from $[0, 1]$ to Y. Since, for f in F', $\varphi^k(f, .)$ is continuous when Q is endowed with the weak topology, for which it is compact, and moreover φ^k is affine in each variable, Proposition I.1.3, p. 6, implies that $\underline{v}'(p) = \overline{v}'(p)$. Obviously $\overline{v}'(p) \geq \overline{v}(p)$; hence it is enough to prove that $\underline{v}(p) \geq \underline{v}'(p)$. For each ρ in Q and f in F there exists by Lusin's theorem a sequence in F' converging to f, a.e. w.r.t. ρ and ℓ. Hence the result follows by Lebesgue's dominated convergence theorem. ∎

We now prove that Γ is a good representation of $\lim \Gamma_n$ (and $\lim \Gamma_\lambda$).

Theorem VIII.4.3. *$\lim v_n$ and $\lim v_\lambda$ exist and both are equal to v on Π.*

Proof. We first show $\limsup v_n(p) \leq \overline{v}'(p)$. Let f in F' be ε-optimal for player II in $\Gamma(p)$ and (by uniform continuity) choose n large enough to have $|f(\omega) - f(\omega')| \leq \varepsilon$ for $|\omega - \omega'| \leq 1/n$. Let player II use in Γ_n the following strategy $\tau = (y_1, \dots, y_n)$ with $y_i = f((i-1)/n)$. By the previous remarks, it is enough to consider a pure strategy σ of player I in Γ_n defined by a sequence of moves in S; so let $i_k + 1$ be the first time it induces the move 1 against τ in game k, and take $i_k = n$ if only move 2 is played. The corresponding payoff is then:

$$n\overline{\gamma}_n^k(\sigma, \tau) = \sum_{i=1}^{i_k} G_2^k f\big((i-1)/n\big) + (n - i_k)G_1^k f(i_k/n),$$

so that $\left|\overline{\gamma}_n^k(\sigma, \tau) - \varphi^k(\pi^k, f)\right| \leq \varepsilon$, with π^k being a Dirac mass on i_k/n. Letting $\pi = (\pi^k)$ we obtain:

$$\overline{\gamma}_n(\sigma, \tau) \leq \varphi(\pi, f) + \varepsilon \leq \overline{v}'(p) + 2\varepsilon,$$

and hence the claim.

We now prove $\liminf v_n(p) \geq \underline{v}(p)$. Take ρ optimal for player I in $\Gamma(p)$ (by compactness). For each k, define a sequence $\sigma^k = (x_1^k, \dots, x_n^k)$ with values in X such that one has $P_{\sigma^k}(\theta \leq i) = \underline{\rho}^k(i/n)$, $i = 1, \dots, n$, and let player I use $\sigma = (\sigma^k)$ in $\Gamma_n(p)$, since θ denotes the stopping time at which player I plays 1 for the first time. For each $\tau = (y_1, \dots, y_n)$ take a step function f in F satisfying $f(\omega) = y_1$ on $[0, 1/n]$ and $f(\omega) = y_i$ on $((i-1)/n, i/n]$ for $i = 2, \dots, n$.

We obtain thus:

$$n\overline{\gamma}_n^k(\sigma,\tau) = \sum_{i=1}^{n}\Big[\big\{\underline{\rho}^k(i/n) - \underline{\rho}^k((i-1)/n)\big\}G_1^k y_i(n-i+1) + \big\{1-\underline{\rho}^k(i/n)\big\}G_2^k y_i\Big],$$

and hence $\left|\overline{\gamma}_n^k(\sigma,\tau) - \varphi^k(\rho^k, f)\right| \le 2C/n$, so that for n large enough:

$$\overline{\gamma}_n(\sigma,\tau) \ge \varphi(\rho, f) - \varepsilon \ge \underline{v}(p) - \varepsilon.$$

Finally it is easy to extend these results to Γ_λ: just replace the above uniform partition of $[0,1)$ by the following: $\{[\omega_n,\omega_{n+1})\}_{n\in\mathbb{N}}$, with $\omega_0 = 0$ and $\omega_n = \sum_{i=1}^{n}\lambda(1-\lambda)^{i-1}$. ■

VIII.4.a.3. Maxmin

Consider now the maxmin. The main result of this section is the following:

Theorem VIII.4.4. *$\underline{v}$ exists and equals v on Π.*

Remark VIII.4.1. This result means that player I can play as well in the infinitely repeated game as in a large finite game or, conversely, that he cannot in large games take advantage of the fact that they are finite. This property also holds for the second class we will consider (cf. Section VIII.4.b) and in fact is a conjecture for all games where player I's information σ-field is finer than that of his opponent, i.e., $\mathscr{H}^{\text{II}} \subseteq \mathscr{H}^{\text{I}}$.

Proof. The proof is rather long and split into two parts. We first prove:

Part A. Player II can defend v

Notice that the stochastic aspect of the game prevents us from using the same proof as in Theorem V.3.1, where player II could guarantee even $\lim v_n$. A preliminary result amounts to a remark that the payoff in the auxiliary game $\Gamma(p)$ is the average between 0 and 1 of the expected payoff at time ω. Namely, let:

$$\Phi^k(\rho^k, f, \omega) = \int_0^{\omega} G_1^k f(\omega')\rho^k(d\omega') + (1-\underline{\rho}^k(\omega))G_2^k f(\omega),$$

and $\Phi = \sum_k p^k \Phi^k$; then one has (recall that ℓ is Lebesgue measure):

Lemma VIII.4.5. $\varphi^k(\rho^k, f) = \int_0^1 \Phi^k(\rho^k, f, \omega)\ell(d\omega)$.

Proof. Using Fubini's theorem, the initial definition for φ^k and the above formula are both equal to $\iint_{0\le\omega'\le\omega\le1}\big[G_1^k f(\omega')\rho^k(d\omega') + (1-\underline{\rho}^k(\omega))\, G_2^k f(\omega)\big]\,\ell(d\omega)$. ■

To construct a uniformly good reply of player II in large games, we shall use the following procedure. Given f optimal in Γ and a strategy σ of player I, player II can compute the probability of absorption if he follows f, and hence we can represent σ as a measure on the path defined by f. Since, by the choice of f, the (time) average payoff is less than v, there exists an initial path on which the payoff is at most v, and by keeping f constant thereafter, player II can in fact achieve this payoff. So let us start with an ε-optimal strategy f for player II in $\Gamma(p)$. We first remark that f can be chosen to be a step function, and more precisely there exists a finite family of points ω_r in [0, 1] and of values f_r in Y with:

- $\omega_1 = 0 \le \cdots \le \omega_{R+1} = 1$.
- $f(\omega) = f_r$ on $[\omega_r, \omega_{r+1})$, $r = 1, \ldots, R$.

Given σ and $\varepsilon > 0$, define inductively strategies τ_r, measures $\overline{\mu}_r^k$ and μ_r^k, and natural numbers N_r, as follows (recall that θ denote the stopping time of the first $s = 1$):

- τ_1 is: play f_1 i.i.d.

For each k define: $\overline{\mu}_1^k = \mathsf{Pr}_{\sigma,\tau_1}(\theta < \infty)$, and let μ_1^k and N_1 satisfy $\mu_1^k = \mathrm{P}_{\sigma,\tau_1}(\theta \le N_1) \ge \overline{\mu}_1^k - \varepsilon$.

- Similarly τ_r is: play τ_{r-1} up to stage N_{r-1} (included) and then f_r i.i.d.

Then we let $\overline{\mu}_r^k = \mathrm{P}_{\sigma,\tau_r}(\theta < \infty)$. N_r and μ_r^k satisfy $N_r \ge N_{r-1}$ and $\mu_r^k = \mathrm{P}_{\sigma,\tau_r}(\theta \le N_r) \ge \overline{\mu}_r^k - \varepsilon$, for all k. Define positive atomic measures ρ^k on [0, 1) by $\rho^k(\{\omega_r\}) = \mu_r^k - \mu_{r-1}^k$ so that, by definition of f, $\varphi(\rho, f) \le v(p) + \varepsilon$. This implies that for some ω in [0, 1) $\Phi(\rho, f, \omega) \le v(p) + \varepsilon$. So let r be such that $\omega \in [\omega_r, \omega_{r+1})$ and remark that $\Phi(\rho, f, \omega) = \Phi(\rho, f, \omega_r)$.

We now claim that by playing τ_r, player II can get an asymptotic payoff near v. In fact, for $n \ge N_r$, the payoff at stage n in game k will be of the form:

$$\gamma_n^k(\sigma, \tau_r) = \sum_{m=1}^{r} \alpha_m^k G_1^k f_m + \left(1 - \sum_{m=1}^{r} \alpha_m^k\right) G_2^k f_r,$$

with $\alpha_m^k = P_{\sigma,\tau_r}(N_{m-1} < \theta \le N_m)$ for $m < r$ (with $N_0 = 0$) and $\alpha_r^k = P_{\sigma,\tau_r}(N_{r-1} < \theta \le n)$. Since $\mu_r^k - \mu_{r-1}^k \le \alpha_r^k \le \mu_r^k - \mu_{r-1}^k + \varepsilon$, we obtain $|\gamma_n^k(\sigma, \tau_r) - \Phi^k(\rho, f, \omega_r)| \le 2C\varepsilon$, hence, averaging on k, $|\gamma_n(\sigma, \tau_r) - \Phi(\rho, f, \omega_r)| \le 2C\varepsilon$, and finally $\overline{\gamma}_n(\sigma, \tau_r) \le v(p) + 3C\varepsilon + \varepsilon$ for $n \ge 2N_R/\varepsilon$.

This proves claim A.

Part B. Player I can guarantee $v(p)$.

The idea of the proof relies basically on two facts: first, there exists a pair of "equalizing" strategies (ρ, f) in Γ such that the payoff at ω is constant; the second point is that player I can adapt his strategy, essentially the stopping time θ, to the empirical frequency of moves of II, such that the payoff in Γ_n is equal to the one induced by ρ and f, if II follows f, and is less otherwise. We first prove a preliminary result. Essentially it means that given an optimal strategy of player I, there exists a best reply of player II equalizing in time, i.e., such that the corresponding payoff at ω is constant between 0 and 1.

Proposition VIII.4.6. *Let ρ be optimal in $\Gamma(p)$. There exists $f \in F$ s.t. $\Phi(\rho, f, \omega) = v(p)$, for all ω in* $[0, 1)$.

Proof. Let ρ_ε be a non-atomic ε-optimal strategy for player I in $\Gamma(p)$. We consider an auxiliary game $\mathcal{G}(\rho_\varepsilon)$ where player I chooses at random a point ω in $[0, 1]$ and player II chooses a function in F'. The corresponding payoff is $\Phi(\rho_\varepsilon, f, \omega)$. This game has a value w_ε. Indeed the strategy set of player I, resp. II, is convex and compact, resp. convex. Moreover the mapping $f \mapsto \Phi(\rho_\varepsilon, f, \omega)$ is affine, and the mapping $\omega \mapsto \Phi(\rho_\varepsilon, f, \omega)$ is continuous. Obviously one has $w_\varepsilon \geq v - \varepsilon$, since I can use ℓ to choose ω, and then the payoff is precisely $\varphi(\rho_\varepsilon, f)$. Let us prove that $w_\varepsilon \leq v$. In fact, let m be an optimal (by compactness) strategy of I so that $\int_0^1 \Phi(\rho_\varepsilon, f, \omega) m(d\omega) \geq w_\varepsilon$, for all f in F'. Replacing w_ε by $w_\varepsilon - \delta$, we can assume that $\underline{m}(\omega) = m([0, \omega])$ is a strictly increasing continuous function from $[0, 1]$ to itself with $\underline{m}(0) = 0$ and $\underline{m}(1) = 1$. We can now use $\underline{m}$ to rescale the time; namely, we define $\widetilde{\rho}$ in Q and $\widetilde{f}$ in F by $\underline{\widetilde{\rho}(\underline{m}(\omega))} = \underline{\rho(\omega)}$ and $\widetilde{f}(\underline{m}(\omega)) = f(\omega)$. Hence we obtain:

$$\int_0^1 \Phi(\rho_\varepsilon, f, \omega)\, m(d\omega) = \int_0^1 \Phi(\widetilde{\rho}_\varepsilon, \widetilde{f}, \omega)\, \ell(d\omega).$$

Since m defines a one-to-one mapping on F' this gives: $\varphi(\widetilde{\rho}, f) \geq w_\varepsilon - \delta$, for all f in F', hence $w_\varepsilon - \delta \leq v$. Since δ is arbitrary, the inequality follows. Let now for each $\varepsilon = 1/n$, $\rho_\varepsilon = \rho_n$ and let $f_\varepsilon = f_n$ in F' with $\Phi(\rho_n, f_n, \omega) \leq v + 1/n$, for all ω in $[0, 1]$, and let ρ_n converge weakly to ρ: $\Phi(\rho_n, f_n, \omega)$ converges to $\Phi(\rho, f_n, \omega)$ for all ω. Finally let f in F be such that $\Phi(\rho, f_n, \omega)$ converges to $\Phi(\rho, f, \omega)$ for all ω, so that $\Phi(\rho, f, \omega) \leq v$, hence the equality since ρ is optimal in $\Gamma(p)$. ■

Consider now ρ and f as above and let $\underline{\omega} < 1$ be such that $\rho^k([\underline{\omega}, 1)) \leq \varepsilon/4$, for all k. Note that this implies:

$$\sum_k p^k(1 - \underline{\rho}^k(\underline{\omega}))G_1^k y \geq \sum_k p^k(1 - \underline{\rho}^k(\underline{\omega}))G_1^k f(\underline{\omega}) - \varepsilon C/2 \qquad (1)$$

for all y in Y. Otherwise, one obtains with $g = f$ on $[0, \underline{\omega})$ and $= y$ on $[\underline{\omega}, 1)$ that $\Phi(\rho, g, \omega) = \Phi(\rho, f, \omega)$ on $[0, \underline{\omega})$ and $\Phi(\rho, g, \omega) < v$ on $[\underline{\omega}, 1)$, contradicting the optimality of ρ. Similarly on each atom of $\sum_k p^k \rho^k$, say ω, one has:

$$\sum_k p^k \rho^k(\{\omega\}) G_1^k f(\omega) = \min_y \sum_k p^k \rho^k(\{\omega\}) G_1^k y; \qquad (2)$$

otherwise, by modifying f in some neighborhood O of ω, one obtains a g satisfying $\Phi(\rho, g, \cdot) < \Phi(\rho, f, \cdot)$ on O and equality a.e. otherwise, contradicting again the optimality of ρ. Given $\eta = (1 - \underline{\omega})\varepsilon C/4$, let us now introduce a partition $\omega_1, \ldots, \omega_{R+1}$ with $\omega_1 = 0$, $\omega_R = \underline{\omega}$, $\omega_{R+1} = 1$, and an adapted pair $\widetilde{f}, \widetilde{\rho}$ with:

$$\rho^k(\{\omega_r\}) = \widetilde{\rho}^k([\omega_r, \omega_{r+1})) = \widetilde{\rho}_r^k \text{ and } \widetilde{f}(\omega) = \widetilde{f}_r \text{ on } [\omega_r, \omega_{r+1}), \quad \text{with } \widetilde{f}_R = f(\underline{\omega}), \tag{3}$$

$$\text{if } \sum_k p^k \rho^k(\{\omega\}) > \varepsilon, \text{ then } \omega \in \{\omega_r\}, \widetilde{\rho}^k(\{\omega\}) - \rho^k(\{\omega\}) \le \varepsilon^2 \quad \text{and } \widetilde{f}_r = f(\omega_r), \tag{4}$$

$$\underline{\widetilde{\rho}}^k(\omega) - \underline{\rho}^k(\omega) \le \varepsilon, \ \forall \omega, \tag{5}$$

$$\widetilde{\rho} \text{ is } \eta\text{-optimal in } \Gamma, \quad \text{and } \Phi(\widetilde{\rho}, \widetilde{f}, \omega) \le v + \eta \text{ on } [0, \underline{\omega}). \tag{6}$$

Obviously $\Phi(\widetilde{\rho}, \widetilde{f}, \cdot)$ is piecewise constant on [0, 1) and equal to:

$$\sum_k p^k \left[\sum_{j=1}^r \widetilde{\rho}_j^k G_1^k \widetilde{f}_j + \left(1 - \sum_{j=1}^r \widetilde{\rho}_j^k\right) G_2^k \widetilde{f}_r \right] \quad \text{on } [\omega_r, \omega_{r+1}).$$

Now we claim that for any $y = \{y_r\}_{r<R}$ with y_r in Y:

$$\sum_k p^k \big(1 - \underline{\widetilde{\rho}}^k(\omega_r)\big) G_2^k y_r \le \sum_k p^k \big(1 - \underline{\widetilde{\rho}}^k(\omega_r)\big) G_2^k \widetilde{f}_r + \eta \tag{7}$$

implies:

$$\sum_k p^k \sum_{j=1}^r \widetilde{\rho}_j^k G_1^k y_j \ge \sum_k p^k \sum_{j=1}^r \widetilde{\rho}_j^k G_1^k \widetilde{f}_j - \varepsilon C, \quad \forall r < R.$$

Indeed, if $\sum_k p^k \widetilde{\rho}_j^k G_1^k y_j < \sum_k p^k \widetilde{\rho}_j^k G_1^k \widetilde{f}_j$, defining g as y_j on $[\omega_j, \omega_{j+1})$ and $\widetilde{f}$ otherwise would give $\Phi(\widetilde{\rho}, g, \omega) < v + \eta$ on $[0, \underline{\omega})$, by (6), and $\Phi(\widetilde{\rho}, g, \omega) < v + \varepsilon C/2 - \varepsilon C$ on $[\underline{\omega}, 1)$, by the choice of $\rho, \underline{\omega}$, and (3). Thus, $\varphi(\widetilde{\rho}, g) < v + \eta - \varepsilon C(1 - \underline{\omega})/2 < v - \eta$, which contradicts by (6) the choice of $\widetilde{\rho}$.

We introduce finally a strategy σ for player I by letting σ^k be: play $s = 1$ (for the first time) at stage θ_r, with probability $\widetilde{\rho}_r^k$, where the stopping times θ_r are inductively defined by the following procedure.

We first consider the probability of absorption. If $\sum_k p^k \widetilde{\rho}_1^k \ge 2\varepsilon$, this implies that $\sum_k p^k \rho^k$ is atomic at ω_1 and we let $\theta_1 = 1$. Otherwise, we compute the expected non-absorbing payoff induced by $\widetilde{f}$, i.e., $\psi_1(\widetilde{f}) = \sum_k p^k(1 - \widetilde{\rho}_1^k) G_2^k \widetilde{f}_1 = z_1$, and we consider an optimal strategy α_1 in an associated stochastic game with absorbing states, payoff ψ_1, and level z_1 (cf. VII.4, Ex. 4, p. 417, and VII.4, Ex. 19, p. 422). More precisely, if θ denotes the stopping time of absorption, there exists N_1 such that for all $n \ge N_1$ and every (pure) strategy of II:

$$\psi_1(\bar{t}_n) \le z_1 - C\varepsilon \Longrightarrow P_{\alpha_1}(\theta \le n) \ge 1 - \varepsilon, \quad \text{with } \bar{t}_n = (1/n) \sum_{m=1}^n t_m, \tag{8}$$

$$\big[\mathsf{E}_{\alpha_1}(\psi_1(t_\theta) \mid \theta \le n) - z_1\big] P_{\alpha_1}(\theta \le n) \le \eta\varepsilon. \tag{9}$$

Define similarly $\theta_r = \theta_{r-1} + 1$, if $\sum_k p^k \widetilde{\rho}_r^k \geq 2\varepsilon$; otherwise let $\psi_r(\widetilde{f}) = \sum_k p^k (1 - \sum_{j=1}^{r} \widetilde{\rho}_j^k)\ G_2^k f(\widetilde{\omega}_r) = z_r$, and let α_r and N_r be the corresponding optimal strategies and bound on the number of stages. θ_r then follows the law of θ induced by α_r from stage θ_{r-1} on.

Let us compute the payoff given σ and some pure strategy τ of II (i.e., a sequence of moves in T), at some stage $n \geq RN$, with $N = \max_r N_r$. We first obtain a (random) sequence of blocks B_j, $j = 1, 2, \ldots, r, \ldots$, where player I uses α_1, then α_2, and so on. We shall approximate the average payoff on each of these blocks, except when their length is smaller than N or when the expectation of occurrence is too small: $P(\theta_r \leq n - \sum_{j<r} \theta_j) \leq \varepsilon$. We first notice that on $B_r, r = 1, \ldots, R$, since the length of the block is greater than N and α_r is used, (8) implies that with probability greater than $1 - \varepsilon$:

$$\psi(t(r)) \geq z_r - C\varepsilon\,, \quad \text{where } t(r) = (1/\#B_r) \sum_{m \in B_r} t_m.$$

Note now that the expected absorbing payoff at θ_r, hence on B_{r+1}, is of the form:

$$\sum_k p^k \sum_{j \leq r} \widetilde{\rho}_j^k G_1^k y_j\,, \quad \text{with } y_j = \mathsf{E}(t_{\theta_j}).$$

If ω_r is an atom of $\sum_k p^k \rho^k$, one obtains $\sum_k p^k \widetilde{\rho}_r^k G_1^k y_r \geq \sum_k p^k \widetilde{\rho}_r^k G_1^k \widetilde{f}_r - 2\varepsilon^2 C$ by (2) and (4), and there are at most $1/\varepsilon$ such points. Otherwise α_r is used, and if $\Pr(\theta_r \leq n - \sum_{j<r} \theta_j) \geq \varepsilon$ one has $\psi(y_r) \leq z_r + \eta$ by (9), so that the absorbing payoff is at least:

$$\sum_k p^k \sum_{j \leq r} \widetilde{\rho}_j^k G_1^k \widetilde{f}_j - \varepsilon C, \quad \text{by (7)},$$

and hence by (5) greater than $\sum_k p^k \sum_{j \leq r+1} \widetilde{\rho}_j^k G_1^k \widetilde{f}_j - 3\varepsilon C$. Finally on B_{R+1}, using (1) and (3), the new absorbing payoff is less than $\varepsilon C/4$ and the non-absorbing one greater than or equal to $\sum_k p^k (1 - \underline{\widetilde{\rho}}^k(\underline{\omega})) G_1^k \widetilde{f}(\underline{\omega}) - \varepsilon C/2$. Hence the expected payoff at stage n is greater than or equal to a convex combination of terms of the form:

$$\Phi(\widetilde{\rho}, \widetilde{f}, \omega_r) - 2CRN/n - (1/\varepsilon)\varepsilon^2 4C - 8\varepsilon C,$$

and the result follows from (6).

This completes the proof of Theorem VIII.4.4. ∎

VIII.4.b. A Second Class

A second family of games that we will study here is given by matrices G^k with S lines and T columns but where the first column is absorbing. It is easily seen (compare exercises of Chapter VII) that the values of the (stochastic) n-stage, discounted, or infinite game where player I uses non-revealing strategies are equal, and we will write $u(p)$ for this common value. As in the previous section we will prove here that $\underline{v}(p)$, $\lim v_n$, and $\lim v_\lambda$ exist and are equal. Note that in the current framework also, there is no direct way of proving that player II can defend $\liminf v_n$. Nevertheless the proof will be roughly similar to the previous one.

VIII.4.b.1. Maxmin and $\lim v_n$

Theorem VIII.4.7. $\underline{v}(p) = \lim v_n = \lim v_\lambda = \operatorname{Cav} u(p)$.

Proof. We first remark that player I can concavify as usual (cf. Remark V.1.2, p. 216), so that v_n and v_λ are greater than $\operatorname{Cav} u$ and player I can guarantee $\operatorname{Cav} u$. (Note that he can even get $u(p)$ at each stage.) We prove now that player II can defend $\operatorname{Cav} u$. Basically he will play a best reply to the expected strategy of player I in the non-revealing game at the current posterior after each stage except when the expected variation of this martingale is large. Since this last event has a small expected frequency the result will follow. Let us first consider Γ_∞ and assume that player I is using σ. Let us write $\mathscr{T}'$ for the set of player II's strategies with values having a support included in the set $T \setminus \{1\}$ of non-absorbing columns. Define now τ' in $\mathscr{T}'$ and N in $\mathbb{N}$ satisfying:

$$\mathsf{E}_{\sigma,\tau'} \sum_{m=1}^{N} (p_{m+1} - p_m)^2 \geq \sup_{\tau \in \mathscr{T}'} \mathsf{E}_{\sigma,\tau} \sum_{m=1}^{\infty} (p_{m+1} - p_m)^2 - \varepsilon \qquad (10)$$

and consider τ defined by: play according to τ' up to and including stage N, and thereafter play at each stage m a best reply to $\mathsf{E}(\sigma(h_m) \mid h_m)$ in $D(p_m)$. Note that (10) implies that $\mathsf{E}_{\sigma,\tau}(\sum_{m=N+1}^{\infty} (p_{m+1} - p_m)^2) \leq \varepsilon$. We want to bound from above the average payoff up to some stage $n \geq N$. Letting θ' be the first time where player II is using move 1 and defining $\theta = \min(\theta', n)$, we obtain (as in Section VI.4, p. 357):

$$n\overline{\gamma}_n(\sigma,\tau) \leq 2NC + \mathsf{E}\left(\sum_{m=1}^{\theta} u(p_m) + (n-\theta)u(p_{\theta+1})\right) + CX(p), \qquad (11)$$

with $X(p) = \mathsf{E}\big(\sum_{N+1}^{\theta} |p_{m+1} - p_m| + (n-\theta)\,|p_{\theta+1} - p_\theta|\big)$. Since $\mathsf{E}(\sum_{m=1}^{\theta} p_m + (n-\theta)p_{\theta+1}) = p$ by the martingale property, the second term is bounded from above by $n \operatorname{Cav} u(p)$ (using Jensen's inequality). As for $X(p)$, it can be written as $\mathsf{E}(\sum_{m=N+1}^{\infty} Z_m\, |p_{m+1} - p_m|)$, where:

$$Z_m = \begin{cases} 0 & \text{for } m > \theta \\ n - m + 1 & \text{for } m = \theta \text{ and } p_m \text{ constant for } m > \theta \\ 1 & \text{for } m < \theta. \end{cases}$$

Hence:

$$\begin{aligned} X(p) &\leq \mathsf{E}\big[\sum (p_{m+1} - p_m)^2 \cdot \sum (Z_m^2)\big]^{1/2} \\ &\leq \big[\mathsf{E}(\sum (p_{m+1} - p_m)^2\big]^{1/2} \big[\mathsf{E} \sum (Z_m^2)\big]^{1/2} \\ &\leq \varepsilon^{1/2} n. \end{aligned}$$

We obtain thus $\overline{\gamma}_n(\sigma, \tau) \leq \mathsf{Cav}\, u(p) + C(2N/n + \varepsilon^{1/2})$, and the result follows.

As for Γ_n, recall that for any σ one has: $\mathsf{E}_{\sigma,\tau} \sum_{m=1}^{n} (p_{m+1} - p_m)^2 \leq L$, uniformly in τ (cf. Lemma V.2.1, p. 219); hence the number of stages in Γ_n where $\mathsf{E}(p_{m+1} - p_m)^2 \geq L/n^{3/4}$ is at most $n^{3/4}$. On the other stages, say, m in M, the probability of the set of histories h_m, where $\mathsf{E}((p_{m+1} - p_m)^2 \mid h_m) \geq L/n^{1/2}$, is less than $n^{-1/4}$. Now define τ as being a pure best reply to $\mathsf{E}(\sigma(h_m) \mid h_m)$ in $D(p_m)$ at each stage m in M where the variation $\mathsf{E}((p_{m+1} - p_m)^2 \mid h_m)$ is smaller than $L/n^{1/2}$, and as being any non-absorbing move otherwise. It follows, using the same upper bound as in (11), that:

$$n\overline{\gamma}_n(\sigma, \tau) \leq 2C(n^{3/4} + n.n^{-1/4}) + \mathsf{Cav}\, u(p) + C\big((nL)^{1/2} + nL^{1/2}/n^{1/4}\big),$$

and this completes the proof.

Finally for Γ_λ, let $N = \lambda^{-3/4}$. Then the number of stages where $\mathsf{E}(p_{m+1} - p_m)^2 \geq L/N$ is less than N. On the complement of this set of stages the histories on which the conditional quadratic variation is larger than $L/N^{2/3}$ have a probability less than $N^{1/3}$. Now the weight of these stages is at most $(1 - (1 - \lambda)^{N+1})$, which is of the order of λN; hence we bound from above $\overline{\gamma}_\lambda(\sigma, \tau) - \mathsf{Cav}\, u$ by a term of the order of $\lambda^{1/4}$. ■

VIII.4.b.2. Minmax

We assume from now on $T = \{1, 2\}$.

As in the previous case and as in the next ones, $\overline{v}$ will be obtained through an auxiliary game or, more precisely here, through a sequence of auxiliary games, as in Section VIII.3. (For an alternative approach in special cases, leading to an explicit formula, cf. VIII.4, Ex. 8, VIII.4, Ex. 10, and VIII.4, Ex. 11, p. 478.) For each L in $\mathbb{N}$ define G_L by the following strategy sets Z_L for I and $\mathscr{F}_L$ for II and payoff Ψ_L (G_L should be $G_L(p)$, but we will keep p fixed during the whole section, and so we drop it): $Z_L = (\Delta_L(S))^{K \times L}$, where $\Delta_L(S)$ is the triangulation of the simplex $\Delta(S)$ with mesh $1/L$ and $\mathscr{F}_L$ is the set of mappings f from sequences of length less than or equal to L in $\Delta_L(S)$ to half space s in $\mathbb{R}^S$. The payoff corresponding to a pair (z, f) in $Z_L \times \mathscr{F}_L$ is $\Psi_L(z, f) = \sum_k p^k \Psi_L^k(z^k, f)$, with:

$$\Psi_L^k(z^k, f) = (1/L) \sum_{m=1}^{\ell-1} z_m^k G_1^k + \big(1 - (\ell - 1)/L\big) z_\ell^k G_2^k,$$

where $\ell = \min(\{m \mid z^k_m \notin f(z^k_1, z^k_2, \ldots, z^k_{m-1}\} \cup \{L+1\})$. G_L is thus a matrix game (only finitely many different f give different payoffs) with value w_L. The interpretation is that player I is playing i.i.d. on blocks (his strategy can obviously be assumed to be independent of the moves of player II since it is enough to define it at each stage n, on the event $\theta \geq n$, where θ is the first time II uses $t = 1$, recall that $T = \{1, 2\}$), and player II uses on each block an optimal strategy in the stochastic game with absorbing states defined by the half space at that stage.

Theorem VIII.4.8. $\lim w_L$ *and* $\overline{v}$ *exist and are equal.*

Proof.

Part A. I can defend $\limsup w_L$

We will show that given z for player I in G_L and τ for player II in Γ_∞, there exists f and σ such that for n large enough $\overline{\gamma}_n(\sigma, \tau)$ is near $\psi_L(z, f)$. Given τ, the strategy of player II, we first can assume that one has for all n and all strategies of I, $P(\theta = n) \leq 1/L^2$; in fact, it is easy to see that if player II can guarantee d, she can also guarantee it with such a strategy. We now define a probability induced by τ on a set of f in $\mathscr{F}_L$ (it is sufficient to describe their intersection with $\Delta_L(S)$). Given z in $\Delta_L(S)$ let $\zeta(z) = P_{\sigma(z),\tau}(\theta < \infty)$, where $\sigma(z)$ is: play z i.i.d. Define $\tau(\emptyset) = \{z \in \Delta_L(S) \mid \zeta(z) \geq 1/L\}$, and for z in $\tau(\emptyset)$, let $N(z)$ such that $P_{\sigma(z),\tau}(\theta \leq N(z)) \in [1/L, 1/L + 1/L^2]$. If $z \notin \tau(\emptyset)$, let $N(z) = \infty$.

We first define $f(\emptyset)$: on the extreme points of $\Delta_L(S)$, $\mathbb{1}_{f(\emptyset)} = \mathbb{1}_{\tau(\emptyset)}$. On the one-dimensional faces of $\Delta_L(S)$, z belongs to $f(\emptyset)$ iff there exists an extreme point z' and some z'' both in $\tau(\emptyset)$ with z on $[z', z'']$. $f(\emptyset)$ is now defined on the whole simplex by the half space that coincides with it on the previous one-dimensional faces.

We now define $f(\{z_1\})$. If $z_1 \notin f(\emptyset)$, $f(\{z_1\})$ is arbitrary. If $z_1 \in f \cap \tau(\emptyset)$ we first introduce $\zeta(z_1, z) = P_{\sigma(z_1,z),\tau}(\theta < \infty)$, where $\sigma(z_1, z)$ is the strategy of I defined by z_1 i.i.d. up to stage $N(z_1)$ and then z i.i.d. As above, let $\tau(z_1) = \{z \mid \zeta(z_1, z) \geq 1/L\}$ and for z in this set let $N(z_1, z)$ be such that $P_{\sigma(z_1,z),\tau}(N(z_1) < \theta \leq N(z_1, z)) \in [1/L, 1/L + 1/L^2]$. Now $f(z_1)$ is defined from the set $\tau(z_1)$ exactly as $f(\emptyset)$ is from $\tau(\emptyset)$. Finally, if $z_1 \in f(\emptyset) \setminus \tau(\emptyset)$, there exists $\#S$ points z^i_1 in $f \cap \tau(\emptyset)$ such that z_1 is a barycenter, $z_1 = \sum_i \lambda^i z^i_1$. τ defines then a mixture at z_1: play $f(z^i_1)$ with probability λ^i. For the general construction, given a sequence $(z_1, \ldots, z_\ell)$, consider first the (random) sequence that II has generated: say, $(z^{i_1}_1, \ldots, z^{i_j}_j, \ldots)$ as long as $z_{j+1} \in f(z^{i_1}_1, \ldots, z^{i_j}_j)$ (otherwise f is from then on arbitrary), the $z^{i_j}_j$ being defined from z_j as above. On each path of length j we apply the same construction, introducing first ζ, then τ and N, and finally f. Note that we have described in this way a behavioral strategy F_τ on $\mathscr{F}_L$. Given any array $z = (z_1, \ldots, z_L)$ in $\Delta_L(S)$, we introduce a (non-revealing) strategy σ_z for I in Γ_∞ such that for n large enough the average payoff against τ at state k, namely, $\overline{\gamma}^k_n(\sigma_z, \tau)$, will be near $\int \psi^k_L(z, f) F_\tau(df) = \psi^k_L(z, F_\tau)$. If $z_1 \notin f(\emptyset)$, z_1 can also be written as a barycenter of points

$y_1^i \notin \tau(\emptyset) \cup f(\emptyset)$, say, $z_1 = \sum_i \mu^i y_1^i$. σ_z is then: play with probability μ^i, y_1^i i.i.d. forever. The corresponding expected payoff is then obviously (at each stage) $z_1 G_2^k = \psi^k(z, F_\tau)$ up to $2C/L$ (corresponding to the probability that θ will be finite). If $z_1 \in f(\emptyset)$, consider the same points z_1^i introduced above and let σ_z satisfy: with probability λ^i play z_1^i i.i.d. up to stage $N(z_1^i)$.

Now to define σ_z at some further stage we first consider the (random) sequence generated up to now, say, $z_1^{i_1}, \ldots, z_j^{i_j}$:

- Either $z_{j+1} \notin f(z_1^{i_1}, \ldots, z_j^{i_j})$, then one introduces points $y_{j+1}^i \notin f \cup \tau(z_1^{i_1}, \ldots, z_j^{i_j})$, and σ_z is, from $N(z_1^{i_1}, \ldots, z_j^{i_j})$ on, the corresponding splitting of i.i.d. sequences;
- Or $z_{j+1} \in f(z_1^{i_1}, \ldots, z_j^{i_j})$, and one defines the points $z_{j+1}^i \in \tau \cap f(z_1^{i_1}, \ldots, z_j^{i_j})$ as above, and σ_z is, with probability λ^i (obviously a function of $(z_1^{i_1}, \ldots, z_j^{i_j})$), play z_{j+1}^i i.i.d. from stage $N(z_1^{i_1}, \ldots, z_j^{i_j}) + 1$ to $N(z_1^{i_1}, \ldots, z_{j+1}^i)$.

Thus, for $n \in \underline{N} = L \times \max\{N(z_1, \ldots, z_L) \mid z \in \Delta_L(S)^L\}$, one obtains that the average payoff up to stage n is an expectation of terms of the form (with ℓ being the first time where z_j is not in f):

$$(1/L)\sum_{j<\ell} z_j^{i_j} G_1^k + (1 - (\ell - 1)/L) y_\ell^i G_2^k, \quad \text{up to } 2C(L \times 1/L^2 + 1/L + 1/L),$$

where the first term corresponds to the error on the absorbing payoffs, the second to the non-absorbing payoff, and the third to the stages up to $N(z_1^{i_1}, \ldots, z_{\ell-1}^{i_{\ell-1}})$. Now the expectation of y_ℓ^i is precisely z_ℓ and, moreover, by construction the probabilities of the sequences $(z_1^{i_1}, \ldots, z_j^{i_j})$ are the same under σ_z and F_τ. It follows that for $n \geq \overline{N}$: $\overline{\gamma}_n^k(\sigma_z, \tau) \geq \psi^k(z, F_\tau) - 6C/L$. Finally, given $\varepsilon > 0$, let $L_0 > 6/\varepsilon$ such that $w_{L_0} \geq \limsup w_L - \varepsilon$ and let χ be an optimal strategy for I in G_{L_0}. A strategy σ in Γ_∞ is then defined by: choose $z = (z^k)$ according to χ; given k and z, use the above strategy σ_{z^k}. We thus obtain, for $n \geq \overline{N}$:

$$\overline{\gamma}_n(\sigma, \tau) = \mathsf{E}_\chi \sum_k p^k \overline{\gamma}_n^k(\sigma_{z^k}, \tau) \geq \mathsf{E}_\chi \sum_k p^k \psi_{L_0}^k(z^k, F_\tau) - 6C/L_0,$$

and hence $\overline{\gamma}_n(\sigma, \tau) \geq \psi_{L_0}(\chi, F_\tau) - \varepsilon \geq \limsup w_L - 2\varepsilon$.

Part B. II can guarantee $\liminf w_L$

We will first represent a strategy f in G_L as a strategy $\tau(f)$ in Γ_∞ and then show that for n large enough the payoff it induces against some σ (in Γ_∞) is near a payoff corresponding to f and some $z(\sigma)$ in G_L. The choice of an L realizing the liminf up to some ε, and then of a strategy τ associated to an optimal mixture (with finite support) in G_L, imply the result.

We shall proceed as in part B of the previous Section VIII.4.a.3, and given f, construct a strategy that corresponds to a sequence of optimal strategies in some auxiliary games with absorbing states. The computations being roughly similar we will mainly describe the procedure. To each half space $f(z_1, \dots, z_j)$ is associated a strategy $\tau(z_1, \dots, z_j)$ such that: $P(\theta \le n)$ is near 1 as soon as $n \ge M(z_1, \dots, z_j)$, and the empirical frequency of moves of I up to n is at a distance at most $1/L$ from $f(z_1, \dots, z_j)$; moreover, $\mathsf{E}(s_\theta \mid \theta \le m)$ is with probability near one within $1/L^2$ of $f(z_1, \dots, z_j)$, as soon as the probability of the event $\{\theta \le m\}$ is not too small. Given a (pure) strategy of I (i.e., in this case a sequence of moves), let us introduce a sequence of stopping times. θ_1 follows the law of θ under $\tau(\emptyset)$. Further ω_1 is such that $P(\theta_1 \le \omega_1)$ is near 1 (and ∞ if no such number exists). Finally, if ω_1 is finite, let $x_1 = \mathsf{E}(s_\theta \mid \theta_1 \le \omega_1)$ and choose z_1 as a closest point to x_1 in $\Delta_L(S)$. θ_2 follows the law of θ under $\tau(z_1)$ from stage $\omega_1 + 1$ on. We define similarly ω_2, x_2, and z_2, and θ_j inductively up to $j = L$. τ is obtained by choosing j at random, uniformly in $\{1, \dots, L\}$ and playing $t = 1$ for the first time at stage θ_j. Hence for n large enough (like $L^2 \times \max_z M(z_1, \dots, z_L) = L^2\overline{M}$) the average expected payoff up to stage n given $(s_1, \dots, s_n)$ and τ will be, for any k, near some average of $\Psi^k(y, f)$, with y in $\Delta_L(S)$. In fact, considering the sequence ω_j, one obtains when $\omega_{j+1} - \omega_j$ is large ($\ge\overline{M}$) that the average frequency of moves of player I during these stages is with probability near one, within 1/L of a point y_{j+1} not in f. Moreover, with a probability near 1 the sequence $z_1, \dots, z_j$ is compatible with f; i.e., one has $z_i \in f(z_1, \dots, z_{i-1})$. Since the probability of each event $\{\theta = \theta_i\}$ is $1/L$ we obtain that the average payoff on the stages in $(\omega_j, \omega_{j+1}]$ is roughly (adding another error term of the order of $1/L$), given k: $(1/L)\sum_{i \le j} z_i G_1^k + (1 - (j+1)/L) y_{j+1} G_2^k$, hence in the range of $\Psi^k(\cdot, f)$.

It remains to see that the total weight of the "small blocks" is at most $L \times \overline{M}$ so that by taking expectation over k, $\overline{\gamma}_n(\sigma, \tau)$ will be near the range of $\psi(\cdot, f)$ on Z_L. ■

VIII.4.c. Minmax: Two More Examples

Recall we conjecture that $\lim v_n$, $\lim v_\lambda$ and $\max\min \underline{v}$ exist and coincide in games where one player is more informed than his opponent.

The purpose of this section is thus to give examples where we establish the existence of the minmax, again through an auxiliary game, and, furthermore, we provide an explicit description of the minmax.

VIII.4.c.1. Example A

Let G^k, $k \in K$ be a finite set of 2×2 payoff matrices of the form $G^k = \begin{pmatrix} a^{k*} & b^k \\ c^k & d^k \end{pmatrix}$, where as usual the star * denotes an absorbing payoff.

We first introduce an auxiliary game. The game $G(p)$ is the (one-shot) game in normal form defined by A^K (resp. B) as the strategy set of player I (resp. II) and the payoff f where: $A = \overline{\mathbb{N}} \cup \{\partial\}$ ($\overline{\mathbb{N}}$ is the compactification $\mathbb{N} \cup \{\infty\}$

of the set of positive integers $\mathbb{N}$, and ∂ is some isolated point with $\partial > \infty$), $B = \{0, 1\}^{\mathbb{N}}$, and the payoff f is the average of the state payoff f^k, $f(\alpha, \beta) = \sum_k p^k f^k(\alpha^k, \beta)$, with finally:

$$f^k(n, \beta) = a^k \left(1 - \prod_0^{n-1} \beta'_m\right) + \left(\prod_0^{n-1} \beta'_m\right)(\beta_n c^k + \beta'_n d^k) \quad \text{for } n \in \mathbb{N},$$

$$f^k(\infty, \beta) = a^k \left(1 - \prod_0^{\infty} \beta'_m\right) + \left(\prod_0^{\infty} \beta'_m\right) d^k,$$

$$f^k(\partial, \beta) = a^k \left(1 - \prod_0^{\infty} \beta'_m\right) + \left(\prod_0^{\infty} \beta'_m\right) b^k,$$

where $\beta = (\beta_0, \ldots, \beta_m, \ldots) \in B$, β'_m denotes $1 - \beta_m$, and $\prod_0^{-1} = 1$. Defining $\theta(\beta) = \min\{m \mid \beta_m = 1 \text{ or } m = \infty\}$, it is clear that $\theta(\beta)$ determines the payoff; hence B can also be written as $\overline{\mathbb{N}}$. Then one has, with $\xi \in A$:

$$f^k(\xi, m) = \mathbb{1}_{\xi \leq m-1} d^k + \mathbb{1}_{\xi = m} c^k + \mathbb{1}_{\xi > m} a^k \quad \text{for } m \in \mathbb{N}, \quad \text{and}$$

$$f^k(\xi, \infty) = \mathbb{1}_{\xi \leq \infty} d^k + \mathbb{1}_{\xi = \partial} b^k.$$

We write $\overline{G}(p)$ for the mixed extension of $G(p)$ where player I's strategies are probabilities on A^K (or a K vector of probabilities on A, since f is decomposed on A^K), say, χ in $\Delta(A)^K$, and player II's strategies are probabilities with finite support on B, say, Ψ in $\Delta(B)$.

Proposition VIII.4.9. *$\overline{G}(p)$ has a value $w(p)$.*

Proof. For each β, $f^k(\cdot, \beta)$ is continuous on A. In fact, β corresponds either to some m in $\mathbb{N}$ and f^k is constant on $\alpha^k > m$, or to ∞ and f^k is constant on $\overline{\mathbb{N}}$. Moreover A^K is compact; hence by Proposition I.1.9, p. 9, the game $\overline{G}$ has a value (and player I has an optimal strategy). ∎

Theorem VIII.4.10. *$\min\max \Gamma(p)$ exists and $\overline{v}(p) = w(p)$.*

The proof will follow from the two next lemmas.

Note first that for all $\Psi \in \Delta(B)$ there exists $\delta \in [0, 1]^{\mathbb{N}}$ s.t. $\int f(\alpha, \beta)\Psi(d\beta) = f(\alpha, \delta)$ for all $\alpha \in A^K$. In fact, by the above remarks Ψ can be described as the distribution of the stopping time θ. δ_n is then just the conditional probability on the nth factor, given $\{\theta \geq n\}$.

Lemma VIII.4.11. *Player II can guarantee w.*

Proof. Given $\varepsilon > 0$, let Ψ be an $\varepsilon/4$ optimal strategy of player II for $w(p)$ and as above represent Ψ by some δ in $[0, 1]^{\mathbb{N}}$. Define now τ, the strategy of player II in $\Gamma(p)$, as: play δ_0 i.i.d. until the first Top of player I, then play δ_1 i.i.d. until the second Top, then δ_2, and so on. Let also $\rho = \prod_{m=0}^{\infty} \delta'_m$ and define N such that: if $\rho = 0$, $\prod_{m=0}^{N-1} \delta'_m < \varepsilon/4$, and if $\rho > 0$, $\prod_{m=N}^{\infty} \delta'_m > 1 - \varepsilon/4$.

Let us bound $\overline{\gamma}_n(\sigma, \tau)$ from above for $n \geq N$. It is enough to consider $\overline{\gamma}_n^k(\sigma^k, \tau)$ for each k. Since τ is independent of the previous moves of player II, we can assume that σ^k has the same property (one can replace at each stage σ^k by its expectation w.r.t. τ on J without changing the payoff). Moreover we can consider best replies and assume σ^k to be pure. It follows then that σ^k is completely described by the dates $M_1, \ldots, M_m, \ldots$ of the successive Top. We obtain thus, for $n \in [M_m, M_{m+1}]$, with $M_0 = -1$:

$$\begin{aligned}\gamma_n^k(\sigma, \tau) &= \mathsf{E}_{\sigma^k,\tau}(g_n^k) \\ &= a^k\left(1 - \prod_{\ell=0}^{m-1} \delta'_\ell\right) + \left(\prod_{\ell=0}^{m-1} \delta'_\ell\right)(\delta_m c^k + \delta'_m d^k) \\ &= f^k(m, \delta).\end{aligned}$$

Now for $n \geq M_N$, the expected stage payoff satisfies:

- If $\rho = 0$, $\left|\gamma_n^k(\sigma, \tau) - a^k\right| \leq \varepsilon/2$, thus $\left|\gamma_n^k(\sigma, \tau) - f^k(\infty, \delta)\right| \leq \varepsilon/2$.
- If $\rho > 0$,
  - Either player I plays Bottom, and one has $|\gamma_n^k(\sigma, \tau) - (a^k(1 - \rho) + \rho d^k)| \leq \varepsilon/2$ by the choice of N, thus:
  $$\left|\gamma_n^k(\sigma, \tau) - f^k(\infty, \delta)\right| \leq \varepsilon/2,$$
  - Or player I plays Top, and we obtain similarly:
  $$\left|\gamma_n^k(\sigma, \tau) - f^k(\partial, \delta)\right| \leq \varepsilon/2.$$

It follows that every expected stage payoff, except at most $K \times N$ of them, corresponding to $\{M_m\}$, $m = 1, \ldots, N$, for each σ^k, is within $\varepsilon/2$ of a feasible payoff against Ψ in $\overline{G}(p)$. Hence $n \geq 8KN/\varepsilon$ implies $\overline{\gamma}_n(\sigma, \tau) \leq w(p) + \varepsilon$. ∎

Lemma VIII.4.12. *Player* I *can force* w.

Proof. Consider first χ, the optimal strategy of player I in $\overline{G}(p)$. Given $\varepsilon > 0$, χ, and a strategy τ of player II in $\Gamma(p)$, we shall define a strategy σ of player I in $\Gamma(p)$ by the following procedure (similar to Section VIII.2): we introduce a family, indexed by A, of "non-revealing" strategies in $\Gamma(p)$; i.e., transition probabilities from H to S, say, μ_α. σ^k will then be: select some α according to the probability χ^k on X and play μ_α. Let η be the stopping time of reaching the absorbing entry: $\eta = \min\{\{m \mid i_m = \mathrm{T}, j_m = \mathrm{L}\} \cup \{\infty\}\}$, and define N such that $\chi^k(N) \leq \varepsilon/3$ for all k in K.

For each $m \leq N$, define inductively strategies μ_m and times L_m as follows:

- μ_0 is always Bottom. Given μ_0 and τ, let $t_n^0 = P_{\mu_0,\tau}(j_n = \mathrm{L})$ and L_0 be the first time ℓ where:

$$\sum_k p^k \chi^k(0)(t_\ell^0 c^k + t_\ell^{0\prime} d^k) \leq \inf_n \left[\sum_k p^k \chi^k(0)(t_n^0 c^k + t_n^{0\prime} d^k)\right] + \varepsilon/3.$$

- μ_1 is Bottom up to stage L_0 (excluded), Top at that stage L_0, and always Bottom thereafter.
- Similarly, given μ_m, let $t_n^m = P_{\mu_m,\tau}(j_n = \text{Left} \mid \eta > L_{m-1})$ and let L_m be the first $\ell > L_{m-1}$ where:

$$\sum_k p^k \chi^k(m)(t_\ell^m c^k + t_\ell^{m\prime} d^k) \leq \inf_n \left[\sum_k p^k \chi^k(m)(t_n^m c^k + t_n^{m\prime} d^k) \right] + \varepsilon/3. \tag{12}$$

μ_{m+1} is then μ_m up to stage L_m (excluded), Top at that stage, and Bottom thereafter.

For $m > N$, we introduce a new stopping time L' and a non-revealing strategy μ' satisfying:

$$\pi = P_{\mu',\tau}(\eta \leq L') \geq \sup_{\mu \in M} P_{\mu,\tau}(\eta < \infty) - \varepsilon/9, \tag{13}$$

where M is the set of strategies that coincide with μ_N up to L_{N-1} (included). If $N < m \leq \infty$, let $\mu_m = \mu_\infty$: play μ' up to stage L' (included), and then Bottom forever. Finally we define μ_∂ as: play μ' up to stage L' (included), and then always Top.

Let also δ in $[0, 1]^{\mathbb{N}}$ satisfy:

$$\delta_m = t_{L_m}^m, \quad \text{for } m < N,$$

$$\delta_N = u, \quad \text{where } \pi = 1 - \Big(\prod_{m=0}^{N-1} \delta'_m\Big) u' \ \text{(note that } 1 \geq \pi \geq 1 - \prod_{m=0}^{N-1} \delta'_m),$$

$$\delta_m = 0, \quad \text{for } m > N,$$

and we shall prove that for $n \geq L'$:

$$\gamma_n^p(\sigma, \tau) \geq \int f(\alpha, \delta) \chi(d\alpha) - 2\varepsilon/3. \tag{14}$$

In fact, we can decompose the above payoff on the events $\{\mu_\alpha$ is played$\}$, with α in A, so that:

$$\gamma_n^p(\sigma, \tau) = \sum_k p^k \gamma_n^k(\sigma^k, \tau) = \sum_k \sum_\alpha p^k P_{\sigma^k}(\mu_\alpha) \gamma_n^k(\mu_\alpha, \tau) = \sum_x \varphi_n(\alpha, \tau).$$

For $m \leq N$ we obtain, using (12):

$$\sum_k p^k \chi^k(m) \left[\Big(1 - \prod_0^{m-1} \delta'_\ell\Big) a^k + \prod_0^{m-1} \delta'_\ell (t_n^m c^k + t_n^{m\prime} d^k) \right]$$

$$\geq \sum_k p^k \chi^k(m) \left[\Big(1 - \prod_0^{m-1} \delta'_\ell\Big) a^k + \prod_0^{m-1} \delta'_\ell (\delta_m c^k + \delta'_m d^k) \right] - \varepsilon/3$$

$$\geq \sum_k p^k \chi^k(m) f^k(m, \delta) - \varepsilon/3.$$

For $N < m \le \infty$, we get, using (13):

$$\sum_k p^k \chi^k(m)\big[P_{\mu_m,\tau}(\eta \le n)a^k + \big(1 - P_{\mu_m,\tau}(\eta \le n)\big)(t_n^m c^k + t_n^{m\prime} d^k)\big]$$
$$\ge \sum_k p^k \chi^k(m)(\pi a^k + (1-\pi)d^k) - \varepsilon/3,$$

since the choice of μ' and L' implies $(1 - P_{\mu_m,\tau}(\eta \le n))t_n^m \le \varepsilon/9$. Similarly, when μ_∂ is used the payoff is at least $\sum_k p^k \chi^k(\partial)(\pi a^k + (1-\pi)b^k) - \varepsilon/3$.

It follows that for all $m \in X$, $m \ne N$, $\varphi_n(m,\tau) \ge \sum_k p^k \chi^k(m) f^k(m,\delta) - \varepsilon/3$. Since, by the choice of N, $|\varphi_n(N,\tau)|$ and $\left|\sum_k p^k \chi^k(N) f^k(N,\delta)\right|$ are bounded by $\varepsilon/3$, we obtain (14) by summing. Hence $n \ge 6L'/\varepsilon$ implies $\overline{\gamma}_n^p(\sigma,\tau) \ge w(p) - \varepsilon$.

This completes the proof of Theorem VIII.4.10. ■

For a geometric approach with an explicit description, cf. VIII.4, Ex. 9–VIII.4, Ex. 11.

VIII.4.c.2. Example B

We consider now the case where $G^k = \begin{pmatrix} a^{k*} & b^k \\ c^k & d^{k*} \end{pmatrix}$.

We will prove that $\overline{v}$ is the value $w(p)$ of the one-shot game with incomplete information with payoff matrices:

$$B^k = \begin{array}{c} \\ T\widetilde{T} \\ T\widetilde{TB} \\ T\widetilde{B} \\ B\widetilde{T} \\ B\widetilde{BT} \\ B\widetilde{B} \end{array} \begin{array}{c} \begin{array}{cccccc} L\widetilde{L} & L\widetilde{LR} & L\widetilde{R} & R\widetilde{L} & R\widetilde{RL} & R\widetilde{R} \end{array} \\ \begin{pmatrix} a^k & a^k & a^k & a^k & a^k & b^k \\ a^k & a^k & a^k & a^k & a^k & d^k \\ a^k & a^k & a^k & c^k & d^k & d^k \\ a^k & a^k & b^k & d^k & d^k & d^k \\ a^k & d^k & d^k & d^k & d^k & d^k \\ c^k & d^k & d^k & d^k & d^k & d^k \end{pmatrix} \end{array}.$$

Theorem VIII.4.13. $w(p) = \overline{v}(p)$.

Proof.

Part A. Player II can guarantee w

Let $(\alpha_1, \alpha_2, \alpha_3; \beta_1, \beta_2, \beta_3)$ be an optimal strategy of player II in the auxiliary game. Player II uses it to choose a column and play according to the following dictionary: $L\widetilde{L}$ is Left then always Left, $L\widetilde{R}$ is Left then always Right, and $L\widetilde{LR}$ is Left then $(x, 1-x)$ i.i.d. for any fixed x in $(0,1)$, and similarly for the columns starting with R. Assume that player I plays Top at stage one; then his expected payoff after stage n, where n is such that the stopping time θ of reaching a $*$ is smaller than n with probability near 1 when II plays $(x, 1-x)$, is essentially of the form (with $\alpha = \sum_i \alpha_i$):

$\alpha a^k + \beta_1 a^k + \beta_2 a^k + \beta_3 b^k$ if only Top is played (corresponding to $T\widetilde{T}$),

$\alpha a^k + \beta_1 c^k + \beta_2 d^k + \beta_3 d^k$ if only Bottom is played (corresponding to $T\widetilde{B}$),

and

$$\alpha a^k + \beta_1 a^k + \beta_2(y a^k + (1-y)d^k) + \beta_3 d^k \quad \text{else.}$$

Note now that if $a^k \geq d^k$ the above payoff is maximal for $y = 1$ and corresponds to $T\widetilde{TB}$. Finally, if $a^k < d^k$, player I can obtain, by playing first Bottom and then $(\varepsilon, 1-\varepsilon)$ i.i.d., a payoff near $\alpha_1 a^k + \alpha_2 d^k + \alpha_3 d^k + \beta d^k$, which is a better payoff and corresponds to $B\overline{BT}$. Hence by the choice of τ, for any $\eta > 0$, for n large enough and for all σ: $\overline{\gamma}_n(\sigma, \tau) \leq w(p) + \eta$.

Part B. Player I can defend w

Given τ, player I can compute the probability, say, x, that II will play Left if I plays Top always. Hence, by playing Top a large number of times and then either playing always Top or always Bottom, he can get, at state k, either $xa^k + (1-x)b^k$ or $xa^k + (1-x)d^k$. By playing Top and then always Bottom, he will obtain for n large enough some payoff of the form: $ya^k + zc^k + (1-z-y)d^k$, with obviously $y + z \leq x$. Define then $\alpha' = y$, $\beta'_1 = z$, $\beta'_3 = (1-x)$; note that if player I starts by Bottom, the payoff is d^k with probability $(1-y)$ at stage 1, so that the same analysis starting with Bottom allows us to define α'_i.

This proves that τ gives the same payoff as a strategy in the auxiliary game; hence if $\pi = (q_i^k; r_i^k)$ is an optimal strategy of player I in the auxiliary game, at state k, we define σ, at state k, as: with probability $\underline{q} = \sum_i q_i$, play Top at stage 1, with (total) probability q_3 (that corresponds to $T\widetilde{B}$) play from then on Bottom; otherwise play Top until stage n where $\Pr(\theta \leq n)$ is within ε of its supremum, and from then on keep playing Top (with probability q_1 corresponding to $T\widetilde{T}$) or play Bottom forever (with probability q_2 corresponding to $T\underset{\sim}{T}B$), and similarly with r. The payoff corresponding to σ, τ in Γ_∞ is thus near the payoff induced by π and some (α'_i, β'_i) in the auxiliary game. This completes the proof of the theorem. ∎

EXERCISES

1. A stochastic game with signals. (Ferguson et al., 2003)
We are given two states of nature with the following payoff matrices:

$$G^1 = \begin{pmatrix} 1 & 0 \\ 1 & 0 \end{pmatrix} \qquad G^2 = \begin{pmatrix} 0 & 1 \\ 0 & 0 \end{pmatrix}.$$

The transition from 1 to 2 is a constant $(1-\pi) \in (0, 1)$, independent of the moves. From state 2, one goes to state 1 iff player I plays Bottom. Player I knows everything, and player II is told only the times of the transition from 2 to 1. We will consider Γ_λ, the discounted game starting from $k = 1$, and write v_λ for its value. Let us take as state variable the number m^* of stages since the last transition from 2 to 1.

Consider the following class of strategies for player I:

$$X = \{x = (x_m) \mid x_m = \Pr(\text{play Top} \mid m^* = m)\} \qquad \text{and similarly:}$$

$$Y = \{y = (y_m) \mid y_m = \Pr(\text{play Right} \mid m^* = m)\} \quad \text{for player II.}$$

Given x and y, let U_m (resp. W_m) be the payoff of the λ-discounted game starting at $m^* = m$ and $k = 1$ (resp. $k = 2$).

a. Prove that:

$$U_m = (1 - y_m)\lambda + (1 - \lambda)\big(\pi U_{m+1} + (1 - \pi)W_{m+1}\big),$$

$$W_m = (x_m y_m)\lambda + (1 - \lambda)\big(x_m W_{m+1} + (1 - x_m)U_0\big),$$

and that this system has a unique bounded solution with:

$$U_0 = \lambda \frac{\Big(\sum_{j=0}^{\infty}(1 - y_j)[\pi(1 - \lambda)]^j + (1 - \pi)\sum_{j=1}^{\infty}\{\pi^{j-1}\sum_{m=j}^{\infty}[x_m y_m (1 - \lambda)^m \prod_{l=j}^{m-1} x_l]\}\Big)}{\Big(1 - (1 - \pi)(1 - \lambda)\sum_{j=1}^{\infty}\{\pi^{j-1}\sum_{m=j}^{\infty}[(1 - x_m)(1 - \lambda)^m \prod_{l=j}^{m-1} x_l]\}\Big)}.$$

b. Prove that if the game has a value on $X \times Y$, this value is v_λ (and the corresponding strategies are optimal in Γ_λ).

c. Let r in $\mathbb{N}$ satisfying $\pi^{r-1} > 1/2, \pi^r \le 1/2$ and define $\overline{x}$ in X by:

$$\overline{x}_m = \begin{cases} 1 & m < r \\ \pi^r/(1 - \pi^r) & m = r \\ \pi/(2 - \pi) & m > r. \end{cases}$$

Show that $U_0(\overline{x}, y)$ depends only of (y_l), $0 \le l < r$, that a best reply gives $y_l = 1$, $0 \le l < r$, and that the corresponding payoff is:

$$V = \frac{[1 - (1 - \lambda)^r][1 - \pi(1 - \lambda)] - \lambda\{1 - 2[\pi(1 - \lambda)]^r\}}{[1 - (1 - \lambda)^{r+1}][1 - \pi(1 - \lambda)] + 2(1 - \lambda)^{r+1}\pi^r\lambda}.$$

Define $\overline{y}$ in Y by:

$$\overline{y}_m = \begin{cases} 1 & m < r \\ (1 - \lambda)V & m \ge r. \end{cases}$$

Prove then that $W_m(\overline{x}, \overline{y}) = (1 - \lambda)V$, for $m \ge r$.

To show that $\overline{x}$ is a best reply to $\overline{y}$, assume first that x coincides with $\overline{x}$ from some stage on and then conclude. Deduce then that $v_\lambda = V$.

d. Let $v_0 = \lim_{\lambda \to 0} v_\lambda = \frac{r(1-\pi)-(1-2\pi^r)}{(r+1)(1-\pi)+2\pi^r}$ and define y^* by:

$$y_m^* = \begin{cases} 1 & m < r \\ v_0 & m \ge r. \end{cases}$$

Prove that $\forall \varepsilon > 0$, $\exists \lambda^*$, such that $\forall \lambda \le \lambda^*$, $\forall \sigma \in \Sigma$, $\forall \tau \in \mathscr{T}$:

$$\overline{\gamma}_\lambda(\overline{x}, \tau) \ge v_0 - \varepsilon \text{ and } \overline{\gamma}_\lambda(\sigma, y^*) \le v_0 + \varepsilon.$$

2. Examples of games with no value. (Mertens and Zamir, 1976a; Waternaux, 1983a,b).

We consider games as in Section VIII.2, with $\#K = 2$. $A^\sharp$ means that the entry is revealing; hence the payoff thereafter is 0. Note that the results are more precise than

Theorem VIII.2.2, p. 436, since the auxiliary games $\overline{G}$ or $\underline{G}$ are finite; in particular, minmax and maxmin are algebraic.

a. Let $G^1 = \begin{pmatrix} x_{11}^\sharp & x_{12} \\ x_{21} & x_{22} \end{pmatrix}$ and $G^2 = \begin{pmatrix} y_{11} & y_{12} \\ y_{21} & y_{22}^\sharp \end{pmatrix}$.

Show that the maxmin is the value of the following game:

$$\overline{G} = \begin{array}{c} \widetilde{T} \\ \widetilde{B} \\ \widetilde{1-\varepsilon} \\ \widetilde{\varepsilon} \\ B_1 \\ T_1 \end{array} \overset{\begin{array}{ccc} \widetilde{L} & \widetilde{R} & \widetilde{\beta} \end{array}}{\begin{pmatrix} y_{11} & x_{12}+y_{12} & \beta y_{11}+\beta' y_{12} \\ x_{21}+y_{21} & x_{22} & \beta x_{21}+\beta' x_{22} \\ y_{11} & x_{12} & 0 \\ y_{21} & x_{22} & 0 \\ y_{11} & x_{12} & \beta(\beta y_{11}+\beta' y_{12}) \\ y_{21} & x_{22} & \beta'(\beta x_{21}+\beta' x_{22}) \end{pmatrix}},$$

and obviously a dual result holds for the minmax. $\widetilde{T}$ corresponds to the strategy always Top, similarly for $\widetilde{B}$, $\widetilde{L}$, $\widetilde{R}$; $\widetilde{\beta}$ is playing i.i.d. Left with probability β, and $\widetilde{1-\varepsilon}$ corresponds to the strategy of playing Top and Bottom each infinitely many times with the relative frequency of Top equals 1; T_1 stands for the strategy of playing always Bottom with one exceptional move of Top, and similarly for B_1. Finally β' is $1-\beta'$.

Show that II has an optimal strategy using a single value of β.

b. In the following example:

$$G^1 = \begin{pmatrix} -1^\sharp & 2 \\ 2 & -4 \end{pmatrix}, \qquad G^2 = \begin{pmatrix} -4 & 2 \\ 2 & -1^\sharp \end{pmatrix}$$

show that $\overline{v} = -1/2$ with optimal strategies $(1/4, 1/4, 1/4, 1/4, 0, 0)$ for I and $(1/4, 1/4, 1/2\widetilde{(1/2)})$ for II in $\overline{G}$; $\underline{v} = -2/3$ and $(1/6, 1/6, 2/3\widetilde{(1/2)})$ for I and $(1/6, 1/6, 0, 0, 1/3, 1/3)$ for II are optimal in $\underline{G}$.

c. Let now $G^1 = \begin{pmatrix} x_{11}^\sharp & x_{12} \\ x_{21} & x_{22} \end{pmatrix}$ and $G^2 = \begin{pmatrix} y_{11} & y_{12}^\sharp \\ y_{21} & y_{22} \end{pmatrix}$.

Show that the minmax is the value of

$$\overline{G} = \begin{array}{c} \widetilde{T} \\ \widetilde{B} \\ \widetilde{\varepsilon} \\ T_1 \\ T_2 \end{array} \overset{\begin{array}{ccc} \widetilde{L} & \widetilde{R} & \widetilde{\beta} \end{array}}{\begin{pmatrix} y_{11} & x_{12} & 0 \\ x_{21}+y_{21} & x_{22}+y_{22} & \beta(x_{21}+y_{21})+\beta'(x_{22}+y_{22}) \\ y_{21} & x_{22} & 0 \\ y_{21} & x_{22} & \beta'(\beta x_{21}+\beta' x_{22})+\beta(\beta y_{21}+\beta' y_{22}) \\ y_{21} & x_{22} & \beta'^2(\beta x_{21}+\beta' x_{22})+\beta^2(\beta y_{21}+\beta' y_{22}) \end{pmatrix}},$$

and the maxmin is the value of:

$$\underline{G} = \begin{array}{c} \widetilde{B} \\ \widetilde{\alpha} \end{array} \overset{\begin{array}{cccc} \widetilde{L} & \widetilde{R} & \widetilde{1-\varepsilon} & \widetilde{\varepsilon} \end{array}}{\begin{pmatrix} x_{21}+y_{21} & x_{22}+y_{22} & x_{21}+y_{21} & x_{22}+y_{22} \\ \alpha y_{11}+\alpha' y_{21} & \alpha x_{12}+\alpha' x_{22} & 0 & 0 \end{pmatrix}}.$$

d. For $G^1 = \begin{pmatrix} 7^\sharp & -3 \\ -7 & 3 \end{pmatrix}$ and $G^2 = \begin{pmatrix} -31 & 11^\sharp \\ 31 & -11 \end{pmatrix}$, show that $\overline{v} = 1/4$ with $(0, 0, 0, 2/3, 1/3)$ optimal for I and $(0, 0, \widetilde{1/4})$ optimal for II, and $\underline{v} = 0$, with $(0, \widetilde{1/2})$ and $(0, 0, 0, 1)$ optimal for I and II.

From now on we are in the framework of Section VIII.4

3. Consider the games introduced in Section VIII.4.a and prove that:

$$w(p) = \inf_{F'} \sum_k p^k \max_\omega \Upsilon^k(f, \omega)$$

with:

$$\Upsilon^k(f, \omega) = (1 - \omega) G_1^k f(\omega) + \int_0^\omega G_2^k f(\omega') \ell(d\omega').$$

Assume $\#K = \#S = \#T = 2$. Show that $w(p) = \inf_c [p\, c + (1 - p) J(c)]$ with:

$$J(c) = \max_\omega \{\Upsilon^2(f, \omega) \mid \Upsilon^1(f, \omega') \leq c \text{ for all } \omega'\}.$$

Deduce the existence of optimal strategies for II and an explicit formula for them.

4. Let $G^1 = \begin{pmatrix} 1^* & 0^* \\ 0 & 0 \end{pmatrix}$ and $G^2 = \begin{pmatrix} 0^* & 0^* \\ 0 & 1 \end{pmatrix}$. Show that:

$$u(p) = \operatorname{Cav} u(p) = p(1 - p),$$

$$v(p) = (1 - p)[1 - \exp(-p/(1 - p))],$$

$$f(x) = \begin{cases} L/(1 - x) & \text{on } [0, 1 - L] \\ 1 & \text{on } [1 - L, 1], \end{cases} \quad \text{with } L = \exp(-p/(1 - p))$$

$$\underline{\rho}^1(x) = \begin{cases} -((1 - p)/p) \ln(1 - x) & \text{on } [0, 1 - L] \\ 1 & \text{on } [1 - L, 1], \end{cases}$$

$$\underline{\rho}^2(x) \equiv 0.$$

Note that $\underline{v}$ and $\lim v_n$ are transcendental functions.

In the two following examples ρ has an atomic part.

5. Let $G^1 = \begin{pmatrix} 4^* & -2^* \\ 0 & 0 \end{pmatrix}$ and $G^2 = \begin{pmatrix} 0^* & 1^* \\ -1 & 2 \end{pmatrix}$. Show that:

- For $0 \leq p \leq 1/7 : u(p) = v(p) = v_1(p) = 4p$.
- For $1/7 \leq p \leq 1$:

$$v(p) = (1 - p)\big(1 - (1/3) \exp[(1 - 7p)/3(1 - p)]\big),$$

$$f(x) = \begin{cases} 1/3 + L/(1 - x) & \text{on } [0, 1 - 6L] \\ 1/2 & \text{on } [1 - 6L, 1], \end{cases} \quad \text{with } L = \frac{1}{9} \exp \frac{1 - 7p}{3(1 - p)},$$

$$\underline{\rho}^1(x) = \begin{cases} -((1 - p)/2p) \ln(1 - x) & \text{on } [0, 1 - 9L] \\ 1 & \text{on } [1 - 9L, 1], \end{cases}$$

$$\underline{\rho}^2(x) = \begin{cases} 0 & \text{on } [0, 1 - 9L) \\ 1 & \text{on } [1 - 9L, 1]. \end{cases}$$

6. Let $G^1 = \begin{pmatrix} 3^* & -1^* \\ 2 & 0 \end{pmatrix}$ and $G^2 = \begin{pmatrix} -1^* & 1^* \\ 1 & -1 \end{pmatrix}$. Prove that:

- For $0 \le p \le 1/3$:

$$\begin{aligned} v(p) &= p, \\ f(x) &= 1/2 \text{ on } [0,1], \\ \underline{\rho}^1(x) = \underline{\rho}^2(x) &= 1 - (1-x)^{1/(1-3p)} \text{ on } [0,1]. \end{aligned}$$

- For $1/3 \le p \le 2/3$:

$$\begin{aligned} v(p) &= (1/9)(4-3p), \\ f(x) &= \begin{cases} 1/2 - 2/9(1-x^2) & \text{on } [0,1/3] \\ 0 & \text{on } [1/3,1], \end{cases} \\ \underline{\rho}^1(x) &= (2/3-p)/p \text{ on } [0,1], \\ \underline{\rho}^2(x) &= \begin{cases} [2(2/3-p)+(3p-1)x]/(1-p) & \text{on } [0,1/3) \\ 1 & \text{on } [1/3,1]. \end{cases} \end{aligned}$$

- For $2/3 \le p \le 1$:

$$\begin{aligned} v(p) &= p(1-p), \\ f(x) &= \begin{cases} [1-p^2/(1-x)^2]/2 & \text{on } [0,1-p] \\ 0 & \text{on } [1-p,1], \end{cases} \\ \underline{\rho}^1(x) &= 0 \text{ on } [0,1], \\ \underline{\rho}^2(x) &= \begin{cases} x/(1-p) & \text{on } [0,1-p) \\ 1 & \text{on } [1-p,1]. \end{cases} \end{aligned}$$

7. Consider the game of VIII.4, Ex. 4. Prove that (with $x' = 1 - x$):

$$\begin{aligned} (n+1)v_{n+1}(p) = \max_{s,t} \min_{x} \big\{ &(n+1)psx + p't'x' \\ &+ n(ps' + p't')v_n\big(ps'/(ps'+p't')\big)\big\}, \end{aligned}$$

and deduce the following heuristic differential equation for $\lim v_n(p)$:

$$y(p)(2-p) = 1 - p - (1-p)^2 y'(p).$$

Adding the initial conditions leads to $v(p) = (1-p)\{1 - \exp(-p/(1-p))\}$. Prove by induction, using the recursive formula, that $v_n \ge v - L/n$ and $v_n \le v + L/n^{1/2}$, for some L large enough.

8. Let $G^1 = \begin{pmatrix} 1^* & 0 \\ 0^* & 0 \end{pmatrix}$ and $G^2 = \begin{pmatrix} 0^* & 0 \\ 0^* & 1 \end{pmatrix}$. Prove that:

$$\overline{v}(p) = \inf_{\rho \in Q} \sup_{0 \le t \le 1} \Big[p \int_0^1 (1-s)\rho(ds) + (1-p)t(1-\underline{\rho}(t)) \Big]$$
$$= p\big[1 - \exp(1-(1-p)/p)\big].$$

Note that in this example the minmax is a transcendental function.

9. A geometric approach to the minmax

Player I can *defend a set D* in $\mathbb{R}^K$, if for every $\varepsilon > 0$ and every τ there exists a strategy σ and a number N, such that for all $n \ge N$ there exists d in D with $\overline{\gamma}_n^k(\sigma, \tau) \ge d^k - \varepsilon$, for all k. Prove that if player I can defend the half spaces $H(p, g(p)) = \{t \in \mathbb{R}^K \mid \langle p, t\rangle \ge g(p)\}$ for all $p \in \Pi$, then he can also defend $H(p, \operatorname{Cav} g(p))$.

Player II can *guarantee a point M* in $\mathbb{R}^K$, if for every $\varepsilon > 0$ there exists a strategy τ and a number N, such that for every σ, $n \ge N$ implies: $\overline{\gamma}_n^k(\sigma, \tau) \le M^k + \varepsilon$, for all k (i.e., he can approach $M - \mathbb{R}_+^K$).

Show that the set of points that player II can guarantee is convex.

Denote by D_{I} the intersection of the half spaces of the form $H(p, \alpha)$ that I can defend and by D_{II} the set of points that II can guarantee.

Prove that $\overline{v}(p)$ exists and equals $\min_{d \in D} \langle p, d\rangle \iff D = D_{\mathrm{I}} = D_{\mathrm{II}}$ (D is then called the *minmax set*).

10. Let $G^1 = \begin{pmatrix} 1^* & 0 \\ 0^* & 1 \end{pmatrix}$ and $G^2 = \begin{pmatrix} 0^* & 1 \\ 1^* & 0 \end{pmatrix}$.

Show that the minmax set is $\operatorname{Co}\{M^1, M^2, M\} + \mathbb{R}_+^2$ with:

$M^1 = (1/2, 1)$ (player II plays optimal for $k = 1$),

$M^2 = (1, 1/2)$ (player II plays optimal for $k = 2$),

$M = (2/3, 2/3)$ (player II plays once $(1/3, 2/3)$, then guarantees M^1 (resp. M^2) if $s_1 =$ Top (resp. Bottom).

11. Let $G^1 = \begin{pmatrix} 8^* & -2 \\ -4^* & 1 \end{pmatrix}$ and $G^2 = \begin{pmatrix} -3^* & 2 \\ 6^* & -4 \end{pmatrix}$.

Prove that the minmax set is $D' \cup D'' + \mathbb{R}_+^2$ with:

$$D' = \{(x, f(x)) \mid x \in [0,1], f(x) = 3 - (3/4)x - (1/4)x^{1/5}\}, \quad \text{and}$$
$$D'' = \{(g(y), y) \mid y \in [0,2], g(y) = 4 - (4/3)y - (1/3)(y/2)^{2/5}\}.$$

12. Consider the games introduced in Section VIII.3.a, p. 446, and assume $\#K = 2$.

Prove that the minmax set is the intersection of the positive half spaces (i.e., of the form $H(p, \alpha)$; cf. VIII.4, Ex. 9) that contains one of the following five sets: the point V and the four segments $[C, D]$, $[A, B \vee D]$, $[Q, P]$, and $[Q', P']$, where A (resp. B, C, D) is the point (a^1, a^2), and $V = (v^1, v^2)$ where v^k is the value (minmax would suffice) of $\Gamma_\infty(k)$, $Q = (a^1, c^2)$, $P = (v^1, d^2)$, and similarly $Q' = (a^2, c^1)$, $P' = (d^1, v^2)$ (given two points M and N, $M \vee N$ is $(\max\{m^1, n^1\}, \max\{m^2, n^2\})$.)

Deduce that $\overline{v}$ is the value of a one-shot matrix game.

13. Consider a game as in Section VIII.4.c.1 and VIII.4.c.2 where the matrix G^k is of the form:

$$G^k = \begin{pmatrix} a^{k*} & b^{k*} \\ c^{k*} & d^k \end{pmatrix}.$$

Prove that $\overline{v}$ is the value of the one-shot game with incomplete information and infinite payoff matrices B^k with:

$$B^k = \begin{pmatrix} a^k & b^k & b^k & \cdots & b^k & b^k \\ c^k & a^k & b^k & \cdots & b^k & b^k \\ c^k & c^k & a^k & \cdots & b^k & b^k \\ \vdots & \vdots & \vdots & \ddots & \vdots & \vdots \\ c^k & c^k & c^k & \cdots & a^k & b^k \\ c^k & c^k & c^k & \cdots & c^k & d^k \end{pmatrix}.$$

Show that for any fixed $\#K$, one can replace B^k by finite matrices.

CHAPTER IX

Non-Zero-Sum Games with Incomplete Information

IX.1. EQUILIBRIA IN Γ_∞

In this section, we will study equilibria in games with incomplete information. The analysis will be limited to two players, and some major questions are still open.

As seen in Chapter VI, in the zero-sum case, when there is lack of information on both sides, the value may not exist and hence there is no equilibrium, even in a weak sense; i.e., E_0 is empty. We are thus led to consider games with lack of information on one side. We will moreover assume full monitoring and hence the game Γ_∞ is described by the action sets S and T, the state space K with initial probability p, and, for each k, $S \times T$ vector payoff matrices G^k with elements in $\mathbb{R}^2$.

We shall write $u_{\mathrm{I}}(p)$ (resp. $u_{\mathrm{II}}(p)$) for the value of the game $G^{\mathrm{I}}(p) = \sum p^k G^{k,\mathrm{I}}$ (resp. $G^{\mathrm{II}}(p) = \sum p^k G^{k,\mathrm{II}}$) where player I (resp. II) maximizes. $\gamma_n(\sigma, \tau)$ is the expected (vector) payoff at stage n and $\overline{\gamma}_n(\sigma, \tau)$ the corresponding average up to stage n. Note that the equilibrium condition for I (the informed player) can equivalently be written by using $\overline{\gamma}_n^{k,\mathrm{I}}$, the conditional payoff given the true state, i.e.:

$$\overline{\gamma}_n^{k,\mathrm{I}} = \mathsf{E}^k_{\sigma,\tau}(\overline{g}_n^{\mathrm{I},k}) = \mathsf{E}_{\sigma,\tau}(\overline{g}_n^{\mathrm{I},k} \mid k) = \mathsf{E}_{\sigma^k,\tau}(\overline{g}_n^{\mathrm{I},k}).$$

This leads to a vector payoff for I, and we shall also use this formulation.

We will first prove a partial result[1] concerning the existence of uniform equilibria and then give a complete characterization of E_∞ in Γ_∞.

IX.1.a. Existence

Following Aumann et al. (1968), we define a **joint plan** to be a triple (R, z, θ) where:

- R (set of signals) is a subset of S^m for some fixed m.

[1] The existence Theorem IX.1.3, p. 483, is valid for any K; cf. Simon et al. (1995).

- z (signaling strategy) is a K-tuple where, for each k, $z^k \in \Delta(R)$, and we can always assume:

$$z(r) = \sum_k p^k z^k(r) > 0.$$

- θ (contract) is an R-tuple where, for each r, $\theta(r) \in \Delta(S \times T)$ (correlated move).

To each joint plan is associated a family of probabilities $p(r)$ on $\Pi = \Delta(K)$ where $p^k(r) = \frac{p^k z^k(r)}{z(r)}$ (conditional probability on k given r induced by z) and payoffs:

$$a^k(r) = \sum_{s,t} G^{k,\mathrm{I}}_{st}\theta_{st}(r) \qquad b^k(r) = \sum_{s,t} G^{k,\mathrm{II}}_{st}\theta_{st}(t), \qquad \forall k \in K$$

$$\alpha(r) = \langle p(r), a(r)\rangle \qquad \beta(r) = \langle p(r), b(r)\rangle$$

$$a^k = \sum_r z^k(r)a^k(r) \qquad \beta = \sum_r z(r)\beta(r).$$

Each joint plan will induce a pair of strategies as shown by the following.

Proposition IX.1.1. *A sufficient condition for a joint plan to generate a uniform equilibrium in $\Gamma_\infty(p)$ with payoff $(a = (a^k); \beta)$ is:*

(1) $\beta(r) \geq \mathsf{Vex}\, u_{\mathrm{II}}(p(r)) \quad \forall r \in R,$
(2) $\langle q, \overline{a}\rangle \geq u_{\mathrm{I}}(q) \quad \forall q \in \Pi,$ *where $\overline{a}$ is such that:*
(3) $a^k(r) \leq \overline{a}^k \; \forall r, \forall k$, *and* $\sum_k p^k(r)a^k(r) = \sum_k p^k(r)\overline{a}^k \; \forall r.$

Proof. Player I uses z to select a signal r and plays during m stages according to r. After these stages, both players are required to follow a history $h(r)$ where the empirical distribution of the pair of moves (s, t) converges to $\theta_{s,t}(r)$ (compare Section IV.4, p. 190).

It is thus clear that the corresponding asymptotic payoff, given r, will be $a(r)$, $\beta(r)$ (k-vector payoff for player I, real payoff for player II).

Consider now player II after stage m, given r. Since, from this stage on, player I is playing non-revealing, player II's posterior on K will remain precisely $p(r)$. It follows that, if player II deviates by not following $h(r)$, player I can use a punishing strategy σ satisfying $\tilde{g}_n(\sigma, \tau) \leq \mathsf{Vex}\, u_{\mathrm{II}}(p(r))$, where $\tilde{g}_n$ is the conditional expected payoff given r at each stage n following the deviation. To prove this, consider the zero-sum game with payoff G^{II} starting at $p(r)$ where player I is informed and minimizes, and use Theorem V.3.3. Condition 1 thus implies that there is no profitable deviation for player II.

Consider now player I. He has two kinds of possible deviations:

- First to send a wrong signal, namely, if he is of type k to use some $r' \neq r, r' \in R$ with $p^k(r') = 0 < p^k(r)$. Note that this deviation is not observable by player II, but, by condition (3), player I cannot gain by it, since his (future) payoff will then be $a^k(r') \le \overline{a}^k = a^k(r)$. Similarly I cannot gain by using another signaling strategy z'.

- The second possibility is for player I to make a detectable deviation at some stage. We then require player II to approach, from this stage on, the vector $\overline{a}$, and this is possible due to Section V.3.c, p. 230, and condition (2). It is now easy to see that the above strategies define a uniform equilibrium. ∎

Remark IX.1.1. For an extension of such a construction, cf. Section IX.1.b.

It remains thus to exhibit a joint plan satisfying (1), (2), and (3), i.e., an equilibrium joint plan (EJP for short). We shall use the following notations:

$$Y(p) = \{\, y \in Y = \Delta(T) \mid y \text{ is optimal for player II in } G^{\mathrm{II}}(p) \,\},$$

$$f_y(q) = \max_x xG^{\mathrm{I}}(q)y,$$

$$C(y) = \{\, (q,d) \in \Pi \times \mathbb{R} \mid d \ge f_y(q) \,\},$$

$$D = \{\, (q,d) \in \Pi \times \mathbb{R} \mid d \le \operatorname{Cav} u_{\mathrm{I}}(q) \,\},$$

$$D_{\mathrm{I}} = \{\, (q,d) \in \Pi \times \mathbb{R} \mid d \le u_{\mathrm{I}}(q) \,\}.$$

(Note that these sets are closed and the first two are convex.) By the definition of u_{I}, D_{I} and $C(y)$ have, for all y, an intersection with an empty interior. On the other hand, if D and $C(y)$ have the same property, they can be weakly separated, and the minmax theorem (applied to S and T) implies the existence of x satisfying, for all q, $xG^{\mathrm{I}}(q)y \ge u_{\mathrm{I}}(q)$. Thus:

Lemma IX.1.2. *If $C(y) \cap D$ has an empty interior for some y in $Y(p)$, then there exists an EJP at p.*

Proof. In fact, take $R = \emptyset$ (the joint plan is non-revealing), $\theta = x \otimes y$, where x is as above, and note that (2) follows and (3) is void. Now (1) comes from $y \in Y(p)$, hence $\beta \ge u_{\mathrm{II}}(p) \ge \operatorname{Vex} u_{\mathrm{II}}(p)$. ∎

Denote by SEJP these special EJP, and let $\Pi_1 = \{\, q \in \Pi \mid$ there exists a SEJP at $q \,\}$. It is then clear that Π_1 is closed (and equals Π if u_{I} is concave and in particular if $\#S = 1$).

Now we restrict the analysis to the case $\#K = 2$ and $\#S > 1$.

Theorem IX.1.3. *Assume $\#K = 2$. Then for each p, there exists an EJP at p.*

Proof. Assume $p_0 \in \Pi^\circ \setminus \Pi_1$ and $y_0 \in Y(p_0)$. Since u_{I} is algebraic and $C(y_0) \cap D_{\mathrm{I}}$ has an empty interior, the projection of $C(y_0) \cap D$ on $\mathbb{R}$ is included in some open interval, say, (q_1, q_2), on which $\operatorname{Cav} u_{\mathrm{I}}$ is linear. So there exists c in $\mathbb{R}^2$ with $\operatorname{Cav} u_{\mathrm{I}}(q) = \langle c, q \rangle$ on $[q_1, q_2]$ and $\operatorname{Cav} u_{\mathrm{I}}(q_i) = u_{\mathrm{I}}(q_i)$ for $i = 1, 2$. Define $Q(y) = \{\, p \in \Pi \mid f_y(p) - \langle c, p \rangle = \min_q f_y(q) - \langle c, q \rangle \equiv \zeta(y) \,\}$. Note that Q is a u.s.c. convex-valued correspondence, that ζ is continuous, and that, as above, for each y, there exists some x with, for all

q, $xG^{\mathrm{I}}(q)y - \langle c, q\rangle \geq \zeta(y)$, hence the equality. Finally, $\zeta(y) \geq 0$ implies that the interior of $C(y) \cap D$ is empty.

By definition of y_0, we have $Q(y_0) \subseteq (q_1, q_2)$ and $\zeta(y_0) < 0$.

Let now p_1 and p_2 be in $\Pi_1 \cup \partial\Pi$ with $p_0 \in (p_1, p_2)$ and $(p_1, p_2) \cap \Pi_1 = \emptyset$. Since $Y(p)$ is also an u.s.c. convex-valued correspondence, $Q(Y(p_1, p_2))$ is connected; hence, by the choice of the p_i's, one has:

$$\zeta(y) < 0 \quad \text{and} \quad Q(y) \subseteq (q_1, q_2) \qquad \text{for all } y \in Y(p_1, p_2). \tag{1}$$

By compactness, one gets $y_1' \in Y(p_1)$ and x_1' with:

$$x_1' G^{\mathrm{I}}(q) y_1' - \langle c, q\rangle = \zeta(y_1') \leq 0 \quad \text{and} \quad Q(y_1') \cap [q_1, q_2] \neq \emptyset. \tag{2}$$

Assume first $p_1 \in \Pi_1$. Then either $C(y_1) \cap D$ has an empty interior (write $y_1 = y_1'$, $x_1 = x_1'$), or there exists y_1, a closest point to y_1' in $Y(p_1)$ having this property. But then (1) holds for $y \in [y_1', y_1)$, and one gets (2) for y_1, and some x_1, implying $\zeta(y_1) = 0$. Now, if $p_1 = (1, 0)$, let $y_1' = y_1$. Note first that $f_{y_1} \geq c_1$; hence we can define a supporting hyperplane $c^1 = (c_1, c_2')$ to f_{y_1} with $c_2' \leq c_2$ and $f_{y_1}(q) = \langle c^1, q\rangle$ for some $q \in (q_1, q_2)$. Again this implies the existence of x_1 with $x_1 G^{\mathrm{I}}(q) y_1 = \langle c^1, q\rangle$. A dual analysis holds for p_2. Finally, let $R = 2$, and define z to be the splitting strategy (Proposition V.1.2, p. 216) of player I generating p_1 and p_2. Define now $\theta(r)$ as $x_r \otimes y_r$; then we have an EJP at p. In fact, (1) follows from $y_r \in Y(p_r)$, (2) holds with $\overline{a} = c$, and (3) with $a(r) = c^r$. ■

IX.1.b. Characterization (Hart, 1985)

In the above proof, the splitting property was used to convexify in p the set of non-revealing EJP leading to the same vector payoff for player I. Note also that, for a fixed p, the set of equilibrium payoffs is convex (the players can use their moves to construct a jointly controlled lottery (Aumann et al., 1968); cf. below). The content of the next result is that a repetition of such operations in fact characterizes the set of equilibria; namely, each equilibrium pair generates such a sequence, and any such sequence, leads to an equilibrium.

We first define the set of non-revealing feasible payoffs:

$$F = \mathsf{Co}\{\, G^k_{s,t} \mid s \in S, t \in T \,\} \subseteq \mathbb{R}^K \times \mathbb{R}^K$$

and;

$$W = \big\{ (a, \beta, p) \in \mathbb{R}^K \times \mathbb{R} \times \Pi \;\big|$$

$$\text{i) } \beta \geq \mathsf{Vex}\, u_{\mathrm{II}}(p),$$

$$\text{ii) } \langle q, a\rangle \geq u_{\mathrm{I}}(q)\ \forall q \in \Pi,$$

$$\text{iii) } \exists (c, d) \in F \text{ such that } a \geq c \text{ and } \langle p, a\rangle = \langle p, c\rangle, \langle p, d\rangle = \beta \big\}.$$

(Compare Proposition IX.1.1, p. 482, and note that these conditions correspond to a "non-revealing" joint plan.)

Before introducing the next set, we first define a "W-process" starting at w in $\mathbb{R}^k \times \mathbb{R} \times \Pi$ to be a bounded martingale $w_n = (a_n, \beta_n, p_n)$ from an auxiliary space $(\Omega, \mathscr{F}, Q)$ with an **atomic** filtration $\mathscr{F}_n$ to $\mathbb{R}^k \times \mathbb{R} \times \Pi$ with $w_1 = w$, satisfying, for each n, either $a_{n+1} = a_n$ or $p_{n+1} = p_n$ a.e. (i.e., (a_n, p_n) is a **"bi-martingale"**), and converging to some point w_∞ in W. Define now $W^\star = \{ w \in \mathbb{R}^K \times \mathbb{R} \times \Pi \mid$ there exists a W-process starting at $w \}$. The main result of this section is:

Theorem IX.1.4. *$(a, \beta) \in \mathbb{R}^k \times \mathbb{R}$ belongs to $E_\infty(p)$ iff $(a, \beta, p) \in W^\star$.*

Proof. The proof is divided into two parts:

First, given any $\mathscr{L}$-equilibrium with payoff (a, β), we show that it induces a W-process starting at (a, β, p).

Second, given any W-process starting at (a, β, p), we construct a uniform equilibrium in $\Gamma_\infty(p)$ with payoff (a, β).

Part A. From equilibrium to W-process

A heuristic outline of the proof is as follows. p_n will be the posterior probability on K induced by σ, and hence it is a martingale converging to some p_∞. Thus player I will be asymptotically playing non-revealing, and hence the asymptotic payoffs corresponding to σ, τ, say, c_∞, d_∞, will be in F. In the definition of W, conditions (1) and (2) of Proposition IX.1.1 correspond to the individually rational requirements (cf. Section IV.4.a, p. 190). Remark that the equilibrium condition on the equilibrium path implies that the sequence of conditional future expected payoffs defines a martingale converging to $(c_\infty, \langle p_\infty, d_\infty \rangle)$. Condition (3) indicates that player I cannot cheat (i.e., send a wrong signal), and finally the bi-martingale property will be obtained by conditioning on half histories, i.e., just after a move of player I. Formally, let $H_{n+1/2} = H_n \times S = (S \times T)^{n-1} \times S$, $\mathbb{N}' = \mathbb{N} + 1/2$, $\mathbb{M} = \mathbb{N} \cup \mathbb{N}'$. We define thus H_m and the corresponding σ-algebra $\mathscr{H}_m$ for m in $\mathbb{M}$, and all the martingales will be with respect to this filtration. Fix now a Banach limit $\mathscr{L}$, an initial p in Π, and $\mathscr{L}$-equilibrium strategies (σ, τ) inducing the payoff (a, β) so that $a^k = \mathscr{L}(\overline{\gamma}_n^{\mathrm{I},k}(\sigma, \tau))$, $\beta = \mathscr{L}(\overline{\gamma}_n^{\mathrm{II}}(\sigma, \tau))$, $\langle p, a \rangle = \mathscr{L}(\overline{\gamma}_n^{\mathrm{I}}(\sigma, \tau))$. Define also $p_m^k = P_{\sigma,\tau,p}(k \mid \mathscr{H}_m)$, $\alpha_m = \mathscr{L}(\mathsf{E}_{\sigma,\tau,p}(\overline{g}_n^{\mathrm{I},k} \mid \mathscr{H}_m))$, $\beta_m = \mathscr{L}(\mathsf{E}_{\sigma,\tau,p}(\overline{g}_n^{\mathrm{II},k} \mid \mathscr{H}_m))$, and note the following:

$$p_m \text{ is a martingale in } \Pi \text{ converging to some } p_\infty, \qquad \text{and } p_{n+1/2} = p_{n+1} \text{ for } n \in \mathbb{N}, \tag{3}$$

$$\alpha_m \text{ is a bounded martingale converging to some } \alpha_\infty \text{ with } \alpha_0 = \langle p, a \rangle. \tag{4}$$

The Banach limits commute with conditional expectations, the σ-fields $\mathscr{H}_m$ being finite:

$$\beta_m \text{ is a bounded martingale converging to some } \beta_\infty \text{ with } \beta_0 = \beta. \tag{5}$$

We now define conditional vector payoffs with respect to the marginal distribution E' induced by σ, τ, and p on H_∞ (and not $H_\infty \times K$) conditional on $\mathscr{H}_m$. Since τ is independent of k, this amounts to taking the expectation with respect to $\mathsf{E}_p(\sigma \mid \mathscr{H}_m)$, namely, the average, non-revealing strategy of player I, given $\mathscr{H}_m$, with value $\sum_k p_m^k(h_m)\sigma^k(h_m)$ on h_m. Hence, let $c_m^k = \mathscr{L}(\mathsf{E}'(\overline{g}_n^{\mathrm{I},k} \mid \mathscr{H}_m))$, $d_m^k = \mathscr{L}(\mathsf{E}'(\overline{g}_n^{\mathrm{II},k} \mid \mathscr{H}_m))$. Then we have:

$$c_m \text{ and } d_m \text{ are bounded martingales converging to } (c_\infty, d_\infty)$$
$$\text{with } (c_\infty, d_\infty) \in F \text{ a.s.} \tag{6}$$

The last assertion follows from the fact that, for all m, (c_m, d_m) belongs to the compact convex set F. Moreover, the convergence of p_n implies:

$$\alpha_\infty = \langle p_\infty, c_\infty \rangle \quad \text{and} \quad \beta_\infty = \langle p_\infty, d_\infty \rangle. \tag{7}$$

Proof. Remark that, for n, m in $\mathbb{N}$, $n \geq m$, $\mathsf{E}(g_n^{\mathrm{I},k} \mid \mathscr{H}_m) = \mathsf{E}'(\sum_k p_{n+1}^k g_n^{\mathrm{I},k} \mid \mathscr{H}_m) = \sum_k p_m^k \, \mathsf{E}'(g_n^{\mathrm{I},k} \mid \mathscr{H}_m) + \sum_k \mathsf{E}'((p_{n+1}^k - p_m^k) g_n^{\mathrm{I},k} \mid \mathscr{H}_m)$. Letting $\pi_m = \sum_k \sup_{n \geq m} \left| p_{n+1}^k - p_m^k \right|$, we obtain $|\alpha_m - \langle p_m, c_m \rangle| \leq C \, \mathsf{E}'(\pi_m \mid \mathscr{H}_m)$. Since p_n^k converges to p_∞^k, $\theta_m^k = \sup_{n \geq m} \left| p_{n+1}^k - p_\infty^k \right|$ is a non-increasing positive sequence converging to zero. Hence $\mathsf{E}'(\theta_m^k \mid \mathscr{H}_m)$ is a supermartingale converging to 0. Finally, $\pi_m \leq 2 \sum_k \theta_m^k$ implies the result. The other equality is proved similarly. ∎

We have thus defined some asymptotic payoffs; we use now the equilibrium properties:

$$\beta_\infty \geq \mathsf{Vex}\, u_{\mathrm{II}}(p_\infty) \quad \text{a.s.} \tag{8}$$

In fact, given any history h_m, the posterior probability on K is p_m, and player II can obtain, from this stage on, an asymptotic payoff of $\mathsf{Vex}\, u_{\mathrm{II}}(p_m)$ (cf. Theorem V.2.10, p. 224). It follows that, if for some h_m in H_m with $P(h_m) > 0$, one had $\beta_m(h_m) < \mathsf{Vex}\, u_{\mathrm{II}}(p_m)$, then player II could increase his total payoff $\beta_m = \sum P(h_m)\beta_m(h_m)$ by switching to the previous strategy after h_m. The result follows letting $m \to \infty$, using the continuity of u_{II}.

To get a similar property for player I, we have to consider again the vector payoffs. We start by a sequence that bounds c_m from above. Let first $e_m^k = \sup_{\sigma'} \mathscr{L}(\mathsf{E}_{\sigma',\tau}(\overline{g}_n^{k,\mathrm{I}} \mid \mathscr{H}_m, k)) = \sup_{\sigma'} \mathscr{L}(\mathsf{E}_{\sigma'^k,\tau}(\overline{g}_n^{k,\mathrm{I}} \mid \mathscr{H}_m))$.

Note that the expectation is now given k and that we can assume σ' to be non-revealing:

$$e_0^k = a^k, \qquad e_m \geq c_m, \tag{9}$$

$$e_{m+1/2} = \mathsf{E}(e_{n+1} \mid \mathscr{H}_{n+1/2}) \ \forall n \in \mathbb{N}, \qquad e_n^k(h_t) = \max_s e_{n+1/2}^k(h_t, s) \ \forall k, \forall h_t. \tag{10}$$

Proof. (9) follows from the definition since σ is an equilibrium strategy and the payoff c_m is attainable by player I. The first equality in (10) comes from the fact that player I is a dummy between stages $n + 1/2$ and $n + 1$. The second comes from the fact that, for each k, the player can first choose a move and then play optimally. ■

The previous result proves that e_m is a supermartingale. To get a martingale, we first introduce a sequence λ_n of random variables in $[0, 1]$, $n \in \mathbb{N}'$ with $C - e_n^k = \lambda_{n+1/2}(C - e_{n+1/2}^k)$ $\forall n \in \mathbb{N}$, and we define finally f_m by $C - f_m^k = (C - e_m^k)\prod_{\substack{n\in\mathbb{N}\\ n<m}} \lambda_{n+1/2}$ $\forall m \in \mathbb{M}$. f_m is a bounded martingale converging to some f_∞ with:

$$f_0 = a, \qquad f_n = f_{n+1/2}, \ \forall n, \tag{11}$$

$$f_\infty \geq c_\infty, \quad \text{and} \quad \langle p_\infty, f_\infty \rangle = \langle p_\infty, c_\infty \rangle. \tag{12}$$

Proof. (11) follows from the definitions since λ_n is $\mathscr{H}_n$-measurable, $n \in \mathbb{N}'$. Now $f_m \geq e_m \geq c_m$, $\forall m \in \mathbb{M}$.

Finally, by (3) and (11), (p_n, f_n) is a bi-martingale, and so $\langle p_n, f_n \rangle$ is a martingale:

$$\mathsf{E}(\langle p_\infty, f_\infty \rangle) = \langle p, f_0 \rangle = \langle p, a \rangle = \alpha = \mathsf{E}(\alpha_\infty) = \mathsf{E}(\langle p_\infty, c_\infty \rangle)$$

by (4) and (7), hence (12). ■

It remains to check the individual rationality condition for the payoffs f_∞ of player I:

$$\langle q, f_\infty \rangle \geq u_{\mathrm{I}}(q), \quad \forall q \in \Pi. \tag{13}$$

Proof. At each stage, given any history, player I can, by playing optimally non-revealing in $G^{\mathrm{I}}(q)$, get a stage payoff greater than $u_{\mathrm{I}}(q)$. Thus, for all m:

$$\begin{aligned} u_{\mathrm{I}}(q) &\leq \mathscr{L} \sup_{\sigma'} \sum q^k \, \mathsf{E}_{\sigma'}(\overline{g}_n^{\mathrm{I},k} \mid \mathscr{H}_m) \\ &\leq \langle q, e_m \rangle. \end{aligned}$$

Hence the result since $f_m \leq e_m$. ■

To conclude, (f_m, β_m, p_m) is the required W-process using (c_∞, d_∞) and (3), (5), (6), (7), (8), (12), and (13).

Part B. Second part: from W-process to equilibrium

Observe first that $W^\star$ is not enlarged if one only required the W-process, say, $W_n = (a_n, \beta_n, p)$ on a probability space $(\Omega, \mathscr{F}_n, Q)$, to satisfy "$a_{n+1}$ or p_{n+1} is constant on each atom of F_n" rather than on all of them (adding some intermediate fields reduces to the initial case). Now, the filtration being atomic, it is usefully represented by an oriented tree, where the nodes at distance n from the origin are the atoms of $\mathscr{F}_n$. Such a node, say, w_n, leads to all w_{n+1} in $\mathscr{F}_{n+1}$ with $w_{n+1} \subseteq w_n$, and the corresponding arc has the probability $Q(w_{n+1} \mid w_n)$. Further, we can assume that each w_n has two successors, and, moreover, $Q(w_{n+1} \mid w_n) = 1/2$ for each. In fact, the first assertion is proved by adding intermediate fields (i.e., nodes) with the appropriate probabilities.

For the second point, one can replace the arc between w_n and its successor by an infinite tree corresponding to the first occurrence of 1 in a sequence of i.i.d. centered random variables on $\{-1, 1\}$. Write $Q(w_{n+1} \mid w_n) = \sum_1^\infty \lambda_m/2^m$ and let w_{n+1} be associated to the first 1 at stage m iff $\lambda_m = 1$. It is easy to see how to extend the W-process while keeping all its properties.

We henceforth assume that the W-process possesses the above properties. Basically, the proof will require both players to "follow the above tree," namely:

- To realize the transitions from one node to its successor. This is done by signaling strategies of player I if $p_{n+1} \neq p_n$, and by jointly controlled lotteries if $a_{n+1} \neq a_n$.
- To play a specified sequence of moves between w_n and w_{n+1} in order to realize the required payoff, roughly a_n and β_n.
- To use the parameters at w_n to punish if a deviation occurs between w_n and w_{n+1}.

Step 1. *Preliminary results*

We first represent points in F as payoffs associated to correlated strategies. For all (c, d) in F, there exists $\theta \in \Delta(S \times T)$ with:

$$c^k = \sum_{s,t} G_{st}^{\mathrm{I},k}\theta(s,t), \qquad d^k = \sum_{s,t} G_{st}^{\mathrm{II},k}\theta(s,t),$$

and write $c = G^{\mathrm{I}}\cdot\theta$, $d = G^{\mathrm{II}}\cdot\theta$. We thus obtain, using a measurable selection theorem (cf. Appendix A.7.j, p. 519), that there exists a random variable θ_∞ with values in $\Delta(S \times T)$, s.t. Q-a.s. $a_\infty \geq G^{\mathrm{I}}\cdot\theta_\infty$ and $\langle p_\infty, a_\infty\rangle = \langle p_\infty, G^{\mathrm{I}}\cdot\theta_\infty\rangle$, $\beta_\infty = \langle p_\infty, G^{\mathrm{II}}\cdot\theta_\infty\rangle$.

Approximate now $\mathsf{E}(\theta_\infty \mid \mathscr{F}_n)$ by $\mathscr{F}_n$-measurable random variables θ_n s.t. $n\theta_n$ is integer-valued and $\|\theta_n - \mathsf{E}(\theta_\infty \mid \mathscr{F}_n)\| \leq 1/n$.

We shall also use the following properties. Since $\langle q, a_\infty\rangle \geq u_{\mathrm{I}}(q)$, one has, by taking expectation:

$$\langle a_n, q\rangle \geq u_{\mathrm{I}}(q), \qquad \text{for all } n. \tag{14}$$

Similarly, from $\beta_\infty \geq \operatorname{Vex} u_{\mathrm{II}}(p_\infty)$, one has, using Jensen's inequality:

$$\begin{aligned}\beta_n &= \mathsf{E}(\beta_\infty \mid \mathscr{F}_n) \geq \mathsf{E}(\operatorname{Vex} u_{\mathrm{II}}(p_\infty) \mid \mathscr{F}_n)\\ &\geq \operatorname{Vex} u_{\mathrm{II}}(\mathsf{E}(p_\infty \mid \mathscr{F}_n)) \geq \operatorname{Vex} u_{\mathrm{II}}(p_n).\end{aligned}$$

Step 2. *Construction of the strategies*

As in the previous proofs, the strategies will be defined through a cooperative procedure, master plan, and punishments in the case of detectable deviation. Stages $m = n!$ for n in $\mathbb{N}$ will be communication stages and related to the transition from one node to its successor. The remaining stages will be devoted to the payoffs, while the reference node will be kept fixed. We define now inductively histories consistent with the master plan and a mapping ζ from histories to nodes. Let us write $\{s', s''\}$, $\{t', t''\}$ for two pairs of moves of each player that will be used to communicate. Assume now that $m = n! - 1$, that

h_{m-1} is defined and consistent with the master plan, and that $\zeta(h_{m-1}) = w_{n-1}$. Recall that the successor of w_{n-1} is a random variable w_n with equally likely values w'_n and w''_n.

To define the behavior at stage m, we consider the two cases:

- If $p_n \neq p_{n-1}$, player I uses a signaling strategy with support on $\{s', s''\}$ to generate p_n (cf. Proposition V.1.2, p. 216), namely, $\sigma^k(h_{m-1})(s') = p^k_n/2p^k_{n-1}$, the move of player II is arbitrary, and $\zeta(h_{m-1}, s') = w'_n$.
- If $a_n \neq a_{n-1}$, both players randomize equally on the above moves, namely, $\sigma^k(h_{m-1})(s') = \sigma^k(h_{m-1})(s'') = 1/2$, $\theta(h_{m-1})(t') = \theta(h_{m-1})(t'') = 1/2$, and $\zeta(h_{m-1}, s', t') = \zeta(h_{m-1}, s'', t'') = w'_n$, and w''_n otherwise.

(Note that $P(w'_n \mid w_n) = 1/2$ as soon as one of the players uses the above procedure: no cheating is possible. This is a **jointly controlled lottery.**)

We now look at the payoff stages (from $n! + 1$ to $(n+1)! - 1$). Given w_n, consider $\theta_n = \theta_n(w_n)$ introduced in (b). The players are then requested to play n-cycles of pure moves realizing θ_n during this block n. The node associated to such a history is still w_n.

Let us finally consider deviations and punishments. If $m + 1$ is the first stage where a detectable deviation occurs, define $\zeta(h_{m+1})$ as $\zeta(h_m)$ where h_m precedes h_{m+1} and assume that $\zeta(h_m) = w_n = (p_n, a_n, \beta_n)$:

- If player I is the deviator, player II uses, from stage $m + 1$ on, a strategy that approaches a_n (cf. Section V.2.c, p. 224, and use (14) above), namely, such that, for $\ell \geq N_0$, $\mathsf{E}_{\sigma',\tau}(\rho_\ell \mid \mathscr{H}_{m+1}, k) \leq a^k_n$, for all σ', where ρ_ℓ is the average payoff of player I between stages $m+1$ and ℓ.
- In the case of player II, let player I use a strategy inducing in $G^{\mathrm{II}}(p_n)$ a stage payoff less than or equal to $\mathsf{Vex}\, u_{\mathrm{II}}(p_n)$. (Note that player I is minimizing and use Section V.2.b, p. 222.)

This ends the definition of σ and τ.

Step 3. *Probabilities and payoffs*

We now prove that the probabilities and payoffs induced by (σ, τ) on $\mathscr{H}_\infty \times \wp(K)$ correspond to the arcs and nodes of the initial probability tree. For every $w_n = (a_n, \beta_n, p_n)$ and $n! \leq m < (n+1)! - 1$:

$$P_{\sigma,\tau,p}(\zeta(h_m) = w_n) = Q(w_n), \tag{15}$$

$$P_{\sigma,\tau,p}(k \mid h_m) = p^k_n(\zeta(h_m)). \tag{16}$$

Proof. Both properties are proved by induction. (15) follows from the fact that, at each communication stage, say, $r = \ell!$, $P\big(h_r, \zeta(h_r) = w'_\ell \bigm| \zeta(h_{r-1}) = w_{\ell-1}\big) = \frac{1}{2}$. (16) comes from the fact that player I plays non-revealing during payoff stages and uses the right signaling strategy at the communication stages. ■

Consider now the payoffs. If ϕ_m denotes the empirical distribution of moves up to stage m, and $\lambda_m = n!/m$, one has:

$$\forall s, t, m\,(n! \leq m < (n+1)! - 1),$$
$$\left|\phi_m(s,t) - [\lambda_m \theta_{n-1}(s,t) + (1-\lambda_m)\theta_n(s,t)]\right| \leq 4/n. \tag{17}$$

This follows easily from the fact that most of the stages are in blocks $n-1$ or n where both players play θ_{n-1} or θ_n by cycles.

From the previous properties, we can now deduce

$$\lim \overline{\gamma}_m^{\mathrm{I},k}(\sigma,\tau) = a^k, \tag{18}$$

$$\lim \overline{\gamma}_m^{\mathrm{II}}(\sigma,\tau) = \beta. \tag{19}$$

Proof. Consider first (19). From (17), we obtain, using (15) and conditioning on each history, that $\overline{\gamma}_m^{\mathrm{II}}(\sigma,\tau) = \sum_{h_m} P_{\sigma,\tau,p}(h_m)\,\mathsf{E}(\overline{g}_m^{\mathrm{II},k} \mid h_m) = \sum_{w_n} P_Q(w_n)\,\langle p_n, G^{\mathrm{II}}\cdot\phi_m\rangle$, so that $|\overline{\gamma}_m^{\mathrm{II}}(\sigma,\tau) - \mathsf{E}_Q(\langle p_n, G^{\mathrm{II}}\cdot(\lambda_m\theta_{n-1} + (1-\lambda_m)\theta_n)\rangle| \leq R/n$ with $R = 4C\cdot\#S\cdot\#T$.

Hence as $m \to \infty$, we obtain $\lim \overline{\gamma}_m^{\mathrm{II}}(\sigma,\tau) = \mathsf{E}_Q(\langle p_\infty, G^{\mathrm{II}}\cdot\theta_\infty\rangle) = \mathsf{E}(\beta_\infty) = \beta$.

Similarly, one first gets:

$$\lim \overline{\gamma}_m^{\mathrm{I}}(\sigma,\tau) = \mathsf{E}_Q\langle p_\infty, a_\infty\rangle = \langle p, a\rangle. \tag{20}$$

(Recall that $\langle p_n, a_n\rangle$ is a martingale.)

To get the equality component-wise, we first obtain, from (17), that:

$$\overline{g}_m^{\mathrm{I},k} \leq \left(\lambda_m a_{n-1}^k + (1-\lambda_m)a_n^k\right) + R'/n \quad \text{with } R' = 5C\cdot\#S\cdot\#T, \tag{21}$$

since $\overline{g}_m^{\mathrm{I}} = G^{\mathrm{I}}\cdot\phi_m$ and $a_n = \mathsf{E}(a_\infty \mid \mathscr{F}_n) \geq \mathsf{E}(G^{\mathrm{I}}\cdot\theta_\infty \mid \mathscr{F}_n) \geq G^{\mathrm{I}}\cdot\theta_n - 1/n$. We know that the probability induced by σ, τ, p on the nodes of the tree (through the mapping ζ) coincides with the initial Q. Now, when considering only a_n^k, we have the same property with σ^k and τ, for all k. In fact, σ is non-revealing except at the stages where p_n changes but then a_n is constant. We obtain thus $\overline{\gamma}_m^{\mathrm{I},k} = \mathsf{E}^k(\overline{g}_m^{\mathrm{I},k}) \leq \lambda_m \mathsf{E}^k a_{n-1}^k + (1-\lambda_m)\mathsf{E}^k a_n^k + R'/n \leq a^k + R'/n$, hence (18) by using (20). ■

Step 4. *Equilibrium conditions*

Up to now, σ and τ have been adapted to the tree and define the right probabilities and payoffs. It remains to check the equilibrium conditions.

Consider first player II after some history h_m with $\zeta(h_m) = w_r$. His posterior probability on K is precisely p_r by (16). If $m+1$ is a signaling stage with $p_r = p_{r+1}$, player II can make a non-detectable deviation but without affecting the distribution of outcomes (jointly controlled lottery), and its future payoff will be the same. In other cases, a deviation will be detected and player II punished.

The payoff thereafter will be $\mathsf{Vex}\, u_{\mathrm{I}}(p_r) \leq \beta_r$, while, if player II keeps playing the equilibrium strategy, he could expect $\mathsf{E}\big(\langle p_n, G^{\mathrm{II}}\cdot\theta_n\rangle \bigm| \mathscr{H}_r\big)$ on each of the following blocks n. For n large enough, this in near $\mathsf{E}\big(\langle p_\infty, G^{\mathrm{II}}\cdot\theta_\infty\rangle \mid$

$\mathscr{H}_r) = \mathsf{E}(\beta_\infty \mid \mathscr{H}_r) = \beta_r$. Hence, the above argument shows that (σ, τ) is an $\mathscr{L}$-equilibrium. To get the uniform condition, recall that the punishment strategy of player I is uniform. Since $\langle p_n, G^{\mathrm{II}} \cdot \theta_n \rangle$ converges a.e. to $\langle p_\infty, G^{\mathrm{II}} \cdot \theta_\infty \rangle = \langle p_\infty, d_\infty \rangle = \beta_\infty = \lim \beta_n$, there exists, for every $\varepsilon > 0$, a subset Ω_1 of Ω with probability greater than $1 - \varepsilon$ on which the convergence is uniform.

Define hence N so that, on Ω_1, n and $n' \geq N$ implies:

$$\left|\langle p_n, G^{\mathrm{II}} \cdot \theta_n \rangle - \beta_{n'}\right| \leq \varepsilon.$$

Given any τ', consider the game up to stage $m \geq (N+1)!$ and denote by $X + 1$ the time of the first deviation (with $X = m$ if no deviation occurs before m). Until stage X, the payoffs under τ and τ' coincide, and so we have only to consider the payoffs thereafter. For simplicity, let us write, if $X + 1 \leq m$, $f_\tau(X)$ for $(1/m)\,\mathsf{E}_\tau(\sum_{X+1}^{m} g_n^{\mathrm{II},k} \mid h_X)$ and similarly $f_{\tau'}(X)$. Assume $n! \leq m < (n+1)!$, and from stage $X + 1$ to m, the payoff under (σ, τ) is mainly according to θ_{n-1} or θ_n and we have:

$$\left|f_\tau(X) - (1/m)(m - X + 1)\,\mathsf{E}_{\sigma,\tau}(\beta_n \mid h_X)\right| \leq C P(\Omega_1 \mid h_X) + R/n.$$

Moreover, the conditional expectation, given h_X, depends only on $\zeta(h(X)) = w_\ell$, and hence, since β_n is a martingale, $\mathsf{E}(\beta_n \mid h_X) = \beta_\ell$.

On the other hand, under (σ, τ'), the expected payoff after stage $X + 1$ is at most β_ℓ, so that we get finally $\mathsf{E}_X(f_{\tau'}(X) - f_\tau(X)) \leq \varepsilon + R/n + C/m$, and hence, for m sufficiently large, $\overline{\gamma}_m^{\mathrm{II}}(\sigma', \tau) \leq \overline{\gamma}_m^{\mathrm{II}}(\sigma, \tau) + 2\varepsilon C$.

Consider now player I again after some history consistent with the master plan and with $\zeta(h_m) = w_n$. We claim that, by deviating, player I cannot get more than a_n. This is clearly the case if the deviation is observable since player II can approach a_n. Otherwise, it occurs at some communication stage where either player I cannot cheat or he has to use a signaling strategy; hence $a_{n+1} = a_n$. But, as seen above, the future expected payoff per block is at most a_n. Since a_n is a martingale with expectation a, the result will follow. In fact, consider the average payoff up to stage m, with $n! \leq m < (n+1)!$ under some σ' and τ. Let $X + 1$ be the time of a first observable deviation as before. Write $\zeta(h_X) = w_r$ and let us compute first the payoff until X: then we have, using (21), $\mathsf{E}^k\big((1/m)\sum_1^X g_\ell^{\mathrm{I},k}\big) \leq \mathsf{E}^k\big((X/m)a_r^k\big) + \mathsf{E}^k\big((X/m)((r-1)!/X)(a_{r-1}^k - a_r^k)\big) + \mathsf{E}^k\big((X/m)(1/r)\big)5R'$. Note that the random variable in the last term is always less than $1/n$. For the second term, if $r < n$, the integrand is smaller than $2C/n$, and, finally, by conditioning on $h = h_{(n-1)!}$, one gets $\mathsf{E}^k(\mathbb{1}_{\{r=n\}}(a_{r-1}^k - a_r^k) \mid h) = \mathbb{1}_{\{r=n\}}\ \mathsf{E}^k(a_{r-1}^k - a_r^k \mid h) = 0$ by the martingale property for a_n^k, since the laws induced by (σ, τ) and (σ', τ) coincide until X. Hence:

$$\mathsf{E}^k\left((1/m)\sum_1^X g_\ell^{\mathrm{I},k}\right) \leq \mathsf{E}^k\big((X/m)a_r^k\big) + (5R' + 2C)/n. \tag{22}$$

Finally, for the payoff after $X+1$, we obtain:

$$\mathsf{E}^k_{\sigma'\tau}\left((1/m)\sum_{X+2}^{m} g_\ell^{\mathrm{I},k} \mid \mathscr{H}_X\right) \le \big(m-(X+2)/m\big)a_r^k + (2C/\sqrt{m}) \qquad (23)$$

since player II approaches a_r^k. (22) and (23) together imply:

$$\overline{\gamma}_m^{\mathrm{I},k}(\sigma',\tau) \le \mathsf{E}_{\sigma',\tau}\, a_r^k + (C/m) + (5R+2C)/n + 2C/(\sqrt{m}-1),$$

and, since $\mathsf{E}_{\sigma'\tau}(a_r^k) = a^k = \lim_{m\to\infty}\overline{\gamma}_m^{\mathrm{I},k}(\sigma,\tau)$, we finally obtain:

$$\forall\varepsilon>0,\ \exists M\colon \forall m\ge M,\ \overline{\gamma}_m^{\mathrm{I},k}(\sigma',\tau) \le \overline{\gamma}_m^{\mathrm{I},k}(\sigma,\tau)+\varepsilon.$$

This completes the proof of the second part and of Theorem IX.1.4. ■

IX.2. BI-CONVEXITY AND BI-MARTINGALES

This section is devoted to the study of the new tools that were introduced in the previous section, namely, bi-martingales and the corresponding processes. X and Y are two compact convex subsets of some Euclidian space, and (Z_n) is a bi-martingale with values in $Z = X \times Y$. Namely, there exists a probability space $(\Omega, \mathscr{F}, P)$ and a filtration with *finite* fields $\mathscr{F}_n$, $\mathscr{F}_n \subseteq \mathscr{F}$ such that (Z_n) is a $(\mathscr{F}_n)$-martingale, and, for each n, either $X_n = X_{n+1}$ or $Y_n = Y_{n+1}$. For each $(\mathscr{F}_n)$ stopping time θ, Z^θ is the bi-martingale stopped at θ (i.e., $Z_n^\theta(\omega) = Z_{n\wedge\theta(\omega))}(w))$ and it converges to Z_∞^θ. Given a subset A of Z, we now define the following sets: $A^\star$ (resp. A_f, resp. A_b) $= \{ z \mid$ there exists a bi-martingale Z^n starting at z and a (resp. finite, resp. bounded) stopping time θ such that $Z_\infty^\theta \in A$ a.s.$\}$. Observe that this definition is unambiguous: even if $Z_\infty^\theta \in A$ a.s. was only interpreted in the sense that the outer probability of this event is one, by removing the exceptional set one would obtain another probability space with a filtration of finite fields and a bi-martingale on those, now with $Z_\infty^\theta \in A$ everywhere.

We will give a geometrical characterization of these sets and prove that they may differ. In particular, this will imply that the number of communicating stages needed to reach an equilibrium payoff may be unbounded. (See also IX.3, Ex. 2, p. 508.)

We start with some definitions.

A set A in Z is **bi-convex** if, for all x, resp. y, the sections $A_x = \{ y \mid (x,y) \in A \}$, resp. A_y, are convex. Similarly, a function on a bi-convex set A is **bi-convex** if any of its restrictions to A_x or A_y is convex. Given A in Z, *bico* A is the smallest bi-convex set containing A or, equivalently, *bico* $A = \cup A_n$, where the A_n are constructed inductively from A_{n-1}, by convexifying along X or Y starting from $A_1 = A$. (Note that contrary to the convex hull operator *bico* may require an unbounded number of stages of convexification; cf. example 2.2 in Aumann and Hart (1986).)

Since A_n corresponds precisely to the starting point of bi-martingales $\{Z_m^\theta\}$ with $\theta \le n$, we obtain:

Proposition IX.2.1. $A_b = bico\ A$.

We obtain thus a first distinction between A_b and A_f: in the example of Figure IX.1, $A = \{ z_i \mid i = 1, \ldots, 4 \}$, hence $bicoA = A$. To prove that w_1 belongs to A_f, consider the (cyclic) process splitting from w_i to z_i and w_j with $j \equiv i + 1 \pmod 4$. This induces a bi-martingale and the stopping time corresponding to the entrance in A is clearly finite a.s.

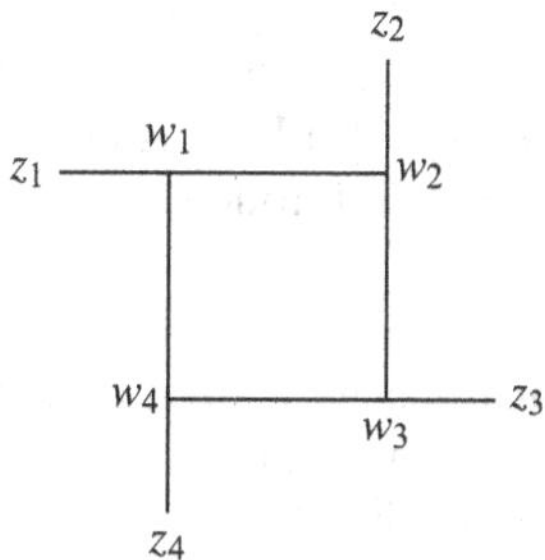

Figure IX.1. An unbounded conversation protocol.

We consider now separation properties. Given a bi-convex set B, a set $A \subseteq B$, and $z \in B$, we say that z is (strictly bi-) separated from A if there exists a bounded bi-convex function f on B such that

$$f(z) > \sup\{ f(a) \mid a \in A \} = f^{\star}(A).$$

We denote by nsB the set of points of B that cannot be separated from A (*n*ot *s*eparated). It is easy to see that nsB is a bi-convex set containing $bicoA$. Note nevertheless that, contrary to the convex case (when the corresponding set nsB equals $\overline{\mathsf{Co}\,A}$), one may have:

- $\overline{bicoA} \subsetneq nsB$ (cf. example IX.1 above)
- The separation by bi-affine functions is not sufficient (Aumann and Hart, 1986, example 3.4)
- The resulting set depends on B (Aumann and Hart, 1986, example 3.5).

We are thus led to apply repeatedly this separating process, and we define inductively $B_1 = Z$ and, for every ordinal α, $B_\alpha = \bigcap_{\beta<\alpha} nsB_\beta$. Hence B_α converges to some set C denoted by $bisA$ (*bi-s*eparated), which satisfies $C = nsC$ and is the largest superset of A having this property. We are now ready to give the second characterization.

Proposition IX.2.2. $A_f = bisA$.

Proof. Let us show that A_f shares the characteristic properties of $bisA$. First, $A_f = nsA_f$. In fact, starting from z in A_f, consider the associated bi-martingale Z_n^θ. Given any bounded bi-convex function f on A_f, $f(Z_n^\theta)$ is then a bounded sub-martingale, and hence, since θ is a.e. finite, we have:

$$f(z) \leq \mathsf{E}(f(Z_\infty^\theta)).$$

Since Z^θ_∞ belongs to A a.s., we obtain:

$$f(z) \leq f^\star(A)$$

and so z belongs to nsA_f.

Assume now that $A \subseteq B = nsB$. Define ϕ on B by:

$$\phi(z) = \inf P(Z_n \notin A, \forall n),$$

where the infimum is taken over all B-valued bi-martingales starting from z. (Observe that, since each Z_n takes only finitely many values, the event considered is measurable, even for non-measurable A.) Clearly, ϕ is bi-convex and equals 0 on A, and hence $\phi(z) = 0,\ \forall z \in B = nsB$. It follows that:

$$1 = 1 - \phi(z) = \sup P(Z^\theta_\infty \in A),$$

where the supremum is taken over all bi-martingales starting from z and all a.e. finite stopping times θ. To prove that the supremum is reached (hence that z belongs to A_f), note that, given any positive ρ and for each z, there exists $m = m(z)$ and an adapted bi-martingale with $P(Z_m \in A) > \rho$. If A is not reached at time m, start a new process adapted to Z_m, and so on. (Recall Z_m takes only finitely many values.) In this way, A will be reached in a finite time with probability one. ∎

To obtain $A^\star$, we have to consider separation by bi-convex functions **continuous** at each point of A. Thus, as above, we define the set $nscB$ of points of B that cannot be strictly separated from A by such functions, and, inductively, $biscA$ as the largest set satisfying $B = nscB$ (c stands for continuous).

Proposition IX.2.3. *Assume A is closed. Then $A^\star = biscA$.*

Proof. First $A^\star = nscA^\star$. Given z in $A^\star$, an associated bi-martingale Z_n, and a bounded bi-convex function f on $A^\star$ continuous at every point of A, one has that $f(Z_n)$ is a submartingale and $Z_n \to Z_\infty \in A$. Hence, $f(Z_n) \to f(Z_\infty)$ so that:

$$f(z) \leq Ef(Z_n) \leq Ef(Z_\infty) \leq f^\star(A),$$

and hence $z \in nscA^\star$. Assume now $B = nscB$. Let $d(\cdot, A)$ be the distance to the (closed) set A and define ψ on B by:

$$\psi(z) = \inf \mathsf{E}[d(Z_\infty, A)],$$

where the infimum is taken over all bi-martingales starting from z. Note that ψ is bi-convex. Now $\psi(\cdot) \leq d(\cdot, A)$ implies that ψ vanishes and is continuous on A, hence $\psi(z) = 0$ for any z in $B = nscB$. To prove that the infimum is actually reached (hence $Z_\infty \in A$ a.e. and $z \in A^\star$), we define, for any z in B and any $\rho > 0$, some $m = m(z, \rho)$ and an adapted bi-martingale satisfying $\mathsf{E}(d(Z_m, A)) \leq \rho$. If A is not reached at stage m $(= m_1)$, start from Z_m with $\rho/2$, and so on. This defines inductively an entrance time θ in A and a sequence of stages m_n with $\mathsf{E}(d(Z^\theta_{m_n}, A)) \leq \rho/n$, hence $\mathsf{E}(d(Z^\theta_\infty, A)) = 0$. ∎

Finally, to prove that A_f and $A^\star$ may differ, consider the following example:

Example IX.2.1. (Aumann and Hart, 1986) $X = Y = [0,1]^2$. Define $T = [0, \varepsilon]$ with $\varepsilon > 0$ small enough, and points in $Z = X \times Y$ by:

$$b_t = (1, 3t - 2t^2; 2t, 4t^2), \qquad c_t = (t, t^2; 1, 3t - 2t^2),$$

$$d_t = (2t, 4t^2; 2t, 4t^2), \qquad e_t = (t, t^2; 2t, 4t^2).$$

Let $B = \{b_t\}_{t \in T}$ and similarly C, D, and E. Define A as $B \cup C \cup \{0\}$ with $0 = ((0,0);(0,0))$. It is easy to see that $D \cup E$ is in $A^\star$ since one has:

$$d_t = \big(t/(1-t)\big)b_t + \big((1-2t)/(1-t)\big)e_t \qquad (y \text{ constant}),$$

$$e_t = \big(t/(1-t)\big)c_t + \big((1-2t)/(1-t)\big)d_{t/2} \qquad (x \text{ constant}),$$

and $d_t, e_t \xrightarrow[t\to\infty]{} 0$. On the other hand, $(D \cup E) \cap A_f = \emptyset$. In fact, consider z in $D \cup E$ and (Z_n^θ) an adapted bi-martingale with θ a.e. finite. Let $F_+ = \{ z \in Z \mid x_2 > 0 \text{ and } y_2 > 0 \}$, $F_0 = \{ z \in Z \mid x_2 = 0 \text{ and } y_2 = 0 \}$, and $F = F_+ \cup F_0$. F is clearly convex and contains A, hence also $A^\star$ and A_f. In particular, $Z_n^\theta \in F$ for all n, but $z \in F_+$ implies moreover $Z_n^\theta \in F_+$ since X_n and Y_n cannot change simultaneously. This implies $z \in (A \cap F_+)_f$. On the other hand, one has $x_1 + y_1 \geq 1$ on $A \cap F_+$, and hence the same property holds for $\mathrm{Co}(A \cap F_+)$, and hence for z, but no point of $D \cup E$ satisfies it.

One can also show that $(A^\star)^\star$ may differ from $A^\star$ (Aumann and Hart, 1986, example 5.3) and that A closed does not imply $A^\star$ closed (Aumann and Hart, 1986, example 5.6).

IX.3. CORRELATED EQUILIBRIUM AND COMMUNICATION EQUILIBRIUM

An r-device ($r = 0, 1, \dots, \infty$) is a communication device (Section II.3.c, p. 105) where players make inputs only until stage r. Thus, for $r = 0$, we obtain the autonomous devices (Section II.3.b, p. 103), and for $r = \infty$ we obtain the communication devices. The corresponding standard devices (Section II.3.c, p. 105) have corresponding sets of inputs I_n (by the players) and of messages M_n (to the players) relative to stage n of the game ($n = 1, 2, \dots$), for $r > 0$:

$$I_0^{\mathrm{I}} = K \quad \#I_0^{\mathrm{II}} = 1$$

$$I_n^{\mathrm{I}} = T \quad I_n^{\mathrm{II}} = S \quad M_n^{\mathrm{I}} = S \qquad M_n^{\mathrm{II}} = T \qquad \text{for } 1 \leq n < r$$

$$\#I_n^{\mathrm{I}} = 1 \quad \#I_n^{\mathrm{II}} = 1 \quad M_n^{\mathrm{I}} = S^{(S\times T)^{n-r}} \quad M_n^{\mathrm{II}} = T^{(S\times T)^{n-r}} \qquad \text{for } n \geq r$$

using (the proofs of) Theorem II.3.6, p. 104, and Corollary II.3.10, p. 107. (One could also use Dalkey's theorem (II.1.2, p. 61) to eliminate redundancies in M_n^{I}, M_n^{II} for $n > r$, thus $S^{T^{n-r}}$ and $T^{S^{n-r}}$, but the present formulation leads, for $r \geq 1$, to a set of pure strategies for the device, $(S \times T)^H$ with $H = K \times \bigcup_{n \geq 0}$

$(S \times T)^n$, which is independent of r, and the canonical device or equilibrium is a probability distribution over this set.) For $r = 0$ we could take $M_n^{\mathrm{I}} = S^{K \times T^{n-1}}$, $M_n^{\mathrm{II}} = T^{S^{n-1}}$, and so we get, as for correlated equilibria, the product of the two pure strategy spaces as the strategy space for the device.

As in Section II.3, p. 101, an r-communication equilibrium is an r-device together with an "equilibrium" of the corresponding extended game. It is called canonical if it uses a canonical r-device and if the equilibrium strategies are to report truthfully and to follow the recommendation. As in Chapter IV, Definition IV.1.9, and Section IX.1 here, we do not in fact define the equilibria, because of the ambiguity of the payoff function, but just the corresponding set of payoffs $E_\infty \subseteq \mathbb{R}^K \times \mathbb{R}$, consisting of a vector payoff to player I and a scalar to player II. Recall that E_∞ "exists" (though conceivably empty) iff any equilibrium payoff corresponding to any Banach limit is also a uniform equilibrium payoff. The corresponding set for r-communication equilibria is denoted D_r. So D_∞ is the set of communication equilibria, and D_0 the set of extensive form correlated equilibria.

We first need the following analogue of Theorem II.3.6, p. 104, and Corollary II.3.10, p. 107:

Lemma IX.3.1. *For any Banach limit $\mathcal{L}$ and any corresponding equilibrium of some r-device, there exists a corresponding canonical $\mathcal{L}$-r-communication equilibrium.*

Proof. Is as in Theorem II.3.6, p. 104, and Corollary II.3.10, p. 107. Observe that the players' personal devices, which handle all communications with the central device and compute the players' strategy, thus receiving from the player as input until stage r his reported signal in the game and giving him as output a recommended action, and which forms the canonical device when taken as a whole with the central device, can be taken to receive, in fact, no inputs from the player from stage r on, by recommending to him an action conditional on the signals he received in the game from stage r on. ∎

IX.3.a. Communication Equilibrium

Let $Z = \{a \in \mathbb{R}^K \mid \langle q, a \rangle \geq u_{\mathrm{I}}(q),\ \forall q \in \Delta(K)\}$. Consider the following class of communication devices: player I first reports $k \in K$ to the device, next $(c, d, z) \in F \times Z$ is selected according to some probability distribution P^k, and (c, d) is transmitted to both players. At every later stage the players' inputs consist of either doing nothing, in which case nothing happens, or of hitting an alarm button, in which case "z" is transmitted to both players. Some Borel map φ from F to $(S \times T)^\infty$ is fixed, yielding for every $f \in F$ a sequence of moves with this average payoff. The players' strategies are the following: player I reports the true state of nature k; both follow the sequence of moves $\varphi(c, d)$, transmitting nothing to the device, until they notice a deviation by their opponent, and in that case they hit the alarm button. As soon as "z" is announced, player I holds player II's payoff down to $(\operatorname{Vex} u_{\mathrm{II}})(p(\cdot \mid c, d, z))$ (Theorem V.3.3, p. 230), and player II holds player I down to z (Corollary V.3.29, p. 258, or Lemma V.3.32.2, p. 264, for the measurability).

Observe that, with such a device, the game remains a game with incomplete information on one side: both players know at every stage the full past history, except for the state of nature and player I's first report, which remain his private information. Let $\overline{D}_\infty = \{p, (a, \beta), (P^k)_{k\in K} \mid$ the above strategies are in equilibrium, with payoff $(a, \beta) \in \mathbb{R}^K \times \mathbb{R}\}$ (with the understanding that P^k and a^k are not to be defined when $p^k = 0$) and $\overline{D}^1_\infty = \operatorname{Proj}_{\Delta(K)\times\mathbb{R}^K\times\mathbb{R}}(\overline{D}_\infty)$, $\overline{D}^2_\infty = \operatorname{Proj}_{[\Delta(F\times Z)]^K}(\overline{D}_\infty)$. Then we have clearly:

Proposition IX.3.2. *$(p, a, \beta, (P^k)_{k\in K})$ belongs to $\overline{D}_\infty$ iff*

(I) $\mathsf{E}^k(c^k) = a^k \quad \forall k \in K \quad s.t. \quad p^k > 0.$
(II) $\mathsf{E}^k \max[c^l, \mathsf{E}^k(z^l \mid c, d)] \le a^l \quad \forall (k, l) \in K \times K \quad s.t. \quad p^k > 0.$
(III) $\mathsf{E}\langle p(\cdot \mid c, d), d\rangle = \beta.$
(IV) $\langle p(\cdot \mid c, d), d\rangle \ge \mathsf{E}[(\operatorname{Vex} u_{\mathrm{II}})(p(\cdot \mid c, d, z)) \mid c, d] \quad a.s.$

More precisely, for every solution, the corresponding strategies form a uniform equilibrium with payoff (a, β).

Remark IX.3.1. In principle, one needs (II) only for those (k, l) such that $p^k > 0$, $p^l > 0$, but one can always set $z^l = a^l = \max_{s,t} G^{\mathrm{I},l}_{s,t}$ under all p^k when $p^l = 0$, and obtain then equivalently the above system. Observe that now a^l is defined, and constrained, even for $p^l = 0$.

Proposition IX.3.3. *Let $\tilde{D}_\infty$ be the set of all $(p, a, \beta, \tilde{P}) \in \Delta(K) \times \mathbb{R}^K \times \mathbb{R} \times \Delta[\Delta(K) \times F \times Z]$ such that, denoting by π, (c, d), and z the random variables under $\tilde{P}$ which are the first, second, and third projections, and by* E *the expectation under $\tilde{P}$:*

(I) $\mathsf{E}(\pi^k c^k) = p^k a^k \quad \forall k \in K.$
(II) $\mathsf{E} \max[\mathsf{E}(\pi^k c^l \mid c, d), \mathsf{E}(\pi^k z^l \mid c, d)] \le p^k a^l \quad \forall (k, l) \in K \times K.$
(III) $\mathsf{E}\langle \pi, d\rangle = \beta.$
(IV) $\mathsf{E}(\langle \pi, d\rangle \mid c, d) \ge \mathsf{E}[(\operatorname{Vex} u_{\mathrm{II}})(\pi) \mid c, d] \quad a.s.$
(V) $\mathsf{E}(\pi^k) = p^k \quad \forall k \in K.$

Also, for $\tilde{P} \in \Delta(\Delta(K) \times F \times Z)$ define $\varphi(\tilde{P}) \in [\Delta(F \times Z)]^K$, where $[\varphi(\tilde{P})]_k$ is the conditional distribution on $F \times Z$ given k, under the distribution $\overline{\tilde{P}}$ on $K \times F \times Z$, induced by $\tilde{P}$. And for $p \in \Delta(K)$, $(P^k)_{k\in K} \in \Delta(F \times Z)$, let $\Psi(p, (P^k)_{k\in K})$ be the distribution on $\Delta(K) \times F \times Z$ of $[p(\cdot \mid f, z), f, z]$ under the distribution on $K \times F \times Z$ induced by p and $(P^k)_{k\in K}$. Then the map $(p, a, \beta, \tilde{P}) \mapsto (p, a, \beta, \varphi(\tilde{P}))$ maps $\tilde{D}_\infty$ onto $\overline{D}_\infty$, and $(p, a, \beta, (P^k)_{k\in K}) \mapsto (p, a, \beta, \Psi(p, (P^k)_{k\in K}))$ maps $\overline{D}_\infty$ to $\tilde{D}_\infty$, and yields the identity on $\overline{D}_\infty$ when composed with the first.

Proof. Is straightforward. Observe that inequalities (I) and (II), being multiplied by p^k, become now valid for all k. Use Jensen's inequality to deduce (IV) in Proposition IX.3.2 from condition (IV) above. ∎

Corollary IX.3.4. *One could equivalently replace* (IV) *by:*

(IV′) $\mathsf{E}[\langle \pi, d\rangle \mid c, d] \geq \mathsf{E}[u_{\text{II}}(\pi) \mid c, d]$.

Or even require in addition that, with probability 1, $u_{\text{II}}(\pi) = \mathsf{Vex}\, u_{\text{II}}(\pi)$.

Proof. Use a measurable version of Carathéodory's theorem (Castaing and Valadier, 1977, Th. IV.11, or Mertens, 2003) to replace π by its image by a transition probability Q from $\Delta(K)$ to itself such that $\forall \pi$, $Q(\{q \mid u_{\text{II}}(q) = \mathsf{Vex}\, u_{\text{II}}(q)\} \mid \pi) = 1$. ∎

Remark IX.3.2. Denote by Z_e the set of extreme points of Z. By Remarks VI.3.15 and VI.3.16, p. 355, which could already have been made after Proposition V.3.39, p. 273, $\mathsf{Co}(Z_e)$ is compact and $Z = \mathsf{Co}(Z_e) + \mathbb{R}^K_+$, and there exists a universally measurable (in fact, one could even have Borel measurability here, due to the finite dimensionality of Z, using a Borel version of Carathéodory's theorem) transition probability Q from Z to Z_e such that $\int y Q(z, dy) \leq z$, $\forall z \in Z$. Such a Q can be used to modify any $\tilde{P}$ in $\tilde{D}_\infty$, without changing the distribution of (π, c, d), and hence (p, a, β), to another one carried by Z_e (in (II), the expectation given any (c, d) is decreased, and in (IV) one uses Jensen's inequality; the new z is less informative). So nothing essential is changed in $\tilde{D}_\infty$ by requiring $\tilde{P}$ to be carried by a compact subset $\tilde{Z}$ of Z containing Z_e (like $\mathsf{Co}(Z_e)$, or $\overline{Z}_e$, or $Z \cap [-C, C]^K$). Similarly, then (cf. Remark IX.3.1, p. 497), $(p, a, \beta, \tilde{P}) \in \tilde{D}_\infty \iff (p, a', \beta, \tilde{P}) \in \tilde{D}_\infty$ with $(a')^k = \min(a^k, \overline{C}^k)$, where $\overline{C}^k = \max_{s,t} G^{\text{I},k}_{s,t}$. Observe that the inequalities (I) and (II) always imply that $a^k \geq \underline{C}^k = \min_{s,t} G^{\text{I},k}_{s,t}$. So, for any closed, convex subset A of $\mathbb{R}^K$ that contains $\prod_{k\in K}[\underline{C}^k, \overline{C}^k]$ and has a maximal point, nothing essential would be changed if we were to restrict a to A in the definition of $\overline{D}_\infty$. Only the coordinates of a corresponding to zero-probability states are possibly restricted.

Proposition IX.3.5.

(1) $\tilde{D} = \{(p, a, \beta, \tilde{P}) \in \tilde{D}_\infty \mid a \in A, \tilde{P}(\tilde{Z}) = 1\}$ *is compact.*
(2) $\tilde{D}_\infty$ *is convex in the other variables both for P fixed and for a fixed.*
(3) $\tilde{D}^1_\infty = \mathsf{Proj}_{\Delta(K)\times\mathbb{R}^K\times\mathbb{R}}(\tilde{D}_\infty)$ *is unchanged if* $\tilde{P}$ *is restricted to have finite support. More precisely, we can assume* $\#\,\mathsf{Supp}(\tilde{P}) \leq [\#K^2 + \#K + 1]^2$ *and* $\tilde{P}(Z_e) = 1$.

Proof. Part (1). The set is a subset of the compact space $\Delta(K) \times (A \cap \prod_{k\in K}[\underline{C}^k, \infty]) \times [-C, C] \times \Delta[\Delta(K) \times F \times \tilde{Z}]$. It is closed because, in conditions (I), (III), and (V), the left-hand expectation is a continuous linear function of $\tilde{P}$, and conditions (II) and (IV) are, by a monotone class argument, equivalent to $\mathsf{E}[\pi^k c^l f(c, d) + \pi^k z^l (1 - f(c, d))] \leq p^k a^l$ and $\mathsf{E}\{[(\mathsf{Vex}\, u_{\text{II}})(\pi) -$

$\langle \pi, d\rangle]f(c,d)\} \le 0$ for every continuous $f\colon F \to [0,1]$, and now the left-hand members are continuous linear functionals of $\tilde{P}$.

Part (2) follows in the same way.

Part (3). Choose first $\tilde{P}$ such that $\tilde{P}(Z_e) = 1$ (cf. Remark IX.3.2, p. 498). Let $q(d\pi, dz \mid c, d)$ be a regular conditional probability distribution under $\tilde{P}$ on $\Delta(K) \times Z_e$ given F (II.1, Ex. 16c, p. 86). Use q to transform the left-hand member of conditions (I), (II), (III), and (V) into expectations of measurable functions of (c, d). There are $\#K \times (\#K + 1)$ such independent equations by deleting one from group (V), and deleting the inequalities of group (II) for $k = l$, since, given those of group (I), these amount to $\mathsf{E}(\pi^k(c^k - z^k) \mid c, d] \ge 0$ a.e. Delete from F the negligible set where one of those conditional expectations, computed with q, is negative, and also those points where condition (IV), computed with q, does not hold. Let F_0 be the remaining set.

We can change the marginal of $\tilde{P}$ on F_0, while keeping the conditional q, preserving the value of those $\#K \times (\#K + 1)$ left-hand members, and such that the new marginal has at most $\#K^2 + (\#K + 1)$ points (of F_0) in its support (cf. I.3, Ex. 10, p. 40). For each of those points, consider now the conditional distribution q on $\Delta(K) \times Z_e$ given this point. It can be changed to any other one provided we preserve the expectations of π^k (conditions (I), (III), and (V)), and of $(\mathsf{Vex}\, u_{\mathrm{II}})(\pi)$. Then condition (IV) is also preserved, and we have now already $\#K$ different expectations, and for condition (II) we just have to preserve in addition the expectations of $\pi^k z^l$, yielding $\#K^2$ more expectations: Again we can do this with $(\#K^2 + \#K + 1)$ points. This completes the proof. ∎

Remark IX.3.3. Part (2) shows something more: let $D = \{(p, y, \beta, \tilde{P}) \in \Delta(K) \times \mathbb{R}^{K \times K} \times \mathbb{R} \times \Delta(\Delta(K) \times F \times \tilde{Z}) \mid$ conditions (I) to (V) are satisfied, using y^{kk} (resp. y^{kl}) in the right-hand member of condition (I) (resp. (II)), and $(\sum_k y^{kl})_{l \in K} \in A\}$. Then D is compact convex, and $\tilde{D} = \{(p, a, \beta, \tilde{P}) \mid (p, (p^k a^l)_{k,l \in K}, \beta, \tilde{P}) \in D\}$; i.e., $\tilde{D}$ is the "linear" one-to-one image by ($p \mapsto p, \sum_k y^{k,l} \mapsto a^l, \beta \mapsto \beta, \tilde{P} \mapsto \tilde{P}$) of $D \cap \{(p, y, \beta, \tilde{P}) \mid y^{k,l} = p^k \sum_n y^{n,l}\}$. It follows in particular that, if $\mu \in \Delta(\overline{D}^1_\infty)$, and if $\beta = \int \hat{\beta}\mu(d\hat{\beta})$, $p = \int \hat{p}\mu(d\hat{p})$, and $p^k a^l \ge \int \hat{p}^k \hat{a}^l \mu(d\hat{p}, d\hat{a})$ with equality if $k = l$, then $(p, a, \beta) \in \overline{D}^1_\infty$, (letting $\tilde{P} = \int \tilde{P}(\hat{p}, \hat{a}, \hat{\beta})\mu(d\hat{p}, d\hat{a}, d\hat{\beta})$, where $\tilde{P}(\hat{p}, \hat{a}, \hat{\beta})$ is a measurable selection). Further, call (p, a, β) "extreme" if such a μ is unique. Then for every (p, a, β) there is such a μ carried by at most $(\#K^2 + \#K + 1)$ extreme points (I.3, Ex. 10, p. 40).

Theorem IX.3.6. *D_∞ exists and equals the projection of $\overline{D}^1_\infty(p) = \{(a, \beta) \mid (p, a, \beta) \in \overline{D}^1_\infty\}$ on $\mathbb{R}^K_0 \times \mathbb{R}$, with $K_0 = \{k \mid p^k > 0\}$.*

Proof. Remark IX.3.1, p. 497, shows that it suffices to prove the theorem when $p^k > 0\, \forall k \in K$. And Proposition IX.3.2 yields that $\overline{D}^1_\infty(p)$ consists of uniform equilibria. So it remains to show, using Lemma IX.3.1, that any canonical $\mathscr{L}$-communication equilibrium payoff (α, β) belongs to $\overline{D}^1_\infty(p)$.

Let $H_n = \prod_{m=1}^{n}(M_m^{\mathrm{I}} \times M_m^{\mathrm{II}} \times (S \times T)_m \times I_m^{\mathrm{I}} \times I_m^{\mathrm{II}})$ for $n = 0, \dots \infty$, with $H = H_\infty$. Our basic probability space is $K \times H$ with the σ-fields $\mathscr{K} \times \mathscr{H}_n$, where $\mathscr{K}$ and $\mathscr{H}_n$ are the (finite) σ-fields generated by K and H_n. K is interpreted as I_0^{I}, the initial report of player I; the actual payoff function (state of nature) is indexed by $l \in L$, a copy of K, as in the inequalities in Proposition IX.3.2 and Proposition IX.3.3. We fix p as the initial probability on K, assuming implicitly that player I always reports the true state of nature. So his strategies have to be specified only after that; we will only use the set Σ of his strategies where he ignores K and L and always reports truthfully player II's move. The strategy of the device p and any pair of strategies σ and τ of the players induce a probability $P_{\sigma,\tau}$ on $K \times H$, with $P_{\sigma,\tau}^k$ conditional on H. For the equilibrium (i.e., truthful and obedient) strategies σ_0 and τ_0, P and P^k will stand for P_{σ_0,τ_0} and P_{σ_0,τ_0}^k, and a.e. for P a.s. $\mathsf{E}_{\sigma,\tau}$, $\mathsf{E}_{\sigma,\tau}^k$, E, and E^k will denote corresponding (conditional) expectation operators. Observe that the posterior probabilities $P_{\sigma,\tau}(k \mid \mathscr{H}_n)$ do not really depend on the pair (σ, τ); hence we can denote them by $p_n^k(h)$, which is a well-defined point in $\Delta(K)$ for every $h \in H_n$ that is reachable (i.e., under some pair σ, τ and for some k) given the strategy of the device. p_n is a $\Delta(K)$-valued martingale w.r.t. $\mathscr{H}_n$, for every $P_{\sigma,\tau}$, and converges, say, to p_∞, $P_{\sigma,\tau}$ a.e. for every (σ, τ).

Part A. Expected payoffs (conditions (I) and (III))

Observe that $(\overline{g}_m^{\mathrm{I},l}, \overline{g}_m^{\mathrm{II},l})_{l \in L}$ is an F-valued random variable on H_m, and thus independent of K. By I.2, Ex. 13f, p. 28, viewing $(\overline{g}_m^{\mathrm{I}}, \overline{g}_m^{\mathrm{II}})$ as elements of $L_\infty^{(2L)}, \sigma(L_\infty, L_1)$, we have an F-valued $\mathscr{H}_\infty$-measurable random variable $(c_\infty, d_\infty) = \mathscr{L}(\overline{g}_m^{\mathrm{I}}, \overline{g}_m^{\mathrm{II}})$, and since $\mathscr{K} \times \mathscr{H}_n$ is finite for $n < \infty$, one has thus for all $n = 0, 1, \dots, \infty$:

$$\mathsf{E}[(c_\infty, d_\infty) \mid \mathscr{K} \times \mathscr{H}_n] = \mathscr{L}\,\mathsf{E}[(\overline{g}_m^{\mathrm{I}}, \overline{g}_m^{\mathrm{II}}) \mid \mathscr{K} \times \mathscr{H}_n]. \tag{1}$$

Further, by definition:

$$a^l = \mathscr{L}\,\mathsf{E}(\overline{g}_m^{\mathrm{I},l} \mid k = l) = \mathsf{E}(c_\infty^l \mid k = l) = \mathsf{E}^l(c_\infty^l), \tag{2}$$

and $\beta = \sum_l p^l \mathscr{L}\,\mathsf{E}(\overline{g}_m^{\mathrm{II},l} \mid k = l) = \sum_l p^l\,\mathsf{E}(d_\infty^l \mid k = l)$. And d_∞^l is $\mathscr{H}_\infty$-measurable, and so $\mathsf{E}(p_\infty^l d_\infty^l) = \mathsf{E}[\mathbb{1}_{\{k=l\}} d_\infty^l] = p^l\,\mathsf{E}[d_\infty^l \mid k = l]$; hence:

$$\beta = \mathsf{E}\langle p_\infty, d_\infty \rangle. \tag{3}$$

Part B. Equilibrium condition for player I (condition (II))

Let $x_n^l = \sup_{\sigma \in \Sigma} \mathscr{L}\,\mathsf{E}_{\sigma,\tau_0}[\overline{g}_m^{\mathrm{I},l} \mid \mathscr{K} \times \mathscr{H}_n]$: x^l is a supermartingale w.r.t. $(\mathscr{K} \times \mathscr{H}_n)_{n \in N}$, under P_{σ,τ_0}, $\forall \sigma \in \Sigma$, by a standard "dynamic programming" argument. So:

$$\mathsf{E}(x_\infty^l \mid \mathscr{K}) \le x_0^l \le a^l, \tag{4}$$

because player I has no profitable deviation. And the definition of x^l implies with (1) that:

$$x_n^l \geq \mathscr{L}[\mathsf{E}(\overline{g}_m^{\mathrm{I},l} \mid \mathscr{K} \times \mathscr{H}_n)] = \mathsf{E}[c_\infty^l \mid \mathscr{K} \times \mathscr{H}_n], \text{ and } \operatorname{so} x_\infty^l \geq c_\infty^l \text{ a.e.} \quad (5)$$

Let also $z_n^l = \sup_{\sigma \in \Sigma} \mathscr{L}\, \mathsf{E}_{\sigma,\tau_0}(\overline{g}_m^{\mathrm{I},l} \mid \mathscr{H}_n)$: z^l is a bounded supermartingale w.r.t. $\mathscr{H}_n$ and P_{σ,τ_0}, $\forall \sigma \in \Sigma$. Further $z = (z^l)_{l \in L}$ is Z-valued. Indeed, after every history $h \in H_n$:

(1) After each stage, I is fully informed of the past, save for $k \in K$, since II uses τ_0.
(2) The pair formed by the device and player II can be considered as a single opponent, whose strategy τ is to first select $k \in K$ with probability $p_n^k(h)$, and next play τ^k.
(3) From this point of view, player II no longer needs I's signals (which are truthful anyway), and we can further worsen I's situation by restricting him to strategies $\sigma \in \Sigma$ that do not listen to the device's messages after h, and he remains fully informed of h.
(4) Therefore $z_n(h)$ is now at least as large as the best vector payoff player I can expect against τ in a zero-sum game $(G^{\mathrm{I},l})_{l \in L}$ with lack of information on one side and standard signaling (by Corollary V.3.29.1, p. 258, $z_n(h) \in Z$).

Further, player I, even when actually forgetting k as here, can try to exhaust the information about k. Indeed, for this problem, the payoff function G^l is irrelevant, and so we can assume that I is ignorant of both k and l. And our fictitious opponent can view $k \in K$ as his initial private information, after which he plays τ^k. So we have again a game with incomplete information on one side, this time the opponent being the informed player.

Here every stage consists of first the opponent sending a message to I, and next both players choosing simultaneously an action ((3) above). When putting such a stage in normal form, one obtains a case of non-standard signaling, but where I's signals are equivalent to knowing $\mathscr{H}_n$ after every stage n ((1) above). Since $\overline{g}_m^{\mathrm{I},l}$ is $\mathscr{H}_\infty$-measurable, we get that, for all σ:

$$\begin{aligned} &p_n^k \left| \mathsf{E}_{\sigma,\tau_0}(\overline{g}_m^{\mathrm{I},l} \mid \mathscr{K} \times \mathscr{H}_n) - \mathsf{E}_{\sigma,\tau_0}(\overline{g}_m^{\mathrm{I},l} \mid \mathscr{H}_n) \right| \\ &\quad \leq C p_n^k \left\| P_{\sigma,\tau_0}(\cdot \mid \mathscr{K} \times \mathscr{H}_n) - P_{\sigma,\tau_0}(\cdot \mid \mathscr{H}_n) \right\|. \end{aligned}$$

Hence, by the definition of x and z, using $x^{l,k}(h)$ for $x^l(k,h)$:

$$p_n^k(h) \left| x_n^{l,k}(h) - z_n^l(h) \right| \leq C' \sqrt{v_n(h)}$$

for $h \in \mathscr{H}_n$, using V.5, Ex. 17, p. 315, in the right-hand member. Therefore, under the strategy $\sigma' = \sigma_\tau$ of that exercise, we get $p_\infty^k x_\infty^{l,k} = p_\infty^k z_\infty^l$, P_{σ',τ_0} a.s. Recall finally from the exercise that the strategy σ' can be chosen to coincide with an arbitrary strategy σ until stage n. So we get, by the supermartingale property of x^l, that $\forall l, \forall k, \forall \sigma, \forall n$, P_{σ,τ_0} a.s.:

$$p_n^k x_n^{l,k} \geq p_n^k \mathsf{E}_{\sigma',\tau_0}(x_\infty^{l,k} \mid \{k\} \times \mathscr{H}_n) = \mathsf{E}_{\sigma',\tau_0}[p_\infty^k x_\infty^{l,k} \mid \mathscr{H}_n] = \mathsf{E}_{\sigma',\tau_0}[p_\infty^k z_\infty^l \mid \mathscr{H}_n]$$
$$= p_n^k \mathsf{E}_{\sigma',\tau_0}[z_\infty^l \mid \mathscr{K} \times \mathscr{H}_n],$$

hence $x_n^l \geq \mathsf{E}_{\sigma',\tau_0}[z_\infty^l \mid \mathscr{K} \times \mathscr{H}_n]$ $\forall l, \forall n$, P_{σ,τ_0} a.s. $\forall \sigma$. Thus, with Q_n the transition probability from $K \times H$ to Z defined by $Q_n(B) = P_{\sigma',\tau_0}(z_\infty \in B \mid \mathscr{K} \times \mathscr{H}_n)$ for every B Borel in Z, we obtain $x_n^l \geq \int_Z z^l Q_n(dz)$ a.s. Select a limit point Q_∞ in the sense of Exercise II.1, Ex. 17b, p. 86, and we have then $x_\infty^l \geq \int_Z z^l Q_\infty(dz)$ a.s., since z^l is continuous on Z and inequalities are preserved under $\sigma(L_\infty, L_1)$ convergence. Denote by $P_\infty(P_n)$ the probability on $K \times H \times Z$ generated by P and $Q_\infty(Q_n)$; the inequality becomes $x_\infty^l \geq \mathsf{E}_\infty(z^l \mid \mathscr{K} \times \mathscr{H}_\infty)$ a.s.

Together with (4) and (5) this yields:

$$\mathsf{E}_\infty(\max\{c_\infty^l, \mathsf{E}_\infty(z^l \mid \mathscr{K} \times \mathscr{H}_\infty)\} \mid \mathscr{K}) \leq a^l. \tag{6}$$

Part C. Equilibrium condition for player II (condition (IV))

Since the variable z constructed in B appears as an information to player II in his equilibrium condition, we have to find a way to give player II access to it. Player I accessed it by using the strategy σ'. So we will here construct a strategy of II that mimics any strategy $\sigma' \in \Sigma$ of player I, in the sense of giving, against σ_0, the same history to the device as (σ', τ_0), and such that player II can reconstruct by some map f, from the full history under (σ_0, τ'), that he knows because of σ_0, the full history under (σ', τ_0) that determined z. It suffices to do this for pure strategies $\sigma' \in \Sigma$, which can by Dalkey's theorem (II.1.2, p. 61) be taken as giving player I's next action as a function of his past messages and of player II's past actions. Player II knows both under σ_0, since player I follows the recommendation and so he can compute this next action s_n recommended by σ'. His strategy $\tau' = \tau(\sigma')$ consists then of reporting always to the device that player I used this computed action, and of always following the device's recommendation. It is clear that (σ_0, τ') will then yield the same history to the device, and hence the same actions by the device, as (σ', τ_0), and hence our map f maps a history of the form $(m_n^{\mathrm{I}}, m_n^{\mathrm{II}}, m_n^{\mathrm{I}}, m_n^{\mathrm{II}}, m_n^{\mathrm{II}}, s_n)_{n=1}^\infty$, which are the only ones arising with positive probability under any (σ_0, τ'), to $(m_n^{\mathrm{I}}, m_n^{\mathrm{II}}, s_n, m_n^{\mathrm{II}}, m_n^{\mathrm{II}}, s_n)_{n=1}^\infty$. Since this map f is independent of the specific σ' used, we can now in the same way transform a mixed strategy σ' into a mixed strategy τ', by transforming all underlying pure strategies, and still use f, thus obtaining $P_{\sigma',\tau_0}^k(E) = P_{\sigma_0,\tau'}^k(f^{-1}(E))$, $\forall k \in K, \forall E \in \mathscr{H}_\infty$. Since σ' can be assumed to coincide with σ_0 during the first m stages, and since then τ' also coincides with τ_0 during those stages, the same result still holds conditional on $h \in \mathscr{H}_m$ with $P(h) > 0$. In particular, with $y_\infty = z_\infty \circ f$:

$$Q_m(B) = P_{\sigma',\tau_0}(z_\infty \in B \mid \mathscr{K} \times \mathscr{H}_m) = P_{\sigma_0,\tau'}(y_\infty \in B \mid \mathscr{K} \times \mathscr{H}_m) \text{ a.s.} \tag{7}$$

Now $\beta_n = \sup_\tau \mathscr{L}\, \mathsf{E}_{\sigma_0,\tau}[\overline{g}_m^{\mathrm{II},k} \mid \mathscr{H}_n]$ is a $P_{\sigma_0,\tau}$-supermartingale w.r.t. $\mathscr{H}_n$, for every τ, because under σ_0 player II is fully informed of $\mathscr{H}_n$. But player

II can also play independently of the device in the future; the game starting after $h \in H_n$ is then an infinitely repeated game with incomplete information on one side and standard signaling, viewing player I together with the device as a single informed opponent, which thus no longer needs player II's input. The initial distribution on K is then $p_n(h)$, so that $\beta_n \geq (\mathsf{Vex}\, u^{\mathrm{II}})(p_n)$, $P_{\sigma_0,\tau}$ a.s. $\forall \tau$, by Theorem V.3.3, p. 230. Hence $\beta_\infty \geq (\mathsf{Vex}\, u^{\mathrm{II}})(p_\infty)$ $P_{\sigma_0,\tau'}$ a.s., so that, since y_∞ is $\mathscr{H}_\infty$-measurable, and using Jensen's inequality (I.3, Ex. 14bα, p. 43):

$$\beta_n \geq \mathsf{E}_{\sigma_0,\tau'}[\beta_\infty \mid \mathscr{H}_n] \geq \mathsf{E}_{\sigma_0,\tau'}\big[(\mathsf{Vex}\, u^{\mathrm{II}})[(P_{\sigma_0,\tau'}(k \mid \mathscr{H}_\infty, y_\infty))_{k\in K}] \bigm| \mathscr{H}_n\big]$$
$$\geq \mathsf{E}_{\sigma_0,\tau'}\big[(\mathsf{Vex}\, u^{\mathrm{II}})[(P_{\sigma_0,\tau'}(k \mid \mathscr{H}_n, y_\infty))_{k\in K}] \bigm| \mathscr{H}_n\big].$$

For $m \geq n$, assume now that σ' coincides with σ_0 until m, hence τ' with τ_0. By (7), the joint distribution of k and y_∞ given $\mathscr{H}_n$ under $P_{\sigma_0,\tau'}$ is the same as that of k and z given $\mathscr{H}_n$ under $P_m (= P.Q_m)$. So we get $\beta_n \geq \mathsf{E}_m\big[(\mathsf{Vex}\, u^{\mathrm{II}})[(P_m(k \mid \mathscr{H}_n, z))_{k\in K}] \bigm| \mathscr{H}_n\big]$, using E_m for the expectation under P_m.

Let now $m \to \infty$. Since the conditional distribution under P_m on $K \times Z$ given $h \in H_n$ has that: under P_∞ as a limit point (weak*), III.4, Ex. 4, p. 167, yields that:

$$\beta_n \geq \mathsf{E}_\infty\big[(\mathsf{Vex}\, u^{\mathrm{II}})[(P_\infty(k \mid \mathscr{H}_n, z))_{k\in K}] \bigm| \mathscr{H}_n\big].$$

So, by the supermartingale property of β, we get for $i \leq n$:

$$\beta_i \geq \mathsf{E}_\infty\big[(\mathsf{Vex}\, u^{\mathrm{II}})[(P_\infty(k \mid \mathscr{H}_n, z))_{k\in K}] \bigm| \mathscr{H}_i\big].$$

Hence, when $n \to \infty$, using the martingale property of conditional probabilities, and the bounded convergence theorem:

$$\beta_i \geq \mathsf{E}_\infty\big[(\mathsf{Vex}\, u^{\mathrm{II}})[(P_\infty(k \mid \mathscr{H}_\infty, z))_{k\in K}] \bigm| \mathscr{H}_i\big],$$

and finally:

$$\beta_\infty \geq \mathsf{E}_\infty\big[(\mathsf{Vex}\, u^{\mathrm{II}})[(P_\infty(k \mid \mathscr{H}_\infty, z))_{k\in K}] \bigm| \mathscr{H}_\infty\big] \quad P_\infty \text{ a.s.}$$

By definition:

$$\beta_n \geq \mathscr{L}\, \mathsf{E}[\overline{g}_m^{\mathrm{II},k} \mid \mathscr{H}_n] = \sum_k p_n^k\, \mathsf{E}(d_\infty^k \mid k, \mathscr{H}_n),$$

so $\beta_\infty \geq \langle p_\infty, d_\infty\rangle$. But, by (3), $\beta = \mathsf{E}\langle p_\infty, d_\infty\rangle \leq \mathsf{E}(\beta_\infty) \leq \beta_0$, and one must have equality since player II is in equilibrium. So $\beta_\infty = \langle p_\infty, d_\infty\rangle$ a.s., and:

$$\langle p_\infty, d_\infty\rangle \geq \mathsf{E}_\infty\big[(\mathsf{Vex}\, u^{\mathrm{II}})[(P_\infty(k \mid \mathscr{H}_\infty, z))_{k\in K}] \bigm| \mathscr{H}_\infty\big] \quad P_\infty \text{ a.s.} \tag{8}$$

Part D. End of the proof

Let $\mathscr{B}_\infty$ be the σ-field generated by (c_∞, d_∞). By Jensen's inequality $\mathscr{H}_\infty$ can be replaced by $\mathscr{B}_\infty$ in (6), and in (8) also, when replacing p_∞ by $[P_\infty(k \mid \mathscr{B}_\infty)]_{k\in K}$ in the left-hand member, by taking first conditional expectations w.r.t. the intermediate σ-field spanned by $\mathscr{B}_\infty$ and z. Now those modified inequalities, together with (2) and (3), can be expressed in terms of the conditional distributions P^k of the $F \times Z$-valued random variable (c_∞, d_∞, z) given k, yielding the conditions of Proposition IX.3.2. ■

IX.3.b. "Noisy Channels"; Characterization of D_r $(0 < r < \infty)$

Let Φ denote the space of continuous convex functions on $\Delta(K)$ that are $\geq u^{\mathrm{II}}$. A "noisy channel" is a 1-device where player I first reports $k \in K$ to the device, next $(c, d, z, \varphi) \in F \times Z \times \Phi$ is selected according to P^k, and (c, d, z) is transmitted to player II while (c, d, φ) is to player I. The corresponding strategies of the players are to play the sequence of moves associated with (c, d) by the same Borel map as in Section IX.3.a until the other deviates from it. From that stage on, player I holds player II down to φ (e.g., in the sense of comments V.3.48 and V.3.49 p. 268), and player II holds player I down to z (Corollary V.3.29, p. 258, or Proposition V.3.41.2, p. 276). Further, player I reports truthfully the state of nature. The device is such that those strategies are in equilibrium.

Let $N = \{\, (p, a, \beta, (P^k)_{k\in K}) \mid$ the above strategies are in equilibrium, with payoff $(a, \beta) \in \mathbb{R}^K \times \mathbb{R}\,\}$ (with the understanding that P^k and a^k are not to be defined when $p^k = 0$). And $N^1 = \mathsf{Proj}_{\Delta(K)\times\mathbb{R}^K\times\mathbb{R}}(N)$. Then we have clearly, as in Section IX.3.a, with the same remark after the proposition:

Proposition IX.3.7. $(p, a, \beta, (P^k)_{k\in K}) \in \Delta(K) \times \mathbb{R}^K \times \mathbb{R} \times [\Delta(F \times Z \times \Phi)]^K$ *is in* N *iff:*

(I) $\mathsf{E}^k(c^k) = a^k \quad \forall k \in K \text{ s.t. } p^k > 0$
(II) $\mathsf{E}^k \max[c^l, \mathsf{E}^k(z^l \mid c, d, \varphi)] \leq a^l \quad \forall (k, l) \in K \times K \text{ s.t. } p^k > 0$
(III) $\mathsf{E}\langle p(\cdot \mid c, d, z), d\rangle = \beta$
(IV) $\langle p(\cdot \mid c, d, z), d\rangle \geq \mathsf{E}[\varphi(p(\cdot \mid c, d, z, \varphi)) \mid c, d, z] \quad$ *a.s.*

More precisely, for every solution, the corresponding strategies form a uniform equilibrium with payoff (a, β).

Proposition IX.3.8. *Let* $\tilde{N}$ *denote the set of all* $(p, a, \beta, P) \in \Delta(K) \times \mathbb{R}^K \times \mathbb{R} \times \Delta[\Delta(K) \times F \times Z \times \Phi]$ *s.t., denoting by* π, (c, d), z, *and* φ *the random variables under* P *that are the successive projections, and by* E *the expectation under* P:

(I) $\mathsf{E}(\pi^k c^k) = p^k a^k \quad \forall k \in K$
(II) $\mathsf{E}\max[\mathsf{E}(\pi^k c^l \mid c, d, \varphi), \mathsf{E}(\pi^k x^l \mid c, d, \varphi)] \leq p^k a^l \quad \forall (k, l) \in K \times K$
(III) $\mathsf{E}\langle \pi, d\rangle = \beta$
(IV) $\mathsf{E}(\langle \pi, d\rangle \mid c, d, z) \geq \mathsf{E}(\varphi(\pi) \mid c, d, z) \quad$ *a.s.*
(V) $\mathsf{E}\pi^k = p^k \quad \forall k \in K.$

Then $\tilde{N}$ *equals* N *in the same sense as* $\tilde{D}_\infty$ *was related to* $\overline{D}_\infty$ *in Proposition IX.3.3.*

Remark IX.3.4. The same remark applies as after Proposition IX.3.3. In addition, for the same reason Φ can be replaced by Φ_e, and all functions in Φ_e

have a uniform norm and Lipschitz constant $\leq C$. So Φ can also be replaced by any compact subset $\tilde{\Phi}$ of Φ that contains Φ_e, like the closure, or the closed convex hull, or like all functions in Φ having a uniform norm and Lipschitz constant $\leq C$.

Proposition IX.3.9.

(1) $\overline{N} = \{(p, a, \beta, P) \in \tilde{N} \mid a \in A,\ P(\tilde{Z} \times \tilde{\Phi}) = 1\}$ *is compact.*
(2) $\tilde{N}$ *(or* $\overline{N}$*) is convex in the other variable both for* p *fixed and for* a *fixed.*
(3) *The same remark applies as after Proposition IX.3.5, p. 498.*

Comment IX.3.5. One cannot show as in Proposition IX.3.5, p. 498, that one can always select P with finite support. Indeed, the analogous procedure would be to first replace π by its conditional expectation given (c, d, z, φ), and then to try to replace the conditional distribution of (z, φ) given (c, d) by one with finite support, and finally to apply Carathéodory's theorem to (c, d). But the second step involves both the conditional distribution of z given φ and that of φ given z. An example is given in Forges (1988a, footnote 3, p. 202) of the difficulties to which such conditions can lead.

Theorem IX.3.10. D_r $(0 < r < \infty)$ *exists and equals the projection of* $N^1(p) = \{(a, \beta) \mid (p, a, \beta) \in N^1\}$ *on* $\mathbb{R}_0^K \times \mathbb{R}$, *with* $K_0 = \{k \mid p^k > 0\}$.

Proof. Again it suffices to prove the theorem in case $K_0 = K$. By Proposition IX.3.7 and Lemma IX.3.1, it suffices to show that any canonical $\mathscr{L}$-r-communication equilibrium payoff (a, β) belongs to $N^1(p)$. We will consider only $n > r$, i.e., all strategies coincide with (σ_0, τ_0) until r, except possibly for player I being untruthful. The notation (including Σ) is the same as in the previous section, except that on H we will, in addition to the σ-fields $\mathscr{H}_n$, consider $\mathscr{H}_n^{\mathrm{I}}$ generated by $\prod_{m\leq n}(M_m^{\mathrm{I}} \times (S \times T)_m \times I_m^{\mathrm{I}})$ and $\mathscr{H}_n^{\mathrm{II}}$ by $\prod_{m\leq n}(M_m^{\mathrm{II}} \times (S \times T)_m \times I_m^{\mathrm{II}})$, and $\mathscr{J}_n = \mathscr{H}_n^{\mathrm{I}} \cap \mathscr{H}_n^{\mathrm{II}}$. Finally, p_n^k stands for $P_{\sigma,\tau}(\{k\} \mid \mathscr{H}_n^{\mathrm{II}})$.

Part A. Expected payoffs

$(c_\infty, d_\infty) \in F$ is defined as previously, and is $\mathscr{J}_\infty$-measurable. It satisfies:

$$\mathsf{E}[(c_\infty, d_\infty) \mid \mathscr{K} \times \mathscr{H}_n] = \mathscr{L}\, \mathsf{E}[(\overline{g}_m^{\mathrm{I}}, \overline{g}_m^{\mathrm{II}}) \mid \mathscr{K} \times \mathscr{H}_n], \tag{9}$$

$$a^l = \mathsf{E}^l(c_\infty^l), \tag{10}$$

$$\text{and} \qquad \beta = \mathsf{E}\langle p_\infty, d_\infty\rangle, \quad d_\infty \text{ being } \mathscr{H}^{\mathrm{II}}\text{-measurable.} \tag{11}$$

Part B. Equilibrium condition for player I

Let now $x_n^l = \sup_\sigma \mathscr{L}\, \mathsf{E}_{\sigma,\tau_0}(\overline{g}_m^{\mathrm{I},l} \mid \mathscr{K} \times \mathscr{H}_n^{\mathrm{I}})$. As before we get:

$$\mathsf{E}(x_\infty^l \mid \mathscr{K}) \leq a^l, \tag{12}$$

$$\text{and} \qquad x_\infty^l \geq c_\infty^l \text{ a.e.,} \quad c_\infty^l \text{ being } \mathscr{H}_\infty^{\mathrm{I}}\text{-measurable.} \tag{13}$$

Consider now the game starting at stage n as a zero-sum game with incomplete information, with $T^{\mathrm{I}} = L \times K \times H_n^{\mathrm{I}}$ as the set of types of player I and $H_n^{\mathrm{II}} \times \prod_{m>n} M_m^{\mathrm{II}} = T^{\mathrm{II}}$ for player II. Further, worsen player I's situation by assuming that the device will not send any messages to him after stage n. Observe that the distribution R on $T^{\mathrm{I}} \times T^{\mathrm{II}}$ is independent of the players' actions in the new game, and that the distribution on T^{II} given T^{I} is independent of L, while the payoff matrix $G^{\mathrm{I},l}$ depends only on L. Player II's strategy τ_0 is a strategy in this game. So x^l has decreased, say, to $\overline{x}^l$; and $\overline{x}^l_n = \mathsf{sup}_\sigma \mathscr{L}\, \mathsf{E}_{\sigma,\tau_0}(\overline{g}_m^{\mathrm{I},l} \mid \mathscr{K} \times \mathscr{L} \times \mathscr{H}_n^{\mathrm{I}})$. By VI.7, Ex. 12b$\beta$, p. 391, there exists a T^{II}-measurable map z_n to Z, such that $\overline{x}^l_n \geq \mathsf{E}[z_n^l \mid \mathscr{K} \times \mathscr{L} \times \mathscr{H}_n^{\mathrm{I}}] = \mathsf{E}(z_n^l \mid \mathscr{K} \times \mathscr{H}_n^{\mathrm{I}})$ (by the conditional independence property of R), and hence $x_n^l \geq \mathsf{E}(z_n^l \mid \mathscr{K} \times \mathscr{H}_n^{\mathrm{I}})$, $\forall n$, for some $\mathscr{H}_\infty^{\mathrm{II}}$-measurable maps z_n to Z.

The supermartingale property of x yields then $x_n^l \geq \mathsf{E}(z_i^l \mid \mathscr{K} \times \mathscr{H}_n^{\mathrm{I}})$ $\forall i \geq n$, and hence for a $\sigma(L_\infty, L_1)$ limit point z we obtain that $x_n^l \geq \mathsf{E}(z^l \mid \mathscr{K} \times \mathscr{H}_n^{\mathrm{I}})$ $\forall n$; hence z is an $\mathscr{H}_\infty^{\mathrm{I}}$-measurable random variable with values in Z such that $x_\infty^l \geq \mathsf{E}(z^l \mid \mathscr{K} \times \mathscr{H}_\infty^{\mathrm{I}})$. Combining this with (12) and (13), we obtain:

$$a^l \geq \mathsf{E}[\max[c_\infty^l, \mathsf{E}(z^l \mid \mathscr{K} \times \mathscr{H}_\infty^{\mathrm{I}})] \mid \mathscr{K}]. \tag{14}$$

Part C. Equilibrium condition for player II

$\beta_n = \mathsf{sup}_\tau \mathscr{L}\, \mathsf{E}_{\sigma_0,\tau}[\overline{g}_m^{\mathrm{II},k} \mid \mathscr{H}_n^{\mathrm{II}}]$ is a supermartingale, $\forall \tau$. Let us bound β_n from below by considering the game with incomplete information starting at date n where this time player II receives no more messages after stage n and player I receives all his future messages immediately; thus $T^{\mathrm{II}} = H_n^{\mathrm{II}}$, $T_n^{\mathrm{I}} = K \times H_n^{\mathrm{I}} \times \prod_{m>n} M_m^{\mathrm{I}}$. Applying now Section VI.7, Ex. 12bα, p. 391, to this new game, we obtain a T^{I}- (hence $\mathscr{K} \times \mathscr{H}_\infty^{\mathrm{I}}$-) measurable transition probability Q_n to Φ, such that, for the induced probability P_n on $K \times H \times \Phi$, we have:

$$\beta_n \geq \mathsf{E}_n[\varphi[(P_n(k \mid \mathscr{H}_n^{\mathrm{II}}, \varphi))_{k\in K}] \mid \mathscr{H}_n^{\mathrm{II}}].$$

So, by the supermartingale property, we get for $i \leq n$:

$$\beta_i \geq \mathsf{E}_n[\varphi[(P_n(k \mid \mathscr{H}_n^{\mathrm{II}}, \varphi))_{k\in K}] \mid \mathscr{H}_i^{\mathrm{II}}],$$

and since, by Jensen's inequality:

$$\mathsf{E}_n[\varphi[(P_n(k \mid \mathscr{H}_n^{\mathrm{II}}, \varphi))_{k\in K}] \mid \mathscr{H}_i^{\mathrm{II}}, \varphi] \geq \varphi[(P_n(k \mid \mathscr{H}_i^{\mathrm{II}}, \varphi))_{k\in K}]$$

we get:

$$\beta_i \geq \mathsf{E}_n[\varphi[(P_n(k \mid \mathscr{H}_i^{\mathrm{II}}, \varphi))_{k\in K}] \mid \mathscr{H}_i^{\mathrm{II}}].$$

We can now let $n \to \infty$ using Section III.4, Ex. 4, p. 167; taking then conditional expectations given $j \leq i$ we obtain:

$$\beta_j \geq \mathsf{E}_\infty[\varphi[(P_\infty(k \mid \mathscr{H}_i^{\mathrm{II}}, \varphi))_{k\in K}] \mid \mathscr{H}_j^{\mathrm{II}}].$$

Let now $i \to \infty$, using the martingale property of posteriors and the dominated convergence theorem:

$$\beta_j \geq \mathsf{E}_\infty[\varphi[(P_\infty(k \mid \mathscr{H}^{\mathrm{II}}_\infty, \varphi))_{k\in K}] \mid \mathscr{H}^{\mathrm{II}}_j],$$

so finally we can let $j \to \infty$:

$$\beta_\infty \geq \mathsf{E}_\infty[\varphi[(P_\infty(k \mid \mathscr{H}^{\mathrm{II}}_\infty, \varphi))_{k\in K}] \mid \mathscr{H}^{\mathrm{II}}_\infty].$$

As in the previous theorem, one obtains now $\beta_\infty = \langle p_\infty, d_\infty \rangle$ a.e., and so:

$$\langle p_\infty, d_\infty \rangle \geq \mathsf{E}_\infty[\varphi[(P_\infty(k \mid \mathscr{H}^{\mathrm{II}}_\infty, \varphi))_{k\in K}] \mid \mathscr{H}^{\mathrm{II}}_\infty]. \tag{15}$$

Part D. End of the proof

Since Q_∞ is $\mathscr{K} \times \mathscr{H}^{\mathrm{I}}_\infty$-measurable, we have that under P_∞, $\mathscr{H}^{\mathrm{II}}_\infty$ and φ are conditionally independent given $\mathscr{K} \times \mathscr{H}^{\mathrm{I}}_\infty$. Therefore, since z is $\mathscr{H}^{\mathrm{II}}_\infty$-measurable, $\mathsf{E}_\infty[z \mid \mathscr{K} \times \mathscr{H}^{\mathrm{I}}_\infty, \varphi] = \mathsf{E}[z \mid \mathscr{K} \times \mathscr{H}^{\mathrm{I}}_\infty]$. So (14) yields:

$$a^l \geq \mathsf{E}_\infty[\max[c^l_\infty, \mathsf{E}_\infty(z^l \mid \mathscr{K} \times \mathscr{H}^{\mathrm{I}}_\infty, \varphi)] \mid \mathscr{K}].$$

Jensen's inequality allows us to decrease here $\mathscr{H}^{\mathrm{I}}_\infty$ to the σ-field generated by (c_∞, d_∞); similarly in (15) we can first reduce the $\mathscr{H}^{\mathrm{II}}_\infty$ appearing in p_∞ and that in the conditional expectation to the σ-field spanned by (c_∞, d_∞, z) (recall that z is $\mathscr{H}^{\mathrm{II}}$-measurable), and then use Jensen's inequality as before to do the same replacement for $\mathscr{H}^{\mathrm{II}}_\infty$ in the conditional probability. This, with conditions (10) and (12), shows that the conditional distributions P^k of $(c_\infty, d_\infty, z, \varphi)$ given k, under P_∞, satisfy the conditions of Proposition IX.3.7. ∎

EXERCISES

1. Incomplete information on the opponent's payoff. (Shalev, 1994); (Koren, 1992); (Israeli, 1999).

Consider a game with incomplete information on one side as in Section IX.1 where moreover G^{II} is independent of k.

a. Prove that $E_\infty(p)$ is the set $L(p)$ of completely revealing E.J.P. payoffs, i.e., satisfying $R = K$ and $p^k(r) = \mathbb{1}_{\{r\}}(k)$ in Proposition IX.1.1, p. 482. (Observe that it depends only on the support of p.)

HINT. To prove that $E_\infty \subseteq L$:

(1) Either use Theorem IX.1.4, p. 485, Proposition IX.2.3, p. 494, and show that L can be strictly separated from any point in its complement by a bi-convex continuous function; or

(2) Define $\theta_{st}(k) = \mathscr{L}(\mathsf{E}_{\sigma^k,\tau}(\bar{l}_n(s,t))$ where $\bar{l}_n(s,t)$ is the empirical frequency of (s,t) up to stage n, and introduce a, b, α, β as in IX.1.a, p. 481.

Note that $\beta_m = \mathscr{L}(\mathsf{E}_{\sigma,\tau,p}(\bar{g}^{\mathrm{II}}_n \mid \mathscr{H}_m)) = \mathscr{L}(\mathsf{E}'_{\sigma,\tau}(\bar{g}^{\mathrm{II}}_n \mid \mathscr{H}_m)) \geq u_{\mathrm{II}}$.

Show that $\mathsf{E}_{\sigma^k,\tau}[\mathscr{L}(\mathsf{E}'_{\sigma,\tau}(\bar{g}^{\mathrm{II}}_n \mid \mathscr{H}_m)) - \mathscr{L}(\mathsf{E}_{\sigma^k,\tau}(\bar{g}^{\mathrm{II}}_n))] \xrightarrow[m\to\infty]{} 0$, so $\beta(k) = G^{\mathrm{II}}[\theta(k)] = \sum_{s,t} G^{\mathrm{II}}_{st}\theta_{st}(k) = \mathscr{L}(\mathsf{E}_{\sigma^k,\tau}(\bar{g}^{\mathrm{II}}_n))$. Use then Proposition IX.1.1, p. 482.

b. Prove that $E_\infty(p) \neq \emptyset$ for all p.

HINT. Use a splitting leading to a S.E.J.P.

c. Prove that $D_\infty = E_\infty$.

HINT. Extend the construction of (2) above.

d. Given two matrices A and B, consider all the games defined as in IX.3, Ex. 1a, above with $G^{1,\mathrm{I}} = A$ and $G^{\mathrm{II}} = B$. Show that there exists ζ (function of the payoff matrices) such that the projection of E_∞ on the (a^1, β) components is the set of feasible payoffs in (A, B) satisfying $a^1 \geq \zeta, \beta \geq u_{\mathrm{II}}$.

Prove that the maximum of such ζ is:

$$\max_{x \in \Delta(S)} \min_{y \in B(x)} xAy, \quad \text{with } B(x) = \{\, y \in \Delta(T) \mid xBy \geq u_{\mathrm{II}} \,\},$$

and is obtained for $K = 2$ and $G^{2,\mathrm{I}} = -B$.

HINT. Use a fully revealing equilibrium with x^k maximizing $\min_{y \in B(x)} xG^{k,\mathrm{I}}y$. For the other inequality, use that a has to be approachable by II.

e. *Incomplete information on both sides.* Consider a non-zero-sum game in the independent case ($K = L \times M$), with standard signaling satisfying:

$$G^{(l,m),\mathrm{I}} = G^{l,\mathrm{I}}, \; G^{(l,m),\mathrm{II}} = G^{m,\mathrm{II}} \text{ and } \#S \geq \#L, \#T \geq \#M.$$

Prove that:

$$\begin{aligned}
\mathsf{E}_\infty(p, q) = \Big\{ &(a, b) \in \mathbb{R}^1 \times \mathbb{R}^m \;\Big|\; \exists \theta(l, m) \in \Delta(S \times T), \\
&x\, c(l, m) \in \mathbb{R}^1, \; d(l, m) \in \mathbb{R}^m, \text{ s.t. :} \\
&\sum_m q^m G^{l,\mathrm{I}}[\theta(l, m)] = a^l, \quad \sum_l p^l G^{m,\mathrm{II}}[\theta(l, m)] = b^m, \\
&a^l \geq \sum_m q^m \max\{G^{l,\mathrm{I}}[\theta(l', m)], c^l(l', m)\}, \; \forall l', \\
&b^m \geq \sum_l p^l \max\{G^{m,\mathrm{II}}[\theta(l, m')], d^m(l, m')\}, \; \forall m', \\
&\forall l, m\colon \; \langle c(l, m), \pi \rangle \geq u_{\mathrm{I}}(\pi) \forall \pi \in \Delta(L), \quad \langle d(l, m), \rho \rangle \geq u_{\mathrm{II}}(\rho) \forall \rho \in \Delta(M) \Big\}.
\end{aligned}$$

HINT. To get equilibrium strategies use a joint plan completely revealing at stage one; then player II approaches $c(l, m)$ if (l, m) is announced, and player I does not follow $\theta(l, m)$. For the other inclusion, define $\theta(l, m)$ as in (a) and introduce:

$$c^l(l', m) = \limsup_t \mathsf{E}_{\sigma^{l'}, \tau^m} \sup_{\sigma'} \mathscr{L}(\mathsf{E}'_{\sigma', \tau}(\bar{g}_n^{l,\mathrm{I}} \mid \mathscr{H}_t)).$$

f. Show in the following example:

$$G^{1,\mathrm{I}} = \begin{pmatrix} 3 & 0 \\ 0 & 1 \end{pmatrix}, \quad G^{2,\mathrm{I}} = \begin{pmatrix} 3 & 3 \\ 1 & 1 \end{pmatrix}, \quad G^{1,\mathrm{II}} = \begin{pmatrix} 1 & 0 \\ 0 & 3 \end{pmatrix}, \quad G^{2,\mathrm{II}} = \begin{pmatrix} 1 & 3 \\ 1 & 3 \end{pmatrix},$$

that $\mathsf{E}_\infty(p)$ is non-empty iff $p^1 \leq 1/6$ or $q^1 \leq 1/6$ or $1/p^1 + 1/q^1 \geq 10$.

2. On the number of revelation stages. (Forges, 1984)
In the notation of Section IX.1, let W_n be obtained from W by n steps of "bi-convexification" (each step is first in p and then in a).

a. Show that in the following game, where the payoff is independent of I's move:

$$G^1 = \big((10, -10); (4, -3); (4, 0); (0, 5); (10, 8); (0, 9); (8, 10)\big),$$

$$G^2 = \big((8, 10); (0, 9); (10, 8); (6, 5); (4, 0); (4, -3); (10, -10)\big).$$

W_2 differs from W_1.

b. In the following example:

$$G^1 = \big((6, -6); (2, 1); (8, 6); (4, 9); (0, -10); (0, -2); (0, 4); (0, 8); (0, 10)\big),$$

$$G^2 = \big((4, 9); (8, 6); (2, 1); (6, -6); (0, 10); (0, 8); (0, 4); (0, -2); (0, -10)\big).$$

$W^\star \neq bico W$ (cf. example of Figure IX.1).

HINT. Look at the points in W with $a^1 + a^2 = 10$.

c. Finally take:

$$G^1 = \big((0, -5); (0, -1); (-1, 2); (3, 4); (1, 5)\big),$$

$$G^2 = \big((1, 5); (3, 4); (-1, 2); (0, -1); (0, -5)\big).$$

and show that $W_2 = bico\ W$ but that W, W_1, W_2, and $W^\star$ all differ: one obtains the configuration of Figure IX.1.

APPENDIX A

Reminder about Analytic Sets

A.1. NOTATION

Denote by $\mathscr{P}$ a *"paving"* (collection of subsets) of a set X. Let $\mathbb{T} = \mathbb{N}^{\mathbb{N}}$, the irrationals (continued fractions), $\mathbb{T}_n = \mathbb{N}^n$, $\mathbb{T}_f = \bigcup_n \mathbb{T}_n$. For $t \in \mathbb{T}$ or $t \in \mathbb{T}_k, k \geq n$, t_n is the natural projection to $\mathbb{T}_n$. A (disjoint) Souslin scheme is a map $t \mapsto P_t$ from $\mathbb{T}_f$ to $\mathscr{P}$ (such that $\left(\bigcap_n P_{s_n}\right) \cap \left(\bigcap_n P_{t_n}\right) = \emptyset\ \forall s \neq t \in \mathbb{T}$) and has as kernel $\bigcup_{t\in\mathbb{T}} \bigcap_n P_{t_n}$. $\mathscr{P}_s$ (resp. $\mathscr{P}_{s_d}$) is the paving consisting of the kernels of all (disjoint) Souslin schemes. $\mathscr{P}_\sigma$, $\mathscr{P}_+$, $\mathscr{P}_\delta$, $\mathscr{P}_c$ denote the pavings consisting, respectively, of the countable unions, the countable disjoint unions, the countable intersections, and the complements of elements of $\mathscr{P}$. $\mathscr{P}_{\sigma\delta} = (\mathscr{P}_\sigma)_\delta$, and so on. $\mathscr{P}_{(\alpha)}$, where α is a string of one or more of the above operations on pavings, denotes the stabilization of $\mathscr{P}$ under the corresponding operations, i.e., the smallest paving $\mathscr{P}^*$ containing $\mathscr{P}$ such that $\mathscr{P}^* = \mathscr{P}^*_O$ for every operation O in the string α. If X is a topological space, $\mathscr{F}$, $\mathscr{G}$, $\mathscr{K}$, $\mathscr{Z}$ will denote the pavings of closed, open, compact, and zero sets (i.e., sets $f^{-1}(0)$ for f real-valued and continuous).[1]

A.2. SOUSLIN SCHEMES

A.2.a. $\mathscr{P}_s = \mathscr{P}_{(s,\sigma,\delta)}$, $\mathscr{P}_{s_d} = \mathscr{P}_{(s_d,+,\delta)}$.

A.2.b. $\mathscr{P}_s$ is the set of projections on X of $(\mathscr{P} \times \mathscr{I})_{\sigma\delta}$ in $X \times \mathbb{T}$ or $X \times [0, 1]$, where $\mathscr{I}$ is the paving of closed intervals (i.e., on $\mathbb{T}$ the subsets with a fixed initial segment in $\mathbb{T}_f$.)

A.2.c. If $\emptyset \in \mathscr{P}$, $\mathscr{P}_s$ is the set of projections on X of $(\mathscr{P} \times \mathscr{F})_s$ in $X \times Y$ if Y is K-analytic (cf. below).

A.2.d. Second separation theorem. (cf. II.2, Ex. 5, p. 97)
Assume $\mathscr{P}_c \subseteq \mathscr{P}_s$. If $C_n \in \mathscr{P}_{sc}$ $(n \in \mathbb{N})$, $\exists D_n \in \mathscr{P}_{sc}$ s.t. $D_n \subseteq C_n$ and D_n is a partition of $\bigcup_n C_n$. In particular:

[1] For a reference book on the material of this chapter see, e.g., Rogers et al. (1980).

Assume $\mathscr{P}_c \subseteq \mathscr{P}_s$. If $A_n \in \mathscr{P}_s$, $A_n \cap A_m = \emptyset$, $\exists B_n \in \mathscr{P}_s \cap \mathscr{P}_{sc}$: $A_n \subseteq B_n$, $B_n \cap B_m = \emptyset$.

A.2.e. Assume $\mathscr{P}_c \subseteq \mathscr{P}_s$. Then $\mathscr{P}_{s_d} \subseteq \mathscr{P}_{sc}$.

A.2.f. Assume $\mathscr{P}_c \subseteq \mathscr{P}_{(\sigma,\delta)}$. Then the σ-field $\mathscr{P}_{(\sigma,\delta)} \subseteq \mathscr{P}_{s_d}$ and every $X \in \mathscr{P}_{(\sigma,\delta)}$ is the kernel of a disjoint Souslin scheme P_t with $\bigcup_{t:\, t_n = s_n} \bigcap_k P_{t_k} \in \mathscr{P}_{(\sigma,\delta)}$ $\forall s_n \in \mathbb{T}_f$. (This hard exercise is an interesting research question in its own right.)

A.3. *K*-ANALYTIC AND *K*-LUSIN SPACES

A Hausdorff topological space X is called K-analytic (K-Lusin) if it is the image of $\mathbb{T}$ by a compact-valued u.s.c. map Γ (with disjoint values). (Γ is u.s.c. (upper semi-continuous) means $\{\, t \mid \Gamma(t) \subseteq O \,\} \in \mathscr{G}^{\mathbb{T}}$, $\forall O \in \mathscr{G}^X$.) Denote by $\mathscr{A}^X$ ($\mathscr{L}^X$) the paving of K-analytic (K-Lusin) subspaces of a Hausdorff space X. $\mathscr{L}i^X$ will denote the Lindelöf subsets (every open cover contains a countable subcover).

A.3.a. Images of K-analytic (K-Lusin) spaces by compact-valued u.s.c. maps (with disjoint values) are K-analytic (K-Lusin). Their countable products and closed subspaces are also K-analytic (K-Lusin); $\mathscr{A}^X \subseteq \mathscr{L}i^X$.

A.3.b. $\mathscr{L} = \mathscr{L}_{s_d} \subseteq \mathscr{F}_{s_d}$. $\mathscr{A} = \mathscr{A}_s \subseteq \mathscr{F}_s$.

A.3.c. For Y K-analytic, $\mathrm{Proj}_X(\mathscr{F}_s^{X\times Y}) = \mathscr{F}_s^X$, and, if X and Y are in addition completely regular: $\mathrm{Proj}_X(\widetilde{\mathscr{Z}}_s^{X\times Y}) \subseteq \mathscr{Z}_s^X$, with $\widetilde{\mathscr{Z}} = \mathscr{Z} \cap \mathscr{L}i$.

A.3.d. $\mathscr{Z}_c \subseteq \mathscr{Z}_{+\delta+}$ (hence $\mathscr{Z}_{(+,\delta)}$ is a σ-field – the Baire σ-field; so any probability μ on it satisfies $\mu(B) = \sup_{Z\subseteq B, Z\in\mathscr{Z}} \mu(Z)$.)

A.3.e. A regular Lindelöf space is paracompact. For X compact, $\mathscr{Z}_{c\delta}^X = \mathscr{L}i^X \cap \mathscr{G}_\delta^X$.

A.3.f. For $X \in \mathscr{A}^X$, denote by G the graph in $\mathbb{T} \times X$ of the corresponding u.s.c. map. G is a $\mathscr{Z}_{c\delta}$-subset of its Stone–Čech compactification $\widehat{G}$.

Hint. First prove G is T_3; by (Appendix A.3.a) G is Lindelöf; use then Appendix A.3.e.

(In particular, K-Lusin spaces are the continuous one-to-one images of the $\mathscr{K}_{+\delta+\delta}$ subsets of compact spaces, and the K-analytic spaces are the continuous images of $\mathscr{K}_{\sigma\delta}$ subsets of compact spaces.)

A.3.g. First Separation Theorem

For $A_n \in \mathscr{A}^X$, $F \in \mathscr{F}_s^X$, with $F \cap \left(\bigcap_{n\in\mathbb{N}} A_n\right) = \emptyset$, $\exists B_n \in \mathscr{G}_{(\sigma,\delta)}^X$, $B_n \supseteq A_n$, $F \cap \left(\bigcap_{n\in\mathbb{N}} B_n\right) = \emptyset$. (So one can increase F to an $\mathscr{F}_{(\sigma,\delta)}$-set.) One could replace $\mathscr{G}$ by any paving $\mathscr{P}$ containing a basis of neighborhoods of every point – in particular, by $\mathscr{F}$ if the space is regular, and by $\mathscr{Z}$ if completely regular. Note the following consequences:

A.3.h. $\mathscr{L}^X \subseteq \mathscr{F}^X_{(\sigma,c)}$ (the Borel sets)
$\mathscr{G}^X \subseteq \mathscr{F}^X_s \Longrightarrow \mathscr{L}^X \subseteq \mathscr{G}^X_{(\sigma,\delta)}$
X regular $\Longrightarrow \mathscr{L}^X \subseteq \mathscr{F}^X_{(\sigma,\delta)}$
X completely regular $\Longrightarrow \mathscr{L}^X \subseteq \mathscr{F}^X_{(+,\delta)}$
X completely regular and $\mathscr{G}^X \subseteq \mathscr{F}^X_s \Longrightarrow \mathscr{L}^X \subseteq \mathscr{Z}^X_{(+,\delta)}$
X completely regular, $L \in \mathscr{L}^X \Longrightarrow [L \in \mathscr{Z}^X_{(+,\delta)} \Longleftrightarrow \exists f : X \to \mathbb{R}^{\mathbb{N}}$ continuous, $f(L) \cap f(L^c) = \emptyset]$.

A.3.i. For $X \in \mathscr{A}^X$, one has:
$\mathscr{F}^X_s \cap \mathscr{F}^X_{sc} = \mathscr{F}^X_{(\sigma,\delta)} \cap \mathscr{G}^X_{(\sigma,\delta)}$ (by Appendix A.3.g) (is a σ-field between Baire and Borel σ-fields.) In particular, $\mathscr{G}^X \subseteq \mathscr{F}^X_s \Longrightarrow \mathscr{G}^X_{(\sigma,\delta)} = \mathscr{F}^X_{(\sigma,\delta)}$ (= Borel sets, $= \mathscr{F}^X_{s_d}$ by Appendix A.2.e and Appendix A.2.f).
X completely regular $\Longrightarrow \mathscr{F}^X_{(+,\delta)} = \mathscr{F}^X_{s_d}$ $(\supseteq \mathscr{F}^X_s \cap \mathscr{F}^X_{sc} = \mathscr{Z}^X_{(+,\delta)})$.
$\mathscr{Z}^X_{(+,\delta)} = \mathscr{Z}^X_s \cap \mathscr{Z}^X_{sc}$ (hence $= \mathscr{Z}^X_{s_d}$ by Appendix A.2.e) (the Baire sets).

A.4. CAPACITIES

E_n and F are Hausdorff spaces.

A *multicapacity* on $\prod_n E_n$ is a map I from $\prod_n \wp(E_n)$ to $\overline{\mathbb{R}}_+$ that is:

- monotone: $X_n \subseteq Y_n \Longrightarrow I(X_1, X_2, \dots) \le I(Y_1, Y_2, \dots)$
- separately left continuous: $X^k_n \uparrow X_n \Longrightarrow I(X_1, X_2, \dots, X^k_n, X_{n+1}, \dots) \uparrow I(X_1, X_2, \dots, X_n, X_{n+1}, \dots)$
- right continuous: for K_n compact and $\varepsilon > 0$ there exist open sets $U_n \supseteq K_n$ with $U_n = E_n$ for all but finitely many indices such that $I(U_1, U_2, \dots) \le I(K_1, K_2, \dots) + \varepsilon$.

A *capacity operation* on $\prod_n E_n$ with values in F is a map I from $\prod_n \wp(E_n)$ to $\wp(F)$ that is:

- monotone
- separately left continuous (i.e., $\forall f \in F, \mathbb{1}_{I(\cdots)}(f)$ is a multicapacity), and
- right continuous: for K_n compact, $I(K_1, K_2, \dots)$ is compact, and for each of its neighborhoods V there exist open sets $U_n \supseteq K_n$ with $U_n = E_n$ for all but finitely many indices, such that $I(U_1, U_2, \dots) \subseteq V$.

A.4.a. If I is a capacity operation (multicapacity) on $\prod_n E_n$, and the J_n's are capacity operations from $\prod_k E_{n,k}$ to E_n, then the composition is a capacity operation (multicapacity).

A.4.b.

A.4.b.1. If Γ is an u.s.c. map from E to $\mathscr{K}^F$, then $I_\Gamma(X) = \bigcup_{x \in X} \Gamma(x)$ is a capacity operation from E to F. (In particular, any K-analytic set A is of the form $I_{\Gamma_A}(\mathbb{T})$.)

A.4.b.2. $\bigcap_n X_n$ and $\prod_n X_n$ are capacity operations J and P. (In particular, $\mathbb{T} = P(\mathbb{N}, \mathbb{N}, \mathbb{N}, \dots)$, and so $A = I_A(\mathbb{N}, \mathbb{N}, \mathbb{N}, \dots)$ for $A \in \mathscr{A}$ and $I_A = I_{\Gamma_A} \circ P$.)

A.4.b.3. Given a capacity operation I with $E_n = \mathbb{N}$, define $\psi_I : \mathbb{T} \to \mathscr{K}^F$ by $\psi_I(n_1, n_2, \dots) = I(\overline{n}_1, \overline{n}_2, \dots)$, with $\overline{n} = \{1, 2, \dots n\}$: $I(\mathbb{N}, \mathbb{N}, \dots) = \sup I(\overline{n}_1, \overline{n}_2, \dots)$, reducing first by evaluation to a multicapacity, then using first left continuity, and finally right continuity. Also ψ_I is u.s.c., and so $I(\mathbb{N}, \mathbb{N}, \mathbb{N}, \dots) = \psi_I(\mathbb{T})$ is K-analytic.

A.4.b.4. It follows thus from (Appendix A.4.a here above) that capacity operations map K-analytic arguments to K-analytic values, and conversely every K-analytic set can be obtained in this way, using just $(\mathbb{N}, \mathbb{N}, \dots)$ as argument.

A.4.b.5. With $E_0 = \{1, 2, 3, \dots\}$, $J(X_0, X_1, X_2, \dots) = \bigcup_{n \in X_0} X_n$ is a capacity operation (so $\bigcup_{n \geq 1} X_i = J(\mathbb{N}, X_1, X_2, \dots)$).

A.4.b.6. With $E_0 = \mathbb{T}$, $E_t = X$ for $t \in \mathbb{T}_f$, $I(X_0, \dots, X_t, \dots) = \bigcup_{x \in X_0} \bigcap_n X_{x_n}$ is a capacity operation, yielding the kernel of the Souslin scheme as $I(\mathbb{T}, \dots, X_t, \dots)$.

A.4.b.7. If μ is a probability measure on the Borel sets, such that $\mu(K) = \inf\{\, \mu(O) \mid K \subseteq O,\ O \text{ open}\,\}$ for any compact set K, the outer measure μ^* is a capacity ($\mu^*(A) = \inf\{\, \mu(B) \mid B \supseteq A,\ B \text{ Borel}\,\}$ for every subset A).

A.4.b.8. For X completely regular, denote by $M^X_{\sigma,+}$ the space of non-negative countably additive bounded measures on the Baire σ-field. For $\mu \in M^X_{\sigma,+}$, denote by μ^* the corresponding outer measure. Endow $M^X_{\sigma,+}$ with the weak*-topology determined by the duality with all bounded continuous functions.

Let $I(A, B) = \sup_{\mu \in A} \mu^*(B)$ for $B \subseteq X$, $A \subseteq M^X_{\sigma,+}$. I is a bi-capacity.

HINT. $\mu^*(K) = \inf\{\, \int f \, d\mu \mid f > \mathbb{1}_K,\ f \text{ continuous and bounded}\,\}$, using Appendix A.3.d. Use Dini's theorem on the compact subset of $M^X_{\sigma,+}$ to select some f_0.

A.4.c. For a capacity operation or a multicapacity I, one has:

$$I(A_1, A_2, \dots) = \sup_{K_n \subseteq A_n} I(K_1, K_2, \dots) = \inf_{B_n \supseteq A_n} I(B_1, B_2, \dots)$$

for A_n K-analytic, K_n compact, $B_n \in \mathscr{G}_{(\sigma,\delta)}$ (or $B_n \in \mathscr{P}_{(\sigma,\delta)}$ where the paving $\mathscr{P}$ contains a basis of neighborhoods of each point) (for a multicapacity, the $\inf$ is obviously achieved).

HINT. It suffices to consider the case of a multicapacity. The first formula follows then from Appendix A.4.a and Appendix A.4.b.4, which reduce the problem to the case $A_n = \mathbb{N}$, which was solved in Appendix A.4.b.3. The second follows now by showing that $J(X_1, X_2, \dots) = \inf_{B_n \supseteq X_n} I(B_1, B_2, \dots)$ is a multicapacity, equal to I on compact sets, and hence by the first formula also equal on K-analytic sets.

(In particular, this yields the first separation theorem (Appendix A.3.g, p. 512), at least for $F \in \mathscr{F}_\sigma$. It suffices indeed to consider $F \in \mathscr{F}$; then $J_F(Y) = \mathbb{1}_{F\cap Y \neq \emptyset}$ is a capacity, and $I(Y_1, Y_2, \dots) = \bigcap_n Y_n$ a capacity operation (Appendix A.4.b.2), and so the above can be applied to the multicapacity (Appendix A.4.a) $J_F \circ I$.)

A.4.d.

A.4.d.1. Given a measurable space $(\Omega, \mathscr{B})$, define the σ-field $\mathscr{B}_u$ of universally measurable sets as consisting of those sets that are μ-measurable for any probability measure, and then for any measure, on $(\Omega, \mathscr{B})$. Then $\mathscr{B}_u = \mathscr{B}_{us}$.

HINT. Since $\mathscr{B}_u = \mathscr{B}_{uu}$, it suffices to show that $\mathscr{B}_s \subseteq \mathscr{B}_u$. Reduce first to the case $\mathscr{B}$ separable, then to $(\Omega, \mathscr{B}) = ([0,1], \mathscr{F}_{(\sigma,\delta)})$, and then use (Appendix A.4.c).

A.4.d.2. A probability as in Appendix A.4.b.7 or Appendix A.4.b.8 on a K-analytic space X is regular.

HINT. Reduce by Appendix A.4.c to the case of a compact space; then use Riesz's theorem.

A.4.d.3. If $A \in \mathscr{A}^X$, X completely regular, and $L \in \mathscr{A}^{M^X_{\sigma,+}}$ are such that $\mu(A) = 0\ \forall \mu \in L$, there exists a Baire set B containing A, such that $\mu(B) = 0$ $\forall \mu \in L$, using Appendix A.4.b.8 and Appendix A.4.c.

A.5. POLISH, ANALYTIC, AND LUSIN SPACES

Definition A.5.1. A Polish space is a regular Hausdorff space that is a continuous, open image of $\mathbb{T}$. An analytic (Lusin) space is a K-analytic (K-Lusin) space where $\mathscr{G} \subseteq \mathscr{F}_s$ and where the Borel σ-field is separable.

A.5.a. The separable metric spaces are the subspaces of the compact metric spaces. If $\overline{X} = P$, P Hausdorff, then $X \in \mathscr{G}_\delta^P$ if X is topologically complete (i.e., can be endowed with a complete metric). Conversely, a metrizable $\mathscr{G}_\delta$ in a compact space or in a complete metric space is topologically complete. A complete separable metric space is homeomorphic to a closed subspace of $\mathbb{R}^{\mathbb{N}}$; conversely, a metrizable space that has a proper map to $\mathbb{R}^{\mathbb{N}}$ is separable and topologically complete. (A map f is proper if it is continuous, maps closed sets to closed sets, and has compact point inverses.) Deduce that X is Polish iff it is separable and topologically complete (cf. II.2, Ex. 8d, p. 100).

A.5.b. The analytic spaces are the continuous, Hausdorff images of $\mathbb{T}$. The uncountable Lusin spaces are the continuous, one-to-one Hausdorff images of $\mathbb{T} \cup \mathbb{N}$.

HINT. To prove separability of the Borel σ-field, use that $(X \times X) \setminus \Delta$ (Δ is the diagonal) is the continuous image of a separable metric space, hence Lindelöf, so there exists a weaker Hausdorff topology with a countable base, and use Appendix A.3.i, p. 513. In the other direction, show that closed subspaces of $\mathbb{T}$ are continuous images of $\mathbb{T}$, and, if uncountable, continuous one-to-one images of $\mathbb{T} \cup \mathbb{N}$. Also, one does not need the Borel σ-field to be separable; it suffices that it contains a separable and separating sub-σ-field; this is then generated by a sequence O_n of open sets and their complements, which separate points and belong to $\mathscr{F}_s$ by assumption. Apply then the following claim:

Claim: *For a K-analytic (K-Lusin) space to be analytic (Lusin), it suffices already that there exists a sequence of pairs (C_n^1, C_n^2) of disjoint sets in $\mathscr{F}_{sc}$, such that $\forall x_1, x_2 \in X, \exists n\colon x_1 \in C_n^1, x_2 \in C_n^2$.*

Indeed, let K_n^i be an u.s.c. map from $\mathbb{T}$ to $\mathscr{K}^X$ corresponding to $(C_n^i)^c$; $L_n\colon \{1,2\} \times \mathbb{T} \to \mathscr{K}^X$, $L_n(i,t) = K_n^i(t)$; $L\colon S = [\{1,2\} \times \mathbb{T}]^{\mathbb{N}} \to \mathscr{K}^{X^{\mathbb{N}}}$, $L(i_1, t_1; i_2, t_2; \ldots) = \prod_n L_n(i_n, t_n)$. L is u.s.c., and $L(S) = X^{\mathbb{N}}$. Denote by Δ the diagonal in $X^{\mathbb{N}}$, and let $\psi(s) = L(s) \cap \Delta$, $F = \{ s \mid \psi(s) \neq \emptyset \}$: F is a closed subset of $\mathbb{N}^{\mathbb{N}}$, and ψ is single-valued on S, thus a continuous map onto Δ (which is homeomorphic to X). This proves the K-analytic case. If X was K-Lusin, the above proves it is analytic, hence, cf. supra, there exists a weaker Hausdorff topology with a countable base O_k. So we can take for (C_n^1, C_n^2) all pairs of disjoint sets O_k. Their complements are then K-Lusin, and so we can choose the maps K_n^i to have disjoint values. The map ψ is then one-to-one. This proves the lemma, and thereby our claim.

A.5.c. For a K-analytic (respectively K-Lusin) space to be analytic (Lusin), it suffices already that there exists a sequence U_n of open sets, such that for every pair of distinct points (x, y), $x \in U_n$ and $y \notin U_n$ for some n.

HINT. Since the projection from the graph G of the correspondence is continuous, and one-to-one in the K-Lusin case, it will suffice to show that G is analytic (Lusin); cf. Appendix A.3.f, p. 512. The u.s.c. character of the map means that the projection π from G to $\mathbb{T}$ is proper. When $\mathbb{T}$ is viewed homeomorphically as the irrationals in $[0, 1]$, this means that the extension $\hat{\pi}\colon \widehat{G} \to [0, 1]$ is such that $\hat{\pi}[\widehat{G} \setminus G]$ is the set of rational numbers. Let thus V_{2n+1} enumerate all open subsets of $\widehat{G}$ of the form $\{ g \mid \hat{\pi}(g) > q \}$ and of the form $\{ g \mid \hat{\pi}(g) < q \}$ for q rational. Let also V_{2n} be the largest open set of $\widehat{G}$ such that $V_{2n} \cap G$ equals the inverse image of U_n in G. The open sets V_n have the property that for any pair of distinct points (x, y) of $\widehat{G}$, such that at least one of them lies in G, one has $x \in V_n$, $y \notin V_n$ for some n. Stabilize the sequence V_n under finite intersections, and consider then all finite open coverings $\left(V_{n_i}\right)_{i=1}^k$ of $\widehat{G}$: there are countably many of them. For each such cover, there exists a corresponding continuous partition of unity, i.e., continuous functions $(f_i)_{i=1}^k$ with $f_i \geq 0$, $\sum_i f_i = 1$, $\{ x \mid f_i(x) > 0 \} \subseteq V_{n_i}$. We claim that the resulting countable family of continuous functions separates points of G: for $x_1, x_2 \in G$, $x_1 \neq x_2$, consider first open sets O_1, O_2, among the V_n with $x_i \in O_i$, $x_j \notin O_i$. For each point $z \in \widehat{G} \setminus (O_1 \cup O_2)$, let O_z^i be an open set among the V_n with $z \in O_z^i$, $x_i \notin O_z^i$, and let $O_z = O_z^1 \cap O_z^2$. Extract by compactness a finite subcovering from O_1, O_2, and O_z: since x_i belongs only to O_i, O_1 and O_2 will belong to the subcovering, and the corresponding continuous functions f_i will satisfy $f_i(x_i) = 1$, and $f_i(x_j) = 0$. Thus we have a one-to-one continuous map φ from G to $[0, 1]^{\mathbb{N}}$. Let W_n be a basis of open sets in the latter: the sets $\varphi^{-1}(W_n)$ are open, and for each pair of distinct points (x_1, x_2) in G there exist two disjoint such sets U_1 and U_2 with $x_i \in U_i$. Since also G is K-analytic (K-Lusin), the assumptions of the claim sub Appendix A.5.b above are satisfied; G is analytic (Lusin).

A.5.d. For any analytic space X there exists a weaker analytic topology with a countable base. If the space is regular, there exists both a weaker and a stronger metrizable analytic topology. The latter also exists if the space has a countable base and can in any case be chosen as being an analytic subset of the Cantor space $\{0, 1\}^{\mathbb{N}}$. Those topologies can further be chosen such as to leave any given sequence of open sets open.

HINT. For the first, use that $(X \times X) \setminus \Delta$ is Lindelöf (by Appendix A.5.b) (and that regularity implies complete regularity (Appendix A.3.e, p. 512); hence, every open set being Lindelöf belongs to $\mathscr{Z}_c$). To get the stronger metrizable topology, use the sequence $(\mathbb{1}_{B_n})$ as a measurable one-to-one map to $\{0, 1\}^{\mathbb{N}}$, with continuous inverse, taking for B_n either the countable base of the space or the closures of the images of a countable base of $\mathbb{T}$. Use Appendix A.5.e below to deduce that the image is analytic.

A.5.e. Let X be K-analytic, with its bianalytic σ-field $\mathscr{B} = \mathscr{F}_s \cap \mathscr{F}_{sc} = \mathscr{F}_{(\sigma,\delta)} \cap \mathscr{G}_{(\sigma,\delta)}$ (Appendix A.3.i, p. 513). Let $(E, \mathscr{E})$ be an analytic space with its Borel sets, and $f : (X, \mathscr{B}) \to (E, \mathscr{E})$ a measurable map. Then $f(X)$ is analytic. If f is one-to-one, it is a Borel isomorphism with $f(X)$ (so X is analytic by Appendix A.5.c and Appendix A.5.d). If furthermore X is Lusin, then $f(X)$ is a Borel set, and even Lusin if E is Lusin.

HINT. Because $\mathscr{E}$ is separable and separating, the graph F of f belongs to $(\mathscr{B} \times \mathscr{E})_{\sigma\delta}$, hence is K-analytic. So $f(X)$ is K-analytic, and hence analytic by Appendix A.5.c. This, applied to elements of $\mathscr{B}$, together with the first separation theorem, yields also the second statement. If E and X are Lusin, then F is Lusin by the above argument as a Borel subset of the Lusin space $E \times X$, so that the one-to-one projection yields that $f(X)$ is Lusin, and in particular Borel (Appendix A.3.b, Appendix A.3.h, Appendix A.3.i). If just X is Lusin, to show that $f(X)$ is still Borel, use Appendix A.5.d above to change the topology of E, without changing its Borel sets, first to an analytic topology with countable base, then to a metrizable analytic topology, which is a subspace of a (Lusin) compact metric space.

Note that the same argument shows that for X Lusin, f one-to-one, $f(X)$ will be Lusin if E is a Hausdorff space, with countable base, or if E is a regular Hausdorff space which is the continuous image of a separable metric space, more generally if there exists a stronger topology on E with the same Borel sets, under which it is a subspace of Lusin space. But for E analytic? The problem reduces to: given a continuous map from $\mathbb{T}$ onto the Cantor space, is the quotient topology Lusin?

A.5.f. Appendix A.3.b, Appendix A.3.h, and Appendix A.3.i imply that, in a Lusin space, the Lusin subsets are the Borel sets. Thus the Lusin subsets of a Hausdorff space are stable under countable unions.

A.5.g. Every bounded Borel measure on an analytic space is regular.

HINT. Use Appendix A.5.d and Appendix A.4.d.2: observe that, in a space where there exists a weaker Hausdorff topology with countable base, $\mathscr{K} \subseteq \mathscr{G}_\delta$.

A.6. BLACKWELL SPACES AND STANDARD BOREL SPACES

A Blackwell (standard Borel) space is a measurable space $(E, \mathscr{E})$ where $\mathscr{E}$ is the Borel σ-field of an analytic (Lusin) topology on E. It follows from

Appendix A.5.b and Appendix A.5.e that all uncountable standard Borel spaces are isomorphic, and from Appendix A.5.d and Appendix A.5.e that every Blackwell space is isomorphic to an analytic subset of the Cantor space.

Given a measurable space $(E, \mathscr{E})$, define the equivalence relation R on E where two points of E are equivalent if they are not separated by $\mathscr{E}$. Call $\mathscr{E}$ a Blackwell σ-field if the quotient space of $(E, \mathscr{E})$ by this equivalence relation is a Blackwell space, and the equivalence classes of E are also called the atoms of $\mathscr{E}$.

Appendix A.5.e implies then that, for X K-analytic with bianalytic σ-field $\mathscr{B}$, all separable sub-σ-fields of $\mathscr{B}$ are Blackwell. And such a σ-field $\mathscr{C}$ contains all elements B of $\mathscr{B}$ that are a union of atoms of $\mathscr{C}$. (Consider the map from $(X, B \vee \mathscr{C})$ to $(X, \mathscr{C})$.) In other words, if f_1 and f_2 are two real-valued random variables on $(X, \mathscr{B})$, functions such that the sets $\{x \mid f(x) \geq \alpha\}$ and $\{x \mid f(x) \leq \alpha\}$ are analytic (i.e., $\in \mathscr{F}_s^X$), and if $f_2(x)$ is a function of $f_1(x)$, then it is a Borel function: $f_2 = h \circ f_1$ with $h\colon \mathbb{R} \to \mathbb{R}$ Borel measurable. Similarly, Appendix A.5.e implies that, if f is a measurable map from a Blackwell space $(B, \mathscr{B})$ to a separable and separating measurable space $(E, \mathscr{E})$, then $f(B)$ is a Blackwell space, f is an isomorphism with $f(B)$ if f is one-to-one, and if in addition B is standard Borel, then $f(B) \in \mathscr{E}$.

A.7. SPACES OF SUBSETS

Given a topological space X, the Hausdorff topology on $\mathscr{K}^X$ has a basis of open subsets $\{K \in \mathscr{K}^X \mid K \subseteq \bigcup_{i \in I} O_i, K \cap O_i \neq \emptyset \, \forall i \in I\}$ for all finite families $(O_i)_{i \in I}$ in $\mathscr{G}^X$.

Also, the Effrös σ-field $\mathcal{E}^X$ on $\mathscr{F}^X$ is spanned by the sets $\{F \in \mathscr{F}^X \mid F \subseteq F_0\}$ $\forall F_0 \in \mathscr{F}^X$.

A.7.a. If Y is a (closed) (open) subspace of X, so is $\mathscr{K}^Y$ in $\mathscr{K}^X$. If X is compact or metrizable, so is $\mathscr{K}^X$. Hence if X is Polish, or locally compact, so is $\mathscr{K}^X$.

A.7.b. If X is compact metric, $\mathcal{E}^X$ is the Borel σ-field of $\mathscr{K}^X$.

A.7.c. $\mathcal{E}^{\mathbb{T}}$ is the Borel σ-field of the topology with a subbase of clopen sets $\{F \in \mathscr{F}^{\mathbb{T}} \mid F \text{ is excluded by } h\}$ for $h \in \mathbb{T}_f$. Define $d(F_1, F_2)$ as k^{-1}, where k is the smallest integer for which there exists $h \in \mathbb{T}_f$ with the sum of its terms $\leq k$ such that either F_1 is excluded by h and F_2, and vice versa. Show that this distance induces the above topology, and that $(\mathscr{F}^{\mathbb{T}}, d)$ is complete: the topology is Polish, and $\mathcal{E}^{\mathbb{T}}$ is standard Borel.

A.7.d. If $f\colon X_1 \to X_2$ is continuous, let $\phi(F) = \overline{f(F)}$, for $F \in \mathscr{F}^{X_1}$. Then $\phi\colon \mathscr{F}^{X_1} \to \mathscr{F}^{X_2}$ is measurable. If f is an inclusion, ϕ is an isomorphism with its image.

A.7.e. If $f\colon X_1 \to X_2$ is open, let $\psi(F) = \overline{f^{-1}(F)}$, for $F \in \mathscr{F}^{X_2}$. Then $\psi\colon \mathscr{F}^{X_2} \to \mathscr{F}^{X_1}$ is measurable. If f is continuous (and so $\psi(F) = f^{-1}(F)$) and onto, ψ is an isomorphism with its image. If furthermore X_1 has a countable base, then $\psi(\mathscr{F}^{X_2}) \in \mathcal{E}^{X_1}$.

A.7.f. Conclude from Appendix A.7.c and Appendix A.7.e that $\mathcal{E}^P$ is standard Borel for any Polish space P.

A.7.g. Conclude from Appendix A.7.d, Appendix A.7.f, and Appendix A.6 that, if S is analytic, all separable sub-σ-fields of $\mathscr{E}^S$ are Blackwell.

(Note that this property of a measurable space $(\Omega, \mathscr{C})$ is sufficient to imply all the nice properties mentioned in A.6 about Blackwell spaces, including that $\mathscr{C}_s \cap \mathscr{C}_{sc} = \mathscr{C}$; this is the property that was obtained for the characterization of the σ-field $\mathscr{B}$ on a K-analytic space: every real-valued random variable on $(\Omega, \mathscr{C})$ has an analytic range.)

A.7.h. Show that the map $c\colon \mathscr{F}^{\mathbb{T}} \to \mathbb{T}$ that selects in each closed set the lexicographically smallest element is Borel measurable (in fact, it is u.s.c. in the lexicographic order, which spans the Borel σ-field).

A.7.i. Kuratowski–Ryll–Nardzewski Selection Theorem

Conclude from Appendix A.7.e and Appendix A.7.h that, for any Polish space P, there exists a Borel function $c\colon \mathscr{F}^P \to P$ such that $c(F) \in F\ \forall F \in \mathscr{F}^P$ s.t. $F \neq \emptyset$.

A.7.j. Von Neumann Selection Theorem

Given a measurable space $(\Omega, \mathscr{C})$ and a Blackwell space $(B, \mathscr{B})$, and given a subset $A \in (\mathscr{C} \times \mathscr{B})_s$, there exists a map $\tilde{c}$ from Ω to B, satisfying $(\omega, \tilde{c}(\omega)) \in A$ whenever possible, which is $((\mathscr{C}_s)_{(\sigma,c)} - \mathscr{B})$-measurable.

Hint. Reduce to $(\Omega, \mathscr{C})$-separable, then a subset of $[0, 1]$, then $[0, 1]$. B can also be viewed as an analytic subset of $[0, 1]$, and so A becomes an analytic subset of $[0, 1] \times [0, 1]$. Let φ be the continuous map from $\mathbb{T}$ onto A, and use $(\pi_B \circ \varphi)\big(c[(\pi_\Omega \circ \varphi)^{-1}(\omega)]\big)$: check that $\omega \mapsto (\pi_\Omega \circ \varphi)^{-1}(\omega)$ is $((\mathscr{A}_s)_{(\sigma,c)} - \mathscr{E}^{\mathbb{T}})$-measurable.

A.8. SOME HARDER RESULTS

A.8.a. Assume Y is a regular Lusin space, and $S \subseteq X \times Y$ is bianalytic for the paving $\mathscr{P} \times \mathscr{F}^Y$, where $\mathscr{P}$ is a paving on X and $S_x \in \mathscr{K}_\sigma^Y\ \forall x \in X$. Then $\mathrm{Proj}_X(S) \in \mathscr{P}_s \cap \mathscr{P}_{sc}$.

A.8.b.

A.8.b.1. In particular, if also $S_x \in \mathscr{F}^Y\ \forall x \in X$, the map $x \mapsto S_x$ is Effrös measurable (cf. Appendix A.7) w.r.t. $\mathscr{P}_s \cap \mathscr{P}_{sc}$. Appendix A.7.i yields then the existence of a $\mathscr{P}_s \cap \mathscr{P}_{sc}$-measurable selection, when Y is Polish, or when $S_x \in \mathscr{K}^Y$.

A.8.b.2. Under the assumptions of Appendix A.8.a, if in addition either Y is metrizable or $S_x \in \mathscr{K}^Y$ $\forall x \in X$, there even exists a sequence of $\mathscr{P}_s \cap \mathscr{P}_{sc}$-measurable selections giving at every x a dense sequence in S_x, so that, if $\mathscr{B}$ is a separable σ-field w.r.t. which these selections are measurable, one can construct a sequence of selections f_n such that the closure of $\{ f_n \mid n \in \mathbb{N} \}$ under a pointwise convergence of sequences equals the set of all $\mathscr{B}$-measurable selections.

HINT. Use, for some weaker metrizable Lusin topology (Appendix A.5), a theorem of Louveau implying that $S = \bigcup_n S^n$, where S^n is bi-analytic and $S^n_x \in \mathscr{K}^Y$ $\forall x$.

A.8.c. Let X be a Polish space and $\Theta\colon \wp(X) \to \wp(X)$.

Θ preserves analytic sets if for any Polish space W and any analytic $A \subseteq X \times W$:

$$\Theta^*(A) = \{ (y, w) \in X \times W \mid y \in \Theta(A_w) \}$$

is again analytic in $X \times W$ (where $A_w = \{ x \in X \mid (x, w) \in A \}$.

Assume Θ is an **analytic derivation,** i.e.:

- Θ is increasing.
- $\Theta(A) \subseteq A$.
- Θ preserves analytic sets.

Let $\Theta^0(A) = A$, $\Theta^{\alpha+1}(A) = \Theta(\Theta^\alpha(A))$, and $\Theta^\beta(A) = \bigcap_{\alpha<\beta} \Theta^\alpha(A)$, if β is a limit ordinal. Let also $\Theta^\infty(A) = \bigcap_\alpha \Theta^\alpha(A)$, which is the largest fixed point of Θ included in A.

MOSCHOVAKIS' THEOREM. (Moschovakis, 1980, 7c.8, p. 414)

- *Θ^∞ is an analytic derivation. In particular, $\Theta^\infty(A)$ is analytic if A is analytic.*
- *If A is analytic, then $\Theta^\infty(A) = \Theta^{\aleph_1}(A)$.*
- *If A is analytic, B is coanalytic, and $\Theta^\infty(A) \subseteq B$, then $\Theta^\alpha(A) \subseteq B$ for some countable α.*

A.9. COMPLEMENTS TO MEASURE THEORY

A.9.a. Any measurable function from a subset of a measurable space to a standard Borel space has a measurable extension to the whole space.

HINT. Take the standard Borel space to be $[0, 1]$: consider then first indicator functions, next step functions, and finally arbitrary measurable functions (use, e.g., $\liminf$).

A.9.b. Assume $f\colon X \to Y$ continuous, Y Hausdorff, and endow the spaces $\Delta(X)$ and $\Delta(Y)$ of regular probability measures on X and Y with the weak* topology (Definition I.1.11, p. 6). Let $\overline{f}\colon \Delta(X) \to \Delta(Y)$ be the induced continuous map (Proposition I.1.8, p. 8).

A.9.b.1. If f is one-to-one, so is $\overline{f}$.

A.9.b.2. If f is an inclusion (i.e., a homeomorphism with $f(X)$) (and $f(X) \in \mathscr{F}^Y$, or $\mathscr{L}^Y$, or $\mathscr{L}^Y_{c\delta}$), so is $\overline{f}$, and $\overline{f}(\Delta(X)) = \{\, \mu \in \Delta(Y) \mid \mu(f(X)) = 1 \,\}$.

A.9.b.3. If X is K-analytic, and f onto, then $\overline{f}$ is onto.

A.9.b.4. If X is K-Lusin, and f is one-to-one and onto, then f is a Borel isomorphism.

HINT. For Appendix A.9.b.1: two different measures already differ on some compact subset.

For Appendix A.9.b.2, the formula for $\overline{f}(\Delta(X))$ is clear. Given that $\overline{f}$ is continuous and one-to-one (Appendix A.9.b.1), it will be an inclusion if we show that the image of a sub-basic open set $\overline{f}\{\, \mu \in \Delta(X) \mid \mu(U) > \alpha \,\}$ with U open in X is open in $\overline{f}(\Delta(X))$: this is because $U = f^{-1}(V)$ for V open in Y, so that our set equals $\{\, \nu \in \overline{f}(\Delta(X)) \mid \nu(V) > \alpha \,\}$. Finally, if X is closed in Y $\Delta(X)$ is closed in $\Delta(Y)$ by definition of the topology; if $f\colon Y \to [0,1]$, $X = f^{-1}(0)$, then $\Delta(X) = \{\, \mu \in \Delta(Y) \mid \mu(f) = 0 \,\}$; and if $X = \bigcap_n O_n$, $O_n = \{\, y \mid f_n(y) > 0 \,\}$ with f_n continuous with values in $[0,1]$, then $\Delta(X) = \bigcap_n \Delta(O_n) = \bigcap_n \bigcap_k \{\, \mu \in \Delta(Y) \mid \lim_{i\to\infty} \mu(f_{n,i}) > 1 - k^{-1} \,\}$ with $f_{n,i} = \min(1, i \cdot f_n)$, and so $\Delta(X) = \bigcap_n \bigcap_k \{\, \mu \mid \varphi_{n,k}(\mu) > 0 \,\}$, where $\varphi_{n,k}(\mu) = \sum_i 2^{-i}[\mu(f_{n,i}) - 1 + k^{-1}]^+$ is continuous.

For Appendix A.9.b.3, fix $\mu \in \Delta(Y)$, and let $I(A) = \mu^*(f(A))$, for $A \subseteq X$: by Appendix A.4.a, Appendix A.4.b.1, and Appendix A.4.b.7, I is a capacity on X. Hence by Appendix A.4.c there exist compact subsets K of X such that $f(K)$ has an arbitrarily large measure. So $\mu = \sum_1^\infty \alpha_n \mu_n$, with $\alpha_n \geq 0$ and $\mu_n \in \Delta(Y)$ carried by some $f(K_n)$, K_n compact in X. It suffices thus that $\mu_n = \overline{f}(\nu_n)$, for $\nu_n \in \Delta(K_n)$: this reduces the problem to the case where X, and hence Y, is compact. Then $\overline{f}(\Delta(Y))$ is compact, as a continuous image of a compact set (Proposition I.1.4, p. 7), and contains all probability measures with finite support, since f is onto. Since those are dense (by the separation theorem (Section I.1.e, p. 9)), the result follows.

For Appendix A.9.b.4, let $F \in \mathscr{F}^X$, F and hence $f(F)$ are K-Lusin (Appendix A.3.a), so $f(F)$ is Borel (Appendix A.3.h).

A.9.c. If X is K-analytic (resp. K-Lusin, resp. a $\mathscr{L}_{c\delta}$ subset of a compact space, resp. analytic, resp. Lusin, resp. Polish), so is $\Delta(X)$.

HINT. For $\mathscr{L}_{c\delta}$ subsets, use Appendix A.9.b.2 above and Proposition I.1.4, p. 7. In the K-analytic (K-Lusin) case, X is a continuous (one-to-one) image of a $\mathscr{L}_{c\delta}$ subset G of a compact space (Appendix A.3.f, p. 512), and so $\Delta(X)$ has the same property, by Appendix A.9.b.3 (and Appendix A.9.b.1) above, and the previous case, hence (by Appendix A.3.a) $\Delta(X)$ is K-analytic (K-Lusin). The argument for the latter three cases is the same, given that the compact space can then be taken to be metrizable (Appendix A.5.a, Appendix A.5.b).

A.9.d. $f\colon X \to Y$, with Y a T_2 space, is *universally measurable* iff it is μ-measurable (cf. Definition I.1.12, p. 7) $\forall \mu \in \Delta(X)$.

$A \subseteq X$ is *universally measurable* iff $\mathbb{1}_A$ is so (recall (Appendix A.4.d.1) that $\mathscr{B}_u$ is the σ-field of universally measurable sets). Then:

A.9.d.1. Universally measurable maps are stable under composition and under countable products (i.e., $\prod_n f_n\colon \prod_n X_n \to \prod_n Y_n$ is universally measurable if each f_n is).

A.9.d.2. If $f\colon X \to Y$ is universally measurable, then $[(\Delta(f))(\mu)](B) = \mu(f^{-1}(B))$ defines $\Delta(f)\colon \Delta(X) \to \Delta(Y)$.

A.9.d.3. If Y is a separable metric space, $f: X \to Y$ is universally measurable iff $f^{-1}(B) \in \mathscr{B}_u$ for every Borel set B.

A.9.e. Endow the space M_X of probability measures on a measurable space $(X, \mathscr{X})$ with the σ-field spanned by the functions $\mu \mapsto \mu(Y)$ for $Y \in \mathscr{X}$.

A transition probability to $(X, \mathscr{X})$ is then just a measurable map to M_X.

If X is analytic, the Borel σ-field on $\Delta(X)$ coincides with the above-defined one for $\mathscr{X}$, which is the Borel σ-field on X. Thus if X is standard Borel, or Blackwell, so is M_X.

HINT. Since $\mathscr{X}$ is separable if X is analytic, our σ-field on M_X will be separable and separating. It is coarser than the Borel σ-field, because $\mu \mapsto \mu(Y)$ is Borel measurable for the weak*-topology. Therefore both coincide by Appendix A.5.e and the analyticity of $\Delta(X)$ (Appendix A.9.c above). Use again Appendix A.9.c for the final conclusion.

A.9.f. For a transition probability P from $(E, \mathscr{E})$ to $(F, \mathscr{F})$, and $X \in \mathscr{F}_s$, the sets $\{ e \in E \mid P_e(X) > \alpha \}$ and $\{ e \in E \mid P_e(X) \geq \alpha \}$ belong to $\mathscr{E}_s$.

Remark A.9.1. Since P can also be viewed as a transition probability from E to $E \times F$, the same result holds if $X \in (\mathscr{E} \otimes \mathscr{F})_s$.

HINT. X already belongs to $(\mathscr{F}_0)_s$ for a separable sub-σ-field $\mathscr{F}_0$ of $\mathscr{F}$; for some separable sub-σ-field $\mathscr{E}_0$ of $\mathscr{E}$, P will still be a transition probability from $\mathscr{E}_0$ to $\mathscr{F}_0$, and it suffices to show the sets are in $(\mathscr{E}_0)_s$. Hence there is no loss of generality in passing to the quotient, and so E and F can be viewed as subsets of $[0, 1]$ with the Borel sets. P can then be viewed as a transition probability from E to $[0, 1]$ (under which F has outer probability one), and so can be extended (by Appendix A.9.a and Appendix A.9.e above) as a transition probability from $[0, 1]$ to $[0, 1]$. X is the trace on F of an analytic subset $\overline{X}$ of $[0, 1]$. Further, $P_e(X) = P_e(\overline{X})$ for $e \in E$; indeed for a Borel set B of $[0, 1]$ with $X \subseteq B$ and $P_e(X) = P_e(B)$ one has $P_e(\overline{X} \setminus B) = 0$, because any compact subset of $\overline{X} \setminus B$ is negligible: $P_e(X) \geq P_e(\overline{X})$. Similarly (with $B \cap F \subseteq X$) one obtains $P_e(X) \geq P_e(\overline{X})$. Therefore, $\{ e \in E \mid P_e(X) > \alpha \} = E \cap \{ e \in [0, 1] \mid P_e(\overline{X}) > \alpha \}$: it suffices to prove the result for E and F compact metric, or (again by Appendix A.9.e) that if X is analytic in a compact metric space F, then $M_\alpha = \{ \mu \in M_F \mid \mu(X) > \alpha \}$ is analytic. Let X be the projection of a Borel set in $F \times [0, 1]$: M_α is the projection of the Borel set $\{ \mu \in M_{F \times [0,1]} \mid \mu(B) > \alpha \}$ (Appendix A.7.j), and hence analytic.

A.10. ∗-RADON SPACES

A.10.a. A *τ-Radon* space is a T_2 space where every probability measure μ on the Borel sets satisfying $\mu(\bigcup_\alpha O_\alpha) = \sup_\alpha \mu(O_\alpha)$ for every increasing net of open sets is regular.

A *quasi-Radon* space is a T_2 space where, for $P \in \Delta(\Delta(X))$, the *barycenter* $\overline{P} = \beta(P)$ defined by $\overline{P}(B) = \int \mu(B) P(d\mu)$ for every Borel set B (observe $\mu(B)$ is a Borel function of μ) is regular.

A.10.a.1. For the regularity of μ (or of $\overline{P}$), it suffices already that $\sup_{K \in \mathscr{K}} \mu(K) = 1$.

A.10.a.2. A τ-Radon space is quasi-Radon.

HINT. Observe that $\mu(O_\alpha)$ is l.s.c.

A.10.a.3. A K-analytic space is τ-Radon.

HINT. Observe that μ also satisfies $\mu(K) = \inf\{\mu(O) \mid K \subseteq O \in \mathscr{G}_X\}$ $\forall K \in \mathscr{K}^X$ (T_2-assumption); hence use Appendix A.4.d.2, p. 515.

A.10.a.4. If A is universally measurable in X, and X is quasi- or τ-Radon, so is A. τ-Radon subspaces are universally measurable.

A.10.a.5. For $f: X \to Y$ universally measurable, $\Delta(f)$ (cf. Appendix A.9.d.2) is universally measurable if X is quasi-Radon.

HINT. For $P \in \Delta(\Delta(X))$, find $K_n \in \mathscr{K}^X$ increasing with $\overline{P}(K_n) \to 1$ and $f_{|K_n}$ continuous: then $\mu(K_n) \nearrow 1$ P a.e. By Egorov's theorem (or Appendix A.9.d.3, with $Y = C(\mathbb{N} \cup \{\infty\})$), it follows that $\exists C \in \mathscr{K}^{\Delta(X)}$ s.t. $P(C) \geq 1 - \varepsilon$ and $\mu(K_n)_{|C}$ (is continuous and) converges uniformly to 1. To show the continuity of $[\Delta(f)]_{|C}$, choose F closed in Y: we have to show that $\mu(f^{-1}(F))$ is u.s.c on C. Since $\mu(K_n) \to 1$ uniformly, it suffices to show that $\mu(K_n \cap f^{-1}(F)) = \mu[(f_{|K_n})^{-1}(F)]$ is u.s.c., which follows from the continuity of $f_{|K_n}$.

A.10.a.6. Quasi- or τ-Radon spaces are closed under countable products.

A.10.a.7. For X quasi-Radon, $\beta: P \mapsto \overline{P}$ is a continuous map from $\Delta(\Delta(X))$ to $\Delta(X)$.

A.10.a.8. If X is quasi-Radon or τ-Radon, so is $\Delta(X)$.

HINT. Assume first X τ-Radon, let μ be an appropriate measure on $\Delta(X)$ (i.e., as in the definition, also called a "τ-smooth" measure in the literature). Then $\overline{\mu}$ is appropriate on X, hence $\overline{\mu} \in \Delta(X)$. Choose $C_i \in \mathscr{K}^X$ disjoint with $\overline{\mu}(K_n) \to 1$, where $K_n = \bigcup_{i \leq n} C_i$. By Egorov's theorem, we have thus that, $\forall \varepsilon > 0$, $\exists \delta_n \searrow 0$: $\mu(C) > 1 - \varepsilon$ with $C = \{\nu \in \Delta(X) \mid \nu(K_n) \geq 1 - \delta_n, \forall n\}$. C is compact in $\Delta(X)$, e.g., as the continuous image of the corresponding set on the (locally compact) disjoint union of the C_i's. Hence, by Appendix A.10.a.1, $\mu \in \Delta(\Delta(X))$: $\Delta(X)$ is τ-Radon.

Assume now X quasi-Radon, and fix $P \in \Delta(\Delta(\Delta(X)))$. Then $\overline{P}$ is an appropriate measure on $\Delta(X)$; hence so is $\overline{\overline{P}}$ on X. Also, for the continuous map β of Appendix A.10.a.7 above from $\Delta(\Delta(X))$ to $\Delta(X)$, we have $[\beta \circ (\Delta(\beta))](P) = \overline{\overline{P}}$; compute for each Borel set B. So $\overline{\overline{P}} \in \Delta(X)$. Complete the proof now as in the τ-Radon case, with $\overline{P}$ instead of μ.

A.10.b. A *countably Radon* space is a τ-Radon space with countable base.

A.10.b.1. In a countably Radon space, every probability measure on the Borel sets is regular (use the countable base to show it is appropriate). (Such spaces are called Radon in Bourbaki (1969).)

A.10.b.2. Countably Radon spaces are closed under countable products, and by taking universally measurable subspaces.

A.10.b.3. If X is a countably Radon space, so is $\Delta(X)$, and the Borel σ-field on $\Delta(X)$ is the smallest one that makes the functions $\mu \mapsto \mu(B)$, B Borel in X, measurable.

HINT. A sub-basis for the topology on $\Delta(X)$ are the sets $\{\mu \mid \mu(O) > \alpha\}$ for O open in X. One can then clearly further restrict α to be rational and O to be a finite union of basic open sets in X: $\Delta(X)$ has a countable sub-basis, hence is countably Radon by Appendix A.10.a.8. Another consequence is that every open set, and hence every Borel set, belongs to the σ-field spanned by the sub-basic open sets, hence to the σ-field making all functions $\mu \mapsto \mu(O)$ measurable.

A.10.b.4. If X is countably Radon, there exists a stronger topology with the same Borel sets under which it becomes a universally measurable subset of the Cantor space.

HINT. Declare all basic open sets to be clopen. To show universal measurability of the image, choose μ that gives outer measure 1 to the image: μ induces a probability measure on the space itself, which is regular (Appendix A.10.b.1), hence carried by a $\mathscr{K}_\sigma$-subset, and the compacts are metrizable by the countable basis assumption. Therefore the $\mathscr{K}_\sigma$ is Lusin (Appendix A.5.f, p. 517), and hence (Appendix A.5.e, p. 517) it is Borel in the Cantor space: the image has also μ-inner probability one.

A.10.b.5. A map from a topological space to a countably Radon space is universally measurable iff the inverse image of every Borel set (and hence also of every universally measurable set) is universally measurable.

HINT. Use Appendix A.10.b.4 and Appendix A.9.d.3.

A.10.b.6. If a map from a countably Radon space to a Hausdorff space is universally measurable, then it is still so for any other countably Radon topology with the same universally measurable sets.

HINT. Apply Appendix A.10.b.5 to the identity from the space to itself, and apply Appendix A.9.d.1. Alternatively, observe that such a map is universally measurable iff $f^{-1}(B) \in \mathscr{B}_u$ for every Borel set B and, $\forall \mu \in \Delta(X)$, there exists a union of a sequence of disjoint compact metric subsets that has measure 1 under $f(\mu)$ (an analytic subset would already be sufficient); use Appendix A.5.d the fact that a compact analytic space is metrizable.

Remark A.10.1. By Appendix A.10.b.1, two countably Radon topologies that have the same Borel σ-field also have the same σ-field $\mathscr{B}_u$. Appendix A.10.b.5 and Appendix A.10.b.6 say that, if they have the same $\mathscr{B}_u$, they have the same universally measurable maps to and from all topological spaces. By Appendix A.10.b.1 they have also the same set $\Delta(X)$, with the same universally measurable sets on $\Delta(X)$ (the sets that are μ-measurable for every probability measure μ on $\Delta(X)$ endowed with the σ-field spanned by the maps $P \mapsto P(B)$, for B universally measurable in X). Also, the σ-field $\mathscr{B}_u$ on a countable product depends only on the σ-fields on the factors (recall the countable base).

Remark A.10.2. To make the picture complete, one would still like an example of such a space, which is not countable, and for which there exists no universally measurable isomorphism with $[0, 1]$ (or a theorem to the opposite effect).

Remark A.10.3. The concept is not quite satisfactory in the sense that analytic spaces have the same properties (Appendix A.5.g for Appendix A.10.b.1; use Appendix A.5.d and Appendix A.10.b.1 to prove Appendix A.10.b.5 and hence Appendix A.10.b.6, Appendix A.10.b.2 for closed, or analytic, subspaces is obvious, and use Appendix A.9.e). In addition, they lead to a more restrictive set of measurable spaces (Appendix A.6), so one would have liked a concept here that would include all analytic spaces, just like K-analytic spaces are τ-Radon (Appendix A.10.a.3).

Remark A.10.4. Appendix A.10.b.2, Appendix A.10.b.3, Appendix A.10.b.5, and Appendix A.10.b.6 remain true for "countably quasi-Radon" spaces, and in Appendix A.10.b.4 one would just have to drop the "universally measurable" property.

APPENDIX B

Historical Notes

CHAPTER I

Section I.1 The original proof of Sion's theorem (1958) (Theorem I.1.1 in this volume) uses the KKM lemma (I.4, Ex. 18) in $\mathbb{R}^n$ (which is equivalent to the fixed point theorem). However, Sion wrote "the difficulty lies in the fact that we cannot use a fixed point theorem (due to lack of continuity) nor the separation of disjoint convex sets by a hyperplane (due to lack of convexity)."

Also in Sion's paper is the proof that his theorem implies Fan's theorem (1953) (cf. the remark after Proposition I.2.7).

The proof of Sion's theorem using Lemma I.1.2, as well as the lemma itself and its proof, appears in Berge (1966, p. 220, resp. p. 172). In fact he wrote: "We note that Sion's proof led us to the statement of the intersection theorem." On the other hand, the original proof of the lemma (Berge, 1959) also uses KKM.

A direct proof of Proposition I.1.9 was obtained by Kneser (1952) (all these results are in the Hausdorff case).

A survey and specific results for games on the square can be found in Yanovskaya (1974).

Section I.2 The proof of I.2, Ex. 17 is due to Karamata (cf., e.g., Titchmarsh, 1939, p. 227).

Section I.3 The original finite minmax theorem (I.3, Ex. 1) can be proved by "elementary tools," namely, the theorem of the alternative (von Neumann and Morgenstern, 1944, pp. 138, 154–155) (also Ville, 1938): the iterated elimination of variables implies the existence of optimal strategies (and a fortiori the value) in the ordered field of coefficients. The first analysis in this framework and Theorem I.3.6 are due to Weyl (1950); cf. I.3, Ex. 13. This elementary aspect was used later by Bewley and Kohlberg (1976a) in analyzing stochastic games.

Another elementary proof by induction on the size of the matrix is due to Loomis (1946).

Section I.4 Theorem I.4.1 was proved in the finite case using Kakutani's (1941) fixed point theorem (Nash, 1950) and Brouwer's fixed point theorem in Nash (1951). He constructed explicitly a "strategy-improving mapping" from σ to τ as follows: $\tau_i(s_i) = \{\sigma_i(s_i) + (F^i(s_i, \sigma_{-i}) - F^i(\sigma))^+\}/\{1 + \sum_{t_i \in S_i}(F^i(t_i, \sigma_{-i}) - F^i(\sigma))^+\}$.

Glicksberg (1952) extends Kakutani's theorem and the first proof of Nash and hence obtains Theorem I.4.1. A similar extension of Kakutani's theorem is due to Fan (1952).

I.4, Ex. 17 bears a clear relation with the fixed point theorems of Eilenberg and Montgomery (1946) and Begle (1950). Debreu (1952) uses this result to prove an equilibrium theorem for a game with constraints, namely, where the set of feasible outcomes is a subset of the product of the strategy spaces.

Other related topics include purification of strategies and equilibria (Aumann et al., 1983), ε-equilibria (cf., e.g., Tijs, 1981), and the study by Blume and Zame (1994) of algebraic-geometrical aspects of the manifold (cf. I.4, Ex. 4) of equilibria.

CHAPTER II

Section II.1 The initial definition of Kuhn (1953) extends the approach of von Neumann and Morgenstern (1944, pp. 67–79). In the former, a sequence of dates is associated to the nodes and is public knowledge: hence it is our model of a multistage game, except that only a single player moves at every node. This means that the following is impossible:

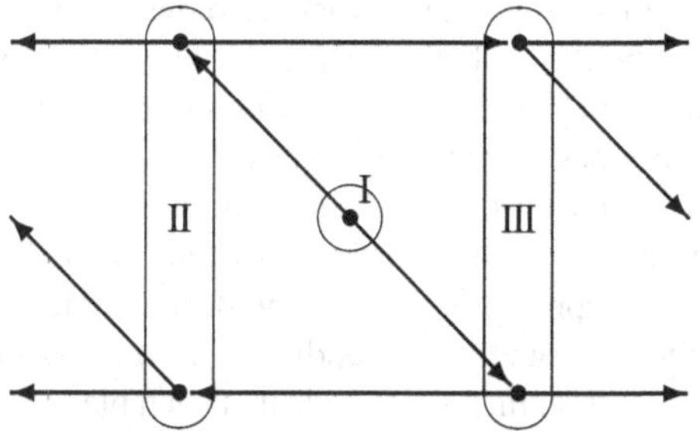

Figure B.1. Perfect recall game that is not multistage.

Isbell's construction (1957) extends Kuhn's definition (which considers only linear games) and essentially corresponds to the notion of the tree described in II.1, Ex. 8 (in the finite case).

An extension of Theorem II.1.3 to the infinite case is in Aumann (1964). Distributional strategies as defined in II.1, Ex. 16c, appear in Milgrom and Weber (1985).

Section II.2 For the use of games with perfect information in descriptive set theory see Jech (cf. 1978, Chapter 7) and Dellacherie et al. (1992, Chapter XXIV).

On topological games, cf. the survey of Telgársky (1987).

Section II.3 Correlated equilibria are due to Aumann (1974). The canonical representation appears explicitly in Aumann (1987) but was known and used before; similar ideas can be found in the framework of coordination mechanisms (cf. Myerson, 1982). Communication equilibria and extensive form correlated equilibria were first introduced in the framework of non-zero-sum repeated games with incomplete information (Forges, 1982b, 1985, 1988b), and then formally defined and studied for themselves in Forges (1986a). They also appear in Myerson (1986).

Section II.4 Blackwell's theorem plays a crucial role in games with incomplete information; cf. Chapters V and VI.

The fact that any set is either weakly approachable or weakly excludable (cf. II.4, Ex. 2) has been proved by Vieille (1992).

The results of II.4, Ex. 8, have been extended to game forms in Abdou and Mertens (1989).

CHAPTER III

Harsanyi (1967, 1968a, 1968b) made precise the difference between games with incomplete information (lack of information about the description of the game) and games with imperfect information (lack of information about the play of the game). In the first framework he remarked that this leads to an infinite hierarchy of beliefs, called the "sequential expectations model." Then he proposed to represent the situation through a consistent probability on the product of the set of types by the set of states, each type being identified with a probability distribution on the product of the other's types and states. He also observed that inconsistent situations may occur. In the first case the above reduction amounts to representing a game with incomplete information as a game with imperfect information, by adding a move of nature. Then several interpretations are possible: the usual one is that each player's type is chosen at random. Another way to look at it is to consider each type as a player, the actual players in the game being chosen at random, one in each "group," according to the initial probability of the types (Selten game).

Böge and Eisele (1979) consider games with unknown utility functions and construct the hierarchy of beliefs under the name "system of complete reflection" (and refer to a previous construction of Böge called the "oracle system"); cf: III.4, Ex. 3b.

The construction of the universal belief space (i.e., part (3) of Theorem III.1.1) is due to Mertens and Zamir (1985), and the content of this paper is the basis of this chapter. They assume that K is compact and proceed as in

III.4, Ex. 2. Further constructions include Brandenburger and Dekel (1993), in the Polish case, and Heifetz (1993), which is similar to the one presented here. The present treatment is the first to offer a characterization (parts (1) and (2) of Theorem III.1.1).

Theorem III.2.4 was given informally in Mertens (1987a). The rest of this chapter is new.

Lemma III.3.2 extends Theorem 2 in Blackwell and Dubins (1962).

Further relations between common knowledge and belief subspaces can be found in Vassilakis and Zamir (1993).

CHAPTER IV

The general model of repeated games appears in Mertens (1987a), and Sections IV.2 and IV.3 are based on this paper. A specific version of Theorem IV.3.2 has been obtained by Armbruster (private communication, 1983).

Section IV.4 The "Folk Theorem" (IV.4.1) was already known in the 1960s by Aumann and Shapley, among others. Theorem IV.4.2 is in Sorin (1986a) (but was probably known before) and so is Proposition IV.4.3.

Most of the results of Section IV.4.b can be found in Lehrer except Proposition IV.4.5. The content of IV.4.b.2 is in Lehrer (1992a), IV.4.b.3 is in Lehrer (1992b), and IV.4.b.4 is in Lehrer (1990).

The notion of subgame (cf. Section IV.1.a) has been emphasized by Selten who introduced the notion of subgame perfection; cf. Selten (1975) and IV.4, Ex. 3–IV.4, Ex. 8.

There has been a large number of papers on refinement of equilibria and their applications to repeated games; cf., e.g., the surveys by Kohlberg (1990) and by van Damme (1992). Somehow the structure of specific, namely, public perfect, equilibrium payoffs in discounted games is easier to characterize (in the spirit of IV.4, Ex. 5); cf. Fudenberg and Levine (1994). IV.5, Ex. 4, is a typical example of "recursive structure" and can be found in Blackwell and Girshick (1954, pp. 69–73).

CHAPTER V

Most of the basic results of this chapter (until Section V.3.c) are introduced and proved by Aumann and Maschler (1966) for the full monitoring case and (1968) for the general case. The construction and proof of Section V.3.d are due to Kohlberg (1975a).

Theorem V.3.1 is new.

Sections V.3.e–V.3.h are new.

Section V.4 is based on the papers of Mertens and Zamir: Theorem V.4.1 from (1976b), Theorem V.4.3 from (1977a), and Section V.4.c from (1995).

The recursive formula (Lemma V.4.2) appears in Zamir (1971–1972).

Section V.5 uses the results of Zamir (1973a) for V.5.a and V.5.b and (1971–1972) for V.5.c.

V.5, Ex. 5 is due to Mertens and V.5, Ex. 7, to Sorin (1979). V.5, Ex. 10, comes in part from Zamir (1971–1972) and (1973b). V.5, Ex. 17, is an extension of Stearns' measure of information (1967).

CHAPTER VI

The basic model and the first results are due to Aumann and Maschler (1967) and Stearns (1967). They considered the independent case with standard signaling and proved Theorem VI.3.1 (existence and computation of the minmax) in this framework. The construction of the strategy exhausting the information (Lemma VI.3.3) is due to Stearns. The extension to the dependent case with a general (state-independent) information structure is due to Mertens and Zamir (1980) and is exposed in Section VI.3.a.

Section VI.3.b is new.

Previously Mertens and Zamir (1971) proved the existence of $\lim v_n$ with standard signaling; then Mertens (1971–1972) proved it for the general case: this is the content of Section VI.4. Corollary VI.4.9 gives a better bound ($n^{1/3}$) on the speed of convergence than the original one ($n^{1/4}$).

Section VI.5 is in Mertens and Zamir (1971) and (1977b).

Part of the results of Section VI.7 can be found in Mertens and Zamir (1981). Example VI.7.4 is in Mertens and Zamir (1971, example 8.5).

VI.7, Ex. 6, is due to Ponssard and Sorin (1980a,b). VI.7, Ex. 7, comes from Sorin (1979) (cf. also Ponssard and Zamir, 1973) and Ponssard and Sorin (1982). VI.7, Ex. 8, comes from Sorin and Zamir (1985).

The material in VI.7, Ex. 9, can be found in Mertens and Zamir (1977b) and Sorin (1984b) for the dependent case.

CHAPTER VII

Section VII.1 Stochastic games were introduced by Shapley (1953) who considered the finite two-person zero-sum case with a strictly positive probability of stopping the game in each state. He proves the existence of a value and of optimal stationary strategies; the result, which basically corresponds to the discounted case, was then extended by Takahashi (1962), Parthasarathy (1973), Couwenbergh (1980), and Nowak (1985a), among others.

The non-zero-sum discounted case was studied by Fink (1964), Takahashi (1964), Federgruen (1978), and Sobel (1971). For a survey cf. Parthasarathy and Stern (1977) and Parthasarathy (1984).

The existence of stationary optimal strategies is still an open problem; cf. Nowak and Raghavan (1992) and Parthasarathy and Sinha (1989). For ε-equilibria cf. Rieder (1979), Whitt (1980), and Nowak (1985b); they basically use approximation by games that do have stationary equilibria.

The content of VII.1.c is due to Mertens and Parthasarathy (2003) and (1991).

Section VII.2 The first papers devoted to the asymptotic analysis developed in this section are due to Bewley and Kohlberg (1976a). They worked in the field of Puiseux series to get Theorem VII.2.3, in the spirit of Theorem I.3.6.

For similar results concerning the limit of finite games, cf. VII.4, Ex. 2, and VII.4, Ex. 6, and (Bewley and Kohlberg, 1976b).

Section VII.3 The non-discounted case was introduced by Everett (1957) who proves the existence of a value in the irreducible case (VII.4, Ex. 10) (cf. also Hoffman and Karp, 1966, and, in the perfect information case, Liggett and Lippman, 1969), and suggests an example that was later solved by Blackwell and Ferguson (1968). The ideas introduced for studying this game ("Big Match," VII.4, Ex. 4) were extensively used in further work: existence of the value for games with absorbing states (Kohlberg, 1974), and finally in the general case. This is the content of Section VII.3 and is due to Mertens and Neyman (1981). Some of the results of Section VII.3.d can be found in Bewley and Kohlberg (1978) and Vrieze et al. (1983).

The content of Section VII.4.a is in Sorin (1986b), and that of Section VII.4.b in Vrieze and Thuijsman (1989).

Part of VII.4, Ex. 9, was in some unpublished notes of Neyman.

More recent results on dynamic programming problems can be found in Lehrer and Monderer (1994), Lehrer and Sorin (1992), Monderer and Sorin (1993), and Lehrer (1993).

CHAPTER VIII

Section VIII.1 is due to Forges (1982a) after a first proof in the deterministic case in Kohlberg and Zamir (1974).

Section VIII.2 corresponds to a class introduced by Mertens and Zamir (1976a) and solved for the minmax and maxmin in a specific 2×2 case. This result was generalized by Waternaux (1983a) to all 2×2 games, and then to the general case (1983b). This is the content of VIII.2.c. (The (1983a) paper contains also a more precise description of optimal strategies.)

Part VIII.2.d is due to Sorin (1989).

Section VIII.3 follows Sorin (1985b), and the content of Section VIII.4 can be found in Sorin (1984a, 1985a) and Sorin and Zamir (1991).

CHAPTER IX

The first approach to non-zero-sum games with lack of information on one side is due to Aumann et al. (1968). They introduced the notions of joint plan and of jointly controlled lottery.

They gave a sufficient condition for equilibria as in Proposition IX.1.1 with condition (3) replaced by the stronger condition $a^k(r) = \overline{a}^k$. They also exhibited examples of equilibrium payoffs that require several stages of signaling.

The content of IX.1.a is in Sorin (1983).

Section IX.1.b follows Hart (1985).

The content of Section IX.2 is taken from Aumann and Hart (1986). The results of Section IX.3 are due to Forges (1988a). More precise results concerning a specific class (information transmission game) can be found in Forges (1985): the set of communication equilibrium payoffs equals the set of (normal form) correlated equilibrium payoffs. For a parallel study in the Selten representation, cf. Forges (1986b).

APPENDIX C

Bibliography

J. Abdou and J.-F. Mertens. Correlated effectivity functions. *Economic Letters*, 30: 97–101, 1989.

D. Abreu. On the theory of infinitely repeated games with discounting. *Econometrica*, 56:383–396, 1988.

D. Abreu, D. Pearce, and E. Stachetti. Towards a theory of discounted repeated games with imperfect monitoring. *Econometrica*, 58:1041–1063, 1990.

L. V. Ahlfors. *Complex Analysis*. McGraw Hill, 1953.

W. Armbruster. Repeated games with unkown utility function. In O. Moeschlin and D. Pallaschke, editors, *Game Theory and Mathematical Economics*, pages 15–26. North-Holland, 1981.

W. Armbruster and W. Böge. Bayesian game theory. In Moeschlin and Pallaschke (1979), pages 17–28.

K. J. Arrow, E. W. Barankin, and D. Blackwell. Admissible points of convex sets. In Kuhn and Tucker (1953), pages 87–91.

R. J. Aumann. Acceptable points in general cooperative n-person games. In Tucker and Luce (1959), pages 287–324.

R. J. Aumann. Acceptable points in games of perfect information. *Pacific Journal of Mathematics*, 10:381–417, 1960.

R. J. Aumann. Almost strictly competitive games. *Journal of the Society for Industrial and Applied Mathematics*, 9:544–550, 1961a.

R. J. Aumann. The core of a cooperative game without side payments. *Transactions of the American Mathematical Society*, 98:539–552, 1961b.

R. J. Aumann. Mixed and behavior strategies in infinite extensive games. In Dresher et al. (1964), pages 627–650.

R. J. Aumann. A survey of cooperative games without side payments. In M. Shubik, editor, *Essays in Mathematical Economics in Honor of Oskar Morgenstern*, pages 3–27. Princeton University Press, 1967.

R. J. Aumann. Subjectivity and correlation in randomized strategies. *Journal of Mathematical Economics*, 1:67–96, 1974.

R. J. Aumann. Agreeing to disagree. *Annals of Statistics*, 4:1236–1239, 1976.

R. J. Aumann. Repeated games. In G. R. Feiwel, editor, *Issues in Contemporary Microeconomics and Welfare*, pages 209–242. Macmillan, 1985.

R. J. Aumann. Correlated equilibrium as an expression of Bayesian rationality. *Econometrica*, 55:1–18, 1987.

R. J. Aumann and S. Hart. Bi-convexity and bi-martingales. *Israel Journal of Mathematics*, 54:159–180, 1986.

R. J. Aumann and S. Hart, editors. *Handbook of Game Theory (with Economic Applications), Vol. 1*. North-Holland, 1992.

R. J. Aumann and S. Hart, editors. *Handbook of Game Theory (with Economic Applications), Vol. 2*. North-Holland, 1994.

R. J. Aumann and S. Hart, editors. *Handbook of Game Theory (with Economic Applications), Vol. 3*. North-Holland, 2002.

R. J. Aumann and M. B. Maschler. Game theoretic aspects of gradual disarmament. In *ACDA Final Report ST-80*, Mathematica (1966), Chapter V, pages V1–V55. Re-edited as Ch. I in Aumann and Maschler (1995).

R. J. Aumann and M. B. Maschler. Repeated games with incomplete information: A survey of recent results. In *ACDA Final Report ST-116*, Mathematica (1967), Chapter III, pages 287–403. Re-edited as Ch. II in Aumann and Maschler (1995).

R. J. Aumann and M. B. Maschler. Repeated games of incomplete information: The zero-sum extensive case. In *ACDA Final Report ST-143*, Mathematica (1968), Chapter III, pages 37–116. Re-edited as Ch. IV in Aumann and Maschler (1995).

R. J. Aumann and M. B. Maschler, with the collaboration of R. E. Stearns. *Repeated Games with Incomplete Information*. MIT Press, 1995.

R. J. Aumann and L. S. Shapley. Long term competition: A game theoretic analysis. In N. Megiddo, editor, *Essays in Game Theory: In Honor of Michael Maschler*, pages 1–15. Springer-Verlag, 1994.

R. J. Aumann and S. Sorin. Cooperation and bounded recall. *Games and Economic Behavior*, 1:5–39, 1989.

R. J. Aumann, M. B. Maschler, and R. E. Stearns. Repeated games of incomplete information: An approach to the non-zero-sum case. In *ACDA Final Report ST-143*, Mathematica (1968), Chapter IV, pages 117–216. Re-edited as Ch. V in Aumann and Maschler (1995).

R. J. Aumann, Y. Katznelson, R. Radner, R. W. Rosenthal, and B. Weiss. Approximate purification of mixed strategies. *Mathematics of Operations Research*, 8:327–341, 1983.

R. Axelrod. *The Evolution of Cooperation*. Basic Books, 1984.

I. Barany. Fair distribution protocols or how the players replace fortune. *Mathematics of Operations Research*, 17:327–340, 1992.

R. A. Becker, J. H. Boyd, and B. Y. Sung. Recursive utility and optimal capital accumulation. I. Existence. *Journal of Economic Theory*, 47:76–100, 1989.

E. G. Begle. A fixed point theorem. *Annals of Mathematics*, 51:544–550, 1950.

J.-P. Benoît and V. Krishna. Finitely repeated games. *Econometrica*, 53:905–922, 1985.

J.-P. Benoît and V. Krishna. Nash equilibria of finitely repeated games. *International Journal of Game Theory*, 16:197–204, 1987.

C. Berge. Sur une propriété combinatoire des ensembles convexes. *Comptes Rendus de l'Académie des Sciences*, 248:2698–2699, 1959.

C. Berge. *Espaces Topologiques, Fonctions Multivoques*. Dunod, 1966.

J. Bergin. A characterization of sequential equilibrium strategies in infinitely repeated incomplete information games. *Journal of Economic Theory*, 47:51–65, 1989.

J. Bergin. Player type distributions as state variables and information revelation in zero-sum repeated games with discounting. *Mathematics of Operations Research*, 17:640–656, 1992.

T. Bewley and E. Kohlberg. The asymptotic theory of stochastic games. *Mathematics of Operations Research*, 1:197–208, 1976a.

T. Bewley and E. Kohlberg. The asymptotic solution of a recursion equation occurring in stochastic games. *Mathematics of Operations Research*, 1:321–336, 1976b.

T. Bewley and E. Kohlberg. On stochastic games with stationary optimal strategies. *Mathematics of Operations Research*, 3:104–125, 1978.

B. J. Birch. On games with almost complete information. *Journal of the Cambridge Philosophical Society*, 51:275–287, 1955.

D. Blackwell. On randomization in statistical games with k terminal actions. In Kuhn and Tucker (1953), pages 183–187.

D. Blackwell. An analog of the minmax theorem for vector payoffs. *Pacific Journal of Mathematics*, 6:1–8, 1956a.

D. Blackwell. Controlled random walks. In J. De Groot and J. C. H. Gerretsen, editors, *Proceedings of the International Congress of Mathematicians 1954 (Amsterdam; September 2–9, 1954)*, Volume 3, pages 336–338. Erven P. Noordhoff N.V., 1956b.

D. Blackwell. Discrete dynamic programming. *Annals of Mathematical Statistics*, 33: 719–726, 1962.

D. Blackwell. Discounted dynamic programming. *Annals of Mathematical Statistics*, 36:226–235, 1965.

D. Blackwell. Infinite games and analytic sets. *Proceedings of the National Academy of Sciences of the U.S.A.*, 58:1836–1837, 1967a.

D. Blackwell. Positive dynamic programming. In Le Cam and Neyman (1967), pages 415–418.

D. Blackwell. Infinite G_δ-games with imperfect information. *Applicationes Mathematicae*, X:99–101, 1969.

D. Blackwell. On stationary policies. *Journal of the Royal Statistical Society. Series A*, 133:33–37, 1970.

D. Blackwell. Borel sets via games. *Annals of Probability*, 9:321–322, 1981.

D. Blackwell. Operator solution of infinite G_δ-games of imperfect information. In K. B. Athreya, D. L. Iglehart, and T. W. Anderson, editors, *Probability, Statistics and Mathematics. Papers in Honor of Samuel Karlin*, pages 83–87. Academic Press, 1989.

D. Blackwell and L. E. Dubins. Merging of opinions with increasing information. *Annals of Mathematical Statistics*, 33:882–886, 1962.

D. Blackwell and T. S. Ferguson. The big match. *Annals of Mathematical Statistics*, 39: 159–163, 1968.

D. Blackwell and M. A. Girshick. *Theory of Games and Statistical Decisions*. John Wiley & Sons, 1954.

D. Blackwell, D. Freedman, and M. Orkin. The optimal reward operator in dynamic programming. *Annals of Probability*, 2:926–941, 1974.

L. Blume and W. R. Zame. The algebraic geometry of perfect and sequential equilibria. *Econometrica*, 62:783–794, 1994.

W. Böge and T. Eisele. On solutions of Bayesian games. *International Journal of Game Theory*, 8:193–215, 1979.

H. F. Bohnenblust, S. Karlin, and L. S. Shapley. Solutions of discrete two-person games. In Kuhn and Tucker (1950), pages 51–72.

N. Bourbaki. *Eléments de Mathématique,* Livre VI: *Intégration,* Chapitre IX: *Intégration sur les espaces topologiques séparés*. Hermann, 1969.

A. Brandenburger and E. Dekel. Hierarchies of beliefs and common knowledge. *Journal of Economic Theory*, 59:189–198, 1993.

C. Castaing and M. Valadier. *Convex Analysis and Measurable Multifunctions*. Lecture Notes in Mathematics, 580. Springer-Verlag, 1977.

G. Choquet. *Lectures on Analysis*. W. A. Benjamin, 1969.

J.-M. Coulomb. Repeated games with absorbing states and no signals. *International Journal of Game Theory*, 21:161–174, 1992.

H. A. M. Couwenbergh. Stochastic games with metric state space. *International Journal of Game Theory*, 9:25–36, 1980.

N. Dalkey. Equivalence of information patterns and essentially determinate games. In Kuhn and Tucker (1953), pages 217–243.

P. Dasgupta and E. Maskin. The existence of equilibrium in discontinuous economic games, I: Theory. *Review of Economic Studies*, LIII:1–26, 1986.

M. Davis. Infinite games of perfect information. In Dresher et al. (1964), pages 85–101.

B. De Meyer. Repeated games and partial differential equations. *Mathematics of Operations Research*, 21:209–236, 1996a.

B. De Meyer. Repeated games, duality and the central limit theorem. *Mathematics of Operations Research*, 21:237–251, 1996b.

G. Debreu. A social equilibrium existence theorem. *Proceedings of the National Academy of Sciences of the U.S.A.*, 38:886–893, 1952.

C. Dellacherie. Capacités, rabotages et ensembles analytiques. *Séminaire d'initiation à l'analyse*, 19, 1980. Édité par G. Choquet, J. Rogalski et J. Saint-Raymond, Université P. et M. Curie, Paris.

C. Dellacherie, B. Maisonneuve, and P.-A. Meyer. *Probabilités et potentiel V*. Hermann, 1992. Processus de Markov (fin). Compléments de calcul stochastique. Chapitres XVII á XXIV.

M. Dresher and S. Karlin. Solutions of convex games as fixed points. In Kuhn and Tucker (1953), pages 75–86.

M. Dresher, L. S. Shapley, and A. W. Tucker, editors. *Advances in Game Theory*. Annals of Mathematics Studies, 52. Princeton University Press, 1964.

M. Dresher, A. W. Tucker, and P. Wolfe, editors. *Contributions to the Theory of Games, Vol. III*. Annals of Mathematics Studies, 39. Princeton University Press, 1957.

L. E. Dubins. A discrete evasion game. In Dresher et al. (1957), pages 231–255.

L. E. Dubins and L. J. Savage. *How to Gamble If You Must. Inequalities for Stochastic Processes*. McGraw Hill, 1965. Second edition under title: *Inequalities for Stochastic Processes*. Dover, 1976.

R. M. Dudley. Distances of probability measures and random variables. *Annals of Mathematical Statistics*, 39:1563–1572, 1968.

D. Duffie, J. Geanakoplos, A. Mas-Colell, and A. McLennan. Stationary Markov equilibria. *Econometrica*, 62:745–781, 1994.

N. Dunford and J. T. Schwartz. *Linear Operators*, Volume 1. Interscience Publishers, 1958.

J. Eatwell, M. Milgate, and P. Newman, editors. *The New Palgrave Dictionary of Economics*. Macmillan Press, 1987.

R. E. Edwards. *Functional Analysis*. Holt, Rinehart and Winston, 1965.

S. Eilenberg and S. D. Montgomery. Fixed point theorems for multi-valued transformations. *American Journal of Mathematics*, 68:214–222, 1946.

H. Everett. Recursive games. In Dresher et al. (1957), pages 47–78.

K. Fan. Fixed point and minimax theorems in locally convex topological linear spaces. *Proceedings of the National Academy of Sciences of the U.S.A.*, 38:121–126, 1952.

K. Fan. Minimax theorems. *Proceedings of the National Academy of Sciences of the U.S.A.*, 39:42–47, 1953.

A. Federgruen. On N-person stochastic games with denumerable state space. *Advances in Applied Probability*, 10:452–471, 1978.

W. Feller. *An Introduction to Probability Theory and Its Applications*, Volume 2. John Wiley & Sons, 1966.

T. S. Ferguson. On discrete evasion games with a two-move information lag. In Le Cam and Neyman (1967), pages 453–462.

T. S. Ferguson and L. S. Shapley. On a game of Gleason. Private communication, 1986.

T. S. Ferguson, L. S. Shapley, and R. Weber. Notes on a stochastic game with information structure. *International Journal of Game Theory*, 31:223–228, 2003.

A. M. Fink. Equilibrium in a stochastic n-person game. *Journal of Science of the Hiroshima University. Ser. A.I. Mathematics*, 28:89–93, 1964.

F. Forges. Infinitely repeated games of incomplete information: Symmetric case with random signals. *International Journal of Game Theory*, 11:203–213, 1982a.

F. Forges. A first study of correlated equilibria in repeated games with incomplete information. Discussion Paper 8218, CORE, Université Catholique de Louvain, Louvain-la-Neuve, Belgium, 1982b.

F. Forges. Note on Nash equilibria in infinitely repeated games with incomplete information. *International Journal of Game Theory*, 13:179–187, 1984.

F. Forges. Correlated equilibria in a class of repeated games with incomplete information. *International Journal of Game Theory*, 14:129–150, 1985.

F. Forges. An approach to communication equilibria. *Econometrica*, 54:1375–1385, 1986a.

F. Forges. Correlated equilibria in repeated games with lack of information on one side: A model with verifiable types. *International Journal of Game Theory*, 15:65–82, 1986b.

F. Forges. Communication equilibria in repeated games with incomplete information. *Mathematics of Operations Research*, 13:191–231, 1988a.

F. Forges. Can sunspots replace a mediator? *Journal of Mathematical Economics*, 17: 347–368, 1988b.

F. Forges. Equilibria with communication in a job market example. *Quarterly Journal of Economics*, 105:375–398, 1990a.

F. Forges. Correlated equilibrium in two-person zero-sum games. *Econometrica*, 58: 515–516, 1990b.

F. Forges. Universal mechanisms. *Econometrica*, 58:1341–1364, 1990c.

F. Forges. Repeated games of incomplete information: Non-zero-sum. In Aumann and Hart (1992), Chapter 6, pages 155–177.

F. Forges, J.-F. Mertens, and A. Neyman. A counterexample to the folk theorem with discounting. *Economic Letters*, 20:7, 1986.

J. W. Friedman. *Oligopoly and the Theory of Games*. North-Holland, 1977.

D. Fudenberg and D. Levine. Subgame-perfect equilibria of finite- and infinite-horizon games. *Journal of Economic Theory*, 31:251–268, 1983.

D. Fudenberg and D. Levine. An approximate folk theorem with imperfect private information. *Journal of Economic Theory*, 54:26–47, 1991.

D. Fudenberg and D. Levine. Efficiency and observability with long-run and short-run players. *Journal of Economic Theory*, 62:103–135, 1994.

D. Fudenberg and E. Maskin. The folk theorem in repeated games with discounting and with incomplete information. *Econometrica*, 54:533–554, 1986.

D. Fudenberg and E. Maskin. On the dispensability of public randomization in discounted repeated games. *Journal of Economic Theory*, 53:428–438, 1991.

D. Fudenberg, D. M. Kreps, and E. Maskin. Repeated games with long-run and short-run players. *Review of Economic Studies*, LVII:555–573, 1990.

D. Gale. The closed linear model of production. In Kuhn and Tucker (1956), pages 285–303.

D. Gale and F. M. Stewart. Infinite games with perfect information. In Kuhn and Tucker (1953), pages 245–266.

D. Gillette. Stochastic games with zero stop probabilities. In Dresher et al. (1957), pages 179–187.

A. M. Gleason. Unpublished example. Oral tradition, 1949.

I. Glicksberg. A further generalization of the Kakutani fixed point theorem, with application to Nash equilibrium points. *Proceedings of the American Mathematical Society*, 3:170–174, 1952.

I. Glicksberg and O. Gross. Notes on games over the square. In Kuhn and Tucker (1953), pages 173–182.

O. Gross. A rational game on the square. In Dresher et al. (1957), pages 307–311.

A. Grothendieck. Sur les applications linéaires faiblement compactes d'espaces du type $C(K)$. *Canadian Journal of Mathematics*, 5:129–173, 1953.

J. Hannan. Approximation to Bayes risk in repeated play. In Dresher et al. (1957), pages 97–139.

J. C. Harsanyi. Games with incomplete information played by "Bayesian" players, part I. *Management Science*, 14:159–182, 1967.

J. C. Harsanyi. Games with incomplete information played by "Bayesian" players, part II. *Management Science*, 14:320–334, 1968a.

J. C. Harsanyi. Games with incomplete information played by "Bayesian" players, part III. *Management Science*, 14:486–502, 1968b.

S. Hart. Nonzero-sum two-person repeated games with incomplete information. *Mathematics of Operations Research*, 10:117–153, 1985.

S. Hart and D. Schmeidler. Existence of correlated equilibria. *Mathematics of Operations Research*, 14:18–25, 1989.

A. Heifetz. The Bayesian formulation of incomplete information: The non-compact case. *International Journal of Game Theory*, 21:329–338, 1993.

M. Heuer. Optimal strategies for the uninformed player. *International Journal of Game Theory*, 20:33–51, 1991a.

M. Heuer. Asymptotically optimal strategies in repeated games with incomplete information. *International Journal of Game Theory*, 20:377–392, 1991b.

A. J. Hoffman and R. M. Karp. On non-terminating stochastic games. *Management Science*, 12:359–370, 1966.

T. Ichiishi, A. Neyman, and Y. Tauman, editors. *Game Theory and Applications*. Economic Theory, Econometrics, and Mathematical Economics. Academic Press, 1990.

A. Ionescu Tulcea and C. Ionescu Tulcea. *Topics in the Theory of Lifting*. Springer-Verlag, 1969.

J. R. Isbell. Finitary games. In Dresher et al. (1957), pages 79–96.

E. Israeli. Sowing doubt optimally in two-person repeated games. *Games and Economic Behavior*, 28:203–216, 1999.

N. Jacobson. *Lectures in Abstract Algebra*, Volume III. D. Van Nostrand Company, 1964.

T. Jech. *Set Theory*. Academic Press, 1978.

S. Kakutani. A generalization of Brouwer's fixed point theorem. *Duke Mathematical Journal*, 8:457–459, 1941.

S. Karlin. Operator treatment of minmax principle. In Kuhn and Tucker (1950), pages 133–154.

S. Karlin. An infinite move game with a lag. In Dresher et al. (1957), pages 257–272.

S. Karlin. *Mathematical Methods and Theory in Games, Programming, and Economics (2 Volumes)*. Addison Wesley, 1959.

J. L. Kelley. *General Topology*. D. Van Nostrand Company, 1955.

J. L. Kelley, I. Namioka et al. *Linear Topological Spaces*. D. Van Nostrand Company, 1963.

H. Kneser. Sur un théorème fondamental de la théorie des jeux. *Comptes Rendus de l'Académie des Sciences*, 234:2418–2420, 1952.

E. Kohlberg. Repeated games with absorbing states. *Annals of Statistics*, 2:724–738, 1974.

E. Kohlberg. Optimal strategies in repeated games with incomplete information. *International Journal of Game Theory*, 4:7–24, 1975a.

E. Kohlberg. The information revealed in infinitely-repeated games of incomplete information. *International Journal of Game Theory*, 4:57–59, 1975b.

E. Kohlberg. Refinement of Nash equilibrium: The main ideas. In Ichiishi et al. (1990), pages 3–45.

E. Kohlberg and J.-F. Mertens. On the strategic stability of equilibria. *Econometrica*, 54:1003–1037, 1986.

E. Kohlberg and A. Neyman. Asymptotic behavior of nonexpansive mappings in normed linear spaces. *Israel Journal of Mathematics*, 38:269–275, 1981.

E. Kohlberg and S. Zamir. Repeated games of incomplete information: The symmetric case. *Annals of Statistics*, 2:1040–1041, 1974.

G. Koren. Two-person repeated games where players know their own payoffs. Mimeo, 1992.

D. M. Kreps and E. L. Porteus. Dynamic choice theory and dynamic programming. *Econometrica*, 47:91–100, 1979.

D. M. Kreps and R. Wilson. Reputation and imperfect information. *Journal of Economic Theory*, 27:253–279, 1982a.

D. M. Kreps and R. Wilson. Sequential equilibria. *Econometrica*, 50:863–894, 1982b.

D. M. Kreps, J. Roberts, P. Milgrom, and R. Wilson. Rational cooperation in the finitely repeated prisoners' dilemma. *Journal of Economic Theory*, 27:245–252, 1982.

H. W. Kuhn. *Lectures on the Theory of Games*. Annals of Mathematics Studies, 37. Princeton University Press, 1952.

H. W. Kuhn. Extensive games and the problem of information. In Kuhn and Tucker (1953), pages 193–216.

H. W. Kuhn and A. W. Tucker, editors. *Contributions to the Theory of Games, Vol. I*. Annals of Mathematics Studies, 24. Princeton University Press, 1950.

H. W. Kuhn and A. W. Tucker, editors. *Contributions to the Theory of Games, Vol. II*. Annals of Mathematics Studies, 28. Princeton University Press, 1953.

H. W. Kuhn and A. W. Tucker, editors. *Linear Inequalities and Related Systems*. Annals of Mathematics Studies, 38. Princeton University Press, 1956.

L. M. Le Cam and J. Neyman, editors. *Proceedings of the Fifth Berkeley Symposium on Mathematical Statistics and Probability*, 1967. University of California Press.

E. Lehrer. A note on the monotonicity of v_n. *Economic Letters*, 23:341–342, 1987.

E. Lehrer. Lower equilibrium payoffs in two-player repeated games with non-observable actions. *International Journal of Game Theory*, 18:57–89, 1989.

E. Lehrer. Nash equilibria of n-player repeated games with semi-standard information. *International Journal of Game Theory*, 19:191–217, 1990.

E. Lehrer. Internal correlation in repeated games. *International Journal of Game Theory*, 19:431–456, 1991.

E. Lehrer. Correlated equilibria in two-player repeated games with nonobservable actions. *Mathematics of Operations Research*, 17:175–199, 1992a.

E. Lehrer. Two-player repeated games with nonobservable actions and observable payoffs. *Mathematics of Operations Research*, 17:200–224, 1992b.

E. Lehrer. On the equilibrium payoffs set of two-player repeated games with imperfect monitoring. *International Journal of Game Theory*, 20:211–226, 1992c.

E. Lehrer. Bounded variation of V_n and its limit. *International Journal of Game Theory*, 22:31–42, 1993.

E. Lehrer and D. Monderer. Discounting versus averaging in dynamic programming. *Games and Economic Behavior*, 6:97–113, 1994.

E. Lehrer and S. Sorin. A uniform Tauberian theorem in dynamic programming. *Mathematics of Operations Research*, 17:303–307, 1992.

C. E. Lemke and J. T. Howson. Equilibrium points of bimatrix games. *Journal of SIAM*, 12:413–423, 1964.

T. Liggett and S. Lippman. Stochastic games with perfect information and time average payoff. *SIAM Review*, 11:604–607, 1969.

L. H. Loomis. On a theorem of Von Neumann. *Proceedings of the National Academy of Sciences of the U.S.A.*, 32:213–215, 1946.

D. Luce and H. Raiffa. *Games and Decisions*. John Wiley & Sons, 1957.

A. Maitra and T. Parthasarathy. On stochastic games. *Journal of Optimization Theory and Applications*, 5:289–300, 1970.

A. Maitra and W. Sudderth. An operator solution of stochastic games. *Israel Journal of Mathematics*, 78:33–49, 1992.

A. Maitra and W. Sudderth. Borel stochastic games with $\limsup$ payoff. *Annals of Probability*, 21:861–885, 1993.

D. A. Martin. Borel determinacy. *Annals of Mathematics*, 102:363–371, 1975.

D. A. Martin. A purely inductive proof of Borel determinacy. In A. Nerode and R. A. Shore, editors, *Recursion Theory*, Proceedings of Symposia in Pure Mathematics, 42, pages 303–308. American Mathematical Society, 1985.

Mathematica, Game theoretical aspects of disarmament – ACDA final report ST-80. Technical report, U.S. Arms Control and Disarmament Agency, Princeton, New Jersey, 1966.

Mathematica, Models of gradual reduction of arms – ACDA final report ST-116. Technical report, U.S. Arms Control and Disarmament Agency, Princeton, New Jersey, 1967.

Mathematica, The indirect measurement of utility – ACDA final report ST-143. Technical report, U.S. Arms Control and Disarmament Agency, Princeton, New Jersey, 1968.

J. P. Mayberry. Discounted repeated games with incomplete information. In *ACDA Final Report ST-116*, Mathematica (1967), pages 435–461. Chapter V.

N. Megiddo. On repeated games with incomplete information played by non-Bayesian players. *International Journal of Game Theory*, 9:157–167, 1980.

C. A. Melolidakis. On stochastic games with lack of information on one side. *International Journal of Game Theory*, 18:1–29, 1989.

J.-F. Mertens. The value of two-person zero-sum repeated games: The extensive case. *International Journal of Game Theory*, 1:217–227, 1971–1972.

J.-F. Mertens. Note on "The value of two-person zero-sum repeated games: The extensive case." *International Journal of Game Theory*, 2:231–234, 1973.

J.-F. Mertens. A note on the characteristic function of supergames. *International Journal of Game Theory*, 9:189–190, 1980.

J.-F. Mertens. Repeated games: An overview of the zero-sum case. In W. Hildenbrand, editor, *Advances in Economic Theory*, Econometric Society Monographs in Quantitative Economics, 1, pages 175–182. Cambridge University Press, 1982.

J.-F. Mertens. The minmax theorem for u.s.c.-l.s.c. payoff functions. *International Journal of Game Theory*, 15:237–250, 1986.

J.-F. Mertens. Repeated games. In A. M. Gleason, editor, *Proceedings of the International Congress of Mathematicians*, pages 1528–1577. American Mathematical Society, 1987a.

J.-F. Mertens. Repeated games. In Eatwell et al. (1987), pages 151–153.

J.-F. Mertens. Supergames. In Eatwell et al. (1987), pages 551–553.

J.-F. Mertens. Stochastic games. In Aumann and Hart (2002), pages 1809–1832.

J.-F. Mertens. A measurable "measurable choice" theorem. In A. Neyman and S. Sorin, editors, *Stochastic Games and Applications*, NATO Science Series C, pages 107–130, 2003.

J.-F. Mertens and A. Neyman. Stochastic games. Discussion Paper 8001, CORE, Université Catholique de Louvain, Louvain-la-Neuve, Belgium, 1980.

J.-F. Mertens and A. Neyman. Stochastic games. *International Journal of Game Theory*, 10:53–66, 1981.

J.-F. Mertens and A. Neyman. Stochastic games have a value. *Proceedings of the National Academy of Sciences of the U.S.A.*, 79:2145–2146, 1982.

J.-F. Mertens and T. Parthasarathy. Nonzero-sum stochastic games. In Raghavan et al. (1991), pages 145–148.

J.-F. Mertens and T. Parthasarathy. Equilibria for discounted stochastic games. In A. Neyman and S. Sorin, editors, *Stochastic Games and Applications*, NATO Science Series C, pages 131–172, 2003.

J.-F. Mertens and S. Zamir. The value of two-person zero-sum repeated games with lack of information on both sides. *International Journal of Game Theory*, 1:39–64, 1971.

J.-F. Mertens and S. Zamir. On a repeated game without a recursive structure. *International Journal of Game Theory*, 5:173–182, 1976a.

J.-F. Mertens and S. Zamir. The normal distribution and repeated games. *International Journal of Game Theory*, 5:187–197, 1976b.

J.-F. Mertens and S. Zamir. The maximal variation of a bounded martingale. *Israel Journal of Mathematics*, 27:252–276, 1977a.

J.-F. Mertens and S. Zamir. A duality theorem on a pair of simultaneous functional equations. *Journal of Mathematical Analysis and Applications*, 60:550–558, 1977b.

J.-F. Mertens and S. Zamir. Minmax and maxmin of repeated games with incomplete information. *International Journal of Game Theory*, 9:201–215, 1980.

J.-F. Mertens and S. Zamir. Incomplete information games with transcendental values. *Mathematics of Operations Research*, 6:313–318, 1981.

J.-F. Mertens and S. Zamir. Formulation of Bayesian analysis for games with incomplete information. *International Journal of Game Theory*, 14:1–29, 1985.

J.-F. Mertens and S. Zamir. Incomplete information games and the normal distribution. Discussion Paper 9520, CORE, Université Catholique de Louvain, Louvain-la-Neuve, Belgium, 1995.

P.-A. Meyer. *Probabilités et Potentiel*. Hermann, 1966.

P.-A. Meyer. Limites médiales, d'après Mokobodzki. In C. Dellacherie, P.-A. Meyer, and M. Weil, editors, *Séminaire de Probabilités VII. Université de Strasbourg*, Lecture Notes in Mathematics, 321, pages 198–204. Springer-Verlag, 1973.

P. Milgrom and J. Roberts. Limit pricing and entry under incomplete information: An equilibrium analysis. *Econometrica*, 50:443–459, 1982a.

P. Milgrom and J. Roberts. Predation, reputation and entry deterrence. *Journal of Economic Theory*, 27:280–312, 1982b.

P. Milgrom and R. Weber. Distributional strategies for games with incomplete information. *Mathematics of Operations Research*, 10:619–632, 1985.

H. D. Mills. Marginal values of matrix games and linear programs. In Kuhn and Tucker (1956), pages 183–193.

J. W. Milnor. *Topology from the Differentiable Viewpoint*. The University Press of Virginia, 1969.

J. W. Milnor and L. S. Shapley. On games of survival. In Dresher et al. (1957), pages 15–45.

O. Moeschlin and D. Pallaschke, editors. *Game Theory and Related Topics*. North-Holland, 1979.

D. Monderer and S. Sorin. Asymptotic properties in dynamic programming. *International Journal of Game Theory*, 22:1–11, 1993.

Y. N. Moschovakis. *Descriptive Set Theory*. North-Holland, 1980.

R. B. Myerson. Optimal coordination mechanisms in generalized principal-agent problems. *Journal of Mathematical Economics*, 10:67–81, 1982.

R. B. Myerson. Multistage games with communication. *Econometrica*, 54:323–358, 1986.

J. Nash. Equilibrium points in n-person games. *Proceedings of the National Academy of Sciences of the U.S.A.*, 36:48–49, 1950.

J. Nash. Non-cooperative games. *Annals of Mathematical Statistics*, 54:286–295, 1951.

D. Naudé. Correlated equilibria with semi-standard information. Mimeo, 1991.

J. Neveu. *Bases Mathématiques du Calcul des Probabilités*. Masson et Cie, 1970.

J. Neveu. *Martingales à Temps Discret*. Masson et Cie, 1972.

A. S. Nowak. Universally measurable strategies in zero-sum stochastic games. *Annals of Probability*, 13:269–287, 1985a.

A. S. Nowak. Existence of equilibrium stationary strategies in discounted noncooperative stochastic games with uncountable state space. *Journal of Optimization Theory and Applications*, 45:591–602, 1985b.

A. S. Nowak and T. E. S. Raghavan. Positive stochastic games and a theorem of Ornstein. In Raghavan et al. (1991), pages 127–134.

A. S. Nowak and T. E. S. Raghavan. Existence of stationary correlated equilibria with symmetric information for discounted stochastic games. *Mathematics of Operations Research*, 17:519–526, 1992.

M. Orkin. An approximation theorem for infinite games. *Proceedings of the American Mathematical Society*, 36:212–216, 1972a.

M. Orkin. Infinite games with imperfect information. *Transactions of the American Mathematical Society*, 171:501–507, 1972b.

M. Orkin. Recursive matrix games. *Journal of Applied Probability*, 9:813–820, 1972c.

D. Ornstein. On the existence of stationary optimal strategies. *Proceedings of the American Mathematical Society*, 20:563–569, 1969.

T. Parthasarathy. Discounted, positive, and noncooperative stochastic games. *International Journal of Game Theory*, 2:25–37, 1973.

T. Parthasarathy. Markov games II. *Methods of Operations Research*, 51:369–376, 1984.

T. Parthasarathy and T. E. S. Raghavan. An orderfield property for stochastic games when one player controls transition probabilities. *Journal of Optimization Theory and Applications*, 33:375–392, 1981.

T. Parthasarathy and S. Sinha. Existence of stationary equilibrium strategies in non-zero-sum discounted stochastic games with uncountable state space and state-independent transitions. *International Journal of Game Theory*, 18:189–194, 1989.

T. Parthasarathy and M. Stern. Markov games. A survey. In E. O. Roxin, P.-T. Liu, and R. L. Sternberg, editors, *Differential Games and Control Theory II*, pages 1–46. Marcel Dekker, 1977.

B. Peleg. Equilibrium points for games with infinitely many players. *Journal of the London Mathematical Society*, 44:292–294, 1969.

J.-P. Ponssard. Zero-sum games with "almost" perfect information. *Management Science*, 21:794–805, 1975a.

J.-P. Ponssard. A note on the L-P formulation of zero-sum sequential games with incomplete information. *International Journal of Game Theory*, 4:1–5, 1975b.

J.-P. Ponssard. On the subject of non-optimal play in zero-sum extensive games: "The trap phenomenon." *International Journal of Game Theory*, 5:107–115, 1976.

J.-P. Ponssard and S. Sorin. The LP formulation of finite zero-sum games with incomplete information. *International Journal of Game Theory*, 9:99–105, 1980a.

J.-P. Ponssard and S. Sorin. Some results on zero-sum games with incomplete information: The dependent case. *International Journal of Game Theory*, 9:233–245, 1980b.

J.-P. Ponssard and S. Sorin. Optimal behavioral strategies in zero-sum games with almost perfect information. *Mathematics of Operations Research*, 7:14–31, 1982.

J.-P. Ponssard and S. Zamir. Zero-sum sequential games with incomplete information. *International Journal of Game Theory*, 2:99–107, 1973.

R. Radner. Collusive behavior in non-cooperative epsilon-equilibria of oligopolies with long but finite lives. *Journal of Economic Theory*, 22:136–154, 1980.

R. Radner. Monitoring cooperative agreements in a repeated principal-agent relationship. *Econometrica*, 49:1127–1148, 1981.

R. Radner. Repeated principal-agent games with discounting. *Econometrica*, 53:1173–1198, 1985.

R. Radner. Repeated partnership games with imperfect monitoring and no discounting. *Review of Economic Studies*, LIII:43–57, 1986a.

R. Radner. Can bounded rationality resolve the prisoners' dilemma? In W. Hildenbrand and A. Mas-Colell, editors, *Contributions to Mathematical Economics in Honor of Gérard Debreu*, pages 387–399. North-Holland, 1986b.

R. Radner. Repeated moral hazard with low discount rates. In W. P. Heller, R. M. Starr, and D. A. Starrett, editors, *Uncertainty, Information and Communication, Essays in Honor of Kenneth J. Arrow, Volume III*, pages 25–63. Cambridge University Press, 1986c.

R. Radner, R. B. Myerson, and E. Maskin. An example of a repeated partnership game with discounting and with uniformly inefficient equilibria. *Review of Economic Studies*, LIII:59–69, 1986.

T. E. S. Raghavan and J. A. Filar. Algorithms for stochastic games, a survey. *Zeitschrift für Operations Research*, 35:437–472, 1991.

T. E. S. Raghavan, T. S. Ferguson, T. Parthasarathy, and O. J. Vrieze, editors. *Stochastic Games and Related Topics – In Honor of Professor L. S. Shapley*. Kluwer Academic Publishers, 1991.

R. Restrepo. Tactical problems involving several actions. In Dresher et al. (1957), pages 313–335.

U. Rieder. Equilibrium plans for non-zero-sum Markov games. In Moeschlin and Pallaschke (1979), pages 91–101.

J. Robinson. An iterative method of solving a game. *Annals of Mathematics. Second Series*, 54:296–301, 1951.

C. A. Rogers, J. E. Jayne, C. Dellacherie, F. Tøpsoe, J. Hoffman-Jørgensen, D. A. Martin, A. S. Kechris, and A. H. Stone. *Analytic Sets*. Academic Press, 1980.

J. L. Rosenfeld. Adaptive competitive decision. In Dresher et al. (1964), pages 69–83.

A. Rubinstein. Equilibrium in supergames with the overtaking criterion. *Journal of Economic Theory*, 21:1–9, 1979.

A. Rubinstein. Strong perfect equilibrium in supergames. *International Journal of Game Theory*, 9:1–12, 1980.

A. Rubinstein. A bargaining model with incomplete information about time preferences. *Econometrica*, 53:1151–1172, 1985.

A. Rubinstein. Equilibrium in supergames. In N. Megiddo, editor, *Essays in Game Theory: In Honor of Michael Maschler*, pages 17–28. Springer-Verlag, 1994.

A. Rubinstein and A. Wolinski. Equilibrium in a market with sequential bargaining. *Econometrica*, 53:1133–1150, 1985.

A. Rubinstein and M. Yaari. Repeated insurance contracts and moral hazard. *Journal of Economic Theory*, 30:74–97, 1983.

J. Saint-Raymond. Jeux topologiques et espaces de Namioka. *Proceedings of the American Mathematical Society*, 87:499–504, 1983.

H. Scarf and L. S. Shapley. Games with partial information. In Dresher et al. (1957), pages 213–229.

R. Selten. Reexamination of the perfectness concept for equilibrium points in extensive games. *International Journal of Game Theory*, 4:25–55, 1975.

J. Shalev. Nonzero-sum two-person repeated games with incomplete information and observable payoffs. *Games and Economic Behavior*, 7:246–259, 1994.

L. S. Shapley. Stochastic games. *Proceedings of the National Academy of Sciences of the U.S.A.*, 39:1095–1100, 1953.

L. S. Shapley. Some topics in two-person games. In Dresher et al. (1964), pages 1–28.

L. S. Shapley and R. N. Snow. Basic solutions of discrete games. In Kuhn and Tucker (1950), pages 27–35.

S. E. Shreve and D. P. Bertsekas. Universally measurable policies in dynamic programming. *Mathematics of Operations Research*, 4:15–30, 1979.

L. K. Simon and W. R. Zame. Discontinuous games and endogenous sharing rules. *Econometrica*, 58:861–872, 1990.

R. S. Simon, S. Spiez, and H. Toruńczyk. The existence of equilibria in certain games, separation for families of convex functions and a theorem of Borsuk-Ulam type. *Israel Journal of Mathematics*, 92:1–21, 1995.

M. Sion. On general minimax theorems. *Pacific Journal of Mathematics*, 8:171–176, 1958.

M. Sion and P. Wolfe. On a game without a value. In Dresher et al. (1957), pages 299–306.

M. J. Sobel. Noncooperative stochastic games. *Annals of Mathematical Statistics*, 42: 1930–1935, 1971.

S. Sorin. A note on the value of zero-sum sequential repeated games with incomplete information. *International Journal of Game Theory*, 8:217–223, 1979.

S. Sorin. An introduction to two-person zero-sum repeated games with incomplete information. Technical Report 312, IMSS-Economics, Stanford University, 1980. Original version in *Cahiers du Groupe de Mathématiques Economiques*, 1, Paris, 1979.

S. Sorin. Some results on the existence of Nash equilibria for non-zero-sum games with incomplete information. *International Journal of Game Theory*, 12:193–205, 1983.

S. Sorin. "Big Match" with lack of information on one side (part I). *International Journal of Game Theory*, 13:201–255, 1984a.

S. Sorin. On a pair of simultaneous functional equations. *Journal of Mathematical Analysis and Applications*, 98:296–303, 1984b.

S. Sorin. "Big Match" with lack of information on one side (part II). *International Journal of Game Theory*, 14:173–204, 1985a.

S. Sorin. On a repeated game with state dependent signalling matrices. *International Journal of Game Theory*, 14:249–272, 1985b.

S. Sorin. On repeated games with complete information. *Mathematics of Operations Research*, 11:147–160, 1986a.

S. Sorin. Asymptotic properties of a non-zero-sum stochastic game. *International Journal of Game Theory*, 15:101–107, 1986b.

S. Sorin. On repeated games without a recursive structure: Existence of $\lim v_n$. *International Journal of Game Theory*, 18:45–55, 1989.

S. Sorin. Supergames. In Ichiishi et al. (1990), pages 46–63.

S. Sorin. Repeated games with complete information. In Aumann and Hart (1992), Chapter 4, pages 71–107.

S. Sorin and S. Zamir. A two-person game with lack of information on 1 1/2 sides. *Mathematics of Operations Research*, 10:17–23, 1985.

S. Sorin and S. Zamir. "Big Match" with lack of information on one side (III). In Raghavan et al. (1991), pages 101–112.

E. H. Spanier. *Algebraic Topology*. McGraw Hill, 1966.

R. E. Stearns. A formal information concept for games with incomplete information. In *ACDA Final Report ST-116* Mathematica (1967), Chapter IV, pages 405–433. Re-edited as Ch. III in Aumann and Maschler (1995).

R. E. Strauch. Negative dynamic programming. *Annals of Mathematical Statistics*, 37: 871–890, 1966.

M. Takahashi. Stochastic games with infinitely many strategies. *Journal of Science of the Hiroshima University. Ser. A.I. Mathematics*, 26:123–134, 1962.

M. Takahashi. Equilibrium points of stochastic non-cooperative n-person games. *Journal of Science of the Hiroshima University. Ser. A.I. Mathematics*, 28:95–99, 1964.

R. Telgársky. Topological games: On the 50th anniversary of the Banach–Mazur game. *Rocky Mountain Journal of Mathematics*, 17:227–276, 1987.

G. L. Thompson. On the solution of a game theoretic problem. In Kuhn and Tucker (1956), pages 275–284.

F. Thuijsman. *Optimality and equilibria in stochastic games*. PhD thesis, Rijksuniversiteit Limburg te Maastricht, The Netherlands, 1989.

F. Thuijsman and O. J. Vrieze. Easy initial states in stochastic games. In Raghavan et al. (1991), pages 85–100.

E. C. Titchmarsh. *The Theory of Functions*. Oxford University Press, 1939.

A. W. Tucker. Dual systems of homogeneous linear relations. In Kuhn and Tucker (1956), pages 3–18.

A. W. Tucker and D. Luce, editors. *Contributions to the Theory of Games, Vol. IV*. Annals of Mathematics Studies, 40. Princeton University Press, 1959.

S. H. Tijs. Nash equilibria for noncooperative n-person games in normal form. *SIAM Review*, 23:225–237, 1981.

S. H. Tijs and O. J. Vrieze. On the existence of easy initial states for non-discounted stochastic games. *Mathematics of Operations Research*, 11:506–513, 1986.

E. van Damme. Refinements of Nash equilibrium. In J.-J. Laffont, editor, *Advances in Economic Theory*, Econometric Society Monographs, 21, pages 32–75. Cambridge University Press, 1992.

S. Vassilakis and S. Zamir. Common belief and common knowledge. *Journal of Mathematical Economics*, 22:495–505, 1993.

N. Vieille. Weak approachability. *Mathematics of Operations Research*, 17:781–791, 1992.

N. Vieille. Solvable states in stochastic games. *International Journal of Game Theory*, 21:395–404, 1993.

J. Ville. Sur la théorie générale des jeux où intervient l'habilité des joueurs. In É. Borel, editor, *Traité du calcul des probabilités et de ses applications*. Vol. IV, Fascicule II: *Applications aux jeux de hasard*, pages 105–113. Gauthier-Villars, 1938.

J. von Neumann and O. Morgenstern. *Theory of Games and Economic Behaviour*. Princeton University Press, 1944.

O. J. Vrieze. Linear programming and non-discounted stochastic games in which one player controls transitions. *OR Spektrum*, 3:29–35, 1981.

O. J. Vrieze. *Stochastic games with finite state and actions spaces*. PhD thesis, Catholic University of Nijmegen, The Netherlands, 1983.

O. J. Vrieze and F. Thuijsman. Stochastic games and optimal stationary stategies. A survey. *Methods of Operations Research*, 57:513–529, 1987.

O. J. Vrieze and F. Thuijsman. On equilibria in repeated games with absorbing states. *International Journal of Game Theory*, 18:293–310, 1989.

O. J. Vrieze, S. H. Tijs, T. E. S. Raghavan, and J. A. Filar. A finite algorithm for switching control stochastic games. *OR Spektrum*, 5:15–24, 1983.

A. Wald. Note on zero-sum two person games. *Annals of Mathematics*, 52:739–742, 1950.

D. W. Walkup and R. J. B. Wets. A Lipschitzian characterization of convex polyhedra. *Proceedings of the American Mathematical Society*, 23:167–173, 1969.

C. Waternaux. Solution for a class of repeated games without a recursive structure. *International Journal of Game Theory*, 12:129–160, 1983a.

C. Waternaux. Minmax and maxmin of repeated games without recursive structure. Discussion Paper 8313, CORE, Université Catholique de Louvain, Louvain-la-Neuve, Belgium, 1983b.

H. Weyl. Elementary proof of a minimax theorem due to von Neumann. In Kuhn and Tucker (1950), pages 19–25.

W. Whitt. Representation and approximation of noncooperative sequential games. *SIAM Journal on Control and Optimisation*, 18:33–48, 1980.

P. Wolfe. Determinateness of polyhedral games. In Kuhn and Tucker (1956), pages 195–198.

E. B. Yanovskaya. Infinite zero-sum two-person games. *Journal of Soviet Mathematics*, 2:520–541, 1974.

S. Zamir. On the relation between finitely and infinitely repeated games with incomplete information. *International Journal of Game Theory*, 1:179–198, 1971–1972.

S. Zamir. On repeated games with general information function. *International Journal of Game Theory*, 2:215–229, 1973a.

S. Zamir. On the notion of value for games with infinitely many stages. *Annals of Statistics*, 1:791–796, 1973b.

S. Zamir. Repeated games of incomplete information: Zero-sum. In Aumann and Hart (1992), Chapter 5, pages 109–154.

E. Zermelo. Über eine Anwendung der Mengenlehre auf die Therie des Schachspiels. In E. Hobson and A. E. H. Love, editors, *Proceedings of the Fifth International Congress of Mathematicians*, Volume 2, pages 501–504. Cambridge University Press, 1913.

APPENDIX D

Updates

D.1. COMPLEMENTS AND ADVANCES

This section describes some of the most important developments of the topics treated in the book.

CHAPTER I

Discontinuous games (I.4, Ex. 13 and 20) have been extensively treated starting with Reny (1999) and Jackson et al. (2002); see Reny (2011) for a recent account.

CHAPTER II

II.2.a (and 2.c, Ex. 4). A number of new results concern infinite games with perfect information, including for n players and requiring subgame-perfection; Flesch et al. (2010b), Flesch et al. (2010a), and Purves and Sudderth (2011).

For continuous games, see Harris et al. (1995).

II.2.b Martin's theorem (Theorem II.2.3) has been extended by Martin to Blackwell's games, Martin (1998), to the framework of stochastic games, Maitra and Sudderth (1998, 2003, 2007), Secchi and Sudderth (2001a,b) (see also VII.5), and to eventual perfect monitoring Shmaya (2011).

Section II.3. The concepts of correlated equilibria, extensive form correlated equilibria, and communication equilibria have been used intensively.

Extension to perfection is described in Dhillon and Mertens (1996); computational aspects are in von Stengel and Forges (2008).

Other properties of correlated equilibria can be found in Myerson (1997) and Viossat (2008).

We refer to Forges (2009) for a recent survey.

II.4. Blackwell's theorem (Theorem II.4.1) is of fundamental importance and has numerous applications, including games with incomplete information and learning procedures (in the spirit of II.4., Ex. 7); see, e.g., Hart (2005).

A necessary condition for approachability is given in Spinat (2002). The analysis has been extended to infinite dimensional spaces, Lehrer (2002), to the case of partial monitoring, Rustichini (1999), Cesa-Bianchi et al. (2006), Lehrer and Solan (2007), Perchet (2009), Perchet (2011a,b), to stochastic games, Milman (2006), and to the space of measures, Perchet and Quincampoix (2010).

CHAPTER III

The construction of the universal belief space has been extended and developed in several directions: Dekel et al. (2006), Heifetz and Samet (1998), Meier (2006), and Pinter (2010).

A general presentation of interactive epistemology is in Aumann (1999a,b).

Developments concerning correlated equilibrium can be found in Forges (2009).

For recent surveys, see Aumann and Heifetz (2002) and Zamir (2009).

CHAPTER IV

IV.4. The literature on supergames is huge; in particular for perfect equilibria in the discounted case, see Fudenberg and Levine (2008), Mailath and Samuelson (2006), and applications in learning, Fudenberg and Levine (1998).

The analog of IV.4, Ex. 9 ("perfect discounted Folk theorem") for finite games is established in Gossner (1995).

For games with signals, several results deal with public signals and public equilibria; see, e.g., Fudenberg et al. (1994), Fudenberg et al. (2007). For the special class of "belief free" equilibria, see Ely et al. (2005).

For the general case of imperfect monitoring, see Compte (1998), Hörner and Olszewski (2006), and Kandori and Matsushima (1998).

The impact of signals on the correlation is studied in Gossner and Tomala (2007) and Heller et al. (2012), and communication equilibrium is analyzed in Renault and Tomala (2004b).

Minority games are treated in Renault et al. (2005) and Renault et al. (2008).

General robust properties are presented in Renault and Tomala (2012). A recent survey is Gossner and Tomala (2009).

CHAPTER V

V.1. The dual game introduced by De Meyer (V.6, Ex. 14) is a fundamental tool in De Meyer (1996a,b), and applies in particular to the value of information in De Meyer et al. (2010).

V.2. Several alternative proofs to the Cav u theorem have been developed: the operator approach, De Meyer and Rosenberg (1999), dual differential game, Laraki (2002), and extensions, Gensbittel (2012a).

V.4. This analysis developed in Mertens and Zamir (1995) has produced a large number of results: De Meyer (1998, 1999, 2010), and Gensbittel (2012b).

V.5. A general result on the speed of convergence is in Mertens (1998).

CHAPTER VI

VI.4. A variational approach to the MZ formula is in Laraki (2001a), with extensions in Laraki (2001b, 2004).

For the associated recursive formula see De Meyer and Marino (2005). Recent advances include Nowik and Zamir (2002) and Neyman (2012a).

CHAPTER VII

Here too the field has been very active.

In the zero-sum case we mention Altman et al. (2005), Coulomb (1996, 1999), and Laraki (2010).

For the non-discounted case with signals, see the important advances in Coulomb (2001, 2003b), and Rosenberg et al. (2003), and a nice presentation in Rosenberg et al. (2006).

For the non-zero sum case, a proof of existence of uniform equilibria for a two player game is due to Vieille, Vieille (2000a,b,c). The general case is still open.

Significant results include Flesch et al. (1997), Flesch et al. (2007), Flesch et al. (2008), Flesch et al. (2009), Jakiewicz and Nowak (2011), Levy (2012a), Simon (2006, 2007), Solan (1998, 1999, 2001a), Solan and Vieille (2002b), and Vieille (2000d), introducing new tools and ideas.

Correlated equilibria are studied in Solan (2001b), Solan and Vieille (2002a), and Solan and Vohra (2002).

Computational aspects are considered in Herings and Peeters (2004), Hörner et al. (2011), and Solan and Vieille (2010).

For a survey, see Mertens (2002), and Vieille (2002), and for a comprehensive treatment Neyman and Sorin (2010).

CHAPTER VIII

VIII.1. The analysis of the symmetric case is developed in Neyman and Sorin (1997, 1998).

Several results involving stochastic aspects and incomplete information include Hörner et al. (2010), Krausz and Rieder (1997), Marino (2005), Rosenberg (2000), and Rosenberg and Vieille (2000).

An important class is studied in Renault (2006), Simon (2003), Marino (2005), and Neyman (2008).

CHAPTER IX

IX.1. The main advance is the proof of equilibria in two-person games with lack of information on one side by Simon, Spiez, and Torunczyk (Simon et al., 1995) and Simon (2002). See also Renault (2000).

Extensions include Renault (2001a,b), and Renault and Tomala (2004a).

The discounted framework is studied in Cripps and Thomas (2003).

There is a strong connection between incomplete information games and reputation effects; see Sorin (1999) and Mailath and Samuelson (2006).

Among the recent active directions of research let us mention:

(1) A unified analysis for the asymptotic approach in the zero-sum case, based on the study of the Shapley operator and its extension (Theorem IV.3.2) that allows us to treat in the same way:
   - Incomplete information games, stochastic games, and mixtures of those.
   - A limit of finitely repeated or discounted games or more general evaluations: Sorin (2003, 2005, 2011), Rosenberg and Sorin (2001), Rosenberg et al. (2002), Sorin and Vigeral (2013), and Vigeral (2010a,b).

   In particular a link is obtained with games in continuous time and corresponding tools: Cardaliaguet et al. (2012).

(2) New connections between the asymptotic and the uniform approaches, especially in the framework of dynamic programming or when one player is more informed that the other: Renault (2011), Rosenberg and Vieille (2000), Renault and Venel (2012), Rosenberg et al. (2002), Rosenberg et al. (2004), and Renault (2012).

(3) The extension to differential games: Buckdahn et al. (2010), Krasovskii et al. (2011), or differential stochastic games: Buckdahn and Li (2008), Hamadène and Lepeltier (1995), or the model of incomplete information. In particular, the results extend the tools of the $\mathsf{Cav}\, u$ theorem and the dual game, and the MZ operator appears as an infinitesimal operator in continuous time: Cardaliaguet (2007, 2008, 2009a,b), Cardaliaguet and Quincampoix (2008), Cardaliaguet and Rainer (2009a, 2012), Cardaliaguet and Souquière (2012), and Grüen (2012).

(4) Games in continuous time and connection with differential games: As Soulaimani (2008), Cardaliaguet and Rainer (2009b), Levy (2012c), and Neyman (2012b); a precursor is Zachrisson (1964).

Finally, nonexistence results have been obtained in a general framework: for incomplete information games, see Simon (2003), and for stochastic games, see Levy (2012b) and Vigeral (2012).

A closely related field that is currently very productive corresponds to stopping games: see the survey Solan and Vieille (2004).

D.2. COMPLEMENTARY BIBLIOGRAPHY

E. Altman, K. Avrachenkov, R. Marquez, and G. Miller. Zero-sum constrained stochastic games with independent state processes. *Mathematical Methods of Operations Research*, 62:375–386, 2005.

S. As Soulaimani. Viability with probabilistic knowledge of initial condition, application to optimal control. *Set-Valued Analysis*, 16:1037–1060, 2008.

S. As Soulaimani, M. Quincampoix, and S. Sorin. Repeated games and qualitative differential games: Approachability and comparison of strategies. *SIAM Journal on Control and Optimization*, 48:2461–2479, 2009.

R. J. Aumann. Interactive epistemology I: Knowledge. *International Journal of Game Theory*, 28:263–300, 1999a.

R. J. Aumann. Interactive epistemology II: Probability. *International Journal of Game Theory*, 28:301–314, 1999b.

R. J. Aumann and A. Heifetz. Incomplete information. In R. J. Aumann and S. Hart, editors, *Handbook of Game Theory, with Economic Applications*, Volume 3, pages 1665–1686. Elsevier, 2002.

R. J. Aumann and M. Maschler. *Repeated Games with Incomplete Information*. MIT Press, 1995.

D. Blackwell. The prediction of sequences. *International Journal of Game Theory*, 31: 245–251, 2003.

R. Buckdahn, P. Cardaliaguet, and M. Quincampoix. Some recent aspects of differential game theory. *Dynamic Games and Applications*, 1:74–114, 2010.

R. Buckdahn and J. Li. Stochastic differential games and viscosity solutions of Hamilton–Jacobi–Bellman–Isaacs equations. *SIAM Journal on Control and Optimization*, 47:444–475, 2008.

P. Cardaliaguet. Differential games with asymmetric information. *SIAM Journal on Control and Optimization*, 46:816–838, 2007.

P. Cardaliaguet. Representation formulas for differential games with asymmetric information. *Journal of Optimization Theory and Applications*, 138:1–16, 2008.

P. Cardaliaguet. A double obstacle problem arising in differential game theory. *Journal of Mathematical Analysis and Applications*, 360:95–107, 2009a.

P. Cardaliaguet. Numerical approximation and optimal strategies for differential games with lack of information on one side. In P. Bernhard, V. Gaitsgory, and O. Pourtalier, editors, *Advances in Dynamic Games and their Applications*, Volume 10 of *Annals of ISDG*, pages 159–176. Birkhauser, 2009b.

P. Cardaliaguet, R. Laraki, and S. Sorin. A continuous time approach for the asymptotic value in two-person zero-sum repeated games. *SIAM Journal on Control and Optimization*, 50:1573–1596, 2012.

P. Cardaliaguet and M. Quincampoix. Deterministic differential games under probability knowledge of initial condition. *International Game Theory Review*, 10:1–16, 2008.

P. Cardaliaguet and C. Rainer. Stochastic differential games with asymmetric information. *Applied Mathematics and Optimization*, 59:1–36, 2009a.

P. Cardaliaguet and C. Rainer. On a continuous time game with incomplete information. *Mathematics of Operations Research*, 34:769–794, 2009b.

P. Cardaliaguet and C. Rainer. Games with incomplete information in continuous time and for continuous types. *Dynamic Games and Applications*, 2:206–227, 2012.

P. Cardaliaguet and A. Souquière. A differential game with a blind player. *SIAM Journal on Control and Optimization*, 50:2090–2116, 2012.

N. Cesa-Bianchi and G. Lugosi. *Prediction, Learning, and Games*. Cambridge University Press, 2006.

N. Cesa-Bianchi, G. Lugosi, and G. Stoltz. Regret minimization under partial monitoring. *Mathematics of Operations Research*, 31:562–580, 2006.

O. Compte. Communication in repeated games with imperfect private monitoring. *Econometrica*, 66:597–626, 1998.

J.-M. Coulomb. A note on "Big Match." *ESAIM: Probability and Statistics*, 1:89–93, 1996.

J.-M. Coulomb. Generalized Big Match. *Mathematics of Operations Research*, 24:795–816, 1999.

J.-M. Coulomb. Repeated games with absorbing states and signalling structure. *Mathematics of Operations Research*, 26:286–303, 2001.

J.-M. Coulomb. Games with a recursive structure. In A. Neyman and S. Sorin, editors, *Stochastic Games and Applications*, pages 427–442. NATO Science Series C570, Kluwer Academic Publishers, 2003a.

J.-M. Coulomb. Stochastic games without perfect monitoring. *International Journal of Game Theory*, 32:73–96, 2003b.

M. W. Cripps and J. P. Thomas. Some asymptotic results in discounted repeated games of one-sided incomplete information. *Mathematics of Operations Research*, 28:433–462, 2003.

B. De Meyer. Repeated games and partial differential equations. *Mathematics of Operations Research*, 21:209–236, 1996a.

B. De Meyer. Repeated games, duality and the central limit theorem. *Mathematics of Operations Research*, 21:237–251, 1996b.

B. De Meyer. The maximal variation of a bounded martingale and the central limit theorem. *Annales de l'Institut Henri Poincaré, Probabilités et Statistiques*, 34:49–59, 1998.

B. De Meyer. From repeated games to Brownian games. *Annales de l'Institut Henri Poincaré, Probabilités et Statistiques*, 35:1–48, 1999.

B. De Meyer. Price dynamics on a stock market with asymmetric information. *Games and Economic Behavior*, 69:42–71, 2010.

B. De Meyer, E. Lehrer, and D. Rosenberg. Evaluating information in zero-sum games with incomplete information on both sides. *Mathematics of Operations Research*, 35:851–863, 2010.

B. De Meyer and A. Marino. Duality and optimal strategies in the finitely repeated zero-sum games with incomplete information on both sides. *Cahiers de la Maison des Sciences Economiques* 2005-27, Université Panthéon-Sorbonne (Paris 1), 2005.

B. De Meyer and H. Moussa-Saley. On the strategic origin of Brownian motion in finance. *International Journal of Game Theory*, 31:285–319, 2002.

B. De Meyer and D. Rosenberg. $\mathsf{Cav}\ u$ and the dual game. *Mathematics of Operations Research*, 24:619–626, 1999.

E. Dekel, D. Fudenberg, and S. Morris. Topologies on types. *Theoretical Economics*, 1:275–309, 2006.

A. Dhillon and J.-F. Mertens. Perfect correlated equilibria. *Journal of Economic Theory*, 68:279–302, 1996.

J. C. Ely, J. Hörner, and W. Olszewski. Belief-free equilibria in repeated games. *Econometrica*, 73:377–415, 2005.

J. Filar and K. Vrieze. *Competitive Markov Decision Processes*. Springer, 1996.

J. Flesch, J. Kuipers, A. Mashiah-Yaakovi, G. Schoenmakers, E. Solan, and K. Vrieze. Perfect-information games with lower-semicontinuous payoffs. *Mathematics of Operations Research*, 35:742–755, 2010a.

J. Flesch, J. Kuipers, G. Schoenmakers, and K. Vrieze. Subgame perfection in positive recursive games with perfect information. *Mathematics of Operations Research*, 35: 193–207, 2010b.

J. Flesch, G. Schoenmakers, and K. Vrieze. Stochastic games on a product state space. *Mathematics of Operations Research*, 33:403–420, 2008.

J. Flesch, G. Schoenmakers, and K. Vrieze. Stochastic games on a product state space: The periodic case. *International Journal of Game Theory*, 38:263–289, 2009.

J. Flesch, F. Thuijsman, and K. Vrieze. Stochastic games with additive transitions. *European Journal of Operations Research*, 179:483–497, 2007.

J. Flesch, F. Thuijsman, and O. J. Vrieze. Cyclic Markov equilibria in a cubic game. *International Journal of Game Theory*, 26:303–314, 1997.

F. Forges. Correlated equilibrium in games with incomplete information revisited. *Theory and Decision*, 61:329–344, 2006.

F. Forges. Correlated equilibrium and communication in games. In M. Meyers, editor, *Encyclopedia of Complexity and Systems Science*, pages 1587–1596. Springer, 2009.

D. Fudenberg and D. K. Levine. *The Theory of Learning in Games*. MIT Press, 1998.

D. Fudenberg and D. K. Levine. *A Long-Run Collaboration on Long-Run Games*. World Scientific Publishing, 2008.

D. Fudenberg, D. K. Levine, and E. Maskin. The folk theorem with imperfect public information. *Econometrica*, 62:997–1039, 1994.

D. Fudenberg, D. K. Levine, and S. Takahashi. Perfect public equilibrium when players are patient. *Games and Economic Behavior*, 61:27–49, 2007.

F. Gensbittel. Extensions of the $\mathsf{Cav}\,u$ theorem for repeated games with one-sided information (preprint). 2012a.

F. Gensbittel. Covariance control problems of martingales arising from game theory (preprint). 2012b.

O. Gossner. The folk theorem for finitely repeated games with mixed strategies. *International Journal of Game Theory*, 24:95–107, 1995.

O. Gossner and T. Tomala. Secret correlation in repeated games with imperfect monitoring. *Mathematics of Operations Research*, 32:413–424, 2007.

O. Gossner and T. Tomala. Repeated games with complete information. In R. Meyers, editor, *Encyclopedia of Complexity and Systems Science*, pages 7616–7630. Springer, 2009.

C. Grüen. A BSDE approach to stochastic differential games with incomplete information. *Stochastic Processes and their Applications*, 122:1917–1946, 2012.

S. Hamadène and J.-P. Lepeltier. Zero-sum stochastic differential games and backward equations. *Systems and Control Letters*, 24:259–263, 1995.

C. Harris, P. Reny, and A. Robson. The existence of subgame-perfect equilibrium in continuous games with almost perfect information: A case for public randomization. *Econometrica*, 63:507–544, 1995.

S. Hart. Adaptive heuristics. *Econometrica*, 73:1401–1430, 2005.

A. Haurie, J. B. Krawczyk, and G. Zaccour. *Games and Dynamic Games*. World Scientific, 2012.

A. Heifetz and D. Samet. Topology-free typology of beliefs. *Journal of Economic Theory*, 82:324–341, 1998.

Y. Heller, E. Solan, and T. Tomala. Communication, correlation and cheap talk in games with public information. *Games and Economic Behavior*, 74:222–234, 2012.

J. J. P. Herings and R. Peeters. Stationary equilibria in stochastic games: Structure, selection, and computation. *Journal of Economic Theory*, 118:32–60, 2004.

J. Hörner and W. Olszewski. The folk theorem with private almost perfect monitoring. *Econometrica*, 74:1499–1544, 2006.

J. Hörner, D. Rosenberg, E. Solan, and N. Vieille. On a Markov game with one-sided incomplete information. *Operations Research*, 58:1107–1115, 2010.

J. Hörner, T. Sugaya, S. Takahashi, and N. Vieille. Recursive methods in discounted stochastic games: An algorithm for delta approaching 1 and a folk theorem. *Econometrica*, 79:1277–1318, 2011.

M. O. Jackson, L. K. Simon, J. M. Swinkels, and W. R. Zame. Communication and equilibrium in discontinuous games of incomplete information. *Econometrica*, 70: 1711–1740, 2002.

A. Jakiewicz and A. Nowak. Stochastic games with unbounded payoffs: Applications to robust control in economics. *Dynamic Games and Applications*, 1:253–279, 2011.

M. Kandori and M. Matsushima. Private observation, communication and collusion. *Econometrica*, 66:627–652, 1998.

N. N. Krasovskii and A. I. Subbotin. *Game-Theoretical Control Problems*. Springer, 2011.

A. Krausz and U. Rieder. Markov games with incomplete information. *Mathematical Methods of Operations Research*, 46:263–279, 1997.

R. Laraki. Variational inequalities, systems of functional equations and incomplete information repeated games. *SIAM Journal on Control and Optimization*, 40:516–524, 2001a.

R. Laraki. The splitting game and applications. *International Journal of Game Theory*, 30:359–376, 2001b.

R. Laraki. Repeated games with lack of information on one side: The dual differential approach. *Mathematics of Operations Research*, 27:419–440, 2002.

R. Laraki. On the regularity of the convexification operator on a compact set. *Journal of Convex Analysis*, 11:209–234, 2004.

R. Laraki. Explicit formulas for repeated games with absorbing states. *International Journal of Game Theory*, 39:53–69, 2010.

R. Laraki and W. D. Sudderth. The preservation of continuity and Lipschitz continuity by optimal reward operators. *Mathematics of Operations Research*, 29:672–685, 2004.

E. Lehrer. Approachability in infinite dimensional spaces. *International Journal of Game Theory*, 31:253–268, 2002.

E. Lehrer and E. Solan. Learning to play partially specified equilibrium (preprint). 2007.

E. Lehrer and L. Yariv. Repeated games with incomplete information on one side: The case of different discounting factors. *Mathematics of Operations Research*, 24: 204–218, 1999.

Y. J. Levy. Stochastic games with information lag. *Games and Economic Behavior*, 74: 243–256, 2012a.

Y. J. Levy. A discounted stochastic game with no stationary Nash equilibrium. Discussion Paper 596, Federmann Center for the Study of Rationality, Hebrew University of Jerusalem, 2012b.

Y. J. Levy. Continuous-time stochastic games of fixed duration. Discussion Paper 617, Federmann Center for the Study of Rationality, Hebrew University of Jerusalem, 2012c.

G. J. Mailath and L. Samuelson. *Repeated Games and Reputations: Long-Run Relationships*. Oxford University Press, 2006.

A. P. Maitra and W. D. Sudderth. *Discrete Gambling and Stochastic Games*. Applications of Mathematics. Springer, 1996.

A. P. Maitra and W. D. Sudderth. Finitely additive stochastic games with Borel measurable payoffs. *International Journal of Game Theory*, 27:257–267, 1998.

A. P. Maitra and W. D. Sudderth. Borel stay-in-a-set games. *International Journal of Game Theory*, 32:97–108, 2003.

A. P. Maitra and W. D. Sudderth. Subgame-perfect equilibria for stochastic games. *Mathematics of Operations Research*, 32:711–722, 2007.

A. Marino. The value and optimal strategies of a particular Markov chain game (preprint). 2005.

D. A. Martin. The determinacy of Blackwell games. *Journal of Symbolic Logic*, 63: 1565–1581, 1998.

M. Meier. Finitely additive beliefs and universal type spaces. *Annals of Probability*, 34: 386–422, 2006.

J.-F. Mertens. The speed of convergence in repeated games with incomplete information on one side. *International Journal of Game Theory*, 27:343–359, 1998.

J.-F. Mertens. Stochastic games. In R. J. Aumann and S. Hart, editors, *Handbook of Game Theory, with Economic Applications*, Volume 3, pages 1809–1832. Elsevier, 2002.

J.-F. Mertens, A. Neyman, and D. Rosenberg. Absorbing games with compact action spaces. *Mathematics of Operations Research*, 34:257–262, 2009.

E. Milman. Approachable sets of vector payoffs in stochastic games. *Games and Economic Behavior*, 56:135–147, 2006.

R. B. Myerson. Dual reduction and elementary games. *Games and Economic Behavior*, 21:183–202, 1997.

A. Neyman. Stochastic games and nonexpansive maps. In A. Neyman and S. Sorin, editors, *Stochastic Games and Applications*, volume 570 of *NATO Science Series C*, pages 397–415. Kluwer Academic Publishers, 2003.

A. Neyman. Existence of optimal strategies in Markov games with incomplete information. *International Journal of Game Theory*, 37:581–596, 2008.

A. Neyman. The value of two-person zero-sum repeated games with incomplete information and uncertain duration. *International Journal of Game Theory*, 41: 195–207, 2012a.

A. Neyman. Continuous-time stochastic games. Discussion Paper 616, Federmann Center for the Study of Rationality, Hebrew University of Jerusalem, 2012b.

A. Neyman and S. Sorin. Equilibria in repeated games of incomplete information: The deterministic symmetric case. In T. Parthasarathy, B. Dutta, J. A. M. Potters, T. E. S. Raghavan, D. Ray, and A. Sen, editors, *Game Theoretical Applications to Economics and Operations Research*, pages 129–131. Kluwer, 1997.

A. Neyman and S. Sorin. Equilibria in repeated games of incomplete information: The general symmetric case. *International Journal of Game Theory*, 27:201–210, 1998.

A. Neyman and S. Sorin. *Stochastic Games and Applications*. NATO Science Series C. Springer, 2003.

A. Neyman and S. Sorin. Repeated games with public uncertain duration process. *International Journal of Game Theory*, 39:29–52, 2010.

A. Nowak. On a new class of nonzero-sum discounted stochastic games having stationary Nash equilibrium points. *International Journal of Game Theory*, 32:121–132, 2003.

A. Nowak. Stochastic games in economics. *Mathematical Methods of Operations Research*, 66:513–530, 2007.

A. Nowak and E. Altman. ε-equilibria for stochastic games with uncountable state space and unbounded costs. *SIAM Journal on Control and Optimization*, 40:1821–1839, 2002.

I. Nowik and S. Zamir. The game for the speed of convergence in repeated games of incomplete information. *International Journal of Game Theory*, 31:203–222, 2002.

M. Oliu-Barton and G. Vigeral. A uniform Tauberian theorem in optimal control. In P. Cardaliaguet, R. Cressman, and T. Basar, editors, *Advances in Dynamic Games*, volume 12 of *Annals of the International Society of Dynamic Games*, pages 199–215. Birkhäuser, 2013.

V. Perchet. Calibration and internal no-regret with random signals. In R. Gavalda, G. Lugosi, T. Zegmann, and S. Zilles, editors, *Algorithmic Learning Theory*, volume 5809 of *LNAI*, pages 68–82. Springer, 2009.

V. Perchet. Approachability of convex sets in games with partial monitoring. *Journal of Optimization Theory and Applications*, 149:665–677, 2011a.

V. Perchet. Internal regret with partial monitoring calibration-based optimal algorithm. *Journal of Machine Learning and Research*, 12:1893–1921, 2011b.

V. Perchet and M. Quincampoix. Purely informative game: Approachability in Wasserstein space (preprint). 2010.

M. Pinter. The non-existence of a universal topological type space. *Journal of Mathematical Economics*, 46:223–229, 2010.

R. A. Purves and W. D. Sudderth. Perfect information games with upper semicontinuous payoffs. *Mathematics of Operations Research*, 36:468–473, 2011.

M. Quincampoix and J. Renault. On the existence of a limit value in some nonexpansive optimal control problems. *SIAM Journal on Control and Optimization*, 49:2118–2132, 2011.

J. Renault. On two-player repeated games with lack of information on one side and state-independent signalling. *Mathematics of Operations Research*, 25:552–572, 2000.

J. Renault. Three-player repeated games with lack of information on one side. *International Journal of Game Theory*, 30:221–246, 2001a.

J. Renault. Learning sets in state dependent signalling game forms: A characterization. *Mathematics of Operations Research*, 26:832–850, 2001b.

J. Renault. The value of Markov chain games with lack of information on one side. *Mathematics of Operations Research*, 31:490–512, 2006.

J. Renault. Uniform value in dynamic programming. *Journal of the European Mathematical Society*, 13:309–330, 2011.

J. Renault. The value of repeated games with an informed controller. *Mathematics of Operations Research*, 37:154–179, 2012.

J. Renault and T. Tomala. Learning the state of nature in repeated games with incomplete information and signals. *Games and Economic Behavior*, 47:124–156, 2004a.

J. Renault and T. Tomala. Communication equilibrium payoffs in repeated games with complete information and imperfect monitoring. *Games and Economic Behavior*, 49:313–344, 2004b.

J. Renault and T. Tomala. General properties of long-run supergames. *Dynamic Games and Applications*, 1:319–350, 2012.

J. Renault, S. Scarlatti, and M. Scarsini. A folk theorem for minority games. *Games and Economic Behavior*, 53:208–230, 2005.

J. Renault, S. Scarlatti, and M. Scarsini. Discounted and finitely repeated minority games with public signals. *Mathematical Social Sciences*, 56:44–74, 2008.

J. Renault and X. Venel. A distance for probability spaces, and long-term values in Markov decision processes and repeated games (preprint), 2012.

P. J. Reny. On the existence of pure and mixed strategy Nash equilibria in discontinuous games. *Econometrica*, 67:1029–1056, 1999.

P. J. Reny. Strategic approximations of discontinuous games. *Economic Theory*, 48: 17–29, 2011.

D. Rosenberg. Duality and Markovian strategies. *International Journal of Game Theory*, 27:577–597, 1998.

D. Rosenberg. Zero-sum absorbing games with incomplete information on one side: Asymptotic analysis. *SIAM Journal on Control and Optimization*, 39:208–225, 2000.

D. Rosenberg, E. Solan, and N. Vieille. Stopping games with randomized strategies. *Probability Theory and Related Fields*, 119:433–451, 2001.

D. Rosenberg, E. Solan, and N. Vieille. Blackwell optimality in Markov decision processes with partial observation. *Annals of Statistics*, 30:1178–1193, 2002.

D. Rosenberg, E. Solan, and N. Vieille. The maxmin value of stochastic games with imperfect monitoring. *International Journal of Game Theory*, 32:133–150, 2003.

D. Rosenberg, E. Solan, and N. Vieille. Stochastic games with a single controller and incomplete information. *SIAM Journal on Control and Optimization*, 43:86–110, 2004.

D. Rosenberg, E. Solan, and N. Vieille. Stochastic games with imperfect monitoring. In A. Haurie, S. Muto, L. A. Petrosjan, and T. Raghavan, editors, *Advances in Dynamic Games*, volume 8 of *Annals of the International Society of Dynamic Games*, pages 3–22. Birkhäuser, 2006.

D. Rosenberg and S. Sorin. An operator approach to zero-sum repeated games. *Israel Journal of Mathematics*, 121:221–246, 2001.

D. Rosenberg and N. Vieille. The maxmin of recursive games with incomplete information on one side. *Mathematics of Operations Research*, 25:23–35, 2000.

A. Rustichini. Minimizing regret: The general case. *Games and Economic Behavior*, 29:224–243, 1999.

G. Schoenmakers, J. Flesch, and F. Thuijsman. Fictitious play in stochastic games. *Mathematical Methods of Operations Research*, 66:315–325, 2007.

P. Secchi and W. D. Sudderth. Stay-in-a-set games. *International Journal of Game Theory*, 30:479–490, 2001a.

P. Secchi and W. D. Sudderth. *n*-person stochastic games with upper semi-continuous payoffs. *International Journal of Game Theory*, 30:491–502, 2001b.

E. Shmaya. The determinacy of infinite games with eventual perfect monitoring. *Proceedings of the AMS*, 139:3665–3678, 2011.

E. Shmaya and E. Solan. Zero-sum dynamic games and a stochastic variation of Ramsey's theorem. *Stochastic Processes and their Applications*, 112:319–329, 2004.

R. S. Simon. Separation of joint plan equilibrium payoffs from the min-max functions. *Games and Economic Behavior*, 41:79–102, 2002.

R. S. Simon. Games of incomplete information, ergodic theory, and the measurability of equilibria. *Israel Journal of Mathematics*, 138:73–92, 2003.

R. S. Simon. Value and perfection in stochastic games. *Israel Journal of Mathematics*, 156:285–309, 2006.

R. S. Simon. The structure of non-zero-sum stochastic games. *Advances in Applied Mathematics*, 38:1–26, 2007.

R. S. Simon, S. Spiez, and H. Torunczyk. The existence of equilibria in certain games, separation for families of convex fuctions and a theorem of Borsuk–Ulam type. *Israel Journal of Mathematics*, 92:1–21, 1995.

R. S. Simon, S. Spiez, and H. Torunczyk. Equilibrium existence and topology in some repeated games with incomplete information. *Transactions of the American Mathematical Society*, 354:5005–5026, 2002.

E. Solan. Discounted stochastic games. *Mathematics of Operations Research*, 23: 1010–1021, 1998.

E. Solan. Three-player absorbing games. *Mathematics of Operations Research*, 24: 669–698, 1999.

E. Solan. The dynamics of the Nash correspondence and n-player stochastic games. *International Game Theory Review*, 3:291–300, 2001a.

E. Solan. Characterization of correlated equilibria in stochastic games. *International Journal of Game Theory*, 30:259–277, 2001b.

E. Solan. Continuity of the value of competitive Markov decision processes. *Journal of Theoretical Probability*, 16:831–845, 2003a.

E. Solan. Perturbations of Markov chains with applications to stochastic games. In A. Neyman and S. Sorin, editors, *Stochastic Games and Applications*, volume 570 of *NATO Science Series*, pages 265–280. Kluwer, 2003b.

E. Solan and N. Vieille. Correlated equilibrium in stochastic games. *Games and Economic Behavior*, 38:362–399, 2002a.

E. Solan and N. Vieille. Uniform value in recursive games. *Annals of Applied Probability*, 12:1185–1201, 2002b.

E. Solan and N. Vieille. Perturbed Markov chains. *Journal of Applied Probability*, 40: 107–122, 2003a.

E. Solan and N. Vieille. Deterministic multi-player Dynkin games. *Journal of Mathematical Economics*, 39:911–929, 2003b.

E. Solan and N. Vieille. Stopping games: Recent results. In A. Nowak and K. Szajowski, editors, *Advances in Dynamic Games*, volume 7 of *Annals of the ISDG*, pages 235–245. Birkhäuser, 2004.

E. Solan and N. Vieille. Computing uniform optimal strategies in two-player stochastic sames. *Economic Theory*, 42:237–253, 2010.

E. Solan and R. Vohra. Correlated equilibrium and public signalling in absorbing games. *International Journal of Game Theory*, 31:91–121, 2002.

S. Sorin. Merging, reputation, and repeated games with incomplete information. *Games and Economic Behavior*, 28:274–308, 1999.

S. Sorin. *A First Course on Zero-Sum Repeated Games*. Mathématiques & Applications #37. Springer, 2002.

S. Sorin. The operator approach to zero-sum stochastic games. In A. Neyman and S. Sorin, editors, *Stochastic Games and Applications*, volume 570 of *NATO Science Series C*, pages 417–426. Kluwer Academic Publishers, 2003.

S. Sorin. Asymptotic properties of monotonic nonexpansive mappings. *Discrete Events Dynamic Systems*, 14:109–122, 2004.

S. Sorin. New approaches and recent advances in two-person zero-sum repeated games. In A. Nowak and K. Szajowski, editors, *Advances in Dynamic Games*, volume 7 of *Annals of the ISDG*, pages 67–93. Birkhäuser, 2005.

S. Sorin. Zero-sum repeated games: Recent advances and new links with differential games. *Dynamic Games and Applications*, 1:172–207, 2011.

S. Sorin, X. Venel, and G. Vigeral. Asymptotic properties of optimal trajectories in dynamic programming. *Sankhya: The Indian Journal of Statistics*, 72A:237–245, 2010.

S. Sorin and G. Vigeral. Existence of the limit value of two-person zero-sum discounted repeated games via comparison theorems. *Journal of Optimization Theory and Applications*, 157:564–576, 2013.

A. Souquière. Approximation and representation of the value for some differential games with asymmetric information. *International Journal of Game Theory*, 39: 699–722, 2010.

X. Spinat. A necessary and sufficient condition for approachability. *Mathematics of Operations Research*, 27:31–44, 2002.

N. Vieille. Equilibrium in 2-person stochastic games I: A reduction. *Israel Journal of Mathematics*, 119:55–91, 2000a.

N. Vieille. Equilibrium in 2-person stochastic games II: The case of recursive games. *Israel Journal of Mathematics*, 119:93–126, 2000b.

N. Vieille. Small perturbations and stochastic games. *Israel Journal of Mathematics*, 119:127–142, 2000c.

N. Vieille. Solvable states in n-player stochastic games. *SIAM Journal on Control and Optimization*, 38:1794–1804, 2000d.

N. Vieille. Stochastic games: Recent results. In R. J. Aumann and S. Hart, editors, *Handbook of Game Theory, with Economic Applications*, Volume 3, pages 1833–1850. Elsevier, 2002.

G. Vigeral. Evolution equations in discrete and continuous time for non-expansive operators in Banach spaces. *ESAIM COCV*, 16:809–832, 2010a.

G. Vigeral. Iterated monotonic nonexpansive operators and asymptotic properties of zero-sum stochastic games (preprint). 2010b.

G. Vigeral. Counter examples in zero-sum repeated games (preprint). 2012.

Y. Viossat. Is having a unique equilibrium robust? *Journal of Mathematical Economics*, 44:1152–1160, 2008.

B. von Stengel and F. Forges. Extensive form correlated equilibrium: Definition and computational complexity. *Mathematics of Operations Research*, 33:1002–1022, 2008.

L. E. Zachrisson. Markov games. In M. Dresher, L. S. Shapley, and A. W. Tucker, editors, *Advances in Game Theory*, pages 211–253. Princeton University Press, 1964.

S. Zamir. Bayesian games: Games with incomplete information. In R. A. Meyers, editor, *Encyclopedia of Complexity and Systems Science*, pages 426–441. Springer, 2009.

Author Index

Subject Index

Other Titles in the Series (*continued from page iii*)

Eric Ghysels, Norman R. Swanson, and Mark Watson, Editors, *Essays in econometrics: Collected papers of Clive W. J. Granger (Volume I)*, 9780521772976, 9780521774963
Eric Ghysels, Norman R. Swanson, and Mark Watson, Editors, *Essays in econometrics: Collected papers of Clive W. J. Granger (Volume II)*, 9780521792073, 9780521796491
Cheng Hsiao, *Analysis of panel data, second edition*, 9780521818551, 9780521522717
Mathias Dewatripont, Lars Peter Hansen, and Stephen J. Turnovsky, Editors, *Advances in economics and econometrics – Eighth World Congress (Volume I)*, 9780521818728, 9780521524117
Mathias Dewatripont, Lars Peter Hansen, and Stephen J. Turnovsky, Editors, *Advances in economics and econometrics – Eighth World Congress (Volume II)*, 9780521818735, 9780521524124
Mathias Dewatripont, Lars Peter Hansen, and Stephen J. Turnovsky, Editors, *Advances in economics and econometrics – Eighth World Congress (Volume III)*, 9780521818742, 9780521524131
Roger Koenker, *Quantile regression*, 9780521845731, 9780521608275
Charles Blackorby, Walter Bossert, and David Donaldson, *Population issues in social choice theory, welfare economics, and ethics*, 9780521825511, 9780521532587
John E. Roemer, *Democracy, education, and equality*, 9780521846653, 9780521609135
Richard Blundell, Whitney K. Newey, and Thorsten Persson, Editors, *Advances in economics and econometrics – Ninth World Congress (Volume I)*, 9780521871525, 9780521692083
Richard Blundell, Whitney K. Newey, and Thorsten Persson, Editors, *Advances in economics and econometrics – Ninth World Congress (Volume I)*, 9780521871532, 9780521692090
Richard Blundell, Whitney K. Newey, and Thorsten Persson, Editors, *Advances in economics and econometrics – Ninth World Congress (Volume I)*, 9780521871549, 9780521692106
Fernando Vega-Redondo, *Complex social networks*, 9780521857406, 9780521674096
Itzhak Gilboa, *Theory of decision under uncertainty*, 9780521517324, 9780521741231
Krislert Samphantharak and Robert M. Townsend, *Households as corporate firms: An analysis of household finance using integrated household surveys and corporate financial accounting*, 9780521195829, 9780521124164
Rakesh Vohra, *Mechanism design: A linear programming approach*, 9781107004368, 9780521179461
Daron Acemoglu, Manuel Arellano, and Eddie Dekel, Editors, *Advances in economics and econometrics – Tenth World Congress (Volume I)*, 9781107016040, 9781107638105
Daron Acemoglu, Manuel Arellano, and Eddie Dekel, Editors, *Advances in economics and econometrics – Tenth World Congress (Volume II)*, 9781107016057, 9781107674165
Daron Acemoglu, Manuel Arellano, and Eddie Dekel, Editors, *Advances in economics and econometrics – Tenth World Congress (Volume III)*, 9781107016064, 9781107627314
Andrew Harvey, *Dynamic models for volatility and heavy tails: With applications to financial and economic time series*, 9781107034723, 9781107630024

Printed in the United States
By Bookmasters